Platter's

SOUTH AFRICAN

WINES

2013

THE GUIDE TO CELLARS, VINEYARDS,

WINEMAKERS, RESTAURANTS

AND ACCOMMODATION

Focus on  Backstories

John Platter SA Wine Guide (Pty) Ltd
www.wineonaplatter.com

PUBLISHER
Andrew McDowall

EDITOR
Philip van Zyl

ASSOCIATE EDITORS
Jos Baker, Tim James, Cathy van Zyl

TASTERS
Michael Fridjhon, Angela Lloyd; Master of Wine Cathy van Zyl; Cape Wine Master Winnie Bowman, Greg de Bruyn, Tim James, Christine Rudman, Meryl Weaver David Biggs, Christian Eedes, Higgo Jacobs, Cathy Marston, Fiona McDonald, Ingrie Motteux, Khuselo Mputa (2010 edition), Jörg Pfützner, James Pietersen & Dave Swingler.

CONTRIBUTORS
Bob Chappell, Christian Eedes, Tony Jackman, Lynne Kloot, Cathy Marston, Lindsaye McGregor, Joanne Gibson & Wendy Toerien

COORDINATORS
Christina Harvett (wine & tasting), Ina Smith (regional tasting), Ina de Villiers (information)

DATABASE, WEB & QR CODES
Sean de Kock, Alex Maughan (Digital Energy Media), Tracy Frayne (Tracy Frayne Digital Design), Ben van Rensburg (Modern Web Presence)

TYPESETTING & MAPS
Gawie du Toit, Ryk Taljaard, Heinrich Schloms (VinPro)

PHOTOGRAPHY
Teddy Sambu & Athol Moult

ADVERTISING
Linda Ransome · T +27 (0)82-412-3048 · lindar@wineonaplatter.com

SALES
Linda Butler · T +27 (0)83-462-8172 · lindab@wineonaplatter.com

© John Platter SA Wine Guide (Pty) Ltd 2013
PO Box 1466 Hermanus 7200
Tel: +27 (0)28-316-3210/+27 (0)82-490-1820 · Fax: +27 (0)86-513-3908
andrew@wineonaplatter.com

🌐 www.wineonaplatter.com
📘 Facebook: http://www.facebook.com/platterswineguide
🐦 Twitter: @wineonaplatter

ISBN 978-0-987-0046-1-1

CONTENTS

PHOTO GALLERY

It is said that every bottle of wine has a tale to tell, and in this edition we dig below the surface to reveal the untold backstories about the cellars, people and brands across South Africa's winelands. We highlight the passions and preoccupations, the dreams, challenges and successes that make South Africa one of the world's most fascinating and dynamic winegrowing areas. See page 246 and following.

The majestic sounds of national anthems, impressive fireworks, smiling athletes, enthusiastic supporters and spectators — all this was imbued in the spirit of London at the end of the 2012 Olympic Games. If it was possible to capture that spirit in a bottle, it would surely have scored 21 points out of 20. For team Great Britain in 1996, only one gold medal was brought home from Atlanta. On home ground in 2012, they raised the bar very significantly to a massive 29 gold medals. This took perseverance, determination and the desire to produce something world class. When thinking about what I might write for this foreword, I found many parallels between the Olympian efforts and the progress in the wine industry since South Africa became a democracy 1994.

It seems aeons ago that I studied winemaking and viticulture with many of the luminaries in our industry at Elsenburg in Stellenbosch and then in Weinsberg, Germany. A French government bursary to spend a year in all the wine regions of France was one of the highlights of my wine career. My only scary experience at that time was finding myself in the middle of a very unfriendly anti-South Africa protest in Paris but that was back in the mid-1980s. We have subsequently witnessed the South African wine industry emerge from the cocoon of the dark days of apartheid into one of the foremost players on the global wine stage.

We have been given lots of advice along the way — some of it bizarre, such as the suggestion that South Africa would never produce a decent chardonnay that could compete with its peers from other countries. The late Tony Lord predicted that pinotage would become a USP for South Africa and that in many cases we were drinking our pinotage too young. A mellow, round and beautifully textured 1983 that I enjoyed recently bore testimony to that. Some visionaries travelled to uncharted territories, bringing back ideas of working with Rhône varieties, and today both red and white Rhône varieties constitute some of South Africa's most exciting wines.

In 1992, when I started to sell South African wines in the UK and Europe, chenin blanc was the £2.99 wine — always cheap and cheerful. It caused us some headaches to try and bust that particular price point, and South Africa was associated with descriptions such as sound, good value and over-delivering at many price points, mainly the lower ones. How times have changed! Thankfully some winemakers dedicated to chenin refused to uproot old vineyards, some of them bushvines, and continued to strive for world-class wines. The results are irrefutable.

It is testimony to a whole new generation of winemakers that in the first decade of the new South Africa they found creative ways to catch up for much lost time in a world of isolation. I recall asking a young winemaker why his wines seemed to have improved exponentially in such a short time. His simple answer was: 'I have worked 18 harvests in nine years and it has helped me to hit the fast-forward button — it was my only option.' Is there still much work to do? Certainly, but then that is a sign of a dynamic, growing and developing wine industry.

A wise author reflecting on life concluded that there are four cornerstones of life — to live, to love, to learn and to leave a legacy. It is important for us as a country not to forget our heroes and honour them, for they provided us with a foundation on which to build — improving nursery practices, introducing fermentation in stainless steel tanks, experimenting with oak, motivating to change the law for the production of noble sweet wines which did not have to be fortified, and many others. At a recent Veritas dinner in Cape Town, I found myself on the dance floor with my old Elsenburg oenology professor, Dr Danie Joubert, who had been honoured for his contribution to the industry. He would not mind me saying that he is a healthy 94-year-old and he danced me off my feet — clearly the numerous benefits of wine are encapsulated in him.

During all my time selling wine in Europe I cannot recall ever going into a buyer's office without seeing the Platter guide on their shelves — from Waitrose to Kaufhof and Systembolaget, they always had the latest edition. The inaugural edition in 1980 included 1,250 wines. This edition includes over 7,000 wines, so it is hardly a pocket book any longer, almost requiring its own briefcase! Our friend Hugh Johnson, whose Pocket Wine Book inspired journalists and winelovers John and Erica Platter to create their own South African wine guide, always remarks on the consistently high standard which Platter's has maintained. One thing is certain — it provides an incredible service to the South African wine industry, locally and abroad, and long may it continue to flourish.

Lynne Sherriff MW
Chair, Institute Masters of Wine (2010–2012)

EDITOR'S NOTE

Regular readers will have noted that the most recent editions of this guide have focused on particular themes — 'Sustainability' in 2011 and 'Innovation' in 2012. For this book, the 33rd since inception in 1980, we were inspired by the oft-repeated phrase, that 'every bottle of wine has a tale to tell', to choose the theme 'Backstories'. The idea (as detailed on page 3) is to dig below the surface of South Africa's wine industry and reveal some of the untold narratives behind its cellars, people and brands. It's been a truly fascinating exercise, and a vivid reminder that South Africa's wine culture, generally considered 'New World' and by implication 'young', is in fact more than three centuries old. For those who hold that the past is passé, this is of course a complete irrelevance. But for those winelovers and hopefully soon-to-be-winelovers in Asia and other growth markets, for whom tradition and heritage in wine are real and meaningful, it's potentially hugely significant that winegrowing in this country stretches back more than 350 years. Not only that, but unlike most countries' wine chronicles, which begin with a vague 'Once upon a time', South Africa's commences — with the joyful exclamation 'Praise be to God!' — on an actual day: February 2nd 1659. What a great backstory! The long tradition of individuals and families paying homage to the vine at the southern tip of Africa continues unbroken, and we're hopeful that our focus on backstories will help to convey something of the passion and dedication which today's winegrowers, like their predecessors, bring to their craft.

Talking of backstories, a series of happy coincidences caused our path to intersect with that of a gifted young photographer from Cape Town's Khayelitsha neighbourhood, Teddy Sambu, whose acuity and imagination have transformed this edition's full-colour Photo Gallery into something truly special. Inspired by feedback from an image of his mother taken in boyhood with his first camera, and displayed some years later at her funeral, the enterprising Teddy disregarded the advice of a career counsellor and set himself up as a photographer under the banner Khaya Productions. With a canvas backdrop pegged to a barbed wire fence, Teddy had been photographing Learn-to-Earn graduates for R50 an A4 enlargement. Cape Town artist and photographer Athol Moult had founded a photography mentorship initiative Lightwarriors when serendipitously he discovered Teddy. More recently, Lightwarriors has been underpinned by a bursary from the African investment banking group, Imara Holdings. With Imara's backing and mentored by Athol, Teddy has been able to enrol at the Cape Town School of Photography and over a two-year scholarship period, is honing his craft and realising his enormous potential. Teddy entered our orbit when, over a plate of sushi, Athol (who is

part of the Pitchblack team responsible for Platter's smartphone/tablet Apps) in passing mentioned the Imara Lightwarriors project and his delight about Imara coming on board with a substantial sponsorship. The rest, as they say in some of the best backstories, is history.

Regarding the tastings for this edition, our aim and approach have remained unchanged, namely to taste, rate and describe as many as possible South African-made wines available during the currency of the book, both locally and overseas.

Much as we'd like to, the number of individual wines precludes us from re-tasting/rating vintages which have been submitted previously yet will still be available for sale during the book's currency. Only wines which last year were reviewed as tank or barrel samples, and thus rated provisionally (or considered too young and unformed to rate), or wines we believe we may have miscalled last time, are revisited for the current book. New and previously untasted vintages are, of course, reviewed as normal.

It bears repeating that the rankings reflected in the book are the result of a process beginning towards the end of June, when we mobilise our team of tasters. The results of their work are reflected in the A–Z section, along with news about the wineries and winemakers, general information about products, vinification facilities, vineyards, amenities available to visitors and more. (Scores for all wines in the A–Z are also listed separately for convenience in the section named 'This Year's Ratings Summarised' on page 506.)

For visitors in search of wine-route information, we've incorporated GPS coordinates for as many as possible of the wineries open to the public at set hours or by appointment. The maps have again been fully updated, along with the quick-lookup tables which furnish key visitor information about the wineries of a particular area, such as whether or not they are open on weekends and public holidays, offer meals or refreshments, specifically cater for children, or are friendly to individuals with reduced mobility. The maps and tables have been moved to the very back of the book, where hopefully they will be easier and quicker to find.

Our initiative to provide professionally conducted audits of winetasting areas, cellar tours and other visitor facilities in the winelands in conjunction with accessibility specialist Guy Davies is highlighted on page 588.

Also of interest to tourists and wine-ramblers are the Restaurants and Accommodation sections, featuring hotels, B&Bs, restaurants, delis and a plethora of other dining and unwinding venues among the vines. Well-qualified Jos Baker edits the (sponsored) entries.

Our wine ranking system remains the same as last year. We cover the full spectrum, from wines we consider 'somewhat less than ordinary' (and award 0 stars) to 'superlative Cape classics', worthy of a full 5 stars. Wines rated ★★★★ or higher are usually listed first in each entry, and set in red type. However, wines debuting as barrel/tank previews and therefore provisionally rated 4 or more stars remain in black type. Vintages deviating from the general rating are individually starred in the text. Very good/promising wines and more modest examples (★★★★ or fewer) are included in the 'run-on' listings at the end of entries. For easy identification, the quaffing best-buys are boxed together and individually labelled with the wallet-cordial ☺ sign. See also the section 'How to Use the Guide' on page 7.

Because of deadlines, many wines in the guide are tasted freshly bottled or as works-in-progress; any considered unrateable as a result are noted as such in the text. It's worth mentioning that we taste from the end of June to mid-August. Except for the bottlings assessed for five stars (see the preamble to the Wines of the Year on page 10), all wines are tasted 'sighted' (with labels exposed) and the name of the producer known. As a control, we also double-blind taste hundreds of wines in the course of our assessments. In these corroborative reviews, tasters have no information about the wine save what's in the glass. Because of the subjective element associated with wine assessment, we strongly recommend you view our rankings as adjuncts to the tasting notes rather than as oracular pronouncements. And we continue to urge you, in the words of a local winery's marketing slogan, to 'trust your taste'.

Wines featured in this edition were assessed by a team whose professionalism and unflagging enthusiasm we gratefully acknowledge. Their initials appear below the wines they tasted, as follows: Michael Fridjhon (MF), Angela Lloyd (AL); Master of Wine Cathy van Zyl (CvZ); Cape Wine Masters Winnie Bowman (WB), Greg de Bruyn (GdB), Tim James (TJ), Christine Rudman (CR), Meryl Weaver (MW); also David Biggs (DB), Christian Eedes (CE), Higgo Jacobs (HJ), Cathy Marston (CM), Fiona McDonald (FM), Ingrid Motteux (IM), Khuselo Mputa (KM, 2010 edition), Jörg Pfützner (JPf), James Pietersen (JP) and Dave Swingler (DS). For potted biographies of the tasters, see page 504.

In a further endeavour to ensure the fairest possible ratings for wines debuting this edition, or returning after a gap, we've again assembled small panels of tasters to carry out the reviews. Regional tastings (in Worcester, Robertson, Olifants River, Klein Karoo, Tulbagh and the southern Cape/Elim) are also done by small teams.

Warm thanks to the rest of the splendid team, specially to associate editors Tim James (also proof-reader) and Jos Baker; contributors Bob Chappell, Christian Eedes, Tony Jackman, Lynne Kloot, Cathy Marston, Lindsaye McGregor, Joanne Gibson and Wendy Toerien; information coordinator Ina de Villiers, regional tasting coordinator Ina Smith, wine coordina-tor Christina Harvett and assistants Deon Boonzaier, Bettina Botha, Jose du Toit, Wilbe Myburgh, Alex Reichle, MF Schoeman, Wilhelm Schultz, Duncan Thokoane and Carami van der Merwe; map and typesetting guru Gawie du Toit; light warriors Teddy Sambu and Athol Moult; the two Lindas (Ransome and Butler) for advertising and sales respectively; Lara Philp and Johan Rademan of Vineyard Connection for the use of their excellent facilities; Lauren de Kock for fact-checking; Mark Whyte and XtraSmile Couriers; Ryk Taljaard (Geo-Logic Mapping) and Heinrich Schloms (VinPro) for the Wine of Origin maps; Ben van Rensburg (Modern Web Presence) for QR code; Alex Maughan (Digital Energy Media) and Tracy Frayne (Tracy Frayne Digital Design) for web/mobi site design; the ever-helpful SAWIS; and Michael Bucholz for the calibration samples. Special thanks to Sean 'Anything Is Possible' de Kock for 24 x 7 help with the database, intranet and website.

Most of all, loving thanks to Superwoman, aka wife, associate editor and regional tasting team leader Cathy, whose ability to get the impossible done, on time, continues to baffle, astound and delight; and to son Luke, 16 this year and suddenly taller than dad, with a Private Pilot Licence in his sights.

Certainly not least, sincere thanks to South Africa's wine producers and negociants, without whose support the book could not be produced.

Finally, an invitation to join us on the web, Facebook and Twitter (see page 2 for details), and to check out the seriously cool Platter's Apps for Apple and Android devices — see the display advertisement on page 627 for details.

Philip van Zyl

Our Track-Record-Based Rating System

All wines rated 4 stars or more are set in red type

General rating ★★★★ **Caldera**

For 4-star or better wines, we give the 'track-record rating' over two or more vintages in the margin.

Vintage-specific rating **06 (★★★★)**

Any differences from the general rating noted in brackets beside the particular vintage

★★★★★	Superlative. A South African classic
★★★★★	Outstanding
★★★★	Excellent
★★★★	Very good/promising
★★★	Characterful, appealing
★★★	Good everyday drinking
★★	Pleasant drinking
★★	Casual quaffing
★	Plain and simple
★	Very ordinary
No star	Somewhat less than ordinary

Abbreviations

% alc	Percentage alcohol by volume
1stB	First bottled vintage
BEE	Black Economic Empowerment
BWI	Biodiversity & Wine Initiative
BYO	Bring your own (wine, picnic)
Cs	Cases
CWG	Cape Winemakers Guild
CWM	Cape Wine Master
Est	Date established
g/l	Grams per litre
IPW	Integrated Production of Wine
IWC	International Wine Challenge
IWSC	International Wine & Spirit Competition
LBV	Late Bottled Vintage
Malo	Malolactic fermentation
MCC	Méthode cap classique
MW	Master of Wine
NLH	Noble Late Harvest
NV	Non-vintage. Year of harvest not stated on label
RS	Residual sugar
SAA	South African Airways (selected for First or Premium Class)
SLH	Special Late Harvest
Veritas	SA National Bottled Wine Show
WIETA	Wine & Agricultural Ethical Trade Association
Wine	Wine magazine (South African)
WO	Wine of Origin

cabernet/cab	cabernet sauvignon
pinot	pinot noir
chenin	chenin blanc
sauvignon/sauv	sauvignon blanc
touriga	touriga nacional
tinta	tinta barocca

Symbols

Winery symbols

▲	Bottles own wine on property
▌	Open for tasting (no fee unless noted)
🍴	Restaurant/refreshments
⌂	Accommodation
📷	Other tourist attractions/amenities on the property
⊼	Bring your own (BYO) picnic
🧒	Child friendly
♿	Wheelchair friendly (see page 588)

Wine symbols

📰	Screwcapped
✓	Good value
☺	Exceptionally drinkable and well priced
NEW	New wine
⊕	Wine still selling, not retasted
✿	Organic
◎	Biodynamic
▨	Certified as sustainable (see www.swsa.co.za)

Location: nearest major centre to winery, vyd, head office. Map: See Maps section for winery's position. WO: Wine of Origin geographical unit, region, district or ward; wines described/rated bear the first-mentioned WO certification unless noted.

Total hectares/hectares under vine (not necessarily in production); main varieties planted

GPS coordinates, based on Datum WGS 84

Our track-record-based rating system
See previous page for an explanation

Unless noted, red wines wooded; whites unoaked

Wine name, vintage, colour & style

Listings of wines available during the currency of the book

Symbols
See previous page for a complete list

See previous page for a list of abbreviations

Date established

T = Telephone number
F = Fax number

Producer's name

The text used here is illustrative art not complete. See A–Z for full details.

Fairview

Location/WO: Paarl ▪ Map: Paarl & Wellington ▪ 30min before closing ▪ Fee R25 or R60 ▪ Closed Ea Groups by appt only ▪ Tasting & sales of Fairview Anthony de Jager (Dec 1996), with Adele Dunbar Mouton ▪ 500ha/300ha (cab, barbera, merlot, n sauv, viog) ▪ 1 850t 80% red 15% white 5% rosé accredited ▪ Export brand: Six Hats ▪ PO Box 583 S S 33° 46' 19.5" E 018° 55' 28.0" ▪ **T 021-863-2**

Fresh life is being fed into the ent Paarl's distinctive granite dome an form of uprooting blue gum trees a dry as long as Charles Back can rec plantings of Grenache blanc and rou first tempranillo went to barrel.

Fairview range

★★★★ Cabernet Sauvignon ✓ Renamed ' some & approachable. Silky tannin frame from

★★★★ Cyril Back Flagship homage to Back but gentle texture. Complex, dense & concentr fruit 18 mths in 30% new Fr oak. Needs time.

★★★★ Sauvignon Blanc ✓ 🗒 🗟 Fig & g tact adds body to mid-palate. All Darling fruit.

Darling Chenin Blanc 😊 🗒 🗟 ★★★ minerality with honeysuckle hint. Broad palate

Barbera ★★★★ 08 has ripe mulberry succulenc mths old Fr oak. **Stellenbosch Merlot** 🗒 ★★ tar intensity. Fr oak, 20% new, yr. **Mourv NEW** "c 08. Concentrated & slightly chunky but elegant. 08's bold structure & density tempered by plum **Straw Wine ✓ ★★★★** Exotic lavender floral no Vanilla wafer too. Sweet (136g RS) but long, dry '

False Bay Vineyards

Location: Somerset West ▪ WO: Coastal/Wester Boutinot ▪ Winemaker(s) Werner Engelbrecht (2 70% white ▪ PO Box 2093 Somerset West 7129 ▪ **T 021-858-1292** ▪ F 021-858-1293

A consistent range for the UK-owne lar of sibling Waterkloof – with the and often with the natural ferm Engelbrecht. The grapes are, howeve

Tastings, sales & cellar tour times (closed Saturdays & Sundays but open public holidays unless noted)

Symbols
See previous page for a complete list

Other attractions or activities available on the property

stB 1974 ▪ Tasting & sales daily 9–5, last tastings 5, Jan 1 ▪ The Goatshed (see Restaurants section) ▪ er(s) Charles Back ▪ Winemaker(s) Charles Back & ohanie Betts (2010) ▪ Vineyard manager(s) Donald irah, ptage, chard, chenin, grenache b&n, 01 & HACCP certified; IPW & BWI member; WIETA 624 ▪ info@fairview.co.za ▪ www.fairview.co.za ▪ 363-2591

Names of owner, winemaker, viticulturist & consultant/s; year/month of appointment in brackets

Postal & email address, website
(see www.wineonaplatter.com for social media details)

ew ecosystem on the rear slopes of ain. On the natural front it took the egetation that has seen riverbeds — with water again. In the cellar, new ere vinified for the first time, and the

All wines dry unless noted

08 is bold, leafy cassis & fruitcake galore. Sleek, lis- rl-ferm fruit. 16 mths in 25% new Fr oak.

7's waxy plum segues to blueberry & pepper. Firm et full-bodied. Basket-pressed Paarl & Swartland

spness on **10**. Lemon & flint minerality. Lees con-

adilla & grapefruit zip on unoaked **10**. Fresh ntact.

Exceptionally drinkable & well priced

on spice over cocoa oak notes. Fine tannin from 12 ng 08. Cocoa earthiness set against ripe mulberry, ★ Savoury soy & earth over black pepper & plum on **Petite Sirah** ★★★★ Floral lavender & blueberry. ong mocha tail. Yr Fr oak, 40% new. **Hanepoot** sugar, jasmine, ginger & peach abundance on **08**. poot grapes ex-swartland. — FM

Taster/s initials

1stB 2000 ▪ Tasting at Waterkloof ▪ Owner(s) Paul lturist(s) Werner Engelbrecht ▪ 60,000cs 30% red rkloofwines.co.za ▪ www.waterkloofwines.co.za ▪

Production, in tons and/or 12-bottle cases (cs) and red:white ratio

utinot portfolio and made in the cel- ention to detail as the estate's wines favoured by winemaker Werner widely sourced.

Brief introduction/news update

In the course of tasting and rating more than 7,000 wines for this edition, the members of our team individually identified a limited number of bottlings showing exceptional quality. These were entered into a second round of tasting, open only to finished/bottled wines, available during the currency of the book. The short-listed wines were tasted 'blind' (without sight of the label) by an assembled panel, and those regarded as superlative in a South African context awarded the guide's highest grading — five stars. These standouts are listed below under the heading 'Five Stars'. The highest-scoring five star wines were subjected to a further evaluation to determine the overall top scorer. The two wines which emerged this year from the stringent selection represent the pinnacle of SA winemaking and are the joint recipients of the guide's highest accolade: Wines of the Year.

The wines which did not make the five star selection, but which are extremely fine and collectible in their own right, are listed immediately below the Five Stars under the heading 'Highly Recommended'.

Implicit in wines of this calibre is the potential to improve with further bottle-maturation — say 8–10 years, perhaps more, in the case of the reds and fortifieds, and around 4-6 years for the whites. (Proper storage is, of course, vital for sound maturation.) During the cycle of tasting, our team identified a number of bottlings, over and above the candidate five stars, which show particular potential for cellaring. These ageworthy wines are listed separately under the heading 'Buy Now, Drink Later'.

Also listed is a selection of entry-level wines offering exceptional drinkability at budget prices. The 'Superquaffer of the Year' provides the best overall value and quaffability in this category.

There is, too, the prestigious 'super award', Winery of the Year, in recognition of a winegrowing team who, in the opinion of the editor, are ambassadors par excellence for South African wine.

Further details about all releases listed in this section will be found under the names of the relevant producers in the A–Z directory. The five-star tasting is audited by PKF (Cpt) Inc.

Winery of the Year

Cape Chamonix Wine Farm

The overarching theme for this edition is 'Backstories', and it's particularly apt that our Winery of the Year has not only a compelling background narrative but one that can be handily summarised in one word — kaizen — the Japanese idea of continuous betterment through ongoing focus on key processes. Whether by design or intuition, this Franschhoek winery has embraced kaizen while achieving a seamless integration of viticulture and winemaking (it helps that the same person, the unassuming outdoorsman Gottfried Mocke, is responsible for both). The result is such an astounding growth in quality over the past decade-plus, culminating in no fewer than four 5 star ratings this edition, that Gottfried and his team at Cape Chamonix Wine Farm must now be recognised as among South Africa's top handful of winegrowers. We salute and congratulate them, and trust that the fruits of their change-for-the-better will provide winelovers with continuing pleasure and joy.

Platter's SOUTH AFRICAN WINE GUIDE — WINERY OF THE YEAR

Wines of the Year

FIVE STARS & RED WINE OF THE YEAR

Shiraz
- Mullineux Family Syrah 2010

FIVE STARS & WHITE WINE OF THE YEAR

Dessert Wine Unfortified
- Paul Cluver Noble Late Harvest 2011

Platter's SOUTH AFRICAN WINE GUIDE — WINES OF THE YEAR

Five Stars

Cabernet Franc
- Raka 2009
- Von Ortloff Quintessence 2008
- Warwick 2009

Cabernet Sauvignon
- Delaire Graff Laurence Graff Reserve 2009

Pinotage
- Cape Chamonix Greywacke 2010
- Kanonkop 2010

Pinot Noir
- Cape Chamonix Reserve 2011
- Newton Johnson Family Vineyards 2011

Platter's SOUTH AFRICAN WINE GUIDE — ★★★★★

Five Stars *(continued)*

Shiraz
- Boschendal Cecil John Reserve 2010
- Cederberg CWG Auction Reserve Teen die Hoog 2010
- Delheim Vera Cruz 2009
- Fable Bobbejaan 2010
- Fairview Jakkalsfontein 2009
- Mullineux Family Schist 2010
- Raka Biography 2010
- Saronsberg 2010
- Simonsig Merindol Syrah 2010

Red Blends
- Dalla Cia Wine & Spirit Company Giorgio 2007
- Fleur de Cap Lazlo 2008
- Keets First Verse 2010
- Ken Forrester The Gypsy 2009
- La Motte Pierneef Shiraz-Viognier 2010
- Mvemve Raats MR De Compostella 2009
- Nico van der Merwe Mas Nicolas Cape 2007
- Sadie Family Columella 2010

Chardonnay
- Boschendal Reserve 2011
- Cape Chamonix Reserve 2011
- Hamilton Russell 2011
- Jordan CWG Auction Reserve 2011
- Jordan Nine Yards 2011

Chenin Blanc
- Alheit Cartology 2011
- Beaumont Hope Marguerite 2011
- Botanica 2011
- DeMorgenzon Reserve 2010
- Jean Daneel Signature 2011

- KWV Cathedral Cellar 2011
- Sadie Family Skurfberg 2011
- Spice Route 2011

Sauvignon Blanc
- Fryer's Cove 2011
- Graham Beck Pheasant's Run 2012
- Tokara Walker Bay 2012

White Blends
- AA Badenhorst Family 2010
- Cape Chamonix Reserve 2011
- Cape Point CWG Auction Reserve 2011
- David Aristargos 2011
- Fairview Nurok 2011
- Flagstone Treaty Tree Reserve 2010
- Miles Mossop Saskia 2011
- Nederburg Ingenuity 2011
- Nederberg Sauvignon Blanc-Semillon Private Bin D252 2012
- Nitida Coronata Integration 2011
- Rall 2011
- Tokara Director's Reserve 2011

Méthode Cap Classique
- Bon Courage Jacques Bruére Brut Reserve 2008
- Villiera Monro Brut 2007

Dessert Wine Unfortified
- Fairview La Beryl Blanc 2011
- Fleur du Cap Noble Late Harvest 2011
- Mullineux Family Straw Wine 2011
- Nederburg Winemaster's Reserve Noble Late Harvest 2011

Port
- De Krans The Last Cape Vintage Reserve Port 2010

Highly Recommended

Cabernet Franc
- Buitenverwachting 2009
- Raats Family 2010

Cabernet Sauvignon
- Cederberg Five Generations 2010
- Ernie Els 2010
- Glen Carlou Gravel Quarry 2009
- Glenelly Lady May 2010
- Le Riche CWG Auction Reserve 2009
- Meerlust 2010
- Neil Ellis Vineyard Selection 2009
- Rickety Bridge Paulina's Reserve 2009
- Stark-Condé Three Pines 2010
- The Butcher Shop & Grill Teddy Hall 2007
- Webersburg 2007

Cinsaut
- Sadie Family Pofadder 2011

Merlot
- Eagles' Nest 2008
- Hartenberg CWG Auction Reserve Loam Hill 2009

Platter's
SOUTH AFRICAN WINE GUIDE
HIGHLY RECOMMENDED

Pinotage
- Durbanville Hills Rhinofields 2011
- Meerendal Heritage Block 2010
- Rijk's Private Cellar 2008
- Spier 21 Gables 2010

Pinot Noir
- Crystallum Cuvée Cinéma 2011
- Iona Limited Release 2010
- Meerlust 2011
- Shannon Rockview Ridge 2011
- The Winery of Good Hope AD 2010

Highly Recommended (continued)

Shiraz
- Boekenhoutskloof Syrah 2010
- Eagles' Nest 2009
- Fairview The Beacon 2009
- Graham Beck The Joshua 2009
- Graham Beck The Ridge Syrah 2009
- Hartenberg Gravel Hill 2008
- Hartenberg The Stork 2009
- Hartenberg CWG Auction Reserve 2009
- Julien Schaal Syrah 2011
- Lomond Conebush Syrah 2009
- Mullineux Family Granite 2010
- Rustenberg Syrah 2010
- Saxenburg Select 2009
- Simonsig CWG Auction Reserve Heirloom 2010
- Stark-Condé Three Pines Syrah 2010
- StellenRust Peppergrinder's 2009

Tinta Barocca
- Sadie Family Treinspoor 2011

Red Blends
- AA Badenhorst Family 2009
- Anthonij Rupert Optima 2008
- Beaumont Ariane 2010
- Bouchard Finlayson Hannibal 2009
- Cape Chamonix Troika 2010
- Diemersdal MM Louw 2010
- Eikendal Classique 2009
- Ernie Els CWG Auction Reserve 2010
- Fable Lion's Whisker 2010
- Hartenberg The Mackenzie 2009
- Iona One Man Band 2008
- Jordan Cobblers Hill 2009
- Jordan Sophia 2009
- Meerlust Rubicon 2008
- Miles Mossop Max 2009
- Mulderbosch Faithful Hound 2010
- Rupert & Rothschild Baron Edmund 2010
- Strandveld The Navigator 2010
- Thelema Rabelais 2008
- Tokara Director's Reserve 2009
- Waterford The Jem 2009
- Woolworths Allan Mullins 'My Song' 2009

Chardonnay
- Ataraxia 2011

- De Wetshof The Site 2011
- Mulderbosch Barrel Fermented 2010
- Rustenberg Five Soldiers 2010
- The Winery of Good Hope Radford Dale 2011
- Vins d'Orrance Cuvée Anaïs 2011

Grenache Blanc
- KWV The Mentors 2011

Riesling
- Groote Post 2012

Sauvignon Blanc
- Buitenverwachting Husseys Vlei 2011
- Cape Point Reserve 2011
- Constantia Uitsig 2012
- Corder Family Cool Climate 2011
- Diemersdal 8 Rows 2012
- Quoin Rock The Nicobar Reserve 2011
- Steenberg Reserve 2011

White Blends
- Anatu Fugue 2011
- Cape Point Isliedh 2011
- Fable Jackal Bird 2011
- Mullineux Family 2011
- Sijnn 2011
- Strandveld Adamastor 2011
- The Berrio The Weathergirl 2011

Méthode Cap Classique
- Colmant Brut Reserve NV
- Colmant Brut Chardonnay NV
- Graham Beck Cuvée Clive 2007
- Simonsig CWG Auction Reserve Cuvée Chêne 2007

Dessert Wine Unfortified
- Boekenhoutskloof Noble Late Harvest 2009
- Nederburg Edelkeur 2011
- Neethlingshof Maria 2012
- Quoin Rock Simonsberg Vine Dried Sauvignon Blanc 2011
- Rudera Noble Late Harvest 2010

Dessert Wine Fortified
- Signal Hill Pineau de Ludovic NV

Port
- Boplaas Family Cape Vintage Reserve 2010
- Boplaas Family Cape Tawny Reserve 1995

Buy Now, Drink Later

Barbera
- Hofstraat 2011

Cabernet Franc
- La Petite Ferme 2011

Cabernet Sauvignon
- AntHill Entre Nous 2009
- Bartinney 2010

- Bergsig Reserve 2010
- Dalla Cia Wine & Spirit Company Classico 2010
- De Trafford 2010
- Edgebaston GS 2010

Platter's SOUTH AFRICAN WINE GUIDE
BUY NOW, DRINK LATER

Buy Now, Drink Later — Cabernet Sauvignon (continued)

- Lanzerac 2010
- Le Riche Reserve 2009
- Nuy Barrel Selection 2010
- Rainbow's End 2010
- Saxenburg 2009
- Thelema 2009
- Thelema The Mint 2010
- Waterford 2009

Durif/Petite Sirah
- Fairview 2010

Merlot
- Anura Reserve 2009
- GlenWood 2009
- Groot Constantia 2010
- Lanzerac 2010
- Nabygelegen 2011
- Nederburg Private Bin R181 2009
- Saxenburg 2009

Petit Verdot
- Raka 2010

Pinotage
- Beyerskloof Reserve 2009
- Fairview Primo 2010
- Hidden Valley 2011
- L'Avenir Grand Vin 2009
- Lanzerac 2010
- Lanzerac Pionier 2009
- Neil Ellis Vineyard Selection 2010
- Rijk's Reserve 2008
- StellenRust Cornerstone 2009
- Windmeul Reserve 2011

Pinot Noir
- Botanica 2011

Shiraz
- Andreas 2010
- Annandale 2004
- Bon Courage Inkara 2010
- Cederberg Private Cellar 2010
- De Trafford CWG Auction Reserve 2009
- Fairview Eenzaamheid 2010
- Lammershoek 2010
- Land's End 2009
- Muratie Ronnie Melck 2010
- Nederburg Private Bin R121 2009
- Neil Ellis Vineyard Selection 2010
- Nuy Barrel Selection 2010
- Post House 2009
- Saxenburg 2009
- Spice Route Flagship 2010
- Waterford Kevin Arnold 2009

Red Blends
- Anatu Family Blend 2010
- AntHill The Davey Jones Locker 2009
- Axe Hill Machado 2011

- Bartinney Elevage 2009
- Cloof Duckitt Merlot-Cabernet Sauvignon 2009
- Constantia Glen Three 2009
- Darling Cellars Sir Charles Henry Darling 2009
- Dornier Donatus 2009
- Druk My Niet Invictus 2009
- Druk My Niet T3 2009
- Ernie Els Signature 2009
- Fairview Caldera 2010
- Gabriëlskloof Five Arches 2009
- Hermanuspietersfontein Kleinboet 2009
- Hillcrest Hornfels 2010
- Hughes Family Nativo 2010
- Keermont 2009
- Klein Constantia Marlbrook 2009
- KWV Orchestra 2010
- Lammershoek Roulette 2010
- Landskroon Paul de Villiers Reserve 2010
- Lourensford Winemaker's Selection Reserve 2009
- Meinert Synchronicity 2008
- Môreson Mata Mata 2010
- Nederburg Ingenuity 2009
- Neil Ellis Aenigma 2009
- Nico van der Merwe 2007
- Overgaauw Tria Corda 2009
- Post House Missing Virgin 2010
- Raats Family Red Jasper 2010
- Reynecke Cornerstone 2010
- StellenRust Timeless 2009
- StellenRust JJ Handmade Reserve 2009
- Val de Vie Ryk Neethling 2010
- Warwick Trilogy 2009
- Waterford CWG Auction Reserve BB 2009

Chardonnay
- Eikendal 2011
- GlenWood Vigneron's Selection 2011
- Groot Constantia 2011
- Julien Schaal 2011
- KWV The Mentors 2011
- Lanzerac Mrs English 2011
- Lourensford Winemaker's Selection 2011
- Môreson Premium 2011
- Saxenburg 2010
- Windmeul Reserve 2011

Chenin Blanc
- Cederberg Private Cellar 2012
- David 2011
- De Trafford 2011
- Druk My Niet C68 2012
- Eenzaamheid 2011
- Graham Beck Bowed Head 2011
- Ken Forrester The FMC 2010
- Post House Stamp of Chenin 2011
- Remhoogte Honeybunch Reserve 2011
- Rijk's Private Cellar 2009

Buy Now, Drink Later — Chenin Blanc *(continued)*
- Sadie Family Mev Kirsten 2011
- Windmeul 2011

Riesling
- Nitida 2012
- Spioenkop 2011

Sauvignon Blanc
- Cederberg David Nieuwoudt Ghost Corner 2012
- De Grendel Koetshuis 2012
- Spioenkop 2011
- Strandveld Poffadderbos 2011
- The Berrio 2011

Semillon
- Cederberg David Nieuwoudt Ghost Corner 2011
- Fairview Oom Pagel 2011
- GlenWood Vigneron's Selection 2010

Viognier
- Lourensford Winemaker's Selection 2011

White Blends
- Anatu Family Blend 2011
- Bizoe Henriëtta 2011
- DeMorgenzon Concerto 2011
- Ernst Gouws & Co Depth 2011
- Lourensford Winemaker's Selection Reserve 2011
- Nico van der Merwe 2011

Méthode Cap Classique
- Sterhuis Blanc de Blancs 2009

Dessert Wine Unfortified
- Miles Mossop Kika 2011

Dessert Wine Fortified
- Nuy Red Muscadel 2012
- Nuy White Muscadel 2010
- Opstal Hanepoot 2011

Port
- De Krans Cape Vintage 2011
- Landskroon Cape Vintage 2008

Superquaffer of the Year

Red Blends
- Muratie Melck's Shiraz-Cabernet Sauvignon 2011

Exceptionally Drinkable & Well Priced

Pinotage
- Teubes Family Malkopbaai 2011

Red Blends
- Doolhof Cape Boar 2010
- Kanu Rifle Range NV
- Raka Spliced 2010
- Stettyn Stone Red NV

Chardonnay
- Vriesenhof Paradyskloof 2011
- Zonnebloem 2011

Chenin Blanc
- Pulpit Rock Brink Family 2012

Sauvignon Blanc
- Zorgvliet Silver Myn 2012

White Blends
- De Zoete Inval Chenin Blanc-Viognier-Semillon 2011

AA Badenhorst Family Wines

Location: Malmesbury ▪ Map: Swartland ▪ WO: Swartland/Coastal ▪ Est 2007 ▪ 1stB 2006 ▪ Tasting, sales & tours by appt ▪ Closed all pub hols ▪ Conferences ▪ Function venue for 130 people ▪ Conservation area ▪ Guest cottages ▪ Owner(s) Adi & Hein Badenhorst ▪ Winemaker(s) Adi Badenhorst (2006), with Jasper Wickens (2008) ▪ Viticulturist(s) Pierre Rossouw (Jan 1975) ▪ 60ha/23ha (cinsaut, grenache, shiraz, chard, chenin, rouss) ▪ 24,000cs own label 60% red 40% white ▪ PO Box 1177 Malmesbury 7299 ▪ adi@iafrica.com ▪ www.aabadenhorst.com ▪ S 33° 32' 38.01" E 018° 49' 7.42" ▪ **T +27 (0)82-373-5038** ▪ F +27 (0)21-794-5196

They've gone batty at Kalmoesfontein farm on Perdeberg. No, it's not (entirely) co-owner Adi Badenhorst's experiments with soleras or skin-fermented whites, nor his quip about the upgrading of their tasting room (now with running water!). We mean the bats that have taken up residence in his underground bottle maturation cellar. 'They either like the wine, or maybe the wynvlieggies (wine midges) that come after the wine,' muses Adi. 'Whatever it is, there's lots of them!' While bats may be in oversupply, grenache and cinsaut — from vines planted in 1950 and 1957 respectively — have been bottled solo for limited release. Also restricted are places at his monthly Saturday morning tastings, followed by brunch, Swartland style: Eggs Benedict, waterblommetjie quiche and boerewors. And wine.

AA Badenhorst range

★★★★☆ **CWG Auction Reserve Shatoe Ramnasgras Cinsaut** NEW Translucent & light-footed **11** charms with strawberry & floral typicity, crystal pure fruit & cheeky nudge tannin. Clever & intuitive; quite the opposite of the often oak-dominated, powerful wines on the Auction. 12.8% alcohol, large old oak.

★★★★ **Red** Shiraz-led **09** (★★★★★), with cinsaut, grenache & mourvèdre cosseted by large older oak. Seamless, restrained, understated. Similar styling to disarmingly fruity, delightfully savoury **08** — oh-so effortless, unforced. Does have a few grams of sugar.

★★★★ **White** A new SA classic: **10** (★★★★★) remarkably unshowy yet rich, flavoursome courtesy one third chenin & drop each of 8 other varieties, fermented/aged in 60 year old casks. Subtle sense of gravitas & purpose. Like smooth & complex **09**, held together by minerality. Some Voor Paardeberg grapes.

★★★★ **Funky White Wine** NV from 11 varieties inspired by 'vin jaune' (Jura, France); utilising a solera (Jerez, Spain). Differences? No flor (as yet); no fortification as in Jerez. Similarities? Nutty, salty & 'umami' savouriness; cleansing acidity, length & dry persistence. Only 500L drawn off/replaced annually. Truly funky.

Secateurs range

Red Blend ▤ ★★★★ **11** even better than **10** (★★★★). Only large old oak for shiraz-led 5-way blend (with drop pinotage); spicy, with 'oystershell' minerality & a bracing seaside rockpool freshness. Graceful 12.5% alcohol. **Rosé** ▤ ★★★★ Punchy pink **12** from cinsaut, shiraz & grenache; delivers oodles of flavour without much help from sugar. **Chenin Blanc** ▤ ★★★★ Mostly natural ferment in concrete tanks & old casks. Stonefruit, lemon appeal on soulful & versatile **12**; masterly balance. Improves on ripe & full **11** (★★★★). Like Red Blend, some Voor Paardeberg grapes. Range previously listed separately. — CvZ

Aaldering Vineyards & Wines

Location/map: Stellenbosch ▪ WO: Devon Valley ▪ Est 2004 ▪ 1stB 2007 ▪ Tasting & sales Mon-Fri 9-5 Sat 9-3 ▪ Closed all pub hols ▪ Cellar tours by appt ▪ Owner(s) Marianne & Fons Aaldering ▪ Cellarmaster(s)/winemaker(s)/viticulturist(s) Dustin Osborne (Jul 2011) ▪ 20ha/19.7ha (cab, merlot, ptage, syrah, chard, sauv) ▪ ±120t/±9,150cs own label 70% red 30% white ▪ IPW ▪ PO Box 1068 Stellenbosch 7599 ▪ estate@aaldering.co.za, dustin@aaldering.co.za ▪ www.aaldering.co.za ▪ S 33° 55' 9.81" E 018° 49' 8.14" ▪ **T +27 (0)79-526-8026**

Is this Devon Valley winery about to go to the next level? Dutch businessman Fons Aaldering enticed winemaker Dustin Osborne over from Franschhoek in mid-2011 and a new cellar (and tasting venue) was completed for the 2012 harvest. 'We focused on keeping it simple, no architectural boundaries were pushed,' says Dustin, 'but we now have a fully functional and technologically advanced facility.'

★★★★ **Shiraz** **09** (★★★★) shows red & black fruit, some fragrance, but less of the generosity & longevity of **07**. No **08**.

Pinotage ★★★ Somewhat rustic, unfocused **09** marked by very ripe, almost raisined fruit, toffee note. Also some savoury, evolved character. **Cabernet Sauvignon-Merlot** ★★★ Modest **09** shows red & black fruit, slight green edge. Medium bodied with fresh acidity, fine tannins but no great complexity. **Chardonnay** ▨

★★★ Now bottled, **11** is medium bodied, with slight citrus & vanilla notes. **Sauvignon Blanc** NEW ⓦ **12** not ready for tasting. — CE

Aan de Doorns Cellar

Location/map/WO: Worcester ▪ Est 1954 ▪ Tasting & sales Mon–Fri 8–5 Sat 10-1 ▪ Closed all pub hols ▪ Tours during harvest by appt ▪ Owner(s) 58 members ▪ Cellarmaster(s) Johan Morkel (Nov 1993) ▪ Winemaker(s) Gert van Deventer (Sept 1997) & Ryno Booysen (Jan 2007) ▪ Viticulturist(s) Pierre Snyman ▪ 1,494ha (cab, ptage, chard, chenin, cbard) ▪ ±29,000t/11,200cs own label ▪ PO Box 235 Worcester 6849 ▪ info@ aandedoorns.co.za ▪ www.aandedoorns.co.za ▪ S 33° 41'47.0" E 019° 29'26.2" ▪ **T +27 (0)23-347-2301** ▪ F +27 (0)23-347-4629

This Worcester grower-owned winery's principal customer is FirstCape, major UK supermarket supplier, in turn a conduit for news of the growing trend towards lower-alcohol wines reaching cellarmaster Johan Morkel's ears. Drinkable reds below 13% and whites below 12% are, he reckons, a challenge in this warm area, but achievable with work.

Doornroodt ☺ ★★★ Equal combo ruby cab & merlot, **10** slips down easily with cranberry/tealeaf charm. **Chenin Blanc** ☺ 🍽 ⓦ ★★★ Stonefruit & quince, **12** nicely padded & not as steely-dry as previous.

Pinotage ⓦ ★★★ Boiled sweets, caramel & star anise, **11** casual sipper with bitter trace on finish. **Blanc de Noir** ⓦ 🍽 ⓦ ★★★ Grapey & slightly sweet **11** quick-quaff, perfect curry companion. **Colombar Semi-Sweet** 🍽 ⓦ ★★ Soft & floral **12**, enjoy well chilled. **Sauvignon Blanc** 🍽 ⓦ ★★★ Shy **12** has grass & thatch, lightish 12% alcohol for lunchtime fun. **Sparkling Demi Sec** ★★★ Listed as 'Sparkling' last time. Frothy, sunset-hued **NV (12)** party starter with kiss of sweetness. **Muscat d'Alexandrie** ⓦ ⓦ ★★★★ Aromatic **10** fortified dessert, unctuous & rich yet wonderfully fresh & zippy, more layered than **09** (★★★). **Red Muscadel** ★★★★ Step-up **11** after-dinner fortified, spice, tealeaf & raisin complexity, syrupy flavours freshened by spirity bite. **Cape Ruby** ⓦ ★★★ Uncomplex port-style fortified from tinta & touriga. Dark & plummy **10** has liquorice accent, ready now. — HJ/CvZ

■ **Abbotsville** *see Org de Rac*

Abbottshill

Location: Malmesbury ▪ Map/WO: Swartland ▪ Est/1stB 2004 ▪ Tasting, sales & tours by appt ▪ BYO picnic ▪ Owner(s) Dynadeals One (Pty) Ltd ▪ Winemaker(s)/viticulturist(s) CA Bain ▪ 112ha/10ha (cab, mourv, shiraz) ▪ 625cs own label 100% red ▪ PO Box 433 Malmesbury 7299 ▪ cameron@empa.co.za ▪ S 33° 29'26.4" E 018° 39'25.3" ▪ **T +27 (0)82-492-0692**

Winemaker/viticulturist Cameron Bain has subscribed to Swartland Independent's natural winemaking code and future Abbottshill releases will feature the association's 'proudly bushvine' seal. He intends to carry the philosophy through to a méthode cap classique bubbly currently on lees, using grape concentrate instead of the more usual sugar for the dosage.

Cabernet Sauvignon ⓦ ★★★ Mid-2010 unwooded preview **09** looked promising, yet needed time to show it's best. **Shiraz** ⓦ ★★★ Rich, powerful **09** ripe blackberry & tar, high alcohol adding to sweet impression & warming (slightly bitter) end. **Shiraz-Cabernet Sauvignon** Await new, as for **Rosé**. **Bosstok Boogie** ⓦ ★★ Off-dry red blend **10** alcoholic, oaky & awkward. — DB

Abingdon Wine Estate

Location: Lions River ▪ Map/WO: KwaZulu-Natal ▪ Est 2004 ▪ 1stB 2007 ▪ Tasting room & restaurant open Sat/ Sun & pub hols 10-5 for personalised tastings & fresh country meals ▪ Weekday visits by appt ▪ Weddings & corporate functions ▪ Self-catering accommodation ▪ Owner(s) Ian & Jane Smorthwaite ▪ Winemaker(s)/viticulturist(s) Ian Smorthwaite ▪ 7ha/3ha (cab, shiraz, chard, sauv, viog) ▪ Lions River KZN Midlands ▪ jane@ abingdonestate.co.za, ian@abingdonestate.co.za ▪ www.abingdonestate.co.za ▪ S 29° 26'36.71" E 030° 09' 14.18" ▪ **T +27 (0)33-234-4335/+27 (0)83-463-8503 (Jane)** ▪ F +27 (0)86-572-6877

Lions River, between Howick and Balgowan in the KwaZulu-Natal Midlands, is not your typical wine region, but the unusualness is no impediment to commercial success for Ian and Jane Smorthwaite, whose only registered single-vineyards in the province battle to meet demand, pushing the couple 'to plant further'. Summer rainfall 'is a manageable problem and because of our high altitude (1,140m) we do not have to deal with humidity'. Terroir and climate dictate a restrained style, to show off in their expanded tasting room and restaurant.

Cabernet Sauvignon Await new vintage, as for **Syrah**, **Sauvignon Blanc**, **Viognier Unwooded** & **Chardonnay-Viognier**. **Blanc de Noir** NEW 🌣 ★★ 11 gentle savoury-toned sunset tipple. **Chardonnay** NEW 🌣 ★★ 11 demure, ripe quaffer. Creamy pear flavours with a twist of lime. **Viognier** NEW 🌣 ★★★ 11 exudes varietal perfume & plump almond/quince flavours, pithy finish invites fusion fare. Discontinued: **Rosé**. — MW

■ **Above the Mist** *see* Retief Wines

Accolade Wines South Africa

Stellenbosch ▪ Owner(s) Champ Private Equity based in Australia ▪ Winemaker(s) Bruce Jack, Gerhard Swart, Ben Jordaan & Karen Bruwer ▪ Viticulturist(s) Chris Keet ▪ 3.2m cs own label ▪ PO Box 769 Stellenbosch 7599 ▪ hannelize.mouton@accolade-wines.com ▪ www.accolade-wines.com ▪ **T +27 (0)21-882-8177** ▪ F +27 (0)21-882-8176

Owned by Champ Private Equity of Australia, Accolade Wines South Africa is part of the global drinks company, Accolade Wines, whose portfolio contains some of the world's best-known wine brands including Hardys, Houghton, Echo Falls and Banrock Station. The South African business, headquartered in Stellenbosch, is responsible for phenomenally successful entry-level brand Kumala, mid-tier Fish Hoek, and highly regarded Flagstone pinnacle wines. See separate listings.

Adoro Wines

Location: Stellenbosch ▪ WO: Western Cape ▪ Est 2005 ▪ 1stB 2004 ▪ Closed to public ▪ Owner(s) Intra International ▪ Winemaker(s) Ian Naudé (May 2005) ▪ Viticulturist(s) Lucas de Kock (Aug 2005) ▪ 40% red 60% white ▪ PO Box 982 Stellenbosch 7599 ▪ adorowines@iafrica.com ▪ www.adorowines.co.za ▪ **T +27 (0)83-630-3794** ▪ F +27 (0)21-880-1585

Adoro Wines was born of the view that blended wine — mindful of the influence of soil, grape and man — is greater than the sum of its parts. It owns no vines but has long-term relationships with grape growers in a wide variety of regions. Each parcel is vinified separately, giving vintner Ian Naudé a multitude of elements with which to build his compositions.

★★★★ **Red Blend** 🥂 Soft & accessible 06's (★★★★) overt oak previously masked the delicate red-berry fragrance we admired in **05**.

★★★★ **Sauvignon Blanc** 🥂 🍃 **10** (★★★★) was steely last time but not as penetrating as **09**, thanks to fleshy fruit & the softening effect of bottle-maturation at the cellar.

★★★★☆ **Naudé White** 🥂 🍃 Lightly oaked chenin, semillon, sauvignon, roughly equal portions. **10**'s chalk, mineral, floral & fruity elements held together by fresh acidity, & background wood.

Natural Sweet Mourvèdre 🥂 ★★★★ The brief: a made-for-cheese wine, 'neither fortified nor overly dry or sweet'. The **09** reply: jostling ripe fruit, sweetness & oak. Singular, & (atypically for this producer) unsubtle. — DS

Aeternitas Wines

Location: Strand ▪ Map: Helderberg ▪ WO: Swartland ▪ Est 2005 ▪ 1stB 2007 ▪ Tasting by appt ▪ Closed all pub hols ▪ Owner(s) Johan & Michelle Grimbeek ▪ Cellarmaster(s)/winemaker(s) Johan Grimbeek (Jan 2002) ▪ Viticulturist(s) Various ▪ 4t/320cs own label 50% red 45% white 5% rosé + 4,000cs for clients ▪ 21 Livingstone Street, Strand 7140 ▪ aeternitaswines@telkomsa.net ▪ S 34° 6' 3.3" E 018° 49' 35.6" ▪ **T +27 (0)82-714-2095**

The demands of his day job as Kanu winemaker mean that Johan Grimbeek and wife Michelle have had to mark time with their own brand, not crushing again in 2012. With a Syrah in barrel, they hope to be back as suburban vintners in 2013.

Syrah ✓ ★★★★ Delectable 08 is plush & utterly moreish. Heaped with sweet mulberry fruit, it has poise & finesse, despite 15% alcohol. Half-new oak 2 years, & wild ferment, like **07** (★★★★). **Blanc** 🥂 🍃 🌣 ★★★★ **10** billows summer fruit, shows amazing balance considering ripeness, oak & 14% alcohol. Ex chenin. — DS

■ **A Few Good Men** *see* Riebeek Cellars
■ **Africa** *see* Waterstone Wines
■ **Africa Five** *see* Waterstone Wines
■ **African Dawn** *see* Rooiberg Winery
■ **African Gold** *see* Old Bridge Wines
■ **African Lizard** *see* Waterstone Wines

African Pride Wines

Location: Constantia ▪ WO: Western Cape/Coastal ▪ Est/1stB 2002 ▪ Closed to public ▪ Owner(s) Afrifresh Group ▪ Winemaker(s) Mike Graham (May 2002) ▪ 240,000cs ▪ PO Box 518 Constantia 7848 ▪ info@ africanpridewines.co.za ▪ www.africanpridewines.co.za ▪ **T +27 (0)21-887-2204** ▪ F +27 (0)21-887-2204

Now into its second decade in the wine export business, and markets in more than 30 countries, African Pride is still expanding (over 240,000 cases made annually) and adding new outlets, including Latvia, Estonia and Turkey. Stalwart Mike Graham's wines can also be enjoyed on Etihad Airways and Windstar cruise liners.

Lady Anne Barnard range

★★★★ **Cabernet Sauvignon** ✓ ⊘ **11** (★★★☆) a tad off last-tasted **08**, bold & rustic with intense cassis & dried herb flavours, chunky tannins & dry finish. Stellenbosch vines.

★★★★ **Sauvignon Blanc** ⊕ ⊘ Serious cooler-climate expression, **10** vibrant capsicum & tropical fruit in luscious (lees-influenced) & textured frame last time. Firm & generous. From Darling vines.

Syrah ⊘ ★★★ **11** lacks luscious concentration of previous, offers vibrant & spicy dark berries but essentially an easy-drinker. WO Coastal.

Footprint range

Merlot-Pinotage ▤ ⊘ ★★★ Unoaked **12** a notch up, ripe, more body; fun & fruity, a summer sipper.
Chenin Blanc-Semillon ⊕ ▤ ⊘ ★★ Fruity & zippy **11** last edition noted as perfect for picnics.

Cape Grace Sugarbird range

Pinotage ▤ ⊘ ★★ Unoaked, as next, perky **11** with understated dry plum flavours. **Shiraz** ▤ ⊘ ★★☆ Improved **11** offers ripe dark fruit & fynbos, smoky end. **Chenin Blanc** ▤ ⊘ ★★ Summery, light & fruity **11**, easy sipper.

Footprint Long Walk NEW

Cabernet Sauvignon ☺ ⊘ ★★★ Berry fruit & fresh herb appeal, unoaked (as all in this range) **11** firm tannins plumped by juicy fruit.

Merlot ⊘ ★★ Less complex **11**, upfront fruit yet a dry, very firm finish. **Shiraz** ⊘ ★★ Juicy-fruity **11** is ripe but firm, smoky & brambly. Perfect for the braai. **Pinotage Rosé** ▤ ⊘ ★★ **12** bright pink, fruit-shy & dry. **Chardonnay** ⊘ ★★★ Citrus & ripe yellow peaches, zesty & mouthfilling, **12** well structured & balanced for no-worries sipping. **Sauvignon Blanc** ⊘ ★★★ Fragrant tropical fruit aromas on **12**, lean & dry finish.

Footprint Impression range
Discontinued: **Shiraz-Mourvédre-Viognier**, **Viognier**. — WB

■ **African Roots** *see* Seven Sisters
■ **African Star** *see* Stellar Winery

African Terroir

Location: Paarl ▪ Map: Paarl & Wellington ▪ WO: Western Cape/Paarl/Elgin ▪ Est/1stB 1991 ▪ Tasting, sales & cellar tours Mon-Fri 8.30-4 strictly by appt ▪ Closed all pub hols ▪ Conferences ▪ Functions ▪ Conservation area ▪ Owner(s) Jacques Germanier ▪ Winemaker(s) Alain Cajeux (Nov 2011), with Marco Swartz (Feb 2009) ▪ Viticulturist(s) Johar Barnard (Nov 2009) ▪ 118ha/75ha (cab, merlot, ptage, shiraz, chard, cbard, sauv, viog) ▪ 540t ▪ Brands for clients Hunting Owl (Woolworths), Mwitu (USA), to name a few ▪ ISO 22000, BWI, BRC, Fairtrade, FFF, FOA, HACCP, IPW, Organic ▪ PO Box 2029 Windmeul Paarl 7630 ▪ office@african-terroir.co.za ▪ www.african-terroir.co.za ▪ S 33° 37' 1.8" E 018° 50' 38.4" ▪ **T +27 (0)21-869-8103 (Terrance)** ▪ F +27 (0)21-869-8104

This winery on the farm Sonop near Paarl is Swiss owned but it incorporates the 'spirit of Africa' – compassion for the environment and those who inhabit it – into everything it does. Hence its commitment to organic grape growing and its upliftment project, the Winds of Change/Communal Property Association. Previously focused on the international market, it's striving to share more of its spirit locally.

Azania range

Shiraz ★★★ Some oak on dark plum-fruited **11** adds form, spice. Not ripe/malty like previous but step up. **Sauvignon Blanc** NEW ★★★ Food-friendly **11** unassuming, with quiet grass & mineral undertones. Balanced; light oaking extends the finish.

Big Five range

Cabernet Sauvignon ⓘ ★★★ Lush red berries, firm tannin on **10**. **Pinotage** ⓘ ★★ **10** strawberry-toned sipper. **Shiraz** ⓘ ★★ Shy **10** has dusty red fruit, is tad bitter. **Chardonnay** ⓘ ★★★ Brisk **10** has baked apple nuance. **Sauvignon Blanc** ⓘ ★★ Pear drop **10** has lunchtime-friendly 12% alcohol.

Lo Splendore del Sole NEW

Cabernet Sauvignon 🌣 ★★★ Generously fruited **11** has freshness, light tannins. From Perdeberg vines, as next. **Viognier** ★★★ **12** faint almonds, boiled sweets & fine butter note from brush oak.

Out of Africa range

> **Chardonnay** ☺ ★★★ Attractive nut & lemon bouquet on zingy, lightly oaked & satisfying **12** sipper.

Cabernet Sauvignon ⓘ ★★★ Unoaked **11**, ex-tank mid-2011, strawberry toned with affable grip. WO Elgin. **Shiraz** 🗐 ★★ **11** comfortingly familiar: savoury, ripe & very gruff. **Sauvignon Blanc** Not tasted.

Sonop Organic range

Cabernet Sauvignon ⓘ 🌣 ⍟ ★★★ Juicy, red berry-nuanced **11** unoaked, like all reds in range, for immediate enjoyment. **Merlot** ⓘ 🌣 ⍟ ★★ Demure **11** zesty acidity, tad stalky end. **Pinotage** ⓘ 🌣 ⍟ ★★ Lemony acidity on strawberry-infused **10**. **Shiraz** ⓘ 🌣 ⍟ ★★★ Appealing tealeaf & cranberry aromas, firm tannins on unassuming **10**. **Viognier-Merlot Rosé** ⓘ 🗐 🌣 ⍟ ★ Perfumed **10** lacks verve. **Chardonnay** ⓘ 🌣 ⍟ ★★★ **10** wallet-friendly easy drinker. **Sauvignon Blanc** ⓘ 🌣 ⍟ ★★ **10** is zesty, with khaki bush notes. WO Paarl, as for all. **Viognier** ⓘ 🌣 ⍟ ★★★ Best-in-line-up **11** engaging orange & apricot, good weight & length.

Tribal range

Cabernet Sauvignon NEW 🗐 ⍟ ★★ **11** blueberry-flavoured, just-dry quaffer with tannic tug. As all reds below, unoaked. **Merlot** 🗐 ⍟ ★★ New bottling of **11**, preview is fruity with rustic tannins. **Pinotage** 🗐 ⍟ ★★ **11**'s firm tannin softened by some sugar. **Shiraz** NEW 🗐 ⍟ ★★ Nice sweet red fruit, warm bread character on **11**. **Dry Red** ⓘ Unwooded NV ex cinsaut, pinotage & shiraz. **Semi Dry Red** NEW 🗐 ⍟ ★★ **11** red berry, lowish 12% alcohol. **Rosé** Await next. **Chardonnay** NEW 🗐 ⍟ ★★ Lightly wooded **11** tank sample's light fruit still meshing with oak mid-2012. **Chenin Blanc** NEW 🗐 ⍟ ★★ Khaki bush aroma on sweet-fruited **11** preview. **Sauvignon Blanc** NEW 🗐 ⍟ ★★ **11** ex-tank pungent, almost sweaty; brief & pithy. **Dry White** 🗐 ★★ Muscat high notes on fresh NV sipper. Serve well chilled. **Sauvignon Blanc-Colombard Fairtrade** ⓘ ★★ Ex tank, last-tasted **10** brisk, light & grassy. **Chenin Blanc-Colombar** ⓘ ★ Reticent **10** previewed mid-2011. **African White** NEW ★★ Grapey, bright & breezy summer NV. **Semi Dry White** NEW 🗐 ⍟ ★★ Faintly floral, gently sweet NV. **Sparkling Rosé Dry** ⓘ Await next, as for **Sparkling White Dry** & **Sparkling Semi-Sweet**.

Winds of Change Fairtrade Organic range

Cabernet Sauvignon ⓘ 🌣 ★★★ **10** has spice highlights to red fruit. WO W Cape for all unless noted. **Merlot** ⓘ 🌣 ★★ **10**'s soft plums offset by firm tannins. **Pinotage** ⓘ 🌣 ★★ Lemon acidity adds zest to strawberry flavours in **10**. **Shiraz** ⓘ 🌣 ★★★ Scrub & sour cherry notes, firm tannins on **10**. **Pinotage-Shiraz** ⍟ 🌣 ★★★ Friendly **11** supple & juicy, slips down easily. **Chardonnay** 🌣 ⍟ ★★ New bottling of **11** is nutty, some woody notes, brief. **Sauvignon Blanc** ⓘ 🌣 ★★ Grassy **10** tangy & dry. **Chardonnay-Viognier** ⓘ 🌣 ⍟ ★ Last edition, fragrant **11** preview had bold, plump palate. WO Paarl. **Sparkling Cabernet Sauvignon Rosé** ⓘ 🌣 ★★ NV sparkler an appealing celebration package. — CvZ

African Wines & Spirits

Cape Town ▪ Est 1999 ▪ Closed to public ▪ Owner(s) Edward Snell & Co ▪ Directors D Asherson, DV Hooper, IV Hooper, JM Pousson & CC Weeden ▪ 40% red 60% white ▪ PO Box 318 Paarden Eiland ▪ chrisw@esnell.co.za ▪ T +27 (0)21-506-2600 ▪ F +27 (0)21-510-4560 / +27 (0)86-682-4922

This wholesaling and marketing company is owned by Edward Snell & Co, and responsible for the separately listed good-value range, Craighall, among others.

■ **Agterkliphoogte** *see* Wandsbeck Wyne Koöp Bpk

Agterplaas Wines

Location: Stellenbosch ▪ WO: Western Cape/Stellenbosch ▪ 1stB 2003 ▪ Tasting by appt ▪ Owner(s)/ winemaker(s) James Basson ▪ 2t/150cs own label 60% red 40% white ▪ PO Box 863 Stellenbosch 7599 ▪ agterplaas@adept.co.za ▪ **T** +27 (0)21-886-5446 ▪ F +27 (0)21-886-5446

Having started out making wines in his backyard (agterplaas), architectural designer James Basson once had dreams of building his own winery. But he's now perfectly happy to be renting cellar space at Lievland Estate: 'My production is still very small so it's cheaper and much more convenient to rent.'

Cabernet Sauvignon ★★★★ Fruit-forward & rounded **10**, mocha & blackberry juiciness, friendly ripe tannins on finish. **Agterplaas ④ 🍴 ★★★** Mainly cab & merlot, dashes cab franc, malbec & petit verdot. When last tasted, **06** savoury plum spice, silky tannin & integrated oak. **Chenin Blanc ④ ★★★** Oatmeal & apricot on toasty backing of wooded **10**. Good length & structure, tangy acidity adds freshness. — DB

Akkerdal Wine Estate

Location/map/WO: Franschhoek ▪ Est 2000 ▪ 1stB 2001 ▪ Tasting & sales Mon-Fri 10-4 ▪ Fee R20pp ▪ Closed all pub hols ▪ Akkerdal self-catering chalet (see Accommodation section) ▪ Owner(s)/cellarmaster(s)/ winemaker(s) Pieter Hanekom ▪ Viticulturist(s) Pieter Hanekom, advised by Eben Archer, Bennie Liebenberg & Dawid Saayman ▪ 18ha (barbera, cab f, carignan, durif, grenache, malbec, merlot, mourv, p verdot, roobernet, shiraz, tannat, tempranillo, chard, nouvelle, sauv, sem, viog) ▪ 3,000cs own label 95% red 4% white 1% rosé ▪ IPW ▪ PO Box 36 La Motte 7691 ▪ wine@akkerdal.co.za ▪ www.akkerdal.co.za ▪ S 33° 52' 50.9" E 019° 3' 3.8" ▪ **T** +27 (0)21-876-3481 ▪ F +27 (0)21-876-3189

Pieter Hanekom, owner and winemaker at this small Franschhoek property, reports some new additions to the viticultural team, namely his two Jack Russells and two Alsatians. They've learnt to taste grapes for phenolic ripeness, and so impressed with their acuity is Hanekom that he's credited them as 'wine masters' on the back label of new red blend TDT 2010.

Limited Release range NEW
★★★★ Kallie's Dream 📖 Shiraz-led blend, rest mourvèdre, grenache, carignan, viognier. Pure & very expressive **10** with red fruit, fynbos & some toasty oak. Permeated with fresh acidity & fine spicy tannins.
TDT 📖 ★★★★ Big & brooding **10** is a singular blend of near equal tempranillo & durif, 26% tannat. Lots of dark fruit, toasty oak but bright acidity lends balance.

Akkerdal range
★★★★ Wild Boar ④ 09 conforms to no conventional template, with 5 different varieties inc roobernet & tempranillo. Fruit driven but not facile, with fresh acidity, dry finish. No **07**, **08**.
Petit Noir ④ 📖 ★★★ Malbec-led **10** shows dark fruit, herbal note on nose & palate. Rustic but not without charm. **Passion Red ④ ★★★★** Intriguing 5-way, shiraz-led **08** shows red fruit & spice on palate. Medium bodied with well-judged oak. **Kallie's Dream Red ④ ★★★** **06** blend shiraz, mourvèdre, merlot, malbec. Sweet fruited, with serious oak when last tasted. **Sauvignon Blanc ④ ★★** **10** understated herbal quality, gentle acidity last edition. — CE

Akkerdraai

Location/map/WO: Stellenbosch ▪ Est 1956 ▪ 1stB 2007 ▪ Tasting Mon-Fri 9-5 Sat 9-12:30 ▪ Closed Easter Fri-Mon, Dec 25 & Jan 1 ▪ Fee R20, waived on purchase ▪ Walks/hikes ▪ Owner(s)/cellarmaster(s) Salie de Swardt ▪ Winemaker(s) Marius Malan (consultant), with Salie de Swardt (both Jan 2004) ▪ Viticulturist(s) Marius Malan (Jan 2004, consultant) ▪ 1.75ha (cab) ▪ 12t 100% red ▪ PO Box 22 Lynedoch 7603 ▪ saliedes@mweb.co.za ▪ S 33° 59' 53.52" E 018° 49' 50.94" ▪ **T** +27 (0)21-881-3861/+27 (0)83-264-1463 ▪ F +27 (0)21-881-3861

Time will tell if the 2009 cabernet from this boutique winery on Stellenbosch's Annandale Road lives up to the vintage hype. But retired media man Salie de

Swardt is happy for the wine to rest quietly in barrel until he and consultant winemaker Marius Malan feel it's ready for release.

★★★★ **Cabernet Sauvignon** Fynbos whiff to richly fruited **08** last time, with blackcurrant, white pepper, cigarbox complexity. Sleek & lithe, well-judged oak (30% new) provided firm grip. — FM

■ **Alexanderfontein** *see Ormonde Private Cellar*

AlexKia Estate

Location/WO: Robertson ▪ Est 2004 ▪ 1stB 2006 ▪ Tasting by appt at La Verne Wine Boutique, Robertson ▪ Owner(s) Carla Maestroni ▪ Winemaker(s) André van Dyk (Rooiberg) ▪ ±90ha/7ha (cab, chard) ▪ ±70t/ 5,000cs own label 50% red 50% white + 4,000cs for clients ▪ PO Box 101 Robertson 6705 ▪ franco@alexkia. co.za ▪ www.alexkia.co.za ▪ **T +27 (0)82-575-9578, +27 (0)82-783-9825**

'A marriage of Mediterranean heritage and modern taste' is how Franco and Carla Maestroni describe their wine and rosemary farm — named after granddaughters Alexandra and Chiara — in Robertson's Eilandia Valley. Designed by renowned architect Revel Fox, the homestead's winged roof was inspired by resident swooping African Black Swifts, also featured on the label.

Alexandra Cabernet Sauvignon This & **Merlot Reserve** not tasted. **Chiara Chardonnay** ★★★ Much-improved **11** acacia & thatch bouquet, unoaked with zesty acidity for seafood. — JP/CvZ

Alheit Vineyards NEW

Location: Hermanus ▪ Map: Elgin, Walker Bay & Bot River ▪ WO: Western Cape ▪ Est 2010 ▪ 1stB 2011 ▪ Tasting by appt only ▪ Owner(s)/winemaker(s) Chris & Suzaan Alheit ▪ Cellarmaster(s) Chris Alheit ▪ 10.5t/410cs own label 100% white ▪ PO Box 711 Hermanus 7200 ▪ chris@alheitvineyards.co.za ▪ www.alheitvineyards.co.za ▪ S 34° 20' 35.56" E 019° 18' 11.30" ▪ **T +27 (0)83-274-6860**

They met while studying oenology in Stellenbosch, fell in love, married, and now Chris and Suzaan Alheit are vinifying on their friends Hans and Mary-Anne Evenhuis's Hemelrand property in Walker Bay. 'Our entire business revolves around blocks that are old, unique and unusual,' says Chris. 'The youngest represented in our Cartology is 26 years old, the oldest 75.' Well travelled (Napa, Western Australia, Clare, St Emilion, Mosel), they came home with 'a tremendous respect for the great wines of Europe'. Lessons learnt have everything to do with their ambition to make wine that is authentically 'Cape' and cannot be mimicked.

★★★★★ **Cartology** Our unofficial Newcomer of the Year, **11** special & exciting in every way: provenance of old chenin bushvines (& dash semillon) ex 5 far-flung sites; natural older-barrel ferment; stylish extrinsics (wax-sealed bottle, thoughtful website); oxidative melt-in-mouth opulence. Place your order today! — FM/GdB

Alkmaar Boutique Vineyard

Location/WO: Wellington ▪ Map: Paarl & Wellington ▪ Est 2001 ▪ 1stB 2005 ▪ Tasting & sales Mon-Fri 10-4 Sat 10-2 ▪ Closed all religious pub hols ▪ Cellar tours by appt ▪ Walks (part of Wellington Wine Walk) ▪ Owner(s) Bouwer & Janet Nell ▪ Winemaker(s) Pieter-Niel Rossouw (Jan 2010, consultant), with Dawid Futhwa (Jan 2010) ▪ Viticulturist(s) Dawid Futhwa (Jan 2003) ▪ 9.9ha (cab, merlot, mourv, p verdot, ptage, shiraz, chard, viog) ▪ 50t/380cs own label 83% red 17% white + 12,000L bulk ▪ PO Box 1273 Blouvlei Road Wellington 7654 ▪ janet@alkmaarwines. co.za ▪ www.alkmaarwines.co.za ▪ S 33° 39' 37.98" E 019° 1' 55.14" ▪ **T +27 (0)21-873-0191**

This Wellington property, originally a 19th century school, was acquired by current owners Bouwer and Janet Nell ten years ago and a process of renewal was begun. Vineyards were extended, the original homestead (now the family home) and some of the other older buildings converted into a working cellar — 2010 the first vintage to be made entirely onsite.

The Old School Master ★★★ Bordeaux-style red **10** ultra-ripe to the point of jammy, also slightly minty, finishes a little short. **The Old School Mistress** NEW ★★★★ Well-assembled Rhône-style red, **10** is medium bodied with red fruit & touch of spice, fresh acidity & fine tannins. **The Old School Reunion** ★★★ Shy, unevolved **10** unoaked chardonnay with citrus flavour, bright acidity, appealing if not hugely complex. — CE

Allée Bleue Wines

Location/map: Franschhoek ▪ WO: Franschhoek/Walker Bay/Coastal/Western Cape/Piekenierskloof/ Stellenbosch ▪ Est 1690 ▪ 1stB 2001 ▪ Tasting & sales Mon-Fri 9-5 Sat 10-5 Sun 10-4 ▪ Fee R20/4 wines ▪ Closed Good Fri ▪ Cellar tours by appt ▪ Bistro Allée Bleue (see Restaurants section) ▪ Wine tasting courtyard with kiddies corner, light lunches in summer ▪ Picnics — booking required ▪ Jungle gym ▪ Tour groups by appt ▪ Gifts ▪ Farm produce ▪ Conferences ▪ Weddings ▪ Allée Bleue Kendall Cottage & Manor House (see Accommodation section) ▪ Owner(s) DAUPHIN Entwicklungs-und Beteiligungs GMH (Germany) ▪ Winemaker(s) Van Zyl du Toit (Jul 2009) ▪ Viticulturist(s) Douw Willemse (Sep 2008) ▪ 135ha/30ha (cab, merlot, ptage, pinot, shiraz, chard, chenin, sauv, viog) ▪ 380t/18,000cs own label 34.5% red 55% white 5% rosé 5% MCC 0.5% fortified ▪ IPW ▪ PO Box 100 Groot Drakenstein 7680 ▪ info@alleebleue.com ▪ www.alleebleue.com ▪ S 33° 51' 29.0" E 018° 59' 12.9" ▪ **T +27 (0)21-874-1021** ▪ F +27 (0)21-874-1850

The highlight of the past year for winemaker Van Zyl du Toit was becoming a father again. 'In the middle of harvest!' he laughs. It has been a very busy time for the German-owned Franschhoek property. 'Exports are doing well and our new personal approach in local sales is starting to bear fruit. Our premium wines are performing well in competitions and that also aids sales. Wine keeps us sane and it makes one healthy and happy — and it is cheaper than a visit to the doctor!'

Allée Bleue range

★★★★ **Pinotage** Juicy plums, berries & lively spice, punchy **09** bursts with luscious flavour through to a firm but amenable conclusion. WO Piekenierskloof.

★★★★ **L'Amour Toujours** Red flagship. Cab, merlot & cab franc blend **09** has intense ripe berry flavours, super oak balance & structure. Dollop of grenache adds an earthy spice lift. WO Coastal, like Starlette Rouge.

★★★★ **Sauvignon Blanc** ✓ 🍷 **12** from Walker Bay, like **10**, showing similar tropical, herbal & mineral notes, lipsmacking acidity & silky mouthfeel plumped by some sugar. **11** sold out untasted.

★★★★ **Isabeau** 🍷 Flagship white is a perfumed blend of chardonnay, semillon & viognier. **11** rich, silky mouthfeel with creamy texture, a livening citrus tang in the dry finish. WO W Cape.

Shiraz ⓘ 🍷 ★★★☆ Fruit-driven **10** offers ripe dark berries & spice in rich & balanced offering. **Cabernet Sauvignon-Merlot** ✓ ★★★★ Blueberry, chocolate & plum complement harmonious oaking, **10** a balanced & versatile food/solo offering from Stellenbosch grapes. **Chenin Blanc** 🍷 Await next. **Brut Rosé Méthode Cap Classique** ★★★★ Dry bottle-fermented sparkling from pinotage, chenin & pinot noir. **11** onionskin hue with strawberry & green apple, fine creamy mousse & zesty finish. Franschhoek & Walker Bay vines. **Brut Méthode Cap Classique** NEW ★★★★ Creamy-dry bubbly **10** from pinot & chardonnay with Golden Delicious apple & vanilla biscuit flavours. WO Walker Bay. **Cape Ruby** 🍷 ★★★ Port-style **11** from pinotage is light & full-fruited, with a spirited finish. Discontinued: **Cabernet Sauvignon.**

Starlette range

Pinotage ☺ 🍷 🍷 ★★★ Easy-drinking **11**, juicy, ripe cherry, strawberry & spice balanced by soft tannins. **Rouge** ☺ ★★★ Cab, merlot & shiraz blend for early consumption. Bright berries & spice, **10** harmonises soft tannins & fresh acidity. **Rosé** ☺ 🍷 🍷 ★★★ Strawberry & spice on bright pink **12**, from shiraz & sauvignon. Just off-dry, vivacious & delightful. **Blanc** ☺ 🍷 🍷 ★★★ Tropical fruit salad aromas leap out the glass; just-dry **12** sauvignon & chenin mix is bright & focused. Perfect summer sipper. — WB

Allegria Vineyards

Location/map: Stellenbosch ▪ WO: Polkadraai Hills ▪ Est 2005 ▪ 1stB 2010 ▪ Tasting by appt ▪ Conferences ▪ Allegria Guest House ▪ Owner(s) Jan & Annemarie Zevenbergen ▪ Winemaker(s) Louis Nel (Nov 2009, consultant) ▪ Viticulturist(s) Francois Hanekom (Sep 2009, consultant) ▪ 2ha/0.5ha (shiraz) ▪ ±3,500kg/±80cs own label 100% red ▪ PO Box 24 Vlottenburg 7604 ▪ wine@allegria.co.za ▪ www.allegriavineyards.co.za ▪ S 33° 57' 29.79" E 018° 45' 31.63" ▪ **T +27 (0)21-881-3389** ▪ F +27 (0)21-881-3210

Jan and Annemarie Zevenbergen arrived from Holland in 2003 and bought this Stellenbosch smallholding, renovating its residence to become a guest house and, two years later, replacing blueberry crops with vines. With soils identified as perfect for shiraz, and consultant viticulturist Francois Hanekom and winemaker Louis Nel on board, 2010 saw their first 'modest' harvest and Louis's maiden two-barrel vintage. He's excited to get 'such good flavours from a vineyard so young'. To taste it, check into their guest house or find it on a select wine list.

★★★★ **Shiraz** From tiny block next to property's guest house. **11** preview younger version of opulently spiced yet still elegant **10**; both with mineral thread & pleasing savouriness supported by older oak. — WB/IM

Allesverloren

Location: Riebeek West ▪ Map/WO: Swartland ▪ Est 1704 ▪ Tasting & sales Mon-Fri 8.30–5 Sat 8.30–2 ▪ Fee charged only for groups of 10 & more R15pp ▪ Closed Easter Fri/Mon, Dec 25 & Jan 1 ▪ Cellar tours by appt ▪ Pleasant Pheasant Restaurant Tue 10.30-3 Wed-Sat 9-3 & 6-10 Sun 9-4 ▪ Facilities for children ▪ Conferences ▪ Weddings/functions ▪ Owner(s) Malan Boerdery Trust ▪ Cellarmaster(s) Danie Malan (Nov 1987) ▪ Winemaker(s) Danie Malan (Nov 1987), with Armand Lacomme (Aug 2012) ▪ 227ha/187ha (cab, shiraz & various port varieties) ▪ 50,000cs own label 100% red ▪ PO Box 23 Riebeek West 7306 ▪ info@allesverloren.co.za ▪ www.allesverloren.co.za ▪ S 33° 21'32.5" E 018° 52'24.1" ▪ **T +27 (0)22-461-2320** ▪ F +27 (0)22-461-2444

Allesverloren, in the Malan family since 1872, has long seen the cultivation of red varieties, in particular those associated with port. As of 2012, however, the cellar's celebrated fortified offering is no longer called 'port' in line with EU regulations and is now labelled 'Fine Old Vintage'. Cellarmaster Danie Malan is, if anything, delighted by this: 'I've always considered what we make here a unique product and could see no reason why it should have, through the name, an association with a product from another country.'

★★★★ **Shiraz** ⓐ Understated **10**, berries, vanilla & fynbos; medium bodied & well balanced with juicy fruit, fresh acidity & fine tannins.

★★★★☆ **Fine Old Vintage** Was 'Port'. **08** (★★★★) mainly tinta, souzão, & rare pontac, spiritous on the nose; rather light bodied, with red & black fruit, some Xmas pudding spice & too much warmth on finish. Not as complex as **07**.

Cabernet Sauvignon ★★★ **10** is rich & full but lacks focus & purity as result of slightly raisined fruit, drying on finish. **Tinta Barocca** ★★★ **10** lightly fruity, hint of spice but rather plain, bare boned. **Touriga Nacional** ★★★ Straightforward **10** shows dark fruit, firm tannins, tart acidity. **Danie's Backyard Blend** NEW ★★★ Tinta-based combo, **10** features funky packaging & is priced to go. Fresh & dry, but slightly dilute. — CE

Alluvia Winery & Private Residence Club

Location/map: Stellenbosch ▪ WO: Banghoek/Stellenbosch ▪ Est 2002 ▪ 1stB 2005 ▪ Tasting & sales daily 9-5 ▪ Fee R30 ▪ Closed Good Fri & Dec 25 ▪ Cellar tours by appt ▪ Two 5-star self-catering houses & five 4-star suites ▪ Breakfast & picnic baskets for stay-over guests ▪ Day & estate spa ▪ Facilities for children ▪ Tour groups ▪ Gift shop ▪ BYO picnic ▪ Conferences ▪ Hiking & mountain biking trails ▪ Helipad ▪ Fly fishing ▪ PGA golf tee & green ▪ Owner(s) Brugman family ▪ Cellarmaster(s) Delarey Brugman ▪ Winemaker(s) Delarey Brugman & Neil Moorhouse ▪ Viticulturist(s) Bennie Booysen (Jan 2009, consultant) ▪ 11ha/7ha (cabs s/f, sauv) ▪ 30t/1,800cs own label 85% red 10% white 5% straw wine ▪ PO Box 6365 Uniedal 7612 ▪ wine@alluvia.co.za ▪ www.alluvia.co.za ▪ S 33° 55'4.7" E 018° 55'37.1" ▪ **T +27 (0)21-885-1661** ▪ F +27 (0)21-885-2064

Learning in 2002 that his wife Sandie was expecting twin girls, co-owner/cellarmaster Delarey Brugman decided to create a legacy and safe, nurturing environment for them, one of integrity and community involvement — and Alluvia is the result. The wines are named after family members and the residence club has attracted like-minded people. The Give Me A Chance range funds a social upliftment programme.

Princess range

★★★★ **Ilka Cabernet Sauvignon** Riveting fruit intensity in succulent berry-rich **10**. Masterly oaking (18 months new French) adds structure & spice but no edges. Delicious now or age 3-4 years. **09** sold out untasted.

★★★★ **Lisa Vineyard Cabernet Franc** One of very few varietal bottlings. Again offers varietal purity, **10** with tobacco, brambleberry & herbal notes. Supported by a svelte body & polished tannins.

★★★★ **Ilka Sauvignon Blanc** Ex-tank **12** (★★★★) shows house-style yellow apple & melon, palate less focused than **11**. Could rate better once bottled.

Queen range

★★★★ **Sandie Viognier Straw Wine** ⓐ Tasted from barrel, **10** (★★★★★) is richer than **09**, reflects apricot, peach & quince preserves — & barley sugar. Syrupy in its richness, it has an intriguing olive oil note at the end. Superb. 375 ml. WO Stellenbosch for this range & next.

Give Me A Chance range

Red Blend ⊕ 🍽 ★★★ Last was easy-drinking **07** mix Bordeaux varieties; packed with red & black berries, dusty note from year oak-staving. **Sauvignon Blanc** 🍽 Await next. — CR

■ **Almara** *see Southern Sky Wines*

Almenkerk Wine Estate

Location/WO: Elgin ▪ Map: Elgin, Walker Bay & Bot River ▪ Est 2004 ▪ 1stB 2009 ▪ Tasting, sales & cellar tours Wed-Sun 10-4 ▪ Open pub hols except on Mon/Tue ▪ Meals/picnics by prior booking (min 20 pax) or BYO picnic ▪ Walking/hiking trails ▪ Conservation area ▪ Heliport ▪ Boules court ▪ Owner(s) Van Almenkerk family ▪ Cellarmaster(s) Joris van Almenkerk ▪ Winemaker(s) Joris van Almenkerk, with Danver van Wyk (Feb 2009) ▪ Viticulturist(s) Neil de Beer (May 2010) & Kevin Watt (consultant) ▪ 104.2ha/15ha (cabs s/f, malbec, merlot, mourv, p verdot, shiraz, chard, sauv, viog) ▪ 100t/800cs own label 65% red 30% white 5% rosé ▪ Brands for clients: De Mikke Patron ▪ BWI ▪ PO Box 1129 Grabouw 7160 ▪ info@almenkerk.co.za ▪ www.almenkerk.co.za ▪ S 34° 12′ 55″ E 019° 01′ 57″ ▪ **T +27 (0)21-848-9844** ▪ F +27 (0)86-523-0877

The young and energetic cellarmaster of this showpiece Elgin winery, Joris van Almenkerk, is determined to take the area's reputation — already high courtesy the established producers — into the stratosphere. Every activity is geared to raising the bar: experimentation in the vineyards and cellar, adding new labels to the portfolio, and opening on Sundays to boost the flow of visitors. As a result, sales are rising and the trophy cabinet is filling up with awards.

Almenkerk Estate range

★★★★ **Sauvignon Blanc** 🍽 🔲 **11** (★★★) shares Elgin's typical 'wet stone' minerality with understated **10**, but also has a racy lemon freshness, leesy-nutty overlay that makes it a food wine.

Chardonnay 🔲 ★★★★ Pale straw hue on step-up **11** belies intensity, complexity, of this barrel-fermented offering. Vanilla, buttery oak currently in the fore, but there's poise, grace waiting in the wings. Like **10** (★★★★), brisk acidity refreshes few grams sugar.

Lace range

Red Blend 🍽 🔲 ★★★ **09** Bordeaux red tasted last edition as unlabelled wine never released, thus **10** 'official' maiden. Delivers berry-infused sipping courtesy mainly shiraz; seamless & smooth for everyday pleasure. **Rosé** NEW 🍽 🔲 ★★★ **11** From early-picked cab (60%) & barrel-fermented chardonnay. Attractive **11** focuses more on freshness & texture than overt fruitiness. **White** NEW 🔲 ★★★ **11** 100% sauvignon, but a less complex vinification & assembly than senior version. **11** austere, with intriguing earth, nutty notes. — CvZ

■ **Alta Casa** *see Darling Cellars*

Alto Wine Estate

Location/map/WO: Stellenbosch ▪ Est 1693 ▪ 1stB 1921 ▪ Tasting & sales Mon-Fri 9–5 Sat/Sun10–4 ▪ Fee R10 wine tasting/R10 port tasting ▪ Closed Good Fri & Dec 25 ▪ Pâté & wine pairing R50pp, advance booking required ▪ Hiking trail ▪ Owner(s) Lusan Premium Wines ▪ Cellarmaster(s)/winemaker(s) Schalk van der Westhuizen (Jun 2000) ▪ Viticulturist(s) Schalk van der Westhuizen & Danie van Zyl ▪ 191ha/93ha (cabs s/f, merlot, shiraz) ▪ 800t/50,000cs own label 100% red ▪ PO Box 104 Stellenbosch 7599 ▪ info@alto.co.za ▪ www.alto.co.za ▪ S 34° 0′ 10.4″ E 018° 50′ 49.4″ ▪ **T +27 (0)21-881-3884** ▪ F +27 (0)21-881-3894

The original farm was granted in 1693, but the title 'oldest red wine estate in South Africa' refers to a subdivided portion on which the Malans first made wine in the 1920s. They named it Alto, alluding to the farm's altitude on the slopes of Helderberg Mountain and their aspirations. Under Lusan Premium Wines' ownership, the property maintains its reputation for classically styled red wines, including Alto Rouge, a popular label for more than 50 years.

★★★★ **Cabernet Sauvignon** Dark & dense in warmer **10** (★★★★) vintage, with molten liquorice & cassis in firm tannic embrace. Sacrifices some of the classical elegance of **09** & previous. Needs time's smoothing hand.

★★★★ **Alto Rouge** Return to form for shiraz-led **09** blend with cab franc, merlot & cab after dip in **08** (★★★★). Hallmark elegant understatement without austerity. Cedary dark fruit, supple tannins still unfolding.

Shiraz ★★★★ Two vintages tasted: **10** riper, big boned & robust, will mature earlier. Youthful **09** (★★★★) has tightly coiled fruit, more structure & refinement. Both deserve lengthy cellaring & hearty fare. **MPHS** Not tasted. **Port** ⊕ ★★★★ **06** from shiraz, previously was light with gentle grip. — MW

Altydgedacht Estate

Location/WO: Durbanville ▪ Map: Durbanville, Philadelphia & Darling ▪ Est 1698 ▪ 1stB 1981 ▪ Tasting & sales Mon-Fri 9–5 Sat 9–3 ▪ Closed Easter Fri/Sun, Dec 25 & Jan 1 ▪ Cellar tours by appt ▪ B'fast & light lunches Mon-Sat 9.30-4 (T +27 (0)21-975-7815/eat@altydgedacht.co.za) ▪ Facilities for children ▪ Conferences ▪ Weddings/functions ▪ Conservation area ▪ Owner(s) Parker family ▪ Cellarmaster(s) Oliver Parker (1981) ▪ Winemaker(s) Etienne Louw (Jan 2006) ▪ Viticulturist(s) John Parker (1981) ▪ 412ha/180ha (16 varieties, r/w) ▪ 1,500t total 160t/11,000cs own label 30% red 65% white 5% rosé ▪ Other export brand: Ralph Parker ▪ PO Box 213 Durbanville 7551 ▪ altydgedacht@mweb.co.za ▪ www.altydgedacht.co.za ▪ S 33° 50' 46.6" E 018° 37' 26.4" ▪ **T +27 (0)21-976-1295** ▪ F +27 (0)21-976-4318

The Parker family have been farming their enviable 400ha-plus spread, tucked into the suburban edge of Durbanville, since 1852. Fifth-generation Oliver (cellarmaster) and John (viticulturist) have always taken roads less travelled: dry gewürztraminer, varietal barbera, aromatic blends for spicy food; these were their hallmarks of the early 1990s. Things are not much different now, with three promising new labels in this year's range, all tending to the spicy and herbaceous.

Parker Family Reserve range

★★★★ **Tintoretto** Estate flagship. Unique, characterful Cape Blend with barbera, **11** is dark & intense. Opulently ripe, finely balanced & smoothly textured, demanding attention.

★★★★ **The Ollo Estate White** ⏱ Aromatic viognier adds charm to dry **11** top-tier semillon-led blend, with chardonnay & chenin. Fermentation in barrel broadens flavours, provides weight & firm texture.

★★★★ **Méthode Cap Classique Blanc de Blanc** ⏱ All-chardonnay maiden **08** bubbly is commendably complex with attractive yeastiness & refreshing thread of acidity throughout.

Weisser Riesling NEW ✓ 🍴 ★★★☆ Promising debut for **12** single-vineyard selection. Dry & tangy, with piercing acidity, hints of marmalade & lemon. **Semillon NLH** ⏱ ★★★ Lightly spicy, soft **11** botrytis dessert wine has easy, pleasingly sweet & simple charm balanced by sufficient acidity to prevent cloying finish.

Altydgedacht Estate range

★★★★ **Cabernet Sauvignon Limited Release** Leafy, nervous **10** (★★★★) offers succulent, juicy fruit but lacks ripeness & intensity, possibly reflecting challenging vintage after classic **09**.

★★★★ **Barbera** Pioneers of Piedmont's prolific variety, 19th vintage **11** improves on lighter **10** (★★★★). Shows mocha-toffee aromas, but delivers spicy, flavoursome palate with distinctive fragrance & fine acidity.

★★★★ **Pinotage** Dense, tightly woven **11**, pretty floral scents on layered plummy, jammy fruit. Forceful but elegant expression of variety. Try pairing with venison.

★★★★ **Sauvignon Blanc** 🍴 Typically pungent, aromatic Durbanville **12** is bolstered by ripe healthy fruit. Nervously poised, vibrant, should settle with time in bottle. Back up to speed after **11** (★★★★) dip.

Merlot Limited Release ★★★ Full-bodied with lush black fruit & gentle tannins, **10** presents pleasing leafy, minty notes on nutty oak mantle. **Shiraz** ★★★ Smoky, meaty **10**, red sour cherries toned with wild herbs, sweet oak vanilla spiciness. **Gewürztraminer** 🍴 ★★★ Persistently dry **12** is light & fragrantly aromatic. Uncomplicated, refreshing; definitive spicy food accompaniment. Note: range last listed as 'Altydgedacht Cultivar'.

Tygerberg range

Cabernet Franc Blanc de Noir NEW ☺ 🍴 ★★★ Replaces 'Rosé'. Pale blush **12** has dusty, earthy tones & lean, dry blackcurrant fruit. Real character, real summertime appeal. **Blanc de Blanc** ☺ 🍴 ★★★ Aromatic sweet spices & rosepetals on **12** all-sorts dry blend add a food dimension to price-wise entry level quaffer. **Chatelaine** ☺ 🍴 ★★★ Bright, aromatic off-dry **12** riesling/gewürztraminer with splash of muscat for fragrance. Try with Thai food.

Gamay Noir 🍴 ★★ Funky whiff on **12** mars spicy cherry fruit. **Blanc de Blanc Sparkling** NEW ★★★ Aromatic 8-way fizzy cocktail, carbonated **11** is off-dry, spicy & light. — GdB

Alvi's Drift Private Cellar

Location/map: Worcester ▪ WO: Worcester/Western Cape ▪ Est 1928 ▪ 1stB 2004 ▪ Tasting, sales & tours by appt ▪ Closed all pub hols ▪ Farm produce ▪ Owner(s) Bertie, Alvi & Johan van der Merwe ▪ Cellarmaster(s) Henk Swart ▪ Winemaker(s) Henk Swart, Alvi van der Merwe & Linley Schultz, with Anton Trollip ▪ Viticulturist(s) Pierre Snyman (consultant) & Jan du Toit ▪ 6,000ha/420ha (ptage, shiraz, chard, chenin, muscat de F) ▪

±7,500t/200,000cs own label ▪ IPW ▪ PO Box 126 Worcester 6850 ▪ info@alvisdrift.co.za ▪ www.alvisdrift.co.za ▪ S 33° 46′ 25.8″ E 019° 31′ 53.7″ ▪ **T +27 (0)23-340-4117** ▪ F +27 (0)86-654-9425

Alvi van der Merwe was a doctor who always loved working in the vineyards established by his grandfather on the family farm near Worcester. His brother Johan was a lawyer with a particular interest in business. Linley Schultz was chief winemaker at Distell with a yearning for a brand of his own. After they got talking, it was only a matter of time before they made it happen: an integrated wine business based on family values, business acumen and innovative use of production facilities. Having grown off a small base, cellar capacity is now steadily increasing to accommodate increased output.

AD range

★★★★ **Drift Fusion** Suave combo cab, pinotage &, in 09, shiraz. Berry & clove appeal, supportive tannins, savoury & dry finish despite grain sugar & dash new American oak.

★★★★ **Chardonnay** 🍃 🊠 Oak-touched 11 continues upward quality trajectory set by citrus-toned 10. Emphatic & boldly flavoured, soupçon of sugar well disguised. WO W Cape.

★★★★ **CVC** 🍃 🊠 Pleasing blend chenin & viognier (50/30) with chardonnay; latter variety & 30% new oak play big role in 11: lemon, vanilla & floral aromas, plush & creamy texture. To sip attentively, like 10. Discontinued: **SVC**.

Premium Selection

★★★★☆ **Muscat de Frontignan White** ⱱ Alluring fortified dessert with sherry-like oxidative notes. Sweet & viscous 07 delightfully clean & fresh.

Signature range

★★★★ **Viognier** ✓ 🍃 🊠 Once again, deft handling of a variety that can be blowsy. 12 lightly oaked (as are the reds & chardonnay blend in this range), similar ginger spice & stonefruit as last-tasted 10.

> **Sauvignon Blanc** ☺ 🍃 🊠 ★★★ 12 punches above its price with nettle & khaki bush aromas, good weight (though moderate 13% alcohol) & vinosity.

Cabernet Sauvignon ⱱ 🍃 🊠 ★★★ Fruit-bomb 10 dusted with oak spice, very drinkable. **Pinotage** ⱱ 🍃 🊠 ★★ Vanilla-toned 10 for early drinking. **Shiraz** ⱱ 🍃 🊠 ★★★ Faint 'wild' hint on cherry-fruited 10. **Chenin Blanc** 🍃 🊠 ★★★ 12 drops the previous 'Unwooded' suffix & the oxidative styling. Clean & fresh stonefruit, bit shy, firm conclusion from 3 months lees-ageing. **Chardonnay-Viognier** **NEW** 🍃 🊠 ★★★ Tad confected sugar almonds on 11, lemony conclusion is more convincing, satisfying.

Alvi's Drift Private Cellar range

Naughty Girl ⱱ ★★★ Charming off-dry **NV** rosé sparkler, just 7.5% alcohol & 'berryful'. — HJ/CvZ

■ **Amalienstein** *see* Ladismith Cellar – SCV
■ **Amandalia** *see* Rooiberg Winery

Amani Vineyards   🎡 🏠 ♨ ⎈

Location/map: Stellenbosch ▪ WO: Stellenbosch/Coastal/Western Cape ▪ Est/1stB 1997 ▪ Tasting, sales & cellar tours Mon-Fri 9–4.30 Sat 10-4 ▪ Closed Easter Fri-Mon, Dec 25/26 & Jan 1 ▪ Facilities for children ▪ BYO picnic ▪ Walks/hikes ▪ Owner(s) Lynde & Rusty Myers ▪ Cellarmaster(s) Carmen Stevens (Jul 2005) ▪ Winemaker(s) Carmen Stevens (Jul 2005), with Chris van Reenen (Jan 2011) ▪ Viticulturist(s) JD Stassen (Apr 2006) ▪ 38ha/32ha (cabs s/f, merlot, mourv, shiraz, chard, sauv, viog) ▪ 217t/10,000cs own label 70% red 29% white 1% rosé ▪ EnviroWines ▪ PO Box 12422 Die Boord 7613 ▪ wine@amani.co.za ▪ www.amani.co.za ▪ S 33° 57′ 54.3″ E 018° 43′ 59.5″ ▪ **T +27 (0)21-881-3930** ▪ F +27 (0)21-881-3931

There's a clear aesthetic at this Stellenbosch boutique winery, skilfully expressed by winemaker Carmen Stevens. The wines are generally richly fruited and powerful, with a touch of gratifying sweetness; oaking is masterly and restrained. Ready for early drinking, they have enough structure to age — but not enough to alienate. Sentiment is not forgotten, with wines named for the children of owners Lynde and Rusty Myers: Kenzie (only in US), Jordan, and the late Forest Myers.

Amani range

★★★★☆ **Merlot** 🊠 10 (★★★★) plummy & savoury like 09; big, heavy textured & flavoursome, the sweet ripeness balanced by acid, firm & cushiony tannin structure, cleverly restrained oaking. WO Coastal.

★★★★ **Cabernet Franc-Merlot** Enticing **10** (★★★★), with dollops cab & malbec, but less classic than **09**. Fresh, spicy-leafy aromas; succulent flavours with modest savoury grip from tannin. WO W Cape.

★★★★ **Forest Myers** **10** from shiraz & mourvèdre, the blend making for greater complexity. Rich, sweetly fruity & powerful (around 15% alcohol, like many of these), but well focused & structurally supported.

★★★★ **I Am 1** **10** cab-based Bordeaux blend with a little shiraz. Nice herbal element, fresh & bright — the least sweetly rich of all the reds, with disciplined fruit, intelligent oaking. WO W Cape.

★★★★ **Chardonnay** Lively, well-textured & attractively balanced **11**, naturally fermented & with only older barrels used for maturation. Broad, soft richness makes for easy approachability.

★★★★ **Kamili Chardonnay-Viognier** **11** (★★★★) almost semi-sweet, unlike **10** (wrongly noted last year as **11**), with easy charm. Structure from chardonnay & light oaking, with viognier's peachy, oily richness, but no intensity.

Pendana Shiraz ★★★★ Good varietal aromas/flavours on **10**, with dollops cab & mourvèdre. Lipsmacking structure copes happily with big flavours & soft fruit. **Jordan Myers** Occasional release. **Poppy Blush** ★★★ Weighty, flavourful preview **11** from shiraz, dollop viognier. Sweet impression from sugar & 15% alc. **Sauvignon Blanc** ★★★★ A little oak influence adds broadness to the grassy-tropical flavour mix on lightish, fresh **11**, now bottled. **09** (★★★★) was bigger. Discontinued: **Chardonnay Reserve**.

Atkinson Ridge range
Discontinued: **Chardonnay**, **Sauvignon Blanc**. — TJ

Amares Wines

Location/map: Stellenbosch ▪ WO: Simonsberg-Stellenbosch/Stellenbosch ▪ Est 2005 ▪ 1stB 2006 ▪ Tasting, sales & cellar tours Mon-Sat by appt ▪ Closed all pub hols ▪ Cheese & olive platters by appt ▪ Owner(s) Amares Wines (Pty) Ltd ▪ Winemaker(s) Neville Koudstaal (Mar 2006), Sally Noel & Renier Pienaar ▪ Viticulturist(s) Amares Wines ▪ 5ha/2ha (cab) ▪ 4t/375cs own label 100% red ▪ PO Box 7253 Stellenbosch 7599 ▪ info@amares.co.za ▪ www.amares.co.za ▪ S 33° 54' 30.30" E 018° 53' 27.21" ▪ **T +27 (0)21-887-9414** ▪ F +27 (0)21-413-0854

It's not only vines on this small farm where a group of family and friends strive 'to live the good life'. 'The veggie garden is producing abundantly and the chickens ranging freely,' says part-owner Renier Pienaar. The vineyard, he adds, was 'converted to organic by a leap of blind faith that would scare any viticulturist'.

Cabernet Sauvignon ★★★★ Like previous vintage, **09** solid, sweet-fruited, powerful & oak-influenced; a few years should help soften the slightly drying finish. **Syrah** ★★★★ Big, exuberant, deep-coloured **09**; lots of savoury-edged ripe fruit, lots of power. High alcohol adds sweetness. WO Stellenbosch. — TJ

■ **Ama Ulibo** *see* Goedverwacht Wine Estate

Ambeloui Wine Cellar

Location: Hout Bay ▪ Map: Cape Peninsula ▪ WO: Western Cape ▪ Est 1994 ▪ 1stB 1998 ▪ Tasting by appt ▪ Owner(s) Nick & Ann Christodoulou ▪ Cellarmaster(s)/viticulturist(s) Nick Christodoulou (1994) ▪ Winemaker(s) Nick Christodoulou (2005), with Alexis & Christo Christodoulou ▪ 1ha/0.5ha (pinot, chard) ▪ 15t/1,500cs own label 5% white 95% MCC ▪ PO Box 26800 Hout Bay 7872 ▪ wine@ambeloui.co.za ▪ www.ambeloui.co.za ▪ S 34° 0' 49.5" E 018° 22' 55.4" ▪ **T +27 (0)21-790-7386/+27 (0)82-880-1715/+27 (0)82-460-8399** ▪ F +27 (0)88-021-790-7386

Nick and Ann Christodoulou have found themselves in the enviable position of selling all their specialist bubbly cellar's stock, which good fortune they ascribe to niche-ing wisely in an over-producing industry. Increased capacity will allow them to mature better vintages for longer — a four-year-old MCC is promised next.

★★★★ **MCC Rosanne Rosé** Chardonnay-led, lightly oaked **NV** with pinot noir, offers delicate red fruit flavours & softly persistent mousse. Tad less thrilling than previous, but appealing & harmonious.

★★★★☆ **MCC** Classy & stylish chardonnay-pinot blanc sparkler, including grapes from other areas. Richly aromatic **09** 'Nicholas' followed by **10** 'Miranda' with complex brioche aromas & baked apple flavours in tightly wound core, carried by fine mousse to exquisitely focused, mouthwatering conclusion. — IM

■ **Amera** *see* StellenRust
■ **Amistad Wine Company** *see* The Amistad Wine Company

Anatu Wines

Location: Stellenbosch ▪ Map: Helderberg ▪ WO: Coastal ▪ Est/1stB 2002 ▪ Tasting, sales & cellar tours by appt ▪ Closed all pub hols ▪ Owner(s) André & Freda Hamersma ▪ Winemaker(s) Micu Narunsky (Jan 2009) ▪ 40t/ 2,800cs own label 40% red 40% white 20% rosé ▪ Other export brand: Sereia ▪ Postnet Suite 246 Private Bag X5061 Stellenbosch 7599 ▪ sales@anatu.co.za ▪ www.anatu.co.za ▪ S 34° 1'52.20" E 018° 50' 46.73" ▪ **T +27 (0)83-307-9333** ▪ F +27 (0)86-577-5019

Anatu is a story of two people from different backgrounds and careers drawn together by a passion for wine: former banker André Hamersma and Micu Narunsky, jazz pianist who fell in love with wine while touring the French vineyards. They make a formidable pair, believing that blending — not only complementary varieties but also grapes from different areas — gives best results.

Family Blend range

★★★★☆ **Red** ✓ Full-bodied **10** (★★★★) mix grenache & shiraz from Wellington & Stellenbosch, concentrated black fruit & good oaking, with warmish finish. Attractive, but misses the complexity of **08**.

★★★★ **White** NEW ✓ Delicious **11** from chenin, grenache blanc & roussanne, shows stonefruit, melon & apple pie. Well rounded & harmonious, with excellent freshness & hint of vanilla oak.

Rosé NEW ★★★ Richly fruited, dry **11** from grenache, mourvèdre, cinsaut. Crisp acidity & light tannins give grip & focus.

Fugue range

★★★★☆ **Red** NEW Super debut **10**, shiraz & grenache from Stellenbosch & Wellington, is restrained, combining clean black fruit, meat & wild game aromas. Full-bodied, concentrated fruit flavours with a delicious core of well-judged oak. Alcohol (15.5%) well hidden.

★★★★☆ **White** ✓ Was 'Fugue'. **11** blend of roussanne, chenin & grenache blanc; rich, vibrant & full bodied, waxy ripe-fruit flavours supported by precise oaking & firm minerality. Elegant, with an unflagging end.

Rosé ★★★★ Shiraz & grenache-led WO Coastal blend. **11** intensely flavoured red fruit with light oaking adding interest. Range was 'Anatu' last time. Discontinued: **Shiraz**. — WB

Andersons Wines

Location/WO: Plettenberg Bay ▪ Map: Klein Karoo & Garden Route ▪ Est 2008 ▪ 1stB 2011 ▪ Tasting by appt ▪ Fee R5/wine ▪ Closed all pub hols ▪ Owner(s) Ian & Bruce Anderson ▪ Winemaker(s) Anton Smal (Bramon Wines) ▪ Viticulturist(s) Bruce Anderson (2008) ▪ 22ha/2.5ha (sauv) ▪ 5.5t/600cs (6btl) own label 100% white ▪ PO Box 2146 Plettenberg Bay 6600 ▪ andersonswine@gmail.com ▪ S 33° 59' 17.7" E 023° 27' 15.1 ▪ **T +27 (0)44-533-5020** ▪ F +27 (0)44-533-5020

'Wine from Plettenberg Bay' is no longer an idea greeted with incredulity. In fact, this Garden Route playground, its neighbour Knysna and environs are among South Africa's fastest growing wine areas. Bruce and Ian Anderson's venture is a retirement project which has progressed from the establishment of a small vineyard block in 2008 to having Anton Smal from up-the-road Bramon Wines vinify and bottle a maiden Leto Venus Sauvignon Blanc (honouring the endemic Ghost Moth). There's a tasting room on the property, so those visiting Plett for the usual swimming and watersports can take in a not-so-unexpected spot of winetasting.

Leto Venus Sauvignon Blanc 🍸 ★★★ **12**, 2nd crop from young block, elegant green flavours & minerality, lightish, brisk & fresh. Everything attractively in place — greater intensity will come as vines mature. — FM/GdB

Andreas Wines

Location/WO: Wellington ▪ Map: Paarl & Wellington ▪ Est 2003 ▪ 1stB 2004 ▪ Tasting & sales by appt Mon-Fri 9–5 ▪ Fee R10 ▪ Closed all pub hols ▪ Cellar tours by appt ▪ Accommodation ▪ Weddings/functions ▪ Owner(s) Jan & Anita Bokdal ▪ Cellarmaster(s) Howard Heughs & Eugenie Ellis ▪ Winemaker(s) Howard Heughs & Ettienne Malan (consultant) ▪ Viticulturist(s) Howard Heughs ▪ 6ha/4.5ha (mourv, shiraz) ▪ 48t/1,584cs own label 100% red ▪ PO Box 892 Wellington 7654 ▪ andreas@ezinet.co.za ▪ www.andreas.co.za ▪ S 33° 37'52.0" E 019° 2'50.1" ▪ **T +27 (0)21-873-2286** ▪ F +27 (0)86-664-5087

Jan and Anita Bokdal have added an Andreas olive oil to the successful shiraz from their tiny Wellington property. The Swedish owners' goal is for their wine to attain cult status, something 'which we are finally seeing evidence of, from the client base we have built up over the years', says farm manager Eugenie Ellis.

★★★★ **Andreas Shiraz** Distinctive super-silky styling continues in **10**, intense choc-dipped wild berry & liquorice, well-judged oak & wine's signature spicy blackberry liqueur aftertaste. — WB

Andy Mitchell Wines

Location: Greyton ▪ Map: Southern Cape ▪ WO: Elgin/Stellenbosch/Swartland ▪ Est/1stB 2003 ▪ Tasting, sales & tours by appt ▪ Closed Easter Fri/Sun & Dec 25 ▪ Owner(s) Andy & Vikki Mitchell ▪ Cellarmaster(s) Andy Mitchell (Jan 2003) ▪ Winemaker(s) Andy Mitchell (Jan 2003), with Olivia Mitchell (Jan 2008) ▪ 10.5t/766cs own label 42% red 21% white 13% rosé 24% MCC + 100cs for clients ▪ PO Box 543 Paarden Eiland 7420 ▪ andy@andymitchellwines.com ▪ www.andymitchellwines.com ▪ S 34° 2' 26.3" E 019° 37' 2.6" ▪ **T +27 (0)28-254-9045** ▪ F +27 (0)86-611-3106

This tiny family winery reached its capacity last year, says 'chief tankwasher' Andy Mitchell, who sources grapes from cool-climate areas (Elgin, Walker Bay), Swartland and elsewhere. With the first MCC sparkling in bottle and maiden southern Rhône blend in cask, and the chenin now recognising its fruit source on the label, they're 'desperately needing a bit more space' and may move the cellar.

★★★★ **Crooked Path Shiraz** ⓘ Ripeness on **06** reined in by savoury acidity & tannin backbone, lifted by dash viognier. Stellenbosch WO, as for Rosé.

★★★★ **Swartland Chenin Blanc** 🗃 40 year old Malmesbury bushvines; cask-fermented **11** generously fruited yet with appealing minerality, lees complexity, dry tail. Greater dimension than **09** (★★★★). No **10**.

Elgin Pinot Noir ✓ 🗃 ★★★★ Was 'Pinot Noir'. One of two Elgin pinots from **11** vintage, this 75% new oak, aromatic & fresh with elegant tannins for solo sipping or mealtime enjoyment. Step up on **09** (★★★), from Bamboes Bay fruit. No **10**. **Crooked Path Pinot Noir** NEW 🗃 ★★★ Only older barrels for this **11** Elgin version. Bright red cherries & raspberries; light footed, with pleasing form & texture. **Breakfast Rock Syrah** ⓘ ★★★★ **07** dark fruited & lithe but bold courtesy 15.2% alcohol, so not as balanced as **05** (★★★★). **Nerina Shiraz Rosé** ⓘ 🗃 ★★★ Summer refreshment from berry-toned & dry **10**. — WB/GdB

Angels Tears Wines

Location: Franschhoek ▪ WO: Western Cape/Franschhoek ▪ Closed to public ▪ Owner(s) Dutch & Belgium consortium ▪ Cellarmaster(s)/winemaker(s)/viticulturist(s) Karl Lambour (Jul 2012) ▪ 32ha/22ha (cab, merlot, chard, sauv) ▪ 600t/30,000cs own label 30% red 60% white 10% rosé ▪ PO Box 102 Franschhoek 7690 ▪ enquiries@ grandeprovence.co.za ▪ www.angelstears.co.za ▪ **T +27 (0)21-876-8600** ▪ F +27 (0)21-876-8601

The name of this big-selling second-tier range from Grande Provence first appeared in the 1989 edition of the guide under the Haute Provence label, as Larmes des Anges, with the explanation: 'Legend has it that on tasting the fruits of a fine vintage, the angels wept for joy'.

Merlot-Cabernet Sauvignon-Shiraz-Petit Verdot ☺ 🗃 ★★★ **11** another notch up, showing light, juicy fruit. **Muscat d'Alexandrie-Chenin Blanc** ☺ 🗃 ⌀ ★★★ The original, since 1989 aromatic semi-sweet. Spicy **11** (as we said then) 'could have [the angels] reaching for their wingkerchiefs'.

Rosé ⓘ 🗃 ★★ Uncomplicated, tutti-frutti **11** off-dry quaffer. **Sauvignon Blanc** 🗃 ★★★ Light-bodied **11** is likeable & refreshing anytime tipple. Franschhoek WO. — GdB

■ **Ankerman** *see* uniWines Vineyards

Annandale Wines

Location/map: Stellenbosch ▪ WO: Stellenbosch/Coastal ▪ Est/1stB 1996 ▪ Tasting, sales & cellar tours Mon-Sat 9-5 ▪ Fee R20 ▪ Closed Easter Fri-Mon, Ascension Day & Dec 25 ▪ Farm produce ▪ BYO picnic ▪ Owner(s) Hempies du Toit ▪ Winemaker(s)/viticulturist(s) Hempies du Toit (1996) ▪ 72ha/45ha (cabs s/f, merlot, shiraz) ▪ 250t/5,000cs own label 100% red ▪ PO Box 12681 Stellenbosch 7613 ▪ info@annandale.co.za ▪ www. annandale.co.za ▪ S 33° 59' 49.2" E 018° 49' 50.9" ▪ **T +27 (0)21-881-3560** ▪ F +27 (0)21-881-3562

'I make "soul wine",' says ever-exuberant rugby legend and Helderberg boutique-scale vintner Hempies du Toit, who forged his reputation at then Du Toit family owned Alto Estate nearby. 'Soul wine because very few winemakers leave their wines in barrels for up to eight years! It is the love for winemaking, my passion and commitment extraordinaire that drives me, and I hope that my passion will spill over to my family that will come here after me.'

★★★★ **Cabernet Sauvignon** Serious-minded & classically styled. A melange of dark cherry & cassis on bold, spicy **04**, now bottled (after 7 years in barrel) & showing similar fine form to previous.

★★★★ **Shiraz** Spicy, oaky complexity adds to black pastille fruit on solid, unshowy & firmly structured **04**. Made to last.

★★★★ **Nostalgia** Tribute to old-style Cape reds & the founders of Alto Estate. From cab, shiraz & cinsaut — latter adding charming wild, raspberry notes in now-bottled **NV**. From various years, is mature but still vibrant. **Merlot** ★★★★ **05**'s herbal-edged fruit has survived 6 years in oak, still some freshness. Ready now, but like all these should keep well. **Cavalier** ★★★★ **04** Bordeaux-style blend with shiraz oozes spice & black fruit. Big & sturdy, yet balanced & smooth with lots of life after 7 years in barrel. More complex than **01** (★★★★). Great with a roast. **Sauvignon Blanc** ⊕ ★★★★ Unusual, successful take on variety in **11**. Oxidative styling lessens fruitiness, not flavour. Lightly rich, dry, savoury. Coastal WO. **CVP** ★★★★ 'Cape Vintage Port' from shiraz; **04** offers spicy fruitcake flavours, vibrant raisins & spirity grip. — WB

Annex Kloof Wines

Location: Malmesbury ▪ Map: Swartland ▪ WO: Swartland/Western Cape ▪ Est/1stB 2006 ▪ AnnexKloof stall on N7: sales daily; tasting Fri 8-5.30 Sat 8-3 Sun 9-5 ▪ Farm: tasting, sales & cellar tours by appt only ▪ Closed Easter Fri-Mon, Ascension day, Pentecost, Dec 16/25/26 & Jan 1 ▪ BYO picnic ▪ Walks/hikes ▪ 4x4 trail ▪ Conservation area ▪ Owner(s) Toeloe Basson with sons Thys, Hugo & Tobie Basson ▪ Winemaker(s) Hugo Basson (Jan 2006) ▪ 450ha (cab, malbec, merlot, ptage, shiraz, chard, chenin, sauv) ▪ 4,300t/625cs own label 95% red 5% white ▪ PO Box 772 Malmesbury 7299 ▪ hugo@annexkloofwines.co.za ▪ www.annexkloofwines.co.za ▪ S 33° 30'39.1" E 018° 48'22.5" (estate), S 33° 21'5.69" E 018° 42'36.87" (farmstall) ▪ **T +27 (0)22-487-3870** ▪ F +27 (0)86-569-3957

It was a trip to Argentina in 1993 that inspired Hugo Basson to plant malbec on his family farm, despite his fellow Swartlanders laughing at him for introducing a variety unknown to South African consumers. Today all five locally available clones are planted on Annex Kloof, and the wine has enjoyed local and international success. All the wines, including the new value range, Xenna (Annex reversed), are also available from the new Annex Kloof farmstall on the N7 between Malmesbury and Moorreesburg.

Annex Kloof Wines range
Malbec Await next. **Red Blend** ✓ ★★★★ **10** from shiraz, mourvèdre & grenache. Pleasant gamey, truffly features with rounded, ripe-fruited tail. Last tasted was **07**. **Port** NEW ★★★★ Maiden **09** tinta/shiraz blend tasted from tank. Rich fruitcake flavours, not too sweet, balanced grip from tannin & unusually low 15.5% alcohol. Discontinued: **White Blend**.

Xenna range NEW
★★★★ **Chenin Blanc** ✓ 📖 📷 **12** (tank sample, so rating provisional) unoaked to highlight ripe pear & spice concentration of old-vine fruit. Ripe & forceful yet also wonderfully fresh, unheavy & dry. Memorably long.

Cabernet Sauvignon ☺ 📷 ★★★ **10** forthcoming red berry, tomato leaf features, fresh, unaggressive grip. WO W Cape.

Pinotage ✓ 📷 ★★★★ **10** a good reflection of the area's ripe, hearty generosity. Lifted mulberries, red earth aromas; dense yet lively & roundly dry. **Shiraz** ✓ 📷 ★★★★ **11** in honest, rustic style. Rich, savoury flavours backed by rumbling tannins. Rounded by older oak for a warming winter red. — AL

AntHill Wines

Location: Somerset West ▪ WO: Stellenbosch ▪ Est 1999 ▪ 1stB 2000 ▪ Tasting by appt ▪ Owner(s) Mark Howell & Hylton Schwenk ▪ Winemaker(s) Mark Howell (Feb 2000) ▪ 300cs own label 100% red ▪ 19 Immelman Rd Somerset West 7130 ▪ anthill@absamail.co.za ▪ S 34° 4'30.8" E 018° 52'37.6" ▪ **T +27 (0)82-895-9008** ▪ F +27 (0)21-851-5914

'We remain a small garagiste operation selling our wines to family, friends and loyal followers,' says co-owner and winemaker Mark Howell, adding somewhat cryptically: 'At the moment the road to the winery can only be accessed in a 4x4 vehicle, but boasts one of the best views in the world.'

★★★★ **Cabernet Sauvignon Entre Nous 09** is a bold Helderberg cab with pure, lush, minty blackcurrant fruit. Careful oaking adds complexity & harmony. Charming, with lots of life & a fine tannin grip.

★★★★ **Davey Jones Locker** NEW ✓ Rhône-style blend **09** knocks you out with viognier-lifted bouquet of brambleberries & violets. Well structured, elegant, shows balance & presence, appealing earthy end.

The Persian Shiraz ⓟ 🍴 ★★★ Deep, dense smoky black fruit, **08** rich & sweet with supporting round spicy tannins. For early enjoyment. Discontinued: **Shiraz Entre Nous**, **Whitestone Sauvignon Blanc**. — WB

Anthonij Rupert Wines   22-12-12   lunch 🍴🍷📷♿

Location/map: Franschhoek ■ WO: Coastal/Western Cape/Citrusdal Mountain/Stellenbosch/Swartland/Overberg/Elandskloof ■ Est 1714 ■ 1stB 1982 ■ Tasting Mon-Fri 9-4.30 Sat/Sun 10-3 ■ Fee R30 ■ Closed Good Fri & Dec 25 ■ Light meals & refreshments (gourmet sandwiches; cheese & meat platters) ■ Cheese, olive oil & honey ■ Franschhoek Motor Museum Mon-Fri 10-4 Sat/Sun 10-3; admittance R60 adults R50 senior R30 kids (3-12) ■ Owner(s) Johann Rupert ■ Winemaker(s) Dawie Botha (Jan 2005) & Zanie Viljoen (Jan 2007) ■ 4 farms: total ±1,100ha/±210ha (cabs s/f, carignan, cinsaut, grenache, merlot, mourv, pinot, sangio, shiraz, chard, chenin, pinot grigio, rouss) ■ ISO 14001:2009 ■ PO Box 435 Franschhoek 7690 ■ tasting@rupertwines.com ■ www.rupertwines.com ■ S 33° 52′ 47.36″ E 019° 0′ 10.91″ ■ **T** +27 (0)21-874-9000 ■ **F** +27 (0)21-874-9111

It's 10 years since Johann Rupert took over the reins at his late brother's winery at the foot of the Groot Drakenstein Mountains in Franschhoek. Since then he has built on his sibling's work, and now produces several ranges from different sites around the Cape. The flagship line-up has it all — sites, grapes, barrels and winemaking — to create wines worthy of the vision of Anthonij Rupert. He was a longtime Italophile, and one of the pioneers of sangiovese and pinot grigio for his Terra del Capo wines. The Protea range offers good-value, everyday drinking. Strongly flying the terroir flag are the Cape of Good Hope bottlings (previously listed separately), recognising the Cape's vinous heritage and its old vineyard sites. Respect and love for the land guide every decision affecting these wines; they're worth seeking out as much for the stories they tell as their expression of the soil.

Anthonij Rupert range

★★★★ **Cabernet Franc** ⓟ Accomplished & polished modern take on the variety, **07** black fruit & echoes of scrub & forest floor, tad confected finish. Powerful, tight, would benefit from decanting, as all these.

★★★★ **Merlot** ⓟ **07** silky & hedonistic, noticeable fruit & oak sweetness balanced by savoury tomato-like hint & mineral texture. WO W Cape, like next.

★★★★ **Optima 08** (★★★★★) intensely pleasurable black fruit wrapped up in chocolate & cream. Sweet spiced notes (cloves/cedarwood) show in robust tannins but fruit concentration & lengthy liquorice finish suggest, as with **07**, that this can be a keeper. *purchased*

Cabernet Sauvignon ⓟ ★★★★ Recent releases emphasise power, structure & opulent oak seasoning, so **07**'s blackcurrant fruit broods in a savoury, almost malty cocoon, waiting to emerge. **Syrah** ⓟ ★★★★ **07** lovely lily/blackcurrant aroma, broad & generous flavours, let down a bit by overt oak char in conclusion.

Cape of Good Hope range

★★★★ **Parel Vallei Farmstead Merlot** Like step-up **07**, **08** intensely perfumed & flavoured, richness curtailed by lively acidity, firm tannins. Hedonistic, but retains poise & focus. Helderberg vines.

Basson Pinotage ★★★ Perdeberg grapes in faintly strawberry/acetone **09**. Marked acidity detracts from soft fruit, finish. **Serruria Chardonnay** ⓟ ★★★★ Faint lemon & oatmeal on **10** from 10 year old Elandskloof vines. Satisfying without being contrived; nudges next level with 11 months older oak adding weight, subtle seasoning. **Van Lill & Visser Chenin Blanc** ⓟ ★★★★ Taut & tempered **10** hints at what this Citrusdal vineyard can achieve. Like exceptional Loire examples & **09** (★★★★), focus is on structure, not aroma, with older oak in supportive role. **Sauvignon Blanc** NEW ✓ ★★★★ **12** preview reveals blackcurrant aromas on a bed of green fruit, reflecting the cool Elandskloof provenance. Vibrant acidity & concentration mask 14% alcohol; 6 months lees-ageing adds weight, extends the confident mineral end. **Laing Semillon** ⓟ ★★★★ Judiciously oaked **10** from Citrusdal Mountain raised bar on soft **09** (★★★★) with greater intensity, structure. Yellow peach/fennel hints, fine acid thread, presence & poise at moderate 13% alcohol.

Terra Del Capo range

Sangiovese ★★★★ Subtle whiffs of black & red fruit in **09** outlined by firm tannins, lively acidity & dry finish. As per all Italian varieties — needs food. **Arné ★★★★** Successful blend **09** of merlot & sangiovese (50/50) balances forthright dark chocolate notes with gritty black fruit & spice. Last-tasted **07** (★★★★) raised the bar. **Pinot Grigio ✓ 🍷 ★★★★** Bags of character on previewed **12**, combo crunchy green apples/soft aromatic pear fruit. Balanced acidity, weightier than most Italian versions at modest 12% alcohol.

Protea range

Merlot ☺ 🍷 ★★★ Friendly choc-mint quaffer **11** with soft, sweet black plums & cherries mid-palate & dry finish. *purchased*

Cabernet Sauvignon ⓟ 🍷 ★★★★ Improved **09** greets with blackcurrant & liquorice, follows with restrained fruitiness, gentle but firm grip. Able flag waver for this well-priced range targeting wine-by-the-glass market. WO W Cape. **Shiraz ✓ 🍷 ★★★★ 11** an over-deliverer of note. Perfume, black pepper, cinnamon-spiced plums with whiffs of orange peel & cloves. **Reserve ⓟ ★★★★** Ready-to-drink combo shiraz, mourvèdre & drop viognier. Preview **09** food-friendly savouriness & restraint, hint strawberry fruit. **Chardonnay ⓟ ★★★ 10** carbon copy of debut **09**: timid lemon blossom aroma followed by burst of flavour, freshness, even some tannin. WO W Cape, like next two. **Chenin Blanc 🍷 ★★★** Floral & attractive **11** has creamy undertones from extended lees-ageing. Finishes warmer than previous. **Sauvignon Blanc ✓ 🍷 ★★★★** Lively & zesty **12**, more concentrated fruit (lemons, limes, papaya) than expected for the price. Balanced acidity, long length. — CM/CvZ

Anthony Smook Wines

Location/WO: Paarl ▪ Est/1stB 2000 ▪ Tasting by appt ▪ Owner(s) Tresso Trading 532 (Pty) Ltd ▪ Cellarmaster(s) Anthony Smook ▪ Viticulturist(s) Johan Wiese (2001, consultant) ▪ 30t from various vyds ▪ PO Box 7038 Northern Paarl 7623 ▪ anthony@smook.co.za ▪ www.smookwines.co.za ▪ **T +27 (0)21-872-3232** ▪ F +27 (0)21-872-3235

Paarl negociant Anthony Smook made no own-label wines last year as he couldn't find the grape quality he sought. To crown it all, ribbok ate the leaves off an experimental vineyard among fynbos on his Du Toitskloof Mountain farm, Elandsjacht. 'The first vintage of this Biodiversity Fynbos Shiraz is going be very special to me!'

Shiraz Reserve Await next, as for **Shiraz**. **Chardonnay ⓟ ★★★** Ripe pear nuances & integrated oak detail on approachable **06**. — DB

Anura Vineyards

Location: Paarl ▪ Map: Paarl & Wellington ▪ WO: Simonsberg-Paarl/Western Cape/Coastal/Darling/Swartland/Paarl ▪ Est 1990 ▪ 1stB 2001 ▪ Tasting, sales & cellar tours daily 9.30–5 ▪ Closed Good Fri, Dec 25 & Jan 1 ▪ Fee R30 (cheese & wine) ▪ Lilly Pad Restaurant ▪ Tour groups ▪ Farm produce ▪ Conferences ▪ Owner(s) Tymen Bouma ▪ Cellarmaster(s) Tymen Bouma (1990) ▪ Winemaker(s) Johnnie Calitz & Lance Bouma (Jan 2007) ▪ Viticulturist(s) Hannes Kloppers (Oct 1997) ▪ 240ha/120ha (cab, carignan, grenache, malbec, merlot, mourv, nebbiolo, p verdot, ptage, pinot, sangio, shiraz, tempranillo, chard, chenin, nouvelle, pinot gris, sauv, verdelho) ▪ 750t/50,000cs own label 80% red 17% white 2% rosé 1% fortified + 10,000cs for clients ▪ Other export brand: Zee ▪ Brands for clients: Heart & Soul, Joy, Kiss My Springbok, Wine Lover's Collection ▪ IPW ▪ PO Box 244 Klapmuts 7625 ▪ info@anura.co.za, wine@anura.co.za ▪ www.anura.co.za ▪ S 33° 48' 41.4" E 018° 53' 19.8" ▪ **T +27 (0)21-875-5360** ▪ F +27 (0)21-875-5657

Anura (Latin for tailless amphibians) celebrate their considerable resident frog community in all their branding. Diversity remains the catchword at this dynamic estate, founded by Tymen Bouma after a successful optometry career, with even more new cultivars planted — see the list above — a conference centre on the drawing boards and a residential estate development adjoining Klapmuts. Keep an eye on the innovative and promising remake of their signature range, 'LB'.

LB Series

★★★★ Shiraz NEW Subtle, smooth & rounded, with floral scents & peppery spices, first-release **09** augurs well. Hints of Rhône with solid New World ripeness.

Sangiovese ★★★★ Previously in 'Signature Series'. **07** shows maturity, but offers sunshiny ripe fruit, brisk acidity with dried tomato & hints of cherry. Better than **06** (★★★★). **Verdelho** NEW ★★★★ Tiny first release of barrel-fermented Madeira rarity in dry white guise, **10** has body & finesse. Should appeal to the adventurous. WO Paarl. **La Traviata** ⚱ ★★★★ 'La Traviata White' under 'Signature Series' previously. Oaked **09** based on roussanne, grenache blanc, with chenin & telling 8% viognier. WO Coastal.

Reserves & Limited Releases

★★★★ **Merlot Reserve** Satisfyingly full-bodied **09** reflects fine balance of vintage. Supple & finely textured, gushing with ripe, juicy berries. Should improve with time in bottle.

★★★★ **Syrah Limited Release** ⚱ **07** on review was big yet rich & multi-dimensional; tannins, oak integrated, allowing peep of sombre, unevolved dark chocolate & spice.

Cabernet Sauvignon Reserve ★★★★ Listed without 'Reserve' suffix last time. Rich, ripe porty notes underpinned by strident oak spiciness on big, bold **08**. Unsubtle, but should integrate in time. **Malbec Limited Release** ⚱ ★★★★ **08** improves on tangy **07** (★★★★), shows lots of concentration, honest black fruit & elegant structure. **Petit Verdot Limited Release** ⚱ ★★★★ Elegantly handled varietal rarity, **08** has rich exotic fruit & thick tannin cloak. **Pinotage Reserve** ⚱ ★★★★ When last tasted, **09** boasted fresher raspberry focus than **08** (★★★★). Concentrated & creamy, with supportive structure. Coastal WO. **Chardonnay Limited Release** 🍷 ★★★★ Seriously conceived top-of-range label gets full oak treatment in **11**, but rich, ripe fruit copes better than **10** (★★★★). Tight, nutty & solidly structured. Should unfurl in a year or two. **Chenin Blanc Limited Release** 🍷 ★★★★ Big & bold **11** struggles with overwhelming oak, but still delivers ripe, honest fruit & creamy, lees-rich texture. WO Coastal. **Sauvignon Blanc Unfiltered Reserve** ⚱ 🍷 ★★★★ Stylish flag-bearer from Darling vineyards, previewed **11** shows greater depth & complexity than siblings. Notch up on **10** (★★★★), with focused fruit & lingering finish. **Méthode Cap Classique Brut** ⚱ ★★★★ Was in 'Anura' range. Like **06** (★★★★), previously tasted bottle-fermented sparkling **08**, classic chardonnay, pinot noir mix. Generous brioche, bruised apple aromas, oak-enriched. WO W Cape. Discontinued: **Syrah-Mourvèdre**.

Anura range

Merlot 🍷 ★★★ Supple, fruity **10** shows better ripeness than **09**, from vaunted vintage. Modest but appealing weight & finish. **Pinotage** 🍷 ★★★ Overtly savoury **10** has some hard edges, but still delivers solid fruit core & typical varietal aromatic punch. **Legato** ✓ 🍴 🍷 ★★★★ **10** merlot/cab blend follows previous form with aromatic oaky spices & bright, ripe fruit. Supple & appealing. **Pinotage-Syrah** 🍴 🍷 ★★★ Compatible blending partners combine in juicy berry compote, with hints of coffee in **11**. Spicy & aromatic if not subtle. **Rosé** ⚱ 🍴 🍷 ★★★ Impressive previewed **11**. Grenache with splash hanepoot, from Darling vineyards. Dry, fullish, fruity & satisfying. **Chardonnay** 🍷 ★★★ Appealing, approachable style continues in **11**, with crisply acidic citrus zest on restrained oak. Own & Tradouw Highlands grapes. **Sauvignon Blanc** 🍴 🍷 ★★★ Refreshing, undemanding **12** shows gentle acidity & ripe fruit. WO Coastal. **Viognier Barrel Selection** ⚱ 🍷 ★★★ Rather heavy oaking on **10**, from Swartland vines, mars otherwise promising fruity & aromatic profile. **Cape Ruby Port** ⚱ ★★★ When last tasted, **08** was suitably if not classically from ruby cab. Fruity, smoothed by noticeable brandy spirit.

Frog Hill range

Cabernet Sauvignon-Merlot ☺ 🍴 🍷 ★★★ Entry-level picnic hamper filler **10** offers commendable ripe fruit.

Pinotage 🍴 🍷 ★★★ Oak-spiced fruit bomb, **11** offers solid entry-level enjoyment. Discontinued: **Sauvignon Blanc**. — GdB

Anwilka   🍴🍷

Location: Somerset West ▪ WO: Stellenbosch ▪ Est 1997 ▪ 1stB 2005 ▪ Tasting & sales by appt at Klein Constantia ▪ Closed all pub hols ▪ Cellar tours by appt ▪ Owner(s) Zdenek Bakala, Charles Harman, Bruno Prats & Hubert de Boüard ▪ Cellarmaster(s) Bruno Prats & Hubert de Boüard (both Oct 2004) ▪ Winemaker(s) Jean du Plessis (Aug 2008) ▪ Viticulturist(s) Piet Neethling, with Johan Wiese (consultant, both 1997) ▪ 48ha/ ±39ha (cab, merlot, p verdot, shiraz) ▪ 200t/±12,000cs own label 100% red ▪ PO Box 5298 Helderberg 7135 ▪ anwilka@mweb.co.za ▪ www.anwilka.com ▪ T +27 (0)21-842-3225 ▪ F +27 (0)21-842-3983

With the departure of Lowell Jooste, one of the founder-owners of Anwilka, it was decided in 2012 to merge with Klein Constantia (with which there had always been ties). The other two owners, Bruno Prats and Hubert de Boüard of Bordeaux, remain fully involved, now as KC minority shareholders. Anwilka's independence is sacrosanct, however, so don't expect change. Quite apart from human shuffling, nature persists, and is being invoked to help environmentally responsible farming. Owl boxes in the Anwilka vineyards are encouraging Barn and Cape Spotted Eagle Owls to control rodents, while an international bat expert is advising on using those fluttering creatures to help with biological insect control.

★★★★★ **Anwilka** ⏰ **09** a break-through vintage — adding more depth, seriousness & structure to usual ripe, dense fruit. From 56% shiraz + cab (**08** included merlot). Plenty of new oak used, but integrated. Supple & flowing, on implacable but graceful infrastructure. A modern classic; will mature many years.

★★★★ **Ugaba** ⏰ **09** from same grapes as senior, with 69% shiraz & just 25% new oak. Less intense & deep, but lovely & seamless; smooth, sweet-fruited, dry-finishing (a touch too drying). — TJ

■ **Arbelos Wines** *see* Botha Wine Cellar

Arendsig Handcrafted Wines

Location/map: Robertson ▪ Est/1stB 2004 ▪ Tasting & cellar tours by appt ▪ Tour groups ▪ BYO picnic ▪ Wedding/function venue ▪ Farmhouse (sleeps up to 10 people) ▪ Owner(s) Lourens & Frikkie van der Westhuizen ▪ Cellarmaster(s)/viticulturist(s) Lourens van der Westhuizen (2004) ▪ 95ha/12ha (cab, shiraz, chard, sauv, viog) ▪ 80t/3,000cs own label 50% red 50% white + 100t/3,000cs for clients ▪ Brands for clients: Esona, Mimosa, Star Hill ▪ PO Box 170 Robertson 6705 ▪ info@arendsig.co.za ▪ www.arendsig.co.za ▪ S 33°55'37.9" E 020°0'47.6" ▪ **T +27 (0)84-200-2163/+27 (0)23-616-2835** ▪ F +27 (0)86-535-0693/+27 (0)23-616-2090

Arendsig co-owner and cellarmaster Lourens van der Westhuizen, who also vinifies for Esona, Mimosa and Star Hill, makes only single-vineyard wines in the small cellar on the Robertson family farm. His latest offering, untasted, is a chenin blanc from a 41-year-old bushvine block near Rawsonville.

■ **Arendskloof** *see* Eagle's Cliff Wines-New Cape Wines
■ **Are We Having Fun Yet** *see* Wine Village-Hermanus

Arniston Bay

Think 'Arniston', a resort close to Africa's southern tip, and you think of relaxed holidays and beach living, hence this accessible brand, one of The Company of Wine People's best export sellers. The trend's towards lighter wines, so there's now a Light range in white, rosé and red.

Bush Vine range

Pinotage 🏠 📖 ★★★ Sappy & bright **10** has appealing red berries & spice with creamy vanilla undertone. Firm but supple. WO W Cape, as for all following. **Chenin Blanc** ✓ 🏠 📖 ★★★★ **11** rich toasted nut nuance to bright apple flavours. Clean-cut & quite feisty, with good food-pairing length.

Arniston Bay range

Cabernet Sauvignon ☺ 🏠 📖 ★★★ **11** tank sample shows good varietal character in supple, juicy style. Easy-drinking, but enough structure for a meal. **Shiraz-Pinotage** ☺ 🏠 📖 ★★★ Friendly **11** is a smooth, spicy duo, with smoky berry tone. **Shiraz-Merlot** ☺ 🏠 📖 ★★★ **11** more engaging than previous. A bright, sappy 60/40 blend, with dryfood-friendly conclusion. **Cabernet Sauvignon-Shiraz** ☺ 🏠 📖 ★★★ Savoury & dark-fruited **11** preview is balanced, with succulent drinkability.

Merlot 🏠 📖 ★★ Light & bright **11** has a cool red berry tone. **Shiraz** 🏠 📖 ★★★ Preview of **11** reveals smoky bacon flavours. Spicy & warm BBQ quaffer. **Cabernet Sauvignon-Merlot** 🏠 📖 ★★★ **11** is a satisfying equal blend, with juicy dark fruit & some underlying seriousness from supple tannins. **Rosé** 🏠 📖 ★★ Fragrant off-dry **12** ex-tank, mostly shiraz, with sweet/sour balance. **Chardonnay** ✓ 🏠 📖 ★★★★ Unwooded **12** tank sample shows succulent stonefruit & pineapple freshened by clean limy acidity. Satisfying & flavoursome. **Sauvignon Blanc** 🏠 📖 ★★★ Fresh grassy, granadilla tone to lean & flinty **12**. **Sauvignon Blanc-Semillon** 🏠 📖 ★★★ Waxy & herbaceous **12** in leaner style, with crisp almond tone. **Chenin Blanc-Chardonnay** 🏠 📖 ★★★ Brisk & tangy **12** with ripe but low-key melon/apple flavours. Note: range previously listed as 'Original'.

The Shore range

White ☺ 🍷 ★★★ NV ex-tank, semi-dry, aromatic & fresh glassful with peachy/tropical tone.

Red 🍷 ★★ Undemanding **NV** preview is smooth with berry jam flavours. **Rosé** 🍷 ★★ Just off-dry, **NV** tank sample is light & crisp for sunset sipping.

Sparkling range

Méthode Charmat Rosé ⓕ ★★ Pretty packaging reflects in gently frothy, fruitily sweet **NV**. **Sparkling Brut** ★★ **NV** gentle stonefruit & apple on zesty, easy-drinking summer fizz from 3 varieties.

The Light range NEW

Red 🍷 ★★ Smoky savoury-sweetness on amiable **NV** sipper. **Rosé** ★★ **NV** has piquantly sweet berry tone for sunset quaffing. **White** 🍷 ★★ Delightfully light (5.5%, as all these), tropical & crisply sweet **NV**. — MW

Arra Vineyards

Location: Paarl ▪ Map: Paarl & Wellington ▪ WO: Paarl/Coastal ▪ Est 1998 ▪ 1stB 2001 ▪ Tasting & sales Mon-Sat 9-4.30 ▪ Owner(s) Arra Vineyards (Pty) Ltd ▪ Cellarmaster(s) Dee Wentzel (2006) ▪ Viticulturist(s) Johan Southey (2000) ▪ 72ha/30ha (cab, merlot, mourv, ptage, ruby cab, shiraz, viog) ▪ 10,000cs ▪ PO Box 298 Klapmuts 7625 ▪ info@arrawines.com ▪ www.arrawines.com ▪ S 33° 49′ 25.9″ E 018° 51′ 47.7″ ▪ **T +27 (0)21-875-5363** ▪ F +27 (0)21-875-5866

Cellar manager Dee Wentzel's enthusiasm for viognier shows no signs of slowing. She admits the variety is 'a demanding mistress' and her main concern is to be 'mindful of the acid; I don't like too much. It's never going to be a light, crisp, easy drinking wine, something we won't achieve in our hot climate.' Dee believes the maturing vineyard naturally produces rich, intense and creamy wines well suited as a food partner. She will next attempt a fortified version, 'if time allows'.

Reserve range

★★★★ **Cabernet Sauvignon** Lighter feel, more evolved savouriness, smooth tannins, leave **07** satisfying if not very complex drinking now.

★★★★ **Shiraz** Deep-hued & dark-fruited **07** bears a rich & supple texture with some still evident sweet oak flavours. Good fresh core should allow for more harmony over next year/2.

★★★★ **Viognier** 🥂 Evident oak spice on **11** (★★★★), may still meld with peachy, ginger fruit. Medium bodied, smooth & silky, fruitily dry finish. **09** more expressive; **10** not made.

Nobility 🥂 ★★★★ Sweetest, most unctuous viognier in range. **11** laced with plentiful spiced crème brulée appeal; richly textured with lingering honeyed tones.

Barrel Select range

★★★★ **Cabernet Sauvignon** ⓕ For those who enjoy reds with some age, traditionally styled **06** shows some meaty, savoury evolution, complexity. Harmonious but no hurry to drink up.

★★★★ **Pinotage Barrel Select** ⓕ One to please even non-pinotage lovers. **08** understated, more savoury spice than sweet red fruits; quite dense but fresh, beautifully polished tannins. Subtly oaked (20% new).

Arra Vineyards range

Blanc de Noir ☺ 🍷 🥂 ★★★ As fresh & fruity as a good dry blusher should be, shiraz-based **12** delivers smooth mouthful of spicy red berries designed for summer sipping.

Cabernet Sauvignon ⓕ ★★★★ **09** fresh, ripe blackberry scents, firm but not intimidating. Dashes merlot & malbec add interest. **Merlot** ⓕ ★★★ **09** uncomplicated drinking. Ripe dark berry aromas; very fresh, simple flavours. **Pinotage** ⓕ ★★★ **08**'s earthy nose refrained on **09** palate. Plainer, sweetish red fruit, soft, ready. **Shiraz** ⓕ ★★★ Blended with grenache noir, mourvèdre & noticeably peachy viognier in tail, **09** ripely juicy & ready. WO Coastal. **Cabernet Sauvignon-Merlot** ⓕ ★★★ unoaked 85/15 blend; satisfying ripe fruit, structure for current enjoyment. **Red Blend** ⓕ 🍷 ★★★ Hearty, country-style **09** headed by well-disguised pinotage with shiraz, cab, merlot. Richly flavoured, chewy tannins. **Shiraz-Cabernet Sauvignon** ⓕ ★★★★ Usual happy pairing of bright cassis fruit overlay to textured savouriness in **09**. Beneficial French oak, 10% new. **Shiraz-Mourvèdre-Carignan** ⓕ ★★★★ Comfortably padded **09** with rich yet fresh gamey, spicy flavours & tasty savoury tail. WO Coastal. **Chenin Blanc** NEW ★★★★ Assertive **11** with oxidative, honeyed concentration; grippy close leaves drier sensation than 4.4g/l sugar suggests. WO Coastal. **Viognier** ★★ Slight, rather funky features on **11**. Modest texture with alcohol glow edging semi-sweet tail. **Natural**

Sweet Viognier 🎗 ★★★ Modest fruit on sweet & silky **11**. Medium bodied; just enough cleansing acid on tail. **Natural Sweet Red Blend** ⏱ ★★★ **09** spicy shiraz-led septet; ideal candidate for mulled wine. — AL

Arumdale Cool Climate Wines

Location/WO: Elgin ▪ Map: Elgin, Walker Bay & Bot River ▪ Est 1962 ▪ 1stB 2003 ▪ Tasting & sales by appt Mon-Sat 8-5 Sun 10-5 ▪ Fee R15/5 wines, waived on purchase of 2/more bottles ▪ Closed Easter Fri-Mon, Dec 25/26 & Jan 1 ▪ Owner(s) Mark Simpson ▪ Cellarmaster(s) Ian Nieuwoudt (2012) ▪ Viticulturist(s) Paul Wallace (Nov 2008, consultant) ▪ 90ha/10ha (cab, merlot, shiraz, sauv) ▪ 70t/4,000cs own label 80% red 10% white 10% rosé ▪ PO Box 2 Elgin 7180 ▪ royalwine@arumdale.co.za ▪ www.arumdale.co.za ▪ S 34° 13'11.3" E 019° 2'31 3" ▪ **T** +27 (0)21-848-9880 ▪ F +27 (0)21-848-9683

After the launch of the (untasted by us) Robin Hood Legendary Wine series last year, owner Mark Simpson realised a long-held dream and transformed his Elgin visitor venue into a medieval 'tasting palace'. Visitor numbers are up and the plan is to move to larger premises soon, so more people can enjoy the wines.

Shiraz NEW ★★★ Meaty sweetness on nose of **07** with some liquorice, fennel & smoke. Stewed black fruit & chewy texture. **Pink Shiraz** NEW 🍷 ★★★★ Attractive strawberry/raspberry notes on **12**, lowish alcohol (12%) & lively 'pink fizzer' confection. All very delicious & summery. **Special L.Y.C. Sauvignon Blanc** NEW 🍷 ★★★★ Unusual flavours on **12** from 4 months on chardonnay lees — fragrant melons & white peach. Confected fruit, balanced acidity. Discontinued: **St. Andrews Blend**. — CM

Asara Wine Estate & Hotel

Location/map: Stellenbosch ▪ WO: Stellenbosch/Western Cape ▪ Est/1stB 2001 ▪ Tasting Mon-Sat 10-6 Sun 10-4 ▪ Fee R30/3 wines, R50/5 wines ▪ Sales 10-5 ▪ Closed Good Fri & Dec 25 ▪ Tasting centre ▪ Cellar tours by appt ▪ Tour groups ▪ Five star hotel ▪ Raphael's restaurant ▪ Sansibar Cigar & Whisky Lounge ▪ Deli ▪ Gift shop ▪ Function & banqueting facilities ▪ Conferences ▪ Weddings ▪ Owner(s) Markus & Christiane Rahmann ▪ Cellarmaster(s) Francois Joubert (Sep 2009) ▪ Winemaker(s) Francois Joubert (Sep 2009), with Tanja-Mari Goedhart (Oct 2010) ▪ Viticulturist(s) Henk Agenbach (Oct 2009) ▪ 180ha/102ha (cab, merlot, p verdot, chard, sauv) ▪ 800t/35,000cs own label 73% red 25% white 2% rosé ▪ IPW ▪ PO Box 882 Stellenbosch 7599 ▪ info@asarawine.com ▪ www.asarawine.co za ▪ S 33° 56'35.00" E 018° 48'31.00" ▪ **T** +27 (0)21-888-8000 ▪ F +27 (0)21-888-8001

When Markus and Christiane Rahmann acquired this historic property — first granted in 1691 — in 2001, they named it Asara, 'the meeting point of the African gods Astar (earth), Asis (sun) and Asase (sky)'. Strategically situated at the confluence of two major access roads into Stellenbosch, they then set about creating an abundance of upmarket hospitality offerings for 'the discerning traveller', wine amongst them. More recently the tasting centre has been moved to overlook the barrel cellar, resplendent with beautiful chandeliers.

Bell Tower Collection

★★★★☆ **Petit Verdot** Back after hiatus (no **07**, **08**), previewed **09** (★★★★) peculiarity for jaded palates: intense 'green' tension to cranberry fruit, austere yet manages balance. Shade less exhilarating than **06**.

★★★★ **Estate Wine** ⏱ Malbec-led blend of 5 Bordeaux red varieties; **07** 'wet leaf' character when last tasted, but enough bramble fruit to balance pliable tannins. WO W Cape.

★★★★ **Avalon** Remarkable vine-dried shiraz (& 7% pinotage) in Amarone style; long oaking, 30% new. **08** (★★★★★) rich & robust fruitcake, more silky, better integrated than warmly alcoholic **07**, led by pinotage.

Asara Wine Estate & Hotel range

★★★★ **Cabernet Sauvignon** ⏱ **09** tightly wound — even a tad angular — mid-2011 but promises elegance 5-7 years from harvest. Improves on softer, less enduring **08** (★★★★). WO W Cape.

Nouveau NEW ☺ 🍷 ★★★ 'Be Jolly Now Wow!' is marketing's onomatopoeic reference to the French origin of the style; fresh **12** gamay tastes like red berries dancing with watermelon. **Ebony** ☺ 🍷 🎗 ★★★ Mulberry-laden **10** merlot-cab a bit brash but utterly drinkable. **Rosé** ☺ 🍷 🎗 ★★★ Coralhued **12** proffers ripe bonbon fruit in just-dry finish, from pinotage. **Chardonnay Unwooded** ☺ 🎗 ★★★ Lipsmacking citrus focus of pre-bottling **12** fresher & fuller than previous, bristles with lemon & lime. Moderate 13% alcohol.

Merlot ⊕ ★★★★ Scrumptious **09**, succulence & meaty flesh are like a bear hug, with big tannins, too, when last we tasted. WO C Cape, as next 2. **Shiraz** ⊕ ★★★★ **09** back to form after barnyardy **07**, (no **08**), polished spice & savoury fruit limited only by 'wild' edginess. **Cape Fusion** ⊕ ★★★ Cape Blend of pinotage, merlot, shiraz & cab, **09** plummy & touch rustic previously, just-dry. **Cabernet Sauvignon Blanc** ⬚ ★★★ Novel white wine from black grape. Lightish, capsicum-crisp **12** tank sample has nutty interest. **Chardonnay Reserve** ⊕ ⬚ ★★★★ Obvious oak shielded promising lemony fruit from view in previewed **11**, should integrate in time. **Sauvignon Blanc** ⬚ ★★★ Uncomplicated **12** preview, clean & dry, tropical features & gentle 12.3% alcohol for summer lunches. **Ivory** ⊕ 🍴 ⬚ ★★★ **11** refreshing, fruity chenin fleshes out steely sauvignon for poolside pleasure. WO W Cape. **Noble Late Harvest** Next awaited. Discontinued: **Spirit of Chenin**. — DS

Ashbourne

Location: Hermanus ▪ Map: Elgin, Walker Bay & Bot River ▪ WO: Hemel-en-Aarde Valley/Walker Bay ▪ Est 1996 ▪ 1stB 2001 ▪ Tasting, sales & tours by appt ▪ Owner(s) Anthony Hamilton Russell ▪ Winemaker(s) Hannes Storm (2004) ▪ Viticulturist(s) Johan Montgomery (2005) ▪ 113ha/24.35ha (cabs s/f, malbec, p verdot, ptage, shiraz, sauv, sem) ▪ 20t/1,000cs own label 50% red 50% white ▪ PO Box 158 Hermanus 7200 ▪ hrv@hermanus.co.za ▪ S 34° 23'09.25" E 019° 14' 29.90" ▪ **T +27 (0)28-312-3595** ▪ F +27 (0)28-312-1797

For owner Anthony Hamilton Russell, alcohol is one of the last socially acceptable euphorics, and wine is without doubt the most beautiful and beneficial way of enjoying it. However, given his (admitted) bias towards classic European wine styles, is it inappropriate for Ashbourne to pay homage to wine through pinotage — South Africa's 'own' grape, but one not generally recognised for its finesse and refinement? Not so, he insists. Cape wines of the early 1970s, for example, were strongly European in their leanings, and great wines to boot. 'Making European-styled wine in South Africa is a very South African thing to do; this is the stylistic flag we will always fly with Ashbourne.'

★★★★☆ **Ashbourne** ⊕ Pinotage-led **07** (★★★★) enriched with equal dabs (9%) shiraz & cab. Cool black cherry & clean leather coupled with Old World savouriness, subtle oaking & leafy tannins. Previous vintages 100% pinotage. Moderate ±13% alcohol for this & stablemate.

★★★★☆ **Sandstone** ⊕ Masterly **08** blends sauvignon (77%), chardonnay & semillon fermented in clay amphoras. Enticing, with vibrant acid structure & flavour depth to reward further ageing. Walker Bay WO. — CvZ

Ashton Wynkelder 🍴🏠📷🎿♿

Location: Ashton ▪ Map/WO: Robertson ▪ Est 1962 ▪ 1stB 1970 ▪ Tasting & sales Mon-Fri 8-5 Sat 9-2 (summer) & 10-2 (winter) ▪ Closed Easter Fri/Sat & Dec 25/26 ▪ Cellar tours by appt ▪ Facilities for children ▪ Tour groups ▪ Farm produce ▪ Conferences ▪ Walks/hikes ▪ 4x4 trail ▪ Mountain biking ▪ Conservation area ▪ Accommodation ▪ Owner(s) 52 shareholders ▪ Cellarmaster(s) Sterik de Wet (Oct 2009) ▪ Winemaker(s) Simon Basson (Nov 2007) & Roy Thorne (Oct 2011) ▪ Viticulturist(s) Hennie Visser (Vinpro) ▪ 1,200ha (cab, ruby cab, shiraz, chard, chenin) ▪ 23,079t/10,000cs own label 42% red 50% white 6% rosé 2% other; 3,300cs for clients & 12m L bulk ▪ Other export brands: Berryfields, Mountain Stream ▪ ISO 22000, BWI, HACCP ▪ PO Box 40 Ashton 6715 ▪ info@ashtonkelder.co.za ▪ www.ashtonkelder.co.za ▪ S 33° 50'12.1" E 020° 1'48.3" ▪ **T +27 (0)23-615-1135** ▪ F +27 (0)23-615-1284

A happy 50th birthday in May 2012 saw this Robertson Valley grower-owned cellar going greener, with solar panels installed in staff houses and effective recycling procedures put in place. They aim to offer something for everyone, from grape juice for the kids, the Satyn range for the young at heart, 'mealtime wine', a Reserve line for the sophisticate, and fortified wine 'for the sweeter, older palate'.

Reserve range

Shiraz Reserve ⊕ ★★★ Aromatic **07** previously showed weighty oak spices & solid tannins, from which fruit may emerge given time. **Roodewal** ⊕ ★★★★ **10**'s cab (60%), pinotage & dash merlot deliver rich, well composed & smooth sipping. **Chardonnay Limited Release** NEW ⬚ ★★★ Barrel-fermented **12** preview, understated fresh lime flavours, elegance expected at Reserve level compromised somewhat by obvious sweetness.

Ashton range

Satynwit ☺ 🍴 ⬚ ★★★ Chenin & sauvignon partnership raise the bar in crisp, friendly **12**.

Cabernet Sauvignon 🈂 ★★★ Fruity blackberries & idiosyncratic Turkish Delight note on frisky party animal **11**. **Pinotage** ⓘ 🈂 ★★ Blackberry jam, savoury spice & banana tones on **11** glugger. **Shiraz** 🈂 ★★★ Friendly steak dinner companion **11** offers lovely shiraz typicity: red fruit, black pepper dusting. **Cabernet Sauvignon-Merlot** Await new vintage. **Satynrooi** ⓘ 🍴 ★★ **11** unoaked & uncomplicated for everyday enjoyment. **Satynrosé** 🍴 🈂 ★★ **12** repeats successful recipe: light-bodied rosé for the sweet-toothed, from pinotage. **Chardonnay Unwooded** 🍴 Not ready at press time. **Chenin Blanc** 🍴 🈂 ★★ Step-up **12** easygoing peachy sipper. **Sauvignon Blanc** 🍴 🈂 ★★ Early picked **12** pineapple & melon quick-sip. **Satynperlé** 🍴 🈂 ★★ Tiny bubbles provide zing & lift in improved **12** sweet perlé chenin & sauvignon. **Bonica Vin Doux** Not tasted. **Red Muscadel Jerepigo** Await new. Discontinued: **White Muskadel Jerepiko**. — DB/JP

Assegai Selection

Location: Somerset West ▪ Est 1999 ▪ Sales by appt ▪ Owner(s) Woodlands Import Export ▪ 67 Oakbridge Village Bizweni Ave Somerset West 7130 ▪ rbuchner@worldonline.co.za ▪ S 34° 3'9.2" E 018° 49'58.3" ▪ **T +27 (0)21-851-0552** ▪ F +27 (0)86-616-1743

Assegai's Raimund Buchner reports that his export-only sparkling wine brand is to all intents and purposes 'in limbo', the rand exchange rate and the economic woes of the Eurozone having stopped off channels into his native Germany. With other fish to fry, he's resigned to biding his time.

Ataraxia Wines

Location: Hermanus ▪ Map: Elgin, Walker Bay & Bot River ▪ WO: Western Cape ▪ Est 2004 ▪ 1stB 2005 ▪ Tasting & sales Mon–Fri 9-4 Sat 10-5 Sun in season only ▪ Fee R15pp for groups of 10 or more, refunded with individual purchase ▪ Closed Easter Fri/Sun, Dec 25 & Jan 1 ▪ Art exhibition ▪ Charcuterie platters available during holiday season ▪ Owner(s) Kevin Grant Wines (Pty) Ltd ▪ Cellarmaster(s)/winemaker(s)/viticulturist(s) Kevin Grant (Sep 2004) ▪ 47ha/12ha (pinot, chard) ▪ 83t/6,000cs own label 40% red 60% white ▪ PO Box 603 Hermanus 7200 ▪ info@ataraxiawines.co.za ▪ www.ataraxiawines.co.za ▪ S 34° 20'27.0" E 019° 18'30.8" ▪ **T +27 (0)28-212-2007** ▪ F +27 (0)28-212-1921

Chardonnay and pinot noir are Kevin Grant's passions. He has received acclaim for the former since his maiden vintage in 2005 but only in 2011 was he able to include fruit from his own maturing vineyards — the 2012 coming entirely from homegrown grapes. Pinot noir remains a work in progress from his young vines, with no date set for a maiden release. In the meantime, activity has centred on expanding sales on both local and international markets; an iPad in the Wine Lounge allows overseas clients to place orders in their own country. To accompany the wines for holiday-season visitors, Grant has lined up charcuterie from a renowned Cape Town charcutier, with local breads and cheeses.

★★★★ **Serenity** Unspecified Elgin, Walker Bay fruit in fulsome **09**. Very ripe with soft-fruited core; fine tannin trim lends focus & some freshness but not as impressive as **08** (★★★★★).

★★★★☆ **Chardonnay 11** first from 100% Hemel-en-Aarde area fruit. Elegant & precise, with tense minerality restraining delicious leesy richness. Oak subtle extra to oatmeal & lime complexity. Very classy. Impressive potential.

★★★★☆ **Sauvignon Blanc** Cool, steely yet ripe feel to **12** from Elgin/Walker Bay fruit. Well weighted, quite intense; its undeniably sauvignon face presented with restraint, sophistication. — AL

■ **Atkinson Ridge** *see* Amani Vineyards
■ **Attie's Long Shadow** *see* Opstal Estate
■ **Auberge du Paysan** *see* L'Auberge du Paysan

Auction Crossing Private Cellar

Location: De Doorns ▪ Map: Worcester ▪ WO: Western Cape ▪ Est 2003 ▪ 1stB 2004 ▪ Tasting & sales Mon–Fri 9-5 Sat 9-2 ▪ Closed all pub hols ▪ Cellar tours by appt ▪ Bistro 'Inspirati' ▪ Facilities for children ▪ Tour groups ▪ Gifts ▪ Farm produce ▪ Owner(s) De Villiers Graaff, AJ Reyneke & Leon Dippenaar ▪ Cellarmaster(s)/winemaker(s)/viticulturist(s) Leon Dippenaar (Aug 2004) ▪ ±41ha/2ha (mourv, shiraz, viog) ▪ 10t/2,000cs own label 75% red 25% white ▪ The Pines PO Box 5 Hex River 6855 ▪ auctioncrossing@hexvalley.co.za ▪ www.auctioncrossing.co.za ▪ S 33° 29'42.8" E 019° 34'32.7" ▪ **T +27 (0)23-357-9655** ▪ F +27 (0)23-357-9255

Formerly listed as Hex River Crossing, though Auction Crossing is on the label — and the name of the 1938 cellar which, refurbished, saw the first modern vintage in 2004. Part-owner and winemaker Leon Dippenaar takes grapes from different regions, one being Durbanville — De Grendel's De Villiers Graaff is also a co-owner.

Syrah-Viognier ⚑ ★★★★ Co-fermented, aromatic **09** well made & accessible, pleasingly positive spicy finish as tannins tug sweetly ripe dark fruit. **Viognier** ⚑ 🗒 🖾 ★★★ Variety's exotic fruity, floral aromas belie bone-dry savouriness in lightly oaked **10** with nice underlying pithiness. — IM

Audacia Wines

Location/map/WO: Stellenbosch ▪ Est 1930 ▪ Tasting & sales Mon-Sat 9-5 ▪ Fee R20, waived on purchase ▪ Closed Easter Fri/Sun, Dec 25 & Jan 1 ▪ Owner(s) Strydom & Harris families ▪ Cellarmaster(s)/winemaker(s)/viticulturist(s) Michael van Niekerk (Aug 2009) ▪ 32ha/20ha (cabs s/f, malbec, merlot, p verdot, roobernet, shiraz) ▪ 120t/9,000cs own label 100% red ▪ IPW ▪ PO Box 12679 Die Boord 7613 ▪ info@audacia.co.za ▪ www.audacia.co.za ▪ S 33° 59' 45.7" E 018° 50' 2.9" ▪ **T +27 (0)21-881-3052** ▪ F +27 (0)21-881-3137

The specialist red wine boutique cellar on the increasingly busy Route 44 between Stellenbosch and Somerset West is raising its profile with what they describe as 'a new cosy tasting venue' and an all-weather weekend family market, cleverly named Root 44. In the vineyard, worm tea irrigation is boosting nutrients and microbial activity in the soil, with a 'positive impact on our vines and wines'.

Cabernet Sauvignon ★★★ Previously noted as discontinued, returns in **10** with food-styled firm blueberry flavours & spicy notes. **History** NEW ★★★ Spice & cocoa richness on **10**, from cab franc, oak still prominent & firm mid-2012. Allow year/2 to sync with the fruit. **Malbec** Await new vintage. **Merlot** ★★★ Juicy black berry on **10**, brisk freshness & chalky length. **Shiraz** ⚑ ★★★ Ripe but restrained **09**, savoury & straightforward, lighter than previous. **Rouge Noble** ★★★ Meaty salami on **NV** blend. Structured & long. **Jeté** ★★★ Leathery cherry on this **NV** off-dry blend from unspecified grapes. — FM

Aufwaerts Co-operative

Location: Rawsonville ▪ Map: Breedekloof ▪ Tasting by appt ▪ Winemaker(s) Hennie de Villiers ▪ PO Box 51 Rawsonville 6845 ▪ aufwaerts@breede.co.za, hanepoot39@gmail.com ▪ S 33° 41' 42.4" E 019° 17' 33.7" ▪ **T +27 (0)23-349-1202** ▪ F +27 (0)23-349-1202

This is a small family co-operative, situated on a Breedekloof property owned by the De Villiers family since the 1800s. Planted with a wide array of grape varieties, the estate also features a brandy distillery, declared a National Monument in the 1940s. 'Anybody can visit us by appointment,' says winemaker Hennie de Villiers.

Austin *see* Noble Hill Wine Estate

Autumn Harvest Crackling

One of South Africa's top-selling brands, this perlé range is made by Distell from grapes sourced across the Western Cape.

White 🗒 ★★ Previously listed as 'Crackling'. A fun all-sorts blend, lots of sugar but citrus zestiness & zingy bubbles taste crisp rather than sweet. **NV**. **Rosé** 🗒 ★★ Blend of red & white wine, newest **NV** fresh & crisp, sweetness balanced by bouncy bubbles. **Red** NEW 🗒 ★ **NV** from multitude of varieties starts off savoury then surprises with lots of sweetness, rescued by zesty bubbles. Lightish ±12% alcohol for all these. — DB/HJ

Avondale

Location: Paarl ▪ Map: Paarl & Wellington ▪ WO: Paarl/Coastal ▪ Est 1996 ▪ 1stB 1999 ▪ Tasting & sales Mon-Sat by appt ▪ Tasting R50pp, Eco Tour R200pp ▪ Closed Easter Fri-Mon, Dec 25 & Jan 1 ▪ Cellar & eco tours by appt only ▪ Art exhibit ▪ Owner(s) Grieve Family / The Avondale Trust ▪ Winemaker(s) Corné Marais (Sep-tember (Jan 2012) ▪ Viticulturist(s) Johnathan Grieve (Jul 1999) ▪ 300ha/100ha (cabs s/f, grenache, merlot, mourv, shiraz, chard, chenin, rouss, sem, viog) ▪ 500t/25,000cs own label 50% red 38% white 2% rosé 10% MCC ▪ EU Organic & USDA NOP organic, LEAF ▪ PO Box 602 Paarl South 7624 ▪ wine@avondalewine.co.za ▪ www.avondalewine.co.za ▪ S 33° 45' 52.9" E 019° 0' 4.7" ▪ **T +27 (0)21-863-1976** ▪ F +27 (0)21-863-1534

For a while now, Avondale GM and viticulturist Johnathan Grieve has advocated an approach to farming which combines organic and biodynamic farming principles with the best that modern science has to offer. It's a philosophy that's evolved since he arrived at the family's Paarl farm in 1999 and realised that it had been thrown out of balance by years of conventional farming. By taking account of everything from the smallest microbes in the soil to planetary influences, he's steadily rejuvenating the property and, as the land regenerates, so the wines are improving and becoming more expressive of their origin, Johnathan believes.

★★★★ **Samsara** 🌿 100% shiraz, **06** well rounded with moderate acidity, smooth tannins. Notes of red & black fruit, white pepper, cinnamon. Arguably lacks punch so don't keep too long.

★★★★ **La Luna** 🌿 **06** serious Bordeaux-style red blend is probably at peak. Red & black fruit, dried herbs, savoury edge. Rich but not bulky, soft tannins.

★★★★ **Navitas** 🌿 Well-assembled, understated **08** is shiraz-led, rest mourvèdre, grenache. Now bottled, it's medium bodied with notes of red fruit & white pepper before a long, dry finish.

★★★★ **Cyclus** 🌿 🈯 Imaginative **10** (★★★★★) white blend is viognier led, rest chenin, roussanne, semillon. Complex, with aromas & flavours of citrus through peach plus waxy, leesy notes. Rich & full, creamy texture offset by zingy acidity. Less oak than **09**.

★★★★ **Armilla Méthode Cap Classique Brut** 🌿 **NV** sparkling from chardonnay, 10% oaked, 2 years on lees. Citrus, subtle biscuit note. Rich & full, fine mousse, bright acidity. Latest is more intensely flavoured, precise.

Camissa 🌿 🈯 ★★★ Rosé from unconventional combo muscat de Frontignan & mourvèdre. **11** subtle red fruit, slight spicy note lends interest. Ideal with seafood. **Anima** 🌿 🈯 ★★★★ 100% chenin, composed **10** has good intensity, tangy acidity. Peach flavour to the fore but also honey, vanilla. Year in oak, 20% new, adds just the right amount of heft. Tad more poise than **09** (★★★★). — CE

Avondrood Vineyards

Location: Rawsonville ▪ Map: Breedekloof ▪ Est/1stB 2005 ▪ Tasting, sales & cellar tours Mon-Fri 8-12 & 1.30-5 Sat by appt (phone +27 (0)82-578-6841) ▪ Closed most pub hols ▪ Refreshments/food-and-wine tastings by appt or BYO picnic ▪ Conferences ▪ Walks/hikes ▪ Facilities for children ▪ Hewn-stone mountain cottage ▪ Owner(s) Albertus van Rensburg ▪ Winemaker(s) Albertus van Rensburg, with Johannes Damane ▪ Viticulturist(s) Pierre Snyman ▪ 80ha (cab, ptage, shiraz, chard, sauv, viog) ▪ 30t/2,100cs own label 40% red 60% white ▪ PO Box 277 Worcester 6849 ▪ vineyards@avondrood.co.za ▪ www.avondrood.co.za ▪ S 33° 43'32.9" E 019° 20'18.7" ▪ **T +27 (0)23-349-1858** ▪ F +27 (0)86-210-5806

No major changes at this small Breedekloof family winery, from where Albertus and Minett van Rensburg target the Pretoria-Johannesburg market, in particular, in collaboration with a local agent. Plans for this year include the addition of a limited-release malbec to their range.

Avondvrede

Location: Paarl ▪ Map: Paarl & Wellington ▪ Est 1995 ▪ 1stB 1999 ▪ Tasting, sales & light lunches by appt ▪ Owner(s) John & Christine Enthoven ▪ Winemaker(s) John Enthoven ▪ Vineyard manager(s) Gerardus van Zyl ▪ 3ha (cabs s/f, merlot) ▪ PO Box 152 Klapmuts 7625 ▪ S 33° 49'47.2" E 018° 53'8.3" ▪ **T +27 (0)83-658-0595** ▪ F +27 (0)21-875-5609

The Enthoven family vinify tiny quantities of cab and merlot (2011 is the current vintage) exclusively for the export market.

Avontuur Estate

Location: Somerset West ▪ Map: Helderberg ▪ WO: Stellenbosch ▪ Est 1850 ▪ 1stB 1990 ▪ Tasting & sales Mon-Fri 8. 30-5 Sat/Sun 9-4 ▪ Fee R20/5 wines, R40/Premiere range, brandy & bubbly ▪ Closed Good Fri, Dec 25 & Jan 1 ▪ Cellar tours by appt ▪ Avontuur Estate Restaurant (see Restaurants section) ▪ Conference venue ▪ Thoroughbred stud ▪ Owner(s) Taberer family ▪ Winemaker(s) Jan van Rooyen (Jan 2011) ▪ Viticulturist(s) Pippa Mickleburgh (Sep 1999) ▪ 104ha/51ha (cabs s/f, merlot, ptage, pinot, shiraz, chard, chenin, sauv, viog) ▪ 260t/18,000cs own label 60% red 40% white ▪ PO Box 1128 Somerset West 7129 ▪ info@avontuurestate.co.za ▪ www.avontuurestate.co. za ▪ S 34° 1'33.2" E 018° 49'23.8" ▪ **T +27 (0)21-855-3450** ▪ F +27 (0)21-855-4600

The Taberer family's prominent Helderberg estate is inextricably interwoven with their famed racehorse stud, which the late founder, Tony Taberer, relocated from Zimbabwe in the 1980s. The labels of their Premiere range honour past champion alumni and bloodstock. Now in the hands of next generation Michael and Philip, with enthusiastic input from the new broom in the cellar, Jan van Rooyen, they intend restoring their former status in this prestige red-wine area. The cellar is undergoing an equipment upgrade to facilitate new winemaking philosophies emphasising terroir and varietal character, while reducing the carbon footprint.

Avontuur Premiere range

★★★★ **Dominion Royale (Shiraz Reserve)** Dense, concentrated & ripe 09 (★★★★) outperforms 08, fully deserves Reserve status. Brooding dark power with satin tannins, easily tames new oak regime. Appealing wild herb & meaty notes round out substantial body.

Minelli (Pinot Noir Reserve) ⓘ ★★★★ Fresh & food-friendly 09 offers delicate cherry & raspberry. Modest alcohol, unobtrusive oaking & soft tannin make it very accessible. **Baccarat** ⓘ ★★★★ When last tasted, 08 Bordeaux blend was just-dry, with ripe fruit & spicy notes, the finish a bit warm from 14.5% alcohol. **Luna de Miel (Chardonnay Reserve)** ★★★ Toasty oak dominates 10, masks well-formed, ripe fruit profile on slender body. Unlikely to evolve. **Sarabande (Sauvignon Blanc Reserve)** ⓘ ★★★★ 10, with mineral-toned blackcurrant flavours, was fresh & dry, last year looked likely to gain complexity with time.

Avontuur Estate range

★★★★ **Brut Cap Classique** ⓘ Traditional-method sparkling, **NV** from chardonnay, tasted previously. Aromas of ripe apple, pear & spicy gingerbread; creamy mouthfeel, showing yeasty notes & a good dry finish. **Cabernet Sauvignon** ★★★★ Medium bodied, more focused than previous, previewed 09 ticks the boxes but falls short of impressing. **Cabernet Franc** ★★★★ Steely varietal grip & layered fruit on 09 reflect stellar vintage. Lean & linear, showing more supple body, tempered alcohol than previous 08 (★★★★). **Pinotage** ⓘ ★★★ 08 sampled previously, raspberry fruit dominated by oak & dry tannin. **Shiraz** ⓘ ★★★ On review, 08 loaded with jammy fruit & spicy oak. Dry, but big alcohol left sweet impression. **Cabernet Sauvignon-Merlot** ⓘ ★★★ Just-off-dry 08, firmly built, with support from older oak, awkward acid balanced by sweetness on satisfying finish. **Sauvignon Blanc** 🍷 🖾 ★★★★ Previewed 12, designated 'Sur Lie', a welcome change in direction. Fatter, with better focus, finer detail. **Above Royalty (Noble Late Harvest)** Await new vintage.

Vintner's range

Red 🍷 ★★★ Previously in 'Avontuur Estate' line-up, as for Blend. Bright & sprightly cab-shiraz blend, **10** leads low pocket-friendly range. Decent body & supple fruit. **Blend** 🍷 🖾 ★★★ Previewed 12 dry blush from chardonnay & pinot. Refreshingly light. **White** 🍷 🖾 ★★★ Returns to the guide with 12, tank sample mostly sauvignon, vibrantly fruity & fresh. — GdB

Awendland

Location: Rawsonville ▪ Map/WO: Breedekloof ▪ Est/1stB 2006 ▪ Tasting, sales & tours by appt ▪ Owner(s) André van der Walt ▪ Cellarmaster(s)/winemaker(s) André van der Walt (Jan 2009) ▪ Viticulturist(s) Peet Smith (Jan 2009) ▪ 10ha total ▪ 10t/2,000cs own label 50% red 50% white ▪ PO Box 237 Rawsonville 6845 ▪ utilitas@iafrica.com, dagbreek@compnet.co.za ▪ S 33° 39'57.7" E 019° 18'8.43" ▪ **T +27 (0)21-887-2713** ▪ F +27 (0)21-887-2710

'The queen' is still resting, this time in bottle, says André van der Walt, who intends leaving his nebbiolo to mature for at least a year before releasing it. 'I check up on it and taste it regularly though,' notes the semi-retired Breedekloof farmer with a twinkle.

Nebbia Reserve Await next, as for **Shiraz, Cabernet Sauvignon-Merlot Unfiltered, Cabernet Sauvignon-Merlot** & **Sauvignon Blanc. Chenin Blanc Reserve** ⓘ ★★★★ Previously, seriously styled 10 preview had rich glacé pineapple & lime flavour balanced by tangy acid. — MW

Axe Hill

Location/WO: Calitzdorp ▪ Map: Klein Karoo & Garden Route ▪ Est 1993 ▪ 1stB 1997 ▪ Tasting, sales & cellar tours by appt Mon-Sat ▪ Owner(s) Axe Hill Winery (Pty) Ltd ▪ Cellarmaster(s)/winemaker(s) Mike Neebe (Oct 2007) ▪ Viticulturist(s) Johannes Mellet (Aug 2009, consultant) ▪ ±60ha/1.3ha (souzão, tinta barocca, touriga nacional) ▪ ±5t/±2,000cs own label 70% red 30% white ▪ Wesoewer Road Calitzdorp 6660 ▪ info@axehill.

co.za ▪ www.axehill.co.za ▪ S 33° 30' 54.6" E 021° 41' 23.0" ▪ **T** +27 (0)11-447-4366, +27 (0)44-213-**3585** ▪ F +27 (0)11-447-3219

This premium port producer in Klein Karoo's Calitzdorp is looking at 'new areas of focus without harming our legacy of premium port production'. One obvious avenue is the unfortified 'Calitzdorp Blend' of classic Portuguese varieties currently generating much excitement locally, but cellarmaster Mike Neebe says Axe Hill wants to keep its options open and, in partnership with a neighbour, has planted small blocks of southern Rhône varieties grenache noir and viognier (and port variety tinta roriz, aka tempranillo). The preference is to use own and Calitzdorp-area grapes but, again, market demand might necessitate sourcing more widely.

★★★★ **Shiraz** ⊕ Cellar's first unfortified red impresses in **10** with dark fruit & bouillon, 50% new oak deftly judged, adds structure & light seasoning.

★★★★☆ **Cape Vintage Port** ⊕ Classic Cape port-style, with souzão (39%) leading touriga & tinta for 1st time in **09** (★★★★), also one of their driest (mere 88g/l sugar). Plump fruit, dried herb & spice overlay, good complexity but shade off **08**.

★★★★ **Cape Ruby Port** ⊕ Ripe & rich **NV** from touriga permeated by Karoo scrub, buoyed by exceptionally pure fruit, elegant & accessible — & delicious!

Distinta NEW ✓ ★★★★ 'Different' in name & make-up: **11** vibrant blend shiraz (68%) & tinta, matured in older French barrels. Floral dark berries, smooth & lipsmackingly dry. **Machado** ✓ ★★★★ Rung up in ageworthy **11** touriga-led (just) combo with equal shiraz & tinta. Intense aromas, rich Christmas cake flavours flesh out firm tannins. More open & showy on review than **10** (★★★). **Cape White** ★★★ Fortified chenin aged in a solera, hence oxidative styling of latest **NV**. Attractive nutty/savoury conclusion & tapas-friendly grip. — WB/JP

Ayama Wines

Location: Paarl ▪ Map: Paarl & Wellington ▪ WO: Western Cape/Paarl/Voor Paardeberg ▪ Est 2005 ▪ 1stB 2006 ▪ Tasting by appt ▪ Closed all pub hols ▪ Meals/refreshments by appt; or BYO picnic ▪ Walks/hikes ▪ Conservation area ▪ Owner(s) Slent Farms (Pty) Ltd (6 partners) ▪ Cellarmaster(s)/winemaker(s) Michela Sfiligoi (2005) ▪ Viticulturist(s) Attilio Dalpiaz (2005) ▪ 172ha/37ha (cab, merlot, shiraz, chenin) ▪ 300t/20,000cs own label 30% red 68% white 2% rosé ▪ WIETA ▪ Suite 106 Private Bag X3041 Paarl 7620 ▪ info@slentfarms.com ▪ www.ayama.co.za ▪ S 33° 37' 22.5" E 018° 49' 19" ▪ **T** +27 (0)21-869-8313 ▪ F +27 (0)21-869-8313

Ayama ('Someone To Lean On') brings together Italian family and friends with enthusiastically patriotic views about their adopted country. They plunge headlong into the winelands life experience at Slent Farm in the Perdeberg foothills, engaging, experimenting and celebrating their good fortune (lately with their first méthode cap classique sparkling).

Leopard range

★★★★ **Shiraz-Pinotage-Mourvèdre** ⊕ 🍖 🍷 Appealing blend with ripe dark berry fruit & soft texture, **10** shows classic Old World touch. Elegant & balanced, eminently drinkable.

Chardonnay-Chenin Blanc-Viognier ⊕ 🍖 🍷 ★★★★ First tasting, alluringly scented **10** shows richly ripe fruit, thick texture & elegantly balanced acidity.

Ayama Wines range

★★★★ **Méthode Cap Classique Rosé** NEW Pretty tinsel-pink dry **09**, champagne-method sparkling mostly from pinot noir, shows satisfying yeasty notes on red berry fruit & shortbread, all nicely judged.

Chenin Blanc ☺ 🍖 🍷 ★★★ Dry **12** resolutely fruit-driven, unpretentious & generous. Cheerful, sunny poolside delight. Voor Paardeberg WO.

Cabernet Sauvignon 🍷 ★★★ Simonsberg-sourced **11** tank sample offers ripe blackcurrant fruit spiced with oak. Thick tannins lend bitter twist at finish. **Merlot** ⊕ 🍖 ★★★ Reticent, lean **10** shows restrained handling, cooler vintage. Still appealing, but begging meaty, saucy dishes. **Pinotage** 🍷 ★★☆ Rustic, funky aromas on **10** mask ripe, appealing fruit. **Shiraz** ⊕ ★★★★ When last tasted, fruit-driven unwooded **09** had depth & substance, appealing peppery centre & black cherries. **Baboon's Back Shiraz** 🍷 ★★★★ Partially oaked **11**, pre-bottling expresses fruit-driven, easy-drinking style. Unpretentiously soft, ripe & eminently moreish. Voor Paardeberg WO. **Pinotage-Shiraz** 🍷 ★★★ **11** Cape Blend has appealing savoury stewed fruit with silky texture. Ripe, juicy & generous. **Rosé** ⊕ 🍖 ★★ Spicy, fruity **10** from pinotage previously showed variety's brisk acidity. **Chardonnay** ⊕ 🍖 ★★☆ Unoaked **10**, fullish body with ntense apricot notes. WO Swartland. **Sauvignon Blanc** ⊕ 🍴 ★★★ Waxy, mineral **10** has distinctive fla-vour profile nodding at Swartland new-wave. Fullish, gently acidic & appealing. **Viognier** 🍴 🎨 ★★★ Full, ripe & unoaked, **10** has honest fruit, but beginning to show age development. Drink now. Paarl WO. **Chenin Blanc-Sauvignon Blanc** 🍴 🎨 ★★★ Mostly chenin, **11** shows oxidative almond notes with appealing muted white fruit & dry, mineral finish. **Méthode Cap Classique Brut** NEW ★★★ First-release trio of bot-tle-fermented bubblies, all from Elgin grapes. **08** pinot/chardonnay has lees richness on salty-savoury, just-dry palate. **Méthode Cap Classique Blanc de Blancs** NEW ★★★★ Dry, austere **08** chardonnay sparkler has purity of form, subdued baked apple aromas under mineral-lime lees mantle. — GdB

■ **Azania** *see* African Terroir

Baarsma Wine Group

Stellenbosch ▪ Closed to public ▪ Owner(s) Baarsma Wine Group BV ▪ MD Chris Rabie ▪ Cellarmaster(s) Hannes Louw (since Jan 2005) ▪ PO Box 7275 Stellenbosch 7599 ▪ info@baarsma.co.za ▪ www.baarsma.co.za ▪ **T +27 (0)21-880-1221** ▪ F +27 (0)21-880-0851

Stellenbosch-based Baarsma SA is a major export marketer of South African wines, shipping more than 1 million cases a year to the major international wine markets. The group's Lyngrove brand is listed separately.

BABISA — Born & Bred in South Africa

Location/WO: Paarl ▪ Est 2008 ▪ 1stB 2007 ▪ Tasting by appt ▪ Tours to estates producing BABISA wines by prior arrangement ▪ Owner(s) BABISA Brand Innovation Holdings Ltd ▪ Cellarmaster(s)/winemaker(s)/viticultur-ist(s) Various ▪ 5,000cs own label 60% red 30% white 10% rosé ▪ PO Box 52185 Waterfront 8002 ▪ wines@babisa.com ▪ www.babisa.com ▪ **T +27 (0)21-232-8840** ▪ F +27 (0)86-616-2794

BABISA prime mover Paul Burger, born and bred in South Africa like the epony-mous brand, is bullish about prospects for a BABISA wine collection, but it's just one of the strands in the brand portfolio, and roll-out timing requires that the Valerie red blend remains just a little longer in its current maturation cellar home.

★★★★ **Valerie Reserve** ⊕ Serious shiraz-led 6-way blend from Paarl. Lingering **09** repeats previous for-mula: ripe & heavily oaked, but should evolve. — GdB

Babylon's Peak Private Cellar

Location: Malmesbury ▪ Map: Swartland ▪ WO: Swartland/Western Cape ▪ Est/1stB 2003 ▪ Tasting, sales & cel-lar tours by appt ▪ Closed Easter Fri-Mon, Dec 25 & Jan 1 ▪ Pre-booked light refreshments for groups ▪ Olives ▪ BYO picnic ▪ Walking/hiking trails ▪ Conservation area ▪ Self-catering cottage ▪ Dams for fishing ▪ Owner(s) Stephan Basson ▪ Cellarmaster(s)/winemaker(s)/viticulturist(s) Stephan Basson (Jan 2003) ▪ 580ha/230ha (carignan, grenache, mourv, ptage, shiraz, chenin, rouss, viog) ▪ 10,000cs own label 65% red 35% white ▪ 500,000L bulk ▪ PO Box 161 Malmesbury 7299 ▪ info@babylonspeak.co.za ▪ S 33° 33'40.8" E 018° 48'38.6" ▪ **T +27 (0)21-300-1052** ▪ F +27 (0)86-518-3773

The name derives from the granite thumb on the eastern slope of the Perdeberg, locally known as Babylonstoren. This large farm has been in the Basson family since 1919, sending grapes to the big houses. In 2003, fourth-generation scion Stephan, with the 'Swartland revolution' happening all around, set out to make wines on his own account, from some of the highest vineyards in the Swartland.

Babylon's Peak range

★★★★ **Shiraz-Mourvèdre-Grenache** ⊕ Good exposition of modern Swartland Rhône-blend style. **09** 87% shiraz. Savoury spice, fynbos & contained ripe berries meld into rich, dry palate. WO W Cape.

★★★★ **Chenin Blanc** ✓ 🍴 39 year old bushvines still produce the goods. Rich poised peach & granadilla harmonised by fresh acid on lively crisp **12**. 6 months lees-ageing aids complexity. Modest 13% alcohol.

★★★★ **Viognier-Roussanne** NEW **11** 80% off young viognier bushvines. Complex, perfumed aromas lead to floral & potpourri flavours. Focused, pithy & clean, with verve & integrated oak support.

Syrah ★★★★ Ripe bold style, densely layered with savoury liquorice, dark fruits, coffee & tar intensity. **09** has firm serious send-off. **Shiraz-Carignan** ✓ 🍴 ★★★★ **10** modern in style with spice, smoked meats jostling with sweet ripeness to end dry & savoury. Bouncy freshness adds zip. Discontinued: **Babylon, Viognier.**

Coded range NEW

Red ☺ 🍴 ★★★ These labels show big QR-coded vineleaf. Easy-drinking, dark-berried & juicy NV (11) offering. Just about dry. Some oak for gravitas. White ☺ 🍴 ★★★ NV (12) blend offers crisp & fruity (just as the label says) everyday drinking. Dry, but a few grams sugar for softness. — JP

Babylonstoren

Location: Paarl ▪ Map: Paarl & Wellington ▪ WO: Simonsberg-Paarl/Western Cape ▪ Est 2011 ▪ Tasting & sale daily 10–4 ▪ Tour groups ▪ Gift shop ▪ Hiking/walking trails ▪ Guided garden tours ▪ Hosted wine tasting wit' cellar tour to be pre-booked ▪ Babylonstoren Farm Hotel (see Accommodation section) ▪ Babel Restaurant (see Restaurants section); Garden glasshouse for teas & light meals ▪ Winemaker(s) Charl Coetzee (Nov 2010) with Wian Mouton (Jan 2011) ▪ Viticulturist(s) Hannes Aucamp (Jan 2010) ▪ 200ha/±62ha (mourv, shiraz chard) ▪ PO Box 167 Simondium 7670 ▪ cellar@babylonstoren.com ▪ www.babylonstoren.com ▪ S 33° 49' 26 73" E 018° 55' 39.08" ▪ **T +27 (0)21-863-1804** ▪ F +27 (0)21-863-1727

The Paarl showpiece estate that has lovers of food, decor and gardens agog has se' winemakers Charl Coetzee and Wian Mouton standards as high as the profiles of it' owners, communications mogul Koos Bekker and media personality Karen Roos Immediate aims are to expand the range, now including a Bordeaux blend and a chardonnay, and establish an export market in China. Smaller projects are experi ments with low-alcohol and low-sulphur wines, and trying out labelling ideas.

Babylonstoren range NEW

Shiraz 🖾 ★★★★ Barrel sample 11 shows promise despite being tad unsettled mid-2012. Brooding frui lifted by hints scrub & spice, oak tannin courtesy 18 months in new barrels still meshing. **Babel** 🖾 ★★★ Gutsy merlot-led blend with cab (38%) & cab franc (12%); 11 dark meaty blackcurrant aromas, tightl' clenched fist of tarry fruit still some way off opening, integrating with (mostly new) oak. Previewed, so ratin provisional, but looks like a worthy flagship. WO W Cape. **Mourvèdre Rosé** 🖾 ★★★ Pleasant, lightish 11 slightly sweet strawberry aromas & flavours offset by tingling acidity for amiable summer quaffing. **Char donnay** 🖾 ★★★★ Barrel-fermented 11 restrained on nose but exuberant on palate: generous citrus frui creamy lees, subtle vanilla & refreshing marmalade twist. **Chenin Blanc** 🖾 ★★★★ 'Great match with any thing as long as the sun is out' enthuses winemaker. 11 is appropriately bright & fruity, with vivacious minera seam. WO W Cape. **Viognier** 🖾 ★★★★ Burst of peach & honey on 11 precedes plump & sleek palate; seri ous expression of variety, judiciously (25%) oaked but ripe-picked style (15% alcohol) forfeits elegance. — FM/GdB

■ **Babylons Toren** see Backsberg Estate Cellars
■ **Babylon's Vineyards** see Mount Babylon Vineyards

Backsberg Estate Cellars

Location: Paarl ▪ Map: Paarl & Wellington ▪ WO: Paarl/Western Cape/Elgin ▪ Est 1916 ▪ 1stB 1970 ▪ Tasting & sale Mon–Fri 8–5 Sat 9.30–4.30 Sun 10.30–4.30 ▪ Fee R15 ▪ Open 365 days a year ▪ Cellar tours by appt ▪ Backsberg Res taurant (see Restaurants section) ▪ Tour groups ▪ Gift shop ▪ Figs & preserves for sale ▪ Conferences ▪ Weddings & functions ▪ Conservation area ▪ Sunday picnic concerts (Jan–Mar) ▪ Owner(s) Michael Back ▪ Winemaker(s) Alici Rechner (Jun 2012) ▪ Viticulturist(s) Clive Trent (Jul 1992) ▪ 130ha (cab, merlot, shiraz, chard) ▪ 900t/80,000c own label 65% red 30% white 5% rosé ▪ PO Box 537 Suider-Paarl 7624 ▪ info@backsberg.co.za ▪ www.backsberg co.za ▪ S 33° 49' 42.9" E 018° 54' 56.9" ▪ **T +27 (0)21-875-5141** ▪ F +27 (0)21-875-5144

'You start doing what you really want, then do things you like less and ultimately end up going back to where you began,' says Michael Back, patriarch of this long established family winery near Paarl. Son Simon has taken over the reins after time abroad and Michael now focuses on his passion: renewable energy, biomass development and farming. The duo intend taking Backsberg off the grid by becoming energy self-sufficient. Alicia Rechner is back in the revamped cellar and has not only seen all the red wine tanks lifted (no mean feat!) but a new upgrade embarked on to make everything fully gravitational. Next up is a com prehensive overhaul of the visitor offering and tasting room.

Flagship — Backsberg Family Reserve range

★★★★ **Red Blend** Cab leads the merlot/shiraz chorus in **08** blend. Rich & spicy, with black fruit. Nutty appeal from prominent oak. Big, firm & ripe with long fruity finish. No **06** or **07**.

★★★★ **White Blend** ⊕ 🍽 Chardonnay/roussanne-driven **09**'s waxy overlay complements boldly flavoured yet balanced profile, refreshing acid zing. Drop viognier gives floral lift.

Black Label range

★★★★ **Klein Babylons Toren** Classically styled blend of cab & merlot with dab malbec. **07** black fruit with cedar & cigarbox lift. Lithe frame provided by 18 months in small oak. **06** sold out untasted.

★★★★ **Elbar** ⊕ Malbec & mourvèdre 70% of **07**'s 7-way blend, tasted from barrel last time. Hedgerow fruit, sprinkle of dried herbs, supple oak add savoury flavours, long silky finish.

★★★★ **John Martin Sauvignon Blanc** 🍽 🖉 'Reserve' dropped from name in **12** (★★★☆), tangy grapefruit succulence less intense than last-tasted **10**. Smoother & more rounded, with good fruit/acid balance.

★★★★ **Hillside Viognier** ⊕ 🍽 Vanilla notes to **09**'s peach/apricot medley. Delicately textured, smooth balanced acidity from 14% roussanne; lingering nutty finish.

Beyond Borders Pinot Noir NEW 🍽 🖉 ★★★★ Maiden **10** still young & brash. Raspberry fruit gawky & not mingling with spicy oak mid-2012 but shows promise & oodles of appeal. **Pumphouse Shiraz** ★★★★ **08** a step up on **07** (★★★). French-styled delicacy & refinement yet power too. Body & depth yet gentle texture. Fine tannins, excellent balance & lingering aftertaste. **Brut Méthode Cap Classique** ⊕ ★★★★ Traditional-method sparkling, **08** a blend of chardonnay & pinot; yeasty biscuit aromas, vibrant melon/apple flavours, persistent lemon drop conclusion. Discontinued: **Bella Rosa, Aldorina**.

Premium range

★★★★ **Special Late Harvest** Litchi floral abundance on **12** (★★★☆), first since **07**. Simple sweet appeal to 70/30 viognier & gewürztraminer mix.

Cabernet Sauvignon ✓ ★★★★ **09** a notch up. Depth & intensity to ripe cassis & cigarbox spice. Elegant, refined & long. **Merlot** ★★★★ Splash of malbec (10%) livens **11** barrel sample with cocoa depth & grip. Perky & fresh, lovely texture & fruit. **Pinotage** 🖉 ★★★ Somewhat straightforward **11**. Lightweight, with generic red fruit. **Dry Red** 🍽 ★★★ Plum & berry appeal to **NV** blend of unspecified red grapes, step up on previous. **Rosé** ⊕ 🍽 ★★★ Semi-sweet **NV** from white aromatic varieties with shiraz; gentle & charming. **Chardonnay** 🍽 🖉 ★★★ **11** pre-bottling sample light citrus tang with medium body & length. **Chenin Blanc** 🍽 🖉 ★★★ Previewed **12** pear drop & apricot typicity, good juicy freshness & appeal. **Sauvignon Blanc** 🍽 🖉 ★★★ Tangy lemon/lime crispness on **12**. Vibrant acidity with nice body & flinty note on the finish.

Kosher range

Merlot ★★★ Chunky sweet fruit, **11** showing its light oak cloak now. **Pinotage** ★★★ Raspberry & spice appeal, **11** touch short overall. **Chardonnay** ★★★ **11** improves on previous with creamy citrus freshness. **Brut Méthode Cap Classique** ⊕ ★★★ 1st kosher bubbly in SA. 100% chardonnay **08** frothy, light & fruitily crisp. **Kiddush Natural Sweet** NEW 🖉 ★★ Sweet sugary clove spice & caramel on **11**, juicy grape syrup character.

Fortified range

Pinneau ⊕ ★★★ Fortified semillon grape juice; last tasted was **04** with fruit, toffee, medicinal notes. **Cape Ruby** ⊕ ★★★★ Previously listed as 'Port'. From cab franc, **06** on review was like drinking brandy-doused fruitcake: full bodied & rich. — FM

■ **Badenhorst Family Wines** *see* AA Badenhorst Family Wines

Badgerberg Estate

Location/map: Villiersdorp • WO: Overberg • Est 2000 • 1stB 2009 • Tasting & sales Mon-Thu by appt Fri 3-6 Sat 10-4 (Sep-May) • Light German refreshments, sausages, cheese breads, cold cuts • German Octoberfest & Maibaumfest annually • Owner(s) Heinz & Lynnette Mederer • Winemaker(s) Ryan Puttick • Matthew Krone MCC consultant • 35ha/9ha (cab, merlot, shiraz, sauv) • 100t/634cs own label 53% red 47% white • PO Box 1605 Somerset West 7129 • info@badgerberg.co.za, lynnettem@badgerberg.co.za • www.badgerberg.co.za • S 33°57′07.5″ E 19°19′29.5″ • **T +27 (0)21-852-1150/+27 (0)83-263-2783** • F +27 (0)86-586-2237

A 'retirement project' farming apples and grapes at Badgerberg has evolved into wine production (at Villiersdorp Cellar) and export. 'The first shipment to Germany was sold out before landing,' owner Lynnette Mederer reports delightedly – as did their first batch of bubbly. Their annual Oktoberfest and Maibaumfest are highlights on the German community calendar.

Prima ⓟ ★★★ 09 merlot, cab blend oozes red fruit. Bright & uncomplicated, supple fruit flavours balanced by fresh acidity & firm vanilla oak. **Sauvignon Blanc** Next awaited. **Aquarius Cuvée Brut** NEW 🚫 ★★★★ Méthode cap classique sparkling from sauvignon, **10** shows variety's grapefruit lift & appley 'sea breeze' character. Lightish, clean & crisp. — FM

Badsberg Wine Cellar   🍴 ☕ 🎋 📷 🎿 ♿

Location: Rawsonville ▪ Map/WO: Breedekloof ▪ Est 1951 ▪ 1stB 1958 ▪ Tasting & sales Mon-Fri 8–5 Sat 10–1 ▪ Fee R20pp for groups of 8+ ▪ Closed all pub hols ▪ Cellar tours Mon-Fri 2-3 (Feb-Mar only) ▪ Picnics by appt during harvest; or BYO picnic ▪ Facilities for children ▪ Farm produce ▪ Conferences (40 pax) ▪ Conservation area ▪ Cloudy Nouveau (Mar), Soetes & Soup (Jul) & Outdoor festivals (Oct) ▪ Owner(s) 26 members ▪ Cellarmaster(s) Willie Burger (1998) ▪ Winemaker(s) Henri Swiegers (2002) & De Wet Hugo (Dec 2006), with Jaco Booysen (Jan 2007) ▪ Viticulturist(s) De Wet Hugo (Dec 2006) ▪ ±1,500ha/±1,300ha (ptage, shiraz, chenin, cbard) ▪ ±23,000t own label 15% red 60% white 10% rosé 15% fortified ▪ ISO 22000:2009 ▪ PO Box 72 Rawsonville 6845 ▪ enquiries@badsberg.co.za ▪ www.badsberg.co.za ▪ S 33° 39' 40.1" E 019° 16' 9.2" ▪ **T +27 (0)23-344-3021** ▪ F +27 (0)23-344-3023

'Give the customer what the customer wants' is the mantra at this large-scale producer and exporter supplied by Breedekloof grape growers. It appears this would also apply to wine judges: our White Wine of the Year in 2012, the 2009 Badslese, took double gold at both the Michelangelo and Veritas competitions.

★★★★★ **Badslese** 🍴 🚫 Natural Sweet dessert from chenin, splash muscat d'Alexandrie; only in best years (no **10, 11**). Preview **12** (★★★★★) ups muscat portion to 30%; melon, quince & grapey complexity & length; gorgeous wine, if perhaps shade less thrilling than **09**, our White Wine of the Year last edition.

★★★★ **Noble Late Harvest** ⓟ Soft & sweet after-dinner treat in 375ml from (unwooded) chenin; **07** lots of good things — honey, apricot, marmalade — to smell & taste; clean & uplifting.

★★★★ **Noble Late Harvest Limited Edition** ⓟ Wooded version, also chenin. **05**'s 3 years in oak add caramel tone to fruit (fresh, dried & candied!) & palate-cleansing freshness. 750ml.

★★★★ **Red Muscadel** 🚫 Tealeaf-nuanced **11** unashamedly raisin-sweet & slippery; perfect for winter fires or — over ice — summer sunsets.

★★★★ **Red Jerepigo** 🚫 Effortless & classy fortified pinotage for the sweet-toothed. **11** has molasses & caramel overtones, liqueur cherry fruit.

Rosé ☺ 🍴 🚫 ★★★ From merlot, **12** pretty berry-toned party companion. **Chenin Blanc** ☺ 🍴 🚫 ★★★ Pear drops & dried grass on appealing **12**, lightish 12.5% alcohol for lunchtime sipping.

Merlot 🍴 🚫 ★★★ Plummy **11** supple & refreshing, light textured for summer sipping. **Pinotage-Mocha Fusion** 🚫 ★★★★ Strawberry base, choc-mocha top notes on lightly oaked **11**. Juicy, fresh & commendably dry; for youthful enjoyment. **Belladonna** ⓟ ★★★ Shiraz plus three Bordeaux reds in dusty & dry **09**; tad chunky. **Chardonnay Sur Lie** ⓟ 🚫 ★★★★ Tangy lime acidity good counterpoint to barrel-fermented **11**'s buttery, oaky richness. **Sauvignon Blanc** 🍴 🚫 ★★ Uncomplicated just-off-dry **12** soft & fruity middle, zesty tail. **Vin Doux** 🚫 ★★★ Sweet, frothy & grapey **11** sparkling from muscat d'Alexandrie. 'Makes a great palate-cleansing sorbet' say the team. **Special Late Harvest** 🚫 ★★★ Equal mix chenin, hanepoot in **11**, faintly aromatic, gently sweet to pair with Indian curries. **Hanepoot Jerepigo** 🚫 ★★★★ Spirity upliftment from **11** fortified dessert Sweet & grapey but not cloying. **Cape Vintage** 🍴 ★★★ Previously 'Vintage Port'. **09** preview from touriga, shiraz, ruby cab. Dense & fiery; Turkish Delight aromas/flavours, charry tannins. — CvZ

▪ **Bain's Way** *see Wellington Wines*
▪ **Bakenskop** *see Jonkheer*
▪ **Balance** *see Overhex Wines International*
▪ **Balthazar** *see Roodezandt Wines*
▪ **Bandana** *see Klein Roosboom*
▪ **Barber's Wood** *see Celestina*

Barista

Location: Paarl/Robertson ▪ WO: Western Cape ▪ Est/1stB 2009 ▪ Tasting at Val de Vie & Robertson Winery ▪ Owner(s) Vinimark ▪ Winemaker(s) Bertus Fourie ▪ 600t/30,000cs own label ▪ PO Box 6223 Paarl 7620 ▪ info@ vinimark.co.za ▪ www.baristawine.co.za ▪ **T +27 (0)21-883-8043** ▪ F +27 (0)21-886-4708

In this age of diversity, multiple choice and instant gratification, it's not easy just having one apple in your basket, the Barista team concede, even if that apple is a crowd-pleasing popular coffee-style pinotage. Nonetheless, punters love its in-your-face mocha aromas and flavours, and sales are ticking along nicely.

Pinotage 🍴 📷 ★★★ **11** continues the in-your-face coffee boldness & blueberry fruit of previous, along with a smoky meat note. Lightish & easy drinking. —FM

- **Barn Find** see Franki's Vineyards
- **Baroness** see Oudtshoorn Cellar — SCV
- **Barony** see Rosendal Winery

Barrydale Cellar — SCV

Location: Barrydale ▪ Map: Klein Karoo & Garden Route ▪ WO: Tradouw/Western Cape/Klein Karoo ▪ Est 1941 ▪ 1stB 1976 ▪ Tasting & sales Mon-Fri 9-5 Sat 9-3 ▪ Fee R25 for groups of 5 or more ▪ Closed Easter Fri-Mon, Dec 25/26 & Jan 1 ▪ Book ahead for cellar tours ▪ BYO picnic ▪ Conservation area ▪ Owner(s) 75 members ▪ Production Manager Ferdi Smit (May 1985) ▪ Winemaker(s)/viticulturist(s) Marius Prins (Oct 2011) ▪ ±102ha (cab, merlot, shiraz, chard, cbard, sauv) ▪ ±997t/5,000cs own label 56% red 43% white 1% rosé + 500cs for clients ▪ Other export brand: Joseph Barry ▪ PO Box 59 Barrydale 6750 ▪ sales@scv.co.za ▪ www.barrydalewines.co.za ▪ S 33° 54'35.83" E 020° 42'45.20" ▪ **T +27 (0)28-572-1012** ▪ F +27 (0)28-572-1541

With Oudtshoorn and Ladismith cellars also under his aegis, CEO Riaan Marais no longer has the time for cellar duties. Filling the gap is winemaker Marius Prins, ex Delheim, whose first season coincided with the second bottling of a Joseph Barry 10 Year Pot Still Brandy. Hopes are that it will garner the awards of its predecessor.

Merchant's Mark range

Chardonnay-Viognier ☺ 📷 ★★★ Ripe apple & peach complexity, floral lift & smooth vanilla oak raise the bar in **11**. Enjoy chilled.

Cabernet Sauvignon 🕐 ★★ Dry & medium-bodied **08** soft & approachable for solo sipping. **Merlot** 🕐 ★★ **10** fresh & fruity fun, but brief. **Pinot Noir** 🕐 ★★★ **10** first since **05**; dark cherry/earth fragrance & good varietal flavours easy to like, linger pleasantly. WO W Cape. **Ruby Cabernet** 🕐 🍴 ★★ Friendly **09** upbeat & rounded quick-sip. WO Klein Karoo. **Shiraz** 🕐 ★★ From Klein Karoo vineyards **08** has black pepper dusting, softer mouthfeel. **Chardonnay** NEW 📷 ★★ **11** ripe apple tones seamed with vanilla & wood char. For fans of an oakier style. **Sauvignon Blanc** 🕐 ★★ Light acid bite to breezy **11**. **Brut Rosé** NEW ★★★★ Pale pink NV méthode cap classique from pinotage and chenin ex Stellenbosch. Cheerful strawberry & shortbread aromas mingle with faint almond oxidative notes; lively fruit & tangy finish. Enjoy soon.

Decent range

Decent Red 🕐 🍴 ★★ Uncomplicated fun from NV combo red varieties. **Decent White** 🕐 🍴 ★★ Potpourri bouquet on gently sweet NV trio white varieties. —WB/JP

Barry Gould Family Wines

Location/WO: Elgin ▪ Map: Elgin, Walker Bay & Bot River ▪ Est 2003 ▪ 1stB 2004 ▪ Tasting, sales & cellar tours by appt ▪ Closed Good Fri, Dec 25 & Jan 1 ▪ Meals/functions by arrangement (up to 20 pax) ▪ Wildekrans Country House (B&B) + self-catering cottage ▪ Child-friendly ▪ Gifts ▪ Farm produce ▪ Conference venue (20 pax) ▪ 4-day fully guided slack-packing trail ▪ Owner(s) Barry Gould & Alison Green ▪ Cellarmaster(s) Barry Gould (2003) ▪ Winemaker(s) Barry Gould (2003), with family (2004) ▪ Viticulturist(s) Grapes bought in from various sources ▪ ±2t/160cs own label 70% red 30% white ▪ PO Box 7 Elgin 7180 ▪ gould.arc@wildekrans.co.za ▪ S 34° 12'12.7" E 019° 8'53.6" ▪ **T +27 (0)21-848-9788 / +27 (0)82-901-4896** ▪ F +27 (0)21-848-9788

'My wines are what they are,' says Barry Gould, cellarmaster and co-owner of this low-tech family winery in Elgin. 'They're the end product of a hands-in, hands-on, home-made process — not "tweaked" using additives and chemical enhancers.' Barry also remains a great believer in traditional cork and glass: 'A well-washed reused bottle is hard to beat in enviro terms.'

A Simple Red ★★★ Equal cab & merlot in **06**, with spices dominating stewed plum fruit. Tasty, & more interesting than name suggests. **Chenin Blanc** Await next. **Sauvignon Blanc** Untasted. —DB

Bartinney Private Cellar

Location/map: Stellenbosch ▪ WO: Stellenbosch/Banghoek ▪ Est 2006 ▪ 1stB 2008 ▪ Tasting & sales Mon-Fr
10-4 ▪ Closed all pub hols ▪ Cellar tours by appt ▪ Owner(s) Rose & Michael Jordaan ▪ Winemaker(s) Rone
Wiid (consultant) ▪ Viticulturist(s) Ryno Maree (Oct 2010) ▪ 38ha/±17ha (cab, chard, sauv) ▪ 118t/2,000c
own label 70% red 30% white + 20,000L bulk ▪ BWI champion ▪ Postnet Suite 231 Private Bag X506
Stellenbosch 7599 ▪ info@bartinney.co.za ▪ www.bartinney.co.za ▪ S 33° 55'34.66" E 018° 55'56.79" ▪ **T +2.
(0)21-885-1013** ▪ F +27 (0)21-885-2852

Taking up the winemaking reins at this boutique cellar in the heights o
Banghoek is consultant Ronell Wiid, who brings a wealth of knowledge and
enthusiasm with her. That experience is invaluable to owners Michael and Rose
Jordaan for whom making wine at Bartinney is a matter of 'capturing history in
the bottle' as the family celebrates its fourth generation of living on the farm
Their fun, easy-drinking label, Noble Savage, is listed as a separate entry.

★★★★ **Cabernet Sauvignon** 🧬 Upfront aromas of blackberries & cassis on **10**. Spiced fruitcake & velvet
plummy softness with more than a hint of mint. Well-integrated tannins & oak, should improve.

★★★★☆ **Elevage** Not new, but our first taste of outstanding cab-based Bordeaux blend reveals polishe
black fruit nose, darkly concentrated bitter chocolate edge. **09** minty overtones wrapped around black cherr
fruit with plushy tannins & exotic perfumes. A keeper. WO Stellenbosch.

★★★★ **Chardonnay** Sweet baked peaches & toasted apricots, hints of buttery crumble & spice. **11** concen
trated flavours of lime/lemon meringue pie, balanced acidity, long finish. **10** sold out untasted.

★★★★ **Sauvignon Blanc** 🧬 Improved **10** goes up further notch with multi-layered **11** (★★★★★), onl
now coming into its own. Figs & guavas on the nose before flavours of green gooseberries, tropical fruit & citru
flood in, backed up by discreet acidity. Also-reviewed **12** still tight, needs the extra year. — CM

Barton Vineyards

Location: Bot River ▪ Map: Elgin, Walker Bay & Bot River ▪ WO: Walker Bay ▪ Est 2001 ▪ 1stB 2003 ▪ Tastinc
sales & cellar tours Mon-Fri 9-5 Sat 11-4 ▪ Fee R20/6 wines ▪ Closed Easter Sun, Dec 25 & Jan 1 ▪ Lavende
products, olive oil, marinated olives & proteas ▪ Four 4-star self-catering villas (www.bartonvillas.co.za)
Owner(s) Peter J Neill ▪ Cellarmaster(s)/winemaker(s)/viticulturist(s) PJ Geyer (Oct 2010) ▪ 200ha/30ha (cab
malbec, merlot, mourv, pinot, shiraz, chenin, sauv, sem) ▪ 100t/5,500cs own label 40% red 50% white 10%
rosé ▪ IPW ▪ PO Box 100 Bot River 7185 ▪ info@bartonvineyards.co.za ▪ www.bartonvineyards.co.za ▪ S 34° 1!
43.8" E 019° 10'29.2" ▪ **T +27 (0)28-284-9283** ▪ F +27 (0)28-284-9776

Increasing yield is the current focus for winemaker PJ Geyer and the team: 'With
the 2.2 tons per hectare we had, both profit margin and quality are in jeopardy', he
explains. Their two-year goal of 6 tons/ha on the sandy soils requires careful wate
and fertiliser management; so far it's proving successful. Changing wine style is an
equally slow process, with Geyer looking to his French training for inspiration.

★★★★ **Shiraz-Cabernet Sauvignon** Delicious **10** a little riper, with more truffly, gamey flavours than **09**
with deep, crushed velvet texture. Supple but with sufficient form, freshness for now or years ahead.

Merlot ★★★★ Ripe, full-bodied **10**, its sweet flesh lifted by tasty savouriness. Balanced, supple grip allow
for current drinking or few further years. **09** (★★★★) riper, simpler. **Shiraz Rosé** 🍴 🧬 ★★★ Electric pin
from shiraz; equally vivid spicy features in refreshing, food-friendly **12**. **Chenin Blanc** 🍴 🧬 ★★★★ Tastec
mid-2012, unoaked **12** still shut down; very tight & fresh; hint of lees richness, fruit before bracing acid close
Sauvignon Blanc 🍴 🧬 ★★★★ Tangily fresh **12** (tank sample) in greener spectrum with tense mineralit
bone-dry finish — but balancing lees richness lurks. **Sauvignon Blanc-Semillon** ★★★ Unwooded just-dr
blend; shy-fruited, waxy **11** shows some evolved characters. — AL

◼ **Basco** see Blomendahl Vineyards

Bayede!

Location: Paarl ▪ Map: Paarl & Wellington ▪ WO: Western Cape/Paarl/Franschhoek ▪ Est 2009 ▪ Tasting & sale
in showroom/office at 510 Main Road Paarl Mon-Fri/by appt ▪ Fee R30 ▪ Private VIP tastings at Villa Beant
Winelands Estate by appt only ▪ Closed all pub hols ▪ Tour groups by appt ▪ 60% red 30% white 10% rosé
510 Main Road Paarl 7646 ▪ anto@bayede.co.za ▪ www.bayede.co.za ▪ S 33° 42'30.46" E 018° 57'42.92"
T +27 (0)21-870-1686, +27 (0)83-650-3585 ▪ F +27 (0)21-871-1105

Named for the traditional greeting 'Hail the King!', the Bayede! job-creation initiative includes South Africa's first 'by royal appointment' range of wines, selected from across the Western Cape and sold in bead-adorned bottles. 'The project puts people to work, shares expertise and resources and, as a result of combined input, produces unique goods,' says Zulu monarch Goodwill Zwelethini.

IM King Goodwill range

★★★★ **Pinotage Reserve** ⓟ ⃠ Hinting at blackcurrant & lavender, **10** showed promise last edition, deserved more time for oak to fully integrate.

Merlot ⓟ ★★★ Ripe **09** needed time to settle mid-2011, earthy & savoury styling with hints of dark chocolate. Discontinued: **Shiraz, Chardonnay**.

Royal Signature range

> **The Prince Red** ☺ ⃞ ★★★ Juicy, fruity off-dry cab/shiraz, **11** a real crowd pleaser. **The Prince White** ☺ ⃞ ★★★ Fresh, grassy melon fruit on **12**, accessible, easy-drinking chenin & sauvignon.

IM King Goodwill Shiraz NEW ✓ ⃠ ★★★★ Most serious wine in this range. **10** savoury aromas, ripe berry flavours on a peppery, well-managed tannin base. **King Shaka Jubilee** ★★★ Bordeaux-style red, mainly cab & merlot, **09** with developed stewed fruit flavours best enjoyed soon. WO Franschhoek. **Queen Thomo Sauvignon Blanc** ⃞ ⃠ ★★ Easy, uncomplicated & lightish **11**, with nettle & fynbos hints. **Queen Mantfombi Dry MCC Sparkling Rosé** ⃠ ★★★ Listed as 'Queen Mantfombi Brut Rosé' last time. Fairly refined & understated **11**, pale pink colour, delicate fruit & lively mousse. Ends crisp & dry. Note: this range appeared under 'Bayede!' heading last edition.

The Shield range NEW

> **The Prince Cabernet Sauvignon-Shiraz-Merlot** ☺ ⃠ ★★★ Shiraz component dominates ripe & approachable **11**, with spicy berry aromas adding to the easy appeal.

The Prince Cabernet Sauvignon ★★★ Savoury dark chocolate & plums, **11** good with a juicy steak. **The Prince Merlot** ⃠ ★★★ Spicy berries on **11** lead to a firm peppery conclusion. **The Prince Pinotage** ⃠ ★★ Robust **11**, white pepper notes, crisp berry flavours. **The Prince Chenin Blanc** ⃠ ★★ Lightish, crisp & dry **12**, with herbal flavours. **The Prince Sauvignon Blanc** ⃠ ★★ Lean & dry **12** needs a food partner. — DB

▮ **BC Wines** *see* Brandvlei Cellar
▮ **Beacon Hill** *see* Jonkheer

Beau Constantia

Location/WO: Constantia ▪ Map: Cape Peninsula ▪ Est 2003 ▪ 1stB 2010 ▪ Tasting & sales Wed-Sun 10-4.30, Mon-Tue by appt ▪ Closed all pub hols ▪ Spa by appt, T +27 (0)21-794-3376 (Anda) ▪ Owner(s) Dormell Properties 139 (Pty) Ltd ▪ Winemaker(s) Justin van Wyk (Sep 2010) ▪ Viticulturist(s) Japie Bronn (Sep 2002) ▪ 22ha/±11ha (cabs s/f, malbec, merlot, p verdot, shiraz, sauv, sem, viog) ▪ 20t/900cs own label 80% red 20% white ▪ 1043 Constantia Main Road Constantia 7806 ▪ justin@beauconstantia.com ▪ www.beauconstantia.com ▪ S 34° 0' 48.57" E 018° 24' 21.67" ▪ **T +27 (0)21-794-7061** ▪ F +27 (0)21-794-0534

Cecily is named for co-owner of this, the newest estate in venerable Constantia, Cecily du Preez. The names of Lucca and Aidan, the Du Preez children, will appear on the first red blends under the Beau Constantia label. But 'Pas de Nom', or 'No Name'? 'It honours Japie Bronn, our viticulturist,' explains winemaker Justin van Wyk, 'who's worked in the valley for over 30 years. Many know this humble man's face and beard, as on the label, rather than his name.'

★★★★ **Cecily** ⃞ **11** builds on **10** with more concentration, but not at the expense of elegance. Natural freshness, bone-dry finish lengthen viognier's fine apricot-peach tones & oak-enriched silkiness.

Pas de Nom Red NEW ⃞ ★★★★ Whiffs of cedar & greenleaf spice on cab franc-led **10**. Simple yet tasty ripe fruit & a gentle grip encourage early drinking. **Pas de Nom White** NEW ⃞ ★★★★ Sauvignon's clean, invigorating fruit effectively augmented by drops semillon, oaked viognier. **11** a satisfying easy-drinker. — AL

Beau Joubert Vineyards & Winery

Location/map: Stellenbosch ▪ WO: Polkadraai Hills/Stellenbosch ▪ Est 1695 ▪ 1stB 2000 ▪ Tasting & sales Mon-Fri 8-5 Sat by appt ▪ Fee R15 ▪ Closed all pub hols ▪ Cellar tours by appt ▪ BYO picnic ▪ Walks/hikes ▪ Bird watching ▪

Self-catering guest cottage ▪ Owner(s) MD Andrew Hilliard ▪ Cellarmaster(s)/winemaker(s) Christian Kuun (De 2006) ▪ Viticulturist(s) Ian Engelbrecht (Nov 2010) ▪ 105ha/50ha (cabs s/f, merlot, pinot, shiraz, chenin, sauv) 280t/20,000cs own label 60% red 35% white 5% rosé + 10,000L for clients ▪ Other export brand: Joubert Brothers ▪ Ranges for customers: Infusino's, Polkadraai Road ▪ PO Box 1114 Stellenbosch 7599 ▪ info@beaujoubert.com ▪ www.beaujoubert.com ▪ S 33° 57' 11.6" E 018° 44' 25.5" ▪ **T +27 (0)21-881-3103** ▪ F +27 (0)21-881-3377

The process of beau-tification and revitalisation continues at this auspiciously sited property in Stellenbosch's Polkadraai Hills wine ward overlooking False Bay. Viticulturist Ian Engelbrecht has been 'delicately managing' 30+ year old vineyards to enhance their fruit quality, and the natural spring in the centre of the property has been cleared, revealing a 'peaceful, tranquil' area with sweeping vistas. Next are the old cellar, tasting room and original barn dating from the 1700s.

Beau Joubert range

★★★★ **Ambassador** ⓐ Was 'Reserve'. Elegant merlot blend (81%), plus cab & shiraz, **09** bright ripe berries, soft spice. Balanced & understated on debut last year. Ageworthy.

Cabernet Sauvignon ⓐ ★★★★ **09** seduces with upfront blackcurrant & fresh herbal notes, balanced by spicy oaky grip. Needs year/2 for optimum enjoyment. **Christmas Cabernet** ⓐ ★★ Sweet black fruit with charry grip on easy **NV** quaffer previously. **Merlot** ⓐ ★★★ Smoky mulberry, plum & cocoa richness on soft & succulent **08** last time. **Shiraz** ⓐ ★★★ **09** a step up last time; sweet earthy black fruit, vanilla oak flavours & a sprinkle of dry herbs. **Rosé** 🍴 ★★★ Ex-tank **12** from merlot trumps previous with juicy-dry strawberry & candyfloss flavours. **Old Vine Chenin Blanc** NEW 🍴 ★★★★ Lipsmacking **12** oozes tropical fruit, creamy vanilla oak from barrel-fermented portion & refreshing acid. Made in serious style. **Sauvignon Blanc** 🍴 ★★ Fresh greenpepper & zingy lemon appeal on tasty **12** preview. **Fat Pig** ⓐ ★★★ Light-bodied port from pinotage. Sweet fruitcake & cinnamon on previewed **07**, for fireside enjoyment. Discontinued: **Chardonnay**.

Oak Lane range

Merlot-Cabernet Sauvignon ✓ 🍴 ★★★★ Sweet plums, herbs & spice on **11**. Smooth, ends with light grip; lovely balance for early drinking. **Shiraz-Cabernet Sauvignon** 🍴 ★★★ **11** appealing earthiness & spice, blackcurrant pastilles & dusty notes, silky texture. For easy sipping. **Chenin Blanc-Sauvignon Blanc** 🍴 ★★★ Pre-bottling, **12** juicy & fruity with smooth mouthfeel & citrus finish. Discontinued: **Pinot Noir**. — WB

Beaumont Wines   🍴🍷⛺📷♿

Location/WO: Bot River ▪ Map: Elgin, Walker Bay & Bot River ▪ Est 1750 ▪ 1stB 1994 ▪ Tasting, sales & cellar tours Mon-Fri 9.30-4.30 Sat 10-3 ▪ Fee R20pp for groups of 10+ ▪ Closed Easter Sun, Dec 25 & Jan 1 ▪ Light seasonal dishes Thu-Sat 11-2 ▪ Farm produce ▪ Walking/hiking trails ▪ Conservation area ▪ 200-year old watermill ▪ Art/jewellery exhibits ▪ 2 historic self-catering guest cottages ▪ Owner(s) Beaumont family ▪ Cellarmaster(s) Sebastian Beaumont (Jun 2003) ▪ Winemaker(s) Marelise Jansen van Rensburg (Jan 2007) ▪ Viticulturist(s) Sebastian Beaumont (Jun 1999) ▪ 500ha/31ha (mourv, ptage, chenin) ▪ 150t/10,000cs own label 45% red 50% white 5% rosé ▪ BWI, IPW ▪ PO Box 3 Bot River 7185 ▪ info@beaumont.co.za ▪ www.beaumont.co.za ▪ S 34° 13' 27.2" E 019° 12' 24.9" ▪ **T +27 (0)28-284-9194** ▪ F +27 (0)28-284-9733

Once upon a time there was a fruit-farming family in Bot River who loved wine. They decided to add wine-grapes to their crop. Although the path they chose was initially easy (there was a century-old dormant winery on the property they renovated without too much expense), it soon turned difficult. Farming had taught them about the unpredictability of the weather and the seasons, but they were unprepared for the dynamic nature of the wine business: new trends, changing styles, and so on. The family came to realise that getting the wine to market was once thing, getting it consumed was another. This complexity changed them, so they are now a wine business that is family run... and living happily ever after.

Beaumont range

★★★★☆ **Mourvèdre** ⓐ SA benchmark, usually aged 2 years mainly older French oak. Preview **10** shows charry oak, candied orange-peel whiffs; ripe but not heavy. On path blazed by **09**, **08**.

★★★★☆ **Ariane** ⓐ Always a well-composed Bordeaux blend. Still-unfolding aromas & flavours but fine tannins, refreshing acidity in **10** bode well; lithe & confident conclusion. **09** sold out untasted.

★★★★☆ **Vitruvian** ⓐ **08** authoritative mix mourvèdre & pinotage, dashes shiraz, cab franc, petit verdot (latter not in fine **06**; **07** not reviewed). Well composed, with firm tannin grip, subtle sour cherry tones.

★★★★ **Shiraz-Mourvèdre** Sweet mulberry & red berry, mineral/'graphite' tannins on **10** (★★★★) preview. Satisfying & soulful; in line with house style & **08**, but expressing less fruit. **09** cask sample unrated.

★★★★★ **Hope Marguerite Chenin Blanc** Benchmark barrel-fermented/aged chenin crafted for ageing. **11** leads the Beaumont white pack by some way: fruit-full but not sweet (despite 6g/l sugar); smooth, serious & complex, with reined-in oaking (only 15% new).

★★★★ **Chenin Blanc** **12** rings the changes from bone-dry styling to off-dry & lower alcohol. Balanced & expressive, with thatch, quince & racy acidity but shade off steely **11** (★★★★).

★★★★ **Goutte d'Or** Consistently luscious botrytised dessert from oaked semillon & sauvignon. Marzipan & rosepetal appeal in **11** (no **09** or **10**); as always neither overtly sweet nor heavy.

Pinotage ★★★★ not your quintessential version: savoury, earthy as opposed to strawberry, acetone. **09** (★★★★) was more typical & generously fruited. **Cape Vintage** ★★★★ Sample **08** equal marriage tinta/pinotage drier than most local ports (only 80g/l sugar); combines firmness & generosity.

Raoul's range

Constable House Shiraz-Cabernet Sauvignon ⊟ ★★★ Low-yielding vineyards provide fruit for warm-hearted (big alcohol but dry) **10** blend. **Red** ⊕ ⊟ ★★ **10** blend offers berry flavours, firm smoky end. **Shiraz Rosé** ⊟ ★★★ Bubblegum & red cherry boiled sweets on just-dry **12**; sip well chilled. **Jackals River White** ⊟ ★★★ Friendly, just-off-dry **12** chardonnay-based blend; unoaked & tasty. — CvZ

Bein Wine Cellar

Location/map/WO: Stellenbosch ▪ Est 2002 ▪ 1stB 2004 ▪ Tasting, sales & cellar tours Mon-Sat by appt only ▪ Owner(s)/cellarmaster(s)/winemaker(s) Luca & Ingrid Bein ▪ Viticulturist(s) Luca Bein ▪ 3ha/2.2ha (merlot) ▪ 16t/1,200cs 750ml, 80cs 375ml & 290 magnums own label 80% red 20% rosé ▪ IPW ▪ PO Box 3408 Matieland 7602 ▪ lib@beinwine.com ▪ www.beinwine.com ▪ S 33° 57'40.0" E 018° 44'12.0" ▪ **T +27 (0)21-881-3025** ▪ F +27 (0)88-021-881-3025

Qualified vets and oenologists, Ingrid and Luca Bein are involved in every step of their Polkadraai Hills boutique winery's production. Many of their followers are self-confessed merlot freaks, and their maiden 08 Reserve has become something of a legend. Sadly, the 2012 vintage of this and their flagship Merlot will not be released: a carelessly tossed cigarette from a passing vehicle set the heart of their perfectly maintained 2.2ha of vines ablaze.

★★★★ **Little Merlot** Flagship's 'little brother'; delightful fresh, lithe **11** (with a splash of cab) accessible in youth, but structural credentials for 5 or so years ageing.

★★★★☆ **Merlot** Satisfyingly delicious **10** ticks all boxes of classic, polished style. Splashes cab, malbec, petit verdot emphasise structure & complexity, while succulent fleshy merlot fills in outline of remarkably fine tannins supported by oaking, half new barrels.

★★★★☆ **Merlot Reserve** From tiny yields. All new oak judiciously employed in **10** to add polish & grip to ample rich plummy fruit. Other Bordeaux grapes enhance complexity, structure, to produce a wine which stylishly straddles classic/modern divide. No **09**.

Pink Merlot ☺ ★★★ Splash muscat adds character & fragrance to richly fruity but dry & zippy rosé. **12** charming, satisfying summer sipper. — IM

Belbon Hills Private Cellar

Location: Cape Town ▪ WO: Western Cape ▪ Est/1stB 1999 ▪ Closed to public ▪ Owner(s) Pedro Estrada Belli ▪ Winemaker(s) Outsourced, with Pedro Estrada Belli ▪ 10,000cs own label 70% red 25% white 5% dessert ▪ Other export brand: Gugu ▪ PO Box 457 Bloubergstrand 7436 ▪ info@belbonhills.com ▪ www.belbonhills.com ▪ **T +27 (0)21-557-7143** ▪ F +27 (0)21-557-1351

After his many years in the wine business, Cape Town-based Italian importer/exporter Pedro Estrada Belli believes the answer isn't following new fashions: 'Trends are only temporary; quality and tradition set the image of the industry.' However, he wants to offer consumers a broader experience. 'So I will definitively increase the Italian cultivars in my range.'

Belbon Hills range

Cabernet Sauvignon ⓟ ★★★ Easy-drinking **08** had red cherry & mulberry appeal previously. **Shiraz** ⓟ ★★★ Spicy nuances, juicy finish to last-tasted **08**. **Red** Await new release, as for **White**, **Chenin Blanc** & **Sauvignon Blanc**.

South African Soul range

Gewürztraminer New bottling of this & **Passito** not available at press time. — DB

Belfield Wines

Location/WO: Elgin ▪ Map: Elgin, Walker Bay & Bot River ▪ Est 2000 ▪ 1stB 2005 ▪ Tasting, sales & tours by appt ▪ Closed Dec 25 ▪ Owner(s) Mike & Mel Kreft ▪ Cellarmaster(s)/winemaker(s)/viticulturist(s) Mike Kreft ▪ 5.5ha/2. 5ha (cab, merlot, shiraz) ▪ 20t/1,000cs own label 100% red ▪ PO Box 191 Elgin 7180 ▪ mike@belfield.co.za ▪ www. belfield.co.za ▪ S 34° 10' 20.9" E 019° 1' 45.8" ▪ **T +27 (0)21-848-9840** ▪ F +27 (0)86-613-3108

'There was no passion for winemaking,' recalls co-owner Mike Kreft of his days as a boy, kicking up dust, barefoot, while eating grapes on his grandparents' Durbanville wine farm. It was the pioneering challenge of crafting red wine in Elgin — commonly seen as a white-wine area — that fired his spirit. This boutique clutch of reds has proved doubters wrong.

★★★★☆ **Magnifica** ✓ Flagship bears Queen Protea moniker; previously all-cab, **09** with splashes shiraz & merlot. Bounces back to elegant form with fabulously silky, balanced composure (& gentle oaking: only 20% new, 12 months) after tad less intense **08** (★★★★).

★★★★☆ **Syrah** NEW ✓ Exhilarating debut **09** bolts out of the blocks with delicate pimento spice, a bounty of elegant violet flavours, supple tannins & power without heaviness. A tour de force!

★★★★ **Aristata** ✓ Bordeaux-style red named for an indigenous aloe; coolly aligned merlot, cab, cab franc & soupçon shiraz. **09** generous yet measured, offers plump fruit with restraint. No **08**.

Discontinued: **Merlot**. — DS

◼ **Bellemore** see Bellevue Estate Stellenbosch

Bellevue Estate Stellenbosch

Location/map: Stellenbosch ▪ WO: Bottelary/Stellenbosch ▪ Est 1701 ▪ 1stB 1999 ▪ Tasting & sales Mon-Fri 10–4 Sat 10–3 ▪ Closed Good Fri, Dec 25 & Jan 1 ▪ Owner(s) Dirkie Morkel ▪ Winemaker(s) Wilhelm Kritzinger (Feb 2002) & Anneke Potgieter (Feb 2003) ▪ Viticulturist(s) Dirkie Morkel (Jan 1979) ▪ 291ha/151ha (cabs s/f, cinsaut, malbec, merlot, p verdot, ptage, pinot, shiraz, chenin, sauv) ▪ ±750t/±10,000cs own label 97% red, 3% white; ±20,000cs for clients; balance in bulkwine & grapes ▪ Export brands: Bellemore, Bellemore Family Selection, Houdamond, Morkel, Tumara ▪ Labels for clients: Cap du Vin, Marks & Spencer, Provoyeur, Pure African, Sizanani, Woolworths ▪ BWI, IPW, WIETA ▪ PO Box 33 Koelenhof 7605 ▪ info@bellevue.co.za ▪ www. bellevue.co.za ▪ S 33° 52' 48.48" E 018° 45' 50.40" ▪ **T +27 (0)21-865-2055** ▪ F +27 (0)21-865-2899

Bellevue winemaker Wilhelm Kritzinger can hardly contain his excitement when talking about the release of Eselgraf Chenin Blanc, a wine made for the first time last year from a 36-year-old block of dryland bushvines on the property. The Afrikaans word 'eselgraf' literally means 'donkey's grave', the name given to the vineyard by workers on account of it being established on an old donkey burial ground, the beasts of burden used to tend the land in the era before tractors. The 2012 yield of this 2.29ha parcel was a mere 3.5t/hectare so only about 350 cases were bottled.

PK Morkel range

Petit Verdot ★★★ Now bottled, **09** shade less seductive than it was on preview. Full-bodied, with subdued sour cherry fruit, plenty of chocolate & coffee character, drying on finish. **Pinotage** New bottling not ready. **Tumara** ★★★ Bordeaux red blend **06** lacks fruit weight, dominated by oak. Stellenbosch WO.

Morkel range

★★★★ **Pinotage** Sweet red & black fruit, malty note on **09** (★★★), now bottled. Big & rich, not as fresh or poised as **08**.

Malbec ★★★ Last time a preview, **09** now shows ultra-ripe dark fruit, chocolate & mint. **Shiraz** 🖉 ★★★★ Now bottled, **10** looking much more settled. Red fruit & fynbos, good concentration, fresh acidity & firm but fine tannins. **Atticus Cape Blend** Await new vintage. **Eselgraf Single Vineyard Chenin Blanc** NEW 🖉

⌥ ★★★★ Tank sample of unwooded **12** appealing if very youthful, with notes of pear & guava. Lightly fruity, bright acidity, needs time to settle. **Sauvignon Blanc** 🍴 ⌥ ★★★ Tasted pre-bottling, **12** is very bold with pronounced granadilla plus slight sweaty character & tangy acidity. — CE

Bellingham

Location: Wellington ▪ WO: Coastal/Western Cape/Paarl ▪ Est 1693 ▪ 1stB 1947 ▪ Closed to public ▪ Owner(s) DGB ▪ Winemaker(s) Niël Groenewald (Jul 2004), with Mario Damon (Jan 2002) ▪ Viticulturist(s) Stephan Joubert (2006) ▪ 4,000t/280,000cs own label 50% red 49% white 1% rosé ▪ ISO 9001:2000, HACCP, IPW, WIETA ▪ Private Bag X03 Groot Drakenstein 7680 ▪ bellingham@dgb.co.za ▪ www.bellinghamwines.com ▪ **T +27 (0)21-870-4200** ▪ F +27 (0)21-874-1531

Founded by Huguenots in 1693, Bellingham was known as 'Belle en Champ', meaning 'beautiful fields'. Some of the history relating to this enduring brand's modest beginnings on the farm are now being highlighted in the realignment and launch of four distinct ranges: Bernard Series honours maverick vintner Bernard Podlashuk, who revitalised Bellingham and started the brand in the 1940s; Tree Series alludes to the beautiful shaded gardens in which the Podlashuks entertained family and friends; Insignia Series recalls the property's fruit-growing origins and the flavours associated with the farmhouse kitchen; Ancient Earth acknowledges the foundation of the industry — its soils.

The Bernard Series

★★★★ **Basket Press Syrah** ⌥ **10** powerful, modern style but with fruit (including viognier) & structure to back it. Ripe vintage well concealed in balanced profile. Ageworthy, although earlier maturing than **09**.

★★★★ **Small Barrel SMV** Shiraz (80%), mourvèdre & viognier; modern style-change & quite ripe for **09**, with sleek, muscle-rippling structure & rich- textured, dark & spicy fruit. Ageworthy & powerful. No **08**.

★★★★ **Old Vine Chenin Blanc** 🍴 ⌥ Step up on **10** (★★★★), though not as vibrant as **09**, **11** shows rich, honeyed dried peach tone, good texture & tangy grip from low yields. Contemplative, food wine.

★★★★ **Whole Bunch Roussanne** ⊕ 🍴 ⌥ Rare-in-Cape Rhône white grape, reticent in **10** (★★★★), gently aromatic, with silky texture. Less tangy than **09**, still appealing. Voor Paardeberg vines.

Bush Vine Pinotage ⌥ ★★★★ Big-boned, riper **10** has more fruit-filled gravitas in warmer vintage. Dark, smoky plum just restrained by dry tannins & structure. **Hand Picked Viognier** 🍴 ⌥ ★★★★ **11** a fresher step up on previous. Rich & aromatic fruit profile, both crisp & succulent, with feisty grip & pithy almond fare-well. **Whole Bunch Grenache Blanc-Viognier** 🍴 ⌥ ★★★★ **11**, with 20% viognier, raises the bar on maiden **10** (★★★★). Tangy dried apricot & almond flavours enliven waxy, lanolin-rich texture from low yield. Serious, food-styled.

Insignia Series

Mocha Java Merlot 🍴 ⌥ ★★★ **11** retains previous creamy mocha tone, with extra dash of crema & dry bitter chocolate farewell. Balanced 'café culture' style. **Citrus Grove Chenin** NEW 🍴 ⌥ ★★★ **12** pungent herb & citrus oil nuance, though riper & rounder mouthfeel. Fresh pithy farewell favours food.

Ancient Earth range NEW

Cabernet Sauvignon ⌥ ★★★ **10** preview a tad lean & tight. Dry, dusty tannins restrain fresh fruit pastille & leafy flavours. Should mellow once bottled. **Merlot** ⌥ ★★★ **10** tank sample shows appealing freshness. Bright red berry fruit & firm food-pairing tannins. **Pinotage** 🍴 ⌥ ★★★ Preview **10** is accessible, balanced & creamy, with ripe spicy mulberry & sweet tobacco flavours. WO W Cape. **Shiraz** 🍴 ⌥ ★★★ **11** youthful pre-bottling sample shows drier vintage in leaner & savoury styling. **Chardonnay** 🍴 ⌥ ★★★★ New World styling on succulent **11** preview. Oak masks lime/pear core, enveloped in creamy texture. Needs time. **Sauvignon Blanc** 🍴 ⌥ ★★★ Pre-bottling, **12** dusty herbaceous tone though quite ripe & mouthfilling. Balanced but feisty.

The Tree Series NEW

Big Oak Red ⌥ ★★★ Was 'Shiraz-Cab'. **11** preview not named for wooding, which is modest. Savoury, sweet tobacco & spice, courtesy dab of malbec, with firm dry tannins. Balanced braai mate. WO Cape, as for all these. **Berry Bush Rosé** 🍴 ⌥ ★★ Was 'Pinotage Rosé'. Tank sample **12** still from pinotage, crisply smooth & strawberry toned. **Pear Tree White** ✓ 🍴 ⌥ ★★★★ Was 'Chenin-Viognier'. Lively **12** preview shows nectarine, pear & quince with delicious tangy acidity. Well-crafted, elegant entertainer. Range was 'The Blends'. — MW

Bellpost

Location: Vredendal • Map/WO: Olifants River • Est/1stB 2005 • Tasting, sales & cellar tours by appt • Owner(s) Lollies Thiart • Winemaker(s) Koos Thiart (Jan 2005) • Viticulturist(s) Nico Thiart (Jan 2005) • 5ha/2ha (merlot, ruby cab, shiraz, chard, nouvelle, viog) • 12t/900cs own label 80% red 20% white • PO Box 39 Vredendal 8160 • bellpost@starmail.co.za • www.bellpost.co.za • S 31° 36'24.1" E 018° 25'0.6" • **T +27 (0)27-213-2562, +27 (0)82-619-2428** • F +27 (0)27-213-2562

A concerted marketing effort is bearing fruit for the Thiart family owners, and scion Koos Thiart notes that sales are growing particularly rapidly in Cape Town. Welcome news for a young winemaker who says the opportunity to vinify on the home farm with terroir-appropriate varieties such as ruby cabernet and nouvelle, in a region traditionally known for brandy-wine, is the realisation of a life's dream.

Merlot ★★★ Appealing vanilla & plum sweetness on ready-to-drink **11**. **Ruby Cabernet** ⓦ ★★★ Step-up **08**, expressive & packed with mulberry flavour, engaging despite slight bitter edge. **Shiraz** ⓦ ★★★★ **08** typical leather, bacon & smoke character, producer's signature big alcohol (15%) well contained. **Chardonnay** ★★★ Restrained **11** back on track, satisfying vinosity & fresh limy conclusion. **C'est la Vie** ★★★ Apricot-toned **11** mouthfilling mix of nouvelle & barrel-fermented chardonnay/viognier, for fans of oak-driven style. — DB/CvZ

■ **Bell Tower** see Asara Wine Estate & Hotel

Benguela Cove

Location: Bot River • Map: Elgin, Walker Bay & Bot River • WO: Overberg/Walker Bay • Est 2004 • 1stB 2007 • Tasting Mon-Sat 10-5 (mid Sep-Apr); Fri-Sat 10-5 (May-mid Sep), other days by appt with 24 hrs notice • Fee R30pp, waived on purchase • Sales Mon-Sat 10-5 • Closed Easter Fri/Sun, Dec 25/26 & Jan 1 • BYO picnic • Owner(s) Benguela Cove Investments (Pty) Ltd (Flora Drummond) • Winemaker(s) Niels Verburg (2010, Luddite) & Kevin Grant (2012 Ataraxia) • Viticulturist(s) Paul Wallace (2011, consultant) • 206ha/66ha (cabs s/f, malbec, merlot, p verdot, pinot, shiraz, chard, sauv, sem, viog) • 600t/2,200cs own label 50% red 40% white 10% rosé • PO Box 112 Onrusriver 7201 • info@benguelacove.co.za • www.benguelacove.co.za • S 34° 20'45.0" E 019° 8'15.7" • **T +27 (0)83-645-6198** • F +27 (0)21-671-5229

This is a residential as well as a wine estate, and sustainability and working in harmony with nature is high on the agenda. Alien plant species are being removed and attention focused on natural fauna and flora. Next is lighter wine bottles to reduce the carbon footprint. The string of consultant winemakers has been reduced to two, but others can be drawn in when needed. A new wine range, Moody Lagoon (white and red) created for the Chinese market, is also available cellar door, as is Catalina, a Bordeaux blend.

★★★★ **Sauvignon Blanc** 🍽 📷 Ex-tank **12** already shows its class, prominent minerality & a leafy edge, seamed with tangy acidity that awakens the senses. From a single vineyard. Could rate better once bottled. **Cabernet Sauvignon** Await next, as for **Rosé** & **Chardonnay-Semillon**. **Cabernet Franc** 📷 ★★★★ Preview **11** rich & dense, with mocha chocolate & dark plums. Tannins firm & dry, showing some integration but needing time to complete. **Shiraz** ⓦ ★★★★ Rich & ripe, mocha choc & vanilla-toned **10** ex barrel is warm hearted, generous; supple tannins allow early enjoyment. — CR

■ **Ben Hur** see Blomendahl Vineyards
■ **Berg en Dal** see Wine-of-the-Month Club

Bergheim

Location: Paarl • Map: Paarl & Wellington • WO: Western Cape/Paarl • Est/1stB 2000 • Tasting by appt • Owner(s) Edwin Jordaan • Cellarmaster(s)/winemaker(s) Edwin Jordaan (Jan 2000) • 4-6t/500cs own label 66% red 34% white • PO Box 6020 Paarl 7622 • drjordaan@gmail.com • S 33° 45'20.2" E 018° 57'42.5" • **T +27 (0)82-923-3115, +27 (0)21-863-1529** • F +27 (0)21-862-7852

After missing out due to illness, Paarl one-man-show Edwin Jordaan felt blessed to make wine again last year: 'The grapes were better than ever; the pleasure was greater than ever. Every bottle of wine wants to tell a story about terroir, cultivar and/or harvest. My passion is seeing this happen with minimum interference.'

Bergheim range

★★★★ **Mignon** ⊕ Vibrant **10** marries 80% semillon with sauvignon, all barrel fermented. Restrained but complex: interwoven oatmeal, minerality & lemongrass. WO W Cape, as for Couple's duo.

Pinotage ⊕ ★★★ Only 2 barrels made, **08** full-ripe plums, older-oak-spiced. Paarl vines, as for Shiraz. **Shiraz** ⊕ ★★★★ **08**'s tannins fully integrated, exuberant fruit & spice. Drink up.

Couple's Wine range

Dry Red Ben ⊕ ★★★★ Same wine as **08** Shiraz. Tall 500ml bottle to partner Celia when couples want different wines. **Dry White Celia** ⊕ ★★★ Friendly 12% alcohol on appley, leafy & bone-dry **10**. 500ml. —CR

■ **Berghuis** *see* Groupe CDV
■ **Bergkelder** *see* Die Bergkelder Wine Centre

Bergsig Estate

Location: Worcester ▪ Map/WO: Breedekloof ▪ Est 1843 ▪ 1stB 1977 ▪ Tasting & sales Mon-Fri 8–5 Sat & pub hols 9–5 ▪ Fee R20 for groups of 10+ ▪ Closed Good Fri, Dec 25 & Jan 1 ▪ Cellar tours by appt ▪ Bergsig Bistro ▪ Facilities for children ▪ Farm produce ▪ Conferences ▪ Self-guided birdwatching route ▪ Conservation area, visits by appt ▪ Lategan family history & historical artefacts on display ▪ Festivals: Cloudy Nouveau (Apr); Soetes & Soup (Jul); Outdoor (Oct) ▪ Owner(s) Lategan family ▪ Cellarmaster(s) De Wet Lategan (Jan 1989) ▪ Winemaker(s) Chris du Toit (Jul 2003) ▪ Viticulturist(s) Louis & Plum Lategan (1991) ▪ ±400ha/253ha (cab, ptage, shiraz, touriga, chard, chenin, sauv) ▪ 3,200t/50,000cs own label 35% red 60% white 4% rosé 1% other + 70,000cs for clients ▪ Other export brand: White River ▪ Brand for clients: Woolworths ▪ BWI, BRC, Fairtrade, IPW ▪ PO Box 15 Breërivier 6858 ▪ wine@bergsig.co.za ▪ www.bergsig.co.za ▪ S 33° 31'9.4" E 019° 11'38.7" ▪ **T +27 (0)23-355-1603** ▪ F +27 (0)23-355-1658

A leopard was recently spotted among the vines on the Lategan family's estate — a remarkable occurrence and also a reminder that winegrowing and the preservation of the natural environment are equally important here. In fact, in line with their eco policy, a larger part of the Breedekloof farm is under conservation than under vine. It's no surprise, then, that winemaker De Wet Lategan and his viticulturist brothers Louis and Plum were the first to receive Woolworths' Farming for the Future sustainability accreditation.

Limited Editions

★★★★ **Cabernet Sauvignon Reserve** √ ▨ Lower yield, longer small-oak ageing for this version. Understated but serious **10**, firm but ripe tannins provide excellent balance. Will reward ageing. **09** held back.

Bergsig Estate range

★★★★ **Icarus** ▨ **10** from cab & touriga seduces with sweet blackcurrant & exotic spice profile. Modern & lush, lifted by bright fruit, vibrant acidity, smart oaking. **09** held back.

★★★★ **Chardonnay** √ ▨ **11** back to form after oakier **10** (★★★★), oozes lemon cream & lime with reined-in balanced wood. Smooth & rich, vanilla-kissed fruit tempered by citrus freshness.

★★★★ **Cape Vintage** ⊕ Succulent, smooth & spicy port from tinta. **04** similar to last-tasted **00**, generously flavoured but not sweet, sufficient fire to warm a winter night.

★★★★ **Cape LBV** ⊕ **01** port from tinta entices with molasses & nut bouquet, charms with well-knit tannins & alcohol, seduces with chocolate-orange aftertaste. At 88g/l sugar, drier than most. Drinking well.

> **Cabernet Sauvignon** ☺ ▨ ★★★ **11** dark fruited & youthful, smooth & savoury, firm toasty conclusion. Alcohol is a friendly 12.8%. **The Family Friend** ⓃⒺⓌ ☺ 🍴 ▨ ★★★ Merlot & pinotage-driven multi-variety red blend **11** is lightish, succulent & smooth, bright black fruit for fireside enjoyment. **Gewürztraminer** ☺ 🍴 ▨ ★★★ **12**'s intense litchi & rosepetal fragrance, soft sweetness & light grip as always tick all the right drinkability boxes. **Sauvignon Blanc** ☺ 🍴 ▨ ★★★ Fragrant fruit salad & lively acidity on amenable **12** (12.4% alcohol), perfect just-dry summer sipping.

Pinotage √ ▨ ★★★ Juicy spicy plum character, improved **10** good sweet-sour balance, more body than previous. For early enjoyment. **Bulldozer Pinotage** ⊕ ★★★ Exuberant **10**, when previewed was unfettered by oak, enlivened by zesty acidity. **Touriga Nacional** ⓃⒺⓌ ★★★ Rare unfortified bottling of port grape. Ripe dark fruit with earthy tones, medium-bodied **11** hints of fynbos & spice, drinks easily. **Shiraz Rosé** 🍴 ▨ ★★ Off-dry **12**, lightish, with soft red fruit & spice flavours. **Chenin Blanc** 🍴 ▨ ★★★ Crunchy green apple, crisp acidity, **12** uncomplicated sipping. **White River Chenin Blanc** ⊕ ★★★ **10**

engaging marriage crackling acidity & pithy goodbye. **Bouquet Light** ⓐ 📖 ★★ Sweet, tingly perlé **NV** from muscat. **Sauvignon Blanc Brut** Await new vintage. **Special Late Harvest** ⓐ ★★★ Previously reviewed was **07** from botrytised chenin. **Cape Ruby** ⓐ ★★★★ Unoaked **NV** port from tinta, delicious, approachable as this style should be. Discontinued: **Ruby Cabernet-Merlot**.

Lategan Family Reserve range
Discontinued: **Barrel Aged Chardonnay**. — WB

Bergwater Winery

Location: Prince Albert • Map: Klein Karoo & Garden Route • WO: Prince Albert Valley/Western Cape • Est 1999 • 1stB 2003 • Tasting & sales Mon-Thu 8–4.30 Fri 8-4 Sat/Sun 10-3 • Fee R15 for groups, free for individuals • Cellar tours by appt • Meals by prior arrangement • BYO picnic • Gifts • Olives & olive oil • Wedding/conference/function venue (up to 250 pax) • 2 x self-catering guesthouses • Gravel airstrip for light aircraft (phone ahead) • Hiking/mountain biking & 4x4 trail by arrangement • Owner(s) Heimie & Stephan Schoeman • Cellarmaster(s)/winemaker(s) Mariska Vorster (Jan 2003) • 1,500ha/72ha (cab, merlot, shiraz, chard, sauv) • 126t/±1,000cs own label 80% red 15% white 5% rosé + 70,000L bulk • PO Box 40 Prince Albert 6930 • wine@bergwater.co.za • www.bergwater.com • S 33° 16'46.3" E 022° 13'55.7" • **T +27 (0)23-541-1703** • F +27 (0)23-541-1081/+27 (0)86-541-7335

Set in the Groot Karoo's scenic Prince Albert Valley, some 20km from the hamlet of Prince Albert — recently something of a magnet for food lovers — this family-owned winery has opened a curio/gift shop selling local products such as olives and olive oil from the farm, fig preserves, jams and dried fruit.

Reserve range
Cabernet Sauvignon ⓐ 📖 ★★ Mid-2010, blackcurrant-infused **09** needed time to mellow, should be ready now. **Merlot** ⓐ 📖 Tank sample **09** fresh & fruit-filled; too unformed to rate mid-2011. **Shiraz** ⓐ 📖 ★★★ Pre-bottling, **09** supple, red-fruited & crisp but needs year/2 to show its best. **Royal Reserve** Await new vintage. **Sauvignon Blanc** ⓐ 📖 ★★★★ Appealing **11** preview shows Karoo scrub, lime & grapefruit flavours, zesty acidity & long aftertaste.

Bergwater range
Merlot ⓐ 📖 ★★ Blackcurrant & vanilla **08**, chunky, brisk & dry. **Shiraz** 📖 Await next, like **Organic Shiraz, Chardonnay & Rendezvous White**. **Rendezvous Red** ⓐ 📖 ★★ Plummy **08** merlot & shiraz mix previously harmonious & earthy. **Muscat D'Alexandrie** ⓐ ★★★ Spicy highlight, lovely length & light texture to grapey **10** fortified dessert. WO W Cape.

Pienk Pikkewyn range
Pienk Pikkewyn 📖 Await next. **Sparkling Brut Rosé** ⓐ ★★ Ebullient **10** bubbly with faint red-berry notes & lowish alc (12%) for anytime fun. — CE/JP

Bernheim Wines

Location: Paarl • Map: Paarl & Wellington • WO: Paarl/Voor Paardeberg • Est/1stB 2004 • Tasting, sales & tours by appt • Closed all pub hols • Conservation area • Owner(s) Pacas Winery (Pty) Ltd (Pieter Taljaard, Hermann Helmbold, Jacques Kruger) • Cellarmaster(s)/winemaker(s) Jacques Kruger (Feb 2004) • Viticulturist(s) Morné van Greunen (Feb 2009) • 133ha/50ha (cabs s/f, merlot, ptage, p verdot, shiraz) • 6,000cs own label 95% red 5% rosé & less than 1% port • BWI, IPW • PO Box 7274 Noorder-Paarl 7623 • bernheim@iafrica.com • www.bernheimwines.com • S 33° 35'22.5" E 018° 52'45.0" (VP), S 33° 40'54.73" E 018° 58'20.92" (P) • **T +27 (0)21-869-8384** • F +27 (0)21-869-8365

This Paarl winery may have had its ups and downs since establishment in 2004 but it's now demonstrably on the up and up, the three partners say, citing revamped labels, new cab and shiraz for the Bernheim range awaiting roll-out, and a listing by British Airways. They see only success in their future, and they intend to use new marketing methods to ensure their passion wins through.

JH Pacas & Co range
Cabernet Sauvignon ★★★★ **05** is for lovers of mature cab, with cedar, tobacco & good dark-fruit support, earthy complexity. **Shiraz** ⓐ ★★★★ **05** long & firm flavours, lavender & red berry hints, 14.5% alc hardly noticeable.

Vintners Selection
Cabernet Sauvignon Await new vintage.

Bernheim range
Merlot NEW 🗄 📷 ★★ Savoury **11**, blackcurrant jam & racy acidity. **Merlot-Cabernet Sauvignon** ⚡ ★★★ **06** noted previously as light & uncomplicated, with herbal edge to mulberry fruit. **Classique** 🗄 Not tasted. **Dry Red** ⚡ Await next. **Shiraz-Cabernet Sauvignon** ⚡ 🗄 ★★★ Cheery cranberry & salami combo on still-selling **08**. Shiraz edges cab in the blend, adding pepper spice. **Cape Vintage** ⚡ ★★★ 5 barrels of cab & shiraz, **08** fiery cherry plum & spice.

Casual Collection
Pinotage ⚡ ★★★ **10** a step up, offers smoky plum & spice appeal. **Red Select** ⚡ 🗄 ★★★ NV merlot, pinotage & cab blend mirrors its fun label. Light red fruit, cinnamon & a touch of dry tannin. **Pinotage Rosé** 🗄 📷 ★★ Moves here from Bernheim range. **11** dry, with raspberry & spice. — HJ

BerRaz

A shiraz aimed at young people just getting into wine. The cheerful back label of this KWV brand makes many suggestions of where and how it can be enjoyed.

BerRaz 🗄 ★★ Cheerfully packaged spicy, sweet shiraz. **NV** best chilled. Sourced around Western Cape. — AL

- ▦ **Berrio** *see* The Berrio Wines
- ▦ **Berryfields** *see* Ashton Wynkelder
- ▦ **Bestvino Cape** *see* Boutique Baratok

Beyerskloof   🍴 🍷 📷 ♿

Location/map: Stellenbosch • WO: Stellenbosch/Western Cape/Coastal • Est 1988 • 1stB 1989 • Tasting & sales Mon-Fri 8.30-4.30 Sat 10-4.30 • Closed Easter Fri-Mon, Dec 25/26 & Jan 1 • Cellar tours by appt • Red Leaf Restaurant (see Restaurants section) • Farm produce • Conferences (30 pax) • Owner(s) Beyers Truter & Simon Halliday • Cellarmaster(s) Beyers Truter (Jan 1988) • Winemaker(s) Anri Truter (Jan 2004) & Travis Langley (Jan 2009), with Buddy Hendricks (Jan 2010) • Viticulturist(s) Johan Pienaar (2000, consultant) • 130ha/94ha (cab, merlot, ptage) • 750t/120,000cs own label 96% red 2% white 2% rosé + 5,000cs for clients • Brands for clients: Pick's Pick, Tesco • WIETA • PO Box 107 Koelenhof 7605 • wine@beyerskloof.co.za • www.beyerskloof.co.za • S 33° 53'28.0" E 018° 49'23.6" • **T +27 (0)21-865-2135** • F +27 (0)21-865-2683

The iconic name of Beyers Truter, raconteur extraordinary, is synonymous with the highest aspirations of pinotage. He came to prominence during the rise and rise of Kanonkop's fame, but also through his abiding belief in the variety's potential and in his work with bodies and movements promoting it. However, his community work possibly outshines this reputation, with his foetal alcohol syndrome fund, Faith, his years of service as a Stellenbosch town councillor, and education and social mentorship through, among others, the Cape Winemakers Guild. The estate, now in its 24th year of bottling, has steadily focused attention on pinotage, its innate qualities, its versatility (the estate restaurant even offers pinotage burgers) and its lifestyle image.

★★★★☆ **Pinotage Reserve** Eagerly awaited standout-vintage **09** refinement without overt power or heaviness. Elegantly spicy mulberry compote on velvet tannins defines variety, but deftly avoids pitfalls. Track record shows great ageing potential.

★★★★☆ **Field Blend** Finely-crafted cab-merlot from a very special mixed vineyard. **08** (★★★★) is more subtle, less emphatic than **07**, but offers finesse & herbaceousness, reflecting lighter vintage.

★★★★ **Synergy Cape Blend** ✓ Definitive pinotage-led Cape Blend, **10** maintains high standards of previous. Elegance balanced against weight, with beguiling juicy berries cloaked in satin tannins.

★★★★☆ **Faith 09** Cape Blend, 37% pinotage with cab, merlot & shiraz, plays down blockbuster reputation in favour of finesse & sculpted fruit profile. Ripeness is reflected in elegance & balance, with layered fresh berry & compote flavours.

Pinotage ✓ 🗄 📷 ★★★★ Industry standard, produced in awesome volumes, never disappoints. **11** gushes with red berry fruit & good cheer. **Diesel Pinotage** Await new vintage. **Cabernet Sauvignon-Merlot** NEW 🗄 ★★★ New entry-level Bordeaux-style blend from Paarl vineyards, **11** offers refined nuances with generous, easy-drinking fruitiness. **Pinotage Rosé** 🏠 🎨 ★★★ **12** is true to form, with generous berry fruit on crisply dry acidity & welcome 11.5% alcohol. **Chenin Blanc-Pinotage** 🏠 🎨 ★★★ **12**, mostly Swartland chenin, light & breezy with zesty fruit. **Pinotage Rosé Brut** ★★★☆ **10** charmat (tank-fermented) sparkling shows higher aspirations than last, with elegant leesy body & creamy mousse. Satisfyingly dry. **Lagare Cape Vintage** ★★★☆ Port-style fortified from touriga & pinotage. Tuned-down sweetness on foot-stomped **10** suits plummy fruit & appealing brandy-spirit. Discontinued: **Bouwland Cabernet Sauvignon-Merlot.** — GdB

Bezalel-Dyasonsklip Wine Cellar

Location: Upington ▪ Map: Northern Cape, Free State & North West ▪ Est 1949 (farm)/1997 (cellar) ▪ 1stB 1998 ▪ Tasting, sales & cellar tours Mon-Fri 9–5 Sat 9–1 ▪ Fee R15pp ▪ Professional tasting by appt ▪ Closed Easter Fri-Sun, May 1, Dec 16/25 & Jan 1 ▪ Green Fig Café — breakfast & light meals ▪ Venue for conferences & weddings up to 250 people ▪ Owner(s) Bezuidenhout family ▪ Cellarmaster(s)/winemaker(s)/viticulturist(s) Inus Bezuidenhout (1989), with Jan-Adriaan Bezuidenhout (2005) ▪ 60ha/44ha (cab, cornifesto, merlot, pinot, ptage, sangio, shiraz, touriga, chard, cbard, gewürz, merbein, sultana) ▪ ±500cs own label 100% red ▪ Eurogap certified ▪ PO Dyasonsklip 8805 ▪ info@bezalel.co.za ▪ www.bezalel.co.za ▪ S 28° 36' 28.69" E 021° 6' 19.01" ▪ **T +27 (0)54-491-1325, +27 (0)83-310-4763** ▪ F +27 (0)54-491-1141

A visit from the Pasella team, and featuring in an episode of this Afrikaans lifestyle television programme, were highlights at this Northern Cape family farm, where father-and-son team Inus and Jan-Adriaan Bezuidenhout produce a range of boutique wines, a potstill brandy and various liqueurs.

■ **Big Five** see African Terroir
■ **BIG Flower** see Botanica Wines
■ **Big Six** see Old Bridge Wines

Bilton Wines

Location/map/WO: Stellenbosch ▪ Est 1964 ▪ 1stB 1998 ▪ Tasting & sales Mon-Sun 10–5 ▪ Fee R35/6 wines, R50 dark Belgian chocolate & wine pairing (6 wines) ▪ Closed Good Fri, Dec 25/26 & Jan 1 ▪ Cellar tours Mon-Fri by appt ▪ Bilton restaurant Tue-Sun 12-4; also picnics by appt ▪ Jungle gym & play area for children ▪ Vineyard walk ▪ Mountain bike route — booking required ▪ Owner(s) Mark Bilton ▪ Winemaker(s) Rudolf de Wet (Nov 2005) & Elizma van der Mescht (Jan 2010), with Giorgio Dalla Cia (consultant) ▪ Viticulturist(s) Ruan du Plessis (Dec 2004) ▪ 377ha/80ha (cab, merlot, mourv, p verdot, pinot, shiraz, sauv, viog) ▪ 100t/8,000cs own label 90% red 10% white ▪ BWI, IPW ▪ PO Box 60 Lynedoch 7603 ▪ info@biltonwines.com ▪ www. biltonwines.com ▪ S 33° 59' 52.9" E 018° 50' 58.3" ▪ **T +27 (0)21-881-3714** ▪ F +27 (0)21-881-3721

Behind the impressive flagship wine of this Helderberg estate is the story of owner Mark Bilton's entrepreneurial great-grandfather, Sir Percy Bilton. Youngest of 11 children, Percy went from a lad hand-selling grease remover to the head of a listed property group and, via the Percy Bilton Charity, a noted philanthropist. Each vintage of the wine that honours him tells a tale through a different type of hat, the most recent being a ship's captain's, doffing a cap to Mark's love of the sea.

Private Collection

★★★★ **The Bilton** ⊕ 100% cab, **06** matured 3 years in '500% new oak' produced porty, inky, tannic leviathan, hopefully to emerge with grace.

★★★★☆ **Sir Percy** Refined but richly fruited **08** Bordeaux-style red blend maintains the standard of **07**. Dab mourvèdre adds spice to the refined, classic blackberry flavours. Lithe frame, fine tannin & harmonious balance. Complex & substantial.

★★★★ **Viognier** ⊕ Pricey **08** white flagship was impossibly spicy & intense when last tasted, with ripe peach fruit.

Cellar Selection

★★★★☆ **Cabernet Sauvignon 08** cements this label's claim to higher general rating. Bold, ripe cassis fruit with silky glissade of tannins. Structured & firm but beautifully smooth & rich overall. Light, tasty cocoa note adds complex nuance to the layered palate.

★★★★ **Shiraz** ✓ Lovely concentration of **08** on par with **07**. Intense but seamlessly elegant, ripe blue/black berries & char hint from 80% new oak. Silky smooth texture, long rich tail.

Merlot ★★★ Tangy fynbos, herbal edge to **08**, lighter than previous but rich dark berry/chocolate mouthfeel pleases. Discontinued: **Pinotage**.

Bilton range

Matt Black Red Blend 🔲 ★★★★ Merlot toned down on 5-way **09** blend, shiraz now leads ample ripe fruity appeal. Rounded, textured palate & structure. **Bonnie Anne** 🔲 🈂 ★★☆ Changes name from 'Sauvignon Blanc' but **12** still made from that variety, remains soft styled, light, crisp & easy. — FM

▪ **Birdfield** *see* Klawer Wine Cellars
▪ **Birkenhead Estate & Brewery** *see* Walker Bay Vineyards
▪ **Bistro** *see* Zandvliet Wine Estate & Thoroughbred Stud

Bizoe Wines

Location: Somerset West ▪ WO: Western Cape ▪ Est/1stB 2008 ▪ Tasting & sales by appt or during tailor-made tours — booking essential ▪ Fee R1,500 pp incl transport & lunch ▪ Owner(s)/cellarmaster(s)/winemaker(s) Rikus Neethling ▪ Viticulturist(s) Org Viljoen ▪ 1,000cs ▪ Unit 189 Croydon Vineyard Estate Somerset West 7130 ▪ info@bizoe.co.za ▪ www.bizoe.co.za ▪ **T +27 (0)21-843-3307** ▪ F +27 (0)86-653-8186

Asked what he'd like to change in business if he could, boutique-scale winemaker and conductor of upscale wine tours Rikus Neethling answers: 'Nothing. I enjoy every minute of my wine life and, should circumstances demand that I change, I'll do so then, but not now.'

★★★★ **Estalet Syrah** Seamless **10** boasts cassis, lily & house's fynbos aromas. Dense but fresh, with bright acidity, good grip & modest 13% alcohol. Stellenbosch, Breedekloof grapes (**09** only the latter).

★★★★☆ **Henriëtta** Smartly oaked 70% semillon, sauvignon in **11**. Savoury expression, with faint quince, lemon & bruised apple fruit notes; immensely satisfying weight, dry tail. Franschhoek, Elgin fruit. — CvZ

Blaauwklippen Vineyards

Location/map: Stellenbosch ▪ WO: Stellenbosch/Western Cape ▪ Est 1682 ▪ 1stB 1974 ▪ Tasting & sales Mon-Fri 10-6.30 (summer) & 10-5 (winter) Sat 10-5 Sun & pub hols 10-4 ▪ Fee R30/informal, R40/formal, R50/tour & formal tasting, R75 unique chocolate & (fortified) wine & brandy pairing ▪ Closed Dec 25 & Jan 1 ▪ Cellar tours by appt (48-hr advance notice) ▪ Family market every Sun 10-3 ▪ Mini cheese boards in Wine Centre ▪ Barouche Restaurant (see Restaurants section) ▪ Facilities for children ▪ Pony & carriage rides ▪ Gift shop ▪ Conferences ▪ Weddings/functions ▪ Walks/hikes & mountain biking by appt ▪ Permanent carriage museum ▪ Distillery ▪ Coffee roastery ▪ Owner(s) Blue Lion GmbH ▪ Winemaker(s) Rolf Zeitvogel (Sep 2003), with Albert Basson (Jul 2007) ▪ Viticulturist(s) Christo Hamman (Jan 2009) ▪ 180ha/103ha (cabs s/f, malbec, merlot, p verdot, shiraz, zin, viog) ▪ 550t/35,000cs own label 89% red 3% white 6% rosé 2% other & 11,000cs for clients ▪ Brands for clients: Blue Rock (Germany), Eagle Canyon (China) ▪ IPW ▪ PO Box 54 Stellenbosch 7599 ▪ marketing@blaauwklippen.com ▪ www.blaauwklippen.com ▪ S 33° 58' 23.3" E 018° 50' 51.0" ▪ **T +27 (0)21-880-0133** ▪ F +27 (0)21-880-0136

Popular demand has seen this large wine farm (±100ha of vineyard) on the fringes of Stellenbosch up the frequency of its family market to every Sunday. It celebrated its 330th anniversary last year, while the popular Blaauwklippen Blending Competition is staged for the 30th time this year. Never short of visitor attractions, the constantly evolving modern operation now boasts a distillery, coffee roastery and high teas and tapas in summer. One thing that won't change however, is the property's association with zinfandel — in many forms.

Reserve Selection

★★★★ **Shiraz 10** powerful but restrained, with herbal edge to plum, chocolate & charry fruit. Pancetta whiff adds savoury note on soft-textured palate. This range listed as 'Icon' last time.

★★★★ **Zinfandel** ④ Although still youthful, with 6+ years potential, **09** shows fruit purity & concentration, proving how good this variety can be with grape selection & careful handling.

Merlot NEW ★★★★ Prominent mulberry & cocoa on debut **10**. Wood bold too but will soften in time. Dry, chalky texture on serious frame.

Blaauwklippen Vineyard Selection (BVS)

★★★★ **Cabriolet** ④ Changing blend, malbec with cab, petit verdot in **07**. Last year showed deepened, darkened succulent fruit. Built to age 8+ years, mainly new barrels 17 months but deftly done, approachable.

Shiraz ⓘ ★★★★ Last **07** had blackberries & fennel, elegant oak & Rhône-style peppery complexity. Improved on jammy **06** (★★★★). **Zinfandel** ⓘ ★★★★ Dusty cranberries, intense & insistent, anchored by **08**'s youthfully firm tannins, ideal for rich stews or further cellaring. **White Zinfandel** ⓰ ★★★ **11** continues theme of previous **10**, distinctive cherry spice & faint pink hue. Discontinued: **Cabernet Sauvignon**.

Blaauwklippen Blending Competition (BBC)

BBC 29th Barouche NEW ★★★ Winner of 29th annual wine club blending competition. Shiraz & zinfandel battle for supremacy in 4-way blend with petit verdot & cab franc. **11** preview has inky graphite & spicy grip. 1.5L magnum, as all. **BBC 27** ⓘ ★★★★ Zinfandel/shiraz mix, dab others, **09** shows fruitcake ripeness, retains balance, succulence, making drinking this 1.5L easy. **BBC 28th Barouche** NEW ⓰ ★★★ Merlot leads zinfandel, malbec & petit verdot in 4-way blend, **10** uncomplicated black fruit & cocoa appeal, dry texture.

Blaauwklippen Cultivar Selection

Cabernet Sauvignon ⓘ ★★★ Last was **07**, showed black plums & liquorice, trademark dry tannins. **Malbec** ★★★★ Tobacco leaf & blueberry, **09** preview offers meaty savouriness yet plush mouthfeel. Soft & approachable, with deep, long finish. **Merlot** ★★★ Powerful earthy dark chocolate on improved **09**, dry texture but lots of ripe black fruit. Elegant & persistent. **Shiraz** ⓰ ★★★★ **10** ups the ante with juicy plum intensity & power, inky depth & concentration. Natural ferment in barrel. **Rosé** ⓰ ★★★ Shiraz & zinfandel combo in off-dry **12** tank sample delivers raspberry/cherry succulence. **Chenin Blanc** ★★★ Floral stonefruit appeal on **12** preview, melon & peach simplicity. WO W Cape, like next. **Sauvignon Blanc** ▤ ★★★ Grassy granadilla zip to spirited **12**, pre-bottling zesty fullness on palate ups ante on previous. Good body & long tail. **Viognier** ⓰ ★★★ **12** preview offers lemongrass & peach richness, lees-ageing adds some body & fullness.

Noble Late Harvests

★★★★ **Malbec** Tiny yields for all of the unusual botrytised dessert wines in this range. Chalky feel to **11** (★★★★), tad more restrained plum & blueberry flavours than **10** but attractive, succulent long-fruited finish.
★★★★ **Viognier** Sundried pineapple & peach on rich, honeyed **12** (★★★★), light & tangy, dry-seeming finish. Last was scented **07**.
★★★★ **Zinfandel** Hugely sweet (316g sugar) red & black cherry syrup with a tangy edge, **11** pecan nut nuance from 100% new wood. Spicy too. Balanced & clean, not cloying. Previewed, as for Malbec.

Aperitif range

★★★★☆ **Before & After** ⓘ Handsome packaging for aptly named berry & spice saturated beauty; cloves, cinnamon, palate silky sweet & very moreish. Fortified to 16% alcohol, brandy-like notes on finish. NV. — FM

▪ **Black Box** *see* Wineways Marketing
▪ **Black Forest** *see* Louis
▪ **Black Granite** *see* Darling Cellars
▪ **Black Label** *see* Backsberg Estate Cellars

Black Oystercatcher Wines

Location/WO: Elim ▪ Map: Southern Cape ▪ Est 1998 ▪ 1stB 2003 ▪ Tasting, sales & cellar tours Mon-Fri 9-5 Sat/Sun 10-3.30 ▪ Closed Good Fri & Dec 24/25 ▪ Restaurant, function & wedding venue: kitchen open Mon-Sun 11-2.30, booking essential ▪ Facilities for children ▪ Tour groups ▪ Conferences ▪ Conservation area ▪ Cycling route ▪ Annual sauvignon blanc & oyster festival (Dec); peak season programme ▪ Owner(s)/cellarmaster(s)/winemaker(s)/viticulturist(s) Dirk Human ▪ 1,550ha/18.5ha (cab, merlot, shiraz, sauv, sem) ▪ ±90t/±8,500cs own label 12% red 76% white 12% rosé ▪ BWI, IPW, WIETA ▪ PO Box 199 Bredasdorp 7280 ▪ venue@blackoystercatcher.co.za, wine@blackoystercatcher.co.za ▪ www.blackoystercatcher.co.za ▪ S 34° 37' 58.0" E 019° 49' 39.9" ▪ T +27 (0)28-482-1618 ▪ F +27 (0)86-666-7954

The Black Oystercatcher home farm is on the windy Agulhas plain at the southernmost tip of Africa, and a multitude of adaptations have had to be found to meet the often extreme climate conditions and the diverse and distinctive soil types. The property is also in the Nuwejaars Wetland Special Management Area, and conservation runs like a thread through everything its sixth-generation Human family custodians do, from viticulture and winemaking to the fare in the restaurant.

★★★★ **Triton** ⓘ ▤ Liquorice-toned **08** mixes shiraz (41%), cab & merlot to deliver impressive, restrained & cellarworthy red. Still tightly wound mid-2011, as was cab-dominated **07** (★★★★).
★★★★ **Blanc Fumé** NEW ▤ ⓰ Barrel-fermented sauvignon, from special site within a top block. **10** intensely aromatic, vanilla/nut highlights from (600L) cask, glorious rounded mouthfeel ex year lees-ageing.

Love it *Red or White?*

Pick n Pay

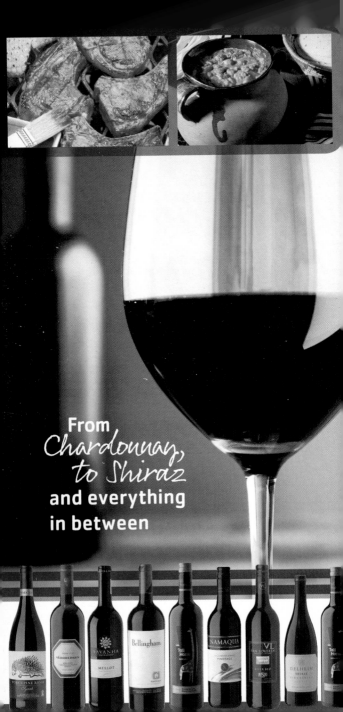

From *Chardonnay,* *to Shiraz* and everything in between

Pick n Pay

Alcohol Not for Sale to Persons Under the
Age of 18. Drink Responsibly.

★★★★ **Sauvignon Blanc** √ 🍶 📖 **11** (★★★★) shows limy minerality, fair substance & weight though arguably too bracingly fresh for solo. **10** fine effort in difficult vintage.

★★★★★ **White Pearl** ⏱ 🍶 Partly oaked semillon & sauvignon blend (70/30) leads the line-up. **09** with khaki bush & white peach notes, extra heft from older oak, endless finish. Will reward patience.

Cabernet Sauvignon-Merlot ⏱ 🍶 ★★★ Fruit-filled & satisfying **08**, mineral & cedar notes from French oak, cab's drying tannin & merlot's plum fruit. **Rosé** 🍶 📖 ★★★ Zesty, dry, lightish merlot-led **12** 'perfect with watercress, goat's cheese & peppered strawberry salad' says owner-winemaker Dirk Human. — WB/GdB

Black Pearl Vineyards

Location/WO: Paarl ▪ Map: Paarl & Wellington ▪ Est 1998 ▪ 1stB 2001 ▪ Tasting, sales & tours just about anytime but phone ahead (no credit cards) ▪ Closed Dec 25 ▪ Walks ▪ Lapa & camping facilities ▪ Self-catering cottage ▪ Conservation area ▪ Owner(s) Lance & Mary-Lou Nash ▪ Winemaker(s)/viticulturist(s) Mary-Lou Nash ▪ 240ha/7.2ha (cab, shiraz) ▪ ±2,500cs 90% red 10% white ▪ BWI, IPW ▪ PO Box 609 Suider-Paarl 7624 ▪ info@ blackpearlwines.com ▪ www.blackpearlwines.com ▪ S 33° 44' 10.5" E 018° 53' 40.8" ▪ **T +27 (0)83-297-9796/+27 (0)83-395-6999** ▪ F +27 (0)86-617-8507

Cape Wine Master Mary-Lou Nash came to wine, and indeed South Africa, purely by chance when, in 1995, she dropped in en route home to the US from an extended stay in Asia, to see her father's newly acquired Paarl farm, Rhenosterkop. She's still there, running her boutique-scale winery in bucolic bliss.

Black Pearl range

★★★★ **Shiraz** √ 🍶 📖 Heavily toasted oak on big-bodied **10** yields in time to spicy, richly ripe black fruit with earthy overtones. Showy, opulent style eschews finesse.

★★★★ **Oro** √ 🍶 📖 **10** cab/shiraz blend has beguiling black fruit lifted by maraschino & liquorice notes. Improves on **09** (★★★★), shows poise & character on quite supple structure.

Cabernet Sauvignon 🍶 Await new vintage. **Chenin Blanc** NEW √ 🍶 📖 ★★★★ Maiden venture into white wine, **11** shows serious intent. Dipped in oak, lees-rich with creamy texture & resonating nutty fruit.

Conservation range
Nash Family Vineyards Rhinoceros Shiraz 🍶 New bottling not ready. — GdB

■ **Black Tie** see Wineways Marketing

BLANKbottle

Location: Somerset West ▪ Map: Helderberg ▪ WO: Stellenbosch/Western Cape/Wellington/Swartland/ Piekenierskloof/Breede River Valley ▪ Est 2005 ▪ 1stB 2003 ▪ Tasting & sales Mon-Sat by appt ▪ Sales also via website ▪ Owner(s)/cellarmaster(s)/winemaker(s) Pieter H Walser ▪ Viticulturist(s) Various ▪ 5,000cs (6btl) own label 70% red 30% white ▪ Lanrust Wine Estate, Winery Road, Somerset West 7129 ▪ pieter@ blankbottle.co.za ▪ www.blankbottle.co.za ▪ S 34° 2'41.1" E 018° 47'16.0" ▪ **T +27 (0)21-842-2747/+27 (0)82-872-8658** ▪ F +27 (0)86-503-0974

Pieter Walser is an adventurous spirit whose production has evolved from opportunistic bought-in batches blended into good-value originals, to an impressive range of area-specific studies. He has made his mark for innovative thinking in an industry awash with marketing gurus, through a combination of intelligent sourcing and blending, striking branding and resolutely single-minded independence. Over the past decade, his growing e-market following has been treated to many ambitious experiments, each with its own intriguing backstory.

BLANKbottle range

★★★★★ **My Eie Stofpad** NEW Focused & eminently satisfying, **11** Stellenbosch cab franc is vibrantly youthful but promises finer things to come. Complex aromas, velvet texture & lingering finish; a complete package.

★★★★ **The Bomb** NEW Aptly named cab-merlot blockbuster from Stellenbosch vineyards, **10** is for fans of muscle-bound physiques with massive (16%) alcohol. Daunting, but still very appealing.

★★★★ **The Big Spaniard** ⏱ Rhône-style 4-way red blend is serious, full, **09** shows dividends from ripe vintage & longer oaking.

★★★★ **Moment of Silence** 📖 Spicy, opulent & expressive **11** Wellington chenin, chardonnay, viognier blend follows **10**'s improved form. Older oak fleshes out body, lees-ageing adds texture. Solidly satisfying.

The Misfit Await new vintage. **My Koffer** NEW ★★★ Serious & pricey artisanal effort with Breedeklo cinsaut, 11 is pleasantly silky but lacks focus or intensity. **E.K.G.** NEW ✓ ★★★★ Concentrated, in standalone petit verdot, 11 from Stellenbosch over-delivers at price. Worthy varietal illustration. **Midnig Call** ★★★★ Classic 5-way Bordeaux-style red blend, 11 from Stellenbosch fruit is opulently ripe & roun with silky texture. **Mnr Professor** Next awaited, as for **Batavia** & **Nothing To Declare**.

Black & The White Black range

★★★★ **Black** Shiraz-based Rhône-style blend from Swartland vineyards. 10 shows meaty herbaceousne & floral hints. Plush, well-rounded plum/damson fruit with solid tannin coating.

★★★★ **The White Black** Recipe change for 10 to Perdeberg-sourced roussanne, clairette, grenache bla & viognier brings trendy oxidative, leesy notes to the fore. Rich & creamy, with subtlety & length.

Educational range

Occasional releases. — GdB

Bloemendal Estate

Location/WO: Durbanville ▪ Map: Durbanville, Philadelphia & Darling ▪ Est 1902 ▪ 1stB 1987 ▪ Tasting & sales Mo Fri 9–5 Sat 9–4 Sun 11–3 ▪ Fee R14pp tasting, R25 cellar tour & tasting ▪ Bon Amis Bistro: weddings, evening fun tions & conferences ▪ Owner(s) Spirito Trade 82 (Pty) Ltd ▪ Winemaker(s) Christie Langeveld & Rianie Strydo (consultant) ▪ Vineyard manager(s) Lombard Loubser ▪ 154ha (cab, malbec, merlot, shiraz, chard, sauv, sem) 5,000cs own label 75% red 25% white ▪ PO Box 466 Durbanville 7551 ▪ mike@bloemendalwines.co.za ▪ ww bloemendalwines.co.za ▪ S 33° 50′ 22.1″ E 018° 36′ 1.4″ ▪ **T +27 (0)21-975-9591** ▪ F +27 (0)86-615-7020

Last seen in the guide a decade ago, Bloemendal's 'regular' Sauvignon Blanc wit its distinctive and pungent 'dusty' character helped build former owner-cella master Jackie Coetzee's (and Durbanville's) reputation for sauvignon. It's no been revived by incumbent winemaker and Coetzee protégée Christie 'Boetma Langeveld, whose first solo vintage, 2009, earned top marks for the senior Suide Terras version at the Terroir Awards. With five star winemaker Rianie Strydo advising, junior is back and the story continues…

Bloemenblanc ☺ ▤ ★★★ Sauvignon/semillon combo, typically more of the former. Two tasted: 12 less ripe therefore more zesty & expressive, showing greater varietal character, hints of 'Durbanville dust'. 11 (★★★) more muted but lipsmackingly dry; big alcohol well hidden.

Cabernet Sauvignon ★★★ Leafy edge to 10's dark fruit & clean leather. Commendably dry, with terse pe sistent tannic grip. Like Merlot, first since 05. **Merlot** ★★☆ Fruit compote 10 has (not unpleasant) toma leaf notes, some chocolate & coffee; tad bitter conclusion. **Pinotage** ⊕ ★★★ 10's fruit-filled palate enli ened by bright acidity; a slightly bitter nudge on finish. **Chardonnay** Await next. **Sauvignon Blanc Suide Terras** ★★★★ 11 shows riper sauvignon aromas, flavours: white peach, papaya, melon; also softer acidity big alcohol. Step up on other 11 whites reviewed, yet lacks verve of some previous vintages. **Sauvigno Blanc** NEW ▤ ★★★ Nettle-nuanced, lightly cropped 12 in delicate vein: balanced moderate alcohol & grain of sweetness. Heavily cropped 11 (★★★) faintly herbal; very dry, with big alcohol slightly bitter. **Semi lon** ⊕ ★★★★ Unwooded & undemanding 10 previewed mid-2011 was for youthful enjoyment. — CvZ

Blomendahl Vineyards

Location: Elgin ▪ Map: Elgin, Walker Bay & Bot River ▪ WO: Elgin/Simonsberg-Paarl/Coastal/Stellenbosc Western Cape ▪ Est 2003 ▪ 1stB 2006 ▪ Tasting by appt ▪ Owner(s) Blomendahl Trust ▪ Cellarmaster(s winemaker(s)/viticulturist(s) Franz Josef Blomendahl ▪ 126ha (cab, merlot, ptage, shiraz, chard, chenin) 480t/35,000cs own label 90% red 10% white ▪ PO Box 52019 Waterfront Cape Town 8002 ▪ info@basco.co.z ▪ www.blomendahl.de ▪ S 34° 13′ 12.2″ E 019° 2′ 28.8″ ▪ **T +27 (0)21-859-2937/+27 (0)72-692-6229** F +27 (0)21-859-1411

While overseeing construction of a new boutique winery and tasting room i time for harvest 2013, Franz Blomendahl has been sourcing icon wines fro France, Italy and Spain against which to benchmark some 'Gran Reserva-styl reds he's been maturing in barrel for up to 48 months. 'We're focusing on th high-end now.'

Ben Hur range

Shiraz NEW ★★ Herbaceous seam to wild berry fruit on medium-bodied **07**. **Quadrega** ⓣ ★★★ Black-fruited **06** trio cab, merlot & shiraz showed sleek oak tannins when last tasted.

Estate Collection

Basco Cabernet Sauvignon NEW ★★ Hints of cedar & sweet berries, **10** soft & fruity. WO W Cape. **Basco Merlot** ⓣ ★★★ **07** for early enjoyment, sweetness held in firm tannic grip when last we tried. **Môrewag Pinotage** ⓣ ★★★ **06** demure compared with previous, less extracted, with firm tannins. Simonsberg-Paarl WO, as for all Môrewag wines. **Basco Pinotage** ⓣ 🍴 ★★ Acid dominated youthful, magenta-hued, spicy **10** when last tasted. **Blue Bay Shiraz** ⓣ ★★★ Ripe, dark fruit in juicy, accessible **06**. Ex West Coast vines. **Môrewag Rosé** ⓣ 🍴 **09** sweet impression from fruitiness but dry & nicely structured. **Basco Rosé** ⓣ 🍴 ★★★ Light pink **10** delighted with off-dry fruity flavours when reviewed. **Basco Chardonnay** ⓣ 🍴 ★★★ Green-apple toned **10** was pleasant summertime sipper mid-2010. Simonsberg-Paarl WO. **Bonny Bay Bushvine Chenin Blanc** ⓣ 🍴 ★★★ Noted previously as tad unexpressive for bushvines, but **09** pleasantly dry food wine. WO Stellenbosch. **Basco Sauvignon Blanc** ⓣ 🍴 ★★★★ **09** attractive stony acidity & minerality when tasted mid-2010. Good table companion. **Môrewag Shiraz** ⓣ ★★★ Natural Sweet **08** had savoury hints last time; sweet, but good grip added balancing savouriness. **Môrewag Cabernet Sauvignon** ⓣ ★★★ Natural Sweet **08** brimmed with fruit, sweetness checked by leafy dry savouriness.

Prime Bin range

Cabernet Sauvignon-Merlot ⓣ ★★★ Mix cab & merlot in black-fruited **06**, was dense & closely knit, must since have softened. **Lady in Red Rosé** ⓣ 🍴 ★★★ Attractively different: more 'light red' than 'rosé', **09** had plenty cab fruit for flavour & structure. Simonsberg-Paarl WO.

Bonolo range

Cabernet Sauvignon Not tasted. — DB

■ **Blouberg** see Graça

Blouvlei Wyne

Location: Wellington ▪ Map: Paarl & Wellington ▪ WO: Paarl ▪ Est/1stB 2003 ▪ Tasting, sales & cellar tours Mon-Fri 9-4.30 Sat by appt ▪ Fee R15 ▪ Closed all pub hols ▪ Picnic area by arrangement ▪ Owner(s) BEE Company ▪ Winemaker(s) Abraham Cloete & Chris Roux ▪ Viticulturist(s) Ettienne Barnard (Oct 2010) ▪ ±40ha/28ha (alicante bouschet, cabs s/f, merlot, mourv, p verdot, shiraz, tinta barocca) ▪ ±150t/5,000cs own label 70% red 30% white ▪ IPW ▪ PO Box 817 Wellington 7654 ▪ blouvlei@cknet.co.za ▪ www.montdutoit.co.za ▪ S 33° 39'31.3" E 019° 2'2.6" ▪ **T +27 (0)21-873-7745** ▪ F +27 (0)21-864-2737

The workers of Mont du Toit winery in Wellington are shareholders in this enterprise making wines for easy, everyday drinking. Red grapes come partly from the parent farm (which shares its production and sales facilities with Blouvlei) but, as Mont du Toit is all-red, the sauvignon blanc grapes must be bought in.

Red ☺ 🍴 ★★★ Light but flavourful **10** cab-based blend. Dry tannins firm up easygoing charm.

Rosé ⓣ 🍴 ★★★★ Uncomplicated **10** dry, zesty & fruity. **Sauvignon Blanc** ⓣ 🍴 🍸 ★★★ **11** tends to the greener side of the sauvignon spectrum, but has a bit of weight & is crisply & tastily succulent. WO Paarl. Discontinued: **Klassique**. — TJ

■ **Blue Bay** see Blomendahl Vineyards

Blueberry Hill Estate

Location/map/WO: Franschhoek ▪ Est 1998 ▪ 1stB 2005 ▪ Tasting & sales by appt ▪ 3 self-catering cottages (T +27 (0)78-148-2749 Claire van Zyl) ▪ Owner(s) Proximitas Investments 106 (Pty) Ltd ▪ Winemaker(s)/viticulturist(s) Oswald Sauermann (Nov 2008) ▪ 0.6ha (merlot) ▪ 4t/250cs own label 100% red ▪ PO Box 383 Franschhoek 7690 ▪ blueberryhill@telkomsa.net ▪ www.blueberryhillcottages.co.za ▪ S 33° 55'19.14" E 019° 8'4.92" ▪ **T +27 (0)21-876-3362** ▪ F +27 (0)21-876-3341

When it comes to winefarming you don't get much smaller — more boutiquish? — than this little block of merlot vines on a slope in the lovely Franschhoek Valley where, though not officially organic, they like 'to let nature take its course'. The grapes are taken offsite for vinification and bottling.

Merlot ★★★★ 07 dark fruit mingled with herbal notes; rounded, with signs of pleasant evolution adding a savoury nuance. Ready to enjoy. — JP

Blue Crane Vineyards

Location/map/WO: Tulbagh ▪ Est 2001 ▪ 1stB 2004 ▪ Visitors welcome but phone ahead ▪ Owner(s) Fred & Manuela Crabbia ▪ Cellarmaster(s)/winemaker(s) Zia Pienaar ▪ Viticulturist(s) Chris Fox, advised by Andrew Teubes & suppliers ▪ 138ha/6ha (cab, merlot, shiraz, sauv) ▪ 2,000cs own label 75% red 25% white ▪ BWI ▪ PO Box 306 Tulbagh 6820 ▪ info@bluecrane.co.za ▪ www.bluecrane.co.za ▪ S 33° 14' 34.7" E 019° 9' 49.4" ▪ **T +27 (0)23-230-0823** ▪ F +27 (0)23-230-0825

It's all smiles at this Tulbagh family wine and olive farm. Wine exports have been successful, says cellarmaster Zia Pienaar, vintage 12 shows a lot of promise, and their first olive harvest yielded an extra virgin oil.

Blue Crane range

Cabernet Sauvignon ★★ Now bottled, **10** shows oaky stewed fruit. **Merlot ⓟ ★★★** Rounded **10**, attractive cherry fruit & lightly spiced vanilla notes. **Shiraz ★★★** Previewed last edition, burly **10** ideally needs further year/2 to mellow. **Full Flight ⓟ 🍽 ★★★** Food-friendly combo cab, shiraz & merlot, **08** chunky but well fleshed, blackcurrant flavour & savoury spice. **Sauvignon Blanc** NEW 🍽 **★★★** Grassy **11** fresh & uncomplicated, lightish body for al fresco imbibing.

Strelizia range

Shiraz-Merlot ⓟ 🍽 ★★★ Juicy **NV** easy sipper with earthy aftertaste. **Shiraz-Cabernet Sauvignon-Merlot ⓟ 🍽 ★★★** Evident tannins in dry & spicy **07** blend. **Sauvignon Blanc ⓟ 🍽 🌿 ★★★** Greengage, citrus & mineral flavours on zingy **10**. — CE/CvZ

▪ **Blue Rock** see Blaauwklippen Vineyards
▪ **Bob's Your Uncle** see Boer & Brit

Boekenhoutskloof Winery

Location/map: Franschhoek ▪ WO: Western Cape/Franschhoek/Coastal/Swartland ▪ Est 1994 ▪ 1stB 1996 ▪ Tasting & sales Mon-Fri 9–5 ▪ Closed all pub hols ▪ Owner(s) Boekenhoutskloof Winery (Pty) Ltd ▪ Cellarmaster(s) Marc Kent (1994) ▪ Winemaker(s) Jean Smit, Johan Nesenberend & Elsabé Engelbrecht ▪ Viticulturist(s) Heini Tait ▪ 71ha/20ha (cabs s/f) ▪ 3,000t/250,000cs own label 60% red 39% white 1% rosé ▪ BDOCA, BRC, HACCP ▪ PO Box 433 Franschhoek 7690 ▪ info@boekenhoutskloof.co.za ▪ www.boekenhoutskloof.co.za ▪ S 33° 56' 33.0" E 019° 6' 28.0" ▪ **T +27 (0)21-876-3320** ▪ F +27 (0)21-876-3793

This go-getting winery was established nearly two decades ago by a group of business and advertising executives and impassioned Francophile winemaker Marc Kent. (It is rumoured that each of the antique chairs on their label represents a partner.) Since announcing themselves serious players through a maximum five star rating in our 2000 edition for the now legendary Syrah 1997, they have led viti/vinicultural and market trends — from their idyllic home in the hills outside Franschhoek to the cutting edge of Swartland's terroir initiatives, Firgrove's trove of fine red vineyards (via recently acquired Helderberg Wijnmakerij) and veteran blocks around Wellington. Their premium wines deservedly get applause at home and around the world, yet equally impressive in their own way are the amazing quality, typicity and value on offer in the Porcupine Ridge and Wolftrap ranges.

Boekenhoutskloof range

★★★★★ Cabernet Sauvignon Nervous leafy notes on **10** (★★★★★) hint at lesser ripeness than great **09** vintage. Stately & finely crafted, but missing classic black-fruit core & earthy nuances. Thick tannic cloak needs time to unravel. Franschhoek grapes, as all these unless noted.

★★★★☆ Syrah Iconic label & industry benchmark. Always focused, classical, tending towards Old World styling, but proudly individual. **10** from Wellington vines upholds lofty reputation. Follows **09** (★★★★★), which revelled in ripeness of standout vintage.

★★★★ The Chocolate Block Crowd-pleasing shiraz-led 5-way blend, **11** (★★★★★) is enigmatic, yet seductively appealing. Rhône-like spiciness with exotic herbs, sweet berry fruit & ethereal aromas on finish defy pigeon-holing. Upstages already impressive **10**. WO W Cape.

★★★★ **Semillon** Oaky & lees-rich, barrel-fermented **10** in Bordeaux style offers thought-provoking complexity. Spicy minerality with roasted nuts & fascinating aromatic finish.

★★★★☆ **Noble Late Harvest** Barrel-fermented **09** semillon is elegantly weighted, showing restraint & control, but complex & fascinating, unfurling all the subtle nuances of botrytis. Follows less-syrupy Sauternes style of exceptional **08** (★★★★★).

The Wolftrap range

The Wolftrap ☺ 🍴 ★★★ Base range of classy, Rhône-styled blends, WO W Cape. No shortcuts on elegant, oak-matured **11** shiraz/mourvèdre/viognier, in spite of bargain price.

The Wolftrap White ✓ 🍴 ★★★☆ Over-performing entry level viognier-led blend with chenin, grenache blanc, **11** is richly ripe & satisfying.

Porcupine Ridge range

Sauvignon Blanc ☺ 🍴 📖 ★★★ As always, **12** is light, refreshing & uncomplicated, avoiding aromatic clichés. Ex Stellenbosch & Robertson fruit.

Cabernet Sauvignon ✓ 🍴 ★★★☆ Leafy, herbaceous notes on **11** give way to ripe blackcurrant fruit. Generously ripe & full. Over-delivers at price. **Merlot** 🍴 📖 ★★★☆ Earthy, ripe & juicy **11** from Swartland & Stellenbosch vines (as for Cab) is better than price or provenance suggest. **Syrah** ✓ 🍴 📖 ★★★☆ Elegant Swartland-sourced, keenly-priced charmer. **11** is modestly oaked to express typical peppery spices & Rhône-like profile. **Syrah-Viognier** ✓ 🍴 📖 ★★★☆ Enticing middleweight with satin texture & juicy ripeness, violet & fynbos scents. **11** from Swartland vines. **Viognier-Grenache Blanc** ✓ 🍴 📖 ★★★☆ Swartland/Piekenierskloof blend uses innovative winemaking to produce complex **11**. Restrained oak, sunny ripeness, textured body contribute to fine balance. Great-value wine improves on impressive **10** (★★★☆). — GdB

Boer & Brit

Location: Paarl ▪ Map: Paarl & Wellington ▪ WO: Western Cape ▪ Est 2010 ▪ 1stB 2008 ▪ Tasting & sales at Bovlei Cellar (see entry) ▪ Owner(s) Stefan Gerber & Alexander Milner ▪ Winemaker(s) Stefan Gerber, Alex Milner (both Jul 2010) & Marco Benjamin (2011) ▪ 30t own label 60% red 40% white ▪ Other export label: Bob's Your Uncle ▪ PO Box 4 Klapmuts 7625 ▪ alex@boerandbrit.com ▪ www.boerandbrit.com ▪ S 33° 38′ 18.4″ E 019° 1′ 54.2″ ▪ **T +27 (0)21-807-3331** ▪ F +27 (0)86-531-7137

Stefan Gerber and Alex Milner are direct descendants of two major protagonists in the Anglo-Boer War, Gerber of President Paul Kruger, Milner of Field Marshal John French and hence the name of this maverick operation. Their wines are currently available from Bovlei Cellar in Wellington while they rent office space at KWV head office La Concorde in Paarl.

Boer & Brit range

★★★★ **The General** 🍴 📖 **10** (★★★★) Bordeaux-style red led by cab franc, with merlot & petit verdot. Tad sullen meat & coriander notes, challenging tannins. Less accessible, complex than violet & herb **09**.

The Field Marshal 🍴 📖 ★★★☆ Increasingly sophisticated blend, **10** includes 4 Rhône varieties & 12% pinta amarela. Rich & full with fresh acidity, crunchy tannins. **Gezina** 🍴 **12** not ready for tasting.

Suikerbossie Ek Wil Jou Hê range
Cap Classique Brut Await new vintage.

Transkaroo-Bring My Huis Toe/Take Me Home range
Pinotage ⑪ ★★★ Earthy banana notes, **08** gentle tannins, hints of elegant pinot parentage last time. — CE

▨ **Boland Cellar** see Boland Kelder

Boland Kelder

Location/WO: Paarl ▪ Map: Paarl & Wellington ▪ Est/1stB 1947 ▪ Tasting & sales Mon-Fri 8-5 Sat & pub hols 9-1 ▪ Closed Easter Fri-Sun, Ascension day, Sep 24, Dec 25/26 & Jan 1 ▪ Cellar tours by appt ▪ Wynvlieg cellar theatre (www.ticketbreak.co.za) ▪ Owner(s) 96 producing shareholders ▪ Cellarmaster(s) Bernard Smuts (Feb 2012) ▪ Winemaker(s) JD Rossouw (Sep 2007) & Bernard Smuts (Dec 2001), with Heidi Dietstein, Burger Badenhorst & Handré Barkhuizen (all Dec 2009) ▪ Viticulturist(s) Jaco Engelbrecht (Feb 2012) ▪ 2,210ha (cab, merlot, ptage, shiraz, chard, chenin, nouvelle, sauv, viog) ▪ 21,976t/120,000cs own label 50% red 40% white

10% rosé + 200,000cs for clients ▪ Other export brands: Lindenhof, Montestell ▪ WIETA ▪ PO Box 7007 Noorder-Paarl 7623 ▪ info@bolandkelder.co.za ▪ www.bolandcellar.co.za, www.bolandkelder.co.za, www.bolandwines.co.za ▪ S 33° 41' 19.6" E 018° 57' 20.1" ▪ **T +27 (0)21-862-6190** ▪ F +27 (0)21-862-5379

There's lots of energy and enthusiasm at this well-organised grower-owned Paarl winery these days. Their innovative eco-friendly Flutterby range in plastic (PET) bottles has been a big hit with local customers and the plan is to roll it out overseas as well. Their core premise remains the five very different meso-climates from which they source their grapes — hence the Five Climates range — and they have access to a wide variety of different parcels of fruit. New viticulturist on/in the block is Jaco Engelbrecht, an all-round botany enthusiast who cultivates seawater coral in his spare time and believes the vine is the most intricate and interesting plant on the planet. His mission — to continue to supply cellarmaster Bernard Smuts with the same award-winning standard of grapes.

Cellar Reserve range

★★★★ Shiraz 🅰 Sweet/savoury **10** with whiffs of aromatic spices, blackcurrants & plums. Soft black berries & cherries on palate, plenty of drinkability & charm.

Cabernet Sauvignon ★★★ 09 showing upfront minty/herbal notes on nose with dry raisined black fruit. Somewhat shy, may speak up given time. **Merlot** ⓘ **★★★★ 09** ripe mulberry & some beetroot earthiness. Intense, concentrated & long but textured. **Pinotage** ⓘ **★★★★ 09** raspberry with earthy overlay, tangy succulence & softness. Not quite as delicious or persistent as **08** (**★★★★**) (both vintages tasted). **Chardonnay** ⓘ 🅰 **★★★★** Appetising & rich combo marmalade & banana toast, yet **10** is light, zesty & fresh too. Oaking shows restraint. **Chenin Blanc** NEW 🅰 **★★★★** Promising debut in **11**, ripe honeyed apricots & limes with well-integrated spicy oak (naturally barrel-fermented/aged 9 months).

Five Climates Single Varietal range

> **Cabernet Sauvignon** ☺ 🍴 🅰 **★★★** Pleasant black-fruit mouthful **10** with some elegance & spice. Easy-drinking tannins, youthful & cheerful. **Chenin Blanc** ☺ 🍴 🅰 **★★★** Appetisingly fresh **12** has pineapple cake notes, hints of toffee apple & a crisp finish.

Merlot 🍴 🅰 **★★★** Chocolate/coffee nose **11** gives way to ripe, soft black berries, plums & black cherry yoghurt. Well-managed tannins, mass appeal. **Pinotage** 🍴 🅰 **★★★** Forthright medicinal aromas relaxing into sweet cherries, **10** nicely balanced wood/alcohol, sweet fruit finish. **Shiraz** ⓘ 🍴 **★★★★ 09** retains standard with its accessible black cherry fruit. Good body, density & depth. Light oak sheen. **Chardonnay** 🍴 🅰 **★★★ 12** has plenty of pineapples & crunchy apples for comfortable quaffing. **Sauvignon Blanc** 🍴 🅰 **★★★** Grapefruit & gooseberry on **12** giving way to tropical fruit mix. Crisp finish, light in body, pleasant sipper. **Red Muscadel** ⓘ 🅰 **★★★** Lovely lavender & jasmine perfume on **11** fortified dessert. Barley sugar sweetness, full flavoured but ends clean, dry. **Cape Ruby Port** ⓘ **★★★** Return to form in **09** from shiraz. Plum & tealeaf mouthful of sweetness, spice & fire with chalky texture.

Cappupinoccinotage range

Cappupinoccinotage 🍴 🅰 **★★★** Sweet coffee aromas with savoury ham edge on **11**, now bottled. Spiced meats & peppery biltong flavours to watch rugby by.

Sixty 40 Blend range

Cabernet Sauvignon-Shiraz 🍴 🅰 **★★** Sweeter style makes for general crowd pleaser **11**, with smoky black fruit. **Chenin Blanc-Sauvignon Blanc** 🍴 🅰 **★★★ 12** zippy off-dry raft of tropical fruit, lashed together with lively acidity. Discontinued: **Rosé**.

Flutterby range

> **Sauvignon Blanc** ☺ 🍴 🅰 **★★★** Tangy summer white **12** in picnic-friendly PET bottles (as is Merlot). Fresh lemons & limes.

Merlot 🍴 🅰 **★★★** Uncomplicated everyday drinker offering charry black fruit in **11**. — CM

Bon Cap Organic Winery

Location/map: Robertson ▪ WO: Eilandia ▪ Est 2001 ▪ 1stB 2002 ▪ Tasting & sales Mon-Fri 8–5 Sun 8–4 ▪ Closed Sat due to weddings & functions ▪ Cellar tours by appt ▪ Bon Rouge Bistro ▪ Facilities for children ▪ Gifts ▪ Cheese platters ▪ Guest house ▪ Owner(s) Roelf & Michelle du Preez/SHZ Winery (Pty) Ltd ▪ Winemaker(s) Marinus otgieter (Jan 2008) ▪ Viticulturist(s) Roelf du Preez ▪ 460ha/40ha (cab, p verdot, ptage, shiraz, chard, cbard, auv, viog) ▪ 295t/21,000cs own label 60% red 35% white 5% rosé ▪ Other export brand: The Greenhouse ▪ rand for client: The UK Societies ▪ SGS ▪ PO Box 356 Robertson 6705 ▪ info@boncap.co.za ▪ www.oncaporganic.co.za ▪ S 33° 47' 1.0" E 019° 40' 53.2" ▪ **T +27 (0)23-626-2073** ▪ F +27 (0)23-626-5789

One of the country's largest privately owned organic wineries, Bon Cap welcomes family visits, even families in the making — its wedding venue is now booked 90% of the year. Michelle du Preez, owner with husband Roelf of the sixth-generation Robertson farm, notes that their pinotage (which accounts for a third of production) is a favourite with their UK importer, who buys 70% of their wines, as it is with their Canadian and Scandinavian customers.

Bon Cap range

★★★★ **Cape Blend** ⓔ 🌺 Unusual combo pinotage, petit verdot, cab works in polished & fresh **07** (★★★★). 1st tasted since **05** (**06** sold out untasted).

The Perfect Blend Await next, as for **Viognier**. **Méthode Cap Classique** ⓔ 🌺 ★★★★ Butterscotch & emon zest on **06** bottle-fermented bubbly from chardonnay (82%) & pinot. Rich & satisfying, attractively dry elebrator. **Cape Ruby** NEW 🌺 ★★ NV port-style fortified from touriga only available from cellardoor. With arnet hue & savoury tone more 'Late Bottled' than fruity 'Ruby'.

The Ruins range

★★★★ **Syrah-Cabernet Sauvignon** ✓ 🍴 🌺 🅿 Wallet-friendly **11** nod to the Rhône: scrub & black pepper highlights, flexible backbone from majority shiraz. Worthy successor to accomplished & vivacious **10**.

Pinotage ⓔ 🍴 🌺 🅿 ★★★ **10**'s mulberry jam, smoky overlay, crisp acidity hit right drinkability notes.
Rosé 🍴 🌺 🅿 ★★★ From shiraz, **12** savoury, fresh & dry for al fresco sipping. **Sauvignon Blanc** 🍴 🌺 🅿 ★★★ **12** weighty despite lowish 12% alcohol, with Granny Smith apple zing. **Chardonnay-Viognier** 🍴 🌺 🅿 ★★★ Aromatic, lightly oaked **12**, similar dry tail to previous but less well-contained alcohol.
Sparkling Brut 🌺 🅿 ★★ Gently sweet **11** uncomplicated sparkler from colombard. — CvZ/MW

Bon Courage Estate

.ocation/map/WO: Robertson ▪ Est 1927 ▪ 1stB 1983 ▪ Tasting & sales Mon-Fri 8–5 Sat 9–3 ▪ Fee R10pp for groups of 10+ ▪ Closed Good Fri, Dec 25 & Jan 1 ▪ Café Maude T +27 (0)23-626-6806 ▪ Facilities for children ▪ Owner(s) André & Jacques Bruwer ▪ Winemaker(s) Jacques Bruwer ▪ Viticulturist(s) André Bruwer ▪ 150ha (cab, pinot, shiraz, chard) ▪ 40% red 50% white 10% rosé ▪ Export brand: Three Rivers ▪ PO Box 589 Robertson 6705 ▪ wine@boncourage.co.za ▪ www.boncourage.co.za ▪ S 33° 50' 43.8" E 019° 57' 38.0" ▪ **T +27 (0)23-626-4178** ▪ F +27 (0)23-626-3581

Redesigned labels for the méthode cap classique sparklings, which regularly bring awards back to the third-generation Bruwer family estate in Robertson, are 'classic but modern' notes PR Bea Eillert. She describes the new Cuvée Rosé Brut, which was on the lees for 48 months, as 'a special lady, very feminine'. Winemaker Jacques Bruwer had to exercise considerable restraint: 'It was very tempting to release it earlier with all the other rosé MCCs coming onto the market.'

nkará range

★★★★ **Cabernet Sauvignon** Smoke & cassis infused **10** has firm tannin frame on which to hang succulent fruit. Like **09**, signature sweetness lifted by minerality, persistent savouriness.

★★★★☆ **Shiraz** Classic from the region. Perfumed **10**'s (★★★★☆) plush red fruit graciously cradled in soft, sweet new oak. Long & concentrated, just shy of sense of accomplishment of full & bold (±15% alcohol) **09**.

Pinot Noir ★★★ Name changed from 'Bruére Gold Reserve' & moved to this top range. Earthy, gamey notes in limited-edition **10**; smooth & supple, very ripe; a crowd- rather than purist-pleasing version of the grape.

Bon Courage range

★★★★ **Jacques Bruére Cuvée Rosé Brut** NEW ✓ Salmon-hued sparkling, **06** entices with whoosh of tiny cranberry bubbles, silk texture ex pinot (80%), zing from chardonnay. Portion oaked, 4 years on lees.

★★★★ **Cap Classique Jacques Bruére Brut Reserve Blanc de Blancs** Consistently excellent sparkling from chardonnay, **08** as sophisticated & balanced as **07**. Delicious lemon-biscuit snap & persistent creamy finish. 10% oak, 2 years sur lie in bottle.

★★★★☆ **Cap Classique Jacques Bruére Brut Reserve** Ever-superb pinot/chardonnay sparkling which, like all-chardonnay version (& **07**) is partly oaked, but spends extra ±36 months in bottle. Exceptional **08** (★★★★★) well worth the effort! Invigorating from start to finish, coiled & engaging, still has much to give.

★★★★ **Noble Late Harvest** ✓ Unoaked botrytised riesling. Elegant **11** almonds, apricot preserve & choco-late-dipped citrus; succulent, super-concentrated, just misses perfect seam of acidity of **10** (★★★★★).

★★★★ **White Muscadel** Grapey **12** (★★★★) is liquidised barley sugar, hugely appealing if lacking **11**'s perfect marriage of fruity sweetness, zingy acidity & integrated spirit.

André's Fame Colombard ☺ 🍴 ★★ Packed with guava & wild herbs, lively acidity, characterful **12** is an invigorating summer tipple. **Gewürztraminer Special Late Harvest** ☺ ★★★ Shy on nose, **12** expands on palate into a litchi/melon delight, with dainty sweetness, tangy & moreish farewell.

Cabernet Sauvignon ★★★ Whole-berry ferment for all single-variety reds reviewed this year. Spice high-lights on black berry compote, **11** supple & dry, with evident acidity inviting early drinking. **Pinotage** ★★★ Intense banana & acetone bouquet let down by ungenerous, dusty palate in **10**. **Shiraz** ★★★★ Cream & vanilla invitation on juicy **11**. Fresh & light-textured for uncomplicated early enjoyment. **Hillside Red** ★★★ 60/40 cab/shiraz happy marriage in supple **11** sipper. Enjoy in youth. **Chardonnay Prestige Cuvée** ✓ ★★★★ Smart lees-ageing (8 months older barrels) on suave **11**. Buttery & rich yet with lemon & spice uplift. **Chardonnay Unwooded** 🍴 ★★★ **12** subtle pear & citrus, soft, refreshing & modestly satisfying. **Sauvignon Blanc** 🍴 ★★★ **12** all figgy freshness but misses the layered concentration of previous. **Hillside White** 🍴 ★★★ Fruit-filled quaffing from colombard & chardonnay combo in **12**. **Blush Vin Doux** ★★★ Floral, grapey & frothy flirtation in sweet **NV** sparkling from red muscadel. **Red Muscadel** ★★★★ Sunset-hued **12** reticent on the nose but pops with flavours of honeyed mulberry jam; decadent but balanced fortified dessert. **Cape Vintage** ★★★ Brooding port-style **11**, tinta (80%) & touriga, offers plums, prunes & lovely dry finish; lowish 16% fortification.

Like Father Like Son range

Cabernet Sauvignon-Merlot 🍴 ★★★ Budget range providing fruit-filled early enjoyment. **11** cocoa-dusted, packed with red berries. **Pinotage Rosé** 🍴 ★★ Was 'Rosé'. **12** is sweet but has a savoury smoked bacon character. **Chenin Blanc** 🍴 ★★ Previous featured colombard. **12** is off-dry & peachy. — CvZ/MW

Bonfoi Estate

Location/map: Stellenbosch ▪ Est 1699 ▪ 1stB 1974 ▪ Tasting & sales by appt only ▪ Closed all pub hols ▪ BYO picnic ▪ Walks ▪ Conservation area ▪ Owner(s)/winemaker/viticulturist(s) Johannes van der Westhuizen ▪ 200ha/101ha (cabs s/f, merlot, pinot, pinot meunier, ptage, shiraz, chard, chenin, sauv, sem) ▪ 700t/3,000cs own label 60% red 40% white ▪ BWI ▪ PO Box 9 Vlottenburg 7604 ▪ bonfoi@mweb.co.za ▪ www.bonfoiwines. co.za ▪ S 33° 56′ 29.1″ E 018° 46′ 29.8″ ▪ **T +27 (0)21-881-3774** ▪ F +27 (0)21-881-3807

Nothing new this year, but those older wines available should be nicely matured. Good faith in them seems appropriate, anyway, seeing that's the meaning of the name of this boutique Stellenbosch outfit — the name given by two French ladies who purchased the farm in the 18th century.

★★★★ **Cabernet Sauvignon** ⑫ **04** previously tasted, still available at time of press.

★★★★ **Ouverture** ⑫ Previously reviewed was stylish **04**, still selling.

Merlot Not tasted, as for **Shiraz**, **Chardonnay** & **Sauvignon Blanc**. — JP

Bonne Esperance

KWV brand Bonne Esperance ('Good Hope') or 'Bonnies' as it is fondly known, was introduced in the early 1960s. After a break on the local market it has been re-introduced at entry level. Sales are currently focused throughout Africa as well.

Red ★★ Easy-drinking **NV** with sweet red berry flavours. **White** ★★ Lightly fruited **NV**, crisp & gently sweet. WO W Cape for both. — AL

Bonnievale Cellar

Location: Bonnievale ▪ Map: Robertson ▪ WO: Robertson/Bonnievale ▪ Est 1951 ▪ 1stB 1977 ▪ Tasting & sales Mon-Fri 8-5 Sat 10-1 ▪ Closed Easter Fri-Mon, Dec 25/26 & Jan 1 ▪ Cheese straws, biltong/droëwors & mini cheese plat-ters ▪ Facilities for children ▪ Tour groups ▪ Conferences (12 pax) ▪ CCC Christmas Market ▪ Owner(s) 110 members ▪ Winemaker(s) Esmarie Smuts, Jolene le Roux & Eduard Malherbe (Jan 2002/Aug 2007/Dec 2007), with Marthinus Rademeyer (Dec 2009) ▪ Viticulturist(s) Sakkie Bosman (Nov 2006) ▪ 1,780ha (cab, shiraz, chard, che-nin, sauv) ▪ 30,000t/40,000cs own label 30% red 55% white 10% perlé 5% juice + 60,000cs for clients ▪ IPW

WIETA ▪ PO Box 206 Bonnievale 6730 ▪ sales@bonnievalecellar.co.za ▪ www.bonnievalecellar.co.za ▪ S 33° 57′ 26.2″ E 020° 6′ 7.6″ ▪ **T +27 (0)23-616-2795/2800/2359** ▪ F +27 (0)23-616-2332

In the spirit of continuing to provide 'something for every taste', this grower-owned winery consulted its regional agents on trends. 'Something sweet, a rosé and a low-alcohol wine,' they choused. The new perlé Dusk and Dawn, names inspired by 'the beauty of Bonnievale', tick the boxes. CEO John Barnardt celebrated 'excellent' 2012 national sales growth, prompting an increase in sales staff.

Vertex Reserve range

Cabernet Sauvignon 🄿 ★★★ Barrel sample **10** is well made, with hint tobacco & dark chocolate to plush blackberry fruit. **Shiraz** 🄿 ★★★ Medium-bodied **10** preview delivers roasted nuts, mulberry & spice complexity, fair tannic grip.

Bonnievale range

Shiraz 🍴 🄿 ★★ Spices & mulberries, twist of black pepper on lean, food-styled **10** work-in-progress. **Cabernet Sauvignon-Merlot** ⓘ 🍴 ★★ Cab's bold tannins dominate lavender-infused & juicy **11**. **Cabernet Sauvignon-Shiraz** 🍴 🄿 ★★ Dry tannins follow 10's red plum & sour cherry charm. **Chardonnay** ⓘ 🍴 ★★ Faint lemon & beeswax on reticent **11**. **Sauvignon Blanc** ✓ 🍴 🄿 ★★★ Crisp & flavoursome **12** has unusual white pepper top notes as well as variety's typical grass, greenpepper & tropical fruits. Also in 3L box for even more fun. **Sauvignon Blanc Brut** ★★ NV party-starting bubbly with frothy mousse, lively acidity. **Cape Ruby** 🄿 ★★ Savoury port-style **10** from tinta still cloaked with oak mid-2012, needs year/2 to settle.

CCC range

Red 🍴 🄿 ★★ Two cabs & cinsaut, **11** slips down easily, ideal braai quaffer. Also in 3L bag-in-box, as for next. **White** 🍴 🄿 ★★ **12** preview is cheerful, dry & peachy. **Semi-Sweet** 🍴 ★ NV sipper with faint melon tone, gently sweet tail, 'for Thai green curry'.

Perlé range NEW

Dusk 🍴 ★ Pink NV with teeny soft bubbles, not too sweet, low 8.5% alcohol. **Dawn** 🍴 ★★ Perfumed sweet pétillant chenin, **NV** just ±9% alcohol for all-day enjoyment. — DB/JP

▮ **Bonny Bay** see Blomendahl Vineyards
▮ **Bonolo** see Blomendahl Vineyards

Bon Terroir

Location/WO: Stellenbosch ▪ Est 2002 ▪ 1stB 2007 ▪ Closed to public ▪ Owner(s) Agri Marketing Exchange (Pty) Ltd, with shareholder Will-Mag Holdings Ltd ▪ Winemaker(s) Bruwer Raats (2007, consultant) ▪ 15.5ha/4ha (cabs s/f) ▪ 5t/300cs own label 100% red ▪ PO Box 12511 Die Boord 7613 ▪ willie@willmag.co.za ▪ www.bonterroir.co.za ▪ **T +27 (0)82-445-3440** ▪ F +27 (0)86-622-8254

There's not too much yet in the way of vinegrowing at this Stellenbosch estate ('boutique' the word), but the soil analysis made at the time the vineyard was planted revealed that the terroir would be particularly 'bon' for rouge. So cabernet sauvignon it was, and the eminent Bruwer Raats was given the task of making it.

★★★★☆ **Cabernet Sauvignon** ⓘ Modern, big, sweet-fruited **09** (★★★★), showing tobacco & spice from effective oaking, last year seemed riper, bolder & heavier than **08** — & a touch clumsier. — TJ

Bonview Wines NEW

Location: Somerset West ▪ WO: Western Cape/Stellenbosch ▪ Est 2011 ▪ 1stB 2012 ▪ Closed to public ▪ Owner(s) Teuns Keuzenkamp ▪ 1,390cs own label 95% red 5% white ▪ PO Box 1977 Somerset West 7129 ▪ bonview@telkomsa.net ▪ **T +27 (0)21-887-5812** ▪ F +27 (0)86-224-9348

Negociant business Bonview was established in 2011 to produce wine and grape juice for export. Owner Teuns Keuzenkamp has long-term contracts with various Cape cellars, and targets mainly West Africa and China with 'quality wines that are affordable and attuned to the tastes of everyday wine consumers'.

Pegalle range

Cabernet Sauvignon 🄿 ★★★ 11's creamy oak-seamed plum character is quite serious yet very easy to drink. **Merlot** 🄿 ★★ A savoury food wine, **10** has dusty & leafy overtones, firm green olive-like flavours. WO

Stellenbosch. **Shiraz** ★★★ **11** perfect for times when all you want is a tasty food/solo glass of red with generous fruity flavour — nothing challenging or out there. — HJ/JP

■ **Bon Vino** *see* Boland Kelder

Boplaas Family Vineyards

Location: Calitzdorp ▪ Map: Klein Karoo & Garden Route ▪ WO: Calitzdorp/Coastal/Western Cape ▪ Est 1880 ▪ 1stB 1982 ▪ Tasting & sales Mon-Fri 8-5 Sat 9-3 ▪ Fee R20pp ▪ Closed Good Fri & Dec 25 ▪ Cellar tours by appt ▪ Facilities for children ▪ Gifts ▪ Farm produce ▪ Walks/hikes ▪ Conservation area ▪ Ring of Rocks ▪ Owner(s) Carel Nel ▪ Cellarmaster(s) Carel Nel (1982) ▪ Winemaker(s) Margaux Nel (Dec 2006) ▪ Viticulturist(s) Johannes Mellet (Vinpro) ▪ 2,300ha/70ha (cab, ptage, shiraz, tinta, touriga, chard, cbard, sauv) ▪ 55% red 45% white ▪ BWI, IPW ▪ PO Box 156 Calitzdorp 6660 ▪ info@boplaas.co.za ▪ www.boplaas.co.za, www.coolbay.co.za ▪ S 33°32'8.0" E 021°41'1.9" (Boplaas), S 34°4'45.40" E 022°8'25.22" (Cool Bay) ▪ **T +27 (0)44-213-3326** ▪ F +27 (0)44-213-3750

The name says it all. 'We're a wine family,' asserts quietly spoken Carel Nel, Cape port champion (title holder and advocate). Daughters Margaux (winemaker) and Rozanne (wine marketer) concur. A strong sense of tradition coexists with eagerness to innovate, most recently illustrated by a packaging revamp, trendily retro in recalling the 1980s when Carel and late father Danie started bottling wine. They continue, with their ports, muscat wines and potstill brandies, Carel's great grandfather's legacy of exporting brandy abroad. But they keep abreast of changing tastes (witness their new Moscato Light and Tinta Chocolat). Embracing terroir wines in Calitzdorp's semi-arid, Douro-like environment, the conservation-conscious family is now also focusing on port varieties for unfortified wine to enrich their extensive portfolio: again, spot-on with trends.

Family Reserve range

★★★★ **Shiraz 10**'s bramble berry & spice, fynbos & pepper notes followed by plump sweet fruit, gutsy tannins. Shade off svelte & balanced **09**; similarly needs year/2 to settle & integrate.

★★★★ **Cabernet Sauvignon-Shiraz** ⓘ 60/40 duo from Bo-Langkloof/home vineyards, **07** elegant without sacrificing ripeness.

Cabernet Sauvignon ★★★ Cassis, touch of cocoa on **09** medium-bodied & easy-drinking dinner companion. Oak tannins well knit (year French cask), perfect now. WO W Cape for all these. **Ring of Rocks** ✓ ★★★★ Earthy, meaty **10** mixes shiraz, touriga & year French oak seasoning in a punchy country-style red. First since **07**, from cab, merlot & touriga. **Pinot Noir Méthode Cap Classique** ⓘ ★★★★ Pale pink **09** champagne-method sparkling with bready/honeyed bottle-age notes; lovely pinot noir weight but tad sweeter than usual for this style. Discontinued: **Pinotage**.

Boplaas range

★★★★ **Hanepoot Reserve** ⓘ **11** (★★★★★) fortified dessert more complex than last **09**. Litchi, orange & raisin flavours coupled with measured sweetness for uncloying enjoyment.

★★★★☆ **Red Muscadel Vintners Reserve** ⓘ Senior citizen **75** suave, engaging, with fully integrated dried fruit flavour, tannin & alcohol.

★★★★☆ **Muscadel Reserve** ⓘ Gingery/grapey **10** fortified dessert is beautifully structured with crisp acid, silky fruit & spicy sweetness (213g/l sugar). Poise in a glass.

★★★★★ **Cape Vintage Reserve Port** Cape flagship for this style. **10** (★★★★★) repeat performance of **09**'s Old World restraint, ageability. Touriga, tinta & droplet souzão deliver tealeaf top notes, depth & richness, endless savoury conclusion. WO W Cape.

★★★★☆ **Cape Tawny Port** ⓘ NV from tinta, touriga, souzão. Nutty & spicy from long ageing in barrel, wonderfully balanced, shows mere hint of sweetness on the aftertaste. WO W Cape.

★★★★☆ **Cape Vintage Port** ✓ Ready-to-drink **11** (★★★★) raisined & spiced fruitcake, concentrated bright red fruit, well-judged spirit; polished, though shade less powerful than also-reviewed **10**, proverbial iron fist in a velvet glove. Combo touriga, tinta & souzão.

★★★★ **Cape Ruby Port** ⓘ Shy NV raises the bar on previous bottling but needs time to realise its full potential; soft, sweet & juicy, with just a nip of tannin on finish.

★★★★ **Cape Tawny Port Vintners Reserve** ⓘ Tinta & touriga duo in NV 375ml bottle. Mocha flavours spiked with tangy citrus rind & deliciously warming swirl of peppery spirit.

★★★★★ **Cape Tawny Port** ⓐ A tinta, touriga, souzão mix (90/8/2), **97** exceptionally classy. Rich & sleek, infused with caramel, chocolate, orange & cinnamon; superb spirit integration (±19%) from 12 years in old barrels. W Cape WO.

★★★★ **Cape Tawny Show Reserve** ⓐ Nut & citrus melange **NV** from tinta, touriga, souzão. Slightly more sweetness than others in line-up; also greater richness, creamier tones.

★★★★ **Chocolate Cape Vintage Port** After hedonistic **09**, tinta (70%), touriga **10** (★★★★) shows similar lushness on nose, vivid flavours but tannins still obvious, need more time to settle. WO W Cape.

★★★★☆ **Cape Tawny Reserve** NEW Masterly **95** fortified from tinta (90%) & touriga 'made before Calitzdorp even became a WO district' says cellarmaster Carel Nel. 12 years in cask yield complex, intense medley of nuts, toffee, orange marmalade, lingering dry conclusion. 375ml. WO Klein Karoo.

Hanepoot ☺ ★★★ Charming & fragrant fortified dessert, **12** all jasmine & honeysuckle prettiness, easy drinkability assured by tangy acidity.

abernet Sauvignon ★★ **10** lean & firm, with herbal nuance. **Merlot** 🗄 ★★ Mediumweight **11** sweet lum fruit & charry tannins, for early drinking. **Pinotage** 🗄 ★★★ **11** is accessible, juicy, chocolate-laced, hough perhaps shade less textured & complete than previous. **Shiraz** ⓐ ★★★★ Polished tannins, dense lum centre, earth & floral notes on peppery **08**. **Tinta Barocca** ⓐ ★★★ Lightly wooded **09** is savoury, efreshing & friendly. **Tinta Chocolat** 🗄 ★★★ Full bodied & unashamedly riding the 'choc-mocha' wave, **1** tinta is rich & plummy, saturated with chocolate & vanilla. WO W Cape. **Touriga Nacional** ⓐ ★★★★ ragrant **09**, orange peel hint, vibrant red-berry acidity & fair grip. **Chardonnay Unwooded** 🗄 📶 ★★ **12** oneysuckle taste & lowish 11.5% alcohol for al fresco sipping. **Moscato Light** NEW 🗄 ★★ Light (±9% cohol), grapey & off-dry **12**, perfect foil for Asian cuisine. **Sauvignon Blanc** 🗄 ★★ Gooseberry & Golden elicious apple in lightish **12**. **Viognier** ⓐ ★★★ Apricot & rosepetal on aromatic **10**, attractive, not blowsy; ry & zesty early drinking. **Pinot Noir Sparkling** ⓐ ★★ **11** pink & frothy cherry-flavoured bubbly with weetish tail. **Red Muscadel Reserve** NEW ★★★ Young vines pack quite an aromatic punch! Intense raisin, innamon & clove highlights to **11**'s lanolin bouquet, smooth palate. 375ml. **Red Muscadel** NEW ★★★★ ank sample **12** is zesty & fresh, with plum & raisin appeal, pleasantly fiery conclusion. **Muscadel** ★★★★ rapey & caramel-toned **12** is light bodied & spicy, quite sweet on the aftertaste though. **Pink Port** ⓐ ★★★ nta, touriga, souzão **NV** combo. Tangy, with interesting watermelon nuance. **Cape White Port** ⓐ ★★★ **V** from chardonnay, with ginger & melon appeal.

ool Bay range

★★★★ **Sauvignon Blanc Reserve** 🗄 From old Darling bushvines (WO Coastal), tank sample **12** rated provisionally. Bright & effusive: gooseberry, fig, tropical fruit; gorgeous texture & seamless acidity.

auvignon Blanc ⓐ ★★★ Cool, green **11**, similar pebbly notes to sibling but fruitier. Discontinued: **teserve Shiraz**. — WB/JP

■ **Borg Family Wines** *see* Painted Wolf Wines
■ **Born & Bred in South Africa** *see* BABISA — Born & Bred in South Africa

Boschendal Wines

ocation/map: Franschhoek ▪ WO: Coastal/Western Cape/Stellenbosch ▪ Est 1685 ▪ 1stB 1975 ▪ Tasting & sales aily May-Oct 9-4.30 Nov-Apr 10-6 ▪ Fee R20pp ▪ Closed Mar 21, Good Fri, May 1 & Dec 25 ▪ Cellar tours daily 10. 0, 11.30 & 3 ▪ Cheese platters on request ▪ Restaurant ▪ Facilities for children ▪ Tour groups ▪ Gifts ▪ Farm produce ▪ onservation area ▪ Museum ▪ Owner(s) DGB (Pty) Ltd ▪ Cellarmaster(s) JC Bekker (1986) ▪ Winemaker(s) Lizelle erber (whites, 2006) & Thinus Kruger (reds, 2008), with Lionel Leibrandt (1999) ▪ Viticulturist(s) Stephan Joubert 2006) ▪ 2,240ha/200ha (shiraz, sauv) ▪ 3,100t/250,000cs own label 32% red 43% white 14% rosé 11% sparling ▪ WIETA ▪ Private Bag X03 Groot Drakenstein 7680 ▪ cellardoor@dgb.co.za ▪ www.boschendalwines.com ▪ S 3° 52' 27.5" E 018° 58' 34.4" ▪ **T** +27 (0)21-870-4200 ▪ F +27 (0)21-874-5130

ife has a way of coming full circle, especially in a place with as much history and llure as this showpiece for the traditional heritage of the South African wine ndustry. Established in 1685, Boschendal is one of the oldest farms in South Africa. irst granted to French immigrant Jean le Long, it was soon acquired by Abraham le Villiers, and remained in his family for around 160 years. Paul de Villiers, who vas responsible for building the Boschendal homestead and famous gable, was one f the last De Villiers owners. With 22 children, he no doubt would have appreciated the family atmosphere created at modern day Boschendal with its restaurants, wine bar and 'Le Pique Nique', sunlit or starlit picnics on the pavillion lawns.

Cecil John Reserve range

★★★★★ **Shiraz** 🅥 Accomplished, mostly older oak matured flagship from Stellenbosch vineyards. 1C composed & restrained, with white pepper nuances to tightly wound red fruit. Far sterner & less accessible now than Reserve version; poise & concentration hint at its huge potential.

Sauvignon Blanc Await next.

Reserve Collection

★★★★☆ **Shiraz** 🅥 All-new oak sets this apart from siblings. **10** indisputably, fragrantly shiraz: black pepper, lilies, red plum fruit, all supported by supple, well-tailored tannin. From Stellenbosch fruit.

★★★★ **Grande Reserve** ⏱ Ripe-fruited **09** blend cab & shiraz is fleshier than previous. Composed & plush, the palate evolves to a fine tannin finish, polished oaking adds weight & texture.

★★★★ **Chardonnay** This version fermented & aged in oak (a third new). Well-measured **11** (★★★★★ step up on bright, also sophisticated **09**. Intensity of vanilla & toasted nut aromas belies a palate which is rendered light, almost delicate by a vibrant lemony acidity & poised finish. From Stellenbosch grapes. **10** untasted.

★★★★☆ **MCC Grande Cuvée Brut** This handsomely packaged chardonnay/pinot noir sparkling a sentimental favourite of many. **08** shows usual brioche notes & tiny bubble from extended ageing on lees; rich flavours buoyed by zesty acidity.

★★★★ **Vin d'Or** Natural Sweet dessert from chenin & riesling. **11** (★★★☆) pineapple & quince flavours uncloying but lacking vibrancy of **09** (no **10** made). WO W Cape

Sauvignon Blanc 🍴 ★★★★ Improved **12** has greater presence than **10** (★★★☆). Cool green fruit & blackcurrant appeal, pinpoint acidity in fruit-filled but dry finish. Fine-dining companion. **11** untasted. WO W Cape. **MCC Le Grande Pavillion Brut Rosé** ⏱ ★★★★ Last-tasted **NV** had salmon hue, red berry lift to well balanced lively mousse & rounded softness. Discontinued: **Cabernet Sauvignon**.

1685 range

Merlot ★★★★ Sugared plum fruit, vanilla highlights, mulberry notes on inviting **10**. Succulent, refreshing. Some new oak, but also an unoaked portion for freshness. **Shiraz** ✓ 🅥 ★★★★ Improved **10** very ripe but smartly oaked, with plump red plum centre; for dining. **Shiraz-Cabernet Sauvignon** 🅥 ★★★★ **10** blend has tarry oak appeal from the 20% new wood; red fruit & a solid tannin structure need year or 2 to meld. **Chardonnay** 🍴 ★★★★ **11** in usual oaky style; creamy, buttery with mouthcoating richness, enlivening lemon acidity. WO W Cape. **Sauvignon Blanc Grand Vin Blanc** ★★★★ Restrained acacia/khaki bush nose, piercing acidity & 'oystershell' mineral finish on **12**. Tad brief, but a classy version — nudges next level. **Chardonnay-Pinot Noir** ★★★★ Faint pink tinge, earthy finish from 41% pinot on nearly dry **12**. Silky, vibrant; won't disappoint its fans.

Boschendal Favourites

Lanoy ☺ 🅥 ★★★ Charry **10** mainly cab with merlot & others; plush ripe fruit layered with vanilla & honey from light oaking. **Chenin Blanc** ☺ 🍴 🅥 ★★★ Shy & uncomplex, just-off-dry **12** preview has tropical hints, ripe fruit; lightish feel yet satisfying. **Le Bouquet** ☺ 🍴 🅥 ★★★ All about fragrance & balanced sweetness; **12** offers grapey aromas & dulcet musky flavours; enjoy well chilled.

Blanc de Noir 🍴 🅥 ★★★ Effortless, just-dry **12**'s pale salmon hue belies its depth of flavour & lipsmacking appeal. Just the right amount of tannin for food. Undisclosed varieties. **Boschen Blanc** 🍴 🅥 ★★★ Tank sample **12** is a fresh & fruity picnic basket filler. WO W Cape.

The Pavillion range

Shiraz-Cabernet Sauvignon 🅥 ★★★ **11** very ripe & oaky sweet, shows a hint rusticity. These both WO W Cape. **Pavillion Blanc** 🍴 🅥 ★★★ Tank sample **12** from unspecified varieties, pineapple, pear & passionfruit notes, sippability enhanced by few grams sugar. Discontinued: **Rosé**. — CvZ

■ **Boschetto** *see Stellakaya Winery*

Boschheim

Location/map/WO: Stellenbosch ▪ 1stB 2003 ▪ Tasting & sales by appt ▪ Owner(s)/winemaker(s) Andy Roediger ▪ 900cs own label 85% red 15% white ▪ PO Box 3202 Matieland 7602 ▪ andy@roedigeragencies.co.za ▪ S 33° 55′ 54.9″ E 018° 50′ 10.5″ ▪ **T +27 (0)21-887-0010** ▪ F +27 (0)21-886-4731

Despite a busy year of travelling internationally for his phenolic ripeness specialisation, Stellenbosch owner-winemaker Andy Roediger hasn't neglected his boutique winery. A sorting table and pneumatic basket press have been installed in an ongoing drive for improved quality, and with a quieter schedule for the next year, he's looking forward to getting back to what he likes best, making wine.

Cabernet Sauvignon ⊕ ★★★★ 09 savoury & grassy rather than fruity, still withdrawn previously; we noted would benefit from year/2. **Muse** ⊕ ★★★★ Lots on offer in 100% cab 09, including cassis & nutmeg spicing, supple tannins. **Elemental Shiraz** ⊕ ★★★ Plums & white pepper, sprinkle dried herbs, 09 has the palate freshness for food, but dry tannins require rich dishes. **Ella Marie** ⊕ ★★★ Previous 07 shiraz/cab blend (plus dollop merlot) was soft & easy, with attractive cedar aroma. Discontinued: **Merlot, Verdelho, Viognier.** — CR

Boschkloof Wines

Location/map: Stellenbosch ▪ WO: Western Cape/Stellenbosch ▪ Est/1stB 1996 ▪ Tasting, sales & cellar tours Mon-Fri 9-5 Sat 9-1 ▪ Fee R20 ▪ Closed Easter Fri-Sun, Dec 25 & Jan 1 ▪ BYO picnic ▪ Owner(s)/cellarmaster(s)/viticulturist(s) Jacques Borman ▪ Winemaker(s) Jacques Borman, with Reenen Borman (Jun 2010) ▪ 30ha/19ha (cabs s/f, merlot, shiraz, chard) ▪ ±80-120t/3-4,000cs own label 90% red 10% white ▪ PO Box 1340 Stellenbosch 7599 ▪ boschkloof@adept.co.za, info@boschkloofwines.com ▪ www.boschkloofwines.com ▪ S 33° 57′ 37.0″ E 018° 46′ 11.8″ ▪ **T +27 (0)21-881-3293 (office)/+27 (0)21-881-3268 (cellar)** ▪ F +27 (0)21-881-3032

When asked to describe what wines this Stellenbosch property will make in five years' time, cellarmaster and co-owner Jacques Borman says evolving tastes have already prompted a move to fruitier, less oaky styles. He anticipates the trend will pick up pace, and be complemented by a growing desire for new varieties. All this will provide ample opportunity to continue the quest for the perfect wine and live the Boschkloof creed — 'Inconcessum persequor' or 'I pursue the unattainable'.

★★★★ **Syrah** Appealing cassis-choc aromas on forceful 09 (★★★) from Stellenbosch grapes, but oak overpowers the fruit, extends the finish. 08 bold too, but better balanced.

★★★★ **Conclusion** Cab-led Bordeaux combo; none in 07, 08. On-form 09's intensity enhanced by 'bleeding off' 30% of juice; astringent tannins & refreshing acidity good counterpoint for sweet fruit.

★★★★ **Chardonnay** Barrel-fermented 11 (★★★★) is rich & buttery; has less citrus fruit & refreshment than 10 or 09; lacks preceding vintages' tang.

Cabernet Sauvignon ★★★ Commendably dry 09, powerful with big alcohol, needing year or 2 for plush fruit to meld with terse tannins. WO Stellenbosch. **Merlot** ⊕ ★★★ 07 not for the faint-hearted: big tannins & 14.8% alcohol; gentle prune, malt & clean leather flavours. **Cabernet Sauvignon-Merlot** ★★★ Sugared plum fruit & very firm tannins on 09; tad green though nearly off-dry. WO Stellenbosch. **Sauvignon Blanc** NEW 📖 ★★★ Tropical-toned 12 balanced & refreshing, satisfying weight courtesy time on lees & a little sugar. — CvZ

Boschrivier De Villiers Family Vineyards

Location: Stanford ▪ Map: Elgin, Walker Bay & Bot River ▪ WO: Klein River ▪ Est 1998 ▪ 1stB 2002 ▪ Tasting & sales Mon-Fri 8-5 Sat 9-5 Sun 10-1 ▪ Fee R5 ▪ Closed Dec 25 ▪ Restaurant (see Restaurants section) ▪ BYO picnic ▪ Gift shop ▪ Farm produce ▪ Conference facilities (20 pax) ▪ Walking/hiking & 4x4 trails ▪ Self-catering farm house (see Accommodation section) ▪ Owner(s)/viticulturist(s) Theodore de Villiers ▪ Winemaker(s) Mike Dobrovic ▪ 14ha (cab, shiraz) ▪ 7t/ha 464cs own label 100% red ▪ Remhoogte Caledon p/a 70 Fairbairn Street Worcester 6850 ▪ drnjtdevilliers@mweb.co.za ▪ www.boschrivier.co.za ▪ S 34° 23′ 19.4″ E 019° 37′ 51.0″ ▪ **T +27 (0)23-347-3313/2 ext 3; +27 (0)76-736-0351** ▪ F +27 (0)23-342-2215

Worcester paediatrician Theo de Villiers insists that when he inherited land near Stanford in the late 1990s, he couldn't possibly imagine becoming a wine producer. 'My father always said a wine farm was a sure way to go bankrupt and initially I sold all our grapes.' His great-grandfather, however, used to make 'vaaljapie' in a small cellar that still exists on the property and clearly it is his grape-encoded genes that Theo inherited.

★★★★ **Shiraz** 09 (★★★★) slightly off usual high standard, with tart acidity, lots of toasty oak to go with black cherry fruit. Not the finesse we admired in 08 & previous. — CE

Bosman Family Vineyards

Location: Wellington ▪ Map: Paarl & Wellington ▪ WO: Wellington/Western Cape/Upper Hemel-en-Aarde Valley ▪ Est 1699 ▪ 1stB 2004 ▪ Tasting by appt ▪ Fee R50pp, waived on purchase ▪ Closed Easter Fri-Mon, Dec 21-Jan 7 ▪ Sales Mon-Thu 8-5 Fri 8-4.30 ▪ Cellar tours by appt ▪ Conservation area ▪ Festivals: 'Bosman Long Lunch' (Mar) & 'Bosman Release Weekend' (Sep) ▪ Owner(s) Bosman Family & Adama Workers Trust ▪ Cellarmaster(s) Petrus Bosman (Nov 2003) ▪ Winemaker(s) Corlea Fourie (Nov 2006), with Charlene Ferreira (Nov 2006) ▪ Viticulturist(s) Heinie Nel & Pierre Carstens (Jan 2000) ▪ 1,000ha/280ha (47 varieties r/w) ▪ 3,000t/10,000cs own label 70% red 25% white 5% rosé ▪ Other brand: Appollis Fairtrade ▪ Brands for clients: Checkers; Sainsbury Supermarkets; The Cooperative ▪ BWI, Fairtrade ▪ PO Box 9 Wellington 7654 ▪ info@bosmanwines.com ▪ www.bosmanwines.com ▪ S33° 37'34.7" E019° 01'28.9" ▪ **T +27 (0)21-873-3170** ▪ F +27 (0)21-873-2517

Western Cape Best Young Farmer for 2012 was 8th generation family member Petrus Bosman, and he's making up for lost time at historic Wellington property Lelienfontein. No wine was made between here from 1957 till 2007 but now there's innovation aplenty. Erfenis, a nod to the family heritage, is joined by a new range: De Bos, handcrafted wines with fruit from their Hermanus property, blended with the home-farm grapes. Fairtrade accredited too, celebrating their ethical initiative with the Adama Workers Trust.

Unique Innovation range

★★★★ **Adama Red** ⊕ Shiraz (81%) leads 5-way blend in **09**. Velvety mouthful of spicy plum compote, French/American oak, half new, adds backbone, exotic edge from mourvèdre & primitivo.

★★★★ **Adama White** ⊕ ▨ Full bodied but lithe, dry & structured blend of chenin & 4 other varieties. **10** nectarine & lemongrass with light oak sheen, 30% new. Zesty nettle liveliness, long peppery finish. WO W Cape.

Bosman Family Vineyards range

★★★★☆ **Erfenis** NEW ▨ 'Heritage' makes stellar debut with intriguingly complex **10** pinotage, cab franc, petit verdot, shiraz & cinsaut mix — best barrels only. Flirtatiously sexy yet serious. Cherry fruitcake generosity with depth & density. Layered, rounded & succulent. Lingers long.

30 Rosé ⊕ 🍴 ▨ ★★★ Ruby grapefruit & cranberry **10**, mix of 30 different varieties! Dry & zesty. Upper Hemel-en-Aarde Valley WO.

De Bos Handpicked Vineyards range NEW

Handpicked Red Blend ✓ ▨ ★★★★ Sweet fruity appeal to bold maiden **10** cab-led Bordeaux-style blend. Structured, with light tannic grip. Over-delivers. **Walker Bay Sauvignon Blanc** Missed our deadline

Special Vineyard Selection NEW

★★★★ **Pinotage** ▨ **10** shows return to form after slight dip in **09** (★★★★). Tangy blue & black berry vibrancy with spice highlights. Softly, elegant, with smooth, silky mouthfeel. Harmonious & integrated. **Cabernet Sauvignon** ⊕ ★★★★ **07** notch up on previous. Cassis & fynbos overlay, previously showed posture & elegance from French oak, 33% new. **Optenhorst Chenin Blanc** ⊕ ★★★★ From chenin vineyard planted 1952, 4th oldest in SA. When tasted, creamy apricot & oatmeal on naturally fermented **09**, step up on previous. **Dolce Primitivo** ⊕ ★★★ Unusual sweet red from botrytised primitivo. Last time **07**'s spicy black currant & cherry got dry tannin backbone from 2 years all-new extra-charred oak. — FM

■ **Bosman's Hill** *see* Saxenburg Wine Farm

Botanica Wines

Location/map: Stellenbosch ▪ WO: Stellenbosch/Walker Bay/Citrusdal Mountain ▪ Est/1stB 2008 ▪ Tasting b appt ▪ Wine sales Mon-Fri 8-5 ▪ Farm produce ▪ Conferences ▪ Walks/hikes ▪ Mountain biking trail ▪ Refreshments offered at Sugarbird Manor guesthouse (see Accommodation section) ▪ Owner(s) Virginia C Povall ▪ Winemaker(s) Virginia Povall (Jan 2008) ▪ Viticulturist(s) Johan Viljoen (Jul 2008, consultant) ▪ 21.6ha/5h (cabs s/f, merlot, p verdot, pinot) ▪ PO Box 12523 Die Boord 7613 ▪ ginny@botanicawines.com ▪ www. botanicawines.com ▪ S 33° 54' 18.5" E 018° 49' 25.4" ▪ **T +27 (0)21-865-2313**

American owner Ginny Povall has truly embraced South Africa and its people With the help of Habitat for Humanity in Jamestown she has completed buildin new homes on her Devon Valley property and moving six families into them. He obsession with being innovative in the way both vines and flowers are farme has led to experiments with unique vine trellising, tackling vineyard diseases

over crop usage and the deployment of alternative equipment to overcome the
pace limitations imposed by high-density vineyards.

otanica range

★★★★☆ **Pinot Noir 11** (★★★★), from Walker Bay, tad off super Elgin-sourced **10**. A very delicate wine,
elegant & soft structured, with spicy strawberries to lingering savoury conclusion.

★★★★★ **Chenin Blanc** ✓ From ±50 year old bushvines near Clanwilliam. Off-dry **11** is delicate, with
sweet floral & honeyed tones, minerality building in the mouth, part barrel ferment adding to harmony & prom-
se of greater pleasure with time. Super varietal expression, like only marginally less brilliant **10** (★★★★☆).

IG Flower range

★★★★ **Cabernet Sauvignon** ✓ Bright character of ripe dark berry fruit, sweet spice & tobacco hint. **09**
from Stellenbosch vines is rich, medium bodied yet complex with a dusty, savoury finish.

Merlot NEW ★★★★ Intricate aromas of spiced dark berry fruit, **10** rounded mouthfeel & carefully managed
annins. From Devon Valley vines. — WB

Botha Wine Cellar

ocation: Worcester ▪ Map: Breedekloof ▪ WO: Breedekloof/Breede River Valley ▪ Est 1949 ▪ 1stB 1974 ▪ Tasting
& sales Mon-Fri 8–5 Sat 10–1 ▪ Closed Easter Fri-Sun & Dec 25 ▪ Cellar tours by appt ▪ BYO picnic ▪ Conservation
rea ▪ Breedekloof Soetes & Soup and Outdoor & Wine festivals ▪ Owner(s) Botha Wynkelder (Edms) Bpk ▪
ellarmaster(s) Gerrit van Zyl (Nov 2007) ▪ Winemaker(s) Johan Linde & Michiel Visser (Nov 1996/Nov 1999),
with Annamarie van Niekerk & Pierre Hugo (Dec 2009/Jan 2001) ▪ Viticulturist(s) Jan-Carel Coetzee (Nov
010) ▪ 1,969ha (cab, merlot, ptage, shiraz, chard, chenin, cbard) ▪ 37,540t/7,500cs own label 75% red 20%
white 1% rosé 4% fortified; 900cs for clients ▪ ISO 22000:2009 ▪ BWI, IPW, WIETA ▪ PO Box 30 PK Botha 6857 ▪
dmin@bothakelder.co.za ▪ www.bothakelder.co.za ▪ S 33° 34' 1.5" E 019° 15' 27.5" ▪ **T +27 (0)23-355-
740** ▪ F +27 (0)23-355-1615

With only 1% of its massive 37,000+ ton harvest going into bottle under an own
abel, this Breedekloof bulk-wine specialist has the double advantage of unlim-
ted scope for selection and minimal dependence on sales volumes. The result is
mpressive quality at the price (especially the whites) together with a happy
▪and of shareholders.

eserve range

abernet Sauvignon Sold out, await new release.

assie's Reserve range

assie's Rood ⊕ 🍴 ★★★ Juicy cranberries on **09** last year, with dash sweetness adding drinkability.
assie's Rosé ⊕ 🍴 🗱 ★★ Semi-sweet **10** has floral scents with light berry fruit. **Dassie's Blanc** 🍴
wait new vintage.

otha range

★★★★ **Hanepoot Jerepigo** ✓ 🗱 Stripped-down, focused muscat-raisin fragrance on delicious **12** shows
stylish handling. Purity & intensity of fruit allowed to take centre-stage. First since **08**.

> **Chenin Blanc** ☺ 🍴 🗱 ★★★ Generously fruity **12** is just off-dry, totally cheerful. Modest 12.2% alco-
> hol. **Chardonnay Brut** ☺ ★★★ Nearly-dry **NV** sparkler is fun loving & unfussy.

abernet Sauvignon ★★★ Tangy stewed prunes & oak spices on **09**, with hint of rustic farmyard. Drink
ow. **Merlot** ⊕ 🗱 ★★★ Sweet-spicy **10** still oak dominated but shows underlying ripe berry fruit. Light,
nserious quaffer. **Pinotage** ⊕ ★★★ Ripe plum-fruited **09** previously was pleasingly juicy & drinkable.
hiraz 🗱 ★★★ Candy-drop humbugs & blackcurrants, chewy texture on **10**. **Sauvignon Blanc** ⊕ 🍴
🗱 ★★★ **11** fresh & vibrant, with aromatic fruitiness. Appealing rounded ripeness & solid body. **White
ight** 🍴 Next awaited. **Red Jerepigo** ⊕ ★★★ Oddly structured pinotage fortified dessert, **08** somewhat
wild', with green grass notes. **Cape Vintage Reserve** ★★★ Last-featured port-style offering was LBV **04**.
arrel-matured **10** is from shiraz, offers spicy brandy spirit & dark baked plum fruit, hint of racy acid. — GdB

▪ **Bottega Family Wines** see Idiom & Whalehaven

Bottelary Hills Wines

Location/map: Stellenbosch ▪ WO: Bottelary ▪ Tasting & sales Mon-Sat 9-5 Sun & pub hols 10-3 ▪ Close
Easter Fri, Dec 25/26 & Jan 1 ▪ Owner(s) Bottelary farmers ▪ Cellarmaster(s) Danie Steytler ▪ PO Box 4
Koelenhof 7605 ▪ bhwc@telkomsa.net ▪ www.bhwc.co.za ▪ S 33° 52'34.6" E 018° 48'47.2" ▪ T +27 (0)2¹
865-2955 ▪ F +27 (0)21-865-2885

This loose association of winemakers and growers, based at the Bottelary Win
Centre in Koelenhof, have the terroir of their appellation as their common inte
est. The wines are made under the aegis of Kaapzicht cellarmaster, Dani
Steytler, and mostly styled as unpretentious everyday enjoyment.

Chenin Blanc NEW ☺ 🍸 ★★★ Vibrantly fresh **12** has ripe tropical fruit rush, balanced by crisp acidity.

Pinotage Await new vintage, as for **Chenin Blanc-Sauvignon Blanc** & **Natural Sweet Chenin Blanc. Sh**
raz ★★★★ Latest release **07** is still fresh & vibrant. Medium bodied, with juicy cherry fruit. Sunny & cheerful
refreshing. **Merlot-Cabernet Sauvignon** ✓ ★★★★ **09** is a far cry from last-tasted **02** (★★). Ripe, concen
trated red berry fruit, made supple by extended barrel maturation, rounded by smooth tannins. **Cabernet Sauv**
gnon-Pinotage ★★★★★ Deep, dark & intense **07** Cape Blend in a different class to rest of range or previous **0**
(★★★★). All-new French barrels elevate & refine dense fruit, smooth out tannin structure. Shows the expe
Steytler touch. **Hillside Red** 🍸 ★★★ Deliciously fruity unwooded cab-led 4-way blend, **10** is soft & juicy. Sol
everyday enjoyment. **Sauvignon Blanc** ✓ 🍸 ★★★★ Striking herbaceous, grassy aromas on **12** tank samp
deliver on palate too. Generous in body, fruit & value. Discontinued: **Limerick**. — GdB

Bottelary Winery

A Perdeberg Winery value-for-money brand, the wines mostly going to China.

Classic Red ☺ 🍸 🖉 ★★★ Appealing, dry **11** cab, merlot, cinsaut, with hint of oak on ripe, dark fruit
centre. Balanced & smooth everyday drinking.

Merlot 🍸 🖉 Await new vintage. **Velvet Red** NEW 🍸 🖉 ★★ Newcomer **11** is lightly quaffable off-d
shiraz-cab blend. **Rosé** 🍸 New bottling not ready. **Chenin Blanc** ☻ 🍸 🖉 ★★★ Apple & pear freshne
in **10** makes for perky summer fare. **Semi-Sweet** 🍸 🖉 ★★ Modestly sweet, mildly fruity **11** Paarl cheni
Fresh & light. **Satin White** NEW 🍸 🖉 ★★ Clone of semi-sweet above, **11** shows slightly less sugar. **So**
Smooth Red 🍸 🖉 ★★ Semi-sweet **11** cinsaut, shiraz, cab mix has berry-jam fruitiness. — GdB

Bouchard Finlayson

Location: Hermanus ▪ Map: Elgin, Walker Bay & Bot River ▪ WO: Walker Bay/Overberg/Hemel-en-Aarde Va
ley/Western Cape ▪ Est 1989 ▪ 1stB 1991 ▪ Tasting, sales & cellar tours Mon-Fri 9-5 Sat 10-1 ▪ Fee R40pp f
groups of 6+ ▪ Closed all pub hols ▪ Cheese & salami platters ▪ Gift shop ▪ BYO picnic ▪ Conservation area
Nature walks by appt (guided & self-guided) ▪ Owner(s) The Tollman Family Trust ▪ Winemaker(s) Peter Finlayson (1989), with Chris Albrecht (Nov 2010)
turist(s) Peter Finlayson (1989) ▪ Winemaker(s) Peter Finlayson (1989), with Chris Albrecht (Nov 2010)
125ha/20ha (barbera, nebbiolo, pinot, sangio, chard, sauv) ▪ 210t/16,500cs own label 25% red 75% white
BWI, IPW ▪ PO Box 303 Hermanus 7200 ▪ info@bouchardfinlayson.co.za ▪ www.bouchardfinlayson.co.za ▪
34° 22'54.0" E 019° 14'30.9" ▪ T +27 (0)28-312-3515 ▪ F +27 (0)28-312-2317

With a sense of bemusement, winemaker Peter Finlayson comments that he has
challenger to pinot noir's pre-eminence here, in his chardonnays. It has been a par
ticularly successful year for them, including a Decanter gold for Kaaimansgat Lim
ited Edition 2010 and having two of his wines on German magazine Weinwelt's lis
of top ten in the world out of 324 tasted. Then he uses a Burgundian quote of cha
donnay being the 'courtesan of the world', which shows how well he understand
the seduction and success. Further proof is the new French trellising and trainin
system used here for all new chardonnay vines, to improve flowering and mor
fruiting bunches, offsetting the moderating ocean proximity for a variety that pre
fers much colder winters. Likely to give yet another quality hike...

★★★★★ **Galpin Peak Pinot Noir** 🖉 Now bottled, **10** is sleekly curvaceous, the succulent red berrie
spice dusted with espresso notes. Supported by harmonious tannins, it finishes dry, savoury & long. No fore
floor here, just superb fruit, expertly oaked.

★★★★☆ **Tête de Cuvée Galpin Peak Pinot Noir** ◻ Barrel selection & double new oak (75%) of siblings. Now bottled & showing the benefit of the extra year, **10**'s dark fruit & mocha, scrub notes reflect a bold version of pinot noir, but keeps the supple polish of the variety at its best.

★★★★☆ **Hannibal** A 6-part marriage of Italian & French varieties, none of them Bordeaux. Unusually, **09** released after **10**, & worth the wait. An assault on the senses, morello cherries, scrub, prosciutto, deep & layered, with a lovely silky savoury elegance.

★★★★☆ **Kaaimansgat/Crocodile's Lair Chardonnay** From reputed Elandskloof vines. With limy fruit to back it, **11** has showy oak, hazelnuts & toasted brioche, but the wine's seductive appeal is the unfolding layers as you drink it, including a lovely salty minerality at the end.

★★★★☆ **Kaaimansgat Chardonnay Limited Edition** ⓣ Citrus rind & buttered toast, **10** has forthcoming perfume but flavours are subtler: crushed almonds, a slatey note. Textured mouthfeel from 60% new oak portion. Masterly construction, layers of interest, speaks in a quiet but authoritative voice.

★★★★ **Missionvale Chardonnay** ⓣ ◻ A different style to other chardonnays from this cellar, upfront, more New World, **10**'s toastiness from barrel ferment/maturation a strong component, tropical fruit in support.

★★★★ **Sauvignon Blanc Reserve** ⓣ **10** continues to impress with its gooseberry flavours, gunflint smokiness. Bone-dry but palate weight & finish are extended by 14% semillon.

★★★★ **Sauvignon Blanc** ◻ Pre-bottled **12** combines greengage & litchi with a leafy, fennel tone to give fresh-fruity layers designed for pleasurable drinking, broad food matching.

Galpin Peak Pinot Noir Unfiltered Limited Edition Await new vintage. **Sans Barrique Chardonnay** ★★★★ Showing chardonnay's unadorned face, **11** is worthy in its own right: lime peel, underlying tropical tones, tangy fresh. **Blanc de Mer** ✓ ◻ ★★★★ With riesling leading 6-variety blend, bottled **11** aromatic delight, improves on **10** (★★★☆). Floral & tropical scents promise richness, but flavours are dry, long. WO W Cape. — CR

Boucheron Wines   NEW

Location: Randburg ▪ WO: Stellenbosch ▪ Est 1996 ▪ 1stB 2012 ▪ Closed to public ▪ Cellarmaster(s) Nicholas Ridley (Sep 2011) ▪ 7t/325cs ▪ PO Box 870 Strathavon 2031 ▪ info@boucheron.co.za ▪ www.boucheron.co.za ▪ **T** +27 (0)11-708-3444 ▪ F +27 (0)11-708-3615

Such has been the success of Gauteng-based wine merchants Boucheron that they have decided to extend their ambit from simply sourcing exciting parcels of boutique wines for their customers, to now include wines made exclusively to their specifications. Their White Merlot, vinified under the aegis of Nicholas Ridley, is exclusive indeed, being one of only three wines of this style in the guide.

White Merlot ▤ ◻ ★★ The merest hint of blush on **12** draws you in, leads on to a whisper of red berries in a pure, clean & austerely dry wine, perfectly styled for delicately flavoured food like sashimi. — JP/CvZ

Boutique Baratok   NEW

Location: Paarl ▪ Map: Paarl & Wellington ▪ WO: Western Cape/Stellenbosch ▪ Est 2012 ▪ Tasting, sales & cellar tours daily ▪ Fee R20pp ▪ Closed all pub hols ▪ Restaurant ▪ Tour groups ▪ Farm produce ▪ Conferences ▪ Owner(s) Alex Boraine & Daniël Langenhoven ▪ Cellarmaster(s)/winemaker(s)/viticulturist(s) Daniël Langenhoven & Alex Boraine ▪ (cinsaut, grenache, ptage, shiraz, chard, chenin, viog) ▪ 27t/200,000L own label 60% red 40% white; 90,000L for clients + 480,000L bulk ▪ Brands for clients: Bestvino Cape, Roulou, Welgegund ▪ PO Box 668 Wellington 7654 ▪ admin@smlwines.com ▪ www.laskawine.com ▪ S 33° 44'34.93" E 018° 57'44.98" ▪ **T** +27 (0)84-582-6376/+27 (0)82-375-0519/+27 (0)78-154-8929 ▪ F +27 (0)86-675-4372

Aptly named Baratok ('Friends' in Hungarian) is a partnership between good mates Alex Boraine and Daniël Langenhoven, co-owner and cellarmaster respectively of Welgegund, who after years of renting cellar space have found a home on Main Street, Paarl, at the premises of Zomerlust guest house and restaurant. Welgegund's wines are now made here, along with Boraine-Langenhoven joint venture ranges and third parties'. The 'picture perfect' cellar is housed in a converted cowshed, and 'man power' rules: there's only one electric machine (a destalker). A convivial tasting experience is promised, and if you're a buyer or a potential client you'll get 'eye-to-eye' service and be treated like... barátok.

Diamant & Son range

Cabernet Sauvignon ★★ **11** shows some of variety's berry fruit but much more of its tannin. Time or juicy steak needed. **Pinotage** ★★ Spicy, fruit-filled **11** leads the range with coffee-oak tone, tangy finish. **Cinsaut-Pinotage** ★★ Not all that fruity given varieties, but **12** pleasantly & sweetish for casual quaffing.

Kipepeo range

Merlot ★★ Export-only range. Easy sipper **11** savoury overlay to juicy finish. **Sauvignon Blanc** ★★ Tropical fruit & greenpepper combo, **11** touch too fresh for solo.

Laska range

The One ▦ ★★ House's booming, food-craving tannins on display, with some ripe plums, spice & freshness in **09**, from pinotage. **Cabernet Sauvignon-Merlot** ▦ ★★ Foursquare **10** is ripe & rustic. **Chenin Blanc** ▦ ★★ **11** brisk & zingy, has a brush of sweetness but rather more racy acidity. **Sauvignon Blanc** ▦ ★ Grassy toned **11** is ultra-dry & bracing.

Roulou range

Cabernet Sauvignon ▦ ★★ **08**'s ripeness cut by brisk acidity. Stellenbosch WO for this range. **Merlot** ▦ ★ **08** has unlingering baked prune flavours. **Shiraz** ▦ ★★ The softie in the Boutique, **08** amenable tannins & smoke-laced savoury fruit. — WB/IM

Boutros Wine

Location: Bot River ▪ Map: Elgin, Walker Bay & Bot River ▪ 1stB 2006 ▪ Tasting & sales Mon-Fri 9-4 Sat 9-1 ▪ Closed Easter Fri/Sun, Dec 25 & Jan 1 ▪ Owner(s) Pieter & Bonnie Meiring ▪ Winemaker(s) Niels Verburg (consultant) ▪ 2.6ha (cab, shiraz) ▪ 14t 100% red ▪ PO Box 622 Bot River 7185 ▪ meiringp@mweb.co.za ▪ S 34° 10' 31.63" E 019° 13'33.95" ▪ **T +27 (0)28-284-9871** ▪ F +27 (0)28-284-9871

This boutique winery in Bot River has as yet released only one vintage of its red. The blend was chosen both because neighbours were successful with the style, 'and it is one we both enjoy', say Pieter and Bonnie Meiring.

Shiraz-Cabernet Sauvignon ⓧ ★★★★ **06** tasted 2009 refreshing, with fine tannins & rich, sweet fruit. — AL

Bovlei Cellar

Location: Wellington ▪ Map: Paarl & Wellington ▪ WO: Wellington/Coastal ▪ Est 1907 ▪ Tasting & sales Mon-Fri 9-5 Sat 9-1 pub hols 9-4 ▪ Closed Easter Fri/Sun, Dec 25/26 & Jan 1 ▪ Owner(s) 32 members ▪ Cellarmaster(s) Frank Meaker ▪ Winemaker(s) Frank Meaker, with Jacques Theron ▪ Viticulturist(s) Dawie le Roux (consultant) ▪ 920ha ▪ 8,000t/7m L 52% red 48% white ▪ PO Box 82 Wellington 7654 ▪ info@bovlei.co.za, wines@bovlei. co.za ▪ www.bovlei.co.za ▪ S 33° 38'18.4" E 019° 1'54.2" ▪ **T +27 (0)21-873-1567/+27 (0)21-864-1283** ▪ F +27 (0)21-864-1483

Bovlei, the second oldest member-owned winery in the Cape, was founded in 1907 and has operated continuously ever since, through two World Wars, the KWV era and the modern global expansion of wine. Its present 32 members still operate it as a 'cooperative estate' whereby each batch of fruit brought in is handled individually for the supplier.

Bovlei Vineyard Selected range

★★★★ **Shiraz-Mourvèdre** ✓ Plenty of fruit & body on this New World-styled variation on a Rhône theme. **10** has 71% shiraz, elegantly plumped out by ripe, dark partner.
Cabernet Sauvignon ✓ ★★★★ **10** expresses ripeness in well-weighted & balanced structure. Approachable, unpretentious but satisfying. **Merlot** ✓ ★★★★ Focused, richly fruity **10** offers elegance, balance & good varietal character. Laudable effort at the price. **Pinotage** ✓ ★★★★ Subtlety triumphs over power in this well-restrained interpretation of variety; **10** is light bodied & fragrant. **Shiraz** ★★★★ **10** top-range release is a cut above previous, showing substance & elegance. Riper & fruitier than Winemakers Selection version.

Bovlei Winemakers Selection

Cabernet Sauvignon ☺ ★★★ Earthy centre brings authenticity to unassuming, quaffable **10**. Hints of varietal leanness couched in ripe, juicy fruit. **Shiraz** ☺ ★★★ **10** offers appealing Rhône-style peppery notes in a gently textured middleweight body. **Chenin Blanc** ☺ ▦ ▨ ★★★ **12** shows typical gush of fruit on dry, fresh platform. **Sparkling Brut** NEW ☺ ★★★ Light & delightfully unpretentious NV (**12**) chenin-sauvignon with frothy mousse. **Cape Ruby** ☺ ★★★ 'Port' previous edition. Pleasant if very sweet NV fortified winter warmer from classic port varieties.

Merlot ★★★ Vanilla-toffee oak flavours & modest fruit mar otherwise attractive **11**. **Pinotage** ⓐ ⓩ ★★★ **10** shows lively wild berry fruit with steely edge. **Vin Rouge** ⓐ 🖩 ★★ Ebullient **NV** poolside quaffer from pinotage in 500ml bottle. Not retasted. **Pinotage Rosé** 🖩 ★★★ Lightish, off-dry **12** is crisply fruity & cheerful. **Rosé** ⓐ 🖩 Untasted. **Chardonnay** 🖩 ★★ Refreshing **11** shows hint of development & crisp acid. **Gewürztraminer** 🖩 ★★ Off-dry & spicy **11** shows unmistakable floral scent. **Sauvignon Blanc** 🖩 ⓩ ★★ Unassuming, light **12** for casual quaffing. No frills. **Vin Blanc** ⓐ 🖩 ★★ **NV** easy picnic-style dry white in 500ml format. **Beaukett** 🖩 ★★ Off-dry **NV** (**11**) from undisclosed varieties has pleasant fruity body. **Sparkling Pinotage Rosé** ★★ **11** entry-level, light & modestly sweet. **Special Late Harvest** ⓐ 🖩 ⓩ ★★★ Straightforward, honest sweet chenin, **11** is fresh & crisp. **Hanepoot Jerepiko** ⓐ ★★★ Opulent, spicy muscat fruit on **10** borne on honeyed sweetness. Satisfying fortified winter warmer.

Mad Hatter's range NEW
Modestly priced range of lesser-known varieties in a light-hearted vein.

> **Barbera** ☺ 🖩 ⓩ ★★★ Most widely planted black grape of Piedmont, Italy. Local interpretation **10** is deep coloured & fruity over gentle oak. Coastal WO. **Carignan** ☺ 🖩 ⓩ ★★★ Oaked **10** shows typical crushed red berry fruit & bold acidity. Light but attractive example of mainstay Mediterranean variety. **Mourvèdre** ☺ 🖩 ⓩ ★★★ **10** is a lighter, fruitier version of the originally Spanish black grape, but charming in its own right. **Sangiovese** ☺ 🖩 ⓩ ★★★ **10** offers hints of Tuscany's finest red-wine variety, but doesn't tell all the story. Coastal WO. **Roussanne-Grenache Blanc** ☺ 🖩 ⓩ ★★★ Waxy, mineral & well-rounded **11** white blend of southern French varieties is a welcome newcomer in a sea of conformity. WO Coastal.

Malbec 🖩 ⓩ ★★☆ The Bordeaux black grape that Argentina adopted. This **10** from Wellington is rather lighter & leaner. — GdB

- ◼ **Bowwood** *see* The Drift Farm
- ◼ **Bradgate** *see* Jordan Wine Estate
- ◼ **Brahms** *see* Domaine Brahms Wineries

Bramon Wines

Location/WO: Plettenberg Bay ▪ Map: Klein Karoo & Garden Route ▪ Est 2000 ▪ 1stB 2004 ▪ Tasting & sales daily 9-5.30 ▪ Fee R5/tasting glass ▪ Closed Dec 25 ▪ Cellar tours by appt ▪ Restaurant (see Restaurants section) ▪ Facilities for children ▪ Southern Crags Conservancy ▪ Owner(s) Private company ▪ Cellarmaster(s)/winemaker(s) Anton Smal (Feb 2010) ▪ Viticulturist(s) Peter Thorpe (2000) ▪ 26ha/13ha (chard, sauv) ▪ 21t/2,200cs own label 100% white ▪ PO Box 1606 Plettenberg Bay 6602 ▪ accounts@bramonwines.co.za ▪ www.bramonwines.co.za ▪ S 33°57'20.30" E 023°28'45.02" ▪ **T +27 (0)44-534-8007** ▪ F +27 (0)86-589-6816

Most of the fruit from the ±40ha of vineyards in the Plettenberg Bay area passes through the hands of winemaker Anton Smal at Bramon, the Western Cape's most easterly winery. He's a keen sauvignon blanc man, pleased to be sending a fresh disgorgement of the 08 out to bubbly lovers — he arrived in time for vintage 10.

The Crags Sauvignon Blanc ★★★★ Arrestingly fresh, impressive **12** needs time to unfurl its herbaceous, minerally charms, concealed by rapier-like acidity & pithy grip. More concentration than light **11** (★★★). **Méthode Cap Classique** 🖩 ★★★★ New disgorgement of **08** bone-dry sauvignon bubbly has benefited from extra year: more complex, settled & integrated. — IM

Brampton

Location/map: Stellenbosch ▪ WO: Coastal/Western Cape/Stellenbosch ▪ Est/1stB 1996 ▪ Tasting & sales Mon-Sat 10-7 ▪ Fee R25/3 wines R50/7 wines R45 food & wine pairing ▪ Closed Dec 25 ▪ Light lunches 10-4.15; snacks (cheese platters, pistachio nuts, biltong, olives, etc) & refreshments all day ▪ Owner(s) DGB (Pty) Ltd ▪ Winemaker(s) Thinus Krüger (Sep 2007) ▪ Viticulturist(s) Stephan Joubert (Nov 2006) ▪ 500t/40,000cs own label 40% red 55% white 5% rosé ▪ WIETA ▪ Private Bag X3 Groot Drakenstein 7680 ▪ brampton@dgb.co.za ▪ www.brampton.co.za ▪ S 33°56'17.42" E 018°51'38.08" ▪ **T +27 (0)21-883-9097**

This DGB brand attracts the trendy, creative and 'green' to Brampton Wine Studio in the historic university town of Stellenbosch. More seating, a fireplace and deli foods join wine-and-food pairing, snacks and board games offered during extended trading hours. 'New, 100% recyclable packaging and new varieties to come,' promises manager Harry Joubert.

★★★★ **Cabernet Sauvignon** √ 🗄 🖾 **10** (★★★★) sumptuously ripe, framed by dusty tannins. Heart-warming alcohol adds weight, but lacks focus & structure of **09**.

★★★★ **OVR** √ 🗄 🖾 Sappy **10** now shiraz-led blend. Supple, structured & balanced, with appealing dusty spice undertone. Accessible earlier than **09**, with 3-4 years development.

> **Rosé** ☺ 🗄 🖾 ★★★ Quaffable **12**, tangy red fruit in merlot-led, multi-variety mix. Balanced & crisp summer pleasure.

Shiraz √ 🗄 ★★★★ **09** savoury pepper & spicy red fruit. Balanced structure ensures friendly drinkability intact now & for a few years. Stellenbosch WO. **Unoaked Chardonnay** √ 🗄 🖾 ★★★★ **12** is satisfying & juicy. Ripe pear & tropical flavours threaded with limy freshness for solo or light meal entertainment. WO W Cape, as next. **Sauvignon Blanc** √ 🗄 🖾 ★★★★ Zesty **12** bursts with vitality. Peach & passionfruit in tangy mix for early enjoyment. **Viognier** ⏱ 🗄 ★★★ When last lasted, **09** shade less harmonious & engaging than previous, gentle & understated. — MW

Brandvlei Cellar

Location/map/WO: Worcester ▪ Est 1955 ▪ Tasting & sales Mon-Thu 8–5 Fri 8–4.30 Sat 9-1 ▪ Closed all pub hols ▪ Conferences ▪ Owner(s) 19 members ▪ Cellarmaster(s) Jean le Roux (Aug 1995) ▪ Winemaker(s) Willie Biggs (Sep 2009) & Daneel Jacobs (Sep 2007) ▪ Viticulturist(s) Danie Conradie (Sep 2004) ▪ 1,630ha (cab, ptage, chard, chenin, cbard, sauv) ▪ 28,500t 20% red 80% white ▪ PO Box 595 Worcester 6849 ▪ sales@bcwines.co.za ▪ www.bcwines.co.za ▪ S 33° 48' 19.5" E 019° 28' 8.1" ▪ **T +27 (0)23-340-4215, +27 (0)23-340-4332 (Emma)** ▪ F +27 (0)23-340-4332

Baking under the Worcester sun, yet chilly in winter when snow caps the Jonaskop peak that towers above it, Brandvlei Cellar lies in a valley of fine-weather wines. The credo: quality wines that everyone can enjoy and afford. Four-fifths of their production is white wine, including a hanepoot jerepigo whose sweetness owes everything to that summer sun.

BC Wines range

> **Shiraz Rosé** ☺ 🗄 🖾 ★★★ **12** cheerful pink sipper with off-dry berry flavours.

Cabernet Sauvignon 🖾 ★★★ Improved **11** more serious & structured than previous, ripe prune-like flavours, firm tannins need time or food. **Ruby Cabernet-Merlot** ⏱ 🗄 🖾 ★★ When last tasted, rum & raisin nuanced **10** had hard tannin, acid end. **Chardonnay** 🗄 🖾 ★★★ Satisfying vinosity, melon & lime notes on brief **12**. **Chenin Blanc** 🗄 🖾 ★★★ Green-fruited **12**, lightish, uncomplicated but zippy. **Bacchanté** ⏱ 🗄 ★★★ Perfect budget summer sipping **NV (11)** from gently sweet chenin. **Sauvignon Blanc** 🗄 🖾 ★★ Light-textured **12** has grassy appeal, tangy freshness. **Hanepoot Jerepigo** ⏱ 🖾 ★★★ **11** fortified dessert is intensely raisined but uncloying. — HJ/CvZ

▪ **Bredell's** see JP Bredell Wines
▪ **Breede Valley Wines** see Wedgewood Wines

Breëland Winery

Location: Rawsonville ▪ Map: Breedekloof ▪ WO: Slanghoek ▪ Est 1825 ▪ 1stB 2010 ▪ Tasting, sales & cellar tours Mon-Sat by appt ▪ Fee R10pp tour & tasting ▪ Closed Ash Wed, Easter Fri-Mon, Ascension day, Dec 25 & Jan 1 ▪ Pre-booked lunches (5 days prior notice) ▪ BYO picnic ▪ Walks/hikes ▪ Mountain biking & 4x4 trails ▪ Conservation area ▪ Guest accommodation (mountain hut/farm house/camping) ▪ Owner(s) Kosie & Lizelle Marias ▪ Cellarmaster(s) Wickus Erasmus (Dec 2008) ▪ Winemaker(s) Wickus Erasmus (Dec 2008), with Jefry Fry (Jan 2009) ▪ Viticulturist(s) Wickus Erasmus, Kosie Marais ▪ 1,000ha/100ha (cab, cinsaut, ptage, shiraz, chenin, cbard, hanepoot, sauv, sem) ▪ 1,750t/250cs own label 20% red 80% white + 250cs for clients ▪ Brands for clients: Kaap Agri ▪ PO Box 26 Rawsonville 6845 ▪ wine@boegoekloof.co.za ▪ www.buchukloof.co.za ▪ S 33° 39' 2.87" E 019° 13' 40.08" ▪ **T +27 (0)23-344-3129** ▪ F +27 (0)23-344-3671

In the middle of last season, lightning struck the roof of the cellar on the large, recently renovated Slanghoek Valley family farm and took out the electronics and electrical equipment, damage that reverberated for some months. The weather favoured the vines, though — production volumes were up and co-owner Kosie Marais is buoyed up by the promise of the wines.

Cabernet Sauvignon ⊕ 🍴 ★★★ Big & bold 09 attractive mulberry flavour, racy freshness good foil for meaty stews. **Pinotage** ⊕ 🍴 ★★★ Effortless 09 juicy plum, mocha & hint vanilla; perfect pepperoni pizza partner. **Sauvignon Blanc-Chenin Blanc** ⊕ 🍴 ★★ 10 easy-sipper has guava & other ripe tropical fruit flavours, refreshing sherbety goodbye. — HJ

Brenaissance 🍷 🎄 🏕 **NEW**

Location/map/WO: Stellenbosch ▪ 1stB 2010 ▪ Tasting by appt ▪ BYO picnic ▪ Conferences/functions ▪ Wedding chapel ▪ B&B (9 rooms) ▪ Owner(s) Tom & Hayley Breytenbach ▪ Winemaker(s) Various ▪ 58.23ha/31.65ha (cab, malbec, merlot, shiraz) ▪ 2,529cs own label 70% red 30% white ▪ Suite 3, Private Bag X4, Die Boord, Stellenbosch 7613 ▪ wine@brenaissance.co.za ▪ www.brenaissance.co.za ▪ S 33° 55'4.85" E 018° 49'3.17" ▪ **T +27 (0)76-400-0175** ▪ F +27 (0)86-573-1119

High Mead, formerly an anonymous Stellenbosch grape-growing property, has been granted a new lease of life as Tom and Hayley Breytenbach's 'Brenaissance'. Tom felt that the property's grapes had more potential than was being realised, and, with farm manager Johan Kriek's help, individual varieties are now paired up with specialist wineries for vinification: Clos Malverne (cab, shiraz, Bordeaux-shiraz blend, latter with Hidden Valley), Marklew (merlot, Bordeaux red) and Longridge (chardonnay and sauvignon blanc).

★★★★ **King of Clubs Cabernet Sauvignon** Focused 09 shows considerable complexity: mint, cedar, cassis, black olive, tobacco, cigarbox — you name it; ripe & supple tannins for youthful enjoyment or cellaring. **Queen of Hearts Merlot** ★★★ Plum & meat 10 juxtapositions ripe fruit & green leafy characters. **Jack of Diamonds Shiraz** ★★★★ Pepper & liquorice intro to 09, brooding, tarry & smoky — needs time for dark fruit, muscular tannins to knit & develop. **Full House Bordeaux Style Blend** 🚫 ★★★ Herbaceous cab-led 10 leaner, more elegant than single-variety reds in range; ready now. **Lord T Secret Blend** ✓ ★★★★ Engaging NV, heady spice & red fruit from 49% shiraz supported by acidity & tannins of malbec (31%), cab. Delivers a lot of bang for your buck. **Knight of White Chardonnay** ★★★★ 10 for lovers of oak-driven style. Vanilla & butterscotch overlay to apple pie flavour; rather broad conclusion, could do with touch more acidity to boost vibrancy. **Lady H Sauvignon Blanc** ★★★ Food-friendly 11, green apple & lime, lively & bright, with firm ripe flavours. — HJ/JP

▪ **Brendel Collection** see Le Manoir de Brendel

Brenthurst Winery 🍷

Location: Paarl ▪ Est 1993 ▪ 1stB 1994 ▪ Open to public only by special appt ▪ Owner(s) José Jordaan ▪ Winemaker(s) José Jordaan with advisers ▪ Viticulturist(s) Johan Wiese (1991, consultant) ▪ 5ha (cabs s/f, merlot, p verdot) ▪ 50-70t ▪ PO Box 6091 Paarl 7622 ▪ **T +27 (0)21-863-1154/1375** ▪ F +27 (0)21-424-5666

Cape Town advocate and winegrower José Jordaan is rejuvenating his small Paarl vineyard in order to focus on limited bottlings of special-interest, unusual varieties (like his own petit verdot and other bought-in grapes) in collaboration with young consultant winemaker Martin Fourie. The new cost-effective Australian Flexcube maturation vessel will play a role.

▪ **Brink Family** see Pulpit Rock Winery
▪ **Broad Reach** see Devonvale Golf & Wine Estate
▪ **Broken Rock** see Riebeek Cellars
▪ **Broken Stone** see Slaley

Brothers Wines **NEW**

Location: Cape Town ▪ WO: Western Cape ▪ Est/1stB 2005 ▪ Closed to public ▪ Owner(s) Greg Castle ▪ Cellarmaster(s)/winemaker(s) Greg Castle (2005) ▪ 10t/833cs own label 55% red 45% white ▪ PO Box 21681 Kloof Street Cape Town 8008 ▪ info@brotherswines.co.za ▪ www.brotherswines.com ▪ **T +27 (0)82-600-2555** ▪ F +27 (0)86-528-6081

Capetonian Greg Castle's hobby has become a niche wine brand, established in 2005 and named for sons Dylan and Alex (whose silhouetted images as little boys appear on the charming label). Winemaking courses by the strategy and marketing specialist have translated into vinifying 10t of premium grapes from top Constantia, Paarl and Swartland growers for his fewer than 1,000 cases, now available in local wine shops and selected eateries, and overseas.

Shiraz ★★★☆ Attractive light feel to **09** is accentuated by pepper & floral notes, nice chalky-dry tannins, but shade less complexity & elegance than savoury-tinged, medium-bodied **07** (★★★★). Both equally good with suggested osso bucco accompaniment. **Legacy** ★★★★ Well-crafted red blend **08** showing fine oak detail (100% new for the 33% cab portion, 50% new for shiraz), plush fruit & supple tannins. For fireside philosophising. **Chardonnay** 🍽 ★★★★ Chardonnay for the grown-up brother. **11** socks it to you with butter, caramel (from oak fermentation, third new), lime pie & a lingering sweet aftertaste. 'Unfiltered to retain full flavour.' We noticed! **Sauvignon Blanc** 🍽 ★★★ Successfully aiming for lower-acid, riper tropical profile, **11** is fattish, well padded, more about mouthfeel than zip & pyrotechnics. — FM/GdB

Brunia Wines

Location: Stanford ▪ Map: Southern Cape ▪ WO: Walker Bay ▪ Est 2005 ▪ 1stB 2009 ▪ Tasting & sales by appt Tue-Sun 10-4 & daily during holidays ▪ Closed Dec 25/26 ▪ Light lunches, picnics & tractor rides ▪ Self-guided hiking trails ▪ Mountain biking ▪ Conservation area ▪ Owner(s) W P du Preez ▪ Winemaker(s) Kobie Viljoen (Gabriëlskloof) ▪ Viticulturist(s) Andrew Teubes (consultant) ▪ 417ha/17ha (pinot, shiraz, chard, sauv, sem) ▪ 75t/2,800cs own label 16% red 84% white ▪ PO Box 368 Stanford 7210 ▪ info@bruniawines.co.za ▪ www.bruniawines.co.za ▪ S 34° 28' 9.25" E 019° 39' 42.60" ▪ **T +27 (0)28-341-0432** ▪ F +27 (0)86-669-6064

'We're running out of money,' chortles former stock farmer Willie du Preez, nine years after purchasing his dream wine farm, Cold Mountain, south of Stanford. But the hardest work is done — clearing alien vegetation, installing irrigation, planting vineyards, building a stylish homestead and tasting venue — and he's now anticipating the maiden vintage of a chardonnay and white blend.

★★★★ **Shiraz** Peppery **10** (★★★) generously proportioned but short somewhat on finish & complexity compared with elegant & suave **09**.

Sauvignon Blanc ✓ 🍽 ★★★★ Lime-scented **11** raises the bar with fine mineral fruit core, chalky finish & a steely dryness that shouts 'oysters!'. **10** (★★★★) flew with/to British Airways & UK's Wine Society. — WB/GdB

◼ **Buckleberry** see Louis
◼ **Buddy** see Overhex Wines International

Buffalo Creek Wines

Location: McGregor ▪ Map: Robertson ▪ Est/1stB 2005 ▪ Tasting, sales & cellar tours Mon-Fri 9-6 Sat 9-12.30 Sun by appt only ▪ Closed Easter Sun, Dec 25 & Jan 1 ▪ Owner(s) Leroy & Mark Tolmay ▪ Cellarmaster(s)/winemaker(s) Mark Tolmay (Jun 2005) ▪ 1,328ha/30ha (p verdot, ptage, pinot, merlot, chard, chenin, cbard, sauv) ▪ ±350-380t/250-300cs own label 65% red 25% white 10% rosé ▪ PO Box 124 McGregor 6708 ▪ info@buffalocreek.co.za ▪ S 34° 0' 2.97" E 019°53'11.94" ▪ **T +27 (0)23-625-1727** ▪ F +27 (0)23-625-1727

There are now three generations of Tolmays involved in this boutique winery in McGregor, all of them committed to delivering quality wines at reasonable prices — something grandfather Leroy believes the bigger brands are letting slide. Expansion into the UK is planned, though the cellar will still remain small and focused.

Merlot Selling but not tasted, as for **Pinotage, Sweet Rosé, Chardonnay, Sauvignon Blanc** & **Crispy Dry White**. **Dry Red** Await next.

Buitenverwachting

Location: Constantia ▪ Map: Cape Peninsula ▪ WO: Constantia/Coastal/Western Cape ▪ Est 1796 ▪ 1stB 1985 ▪ Tasting & sales Mon-Fri 9-5 Sat 10-3 ▪ Closed all pub hols ▪ Cellar tours by appt ▪ Buitenverwachting Restaurant (see Restaurants section) ▪ Deli & coffee shop ▪ Picnic area ▪ Conferences ▪ Owner(s) Richard & Sieglinde (Christine) Mueller, Lars Maack ▪ Cellarmaster(s) Hermann Kirschbaum (Jan 1993) ▪ Winemaker(s) Brad Paton (Jan 2005) ▪ Viticulturist(s) Peter Reynolds (Jan 2001) ▪ 147ha/105ha (cab, chard, sauv) ▪ 500t/100,000cs own label 8% red 90% white 2% rosé ▪ PO Box 281 Constantia 7848 ▪ info@buitenverwachting.com ▪ www.buitenverwachting.com ▪ S 34° 2' 30.4" E 018° 25' 1.5" ▪ **T +27 (0)21-794-5190/1** ▪ F +27 (0)21-794-1351

It's back to the future for this gracious old Constantia property: cement, rather than stainless steel tanks are being installed; these allow for a more hands-on punchdown and better aeration. Also, a wider spectrum of wood is being trialled to reduce the oak flavour in the wine and gain the full effect of evaporation. In the vineyards, the focus is on maximising the farm's strengths via new plantings (especially sauvignon blanc), selecting variety and clone according to the specific conditions of each site — in some instances this means reducing the size of the block. The end goal is to emphasise the unique 'Constantia — Buitenverwachting' style, something diligently and passionately followed by Hermann Kirschbaum, celebrating 20 years as cellarmaster.

★★★★ **Cabernet Sauvignon** ⓘ Last-tasted austere **07** with fine, dark-berried fruit & tannic grip promised to benefit from few years in bottle.

★★★★ **Cabernet Franc 09** (★★★★★) shows strength of vintage in its rich spicy concentration, wreath of stern but fine tannins, & its ability to soak up nearly two years in 90% new French oak. Great now; better still with time it deserves. **08** attractive if less complex.

★★★★ **Merlot** Less flashy than many. **09** ripe spice, dark plum, bitter choc features welded & gripped by tight tannin. Well judged oak; fresh, dry-finishing. Should age well. Quieter **08** (★★★★).

★★★★☆ **Christine** ⓘ Refined benchmark Bordeaux red. Cab, cab franc, merlot & petit verdot convincingly blended in **08**. Subtly complex; sweet flesh contrasted by balanced freshness, fine tannin. All-new oak seamlessly absorbed.

★★★★ **Chardonnay 11** follows in footsteps of **10** but with more oatmeal, fruity substance, limy freshness to balance toasty oak. Well-sustained, dry finish. Promising future.

★★★★ **G** 🍷 📖 🌿 G for gewürztraminer; typical but unblowsy aromas on **10**; smoothed by older oak, persistent & bone-dry. WO Coastal.

★★★★☆ **Husseys Vlei Sauvignon Blanc** Slower developer than standard version, **11** reaps benefits of release year after vintage. Sophisticated & elegant, impresses through subtlety, complexity rather than power. Intricate weave chalky tones, lime/minerals with ripe fruit, lengthily refrained. Plenty still to give.

★★★★ **Sauvignon Blanc** ⓘ 📖 🌿 **11** shows the fruity succulence of the year; a bone-dry, bracing finish lengthens those juicy lime, grassy tones.

★★★★☆ **1769** ⓘ Natural Sweet dessert from oaked muscat de Frontignan. Clean, long **08** tasted previously. **07** (★★★★★) amazingly elegant.

Meifort ⓘ ★★★★ Dusty overlay to spicy, fresh red fruit attractions on **08** Bordeaux-style blend. Bone-dry with savoury richness aiding accessibility. **Blanc de Noir** Await next. **Buiten Blanc** 📖 ★★★★ Ever-popular sauvignon-led blend with chenin, splashes viognier, semillon. **12** brims with delicious fruity acids, extra breadth from minor partners. WO W Cape. **Batavia** ⓘ ★★★★ Experimental, one-off riesling, oaked viognier, chenin blend. Freshness & silken viscosity on off-dry **09**. **Maximus** ⓘ ★★★★ Ripe tangerine flavours, sumptuous texture feature on persistent, just-dry **09** from lightly oaked sauvignon/semillon. **Brut MCC** ★★★★ Invitingly fresh, citrusy aromas on latest **NV** sparkling from chardonnay & pinot noir. Light & creamy, with complementary gentle pinprick mousse. Great for 'champagne' breakfasts or sundowner sipping. Discontinued: **Rough Diamond**, **White Blend**. — AL

■ **Bundustar** *see* Origin Wine

BurCon Wines

Location/map/WO: Robertson ▪ 1stB 2004 ▪ Tasting Tue-Fri 9-4 Sat 10-2 Sun by appt only ▪ Restaurant ▪ Conferences ▪ Farm produce ▪ Facilities for children & tour groups ▪ Walks/hikes ▪ Mountain biking & guided horseback trails ▪ Owner(s) Frans & Amanda Conradie, Renée Burger ▪ Winemaker(s) Christie Steytler (Feb 2004, Roodezandt) ▪ 234ha/25ha (ptage, shiraz, muscadel) ▪ 16t/1,250cs own label ▪ PO Box 86 Robertson 6705 ▪ info@nerinaguestfarm.com ▪ www.nerinaguestfarm.com ▪ S 33° 50′ 5.2″ E 019° 45′ 55.3″ ▪ **T +27 (0)23-626-2012/+27 (0)82-823-4231** ▪ F +27 (0)23-626-2012

Nerina Guest Farm's BurCon house wines aren't taken too seriously, Amanda Conradie reports, except perhaps by the bank manager, who, she says, feels ill every time he thinks about them. The labels feature illustrations an old school friend of Amanda's drew for the children's stories she wrote, and the peculiar brand name commemorates the marriage of a Burger into the Conradie family.

Oompie se Oeps ⊕ 🍷 ★★ NV (09) pinotage (85%) & shiraz (co-planted in error!) unwooded plummy fruit & spice mix. **Miskien Christien** ⊕ ★★★ Rich fortified red muscadel, 09 unctuous raisined & honeyed, in 2L pack. — JP/CvZ

Burgershof

Location/WO: Robertson ▪ Est 1864 ▪ 1stB 2000 ▪ Closed to public ▪ Sales at La Verne, Robertson & Wine Boutique, Ashton ▪ Owner(s) HJ Reynecke ▪ Cellarmaster(s)/winemaker(s)/viticulturist(s) Hennie Reynecke (Jan 1979) ▪ 68ha (cab, merlot, muscadel r/w, ptage, ruby cab, shiraz, chard, chenin, cbard, sauv) ▪ IPW ▪ PO Box 72 Klaasvoogds River 6707 ▪ burgershof@barvallei.co.za ▪ **T +27 (0)23-626-5433** ▪ F +27 (0)23-626-5433

Fourth-generation owner Hennie Reynecke's winemaking philosophy remains unchanged: 'The quality of wine lies in the vineyards that you nurture and care for all year.' Dutch supermarket chain Jumbo leaves only smidgens of his wine for sale locally: sole stockists are The Wine Boutique in Ashton and La Verne in Robertson.

Pinotage ☺ 🍷 🎞 ★★★ Supple & fresh 11 has friendly tannins, lipsmacking dry end for outdoor fun. **Chardonnay** ☺ 🍷 🎞 ★★★ Cardamom & coriander nuances on lemon-toned 12 fusion food partner.

Merlot ⊕ ★★ Forest floor, bouillon overlay to plum jam fruit on 08, best enjoyed soon. **Cabernet Sauvignon- Shiraz** ⊕ ★★ Plum & prune-toned 09 for campfires & winter casseroles. **Sauvignon Blanc** 🍷 🎞 ★★ Crisp & herbaceous 12, lowish 12.5% alcohol extends the summer fun. — CvZ/MW

▪ **Bush Camp** see Landskroon Wines

Bushmanspad Estate

Location: Bonnievale ▪ Map/WO: Robertson ▪ Est 2000 ▪ 1stB 2006 ▪ Tasting & sales Mon-Fri 8.30-5 ▪ Fee R15/ 6 wines ▪ BYO picnic ▪ Walks/hikes ▪ 4-star B&B/self-catering cottages (see Accommodation section) ▪ Owner(s) Menno Schaafsma ▪ Cellarmaster(s)/winemaker(s)/viticulturist(s) Arthur Basson ▪ 52ha (cabs s/f, malbec, merlot, mourv, shiraz, sauv) ▪ 400t own label 80% red 15% white 5% rosé ▪ PO Box 227 Bonnievale 6705 ▪ info@bushmanspad.co.za ▪ www.bushmanspad.co.za ▪ S 33° 53'55.0" E 020° 11'46.7" ▪ **T +27 (0)23-616-2961** ▪ F +27 (0)23-616-3714

The Bushmanspad vineyards in the Langeberg foothills are fringed by fynbos, and winemaker Arthur Basson believes these aromatic plants lend a special character to the fruit, which he tries to capture using 'Old World winemaking techniques'. Some of the wines recently performed well in professional tastings, while others flew business class with KLM. A thrust is planned into China which, if successful, will mean 'we will harvest more than just grapes!'

Bushmanspad range

★★★★ **The Menno** ⊕ Flagship 09 red fruit & spice, medium bodied & elegant, chewy tannins to accompany red meat dishes.

Cabernet Sauvignon ⊕ ★★★★ Well-constructed 09 judiciously oaked; a satisfying & refreshing everyday red. **Cabernet Franc** ⊕ ★★★ 09 herbal edge to red fruit, unyielding tannins may have softened. **Malbec** NEW 🎞 ★★★ 09 supple & generous 11 supple, pleasantly rounded; amenable outdoor companion. **Rosé** 🍷 ★★★ Attractive strawberry & floral notes on dry, crisp 12, satisfying summer sipper. **Sauvignon Blanc** 🍷 ★★★★ Aromatic bouquet & lemongrass flavour on a solid acid platform give 12 real charm. Balanced & lipsmacking.

Red Gold range

Cabernet Sauvignon ⊕ ★★★ Appealing 07 with red fruit, fresh acidity, soft tannins. **Shiraz** 🎞 ★★★ 11 oaky & sombre, with dense black cherry & biltong notes, firm tannins for game dishes. — GdB

▪ **Butcher Shop & Grill** see The Butcher Shop & Grill
▪ **Buthelezi** see Signal Hill Wines
▪ **BWC Wines** see Catherine Marshall Wines
▪ **Cabrière** see Haute Cabrière
▪ **Café Collection** see FirstCape Vineyards

Café Culture

A still and a sparkling wine now make up this KWV 'coffee pinotage' label. With its bright, funky packaging, ChocMousse has caught consumers' attention; 'making a statement is what the brand is all about', confirms brand manager Karen Kruger.

Pinotage 🗄 📷 ★★ **11** hearty red from pinotage but more evident espresso flavours from oak. WO W Cape. **ChocMousse** NEW ★ Sweetish & frothy **NV** fizz from pinotage with mocha overtones. — AL

Calais Wine Estate

Location/WO: Paarl ▪ Map: Paarl & Wellington ▪ Est/1stB 2000 ▪ Tasting by appt ▪ Sales daily 8-4 ▪ Guest accommodation ▪ Owner(s) Calais Wine Estate shareholders ▪ Winemaker(s)/viticulturist(s) Helene van der Westhuizen ▪ 28ha (cab, malbec, merlot, p verdot, ptage, shiraz, chard) ▪ 50t/1,500cs own label 90% red 10% white ▪ PO Box 9006 Klein Drakenstein 7628 ▪ info@calais.co.za ▪ www.calais.co.za ▪ S 33° 42' 32.1" E 019° 1' 4.6" ▪ **T +27 (0)21-868-3888** ▪ F +27 (0)21-868-1400

Part of the original Berg River Valley farm established in 1692 by French Huguenot Jean Manjie, who named it after his home town, Calais has several new staff members, including winemaker Helene van der Westhuizen. 'New developments are most likely,' they say, though the warm welcome remains unchanged: 'Every visit is a special occasion.'

Cabernet Sauvignon ⓣ ★★★ Unwooded '& unplugged' **06** showed succulent, lively fruit when tasted mid-2009. **Merlot** Next awaited, as for **Petit Verdot, Pinotage, Applause, Bel Canto** & **Chardonnay.** **Shiraz** ⓣ ★★★ Unadorned fruit in **06**, juicy smooth drinking. **Cape Riesling** ⓣ ★★ Delicate **08**, crisp & dry. WO Wellington. **Chenin Blanc** ⓣ ★★ Easy **10** attractive & restrained, but a warming finish. **Sauvignon Blanc** ⓣ ★★★ Light & easy, yellow-fruited, softish **11** from Stellenbosch. Also light, but greener **10** (★★) ex Paarl, with awkward acidity. — JPf

Calitzdorp Cellar 🍴 🍷 🌳 📷

Location/WO: Calitzdorp ▪ Map: Klein Karoo & Garden Route ▪ Est 1928 ▪ 1stB 1976 ▪ Tasting & sales Mon-Fri 8-5 Sat 8-1 ▪ Closed Good Fri & Dec 25 ▪ Cellar tours by appt ▪ Tour groups ▪ Farm produce ▪ Picnics/meals by appt; or BYO picnic ▪ Conferences ▪ Succulent garden ▪ Owner(s) 39 members ▪ Cellarmaster(s)/winemaker(s) Alwyn Burger (1990) ▪ Viticulturist(s) Johannes Mellet (2005, consultant) ▪ 286ha (13 varieties, r/w) ▪ ±4,000t/3,500cs own label 34% red 17% white 11% rosé 38% other ▪ IPW ▪ PO Box 193 Calitzdorp 6660 ▪ manager@calitzdorpwine.co.za ▪ www.calitzdorpwine.co.za ▪ S 33° 32' 18.9" E 021° 41' 10.6" ▪ **T +27 (0)44-213-3301** ▪ F +27 (0)44-213-3328

Calitzdorp Cellar is on a roll, says winemaker Alwyn Burger. 'We had our biggest harvest ever — and quality fruit, too.' Calitzdorp continues to maintain its presence in the South African port-style leaderboard, but, like others, is discovering the potential of unfortified touriga nacional, a Veritas gold medal auguring well.

★★★★ **Hanepoot** ✓ Attractive fortified dessert; **10** tasted out of vintage sequence, lovely pear & white peach bouquet, uncloying sweetness through to tangy farewell. Improves on **11** (★★★) previewed last edition.
★★★★ **Hanepoot-Muskadel Reserve** ⓣ 📷 Fortified delight from equal portions muscats de Frontignan & d'Alexandrie, **10** pure fruit, great intensity & poise courtesy zesty acidity. Rivals the region's finest.
★★★★ **Red Muscadel** ✓ Tealeaf-toned **NV** (**11**) fortified muscat similar to geranium-scented **10** in its mouthcoating but uncloying sweetness. Goes well with cheesecake, nuts, preserved figs, cellar says.
★★★★ **White Muscadel** 📷 Fragrant & spicy fortified dessert. Revisited **10** has blossomed, shows same liquid sunshine character as **09**, acidity more balanced now but still wide awake.

Pinotage ☺ 📷 ★★★ Unusual (but tasty) curry-spiced strawberry jam character on **11**, soft, juicy & affordably priced. **Golden Jerepigo** ☺ ★★★ Junior version of Hanepoot-Muskadel Reserve. Spirited **NV** with raisin sweetness which glides down oh-so-easily.

Cabernet Sauvignon 📷 ★★ **10** straightforward & unyielding, needs hearty ostrich stew. **Merlot** 📷 ★★ Brief **11** mainly spicy oak aromas, some plums peeping through. **Shiraz** 🗄 ★★ Floral lily perfume, red fruit & pleasant tannic bite in **10**. **Touriga Nacional** 📷 ★★★ New bottling of **10** is fresher, scented with roses & vanilla, firm tannins cushioned by actual sugar & sweetening effect of high alcohol. **Rosé** 🗄 Await next.

Chardonnay ⊕ 🍴 🏵 ★★★ Very subdued **11** not quite up to speed of previous. **Sauvignon Blanc** 🍴 🏵 ★★ Grassy **12**, more body & zing than previous. **White Muscadel** Not tasted. **Vintage Port** ★★★★ Equal touriga & tinta in **09**, Portuguese-style higher fortification, lower sugar. Improving in bottle, offers generous fruit & good concentration, extended dry finish. **Cape Ruby** ★★★ Was 'Ruby Port'. Equal tinta, touriga in latest **NV**; very tarry, with medicinal hint & cloves, misses the affability of the ruby style. — GdB/CvZ

Callender Peak

Location: Ceres • WO: Western Cape • Est/1stB 2007 • Closed to public • Owner(s) MacDonald & Jeffrey families • Cellarmaster(s)/winemaker(s) Johan Kruger (whites, Sterhuis 2007) & Clive Torr (reds, Topaz 2007) • Viticulturist(s) Willem Mouton (1990) • 2ha (cab, merlot, pinot, chard) • 2t/200cs own label 50% red 50% white • clivetorrwines@mweb.co.za • **T** +27 (0)82-557-0826

The extreme conditions prevailing in these far-flung vineyards, near the snow-line above Ceres, mean there's great quality potential, but also great risk to the crop. Last year, the birds got it, so there was no vintage. This year sees the launch of the second-tier Winterhoek range of exciting, individualistic wines.

Winterhoek range

★★★★ **Chardonnay** 🍴 Previously in Callender range. **10**'s beeswax & honey from oxidative styling; nutty oak spices integrate well with ripe fruit from Koue Bokkeveld (Ceres) vines. **09**, too, had serious intent.
Sauvignon Blanc NEW ✓ ★★★★ Pungent, slightly sweaty **11** shows satisfying fullness with spicy tropical fruit-salad.

Callender Peak range

Cabernet Sauvignon ⊕ ★★★★ Leafy, savoury **07** dominated previously by all-new oak & astringent tannins — but had fruit to balance, given time. **Merlot** Await new, as for **Pinot Noir**. — GdB

Camanga Wine & Olives

Location: Tulbagh • Est 2003 • 1stB 2005 • Closed to public • Owner(s) Colin & Charlotte Richardson • Winemaker(s) Dewaldt Heyns (Feb 2010, Saronsberg) • Viticulturist(s) Grant Clack (Jun 2003, consultant) • 34ha/1ha (shiraz) • 3t/200cs own label • info@camanga.co.za • www.camanga.co.za

Back on track after human error and animal escapades derailed two vintages, Britons Colin and Charlotte Richardson have bottled their 11 Shiraz for release end 2013. Now nurtured by neighbouring Saronsberg's award-winning vintner Dewaldt Heyns, their wines should again set sail abroad through mega-yacht captain Colin's Caribbean, Mediterranean and UK contacts.

Camberley Wines

Location/map/WO: Stellenbosch • Est 1990 • 1stB 1996 • Tasting & sales Mon-Sat & pub hols 9–5 Sun 9-3 • Fee R40 max (depending on wine choice), waived on purchase • Closed Dec 25 & Jan 1 • Cellar tours by appt • Lunch/refreshments by appt; or BYO picnic • Boule court for hire • B&B guest cottage • Owner(s) John & Gaël Nel • Winemaker(s) John Nel, with Louis Koch • Viticulturist(s) Bennie Booysen • 7ha (cabs s/f, merlot, p verdot, ptage, shiraz, touriga) • ±35t/3,200cs own label 100% red • PO Box 6120 Uniedal 7612 • john@ camberley.co.za • www.camberley.co.za • S 33°55'8.9" E 018°55'58.3" • **T** +27 (0)21-885-1176 • F +27 (0)21-885-1822

Ebullient Johnny Nel and family have followed a passionate hobby that has slowly evolved into a wine destination in Stellenbosch. The recently completed bar cum tasting room attached to their house is a cosy, homely spot for enjoying these dark-fruited and ripely voluptuous wines — while catching up with a bit of quality sport. Even a cleansing ale is on hand to provide alternative refreshment for tiring palates at the end of a long day of wine indulgence.

Camberley Wines range

★★★★ **Shiraz** Inky, ultra-ripe & huge **10** (★★★☆), still all oak & alcohol sweetness mid-2012. Opulent like bold & robust **09**.

★★★★☆ **Philosophers' Stone** Cab franc with merlot, cab. **09** (★★★★) has lovely extracted richness round full body, layers of black tarry fruit. Not for the faint hearted, given 15.5% alcohol. **08** was merlot-led.

★★★ **Cabernet Sauvignon-Merlot** ⊕ **09** upfront bright New World fruit, bold & sweet, balanced oak & smoky conclusion, firm tannin grip. Needs time to develop & show charms.

★★★ **Charisma** ⊕ Gorgeous mint, herbs & red berry flavours on classy **08** blend cabs sauvignon & franc. uicy & balanced, smooth vanilla finish. Should age well.

abernet Sauvignon Reserve Await next. **Elm Tree Merlot** Not tasted. **Pinotage** ★★★★ **11** in usual ch vein, almost porty intensity of ripe plump fruit ensconced in obvious oak. 15.5% alcohol glows on sweet-h end. **Sparkling Shiraz** ⊕ ★★★ Rare shiraz bubbly. **04** bright cherry flavours, light & elegant, savoury & usty finish. **Elixir Fortified Red** ⊕ ★★★ Spirited port-style dessert from shiraz with a sweet finish on last-sted **05**.

rohibition range

ed ⊕ 🍷 ★★★ **NV** quaffer from shiraz & pinotage, juicy & soft with earthy finish. **White** ⊕ 🍷 ★★★ ight & crisp **NV** from sauvignon; full-flavoured grassy, lemony freshness; slips down easily. — JP

Cameradi Wines

ocation: Wellington ▪ Est 1999 ▪ 1stB 2000 ▪ Closed to public ▪ Owner(s) Stelvest cc (Nic Swingler, Hendrik du eez & Casper Lategan) ▪ Winemaker(s) Casper Lategan (Jan 1999) ▪ 2t/130cs own label 100% red ▪ 48 Bain r Wellington 7655 ▪ cas@lategans.co.za ▪ **T +27 (0)21-873-1225** ▪ F +27 (0)21-873-4910

here's talk of a new ageing cellar for this garagiste brand at co-owner/ inemaker Casper Lategan's Wellington premises, and we look forward to new fferings.

Capaia Wine Estate

ocation/WO: Philadelphia ▪ Map: Durbanville, Philadelphia & Darling ▪ Est 1997 ▪ 1stB 2003 ▪ Tasting, sales & ellar tours Mon-Fri 8-5 Sat/Sun on request ▪ Closed all pub hols ▪ Tour groups ▪ Owner(s) Ingrid & Alexander aron von Essen ▪ Cellarmaster(s) Bernabé Strydom (Oct 2006), assisted by Stephan von Neipperg (consul-nt) ▪ Winemaker(s) Adriaan Burger (Oct 2010) ▪ Viticulturist(s) Schalk du Toit (2009, consultant) ▪ 140ha/ 0ha (cabs s/f, merlot, p verdot, shiraz, sauv) ▪ 260t/13,000cs own label 85% red 15% white ▪ IPW ▪ PO Box 5 Philadelphia 7304 ▪ info@capaia.co.za ▪ www.capaia.co.za, www.capaia.com ▪ S 33° 42'45.9" E 018° 34' 9" ▪ **T +27 (0)21-972-1081** ▪ F +27 (0)21-972-1894

's a decade worth celebrating at this Philadelphia winery, owned by Germans Ing-d and Alexander von Essen. 2003 saw the first vintage off their superb young vine-ards, vinified in the magnificent new cellar. No expense had been spared in stablishing a wine farm and winery where only wheat had grown before. There ave been ups and downs (we recall the tragic 2005 death of the man responsible or that first vintage, the great Hungarian winemaker Tibor Gál), but stability has een achieved and the results of it (and of that initial planning) show in the wines.

★★★★ **Merlot-Cabernet Sauvignon** ✓ 🖼 Intense & plush **10**, demure dark fruit, beautifully managed tannins, some spice, textured elegance. Showy yet restrained. Firmer than softly ripe **09** (★★★★).

★★★★☆ **ONE** ⊕ ✓ 🖼 Brooding **09** (★★★★) from merlot, cab, cab franc, petit verdot plus 5% shiraz. Unyielding tannins mask ultra-ripe fruit, lacks freshness. **08** more impressive.

auvignon Blanc ⊕ ✓ 🖼 ★★★★ Herbaceous previewed **11** big step-up from **10** (★★★). Has steely resolve. rm acid controls fruit, light oaking adds dimension to austere food-style intended by winemaker. — MF

▪ **Cap du Vin** see Bellevue Estate Stellenbosch
▪ **Cape Elephant** see Lutzville Cape Diamond Vineyards
▪ **Cape Auction** see Jonkheer
▪ **Cape Avocet** see Rooiberg Winery

Cape Chamonix Wine Farm

ocation/map/WO: Franschhoek ▪ Est 1991 ▪ 1stB 1992 ▪ Tasting & sales Mon-Sat 9.30-4.30 Sun 9.30-4 ▪ Fee 20 ▪ Closed Dec 25 & Jan 1 ▪ Cellar tours by appt ▪ Mon Plaisir Restaurant T +27 (0)21-876-2393 ▪ Conserva-ion area ▪ Fully equipped self-catering cottages ▪ Owner(s) Chris Hellinger ▪ Cellarmaster(s)/viticulturist(s) ottfried Mocke (Sep 2001) ▪ Winemaker(s) Gottfried Mocke (Sep 2001) & Emul Ross (Jun 2011) ▪ 300ha/ 0ha (cabs s/f, malbec, merlot, p verdot, ptage, pinot, chard, chenin, sauv, sem) ▪ 220-250t/20,000cs own label 60% red 40% white ▪ IPW ▪ PO Box 28 Franschhoek 7690 ▪ marketing@chamonix.co.za ▪ www.chamonix.co.za ▪ S 33° 53'60.0" E 019° 7'34.0" ▪ **T +27 (0)21-876-8400** ▪ F +27 (0)21-876-3237

The almost unprecedented growth in quality from this Franschhoek producer – our Winery of the Year this edition – in the decade-plus since Gottfried Mock took charge of grape-growing and wine-making has been so remarkable that it' almost alarming that more is planned. 'We have changed the cellar layout t allow for more space to enable us to be more creative in our winemakin approach,' says Gottfried. (The thoughtful originality of his work in the cellar i exemplified by his uniquely-vinified pinotage.) And in the vineyard – the rea source of the great transformation in, particularly, Chamonix's reds – mor virus-infected vineyards have been ripped out and replanted. If anyone doubt that this is one of the Cape's top handful of winegrowers, they can't remai unconvinced for much longer.

Reserve range

★★★★★ **Pinot Noir Reserve** Proving itself one of the Cape's leaders. Flamboyant **11** shows ripe raspberr & cherry aromas but also rosepetals, cinnamon & a hint of pepper. Natural ferment, integrated oaking (65% nev French) give great succulence, with a fine soft tannin structure. Immediate appeal, but should age.

★★★★★ **Troika 10** from cab franc & cab plus a little merlot. Lovely fruit definition untrammeled by the 60% new oak. Shows some early drinkability, though slightly astringent in youth, needing some years to integrat the ripe fruit fully with the oak & the herbaceous element.

Liam likes

★★★★☆ **Chardonnay Reserve** Subtle, classic & deep **11** (★★★★★) shows tropical & stonefruit, th intense flavour easily absorbing 80% new oak. Mouthfilling palate flirts with intricate minerality in long, com plex finish. Natural ferment; matured in oak & concrete 'eggs'. Many years maturation will benefit – as with **10**.

★★★★☆ **Sauvignon Blanc Reserve** ⓦ A top example of oaked sauvignon. **10**'s white peach & vanill aromas herald profound, harmonious flavours. Ageworthy, with 13% semillon contributing vitality, length. Les exuberance than **09**.

★★★★★ **Reserve White [NEW] 11** blend 60% sauvignon with semillon offers wonderful acidity, body & texture; aromas reminiscent of lemon oil, green fig, crushed stones & oak. Substantial & mouthfilling, with fin palate weight – but needs & deserves at least a few years, which will integrate the wood (50% new).

Cape Chamonix range

Liam no like – too young

★★★★ **Cabernet Sauvignon** ⓦ Blackcurrant, lead pencil & leafy notes dominate this austere, fragrant spicy & classic **09**, with an extra green lift from 10% cab franc. 50% new oak evident, but integrating.

★★★★★ **Greywacke Pinotage 10** (★★★★★) shows great tension between vibrant red bramble fruits & dark super-ripe blackberries. Like **09**, complex winemaking mixes early-picked & desiccated grapes. Full fla voured, with integrated oak; long finish framed by fine tannin. Brilliant 10% pinot noir inclusion.

★★★★ **Chardonnay 11** has intense ripe honey-melon, pineapple & lemon, oak integrated & contributin a vanilla hint. Some emergent complexity on the palate, with minerality on the lemon-twist finish.

★★★★☆ **Sauvignon Blanc** 🍶 **12** tank sample shows ripeness but stays on the mineral side with aroma of crushed stone, green fig, nettle dominating any tropical fruit. Intense but subtle, showing length & complex ity. Includes small oak-fermented portion. **11** (★★★★) was a touch off standard.

★★★★ **MCC Blanc de Blancs** ⓦ Finely styled **06** sparkling from chardonnay, tasted last year. Restrained classical freshness, with zesty citrus notes, stony fragrance.

Rouge ⓦ ★★★★ **09** as usual a savoury, merlot-led Bordeaux blend, showing tobacco, tealeaf & plum, wit a fine-tannined structure. **Blanc** ✓ 🍶 ★★★★ **12** tank sample from chardonnay, chenin, sauvignon show array of tropical & green aromas. Quite serious for an entry-level wine! — JPf

Cape Classics

Location: Somerset West ▪ Map: Helderberg ▪ WO: Western Cape ▪ Est 1991 ▪ 1stB 1996 ▪ Tasting by appt only Owner(s) André Shearer ▪ Winemaker(s) Bruwer Raats (May 2010) ▪ 120,000cs own label 45% red 55% white ▪ Other export brands: Indaba, Jam Jar ▪ PO Box 1695 Somerset West 7129 ▪ info@capeclassics.com ▪ www.capeclassics.com, www.indabawines.com ▪ S 34° 4'5.9" E 018° 53'38.2" ▪ **T +27 (0)21-847-2400** ▪ F +2 (0)21-847-2414

This respected importer and distributor of South African wine into the US repres sents many high-profile Cape estates and labels, and enjoys enviable marke penetration through nation-wide chains and networks, currently supplying 4 tates with their own Indaba range. Following current marketing trends, their weet red, Jam Jar Shiraz, is the biggest-selling SA wine brand in the US market, artnered now by the sweet white Jam Jar Moscato. Founder/owner André hearer records their progress from apartheid-era pariah in the early 1990s to MPACT Newsletter's '2011 Hot Prospect' and Food & Wine's 'Best Wine mporter' and 'Name You Can Trust', with some satisfaction.

ndaba range

Merlot 🍴 🈂 ★★★ Mocha-tinted **11** offers sweet berry fruit on base of oaky tannins, good body & length. **hiraz** ⊕ 🍴 ★★★ Focused on enjoyment & texture, **10** tenders blackberry & earth, middling body & grip rom 5 months oak. **Jam Jar Sweet Shiraz** 🍴 🈂 ★★ Undemanding candy-sweet offering, **11** is true to ame. **Chardonnay** √ 🍴 🈂 ★★★★ Impressively poised & elegant **11** shows a tiny hint of oak, but mphasises ripe citrus fruit. **Chenin Blanc** ⊕ 🍴 🈂 ★★★ **11** fig & apricot zip, ideal zesty summer food pper. **Jam Jar Moscato** NEW 🍴 🈂 ★★ Spicy, low-alcohol **11** non-spritzy muscat for the sweeter tooth. **auvignon Blanc** 🍴 🈂 ★★★ Multi-regional **11** composition has a hint of sweetness. — GdB

■ **Cape Diamond** *see Lutzville Cape Diamond Vineyards*
■ **Cape Discovery** *see Waterstone Wines*
■ **Cape Diversity** *see Withington*

Cape Dreams

ocation/map/WO: Robertson ▪ Est/1stB 2009 ▪ Tasting & cellar tours by appt ▪ Owner(s) Bunty Khan ▪ Cellar-naster(s) André van Dyk ▪ 600ha (cab, merlot, ptage, shiraz, chard, chenin, sauv) ▪ 60% red 40% white ▪ ISO 001, HACCP, BEE, BWI ▪ croftsales@telkomsa.net, info@croftsales.co.za ▪ www.croftsales.co.za ▪ S 33° 46' 35. " E 019° 45' 42.9" ▪ **T +27 (0)21-531-2016, +27 (0)83-792-7638**

our years on, Cape Dreams wines are listed with local retailers Makro and Game, nd imported into (among others) Belarus, Finland, Singapore, Malaysia, China, Nigeria, Zimbabwe and Italy. The last surprised Bunty Khan, who has realised her dream of owning an own wine brand and supporting community upliftment pro-ects: 'I thought I was wasting my time there but the response was amazing.'

abernet Sauvignon 🈂 ★★★ Dinner companion **11**, ripe berry flavours lightly seasoned with vanilla rom combo oak barrels & staves (like all these reds). **Merlot** 🈂 ★★ Dusty plum fruit on stalky, lightish **11**. **inotage** 🈂 ★★★ **11** star in the line-up. Vanilla highlights, blackcurrant & strawberry perfume, dry & satis-ying. **Shiraz** 🈂 ★★★ 10's mix dark & red fruits, bright acidity for uncomplicated enjoyment. **Pinotage Rosé** 🍴 Await next. **Chardonnay** 🍴 🈂 ★★★ Unwooded **12** preview faint lemon & stonefruit, pleas-ntly soft for solo sipping. **Chenin Blanc** 🍴 Await next. **Sauvignon Blanc** 🈂 ★★ **12** crisp if brief appley avours, hint of sweetness in tail. — JP/CvZ

■ **Cape Elements** *see Nico van der Merwe Wines*
■ **Cape Grace** *see African Pride Wines*

Cape Hutton

ocation/map: Stellenbosch ▪ WO: Stellenbosch/Western Cape ▪ Est 2003 ▪ 1stB 2004 ▪ Tasting, sales & cellar ours by appt ▪ Deli & wine tasting 8-5 by appt (incl cheese, meats, jams & olives) ▪ Weddings/functions ▪)wner(s)/viticulturist(s) Gerrit & Lesley Wyma ▪ Winemaker(s) Piet Smal (cab), Wynand Hamman (sauv) & iilko Hegewisch (merlot) ▪ 4ha (cab, merlot) ▪ PO Box 2200 Somerset West 7129 ▪ lesley@capehutton.com ▪ vww.capehutton.com ▪ S 33° 58' 27.6" E 018° 51' 10.3" ▪ **T +27 (0)21-880-0527** ▪ F +27 (0)21-880-0666

ounded to indulge the wine passion of oral and maxillofacial surgeon Gerrit Wyma and wife Lesley, this Blaauwklippen Valley estate is taking advantage of ts location, offering wedding and corporate facilities in their brand-new func-ions venue. The wine continues to be made to order by handpicked winemakers.

★★★★ **Cabernet Sauvignon** Smooth, ripe & concentrated **09** reflects good vintage. Elegantly oaked, with subtle spices filling out healthy fruit profile.

auvignon Blanc √ 🍴 🈂 ★★★★ **11**, ex West Coast vines, intense, complex aromatic profile & steely lees ninerality. Fine expression of cool maritime climate. Step up from **09** (★★★). Discontinued: **Veri Beri**. — GdB

Capelands Estate

 NEW

Location: Somerset West • WO: Stellenbosch • Est 2004 • 1stB 2010 • Closed to public • Tasting at Capelands Restaurant available to patrons • Guest house • Owner(s) Capelands Estate (Pty) Ltd • Cellarmaster(s) Louis Nel (Feb 2010, consultant) • Viticulturist(s) Francois Hanekom (Feb 2009, consultant) • 12.5ha/2.5ha (cab) • 6t/400cs own label 100% red • 3 Old Sir Lowry's Pass Road Somerset West 7130 • restaurant@capelands.com • www.capelands.com • **T +27 (0)21-858-1477** • F +27 (0)86-299-3905

Johann Innerhofer and Laura Mauri's tiny walled vineyard near Somerset West has been something of a sleeping beauty waiting for a prince to bring it to life. Enter seasoned consultant Louis Nel, with a winemaking philosophy of 'expression of the vineyard' — balanced wine from old vines, no irrigation, early harvesting and no new oak — and voila! a very special result. The first wine only from the 15-year-old unirrigated domaine vines, it's being exported to Europe (though total output is a mere 400 cases). Next step is to 'take our product to the top of the market'.

★★★★☆ **Redstone** Impressive debut from 2.5ha 'clos' on vaunted Schapenberg. **10** from 85% cab, malbec; ripe blackcurrant, dried herbs & earth give way to firm but yielding tannins, fresh acidity, integrated oak. Harmonious & built to last 5+ years. — WB/IM

■ **Cape Nelson** see uniWines Vineyards

Capenheimer

South Africa's original perlé wine, launched in 1962. Made by Distell.

Capenheimer ▦ ★★ Lightish, off-dry, easy-sipping chenin & colombard blend with a tingle on the tongue to add interest. Widely sourced **NV**. — DB/HJ

■ **Cape of Good Hope** see Anthonij Rupert Wines
■ **Cape Orchards & Vineyards** see COAV
■ **Cape Original** see Origin Wine

Cape Point Vineyards

Location: Noordhoek • Map: Cape Peninsula • WO: Cape Point/Coastal/Western Cape • Est 1996 • 1stB 2000 • Tasting & sales Mon-Fri 9-5 Sat 10-5 Sun 10-4 • Fee R15-R60 • Closed Good Fri, Dec 25 & Jan 1 • Cheese/ antipasti platters available during tasting hours • Weddings & events • Picnics & sundowners • Nature trails & vineyard walks • Facilities for children • Farm produce • Conservation area • Owner(s) Sybrand van der Spuy • Cellarmaster(s) Duncan Savage (Dec 2002) • Winemaker(s) Duncan Savage (Dec 2002), with Jeremiah Mkhwanazi (Oct 2005) • Viticulturist(s) Duncan Savage (Dec 2002), with Hendri Burger (Sep 2010) • 22ha (chard, sauv, sem) • 8,000cs own label 100% white; Splattered Toad ±25,000cs + 2,000cs for clients • Brands for clients: Foodbarn Restaurant, Woolworths • BWI, IPW, Farming for the future • PO Box 100 Noordhoek 7985 • info@cape-point.com • www.capepointvineyards.co.za, www.splatteredtoad.co.za • S 34° 5'41.82" E 018° 22'17.28" • **T +27 (0)21-789-0900** • F +27 (0)21-789-0614

Talking extreme vineyards, here's a reality check from viticulturist/winemaker Duncan Savage: 'We nurse our vines back to health every year in the wind here!!!' Clearly this terroir on the southern extreme of the Cape Peninsula isn't for the faint of heart, but despite (because of?) its challenges, and the team's virtuosity, the wines to many have already achieved the goal implied in their narrowed focus on essentially four premium labels: 'When someone thinks of South African white wine, Cape Point Vineyards must be the first name that comes to mind.' To that end, they're happy to acknowledge the role of happenstance: 'For practical purposes, we have always aged in barrel for 10-11 months, but in 2011 we had a delay and ended up bottling some of the wines only after 14 months. The results are amazing! As human beings, we like to claim the glory but the best results come when we interfere the least.'

Cape Point Vineyards range

★★★★ **Chardonnay** 🌐 **11** already beguilingly rich & smooth. Ample tangerine & stonefruit tailored into fresher, sleeker form by limy acidity. Balanced & approachable but will improve for good few years.

★★★★☆ **Sauvignon Blanc Reserve** 🏅 Classy **11** continues fine form. More brioche & aromatics than ordinary version, with similar waxy nuance from dash of semillon. Seamless integration of fruit, acidity & oak — showing elegant restraint in youth.

★★★★ **Sauvignon Blanc** 🏅 **11** consistently refined, smooth textured from dab semillon & concentration ex low yields (as for all here). Clean-cut freshness, with the least oak of the range & structure for 3-5 years.

★★★★★ **CWG Auction Reserve White** NEW 🏅 Benefit of lowest yields (2.3t) evident in superlative **11**, 70% sauvignon, with semillon. Vivacious balance to generous stonefruit, with oak (20% new) & the semillon component adding a rich texture. Youthful bonhomie belies a profound wine deserving time to express itself.

★★★★☆ **Isliedh** 🏅 Acclaimed Bordeaux-style white blend more concentrated in **11** than **10**. Sauvignon's spicy melange of stonefruit & herb flavours enhanced by semillon (most ever — 30%) & new oak. As always, complexity, depth & balance for a rewarding future.

Splattered Toad range

Shiraz-Cabernet Sauvignon 🍷🏅 **11** tank sample still a tadpole, too young to rate. Sales of bottled version will help save Western Leopard Toad. WO Coastal. **Sauvignon Blanc** 🍷 🏅 ★★★ **12** crisp & tangy, crunchy apple tone for summer picnics. WO W Cape. — MW

■ **Cape Promise** *see* uniWines Vineyards

Cape Rock Wines

Location: Vredendal ▪ Map/WO: Olifants River ▪ Est 2001 ▪ 1stB 2002 ▪ Tasting, sales & cellar tours by appt ▪ closed Good Fri, Dec 25 & Jan 1 ▪ BYO picnic ▪ Owner(s) Willie Brand ▪ Cellarmaster(s) Willie Brand (Jan 2001) ▪ Winemaker(s) Willie Brand (Jan 2001) & Gavin Brand ▪ Viticulturist(s) Jeff Joubert (Jan 2001, consultant) ▪ 2ha/32ha (cab, grenache, merlot, mourv, ptage, roobernet, ruby cab, shiraz, chard, chenin, cbard, rouss, sauv, viog) ▪ 480t/250cs own label 75% red 25% white + 32,000 litres bulk ▪ PO Box 261 Vredendal 8160 ▪ caperockwines@gmail.com ▪ www.caperockwines.co.za ▪ S 31° 37′ 24.0″ E 018° 24′ 52.9″ ▪ **T +27 (0)27-213-2567** ▪ F +27 (0)27-213-5567

The father-and-son team of Willie and Gavin Brand are emerging as leaders of the Olifants River Valley's nascent fine-wine making movement, their increasingly Rhône-influenced varietal bottlings and (somewhat inscrutably named) blends improving by the vintage, while reflecting the ability to innovate. The new GRV, their first white wine listed in these pages, is a case in point: smart, flavourful and unusual within a broader South African context, let alone traditionally bulk/brandy focused Olifants River.

★★★★ **SMV** ⓧ Step-up **09**, shiraz, mourvèdre & viognier co-fermented, elegant & composed mid-2011, with good maturation potential.

★★★★ **GRV** NEW √ Waxy, lemon-toned **11**, sophisticated near-equal blend of grenache blanc, roussanne & viognier (36/33/31) kissed by older oak; leesy richness enlivened by zesty tail.

Cabernet Sauvignon ⓧ ★★ On review mid-2010, **09** needed year/2 to integrate, should be ready now. **Shiraz** √ 🍷 ★★★★ Satisfying, spicy & floral **11** is lightly oaked, fruit-filled for early enjoyment. **SGMV** ⓧ ★★★★ When last tasted, **08** was a characterful & expressive blend of shiraz, grenache, mourvèdre & viognier. **Capa Roca** New bottling not ready, as for **Red Shoe Cabernet Sauvignon-Ruby Cabernet**. — DB/CvZ

■ **Cape Roots** *see* Quest Wines
■ **Cape Sparrow** *see* TCB Wines
■ **Cape Style** *see* Paarl Wine Company

Cape to Cairo Wines

Location: Cape Town ▪ Map: Cape Peninsula ▪ WO: Breede River Valley ▪ Est 2007 ▪ 1stB 2008 ▪ Tasting by appt ▪ Owner(s) Trans-Scripto (Pty) Ltd ▪ Winemaker(s) Nico van der Merwe (consultant) & Jolene Calitz-Le Roux ▪ 3,500cs 100% red ▪ PO Box 1358 Cape Town 8000 ▪ info@capetocairo.net ▪ www.capetocairowines.com ▪ S 33° 56′ 29.06″ E 018° 23′ 47.76″ ▪ **T +27 (0)82-579-4849** ▪ F +27 (0)86-660-4323

The Cape to Cairo brand, with its distinctive packaging suggesting the mystique of Africa, is at the start of a significant growth phase after the owners concluded agreements with importers in various countries. Design changes are afoot to reflect the varying cultures in which the brand will be marketed, and 'concrete interest' is reported in shareholding and participation in the venture.

Syrah ① ★★★ Accessible **07**'s very ripe fruit wrapped in sweet oak, pleasing lingering savouriness. — KM/CvZ

■ **Cape Tranquility** see Pulpit Rock Winery
■ **Cape View** see Kaapzicht Wine Estate
■ **Cappupinoccinotage** see Boland Kelder
■ **Cap Vino** see Winkelshoek Wine Cellar

Carisbrooke Wines

Location/map/WO: Stellenbosch ▪ Est 1989 ▪ 1stB 1996 ▪ Tasting & sales Mon-Fri 10-2 ▪ Closed all pub hols ▪ Owner(s) Willem Pretorius ▪ Cellarmaster(s)/winemaker(s) Kowie du Toit (1997), Willem Pretorius ▪ Viticulturist(s) Kowie du Toit (1997) ▪ 19ha/6ha (cab, sem) ▪ 50t/400cs own label 100% red ▪ PO Box 25 Vlottenburg 7604 ▪ willem@carisbrooke.co.za ▪ C6 ▪ **T +27 (0)21-881-3798** ▪ F +27 (0)21-881-3796 / +27 (0)86-518-8767

The brand from lawyer-winegrower Willem Pretorius' Stellenboschkloof farm takes its name from the little train station of Carisbrooke, made famous by Alan Paton's masterpiece Cry, the Beloved Country.

Alan Paton Cabernet Sauvignon ▥ ★★★★ Seriously styled & elegant **10** savoury, spicy, with fine acid backbone & judicious oaking (75% new). — IM

■ **Carnival** see Orange River Wine Cellars
■ **Carpe Diem** see Diemersfontein Wines

Casa Mori

Location/map/WO: Stellenbosch ▪ Est 1995 ▪ 1stB 2009 ▪ Tasting, sales & tours by appt ▪ Meals/refreshments by appt ▪ Farm produce ▪ Conferences/functions ▪ Artichoke festival ▪ Owner(s) Eugene Mori ▪ Cellarmaster(s)/viticulturist(s) Bruno Julian Mori (1997) ▪ Winemaker(s) Bruno Julian Mori (1997), with Mori family ▪ 4.4ha/2.3ha (cab, malbec, sangio, shiraz, viog) ▪ 5-8t/200cs own label 97% red 1% white 2% rosé ▪ Other export label: Mori ▪ PO Box 71 Koelenhof 7605 ▪ mori.wines@gmail.com, casamori@mweb.co.za ▪ www.casamori.co.za ▪ S 33° 53' 15.28" E 018° 48' 27.64" ▪ **T +27 (0)83-620-0016** ▪ F +27 (0)86-625-0080

At the Mori family's boutique winery in Stellenbosch, wine and food are inseparable, so cellarmaster Bruno Julian Mori's plans include: a sangiovese-based blend called Pietro after his great-grandfather; adding olives to the bountiful artichoke crop; and bottling red wine vinegar put in barrel over 30 years ago by his father: 'It's so old, it's lost its colour, but tastes fantastic!'

Bruno ① ★★★★ Unfiltered **NV** combo sangiovese/cab (78/22) elegant & dry, attractive polished leather nuance, firm food-pairing tannins. — CvZ

■ **Casual Collection** see Bernheim Wines

Catch Of The Day

Location: Cape Town ▪ WO: Stellenbosch/Paarl ▪ Closed to public ▪ Owner(s) Cuniscar Vintners cc t/a Rainbow Nation Wines ▪ PO Box 44852 Claremont 7735 ▪ kc5@pixie.co.za ▪ www.rainbownationwines.com ▪ **T +27 (0)21-671-6024/+27 (0)82-577-1608** ▪ F +27 (0)21-671-6036

As far as these Cape Town-based negociants for the restaurant trade are concerned, the way forward is deposit-based, returnable, lightweight bottles transported in re-usable plastic crates — and not only because it's green. 'By passing our dry goods cost savings onto the restaurants, our prices are currently lower than they were in 2008,' reveals managing member Keith Cronwright.

Cabernet Sauvignon NEW ▥ ★★★★ Robust **09**, firm red berry flavours perfect for winter stews or fireside contemplation. **Shiraz** ▥ ★★★ Toasty dark berry fruit, satisfying palate weight on easy-drinking **09** pizza partner. WO Paarl. **Chenin Blanc** Await new vintage. **Sauvignon Blanc** ① ▥ ★★★ Fresh & lively **11**, attractive perfumes & crisp apple aftertaste. — DB

■ **Cathedral Cellar** see KWV Wines

Catherine Marshall Wines

Location: Elgin ▪ Map: Elgin, Walker Bay & Bot River ▪ WO: Elgin/Swartland ▪ Est/1stB 1997 ▪ Tasting, sales & cellar tours by appt ▪ Closed Easter Fri-Sun, Dec 25 & Jan 1 ▪ Meals/refreshments by appt ▪ Owner(s) Cathy Marshall, Greg Mitchell, Jonathan Oxenham & Jeff Jolly ▪ Cellarmaster(s) Catherine Marshall (Oct 1996) ▪ Winemaker(s) Shawn Fortuin (Jan 2010) ▪ Viticulturist(s) Various ▪ 40-50t/3,000cs own label 60% red 35% white 5% fortified ▪ IPW ▪ PO Box 30913 Tokai 7966 ▪ cathy@cmwines.co.za ▪ www.cmwines.co.za ▪ S 34° 10' .7" E 019° 0' 29.8" ▪ **T +27 (0)83-258-1307** ▪ F +27 (0)86-523-7479

Pinot noir has always been Catherine Marshall's first love, and she found a 2012 visit to top Burgundy domaines motivating. 'The passion for pinot displayed by those vignerons has inspired me to push the envelope of fruit purity even more', she enthuses; 'to find this great variety's energy and the true expression of vines grown in soils not tainted by antibiotic-type chemicals.' To this end, she is turning over the pinot vineyard at her Valley Farm base in Elgin to biodynamics, planning 'a special bottling attributing soil specifics'.

★★★★ **Pinot Noir** 🍴 **11** a favourite vintage of Marshall's, notable for its fragrance, fruit purity, delicate freshness, silky mouthfeel & enough of each to charm over several years.

★★★★ **Pinot Noir 6 Barrels Reserve** ⏺ **10** more introvert, viscous than regular version. Earthy notes, oak spice temper palate's brighter cherry flavours but ends distinctly savoury. Worth few years ageing.

★★★★ **SMG** ⏺ Shiraz-led, homogenous trio (with mourvèdre, grenache). **09** shows freshness, purity associated with range. Ripe but unhealthy; tasty savoury thread grows to expansive finish. WO Swartland.

★★★★ **Sauvignon Blanc** ⏺ 🍴 Tasted just post-bottling in 2010, **11** captures Elgin's poise, minerality. Has weight to balance vivacity without spoiling fruit purity, length. **10** (★★★★) from Durbanville less balanced.

Imatra Merlot 🍴 🈵 ★★★★ Adds name for Persian storage vessel as from charming & gently persuasive **11** (no **10**). Fragrant & juicily fresh red plums with merest hint of forming grip. **Myriad** ⏺ ★★★★ Unheavy, lean fortified merlot/pinot; 3 years older oak. **07** showed toffee, nut tones a few years back. — AL

▪ **CCC Wines** see Bonnievale Cellar

Cecilia Wines

Location: Klawer ▪ Map: Olifants River ▪ WO: Western Cape ▪ Est 2010 ▪ 1stB 2007 ▪ Tasting by appt ▪ Owner(s) Cerina van Niekerk ▪ Cellarmaster(s)/winemaker(s) Cerina van Niekerk (2007) ▪ 2t/125cs own label 100% red ▪ PO Box 23 Trawal 8147 ▪ cecilia@mylan.co.za ▪ www.ceciliawines.co.za ▪ S 31° 51'32.16" E 018° 36' 13.37" ▪ **+27 (0)82-334-9422** ▪ F +27 (0)86-617-0101

Named after the patron of music, Cecilia is Klawer Cellars winemaker and trained concert pianist Cerina van Niekerk's own label, and the embodiment of her dream of vinifying exceptional wine, interweaving it with music and thereby offering 'a unique wine experience'. Dreams, Cerina soberly observes, require effort, time and money, and are realised in the fulness of time. The 2012 vintage of her red blend, still incubating at press time, is 'heading in the right direction'. Next steps include label/packaging design, and, hopefully, local community participation.

Shiraz-Mourvèdre ⏺ ★★★★ Last edition, previewed **11** lost its malbec component & was very ripe but balanced, not warming like last **06** (★★★★), with oak in supporting role. — DB/CvZ

▪ **Cecil John** see Boschendal Wines

Cederberg Private Cellar

Location: Citrusdal ▪ Map: Olifants River ▪ WO: Cederberg/Elim ▪ Est 1973 ▪ 1stB 1977 ▪ Tasting Mon-Sat 8–12; 2–4.30 pub hols 9–11.30; 4-5.30 Fee R20 ▪ Closed Easter Fri/Sun, Dec 25 & Jan 1 ▪ Sales Mon-Sat 8-12.30; 2-5 Sun/pub hols 9-12; 4-6 ▪ BYO picnic ▪ Sanddrif Holiday Resort self-catering cottages; camping ▪ Walks/hikes ▪ Mountain biking ▪ Conservation area ▪ Rock climbing ▪ Sport climbing ▪ Observatory ▪ Owner(s) Nieuwoudt family ▪ Cellarmaster(s) David Nieuwoudt (Jan 1997) ▪ Winemaker(s) David Nieuwoudt (Jan 1997), with Alex Nel & Tammy Turck (Aug 2011) ▪ Viticulturist(s) Ernst Nieuwoudt (Jan 1960) ▪ 5,500ha/53ha (cab, shiraz, bukettraube, chenin, sauv) ▪ 480t/26,000cs own label 50% red 50% white ▪ PO Box 84 Clanwilliam 8135 ▪ info@cederbergwine.com ▪ www.cederbergwine.com ▪ S 32° 30'12.8" E 019° 15'27.7" ▪ **T +27 (0)27-482-2827** ▪ F +27 (0)86-531-0491

The Nieuwoudt family vineyards qualify for 'extreme' status in many respects: remote (in the Cederberg Wilderness Area some 150 km from Cape Town), high (their mountain location among the loftiest in the Cape) and, given the extremely rocky terroir, fiendishly difficult to establish. 'Site preparation included not just the moving of boulders and rocks, but also collecting soil for each vine,' says co-owner and cellarmaster David Nieuwoudt. They are now reaping the rewards of this arduous endeavour, however: the vines are thriving and acclaim keeps coming in from around the world. The cellar is being expanded to cope with increased production of mainly sauvignon and chenin. A new tasting room and barrel storage area are next. And look out for a 'cool-climate Pinot Noir, New World style'.

Five Generations range

★★★★ **Cabernet Sauvignon** 🔲 **10** (★★★★★) rises above **09** with sweet ripe black cherry fruit, dried herbs, whiff of tobacco. Impressive structure, lush & harmonious, with intense fruit concentration. Plenty of ripe tannin to give body & grip. A wine with personality.

★★★★ **Chenin Blanc** ⊕ 🔲 🔲 **10** (★★★★★) even finer than **09**. Richer, rounder than standard version, with floral complexity to the tropical notes, well supported by sensitive oaking (which adds a little nuttiness). Clean, dry & elegantly balanced, with a lovely ripple of fresh acidity.

David Nieuwoudt Ghost Corner range

★★★★ **Sauvignon Blanc** 🔲 🔲 This pair from Elim. **12** is steely, with a distinct mineral edge, dusty & complex with mouthfilling racy grapefruit & lime flavours. Lush & rounded with great depth on the finish.

★★★★ **Semillon** 🔲 **11** (★★★★★) easily outdoes **10** (★★★★) & **09** with a peacock's tail of aromas: crushed stone, dusty green capsicum, grass with a hint of smoke & sea breeze. Well-judged oak fills out the palate. Elegant & harmonious now & for several years.

Cederberg Private Cellar range

★★★★ **Cabernet Sauvignon** 🔲 Youthful **10** shows sweet ripe fruit & vanilla oak. Supple & mouthfilling, with a firm tannin bite & same build as premium version, a little more approachable in youth.

★★★★☆ **CWG Auction Reserve Teen die Hoog Shiraz** 🔲 Knockout **10** (★★★★★) is ripe fruited with concentrated flavours, impressive chewy structure. Big, but well balanced, with a superb flavour complexity. Persistent firm dry finish. It has depth to age for those who can wait. **09** also impressive.

★★★★ **Shiraz** 🔲 Big, ripe, black-fruited **10** is generous & juicy for lovers of fruit-driven style. Serious & rounded, with vanilla oak spice balancing luscious fruit.

★★★★ **Sauvignon Blanc** 🔲 🔲 Racy lime & orchard fruit flavours on **12**. More fruity than Elim partner. Generously textured & elegant with palate-saturating citrus finish.

★★★★ **Blanc de Blancs** MCC sparkling from chardonnay in extra-dry style. Mature biscuity notes from 4 years on lees mingle with citrus & baked apple aromas on fresh **07**; creamy texture, moderate depth & length.

Merlot-Shiraz ✓ 🔲 ★★★★ **10** is fresh & savoury with intense spicy fruit flavours. Oaking rounds off good structure. **Sustainable Rosé** ✓ 🔲 🔲 ★★★★ Charming candyfloss pink **12** from shiraz raises the bar with perfumed ripe strawberry & spice flavours. Light, dry & fruity — perfect for the patio. **Bukettraube** 🔲 🔲 ★★★ Fragrant Turkish Delight on **12**, charms with semi-sweet mouthfilling flavours yet finishes dry. Begs for Cape Malay curries. **Chenin Blanc** ✓ 🔲 🔲 ★★★★ **12** is serious & more layered than **11** (★★★★). Intense tropical flavours are bright & focused, with mouthwatering succulence. Good cool-climate expression. — WB

Celestina   [NEW]

Location: Gansbaai ▪ WO: Cape Agulhas ▪ Est 2004 ▪ 1stB 2009 ▪ Closed to public ▪ Owner(s) Caroline Rillema ▪ Winemaker(s) Dirk Human (Black Oystercatcher) ▪ Viticulturist(s) Caroline Rillema & Ray Kilian ▪ 3.4ha/1.85ha (sauv, sem) ▪ 1t/46cs own label 100% white ▪ c/o Caroline's Fine Wine Cellar, Shop 44, Matador Centre, 62 Strand Street, Cape Town 8001 ▪ carowine2@mweb.co.za ▪ **T +27 (0)21-419-8984** ▪ F +27 (0)21-419-8985

Over three decades Caroline Rillema has built up a classy Cape Town wine merchant business, but has always wanted her own vineyard small enough to be managed over weekends. On a cool, scenic ±3ha slice of land at Baardskeerdersbos near Gansbaai, she and partner Ray Kilian planted sauvignon blanc and semillon, vinified by Dirk Human of Black Oystercatcher. Caroline's 'over the moon' with the elegance, typicity and minerality of the result noting poetically, that the 'white diamonds' which might form in the unfiltered and fined wine are harmless.

★★★★ **Sauvignon Blanc-Semillon** Barrel-fermented **11** 60/40 blend beautifully restrained & mineral, overlain with gunflint & white flowers; taut & focused — perfect dinner companion. — WB/IM

Cellar Cask

South Africa's first bag-in-box, launched in 1979, styled by Distell to meet rising demand for Natural Sweet wines with lower alcohol levels.

Select Johannisberger Rosé ★★ Sweet, bright & friendly **NV**, dollops ruby cab, shiraz & merlot for colour. Widely sourced, as all these. **Select Johannisberger White** ★ Delicate raisiny fruit flavours for the sweet toothed. **NV** from mainly chenin & colombard. **Select Johannisberger Red** ★ Contrasting sweet-savoury combo in latest **NV**, chiefly shiraz, merlot & ruby cab. Lightish ±11.5% alcohol for all these. — DB/HJ

Chabivin Champagne & MCC House

Location/map: Stellenbosch ▪ WO: Breedekloof/Franschhoek/Western Cape ▪ Est 2008 ▪ Tasting & sales Tue-Fri 9-5 Sat 10-4 ▪ Fee R30/3 MCC, R100/4 Champagnes ▪ Light lunches/platters & refreshments ▪ Winemaker(s)/viticulturist(s) Hendrik Snyman ▪ 3ha/0.4ha (pinot, chard) ▪ ±8t/±620cs own label 100% MCC ▪ PO Box 12456 Die Boord Stellenbosch 7613 ▪ info@chabivin.co.za ▪ www.chabivin.co.za ▪ S 33°58'24. 27" E 018°51'8.17" ▪ **T +27 (0)21-880-1643** ▪ F +27 (0)86-540-6237

Schooled in the Cape, seasoned in Napa, Marlborough and Mareuil-sur-Aÿ, Hendrik Snyman has joined Jean-Pierre and Brigitte Charbaut of the eponymous Reims champagne house (where he was welcomed as a 'foreign son' in 2007) in converting a garden cottage and 'small chaotic forest' in Stellenbosch into a postage stamp vineyard, maturation cellar, and tasting, lunching and live music venue, dedicated to their bottle-fermented bubblies: fledgling Chabivin Diary and Signature Series, a future 'estate' MCC and imported Champagnes Guy Charbaut.

Diary Series

★★★★ **Mademoiselle Mégane** Perfectly poised **NV** cap classique from chardonnay, attractive savoury & biscuit tones, steely 'oystershell' minerality from Breedekloof limestone soil. Classy special occasions celebrator.

★★★★ **Adémée 05** traditional-method dry sparkler from Franschhoek semillon, distinctive varietal characteristics of hay, green citrus & lively acidity. Impressive length, texture add to appeal. Ideal partner for oysters.

Cuvée Jean-Michel ★★★★ Classic champagne blend (pinot noir, chardonnay 50/50), but unusual (attractive) pineapple/baked lime hints. **07** touch more evolved than siblings, for earlier drinking (no hardship!). — HJ/JP

Charles Fox Cap Classique Wines

Location: Elgin ▪ Map: Elgin, Walker Bay & Bot River ▪ Est 2007 ▪ 1stB 2010 ▪ Tasting, sales & cellar tours Mon-Thu by appt Fri 12-5 Sat 10-5 Sun 11-4 ▪ Fee R50 ▪ Closed Easter Fri/Sun, Dec 25/26 & Jan 1 ▪ Play area for children ▪ Owner(s) Charles & Zelda Fox ▪ Cellarmaster(s) Charles Fox (2010) ▪ Winemaker(s) Nicolas Follet (2010, consultant) ▪ Viticulturist(s) Kevin Watt (2008, consultant) ▪ 33.4ha/6.3ha (pinot meunier, pinot, chard) ▪ 480cs (2010)/ 1,680cs (2011) own label 100% MCC ▪ PO Box 105 Elgin 7180 ▪ charlesfoxmcc@gmail.com ▪ www.charlesfox.co. za ▪ S 34° 14' 14.38" E 019° 04' 41.99" ▪ **T +27 (0)21-300-1065** ▪ F +27 (0)86-536-2924

Charles and Zelda Fox left Johannesburg big city life in 2005 for 'a better lifestyle for us and our children'. They found it in Elgin on an old fruit farm they renamed Furneaux (after Charles' mother). They've been guided by 'the soils and climate'

(and adviser Kevin Watt) to plant some 6ha of champagne varieties. Cape-base
Champenois Nicolas Follet consults. Small maiden disgorgements end 2012 will b
doubled this year, gradually increased production eventually allowing for exports.

Chateau Beau Belle

Location/map/WO: Stellenbosch ▪ Est 2009 ▪ 1stB 2010 ▪ Tasting, sales & cellar tours by appt Mon-Fri 8-5
weekends by special arrangement ▪ Closed Ash Wed, Easter Fri-Sun, Ascension day, Pentecost, Dec 25/26
Jan 1 ▪ Meals/refreshments for groups of 10-50 by arrangement ▪ Olive oil ▪ BYO picnic ▪ Mountain biking tra
▪ Weddings ▪ Chapel ▪ Self-catering guest cottage (max 4 people) ▪ Owner(s) Lindeque Family Trust ▪ Direc
tors Tienie & Estelle Lindeque ▪ Cellarmaster(s) Johann Visagie (Apr 2009) ▪ Winemaker(s) Johann Visagi
(Mar 2009) ▪ Viticulturist(s) Johann Visagie (Mar 2009) & Tienie Lindeque, advised by Johan Pienaar (consul
tant) ▪ 36ha/23ha (shiraz) ▪ 208t/750cs own label 77% red 23% rosé + 125,000 L bulk ▪ PO Box 15
Lynedoch Stellenbosch 7603 ▪ tienie@beaubelle.co.za ▪ www.beaubelle.co.za ▪ S 33° 59′ 47.30″ E 018° 4(
45.69″ ▪ **T +27 (0)21-881-3808** ▪ F +27 (0)86-670-6720

After 30 years of hard work in Gauteng, Tienie Lindeque decided to move his famil
to the Western Cape. A wine enthusiast for many years, it was long a dream to ow
a farm and in 2008 he acquired 36ha of vineyard in Stellenbosch. All buildings o
the property have been built from scratch, the main house in the style of a Frenc
château completed in 2011 and set to become a landmark for the Lynedoch area.

Shiraz ★★ Pleasantly lean **10** easy-sipper with smoke, tar & meaty notes; only older (3rd fill) oak
Reserve Shiraz ★★★ Riper & more extracted than regular bottling, **10** has similar savoury over
tones; portion younger oak (some 2nd fill) showing in coconut sweetness, slight astringency. **Pink**
★★ Baked plum & confectionery nuances on sweetish **11** rosé from shiraz. — HJ/JP

Chateau Libertas

Among South Africa's longest-established red blends, available every year sinc
1932 and still a paragon of value and drinkability. By Distell.

Chateau Libertas ☺ ★★★ Reliable & consistent mix of Bordeaux grapes plus shiraz & ruby cab. **11** touch
more serious but still very easy to like, attractive freshness to the dark fruit flavours. WO W Cape. — DB/HJ

Chateau Naudé Wine Creation

Location: Stellenbosch ▪ WO: Wellington/Stellenbosch/Bot River ▪ Est 2006 ▪ 1stB 2007 ▪ Closed to public
Owner(s) Francois Naudé snr, Magda Naudé, Francois Naudé jnr, Melissa Naudé ▪ Cellarmaster(s) Francoi
Naudé (Jul 2007) ▪ 520cs own label 65% red 35% white ▪ 11 Weidenhof Street Stellenbosch 7600 ▪ naude@
levindefrancois.co.za ▪ www.levindefrancois.com ▪ **T +27 (0)21-883-8469** ▪ F +27 (0)86-651-3192

It's not everyone who has the pick of several crops for their pinotage, but that'
the good fortune of Francois Naudé, who consults to a number of top producer
as well as running his Stellenbosch-based family concern. Since 2007, with Vi
de Francois, he has been pursuing his quest for 'the ultimate wine of a specifi
vintage; something unique, exclusive and with a touch of magic!' In 2010 ('trick
in the vineyard, great in the cellar') he selected 10 barrels, from six producers i
Stellenbosch and one in Bot River. Sold only on the Naudé family's annual auc
tion, the 2010 went for an enviable R1,200 a bottle.

Chateau Naudé Wine Creation range
★★★★☆ **Le Vin de François** 100% pinotage, from 7 Stellenbosch & Bot River producers. Less concen
trated **10** (★★★★), though it still tips evident 15% alcohol. Very ripe mulberries & plums with a touch c
jamminess; tannins well managed to allow for current drinking. Doesn't have the legs or substance of sleek **09**.

The Wingnut range
★★★★ **Cabernet Sauvignon** Classic style & vintage; **09**'s (★★★★★) cedary, black berry fragrance offer
instant appeal but tannin armour is serious enough to warn 'hands off' for year/2; will reward with deliciou
savoury harmony to ripe flesh beneath. **08** was a lighter vintage. Stellenbosch WO, like next.
Chardonnay ★★★★ Intense **10**'s upfront lemon-cream; oak spice features held by very zesty acid; sweetis
close. **Chenin Blanc Barrel Fermented** NEW ★★★★ Just-dry **11** fermented in larger oak for spice & extr

weight but not to overshadow the quiet mineral-edged fruit. A little one-dimensional mid-2012, has substance to grow. WO Wellington. **White Port** ① ★★★ Fruity, sweetish lightly oaked **10** from chenin.

Nuts About range

Shiraz ★★★★ Naudé's deft touch evident in previewed **11**. Medium body, fresh ripe fruit, tempered tannins suggest good medium-term drinking. WO Wellington. **Chenin Blanc** ✓ 🍽 ★★★★ Unshowy yet persuasive **11** from Wellington; cool, clean lines, complementary textural bounce, smooth yet long close. — AL

■ **Chatta Box** see Distell

Chennells Wines

Location: Somerset West ▪ Map: Helderberg ▪ WO: Stellenbosch/Western Cape ▪ Est 2004 ▪ 1stB 2008 ▪ Tasting, sales & cellar tours by appt Mon-Sun 9-5 ▪ Closed all pub hols ▪ Owner(s) Jeremy & Colleen Chennells ▪ Cellarmaster(s)/winemaker(s) Chris Keet (Jul 2009, consultant) & Jeremy Chennells ▪ Viticulturist(s) Chris Keet (Jul 2009, consultant) & Colleen Chennells ▪ 5ha/3.2ha (cab, shiraz, viog) ▪ 26t/230cs own label 85% red 15% white ▪ Romond Vineyards, Klein Helderberg Road, Somerset West 7130 ▪ chennell@iafrica.com ▪ S 34° 1' 52.61" E 018° 49' 59.67" ▪ **T +27 (0)21-855-3905** ▪ F +27 (0)21-683-6280

In 2003 Jeremy and Colleen Chennells decided to replace their smallholding's unproductive fruit trees with vines. Their journey of soil analysis and preparation, planting and nurturing of vines and making wines that express their philosophy of vivimus vivamos (whilst we live, let us truly live), has been 'truly fulfilling'; the care and support of 'mentors and coaches' like neighbour Helderberg winegrower André Liebenberg (Romond Vineyards) and consultant viticulturist/winemaker Chris Keet (Keets Wines), 'humbling'. It's an experience they'd love to share.

Cabernet Sauvignon 🖾 ★★★★ Bold & robust **10** aims for seriousness in riper vintage, achieves good concentration of savoury dark berry fruit, supportive acid backbone & firm dry tannins; 15% alcohol obvious in youth, though, might integrate in time. **Shiraz** 🖾 ★★★ Ripe black berries & spice, some earthiness & tobacco on **10**, otherwise attractive wine somewhat unbalanced by 15% alcohol. WO W Cape. **Viognier** 🖾 ★★★ Classic varietal traits of fresh peach, apricot pip & flowers on older oak fermented **11**, tasty savoury flavours with food-friendly pithy grip & laudably modest 13.5% alcohol. — WB/IM

■ **Chris Keet** see Keets Wines
■ **Christina Van Loveren** see Van Loveren Family Vineyards
■ **Christine-Marié** see Niel Joubert Estate
■ **Cilliers Cellars** see Stellendrift — SHZ Cilliers/Kuün Wyne
■ **Circumstance** see Waterkloof

Cirrus Wines

Location/map/WO: Stellenbosch ▪ Est/1stB 2003 ▪ Tasting & sales at Guardian Peak (see entry) ▪ Owner(s) Jean Engelbrecht & Ray Duncan ▪ Cellarmaster(s)/winemaker(s) Coenie Snyman (Jun 2010) ▪ Viticulturist(s) Dirkie Mouton (Jun 2010) ▪ 5t/280cs own label 100% red ▪ IPW ▪ PO Box 473 Stellenbosch 7599 ▪ info@cirruswines.com ▪ www.cirruswines.com ▪ S 34° 0' 44.31" E 018° 50' 33.22" ▪ **T +27 (0)21-881-3899** ▪ F +27 (0)21-881-3000

2013 marks the decade milestone of this transcontinental joint venture between the owner of Silver Oaks Cellars in California, Ray Duncan, and Jean Engelbrecht of Stellenbosch's Rust en Vrede. With its larger-than-life American styling garnering plaudits locally and abroad, there are plans for a second wine produced Stateside.

★★★★ **Cirrus Syrah** ① Opulent & polished **09**'s super-ripe fruit intensity holds the oak (60% new) & high alcohol (15.5%) with savoury aplomb, has dab viognier for extra perfume. — MF

■ **Citrusdal Wines** see Six Hats

CK Wines

Location/WO: Stellenbosch ▪ Est 2009 ▪ 1stB 2010 ▪ Tasting by appt ▪ Fee R50 ▪ Sales via Personal Wines T +27 (0)21-552-6280, sales@baypointtrading.co.za ▪ Owner(s)/cellarmaster(s)/winemaker(s) Christian Kuun ▪ 300cs own label 100% red ▪ gumbootkuun@hotmail.com ▪ **T +27 (0)82-615-8105** ▪ F +27 (0)86-671-3363

A self-confessed 'bushveld boykie' from Polokwane, Christian Kuun was bitten by the grape bug after his first ever wine tasting just weeks after starting stock farming studies at Elsenburg College. He changed direction and never looked back. Also cellarmaster at Beau Joubert near Stellenbosch, Christian says production — and sales — of his own brand doubled last year. 'We can't keep up.'

Sincera NEW ★★★★ Appealing rich cocoa & oodles of succulent black fruit on pre-bottling **11**, 100% cab franc. Yielding & plush textured; harmonious oaking with long star anise & liquorice finish. **Integra** ★★★★ Switches from varietal cab to 60/40 blend cab & cab franc in **10**, goes up notch on **09** (★★★★). Rich & ripe yet gently soft, heaps of cassis flavour, lovely mouthfeel & balance. Structured & elegantly long. — FM

Claime d'Or

Location: Robertson ▪ WO: Robertson/Western Cape ▪ Est/1stB 2008 ▪ Tasting & sales at Rietvallei Wine Estate (see entry) ▪ Owner(s) Magriet de Wet & Bernardo Rapoport ▪ Cellarmaster(s)/winemaker(s) Kobus Burger (2002, Rietvallei) ▪ Viticulturist(s) Wilhelm Treurnicht (2007, Rietvallei) ▪ 10ha (cabs s/f, sauv) ▪ 30% red 60% white 10% rosé ▪ PO Box 2040 Parklands 2121 ▪ info@claimedorwines.co.za ▪ www.claimedorwines.co.za ▪ **T +27 (0)23-626-3596/+27 (0)82-444-5473/+27 (0)82-567-5197** ▪ F +27 (0)23-626-4514/+27 (0)11-788-7346

'The pride and satisfaction we get from consumers who do research on our wines and where they can get their hands on some is unbelievable!' say Bernardo Rapoport and Magriet de Wet, owners of this Robertson boutique venture, where production remains limited and each bottle is numbered to convey its exclusivity.

★★★★ **Cabernet Franc** Perfumed **09** attractive dark fruit, supple tannin; same vibrant acid balance & fruit-filled conclusion as delightful chocolate-berry laden **08**.

★★★★ **Cabernet Sauvignon-Cabernet Franc** Initially shy, **09** opens up to reveal black berries, subtle oak spice. Like herbal **08**, suave, smooth & finely structured for contemplative sipping or cellaring a few years. **Shiraz** NEW ★★★★ Succulent **10** has peppery top notes, friendly tannins & sweet-sour persistence. Great with a steak. **Cabernet Sauvignon Rosé** ⊛ 🍴 ★★★ Floral berry aromas & flavours on dry & savoury **11**. **Chardonnay** NEW 🍴 ⌀ ★★★ Oak aromas/flavours dominate **11** mid-2012, needs year/2 to harmonise with lemon-lime fruit. **Sauvignon Blanc** 🍴 ★★★★ Previewed last edition, **11** now less effusive but still crisp & gravelly, with long mineral finish. WO W Cape. — CvZ/MW

Clairvaux Private Cellar

Location/map/WO: Robertson ▪ Est/1stB 2000 ▪ Tasting & sales Mon-Fri 8-5 ▪ Closed all pub hols ▪ Cellar tours by appt ▪ BYO picnic ▪ Sales (at cellar price) also from La Verne Wine Boutique Mon-Thu 9-5.30 Fri 9-6 Sat 9-5 ▪ Owner(s) Wouter J de Wet snr & jnr ▪ Cellarmaster(s) Jaco van der Merwe (Oct 2011) ▪ Winemaker(s) Jaco van der Merwe (Oct 2011), with Coenraad Groenewald (Jan 2010) ▪ 200ha (cab, merlot, ptage, shiraz, chard, chenin, cbard, muscadel, sauv) ▪ 4,000t/3.2m L bulk ▪ PO Box 179 Robertson 6705 ▪ appelsdrift@lando.co.za ▪ www.clairvauxcellar.co.za ▪ S 33° 48' 13.8" E 019° 52' 21.1" ▪ **T +27 (0)23-626-3842** ▪ F +27 (0)23-626-1925

This Robertson family winery produces mainly bulk wine while emphasising accessibility (in both style and packaging — the shiraz and cab now also under screwcap) under its own label. Last year newcomer Jaco van der Merwe was grateful for Coenraad Groenewald's seasoned hands during the 'biggest harvest ever'.

Cabernet Sauvignon 🍴 ★★★ A poster for the variety, step-up **10** drinks early & well. **Shiraz** 🍴 ★★ Prunes & lilies on quick-sip **10**. **Sauvignon Blanc** 🍴 ★★ Nettly **12** fresh & tangy, with sweet & sour acid bite. **Good Night Irene** ⊛ ★★★ Fortified fireside charmer from hanepoot. **10** honey & full-ripe raisins lifted by zesty citrus. **Red Muscadel** NEW ✓ ★★★★ **10** fortified dessert a happy marriage of raspberry cordial richness & brandy-spirit bite, spicy top notes, appealing tannin grip. **Madonna's Kisses Golden Muscadel** ⊛ ★★★ Fortified white muscadel, **10** bursts with uncomplicated sunny sweetness. **Port** ⊛ ★★★ Ruby cab stars in step-up **07**, savoury nuance to dark chocolate & brandy pudding flavours. Discontinued: **Sandberg Purple, Chardonnay, Appelsdrift Dry White, Soleil, Rosé**. — JP/CvZ

Cloof Wine Estate

Location/WO: Darling ▪ Map: Durbanville, Philadelphia & Darling ▪ Est/1stB 1998 ▪ Tasting & sales Mon-Sat 10–4 ▪ Closed Easter Fri-Sun, Dec 25 & Jan 1 ▪ Cellar tours by appt ▪ Meals/refreshments Tue-Sat 10-3 ▪ Farm produce ▪ Conservation area ▪ Game & eco drives by appt ▪ Owner(s) Cloof Wine Estate (Pty) Ltd ▪

Winemaker(s) Christopher van Dieren (Jan 2002), with Frederick Kalumpie (Apr 1999) ▪ Viticulturist(s) Peter Duckitt (May 2004) ▪ 1,300ha/166ha (cabs s/f, cinsaut, merlot, ptage, shiraz, chard, chenin, viog) ▪ 600t/50,000cs own label 88% red 12% white ▪ BWI champion ▪ PO Box 269 Darling 7345 ▪ info@cloof.co.za ▪ www.cloof.co.za ▪ S 33° 28' 58.1" E 018° 31' 23.4" ▪ **T +27 (0)22-492-2839** ▪ F +27 (0)22-492-3261

The cellar has been enlarged and new tanks installed to cope with increased production volumes. Hosting the Rocking the Daisies festival, now in its 7th year, this Darling property entertains in excess of 15,000 music fans annually and, thanks to a philosophy of sustainable farming, garners many eco awards in the process. A wedding venue, lunches at Cloof Kitchen, game drives and accommodation are available to visitors in conjunction with sister and neighbour farm Burgherspost.

Cloof range

★★★★☆ **Crucible Shiraz** ⊕ 06 (★★★★) last impressed with peppery dark fruit, prosciutto layers but was less harmonious than concentrated 04; no 05.

★★★★ **Lynchpin** ⊕ Named for vital cab franc role in merlot-led blend: 29% in last-tasted 06. Interesting sipper, should be showing well now.

Cab Cult Cabernet Sauvignon ⊕ ★★★ Bright cassis, juicy blackberry, smoky oak on smooth & easy-drinking 09. **The Very Posh Pinotage** ⊕ ★★★ 09 offers juicy plums, spice & chocolate notes, mouthfilling & silky with perky smoky end. Good everyday drinking. **Cellar Blend** ⊕ 🍽 ★★★ All-sorts red blend from press juice in preview 09; dark, brooding berries, chunky dried finish; extracted fruit needs hearty food. **Inkspot Vin Noir** ⊕ 🍽 ★★★★ Ever-popular pinotage, shiraz, cinsaut mix, 09 delights with succulent plums, fresh berries & vanilla oak conclusion. **The Dark Side Cabernet Sauvignon-Shiraz** ⊕ 🍽 ★★★★ Smoke-infused 08 nicely structured: fleshy, rich black berry fruit, smooth entry, firm finish. Appealing savoury tone. **Rosy Darling** 🍽 Next awaited. **Happy Dragon Chenin** ⊕ ★★★ Gentle apple & marzipan on friendly 10 picnic sipper. **40 Days Natural Sweet** ⊕ 🍽 ★★★★ Previously noted as exuding barley sugar, peach & lime, barrel-aged 09's richness lifted by tangy acidity. Discontinued: **Kalumpie & Co.**

Fancy range

★★★★ **Duckitt Cabernet Sauvignon-Merlot-Cabernet Franc** ✓ 09 well crafted, cedar infused from serious oaking. Just off-dry with a lovely freshness. Harmonious tannins should support 6+ years ageing.

Summertime Sauvignon Blanc ☺ 🍽 🖼 ★★★ Funky packaging a feature of breezy 12, tropical fruity, zippy & fresh beach sipper.

Pinotage ✓ ★★★☆ 10 from Darling bushvines is mouthfilling & rounded. Deep, dark chocolate-dipped plums with a savoury end. Balanced & smooth. **The Very Sexy Shiraz** ✓ 🍽 🖼 ★★★★ Succulent 10 packed with sweet spicy black fruit, dusted with fynbos, pepper & vanilla. Needs time for tannins to meld. **The Very Vivacious Viognier** ⊕ ★★★ Fragrant peach & apricot intermingle with creamy vanilla on part-oaked off-dry 11. All these previously in Cloof range.

Darling range

Ruby Darling ☺ 🍽 🖼 ★★★ Was 'Happy Dragon Pinotage-Shiraz'. Same varieties, unoaked, in easy-sipping 11. Plummy, with good grip. **Daisy Darling Chardonnay** NEW ☺ 🍽 🖼 ★★★ Crunchy apple & floral notes & bright acidity on cheeky 12. **Daisy Darling** ☺ 🍽 🖼 ★★★ Varieties no longer identified in name but chenin & sauvignon still the partners in bouncy 12 summer's day delight: tropical fruit, zippy acidity, dry tail. All except Chardonnay previously in Cloof range. — WB

Clos Malverne

Location/map: Stellenbosch ▪ WO: Stellenbosch/Western Cape ▪ Est/1stB 1986 ▪ Tasting & sales Mon-Sat 10–5 Sun 10-4.30 ▪ Fee R25/4 wines ▪ Closed Good Fri, Dec 25 & Jan 1 ▪ Cellar tours Mon-Fri ▪ The Restaurant @ Clos Malverne (see Restaurants section) ▪ Tour groups ▪ Gifts ▪ Farm produce ▪ Conferences ▪ Weddings/functions ▪ Walks/hikes ▪ Wellness Day Spa ▪ Owner(s) Seymour & Sophia Pritchard ▪ Cellarmaster(s)/viticulturist(s) Suzanne Coetzee (Oct 2010) ▪ Winemaker(s) Suzanne Coetzee (Oct 2010), with Mynardt Hitchcock (1999) ▪ 27ha/18ha (cab, ptage, sauv) ▪ ±200t/40,000cs own label 50% red 50% white ▪ PO Box 187 Stellenbosch 7599 ▪ info@closmalverne.co.za ▪ www.closmalverne.co.za; www.capeblend.co.za ▪ S 33° 54' 38.0" E 018° 48' 49.2" ▪ **T +27 (0)21-865-2022** ▪ F +27 (0)21-865-2518

Pinotage remains this Devon Valley family wine farm's strong suit — but the whole visitor experience is a strong one, too. The restaurant is now sheltered from the elements by frameless glass, and the food-and-wine pairing menus along with the wine-and ice-cream combos have been a hit, says cellarmaster Suzanne Coetzee, as has the new sauvignon bubbly, already the second-biggest seller off the farm.

Clos Malverne range

★★★★ **Pinotage Reserve** 🕸 Lovely balance of ripeness & dark intensity on **10**, with 10% cab. Layers of cherry & plum flavour with dry fine tannin. Complex & firm.

★★★★ **Auret** 🕸 Pioneer Cape Blend in **10** retains soft mouthfeel & silky refinement of **09**. Textured, dense, stratified concentration to classy & elegant 4-way blend of cab, pinotage, merlot & shiraz.

★★★★ **Auret Limited Release** ⏱ Small-production reserve release, **08** (similar ratios to sibling) shows little more weight, lots more oaky spiciness. Hard to justify extra cost, but honest effort to raise bar.

Merlot 🕸 ★★★★ **10** has dense dark fruit & wonderful length. Rich & structured but with velvet texture & spicy highlights. **Le Café Pinotage** 🕸 ★★★ Popular mocha style doesn't overwhelm varietal typicity of **11**, fruity & soft but appealingly so. **Cabernet Sauvignon-Merlot** 🕸 ★★★★ Chalky grip to **10**'s 60/40 mix, tarry density to layered cassis-filled palate. Balanced & supple, harmonious to end. **Cabernet Sauvignon-Shiraz** 🕸 ★★★ On paper & in glass cab leads 60/40 mix but shiraz offers spicy grip on step-up **10**, softly chunky with rich long tail. **Chardonnay** 🍷 🕸 ★★★★ Tangerine zestiness mingles with leesy roundness, **11** is creamy & medium bodied but also refined & framed in light oak. WO W Cape. **Sauvignon Blanc** 🍷 🕸 ★★★★ Flinty grass with tropical granadilla lift, **11** is juicy but gains breadth from lees-ageing. **Sauvignon Blanc Brut** NEW ★★★ Broad crisp grapefruit tang on **NV** sparkler. Acidity a touch spiky but adds succulence, freshness & verve to the bubbles.

Devonet range
Merlot-Pinotage Await new vintage. — FM

Clouds Wine Estate 🍷 🏠 📷

Location/map/WO: Stellenbosch ▪ Est/1stB 1993 ▪ Tasting & sales Mon-Sat 10-5 ▪ Fee R10 ▪ Closed Dec 25 & Jan 1 ▪ Breakfast, lunch & dinner by appt for non residents/visitors ▪ Clouds Wine & Guest Estate self-catering chalets (see Accommodation section) ▪ Conferences ▪ Weddings & functions ▪ Owner(s) Paul Burema & Jolanda van Haperen ▪ Cellarmaster(s) Neil Moorhouse (Jan 2010, Zorgvliet) ▪ Winemaker(s) Neil Moorhouse (Jan 2010, Zorgvliet), with Paul Burema (Jan 2012) ▪ Viticulturist(s) Wynand Pienaar (Aug 2009, consultant) ▪ 4.5ha/2.7 ha (cab, sauv, chard) ▪ 24t/1,250cs own label 100% white ▪ PO Box 540 Stellenbosch 7599 ▪ info@cloudsestate.co.za ▪ www.cloudsestate.co.za ▪ S 33°55'23.9" E 018°55'29.7" ▪ **T +27 (0)21-885-1819** ▪ F +27 (0)21-885-2829

A new broom is sweeping clean at this guest house and winery near the summit of Helshoogte Pass. After changing hands in January 2012, an extensive modernisation was undertaken — and it didn't only involve the accommodation: two hectares of sauvignon blanc made way for cab and chardonnay to broaden the range.

Clouds Vineyards range

★★★★ **Sauvignon Blanc** 🍷 Punch of intense lemon, fig & gravel on **12**, showing focused structure & lively concentration, & good minerality on long aftertaste.

Pink Sauvignon Blanc ☺ 🍷 ★★★ Grapefruit zip of **12** preview fleshed out by dab shiraz, adding rounded sour plum note. Light & undemanding but fresh. — FM

Clovelly Wines

Location/map/WO: Stellenbosch ▪ Est/1stB 2000 ▪ Tasting, sales & tours strictly by appt ▪ Owner(s) York Partnership t/a Clovelly Wines ▪ Winemaker(s)/viticulturist(s) Jacques Fourie ▪ 4ha/3ha (cab) ▪ 90% red 10% white ▪ Postnet Suite 215 Private Bag X5061 Stellenbosch 7599 ▪ info@clovellywines.com ▪ www.clovellywines.com ▪ S 33° 53'54.1" E 018° 47'52.3" ▪ **T +27 (0)82-853-7190** ▪ F +27 (0)21-865-2511

Jacques Fourie is the ever-thoughtful winemaker on this Devon Valley family farm. Facing absurd prices for wine (some too low, given production costs; some too high, given what winelovers can afford), rules and regulations, the high costs of competitions etc — he can still say: 'I work in a wonderful industry!'

★★★★ **Cabernet Sauvignon** ⏱ Full-bodied **08** boasts blackcurrant, toasty oak & scorched earth. Impressive & concentrated, plush & rounded with ripe tannins, but the acidity is rather marked.

Patina Shiraz ⓟ ★★★★ **05** dense & brooding. Like others below, tasted a few years back. **The Three Sides Vineyard Blend** ⓟ ★★★★ Firm, tasty **05** cab, merlot, shiraz blend has concentrated fruit & characterful rusticity, with a warming finish. Last was lean **NV (★★★)**. **Chardonnay** Not tasted. —JPf

Cloverfield Private Cellar

Location/map/WO: Robertson ▪ Est 1945 ▪ 1stB 2002 ▪ Tasting & sales Mon-Fri 9-5 ▪ Closed Easter Fri-Mon, Dec 25 & Jan 1 ▪ Owner(s)/viticulturist(s) Pieter Marais ▪ Cellarmaster(s) Cobus Marais (2002) ▪ Winemaker(s) Cobus Marais (2002), with Gerald Smith (Jun 2009) ▪ ±200ha total (shiraz, chard, chenin, sauv) ▪ 40% red 60% white ▪ PO Box 429 Robertson 6705 ▪ info@cloverfield.co.za ▪ www.cloverfield.co.za ▪ S 33° 49′57.3" E 019° 55′34.1" ▪ **T +27 (0)23-626-4118** ▪ F +27 (0)23-626-3203

Family history has an honoured place for the much-loved Irish lass — honoured in the winery branding and the name of the Shamrock Red — who bore Cloverfield patriarch Pietie Marais three sons and brought hope, love as well as luck to the Robertson farm.

Winemaker Selection

Shiraz ⓟ ★★★ Smoke & red fruit, pleasant firm tannin grip on satisfying **09**. **Chardonnay Wooded** 🍴 🖻 ★★★ Subtle vanilla spice on muted **12**, sweet-fruit finish, less focused & concentrated than previous.

Vineyard Selection

> **Chardonnay Unwooded** ☺ 🍴 🖻 ★★★ Tropical-toned **12** zesty & fresh pear drop & melon taste, understated — but no quibbles at the price!

Shamrock Red 🍴 ★★ Oak-brushed three-way blend, **NV** glugger is budget priced & light in all respects, as most here. **Chenin Blanc** 🍴 🖻 ★★★ Thatchy rather than fruity, **12** satisfies & seems dry despite sprinkle of sugar. **Sauvignon Blanc** 🍴 🖻 ★★ Slimmer's friend **12** is light in both alcohol & sugar. —CvZ/MW

▪ **Coast** see PicardiRebel

COAV

Location/WO: Elgin ▪ Map: Elgin, Walker Bay & Bot River ▪ Est 2005 ▪ 1stB 2009 ▪ Open by appt ▪ Owner(s) James & Mark Simpson, James Craven ▪ Cellarmaster(s)/winemaker(s) Joris van Almenkerk (consultant) ▪ Viticulturist(s) Hannes Louw (Jun 2005) ▪ 165ha/11ha (cab, shiraz, sauv) ▪ 36t/1,000cs own label 100% white + 1,000cs for clients ▪ Viljoenshoop Road 50, Elgin Valley 7180 ▪ james@thecravens.co.za ▪ www.coav.co.za ▪ S 34° 14′14.08" E 019° 00′00" ▪ **T +27 (0)82-801-8811** ▪ F +27 (0)21-683-0776

James Craven, co-owner of COAV (Cape Orchards & Vineyards) is perplexed by the local predisposition to drink sauvignon blanc young. 'Elgin is a cool climate which means our wines have the ability to improve in bottle.' Even so, he's fully aware of the commercial imperative to give customers what they want, and to that end he intends skipping the 2012 vintage and moving straight on to 2013.

Sauvignon Blanc 🍴 ★★★ **11** plenty of cool-climate character with notes of asparagus & greenpepper. Juicy, with well integrated acidity. —CE

▪ **Cocoa Hill** see Dornier Wines
▪ **Coded** see Babylon's Peak Private Cellar
▪ **Cogmanskloof** see Zandvliet Wine Estate & Thoroughbred Stud

Cold Duck (5th Avenue)

Enduring, sweet, low-alcohol carbonated sparkling brand owned by Distell.

5th Avenue Cold Duck ★★ Strawberry richness in new **NV** version of charming sparkling rosé. Light, sweet, but really well balanced, so it's not cloying. Grapes (including pinotage for colour) widely sourced. —DB/HJ

▪ **Cold Mountain** see Brunia Wines
▪ **Collaboration** see Louis

Colmant Cap Classique & Champagne

Location/map: Franschhoek ▪ WO: Western Cape ▪ Est 2005 ▪ 1stB 2006 ▪ Tasting & cellar tours daily by appt ▪ Fee R10 per ½ glass MCC ▪ Sales Mon-Fri 9-4.30 Sat 10.30-1 ▪ Owner(s) Jean-Philippe & Isabelle Colmant ▪ Cellarmaster(s) Jean-Philippe Colmant ▪ Viticulturist(s) Paul Wallace (consultant) ▪ 5ha/3ha (pinot, chard), 3,400cs own label 100% MCC ▪ PO Box 602 Franschhoek 7690 ▪ info@colmant.co.za ▪ www.colmant.co.za ▪ S 33°55'22.4" E 019°7'37.3" ▪ **T +27 (0)21-876-4348/+27 (0)72-368-4942** ▪ F +27 (0)21-876-3732

Late 2012 saw the turn of the decade since Jean-Philippe and Isabelle Colmant 'landed in unknown territories from our native Belgium, with luggage, five children and a passion for bubbly...' Now, drawing on grapes from their own tiny vineyard as well as from other regions, they have one of the Cape's few wineries totally focused on making sparkling wine in the classic manner from the classic varieties. Intent on quality above all, they have not (yet) made any vintage wines, preferring to blend in reserves from previous years. The wines are then kept for unusually long periods on their lees before disgorging, which adds to their finesse and subtle richness of flavour. The quality, and value for money, are remarkable.

★★★★ **Brut Rosé** Pale pink with a gleam of copper, this refined NV from chardonnay & pinot has the most obvious charm of these sparklers, with its richness & customary raspberry & baked bread notes.

★★★★☆ **Brut Reserve** ✓ Superbly elegant, a touch more expressive, generous than the Brut Chardonnay, with a hint of red fruit to the riper citrus & green apple notes. Long, long silky finish. Current NV as usual blends pinot & chardonnay, with 25% from previous vintages; 32 months on lees.

★★★★☆ **Brut Chardonnay** ✓ Few locals achieve such finesse, in the current NV again combined with a subtle lime-lemon deliciousness holding it back from the fine austerity of its stony penetration. Brioche aromas point to 45 months maturation; 8% from earlier vintages. Very dry & serious, but lovely. — TJ

■ **Commonwealth** see Origin Wine
■ **Compagnies Wijn** see Oude Compagnies Post Private Cellar
■ **Condé** see Stark-Condé Wines

Conradie Family Vineyards

Location/map: Worcester ▪ WO: Nuy/Western Cape ▪ Est/1stB 2004 ▪ Tasting, sales & cellar tours Mon-Fri 9-5 Sat 9-3 Sun 11-2; after-hours by appt ▪ Closed Good Fri, Ascension Day, Dec 25 & Jan 1 ▪ Nuy Vallei Restaurant & Guest House: meals daily 8-5, or by appt ▪ Facilities for children ▪ Tour groups ▪ Gift shop ▪ Farm produce ▪ BYO picnic ▪ Conferences ▪ Walks/hikes ▪ Mountain biking & 4x4 trails ▪ Conservation area ▪ Annual Nuy Valley Feast (May) ▪ Owner(s) Conradie family ▪ Cellarmaster(s) CP Conradie (Jan 2004) ▪ Winemaker(s) CP Conradie (Jan 2004), Colin Cilliers (Jan 2004) & Ronwan Griffiths (Sep 2009) ▪ Viticulturist(s) Riaan Lambrechts (Aug 2011) ▪ 4,500ha/83ha (cab, ptage, chenin, cbard, crouchen, muscadel w, pinot gris, sauv) ▪ 1,840t total 70t/2,700cs own label 50% red 25% white 25% rosé ▪ BWI ▪ PO Box 5298 Worcester 6851 ▪ wine@conradievineyards.co.za ▪ www.conradie-vineyards.co.za ▪ S 33°39'28.0" E 019°37'59.6" ▪ **T +27 (0)23-342-7025** ▪ F +27 (0)86-509-4911

Winemaking sister Elsabé having married, CP Conradie — of the family which has farmed in Worcester's Nuy Valley for generations — is now working in the cellar full-time, aided by Colin Cilliers and Ronwan Griffiths. At time of writing, the assistants were finalists in a contest offering a prize of six weeks internship in France.

Sweet Rosaline Perlé Rosé ☺ 🍴 📖 ★★★ Refreshing limy tang adds to the fun in petillant NV party starter, from sauvignon, pinotage & muscadel.

Single Vineyard Barrel Selection Reserve Cabernet Sauvignon 🍷 ★★★★ Step-up 11 lighter textured & fresher, firm tannins provide counterpoint to sweet plump fruit. WO W Cape. **Single Vineyard Barrel Selection Reserve Pinotage** ✓ 🍷 ★★★★ 11 continues upward path set by last-tasted 09 (★★★★); latest has similar banana/acetone notes but not the overripe fruit. Quintessential pinotage — will please the variety's fans. 10 sold out untasted. **Pinotage-Cabernet Sauvignon** 🍴 ★★★ Sweet & uncomplicated 11, lightish sipper with brief farewell. **Single Vineyard Chardonnay** ⊕ 🍴 🍷 ★★★ 10 well-judged coconut oak, slightly warm tail & sweet impression. **Sauvignon Blanc** ✓ 🍴 🍷 ★★★★ Tropical-toned 12 preview bright & balanced, easy-drinking with food or solo. — HJ/CvZ

Conspirare

Location: Somerset West ▪ Map: Helderberg ▪ Est/1stB 2002 ▪ Tasting by appt ▪ Owner(s) HB Dowling/LRD Trust ▪ Winemaker(s) Henry Dowling ▪ Viticulturist(s) Francois de Villiers ▪ 24ha (cab s/f, merlot, shiraz, cherain) ▪ 250t/425cs own label 100% red ▪ PO Box 1210 Stellenbosch 7599 ▪ dowls@mweb.co.za ▪ S 34° 1' 18.4" E 018° 50' 54.6" ▪ **T +27 (0)21-855-0706** ▪ F +27 (0)86-516-3086

Boutique winemaker Henry Dowling hasn't vinified his blended red Conspirare ('Breathing Together') in several years, but the 02 is still available from the farm in the Helderberg heights.

Constantia de Tulbagh

Location/map/WO: Tulbagh ▪ Est 1965 ▪ 1stB 2000 ▪ Tasting, sales & tours by appt ▪ Closed all pub hols ▪ Owner(s) Lucas J van Tonder ▪ Cellarmaster(s) Theo Brink (Jan 2008) ▪ Winemaker(s) Theo Brink (Jan 2008), with Niël Russouw (Dec 2011) ▪ Viticulturist(s) Theo Brink (Jan 2008), Niël Russouw (Dec 2011) ▪ 330ha/35ha (cab, merlot, pinot, chenin, riesling, sauv) ▪ 3–5,000cs own label 20% red 80% white ▪ PO Box 79 Tulbagh 6820 ▪ montpellier@montpellier.co.za ▪ www.montpellier.co.za ▪ S 33° 17' 21.3" E 019° 6' 30.7" ▪ **T +27 (0)23-230-0656** ▪ F +27 (0)23-230-1574

Since its purchase in 2004 by Montpellier's Lucas van Tonder, the emphasis at neighbour farm Constantia de Tulbagh has been on raising quality standards in the vineyards, and results are now coming through — Constantia wine is once more in barrel and a Bordeaux blend is promised in the very near future.

Cabernet Sauvignon ⓟ ★★★★ When last tasted, **04** showed integrated toasty aromas, dark berries, firm but yielding tannins. — GbB

Constantia Glen

Location/WO: Constantia ▪ Map: Cape Peninsula ▪ Est 2000 ▪ 1stB 2005 ▪ Tasting & sales Mon-Fri 10-5 Sat/Sun 10-4 ▪ Fee R30, waived on purchase ▪ Closed Good Fri & Dec 25 ▪ Coffee & hot chocolate R15/cup; cheese & charcuterie platters; various soups during winter ▪ Owner(s) Tumado Investments (Pty) Ltd ▪ Winemaker(s) Justin van Wyk (Dec 2011) ▪ Viticulturist(s) Andrew Teubes (consultant) ▪ 60ha/28.5ha (cabs s/f, malbec, merlot, p verdot, sauv, sem) ▪ 160t/10,000cs own label 70% red 30% white ▪ PO Box 780 Constantia 7848 ▪ wine@constantiaglen.com ▪ www.constantiaglen.com ▪ S 34°0'39.6" E 018° 24'30.6" ▪ **T +27 (0)21-795-6100** ▪ F +27 (0)21-795-6101

Originally part of Simon van der Stel's Constantia farm, the portion now called Constantia Glen was covered by forest or grazed by cattle before the Waibel family joined it to the valley's great tradition of winegrowing in 2000. Thanks to the longer sunlight hours at this northern end of the valley, their favourite Bordeaux-style wines, both white and red, flourish. With the help of consultant Dominique Hebrard from Bordeaux, every year sees a better understanding of how each vineyard block performs and into which blend it best fits. The wines' names, Two, Three and Five, are less complicated: 'Consumers asked for the wine with three or five varieties, which gave us the idea,' explains winemaker Justin van Wyk; 'this also allows us to focus on our brand name.'

★★★★☆ **Constantia Glen Five** ⓟ Used to just bear estate name. New one, with **08**, refers to Bordeaux quintet make-up. Deep, spice-laden fragrance sets classy tone for this sleek, cab franc-led blend. Ample sweet flesh, complexities need further 4-6 years to emerge from vibrant, taut structure.

★★★★☆ **Constantia Glen Three** ✓ More precision, greater character in **09**. Merlot-led (41%), as were previous, but fresher, more enticingly fragrant; its ripe flavours balanced, bolstered by cab & cab franc's succulent tannins. Polished with 100% new French oak. Deserves 5-8 years.

★★★★☆ **Sauvignon Blanc 11** reverts to usual bracing style after riper, more gentle **10** (★★★★). Aromatically appealing: fresh Granny Smith apples with tangerine peel & textural extras from drop semillon. Deep, long flavours; incisively dry. Lovely potential.

★★★★ **Constantia Glen Two** NEW Harmonious 60:40 sauvignon-semillon combo joins ranks of area's signature white blend style. **11**'s classic restraint, vinosity, well-judged oak, structure & freshness augur well. — AL

Constantia Mist

Location/WO: Constantia ▪ Map: Cape Peninsula ▪ Est 2004 ▪ 1stB 2009 ▪ Tasting by appt only ▪ Fee R30 ▪ Sales daily 10–5 ▪ Closed Good Fri & Dec 25 ▪ BYO picnic ▪ 4-star guest house (self-catering) ▪ Owner(s) Eagles Nest Property Investments (Pty) Ltd ▪ Cellarmaster(s) John Schooling (2009) ▪ Winemaker(s) Karl Lambour (2009 & 2010 vintages), with Justin van Wyk ▪ Viticulturist(s) Alan Cockroft (2009) ▪ 6.6ha/2.8ha (sauv) ▪ 6t/ha 560cs own label 100% white ▪ Postnet Suite 96, Private Bag X16, Constantia 7848 ▪ johns@stagprop.com ▪ www.constantiamist. co.za ▪ S 34° 1'0.48" E 018° 24'58.32" ▪ T +27 (0)21-794-0904 ▪ F +27 (0)21-794-4123

Pressure of work means John Schooling has for now halted production of this tiny Constantia property's only wine. Grapes from the 'high quality' 2012 harvest were sold to a local winery. In the meantime, the 2010 is still available from the farm.

★★★★☆ **Sauvignon Blanc** Ⓟ Riper tropical profile on **10** (★★★★), misreported as **11** last time. Bone-dry & bracing, with some toasty lees extras, but it lacks the intensity & length of **09**. — AL

Constantia Uitsig

Location/WO: Constantia ▪ Map: Cape Peninsula ▪ Est 1980 ▪ 1stB 1988 ▪ Tasting Mon–Fri 9–5 Sat/Sun & pub hols 10–5 ▪ Fee R25 ▪ Closed Good Fri, Dec 25/26 & Jan 1 ▪ Wine Shop: cheese platters, deli items, gifts ▪ Hanepoot grapes sold annually ▪ Tour groups ▪ Conferences ▪ Horse livery facilities ▪ Cricket oval ▪ La Colombe, Constantia Uitsig Restaurant & The River Café (see Restaurants section) ▪ Constantia Uitsig Country Hotel & Spa (see Accommodation section) ▪ Owner(s) Constantia Uitsig Wine Estate (Pty) Limited ▪ Cellarmaster(s) JD Pretorius ▪ Winemaker(s) André Rousseau (2003) & JD Pretorius ▪ Viticulturist(s) André Rousseau (1997) ▪ 60ha/32ha (cabs s/f, merlot, chard, Muscat d'A, sauv, sem) ▪ 120t/10,000cs own label 10% red 90% white ▪ WIETA ▪ PO Box 32 Constantia 7848 ▪ marketingmanager@uitsig.co.za, andre@uitsig.co.za ▪ www. constantia-uitsig.com ▪ S 34° 2'51.9" E 018° 25'27.5" ▪ T +27 (0)21-794-6500 ▪ F +27 (0)21-794-7605

André Rousseau joined Constantia Uitsig as viticulturist in 1997 and took on joint winemaking responsibilities in 2003. He counts the production of a Bordeaux-style white blend and a méthode cap classique from 100% chardonnay, the former made for the first time in 2003 and the latter in 2005, as 'a life dream realised' but really all of the wines during his tenure have been of a consistently high quality, perhaps because he lives out the mantra that 'quality starts in the vineyards' more than most. This is a property known first and foremost for its whites and chardonnay fans should look out for the return of a wooded version to the range later this year.

★★★★ **Constantia Red** Merlot-driven Bordeaux blend, **09** shows ripe dark fruit, notable oak character. Big & textured, doesn't have quite the elegance of **07** (★★★★★). **08** sold out untasted.

★★★★ **Sauvignon Blanc** 🖿 🖾 Immaculate **12** (★★★★★) is pure & poised, has great fruit intensity without being heavy. Broad range of flavours including subtle fynbos, bellpepper & green melon. Bright but by no means sharp acidity. Even more class than **11**.

★★★★ **Constantia White** 🖿 🖾 Carefully assembled **11** (★★★★★) has weight from 60% barrel-fermented semillon, freshness from 40% sauvignon. Rich but not unctuous, again a wide spectrum of flavour, acidity well integrated. Has real substance while retaining balance & finesse. Hangs together better than **10**.

★★★★ **Méthode Cap Classique** **09** (★★★★) from chardonnay, clean & fresh with ultra-fine mousse bright acidity. Appears light bodied, with sherbet-like sensation in the mouth. Not as rounded aa **08**.

★★★★☆ **Red Muscat d'Alexandrie** Ⓟ Irresistible fortified dessert from 40 year old block of rare-in-Cape red hanepoot. Current incarnation (**NV** blend of 2008, 2010 & 2011) relatively light body but intense red fruit & spice flavour. Even more wow-factor than previous bottling.

Chardonnay Unwooded 🖿 🖾 ★★★★ Subtle, refined **12** is medium bodied with moderate acidity. Slight citrus character but more about texture. Lacks intensity of **11** (★★★★). **Semillon** 🖿 🖾 ★★★★ Typically requiring a few years to unfold, **11** very tight on tasting. Subtle tangerine & green melon notes plus vanilla. — CE

▪ **Constitution Road** *see* Robertson Winery

Conviction

Location: Somerset West ▪ WO: Elgin ▪ Est/1stB 2009 ▪ Closed to public ▪ Winemaker(s) Clive Torr & David Brown, with Anne Howell ▪ 10ha ▪ 50cs ▪ 26 Topaz Street Heldervue 7130 ▪ clivetorr@bigfoot.com ▪ T +27 (0)82-557-0826

David Brown, now de facto winemaker, takes Elgin grapes to Romond in the Helderberg and there makes wines 'to be consumed, not collected'. Partner Clive Torr says he's found Elgin's best site for ripening cab — ripe enough to translate into higher alcohol, in fact. 'It is what it is,' he shrugs.

★★★★☆ **Cabernet Sauvignon** 🏼 🖉 Temptingly ripe, perfumed, sweet berry fruit in abundance amongst silky smooth tannins, **11** back on form after **10** (★★★★). Deliciously drinkable now but has depth to age; higher alcohol fits snugly into this Elgin cab, managing to retain elegance. — IM

■　**Cool Bay** *see* Boplaas Family Vineyards
■　**Coral Reef** *see* Wineways Marketing

Corder Family Wines

Location/WO: Elgin ▪ Map: Elgin, Walker Bay & Bot River ▪ Est 2003 ▪ 1stB 2007 ▪ Tasting & sales Mon-Fri 9-2 Sat/Sun by appt ▪ Closed all pub hols ▪ Owner(s) Ian & Anette Corder ▪ Cellarmaster(s)/winemaker(s) Joris van Almenkerk (Mar 2010) ▪ Viticulturist(s) Kevin Watt (2004) ▪ 40ha/14ha (pinot, shiraz, chard, sauv) ▪ 90t ▪ own label 20% red 80% white ▪ PO Box 169 Elgin 7180 ▪ ian@corderwines.co.za ▪ www.corderwines.co.za ▪ S 34° 12'8.10" E 019° 0'47.46" ▪ **T +27 (0)21-846-8083** ▪ F +27 (0)21-846-8460

Co-owner Ian Corder last year decided to change the name from Elgin Valley Vineyards to Corder Family Wines due to confusion with other Elgin brands. An advertising man, Corder knows the value of a good yarn and will soon launch a new line called Poor Corder, recalling his great-great-grandfather, a central character in the notorious Suffolk 'red barn' murder and subsequent public hanging in 1828.

Corder Family Wines range

★★★★☆ **Corder Barrel Crafted Viognier** ⓧ 🏼 Simply 'Viognier' last time. Peach & hint of spice, **10** preview (★★★) is creamy but lacks intensity & freshness of last **08**.

Corder Special Reserve Shiraz 🏼 Await new vintage. **Cool Climate Sauvignon Blanc** ✓ 🏼 🖉 ★★★★ Gets 'Cool Climate' prefix in distinguished **11**, huge step up on **10** (★★★). Great intensity, balance, length. Lime, yellow apple, honey, some herbal bite on finish & all this at only 12.5% alcohol. Tantalising acidity, good texture thanks in part to 6% semillon.

Lorry range

Red Lorry Easy Red 🏼 ★★★ From shiraz, this bottling of NV big improvement on previous. Uncomplicated but appealing black cherry fruit, good freshness. **Yellow Lorry Sauvignon Blanc** 🏼 🖉 ★★ Now bottled, **11** sweet, otherwise simple & short. — CE

■　**Country Cellars** *see* Orange River Wine Cellars
■　**Couple's Wine** *see* Bergheim

Craighall

These easy-drinkers by African Wines & Spirits have been perennial favourites and stalwarts since 1994, and the chardonnay/sauvignon blanc was one of the first such blends in South Africa.

Chardonnay-Sauvignon Blanc ☺ 🏼 ★★★ Brand on cusp of 20th birthday in **12** still delivers juicy lime quaffability gussied up with feather brush of oak.

Cabernet Sauvignon-Merlot 🏼 ★★ Plummy, fruity **11**, undemanding everyday red. **Sauvignon Blanc** 🏼 ★★ Light & dry **12** summer quaffer. WO W Cape for all. — JP

Cranefields Wine

Location/map: Villiersdorp ▪ WO: Overberg ▪ Est/1st B 1995 ▪ Tasting by appt only ▪ Owner(s) SJ Greve & CJ Roux ▪ Winemaker(s) Riaan Wassüng (Jan 2005, consultant) ▪ Viticulturist(s) Charl Roux (Feb 1998) ▪ 35ha (cab, merlot, shiraz) ▪ 220t/3,000cs own label 100% red ▪ PO Box 417 Villiersdorp 6846 ▪ info@cranefields.com ▪ www.cranefields.com ▪ S 34° 2'45.99" E 019°13'59.64" ▪ **T +27 (0)28-840-2565** ▪ F +27 (0)28-840-0440

Vinification (by Riaan Wassüng) has moved to Villiersdorp Cellar, but this brand continues to celebrate South Africa's national bird, the Blue Crane, at home in the Overberg wine district. Co-founder and viticulturist Charl Roux has 'loved these hills since boyhood', marketing their beauty and bounty overseas too (Hamburg-based merchant Siegfried Greve is co-owner).

Cabernet Sauvignon ★★ 07 true to variety with blackberry fruit, juicy acidity, but straightforward flavours don't linger. **Merlot ★★ 07** food wine has a herbal character with perhaps too much freshness. **Shiraz ★★** Ripe, savoury & very fresh **07** needs drinking soonest. **Red Bishop ★★** Cab-led blend with dollop shiraz, drop merlot, **07** misses harmony of previous vintage. — WB/IM

Creation Wines

Location: Hermanus ▪ Map: Elgin, Walker Bay & Bot River ▪ WO: Walker Bay ▪ Est 2002 ▪ 1stB 2006 ▪ Tasting, sales & cellar tours daily 10-5 ▪ Closed Dec 25 & Jan 1 ▪ Lunch: wine & canapés; secret food & wine pairing; 'éclat de chocolat' pairing ▪ Kiddies menu & designated play area ▪ Tour groups ▪ Wine accessories, books & souvenirs on sale ▪ Walking/hiking trails ▪ Conservation area ▪ Art exhibition (paintings & sculptures) ▪ Events: blend your own bottle; barrel/true terroir tasting; vineyard safari on foot; regular musical performances & themed cultural events ▪ Owner(s) Jean-Claude & Carolyn Martin ▪ Cellarmaster(s) Jean-Claude Martin (Jan 2006) ▪ Winemaker(s) Jean-Claude Martin (Jan 2006), with Werner du Plessis (Jan 2012) ▪ Viticulturist(s) Jean-Claude Martin & Peter Davison (consultant), advised by Johan Pienaar (all 2002) ▪ 35ha (cab, grenache, merlot, p verdot, pinot, shiraz, chard, sauv, sem, viog) ▪ 220t/18,000cs own label 65% red 35% white ▪ BWI, IPW ▪ PO Box 1772 Hermanus 7200 ▪ info@creationwines.com ▪ www.creationwines.com ▪ S 34° 19'51.90" E 019° 19'35.53" ▪ **T** +27 (0)28-212-1107 ▪ F +27 (0)28-212-1127

Just over a decade ago Carolyn Martin and her Swiss winemaker husband Jean-Claude found their ideal tract of virgin land in the Hemel-en-Aarde area, and with enviable vision and acumen set about developing its potential. The phrase 'not resting on laurels' gets new meaning here, as the marketing and cellardoor trend setters keep adding to an already irresistible visitor offering — latest attraction being walks through the vineyards and fynbos to admire the biodiversity and natural beauty. For the less physically inclined, hands-on blending sessions have joined the oh-so-tasty food-and-wine pairings... Which all explains why more chairs had to be bought for the tasting room!

★★★★ **Merlot** ⏱ 📖 **10** (★★★★☆) ratchets the bar higher still, improving on **09**. Rich, rounded & restrained, it's pure black-fruit elegance. Succulent & integrated, with structure to last for 5+ years.

★★★★ **Pinot Noir** 📖 **11** tangy cranberry vibrancy highlights earthy char notes. Silky & poised but with concentration & power. Elegant.

★★★★☆ **Pinot Noir Reserve** 📖 Similar specs to standard version, slightly more new oak (30%) in second-vintage **11**. Initially shy, grows in stature to a big, perfumed musk & earthy mouthful. Abundant forest fruit & smoky notes with elegance, purity & succulent generosity. Beautiful satiny finish that goes on & on.

★★★★ **Syrah** ⏱ 📖 Soft black berry fruit with fynbos overlay on **10**. Gymnastic sleekness & pure fruit concentration. Length, body & integrated oak (25% new). Supple & rewarding. Like **09**, will age well.

★★★★ **Merlot-Cabernet Sauvignon-Petit Verdot** 📖 Rich, brooding **10** returns to heights of cab-led **08**, after flamboyant but lesser **09** (★★★★). Depth & concentration of black berries & chocolate flavours mingle harmoniously with light sheen of oak.

★★★★ **Syrah-Grenache** ⏱ 📖 Delicious **10** (★★★★★) improves on perfumed **09**. Rich spice lifts red & black berry succulence. Plump & full, but with firm oak backbone, just 25% new.

★★★★ **Chardonnay** 📖 Toasty melange of citrus & vanilla on **11**. Firm Old World styling with New World succulence & fruit. Rewarding rounded creamy richness which lingers long.

★★★★ **Sauvignon Blanc** ⏱ 📖 **11** typical pungent flint, lemon & herb but good length. Body & acidity to comfortably take it beyond cricket season.

★★★★ **Viognier** ⏱ 📖 **11** whispers its typicity: nuanced nectarine, peach richness, poised flinty minerality & zesty lightness, lingering elegant spicy aftertaste.

Sauvignon Blanc-Semillon ⏱ 📖 ★★★★ Gravel minerality to **11**, tangy nettle & herb zestiness. No rush: it'll gain complexity with age. Discontinued: **Semillon**. — FM

Credo

This quality brand, first launched in 2002, featured three single-variety wines, before being taken over by the group now known as The Company of Wine People. They are now relaunching Credo with the release of Quattuor and Quinque, a red and white blend, using the Latin names for the fourth and fifth wine styles to appear under the brand.

Quattuor ★★★★ NEW Elegant & ageworthy blend mostly cab with petit verdot & pinotage, from Helderberg & Darling vines. **09** barrel sample dark, juicy fruit complemented by oak — all streamlined by supple dry tannin structure. **Quinque** ★★★☆ NEW Stylish **11** preview of sauvignon-led blend. Succulent balance, with aromatic lift courtesy dab of viognier/semillon & subtle oaking. WO Coastal. — MW

Crios Bríde

Location: Stellenbosch ▪ Est/1stB 2007 ▪ Closed to public ▪ Owner(s) Yorke-Smith Family & Martin Bates ▪ Winemaker(s) Carla Pauw (Jan 2007, consultant) ▪ 1,250cs own label 15% red 25% white 60% MCC ▪ PO Box 2290 Dennesig Stellenbosch 7601 ▪ info@criosbride.com ▪ T +27 (0)21-883-9568 ▪ F +27 (0)88-021-883-9568

This year sees (finally!) the release of consultant winemaker and bubbly aficionado Carla Pauw's new MCCs under this boutique wine label, after five years on the lees. Carla is confident the extended bottle-ageing will make the wines worthy additions to the range. We'll have to confirm next year — they missed our deadline.

★★★★ **Syrah-Carignan** ⓐ Powerful **07** concentrated molten dark fruit, good structure & ageability. **Chenin Blanc** ⓐ ★★★★ Sumptuous & robust **07** ex Swartland vines. **Sauvignon Blanc** ⓐ ★★★★ Last was single-vineyard **08** from Darling, with gentle asparagus tone. **Méthode Cap Classique** ⓐ ★★★☆ **07** sparkling from chardonnay & pinot noir, made extra-dry & perfect with oysters. — MW

Cronier Wines   🍷 NEW

Location: Wellington ▪ WO: Coastal/Western Cape ▪ Est 1698 ▪ 1stB 2006 ▪ Tasting by appt only ▪ Owner(s) Johan Cronje ▪ PO Box 1020 Wellington 7654 ▪ info@cronierwines.com ▪ www.cronierwines.com ▪ T 021-863-4145 ▪ F 021-863-3530

Brand owner Johan Cronje, whose ancestors 300 years ago farmed the two original Wellington estates, celebrates the area's rich winegrowing tradition and aims for good-quality wines that are soft, smooth and elegant, and easily drinkable'.

Reserve range

Driebergen ★★★ Bordeaux red honours ship carrying Cronje ancestors, brothers Pierre & Estienne Cronier, to Cape. Soft, plummy **09** is old-school in the best sense, for Sunday roasts. WO W Cape, like next.

Heritage range

Estienne ★★ 100% cab in **09**, at best right now — order in pizza & enjoy.

Cronier range

Merlot ★★ **11**'s vanilla-tinged plums & sweetish flavours make a friendly solo glassful. **Shiraz** ★★★ Easy, fruit-filled **11**, mocha coffee & cherry gateau flavours. Just add Ferrero Rocher & your favourite DVD. **Cabernet Sauvignon-Merlot** ★★★ Bull Terrier in the family, **11** loveable but unbridled, needs a bowl of something solid. **Chenin Blanc** ★★ **12** peach blossom & zingy dried fruit, lightish & charming after-work reviver. **Sauvignon Blanc** 🗃 ★ Dainty **11**, faintly grassy, bone-dry & light bodied. — JP/CvZ

■ **Cross Collection** see Dieu Donné Vineyards

Crows Nest   🍷 ☕ 🌳 📷 🎿

Location: Paarl ▪ Map: Paarl & Wellington ▪ WO: Coastal ▪ Est/1stB 2002 ▪ Tasting, sales & cellar tours Mon-Fri 10-5 Sat/Sun & pub hols by appt ▪ Fee R25, waived on purchase ▪ Meals by appt; or BYO picnic ▪ Facilities for children ▪ Farm produce ▪ Walking/hiking trails ▪ Conservation area ▪ Owner(s) Marcel & Deidre de Reuck ▪ Winemaker(s) Marcel de Reuck ▪ 33.6ha/11.5ha (cab, shiraz) ▪ 60t/5,000cs own label 90% red 5% white 5% port ▪ PO Box 2571 Paarl 7620 ▪ dereuck@mweb.co.za ▪ www.dereuckwines.co.za ▪ S 33° 40'33.0" E018° 54'25.4" ▪ T +27 (0)21-869-8712 ▪ F +27 (0)21-869-8714

Agter Paarl-based Marcel and Deidre de Reuck debuted in our 2004 guide saying: 'We eventually want to produce complex wines for the serious connoisseur.' Nearly a decade on, they're bang on message: 'Our wines are classic, heavier and complex, for the connoisseur.' As expected from one who spent eight years diving off Scotland's oil rigs, Marcel's bottlings are no blushing wallflowers: 'Wine should have a presence, shake you up a bit!'

Marcel de Reuck range

★★★★ **Cabernet Sauvignon** ⓐ Charming red & black cherry fruit, oak spice on firm 07 (★★★), though warming 15.7% alcohol detracts. Less elegant than last-tasted **04**.

Syrah ⓐ ★★★ Ultra-ripe, blockbusterish 07 offers 16% alcohol & sweet raisined black fruit. **Cabernet Sauvignon-Merlot** ⓐ ★★★ Tannins on youthful, bold 07 balance rich fruit but big alcohol evident. **Chardonnay** Await new.

Torres Claude range

Crow's Nest ⓐ ★★★ Rhône-inspired 07 blend with forward fruit; rich, densely packed, sweetish hot finish from 15.4% alcohol. — JPf

Croydon Vineyard Residential Estate

Location: Somerset West ▪ Map: Helderberg ▪ WO: Stellenbosch ▪ Est/1stB 2004 ▪ Tasting & sales Tue-Fri 10-7 Sat 10-1 ▪ Closed all religious holidays ▪ Cellar tours by appt ▪ Meals/refreshments on request ▪ Family dinners every 2nd Wed ▪ Facilities for children ▪ Tour groups ▪ Conferences ▪ Owner(s) Croydon Vineyard Estate Homeowners Association ▪ Cellarmaster(s) Beyers Truter (2004) ▪ Winemaker(s) Corius Visser (2004) ▪ 8ha (cabs s/f, malbec, merlot, ptage, shiraz, chenin) ▪ 65t/2,000cs own label 95% red 5% white ▪ Unit 1 Croydon Vineyard Estate Somerset West 7130 ▪ info@croydon-estate.co.za ▪ www.croydon-estate.co.za ▪ S 34° 2'23.3" E 018° 45'5.5" ▪ **T** +27 (0)21-843-3610 ▪ F +27 (0)21-843-3609

The names of the wines made at this Helderberg residential estate generally reflect the character and story of the place. The Title Deed range confirms that the house-owners are also co-owners of the vineyards and cellar, while the new Portion 20 refers to the original old farm, where the winery is. There's more involvement than mere ownership, however: a port-style wine (sadly not tasted by us) was crushed by foot-stomping householders during a harvest festival.

Title Deed range

★★★★ **Cape Blend** ✓ Chunky & savoury 11 (★★★★) preview (rating provisional) foursquare & earthy, lacking promise of **10**. From pinotage & cab supported by merlot, shiraz.

> **Chenin Blanc** NEW ☺ 🍽 ★★★ 12 pear drop & melon aromas accompanied by a slight earthiness lead on to a lingering palate that is soft & juicy, with good grip.

Rhône Blend Await next. **Rosé** NEW ✓ 🍽 ★★★★ Apricot-edged, strawberryish 12 from shiraz is plush & a little showy. Bright & dry.

Croydon Vineyard Residential Estate range

★★★★ **Covenant** ⓐ Intense fruit & 20 months in new barrels make 09 a serious pinotage. Beautifully made, with a 10 year future. Nudges next level.

Portion 20 NEW ★★★ Ambitious 09 same mix as Cape Blend, but more pinotage, less cab. Already showing some evolution. Substantial & rustic with ample tannin & texture. — MF

Crystallum

Location: Hermanus ▪ WO: Hemel-en-Aarde Ridge/Western Cape ▪ Est 2006 ▪ 1stB 2007 ▪ Closed to public ▪ Owner(s) Crystallum Coastal Vineyards (Pty) Ltd ▪ Winemaker(s) Peter-Allan Finlayson (2006) ▪ 30t/1,850cs own label 60% red 40% white ▪ PO Box 857 Hermanus 7200 ▪ info@crystallumwines.com ▪ www.crystallumwines.com

Peter-Allan Finlayson belongs to a famous Cape winemaking family but, he says, 'I tried my best to get out of the wine industry. I started studying wine science, but changed to philosophy and economics after becoming disillusioned...' Faith returned after he worked a vintage in Burgundy and Priorat: 'My eyes were opened to the richness and depth of the wine world.' So here he is, making wine. Crystallum is now devoted to just pinot noir and chardonnay. The future? 'We will look to have a few more single-vineyard offerings and slightly increase our production, but retain our focus on small bottlings from exceptional sites.'

★★★★☆ **Cuvée Cinéma Pinot Noir** Marvellously perfumed quality on **11**, which continues its graceful seduction with pure fruit in subtle harmony with masterly oaking. Subtly soft tannins; elegant, supple, ingratiating. Remarkably ready for drinking; should keep, but how it will develop is unclear.

★★★★ **Peter Max Pinot Noir 11** (★★★★★) brings in fruit from Elgin, like **10**, & Bot River. Great charm, with beguiling scents & sweet fruit, spicy notes from clever oaking. Harmoniously structured around fresh acidity rather than tannin — though firmer, less ethereal, less lingering than Cinéma. Youthfully approachable.

★★★★☆ **Clay Shales Chardonnay** Forthcoming limy aromas & flavours on modern-style **11**, with notable hints of oak which will complexly integrate with the 5+ years this fine, intense wine deserves. Silky texture & mouthwatering citrus zing on good finish — lime again, but riper mandarin too. No **10** made.

★★★★ **The Agnes Chardonnay** ⓔ Harmonious & consummately crafted **10**, showing dollops of tropical lime fruit, finely layered oak adding grip to plushness. Not simple, but amply fruited. Widely sourced grapes.
Discontinued: **Sauvignon Blanc**. — TJ

■ **Cubana** see Leeuwenjacht

Culemborg

Established range of easy-drinking export wines by DGB, with main markets including the Netherlands and Germany.

Cabernet Sauvignon 🖉 ★★★ **11** is ripe, supple & juicy with friendly dark-berried appeal. **Merlot** 🖉 ★★ **11** has sweet smoky berries; brisk but balanced for pasta/pizza. **Pinotage** 🖉 ★★★ Juicier **11** retains spicy plum flavours. Chill & enjoy. **Cape Red** 🍴 🖉 ★★ Friendly, red-fruited **11** blend. Piquantly sappy & smooth. **Blanc de Noir** 🍴 🖉 ★★★ Bright balance on semi-dry **12** strawberry-toned summer sipper. **Chenin Blanc** 🍴 🖉 ★★★ Light & crisp **12** is ripe & tropically toned. **Muscat du Cap** 🖉 ★★★ **11** crisply balanced, sweet & aromatic aperitif from hanepoot. **Sauvignon Blanc** ⓔ 🍴 🖉 ★★ Previewed **11** ripe & gentle, soft fruity flavour. **Cape White** 🍴 🖉 ★★ **12** light, floral & fresh picnic wine. **Sweet Red** 🖉 ★☆ Smooth & warming **11** is sweet & spicy. WO W Cape for all these. — MW

■ **Cutters Cove** see Robert Stanford Estate

Dâbar

Location/WO: Napier ▪ 1stB 2010 ▪ Closed to public ▪ Owner(s) Kevin Snyman & Jannie Gutter ▪ Winemaker(s) Jean Daneel (Jean Daneel Wines) ▪ Viticulturist(s) Dawie le Roux (consultant) ▪ 50% red 50% white ▪ kevinsnyman@telkomsa.net ▪ **T +27 (0)82-926-8459**

Verdant Napier is the backdrop for this farm of figs, pomegranates, flowers and grapes, where co-owner Kevin Snyman was busy with branding efforts (and fig pruning) as we went to print. They have 25ha of mainly sauvignon with 'a little bit' of chardonnay, semillon, shiraz and pinot noir, the first batch of which is in barrel. The first MCC bubbly from the 2010 harvest is promised for launch with the 2012 sauvignon. Winemaking is outsourced to Napier heavyweight Jean Daneel.

Sauvignon Blanc ⓔ ★★★ **10** in Old World mould with its lightish (12.5% alc) body & tone, racy freshness; hay, wax & cream in satisfying, moreish package. — CvZ/MW

■ **Da Capo Vineyards** see Idiom Wines

Dagbreek

Location: Rawsonville ▪ Map/WO: Breedekloof ▪ Est/1stB 2009 ▪ Tasting, sales & cellar tours Mon-Sat by appt ▪ Closed all pub hols ▪ BYO picnic ▪ Walking/hiking trails ▪ Owner(s) Peet Smith ▪ Cellarmaster(s)/winemaker(s) Peet Smith (2009) ▪ Viticulturist(s) Leon Dippenaar (2009, consultant) ▪ 108ha/48ha ▪ 7t/500cs own label ▪ 70% red 30% white ▪ WIETA ▪ PO Box 237 Rawsonville 6845 ▪ dagbreek@compnet.co.za ▪ www.dagbreek.co. za ▪ S 33° 39' 56.20" E 019°18' 26.99" ▪ **T +27 (0)82-820-2256** ▪ F +27 (0)86-529-2865

'There's a limited market for niche wines,' admits Dagbreek cellar chief Peet Smith, 'but if the quality's there, consumers will buy.' His awarded 09 Nebbiolo is sold out but the 10 is every bit as good, he believes, and the Touriga Nacional shows 'lovely soft tannins — a lot like merlot'.

Nebbiolo ⚘ ★★★ Inky blueberry **10** has variety's typical bright acidity, still unsettled in youth, needs time or food. **Touriga Nacional** ⚘ ★★★★ **10** black fruit plumped by touch sugar, juicy & flavoursome. **Chenin Blanc Barrel Selection** Await next. — MW

Dalla Cia Wine & Spirit Company

Location/map/WO: Stellenbosch ▪ Est 2004 ▪ Tasting, sales & traditional Italian meals at Pane E Vino Food & Wine Bar, Mon-Fri 10-6 Sat 10-5 ▪ Owner(s)/winemaker(s) Giorgio Dalla Cia ▪ 9,000cs ▪ 7A Lower Dorp Street Bosman's Crossing Stellenbosch ▪ info@dallacia.com ▪ www.dallacia.com ▪ S33° 56' 25.8" E018° 50' 50.1" ▪ **T** **+27 (0)21-888-4120** ▪ F +27 (0)21-887-2621

Asked the most significant trend in South African wine today, George Dalla Cia, head of marketing at this family-owned operation, replies 'A return to a classic style of winemaking. We've been following this all along — people are tired of upfront, fruity wines.' Paterfamilias is, of course, Giorgio Dalla Cia, who for many years made the ageworthy wines of Meerlust. Much excitement from both son and father surrounding the launch of the maiden high-end Dalla Cia pinot noir. Grapes from Polkadraai in Stellenbosch, only seven barrels made and a claimed ageing potential of 20 years. 'Burgundian in style of course!'

★★★★ **Classico Cabernet Sauvignon** ✓ Classically styled **10** (★★★★★) still tight mid-2012 with core of dark fruit, bright acidity & tannins which shout for food. Has appealing savoury edge. 18 months in French oak 70% new, underpins a wine that's perhaps even more structured than **06**. No **07**, **08** or **09**.

★★★★ **Pinot Noir** **NEW** **11** is serious & demanding. Red & black fruit, slight toasty oak character. Rich but still balanced thanks to fresh acidity. Extremely youthful when tasted, needs time to marry.

★★★★☆ **Giorgio** Bordeaux blend, masterly **07** (★★★★★) previewed last year now shows real complexity finesse & balance. Red & black fruit, some herbal character, tobacco, attractive oak — 18 months French, 80% new, like **06**. Great concentration, fine but grippy tannins & a certain coolness on the finish. Built to last.

Chardonnay 🍴 📖 ★★★ Remarkably rich & full despite being largely unwooded, **11** shows citrus, yeastiness well integrated acidity. **Sauvignon Blanc** 🍴 ★★★★ **12** whispers rather than shouts class. Lean & fresh with lime, green apple notes, long savoury finish. More focused than **10** (★★★), **11** sold on untasted. — CE

Damarakloof

Location/WO: Paarl ▪ Map: Paarl & Wellington ▪ Est/1stB 2006 ▪ Function venue by appt ▪ Owner(s) Agnes de Vos ▪ Winemaker(s) Carla Pauw (Jan 2006) ▪ 19ha (cabs s/f, merlot, chenin) ▪ 10t/650cs own label 50% red 50% white ▪ PO Box 38 Elsenburg 7607 ▪ agnesdev@telkomsa.net, carlapauw@gmail.com ▪ S 33° 48' 41.79" E 018° 47' 21.19" ▪ **T +27 (0)21-884-4304** ▪ F +27 (0)21-884-4304

The gravelly Paarl-area racetrack turned into a vineyard by Agnes de Vos' grandfather is back in action after a brief hiatus. Agnes' delighted exclamation 'We have wine in the cellar!' refers to a 2012 chenin and the components for the estate's Bordeaux-style red blend, Regale. The former was set for release at press time while the latter incubated a few more years.

Racetrack range

Regale ★★★★ ⚘ When last tasted, **08** Bordeaux red returned to classic form after **06** (★★★★). Very fragrant, refreshingly demure & altogether delightful to drink, even in youth. No **07**. — DS

◼ **Dam Good** see Villiersdorp Cellar
◼ **Danie de Wet** see De Wetshof Estate

D'Aria Winery

Location/WO: Durbanville ▪ Map: Durbanville, Philadelphia & Darling ▪ Est/1stB 2007 ▪ Tasting & sales Mon-Fri 10-6 (Sep-Apr) & 9-5 (May-Aug) Sat 10-5 Sun 10-4 ▪ Fee R10 ▪ Closed Dec 25 & Jan 1 ▪ Cheese platters & deli products served in tasting room ▪ Poplars Restaurant ▪ Conferences/functions ▪ Walks/hikes ▪ Mountain biking trail ▪ 4-star guest cottages ▪ Music concerts (summer months) ▪ Owner(s) Barinor Holdings ▪ Winemaker(s) Rudi von Waltsleben (Nov 2007), with Nicola Viljoen (Apr 2010) ▪ Viticulturist(s) Johan von Waltsleben (1998) ▪ 63ha (cab, merlot, shiraz, sauv) ▪ 400t/30,000cs own label 67% red 30% white 3% rosé + 200cs for clients ▪ Brands for clients: Doilie Klub (Elzabé Zietsman) ▪ M13 Racecourse Road Durbanville 7550 ▪ tasting@daria.co.za ▪ www.dariawinery.co.za ▪ S 33° 50' 28.6" E 018° 36' 32.2" ▪ **T +27 (0)21-801-6772** ▪ F +27 (0)86-539-4519

Musical themes permeate this Durbanville winery, as cellarmaster Rudi von Waltsleben is both musician and winemaker and sees the connection: 'Music is an expression of emotion, so is winemaking; the creative urge in both is always to do something new and better.' His latest creation is a five-year old potstill brandy.

★★★★☆ **The Soprano Shiraz** ⊕ Bold, generously oaked (40% new) **09** (★★★★) a dense pliable mouthful. Good fruit but lacks freshness, with a rather cloying finish. Less successful than powerful **08**.

★★★★ **Songbird Sauvignon Blanc** 🍴 More serious, structured than standard version. **11** invigorating, steely, with mere suggestion of ripe fig flavours & pithy firm finish.

Merlot ★★★ **10** lighterweight in fruit & structure than **09** — but not alcohol. A few grams sugar lift soft red plum flavours. **Cabernet Sauvignon-Merlot** ★★★ Some cassis, greenpepper & oak spice on smooth, sweetish **10**. **Music Red** 🍴 ★★★ Uncomplicated shiraz-based **11** with sweet fruit, gentle tannins. **SV Shiraz** ★★★ Was 'Shiraz-Viognier'. Quite simple **09**; forthcoming floral, red fruits with smoky American oak. Juicy, smooth drinkability. **Blush** 🍴 ★★ Pearly pink **12** from merlot & sauvignon, semi-dry, fruity & lightish. **Sauvignon Blanc** 🍴 ★★★★ **11** easy to enjoy; juicy ripe fig flavours, leesy bounce, balanced by zippy fresh acidity. **The Following White Blend** 🍴 ★★★★ Ripe, flavoursome viognier with semillon, sauvignon &, in **11**, oak vanilla. Plush yet lively, roundly dry. **Music White** 🍴 ★★ Not discontinued after all! Dainty peachy fruit on refreshing, dry **11**. Mainly sauvignon. — AL

Darling Cellars

Location: Darling ▪ Map: Durbanville, Philadelphia & Darling ▪ WO: Darling/Groenekloof/Coastal ▪ Est 1948 ▪ 1stB 1996 ▪ Tasting & sales Mon-Fri 8–5 Sat 10–2 ▪ Closed Good Fri, Dec 25 & Jan 1 ▪ Cellar tours by appt ▪ Wine & food pairing/sampling, no meals ▪ Facilities for children ▪ Owner(s) 20 shareholders ▪ Cellarmaster(s) Abé Beukes (Dec 1997) ▪ Winemaker(s) Welma Visser & Carel Hugo (Nov 2007/Jun 2009) ▪ Viticulturist(s) Gerhard Rossouw (Mar 2012) ▪ 1,300ha (cab, cinsaut, grenache, merlot, ptage, shiraz, chard, chenin, sauv) ▪ 7,500–8,500t/350,000cs own label 70% red 28% white 2% rosé ▪ Export brands: Alta Casa, Black Granite, Cellar Road, Fountain Crossing, Mamre Vale, Victoria Bay ▪ BRC, BWI, WIETA ▪ PO Box 114 Darling 7345 ▪ info@darlingcellars.co.za ▪ www.darlingcellars.co.za ▪ S 33° 26' 25.7" E 018° 31' 25.1" ▪ **T +27 (0)22-492-2276** ▪ F +27 (0)22-492-2647

Wheatfields are punctuated by gnarled bushvines — a signature sight of the Darling region and a combination that allows for a balanced agricultural harmony that reduces disease. The pay-off line 'True to nature' was obvious to cellarmaster Abé Beukes and the team. The bushvine method can produce more intense flavour and in combination with the cooling West Coast breeze gives birth to the characteristic regional expression of elegance with a modern, fruity touch. This large cellar has long been a source of great value, but the greater focus on quality is seen as essential to the perception of the brand.

Limited Releases

★★★★☆ **Sir Charles Henry Darling** ✓ Petit verdot (35%) leads cab, cab franc & merlot in fine flagship. **09** has herbal cool lift, restrained aromas with bright red fruit, leading to fresh & focused fruit expression while balanced by refined tannins & elegant savoury undertone.

★★★★★ **Lime Kilns** ✓ 🈷 Wonderfully executed mix of creamy chardonnay, spicy viognier & rich chenin blanc. **11** exhibits great balance of fruit & Darling saline support. Lovely poised richness from barrel fermentation & fine lees-ageing, with fresh, clean acidity guiding to the finish.

★★★★ **Blanc de Blancs Brut** ✓ Chardonnay **09** bottle-fermented sparkling invites with fine slow bubble, crisp green apple, brioche & lime. Attractive austerity balanced by delightful fresh acidity & focused minerality.

Cellarmaster's Signature Selection No. 1 ⊕ ★★★★ **08**, from petit verdot, bit uncomfortable as standalone when tasted a few years back. Groenekloof WO. **Cellarmaster's Signature Selection No. 2** NEW 🈷 ★★★ Light & delicate **11** from nouvelle shows serious intentions, but ultimately lacks gravitas.

Premium range

★★★★☆ **Cabernet Sauvignon** ⊕ Classy preview **09** (★★★★) ex Groenekloof brims with ripeness, tasted last edition. Classic leafy herbaceousness laced with blackcurrant fruit. Followed finer **08**.

★★★★ **Shiraz** ✓ Brooding black fruits, with spice & savoury support, serve as hint to rich cola-cherry & black berry juiciness on dry & satisfying **09**. Ripe style well executed.

★★★★ **Sauvignon Blanc** ✓ 🈷 Bouncy tropical intro shows off poised granadilla & ruby grapefruit. The rounded palate in modern idiom has fresh citrus finish. **11** less herbal than past regional expressions.

Pinotage 🄴 ★★★ Tart red fruit intro on vibrant **10**, follows to red cherry, earthy & sweet-fruited palate. Rather firm finish detracts. **Kroon** ✓ ★★★★ Chunky **08** Rhône blend plus pinotage & barbera; shines with voluptuous intent, dark-fruited & oaky, but good dry finish. **Noble Late Harvest** Await next.

Reserve range

Terra Hutton Cabernet Sauvignon ☺ 🄳 🄴 ★★★ Cool-climate herbal notes on **11** continue to the savoury palate with green edge; good typicity albeit in older-style mould. **Six Tonner Merlot** ☺ 🄳 🄴 ★★★ Toasty oak combines well with ripe red cherry & vibrant freshness. **11** is inviting & varietally true. **Old Blocks Pinotage** ☺ 🄳 🄴 ★★★ Intensely fruity **10** balanced aromatically by earthy & savoury elements & flavour-wise by fresh crisp acid.

Black Granite Shiraz 🄴 🄳 ★★★ Quaffable **10** softer & lighter than previous, but retaining enticing peppery aromas. **Quercus Gold Chardonnay** 🄴 🄳 🄴 ★★★ Restrained, unassuming **11** but generous in ripeness & body. Atypical yet pleasing white fruit profile. **Arum Fields Chenin Blanc** ✓ 🄳 🄴 ★★★★ The star in this range. Good fruit purity on just-dry **12** matched by rich & weighty palate with excellent texture. Sweet-toned finish well balanced. **Bush Vine Sauvignon Blanc** ✓ 🄳 🄴 ★★★★ **12** less dusty-grassy than expected. Nectarine & green fig balanced by fresh palate with good weight & medium-dry end.

Classic range

Cabernet Sauvignon-Merlot ☺ 🄳 🄴 ★★★ Red fruits meld with smoky thread on soft, appealing **11**. **Merlot Rosé** ☺ 🄳 ★★★ Blazing pink off-dry **12** charms with strawberry perfume. **Chenin Blanc-Sauvignon Blanc** ☺ 🄳 🄴 ★★★ Mostly chenin, **12** proffers expected light crisp fruitiness.

Cinsaut-Cabernet Sauvignon 🄴 🄳 ★★★ A gush of dark berries & oaky spices on **10** emphasise cinsaut drinkability. WO Coastal. Note: range was 'Flamingo Bay'.

Sweet Darling

Rosé 🄳 🄴 ★★ **12** Turkish Delight notes, a sweet pleaser. **White** 🄳 🄴 ★★ **12** bukettraube floral sweetie. **Pettilant White** 🄴 🄳 ★★ Spritzy **11** as above. Range was 'Zantsi Africa Natural Sweet' previously. — JP

▉ **Darlington** *see* Withington
▉ **Daschbosch** *see* uniWines Vineyards
▉ **Dassie's Reserve** *see* Botha Wine Cellar

D'Athis Wines SA Negociants

Location: Stellenbosch ▪ Est 2008 ▪ Tasting & sales by appt only ▪ Owner(s) Marcel du Preez & Jacques du Preez ▪ Winemaker(s)/viticulturist(s) Jan du Preez (consulting) ▪ PO Box 7210 Stellenbosch 7599 ▪ dathiswines@vodamail.co.za ▪ **T +27 (0)82-856-3560** ▪ F +27 (0)86-588-3482

The producer of two brands currently (Headbutt and Leidersburg, made primarily from Robertson grapes and available in supermarkets nationwide), the father-and-son team of Jan and Jacques du Preez are re-evaluating the name and extent of their business. Meanwhile Weinsberg-trained Jacques in 2012 took a position as winemaker for German family estate Schloss Proshwitz.

David

Location: Tulbagh ▪ WO: Swartland/Coastal ▪ Est/1stB 2010 ▪ Tasting by appt T +27 (0)72-375-4336 at Lemberg Wine Estate ▪ Owner(s)/winemaker(s)/viticulturist(s) David & Nadia Sadie ▪ (carignan, cinsaut, grenache n/b, shiraz, chard, chenin, clairette, rouss, viog) ▪ 8t/440cs own label 50% red 50% white ▪ IPW ▪ wine@davidsadie.co.za ▪ www.davidsadie.co.za ▪ **T +27 (0)72-375-4336** ▪ F +27 (0)86-512-4903

Total tonnage for this, David and Nadia Sadie's own boutique label (David also winemaker/viticulturist at resurgent Tulbagh winery Lemberg, where both brands are vinified) has grown by two tons, and David and Nadia are now sourcing from 12 different blocks in the Swartland district. They work with less ubiquitous varieties including carignan, roussanne and clairette blanche, with their first Swartland red blend (which missed our review deadline) debuting this year. They're passionate about being part of the Swartland's wine story, David having rown up there, and are influenced by the classical European way of trying to reate timeless, elegant and expressive wines.

★★★★☆ **Chenin Blanc** NEW Intense & well-defined **11**, white & yellow stonefruit touches, lemony acidity, deft brush older oak & oxidative handling. Delicious now, enough structure for several years fruitful ageing.

★★★★☆ **Aristargos** Five Perdeberg/Kasteelberg vineyards (some old bushvine), native ferment, oxidative styling & older oak make for hedonistic mouthful chenin, roussanne & dash grenache blanc. **11** (★★★★★) integrated & lipsmackingly dry, packed with flavour, structure & freshness to improve good few years, like **10**.

Grenache NEW ★★★ Funky **11** from Perdeberg vines cleverly juxtaposes fruit-sweetness with dry tannins. Only 30 cases made, as for Chenin. — CE/CvZ

David Frost Signature Series

Champion golfer David Frost gives his name to this range, produced by Perdeberg Winery. The wines are available in South Africa exclusively through Pick 'n Pay stores countrywide, and exported to China.

Shiraz ☺ 🍴 🄌 ★★★ Soundly crafted range of pocket-friendly crowd pleasers. Fleshy & intensely fruity **11** is eminently drinkable. **Classic Red** ☺ 🍴 🄌 ★★★ Dash of cinsaut fleshes out **11**'s equal portions cab & merlot. **Chenin Blanc** ☺ 🍴 🄌 ★★★ Easygoing **12** quaffer has pear drop scent & crisp acid.

Soft Smooth Red 🍴 🄌 ★★★ Dash of sugar lends berry-jam fruitiness to undemanding **11**. — GdB

■ **David Nieuwoudt** see Cederberg Private Cellar

DeanDavid Wines

Location: Riebeek-Kasteel ▪ WO: Swartland ▪ Est/1stB 2003 ▪ Closed to public ▪ Wines available at the Wine Collective, Riebeek-Kasteel ▪ Owner(s) Dean Thompson, Roger Clayton, Peter Alexander & John Fulford ▪ Cellarmaster(s)/winemaker(s) Dean Thompson ▪ 8t/400cs own label 100% red ▪ PO Box 56 Green Point 8051 ▪ dean@unwined.co.za, roger@unwined.co.za ▪ www.unwined.co.za ▪ **T +27 (0)71-233-8261 (Dean)/ +27 (0)76-826-8500 (Roger)**

Dean Thompson is the part-time winemaking (and marketing-reluctant) son, David his father who has long had a share in a grape farm just outside Riebeek-Kasteel. A few sometimes delightfully pure wines have emerged, in tiny quantities. The Syrah is off five 'close to organic' blocks.

★★★★ **2 Mile Square Swartland Syrah** There's a sensuality & succulently soft tannic structure on **11** (★★★) — less fresh than last-tasted **09**; but fruit is ultra-ripe & therefore weak. Tasted pre-bottling. — TJ

■ **De B** see De Breede Organic Vineyards

De Breede Organic Vineyards

Location: Worcester ▪ Map/WO: Breedekloof ▪ Est 2006 ▪ 1stB 2009 ▪ Tasting by appt ▪ Owner(s) Tim & Debbie Alcock ▪ Cellarmaster(s)/viticulturist(s) Tim Alcock (2006) ▪ Winemaker(s) Tim Alcock (2006), with Isaac Mabeta (2009) ▪ 26ha/2,5ha (cab, malbec, merlot, p verdot) ▪ 6t/250cs 99% red 1% rosé ▪ Certified organic by BCS ▪ PO Box 511 Worcester 6849 ▪ debreedevineyards@burchells.co.za ▪ www.debreedevineyards.co.za ▪ S 33° 37' 10.69" E 019° 22' 44.79" ▪ **T +27 (0)23-342-5388** ▪ F +27 (0)86-684-7778

'Horrors!' says owner-winemaker Tim Alcock. 'I always saw myself as a garagiste, now I am a confirmed terroiriste.' To express the uniqueness of his Worcester vineyards his approach is non-interventionism in the cellar and organic farming in the vineyards — where, Tim says with relief and pride, 'We have eventually reached some sort of equilibrium between weeds, water usage and yield.'

De B range

1st XI Merlot 🌼 Occasional release. **Little Red Rooster** 🌼 ★★★ Modest, sweet fruit & very strong tannins on **11** merlot-based Bordeaux blend. **The Rooster** NEW 🌼 ★★★★ Barrel selection & an extra year in bottle make a big difference to this cab-based **10** version of Bordeaux blend. Ripe, rich fruit, supported well by oak. — TJ

■ **Debutant** see De Kleine Wijn Koöp
■ **Decent** see Ladismith Cellar — SCV

De Doorns Wynkelder (Koöp) Bpk

Location: De Doorns ▪ Map/WO: Worcester ▪ Est 1968 ▪ Tasting & sales Mon-Fri 8–5 Sat 8–12 ▪ Cellarmaster(s) Danie Koen ▪ Winemaker(s) Danie Koen, with Peter James Thomson ▪ PO Box 129 De Doorns 6875 ▪ ddwk@hexvallei.co.za ▪ www.dedoornscellar.co.za ▪ S 33° 29' 10.3" E 019° 39' 43.2" ▪ **T +27 (0)23-356-2835** ▪ +27 (0)86-579-1310

'All our growers had a bumper season, I almost felt like quitting!' quips cellarmaster Danie Koen with a shake of his head. But being the seasoned veteran he is, he made space in this Hex River Valley cellar and got on with the job of crushing 39,000 tons of grapes, an all-time record.

Cabernet Sauvignon ⓘ ★★★ Sippable **09**, gentle spicy notes, fresh berry centre & slight grip. **Roodeho** ⓘ 📖 ★★ Unoaked & quaffable **10**, mainly cab & pinotage, with smoky bacon savouriness. — GdB/CvZ

Definitum Wines   [NEW]

Location: Strand ▪ WO: Stellenbosch ▪ Est/1stB 2009 ▪ Closed to public ▪ Owner(s) Fritz van der Merwe & De We Schreiber ▪ 260cs own label 100% red ▪ PO Box 917 Strand 7139 ▪ info@definitum.co.za ▪ www.definitum.co.za

Helderberg friends De Wet Schreiber, a project manager, and Fritz van der Merwe, in short-term insurance, are intent on introducing winelovers to the more unusual varieties. Family and friends form a loyal customer base — their first bottling, Carignan 09, sold out and the Petit Verdot 10 looked set to follow Next is a blend, 'one that has not yet been seen in South Africa', they promise.

Petit Verdot 📖 ★★★ More comfortable at table with food than standalone out on the patio, **10** has some plummy flavour but also lots of firm tannin. Time in bottle might settle & soften. — WB/IM

De Grendel Wines

Location: Durbanville ▪ Map: Durbanville, Philadelphia & Darling ▪ WO: Durbanville/Coastal/Western Cape ▪ Est 1720 ▪ 1stB 2004 ▪ Tasting & sales Mon-Fri 9-5 Sat/Sun 10-4 ▪ Closed Dec 25 ▪ Cellar tours by appt ▪ Conferences ▪ De Grendel Restaurant T +27 (0)21-558-7035/restaurant@degrendel.co.za ▪ Owner(s) Sir David Graaff ▪ Cellarmaster(s) Charles Hopkins (Oct 2005) ▪ Winemaker(s) Elzette du Preez (Jan 2006) ▪ Viticulturist(s) Douglas Muzengeza (2008) & Kudzai Mwerenga (2009) ▪ 800ha/110ha (cabs s/f, malbec, merlot mourv, p verdot, ptage, pinot noir/gris, shiraz, chard, sauv, sem, viog) ▪ 550t/25,000cs own label 35% red 50% white 15% rosé ▪ 112 Plattekloof Road Panorama 7505 ▪ info@degrendel.co.za ▪ www.degrendel.co.za ▪ S 33° 51'2.5" E 018° 34' 18.4" ▪ **T +27 (0)21-558-6280** ▪ F +27 (0)21-558-7083

Last year, De Grendel cellarmaster Charles Hopkins was elected chair of the South African National Wine Show Association, the body responsible for the Young Wine Show and Veritas. It's testament to his standing in the industry — a 1986 graduate of agricultural college Elsenburg, he started out at Bellingham before moving to Graham Beck Wines, settling at De Grendel in late 2005. He's worked seasons in Sonoma Valley, California, and Bordeaux, France, as well as conducting numerous international study tours. Needless to say, he's a member of the august Cape Winemakers Guild. The De Grendel wines are, undeniably, among the most technically sound you will encounter. But they are also more than that. They are the wines of a man who thinks and feels deeply about his industry.

★★★★ **Shiraz** ✓ 📖 📖 Pretty **09** is medium bodied, well balanced with notes of red fruit, white pepper & fynbos. Includes mourvèdre, viognier. **10** (★★★★★), also reviewed this edition, from 100% shiraz has more presence. Very aromatic, pristine fruit expression, vivid acidity, firm but fine tannins. Coastal WO, like next.

★★★★ **Rubáiyát** Bordeaux-style red **09** (★★★★) ultra-ripe, rich & broad with soft acidity & smooth texture. Not quite the same focus, structure of **08**.

★★★★ **Sauvignon Blanc** ✓ 📖 📖 Concentrated, rich, full **12** benefits from 9% semillon. Great fruit expression — pear in particular — well integrated acidity, impossible not to like.

★★★★☆ **Koetshuis Sauvignon Blanc** ✓ 📖 📖 **12** reverts to pure, piercing style typical of this label after rounder, riper **11**. Grassy, herbal notes on the nose; lime fruit, racy acidity on the palate before extremely dry, pithy finish. Clean & precise to the point of severe. 55% Darling fruit.

★★★★☆ **Viognier** 📖 📖 **12** (★★★★) in same elegant style as **11** but not quite as arresting. Peach & slight floral note on the nose while the palate is clean & pure, relatively lean for the variety.

Merlot 🏠 ⓘ ★★★ Ripe red fruit, no oak character to speak of on appealing, not overly complex **10** barrel sample. Juicy & smooth. Coastal WO. **Op Die Berg Pinot Noir** 🏠 ⓘ ★★★★ Precise if not profound **10** shows black cherry, hint of oak spice, bright acidity, fine tannins. Not as concentrated as **09** (★★★★). Some Ceres grapes. **Rosé** 🏠 ⓘ ★★☆ Pale pink **12** shows light red cherry flavour, bright acidity. From pinotage & cab. **Pinot Gris** 🏠 ⓘ ★★★★ Subtle lime & pear notes, touch of spice on understated, refined **12**. Bright acidity, pithy finish. 20% barrel fermented for extra structure. Better balance than **11** (★★★). **Winifred** 🏠 ⓘ ★★★★ Non-conformist blend, **11** includes 48% chardonnay, roughly equal semillon & viognier. Subtle pear & peach notes, moderate acidity. WO W Cape, as next. **Méthode Cap Classique Brut** ⓘ ★★★ **10** sparkling (65% chardonnay with pinot noir) overtly fruity with notes of ripe orange & apple, explosive mousse, soft acidity. **Sauvignon Blanc Noble Late Harvest** NEW ⓘ ★★★ **12** displays some yellow fruit but rather soft & short. — CE

■ **De Haas** see Hazendal
■ **Dekker's Valley** see Mellasat Vineyards
■ **De Kleine Leeuwen** see Leeuwenberg

De Kleine Wijn Koöp NEW

Location: Stellenbosch ▪ Est/1stB 2011 ▪ Closed to public ▪ Sales via email 9-5 ▪ Owner(s) Rohan Etsebeth, Jan Solms & Chris Olivier ▪ 200cs own label 100% red ▪ Export brands: Debutant, Steenbok ▪ kantoor@dekleinewijnkoop.co.za ▪ www.dekleinewijnkoop.co.za

The De Kleine Wijn Koöp is owned by Chris Olivier, sommelier and manager at the restaurant on Stellenbosch winery Longridge as well as Rohan Etsebeth and Jan Solms of design studio Fanakalo, wine packaging a particular strength. When they come across small and unusual bottlings, they buy these in and dress them in a more 'flip-flops and boardshorts' than 'power suit' fashion. Current releases include Swartland red blends Debutant 03 and Steenbok 11.

De Krans

Location/WO: Calitzdorp ▪ Map: Klein Karoo & Garden Route ▪ Est 1964 ▪ 1stB 1977 ▪ Tasting & sales Mon-Fri 9-5 Sat 9-3 ▪ Fee R20pp for groups; individuals free ▪ Closed Easter Fri/Sun & Dec 25 ▪ Pick your own apricots last week Nov, 1st week Dec) & hanepoot grapes (±10 Feb-10 Mar) ▪ 'Braaivleis' by Vygieshof Home for the aged available on Wed & Sat during picking season ▪ Facilities for children school hols ▪ BYO picnic ▪ Walking trail ▪ Owner(s) De Krans Wines (MD Boets Nel & Directors Stroebel Nel & René Oosthuizen) ▪ Cellarmaster(s) Boets Nel (Jan 1982) ▪ Winemaker(s) Boets Nel (Jan 1982), Stroebel Nel (Jan 1988) & Louis van der Riet (Aug 2012) ▪ Viticulturist(s) Stroebel Nel (Jan 1988) & Johannes Mellet (2007, Vinpro) ▪ 78ha/45ha (cab, ptage, tempranillo & port varieties, chard, chenin & muscats) ▪ 500t/20–25,000cs own label 50% red 10% white 3% rosé 37% fortifieds ▪ IPW, BWI ▪ PO Box 28 Calitzdorp 6660 ▪ dekrans@mweb.co.za ▪ www.dekrans.co.za ▪ S 33°32'6.3" E 021°41'9.0" ▪ **T +27 (0)44-213-3314** ▪ F +27 (0)44-213-3562

This ever-innovative Calitzdorp winery had a great year, being crowned southern Cape champion for the fourth consecutive year, with awards for their white muscadel jerepigo and various ports. They've long planned a Calitzdorp Blend of solely port varieties, which they're aiming to release in April, in a venture with other local cellars. The dream-come-true-blend is touriga, tinta and tempranillo (tinta roriz), and MD Boets Nel sees this as 'my vision for Calitzdorp for the future'. Finally, The Last Cape Vintage Port 2010 is on Boets' mind, too, 'since we can no longer use the "p" word'. He expects no effect on sales, but, tongue in cheek, certified the wine (as port) just before the 1/1/2012 cut-off. And while labels will no longer carry the 'p' word in tasting notes and talks about De Krans's, um, you know, 'wine formerly known as port'.

★★★ **Touriga Nacional** ⓘ Much lauded flagship, in **10** shows appealing plum & red-berry fruit, savoury touch to plush core; balanced, malleable tannins. Should improve few years in bottle.

★★★ **Red Stone Reserve** ⓘ **06** touriga & 30% cab blend delivers satisfying mouthful. Dark fruit underpinned by tannin, should be drinking well now.

★★★ **Reserve Muscat** ⓘ Very appealing fortified dessert from 30 year old vines. **11**, now bottled, still offers sweet ginger-spiced flavours, good spirit grip & uncloying farewell. More enjoyment than in **10** (★★★).

★★★★★ **The Last Cape Vintage Reserve Port** 🈯 Standout Cape port-style with brilliant track record. **10**, last to be named 'Port', drops souzão for 65/35 touriga/tinta configuration. Aloof on nose, reveals its huge potential on palate: intense, layered, silky, yet with terse grip suggesting stellar 10+ years cellaring.

★★★★☆ **Cape Vintage** ✓ 🈯 Classically styled & ageworthy port-style from touriga (60%) & tinta. **11** bold spirit, intricate plum/date/roasted nut layers, satin texture & endless finish. Like recent vintages, snaps at heels of Vintage Reserve.

★★★★ **Cape Tawny** Latest **NV** shade off previous, drops tinta roriz from usual combo with tinta, touriga but remains delicious; well-judged fortification, burnt toffee & apple persistence. Aged average 8 years.

★★★★ **Cape Ruby** ✓ Attractive cherry, Christmas cake spice on latest **NV** from tinta (60%) with touriga & tinta amarela. As always, over-performs in the category.

> **Tinta Mocha** 😊 🈯 ★★★ The advertised pop-style mocha on **11**, plus ripe plum & mulberry, supple tannins & juicy farewell for easy drinking. **Relishing Red** 😊 ★★★ Budget-priced off-dry **NV** blend, mainly tinta, fresh strawberry taste to relish anywhere, anytime.

Cabernet Sauvignon ⓧ 🍴 ★★★ Tealeaf nuanced **10** deep & brooding with drying tannins, brief end. **Pinotage** ⓧ 🍴 ★★★ Acetone & banana, full body, **10** for solo sipping or venison & casseroles. **Tempranillo** ⓧ 🍴 ★★★ Vanilla top notes ex dab American oak, **10** straightforwardly tasty & appealing. **'Calitzdorp Blend'** NEW ✓ 🍴 ★★★★ Individual dry red from touriga (70%), dollops tinta & tempranillo. **11** aromatic frangipani & Turkish Delight character, fresh core of fruit. **Cabernet Sauvignon Rosé** 🍴 🈯 ★★ Tank sample **12** is sweet-smelling but tastes dry, pleasant if not concentrated. **Chardonnay** 🍴 🈯 ★★★ **12** preview faint lemon, lime; brisk. Should deliver usual pleasant sipping when bottled. **Chenin Blanc** 🍴 🈯 ★★★ Acacia flower, nut & hint guava on **12**, pleasant, smooth & lively. **Golden Harvest** 🍴 ★★ Usual equal muscat d'Alexandrie & chenin in latest **NV**, watermelon & ginger, lightish, softly sweet. **White Muscadel Jerepigo** 🈯 ★★★★ **12** notch down on creamy **11** (★★★★) but still delicious, spice & honey attractions, seamless fortification, shade more sweetness. **Original Espresso** NEW ✓ ★★★★ Billed as 'alternative to coffee' (!), **NV** fortified from tinta & touriga grabs the attention with dried prune, raisin, chocolate &, yes, coffee. Crisp acidity provides verve. **The Original Cape Pink** ★★★ Was 'Pink Port', first of this style. **NV** slight wildness to the berries, green walnut at the end; 'perfect foil for mint in summer cocktails,' says winemaker Boets Nel. **Cape White** ★★★ Port-style sipper from chenin, to be served lightly chilled. **NV** is aromatic, with marzipan & orange peel. Excellent alternative to sherry. Discontinued: **Merlot**. — GdB/CvZ

Delaire Graff Estate   🍴🍷⛺📷♿

Location/map: Stellenbosch ▪ WO: Stellenbosch/Western Cape/Swartland/Coastal ▪ Est 1983 ▪ 1stB 1984 Tasting & sales Mon-Sat 10-5 Sun 10-4 ▪ Fee R30/3 wines R40/4 wines R50/5 wines ▪ Cellar tours by appt (no tours during harvest) ▪ Salads/cheese platters on request ▪ Gifts ▪ Farm produce ▪ Conferences ▪ Walks/hikes ▪ Art collection ▪ Delaire Graff & Indochine Restaurants (see Restaurants section) ▪ 5-star Lodges & Spa (see Accommodation section) ▪ Owner(s) Laurence Graff ▪ Winemaker(s) Morné Vrey (Jul 2009) ▪ Viticulturist(s) Kallie Fernhout (Jun 2010) ▪ 38ha/20ha (cabs s/f, malbec, merlot, p verdot, chard, sauv) ▪ 280t/17,000cs own label 40% red 55% white 5% rosé ▪ WIETA ▪ PO Box 3058 Stellenbosch 7602 ▪ info@delaire.co.za ▪ www. delaire.co.za ▪ S 33° 55' 20.4" E 018° 55' 26.0" ▪ T +27 (0)21-885-8160 ▪ F +27 (0)21-885-1270

It's just ten years since this high-flying, high-lying estate on the Helshoogte Pass just outside Stellenbosch town (it literally looks down on some very classy neighbours!) was bought by diamantaire Laurence Graff — and 30 years since it was founded by John and Erica Platter. A suitable anniversary, then, to introduce a splendid reserve wine named after the owner, whose six-year development programme turned the modest property into a 'leading luxury destination'. All that plushness lies amidst the vineyards that produce some of the grapes for Morné Vrey's wine-cellar — others are sourced elsewhere, some from as far afield as Swartland and Olifants River. Morné turns them into wine that is, if not plush, luxuriously and rather elegantly fine.

★★★★★ **Cabernet Sauvignon Reserve** ⓧ **09** (★★★★★) showed gravitas, dark berry scents & flavour in harmony with the succulent, chalky tannins, fresh acid & oak. Will keep 5+ years, maybe longer than **08**.

★★★★★ **Laurence Graff Reserve** NEW A label for only the very best vintages. Inky dark **09** from this year's best barrels of cab, demure yet not wholly restrained. Bright cassis & mulberry aromas; flashy, well integrated oak. Seamless, with refreshing savoury finish. A 'statement' wine without exaggeration.

★★★★ **Merlot** ✓ Retasted 09 now opened up, showing superbly. Plum & green olive aromas, rich yet savoury, with vibrant, slightly smoky notes. Great vinosity, brooding intensity. Not overdone in any respect; the oak (80% new) promotes the wine's evolution, leaving its purity intact.

★★★ **Shiraz** ✓ 🍴 📖 Bold & brash, all ripe red berry aromas, **10** (★★★★) lacks the purity & plushness of juicier, sweet-fruited 09. But only older oak used.

★★★★ **Botmaskop** ⊕ 09 cab-led Bordeaux quintet with shiraz in seamless, flavoursome composition. More plush, softer tannined than 08. Good in youth, has concentration, firm acid for 5+ years development.

★★★★ **Chardonnay** 📖 Green-edged, vibrant 11 with citrus, iodine notes. Mineral crispness on the palate, unflashy yet intense. One to keep: slow-evolving, potentially profound. More elegant than 10 (★★★★).

★★★ **Chenin Blanc** ✓ 📖 Ripe yet restrained, oak fermented 11 from Swartland with apricot compote & toffee-caramel notes. Finely balanced, with sweet-sour flavours, tangy & fresh.

★★★ **Sauvignon Blanc** 🍴 📖 Widely sourced 12 (half from Olifants River) with a little oaked semillon. In restrained, herbal style, precise & concentrated, offering nettly green aromas.

★★★ **Coastal Cuvée Sauvignon Blanc** 🍴 📖 Classically styled 12 (★★★★★), a step up on 11. With lift from a splash of oaked semillon, has more mineral than fruity character. Intense, flinty; a little angular in youth, but developing weight & pungency.

★★★ **Semillon-Sauvignon Blanc Reserve** 'Reserve' added to **10** name. More flamboyantly aromatic than 09, with butterscotch, grass, ripe melon. Barrel fermented, oak youthfully dominating the waxy fruit notes. Franschhoek semillon, Stellenbosch sauvignon.

★★★★ **Cape Vintage** 📖 Drops 'Port' for **10** (★★★★) from touriga, tinta. Slightly truffly, forest-floor & thyme aromas; spicy, intense, savoury; tannin & alcohol harmonious, but lacks intricacy of 09. Needs time.

Cabernet Franc Rosé ✓ 🍴 📖 ★★★★ Salmon pink 12 tank sample. Pomegranate-sweet fruit reined in by tangy dryness & faint tannic notes. Savoury & expressive, with plush texture & polished finish. 11 (★★★) softer.

Noble Late Harvest Semillon In abeyance. Discontinued: **Red Blend, Chardonnay Reserve**. — MF

■ **De Leuwen Jagt** *see Leeuwenjacht*

Delheim Wines   🍴 🍷 🏬 📷 ✗ 🚹

Location/map: Stellenbosch ▪ WO: Simonsberg–Stellenbosch/Stellenbosch ▪ Est 1971 ▪ 1stB 1961 ▪ Tasting & sales daily 9-5 ▪ Fee R25 tasting/R35 tasting & cellar tour ▪ Closed Easter Fri/Sun, Dec 25 & Jan 1 ▪ Cellar tours daily at 10.30 & 2.30 ▪ Delheim Restaurant (see Restaurants section) ▪ Facilities for children ▪ Tour groups ▪ Gifts ▪ Farm produce ▪ Conferences ▪ Conservation area ▪ Oakleaf Lodge B&B at Delvera ▪ Events: see website for schedule ▪ Owner(s) Sperling family ▪ Winemaker(s) Reg Holder (Jan 2012) ▪ Viticulturist(s) Victor Sperling (Aug 1993) ▪ 375ha/148ha (cab, ptage, shiraz, chard, chenin, riesling, sauv) ▪ 980t/60,000cs own label 50% red 30% white 20% rosé ▪ Brands for client: Woolworths ▪ BWI champion, Level 1 B-BBEE, WIETA ▪ PO Box 10 Stellenbosch 7599 ▪ delheim@delheim.com ▪ www.delheim.com ▪ S 33° 52′ 10.1″   E 018° 53′ 9.8″ ▪ **+27 (0)21-888-4600** ▪ F +27 (0)21-888-4601

This Simonsberg farm, originally 'De Drie Sprong', was acquired by Hans Otto Hoheisen and wife Deli as a retirement property in 1938. In 1944 they built a cellar, considered quite revolutionary at the time, but by the early 1950s realised they could no longer manage the workload on their own. Help soon arrived via the Winchester Castle in the ebullient form of Michael Sperling, Deli's nephew. One of the great characters of South African wine, 'Spatz' Sperling with wife Vera made Delheim their home and the centre of a dynamic wine and tourism business (Delheim a co-founder of the Stellenbosch Wine Route). Children Nora and Victor have taken over and brought fresh energy, as has seasoned new winemaker, Reg Holder. 'Deli's Heimat' continues to attract thousands of visitors, and the marketing slogan, 'Worth the Journey', couldn't be more apt.

Vera Cruz Estate range

★★★★ **Shiraz** A fine 09 (★★★★★) vintage & low-yielding, single-vineyard fruit combine in classic style. Powerful yet well groomed, with savoury dark spicy flavours & supple integration of tannins & oak. Distinguished & ageworthy, as was 08.

Delheim range

★★★ **Cabernet Sauvignon** ⊕ 09 suave & streamlined, good depth of fruit, subtle oaking & long finish. Confident, cellar-worthy style. Upholds estate's reputation for top-quality cab.

★★★★ **Shiraz** 🔲 **10** low yield rewards ample dark fruit & pepper in firm but supple tannin framewor Similar suave elegance to **08**, even in warm vintage. Still youthful, best in 4-5 years. No **09**.

★★★★☆ **Grand Reserve** ⏱ **08** flagship red, mostly cab & dab merlot, classically styled. Inky dark fru leather & cedar oak, all elegantly restrained. So suave & well groomed, disguises inherent power. Cellarworthy

★★★★☆ **Edelspatz Noble Late Harvest** 🔲 **12** riesling preview shows glimpse of **10**'s thrilling balanc Rich & unctuous glacé pineapple, quince & honey threaded with zesty lime-tinged acidity. More elegant vibrant than **11** (★★★★).

Merlot ★★★ Now bottled, **09** less heady & more harmony than preview. Still tightly woven, with minty re berry tone. **Pinotage** 🔲 ★★★★ **11** retains spicy mulberry flavours but all in lighter & juicier mode. Fir food-friendly tannins & silky texture. WO Stellenbosch. **Chardonnay Sur Lie** 🔲 ★★★★ **11**'s tangy lime pear, from old vines, still in oak's toasty hazelnut embrace. Deserves time for fruit to shine (& possible high rating). **Unwooded Chardonnay** ‹NEW› ✓ 🔲 ★★★★ **11** elegant debut shows lovely pear & lemon fru purity, from older vines. Clean-cut freshness, lithe & tangy. **Gewürztraminer** 🔲 ★★★★ A shade c fresh & piquant **10** (★★★★), now-bottled **11** exudes Turkish Delight & rosepetal charm. For spicy fare, aperitif. **Sauvignon Blanc** ✓ 🔲 ★★★★ Bright & crisp, **12** dances with tangy tropical flavours. Deligh ful solo or al fresco partner. **Spatzendreck Late Harvest** 🔲 ★★★★ Bottled **11**, from old chenin vines, le zesty than when previewed last time. Still delicious, uncloying sweetness with dried apricot/floral tone. W Stellenbosch, as for Gewürztraminer. Discontinued: **Chardonnay**.

Lifestyle range

Pinotage Rosé ☺ 🔲 ★★★ Scent of muscat & red berries on amiable off-dry **12**. **Chenin Blanc** ☺ 🔲 ★★★ Crisper **12** has crunchy ripe apple freshness in friendly summer quaffing style. **Heerenwijn Sauvignon Blanc-Chenin Blanc** ☺ 🔲 ★★★ **12** clean apple & almond tone for fresh anywhere/ time enjoyment.

Cabernet Sauvignon-Shiraz 🔲 ★★★ Warm-hearted **11** is riper, less juicy than before. Spicy savoury dark fruit in robust style, good with BBQs. WO Stellenbosch, as for all. — MW

■ **De Liefde** *see* Mountain Ridge Wines

Dellrust Wines

Location: Somerset West ▪ Map: Helderberg ▪ WO: Stellenbosch ▪ Est/1stB 1998 ▪ Tasting & sales by appt Owner(s)/winemaker(s)/viticulturist(s) Albert Bredell ▪ 47ha/25ha (cab, merlot, ptage, shiraz, sauv) ▪ 200t ▪ F Box 5666 Helderberg 7135 ▪ albert.b@dellrust.co.za ▪ S 34° 1′58.7″ E 018° 46′46.9″ ▪ **T +27 (0)82-771-3090**

The beautiful views of False Bay from the Faure hills will hopefully be maximise when Albert Bredell puts into action his plan to erect 'a small boutique cellar'. A the moment it's still conceptual but he continues to keep his brand alive, sellin off stocks of his fortified wines.

Merlot Await new vintage, as for **Shiraz**, **Three Vines Limited Release**, **Sauvignon Blanc** & **Jerepig Cape Vintage** ⏱ ★★★★ Lightish port-style winter sipper **06** from tinta & touriga last had spicy Christma pudding, raisin & chocolate notes, lacked grip & fire. — FM

De Meye Wines

Location/map/WO: Stellenbosch ▪ Est/1stB 1998 ▪ Tasting & sales Mon-Thu by appt Fri 12-5 Sat/Sun & pu hols 11-4 ▪ Fee R15/5 wines ▪ Closed Good Fri, Dec 25/26 & Jan 1 ▪ Cellar tours Mon-Fri by appt ▪ 'The Table De Meye' open for lunch Sat-Sun, booking essential (www.thetablerestaurant.co.za) ▪ Farm produce Owner(s) Jan Myburgh Family Trust ▪ Winemaker(s) Marcus Milner (Sep 1999), with Aby Bodlani (Sep 2000) Viticulturist(s) Schalk Pienaar (Dec 2010) & Johan Pienaar (Jan 2006, consultant) ▪ 100ha/65ha (cabs s▪ merlot, shiraz, chard, chenin) ▪ 300t/18,000cs own label 65% red 25% white 10% rosé ▪ IPW ▪ PO Box 2 Elsenburg 7607 ▪ info@demeye.co.za ▪ www.demeye.co.za ▪ S 33° 49′0.7″ E 018° 49′48.8″ ▪ **T +27 (0)21 884-4131** ▪ F +27 (0)21-884-4154

This family-owned estate is one of the most northerly wine farms i Stellenbosch and altogether as unpretentious and pleasing as the wines — env ronmentally responsible too. The care and craft put into them by Marcus Milne is hinted at by the fact that most of the varietal wines in fact contain splashes c ther varieties. All are properly dry — there's no dumbing down with the showy, heap appeal of sweetness, even with the perennially great-value second tier.

e Meye range

★★★★ **Cabernet Sauvignon ✓** Finely honed with blackcurrant, lead-pencil whiffs reflecting pedigree. Intense yet unflamboyant, oak integrated & filling out the finish. 09 (★★★★★) riper, more generous than herbaceous 08.

★★★★☆ **Trutina** 🖉 Rich & robust 10 (★★★★) from cab with shiraz, merlot, cab franc. Slightly gamey, savoury, a little rustic. Oak evident, but integrated. Harmonious, restrained but less plush than 09.

Chardonnay Unwooded ☺ 🍴 🖉 ★★★ Restrained 12 harmonious & bone-dry; layered, lingering grapefruit, flinty notes; good weight. **Chenin Blanc** ☺ 🍴 🖉 ★★★ Fragrant honeysuckle, pear drop aromas on fresh & almost nettly 12 tank sample, with dry, limy finish.

Merlot ✓ 🖉 ★★★★ Mulberry, mushroom & faintly vegetal notes. 10 nicely unshowy, but unyielding on the nish & lacks full fruit of 09 (★★★★). **Shiraz** 🖉 ★★★ Brooding 10 with dollops cab, cab franc; smoky, beef bouillon & hallmark peppery spice notes; chunky & robust. **Shiraz Rosé ✓** 🍴 🖉 ★★★★ Perfumed, floral otes on salmon-pink 12 tank sample; dry, textured & savoury, offering freshness & length.

ittle River range

Shiraz ☺ 🍴 🖉 ★★★ Quality second tier over-delivering as usual. Red berry notes, quite aromatic; refined but generous & easy-drinking 11, food-friendly finish.

abernet Sauvignon ⓧ 🍴 ★★★ 10 was fresh & juicy, with just a hint of seriousness. — MF

De Mikke Patron see Almenkerk Wine Estate

DeMorgenzon

ocation/map: Stellenbosch ▪ WO: Western Cape/Stellenbosch ▪ Est 2003 ▪ 1stB 2005 ▪ Tasting & sales daily 0–5 ▪ Fee R15-R25 ▪ Closed Good Fri, Dec 25/26 & Jan 1 ▪ Cellar tours on request ▪ Conservation area ▪ wner(s) Wendy & Hylton Appelbaum ▪ Cellarmaster(s) / GM Carl van der Merwe (Jul 2010) ▪ Winemaker(s) arl van der Merwe (Jul 2010), with Vanessa Hoek (Aug 2012) ▪ Viticulturist(s) Louis Buys (Sep 2012) & Kevin Watt (consultant) ▪ 91ha/52ha (cab, grenache, merlot, mourv, shiraz, chard, chenin, rouss, sauv, viog) ▪ 252t/ 5,000cs own label 56% red 33% white 8% rosé 3% other ▪ BWI, IPW ▪ PO Box 1388 Stellenbosch 7599 ▪ fo@demorgenzon.co.za ▪ www.demorgenzon.co.za ▪ S 33° 56'22.99" E 018° 45'0.17" ▪ **T +27 (0)21-881-030** ▪ F +27 (0)21-881-3773

The sound of music echoes off the vineyard-covered slopes of Hylton and Wendy Appelbaum's beautiful Stellenbosch property. If the vines respond to the classical music, their grapes respond to winemaker Carl van der Merwe's care. The early fruits of his tenure show individuality and precision. Now he will have a harvest in China, as one of 10 successful international winemakers in the Ningxia Wine Challenge. 'China is a fascinating country, deeply committed to success,' he says; 'we'd be foolish to ignore its winemaking potential and buying power. The opportunity to meet and work alongside winemakers from around the world will be invaluable, and I look forward to discussing the challenges we all face.'

★★★★ **DMZ Syrah** 🍴 🖉 Characterful shiraz in the making, 11 shows pure spice & ripe red fruit, promising complexity to come. Assertive in youth, with a comfortable suppleness waiting to emerge.

★★★★ **DMZ Chardonnay** 🍴 🖉 12 in crisp, fruit-driven style, oaked portion adding breadth but not interfering with bright limy melon flavours. Good now but has substance for growth. 11 untasted by us.

★★★★☆ **Chenin Blanc Reserve** 🖉 Unforced concentration from 40 year old bushvines shines in this slightly oxidative, richly textured & mineral-core wine. Benefit of maturity emerging in 10 (★★★★★). Natural ferment adds dimension to haunting floral, wet wool character; savoury seduction should develop with age. 11 more of the same, if youthfully unevolved. Both just-off-dry, WO Stellenbosch.

★★★★ **DMZ Sauvignon Blanc** 🍴 🖉 Rush of tropical fruit & hint of sweat on youthful 12. Well-weighted mouthfeel, forming grip from tiny oaked portion to balance overall fresh & lively profile. 11 untasted.

★★★★☆ **DeMorgenzon Concerto White** NEW 🖉 11 beautifully orchestrated roussanne with chenin, viognier & chardonnay. Fine, lengthily sustained floral, spice features with buzz contrasting freshness to full body, textural richness. Lightly oaked. Food & time will bring more pleasure. Stellenbosch WO.

Garden Vineyards Rosé ✓ 🍴 📖 ★★★★ Fermented in older oak, **11**'s peaches & cream savouriness h
more substance & interest than most. Roundly, fruitily dry; mostly from shiraz & other Rhône varieties. Disco
tinued: **DMZ Concerto**. — AL

■ **Denneboom** *see Oude Denneboom*
■ **De Oude Opstal** *see Stellendrift* — SHZ Cilliers/Kuün Wyne

De Redley   `NEW`

WO: Stellenbosch ▪ Est/1stB 2012 ▪ Closed to public ▪ Cellarmaster(s) Nicholas Ridley (Sep 2011) ▪ 7t/175
own label 33% red 66% white ▪ info@deredley.co.za ▪ www.deredley.co.za ▪ **T +27 (0)11-708-3444**
F +27 (0)11-708-3615

Cellarmaster Nicholas Ridley last year released the maiden vintage of an unusua
merlot blanc de noir to a warm reception, locally and overseas, partly because o
its versatility — 'The wine loves sushi!' Based on the success of the small-sca
debut, the plan is to make available at least 2,222 6-bottle cases this year, alon
with 'other exciting wines to be added to the range'.

White Merlot 🍴 📖 ★★ Unlike US examples made sweetish for broader appeal, **12** bone-dry, almost au
tere, mere hint of red berry. Pretty palest onion skin hue, elegant packaging look good at table. — JP/CvZ

Desert Rose Wines

Location: Vredendal ▪ Map: Olifants River ▪ WO: Western Cape ▪ Tasting by appt ▪ Owner(s) Alan van Niekerk
Herman Nel ▪ Winemaker(s) Herman Nel ▪ desertrose@nashuaisp.co.za ▪ S 31° 41′ 33.1″ E 018° 30′ 5.9′
T +27 (0)82-809-2040/+27 (0)82-800-2270 ▪ F +27 (0)27-213-2858

The evocative name comes from 'a song about beauty and love by Sting', explain
Herman Nel, co-owner with Alan van Niekerk of this Olifants River garagist
winery. They now have a sales point and tasting facility at Vredendal Nursery
next step is to join and help develop the Olifants River Wine Route.

Cabernet Sauvignon ★★★ Easy-drinking **10** has refreshing acidity, is less sweet than Winemaker's ve
sion. **Winemaker's Choice Cabernet Sauvignon** `NEW` ★★★ Interesting salty nuance on blackcurran
toned **11**, soft & vanilla-sweet from 100% new American oak. **Winemaker's Choice Merlot** `NEW` ★★
Rum & raisin-infused **10** has charry oak notes, cranberry lift for uncomplicated sipping. **Shiraz** ⑂ ★★★ C
dense & powerful, still tight last edition; structured to develop interestingly. **Jada's Rose** ⑂ ★★★★ C
happy 60/40 mix cab & shiraz, former's taut grip soften by shiraz's raspberry fruit. **Nicola's Rose** `NEW`
★★★★ Succulent mulberry, savoury nuances on silky **10** rosé from cab, merlot & shiraz. Worthy additio
SA's dry pink line-up. — DB/CvZ

De Toren Private Cellar

Location/map/WO: Stellenbosch ▪ Est 1994 ▪ 1stB 1999 ▪ Tasting, sales & cellar tours by appt ▪ Fee R18
waived on purchase ▪ Donkey walk ▪ Owner(s) Edenhall Trust ▪ Cellarmaster(s) Albie Koch (Oct 1998)
Winemaker(s) Charles Williams (Dec 2008) ▪ Viticulturist(s) Ernest Manuel (Mar 2003, consultant) ▪ 25h
±21ha (cabs s/f, malbec, merlot, p verdot) ▪ 150t/8,000cs own label 100% red ▪ PO Box 48 Vlottenburg 760
▪ info@de-toren.com ▪ www.de-toren.com ▪ S 33° 57′ 34.5″ E 018° 45′ 7.5″ ▪ **T +27 (0)21-881-3119** ▪
+27 (0)21-881-3335

In case there's doubt when you speak about the well-known wines from this fam
ily-run winery on Stellenbosch's Polkadraai Hills: the V in Fusion V is not pro
nounced 'Vee' but 'Five' (with a Latin accent, perhaps) while the Z in the othe
wine is 'Zee' (an American tone might be appropriate). The vineyards and wine
have a resolutely South African accent, of course. Emil and Sonette den Dul
acquired the farm primarily for its fine views and only later, they say, realise
that some great terroir was included. The land is treated with great respect, wit
farming done as 'naturally' and responsibly as possible — recycled water efflu
ent, compost production and striving after carbon neutrality all point to this.

★★★★☆ **Fusion V** Cab-based Bordeaux blend often savoury & refined, like **08** & **09** (★★★★★). **1**
(★★★★) raisiny, dried fruit notes. Rich, sweetfruited & soft, but 15% alcohol dulls freshness; oak tannins rule.

★★★★ **Z** Second 5-way blend, this merlot-led. Savoury, restrained & immaculately oaked. Unshowy **10** is lighter & spicier; combines fruit elegance, freshness & tealeaf, tobacco fragrance. Big alcohol in balance. — MF

De Trafford Wines

_ocation/map/WO: Stellenbosch ▪ Est/1stB 1992 ▪ Tasting, sales & tours Fri & Sat 10–1, or otherwise by appt ▪ ee R50, waived on purchase ▪ Closed all pub hols ▪ Owner(s) David & Rita Trafford ▪ Winemaker(s) David rafford ▪ Viticulturist(s) Schalk du Toit (consultant) ▪ 200ha/5ha (cabs s/f, merlot, pinot, shiraz) ▪ 71t/3,500cs wn label 70% red 30% white ▪ PO Box 495 Stellenbosch 7599 ▪ info@detrafford.co.za ▪ www.detrafford.co. a ▪ S 34° 0′ 45.1″ E 018° 53′ 57.8″ ▪ **T +27 (0)21-880-1611** ▪ F +27 (0)21-880-1611

Artisanal winemaker David Trafford was only half joking when he said he'd prob- ably have to walk around with a camcorder linked to YouTube on his head in order to connect with social-media-savvy customers. Not that it's likely to hap- pen at this boutique winery with an international reputation for excellence. 'Perhaps I just lack vision, but I can't see our business changing much — hope- fully just getting better,' he says. Cab, shiraz and chenin remain the focus, ideally suited to his Helderberg terroir. 'Techniques can be copied, vineyard sites can't.' He is also proud of the confidence his fellow serious fine-wine producers have in their own ability to produce world beaters from the Cape but bemoans the specu- atively priced wines which undermine credibility.

★★★★☆ **Cabernet Sauvignon** Continuing stellar orbit of **09**, **10** is textured, complex, layered & concen- trated, shows a fynbos & tealeaf sheen to ripe Christmas cake fruit, ripe dry tannin. Drinkable now, its dense & dark aromas & flavours will unfurl beautifully over many years.

★★★★ **Merlot** Succulent yet polished **10**, savoury tobacco & ripe plum, tannins still perky but elegant, approachable, already drinks well. Naturally fermented, as all De Trafford wines.

★★★★ **Blueprint Syrah** Mainly from neighbour Keermont grapes. Smoky, pancetta veneer to **10**, mara- schino cherry & spice vibrancy. Oakiness should meld. Lighter body than stablemates, but as drinkable.

★★★★ **Syrah 393** From home vineyard, overtly spicy **10** shows blueberries, hedgerow fruit & violets. Plum succulence & Provençal herbs, chalky squeeze of dry tannins add dimension & breadth to concentrated yet lively palate.

★★★★☆ **CWG Auction Reserve Syrah** NEW Cocoa smoky whiffs on big & bold **09** auction offering. Sweet plum & spice handle high alc (15.6%) well, as does the toned oak, 50% new. Intense, as most of their wines are, it's succulent & eminently drinkable but will cellar beautifully.

★★★★☆ **CWG Auction Reserve Perspective** NEW Third each cab franc, merlot & cab. Inky creosote & charcoal intensity vies with spicy black fruit-compote vibrancy, **09** tomato leaf edge to rich ripeness & density on palate. Oak, 50% new, needs time to join the chorus.

★★★★☆ **Elevation 393** ⓧ Barrel selection, named for home-vineyard altitude. Cab-led Bordeaux blend & shiraz, each playing their part in **09**. Plush dark berries, whiffs of salty liquorice, scrub, backed by muscular tan- nins designed for long, slow, bottle evolution.

★★★★ **Chenin Blanc** Brush of oak broadens interest on ripe, leesy & honeyed **11**. Baked apple note deliv- ers on rich promise. Natural fermentation in barrel, as always. Rewards patience too.

★★★★ **Chenin Blanc Four V** NEW A once-off blend of barrel-fermented chenin from 4 vintages. Light tangerine highlight of **NV** offering. Gentle & rounded, with textured, toned oak contribution.

★★★★☆ **Straw Wine** Thatchy brûlée & apricot tang on ambrosial **10** (★★★★) from air-dried, barrel-aged (23 months) chenin. Rich, concentrated & rounded but **09** was slightly fresher & more vibrant. 375ml. — FM

De Villiers Wines

_ocation: Paarl ▪ Map: Paarl & Wellington ▪ Est/1stB 1996 ▪ Tasting & sales by appt ▪ Owner(s) De Villiers Family Trust ▪ Cellarmaster(s)/winemaker(s)/viticulturist(s) Villiers de Villiers (1996) ▪ 25,000cs own label 80% red 20% white ▪ Other export brand: Heeren van Oranje Nassau ▪ PO Box 659 Suider-Paarl 7624 ▪ vadev@mweb.co.za ▪ www.devillierswines.com ▪ S 33° 45′ 43.3″ E 018° 57′ 40.8″ ▪ **T +27 (0)21-863-2175** ▪ F +27 (0)86-653-8988

Brand owner Villiers de Villiers released a new reserve range due to demand from loyal and faithful customers', and available to them directly via the new website, www.devillierswines.com. Villiers' Paarl winery continues to supply wines to 'dis- cerning value-for-money customers' through supermarkets such as Pick 'n Pay.

Cabernet Sauvignon ⑨ ★★★ Intense berry jam flavours, firm tannin on **09** when last tasted. **Merlot** ⑨ ★★★ Berry-toned **09** previously had pleasant roundness & soft structure. **Pinotage** ⑨ ★★★ **09** showed deft touches when last reviewed: enticing spicy wild black fruits & juicy plumpness. **Shiraz** ⑨ ★★★ Smooth **09** previously generous mix black fruit, hint dark choc. **Sauvignon Blanc** ⑨ 🍽 ★★★ Last time, **10** was still quite restrained soon after bottling yet light & refreshing. — GdB

Devonair

Location/map/WO: Stellenbosch ▪ Est 1994 ▪ 1stB 2000 ▪ Tasting & sales by appt ▪ Closed all pub hols ▪ Conferences ▪ 2 self-catering cottages ▪ Owner(s) Leon & Rina de Wit ▪ Winemaker(s) Ernst Gouws (Mar 2006) ▪ Viticulturist(s) Frans Snyman (2011) ▪ 2.2ha (cab) ▪ 10t/460cs own label 100% red ▪ PO Box 1274 Stellenbosch 7599 ▪ info@devonair.co.za ▪ www.devonair.co.za ▪ S 33° 53' 44.45" E 018° 48' 27.46" ▪ **T +27 (0)21-886-6830** ▪ F +27 (0)21-886-6855

Last harvest was a milestone for owners Leon and Rina de Wit who, after 20 years in Johannesburg, had settled in Devon Valley in 2004. The small cabernet block on their property was neglected but had potential, the De Wits believed, and with neighbour and viticulturist Lorna Hughes, was carefully nursed back to award-winning health. With future sustainability in mind, however, the difficult decision was made in 2008 to grub up all the vines and replant. 2012, the much-anticipated 'rebirth' crop, is looking promising and should be released in 2015.

The Cab ★★★★ Medium-bodied **07** shows plush ripe blackberry fruit backed by a fine tannin structure & firm acid balance. **The Cab Family Reserve** ⑨ ★★★★ Good fruit in last **06**, cassis & plums, with sturdy oak providing structure, rewarding future. Own, Grangehurst vines. Discontinued: **The Rosé**. — WB

■ **Devonet** see Clos Malverne

Devon Hill

Location/WO: Stellenbosch ▪ Est 1994 ▪ 1stB 1996 ▪ Closed to public ▪ Owner(s) Geir Tellefsen ▪ Cellarmaster(s)/winemaker(s)/viticulturist(s) Therese de Beer (Jan 2011, consultant) ▪ 10,000cs own label 80% red 15% white 5% rosé ▪ geir@rosendalwinery.com ▪ **T +27 (0)21-424-4498** ▪ F +27 (0)21-424-1571

Though owned by Robertson-based Rosendal Winery's Geir Tellefsen, Devon Hill will continue to feature grapes from the Stellenbosch area, and winemaker Therese de Beer says the team is busy identifying suitable fruit for this purpose.

★★★★ **Bluebird** ⑨ **02** well-knit merlot-led (73%) combo with plummy flavour. Tasted several years back, as for Shiraz.

Cabernet Sauvignon Available but not tasted by us, as for **Pinotage** & **Four Stars**. **Merlot** ⑨ ★★★★ Complex aromas fynbos, wet earth & plum on fruit-filled **10** early sipper. **Shiraz** ⑨ ★★★★ Intense **03**'s ripe mouthful previously reined in by deft oak & tannins, vein of acidity. **Sauvignon Blanc** ⑨ ★★★ Shy tangerine & grass, **10** an appealing food companion. — CvZ

Devon Rocks

Location/map/WO: Stellenbosch ▪ Est 1998 ▪ 1stB 2003 ▪ Tasting, sales & tours by appt ▪ B&B accommodation ▪ Owner(s) Jürgen & Brita Heinrich ▪ Winemaker(s) Simon Smith (Louisvale) ▪ Viticulturist(s) Gawie du Bois & Paul Wallace (advisers) ▪ 4ha/3.5ha (ptage, shiraz) ▪ 2,200cs 57% red 18% white 25% rosé ▪ PO Box 12483 Die Boord 7613 ▪ info@devonrocks.co.za ▪ www.devonrocks.co.za ▪ S 33° 53' 19.9" E 018° 48' 30.1" ▪ **T +27 (0)21-865-2536** ▪ F +27 (0)21-865-2621

A small vineyard in Devon Valley, some occasional labels and ready buyers of finished wine (made at nearby Louisvale); this is the viticultural domain of Jürgen and Brita Heinrich. As currently with many micro-producers, the volumes don't justify the market-spend, so they're biding their time and looking at options.

Devonvale Golf & Wine Estate

Location/map/WO: Stellenbosch ▪ Est 1997 ▪ 1stB 2004 ▪ Tasting by appt ▪ Fee R10pp ▪ Sales Mon-Sat 11–6 ▪ Restaurant open daily for breakfast, lunch & dinner ▪ Tour groups ▪ Golf ▪ Pro shop ▪ Conferences ▪ Devonvale Lodge ▪ Owner(s) Devonmust (Pty) Ltd ▪ Winemaker(s) Wilhelm Kritzinger (2004, Bellevue Estate) ▪ Viticulturist(s) Ruben Nienaber (2000) ▪ 117ha/26.5ha (shiraz) ▪ 14t/950cs own label 100% red ▪ PO Box 77 Koelenhof 7605 ▪ info@devonvale.co.za ▪ www.devonvale.co.za ▪ S 33° 52′59.6″ E 018° 48′15.0″ ▪ **T +27 (0)21-865-2080** ▪ F +27 (0)21-865-2601

Residents of this upmarket Stellenbosch lifestyle estate, with its newly renovated lodge, at harvest time invite family and friends to help bring in the crop from vines fringing some of the fairways, for vinification and bottling at Bellevue. The nautical connotations in the branding are to Devonvale founder and round-the-world yachtsman JJ Provoyeur, and to a particularly favourable angle in sailing.

Owner's Special Reserve range

Shiraz ⓐ ★★★★ Elegant & rounded **08**, good concentration of plums, savoury edge offset by showy oak.

Broad Reach range

Provoyeur Cabernet Sauvignon ⓐ ★★★ When last tasted, **07** earthy notes, plummy centre, toasty new-oak seasoning & support. **Provoyeur Shiraz** ★★★ Fresh-sawn wood scent permeates a plum-pudding, mocha richness, **10** very individually styled. — DB

DeWaal Wines

Location/map/WO: Stellenbosch ▪ Est 1682 ▪ 1stB 1972 ▪ Tasting & sales Mon-Fri 10–12.30 & 2–4.30 Sat 10–4. 30 (Aug-Apr only) ▪ Fee R20 ▪ Closed Easter Fri-Mon, Jun 16, Dec 25/26 & Jan 1 ▪ Owner(s) Pieter de Waal ▪ Winemaker(s)/viticulturist(s) Chris de Waal & Daniël de Waal (whites/reds, consultants) ▪ 154ha/120ha (ptage, shiraz, sauv) ▪ 800t ▪ 50% red 50% white ▪ IPW ▪ PO Box 15 Vlottenburg 7604 ▪ info@dewaal.co.za ▪ www.dewaal.co.za ▪ S 33° 56′29.3″ E 018° 45′59.9″ ▪ **T +27 (0)21-881-3711** ▪ F +27 (0)21-881-3776

Pieter de Waal, brand owner and ninth-generation co-custodian (with brothers Chris and Danie) of lovely Uiterwyk estate in Stellenboschkloof, keeps alive DeWaal Wines' well-established reputation as pinotage specialists. The story goes that forebear CT De Waal was the first person to vinify this local variety with any degree of success, prompting rugby team-mates PK Morkel of Bellevue and Kanonkop's Paul Sauer to plant it too. Fittingly, CT has one of the three DeWaal pinotages named after him. The Top of the Hill version, from one of South Africa's oldest pinotage vineyards, leads the rankings.

DeWaal range

★★★★ **Cabernet Sauvignon** Leafy, herbal **08** (★★★★) from old vineyard in lean, austere style, needing food to accompany. Less richness than **07**.

★★★★ **Merlot** ⓐ Full bodied, resolutely dry **09** shows Old-World styling with solid, ripe black fruit.

★★★★ **CT de Waal Pinotage** From 50 year old vineyard, gets more serious treatment than standard bottling. Handsome **09** lushly rich but not too ripe; well structured by 60% new oak. No **08**.

★★★★☆ **Top of the Hill Pinotage** Amply built, spicy **10** cloaked in all-new oak to deliver seriously structured top-end example of estate's signature variety. Tiny yields from 60 year old bushvines deliver compact dark fruit. Surprisingly accessible, though good potential. No **08** or **09**.

★★★★ **Signal Rock** ⓐ Cab-driven **08** Bordeaux-style blend was big & angular when tasted a few years back; tealeaf & forest floor layers over rich blackcurrant fruit.

Pinotage 🔲 ★★★ Estate's popular, savoury **10** entry-level pinotage bottling made for early uncomplicated drinking. **Viognier** 🔲 🚱 ★★★ **11** unusually crisp & zingy for this variety. Bone-dry, focused, for lightish summer drinking. Discontinued: **Sauvignon Blanc**.

Young Vines range

Merlot ☺ 🔲 🚱 ★★★ Vivacious, youthful **10** is fresh & simply styled for uncomplicated enjoyment. **Sauvignon Blanc** ☺ 🔲 🚱 ★★★ Fresh, zippy **12** reflects charm of vintage with appealing fruitiness & pleasing harmony. Undemanding **11** (★★★) offers crisp, fruity quaffing.

Shiraz 🔲 🚱 ★★★ Popular mocha-styled **10** perfect for smooth quaffing. **Chenin Blanc** 🔲 🚱 ★★★ Preview **12** not quite settled, but previous vintages admired for consistency & over-delivery. — IM

Dewaldt Heyns Family Wines

Location: Tulbagh/Swartland ▪ WO: Swartland ▪ Est/1stB 2006 ▪ Tasting by appt at Saronsberg ▪ Owner(s) Dewaldt Heyns Family Wines ▪ Cellarmaster(s)/winemaker(s)/viticulturist(s) Dewaldt Heyns ▪ (shiraz, chenin) ▪ 15t/550cs own label 50% red 50% white ▪ dewaldt@saronsberg.com ▪ **T +27 (0)82-441-4117**

Joubertskloof, Dewaldt Heyns' father's farm deep in the Perdeberg in the Swartland, is the source of the grapes for his Weathered Hands range. 'A year or so from now,' says the celebrated Saronsberg winemaker, who makes these eponymous wines in his old man's honour, we can expect a pinotage from 39-year-old vines to be added to the range. Planted, doubtless, by the same weathered hands.

Weathered Hands range

★★★★ **Chenin Blanc** From ±1ha Perdeberg block nearly 40 years old, on weathered granite, **10** is elegant, perfumed, pure, its leesy richness tempered by minerality & well-judged spicy French oak (40% new).

Shiraz ★★★★ Very ripe yet unshowy **08** has dark spice & red earth notes, finely judged tannin. — WB/AL

De Wetshof Estate

Location/map/WO: Robertson ▪ Est 1949 ▪ 1stB 1972 ▪ Tasting & sales Mon-Fri 8.30-4.30 Sat 9.30-12.30 ▪ Closed Easter Fri/Sun/Mon, May 1, Dec 25/26 & Jan 1 ▪ Cellar tours by appt Mon-Fri 8.30-4.30 ▪ Conservation area ▪ Owner(s) Danie de Wet, Peter de Wet & Johann de Wet ▪ Cellarmaster(s) Danie de Wet (Jan 1973) ▪ Winemaker(s) Danie de Wet (Jan 1973), Mervyn Williams (2001) & Peter de Wet (2007) ▪ Viticulturist(s) Rudolf Kriel (2012), advised by Phil Freese & Francois Viljoen (both 1997) ▪ 600ha/180ha (cab, merlot, pinot, chard, riesling, sauv) ▪ 1,800t 8% red 90% white 1% rosé 1% cap classique ▪ ISO 9001:2008, ISO 22000:2005, BBBEE Grade 2, BWI, Enviro Scientific, Integrity & Sustainability, IPW ▪ PO Box 31 Robertson 6705 ▪ info@dewetshof.com ▪ www.dewetshof.com ▪ S 33° 52'38.0" E 020° 0'35.1" ▪ **T +27 (0)23-615-1853** ▪ F +27 (0)23-615-1915

'Positioning De Wetshof as a chardonnay house is non-negotiable,' agree Peter and Johann de Wet, co-owners with pioneering father Danie. And what a 'house' it is, replicating buildings designed by 18th century architect Louis Michel Thibault, his vast contributions to Cape culture honoured through a new De Wetshof label. The Bateleur flagship from SA's oldest chardonnay vineyard continues to win international awards, with Danie's belief in terrain-specific production also vindicated by last year's five star rating for The Site 2009, the maiden single-vineyard bottling of vines planted way back in 1987. 'One can well ask what took us so long!'

De Wetshof range

★★★★ **Thibault** NEW Impressive Bordeaux red, one of handful made over the years. **09** merlot, cab, petit verdot & cab franc; plush (15% alc) plum & vanilla but still harmonious. Age or decant now to appreciate fully.

★★★★ **Bateleur Chardonnay** ⓧ Enduring & noble expression of barrel fermented/lees-aged chardonnay always needing few years to show at best. **09** lemon toned & tightly wound.

★★★★★ **The Site Chardonnay** ⓧ 2nd release **11** (★★★★★) confirms this as one of SA's finer barrel-fermented examples. Exudes confidence, big buttery personality, nutty vanilla notes, citrus undertones. Like **09**, for immediate gratification but plenty concentration & structure to improve with cellaring. No **10**.

★★★★ **Rhine Riesling** ⓧ 🍴 Spicy candied fruit character, steely edge on **09** softened by smidgen sugar; commendably moderate 12.5% alcohol.

★★★★★ **Edeloes** ⓧ Exceptional botrytised dessert, occasional release. Last-tasted **05** (★★★★★) was charming & complex; previous was **00**, confirmed by recent tasting as evolved, amber hued, but very much alive, delicious in fact. 500ml.

Chardonnay D'Honneur ⓧ ★★★★ Clotted cream, bruised apple hallmarks of French oak fermented/aged version. **07** preview vanilla & brioche seamed with zingy lime took it step up on **06** (★★★★). Ageworthy, like Bateleur. **Finesse Chardonnay** ⓧ ⓧ ★★★ **10** fatter & more buttery than previous release, engaging citrus zest refreshment, spicy tail. **Bon Vallon Chardonnay** ⓧ ★★★★ Step up for unwooded version. Jasmine-scented **12** has green apple acidity & white peach richness. **11** (★★★★) was equally fresh & supple. **Sauvignon Blanc** ✓ ★★★★ Lime-grapefruit nuanced **12** raises the bar — again — with fine poise, focus & freshness. Takes well-formed **11** (★★★) mouthful to next level. **Méthode Cap Classique Brut** ★★★ NV champagne-method sparkling from chardonnay & pinot noir. Latest version has crisp lemon bite, bready lees touch.

Danie de Wet range

★★★★ **Naissance Cabernet Sauvignon** Leafy **10** (★★★☆) on the austere side of elegant, shade off **09** with lead pencil fragrance, classic firm structure. WO W Cape.

★★★★ **Cape Muscadel** ⊕ Sweetly simple **07** (★★★), missed complexity of **06** & previous. **Nature In Concert Pinot Noir** ⊕ 🍶 ★★★★ Cherry & choc-mocha **09** firm & flavoursome, hides 14.5% alcohol well. **Rosé** ✓ 🍶 ★★★★ Improved **12** has many charms: peach blossom bouquet, fruit-filled yet tangy palate, elegant & dry conclusion. **Chardonnay Sur Lie** ✓ 🍶 🖾 ★★★★ Another step up for unwooded, lees-aged version. **12** effusive biscuit & citrus notes; silky mouthfeel & lemon-lime focus. **11**'s (★★★★) creamy richness was laced with tangy lemon twist. **Limestone Hill Chardonnay** ✓ 🍶 🖾 ★★★★ Unoaked, lees-aged **12** offers summer refreshment with gentle lime notes, lingering chalky conclusion. **Sauvignon Blanc** ✓ 🍶 🖾 ★★★★ Rung-up **12** herbal overtone to tropical fruit, elegant dry conclusion with saline nuance. — DB/JP

De Wet Winery

Location/map/WO: Worcester ▪ Est 1946 ▪ 1stB 1964 ▪ Tasting & sales Mon-Fri 8–5 Sat 9–12 ▪ Fee R1/wine ▪ Closed all pub hols ▪ Cellar tours by appt ▪ BYO picnic ▪ Owner(s) 60 members ▪ Cellarmaster(s) Piet le Roux (Jan 2000) ▪ Winemaker(s) Tertius Jonck (Sep 2007) & Phillip Vercuiel (Dec 2007) ▪ Viticulturist(s) Hennie Visser (Jul 2008, Vinpro) ▪ 1,000ha (cab, shiraz, chard, chenin, sauv) ▪ 15,500t/15,000cs own label 29% red 36% white 5% rosé 30% fortified + 10m L bulk ▪ ISO 22000, SGS ▪ PO Box 16 De Wet 6853 ▪ admin@dewetcellar.co.za ▪ www.dewetcellar.co.za ▪ S 33° 36′ 24.2″ E 019° 30′ 36.5″ ▪ **T +27 (0)23-341-2710** ▪ F +27 (0)23-341-2762

For thoughtful winemaker Tertius Jonck the challenge is balance: between De Wet's role as bulk wine exporter (as main shareholder in SA's top UK brand FirstCape) and nurturing those 'special wines'; between sustainable quality-wine production (now bolstered by monthly vineyard study groups for member growers) and the need for long-term, economically viable returns for farmers.

★★★★ **White Muscadel** ⊕ 🖾 High-toned almond, apricot & tangerine, **10** fortified dessert is sweet but uncloying.

Pinotage ☺ 🍶 🖾 ★★★ Coffee-toned **12** crisp & dry, exuberantly fruity & very drinkable. You could keep it year/2 but we bet you won't!

Cabernet Sauvignon ⊕ 🍶 🖾 ★★ Mulberry, thatch aromas on spicy-sweet **10**, ends tad stalky. Enjoy young, like most of these. **Shiraz** ⊕ 🍶 🖾 ★★ vanilla-infused everyday red. **Dry Red** ⊕ 🍶 🖾 ★★ Enticing berry-honey aroma, candyfloss flavours in **10**. **Chardonnay** ⊕ 🍶 🖾 ★★★ Plenty vanilla & spicy oak on slightly warming **10**. **Chenin Blanc** ⊕ 🍶 🖾 ★★★ Standout **11** a substantial appley mouthful with persistent juicy pineapple aftertaste. **Sauvignon Blanc** ⊕ 🍶 🖾 ★★★ **11** preview pear drop fragrance, 'dusty pebble' flavour & nice lemony bite. **Petillant Fronté** ⊕ 🍶 ★★ Floral, sweetish, spritzy NV from white muscadel, light 8% alcohol. **Cravate** ⊕ 🍶 ★★★★ Among first méthode cap classique sparklings from the region. 100% chardonnay, **09** myriad tiny bubbles, fresh & vibrant. **Rosé** ⊕ 🍶 ★★ Softly sweet NV sparkling from pinotage, with subtle berry taste. **Hanepoot** ⊕ 🖾 ★★★★ **10** fortified dessert with heady muscat aroma, lovely nutty tail. More spiritous & drier than red & white muscadel stablemates. **Red Muscadel** ⊕ 🖾 ★★★★ Charming fortified dessert offering balanced raisin sweetness, cranberry & tealeaf flavours. **10** more complexity than honey-sweet **09** (★★★). **Cape Ruby Port** ★★★ Now with 'Cape' in name. NV soft & comforting as a favourite chair beside a warm fire. Turkish Delight, nutmeg & dried leaves, pleasantly spirituous conclusion. **Cape Vintage** ⊕ ★★★★ Curry spice & Xmas cake, firm structure & luscious lingering flavour on **08** fortified. From now-uprooted, ultra-rare pontac, so has some sentimental value, too. — HJ/CvZ

De Zoete Inval Estate

Location: Paarl ▪ Map: Paarl & Wellington ▪ WO: Paarl/Stellenbosch ▪ Est 1878 ▪ 1stB 1976 ▪ Tastings & sales by appt ▪ Owner(s) DZI Agricultural Investments cc (John Robert & Eulalia Frater) ▪ Cellarmaster(s)/winemaker(s) John Robert Frater (1999) ▪ Viticulturist(s) Dirk Blom (2007) ▪ 80ha/20ha (cab, grenache, malbec, mourv, p verdot, shiraz, chard) ▪ 200t/8,000cs own label 50% red 50% white ▪ Other export brands: Eskdale, Safari ▪ PO Box 591 Suider-Paarl 7624 ▪ info@dezoeteinval.co.za ▪ www.dezoeteinval.co.za ▪ S 33° 46′ 35.9″ E 018° 57′ 50.9″ ▪ **T +27 (0)21-863-1535/+27 (0)82-731-3898** ▪ F +27 (0)21-863-2158

John Robert and Eulalia Frater are the husband and wife owners of one of South Africa's original farms, granted by the father of SA wine himself, Simon van der

Stel, in 1688. The Fraters' natural and minimal approach includes 'biological' farming and *oopkuipe* (traditional open fermentors), the aim being to shepherd the fruit as gently as possible into the bottle and keep the tannins approachable.

★★★★ **Pinotage Reserve** ⊛ When last tasted, spicy oak dominated **08**, with well-layered plummy fruit, meaty savoury notes. Supple body & texture. Simonsberg vines.

> **Chenin Blanc-Viognier-Semillon** NEW ☺ 🍴 ★★★ Soft & accessible **11**, bursting with peach & spice appeal. Well rounded & a pleasure to drink. Stellenbosch WO.

Pinotage Await new vintage. **Cabernet Sauvignon-Shiraz** ⊛ ★★★ **09** medicinal, with sweet berry fruit, heavy & full. **Chardonnay** ⊛ ★★ **10** faint wet-wool notes on lean, mineral body. **Vintage Brut** Not tasted. **Cape Vintage** New bottling not ready. **Sweet Surrender Shiraz** ⊛ ★★★ Fortified campfire warmer, **06** pastille-like blackcurrant flavour & solid spirit grip. — DB

DGB

Wellington ▪ Est 1942 ▪ Closed to public ▪ Owner(s) DGB management, Brait Capital Partners & Kangra ▪ Winemaker(s)/viticulturist(s) see Bellingham & Boschendal ▪ PO Box 246 Wellington 7654 ▪ exports@dgb.co.za ▪ www.dgb.co.za ▪ T +27 (0)21-864-5300 ▪ F +27 (0)21-864-1287

Well-established merchant house with strong portfolio of premium and own-brand ports, sherries and table wines, including Bellingham, Boschendal, Brampton, Culemborg, Douglas Green, Franschhoek Cellar, Legacy, Millstream, Oude Kaap, Tall Horse, The Bernard Series and The Saints, most listed separately.

- ▪ **D'Hero's** *see* Govert Wines
- ▪ **Diamond Collection** *see* Lutzville Cape Diamond Vineyards
- ▪ **Diamond Creek** *see* Wines of Cape Town
- ▪ **Dido** *see* The Township Winery

Die Bergkelder Wine Centre

Location/map: Stellenbosch ▪ All day tasting & sales Mon-Fri 8–5 Sat 9–2 ▪ Tour fee R25 ▪ Open non-religious pub hols ▪ Tours Mon-Fri 10, 11, 2 & 3; Sat 10, 11 & 12; incl AV presentation; bookings: info@bergkelder.co.za ▪ Tel +27 (0)21-809-8025 ▪ Special group tours, private tastings by appt ▪ Owner(s) Distell ▪ Cellarmaster(s) Andrea Freeborough ▪ Winemaker(s) Pieter Badenhorst (whites) & Justin Corrans (reds), with John November & Bradley van Niekerk ▪ Viticulturist(s) Bennie Liebenberg ▪ 2,500t/214,000cs 45% red 55% white ▪ PO Box 184 Stellenbosch 7599 ▪ info@bergkelder.co.za ▪ www.bergkelder.co.za ▪ S 33° 56'8.8" E 018° 50'54.7" ▪ **T +27 (0)21-809-8025** ▪ F +27 (0)21-883-9533

Literally 'Mountain Cellar', after the maturation facilities deep within Stellenbosch's Papegaaiberg, Die Bergkelder is the home of Fleur du Cap, listed separately. FdC wines can be tasted during a cellar tour, while other premium and super-premium wines in the Distell portfolio can be tasted and purchased at Die Bergkelder Wine Centre. The Vinoteque, now in its 29th year, markets fine wines with the option of having purchases stored in perfect cellar conditions. T +27 (0)21-809-8281 • info@vinoteque.co.za • www.vinoteque.co.za.

- ▪ **Die Laan** *see* Stellenbosch University Welgevallen Cellar

---

Die Mas van Kakamas   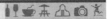

Location/WO: Northern Cape ▪ Map: Northern Cape, Free State & North West ▪ Est/1stB 2005 ▪ Tasting & sales Mon-Fri 8-5 Sat/Sun by appt ▪ Closed Easter Fri-Mon & Dec 25 ▪ 3-hr full farm tour on tractor-pulled wagon during tasting hours ▪ Meals/refreshments by appt; or BYO picnic ▪ Facilities for children ▪ Tour groups ▪ Gift shop ▪ Farm produce ▪ Conferences ▪ Walks/hikes ▪ Mountain biking trail ▪ Conservation area ▪ Camping facilities, 3 self-catering chalets & large lapa/bush pub ▪ Owner(s) Die Mas Boerdery (Pty) Ltd ▪ Cellarmaster(s)/winemaker(s)/viticulturist(s) Danie van der Westhuizen (May 2010) ▪ 1,400ha/80ha (cab, merlot, muscadel r/w, p verdot, pinot, ptage, sangio, shiraz, souzão, tinta, touriga, chard, chenin, cbard, sauv, viog) ▪ 350t/7,000cs own label 50% red 20% white 30% brandy ▪ PO Box 193 Kakamas 8870 ▪ winemaker@diemasvankakamas.co.za ▪ www.diemasvankakamas.co.za ▪ S 28° 45' 48.59" E 020° 38' 26.45" ▪ **T +27 (0)54-431-0245/+27 (0)82-931-5902** ▪ F +27 (0)86-531-9243

our decades ago ex-teachers Vlok and Welna Hanekom started farming a single hectare. Now crowds visiting their Kakamas spread on the Orange riverbanks love the 1,500ha of chalets, campsites, table grapes, raisin production and, of course, wine and brandy — the first of which finished three years' maturation in 2012.

Rooi Kalahari range

Pinotage NEW ☺ ★★★ In-your-face boldness on **12**, ripe, juicy & very friendly with raspberries galore.

Cabernet Sauvignon NEW ★★★ Approachable & gentle **11** has some blackcurrant appeal matched by firm backbone. Good texture to end. **Merlot** ★★★ Soft ripeness on uncomplicated **11**, which ups ante on previous. **Shiraz** ⓐ ⌾ ★★ Sunshiny berry flavours on effortless **10**. **Rooi Jerepigo** NEW ★★ Ruby cab & shiraz in **09** fortified dessert. Spicy & sweet but tad short. **Kalahari Ruby** ★★★★ Listed as 'Port' last time. Fiery spirit adds life & vigour to **NV**. Step up from previous (which was vintage dated), ample spice & pecan nut pie in long tail.

Groen Kalahari range

Chardonnay ⓐ ⌾ ★★ Uncomplicated dry **11** sipper. **Sauvignon Blanc** ★★★ Spanspek & fig on easy-drinking, light & fresh **12**.

Goue Kalahari range

Hanepoot ⓐ ★★★★ Northern Cape sunshine in a bottle. **09** oozes fragrant pineapple & boiled sweets. —FM

Diemersdal Estate

Location: Durbanville ▪ Map: Durbanville, Philadelphia & Darling ▪ WO: Durbanville/Western Cape ▪ Est 1698 ▪ 1stB 1976 ▪ Tasting & sales Mon-Fri 9–5 Sat 9–3 ▪ Closed Easter Fri/Sun, Dec 25 & Jan 1 ▪ Cellar tours by appt ▪ BYO picnic ▪ Walks ▪ Owner(s) Tienie Louw ▪ Winemaker(s) Thys Louw & Mari Branders ▪ Viticulturist(s) Div van Niekerk (1980) ▪ 300ha/165ha (cab, grenache, malbec, merlot, mourv, p verdot, ptage, shiraz, chard, sauv) ▪ 1,750t 70% red 30% white ▪ BWI, BRC, HACCIP ▪ PO Box 27 Durbanville 7551 ▪ thys@diemersdal.co.za ▪ www.diemersdal.co.za ▪ S 33° 48' 6.3" E 018° 38' 25.1" ▪ **T +27 (0)21-976-3361** ▪ F +27 (0)21-976-1810

For Thys Louw, the 6th generation winemaker at this Durbanville property, family and history are entertwined. That's why he rates the birth of his son Tienie — the first of the 7th generation — as the highlight of the past 12 months. 'A Louw has worked the grapes from this farm in the same cellar for over 150 years; it's a very humbling experience. Best of all, I get to share this experience — in a few years, of course — with the 7th generation Louw,' he says.

MM Louw range

★★★★★ **Estate Red** 🌿 Was 'Red Blend'. Restraint & elegance the hallmarks of this Bordeaux blend, revealed again in **10**. Subtly fruited, very dry, & firmly structured for cellaring.

★★★★★ **Sauvignon Blanc** This version of Diemersdal's speciality variety is fermented & aged in new barrels & with 10% semillon; usually the most long-lived. Oak very noticeable on **11** mid-2012 yet exquisite dryness, poise & fruit purity suggest it will deliver same presence, elegance as savoury **09**. No **10**.

Reserve range

★★★★★ **Private Collection** 🌿 Old World-inspired, cab-led 5-way Bordeaux blend. Smart, perfumed **10** in mould of **09**: herbaceous wafts, black fruit/lead pencil whiff, tightly wound tannins.

★★★★ **Chardonnay** 🌿 Oak dominates **11** (★★★★), toasty as well as woody notes permeate aroma & palate; satisfyingly fresh & long but not up to more complex **09**. **10** sold out untasted.

★★★★★ **Sauvignon Blanc** 🌿 From 26 year old single-vineyard, **12** offers concentration & great length with a crystalline finish. The most tropical, sweaty of the three 'serious' versions.

★★★★★ **8 Rows Sauvignon Blanc** 🌿 Moves from Estate range. Selection from 26 year old single-vineyard. Spends 5 months on lees for additional weight, texture. The expression here in **12** is khaki bush, blackcurrant leaf & ruby grapefruit; exceptionally taut but unwinds to reveal 'wet pebble' minerality.

Grenache Await next. **Pinotage** 🌿 ★★★★ As much as Private Collection is Old World, **11** is New World with confected pastille fruit, high alcohol, lavish new oak (60% here). But well done, even better than **10** (★★★★). Best don't broach for 3 years.

Diemersdal Estate range

★★★★ **Pinotage** 🌿 Traditional style very well done. **11** all sweet strawberry fruit, great grip & refreshing acidity.

★★★★ **Chardonnay Unwooded** ✓ 🍷 🅿 **12** neat parcel cool crystalline fruit, flavoursome & dry conclusion, with moderate alcohol. Like limy **11**, brisk aperitif style with structure to improve a year or 2. **Merlot** 🅿 ★★★★ **11** leafy, with lipsmacking acidity & a warm glow from 14.5% alcohol. **Shiraz** 🅿 ★★★★ **10** in similar black pepper & lily vein to **09**; not as plump though, more reined in but with commendably dry finish. **Sauvignon Rosé** 🍷 🅿 ★★★ Idiosyncractic combo sauvignon blanc & cab sauvignon. **12** grassy & slightly sweaty. **Sauvignon Blanc** ✓ 🍷 🅿 ★★★★ **12** a softer delivery than three varietal big brothers thanks to lower acidity & a smidgen of sugar. Faint tropical & nettle aromas, flavours.

Matys range

> **Cabernet Sauvignon-Merlot** ☺ 🍷 🅿 ★★★ Was 'Matys Cape Blend', & in Estate range (as was next). Vibrant, fruity wallet-pleasing **11** combo makes for easy drinking. These WO W Cape. **Sauvignon Blanc** ☺ 🍷 🅿 ★★★ The entry-level offering; crisp **12** still punches above its price point. — CvZ

Diemersfontein Wines

Location/WO: Wellington ▪ Map: Paarl & Wellington ▪ Est 2000 ▪ 1stB 2001 ▪ Tasting & sales daily 10-5 ▪ Closed Dec 25 ▪ Cellar tours by appt ▪ Seasons Restaurant ▪ Tour groups ▪ Conferences ▪ Weddings ▪ Walks ▪ Mountain biking ▪ 3-star Diemersfontein Country House ▪ Owner(s) David & Susan Sonnenberg ▪ Cellarmaster(s) Francois Roode (Sep 2011) & Brett Rightford (consultant) ▪ Winemaker(s) Francois Roode (Sep 2003), with Lauren Hulsman (2011) ▪ Viticulturist(s) Waldo Kellerman (Aug 2007) ▪ 180ha/60ha (cabs s/f, grenache, malbec, mourv, p verdot, ptage, roobernet, shiraz, chenin, viog) ▪ 600t/40,000cs own label 90% red 10% white ▪ ISO 22000 ▪ PO Box 41 Wellington 7654 ▪ wine@diemersfontein.co.za ▪ www.diemersfontein.co.za ▪ S 33° 39'41.1" E 019° 0'31.1" ▪ **T** +27 (0)21-864-5050 ▪ F +27 (0)21-864-2095

Co-owner David Sonnenberg is relieved, when he set up a home-based winery in 2000, he didn't bow to pressure — being told Wellington was no good for white wine — and grub up the chenin vineyard his father planted in the 1980s. It was the source of their first five star garland from this guide last edition, the 2010 Carpe Diem Chenin Blanc. Chenin and pinotage is the duo with which the team seeks to best express itself. The annual Pinotage-on-Tap festival — 'the principal communication with our market', which also travels to Durban, Johannesburg and now the United Kingdom — embodies the fun of wine. 'We take our wines and customers seriously,' says David, 'but we don't take ourselves too seriously!'

Carpe Diem range

★★★★ **Malbec** ✓ Blueberry, roasted coffee & liquorice profile of **10** contrasted & balanced by lithe tannic structure. Needs patience to deliver full potential.

★★★★☆ **Pinotage** ✓ 🅿 Deep, rich & powerful, a super expression of the variety. Oak supports **10**'s fruitcake density — buoyed by hint of coconut — & adds to grace of the ensemble. 80% new oak well integrated.

★★★★☆ **Chenin Blanc** ✓ 🅿 Big, bold & beautiful in New-World style, partly barrel-fermented **11** oozes tropical fruit & creamy oak, tail is viscous but technically dry. Succeeds knockout **10** (★★★★★), whose orange marmalade & vanilla biscuit features especially impressed us last time.

★★★★ **Viognier** 🅿 Peach & apricot kernel flavours glide over fragrant oak (30% cask fermented, 30% new) in upfront **11**, luscious components nicely balanced in dry finish.

Diemersfontein range

★★★★ **Pinotage** ⓣ **11** espresso, tobacco & ripe plum seduced the senses last time. Sweet-savoury moreish finish, brisk tail. Oak dominated, rewarded some patience.

★★★★ **Summer's Lease** ✓ Rhône-style red, shiraz, mourvèdre & drop viognier, only seasoned oak. Muscular tannin tightly grips mulberry flesh of **10** (★★★★) mid-2012, needs time to relax. Not as balanced as **09**.

> **For The Birds White** 〔NEW〕 ☺ 🍷 🅿 ★★★ Perky chenin/sauvignon blend given girth by 13% viognier, **11** ends dry. Sales benefit BirdLife South Africa, as for red partner.

Cabernet Sauvignon ⓣ ★★★ Bright plum, fine spice & cedar prelude to **10**, plush flavour, robust & firm tannin structure begs for food. **Shiraz** ★★★ Jammy (though juicy) black fruit in **11**, firm tannins need time to soften. **For The Birds Red** 🍷 🅿 ★★★ Listed without 'Red' suffix last time. **10** succulent partner for new white quaffer, robust cab leads the brash berry fruit. **Maiden's Prayer Red** ⓣ ★★★ Bordeaux-style blend **10**, well padded with sweet dark fruit, balanced for easy enjoyment. — DS

■ **Die Tweede Droom** *see* Groot Parys Estate

Dieu Donné Vineyards

Location/map: Franschhoek ▪ Est 1984 ▪ 1stB 1986 ▪ Tasting & sales Mon-Fri 9-4 Sat/Sun 10.30-4 ▪ Fee R15 ▪ Closed Dec 25 & Jan 1 ▪ Cellar tours Mon-Fri by appt ▪ Cheese platters ▪ Gifts ▪ Micro beer brewery ▪ Roca Restaurant ▪ Owner(s) Robert Maingard ▪ Cellarmaster(s)/winemaker(s) Stephan du Toit (May 1996) ▪ Viticulturist(s) Hennie du Toit (Apr 1988) ▪ 40ha (cab, merlot, shiraz, chard, sauv, viog) ▪ ±280t/16,500cs own label 60% red 32% white 3% rosé 5% MCC ▪ PO Box 94 Franschhoek 7690 ▪ info@dieudonnevineyards.com ▪ www.dieudonnevineyards. com ▪ S 33° 53' 46.9" E 019° 7' 45.0" ▪ **T +27 (0)21-876-2493** ▪ F +27 (0)21-876-2102

This active Franschhoek exporter's reds continue to impress local and international judges. In 2012 it was long-time cellarmaster and Cape Wine Master Stephan du Toit's 2008 Cabernet and limited-release The Cross Collection Merlot-Cabernet that shone. The mountain eyrie winery's new Mediterranean-style Roca Restaurant features its broad range of wines and bubblies and on-site micro-brewed beers, as well as special Sunday raptor displays.

Diners Club Bartho Eksteen Academy

Location: Paarl ▪ Map: Paarl & Wellington ▪ WO: Overberg/Paarl/Western Cape ▪ Est/1stB 2011 ▪ Tasting, sales & cellar tours by appt ▪ Meals/refreshments by pre-booking ▪ Facilities for children ▪ Farm produce ▪ BYO picnic ▪ Conferences ▪ Walks/hikes ▪ Mountain biking trail ▪ Nature reserve ▪ Owner(s) Bartho & Suné Eksteen ▪ Cellarmaster(s) Bartho Eksteen (Feb 2011) ▪ Winemaker(s) Bartho Eksteen, with Suné Eksteen (both Feb 2011), Pieter Willem Eksteen (Jan 2012) & learners at Hoër Landbouskool Boland ▪ Viticulturist(s) Willie van der Linde (Hoër Landbouskool Boland); Coenie van Dyk & James Downes (bought in grapes) ▪ 20ha (cab, merlot, shiraz, chard, chenin) ▪ 10t/900cs own label 40% red 33% white 13% MCC 14% NLH ▪ PO Box 2244 Hermanus 7200 ▪ info@barthoeksteensavvycelebration.co.za ▪ www.barthoeksteensavvycelebration.co.za ▪ S 33° 39' 11.45" E 018° 52' 59.77" ▪ **T +27 (0)28-312-4612** ▪ F +27 (0)86-554-0896

'Knowledge increases pleasure' is the motto of Paarl-based Boland Agricultural High School, where ex-pupil and Diners Club 2010 Winemaker of the Year, the eminent Bartho Eksteen, founded a three-year winemaking course with sponsorship from Diners Club. Eksteen reasons: 'Our industry is often held responsible for the social problems associated with alcohol; it's a challenge to teach, especially students at secondary level, about social responsibility, responsible alcohol consumption and the role of alcohol in an adult society.'

★★★★ **Wijnskool Sauvignon Blanc** Last year previewed, now bottled. Intense, cool climate **11** off Overberg vines. Ripely fragrant; great vigour balanced by attractively oak-enhanced flavours; brisk, bone-dry.

Wijnskool Shiraz NEW ★★★★ Rich & spicy **11** still flaunting its 16 months in 60% new oak but with sufficient supple fruit, substance to harmonise over year or 2. WO Paarl. **Wijnskool Chenin Blanc** Await next. **Wijnskool Veraison MCC** NEW ★★ Pinky-gold, bone-dry **09** bubbly from classic varieties. WO W Cape. — AL

Director's Choice *see* Wedgewood Wines

Dispore Kamma Boutique Winery

Location: Caledon ▪ Map: Elgin, Walker Bay & Bot River ▪ WO: Paarl ▪ Est/1stB 2002 ▪ Tasting, sales & cellar tours by appt ▪ Owner(s) Philip Mostert & Hannes Coetzee ▪ Winemaker(s) Philip Mostert (Jan 2002), with Hannes Coetzee (Jun 2002) ▪ 75cs own label 100% red ▪ PO Box 272 Caledon 7230 ▪ disporekamma@overnet. co.za ▪ S 34° 13' 40.2" E 019° 25' 10.5" ▪ **T +27 (0)28-212-1096** ▪ F +27 (0)28-214-1077

The story behind this winery's unusual name is that of a father, general practitioner Philip Mostert, many years ago helping one of his children with a project about their spa resort town of Caledon, and discovering its original name was Dispore Kamma — Khoisan for 'Hot Waters'. Philip and orthopaedic surgeon Hannes Coetzee vinify only after hours (from Paarl grapes) but a recent Michelangelo Best Garagiste Wine trophy reflects their aspiration to make 'quality part of our dream'.

★★★★ **Syrah Reserve 10** (★★★★) concentrated flavours & aromas show a little less elegance than **09**. Spiced baked plums, perfume & warm finish.

Syrah ★★★ Shy nose, but plenty of baked black fruit & dark chocolate on palate of **10**. High alcohol (15%) leaves impression of imbalance. — CM

Distell

PO Box 184 Stellenbosch 7599 ▪ info@distell.co.za ▪ www.distell.co.za ▪ **T +27 (0)21-809-7000**

Operating from two corporate-owned cellars in Stellenbosch (Bergkelder and Adam Tas), Distell vinifies some of South Africa's most successful and enduring wine brands. They include: newcomer 4th Street, 5th Avenue Cold Duck, Autumn Harvest Crackling, Capenheimer, Cellar Cask, Chateau Libertas, Chatta Box, Drostdy-Hof, Fleur du Cap, Graça, Grand Mousseux, Grünberger, Ixia, Kellerprinz, Kupferberger Auslese, Libertas, Monis, Obikwa, Oom Tas, Oracle, Overmeer, Place in the Sun, Pongrácz, Sedgwick's, Ship Sherry, Table Mountain, Tassenberg, Taverna, Two Oceans, Virginia and Zonnebloem. Distell also owns the House of JC le Roux, a dedicated sparkling-wine cellar in Devon Valley. Then there are the stand-alone 'estate' labels: Nederburg, Plaisir de Merle and Lomond. Distell is also the co-owner, together with Lusan Holdings, of a handful of top Stellenbosch properties (Alto, Le Bonheur, Neethlingshof, Stellenzicht/Hill & Dale, Uitkyk/Flat Roof Manor), and, with several local growers, of Durbanville Hills. Distell also has agreements with a few independently owned cellars (Allesverloren, Jacobsdal, Theuniskraal) for which it provides a range of services. Finally, there's the black empowerment venture on Papkuilsfontein farm near Darling, source of Tukulu wines. See Die Bergkelder for details about the Vinoteque Wine Bank, and separate entries for most of the above brands and properties.

▪ **Dixon's Peak** *see Waverley Hills Organic Wines & Olives*
▪ **Dolphin Sands** *see Wines of Cape Town*

Domaine Brahms Wineries

Location/WO: Paarl ▪ Map: Paarl & Wellington ▪ Est 1998 ▪ 1stB 1999 ▪ Tasting & tours (vyd/cellar/wine) by appt ▪ Fee R5/wine ▪ Chapel & wedding/function venue ▪ Owner(s) Johan & Gesie van Deventer ▪ Winemaker(s)/viticulturist(s) Gesie van Deventer (1998) ▪ 12ha (cab, merlot, ptage, shiraz) ▪ 30,000L 90% red 10% white ▪ PO Box 2136 Windmeul 7630 ▪ brahms@iafrica.com ▪ www.domainebrahms.co.za ▪ S 33° 40'27.28" E 18° 53'29.24" ▪ **T +27 (0)21-869-8555** ▪ F +27 (0)86-614-9445

In a vote of confidence in their Paarl farm and the industry, Gesie and Johan van Deventer have upgraded the wedding and conference facilities (including a romantic mid-lake island), and have decided to plant more vines, register as organic, and make their operation more sustainable, looking at carbon emissions, conservation and establishing yet more trees, having already planted over 1,000.

★★★★ **Shiraz** ⓣ 08 (★★★★) differs from last big & bold 05: there's more red-fruit tang & chalkiness in the texture, plus a sprinkle of turned earth below. Alcohol is big, though, at 15%. No 06, 07.
Cabernet Sauvignon ⓣ ★★★ 06's fruit very ripe, but rather quiet & lean when last reviewed. **Merlot** ⓣ ★★★ Ripe berry fruit on debut 07, dry spicy oak may have integrated since last tasted. **Pinotage** ★★★★ Prominent clove notes on nose of notch-up 09 giving way to Christmas pudding spices & black fruit. Nicely integrated oak, juicy finish. **Quartet** ⓣ ★★★★ 06 ex-cask last time was ripely fruity pinotage (40%) with cab, merlot, shiraz. Succulent but serious, well oaked. **Sonato** ⓣ ★★★★ 06 cab-based blend last with ripely sweet but modest fruit, charry dry finish. **Chenin Blanc** Not tasted, as for **Unwooded Chenin Blanc**. —CM

Domaine des Dieux

Location: Hermanus ▪ Map: Elgin, Walker Bay & Bot River ▪ WO: Hemel-en-Aarde Ridge/Walker Bay ▪ Est 2002 ▪ 1stB 2006 ▪ Tasting & sales at the vineyards Mon-Sun 10-4.30 (Nov-Feb); off-peak periods by appt — alternatively at La Vierge Cellar ▪ Closed Dec 25 & Jan 1 ▪ Owner(s) Domaine des Dieux (Pty) Ltd ▪ Winemaker(s) John Seccombe (2011) ▪ Vineyard manager Petrus Bothma ▪ Viticulturist(s) Johan Pienaar ▪ 28ha/20ha (pinot, shiraz & other red varieties, chard, sauv) ▪ 15,000cs own label 18% red 25% white 57% MCC ▪ PO Box 2082 Hermanus 7200 ▪ info@domainedesdieux.co.za ▪ www.domainedesdieux.co.za ▪ S 34° 19'35.81" E 019° 19' 50.71" ▪ **T +27 (0)28-313-2126/+27 (0)83-536-5916** ▪ F +27 (0)86-552-9667

Winemaker John Seccombe (ex Iona), who joined owner Sharon Parnell at this boutique winery high on the Hemel-en-Aarde Ridge, appreciates the cool naritime breezes that ensure an extended ripening season. This in turn translates into fruity and aromatic reds, and plenty of acidity for the bubbles.

★★★★ **Syrah-Mourvèdre** Astonishing abundance of pure, beautifully ripe berry fruit in **10**, poised & accessible yet well-structured by one-third mourvèdre & judicious oaking. Thoroughly rewarding.

★★★★ **Sauvignon Blanc** ⊕ Pungent herbaceousness in **10**. Concentration & complexity improve each vintage; flinty minerality & grapefruit pithiness underpin richness from extended lees-ageing.

★★★★ **Rose of Sharon MCC Brut Rosé** ⊕ Steely, mineral **08** pinot-led, chardonnay plumping out austere styling. Oaked portion & 3 years on lees add breadth & creamy length. Some Elgin fruit for these bubblies.

★★★★ **Claudia Brut MCC** Adds 'Brut' to name. Chardonnay-pinot **08** (★★★★) less complex than expected after extended lees maturation, falling short of **07**, but in same bright, bone-dry style.

osephine Pinot Noir ⊕ ★★★★ Earthy **10** up a solid notch on **09** (★★★★) with more substance & pizzazz. Vibrant pure red fruit flavours & harmoniously supple tannins. **Chardonnay** ★★★ Spicily oaked, elegant **11** in trim, flinty style. More depth needed to match serious intent. Attractive citrus twist. — IM

Dombeya Wines

ocation/map/WO: Stellenbosch ▪ Est 2005 ▪ 1stB 2006 ▪ Tasting & sales Tue-Fri 10-4.30 Sat/Sun 10-3 ▪ Closed Mon, Easter Fri-Mon, Dec 25 & Jan 1 ▪ Cellar tours on special request only ▪ The Long Table Restaurant & Café: Tue-Sun 9-5; Fri dinner — booking essential ▪ Facilities for children ▪ Self-catering accommodation in The Residence & The Cottage ▪ Owner(s) Preston Haskell ▪ Cellarmaster(s) Rianie Strydom (Jan 2005) ▪ Winemaker(s)/viticulturist(s) Wikus Pretorius (Dec 2005) ▪ 25ha/13.5ha (cabs s/f, merlot, shiraz, chard) ▪ ±80t/7,500cs own label 80% ed 20% white ▪ PO Box 12766 Die Boord 7613 ▪ info@dombeyawines.com ▪ www.dombeyawines.com ▪ S 34° 0' 13.9" E 018° 51'38.4" ▪ **T +27 (0)21-881-3895** ▪ F +27 (0)21-881-3986

Maintaining a steady course and not fixing anything that ain't broke is the intention of the team at this American-owned Helderberg property. Dombeya remains modest, bottling wines from its prime 'golden triangle' location that many other producers can only dream about. Over-delivery is a cliché but GM/winemaker Wikus Pretorius is adamant that Dombeya's quality outstrips its price point. After all, much-lauded sibling Haskell Vineyards is recognised as the big ticket item.

★★★★ **Boulder Road Shiraz** ⊕ Velvety **08** delivered inviting mouthful of blackberries, plums & meaty savouriness when last tasted; dash mourvèdre added interest & savouriness.

★★★★ **Chardonnay** **11** marries peaches & cream with vibrant citrus so typical of grape. Lively but balanced & elegant. Oak is not overplayed, giving structure & seasoning.

Cabernet Sauvignon ⊕ ★★★★ **08** greater fruit clarity than engaging **07** (★★★★); well-composed tannins, refreshing lift in tail add to cedary charm. **Merlot** ⊕ ★★★★★ **08** last time convincingly trumped **07** (★★★★): concentrated fruit, ripe tannins, balancing spicy freshness. Already complex, should improve 5+ years. **Altus** ⊕ ★★★★ Ripe black fruit & brush of cocoa interest on elegant **07** cab-driven Bordeaux red. A step up on **06** (★★★★). Complex, seamlessly svelte & layered. **Sauvignon Blanc** ★★★★ **12** doesn't quite match **11** (★★★★). Fresh & rounded but touch less intense & concentrated, zesty & succulent nonetheless. — FM

Domein Doornkraal

Location: De Rust ▪ Map: Klein Karoo & Garden Route ▪ Est 1880 ▪ 1stB 1973 ▪ Tasting & sales Mon-Fri 9-5 Sat 9-1 ▪ Closed Easter Fri/Sun & Dec 25 ▪ Light refreshments ▪ Farm produce ▪ Gifts ▪ Conference facility on farm ▪ Self-catering farm cottages & B&B ▪ Owner(s)/winemaker(s) Swepie & Piet le Roux ▪ Cellarmaster(s) Swepie le Roux (Apr 2011) ▪ Viticulturist(s) Danie Theron (2008) & Hugo Steyn (2009, consultant) ▪ 2,000ha/15ha (cab, merlot, muscadel, ptage, chard, chenin, cbard) ▪ 90t/2,000cs own label 15% red 15% white 70% fortified ▪ PO Box 14 De Rust 6650 ▪ wyn@doornkraal.co.za ▪ www.doornkraal.co.za ▪ S 33° 32'43.5" E 022° 26'42. 5" ▪ **T +27 (0)44-251-6715** ▪ F +27 (0)86-528-5633

Legendary septuagenarian Swepie le Roux continues making wine as one of this hospitable, starkly beautiful Klein Karoo family farm's varied enterprises. Daughter Celia Mostert and her husband Christiaan are farming with him, stocking their roadstall between De Rust and Oudtshoorn with regional food and wine (including newly rediscovered, well-aged Doornkraal muscadels, ports and brandies).

■ **Donatus** see Dornier Wines

Donkiesbaai   ♀ NEW

Location/map: Stellenbosch ▪ WO: Piekenierskloof ▪ Est/1stB 2011 ▪ Tasting & sales at Guardian Peak (see entry) ▪ Owner(s) Jean Engelbrecht ▪ Winemaker(s) Coenie Snyman & Philip van Staden (both Jan 2011) ▪ Viticulturist(s) Dirkie Mouton (Jan 2011) ▪ 4.7t/180cs own label 100% white ▪ PO Box 473 Stellenbosch 7599 ▪ info@rustenvrede.com ▪ www.donkiesbaai.com ▪ S 34° 0' 40.19" E 018° 50' 31.99" ▪ T +27 (0)21-881-3881 ▪ F +27 (0)21-881-3000

The Engelbrecht family's holiday home is located in a West Coast area named by Sir Rufane Donkin, Cape acting governor and fledger of the 1820 British Settlers. Locals years ago rechristened the site to Donkiesbaai ('Donkey Bay') — a rustic moniker which Rust en Vrede owner Jean Engelbrecht with gentle irony adopts for his new so-not-bumpkiny chenin blanc. Jean uses the vernacular for chenin ('steen') in the branding, hinting at the elevated age of the Piekenierskloof vines.

★★★★☆ **Steen** Stellar launch for partly barrel-fermented chenin. **11** genteel & elegant, richly fruited, well-mannered wine. Grows in stature to reveal stonefruit, oak sheen & minerality mingling harmoniously on a weighty palate that lingers long. WO Piekenierskloof. — FM

■ **Don Morris** see Govert Wines

Doolhof Wine Estate

Location/WO: Wellington ▪ Map: Paarl & Wellington ▪ Est 1995 ▪ 1stB 2003 ▪ Tasting & sales Mon-Sat 10-5 Sun 10-4 ▪ Fee R20/5 wines ▪ Closed Good Fri, Dec 25/26 & Jan 1 ▪ Cellar tours by appt ▪ Light lunches Tue-Sun 11-3; picnics by appt ▪ Conferences ▪ Walks/hikes ▪ Mountain biking & 4x4 trails ▪ 5-star Grand Dédale Country House (see Accommodation section) ▪ Owner(s) Dennis Kerrison ▪ Cellarmaster(s)/winemaker(s) Friedrich Kühne (Dec 2008) ▪ Viticulturist(s) Hendrik Laubscher (Aug 1996) ▪ 380ha/38ha (cabs s/f, malbec, merlot, p verdot, ptage, shiraz, chard, sauv) ▪ 180-220t/12,000cs own label 73% red 26% white 1% rosé ▪ BWI, IPW ▪ PO Box 157 Wellington 7654 ▪ office@doolhof.com ▪ www.doolhof.com ▪ S 33° 37' 35.6" E 019° 4' 58.7" ▪ T +27 (0)21-873-6911 ▪ F +27 (0)21-864-2321

Doolhof's history dates back to 1707 and current owner Dennis Kerrison has added a new element to its Cape Dutch glory, with the Grand Dédale Country House epitomising luxury. There was no malbec in those olden days, but since being planted here in 2003 it has produced arguably the most successful of the winery's offerings — with many awards augmenting the Wellington estate's growing profile.

Signatures of Doolhof range

★★★★ **Cabernet Franc** NEW ✓ **09** has attractive cedary oak, tart red berry, floral perfume & earthy complexity. Juicy, but balanced by vinous & fine tannin grip. Stays fresh though big alcohol & few grams sugar. **Cabernet Sauvignon** ★★★ **10** rather lean, with some development evident. Big alcohol & some sweetness serve as foil to obvious tannins. **Malbec** ★★★★ Dark fruit expression supported by dry cocoa notes. **10** has lovely fruit-rich appeal with espresso cut to smoothness. **Merlot** ★★★ Red cherry on tangy, medium-bodied **08** with appealing vinosity; juicy-soft entry with slightly tannic end. **Petit Verdot** ★★★★ **09** step up on **08**, with poised ripeness balanced by integrated oak spice & red cherry freshness on finish. **Pinotage** ⑪ ★★★★ **09**'s ripe charry red & black fruit much like **08**. Light bodied but with grip from year French oak, half new. **Shiraz** ★★★★ Good fruit expression & typical varietal black olive & spice, follows to savoury **08**'s palate with ripe polished end. **Renaissance Cabernet Sauvignon-Merlot** ⑪ ★★★★ After generous **06** (★★★★), last-tasted **07** had blackcurrant & cigarbox, ripeness balanced by char from year in 40% new French oak. **Chardonnay Wooded** ★★★★ Barrel-fermented **09** has lovely texture; bruised apple character from bottle-age melds with toasty oak. Ready to enjoy. **Chardonnay Unwooded** ✓ 🏠 🏵 ★★★★ Subtle pear & peach aromas on step-up **11** has cream-textured, dry & focused end. Zingy acid completes ideal food partner. **Sauvignon Blanc** ✓ 🏠 🏵 ★★★★ **11** with moderate 12.5% alcohol appeals with savoury undertone, 'oystershell' whiff & ultra-dry, food-friendly end. Has smidgen semillon for breadth.

Legends of the Labyrinth range

★★★★ **The Minotaur** ⑪ Meaty plum spice when reviewed; **08** (★★★★) soft, light-bodied Bordeaux red, less structure than juicy **07**.
Lady in Red ⑪ 🏠 ★★★★ Unusual jasmine note few years back to juicy mulberry & mocha on seriously oaked **08**, 5-way Bordeaux blend. **Dark Lady of the Labyrinth** 🏵 ★★★ **11** from mostly pinotage in mocha/coffee mould, with shy banana loaf aroma & cherry/chocolate palate. Still very young & needs the new

oak to meld. **Lady in White** ⑦ 🍴 ★★★ Chenin, semillon & sauvignon liaison. Lemon butter & nettle, **10** zingy yet also creamy from year in new oak.

Cape range

Boar ☺ 🍴 ★★★ Perfumed lift to **10**; loads of floral charm with juicy palate. This merlot, cab & petit verdot medley hits the spot. **Roan** ☺ 🍴 ★★★ As name maybe hints, mostly from shiraz plus other Rhône varieties. **10** has spicy counter to ripe, dark-berried sweetness. Just-dry, like Boar. **Loerie** ☺ 🍴 ⓥ ★★★ Clean **11** from sauvignon, splash chenin, is light & dry with fruity fresh appeal. 12% alcohol.

Robin ⑦ 🍴 ⓥ ★★★ **11** from shiraz, a dry spicy & plummy quaffer. **Eagle** ⑦ 🍴 ★★★ Tropical & tangy **10**, lightish unwooded chardonnay with splash of chenin. — JP

Doran Vineyards

Location: Paarl ▪ Map: Paarl & Wellington ▪ WO: Swartland/Voor Paardeberg ▪ Est 2010 ▪ 1stB 2012 ▪ Tasting Mon-Fri by appt Sat/Sun & pub hols 10-4 ▪ Closed Good Fri, Dec 25/26 & Jan 1 ▪ Owner(s) Edwin Doran & André Badenhorst ▪ Winemaker(s) Martin Lambrecht ▪ Viticulturist(s) Basson Potgieter ▪ 170ha/50ha (cabs s/f, merlot, ptage, shiraz) ▪ 450t/15,000cs own label ▪ Other export brand: Thorntree ▪ Suite 310 Private Bag X16 Constantia 7848 ▪ andrebad@iafrica.com ▪ www.horsemountainwines.com ▪ S 33° 35' 15.14" E 018° 52' 06.03" ▪ **T +27 (0)21-869-8328** ▪ F +27 (0)21-869-8329

Edwin Doran, originally from Ireland, and André Badenhorst are two self-proclaimed 'old farts' who have long enjoyed wine, food and rugby together. They've now decided on indulging their mutual passion for the good life by going farming. 'No fancy gabled buildings, lavender or oak trees, but a genuine Swartland farm,' says André. Wine-wise, the focus will be on white and red Rhône-style blends, while there may be a butchery in future, as the farm also has Ile de France sheep and Angus Aberdeen cattle.

Doran Vineyards range NEW

Shiraz ★★★★ Tentatively rated tank sample **12** still unfolding mid-2012 but already bright varietal fruit is peeping out from the deep, brooding structure. May well score higher once bottled. WO Voor Paardeberg. **Chenin Blanc** ★★★★ Barrel-fermented (older oak) **12**, previewed & provisionally rated, as for stablemate, but shows shade more promise: peachy complexity, impressive weight, richness & length, oak already well woven into the structure. One to watch. — JP/CvZ

Dormershire Estate

Location: Kuils River ▪ Map/WO: Stellenbosch ▪ Est 1996 ▪ 1stB 2001 ▪ Tasting, sales & tours Mon-Fri 8-5 Sat 10-1 ▪ Fee R10pp ▪ Closed all pub hols ▪ Farm market on last Sat of every month ▪ Owner(s) SPF Family Trust ▪ Winemaker(s) Michelle Louw (Apr 2007) ▪ Viticulturist(s) Johan Pienaar (consultant) ▪ 8ha/6ha (cab, shiraz, sauv) ▪ ±50t/4,000cs own label 85% red 10% white 5% rosé ▪ PO Box 491 Bellville 7535 ▪ wine@dormershire.co.za ▪ www.dormershire.co.za ▪ S 33° 56' 27.0" E 018° 42' 54.7" ▪ **T +27 (0)21-801-4677** ▪ F +27 (0)86-517-0716

When the first grapes were harvested at this mainly red wine estate, the cellar wasn't ready and the wine barrels ended up maturing on owner Paul Frost's veranda — hence Stoep Shiraz, now reborn only in select vintages. A new monthly food market offers a wide range of local produce, arts and crafts.

Cabernet Sauvignon ⑦ 🍴 ★★★★ As expected, juicier & earlier accessible than the Reserve, a savoury note makes **07** a good food match. **Reserve Cabernet Sauvignon** ⑦ ★★★★ Selection of best barrels, 18 months oak (as for all the reds). Despite big alcohol, **07** achieves elegance & poise. **Shiraz** ⑦ 🍴 ★★★ **07** toasted bread & spicy cherry flavours, ending dry. Ideal winter casserole red. **Stoep Shiraz** ⑦ ★★★ Wood here a toasty backdrop, **07** earthy & savoury blackberry fruit, pepper seasoning. **Cabernet Sauvignon-Shiraz** ⑦ ★★★★ **07** has this estate's Old World character: peppery/dusty notes, cherry flavours & firm tannins. **Rosé** Await new, as for **Sauvignon Blanc**. **Sweet Red** ⑦ ★★★★ NV jerepiko-style fireside snuggler from shiraz, with intriguing savoury overlay. Discontinued: **Reserve Shiraz**. — DB

Dornier Wines   21-12-12 lunch

Location/map: Stellenbosch ▪ WO: Stellenbosch/Western Cape/Swartland ▪ Est 1995 ▪ 1stB 2002 ▪ Tasting & sales daily 11-5 ▪ Cellar tours by appt ▪ Dornier Bodega Restaurant: lunch daily 12-5 dinner (Oct-Apr) Thu-Sat ▪ Facilities for children ▪ Gift shop ▪ Conference venue ▪ Conservation area ▪ Homestead with 6 bedrooms & large entertainment areas offered ▪ Owner(s) Delfinarte Foundation ▪ Winemaker(s) Jeanine Faure (Mar 2012) ▪ Viticulturist(s) Theunis Bell (Sep 2009) ▪ 167ha/60ha (cabs s/f, malbec, merlot, p verdot, ptage, shiraz, tempranillo, chenin, sauv, sem) ▪ 270t 80% red 17% white 3% rosé ▪ PO Box 7518 Stellenbosch 7599 ▪ info@dornier.co.za ▪ www.dornier.co.za ▪ S 33° 59' 31.00" E 018° 52' 19.00" ▪ **T** +27 (0)21-880-0557 ▪ F +27 (0)21-880-1499

Newly appointed winemaker Jeanine Faure comes well experienced both locally and abroad, having worked at Meerlust, Zorgvliet, Camberley and Raats, as well as wineries in Australia, California, Italy and the Rhône. She's impressed with the work done to improve Dornier's vineyards over the past few years by viticulturist Theunis Bell and consultant Kevin Watt, giving her excellent-quality grapes to work with. You can taste the results in soon-to-be-released single varieties malbec, tempranillo and semillon. And the growing interest in chenin finds them well placed, with standalone bottlings plus a chenin-rich blend in the portfolio.

Donatus range

★★★★ **Red** Mainly cab, dashes malbec & cab franc. Now bottled, **09** (★★★★☆) is unfolding into a thing of beauty, improves on last-tasted **07**. Structured for the longer haul, but already drinking well. Offers plush red fruit, cigarbox, whiffs of dried herbs, well-built tannins.

★★★★ **White** 🍷 Chenin-led oaked blend with semillon. The expected sophistication in **11**, everything expertly matched; oak spice, the quince of chenin, sleek & assured. Nudges the next level. WO W Cape.

Dornier range

w/ langoustines

★★★★ **Cabernet Sauvignon** 🍷 Complex **07**'s dark plum centre shows dried herb, allspice, even fynbos nuances. Tannins are supple with a backbone for good few more years.

★★★★ **Pinotage** 🍷 🍷 Individual **10** reveals the finesse pinotage can show in the right hands. Plums, smoke & spice all seamed into a lithe, sleekly muscled form. Tasted from barrel.

★★★★ **Froschkoenig Natural Sweet** 🍷 Occasional release, **09** (1 barrel rack-dried chenin) has melon preserve, baked apple tones in its richness, lovely barley sugar finish that stays. Aged 24 months.

Chenin Blanc Bush Vine ☺ ★★★ Pre-bottled **12** shows crunchy apple & pear fruit salad, fresh & tasty, ending on a mineral note. WO Swartland.

Merlot 🍷 ★★★☆ Previously **07** had berry-rich, herbal-tinged aromas & flavours; was savoury & firm, with modest fruit intensity. **Cabernet Sauvignon-Merlot** 🍷 ★★★☆ A good food match with its dry, savoury tannins, **10** has attractive plummy fruit, complex nuances that open in the glass.

Cocoa Hill range

nice, similar to home

Rosé ☺ 🍴 🍷 ★★★ Combo merlot & sauvignon gives **12** an edge; red berries & a leafy freshness perfect for summer lunches. **Chenin Blanc** ☺ 🍴 🍷 ★★★ Apple & pear fruit salad, infusion of citrus, zesty **12** is ideal for tasty everyday drinking.

Red ★★★ Merlot-led **10** has plummy ripeness, generous curves. WO W Cape. **Sauvignon Blanc** 🍴 🍷 ★★★ Light-textured **12**'s mineral-fresh flavours finish clean & dry. — CR

Douglas Green

Location: Wellington ▪ WO: Western Cape/Wellington ▪ Est 1942 ▪ Closed to public ▪ Owner(s) DGB ▪ Cellarmaster(s) Gerhard Carstens, with Liezl Carstens (2000) ▪ Winemaker(s) Jaco Potgieter (oenologist, 2000) ▪ Viticulturist(s) Stephan Joubert (2006) ▪ 50% red 49% white 1% rosé ▪ ISO 9001:2000, Fairtrade, HACCP, IPW, WIETA ▪ PO Box 246 Wellington 7654 ▪ douglasgreen@dgb.co.za ▪ www.douglasgreenwines.com ▪ **T** +27 (0)21-864-5300 ▪ F +27 (0)21-864-1287

Douglas Green commenced trading from the Stukvat Bottlestore in Main Street, Paarl, in 1938. By 1942 he was making his own wine, negociant style, from grapes carefully sourced around the winelands. His approach and philosophy — good wine, at a good price, that people enjoy — remain the foundation of the DGB-owned brand that bears his name, and which in the 70th anniversary year is being repackaged with a new label honouring the humble but talented founder.

Vineyard Creations

Cabernet Sauvignon ☺ 🏠 🍾 ★★★ **11** subtle but juicy, dark fruit in smooth & friendly easy-drinking style. **Chardonnay** ☺ 🏠 🍾 ★★★ **12** balanced, affable quaffer with pear & melon flavours freshened by a zesty twist of lemon. Previewed, as for next two. **Chenin Blanc** ☺ 🏠 🍾 ★★★ Good vintage shows in crisp & crunchy **12**. Summer picnic styling, with dried apricot & peach/apple flavours. **Sauvignon Blanc** ☺ 🏠 🍾 ★★★ Melange of ripe tropical fruit on vivacious **12**. Tangy, light, a cheerful outdoors sipper.

Merlot 🏠 🍾 ★★★ **11** has smoky nuance to red berries. Bright BBQ/pizza partner. **Pinotage** 🏠 🍾 ★★★ Dapper **11** has firm, supple tannins & tangy fruit, balanced with underlying seriousness. Well-crafted food partner. **Shiraz** 🏠 🍾 ★★ Brusque **11**'s fruit masked by dusty cinnamon-spiced oak.

Diversity range

Merlot-Malbec ☺ 🏠 🍾 ★★★ Juicy **11**, is bright & spicy with smooth-textured quaffability.

Cabernet Sauvignon-Merlot ⓫ 🏠 🍾 ★★★ **10** rich & ripe dark berry fruit in supple accessible style. Balanced, with food-friendly dry finish. **Pinotage Rosé** ⓫ 🏠 🍾 ★★★ Light & tangy **10** still available, not retasted. **Sauvignon Blanc-Chenin Blanc** 🏠 🍾 ★★★★ Sauvignon takes the lead in previewed **12**'s lively blend. Crisp & juicy yellow peach flavours with enough style to grace the table. **Sunkissed Natural Sweet Rosé** ⓫ 🏠 ★★ Sweet low-alcohol pinotage/merlot NV sundowner. **Sunkissed Natural Sweet White** ⓫ 🏠 ★★ NV aromatic charmer is smoothly sweet & tangy.

Douglas Green Signature Brands

Ribshack Red ⓫ 🏠 🍾 ★★★ Savoury, smooth & smoky **10** aptly named, juicy pinotage/shiraz duo, spicy barbecue ribs in a glass! WO Wellington. **St Augustine** ★★ Charry sweet-oak tone to pinotage-led **10**. **The Beachhouse Rosé** ⓫ 🏠 🍾 ★★ **11** a tutti-frutti sundowner. Light & semi-sweet, from pinotage. WO Wellington. **The Delivery Chenin Blanc** ⓫ 🏠 ★★★ Genial **10** preview is smooth, with baked apple flavours. **The Beachhouse** ⓫ 🏠 🍾 ★★★ Fresh & tangy, off-dry **11** white from sauvignon & semillon is tailor-made for summer. **Sprizzo Sweet Rosé** ⓫ 🏠 ★★ NV a sweet, aromatic bouquet that is light, fun & fizzy! **Cape Ruby Port** ⓫ ★★★★ NV blend tinta & souzão with fruitcake sweetness, not retasted. —MW

Douglas Wine Cellar

Location: Douglas ▪ Map: Northern Cape, Free State & North West ▪ Est 1968 ▪ 1stB 1977 ▪ Tasting & sales Mon-Fri 8–5 ▪ Fee R5 ▪ Closed all pub hols ▪ Cellar tours by appt ▪ BYO picnic ▪ Gifts ▪ Owner(s) Shareholders ▪ Cellarmaster(s) Ian Sieg ▪ Winemaker(s) Ian Sieg, with Winston Bailey ▪ Viticulturist(s) Johan Fourie ▪ Douglas + Landzicht GWK: 350ha (cab, ptage, ruby cab, shiraz, chard, chenin, cbard, gewürz, muscadels r/w) ▪ 20,000cs own label 20% red 40% white 5% rosé 35% fortified ▪ PO Box 47 Douglas 8730 ▪ wynkelder@gwk.co.za ▪ www.landzicht.co.za ▪ S 29° 3'57.0" E 023° 46'7.8" ▪ **T +27 (0)53-298-8314/5** ▪ F +27 (0)53-298-1845

After hail damage in 2010 and vineyards under water in 2011, winemaker Winston Bailey welcomed an uneventful 2012 harvest at agribusiness GWK's winery near the confluence of the mighty Orange and Vaal rivers. Cherry on top was the Young Wine Show: two silvers and 16 bronzes for the Northern Cape trophy cabinet.

■ Down to Earth *see Villiera Wines*

Dragonridge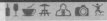

Location: Malmesbury ▪ Map/WO: Swartland ▪ Est 2004 ▪ 1stB 2006 ▪ Tasting, sales & cellar tours by appt ▪ Fee R30, waived on purchase ▪ Closed Easter Fri, Dec 25/26 & Jan 1 ▪ Meals by arrangement ▪ Facilities for children ▪ Farm produce ▪ BYO picnic ▪ Weddings/functions ▪ Conferences ▪ Walks/hikes ▪ Mountain biking trail ▪ Conservation area ▪ Guest house ▪ Owner(s) Fynbos Estate (3 partners) ▪ Cellarmaster(s)/winemaker(s) Johan Simons (Jan 2004) ▪ Viticulturist(s) Johan Simons (Jun 1997) ▪ 320ha/13ha (cab, mourv, ptage, sangio, shiraz, chard, chenin, viog) ▪ 35t/700cs own label 40% red 40% white 20% rosé ▪ P O Box 526 Malmesbury 7299 ▪ info@fynbosestate.co.za, info@dragonridge.co.za ▪ www.dragonridge.co.za ▪ S 33° 33'28.9" E 018° 47'5.6" ▪ **T +27 (0)22-487-1153** ▪ F +27 (0)86-611-5125

Fynbos Estate in the Perdeberg is now an established eco-tourism getaway, with most of the farm formally recognised as a Cape Nature reserve. In these idyllic conditions, winemaker Johan Simons produces his dryland wines with gentle hands, recycling, repairing, reusing; taking the natural options whenever possible.

Sangiovese ⓟ ★★★ 09 last with same dark cherry, pronounced acid & tarry notes as 08. **Jack's Red** ★★ Tasted out of vintage sequence, 08 pinotage-led Cape Blend shows squashed berries & tangy acid. **Cosmos** ⓟ ★★★ 10 dry rosé with delicate red fruits. This & next 2 tasted previously. **Chenin Blanc** ⓟ ★★★ Oxidative almond & baked apple whiffs on 10, long spicy finish. **Galaxy** ⓟ ★★★★ Chardonnay, chenin & viognier blend; apple, honey, blossom & dried apricot on oaked 09, with broad texture & rich finish. — GdB

Driehoek Family Wines 🍷🌲🏔📷🎣

Location: Citrusdal ▪ Map: Olifants River ▪ WO: Cederberg ▪ Est/1stB 2009 ▪ Tasting by appt ▪ Closed Good Fri & Dec 25 ▪ Facilities for children ▪ Gift shop ▪ BYO picnic ▪ Walking/hiking & mountain biking trails ▪ Horse riding ▪ Bird watching ▪ Fishing ▪ Bushman paintings ▪ Conservation area ▪ Self-catering cottages & camping ▪ Beauty treatments ▪ Owner(s) Du Toit Family ▪ Cellarmaster(s)/winemaker(s) David Nieuwoudt (Jan 2008 Cederberg) ▪ Viticulturist(s) Dawie Burger & Hennie Spamer (both Jun 2006), advised by David Nieuwoudt ▪ 375ha/4.5ha (pinot, shiraz, sauv) ▪ 1,250cs own label 50% red 50% white ▪ PO Box 89 Clanwilliam 8135 ▪ driehoekcederberg@gmail.com ▪ www.cederberg-accommodation.co.za ▪ S 32° 26′34.40″ E 019° 11′24.32″ ▪ T +27 (0)27-482-2828 ▪ F +27 (0)86-720-2474

Like their neighbours (Cederberg Private Cellar's David Nieuwoudt makes their wines) the Du Toits have been here in the magnificent Cederberg mountains for five generations. The vineyards, however, date back only to 2006 — amongst the highest in the Cape. The grapes clearly revel in the heady atmosphere.

★★★★☆ **Shiraz** 🫒 Pure, ripe fruit with perfumed floral-herbaceous note on 10 — more modern than classic, on the whole. Oak & a little sweetness (from a touch of sugar & 15% alcohol) show on lingering finish, but pleasingly balanced. Drinkable in youth, but should repay keeping maybe 5 years.

★★★★ **Sauvignon Blanc** 🫒 Interesting ripe aromas & full flavours on 12, tending to the citrus & blackcurrant side of the spectrum. Refined & well balanced. No hurry to drink up, but a tasty treat if you do. — TJ

Drostdy-Hof Wines 🍷♿

Location/map: Tulbagh ▪ WO: Western Cape ▪ Est 1804 ▪ Tasting & sales at De Oude Drostdy Mon-Fri 10-5 Sat 10-2 ▪ Fee R20pp ▪ Closed Good Fri, Dec 25 & Jan 1 ▪ Private functions by arrangement ▪ Owner(s) Distell ▪ Cellarmaster(s) Andrea Freeborough ▪ Winemaker(s) Bonny van Niekerk (reds) & Pieter Badenhorst (whites) ▪ Viticulturist(s) Annelie Viljoen ▪ PO Box 213 Tulbagh 6820 ▪ info@drostdywines.co.za ▪ www.drostdyhof.co.za ▪ S 33° 15′23.3″ E 019° 8′57.5″ ▪ T +27 (0)23-230-0203 ▪ F +27 (0)23-230-0211

The name comes from the drostdy (seat of local government) in Tulbagh, designed by the renowned Louis-Michel Thibault and completed in 1806. Value and a convenient range of pack sizes are attributes of this Distell-owned brand.

Winemaker's Collection

★★★★ **Chardonnay-Semillon** NEW ✓ 🍷 Delightful debut! 12 most attractive pear drop & citrus blossom aromas, well-balanced fruit & oak, clean, moreish. Complexity & structure way above the price.

Pinotage ☺ ★★★ Charming 12 ex tank a step up, lots going on, banana-scented black fruit, nice creamy oak embellishment. Bright & lively, as is 11 (★★), with interesting mulberry & savoury boerewors flavour combo. **Sauvignon Blanc** ☺ 🍷 ★★★ Crushed nettle & pineapple, 12 broad flavours, good mouthfeel, better textured & generous than previous. Also in 3L packs, like Chardonnay.

Cabernet Sauvignon 🍷 ★★★ Two vintages tasted: pre-bottling, 12 big & mocha driven wine, shows variety's firm tannins. Toasty/dusty 11 (★★) even more in need of a country casserole. Also in 3L packs, like Merlot. **Merlot** 🍷 ★★★ Style change from previous softly smooth to (pleasantly) firm & dry 12, on preview offers ripe dusty cherry flavours. 11, also tasted this edition, similar savoury/food-friendly character, plums & bitter chocolate on palate. **Shiraz** ★★★ Lesser 11 (★★) is savoury & leathery, tad astringent whereas 12 pre-bottling, shows more fruit & richness, attractive toasty oak, better-managed tannins. **Shiraz-Pinotage** ★★★ Ex-tank 12 tangy sweet-&-sour character balanced by slight sweetness. Also-tasted 11 (★★) toasty & smoky, honest reflection of the varieties but tannins rather pushy. **Cabernet Sauvignon Rosé** 🍷 Await new vintage. **Chardonnay** 🍷 ★★★ 12 preview is fruity, with nicely judged oak spicing to the zesty lime marmalade flavour. 11 (★★) buttery & overtly woody, shows vanilla-tinged sweetness. **Chardonnay-Viognier** ★★★ Uncomplicated 11, dried pear & apricot nose, stewed fruit flavour, notch down on previous. **Adelpracht** ✓ ★★★★ Seductive, delicious Late Harvest-style 11 from chenin. Botrytis, honey & floral note

- lovely complexity within a light, not over-sweet frame. Perfect rogan josh accompaniment. Also in 2L & 5L packs. Discontinued: **Sparkling Brut**.

Natural Sweet Light range

Xtra Light ★★ NV no-frills crisp white with low alcohol (9%). Also in 2L & 5L packs. **Red ★★** Raspberry cordial character, low alcohol (7.5%), cranberry crispness adds touch of verve to **NV**. Also in 2L packs, as for Natural Sweet White. **Rosé ★★** Strawberries-&-cream in a glass, **NV** fun party wine at low ±7% alcohol. Also in 2L & 5L packs. **White ★★** Sweet & cheerful **NV**, floral/grapey low-alcohol (7%) picnic partner.

Standard range

Claret Select ☺ ★★★ Soft, medium-bodied pizza wine hits the spot. Easy anytime red. **NV**. Also in 2L & 5L packs, as for PGC & Stein Select. **Steen/Chenin Blanc ☺ 🗐 ★★★ 12** liquid salad of ripe peach, pear & apricot, dawn-fresh & highly drinkable.

Cape Red 🗐 ★★★ 12 tank sample, mainly shiraz & merlot, tasty blackcurrant-laced braai wine to be enjoyed early. **11** harmonious & easy drinking, with spiced plum flavours. **Rosé 🗐 ★★** Crisp, frisky **12**, clean & dry, happy summer sipper. **Premier Grand Cru 🗐 ★★** Lightish, fresh & grassy **NV** all-sorts dry white blend. **Stein Select ★** Semi-sweet equivalent of PGC. Latest **NV** very basic chug-a-lug white. — DB/HJ

Druk My Niet Wine Estate

Location/WO: Paarl ▪ Map: Paarl & Wellington ▪ Est 2003 ▪ 1stB 2009 ▪ Tasting, sales & cellar tours by appt ▪ Fee R20pp ▪ Closed all pub hols ▪ Meals/refreshments on request ▪ BYO picnic ▪ Tour groups ▪ Walks/hikes ▪ Mountain biking trail ▪ Conservation area ▪ 3 self-catering cottages (see Accommodation section) ▪ Owner(s) Georg & Dorothee Kirchner, Jens-Peter & Kerstin Stein ▪ Cellarmaster(s)/winemaker(s)/viticulturist(s) Abraham de Klerk (Jun 2008) ▪ 24.5ha/9ha (cabs s/f, malbec, merlot, shiraz, tannat, tempranillo, tinto amerela, chenin, viog) ▪ 60t/1,750cs own label 80% red 20% white ▪ BWI, IPW ▪ PO Box 7383 Paarl 7620 ▪ georg. kirchner@dmnwines.co.za ▪ www.dmnwines.co.za ▪ S 33° 41′ 23.26″ E 019° 1′ 40.23″ ▪ **T +27 (0)21-868-8393** ▪ F +27 (0)21-868-2392

To draw more visitors to one of Paarl Valley's original estates, pizzas are now served from an oven installed on the verandah outside the cellar, which dates from 1692, and food-and-wine pairings are offered in summer. Innovative varietal combinations are already a feature here, and co-owner Dorothee Kirchner envisages more 'great new blends like the T3', along with a continued focus on their flagship wines. Community involvement and eco sensitivity are also high priorities.

Flagship range

★★★★☆ **Invictus ✓** Merlot-led **09** flagship blend (with cabs sauvignon & franc) in classic, plush Bordeaux style; now settled & revealing charm; serious & integrated (40% new oak well judged) with lengthy farewell.

★★★★☆ **T3 ✓** Intriguing red fruit & leafy aromas on creative & unusual **09** equal tannat & tinta amerela blend with tempranillo (25%). Fruit clarity is shining through now in restrained, elegant style. Ripe berries are balanced by savoury acidity & smooth tannins. Handsome packaging a feature of both wines.

Druk My Niet Collection

★★★★ **Cabernet Sauvignon** Boldly fruited **09** exhibits lush dark-toned flavours. Balanced & now-integrated vanilla oak adds complexity. Drinking well.

★★★★ **Cabernet Franc** Excellent varietal expression on **09** — dust, leaf, mint, you name it. Elegant, harmonious & touch savoury. Developed well in the year.

★★★★ **C68 Chenin Blanc NEW** Lightly oaked (6 months) **12** from vines planted in 1968 is understated, with soft flavours of baked apple & vanilla. Well made & structured for a long life.

Malbec ★★★★ Loads of bright cranberry fruit, wild herbs on **09**. Acidity & tannins still a bit gawky. Needs time or food. Note: range was 'Find Art Collection' last time.

Mapoggo range

Cabernet Sauvignon-Merlot-Cabernet Franc ✓ 🗐 ★★★★ 09, 81% cab with dollops merlot & cab franc is fleshy & fruity with a firm, concentrated berry liqueur finish. Food wine. **Cabernet Franc-Cabernet Sauvignon-Merlot 🗐** Next awaited, as for **Sauvignon Blanc-Chenin Blanc-Viognier**. **Chenin Blanc-Sauvignon Blanc-Viognier 🗐 🖉 ★★★** With chenin behind wheel, **10** is fresh with ripe pineapple & floral flavours, balanced & focused with a lipsmacking end. — WB

Dunstone Winery

Location: Wellington ▪ Map: Paarl & Wellington ▪ WO: Wellington/Western Cape ▪ Est/1stB 2006 ▪ Tasting, sales & cellar tours Wed-Sun 10-4 ▪ Fee R10pp, waived on purchase ▪ Closed Dec 25 & Jan 1 ▪ The Stone Kitchen (see Restaurants section) ▪ Facilities for children ▪ Conferences ▪ Bovlei Valley Retreat luxury B&B guesthouse & self-catering cottage (see Accommodation section) ▪ Owner(s) Abbi & Lee Wallis ▪ Winemaker(s) Lee Wallis & Robert Frith, with Neil Marais (Jun 2011) ▪ Viticulturist(s) Johan Viljoen (Jan 2008, Vinpro) ▪ 8.9ha/2.7ha (merlot, shiraz) ▪ 10t/ 1,160cs own label 90% red 10% rosé ▪ PO Box 901 Wellington 7654 ▪ wine@dunstone.co.za ▪ www.dunstone.co.za ▪ S 33° 38'5.3" E 019° 3'36.8" ▪ **T +27 (0)21-873-6770** ▪ F +27 (0)21-873-6770

Lee and Abbi Wallis came to Cape Town from the UK in 2002; falling in love with the country's beauty, climate and people, they purchased Dunstone in Wellington on their return in 2003. Now personal wine tastings are conducted at table at The Stone Kitchen restaurant, which focuses on outdoor family eating. Neil Marais, ex Arendsig, has joined Lee in the cellar, while the range has been expanded by a sauvignon blanc; a viognier (all of one barrel!) will be introduced in 2013.

★★★★ **Shiraz** ⑪ Brooding 09 just wins over-ripeness battle. Rich meaty, spice features in chewily smooth texture. Departs with hint of alcohol glow. Not in league of **08** (★★★★★); up on maiden **07** (★★★).

★★★★ **Sauvignon Blanc** NEW ✓ 🍴 Ripe, figgy profile on big, concentrated **12**; lees richness invigorated by cool linearity, vigour of fruit from a high-altitude Tradauw Highlands vineyard. Very long finish.

Merlot ★★★ Ripe fruit with hint smoky oak on **10**. Simple, juicy backed by neat tannin trim. **Shiraz Rosé** 🍴 ★★★★ Particularly appealing **12**: peachy hue, spicy/savoury distinction set off by medium body & gentle length. Perfect aperitif & food partner. — AL

■ **Du Plessis** see Havana Hills
■ **Du Plevaux** see Imbuko Wines

Du Preez Estate

Location: Rawsonville ▪ Map: Breedekloof ▪ WO: Breedekloof/Western Cape ▪ Est 1916 ▪ 1stB 1998 ▪ Tasting & sales Mon-Fri 8–5 Sat 10–1 ▪ Closed all pub hols ▪ Cellar tours by appt, 2-day prior notice required ▪ BYO picnic ▪ Tour groups (20 pax) ▪ Owner(s) Du Preez family ▪ Cellarmaster(s)/winemaker(s) Kobus van der Merwe (Dec 2008) ▪ Viticulturist(s) Jean du Preez ▪ 400ha (merlot, p verdot, ptage, shiraz, chard, chenin, cbard, nouvelle, sauv) ▪ 6,000t ▪ Other export brand: Martinique ▪ IPW ▪ PO Box 12 Route 101 Rawsonville 6845 ▪ info@dupreezestate.co.za ▪ www.dupreezestate.co.za ▪ S 33° 41'37.1" E 019° 16'59.6" ▪ **T +27 (0)23-349-1995** ▪ F +27 (0)86-654-7337/+27 (0)23-349-1923

This hospitable Breedekloof estate regards all the wines born and bred here for nearly a century by the Du Preez clan as 'love children', says PRO Retha van der Merwe. Export success (note the Martinique addition) is built on market scrutiny, forecasting demand for 'sweet' reds and 'less expensive wines', still with quality.

Hendrik Lodewyk range

★★★★ **Méthode Cap Classique** ⑪ Elegant & layered sparkler, lemon/lime & nutty aromas mingle with rich brioche flavour. 90% chardonnay, with pinot noir, bottle-aged 48 months, **NV**.
Petit Verdot New bottling not ready.

Du Preez Private Cellar range

Cabernet Sauvignon 🈂 ★★★ **10** more serious effort with berry & tealeaf tones, dry tannins invite hearty food. **Merlot** ⑪ 🈂 ★★★★ Warm & alluring texture, dark chocolate & black cherry with mocha overlay. **10** big step up. **Shiraz** ⑪ 🈂 ★★★★ Now from Breedekloof vines, improved **10** ripe mulberry fruit, soft mouthfeel & mocha nuances. **Polla's Red** 🈂 ★★★ Pinotage dominates in smoky **11** blend, with spice & tannic grip. **Chardonnay** 🍴 🈂 ★★★ Uncomplicated citrus-driven **11** with nutty undertones best in light oaking. Breedekloof WO. **Sauvignon Blanc** 🍴 🈂 ★★★ Lightish **12** seamless balance of punchy tropical fruit & crisp freshness. For early drinking. **Maranda Rosé Méthode Cap Classique** Not tasted. **Hanepoot** ⑪ ★★★★ Generous **09** still selling, honey-sweet fortified pudding wine with hint of dried apricot.

Rockfield range

Cabernet Sauvignon 🍴 🈂 ★★★ Light-toned **10** has leafy tones & red berry freshness. WO Breedekloof **Merlot** ⑪ 🍴 🈂 ★★★ Shy & gentle-fruited **10**, milk chocolate & hints coffee. Fresh & tasty table companion. **Shiraz** ⑪ ★★★ Food-friendly **09**, earthy, with ripe & juicy mulberry fruit when reviewed. **Sauvignon**

anc 🍴 🎨 ★★★ Friendly, light-bodied **12** delivers on promise of good anytime companion. Discontinued: **y Creek Red**, **Red Stone Blend**, **Dry Creek Bouquet Blanc**. — HJ

Durbanville Hills

cation/WO: Durbanville ▪ Map: Durbanville, Philadelphia & Darling ▪ Est 1998 ▪ 1stB 1999 ▪ Tasting & sales on-Fri 9–4.30 Sat 10–3 Sun 11–3 ▪ Fee R40/14 wines incl glass ▪ Closed Good Fri, Dec 25 & Jan 1 ▪ Cellar tours on-Fri 11 & 3; groups of 10+ to book ahead ▪ Tapas served Tue-Sun in tasting room ▪ The Eatery Tue-Fri 11-3 t/Sun 8.30-3 ▪ Facilities for children & cyclists ▪ Conferences ▪ Weddings/functions ▪ Owner(s) Distell, 9 mers & workers trust ▪ Cellarmaster(s) Martin Moore (Nov 1998) ▪ Winemaker(s) Wilhelm Coetzee (reds, p 2008) & Günther Kellerman (whites, Jul 2003) ▪ Viticulturist(s) Drikus Heyns (consultant) ▪ 770ha (merlot, uv) ▪ 6,000t/150,000cs own label 40% red 58% white 2% rosé ▪ ISO 9000-1, ISO 14000-1, BWI, BRC, ACCP, IPW, WIETA ▪ PO Box 3276 Durbanville 7551 ▪ info@durbanvillehills.co.za ▪ www.durbanvillehills.co. ▪ S 33° 49' 29.9" E 018° 33' 56.7" ▪ **T** +27 (0)21-558-1300 ▪ **F** +27 (0)21-559-8169

'ith an annual production of around 150,000 cases, it's important to keep con- umer demands front of mind. For cellarmaster Martin Moore and his team, those emands include more tropical flavours in sauvignon blanc, a goal achieved by pening up the vines to more sunlight, and fruitier chardonnay, realised by using ss oak. But such large numbers also demand technology: timers that ensure auto- atic regular pumping over skins of red wine, automatic precision control equip- ient for white wine, which Moore describes as 'like having an extra team of eager ssistant winemakers, one at each fermenting tank'. He admits technology will elp 'make even better wines in the future'. As for 2012 vintage? 'Smooth intake', neventful', 'no peak periods, total control...' says Moore. 'We are pretty excited nd expect the 2012 sauvignon especially to be a real hit.'

ngle Vineyard range

★★★ **Luipaardsberg Merlot** ⚊ Lead player in individual merlot trio. **09** biggest in richness, structure. ucalyptus purity, mineral thread & dry finish add balance. 2 years new French oak seamlessly absorbed.

★★★ **Caapmans Cabernet Sauvignon-Merlot** Big but sleek **09**; well-harmonised cab with 40% nerlot & new oak polish. Freshness & fine grape tannins allow for current drinking but also ageworthy.

★★★ **Biesjes Craal Sauvignon Blanc** ⚊ A sauvignon for every palate from this cellar. This **11** for those vho like it more lively, a hint of maturity softening cool-climate green bean/pea notes. Lacks intensity of **10**.

hinofields Reserve range

★★★ **Merlot** ⚊ **10** introduced by usual minty/leafy fragrance; firm but unforbidding tannins nicely udged for lighter fruit year. Probably ready before **09**.

★★★ **Chardonnay** ⚊ **11** (★★★☆) lacks focus, concentration of **10**. Spicy oak outpacing lighter though till juicy fruit. For early drinking.

★★★☆ **Inner Valley Sauvignon Blanc** ⚊ **12** first since **09**. Great purity & precision with thrilling min- ral tension driving lees-enriched vinosity. Breathtakingly fresh & dry.

★★★ **Outer Valley Sauvignon Blanc** ⚊ **12** (★★★★★) more fruit-expressive of the 'Valley' pair (both asted just post-bottling so will benefit from settling & ageing). Here, passionfruit & green pea aromas reprised vith incisive purity on palate. Clean, natural acid adds to sustained finish. Last **09** earlier ready.

★★★ **Sauvignon Blanc** ⚊ Previewed **12** delights with fruit purity & intensity. Riper fig style; lees-age- ng & big but balanced alcohol give weight, richness. Long, bone-dry finish. **11** (★★★★) lighter.

★★★☆ **Noble Late Harvest** NEW ⚊ This cellar loves sauvignon! **12** makes scintillating debut. Hon- yed botrytis carefully judged not to swamp untamed 'sauvage' varietal edge; great sugar/acid balance too ocuses fruit sweetness rather than sugar. Low 9.5% alcohol cherry on top.

bernet Sauvignon NEW ★★★★ Mint & spicy oak introduce **09**. Still youthful, fresh with underlying eet fruit contained by firm tannins. **Pinotage** ⚊ ★★★★ Cool-climate freshness, fruit purity lifts **11** to gher level. Graceful harmony of ripe cherry/raspberry substance, polished structure & well-judged oak. So nkable now but worth forgetting for few years. **10** (★★★★) more oaky, extravagant. **Shiraz** ⚊ ★★★★ rk-spiced **09** (★★★) a little lean, grippy with sweetish tail. **10** much fuller bodied, more substance & bal- ce. Doubtful if either is a long keeper. **Cape Blend** NEW ⚊ ★★★★ Debut **10** aromatically pinotage-led)%) with cab adding structure, shiraz flesh, drop viognier for 'je ne sais quoi' extra. Whole makes for good, if : complex, drinking.

Durbanville Hills range

Cabernet Sauvignon ★★★ 10 nicely balanced, oaked to take advantage of tasty if simple blackberry fla vours. **Merlot ★★★** Modest sweet minty flavours on **10**, straightforward, short. **Pinotage ★★★** Ripe sweet raspberry/cherry flavours clipped by slightly grippy tannins leaves **10** less elegant than **09**. **Shiraz ★★★** Unpretentious, tasty **10**. Brims with smoked meat, savoury flavours framed by gentle rumble tannin **Bastion √ ★★★★** Cabernet/shiraz happy partners in **11**. A mouthful of berry-lifted savouriness with chewy supple backing. **Merlot Rosé 🍴 🚫 ★★** Spicy plum flavours on juicily smooth **12**; just dry. **Chardonnay 🍴 🚫 ★★★** Easy-drinking, lightly oaked **11**. Lightish ripe melon, orange zest flavours lifted by few gram sugar. **Sauvignon Blanc 🍴 🚫 ★★★** Approachably styled **12** satisfies with plentiful tropical juiciness & easygoing vivacity. — AL

Dusty Heath Vineyard

Location: Hilton ▪ Est 2009 ▪ Closed to public ▪ Owner(s) Mark & Paula Haldane ▪ Cellarmaster(s) Paul Haldane (Aug 2009) ▪ Winemaker(s) Paula Haldane (Aug 2009), with Maqua Madlala (Aug 2009) ▪ Viticultur ist(s) Mark Haldane (Aug 2009) ▪ 20ha/2ha (cabs s/f, merlot, p verdot) ▪ 100% red ▪ dhvineyard@sai.co.za **T +27 (0)33-383-2001/+27 (0)82-901-4304** ▪ F +27 (0)86-542-8704

Though based in the summer-rainfall Midlands of KwaZulu-Natal, Mark and Paula Haldane always fancied making wine. 'When some of our neighbours started doing it successfully, we thought why not?' She describes Dusty Heath, planted to the red varieties of Bordeaux, as a 'retirement project-cum-some thing for the children to get involved in.'

■ **Dusty Rhino** *see* United Nations of Wine

Du'SwaRoo

Location/WO: Calitzdorp ▪ Map: Klein Karoo & Garden Route ▪ Est/1stB 2008 ▪ Tasting & sales by appt Mon-Fri 9-5 Sat 9-1 ▪ Closed all pub hols ▪ Wines also available at Withoek Cellar ▪ Farm produce ▪ Owner(s) Tony Bailey ▪ Cellarmaster(s)/winemaker(s)/viticulturist(s) Tony Bailey (2008) ▪ 1ha (shiraz, tinta, touriga) ▪ 150cs own label 70% red 5% rosé 25% port ▪ 1.5ha/20t hanepoot also grown but delivered to Calitzdorp Cellar ▪ PO Box 279 Calitzdorp 6660 ▪ duswaroo@telkomsa.net ▪ www.kleinkaroowines.co.za/cellars/duswaroo.asp ▪ S 33° 30' 58.7" E 021° 41' 39.5" ▪ **T +27 (0)44-213-3137** ▪ F +27 (0)44-213-3137

Calitzdorp owner Tony Bailey is excited about local cellars' plans to produce an endemic blend, a dry red containing at least 70% traditional port grapes. Mean while he tests various combinations: 'Our Sirocco is an unofficial Calitzdorp Blend, while Shiloh explores the opposite end of the port/other cultivar blend dynamic.'

Shiraz ⓧ ★★★ Lavender & fynbos nuanced **09** had savoury appeal, robust tannins mid-2010. **Shiraz Winemakers Reserve ★★★ 09** previewed last year as 'Shiloh Shiraz Reserve', now bottled & renamed. Bold New World styling with noticeable alcohol & oak. Best enjoyed soon. **Khamsin** Await new. **Shiloh NEW ★★** Uncertified **NV (11)** from 80% shiraz, 15% touriga, drop tinta, named for beloved family Weimaraner. Wild berries & herbs, sips easily. **Sirocco ★★★** Touriga & tinta with 30% shiraz give wild berries & Karoo scrub, frisky acidity energising ripe stewed fruit on uncertified **NV (11)**. **Mistral ⓧ ★★** Savoury rosé from shiraz, **NV (11)** bright & friendly (12.5% alcohol) al fresco sipper. **Cape Vintage ★★★★** Port-style fortified from 66/34 touriga & tinta. New bottling of **09**, year longer in oak, shows tealeaves & Christmas cake, plump raisi flavours, nice balance. Bring on winter! **Cape Ruby ⓧ ★** 60/40 touriga/tinta port-style **10** needs drinking soon. Discontinued: **Cabernet Sauvignon**. — WB/JP

Du Toitskloof Winery

Location: Rawsonville ▪ Map: Breedekloof ▪ WO: Western Cape ▪ Est 1962 ▪ Tasting & sales Mon-Fri 8-5 S 9-3.30 ▪ Closed Good Fri, Dec 25 & Jan 1 ▪ Cellar tours by appt ▪ Cheese platters ▪ BYO picnic ▪ Owner(s) 2 members ▪ Cellarmaster(s) Shawn Thomson (Oct 1999) ▪ Winemaker(s) Chris Geldenhuys (Mar 2005) Willie Stofberg (Feb 2011), with Derrick Cupido (Jan 1993) ▪ Viticulturist(s) Leon Dippenaar (Jan 2005, consul tant) ▪ 900ha (cab, merlot, ptage, shiraz, chard, chenin, cbard, sauv) ▪ 14,000t/±350,000cs own label 40 red 60% white ▪ Fairtrade ▪ PO Box 55 Rawsonville 6845 ▪ info@dutoitskloof.co.za ▪ www.dutoitskloof.com S 33° 42' 9.2" E 019° 16' 8.9" ▪ **T +27 (0)23-349-1601** ▪ F +27 (0)23-349-1581

he sea of good-value smiles for the wines below affirms what budget-minded
undits and punters have been saying for many years now: Du Toitskloof, you
ock! It's not just that cellarmaster Shawn Thomson and team's wines really do
ver-deliver on value and quality, but also their 'Mother Nature directly into the
ottle' philosophy translates into satisfying, convivial glassfuls that are refresh-
ngly free of artifice or confection. Now into their second half-century, our advi-
ory remains: stock up!

eserve Collection

ebbiolo ✓ ★★★★ Bold, just off-dry **10**, earthy dusty berries & variety's naturally firm tannins, good balance
a spicy nut conclusion. **Dimension Red** ⭕ ★★★ Near-equal cab, merlot, shiraz with pinotage. **10** bright,
avoury berry fruit with a smooth core, just misses complexity of previous. **Chardonnay-Viognier** ✓ ★★★★
ungent floral & peach melba notes, vanilla wafts from barrel fermentation. **11** trumps last-tasted **08**
★★★★) with fine structure & balance. Discontinued: **Sauvignon Blanc**.

u Toitskloof range

Cabernet Sauvignon ☺ 🍱 ⭕ ★★★ **10** a step-up: firmer structure but still easy to sip, bright dark
berries & oak spice. **Merlot** ☺ 🍱 ⭕ ★★★ **11** offers dark chocolate & spiced black berries for everyday
quaffing. **Pinotage** ☺ 🍱 ⭕ ★★★ **11** a notch up; fresh & well built, juicy plum fruit is nicely balanced
for early enjoyment. **Cabernet Sauvignon-Shiraz** ☺ 🍱 ⭕ ★★★ Rich berries, smoke & spice seduce
on improved **11**. Well formed, polished, the finish is deliciously firm. **Chardonnay** ☺ 🍱 ⭕ ★★★ Back-
to-form off-dry **12**'s 50% unwooded portion lets the citrus fruit shine while the oaked fraction creates a delicious creaminess in the wine. **Sauvignon Blanc** ☺ 🍱 ⭕ ★★★ Dependable bargain-priced quaffing.
Improved **12** oozes tropical fruit, sprinkle of sugar makes it extra-drinkable. Will thrill its many fans. **Sparkling Brut** ☺ ★★★ Crisp, dry-seeming light-bodied sparkler. Smooth sauvignon-led **NV** offers lemon &
zesty lime to get the party started.

hiraz 🍱 ★★★ Uncomplicated **09** delivers spicy bark berries in a firm structure, harmony slightly disturbed
y some charry oak. **Pinotage-Merlot-Ruby Cabernet** 🍱 ⭕ ★★★ Plump plum fruit on charming **11**,
emi-dry with a tasty savoury conclusion. **Chenin Blanc** 🍱 ⭕ ★★★ Off-dry **12** trumps previous with
reen apple & pineapple refreshment. **Beaukett** ⊕ 🍱 ⭕ ★★ Flamboyant **11** blend with usual rosepetal
orange sweetness. Discontinued: **Rosé**.

essert Wine range

Cape Ruby ☺ ★★★ Ripe raisin & plum pudding flavours on light-bodied port-style **09** from tinta,
souzão, touriga. Not overly sweet.

oble Late Harvest ★★★ Lightish botrytised muscat & chenin. **09** tad off previous, sweet honeyed peach &
pricot tone is charming but straightforward. **Hanepoot Jerepigo** ⭕ ★★★ Super-sweet fortified after-dinner
eat, **12** highly perfumed, billows candied orange & Turkish Delight. **Red Muscadel** ✓ ⭕ ★★★★ Breedekloof
unshine in a bottle! **12** delightful floral & red fruit aromas, lots of sweet flavour, finish needs a bit more zing.

erlé Wines

ape Beach Club Rosé 🍱 ★★ Step-up **NV** spritzy pink, soft, sweet & nice. **Cape Beach Club Blanc** 🍱
★★ Easy & light **NV** with tiny floral bubbles. These listed as 'Cape Secco' last time. — WB

DuVon Private Cellar

ocation/map/WO: Robertson ▪ Est/1stB 2003 ▪ Tasting, sales & cellar tours by appt ▪ Conferences ▪ Weddings
Guest house ▪ Owner(s) Armand du Toit & Alex von Klopmann ▪ Cellarmaster(s)/winemaker(s)/viticultur-
st(s) Armand du Toit ▪ 29.5ha/27ha (cab, ruby cab, shiraz, chenin, cbard, sauv) ▪ 400t/600cs own label 70%
ed 30% white ▪ PO Box 348 Robertson 6705 ▪ info@duvon.co.za ▪ www.duvon.co.za ▪ S 33° 48' 46.8" E 019°
7' 4.1" ▪ **T +27 (0)82-341-1059** ▪ F +27 (0)86-626-1490

ellarmaster Armand du Toit, based on Little Italy farm near Robertson (his
rother owns Little France next door!) sees chenin featuring large in the winery's
uture — he now has vines aged 2 to 32 years old to work with. The US is proving
ertile ground for sales, lately joined in the export melting pot by Romania. No new
intages of his cabernet, shiraz, chenin or sauvignon were ready for tasting.

D' Vine *see* Swartland Winery

- **Dwyka Hills** *see Eagle's Cliff Wines-New Cape Wines*
- **Dyasonsklip** *see Bezalel-Dyasonsklip Wine Cellar*
- **Eagle Canyon** *see Blaauwklippen Vineyards*

Eagle's Cliff Wines-New Cape Wines

Location/map: Worcester ▪ WO: Breede River Valley/Western Cape/Robertson ▪ Est 2000 ▪ Tasting & sale Mon-Fri 8-4.30 ▪ Closed all pub hols ▪ Light meals Mon-Fri 10-2.30 ▪ Facilities for children ▪ Tour groups Owner(s)/winemaker(s) Christiaan Groenewald ▪ 600ha/80ha ▪ 40% red 60% white ▪ PO Box 898 Worcester 6849 ▪ christiaan@ncw.co.za ▪ www.eaglescliff.co.za ▪ S 33° 50' 25.4" E 019° 25' 7.4" ▪ **T +27 (0)23-340 4112** ▪ F +27 (0)23-340-4132

'My two sons are becoming more involved in the winemaking here and their passion is incredible,' says owner-winemaker Christiaan Groenewald. He appear bullish about the future, having doubled the capacity of his cellar and added fou new Arendskloof wines — the need for both quality value-for-money and afford able flagship wines ever in mind.

Arendskloof range

★★★★ **Syrah-Tannat** ⓧ Unusual & ambitious blend. Noble black plum & prune bouquet, firm tannins (a expected from tannat) on **09**. Hedonistic, well composed despite 15% alc. WO W Cape, as for all in this range.

★★★★ **Pinot Grigio** NEW 🍴 Stellar addition to South Africa's limited line-up of this variety. Lime marma lade & green apple flavours have a slight savouriness, making **12** a suave mealtime companion.

Pinotage NEW ★★★★ **08** quintessential pinotage strawberry aroma & flavour, light texture, eas sippability. Toffee bottle-age notes emerging, so best to enjoy soon. **Chardonnay** NEW 🍴 ★★ Rubenesque **12** is easy to drink, with hints of spice & lemon to the plump, slightly sweet flavours. **Sauvigno Blanc** NEW 🍴 ★★★★ Shy in youth, but **12**'s full body, crisp texture & perfect balance mark it as a seriou effort. Worth keeping a few bottles to see how they develop.

Eagle's Cliff range

> **Cabernet Sauvignon-Merlot** ☺ 🍴 ★★★ Exuberant **11** 60/40 combo layered with red berries, vanilla & mint, slides down easily. **Shiraz-Pinotage** ☺ 🍴 ★★★ Savoury appeal on 70/30 harmonious mix in **11**. Bright fruit, just the right amount of grip for mealtime enjoyment.

Pinotage ★★★ **11** a little reticent, very dry, but balanced, with ripe strawberry flavour & supple tannin. **Sh raz Rosé** ⓧ ★★★ Coral-hued **11**, dusty terpene edge, hint of tannin for quaffable semi-dry effect. **Char donnay** In abeyance. **Chenin Blanc** 🍴 ★★★ **12** clean, light & fresh, elderflower nuanced sippe **Sauvignon Blanc** 🍴 ★★★ More vinous than fruity, **12** lightish (12.5% alc) for lunchtime enjoyment.

Dwyka Hills range

Shiraz 🍴 ★★★ **11** pleasantly old school: clean leather, leafy tannins, slightly sweet conclusion. W W Cape. — HJ/CvZ

Eagles' Nest

Location/WO: Constantia ▪ Map: Cape Peninsula ▪ Est 2001 ▪ 1stB 2005 ▪ Tasting & sales daily 10-4.30 ▪ Fe R30pp, waived on purchase of R300+ ▪ Closed Good Fri, Dec 25 & Jan 1 ▪ Light meals ▪ Farm produce Owner(s) Mylrea family ▪ Cellarmaster(s) Martin Meinert (2005) ▪ Winemaker(s) Stuart Botha (2007) ▪ Vit culturist(s) Kobus Jordaan (2008) ▪ 38ha/12ha (merlot, shiraz, viog) ▪ 90t/7,500cs own label 85% red 15% white ▪ PO Box 535 Constantia 7848 ▪ info@eaglesnestwines.com ▪ www.eaglesnestwines.com ▪ S 34° 0' 5 2" E 018° 24' 54.3" ▪ **T +27 (0)21-794-4095** ▪ F +27 (0)21-794-7113

Considering the achievements of the wines here, it's hard to believe it starte with a fire. Until 2000 this family property consisted mainly of a pine forest, an then a devastating fire swept through the area — fortunately sparing the home stead and other buildings. When restoration started, vineyards were considere as a way to combat soil erosion, and advice from Stellenbosch winemaker Marti Meinert and viticulturist Kevin Watt confirmed the soundness of the idea. Direc tor Peter Stewart's love of viognier influenced that choice, in retrospect a inspired one, and the other varieties were chosen to fit the terroir.

★★★ **Merlot** ✓ 🖩 Last was persuasive **06**, then noted by us as discontinued. But now berry-rich **08** ★★★★) confirms how well the variety does in the right terroir. Sugared violets, tobacco spice, creamy succulence & with limber tannins to hold it true till ±2018.

★★★★ **Shiraz** 🖩 Bramleberries & Provençal herbs, white pepper, **09** has more new oak than admirable 08 (★★★★) without losing its fruit focus, supple body. Has the deep muscle tone for long ageing but already gives outstanding drinking pleasure.

★★★ **Verreaux** 🖩 Merlot-led Bordeaux blend from younger vineyards, **09** has lush berries, chocolate tone, curvaceous lines. But it's also complex & involving, there's plenty hidden under the immediate charm.

★★★☆ **Viognier** ✓ 🖩 🖼 Dried peach & melon with a jasmine top note, **11** expertly paired with oak, leaving it deliciously savoury yet fruity. Less austere than **10**, showing more seductive side; fine & impressive.

ttle Eagle ✓ 🖩 🖼 ★★★★ Cab/merlot in **10**, packed with berries but not simple, shows layered spice, ocolate, well supported by ripe tannns. **Sauvignon Blanc** ⓟ ★★★★ Last-tasted **10** had fresh grass-nged passionfruit, was cleanly dry, with penetrating delicacy. — CR

Eaglevlei Wine Estate

ocation/map: Stellenbosch • WO: Stellenbosch/Coastal/Durbanville/Hemel-en-Aarde Valley • Est/1stB 1997 • Tasting & sales Tue-Sun 10-5 • Fee R25 • Eaglevlei Restaurant Tue-Thu 8-8 Fri-Sat 8-9 Sun 8-6 • Facilities for hildren • Tour groups • Conferences • Functions • Owner(s) Rennert van Rensburg • Winemaker(s) Clarise ciocatti-Langeveldt (Jan 2012), with Carlo Sciocatti • Viticulturist(s) Clarise Sciocatti-Langeveldt (Jan 2012) • 0ha/±8ha (cab, merlot, ptage) • 50t/7,000cs own label 90% red 5% white 5% rosé • PO Box 969 tellenbosch 7599 • enquiries@eaglevlei.com • www.eaglevlei.com • S 33° 49' 33.5" E 018° 48' 52.2" • +27 (0)21-884-4713 • F +27 (0)21-884-4716

his family-friendly winery near Stellenbosch has changed hands a few times in ecent years, but new owner Rennert van Rensburg is determined that a new ime of stability and improvement starts now. Winemaking is taking place on the arm again and new labels featuring African eagles are being launched.

★★★ **Tiervoël** NEW ✓ 🖩 Charming & well-priced Cape Blend from pinotage & cab. **08** tobacco & dried ruit, big & bold wine with savoury finish, well-managed juicy tannins.

★★★ **Kroonarend** NEW ✓ 🖩 Shiraz-mourvèdre blend, splash viognier, leads with dark berry flavours, cloves & pepper unfold in layers in aftertaste of serious **09**, worth laying down. WO Coastal.

abernet Sauvignon ⓟ ★★★★ Enticing blackcurrant fruitiness on **07** showed through hefty tannins & ak, needed time to meld when tasted. **Pinotage** ⓟ ★★★★ Full-bodied **07** dominated by heavily toasted ak, but sweet black plum fruit showing through. **Special No 7 Shiraz** Not tasted. **Shiraz** ⓟ ★★★ **07** weet berry fruit couched in heady oak aromas. Neatly formed, lightish body. **Red Affair** ⓟ 🖩 ★★★★ **07** onderous oak over lively, ripe juicy fruit. Blend cab, merlot, shiraz & pinotage. **Berghaan** NEW 🖩 ★★★★ ppealing & serious rosé 'designed to attract attention', which it does. Lots going on in **12**, juicy semi-dry arthy/berry flavours, food-friendly savouriness. Near equal pinotage, cab & merlot. **Breëkop** NEW 🖩 nwooded chardonnay from Hemel-en-Aarde grapes, **12** preview too young to rate but showing promising esh lime character. **Langkuif** NEW 🖩 ★★★ Easy-drinking lightish dry white from Durbanville semillon, **1** filled with dried peach flavour, touch of oak adds weight, interest. **Muscat D' Alexandrie** ⓟ ★★★★ mited-release fortified dessert. **08** unctuous sweetness & intense muscat fruit, gentle spirit tang. Discontin-ed: **Pink**, **Viognier**. — DB

■ **Eden Crest** see Lboursford Wine Estate
■ **Edenhof** see Schalkenbosch Wines
■ **Eden's Vineyards** see Women in Wine

Edgebaston

ocation/map: Stellenbosch • WO: Stellenbosch/Coastal/Western Cape • Est/1stB 2004 • Tasting by appt only • Owner(s) David Finlayson • Cellarmaster(s) David Finlayson (Jan 2004) • Winemaker(s) David Finlayson (Jan 004), with Mark Goldsworthy (Nov 2008) • Viticulturist(s) Mark Goldsworthy (Nov 2008) • 30ha/24ha (cab, iraz, chard, sauv) • 180t/14,000cs own label 60% red 40% white • PO Box 2033 Dennesig 7601 • david@ dgebaston.co.za • www.edgebaston.co.za • S 33° 53'33.82" E 018° 51'17.61" • **T +27 (0)21-889-9572 / 27 (0)83-263-4353** • F +27 (0)21-889-9572

wner David Finlayson founded Edgebaston after the sale of his family's Glen arlou to Hess Family Estates. In the near-decade since, he has established it as a top-rank Stellenbosch producer, and reached his target of annual productio being sold within a year. The next phase is a 'small batch series'; finding parce from selected growers with which to experiment. A pinot noir has been launche and zinfandel, cabernet and chenin are in the works. Tough trading condition will sift the weak out of the industry, David believes, and he's confiden Edgebaston's brand value of over-delivering for its price will prevail.

★★★★☆ **'GS' Cabernet Sauvignon** ✓ Named for wine legend George Spies. **10** is rich & focused, its herbaceous minty fruit crammed into a dense tannic frame mid-2012, much less accessible than **08** when young needs 3-5 years. 100% new oak & 15% alcohol part of a powerful, ageworthy package. No **09**.

★★★★ **Cabernet Sauvignon** ✓ Textbook Stellenbosch cab in contemporary, ripe, generous style. **1** loaded with lush cassis flavours, dusted with herbs & hint of mint, amped by 15% alcohol.

★★★★ **David Finlayson Pinot Noir** NEW ✓ Unabashedly modern **11** oozes red berry charm before silk texture adds gravity to long finish. Two vineyard sites, both 5km from the sea, but 100km apart. WO W Cape

★★★★ **Chardonnay** ✓ 🍷 Masterclass in balancing New & Old Worlds: floral **11**'s lime fruit tucked up tight mineral frame; mouthwatering acidity perfect for food. Wild yeast fermentation in oak (30% new).

The Pepper Pot ✓ 🍷 ★★★★ Eclectic pot-pourri of 6 varieties led by shiraz & mourvèdre. **11** has taut, spic flavours that need time to ease a bit, but still drinkable in youth. WO W Cape. **The Berry Box** ✓ 🍷 ★★★ Juicy counterpart to the piquant 'Pot'; **10** from 5 red varieties, shiraz, merlot & cab in the vanguard. Oodle plump sweet fruit a hip, knock-back glassful in which 14.7% alcohol well hidden. **Sauvignon Blanc** ✓ 🍷 ★★★★ Tropical **12** a tad sweeter & less flinty, but as pleasing as bone-dry **10** (with 10% semillon). No **1** **The Berry Box White** NEW ✓ 🍷 ★★★★ Charming blend sauvignon, semillon & viognier, as fruit-packe as red partner. Semi-sweet **12** shows waxy gloss (27% semillon) while more dominant sauvignon leac melon-fruit appeal of semi-dry **11**. Racy acidity balances both. Discontinued: **Shiraz, Honey Pot**. — DS

Eenzaamheid 🍷🍴📷 NEW

Location/WO: Paarl ▪ Map: Paarl & Wellington ▪ Est 1693 ▪ 1stB 2010 ▪ Tasting by appt only ▪ Conferences Owner(s) Christo & Karina Briers-Louw ▪ Winemaker(s) Janno Briers-Louw (Apr 2008) ▪ Viticulturist(s) And Coetzee (Sep 2003) ▪ 1185ha/380ha (cab, cinsaut, ptage, shiraz, chenin) ▪ ±3,000t/420cs own label 75% re 25% white ▪ PO Box 22 Klapmuts 7625 ▪ wine@eenzaamheid1.co.za ▪ S 33° 44'52.67" E 018° 50'12.06" ▪ **+27 (0)82-493-9930** ▪ F +27 (0)86-583-5741

This 7th-generation farm near Paarl is owned by the Briers-Louw family. Realisin the potential of their dryland vineyards — grapes from which are vinified by sev eral award-winning brands — they decided to bottle wines on a small scale unde their own label. Elsenburg-trained young Janno Briers-Louw makes the wines in a Old World style: 'We prefer to show off the fruit rather than the oak'. A buildin dating back to 1693, when the farm was owned by Sarah Tas, sister of the famou rebel Adam Tas, has been restored to serve as a conference and tasting venue.

★★★★ **Chenin Blanc** Cellar-worthy statement wine, elegant label depicts suitably 'eenzaam' (lonely looking farmhouse. **11** bold but focused apple & citrus array textured & broadened by lees & vanilla oak. Try **Pinotage** ★★★★ Baked plum & meaty notes on very ripe **10**; smidgen new oak & dash shiraz add breadth, com plexity; still a bit chunky, needs time or food. **Shiraz-Mourvèdre** ★★★★ Zesty acidity, robust tannins & hear alcohol need year/2 to settle & mesh in bold, mulberry-toned **10**. **Cuvée 1693** ★★★ Fruity & easy-drinking N combo cab (50%) & equal portions shiraz, mourvèdre. Bright uncomplicated enjoyment. — WB/IM

Eerste Hoop Wine Cellar 🍷🍴

Location: Villiersdorp ▪ Map: Elgin, Walker Bay & Bot River ▪ WO: Western Cape ▪ 1stB 2006 ▪ Tasting, sales cellar tours Mon-Sat by appt ▪ Owner(s) Belgium owners ▪ Cellarmaster(s) Philip Costandius (Mar 2006) Winemaker(s)/viticulturist(s) Philip Costandius (Sep 2012) ▪ 24.5ha/11ha (cab, grenache, mourv, pinot, shi raz, chard, chenin, viog) ▪ 95t/7,000cs 55% red 42% white 3% rosé ▪ Brands for clients: Oggendau, Skoo Vallei, Stilfontein ▪ IPW ▪ PO Box 89 Elgin 7180 ▪ wine@eerstehoop.co.za ▪ www.eerstehoop.co.za ▪ S 34° 23.7" E 019° 11'50.7" ▪ **T +27 (0)28-841-4190/+27 (0)82-802-5267** ▪ F +27 (0)86-625-6028

With the advantage of most of the wine selling in Belgium and the Netherlands including in the Belgian owner's restaurants, there was little need for local mar keting, but that will change now that the winery is in full productio

Improvements in the cellar, now overseen by seasoned Philip Costandius, include a new cooling unit to preserve grape quality. A pinot noir was due at press time.

Lodewijkx range NEW

White Blend ★★★★ Structured **11**, oaked blend of chardonnay, chenin, viognier. Nuts, preserved fruit, limy acidity.

Eerste Hoop range

Cabernet Sauvignon ★★★★ More so than **08** (★★★★), **09** impresses with rich dark fruit, well-judged oaking, juicy accessibility. Integrated tannins promise a few years ageing. **Shiraz** ★★★★ Fruit-rich **09** well bolstered by 18 months oaking, ends firmly dry. Spice an attractive counterpoint. **Blushing Bride Pinot Noir Rosé** 🍷 ★★ 'Blushing Bride Rosé' last edition. Pale blush, muted berries, **11** offers light-textured (12.5% alcohol) dryness. **Wooded Chardonnay** ★★★★ **11** reflects bold toast & citrus styling, well served by crisp, livening acidity. **Viognier** ★★★ Rosewater, gentle peach, **11** is perked by zesty acidity.

Witklip range

Shiraz ☺ 🍷 ★★★ Succulent berries & mint, smooth tannins, **10** is a tasty charmer.

Chardonnay 🍷 ★★★ Peach, melon & bright acidity, unwooded **11** is a flavourful quaffer. —CR

🏛 **1855** *see* Hermanuspietersfontein Wynkelder

Eikehof Wines

Location/map/WO: Franschhoek ▪ Est 1903 ▪ 1stB 1992 ▪ Tasting, sales & tours by appt ▪ Closed Easter Fri/Sat/Sun, Ascension Day, Pentecost & Dec 25 ▪ Function room ▪ Owner(s)/cellarmaster(s)/winemaker(s) Francois Malherbe ▪ 29ha/24ha (cab, merlot, pinot, shiraz, chard, sem) ▪ 28t/1,500cs own label 80% red 20% white ▪ PO Box 222 Franschhoek 7690 ▪ eikehof@mweb.co.za ▪ www.eikehof.com ▪ S 33° 52′ 53.3″ E 019° 3′ 52.0″ ▪ **T +27 (0)21-876-2469** ▪ F +27 (0)21-876-2469

The eponymous oaks (eike) at this Franschhoek family farm, 110 years old, provide a magnificent setting for the function room which recently opened — with encouraging results. Also auspicious for owner/winemaker Francois Malherbe is that he's now exporting red wines to Germany, albeit on a small scale as yet.

Cabernet Sauvignon 🍷 ★★★ Sweet fruit in spicy **08**, charry staves & savoury acid grip. **Merlot** 🍷 ★★★ Earthy **09** in savoury mould with plenty of fresh acidity. **Shiraz** 🍷 ★★★ Smoky mocha dominates sweet spicy fruit in **08**. Slightly astringent finish. **Chardonnay** 🍷 🍴 ★★ Unoaked **10** pleasantly light, crisp quaffing. —IM

Eikendal Vineyards

Location: Somerset West ▪ Map: Helderberg ▪ WO: Stellenbosch/Stellenbosch/Elgin/Western Cape ▪ Est 1981 ▪ 1stB 1984 ▪ Tasting & sales Mon-Sat 9.30-4.30 (Sep-May) & 10-4 (Jun-Aug); Sun 10-4 ▪ Fee R20/5 wines ▪ Closed Good Fri, Dec 25/26 & Jan 1 ▪ Cellar tours Mon-Fri 10 & 2.30 ▪ Restaurant @ Eikendal T +27 (0)21-855-5033: lunch Tue-Sun & dinner Wed ▪ Facilities for children ▪ Tour groups ▪ Gift shop ▪ Conferences ▪ Walks/hikes ▪ Mountain biking trail ▪ Flywaters fly fishing ▪ Cheetah Outreach ▪ Eikendal Lodge (see Accommodation section) ▪ Owner(s) Substantia AG ▪ Winemaker(s)/viticulturist(s) Nico Grobler (2007), with Christo Hanse & Willem van Kerwel (both 2012) ▪ 78ha/±50ha (cabs s/f, malbec, merlot, p verdot, chard) ▪ 250t/35-40,000cs own label 70% red 30% white ▪ IPW ▪ PO Box 2261 Stellenbosch 7601 ▪ info@eikendal.co.za ▪ www.eikendal.com ▪ S 34° 0′ 46.7″ E 018° 49′ 24.5″ ▪ **T +27 (0)21-855-1422** ▪ F +27 (0)21-855-1027

The Swiss Saager family bought portions of Longridge and Mietjiesvlei farms, straddling the Eikendal road on the lower slopes of the Helderberg, in 1981. They consolidated the portions and commissioned a new cellar with the aid and advice of Jan Coetzee (Vriesenhof). Abé Beukes (Darling Cellars) made the first vintages, but he was succeeded shortly after by the long-serving Josef Krammer, who was recruited from Villiera and established the estate's reputation for fine Bordeaux-style red wines and chardonnay. Still in the same hands, their second place overall in the 2012 Trophy Show heralds a return to past glories under current winemaker/viticulturist Nico Grobler.

Limited Releases

★★★★ **Réserve du Patron** ⑨ Dense, concentrated & extracted **05**, last year had very ripe, rich & brooding dark fruit, powdery tannins.

Reserve range

★★★★☆ **Classique** Perennial high-flying flagship label, acclaimed **09** merlot-led Bordeaux blend scales even higher peaks. Intense, precisely modulated, presenting layered ripe fruit & minerality with endless finish.

★★★★ **Chardonnay** 🅥 Beneath a heavy oak mantle lies elegant, supple fruit with mineral notes. Barrel-fermented **11** promises better balance in future. Obvious ripeness despite modest 12.5% alcohol.

★★★★ **Noble Late Harvest** ⑨ Botrytis dessert with classic pineapple & candied peel character previously on **08**, from chenin. Note: range listed as 'Flagship' last time.

Signature range

★★★★ **Cabernet Sauvignon** ✓ Beautiful varietal expression in **09**: iodine, seaweed, leafy herbaceousness, all cosseted in silky tannins & plush blackcurrant fruit. Conspicuous over-performer far outstrips earlier vintages & promising **08**.

★★★★ **Merlot** 🅥 Riper, denser **10** shifts to classic style, with more dark plum-pudding, less mintiness. Noble oak backbone & generously juicy fruit with crisp acidity.

Pinotage ✓ 🅥 ★★★★ **10** is a step up on **09** (★★★☆), with dark, smoky meat tones on heavy Christmas pudding fruit. Muscular body toned with finely judged acidity & subtle long finish. **Shiraz** ⑨ 🅥 ★★★★ Spicy, racy **10** appealing fynbos spice over solid red fruit centre. Shows generous ripeness. Own & Franschhoek grapes. **Cabernet Sauvignon-Merlot** ✓ 🅥 ★★★★ Much fuller **10** has nothing in common with light, juicy **09** (★★★). Focused, dense blackcurrant with liquorice/tarry notes, tapering to long, still tannic finish. Needs time. **Charisma** NEW ★★★★ Debut 5-way almost-Bordeaux-style red blend, **09** shows generous ripeness of vintage through spicy oak mantle. Needs time. **Janina Unwooded Chardonnay** ✓ 🔳 🅥 ★★★★ Primary candyfloss notes on previewed **12** should subside to display honest, complex fruit with creamy lees texture. **Sauvignon Blanc** ✓ 🔳 🅥 ★★★★ New direction in **12** sees West Coast & Elgin grapes blended & partially oaked. Preview is fuller, more complex than **11** (★★★), with lovely mouthfilling flavour, lingering finish.

Cuvée range

Rosé ☺ 🔳 🅥 ★★★ Bright & breezy tinsel-pink merlot/shiraz **12** is just-dry, with generous strawberry fruit. **Blanc** ☺ 🔳 🅥 ★★★ Tank sample of entry-level **12** sauvignon/chardonnay blend has quite sophisticated lees richness, honest ripe fruit.

Rouge 🔳 🅥 ★★★ Generously fruity entry-level quaffer, **11** shiraz-led blend with cab & merlot is a big improvement on previous. Note: range listed as 'Eikendal Wines' last time.

Sparkling Wines

Méthode Cap Classique ⑨ ★★★★ Appealing **08** sparkling from chardonnay shows class, leesy richness on creamy mousse. Improves on previous **05** (★★★★). Delightful aperitif or sunset sipper. — GdB

◼ **Eksteens' Family Vineyards** *see* Stone Ridge Wines
◼ **Elandsberg** *see* Viljoensdrift Wines & Cruises

Elberti Wines

Location: Somerset West ▪ Map: Helderberg ▪ WO: Western Cape ▪ Est 2005 ▪ Tasting & sales by appt ▪ Owner(s)/cellarmaster(s)/winemaker(s)/viticulturist(s) Pieter Steyn ▪ 1,000cs own label 90% red 10% white ▪ PO Box 70 Somerset Mall 7137 ▪ psteyn@elbertiwines.com ▪ www.elbertiwines.com ▪ S 34° 4'39.0" E 018° 49'4.0" ▪ **T** +27 (0)21-851-9540 ▪ F +27 (0)86-540-3334

Though based in Somerset West, the Steyn family's vines are some 50km distant, on the Theewaterskloof lakeshore. The owners' belief in the uniqueness of this terroir has led them to successfully campaign for a Theewater Wine of Origin designation, and to produce the first WO Theewater wines (though export bottles still temporarily bear WO Western Cape). All Elberti wines are now 'estate' certified, and the Elberti whites, furthermore, are single-vineyard.

Merlot Unready. **Cabernet Sauvignon-Merlot** NEW ★★★ Charry oak notes mid-2012 cloak appealing sour cherry & sweet herbal notes on **10**. **Shiraz-Cabernet Sauvignon** NEW ★★★ Brooding dark fruit, sweet vanilla & mocha, racy lean flavours on **10** encourage food partnering. **Sauvignon Blanc** Await next. — HJ

Elemental Bob

Location: Hermanus • WO: Western Cape/Hemel-en-Aarde Ridge • Est/1stB 2004 • Closed to public • Owner(s)/winemaker(s) Craig Sheard • 100-150cs own label 75% red 20% white 5% port • elementalbob@gmail.com • T +27 (0)82-265-1071

Adventurous boutique vintner (and Spookfontein winemaker) Craig Sheard last year suspended rose quartz and amethyst crystals in his wine for their esoteric power. No new oak, cultured yeasts, acid additions or enzymes for him. Keep it natural and let the wine speak with soul, he maintains.

Wood-Cut Series Limited Edition NEW

My SunShine ★★ Idiosyncratic **NV** blend of older-oak-fermented viognier & unwooded sauvignon, offering light, short-lived peachy zest. 'Unfiltered & WILL deposit sediment' notes winemaker.

Sweet Collection Limited Release NEW

My Bauhaus ★★★ Very ripe choc-fruitcake notes on port-style **11** from Hemel-en-Aarde Ridge shiraz. — FM

■ **Elements** *see* Hartswater Wine Cellar
■ **Elephantasy** *see* Groupe CDV

Elgin Grove

Location/WO: Elgin • Est 2004 • 1stB 2007 • Closed to public • Owner(s) Nigel McNaught, Abacus Trust & Tony Davis • Winemaker(s) Nigel McNaught • Viticulturist(s) Paul Wallace (2004, consultant) • 20ha/6ha (sauv) • 40t/500cs own label 100% white • c/o Stony Brook PO Box 22 Franschhoek 7690 • nigel@stonybrook.co.za • T +27 (0)21-876-2182 • F +27 (0)21-876-2182

Commenting that rising costs and consumer resistance to higher prices is making it difficult for smaller producers, co-owner Nigel McNaught of Stony Brook in Franschhoek (where this wine is made by him), says: 'The only response to this is to make quality wines, as these will always sell.' And that neatly sums up his purpose at Elgin Grove.

Sauvignon Blanc ✓ 🏠 ★★★★ Minerality & limy acidity follows **11**'s fynbos-spiked perfume. Admirable intensity, flavour length. — CR

Elgin Heights

Location/map: Stellenbosch • WO: Elgin • 1stB 2007 • Tasting & sales by appt • Conference facilities • Owner(s) Ryk Joubert • Winemaker(s) Andries Burger, Kobie Viljoen & Corne Marais (sauv/shiraz/MCC, consultants) • Viticulturist(s) DD Joubert • 111ha/70ha (cab, merlot, shiraz, chard, sauv, viog) • PO Box 52 Vlottenburg 7604 • mwddj@mweb.co.za • www.elginheights.co.za • S 33° 57' 2.60" E 018° 45' 28.91" • T +27 (0)84-517-9300 • F +27 (0)86-648-1704

When the Joubert family bought Elgin Heights in the mid-1960s, they grew deciduous fruit. Some 30 years later, fifth-generation winefarmer DD Joubert saw how well his neighbours were doing with wine and developed his own vineyards. Early results since the first bottling in 2007 have encouraged expansion of the range with a chardonnay and MCC rosé (the latter not tasted by us) in 2012.

★★★★ **Sauvignon Blanc** 🏠 🐾 **11** lives up to last year's preview with juicy gooseberry, fig flavours, balanced vitality. Easy, characterful drinking.

Shiraz ⊕ 🐾 ★★★★ **10** full of ready, youthful appeal. Crackles with spicy aromas; a touch of sugar emphasises sweet red-fruit flavours; smoothly textured with nip of form-giving tannin. **Chardonnay** 🏠 ★★★ Fruit-forward style; **11** pickled limes & peaches, with zippy freshness, pithily dry. **Emerald Cap Classique Chardonnay** ⊕ ★★★★ Subtle, refreshing **09** traditional-method sparkling from 100% chardonnay. Whiff of cream, ginger biscuit; vivacious bubble leads to clean, tingling departure. — AL

Elgin Ridge

Location/WO: Elgin • Map: Elgin, Walker Bay & Bot River • Est 2007 • 1stB 2009 • Tasting, sales & tours by appt Mon-Fri 10-4 Sat/Sun/pub hols by appt only • Food & wine pairing during Elgin Open Gardens weekends 10-4 • Farm produce • BYO picnic • Owner(s) Brian & Marion Smith • Winemaker(s) Niels Verburg (Aug 2009, consultant), with Brian Smith ▪ Viticulturist(s) Kevin Watt (Apr 2007, consultant), with Marion Smith ▪ 10.2ha/4.5ha (pinot, chard, sauv, sem) ▪ 14.5t/1,000cs own label 100% white ▪ Organic certification ▪ PO Box 143 Elgin 7180 ▪ info@elginridge.com ▪ www.elginridge.com ▪ S 34° 12' 10.68" E 019° 0' 14.34" ▪ **T +27 (0)21-846-8060** ▪ F +27 (0)21-846-8060

Elgin Ridge is now the only certified organic cellar in Elgin, but co-owner/co-winemaker Brian Smith doesn't see it stopping there. Biodynamic trials have begun because Brian and wife Marion, who is in charge of the vineyards, believe that wine quality's most significant advances will be made in the vineyards, as more producers go the same route.

282 Chardonnay 🍴 ❀ ★★★ Peach & citrus, unoaked **11** is gently fruity, drinks easily. Could be enjoyed on its own. **282 Sauvignon Blanc** 🍴 ❀ ★★★★ Crunchy apples & pears, **11**'s limy acidity gives a jolt of freshness, extends the flavours. Ideal dining partner. — CR

■ **Elgin Valley Vineyards** see Corder Family Wines

Elgin Vintners

Location/WO: Elgin ▪ Map: Elgin, Walker Bay & Bot River ▪ Est 2003 ▪ 1stB 2004 ▪ Tasting & sales by appt ▪ Owner(s) Derek Corder, Max Hahn, Alastair Moodie, James Rawbone-Viljoen, Rob Semple & Paul Wallace ▪ Cellarmaster(s)/winemaker(s) Various (Kevin Grant, Gavin Patterson, Jeff Grier, Nico Grobler, Martin Meinert, Niels Verburg, Joris van Almenkerk) ▪ Viticulturist(s) Paul Wallace ▪ 1,379ha/±102ha (cab, malbec, merlot, pinot, shiraz, chard, riesling, sauv, sem, viog) ▪ 1,100t/8,000cs own label ▪ BWI, IPW ▪ PO Box 121 Elgin 7180 ▪ elginvintner@mweb.co.za ▪ www.elginvintners.co.za ▪ S 34° 10' 9.54" S 019° 0' 29.40" ▪ **T +27 (0)21-859-2779/+27 (0)21-848-9587** ▪ F +27 (0)86-646-3693

There's a new wine at this innovative winery with multiple owners and winemakers. The Century pays tribute to Elgin eminence Douglas Moodie, who turned 100 in 2011 — having lived here since arriving on his bicycle in 1930. His pioneering work includes developing irrigation and spraying techniques at his Eikenhof farm, and establishing the Elgin Fruit Company. He also realised the importance of protecting indigenous fynbos: today Eikenhof is a BWI Champion.

★★★★ **Shiraz** ✓ 🍴 **09** big, but with sense of delicacy. Lots of dark spice, smoked meat appeal, gentle tannins & judicious oaking; all provide delicious drinking now, good potential too. Step up on **08** (★★★★).

★★★★ **Chardonnay** ⊕ 🍴 🍷 Expressive limy, buttery nose; good juicy fruit acids with subtle oaking add dimension, weight to **10**. Satisfying rather than complex.

★★★★ **Viognier** ⊕ 🍴 Tasty if simple ripe fruit on dry **10** (★★★★) somewhat overwhelmed by buttery oak (50% new). Cloying farewell despite good acidity. **09** was elegant, aromatic.

Cabernet Sauvignon ★★★ Simple & short fruit on **08**. Balanced freshness, structure for current drinking. **Merlot** ★★★★ Appetising **09**, with splash malbec, pleasingly fresh, fruity with lively & succulent grape tannins. Good now, has staying power too. **Pinot Noir** ⊕ 🍴 🍷 ★★★★ Fresh & fruity style; subtle oaking (30% new) on **10** adds balanced enrichment. **Agama** ★★★ Cab/merlot forge straightforward blend in **08**. Quiet strawberry aromas, flavours in harmony with gentle structure. Not for ageing. **Rosé** 🍴 🍷 ★★★ **12** (ex-tank) charmer, brims with ripe plums, tangy dry freshness. Lovely summer sipper from merlot. **Sauvignon Blanc** ✓ 🍴 🍷 ★★★★ Easy-drinking **11** with bounce, nicely paced vitality to sustain ripe fig, gooseberry flavours. **The Century** NEW 🍷 ★★★★ Bemedalled sauvignon-semillon blend named for Elgin Valley pioneer & centenarian Douglas Moodie. Unoaked **11** bright tangerine, honey notes, creamy texture, overall balance dimmed by hint of alcohol glow. — AL

■ **Embrace** see StellenRust

Emineo Wines

Location: Cape Town ▪ Map: Cape Peninsula ▪ WO: Durbanville/Coastal ▪ Est 2004 ▪ 1stB 2006 ▪ Tasting by appt ▪ Owner(s) Trans-Scripto (Pty) Ltd ▪ Winemaker(s) Nico van der Merwe & Thys Louw ▪ 750cs own label 100% red ▪ PO Box 1358 Cape Town 8000 ▪ info@emineo.com ▪ www.emineo.com ▪ S 33° 56' 29.06" E 018° 23' 47.76" ▪ **T +27 (0)82-579-4849** ▪ F +27 (0)86-660-4323

This legally themed brand, together with sister label Cape to Cairo, is produced on an occasional basis for Cape Town patent attorney Otto Gerntholtz by Nico van der Merwe (Saxenburg, Mas Nicolas) and Thys Louw (Diemersdal). Grapes are sourced from vineyards in Swartland, Durbanville and Stellenbosch.

★★★★ **Liber II JLS** ⊕ Poised **07** cab (65%) with merlot & pinotage. When last tasted, minty chocolate aromas, lively cassis underpinned by acidity & tannin.

★★★★ **Liber III RG** ⊕ **07** big, ebullient shiraz with splash mourvèdre, ex-Durbanville & Swartland. Seriously styled, with polished oak when tasted some time ago.

Liber I OCG ⊕ ★★★★ On review, **06** 5-way Bordeaux blend mostly cab was soft & approachable. — KM/CvZ

■ **Enon** see Zandvliet Wine Estate & Thoroughbred Stud
■ **Enoteca Bottega** see Idiom Wines

Epicurean Wines

WO: Western Cape ▪ Est 2001 ▪ 1stB 2003 ▪ Closed to public ▪ Owner(s) Global Pact Trading 125 (Pty) Ltd ▪ Cellarmaster(s) Mutle Mogase, Mbhazima Shilowa, Moss Ngoaseng, Ron Gault (Nov 2002) ▪ Winemaker(s) Schalk Willem Joubert (consultant) ▪ 250cs own label 100% red ▪ WIETA ▪ PO Box 280 Parklands 2121 Johannesburg ▪ info@epicureanwine.co.za ▪ www.epicureanwine.co.za ▪ **T +27 (0)11-530-9100** ▪ F +27 (0)11-530-9101

'Epicurean is a product of our love and passion for food, wine and the finer things in life,' says Mbhazima Shilowa, one of four partners behind this venture — committed to producing 'elegant, subtle and refined wines'. Working to achieve this is winemaker Schalk-Willem Joubert of Rupert & Rothschild.

★★★★ **Epicurean** ⊕ More lightweight **08** reflects the vintage. Pretty mint-lifted red berry tones are held by a challenging structure. Best opened over next year or two. — AL

Equitania

Location: Somerset West ▪ Map: Helderberg ▪ WO: Stellenbosch ▪ Est 2000 ▪ 1stB 2008 ▪ Tasting & sales by appt ▪ Fee R10 ▪ Closed all pub hols ▪ BYO picnic ▪ Walking/hiking trails ▪ Owner(s) Esme Kruger de Beer ▪ Winemaker(s) Francois Naudé (2012, consultant) ▪ Viticulturist(s) Gavin Dun (May 2007) ▪ 4.65ha/1.38ha (cabs s/f) ▪ 10.54t/6,000cs own label 100% red ▪ PO Box 5308 Helderberg 7135 ▪ esme14@mweb.co.za ▪ www.equitania.co.za ▪ S 34° 2'26.15" E 018° 49'5.51" ▪ **T +27 (0)21-300-1140/1** ▪ F +27 (0)21-300-1092

While plans are still afoot to offer guests a bespoke winelands experience, owner Esme de Beer did secure local winemaking legend Francois Naudé of Chateau Naudé as consultant last year. His first task is to craft just 1,000 bottles of exceptional quality to launch this Helderberg winery's 'Private Collection'.

★★★★ **Flag 08** was serious & savoury new-oaked Bordeaux blend. **10** unrated preview, only older oak. Cab & cab franc with shy lead pencil minerality, stern tannic grip & standout alcohol. No **09**.
Fluke ⊕ ★★★ Appealing creamy berry-mousse character on ripe & rounded cab-led **08**. — CvZ

Ernie Els Wines

Location/map: Stellenbosch ▪ WO: Stellenbosch/Western Cape ▪ Est 1999 ▪ 1stB 2000 ▪ Tasting, sales & cellar tours Mon-Sat 9–5 ▪ Fee R30/4 wines, R60/8 wines ▪ Closed Easter Fri/Sun, Dec 25 & Jan 1 ▪ Light lunches & cheese platters Tue-Sat ▪ Tour groups ▪ Gift shop ▪ Corporate events & functions ▪ Small conference facilities ▪ Mountain biking trail ▪ Ernie Els's Trophy Room ▪ The Big Easy Restaurant at 95 Dorp Str (see Restaurants section) ▪ Owner(s) Ernie Els ▪ Cellarmaster(s) Louis Strydom (Dec 1999) ▪ Winemaker(s) Louis Strydom (Dec 1999), with Klaas Stoffberg (2009) ▪ Viticulturist(s) Charl van Reenen (2008) ▪ 72ha/45ha (cab, merlot, shiraz) ▪ 250t/9,000cs own label 90% red 10% white + 750cs for clients ▪ Brands for clients: SA Rugby ▪ PO Box 7595 Stellenbosch 7599 ▪ info@ernieelswines.com ▪ www.ernieelswines.com ▪ S 34° 0'52.8" E 018° 50'53.5" ▪ **T +27 (0)21-881-3588** ▪ F +27 (0)21-881-3688

The trophy room at this showpiece Stellenbosch cellar has been redesigned and enlarged and a good thing too as owner and top professional golfer Ernie Els last year took his tally of major championship wins to four when he triumphed in The Open at Royal Lytham. The silverware for winning The Open is of course known as the Claret Jug, entirely appropriate as this winery's flagship as made by Louis Strydom is an always outstanding Bordeaux-style red blend. To date, the wines have tended to be big and bold but Strydom increasingly goes in pursuit of elegance. 'It used to be the bigger, the better and we in the Helderberg were well positioned to deliver on that. Now there's a shift to greater refinement and the trick is to step back a little in the winemaking process without losing the essence of place.'

★★★★ **Cabernet Sauvignon** ✓ 📖 It's the precision of viticulture, winemaking on **10** (★★★★★) which elevates it above **09**. Great fruit purity, fresh acidity, oak perfectly judged. Cassis, violets, tobacco, tilled earth, the whole works. Has a great future ahead of it.

★★★★ **Proprietor's Syrah** 📖 Seamless **10** displays concentrated red & black fruit, fresh acidity, firm but fine tannins. Contains 5% viognier.

★★★★☆ **Ernie Els Signature** A shoot-the-lights-out take on the Bordeaux blend since inception, **09** doesn't disappoint. Cab-driven, with notes of ripe dark fruit & toasty oak (20 months French, 80% new), it's super-concentrated & smooth textured. Has real presence.

★★★★ **Big Easy Red** 🍷 **10** (★★★★) is 6-way blend, led by shiraz. Sexy rather than profound, with sweet, juicy red fruit & fine tannins. Includes some Piekenierskloof fruit. Less weight than **08**; **09** not tasted.

★★★★☆ **Proprietor's Blend** 📖 **10** (★★★★) lacks ready charm of **09**. A blend of 59% cab, with shiraz, merlot, cab franc, malbec, petit verdot, has good fruit concentration but currently appears tight, very tannic.

★★★★☆ **CWG Auction Reserve** 📖 Though not fine-boned, **10** is lovely, even so. 60% cab, 30% shiraz, rest merlot, it has big alcohol (just shy of 15%) & few grams of sugar but retains finesse. Red & black fruit, fynbos & lilies, intense spice. Great concentration, freshness, length.

Merlot ★★★ **11** tends to over-reach itself with jammy fruit, tart acidity & drying finish. Has intensity but at expense of balance. **Big Easy White** 🍴 ★★★★ 100% chenin, **12** rich & full, with enticing honeysuckle aroma, lots of yellow fruit on palate. Touch of sugar adds plumpness, soft acidity. WO W Cape, as next. **Sauvignon Blanc** 🍴 ★★★★ **12** is seamless & correct. Wide range of flavour, some sugar (3.9g/l) to fatten out mid-palate, zippy acidity lends balance. More complexity than **11** (★★★). — CE

Ernst Gouws & Co Wines

Location/map: Stellenbosch ▪ WO: Stellenbosch/Malmesbury/Western Cape/Elgin ▪ Est/1stB 2003 ▪ Tasting & sales at Koelenhof Winery Mon-Thu 9-5 Fri 9-4 Sat 10-2 ▪ Fee R15pp ▪ Closed Easter Fri/Sun, Ascension day, Dec 25/26 & Jan 1 ▪ Facilities for children ▪ Owner(s) Ernst & Gwenda Gouws ▪ Cellarmaster(s) Ernst Gouws ▪ Winemaker(s) Ernst Gouws snr, with Ezanne Gouws-Du Toit & Ernst Gouws jnr ▪ 72ha total ▪ 30,000cs own label 40% red 60% white ▪ Other export brands: New Gate, Timbili ▪ IPW ▪ PO Box 7450 Stellenbosch 7599 ▪ ernst@ernstgouws.co.za ▪ www.ernstgouws.co.za ▪ S 33° 50' 3.4" E 018° 47' 52.7" ▪ **T +27 (0)21-865-2895** ▪ F +27 (0)21-865-2894

The Gouws heritage dates back over 300 years to the Huguenots and, with one of the forefathers being a winemaker, co-owner and patriarch Ernst's dream understandably was an own brand. His aspiration became a reality exactly ten years ago. With wife Gwenda and children Ezanne and Ernst junior closely involved, the 'Co' is making inroads into China and Africa, their main focuses for the next year.

★★★★☆ **Depth** NEW ✓ 📖 What a debut! **11** Bordeaux-style white is mouthfilling & harmonious, yet elegant & light on its feet. Subtle wood gives support to textured flavours of white flowers, citrus & lanolin, smoothness to the lingering savoury end. A showstopper. 65% sauvignon, new-oaked semillon, from Elgin.

Merlot ✓ 📖 ★★★★ Ripe black cherry & plum, hints espresso & chocolate, **11** smooth & juicy through to lingering savoury end. **Pinot Noir** 🍷 ★★★ Ripe & big **08** preview reveals earthy, spicy cherry with savoury mushroom & oaky finish. WO W Cape. **Shiraz** 🍷 ★★★★ Friendly & fragrant **09** from Malmesbury vines, fruity, spicy & soft, concludes with lingering savoury creaminess. **Chardonnay** 🍷 📖 ★★★★ From Swartland bushvines, **10** fills the palate with rich & buttery flavour, follows with a delicious citrus & vanilla conclusion. **Chenin Blanc** 🍷 📖 ★★★ Delicate tropical fruit salad & cream, zesty acidity on **11**. **Sauvignon Blanc** ✓ 🍴 ★★★★ Crowd pleasing & dependable. **12** fresh & fruity, shows a succulent fruit/acid balance. — WB

Escapades Winery

Location/map: Stellenbosch ▪ WO: Coastal ▪ Est/1stB 2006 ▪ Tasting by appt ▪ Owner(s) Evangelos Gerovassiliou, Vassilis Tsaktsarlis & Takis Soldatos ▪ Cellarmaster(s) Vassilis Tsaktsarlis & Evangelos Gerovassiliou (both 2006) ▪ Winemaker(s) Chris Kelly (Oct 2010, consultant) ▪ (cab, malbec, merlot, ptage, shiraz, sauv, sem) ▪ 70t/3,000cs own label 30% red 60% white 10% rosé ▪ PO Box 99 Somerset Mall 7129 ▪ info@escapadewinery.com ▪ www.escapadewinery.com ▪ S 33° 54' 47.7" E 018° 44' 7.7" ▪ **T +27 (0)82-569-3371** ▪ F +27 (0)86-585-6549

is is one of the less-observed international ventures (escapades?) in the Cape - t surely a significant one given the eminence of the three Greek friends behind

Highly respected winemakers Evangelos Gerovassiliou and Vassilis aktsarlis tend to take turns in visiting the cellar (where another international ure, New Zealander Chris Kelly, is the permanent presence) and Sweden- sed vintner, connoisseur and marketer Takis Soldatos is ever-alert. The wines from high altitude and older vineyards that the team have sought out — are as phisticated and characterful as might be expected.

★★★ **Semillon-Sauvignon Blanc** 🔲 Delicate, graceful **12** blend works beautifully, semillon adding enerous dimension & lemony complexity to sauvignon brightness. Satiny texture, lingering flavour; a pleasure. **bernet Sauvignon** Awaiting next vintage release, as for **Merlot**, **Pinotage** & **Shiraz**. **Pinotage Rosé** 🔲 ★★ Adds variety to name with pretty, softly textured & quietly flavourful dry **12** from Franschhoek grapes. **Sau- non Blanc** 🔲 ★★★★ Most attractive ripe aromas & flavours on **12**, with no aggressive greenness: floral, tle passionfruit. Not intense but appetising, with sufficient grip. Ready for drinking. Step up on **11** (★★★★). **millon** 🔲 ★★★★ Interesting but understated gentle character on **12** from Franschhoek. Balanced & fresh, less vitality than the blend. Should repay a few years in bottle & maybe then rate higher. — TJ

Eskdale *see* De Zoete Inval Estate

sona Boutique Wine

ation/map/WO: Robertson ▪ Est 2002 ▪ 1stB 2010 ▪ Tasting & sales Mon-Fri 8.30-5 Sat 9.30-1 ▪ Closed Easter Sun, Dec 25 & Jan 1 ▪ Owner(s) Rowan & Caryl Beattie ▪ Winemaker(s) Lourens van der Westhuizen (Jan 2010, ndsig) ▪ Viticulturist(s) Salomè Buys-Vermeulen (Jan 2012) ▪ 17ha/9.83ha (shiraz, chard, chenin, cbard, raisin nc, sauv) ▪ ±250t/3,000cs own label 34% red 66% white ▪ PO Box 2619 Clareinch 7400 ▪ info@esona.co.za ▪ ww.esona.co.za ▪ S 33° 54' 16.14" E 020° 0'38.66" ▪ **T +27 (0)82-417-5362** ▪ F +27 (0)21-787-3792

neyards, the meandering Breede River and a distant chain of hillocks are the arming vista from Rowan and Caryl Beattie's new tasting venue nearing comple- n at press time in the original cellar. Their Esona ('the very one' in Xhosa) bou- que wines are vinified at Arendsig on the opposite riverbank, and marketed with odern aids like social media and direct mail, powered by a burgeoning database.

iraz ⊕ ★★★ Blackcurrant **10** fruit-filled & well balanced, sweet impression on finish. **Chardonnay** ⊕ ★★ Good fruity intro to **10** persists to palate, zippy acidity balances the few grams of sugar & active 14.5% **Sauvignon Blanc** ⊕ ★★★ Honeysuckle & toasty dimension to **10** sipper. Enjoy soon. **11** vintages of all ailable but not tasted. — JP/CvZ

Essay *see* MAN Vintners
Eternal *see* Kumala

ve Bubbly

2006 ▪ Closed to public ▪ Owner(s) Eve Sparkling (Pty) Ltd (6 shareholders) ▪ Cellarmaster(s) Shawn Lucus 009) ▪ PO Box 66442 Highveld 0169 ▪ info@evebubbly.co.za ▪ www.evebubbly.co.za ▪ **T +27 (0)12-661-** 77 ▪ F +27 (0)86-569-3078

's your "go-to" bubbly and wine option — one that fits the South African life- yle like an "I Love Evita" T-shirt,' says brand manager Marisca Biagio. In their etty 250ml slimline aluminium cans, the Eve wines certainly are travel- and casion-friendly. 'Eve gives new meaning to the word "six-pack",' she quips.

e range

y Red ⊕ ★★ Approachable, slightly savoury dry red, **NV**, food friendly & best lightly chilled in summer. **sé** ⊕ ★★ Subtle strawberry hints on gently sweet low-alcohol **NV** sipper. **Dry White** ⊕ ★★ Light, easy dry white for al fresco sipping.

e Bubbly range

sé ⊕ ★★★ The prettiest & tastiest of these: frisky bubbles; sweet strawberry bubblegum flavours. **NV**. ve well chilled. **Brut** ⊕ ★★★ Frothy **NV** sipper, not too dry, refreshing, hint of lemon. **Vin Doux** ⊕ ★★ eet but refreshing **NV** sparkler with low alcohol (8.5%) & lemon-drop flavour. — GdB/MW

Eventide Cellar *see* Mischa Estate

■ **Exact Africa** *see* Stellekaya Winery

Excelsior Estate

Location/map/WO: Robertson ▪ Est 1859 ▪ 1stB 1990 ▪ Tasting & sales Mon-Fri 10-4 Sat 10-3 ▪ Picnics available on request, also BYO picnic ▪ Facilities for children ▪ Conferences ▪ 4-star Excelsior Manor Guesthouse ▪ Owner(s) Freddie & Peter de Wet ▪ Cellarmaster(s) Johan Stemmet (Aug 2003) ▪ Winemaker(s) Johan Stemmet (Aug 2003), with Kelly Gova (2005) ▪ Viticulturist(s) Freddie de Wet (1970) ▪ 320ha/220ha (cab, merlot, p verdot, shiraz, chard, sauv) ▪ 2,200t/160,000cs own label 75% red 25% white ▪ Other export brand: Stablemate ▪ BRC ▪ PO Box 17 Ashton 6715 ▪ info@excelsior.co.za ▪ www.excelsior.co.za ▪ S 33° 51' 15.1" E 020° 0' 25.6" ▪ **T** +27 (0)23-615-1980 ▪ F +27 (0)23-615-2019

'My dad's been farming for 42 years,' says Peter de Wet, co-owner with father Freddie of this picture-perfect, historic Robertson estate, 'and he's never seen a harvest like 2012. Not just high yields but high quality too.' The focus in future will be on chardonnay and cab sauvignon; marketing targets are China and Russia, the latter's bureaucracy 'like trying to get to the bottom of a nest of Russian dolls'.

★★★★ **Evanthuis Cabernet Sauvignon** ✪ Smooth & svelte 07 followed in 06's elegant footsteps; tannin & fruit in perfect balance.

★★★★ **San Louis Shiraz Reserve** ✪ Liquorice & tar 09 (★★★★) tad gruff when last tasted, not as knit as concentrated & smoky 07.

Cabernet Sauvignon ✪ 🍴 ★★★ Everyday companion 09's fruitiness accented by tealeaf & smoky whiffs. **Merlot** 🍴 ★★★ Lightly oak-staved & vanilla-sweet 11, supple & enjoyable young. **Gondolier Merlot Reserve** ★★★★ Notch up 10 intense & dense, with polished but rather firm tannins deserving year/2 to soften & let wine show its potential. **Paddock Shiraz** 🍴 ★★★ Earthy 10 savoury & fresh, lightly oaked for unfettered enjoyment. **Purebred Red** 🍴 ★★★ Fruit-filled 12 drops viognier, adds 25% each of merlot & cab to base of shiraz; slips down easily with smidgen sugar in tail. **Chardonnay** 🍴 ★★★ Made in large quantities (25,000 cases), partially oaked 12 gets crowd appeal from noticeable slick of sugar. **Sauvignon Blanc** 🍴 ★★★★ Upping the likeability level, 12 offers cool green fruit & nettles, light texture, interesting pithy dry farewell. **Viognier** 🍴 ★★★ Perfumed 12 improves on previous with good varietal touches (flowers, apricots) & balance, handles sweetness better than Chardonnay. — CvZ/MW

Excelsior Vlakteplaas

Location: Oudtshoorn ▪ Map: Klein Karoo & Garden Route ▪ Est 1934 ▪ 1stB 1998 ▪ Tasting & sales Mon-Fri 9-5 ▪ Closed Easter Fri-Mon, Ascension Day, Dec 16/25/26 & Jan 1 ▪ Owner(s)/winemaker(s) Danie Schoeman ▪ 41ha (merlot, ptage, ruby cab, chenin, muscadel r/w) ▪ 490t/1,000cs own label 50% red 50% white ▪ PO Box 112 De Rust 6650 ▪ jjschoeman@telkomsa.net ▪ S 33° 29'16.74" E 022° 35' 25.50" ▪ **T** +27 (0)82-821-355 ▪ F +27 (0)44-241-2569

Danie Schoeman won't be bottling under his own label this year. Not because he' superstitious when it comes to the number 13 but because he does so only in ever years. Last harvest was 'a good one' on his Klein Karoo farm. We'll have to wait t taste the resulting red and white muscadel, though — they missed our deadline.

His Master's Choice range
Red Muscadel Await next. **White Muscadel** ✪ ★★★ Sweet but lively 06 is a barley sugar & orange fla voured treat, especially over crushed ice. — JP/CvZ

Fable

Location/map: Tulbagh ▪ WO: Tulbagh/Coastal ▪ Est 1989 ▪ 1stB 2009 ▪ Tasting by appt only ▪ Closed Easter Fr Mon, Dec 25 & Jan 1 ▪ Conservation area ▪ Owner(s) Terroir Capital ▪ Winemaker(s) Rebecca Tanner (Jul 200 ▪ Viticulturist(s) Paul Nicholls (Jul 2009) ▪ 185ha/30ha (grenache, mourv, syrah, viog) ▪ PO Box 12817 D Boord 7613 ▪ info@fablewines.com ▪ www.fablewines.com ▪ S 33° 21'7.9" E 019° 12'46.1" ▪ **T** +27 (0)7 384-2896, +27 (0)78-315-3861, +27 (0)73-768-1600 ▪ F +27 (0)86-660-9288

The branding of this Tulbagh farm (now in the portfolio of California-based Terro Capital) resonates perfectly with the overarching theme of this edition of th guide, namely 'Backstories'. Not only is storytelling implicit in the winery nam but the owners say they want their wines to tell a story as well. 'The vineyards ble are planted in a setting of majestic beauty, in deep shale soils of land dotted th clear blue lakes on westward facing slopes tucked into the foothills of the itzenberg Mountains. It is here that the jackal bird circles above and the baboons ay. For our wines to tell as true a tale as possible about this place, and to really eak of the terroir, we take a minimalistic approach to winemaking, interfering as tle as possible. As part of this philosophy, we use biodynamics as a tool to help the nes develop individual character and tell the story of the seasons.'

★★★☆ **Bobbejaan** 100% shiraz. **10** (★★★★★) as expressive, elegant & delicate as maiden **09** despite ▸vel of ripeness; lovely fresh, cool feel, coriander & white pepper spice, savoury length. Still tight, reticent, ▸eserves 5+ years to show true potential.

★★★☆ **Lion's Whisker** Shiraz (83%) & mourvèdre blend in generous yet unheavy southern French style. ▸Melange roasted nuts, earth, game aromas & well-sustained flavours. **10** fleshy, yet with fine fresh tannin sup-▸ort. Superb now, even better in a few years.

★★★★ **Jackal Bird** 🏠 Another stunning blend of Swartland chenin, chardonnay, roussanne, viognier & ▸renache blanc, **11** (★★★★★) drier, firmer than **10**. Slowly reveals hay, lemon blossom & fynbos scents; admi-▸ble freshness, silky breadth & depth of flavour, savouriness. Individual, worth cellaring. — WB/AL

▮ **Fair Exchange** *see* Origin Wine
▮ **Fairhills** *see* Origin Wine
▮ **Fairtrade Original** *see* uniWines Vineyards

·airvalley Wines

:cation: Paarl ▪ WO: Western Cape ▪ Est 1997 ▪ 1stB 1998 ▪ Tasting by appt only ▪ Fee R25 ▪ Sales daily 9-4.30 ·Fairview ▪ Closed Good Fri, Dec 25 & Jan 1 ▪ Owner(s) Fairvalley Farmworkers Association ▪ Cellarmaster(s) ▸vie Adolf (Feb 1998) ▪ Winemaker(s) Jaco Brand (Nov 2009) ▪ 15,000cs own label 50% red 50% white ▪ ▸rtrade ▪ PO Box 6219 Paarl 7620 ▪ wine@fairvalley.co.za ▪ www.fairvalley.co.za ▪ **T +27 (0)21-863-2450** ▸ +27 (0)21-863-2591

ne of the original farmworker empowerment ventures, Fairvalley marked its ▸th birthday last year amid increasing export sales and, nearer home, news that ▸outh Africa is now the leading market for Fairtrade products in the developing ▸orld, offering 'great opportunities', according to sales and marketing manager ▸och Zaleni, and prompting the team to target new listings in major retailers.

Cabernet Sauvignon ☺ 🏠 ⦰ ★★★ A cheery mouthful of black fruit & some sweet vanilla spice, pre-▸viewed **11** offers plenty of drinking pleasure for the price. **Chardonnay** ☺ 🏠 ⦰ ★★★ Aromatic nose ▸on **11** shows a step up on previous. Toasted hazelnut, citrus, pineapple & creamy notes from light oaking.

▸notage 🏠 ★★★ Well-balanced crowd pleaser, **12** friendly chocolate & coffee with charry, smoky notes ▸cked up by black cherry fruit. **Chenin Blanc** 🏠 ⦰ ★★★ Pretty floral notes with brisk citrus acidity on ▸nk sample of **12**. Discontinued: **Shiraz**, **Sauvignon Blanc**. — CM

·airview

:cation: Paarl ▪ Map: Paarl & Wellington ▪ WO: Coastal/Paarl/Darling/Stellenbosch/Swartland/Western ▸pe ▪ Est 1693 ▪ 1stB 1974 ▪ Tasting & sales daily 9–5, last tasting 30min before closing ▪ R25/standard tast-▸g, R60/master tasting ▪ Closed Good Fri, Dec 25 & Jan 1 ▪ The Goatshed Restaurant (see Restaurants section) ▸our groups by appt only ▪ Farm produce ▪ Museum: history of farm with photos in tasting room ▪ Owner(s) ▸arles Back ▪ Winemaker(s) Anthony de Jager (Dec 1996), with Stephanie Betts (2010) ▪ 500ha/300ha (cab, ▸rignan, grenache, merlot, mourv, petite sirah, ptage, shiraz, tannat, tempranillo, chenin, sauv, viog) ▪ ▸100t/130cs own label 80% red 15% white 5% rosé ▪ ISO 9001:2001, BWI, BRC, HACCP, IPW, WIETA ▪ PO Box ▸3 Suider-Paarl 7624 ▪ info@fairview.co.za ▪ www.fairview.co.za ▪ S 33°46' 19.16" E 018° 55' 25.26" ▪ **+27 (0)21-863-2450** ▪ F +27 (0)21-863-2591

▸othing ever stands still, both in the life of this busy Paarl wine-and-cheesery and ▸f owner Charles Back, one of the most dynamic and energetic figures in South ▸frican wine. Many of the more unusual grape varieties get their first local airing ▸nder a Fairview label, and a reorganisation of brands and vineyards means he is ▸ow able to offer an even wider range of wines, including popular lines such as La ▸apra, Goats do Roam, Leeuwenjacht, Spice Route and Land's End (most listed separately in this guide). The new packaging, reflecting their agricultural roots a... honouring the vineyard workers and part-of-the-furniture winemaker Anthony Jager, signals the farm's commitment to its team members, the heritage of the Ba... family and, of course, the resident goat herd whose averred curiosity and consta... quest for improvement are the essence of the enterprise.

Fairview range

★★★★ **Cabernet Sauvignon** 🍴 🝕 Classic cab character on **10** with cedar, blackcurrant & a somewh... herbaceous edge. Ripe & rounded with good concentration & length. Stellenbosch WO.

★★★★☆ **Primo Pinotage** 🍴 🝕 Concentrated & savoury **10** continues top form of this benchmark fro... dryland vines in Agter Paarl. Smoke, leather & spice enlivened by distinctive floral notes, cured/smoked meat... black fruit weigh in on the palate. Now only American oak, 50% new.

★★★★☆ **Eenzaamheid Shiraz** 🍴 🝕 From Paarl vineyard on shale soils, poised & polished **10** sho... perfumed nose with white pepper & mulberries. Pure red & black berried fruit with seamlessly integrated ta... nins. Needs — & deserves — time to show its best.

★★★★☆ **The Beacon Shiraz** 🍴 From Paarl bushvines, showiest of the shirazes with plenty to sho... about. Meaty cranberries, dried cherry notes on **09** followed by richly spiced palate with flavours of plums, da... chocolate & sweet spice. A touch extra sugar (5.4g/l) adds depth & breadth. **08** (★★★★★) was exceptiona...

★★★★☆ **Jakkalsfontein Shiraz** 🍴 Swartland dryland bushvines; plushness of **07** followed by broodi... black fruit in standout **09** (★★★★★), enhanced by spicy cloves. Powerful & concentrated, giving little away... first, before glorious black fruit supported by gritty, grippy tannins through to an elegant lengthy finish. No **08**.

★★★★ **Cyril Back** ⚡ Flagship homage to Back patriarch, **07** (★★★★★) tasted last edition. From Paarl... Swartland shiraz. Firm but gentle texture; complex, dense, concentrated. Needing time, as did **06**.

★★★★☆ **Caldera** 🍴 🝕 Mainly grenache & shiraz with 14% mourvèdre. Fragrant fruitcake aromas on... (★★★★), a tad shyer than previewed **08**, giving way to cherries, cranberries, leather & cinnamon. Elega... mouthful; should improve.

★★★★★ **Nurok White Blend** NEW Complex & thoughtful (& stellar!) debut **11** is a blend of viognier, ch... nin, roussanne & grenache blanc, each handled separately & with care before merging into glorious mouthful... baked ripe yellow fruit, wild fynbos notes, spice & cream. Impressive wine from Paarl vines.

★★★★★ **La Beryl Blanc** 🍴 🝕 Glorious straw wine from unoaked Paarl chenin. Back-on-song **11** carr... additional sugar — **10** (★★★★★) was 140g/l, now 198g/l — with aplomb. Lavishly unctuous pineapple spon... flavours turn to litchi, toffee apple & cream, as elegant acidity keeps interest going through to lingering finis...

Barbera 🝕 ★★★★ Dark earthy character on the nose of **10** announces step up on **09** (★★★★). Rich & war... ing palate of plums, spice, well-integrated oak & freshening acidity. Paarl WO. **Pegleg Carignan** ★★★☆... Swartland bushvines deliver aromatic **10**, with hints of wild flowers & honey. Bright red fruit, spice & lively acid... make for easier drinking than **09** (★★★★). **Merlot** 🍴 🝕 ★★★★ Pronounced aromas of chocolate/mint on... with some dried prunes. Ripe black fruit, liquorice & vanilla finished off with minty crispness. WO Stellenbosch, l... next. **Mourvèdre** 🍴 🝕 ★★★★ Elegantly styled **10** mixes red fruit & leather to finish with delicious marzip... & slightly jammy plum cake length. **Durif** ★★★★ New name (was 'Petite Sirah') & new oomph in unusua... interesting **10**, up from **09** (★★★★). Violets & crystallised fruit meeting blackcurrants & mint. Lengthy fini... **Pinotage** 🍴 🝕 ★★★ Red berry fruit with smoky coffee lurking in the background of **11**. Damsons & a slig... bitterness at end. **Sangiovese** ⚡ ★★★ Cherry & Glühwein spice on **09** from Darling grapes. Dry, herbal edge... supple body & texture. Year in older oak strengthens structure. **Shiraz** 🍴 🝕 ★★★★ Pungent black pep... spice on **10** with red cherry fruit & whiffs of smoke. Soft, well-integrated tannins & savoury length. **Pinotag...** **Viognier** 🍴 Next awaited. **Extrano** NEW ★★★★ Mediterranean blend of mostly young-vine tranpran... grenache & carignan, **10** has interesting flavours of peppered steak & black fruit. **Darling Chardonnay** 🍴 🝕... ★★★★ Was 'Chardonnay'. Ripe mouthful of tropical fruit, **11** enlivened with citrus & floral notes. Well-integra... oak (10% new) gives creamy weight & spice. **Darling Chenin Blanc** 🍴 🝕 ★★★ Concentrated **12** h... confected apricots & slightly earthy, vegetal undertones. Zippy acidity keeps it fresh. **Darling Riesling** ✅ 🝕... ★★★★ Was 'Riesling'. Crunchy green apple fruit & tangy acidity in **12**, both rounded out by delicious drop... sweetness. Elegantly off-dry. **Darling Sauvignon Blanc** 🍴 🝕 ★★★★ Definitely 'Darling' **12** shows hallma... asparagus & green peas, zesty acidity balances tropical fruit & figs. **Oom Pagel Semillon** 🍴 🝕 ★★★★ Spic... yellow peaches with resinous pine needle character, **11** shows big improvement on **10** (★★★★). Concentra... fruit (pineapples & apples) handles 100% oak (none new) with style. Darling vines. **Viognier** 🍴 🝕 ★★★... Exuberant **11** shows off ripe fresh apricots, perfumed Turkish Delight, basil & thyme. Subtle oak (50% barrel-f... mented) & 8 months lees-ageing add texture & more interest than **10** (★★★★). WO Paarl, as next. **Viogn...** **Special Late Harvest** 🍴 🝕 ★★★ **12** charming glassful of caramelised peaches & grapefruit, the sweetn... perked up by balancing acidity. **Sweet Red** 🍴 🝕 ★★★ Fortified souzão from Swartland. Earthy & rustic no...

10 with sweet berries, boiled sweets & chocolate cake. **La Beryl Rouge** ⊕ ★★★ Shiraz straw wine. **10** oury olive & a touch chalky, with a dry grass undertone to its sweet richness.

Capra range

★★★ **Hanepoot Straw Wine** ⊕ This & rest of range previously listed separately. **09** (★★★★) apricot, utterscotch & ginger zestiness. Touch less complex than **08**. Creamy texture to clean, dry finish.

Malbec ☺ 🍷 🔳 ★★★ Pleasantly fruity **11** with plums, blueberries, mulberries backed up by plushy tannins. WO Paarl. **Merlot** ☺ 🍷 🔳 ★★★ Pale **11** nevertheless packs plenty of juicy, plummy flavours into its punch. Easy-drinking crowd pleaser. **Pinotage** ☺ 🍷 🔳 ★★★ Characterful quaffer **11** maintaining standards with sweet cooked cherry jam nose, raspberries & plums. WO W Cape.

bernet Sauvignon 🍷 🔳 ★★★ Stalky black fruit nose **11** gives way to concentrated blackberries & am. **Shiraz** ✓ 🍷 🔳 ★★★★ Spicy, peppery **10** offers great everyday drinking, with plum cake flavours, 't juicy tannins & dark chocolate finish. **Pinotage Rosé** 🍷 🔳 ★★★ Tank sample **12** shows candyfloss & awberries in dry summer sipper. **Chardonnay** ⊕ 🍷 🔳 ★★★★ Rich citrus fruit & zesty life on **10**. eamy breadth from 4 months on the lees & gentle part-oaking. **Chenin Blanc** ✓ 🍷 🔳 ★★★★ Thoroughly enjoyable **12** fruit salad of apples, pineapples, pears & zippy acidity, all promising many hours of opy drinking. WO Paarl. **Pinot Gris** ⊕ 🍷 🔳 ★★ Lively, tangy simplicity on **11**. **Sauvignon Blanc** 🔳 ★★ Limes & tropical notes on fresh **12** make for pleasant summer sipper. **Viognier** ⊕ 🍷 🔳 ★★★ **11** s tangy peach vibrancy. Pre-bottling sample still on lees last time, so might well have improved. — CM

alse Bay Vineyards

cation: Somerset West ▪ WO: Western Cape/Stellenbosch ▪ Est/1stB 2000 ▪ Tasting at Waterkloof ▪ wner(s) Paul Boutinot ▪ Cellarmaster(s)/viticulturist(s) Werner Engelbrecht (Jun 2004) ▪ Winemaker(s) erner Engelbrecht (Jun 2004), with Nadia Barnard (Dec 2008) ▪ 75,000cs own label 30% red 65% white 5% sé ▪ PO Box 2093 Somerset West 7129 ▪ info@waterkloofwines.co.za ▪ www.falsebayvineyards.co.za ▪ +27 (0)21-858-1292 ▪ F +27 (0)21-858-1293

his range (now including the Peacock Ridge wines previously listed under aterkloof) is the 'pocket-friendly tier' of the Waterkloof-based project of British wine merchant Paul Boutinot. They are made at that estate (with its views cross the eponymous bay) by Werner Engelbrecht, who explains the thinking ehind them: 'We all love fine wine, but we do not always like the price...'

lse Bay Vineyards range

Pinotage ☺ 🍷 🔳 ★★★ Lightly oaked, fruity-savoury **11** tasty & unpretentious, but satisfyingly fresh, lively & dry.

iraz 🍷 🔳 ★★★ Very ripe & fruity **11** much less elegant than previous vintage & a little hollow; neatly ilt — if a tad astringent. **Rosé** 🍷 🔳 ★★ Pre-bottling **11** mostly shiraz; softly dry, fresh & vaguely pleast. **Chardonnay** ⊕ 🍷 🔳 ★★★ **11** preview an unassuming, unimposing & delightful dinner partner. Dry & oaked. Confidently easygoing. **Chenin Blanc** 🍷 🔳 ★★★ Quiet, relaxed, straightforward & light-fruited ▪ has its richness cut by a big acidity. **Sauvignon Blanc** ⊕ 🍷 ★★★ In established style, **11** delivers clean rietal character plus a little more, in a friendly way.

eacock Ridge range

Shiraz NEW ☺ 🍷 🔳 ★★★ Attractive spice, herb & berry aromas lead to fresh, lively mouthful on **11** — though not much stuffing. Well-priced elegance. **Chenin Blanc** NEW ☺ 🍷 🔳 ★★★ **11** riper, intenser fruit & more power than False Bay version; just off-dry — sugar shows on finish despite strong acid.

erlot ✓ 🍷 🔳 ★★★★ Lovely sweet, pure fruit on **11**, mingling with subtle oak influence & a nice herbal ist. Rather elegant; fresh & dry. **Sauvignon Blanc** 🍷 ✓ 🔳 ★★★★ An earthy tug to citrus-dominant ▪ avoiding usual green/tropical Cape style. Big but unaggressive acidity. Stellenbosch WO. — TJ

▪ **Fantail** *see* Morgenhof Wine Estate

Faraway House Wine Estate

cation/map: Villiersdorp ▪ WO: Overberg ▪ Est 2002 ▪ 1stB 2008 ▪ Tasting by appt ▪ Closed Easter Fri-Mon, cension day, Pentecost & Dec 25/26 ▪ Owner(s) Faraway House Estate (Pty) Ltd ▪ Winemaker(s) Nicolas

Follet & David Ciry ▪ Viticulturist(s) Willem Pelser ▪ 90ha/14ha (cab, merlot, ptage, shiraz, sauv) ▪ 50t/2,000 own label 80% red 15% white 5% rosé ▪ PO Box 403 Villiersdorp 6848 ▪ info@farawayhouse.co.za ▪ www farawayhouse.co.za ▪ S 33°56'24.63" E 019°19'39.41" ▪ **T +27 (0)72-342-5052** ▪ F +27 (0)28-840-274

Nicolas Follet, French co-winemaker at this Overberg estate on a magnificer viewsite, wants to convert winelovers from the trend he sees to 'more polishe wine', preferring his 'old French style with light filtration and some sediment For those concerned about sulphur, Follet maintains very low levels.

Faraway House High Overberg Wine Estate range
Shiraz ★★★★ 10 very ripe olive & leather aromas; tightly gripped by assertive grape tannins; lightish, ve fresh feel. **Quadrille ★★★** Merlot-led **10**; ultra ripe, intensely fresh contrast, touch bitter. **09** (★★★★) w better. **Classic ★★★★ 10** similar shiraz, cab, merlot mix as flavoursome **09** (★★★★); bright red fru smoked meat, spice, clamped by firm tannins; briskly dry. — AL

Farm 1120

Location: Riebeek-Kasteel ▪ Map: Swartland ▪ Est 2005 ▪ 1stB 2006 ▪ Tasting facility in The Wine Kollectiv Mon-Sat 10-5 Sun 10-3 ▪ Closed Good Fri, Dec 25 & Jan 1 ▪ Gifts ▪ Farm produce ▪ Bar Bar Black Sheep resta rant adjacent to tasting facility ▪ Owner(s) D Thompson, C Levitan & A Espost ▪ Winemaker(s) Anton Espo (2005) ▪ Viticulturist(s) Thys Greeff (Feb 2008, Outback Viticulture) ▪ 70ha/22ha (ptage, shiraz, chenin) ▪ 18 total 10t/500cs own label 100% red ▪ PO Box 61 Riebeek Kasteel 7307 ▪ espost@telkomsa.net ▪ S 33° 23'1.48 E 018° 53' 46.54" ▪ **T +27 (0)22-448-1008/+27 (0)82-776-9366**

'We love and laugh because of wine,' say the fun-loving 'convenors' of Riebeek Kasteel wine shop The Wine Kollective and adjacent restaurant Bar Bar Blac Sheep, who have a stake in Kasteelberg winefarm Mountain View, from wher limited bottlings of merlot and pinotage emerge under the brand name Farr 1120. 'We believe in the grape,' the stakeholders say of their biodynamic princ ples and of doing everything by hand.

Fat Bastard

What started out as an experimental chardonnay tasted in a dank cellar by tw friends, UK wine brand creator Guy Anderson and French winemaker Thierr Boudinaud, who pronounced it a 'fat bastard', has become a successful range o both sides of the Atlantic. In South Africa, it's made by Robertson Winery.

Cabernet Sauvignon NEW Missed our deadline. **Shiraz ⊛ ⍝ ★★★** Perfumed **10**, ripe & juicy eas sipper with touch coffee. **Chardonnay ⊛ ⍝ ★★★★** Well-handled new oak, smidgen sugar add to th appeal of seductive **10**. Vanilla intro, lemon marmalade, pear & peach middle, generous end. **Sauvigno Blanc ⊛ ⍝ ★★★ 11** preview grassy greenpepper pungency, perky acidity. — DB/WB

Feiteiras Vineyards

Location/WO: Bot River ▪ Map: Elgin, Walker Bay & Bot River ▪ Est 2003 ▪ 1stB 2004 ▪ Tasting & sales by appt Owner(s) De Andrade family ▪ Cellarmaster(s)/winemaker(s) Marelise Jansen van Rensburg (2011, Beaumont) Jose de Andrade ▪ Viticulturist(s) Manuel de Andrade ▪ 16.2ha/4.2ha (cab, merlot, mourv, shiraz, verdelho) ▪ 600 own label 60% red 30% white 10% rosé ▪ PO Box 234 Bot River 7185 ▪ feiteiraswine@icon.co.za ▪ www feiteiraswine.co.za ▪ S 34° 14'3.6" E 019° 12'33.3" ▪ **T +27 (0)82-453-1597** ▪ F +27 (0)28-284-9525

Brothers Manuel and Jose de Andrade brought traditional Portuguese winemakin — including a rare pole-operated basket press — to their Bot River farm a decad ago. Now, to expand production, they've moved operations up the road to Beau mont, where Marelise Jansen van Rensburg crafts the wine under Jose's guidanc

Troca Tintas ☺ ⍝ ★★★ Fragrant grilled meat interest to barrel sample **11**, merlot & cab with slugs o shiraz & petit verdot. Perfect for espetada — even spicy trinchado. **Casa Merlot Rosé NEW ☺ ▤ ★★★** The unwooded edition of cellar's rosé duo; **12** coral hue, lovely dry red-berry zing.

Cabernet Sauvignon ✓ ⍝ ★★★★ Preview **11** robust & brambly, food-friendly tannins add succulenc No **10**. **Côr de Rosa ⊛ ▤ ★★★** Strawberry-pink, bone-dry rosé from merlot; **11** sampled mid-2011 ha grip from seasoned casks that filled out the cherry fruit. **Verdelho ✓ ▤ ⍝ ★★★★** Rare-in-Cape whi grape, a fillip for sauvignon-weary palates; individual **12**'s spice adds zip to fleshy baked quince profile. Moderate 12.5% alc. **Vinho Forte Tinto** ① ★★★★ **06** fortified mourvèdre. Lush, earthy chocolate featured in warm 19% alc bite previously. 375ml for these desserts. **Vinho Forte Branco** ① ★★★★ Fortified **06** verdelho had a clean nutty toffee note to its spiritous aftertaste when last reviewed. — DS

Félicité

Easygoing wines that pass through clever winemaking hands in the Newton Johnson winery — although a new arrangement with Stettyn Cellar sees the chardonnay and rosé vinified in Villiersdorp, for blending in the Hemel-en-Aarde. This follows on the pressure resulting from success with the wines and a cellar with production restrictions — though that will remain the home of the pinot.

Pinot Noir ① 🍷 ★★★ **11** from Robertson & Hemel-en-Aarde grapes. Rustic, moderately fruity aromas; somewhat unharmonious with light boiled-sweet flavours. **Dry Rosé** 🍷 🖉 ★★★ Adds 'dry' to the name in **12** — fairly enough in a category dominated by sweetness. From shiraz & sauvignon, it's also flavourful & fresh, both savoury & fruity. **No Oak Chardonnay** 🍷 🖉 ★★★ Descriptor added to name with pleasant, neat **12**. Lightish, & unpretentious, but not without both forcefulness & elegance. Like Rosé, from Worcester grapes. — TJ

■ **Ferling Noble** *see* Rooiberg Winery

Fernskloof Wines

Location: Prince Albert ▪ Map: Klein Karoo & Garden Route ▪ WO: Prince Albert/Prince Albert Valley ▪ Est 2009 ▪ 1stB 2010 ▪ Tasting & sales Mon-Fri 9-5 Sat 10-5 Sun by appt 10-5 ▪ Closed Good Fri, Ascension Day & Dec 25 ▪ Facilities for children ▪ BYO picnic ▪ Walks/hikes ▪ Mountain biking trail ▪ Conservation area ▪ Angeliersbosch guest house (up to 8 guests) ▪ Owner(s) Le Grange family ▪ Cellarmaster(s)/winemaker(s) Diederik le Grange (2010) ▪ Viticulturist(s) Diederik le Grange (2009) ▪ 1,026ha/8ha (cab, merlot, ptage, shiraz, chard) ▪ 40t/ 950cs own label 42% red 29% white 29% rosé ▪ BWI, SGS ▪ PO Box 41 Prince Albert 6930 ▪ diederiklg@ hotmail.com ▪ S 33° 16'23.77" E 022° 10'55.60" ▪ **T +27 (0)23-541-1702** ▪ F +27 (0)23-541-1702

Diederik le Grange 'learns things the hard way', which may produce some 'unusual' wines from his 1,023ha Groot Karoo farm in the Prince Albert Valley. An interest in dietetics and microbiology dovetails with his new winemaking endeavours (an organic approach is aided by the isolated area's relatively disease-free vines). Visitors are welcomed in the 19th-century main house (for tastings/sales), the old cellar (where grapes were traditionally foot-crushed for brandy), and in the conservation area (for hiking/biking).

Cabernet Sauvignon 🖉 Previewed **11** ample dark berries & tarry oak, too unformed to rate. **Pinotage** 🖉 ★★★ Equal dashes cab & shiraz add panache to exotically spiced **10**. Super-drinkable but note 15% alcohol. **Shiraz** 🖉 ★★ Savoury fruit outgunned by freshness & charry oak (30% new) in **10** food wine. **Barrel Fermented Pinotage Rosé** 🍷 ★★★ **11** sweet plum aroma belies dry savoury palate. Refreshing, with just a hint of oak spice from 2 months in cask. PET (plastic) bottle. **Chardonnay** ★★★ Apple & vanilla **12** barrel sample smooth & juicy, zested with lemon acidity, spiced with brief sojourn older wood. — WB/JP

■ **5th Avenue Cold Duck** *see* Cold Duck (5th Avenue)

Final Cut Wines

Location: Hout Bay ▪ Map: Cape Peninsula ▪ WO: Stellenbosch ▪ Est 2006 ▪ 1stB 2007 ▪ Tasting by appt ▪ Owner(s) Iain & Julie Anderson ▪ Winemaker(s) Teddy Hall (Sep 2006, consultant) ▪ PO Box 12077 Hout Bay 7806 ▪ iain@finalcutwines.co.za ▪ S 34°01'07.26" E 018°22'52.58" ▪ **T +27 (0)21-790-8808**

Hout Bay-based Iain and Julie Anderson continue their love affair with wine, making films about it in the winelands and bottling it under their own label. Last year they didn't manage to secure a shiraz but promise to in future as it was 'a sellout'. 'Chenin continues to deliver!' they enthuse. 'It's our all-star wine.'

Shiraz Await next. **Chenin Blanc** ① ★★★★ **10** in groove of improved **09**: an opulent mouthful, peachy fruit packed into bold finish, enlivened by brisk acidity. — DS

■ **Find Art Collection** *see* Druk My Niet Wine Estate
■ **Finest (Tesco)** *see* Ken Forrester Wines

■ **Firefly** *see* Stellar Winery

FirstCape Vineyards

Location: Paarl ▪ Est 2002 ▪ Closed to public ▪ Owner(s) De Wet, Goudini, Aan de Doorns, Badsberg & Stettyn wineries ▪ Winemaker(s) David Smit ▪ WIETA accredited ▪ PO Box 62 Simondium 7670 ▪ david@firstcape.com ▪ www.firstcape.com ▪ **T +27 (0)21-874-8340** ▪ F +27 (0)21-874-8344

Formed in 2002, this joint venture between five Breede Valley cellars and British marketer BrandPhoenix retains its position as the biggest-selling South African brand in the UK wine market overall. Their offering has been simplified and streamlined, with some second labels dropped and the FirstCape portfolio expanded. On-the-ball marketing, like FirstCape again being one of the main sponsors for the British and Irish Lions for their 2013 tour of Australia, maintains a strong brand presence. All bottling is now done offshore in the UK and Germany. The export-only wines are available as FirstCape (Entry, Limited Release, First Selection, Winemaker's Selection, Sparkling), low-alcohol (5.5%) Café Collection and new Discovery Series (including some low-alcohol bottlings).

■ **First Dawn** *see* Nwanedi Estate
■ **First Sighting** *see* Strandveld Wines

Fish Hoek Wines

Location: Somerset West ▪ Map: Helderberg ▪ WO: Western Cape ▪ Tasting, sales & cellar tours at Flagstone Winery (see entry) ▪ Owner(s) Accolade Wines South Africa ▪ Winemaker(s) Gerhard Swart (Sep 2008) & Bruce Jack (1998) ▪ 50% red 50% white ▪ PO Box 769 Stellenbosch 7599 ▪ hannelize.mouton@accolade-wines.com ▪ S 34° 5′26.38″ E 018° 48′30.04″ ▪ **T +27 (0)21-852-5052** ▪ F +27 (0)21-852-5085

Accolade Wines South Africa, owners of this good-value mid-tier brand, have beefed up the tasting facilities, partly as a welcome to the Cheetah Outreach Project, now open next door. Plans for the future include some lesser-known grape varieties, such as malbec and petit verdot, and a white pinotage is on the cards too.

> **Pinotage Rosé** ☺ 🍷 ★★★ Pleasant & cheery **12** tank sample adds a tad more sugar (now off-dry) & plenty more red berry fruit character with fresh acidity.

Merlot 🍷 🍷 ★★★ Easy-drinker **11** with plenty of soft red berry fruit & a tweak of charred oaky spice at the finish. **Pinotage** 🍷 🍷 ★★★ Pleasant quaffer **11** with a smoky, hammy nose lightened up by some sweet cherry & berry fruit. **Shiraz** ✓ 🍷 🍷 ★★★★ Cut above others in range, **11** offers pungent aromas of black pepper & smoked meat. Leather, spiced blackberries & brambles too. **Chenin Blanc** 🍷 ★★★ Apples & pear drops abound on lively **12**. Brisk tropical flavours & zippy satisfying finish. **Sauvignon Blanc** 🍷 ★★★ Pretty floral notes with guava & pineapple. **12** preview pleasant daytime sipper. — CM

■ **Five Climates** *see* Boland Kelder
■ **Five Generations** *see* Cederberg Private Cellar
■ **Five Girlfriends** *see* Val du Charron

5 Mountains Lodge

Location/WO: Wellington ▪ Map: Paarl & Wellington ▪ Est 2002 ▪ 1stB 2004 ▪ Tasting Tue-Sat 9-5.30 Sun 9-2 ▪ Fee R20 ▪ Closed Easter Fri/Sun/Mon & Dec 25/26 ▪ Cellar tours by appt ▪ Meals & refreshments 9-5 daily ▪ Conference facilities ▪ Guest house & spa ▪ Owner(s) Stuart & Louisa McLachlan ▪ Winemaker(s) Corlea Fourie (2004, Bosman Family Vineyards) ▪ 7.5ha/1ha (chenin) ▪ 2.5t/150cs own label 100% white ▪ PO Box 691 Wellington 7654 ▪ carole@5mountains.co.za ▪ www.exclusiveescapes.com ▪ S 33° 38′43.12″ E 019° 3′26.52″ ▪ **T +27 (0)21-864-3409** ▪ F +27 (0)21-873-7193

'No real changes, just plenty of new guests,' is the bulletin from Carole Rothery, general manager of 5 Mountains boutique guest lodge in Wellington. A few bottles of the maiden 10 Chenin, made by Corlea Fourie of nearby Bosman Family Vineyards, remain and, Carole says, they are ageing with aplomb.

Chenin Blanc ★★★ Attractive barrel-fermented **10** is more mineral than fruity, shows 'stony' aromas, pleasantly textured mouthfeel & a dry finish. — CM

■ **Five's Reserve** *see* Van Loveren Family Vineyards

Flagstone Winery

Location: Somerset West ▪ Map: Helderberg ▪ WO: Western Cape/Breedekloof/Elgin/Tulbagh/Elim ▪ Est 1998 ▪ 1stB 1999 ▪ Tasting & sales Mon-Fri 10-4 Sat 10-3 ▪ Fee R20, waived on purchase ▪ Closed Dec 25-Jan 2 ▪ Cellar tours by appt ▪ Owner(s) Accolade Wines South Africa ▪ Winemaker(s) Gerhard Swart (Sep 2008) & Bruce Jack (1998), with Gerald Cakijana (Jan 2000) ▪ Viticulturist(s) Chris Keet (consultant) ▪ 70% red 30% white ▪ PO Box 769 Stellenbosch 7599 ▪ hannelize.mouton@accolade-wines.com ▪ www.flagstonewines.com ▪ S 34° 5'26.38" E 018° 48'30.04" ▪ **T +27 (0)21-852-5052** ▪ F +27 (0)21-852-5085

'Backstories?' quips winemaker and founder Bruce Jack. 'You've got to be kidding — the Flagstone story is more like a book!' And this talented, ebullient raconteur is never short of a great story, an appropriate word or a pithy comment. Listening to his tales of travelling around the world, spreading the Flagstone philosophy, can while away many a long evening, especially when accompanied by a glass or more from the Somerset West-based team's extensive range. But Bruce's underlying passion is a 'determination and desire to present a South African truth in our bottles.' He believes it is time for South Africans to be confident in their wines and the stories they tell, to stop trying to emulate others' terroir or methodology and instead make wines with integrity and joy.

Flagstone range

★★★★ **Music Room Cabernet Sauvignon** ▣ Much-lauded **09** (★★★★☆) now showing class & elegance — brooding, savoury aromas of leather, spice, some Marmite — giving way to plushy tannins wrapped around blackberries, blackcurrants & spice. Long warm finish. Recalls hedonism of last-tasted **07**.

★★★★ **Fiona Pinot Noir** ▣ Previewed **10** sweet, funky aromas with some eucalyptus, well-hung meat & spice. Soft raspberry & red cherry fruit with plenty of spicy oak. Should improve over next 2 years. No **09**.

★★★★☆ **Writer's Block Pinotage** ▣ ▨ Polished & elegant version from Breedekloof vines. Toasty nose on **10** of baked black fruits with whiffs of coconut from American oak, 40% new. Smooth & silky with dark concentrated fruits, velvety tannins, hints of chocolate, spice & plums.

★★★★ **Dark Horse Shiraz** ▣ **09** on the nose a Black Forest gateau of a wine — sweet black cherries, hints of kirsch & chocolate ganache. Enticing flavours of plum cake & prunes with spice & black pepper.

★★★★ **Dragon Tree** ▣ Cape Blend near-equal cab, shiraz, pinotage in **09**. Plenty of Christmas flavours — cloves, allspice, orange peel — giving way to polished black fruit & grainy tannins, concentrated, savoury finish.

★★★★ **Free Run Sauvignon Blanc** ▣ ▨ A year in bottle has allowed **11** (★★★★★), a preview last time, to open up from **10** with lively herbaceous notes & lime marmalade on the nose. Oodles of citrus with well-judged acidity, serenely poised & confident rather than strident & brash. Both from Elgin.

★★★★ **Word of Mouth Viognier** ▣ ▨ **11** distinctively viognier with tinned & fresh apricots & some underlying gingery notes. Yellow fruit softened by discreet oak (40%) & enlivened by refreshing acidity.

★★★★ **Treaty Tree Reserve White** ▣ ▨ Stunning **10** (★★★★★) from Elim now developed into its full glory. Semillon nose with herbaceous, waxy notes leading into rounded sauvignon mouthful of lemongrass, citrus & coriander all delicately enrobed in creamy, slightly spicy oak. Pure drinking pleasure, as was **09**.

Longitude ✓ ▣ ★★★★ Eminently drinkable & delicious **11**, a step up on **10** (★★★☆). Cabernet, shiraz & malbec combine to show plenty of sweet black fruit with whiffs of coffee/chocolate & chewy tannic finish. **Noon Gun** ✓ ▣ ★★★★ Reliable crowd pleaser, **12** showing more elegance & concentration, tinned grapefruit & tropical fruit from chenin, sauvignon & viognier. **Last Word** ⊛ ▣ ★★★★ Port-style fortified from Tulbagh shiraz, **06** hedonistic, slippery & sweetly delicious, not overly serious. Discontinued: **Treaty Tree Reserve Red**.

Stumble Vineyards range

Malbec ▣ ★★★ Smoky notes on oak-dominated **11**. Stewed black fruit, lacks juiciness of previous. **Merlot** NEW ▨ ★★★ Very pleasant **11** has stewed black fruit, whiffs of fennel & clove. Soft, pliable tannins, fresh & appealing. **Cape Blend** NEW ▣ ▨ ★★★ **11** is cab, pinotage, merlot & shiraz. Cherry/leather nose with concentrated black plum flavours, spicy oak, very drinkable. **Chardonnay** ▣ Not tasted. **Pinot Grigio** NEW ▣ ▨ ★★★ **11** cheery fresh pear & pear drop notes, zingy acidity for early drinking. **Sauvignon**

Blanc ▦ ★★★ **11** shows gassy green notes on the nose, pleasant flavours of yellow fruit with quiet acidity & mouth-filling appeal. **Viognier** ▦ Await new vintage.

Poetry range NEW

Merlot ☺ ▦ ▨ ★★★ Pleasant quaffer **10** has flavours of fat black plums with slightly herbal edge & some spice. Accessible, for current drinking.

Sauvignon Blanc ▦ ▨ ★★★ Light & shy nose of **11** gives way to a zesty mouthful of lemon curd.

Rustler range NEW

Pinotage ▦ ▨ ★★★ Distinctive pinotage nose of sour cherries & liquorice, **11** has plenty of tarry fruit & a little sweet oak spice. **Chenin Blanc** ✓ ▦ ▨ ★★★☆ Well-judged example, **11** crunchy pear drops & tinned pineapples. Slightly off-dry, soupçon sugar fills out mid-palate nicely.

Whispering Jack NEW

Chardonnay ▨ ★★★☆ Soft, spicy, unobtrusive oak (30%) rounds out yellow melon flavours on **11**. Finishes clean with bright tropical fruit. — CM

■ **Flamingo Bay** *see Darling Cellars*

Flat Roof Manor

These are the trendy counterpoint to the more serious Uitkyk Estate offerings. Estelle Lourens is at the helm ensuring that there is a constant tweaking to these bottlings — like a new light rosé. The flat roof in question is that on the elegant Georgian manor house on the Uitkyk property outside Stellenbosch.

Merlot ☺ ▦ ▨ ★★★ Savoury greenpepper edge nicely balanced by vibrant red fruitiness; **11** has leanish, fresh & easy-drinking appeal.

Shiraz-Mourvèdre-Viognier ✓ ▦ ▨ ★★★☆ Successful combination of red cherry bounce with spice & meaty undertone. Subtle oaking lends support to juicy **10**. **Pinot Rosé Light** NEW ▦ ▨ ★★ Pinotage/pinot grigio combo in off-dry **12**. **Pinot Grigio** ▦ ▨ ★★★ **12** touched up with sauvignon & chenin. Easy, lightish (11.8% alcohol) & off-dry. WO W Cape, as is SMV. **Sauvignon Blanc Light** ▦ ▨ ★★ **12** is light in every way. Discontinued: **Pinot Rosé**. — JP

Fleur du Cap

Location: Stellenbosch ▪ WO: Western Cape/Stellenbosch ▪ Est 1968 ▪ 1stB 1969 ▪ Tasting, sales & tours at Die Bergkelder Wine Centre (see entry) ▪ Owner(s) Distell ▪ Cellarmaster(s) Andrea Freebenborough (Aug 2005) ▪ Winemaker(s) Justin Corrans (Aug 2005, reds) & Pieter Badenhorst (Dec 2006, whites), with Christoff de Wet (Sep 2010) & Sanelisiwe (Praisy) Dlamini (Jan 2011) ▪ Viticulturist(s) Bennie Liebenberg (Apr 2001) ▪ ±17,000t/±145,000cs own label 47% red 53% white ▪ ISO 14001, ISO 9001, BRC, HACCP, IFS ▪ info@fleurducap.co.za ▪ www.fleurducap.co.za ▪ **T +27 (0)21-809-8025** ▪ F +27 (0)21-887-9081

There's exciting juxtaposition of old and new at this established Distell-owned brand, based in Stellenbosch: a sense of fresh green shoots sprouting from gnarled old vines. Its 'cellar in the mountain' home, Die Bergkelder, was the first bottle maturation cellar of its kind south of the equator when opened in 1968. Today's visitors can view a history of South African winemaking on carved oak barrels in the Fleur du Cap Room, and then taste the modern Unfiltered wines paired with... salts of the world! In addition to this guide's serial five star stunner, the Noble Late Harvest, the Unfiltered range has been striking gongs for the enthusiastic young team at the Trophy Wine Show, Decanter World Wine Awards and International Wine Review. Cellarmaster Andrea Freebenborough's team manages another notable juxtaposition: high quality wine in generous volumes.

Unfiltered Collection

★★★★☆ **Cabernet Sauvignon** ✓ ▨ Classic, stylish Stellenbosch cabernet at its most dependable. Fine **10** has manicured minty blueberry fruit in a yielding tannic framework with compelling length of flavour. Promises much pleasure over 4-7 years. 100% new French oak 16 months.

★★★★ **Merlot** ✓ 🍷 Sultry dark mulberry fruit is wrapped up in supple tannins with a graceful seam of freshness, **10**'s all-new wood (16 months) unobtrusive. WO Stellenbosch.

★★★★ **Chardonnay** ✓ 🍷 🍷 Full-flavoured yet fine, **11**'s gravelly texture shores up oak (seasoned cask & 30% new) cosseting lime fruit. Nicely balanced so as not to overwhelm food accompaniment.

★★★★☆ **Sauvignon Blanc** ✓ 🍷 🍷 Steely-dry with cool grassy features, tank sample **12**'s lovely texture is given vitality by its racy acidity, & oomph by 14% alcohol in the tail.

★★★★☆ **Sauvignon Blanc Limited Release** ✓ 🍷 🍷 Sleek & as sophisticated as cellar siblings, but richer, more weighty; preview **12** from Agulhas & Darling grapes has mineral structure for development.

★★★★ **Semillon** ✓ 🍷 🍷 Classy, far from simply fruity. **11**'s buffed hay tones cloak a stony mineral heart; well-wielded 8 months oak (20% new) underscores the flavour.

★★★★ **Viognier** ✓ 🍷 🍷 Boisterous **11** as kaleidoscopic as ever; a cornucopia of sweetly-fruited apricot & peach-pip flavours just contained by tangy acid — it ends surprisingly dry. Outlandish, but most enjoyable!

Fleur du Cap Bergkelder Selection

★★★★☆ **Laszlo** Signature blend a homage to legendary cellarmaster Dr Julius Laszlo. Powerful Bordeaux quartet: merlot, cab, petit verdot, malbec. **08** (★★★★★) judiciously oaked, has layers of rich black & blueberry fruit on lattice of fine, powdery tannins. Complex, strikingly elegant. No **07**. **06** 18% shiraz & less oak.

★★★★★ **Noble Late Harvest** ✓ 🍷 Consistently outstanding botrytised dessert from chenin, with sauvignon & chardonnay in **11**; bold orange blossom & tangerine interest to weighty full-sweet profile. Intense flavour & arresting balance, joins its five-star predecessors **10**, **09**, **07** & **06**.

> **Pinotage** ☺ 🍷 ★★★ Uncomplicated **10** in lighter style; cranberry succulence to buffed tannins. WO Coastal. **Chardonnay** ☺ 🍷 ★★★ Oak-vanilla laced **11** enlivened by tangy lemon/lime fruit. **Sauvignon Blanc** ☺ 🍷 ★★★ Grassy features happily cohabit with figgy profile of **12**, nicely judged for wide appeal.

Cabernet Sauvignon 🍷 ★★★ Less compelling than flag bearer above, cheerily generous **10** is plum fruited & open textured — ready for drinking. **Merlot** 🍷 ★★★ Light-styled **10** has chocolate-mocha allure in gentle tannic grip for early access. **Shiraz** 🍷 ★★★ Medium-bodied **10** layered with red berry fruit in savoury, open-grained oak frame. **Chenin Blanc** ✓ 🍷 ★★★★ Less oak & more fruit in recent years, but same old honest reliability. **12** reviewed pre-bottling shows ripe tropical fruit balanced by firm acidity. **Natural Light** 🍷 ★★ Floral **12** fresh & fruity, semi-dry with low ±10% alcohol. Chenin & dollop sauvignon. — DS

■ **Flutterby** see Boland Kelder
■ **Foot of Africa** see Kleine Zalze Wines
■ **Footprint** see African Pride Wines
■ **Forresters** see Ken Forrester Wines
■ **Fortress Hill** see Fort Simon Wine Estate

Fort Simon Wine Estate   🍴 🥄 📷 ♿

Location/map/WO: Stellenbosch ▪ Est 1997 ▪ 1stB 1998 ▪ Tasting & sales Mon-Fri 9.30–5 Sat 10–2 ▪ Fee R15/5wines ▪ Closed all pub hols ▪ Cellar tours by appt ▪ Cheese platters ▪ Farm produce ▪ Venue for after-hours functions/weddings & conferences (120-150 guests) ▪ Owner(s) Renier, Petrus & Michéle Uys ▪ Winemaker(s) Stander Maass (Sep 2006) ▪ Viticulturist(s) Renier Uys ▪ 110ha/80ha (cabs s/f, malbec, merlot, p verdot, ptage, shiraz, chard, chenin, sauv, viog) ▪ 800t/40,000cs own label 60% red 30% white 10% rosé ▪ PO Box 43 Sanlamhof 7532 ▪ accounts@fortsimon.com ▪ www.fortsimon.co.za ▪ S 33°55'9.5" E 018°45'19.4" ▪ **T +27 (0)21-906-0304** ▪ F +27 (0)21-903-8034

Duwisib Castle in Namibia provided the inspiration for this Bottelary Hills cellar, its turrets and ramparts a tribute to late founder Simon Uys and his vision. A conference centre, doubling as a wedding venue, is being added, while on one of the loftiest sites in the area, ±350m above sea level, a young sauvignon block is showing promise and will be treated with kid gloves 'from vine to bottle' this harvest.

Platinum Collection

★★★★ **Viognier** ⏺ Last time, complex & harmonious **09** was layered, appealed with creamy peach & pineapple flavours, lengthy perfumed aftertaste.

★★★★ **Viognier Noble Late Harvest** 🍷 Older-oak-fermented **10** matches intensity of last-tasted **07**. Concentrated but still light on its feet. Long, appealing finish & peach brûlée aftertaste. 375ml.

Fort Simon Estate range

★★★★ **Shiraz** Light-bodied **08** (★★★★) shows herbal edge to plum fruit, gentle savoury texture. Shade off suave & balanced **07**.

★★★★ **Chardonnay** ⓪ Pre-bottling **10** (★★★★) delivers fresh, crunchy apple & citrus with zingy lemon finish. **09** more elegant & stylish, concentrated.

★★★★ **Sauvignon Blanc** ⬚ Lemon curd & grass on lively pre-bottling sample of **12** (★★★). Fresh, zesty & rounded though acidity not as smooth as **10**.

Cabernet Sauvignon ⓪ ★★★★ Tad off well-structured **07** (★★★★), **08** offers rich black fruit & vanilla flavours. **Merlot** ⓪ ★★★★ Delightfully juicy **09**, sampled from barrel; ripe plum & spice cake aromas; soft & balanced for easy drinking. **Pinotage** ⓪ ★★★★ Juicy plum & mocha on **08**. Polished, ripe & rich, lingering savoury farewell. **Rosé** ⓪ ★★★ Previewed from tank, **11** oozes pinotage's ripe strawberries. Easy dry summer sipper. **Chenin Blanc** ⓪ ★★★★ Up a notch from **09** (★★★★), barrel preview **10** is rich & concentrated, lemon & apple with vanilla from well-judged oaking.

Fortress Hill range

Merlot ⓪ ★★★ Delightfully juicy & smooth **09** last was soft & invited early enjoyment, as for all these. **Shiraz** ★★★ Savoury leather & spice on **09** uncomplicated easy-drinker, black berries in abundance, gentle mouthfeel. **Sauvignon Blanc** ⬚ ★★★ Preview of **12** tangy & vibrant with lime zest pungency. Mouthfilling & juicy, lipsmackingly high acidity. Discontinued: **Chardonnay**, **Chenin Blanc**, **Natural Sweet Rosé**. — FM

▪ **Fountain Crossing** *see* Darling Cellars
▪ **Four Cousins** *see* Van Loveren Family Vineyards

Four Fields Vineyards

Location/WO: Durbanville ▪ Map: Durbanville, Philadelphia & Darling ▪ Est/1st B 2004 ▪ Tasting & tours by appt only ▪ Sales mainly via Wine Concepts, Cape Town ▪ Owner(s) 8 shareholders ▪ Cellarmaster(s)/winemaker(s) Chris Kuhn (Sep 2004) ▪ 5t 100% red ▪ 49 Arabella Drive Augusta Place Sunningdale 7441 ▪ dockuhn@gmail.com ▪ S 33° 48′ 56″ E 018° 33′ 15″ ▪ **T +27 (0)83-929-9199** ▪ F +27 (0)21-557-2608

All is quiet at Chris Kuhn's retirement place on the Durbanville hills. He set up his micro cellar after a career in insurance, to indulge his life-long love of wine, but it is in the nature of endeavours like this that innovations and deadlines can wait.

Cabernet Sauvignon-Cabernet Franc ⓪ ★★★ Herbal/perfume contrast on mulberry-fruited **08** previously. **Chardonnay** ⓪ ▤ ★ Barrel-aged **08** had overt oak patina when last tasted. — AL/FM

Four Paws Wines

Location/map: Franschhoek ▪ WO: Western Cape/Franschhoek ▪ Est 2005 ▪ 1stB 2006 ▪ Tasting by appt at La Vigne, Robertsvlei Road, Franschhoek (contact Anne +27 (0)83-447-1376/Gerda +27 (0)82-375-0524) ▪ Owner(s) Rob Meihuizen, Gerda Willers & Anne Jakubiec ▪ Winemaker(s) Gerda Willers (2005) ▪ Viticulturist(s) Gerda Willers ▪ 60t/6,000cs own label 70% red 30% white ▪ PO Box 69 Simondium 7670 ▪ anne@southerntrade.co.za ▪ www.fourpawswines.com ▪ S 33° 53′ 28.0″ E 019° 5′ 0.5″ ▪ **T +27 (0)21-874-1033** ▪ F +27 (0)21-874-2110

A trio of cat lovers with day jobs in the wine trade established this brand in 2005 to offer value-for-money wines for those who drink what they like (not what they're told). They moved the cattery down the Franschhoek valley to La Vigne last year, and launched 'Picatso', a viognier straw wine as sweet as their muses.

★★★★ **Picatso** NEW ✓ Feline theme given cubist edge. **11** naturally dried viognier 8 months in seasoned oak; voluptuous, luxurious & moreish. Pity, only 560L in 375ml format. WO Franschhoek.

Sauvignon Blanc ☺ ▤ ★★★ Now bottled, **11** palate-clucking & steely-fresh; to whet the appetite or revitalise. **Calico** ☺ ▤ ★★★ A preview last time, **11** now a fruit cup of flavours driven by chenin & semillon, ends bone-dry. WO Franschhoek.

Pinotage Await new vintage. **Pablo** ✓ ★★★★ Merlot, cab, grenache & mourvèdre in earthy, rustic **10**, gentle on palate & pocket. **Chardonnay** New bottling not ready. — DS

...th Street [NEW]

..e slogan 'Unashamedly uncomplicated, easy-drinking and flirtatious' typifies ...ese Distell-made, budget-priced, low-alcohol Natural Sweet wines.

...tural Sweet Red 🏠 ★ Unchallenging **NV** from cab & cinsaut, (attractive) Ceylon tea-like character, try ...led. Low ±7% alcohol & WO W Cape, as all. **Natural Sweet Rosé** 🏠 ★★ NV similar 'sweet cuppa' qual-...as Red, but fresher, more fragrant. Chenin & rougeing pinotage. **Natural Sweet White** 🏠 ★★ Sunkissed ...eetness, raisin & honey flavours held together by crisp acidity. **NV** from chenin & colombard. — DB/HJ

...raai Uitzicht 1798

...ation/map: Robertson ▪ WO: Klaasvoogds ▪ 1stB 2000 ▪ Tasting & sales daily 10-6 ▪ Closed Easter Fri/Sun, Dec ...31 & Jan 1 ▪ Restaurant (see Restaurants section) ▪ 4-star guesthouse (see Accommodation section) ▪ Owner(s) ...Uwe Papesch ▪ Winemaker(s) Karl Uwe Papesch (2005) ▪ Viticulturist(s) Michael Marson ▪ 175ha/11ha (gre-...he, merlot, shiraz, viog) ▪ 500cs own label 100% red ▪ PO Box 97 Robertson 6705 ▪ info@fraaiuitzicht.com ▪ ...w.fraaiuitzicht.com ▪ S 33° 47'43.0" E 020° 0'18.2" ▪ **T +27 (0)23-626-6156** ▪ F +27 (0)86-662-5265

...ner-winemaker Karl Uwe Papesch continues amassing building blocks for the ...ône blends he's set his heart on. Replacing touriga in his small vineyard is ...ognier, to join shiraz and grenache (in barrel at time of going to press) and regu-...ly bottled merlots (also on his and wife Sandra's luxury guest house winelist).

...rlot ★★★ Perfumed **10** quite seriously styled, smooth tannins & dark cherry fruit make for elegant sip-...g. **Prima** Ⓟ ★★★★ 100% merlot aged 2 years in French oak. Generous **08** fresh & satisfying. — DB/JP

...rancois La Garde

...ation/map: Stellenbosch ▪ WO: Franschhoek/Western Cape ▪ Est 2004 ▪ Tasting by appt ▪ Owner(s) PL ...tthée ▪ Cellarmaster(s)/winemaker(s) Piet Matthée (Jan 2009) ▪ 15t/1,000cs own label 100% white ▪ PO ...: 12366 Die Boord 7613 ▪ admin@technofill.co.za ▪ www.francois-lagarde.com ▪ E5 ▪ **T +27 (0)21-887-...74** ▪ F +27 (0)21-887-5274

...bbly lover Piet Matthée says he's fulfilling the dream of an ancestor (after whom ...is specialist label is named) to make champagne-methode wine. And he's ...sponding to his own passion too, while his day job remains running his specialist ...ttling and labelling company. The grapes are from Franschhoek, while vinifica-...n happens in the generous space of Zorgvliet's cellar in Stellenbosch.

...ing of Pearls range

★★★ **Blanc de Blancs** Ⓟ Bottle-fermented sparkling from semillon, 48 months on lees. Lemongrass & ...nolin, snaky strings of fine mousse, rich, long lime marmalade flavour. **05** structured for ageing.
★★★ **Brut Méthode Cap Classique** Ⓟ Classic bubbly, equal pinot noir & chardonnay, 36 months on ...es. **07** strawberry flavours, fine yeasty nuance & balance show elegance & class. WO W Cape.
...inette Rosé MCC [NEW] ★★★ Coppery salmon pink **08** brut-style bubbly from mourvèdre, with a fine ...usse but slightly dank, smoky notes, finishing fresh & limy. — MF

...ranki's Vineyards

...ation: Malmesbury ▪ Map: Durbanville, Philadelphia & Darling ▪ WO: Swartland ▪ Est 2004 ▪ 1stB 2007 ▪ Tasting, ...s & cellar tours by appt Mon-Fri 8-5 ▪ Closed all pub hols ▪ Meals by arrangement ▪ Tour groups ▪ BYO picnic ▪ ...ferences ▪ Walks/hikes ▪ Conservation area ▪ Classic car museum ▪ 4-star Franki's Guest Lodge (10 bedrooms) ...olitude @ Franki's B&B (4 bedrooms) ▪ Owner(s) Franco Afrique Technologies (Pty) Ltd ▪ Winemaker(s) Erica ...bert (Jan 2004), with Nicolaas Hanekom (Jan 2004) ▪ 700ha/22ha (grenache, mourv, viog) ▪ 80t/175cs own ...l 100% red ▪ PO Box 972 Malmesbury 7299 ▪ erica.joubert@cropspec.co.za ▪ www.frankisvineyards.com ▪ S ...20°59.5" E 018° 32'12.4" ▪ **T +27 (0)22-482-2837/+27 (0)82-888-3702** ▪ F +27 (0)86-660-3677

...y 'Swartland' today and Rhône varieties immediately spring to mind, but back ...1994 it was a leap of faith for a newcomer to plant grenache, mourvèdre and ...ognier in the region. Winemaker Erica Joubert feels the far-sightedness and ...rd work are being rewarded with unique expressions of variety and terroir.

Barn Find range

Grenache ★★★ Loaded with tobacco perfume & wine gum juiciness, **11** is an unusual wine with individ character. **Joubert Red Blend ★★★** 'Mourvèdre-Grenache' last edition. Friendly **11** packed with mulbe succulence, generous & accessible. — DB

Franschhoek Cellar

Location/map: Franschhoek ▪ WO: Western Cape/Franschhoek ▪ Est 1945 ▪ Tasting & sales Mon-Fri 9.3C (Apr-Sep) & 10-6 (Oct-Mar) Sat 10-3 Sun 11–4▪ Fee R20/6 wines, R35/6 wines with 6 cheeses ▪ Closed Gc Fri, May 1, Jun 16 & Dec 25 ▪ Cheese lunch daily during tasting hours ▪ Farm produce ▪ BYO picnic ▪ Owner DGB (Pty) Ltd ▪ Winemaker(s) Richard Duckitt (Dec 2005) ▪ Viticulturist(s) Stephan Joubert (Nov 2006 300ha (cab, merlot, shiraz, chard, chenin, sauv, sem) ▪ 30,000t 49% red 50% white 1% rosé ▪ ISO 9001:20 IPW ▪ PO Box 52 Franschhoek 7690 ▪ fhcellardoor@dgb.co.za ▪ www.franschhoek-cellar.co.za ▪ S 33° 54' 4" E 019° 6'40.7" ▪ **T +27 (0)21-876-2086** ▪ F +27 (0)21-876-4107

Picturesque Franschhoek is steeped in history, dating back to its French Hugu not founders in the 1680s. Various landmarks around the area honour the pi neers and the village's rich cultural heritage. Franschhoek Cellar shows loyalty and support by naming the wines under The Village Walk range aft some of these historic locations and using mostly locally sourced grapes.

Franschhoek Vineyards range

Shiraz ▤ ⊘ ★★★★ With 'Reserve' suffix when previewed last time, now-bottled **10** has improved bu more withdrawn. Needs time for core of peppery dark fruit, from low yields, to shine. **Semillon ▤ ** **★★★★** Sumptuous **11** a step up on **10** (★★★★), shows good varietal expression & silky texture. Sub creamy oak platform for delicious quince & almond flavours, with fresh, tangy balance.

The Village Walk range

The Churchyard Cabernet Sauvignon ▤ ⊘ 11 tank sample too young to rate, as for **Merlot** & **Shir** This & all below previously listed by their varietal names only. All WO W Cape. **Stone Bridge Pinotage** **NE** ▤ **★★★ 10** reflects hot vintage. Ripe & spicy compote with hint of mocha, sweet tobacco & earthine Warm-hearted, supple structure. **Our Town Hall Chardonnay ✓ ▤ ⊘ ★★★☆ 12** tank sample brigh than previous, with lovely fruit purity, vivacious balance & good length. **La Cotte Mill Chenin Blanc ✓ ▤** ⊘ **★★★☆** Pre-bottling **12** a potential step up. Crisp & crunchy ripe apple with lively balance. Enjoy solo with a meal. **Statue de Femme Sauvignon Blanc ✓ ▤ ⊘ ★★★★** Fresh & tangy **12** has herb & passic fruit flavours with a dusty nuance. Focused, brisk acidity, favours food pairing. **Clubhouse Rosé NEW** tasted. — MW

Freedom Hill Wines

Location: Paarl ▪ Map: Paarl & Wellington ▪ WO: Paarl/Western Cape/Stellenbosch ▪ Est 1997 ▪ 1stB 200 Tasting Mon-Sun 11-3; Sat/Sun by appt in winter ▪ Closed Easter Fri/Sun & Dec 25 ▪ Freedom Hill Country Re taurant ▪ Owner(s) Francois Klomp ▪ Cellarmaster(s) Francois Naudé (Jan 2007, consultant) ▪ Winemaker Kowie du Toit (Feb 2007) ▪ Viticulturist(s) Paul Wallace ▪ 82ha/19ha (cab, ptage, shiraz) ▪ ±70t/6,000cs ov label 100% red ▪ PO Box 6126 Paarl 7620 ▪ info@freedomhill.co.za, suretha@freedomhill.co.za ▪ ww freedomhill.co.za ▪ S 33° 49'48.33" E 019° 0'35.90" ▪ **T +27 (0)21-867-0085** ▪ F +27 (0)21-882-8207

Two wine-men named Francois — Klomp, trained engineer and owner, and Naud seasoned oeno-adviser — are the prime movers behind this southern Paarl wine linked to Nelson Mandela through its proximity to Drakenstein Prison (ex-Vict Verster), from where the global icon walked to liberty 23 years ago. The portfoli heretofore overwhelmingly red, is looking more Rainbow Nation-ish with Stellenbosch chardonnay and Rawsonville chenin debuting this edition.

Freedom Hill range

Pinotage ★★★ Pre-bottling sample of **09** shows plum ripeness vying with big oak flavours which have the ec mid-2012, needing time to settle. **Shiraz ★★★★** Velvety feel to rich & ripe **10** tank sample, vibrant spicy leng Big-boned & chunky but pleasant. **Shiraz Reserve Magnum** Await new vintage. **Cape Blend ★★★** Oak pl major role on cab/pinotage **09**, first tasted since **06**. Heavy clove & cinnamon spice frames ripe blackcurrant fr Chalky feel. **Shiraz-Cabernet Sauvignon ⊘ ★★★** Two-third shiraz edges cab in **10** blend. Black cherry si plicity cloaked in oak veneer. Uncomplicated quaffer. **Chardonnay NEW ⊘ ★★★☆** Toasty, buttery peache cream on oaked **10** from Stellenbosch grapes. Poised & rounded with good length & harmony. **Chenin Bla**

☑ 🍴 ⧈ ★★★ Ripe interplay of tropical notes & zesty freshness, **11** is rounded, with full body & length of fla-
r. WO W Cape. **Sauvignon Blanc** 🍴 ⧈ ★★★ Fresh grapefruit & lemon zest typicity, **12** from Rawsonville
s similar to last-tasted easy-drinking **10**. Discontinued: **Sauvignon Blanc Reserve**.

edom Walk 1335/88 range

otage NEW ⧈ ★★★ Savoury **10** displays smoky, meaty edge on light tarry body. **Shiraz** NEW ★★★
orice & cocoa depth to juicy black fruit, **10** straightforward but ripe & approachable. **Cape Blend** ★★★
/pinotage **09** will appeal to fans of oak, its fragrance & spice pervades the chalky blackcurrant flavours.
continued: **Cabernet Sauvignon-Pinotage**. — FM

Freedom Walk *see* Freedom Hill Wines
French Connection *see* Lynx Wines
Fridham Gaard *see* Migliarina Wines
Friesland *see* Kaapzicht Wine Estate
Frisky Zebras *see* United Nations of Wine
Frog Hill *see* Anura Vineyards
Frost Vineyards *see* David Frost Signature Series

ryer's Cove Vineyards

ation: Doring Bay ▪ Map: Olifants River ▪ WO: Bamboes Bay/Western Cape ▪ Est 1999 ▪ 1stB 2002 ▪ Tasting,
es & cellar tours Mon–Fri 8-5 Sat 10-5 ▪ Fee R15 ▪ Closed Christian hols ▪ Pre-booked cheese platters & pic-
s; or BYO picnic ▪ Farm produce ▪ West Coast walking trail ▪ Owner(s) Jan Ponk Trust, JH Laubscher Family
st & Wynand Hamman ▪ Cellarmaster(s) Wynand Hamman (Apr 1999) ▪ Viticulturist(s) Jan van Zyl (Apr
99) ▪ 10ha/6ha (pinot, sauv) ▪ 50t/3,000cs own label 20% red 80% white ▪ PO Box 93 Vredendal 8160 ▪
onk1@kingsley.co.za, fryerscove@mylan.co.za ▪ www.fryerscove.co.za ▪ S 31° 45'53.1" E 018° 13'55.8"
+27 (0)27-213-2312 **(office)/+27 (0)27-215-1092 (tasting)** ▪ F +27 (0)27-213-2212

Wendy house erected by viticulturist Jan 'Ponk' van Zyl, co-owner with wine-
aking brother-in-law Wynand Hamman, functions as the kitchen for an onsite
afood restaurant run by the local community, serving patrons at sea-facing
les outside the tasting room. 'Now visitors can satisfy their hungry tummies
ile they enjoy a glass of our wine and the beautiful surroundings,' says Jan.
e energy-efficient cellar, also located at the Doring Bay old harbour on the
est Coast, innovatively uses the icy seawater as a refrigerant.

★★★ **Sauvignon Blanc** ✓ 🍴 Only Bamboes Bay grapes for stellar **11** (★★★★★), standout bottling
om consistently excellent producer. Fragrant cool green fruit, layered & restrained, acidity perfectly poised,
ersistent 'oystershell' minerality. More presence, character, than **10** but as lipsmackingly fresh & dry.

★★★ **Bay To Bay Sauvignon Blanc** ✓ 🍴 Portion Lamberts Bay grapes for this. Now bottled, **11** has
tegrated, regained heights of **09**; retains herbaceous character, enduring flavour. Follows lighter **10** (★★★★).

ot Noir ✓ ⧈ ★★★★ One of SA's earthier & more understated examples, revisited **11** savoury, still
htly funky from natural ferment. Bamboes Bay vines. — DB/CvZ

Fugue *see* Anatu Wines

undi

ation: Stellenbosch ▪ WO: Stellenbosch/Coastal ▪ Est 2008 ▪ Closed to public ▪ Owner(s) Section 21 Com-
y ▪ Directors Paul Cluver snr, Tim Rands (Vinimark), Joachim Sa (Amorim Cork), Michael Lutzeyer
ootbos), Valli Moosa & Su Birch (WOSA) ▪ 100% red ▪ PO Box 987 Stellenbosch 7599 ▪ info@fundiwine.co.
▪ www.fundiwine.co.za ▪ **T +27 (0)21-883-3860** ▪ F +27 (0)21-883-3861

e Fundi ('Learner') project aims to plough money earned from sales of the pre-
ium reds listed below into meaningful change in the lives of unemployed South
ricans. To date the project has provided on-the-job training for more than
000 individuals, setting them on track for careers in the hospitality business as
ne waiters. This exceeds the initial target set by generic wine marketing
ganisation Wines of South Africa.

★★★ **Cabernet Sauvignon-Shiraz-Merlot** ⓐ By Anwilka; **07** offers dark, dense black fruit with firm,
gering meaty mocha & oak flavours. Well-made & oaked. Not revisited, as for all.

Cabernet Sauvignon-Merlot ⊕ ★★★★ **06** plummy & ripe, with rich spicy fruit, but dry-finishing Company of Wine People. WO Coastal, as for next. **'Bordeaux Blend'** ⊕ ★★★★ **07** led (unusually) by p verdot. Sweet liquorice aromas; plenty of spicy ripe red fruit; savoury & bright. By Waterkloof/False Bay. M **lot-Cabernet Sauvignon-Pinotage** ⊕ ★★★ Spicy berries & red sour-plums on Stellekaya's access **07**; soft, rich mouthfeel. **Cabernet Sauvignon-Shiraz-Merlot** ⊕ ★★★★ Previously tasted **06** is sup richly fruited & gently savoury with leafy cassis, white choc tones. By Hartenberg.

Gabriëlskloof

Location/WO: Bot River ▪ Map: Elgin, Walker Bay & Bot River ▪ Est 2002 ▪ 1stB 2007 ▪ Tasting & sales Mon 9–5 Sat 11–3 ▪ Fee R15, waived on purchase ▪ Closed Dec 24/25 ▪ Cellar tours by appt ▪ Restaurant Wed–M 9–5 ▪ Deli ▪ Child-friendly & dogs welcome ▪ Weddings (very limited availability) ▪ Annual market (Dec 14– ▪ Owner(s) Bernhard Heyns & shareholders Johan Heyns, Barry Anderson & Wally Clarke ▪ Winemake Kobie Viljoen (Jun 2008), with Christiaan van der Merwe (Jan 2011) ▪ Viticulturist(s) Barry Anderson (200 150ha/68ha (cabs s/f, malbec, merlot, mourv, p verdot, pinot, shiraz, sauv, sem, viog) ▪ BWI ▪ PO Box Kleinmond 7195 ▪ info@gabrielskloof.co.za ▪ www.gabrielskloof.co.za ▪ S 34° 14' 19.89" E 019° 14' 58.68' **+27 (0)28-284-9865** ▪ F +27 (0)28-284-9864

Co-proprietor Bernhard Heyns had long dreamt of owning a wine farm, but was only while holidaying in Pringle Bay in 2002 that he came across th neglected sheep and wheat farm. One month after he'd bought it, his younge son set it and the neighbour farm alight after a fireworks display! Fortunat not too much damage was done and they've since gone from strength strength. Continuing with the green focus, they learnt that their Integrated P duction of Wine review in 2012 was the highest-scoring first audit ever.

Reserve range

★★★★ **Swartriver Shiraz** Listed previously as 'Syrah'. Rich pruney ripeness, **09** (★★★★) has smoky s ing from 2 years barrel but finishes warm from 15.3% alc. Not as fine as **08**.

★★★★☆ **Five Arches** Flagship 5-part Bordeaux red blend. Opulent ripeness in **09**, packed with fruit & v seasoned by 2 years oaking. So well made it's already drinking beautifully but has the credentials & structure a 10+ year future.

Viognier ✓ 📰 ★★★★ Extravagantly perfumed, floral notes, peach pip, roasted almonds, but **11**'s pala all business: savoury-dry with balanced fruit & acid. Drinks very well, more complex than **09** (★★★ Deserves upgrade (as does Magdalena) from Premium range. **Magdalena** 📰 ★★★★ Improving on (★★★★), blend semillon & sauvignon **11** shows 'cool yet ripe' styling, the generous oaking adding oatm biscuit flavours, deliciously savoury & long. **10** untasted. Note: Range listed as 'Ultra Premium' last time.

Premium range

Shiraz ★★★★ With dabs mourvèdre, viognier, dark-toned **10** preview shows scrub, espresso; firm tann need bit of time to meld. **The Blend** 📖 ★★★ Similar blend to Five Arches, half the oaking. Fruit-fresh ' blackcurrant & pepper tones makes it accessible, appealing. **Sauvignon Blanc** ✓ 📖 📰 ★★ Reductively made tank sample **12** offers minerality & grapefruit laced with racy acidity, ends bone-dry. ageing potential. — CR

Galleon Wines

Location/WO: Durbanville ▪ Est 2003 ▪ 1stB 2004 ▪ Tasting by appt at Diemersdal ▪ Owner(s) BK Investme Andries Brink/Thys Louw ▪ Winemaker(s) Andries Brink, Thys Louw & Mari Branders ▪ Viticulturist(s) Div Niekerk ▪ 850cs own label 50% red 50% white ▪ PO Box 62 Durbanville 7551 ▪ info@galleonwines.co. www.galleonwines.co.za ▪ **T +27 (0)21-976-8129** ▪ F +27 (0)21-976-8129

Retired cardiologist Andries Brink is still seeking things that make his heart b faster and 'wine is one of them'. Releasing the maiden Pinotage (post our tasti deadline) was certain to set his pulse racing... The good doctor continues to cr wines from Diemersdal grapes with assistance from the estate's winemakers.

Cabernet Sauvignon ⊕ ★★★ **09**'s subtle oaking supports ripe mulberry aromas & savoury over **Cabernet Sauvignon Reserve** New vintage unready, as for **Shiraz** & **Chardonnay**. **Sauvignon Bl** ⊕ 📖 ★★★ **10** fynbos & herbs, medium body; tad less vivacious than **09** (★★★★). — DB

■ **Ganzekraal** see The Goose Wines

Garden Route

Location: Calitzdorp ▪ Map: Klein Karoo & Garden Route ▪ WO: Outeniqua ▪ Est/1stB 2008 ▪ Tasting & sales at De Krans (see entry) ▪ Wines also available at Outeniqua Wine Emporium, Waboomskraal on N12 between George & Oudtshoorn ▪ Owner(s) Boets Nel ▪ Cellarmaster(s) Boets Nel (2008) ▪ Viticulturist(s) Jean Fourie (Jan 2011) ▪ 9ha (shiraz, chard, sauv) ▪ 80t/±1,500cs own label 40% red 60% white ▪ PO Box 28 Calitzdorp 6660 ▪ dekrans@mweb.co.za ▪ S 33° 32' 6.3" E 021° 41' 9.0" ▪ **T +27 (0)44-213-3314** ▪ F +27 (0)44-213-3562

Inland De Krans' champion port maker Boets Nel revels in working with grapes from a small mountain vineyard in the Outeniqua wine ward on the Cape south coast's famed Garden Route. The 'outstanding cool climate' slow-ripens whites mid-March and shiraz mid-April for 'terroir-specific wines' (available at De Krans and Outeniqua Wine Emporium on the N12).

Shiraz ✓ 🔲 ★★★★ First since savoury **07**, restrained **11** shows faint pepper, spice & light red fruit, firm conclusion. **Sauvignon Blanc** ✓ 🔲 🎋 ★★★★ Asparagus, khaki bush & greengage aromas & flavours on **12**, zingy but focused, benefits from serious food-friendly styling. — GdB/CvZ

■ **Gecko Ridge** *see Long Mountain Wine Company*

Genevieve Méthode Cap Classique

Location: Elgin ▪ Map: Elgin, Walker Bay & Bot River ▪ WO: Overberg ▪ Est 2009 ▪ 1stB 2008 ▪ Tasting by appt ▪ Lunch/picnic by appt ▪ Owner(s) Melissa Nelsen ▪ Viticulturist(s) Leon Engelke (2008) ▪ 16t/950cs own label 100% MCC ▪ PO Box 122 Elgin 7180 ▪ melissa@genevievemcc.co.za ▪ www.genevievemcc.co.za ▪ S 34° 5' 23." E 019° 11' 50.7" ▪ **T +27 (0)83-302-6562**

Melissa Genevieve Nelsen's inspiration for her bubbly comes from her grandmother who was inclined to broach a bottle no matter how minor the occasion. Grapes are from a 2ha block on Van der Stel Pass near Bot River, vinified last year in rented cellar space at Avondale in Paarl for the first time.

★★★★ **Genevieve** NEW **10** from chardonnay (small portion oak fermented) makes a sparkling debut. Fruit-driven, as expected from blanc de blancs, crisp & bright with green apple and floral notes. — HJ/JP

■ **Ghost Corner** *see Cederberg Private Cellar*
■ **Giant Periwinkle** *see The Giant Periwinkle*
■ **Giant's Peak** *see Wine-of-the-Month Club*

Gilga Wines

Location/map: Stellenbosch ▪ WO: Western Cape ▪ Est/1stB 2002 ▪ Tasting & sales by appt ▪ Owner(s) John Rowan ▪ Cellarmaster(s)/viticulturist(s) Stefan Gerber (Jun 2010, consultant) ▪ Winemaker(s) Stefan Gerber (Jun 2010, consultant), with Marco Benjamin (Dec 2010, consultant) ▪ 4ha/3.5ha (grenache, mourv, shiraz, tempranillo) ▪ ±t/550cs own label 100% red ▪ PO Box 871 Stellenbosch 7599 ▪ info@gilga.co.za, stefan@boerandbrit.com ▪ www.gilga.co.za ▪ S 33° 56' 46.1" E 018° 47' 20.6" ▪ **T +27 (0)84-515-6677** ▪ F +27 (0)86-531-7137

Rather like Gilga, the courtesan always overlooked by King Amurabi, so the 2007 vintage of Gilga the wine was 'forgotten' for four years in a cellar. 'Careful attention ensured that even after all that time, it was possible to bottle and sell this vintage,' smiles winemaker Stefan Gerber. The vineyards, meanwhile, have been extensively upgraded, requiring a break in production until 2010. There are also plans for a second wine based on all the Rhône varieties planted on the farm.

★★★ **Gilga Syrah 07** big but better balanced than previous. Some savoury, meaty maturity showing on nose; fresher, more spicy punchy flavours with gentle tannin landing. — AL

■ **Gilysipao** *see Orange River Wine Cellars*
■ **Give Me A Chance** *see Alluvia Winery & Private Residence Club*
■ **Glass Collection** *see Glenelly Cellars*

Glen Carlou   VISITED 23-12-12

Location: Paarl ▪ Map: Paarl & Wellington ▪ WO: Paarl/Coastal/Durbanville/Western Cape/Robertson ▪ Est 1985 ▪ 1stB 1988 ▪ Tasting & sales Mon-Fri 8.30-5 Sat/Sun 10-4 ▪ Fee R25-R50 ▪ Closed Good Fri, Dec 25 & Jan

1 ▪ Cellar tours by appt ▪ Glen Carlou Restaurant (see Restaurants section) ▪ Facilities for children ▪ Tour groups ▪ Gifts ▪ Honey ▪ Conferences ▪ Conservation area ▪ Hess Art Collection Museum ▪ Owner(s) Hess Family Estates Ltd (Switzerland) ▪ Cellarmaster(s)/winemaker(s) Arco Laarman (Jan 2000) ▪ Viticulturist(s) Marius Cloete (2000) ▪ 145ha/62ha (cabs s/f, malbec, mourv, p verdot, pinot, shiraz, chard) ▪ ±700t/50,000cs own label ▪ PO Box 23 Klapmuts 7625 ▪ welcome@glencarlou.co.za ▪ www.glencarlou.co.za ▪ S 33° 48' 44.85" E 018° 54' 12.88" ▪ T +27 (0)21-875-5528 ▪ F +27 (0)21-875-5314

In the Hess Art Museum en route to the cellar, winemaker Arco Laarman wryly notes that wine operations had to give up premium space to these modern exhibits. Nonetheless, with rebuilding completed in 2012, the entire production process is now housed on site. In the cellar, Laarman is particularly proud of his Nomblot concrete fermenters, the basis for the runaway success of his unwooded chardonnay. Made for the cellar's restaurant — both outlet and testing ground for small batches of new wines — in 2011, demand is such that 2012 output doubled and it will be available locally. The 25th harvest here last year was time for a 'complete brand health check': the ranges have been re-stratified and there are subtle label changes, but generous styling and value for money remain the hallmark.

Prestige range

purchased – change in 2014

★★★★☆ **Gravel Quarry Cabernet Sauvignon** Handsome & powerful, farm's top cab in pure-fruited bramble form in **09**. Classy blackcurrant flavours are melded with the pliable tannin frame, giving great grip for cellaring. 100% new wood 18 months.

★★★★☆ **Quartz Stone Chardonnay** Modern **11** a bold romp; oodles of citrus fruit buffed by sweet oak, more plush than mineral **10**. From oldest home vines, wild yeast ferment in new barrels.

The Welder ★★★★ Unwooded sweet chenin named for winemaker who shares first name with US welding supplies company! **11** full & sweet (103 g/l sugar), less complex than strapping **09** (★★★★). No **10**.

Cellar Reserve range NEW

★★★★ **Pinot Noir Reserve** Serious package; dense **11** has forest floor & farmyard richness, with firm grippy tannins. 11 months all new cask. Needs 2-5 years to develop.

★★★★ **Méthode Cap Classique** Exclusive bottling by Bon Courage in Robertson under Glen Carlou finery. Developed **06** sparkling shows broad lines, for current drinking. Barrel-fermented, 4 years on lees.

Classic range

★★★★ **Cabernet Sauvignon** ✓ **10** packed with herbal-scented blackcurrant fruit; polished styling in pliable frame, the flavour lingers. Will amplify over 3-5 years.

★★★★ **Syrah** Broad bacon, pepper & red fruit flavours in open-hearted **07** (★★★★) when last tasted. Less structured than **06** & previous.

★★★★ **Grand Classique** ✓ Svelte cab-led Bordeaux red quintet; vintage-classic **09** is well fruited in elegant style, less oak (18 months, 40% new) & more accessible berry flavour in lovely balance.

★★★★ **Chardonnay** ✓ Cellar's stalwart. **11** rich & creamy, butterscotch nuances (10 months in cask, 30% new) a trademark in broad New World mouthful, snappy acidity balancing lemon preserve profile. **Merlot** NEW ✓ ★★★★ Of velvet texture, sumptuous **10** studded with juicy mulberry-toned fruit in supportive supple tannins. Year old oak. **Pinot Noir** ★★★★ Earthy rather than cherry character, **11** open textured, midweight styling. **Zinfandel** ★★★★ **09** back for final curtain call (no **08**) as vines since removed. Sultry, spice-infused raspberry flavours in generous mouthful. **Unwooded Chardonnay** NEW ✓ ★★★★ Tank sample **12** loaded with fresh citrus fruit, a gentle aperitif option. Untasted maiden **11** only ex cellar's restaurant. Concrete 'egg' fermenters. WO Western Cape. **Sauvignon Blanc** ★★★ Ripe litchi, kiwi fruit-salad flavours take edge off **12**'s zesty tail. Grapes now all ex Durbanville.

Contemporary range

Tortoise Hill Red ☺ ★★★ Cheerful cab/merlot **11** has smoky notes to chunky berry fruits. WO Coastal. **Tortoise Hill White** ☺ ★★★ New chenin/chardonnay blend in rebranded livery, **12** the same juicy pineapple & melon pleasure as before. WO Coastal. — DS

Glenelly Cellars

Location/map/WO: Stellenbosch ▪ Est/1stB 2003 ▪ Tasting & sales Mon-Fri 10-4.30 Sat 10-4 ▪ Closed Easter F Sun, Dec 25/26 & Jan 1 ▪ Cellar tours by appt ▪ Gift shop ▪ Glass museum ▪ Owner(s) May-Eliane de Lencquesain Cellarmaster(s) Luke O'Cuinneagain (Jan 2008) ▪ Winemaker(s) Luke O'Cuinneagain (Jan 2008), with Jero kwa (Jan 2008) ▪ Viticulturist(s) Heinrich Louw (2003) ▪ 128ha/65ha (cabs s/f, merlot, p verdot, shiraz, chard) ▪ 0t/27,667cs own label 95% red 5% white ▪ PO Box 1079 Stellenbosch 7599 ▪ info@glenelly.co.za ▪ www. enellyestate.com ▪ S 33° 55'6.1" E 018° 52'45.1" ▪ **T +27 (0)21-809-6440** ▪ F +27 (0)21-809-6448

he heritage is long (the former owners held this land in one of Stellenbosch's enowned wine valleys for 138 years) but the rest — the owner, young team, ineyards, winery and brand — is more recent. Bordeaux luminary May-Eliane e Lencquesaing, seeing the potential for quality wine in the Cape and wanting contribute to the economic development of a new democracy, set about the ake-over in 2003. She brought too, her antique glass collection. Glass? Apart om being 'perfect partners', fine wine and glass share many attributes, we're ld. Both come from the poorest soils, need heat or sun to take form, are crafted y man and, at their zenith, are an art form.

lenelly range

★★★☆ **Lady May** 🎖 Grace & style defined. Cab with a dash of petit verdot, all the components — precise erry fruit, clean 100% new oak, fine tannins, fresh acid, & even supportive 14.7% alcohol — of **10** are melded nto a glass of seamless class. Follows exceptional & carefully composed **09** (★★★★★).

★★★☆ **Grand Vin de Glenelly** ✓ Elegant & accessible shiraz/Bordeaux blend. **09** back on form with pol-hed, dark berry fruit laced with spice & supple tannins. **08** (★★★★) was lighter. Enjoy while waiting for 'Ma-ame' above to mature.

★★★☆ **Grand Vin de Glenelly Chardonnay** 🎖 Oatmeal texture (ferment/9 months lees-ageing in oak, alf new) gives gravitas to **11**'s vibrant citrus fruit profile; complexity unfolds in length of flavour.

he Glass Collection

abernet Sauvignon ✓ 🍴 🎖 ★★★★ Ripe cassis tightly packed into muscular yet finessed structure. **10** ery taut mid-2012; for 3 years cellaring or with food now. **Merlot** ⓧ 🍴 ★★★★ Full-bodied but demure, **0** sampled last edition had floral violet charm to firm texture. **Shiraz** ⓧ 🍴 ★★★★ **10** more peppery than ch **09**, roasted nut & spicy warmth, dense tannins need time. **Chardonnay** 🍴 🎖 ★★★ **11** loaded with brant citrus flavours unfettered by oak; eminently drinkable. — DS

Glen Erskine Estate

ocation/WO: Elgin ▪ Map: Elgin, Walker Bay & Bot River ▪ Est 2005 ▪ 1stB 2009 ▪ Tasting, sales & cellar tours by ppt ▪ Closed Easter Fri/Sun, Dec 25 & Jan 1 ▪ BYO picnic ▪ Owner(s) Reine & Annalien Dalton ▪ Cellar-aster(s)/winemaker(s) Annalien Dalton ▪ Viticulturist(s) Reine Dalton ▪ 14.6ha/4.93ha (sauv, sem, viog) ▪ 8t/475cs own label 100% white + 115cs for clients ▪ Ranges for customers: Kievits Kroon ▪ PO Box 111 Elgin 180 ▪ annalien.dalton@gmail.com, reinedalton@gmail.com ▪ S 34°10'34.94" E 019° 2'12.75" ▪ **T +27)21-848-9632** ▪ F +27 (0)86-547-4473

wners Reine and Annalien Dalton decided against a formal tasting room, pre-erring instead to receive visitors by appointment in the cellar itself, sampling rom tank and barrel. It's the 'enchanting wine experience of a boutique' they eek to offer and, to this end, they've formed a collaborative marketing venture, lgin Boutique Wines', with Belfield and the Corder family.

auvignon Blanc ✓ 🍴 ★★★★ Cut-grass edginess to greengage fruit of **11**, fuller & less flinty than previ-us, with 2% semillon. **Reserve** ✓ 🍴 ★★★★ Subtle cool-climate elegance. **11** is at ease; hay-like sauvi-non given breadth & added facets by lightly oaked 20% semillon & 10% viognier partners. — DS

Glen Heatlie

ocation: Worcester ▪ Est 2006 ▪ Tasting by appt only ▪ Owner(s) Orange Grove Trust ▪ Winemaker(s) Joan-Marie Heatlie ▪ Viticulturist(s) Charlie Heatlie ▪ 3,100ha/45ha (cab, merlot, shiraz, chenin, chard, cbard, sauv, em) ▪ Orange Grove PO Box 18 De Wet 6853 ▪ joan@glenheatlie.co.za ▪ **T +27 (0)82-364-4702** ▪ F +27)23-341-2708

t would be incredible to go back to the future...' muses winemaker Joan-Marie leatlie, whose Scottish great-grandfather Thomas Tennant Heatlie distilled his irst brandy in 1875. There's a strong inclination to revive the tradition on this fam-y farm near Worcester but for now they're sticking to wine — the small batch of unch-fermented shiraz made last harvest was still incubating at press time.

Glenview Wines

Location: Cape Town ▪ WO: Coastal ▪ Est/1stB 1998 ▪ Closed to public ▪ Owner(s) Robin Marks ▪ Winemaker(s) Frank Meaker (Nov 2010, consultant) ▪ 7,000cs own label 50% red 50% white ▪ PO Box 32234 Camps Bay 8040 ▪ bayexport@kingsley.co.za ▪ **T +27 (0)21-438-1080** ▪ F +27 (0)21-511-2545

Owner Robin Marks has seen his online wine business grow most satisfactorily over recent years, and he ascribes his success to over-delivering on quality. He hopes to continue growth, particularly in Gauteng and Natal, and explore some export opportunities for the brand.

Merlot 🍷 ★★ Pasta pal **11**, facsimile of previous' firm chocolatey flavour, food-friendly savouriness. **Chenin Blanc** 🍷 🏵 ★★★ Fresh & tasty **12**, packed with lingering peachy notes. **Sauvignon Blanc** 🍷 🏵 ★★ Lively **12**, grassy tropical fruit, pleasant lunchtime white. — DB

GlenWood

Location/map: Franschhoek ▪ WO: Franschhoek/Coastal ▪ Est/1stB 2002 ▪ Tasting & sales Mon-Fri 11–4 Sat, Sun (Sep-Apr only) 11-3 ▪ Closed Easter Fri/Sun, Dec 25 & Jan 1 ▪ Tasting R30/R50 incl cellar tour ▪ Tours daily at 11 ▪ Japanese sushi & salads ▪ Hikes ▪ Owner(s) Alastair G Wood ▪ Cellarmaster(s)/viticulturist(s) DP Burger (Apr 1991) ▪ Winemaker(s) DP Burger (Apr 1991), with Justin Jacobs (Jan 2011) ▪ 49ha/30ha (merlot, shiraz, chard, sauv, sem) ▪ 150t/8,000cs own label 50% red 50% white ▪ BWI, IPW ▪ PO Box 204 Franschhoek 7690 ▪ info@glenwoodvineyards.co.za ▪ www.glenwoodvineyards.co.za ▪ S 33° 54' 56.7" E 019° 4' 57.0" ▪ **T +27 (0)21-876-2044** ▪ F +27 (0)21-876-3338

At this scenic Franschhoek winery, cellarmaster and general manager DP Burger strives to make wines of excellent quality using sustainable farming techniques, best winecrafting practice and continuous improvements. And he has succeeded — judging by the numerous accolades won, especially the Vigneron's Selection Chardonnay, a consistent performer. New on the property is a small restaurant, Okamai, serving Japanese cuisine paired with the GlenWood wines.

★★★★ **Merlot** ✓ Mouthfilling **09** is complex & harmonious with ripe plums dipped in dark chocolate. Rich fruit flavours are reined in by dense tannins. Balanced, with good ageing potential.

★★★★☆ **Chardonnay Vigneron's Selection** 🏵 Barrel-fermented **11** back to form after **10** (★★★★) with multidimensional aromas of citrus, pear, white flowers & powdered stone. Wonderfully rich, without being heavy, reflecting the judicious oaking regime (14 months, 100% new). Will reward those who wait.

★★★★ **Unwooded Chardonnay** ✓ 🏵 **12** is a breath of fresh air with vibrant clean citrus & apple flavours. Poised & intense, there's a spicy/creamy element in the finish which is very moreish.

★★★★ **Semillon Vigneron's Selection** Wild yeast fermented **10** shows lingering peach, spice & floral scents. Full & silky, the fruit-filled toasty conclusion invites ageing. Good food partner for the impatient.

Shiraz ⓧ ★★★★★ **08** last edition took a big step up, was much more complex & elegant than **07** (★★★) WO Coastal. **Syrah Vigneron's Selection** Await new vintage. **Shiraz-Merlot** ⓧ 🍷 ★★★ Easy-drinking cheerful **10** is medium bodied, balanced, fruit-sweet & juicy, with soft vanilla wafts. **Sauvignon Blanc** ⓧ ★★★ Ebullient **11**, ripe tropical fruit flavours; crisp & lean, zesty lemon finish, modest 12.5% alcohol. — WB

Goats do Roam Wine Company

Location: Paarl ▪ WO: Coastal/Western Cape ▪ Est/1stB 1998 ▪ Tasting & sales at Fairview ▪ Owner(s) Charles Back ▪ Winemaker(s) Anthony de Jager, with Stephanie Betts ▪ PO Box 583 Suider-Paarl 7624 ▪ info@goatsdoroam.com ▪ www.goatsdoroam.com ▪ **T +27 (0)21-863-2450** ▪ F +27 (0)21-863-2591

A fun brand but serious wines — that's how 'the goats' want this well-established range to be portrayed. Owner (and Fairview proprietor) Charles Back's primary aim is to over-deliver, and now that virtually all the grapes come from his own vineyards, expect to see the standards go even higher.

★★★★ **Goat Roti** 🍷 🏵 Back on track after less sleek **09** (★★★★), **10** shiraz/viognier co-fermented blend delights with coffee, dark chocolate & cherries wrapped up with silky tannins. Spicy tweak at the finish.

Goats do Roam Rosé ☺ 🍷 🏵 ★★★ Delightful summer quaffer. **12** dry, lowish alcohol (12.5%) but with bags of flavour & character — cherry fruit & candied peel.

Goats do Roam Red ✓ 🏠 🔲 ★★★★ Shiraz-led blend **11** packs delicious punch of red & black berries, with attractive peppery nose of leather, violets & spice. **The Goatfather** 🏠 🔲 ★★★★ Unusual mix of sangiovese, barbera & cab, **11** still shy on nose but finishes well, with blueberries & cranberry sauce. **Goats do Roam White** 🏠 🔲 ★★★ **12** tank sample of viognier, roussanne, grenache blanc blend shows aromatic stonefruit in a nicely balanced mouthful of fruit & acidity. WO W Cape. Discontinued: **Bored Doe.** — CM

Goede Hoop Estate

Location/map: Stellenbosch ▪ WO: Bottelary ▪ Est 1928 ▪ 1stB 1974 ▪ Tasting, sales & cellar tours Mon-Fri 9–4 Sat 10-1 ▪ Closed Easter Fri-Sun, Dec 25/26 & Jan 1 ▪ Pieter's Private Cellar: monthly 4-course gourmet meal with wine R305pp, booking essential (12 seats only) ▪ BYO picnic ▪ Conference facilities ▪ Mountain biking trail ▪ Owner(s) Pieter Bestbier ▪ Winemaker(s) Albert Ahrens (Jun 2009, consultant), with Janette Hartshorne (Jan 2012) ▪ Viticulturist(s) Altus van Lill (May 2011) ▪ 122ha/80ha (cab, merlot, ptage, shiraz, chenin, sauv) ▪ ±600t/10,000cs own label 91% red 9% white & ±200,000L bulk ▪ PO Box 25 Kuils River 7579 ▪ goede@adept.co.za ▪ www.goedehoop. co.za ▪ S 33° 54'32.0" E 018° 45' 14.0" ▪ **T +27 (0)21-903-6286** ▪ F +27 (0)21-906-1553

Something of a new-broom situation at this venerable estate on Stellenbosch's Bottelary Hills. Not only new-look labels, and a few new wines, but vintages skipped for the three Estate reds. The 2009s (from the year that Albert Ahrens came as winemaker) reveal the house-style unpretentious elegance, balance and eminent drinkability. The new Heritage label is a joint venture between Albert and Goede Hoop's owner Pieter Bestbier.

Heritage Wines

★★★★ **Estate Wine** NEW **10** harmoniously blends merlot, pinotage, cab, shiraz, malbec & cinsaut! Subtly oaked — no new barrels, so the light, bright herbal elegance & charm is untrammelled. Just 13% alcohol complements well the unassertive but convincing structure. Delicious now, but no hurry to drink up.

★★★★ **Estate Straw Wine** ⏱ **10** from air-dried chenin. Hugely sweet & concentrated, with healthy ripe fruit flavours. To be enjoyed in small helpings.

Domaine range

Red 😊 🏠 ★★★ Ripe & fruity **11** from unwooded cab, shiraz. Amazingly delicate given big alcohol, even insubstantial. Undeniably enjoyable. **White** 😊 🏠 ★★★ Dry but soft-textured **11** sauvignon/chenin blend is easygoing but characterful & not over-fruity, with acid-drop finish.

Goede Hoop Estate range

Cabernet Sauvignon ★★★★ 09 the first vintage since 02. Light-feeling & rather elegant, with intelligently modest use of oak. No great intensity, but balanced & harmonious; very good drinking now. **Merlot** NEW ★★★ Fresh, pleasant 09 offering some charming, bright, sweet fruit; modest & only lightly gripping, making for easy drinkability. **Pinotage** ★★★ Understated 09 has good varietal character. More chunky & sweet-finishing than the other reds, but equally a very pleasing mouthful. **Shiraz** ★★★★ Spicy, smoked meat intro to 09 (first since 03). A little more richness & savoury tannic bite than the other reds, but showing the same satisfactory light touch. **Chardonnay** In abeyance. **Sauvignon Blanc** ⏱ ★★★ Pungent asparagus & mineral/dusty notes on 10 leading onto fruity but crisply tart palate. Needs food. **Shiraz LBV Port** ⏱ ★★★★ Big & ripe maiden 07 emerged after lengthy stay in barrel, revealing modest sweetness & evolved fruit with firm spirit grip. Discontinued: **Merlot-Cabernet Sauvignon.** — TJ

Goedvertrouw Estate

Location: Bot River ▪ Map: Elgin, Walker Bay & Bot River ▪ WO: Overberg ▪ Est 1990 ▪ 1stB 1991 ▪ Tasting & sales by appt ▪ Home-cooked meals & accommodation by appt ▪ Play area for children ▪ Walks ▪ Farm produce ▪ Small conferences ▪ Conservation area ▪ Small art gallery ▪ Owner(s)/winemaker(s)/viticulturist(s) Elreda Pillmann ▪ 8ha (cab, pinot, chard, sauv) ▪ 70% red 30% white ▪ PO Box 37 Bot River 7185 ▪ goedvertrouwwineestate@telkomsa. net ▪ S 34° 9'56.7" E 019° 13'24.1" ▪ **T +27 (0)28-284-9769** ▪ F +27 (0)28-284-9769

If you think cellardoors are becoming too homogenised, program your GPS for Elreda Pillmann's farm, a few kilometres from Bot River on the Van der Stel Pass. The delightful tannie Elreda is a force of nature, making wine, fund-raising for Tommy Prins Foundation, featuring in Elgin Open Gardens Week and Bot River Pink Weekend, running a B&B, and cooking 'boeremeals' for visitors!

Cabernet Sauvignon ⓘ ★★★ **06** yeasty aromas, pure fruit & ripe tannin when last tasted. Should be harmonious now. **Pinot Noir** ★★ Earthy strawberry notes & hint of vanilla on light-hearted **09**. **Chardonnay** ⓘ ★★★ Orange peel & biscuit tones waft out of nicely round **06**. **Sauvignon Blanc** ⓘ ★★★ Previewed **08** finished satisfyingly dry previously. — WB

Goedverwacht Wine Estate

Location: Bonnievale ▪ Map/WO: Robertson ▪ Est 1960's ▪ 1stB 1994 ▪ Tasting, sales & cellar tours Mon-Fri 8. 30-4.30 Sat 10–1 ▪ Closed Easter Fri/Sun, Dec 25/26 & Jan 1 ▪ Mediterranean or quiche & salad platter; picnic basket for 2 (incl sparkling wine) — 2 days prior booking essential ▪ BYO picnic ▪ Tour groups ▪ Conservation area ▪ Owner(s) Jan du Toit & Sons (Pty) Ltd ▪ Winemaker(s) Henry Conradie (Aug 2005), with Charles Petrus Adam (Jan 2003) ▪ Viticulturist(s) Jan du Toit, advised by Francois Viljoen ▪ 220ha/130ha (cab, merlot, shiraz, chard, cbard, sauv) ▪ 1,600t/1m L 43% red 50% white 7% rosé ▪ Other export brands: Ama Ubilo, Misty Kloof's, Mzanzi's, Soek die Geluk ▪ Brands for clients: Vinimark Trading ▪ BEE, BWI, IPW ▪ PO Box 128 Bonnievale 6730 ▪ goedverwachtestate@lando.co.za, info.goedverwacht@breede.co.za ▪ www.goedverwacht.co.za ▪ S 33° 55' 11.3" E 020° 0'19.1" ▪ **T +27 (0)23-616-3430** ▪ F +27 (0)23-616-2073

Co-owner Jan du Toit's son Gawie is joining the team after university, which brings the fifth generation onto the family farm between Bonnievale and Robertson. Acquisition of more land ('virgin soil', says winemaker Henry Conradie) allowed for new vineyards, with durif/petite sirah and nouvelle among the plantings.

Maxim range

★★★★ **Cabernet Sauvignon** 📿 Leafy **10** (★★★★) elegant if slightly austere, with firm tannins for hearty fare. Shade off layered **07**. No **09**, **08**.

Chardonnay 📿 ★★★★ Vanilla biscuit wafts, coconut & butter richness give **11** Californian styling. Bold, could easily pair with spicy dishes.

Goedverwacht Wine Estate range

Shiraz Rosé ☺ 🍴 📿 ★★★ **12** just-off-dry al fresco sipper with lowish alcohol (12.15%) & cranberry zestiness. **Great Expectations Chardonnay** ☺ 🍴 📿 ★★★ Step-up **12** is elegant & understated, has clean citrus lines. Also-tasted **11** (★★★★) greater buttery vanilla intensity, crisp finish. Both part fermented in older oak.

An Acre of Stone Shiraz 🍴 📿 ★★★ Savoury, chocolate-toned **11** takes step up, makes perfect campfire sipper. **Triangle** 🍴 📿 ★★ **10** cab-led Bordeaux blend: loads of berries, commendably dry but tad terse finish. **Pink Shiraz Rosé** NEW 🍴 📿 ★★ **11** spice & savoury, tannin grip on semi-dry canapé companion. **The Good Earth Sauvignon Blanc** 🍴 📿 ★★☆ Improved **12**, gooseberry & herb complexity, tropical richness on palate. **Crane White Sauvignon Blanc** NEW 🍴 📿 ★★★ Lemongrass & lime, guava & apple on crisp & nicely vinous drink-soon **11**.

Crane range

Red Merlot ☺ 🍴 📿 ★★★ Toasty, mocha-infused **12** & **11** in similar style (both tasted this edition); mulberries & plum pudding, friendly & accessible. **Rosé Brut Sparkling** ☺ 📿 ★★★ From shiraz, **11** frothy & fun; party waiting to happen.

White Colombar 🍴 📿 ★★ Pleasingly fruity with guava & pineapple notes, **12** nice dry finish. **Brut Sparkling** Await new. — DB/HJ

▪ **Goeie Tye** *see* Rooiberg Winery
▪ **Golden Triangle** *see* Stellenzicht Vineyards
▪ **Golden Vine** *see* Waterstone Wines

Goudini Wines

Location: Rawsonville ▪ Map: Breedekloof ▪ WO: Goudini ▪ Est 1948 ▪ Tasting & sales Mon-Fri 8–5 Sat 9.30–12. 30 ▪ Closed Good Fri, Dec 25/26 & Jan 1 ▪ Cellar tours by appt ▪ Coffee shop: light meals during tasting hours ▪ Conferences ▪ Owner(s) 40 members ▪ Cellarmaster(s) Hennie Hugo (Dec 1984) ▪ Winemaker(s) Ruaar Terblanche (Nov 2001), with Tinus le Roux (Jan 2010) ▪ Viticulturist(s) Hendrik Myburgh (Nov 2001) ▪ 1,000ha (merlot, ruby cab, shiraz, chard, chenin, sauv) ▪ 20,000t/33,000cs own label 45% red 45% white 10% rosé +

,000cs for clients ▪ PO Box 132 Rawsonville 6845 ▪ winesales@goudiniwine.co.za ▪ www.goudiniwine.co.za ▪ S 33° 41'37.8" E 019° 19'9.5" ▪ **T +27 (0)23-349-1090** ▪ F +27 (0)23-349-1988

Public relations officer Bonita Joubert promises visitors a warm welcome and lovely meal in the renovated coffee house, a remarkably tranquil corner of a winery processing some 20,000 tons of grapes from 40 Breedekloof growers. The extensive Goudini range now boasts an eye-catching new label while the non-vintage Umfiki range continues to be a bestseller.

Goudini range

Ruby Cabernet-Merlot ☺ 🍴 📷 ★★★ **11** balanced & cheery red-berried quaffer for summer chilling. **Unwooded Chardonnay** ☺ 🍴 📷 ★★★ **11** plump & ripe pear/tangy lime, has succulent easy drinkability. **Chenin Blanc** ☺ 🍴 📷 ★★★ Off-dry **12** is a light & crisp tropical charmer.

Pinotage 🍴 📷 ★★★ Fresh & juicy **11** with lightly spiced redcurrant for easy drinking. **Shiraz** 🍴 📷 ★★ Last seen in **07**. Sweet oak spices on bright & tangy **11**. **Rosé** ⊕ 🍴 📷 ★★ **11** from pinotage, light berry tones with sweet-sour twist. **Sauvignon Blanc** ⊕ 🍴 📷 ★★★ **11** soft herb & tropical tones, nice tangy tail. **Brut Sparkling** ⊕ 🍴 ★★ Less fresh appeal than previous, more broad-based waxy, nutty character. **NV**. **Natural Sweet** ⊕ 🍴 📷 ★★ Ripe tropical tones on previewed **11**, fresh & balanced. **Hanepoot** ⊕ ★★★ Previously **06** was a balanced fortified dessert with gentle barley sugar & lemon tastes, best enjoyed soon. Discontinued: **Cape Ruby Port**.

Umfiki range

Cabernet Sauvignon 🍴 ★★ Unoaked **NV** has bright berry fruit. A brisk BBQ partner. **Merlot** 🍴 ★★ **NV** light & tangy red fruit on undemanding & unoaked quaffer. **Dry White** ⊕ 🍴 ★★ **NV** from chenin; softly tropical, gentle yet crisp. **Semi Sweet Chenin Blanc** ⊕ 🍴 ★★ When last tasted, pleasant **NV** semi-sweet white for the poolside. **Sauvignon Blanc** ⊕ 🍴 ★★ Light, tart & tangy **NV** dry white. — MW

▪ **Goue Kalahari** *see* Die Mas van Kakamas
▪ **Gouverneurs** *see* Groot Constantia Estate

Govert Wines   `NEW`

Location: Somerset West ▪ WO: Western Cape/Stellenbosch ▪ Est 2002 ▪ 1stB 2007 ▪ Closed to public ▪ Owner(s) Teuns Keuzenkamp ▪ 90,000cs own label 80% red 5% white 15% rosé ▪ PO Box 1977 Somerset West 7129 ▪ info@govertwines.com ▪ www.govertwines.com ▪ **T +27 (0)21-887-5812** ▪ F +27 (0)86-224-9348

The Keuzenkamp family established Govert Wines in 2002 to produce, market and export their own and clients' brands. Currently they supply countries in Europe and Asia, but it's Nigeria they're keen to highlight: their Don Morris is one of the leading wine and grape juice labels in Africa's most populous country, and a vindication of a decision made in 2004 when, as bulk-wine suppliers to West Africa, they saw an opportunity to add value through an own branded offering.

Loyal Brothers range

Cabernet Sauvignon 📷 ★★★ Dusty oak, charred meat & hint liquorice on very ripe, generous & warming **10** from Stellenbosch.

Charles Borro range

Cabernet Sauvignon-Shiraz 📷 ★★★ **11** 60/40 blend is youthful & well balanced, with cherry & spice appeal from shiraz, fresh acidity from cab.

D'Hero's range

Shiraz-Pinotage 📷 ★★ Briefly oaked shiraz, unoaked pinotage in light & juicy **11** sipper.

Don Morris Cape Red range

Cabernet Sauvignon-Merlot-Ruby Cabernet 📷 ★★★ Minty fruit drops in **11**, light bodied & brief for uncomplicated enjoyment.

Ruby Ridge range

Pinotage 📷 ★★ **11** unoaked, soft & berry toned for anytime quaffing. — FM/GdB

Graça

Inspired by Portugal's vinho verde wines, these popular easy-drinkers are made by Distell and now closed under screwcap.

Rosé ☺ 🍴 **★★★** Acidity masks the sugar to create a balanced, easy-to-quaff **NV** with moderate ±11% alcohol. **Graça** ☺ 🍴 **★★★** Relaxed & cheerful fish-&-chips wine, light-textured **NV** mainly sauvignon, with the variety's crisp kiwifruit freshness. Western Cape grapes, as for Rosé. —DB/HJ

Graceland Vineyards

Location/map/WO: Stellenbosch ▪ Est/1stB 1998 ▪ Tasting & sales Mon-Fri by appt ▪ Fee R30 ▪ Closed all pub hols ▪ B&B, two self-catering cottages ▪ Owner(s) Paul & Susan McNaughton ▪ Cellarmaster(s)/winemaker(s)/ viticulturist(s) Susan McNaughton (2001) ▪ 18ha/10ha (cab, merlot, shiraz) ▪ 55t/4,000cs own label 100% red ▪ Suite 144 Private Bag X4 Die Boord 7613 ▪ graceland@iafrica.com ▪ www.gracelandvineyards.com ▪ S 33° 59′37.5" E 018° 50′3.1" ▪ **T +27 (0)21-881-3121** ▪ F +27 (0)86-556-4600

Fifteen years it is since Paul McNaughton and winemaking wife Susan first bottled (and beautifully packaged) wine from this small but ambitious estate in Stellenbosch's 'golden triangle' of eminent vineyards. A new wine is coming — a red, of course, as that's what they specialise in here: a merlot no doubt, fittingly called 'With Good Grace'.

★★★★ Cabernet Sauvignon ⑨ Opulent, well-groomed **09**. Fine varietal character with cassis & pencil shavings. Harmonious even in youth, with structure for enjoyment over good few years.

★★★★ Strawberry Fields ⑨ **09** shiraz (70%) & cab blend, raises the bar on **08** (**★★★★**), recalls focused **07**. Retro floral label belies gravitas of rich melange of savoury dark fruit. Supple & flavoursome.

★★★★ Three Graces ⑨ **09** first tasted since **06**, captures spirit of Regnault's eponymous painting depicted on label. Barrel selection of cab, merlot & shiraz has layers of flavour in supple & streamlined elegance.

Merlot ⑨ **★★★★** Restrained **09** has a 'graphite' mineral tone. Somewhat unknit in youth, time will reward greater fruit (& rating). **Shiraz** ⑨ 📖 **★★★★** Ripe & unashamedly New World styled **10** has brambly fruit & robust structure, afterglow favours hearty fare. —MW

Graham Beck Wines

Location/map: Robertson ▪ WO: Western Cape/Robertson/Coastal/Stellenbosch ▪ Est 1983 ▪ 1stB 1991 ▪ Tasting & sales Mon-Fri 9–5 Sat/Sun 10–4 ▪ Tasting fees: classic is complimentary; deluxe R50, waived on purchase of R200+; MCC R75 ▪ Closed Good Fri & Dec 25 ▪ Owner(s) Graham Beck Enterprises ▪ Cellarmaster(s) Pieter Ferreira (Aug 1990) & Erika Obermeyer (Jan 2005) ▪ Winemaker(s) Pierre de Klerk (Oct 2010) ▪ Viticulturist(s) Dérick Hamman & Pieter Fouché ▪ 260ha under vine (cab, pinot, shiraz, chard, sauv); Robertson 170ha/ Stellenbosch 90ha ▪ 2,800t/270,000cs own label ▪ ISO 14001, BWI champion, IPW, SABS 1841, WIETA ▪ PO Box 724 Robertson 6705 ▪ cellar@grahambeckwines.co.za, market@grahambeckwines.co.za ▪ www. grahambeckwines.com ▪ S 33° 48′14.95" E 019° 48′1.41" ▪ **T +27 (0)23-626-1214; marketing offices: +27 (0)21-874-1258** ▪ F +27 (0)23-626-5164; marketing ofices: +27 (0)21-874-1712

Well into his third decade at Graham Beck Wines, cellarmaster Pieter 'Bubbles' Ferreira says: 'It has been the greatest blessing to be able to make a career of my passion.' In the face of spiralling production costs, he says specialisation is crucial: 'We are reaping the benefits of concentrating on the things we do best.' Cap classique, in his case, a category enjoying fabulous growth: 'It seems to double every five years, so we are investing to make sure we have more bubbles to take to market.' The team's 'no-compromise' approach to quality extends to the still wines, underwritten by bio-friendly methods and conservation efforts, with super-premium The Game Reserve range poised for expansion (donating a percentage of every bottle towards the Graham Beck Nature Reserve).

Icon range

★★★★★ Ad Honorem Oak-spicy **09** (**★★★★★**) *grand vin* is opulent & tarry, with impressive focused dark fruit, weight & length. Has greater shiraz component than noble & silky **07** cab-shiraz blend (72:28).

★★★★☆ Cuvée Clive Flagship of accomplished méthode cap classique sparklings. **07** is creamy courtesy minimum 5 years on lees; elegant, with lemon persistence & freshness. Follows profoundly mineral **05**. Robertson chardonnay (81%) & Firgrove pinot noir. No **06**.

éthode Cap Classique Sparkling range

★★★ Brut Rosé ⓣ Stylish 09 82% pinot noir, chardonnay co-fermented ('a first for South Africa'). Palest onionskin hue, tiny bubbles & strawberry/cherry vivacity.

★★★ Brut Rosé ✓ Strawberry infused **NV** bubbly; latest equal partners chardonnay & pinot. Creamy mousse, savoury & cherry flavours — 'great for salmon or foie gras' says cellarmaster Pieter Ferreira.

★★★ Brut Blanc de Blancs Inviting brioche, clove, lemon aromas & flavours in oak-influenced (just 7% new) **09** from Robertson grapes. Harmonious, elegant but with verve.

★★★ Brut Zero With less than 2g/l sugar, this ultra-dry version gets all its richness & character from 6 years ageing on lees. Robertson chardonnay only in rapier-like, toasty **06** (**★★★★**); **05** included 15% pinot noir, had greater subtlety & 'oystershell' minerality.

rut ★★★★ The house's mainstay **NV**, more chardonnay than pinot in latest bottling versus previous 'slightly ore pinot noir. Easy-sipping aperitif style, with tangy lime thread, few grams sugar smoothing the finish.

liss Demi Sec ★★★ Latest **NV** 53% chardonnay, pinot noir combo enriched by 40g/l sugar. Shy & smooth njoyment for the sweet-toothed.

ltra Premium range

★★★★ Coffeestone Cabernet Sauvignon Dense **09** from Stellenbosch grapes has cassis, tobacco & mint nuance, chalky tannins. As appealing as pristine **07**; will also reward cellaring 3+ years.

★★★★☆ The Ridge Syrah One of area's & SA's top examples. Rigorous barrel selection from Robertson single-vineyard fruit gives **09** spice, lily, red berry complexity, lovely streamlined body & elegant tannins. As expressive & cellarworthy as opulent **08**.

★★★★☆ The Joshua Co-fermented shiraz, 5% viognier cosseted by new French (90%), American oak. **09** shows pedigree of the vintage in muscular structure underpinned by generous dark berry & spicy fruit. Built to improve 5+ years, more so than svelte **08** (**★★★★**). WO Coastal.

★★★★☆ The William Focused **09** (**★★★★**) Cape Blend from Stellenbosch changes formula, is led by shi-raz (44%) with pinotage (30%) plus cab versus shade more aristocratic **08**'s 70/30 cab/pinotage mix. Excellent expression of savoury-sweet fruit; smart 50% new French/American oak detail. Still tight — needs 5+ years.

★★★★ Bowed Head Chenin Blanc 🝐 Preserved quince & almonds in judiciously oaked **11**. Concentrated apricot, white peach flavours from Agter Paarl dryland vineyards, very long. Less barrel-derived than **10**.

★★★★★ Pheasants' Run Sauvignon Blanc 🝐 Much-lauded version from Coastal vines. **12** immediately appeals with cool grass & blackcurrant plus warmer passionfruit & tropical notes. Attention-grabbing acidity coupled with 'wet stone' minerality completes the package. Structured for 3+ years cellaring.

scontinued: **Lonehill Chardonnay**.

he Game Reserve range

★★★★ Cabernet Sauvignon 🝐 Classy **11** sample's serious intent shows in intense aromas, dense fruit core; needs year/2 to shake off unruly tannins. These, too, evident in herbal, taut **10** (**★★★**).

erlot 🝐 **★★ 10**'s plummy centre overwhelmed by gruff tannins. Seems to be flagging — broach soon. 'O Coastal. **Pinotage** ⓣ 🝐 **★★★★ 10** easy-drinking style: ebullient plummy fruit reined in by endly tannins. **Shiraz ★★★ 09** from Stellenbosch, savoury cranberry fruit, creamy vanilla (30% new oak, ome American) & gutsy tannins. **Shiraz-Viognier** 🝐 Not tasted. **Rosé** 🝐 **★★** Tank sample **12** faint sepetal aroma, tangy flavours. WO Robertson. **Chardonnay** ⓣ 🝐 **★★★★** Step up for **10** ex Robert-on. Vanilla, lemon curd nuances; fresh mouthfilling lime flavours, sympathetic oaking. Finer than **09** **★★★★**). **Chenin Blanc** 🝐 **★★★** Provisional rating for **12** tank sample: thatch & boiled sweet aromas; ttractive vinosity & weight. **11** (**★★★★**) packed with spice, acacia & khaki bush, satisfying dry finish. Both om Paarl fruit; lightly oaked. **Sauvignon Blanc** 🝐 **★★★★** Peppery **12** preview shade off intense & ngthy **11** (**★★★★**). Fresh, full flavoured but lacking weight. WO Coastal. **Viognier** ⓣ 🝐 **★★★** Oak r more in play on peach kernel **10** than gently-brushed **09**. Robertson grapes.

essert Wines

★★★★ Rhona Muscadel 🝐 Glorious frangipan & marzipan, grapey sunshine on **11** fortified sweetie. First since **08**, & not as hedonistic but rather poised & elegant. WO Robertson.

scontinued: **Cape LBV**.

remium range

Pinno 😊 🝐 **★★★** 100% pinotage; friendly **11** is fruity & fresh, with light tannin. Anytime red.

hiraz-Cabernet Sauvignon 🝐 This & **Chardonnay-Viognier** for export only. Not reviewed. **Railroad ed** 🝐 **★★★** Budget-friendly **10** preview blend six varieties, slightly warming on the finish. **Waterside**

Unoaked Chardonnay 🏠 📷 ★★★ Lemon-toned **12** is fresh, dry & pleasantly light (12% alcohol) for summer sipping. WO Robertson. — CvZ/MW

Grande Provence Heritage Wine Estate

Location/map: Franschhoek ▪ WO: Franschhoek/Western Cape ▪ Est 1694 ▪ 1stB 2004 ▪ Tasting & sales Mon-Sat 10-6 (Apr-Oct) & 10-7 (Nov-Mar); Sun 10-6 ▪ Fee R20/4 wines, R40/7 wines, R80/food & wine pairing Group tastings in cathedral extension of art gallery (seat up to 120 pax); winemaker tastings in private tasting room (up to 12 pax) ▪ Cellar tours Mon-Fri 11 & 3 Sat/Sun by appt ▪ Grande Provence — The Restaurant (see Restaurants section) ▪ Tour groups ▪ Gift shop ▪ Farm produce ▪ Conferences ▪ Art gallery ▪ Harvest festival The Owner's Cottage at Grande Provence (see Accommodation section) ▪ Owner(s) Dutch & Belgium consortium ▪ Cellarmaster(s) Jaco Marais (Nov 2003) ▪ Winemaker(s) Jaco Marais ▪ Viticulturist(s) Jaco Marais (Ju 2005) ▪ 32ha/22ha (cab, merlot, chard, sauv) ▪ 120t/5,000cs own label 60% red 40% white ▪ PO Box 10, Franschhoek 7690 ▪ enquiries@grandeprovence.co.za ▪ www.grandeprovence.co.za ▪ S 33° 53'57.6"E 19° 06' 10.5" ▪ **T +27 (0)21-876-8600** ▪ F +27 (0)21-876-8601

A traditionally made sparkling wine was due for release as we went to press in late 2012, and no doubt it will serve the traditional function for Grande Provence, which usually has something to celebrate, as well as its customers and guests. Grande by name and grand by nature and design, this historic estate (dating back to 1694) offers luxury accommodation, fine dining and an art gallery – not to mention wine, with and without bubbles.

Premier range

★★★★ **Pinot Noir** Dark-fruited **10** (★★★★) shows super-ripe aromas, then a surprisingly cool but juicy palate with fine mineral undertones. Voluptuous but shade less impressive than **09**.

★★★★ **Shiraz** Finely structured & savoury **08** in modern style, immediately appeals with bacon & black pepper notes; good lingering flavours, but needs more time to integrate oak. Stellenbosch grapes.

★★★★☆ **The Grande Provence** Opulent & concentrated **07** (★★★★) merlot-cab, like **06**. Flamboyant - even a bit over the top! Ultra-ripe stewed red fruit joined by familiar mint, mocha/chocolate from all-new oak.

★★★★ **Chardonnay** 🏠 Big, ripe, rich & buttery **11** with lots of oak on show. Full body, with gentle acidity, good lingering flavours.

Cabernet Sauvignon ★★★★ Usual leafy, minty aromas accompany red fruit, mocha & toasty oak on **09** - the oak dominating in youth the mild flavours. **Sauvignon Blanc** 🏠 ★★★★ Unpretentious but rather smart **12**, balanced & fresh, with typical aromas of cut grass & green fruits. Durbanville grapes. **Chenin Blanc-Viognier** 🏠 **11** available but not tasted. — JPf

Grand Mousseux

Enduring (launched 1929) budget-priced carbonated sparkling brand by Distell.
Vin Doux ★★ Bubbly that's launched a million brides, **NV** fizzy, grapey, sweet, serve well chilled. — DB/HJ

Grangehurst

Location: Somerset West ▪ Map: Helderberg ▪ WO: Stellenbosch ▪ Est/1stB 1992 ▪ Tasting & sales Mon-Fri 9– Sat/Sun 10-3 (plse phone to confirm) ▪ Fee charged for group tastings depends on wines being presented Closed Easter Fri-Mon, Dec 25/26 & Jan 1 ▪ Self-catering guest cottages ▪ Owner(s) Grangehurst Winery (Pty) Ltd ▪ Cellarmaster(s) Jeremy Walker (Jan 1992) ▪ Winemaker(s) Jeremy Walker (Jan 1992), with Gladys Brown (Jan 2002) ▪ ±13ha/6ha own (cab) + 8ha bought in grapes (merlot, p verdot, ptage, shiraz) ▪ 80t 4,500cs own label 90% red 10% rosé + 1,000cs for clients ▪ Brands for clients: Woolworths ▪ PO Box 20, Stellenbosch 7599 ▪ winery@grangehurst.co.za ▪ www.grangehurst.co.za ▪ S 34° 01'02.9" E 018° 49'50.5" **T +27 (0)21-855-3625** ▪ F +27 (0)21-855-2143

'Handcrafted, traditional, unhurried' is the mantra of Jeremy and Mandy Walker's low-key but upper-echelon boutique winery on the Helderberg. One that is maintained thanks to the limited quantities of classically styled reds released only when they've had time to settle into themselves. The current releases are ready to enjoy but should in most cases give pleasure for many years yet. The one wine that isn't quite as red as the others, the Cape Rosé, started life as the family house wine and, according to Jeremy Walker, fills the gap when

you are in the mood for neither white nor red wine'. It makes an ideal
undowner' he suggests, adding: 'It has made many non-rosé drinkers realise
ow enjoyable this style of wine can be.'

rangehurst range

★★★★ **Cabernet Sauvignon Reserve** ⚓ After charming 05, classic 06 (★★★★★) showed bold ripe
tannins, delicate blackcurrant fruit with extended finish. Tasted a few years back.

★★★★☆ **Pinotage** 05 one of most mature on market, still full of fresh charm. Refined though rather exotic
raspberry, Turkish Delight perfume — more in pinot noir vein, as is light-textured, lively palate with its smooth-
tannined conclusion. Includes 14% cab. No 04 made.

★★★★ **Cabernet Sauvignon-Merlot** ⚓ Increased merlot on 05 (now 32%) lends fleshier, more open
texture to lighter-weight fruit. Poised & balanced for lovely current drinking. No 04. 03 (★★★★★).

★★★★☆ **Grangehurst** Cab-led 06 with merlot, petit verdot. Shows usual house-style restraint, also some
pleasing maturity, immediately noticeable in ruby/garnet hue. Gentle meaty, iron features highlighted by balanced freshness, rounded savoury tannins. Good drinking now & for good few years.

★★★★ **Nikela** ⚓ 05 (no 04) announced by pinotage's sweet raspberry scent. Usual partners cab, shiraz &
merlot imbue savouriness, some richness but lacks depth of 03 (★★★★★). Not for much longer keeping.

★★★★☆ **Shiraz-Cabernet Sauvignon Reserve** ⚓ Complex cassis, red pepper, spice, leather & earthy
notes on 05 (★★★★) after finer 03. Tasted a few years back.

★★★★ **Cape Rosé Blend** ✓ 🍴 'Between a light red and a rosé,' says winemaker Jeremy Walker of 11 soft
yet refreshing, lingering multi-varietal blend. Part oaking adds to red-wine feel, not obscuring red fruit. — AL

▪ **Greendale** see Withington
▪ **Greenfields Organic** see Origin Wine
▪ **Green Shebeen** see Org de Rac
▪ **Grimont** see Tulbagh Winery
▪ **Groblershoop** see Orange River Wine Cellars
▪ **Groen Kalahari** see Die Mas van Kakamas

Groenland   🍴 🎋 📷 ♿

ocation/map/WO: Stellenbosch ▪ Est 1932 ▪ 1stB 1997 ▪ Tasting & sales Mon-Fri 10–4 Sat 10–1 ▪ Fee R10pp
or groups of 6+, waived on purchase ▪ Closed Easter Fri/Sun & Dec 25 ▪ Cellar tours by appt ▪ Gift shop ▪ BYO
icnic by appt ▪ Conference/function venue (20-60 pax) ▪ Owner(s) Kosie Steenkamp ▪ Cellarmaster(s) Kosie
teenkamp (Feb 1975) ▪ Winemaker(s) Kosie Steenkamp (Feb 1975), with Piet Steenkamp (Jan 2001) ▪ Viti-
ulturist(s) Piet Steenkamp (Jan 2001) ▪ 190ha/154ha (cab, merlot, ptage, shiraz, chenin, sauv) ▪ 1,500t/
±6,500cs own label 75% red 25% white ▪ BEE level 3, BWI, IPW ▪ PO Box 4 Kuils River 7579 ▪ steenkamp@
roenland.co.za ▪ www.groenland.co.za ▪ S 33° 53'48.9" E 018° 44'5.3" ▪ **T +27 (0)21-903-8203** ▪ F +27
0)21-903-0250/+27 (0)86-571-4969

Wine may not solve problems, but neither does milk, water or cooldrink, says
Groenland's jovial Kosie Steenkamp who makes wine here with his son Piet.
Groenland is known primarily for its merlot, and with this in mind the
teenkamps decided for the first time to age it in new casks and bottle vintage 09
under a premium label — a significant decision for winemakers who pointedly do
not like to make style changes. Wine brings people together, says Kosie, so why
disconcert them by changing the wine they know and love?

Premium range

★★★★ **Merlot** 09, a year on, early fruit-filled exuberance evolving into greater depth & complexity. Minty
mocha tone in harmony with new oak, giving creamy texture. Inviting now, but life for a good few years.

★★★★ **Antoinette Marié** ⚓ 08 equal blend shiraz, cab, merlot; powerful & enhanced by all-new oak.
Concentrated fruit shows more modern approach than classic-styled Groenland range.

Cabernet Sauvignon ★★★★ 08 has developed handsomely after a year in bottle. Plush, dark fruit with
upportive structure. Integrated new oak adds creamy texture, tempting enjoyment earlier than more
estrained 07 (★★★★). **Shiraz** ⚓ ★★★★ 08 now American oak (100% new), absorbs ripeness of vintage,
ich juicy supple tannins, enjoy with hearty meals.

lassic range

Sauvignon Blanc 😊 🍴 📖 ★★★ 12 appealing green fig & tropical tone on lightish crisp quaffer.

Cabernet Sauvignon ✪ ★★★★ 07 juicy & elegant, slightly dusty tones. Balanced & supple supportive stru ture. **Shiraz** ✪ ★★★★ Tighter 07 shows restraint & cool tones with savoury, dusty overlay; food style. **Anto nette Marié** ✪ ★★★★ 08 half shiraz & equal cab/merlot; ripe, with juicy exuberance, pliable tannins, so easy drink! **Chenin Blanc** ✪ ★★★ Ripe, plump 11, apple & marzipan tones, friendly summer quaffer. — MW

Groot Constantia Estate

Location/WO: Constantia ▪ Map: Cape Peninsula ▪ Est 1685 ▪ 1stB 1688 ▪ Tasting & sales daily 9–6 ▪ Fee R2 R35 incl glass, R40 tasting & tour ▪ Closed Good Fri, Dec 25 & Jan 1 ▪ Cellar tours 10-4 on the hour, every hour Simon's at Groot Constantia Restaurant; Jonkershuis Constantia Restaurant (see Restaurants section) ▪ Facil ties for children ▪ Tour groups ▪ Gifts ▪ Conferences ▪ Walks/hikes ▪ Conservation area ▪ Iziko Museum, Man House, historic buildings & orientation centre ▪ Owner(s) Groot Constantia Trust NPC RF ▪ Estate manag Floricus Beukes ▪ Winemaker(s) Boela Gerber (Jan 2001), with Daniel Keulder (Sep 2009) ▪ Viticulturist(Andrew Teubes (2009) ▪ 170ha/±90ha (cab, merlot, ptage, shiraz, chard, Muscat, sauv, sem) ▪ 483t/34,000 ▪ Private Bag X1 Constantia 7848 ▪ enquiries@grootconstantia.co.za ▪ www.grootconstantia.co.za ▪ S 34° 36.5" E 018° 25' 27.3" ▪ **T** +27 (0)21-794-5128 ▪ **F** +27 (0)21-794-1999

There can be no more illustrious backstory than that of this jewel of the Peninsula the home of Cape wine's founding father, Simon van der Stel. It is at the heart of th narrative from the very beginning, through the great era of Hendrik Cloete world-famous Constantia wines, favoured by Europe's kings and courtiers, to it eventual purchase by the government in 1885 and current stewardship by the G Trust. The vineyards, which weathered the ravages of oidium in 1859 and phyllox era later, have been producing wine since 1688. The modern era has seen substan tial replanting of the vineyards and a steady increase in wine quality. Plans are t optimise the tourism potential, with tasting room upgrades in the pipeline.

Gouverneurs range
★★★★ **Reserve Red** 🎖 Steely minerality on 10 4-way Bordeaux-type blend indicates classical stylin Refined & complex, with dark depths & aromatic lightness, challenging the senses. Fine effort in difficult vintag rewarding attention to detail.

★★★★ **Reserve White** 🎖 Brazenly oaky 11 semillon-dominated Bordeaux-style blend has impressiv creamy/chalky texture, bold floral-tinged passionfruit & persistent bone-dry finish. Should benefit from ageing
Discontinued: **Shiraz**, **Sauvignon Blanc**.

Groot Constantia range
★★★★ **Merlot** 🎖 10 offers earthy, meaty aromas, followed by sweet ripe berry fruit. Classy well-modu lated body & texture suggest good ageing potential.

★★★★ **Shiraz** 🎖 Meaty thumper with liquorice & peppery notes, 10 (★★★★☆) big & bold, with hef tannins wrapped around muscular body. Serious intent showing, but needs time. More defined than 09.

★★★★☆ **Chardonnay** 🎖 Seriously-conceived barrel-fermented 11 beginning to emerge through heav oak mantle, showing appealingly complex citrus fruit mix: marmalade, lime cordial, lemon curd. Neatly avoic New World clichés, shows potential for graceful ageing.

★★★★☆ **Sauvignon Blanc** 🎖 Hot-off-the-press 12 (★★★★) needs time to settle, but already showin forceful pungent nettles on solid structured platform. Less subtle complexity than 11.

★★★★ **Méthode Cap Classique** Distinctive house style beginning to emerge in cream-textured 08 all chardonnay sparkling. Apple tart tinged with brioche, showing extended (3-year) lees-ageing.

★★★★☆ **Grand Constance** Intensely floral, spicy recreation of classic Constantia unfortified/botrytise dessert, 09 flaunts muscat de Frontignan's perfumed sensuality. Seductive yet focused, balanced & finely moc ulated. Partly sun-dried grapes, barrel fermented & matured.

Cabernet Sauvignon 🎖 ★★★★ After classically formed 09 (★★★★), meaty, tarry notes on 10 refle lighter vintage, underscored by honest black fruit & solid structure. Angular tannins should soften with time **Pinotage** Await next. **Constantia Rood** 🎖 ★★★ Six-way lower-tier blend 10 is light bodied & juicy, wit touch of wild berries & oak spiciness. **Blanc de Noir** 🎖 ★★★ 12 dry blush from merlot & cab shows goc fruit intensity, appealing crispness. Fresh & cheerful. **Semillon-Sauvignon Blanc** 🎖 ★★★★ Unoaked 1 Bordeaux-style blend has more immediate appeal than serious big brother. Light & fresh faced. **Cape Rub Port** 🎖 ★★★★ 'Port' last time. Dense & spicy, with tannic grip, 10 from touriga shows tobacco & mulberr syrup on modestly sweet winter warmer. — GdB

■ **Grootdrink** *see* Orange River Wine Cellars

■ **Groot Eiland** *see uniWines Vineyards*

Groote Post Vineyards

ocation: Darling ▪ Map: Durbanville, Philadelphia & Darling ▪ WO: Darling/Coastal ▪ 1stB 1999 ▪ Tasting, sales cellar tours Mon-Fri 9–5 Sat/Sun & pub hols 10–4 ▪ Fee R20 for groups of 10+ ▪ Closed Good Fri, Dec 25 & Jan ▪ Hilda's Kitchen open for lunch Wed-Sun, booking essential ▪ Facilities for children ▪ BYO picnic ▪ Conferences ▪ Walks/hikes ▪ Conservation area & bird hide ▪ Owner(s) Peter & Nicholas Pentz ▪ Winemaker(s) Lukas Wentzel (Nov 2000) ▪ Viticulturist(s) Jannie de Clerk (1999), advised by Johan Pienaar ▪ 4,000ha/107ha (cabs f, merlot, pinot, shiraz, chard, chenin, riesling, sauv, sem) ▪ 580t/32,000cs own label ▪ Brands for clients: Woolworths ▪ PO Box 103 Darling 7345 ▪ wine@grootepost.co.za ▪ www.grootepost.com ▪ S 33° 29'0.5" E 18° 24'35.0" ▪ **T +27 (0)22-492-2825** ▪ F +27 (0)22-492-2693

Within the Old Man's Blend range, a particular success at tastings has been the Rosé sparkling. The 'Old Man' referred to here, and affectionately so called by his children, is co-owner and patriarch Peter Pentz. His role has been particularly crucial in farm affairs, because this was once a large and famous dairy farm, earning Peter the title in 1998 of SA Farmer of the Year. He sold the dairy herd in 2001 to concentrate on winefarming, claiming the decision was helped by the fact that in his 50 years of dairy farming, nobody had ever come up to him in the street to say 'Peter, last night I had a great bottle of your milk!'.

Reserve range

★★★★ **Pinot Noir** ⊕ **09**, now bottled, lost none of its charm or elegance & refinement but quite restrained, has a delicacy that suggests earlier drinking rather than keeping.

★★★★ **Wooded Chardonnay** 🖉 More elegant, restrained than intense **09** (★★★★☆), yet has plenty of interest. **11** shows roasted almonds & stonefruit, gliding to a smooth juicy-fresh conclusion. No **10**.

★★★★ **Sauvignon Blanc Reserve** ✓ 🖉 Selection of top vineyard blocks. Gooseberry & sliced apple, **11**'s extended lees-ageing shows in a palate fullness, light savoury overlay. Nice livening hint of fynbos on the finish.

Groote Post range

★★★★☆ **Shiraz** ✓ 🖉 Going for class rather than show, **11** has the fruit concentration, oak spicing, complex nuances you'd expect, but here it is seamlessly knit into a svelte, harmonious whole with consummate skill.

★★★★ **Unwooded Chardonnay** ✓ 🖉 Catering for a growing market, **11** shows the variety's essential self, a citrus mix & pervading freshness that begs creative food matching. No need for oak trappings, it's lovely.

★★★★ **Chenin Blanc** ✓ 🗏 🖉 Previewed **12** shows a change in style from **11**'s fresh fruit to something richer, riper, melon & stonefruit, without losing the zinging freshness that bodes well for ageing. WO Coastal.

★★★★ **Riesling** ✓ 🖉 **12**'s (★★★★☆) nervy tension shows skilful winemaking to capture such intensity, purity; improves on **10**. Quince & ginger, a tangy texture as the high acid & 21g/l sugar combine, leaving an extended fruitiness. No **11**.

★★★★ **Sauvignon Blanc** ✓ 🗏 Pre-bottling expressive **12** unfolds mineral & gooseberry perfume in the glass, vivid lime-spiked flavours, tangy & long.

Merlot 🖉 ★★★ Grippier than previous, but fruit is there in **11**'s blackberry & cedar profile. Could age 3-4 years, still in its youthful prime. **Noble Late Harvest** Await new vintage.

The Old Man's Blend range

★★★★ **The Old Man's Blend Red** 🗏 🖉 Mainly cab, merlot, giving early-drinking **11** (★★★★) red berries & plums, a soft juicy palate, light grip. Simpler than **10**.

★★★★ **The Old Man's Blend White** ✓ 🗏 🖉 Successful sauvignon, chenin, semillon combo in **12** captures litchi & lime vibrancy, gives the complete drinking enjoyment it was created to do. This, red, WO Coastal.

The Old Man's Sparkle Brut Rosé Méthode Cap Classique ★★★★ Copper-hued latest **NV** now with 12% pinot noir, rest chardonnay. Red berry flavoured & crisply dry, a good anytime sparkler. — CR

■ **Groot Geluk** *see Villiera Wines*

Groot Parys Estate

ocation/WO: Paarl ▪ Map: Paarl & Wellington ▪ Est 1699 ▪ 1stB 1709 ▪ Tasting & sales by appt ▪ Owner(s) Eric Verhaak, Mariëtte Ras & Peter Ras ▪ Viticulturist(s) Gawie Kriel (consultant) ▪ 81ha/45ha (ptage, ruby cab, chard, chenin, cbard) ▪ 105t 90% white 10% rosé ▪ CERES internationally certified organic ▪ PO Box 82 Huguenot 7645 ▪ rootparys@wam.co.za ▪ www.grootparys.co.za ▪ S 33° 44'48.0" E 018° 58'41.6" ▪ **T +27 (0)72-480-9550**

A great love of both chenin and organic farming has become the main driver in the life of Groot Parys' Dutch co-owner, Mariette Ras. Regarding the chenin, she feels that South Africa has only scratched the surface of the variety's potential both locally and internationally. She also thinks that being relatively small inoculates Groot Parys against 'trends', leaving them free to continue pursuing their dream of growing and making wine with integrity and without manipulation.

Die Tweede Droom range

★★★★ **Chenin Blanc Vatgegis** 🏵 Quirky styled, just-dry, smoky **11** (★★★★) not as concentrated & harmonious as **09** (no **10**). Lively acidity provides good food match, oak adds breadth.

★★★★ **Straw Wine** 🏵 Unctuous, characterful, orange marmalade dessert **11** from 30 year old chenin bushvines, air-dried. Integrated all-new oak. Deliciously long finish.

Chardonnay Vatgegis 🏵 ★★★★ Was 'Wooded Wild Yeast' (similarly with Chenin Vatgegis). Rounded peachy **11** has integrated oak, vibrant citrus acidity & focusing steely backbone. **Chardonnay Unwooded** 🍷🏵 Next awaited. **Chenin Blanc Dopkontak** NEW 🏵🌿 ★★★★ **11** made with plenty of skin & lees contact, natural yeast & new oak, resulting in quirky, nutty lowish-alcohol wine, with fino sherry tanginess. **Chenin Blanc Unwooded Wild Yeast** ⊕🍷🏵 ★★★ Unpretentious, light & zesty **11** preview.

Groot Parys range NEW

Rosé Unwooded 🏵 ★★ Adds 'Unwooded' for zingy, dry, characterful **12** preview from ruby cab. **Chenin Blanc Unwooded** 🏵 Tank sample **12** too unsettled to rate. —IM

Groupe CDV

Location: Somerset West ▪ WO: Western Cape/Swartland/Stellenbosch ▪ Est/1stB 2006 ▪ Closed to public ▪ Owner(s) Groupe LFE BV Netherlands ▪ Cellarmaster(s) Nicky Versfeld (consultant) ▪ 600,000c own label 60% red 35% white 5% rosé ▪ Fairtrade ▪ PO Box 88 Somerset Mall 7137 ▪ rob@groupelfe.co.za ▪ www groupelfe.co.za ▪ **T +27 (0)21-850-0160** ▪ F +27 (0)21-851-3578

'Groupe LFE (La Français Expédition), roughly translated as French Wine Exporters, not really appropriate for a South African outfit!' comments MD Rob Coppoolse on the recent name change to Groupe CDV (Cape Dutch Vignerons still part of Groupe LFE, based in the Netherlands). Current production is 9m bottles, having doubled in the last few years, and volumes continue to grow. 'This represents a lot of hard work, it didn't come for nothing!'

Berghuis range

Cabernet Sauvignon ⊕🍷🏵 ★★ Undemanding ripe-fruited **10**, lightly oaked. Stellenbosch WOs for these. **Pinotage Rosé** ⊕🍷🏵 ★★ **10** delicate strawberry notes, satisfactory dry end mid-2011. **Chenin Blanc** ⊕🍷🏵 ★★ Light-textured **11**, peachy lunchtime white.

Centennial 5 Barrel Reserve range

Shiraz ⊕ ★★★ Vibrant **08** red berries & savoury nuances; ripe creamy tannins for early enjoyment.

Elephantasy range

Big Ears Dry Red ⊕ Await new, as for **Long Nose Gewürztraminer**. **Short Tail Rosé** ⊕🍷🏵 ★★ **11** perky dry rosé, light strawberry summer sipper. **Long Nose Dry White** ⊕🍷🏵 ★★ **11** light easy-drinker from chenin, with intriguing dusty herb hint.

Groupe LFE South Africa range

Grâce Blanche Natural Sweet ⊕🍷🏵 ★★★ Juicy, sweet & easy-to-drink **10** from chenin, offers ripe apricot & lime.

Kaaps Geskenk range

Cape Red ⊕🍷🏵 ★ **10** earthy red berries in uncomplicated braai red. **Cape Rosé** ⊕🍷🏵 ★★ **11** dry, strawberry-toned lunchtime sipper. **Cape White** ⊕🍷🏵 ★★ **11** light textured picnic partner from chenin.

Klein Kasteelberg Private Bin range

Merlot ⊕🍷🏵 ★★ Ripe & dark berried, hint of chocolate on **10**. WO Swartland, as all these. **Pinotage** ⊕🍷🏵 ★★★ Fresh mulberry-toned, **10** juicy & accessible. **Expresso Mokka Pinotage** Not reviewed, nor was **Shiraz-Rosé**. **Chardonnay** ⊕🍷🏵 ★★ Brisk & fresh **10** with lemon/lime twist. **Secco** ⊕ ★★★ Bouncy peach-toned **NV**, dry & lightly spritzy.

Klein Kasteelberg range

Merlot ⊕ 🗄 🗵 ★★ **10** plum & milk chocolate on easy quaffer. Swartland WO, as all these. **Pinotage** ⊕ 🗄 🗵 ★★ Plum, prune & pepper combo in **10**, enough tannins for hearty fare. **Shiraz Rosé** ⊕ 🗄 🗵 ★★ Fresh & dry **10** with candyfloss flavour. **Chardonnay** ⊕ 🗄 🗵 ★★★ Unwooded **10**, pleasant melon & marmalade with nutty overlay. **Chenin Blanc** ⊕ 🗄 🗵 ★★★ **10** softly dry & fresh cling peach-toned thirst quencher.

Songloed range

Pinotage-Ruby Cabernet ⊕ ★★ **10**, ripe & dark-berried, nice fruity mouthful. **Shiraz-Merlot** ⊕ 🗄 🗵 ★★★ Earthy & savoury intro, followed by mulberry & black cherry in **10**. **Shiraz-Merlot Rosé** ⊕ 🗄 🗵 ★★ Coral pink **10** fresh & crisp with hints of spicy strawberry. **Colombar-Chardonnay** ⊕ ★★ Accessible **10** crisp with fresh summer fruit. **Chenin Blanc-Viognier** Not ready at press time. — DB

Grünberger

Introduced 60 years ago, the flattish, rounded 'bocksbeutel' flagon, first of its kind in South Africa, remains a feature of this Natural Sweet range by Distell.

> **Freudenlese** ☺ ★★★ Honey-sweet, fragrant mix sauvignon & gewürztraminer, **12** rosewater & Turkish Delight flavours, low 7.5% alc. Perfect wine for korma.

Spritziger ★★ Spritzy **12**, lightish, off-dry yet crisp white from chenin. WO W Cape, as for all. **Spritziger Rosé** ★★ Pinotage does the rouging for lightish, slightly spritzy **12**, fresher than last, berry tang offsets the sweetness. **Rosenlese** ★★★ Very pleasant sweet rosé with colour & wine gum hint from cab, **12** light (8% alcohol), delicate jasmine flavours. — DB/HJ

Grundheim Wines

Location: Oudtshoorn ▪ Map: Klein Karoo & Garden Route ▪ WO: Klein Karoo/Western Cape ▪ Est/1stB 1995 ▪ Tasting & sales Mon-Fri 9-5 Sat 9-1 ▪ Fee R15 for groups of 10+ ▪ Closed Easter Fri/Sun, Dec 25 & Jan 1 ▪ Owner(s) Danie Grundling ▪ Winemaker(s) Dys Grundling (1997) ▪ 25ha (cinsaut, muscadel r/w, ruby cab, tinta, touriga, cbard, hanepoot, palomino) ▪ 360t/10,000L own label 100% fortified ▪ PO Box 400 Oudtshoorn 6620 ▪ grundheim@absamail.co.za ▪ S 33°37'40.1" E 022°3'54.6" ▪ **T +27 (0)44-272-6927** ▪ F +27 (0)86-616-6311

Aside from fortified dessert wines, the Grundling family makes a speciality of witblits, South Africa's fiery eau de vie, with a range which includes buchu- and chilli-infused varieties. If names like 'Bite' and 'Firehose' aren't sufficient warning, the labels additionally portray owner Danie Grundling's Withond (Bull Terrier): 'Once it bites, it doesn't let go,' kindly explains the lady of the house.

★★★★ **Rosyntjiewyn** 🗵 Was 'Red Jerepiko'. **11** (★★★) touriga is very sweet, & though checked by firm tannin, misses crispness & alcohol punch of previous **NV**, which included pinotage. WO W Cape, as next.
★★★★ **Late Bottled Vintage** Commendable & complex winter-warming port-style from touriga & tinta. **09** (★★★★), first since **05** (only touriga), is richly fruity & textured but needs time to settle, harmonise in bottle.
Red Muscadel 🗵 No new vintage dated. Rosepetal-nuanced **11** fortified firesider is extremely sweet, doesn't linger. **White Muscadel** 🗵 ★★★ Clean & pure flavours of fresh grapes & orange rind on satisfying **12** fortified sweetie. **Cape Ruby Port** ⊕ ★★★ Easy-drinking **NV** from touriga, spiced plum jam, balanced finish. **Cape Vintage Port** ⊕ ★★★★ Bit soft for style, but **09** good dense fruit from touriga, layered with chocolate. **White Port** NEW ★★★ Fortified chenin aged year in old brandy barrels. **10** fynbos & almond notes, with honey-slathered yellow plum & pear, lovely sweet/savoury contrast in the tail. — WB/JP

■ **Grysberg** *see* Wandsbeck Wyne Koöp Bpk
■ **G Spot** *see* United Nations of Wine

Guardian Peak Wines

Location/map: Stellenbosch ▪ WO: Stellenbosch/Western Cape ▪ Est 1998 ▪ 1stB 2000 ▪ Tasting & sales Mon-Sun 9-5 ▪ Closed Easter Fri/Sun, Dec 25 & Jan 1 ▪ Guardian Peak Winery & Grill restaurant (see Restaurants section) ▪ Owner(s) Jean Engelbrecht ▪ Winemaker(s) Philip van Staden (Jan 2009), with Jacques Maree (Jan 2009) ▪ Viticulturist(s) Dirkie Mouton (Jun 2010) ▪ 25,000cs own label 100% red ▪ Brands for clients: Pick's Pick ▪ IPW ▪ PO Box 473 Stellenbosch 7599 ▪ info@guardianpeak.com ▪ www.guardianpeak.com ▪ S 34°0'40. 19" E 018°50'31.99" ▪ **T +27 (0)21-881-3899** ▪ F +27 (0)21-881-3388

Entering into long-term contracts with grape growers is a way not only of ensuring longevity and consistency of supply but also enabling this Helderberg winery (and restaurant) to truly reflect a sense of place from vintage to vintage, says owner Jean Engelbrecht (also proprietor of highly regarded Rust en Vrede nearby). The wines below continue their palate-friendly fruit abundance yet alcohol levels are toned down slightly from previous years. The future will still be rampantly red, and the desire remains to turn people on to enjoying the wine lifestyle and culture.

★★★★ **Lapa Cabernet Sauvignon** 10 is once more rich, powerful & elegant. Silky mouthfeel with cassis abundance & spicy nuance. Integration of fruit & wood is superb now but will also reward patience.

★★★★ **SMG** Shiraz-led 10 with mourvèdre, grenache in a minor role (8%). Clove & cherry abundance with grip & power reining it in. Refined yet chunky too. Some Piekenierskloof fruit, as in ultra-ripe 09 (★★★★).

★★★★ **Frontier** 3-way cab, shiraz & merlot blend shows a herbal edge in 11. Plum & tobacco flavours mingle with tar & smoky depth. Body, length & structure are all there. Polished yet savoury.

★★★★ **Tannat-Malbec** Reverses name in 09 for 60% tannat. Sappy yet firm, with juicy edge. Bold, but more classic & dry than some here, grippy & savoury. Wellington/Stellenbosch fruit, plenty of oak (60% new).

Merlot ★★★★ Lithe-but-yielding appeal to approachable 11. Neither too big nor small, ample black fruit, freshness & structure. WO W Cape. **Shiraz** ★★★★ Sweet ripe fruit on 11 impresses, then spice kicks in & ups the attraction. Vibrant, with fine tannin, good body & tasty length. — FM

- **Gugu** see Belbon Hills Private Cellar
- **Guinea Fowl** see Saxenburg Wine Farm
- **Guru** see Hoopenburg Wines
- **Gwendolyn** see Saxenburg Wine Farm
- **Hagelsberg** see Middelvlei Estate

Halala Afrika Wines

These are the export wines (the name means 'Celebrate Africa') of highly rated Paarl producer Rudera, intended for early and easy drinking.

Shiraz ★★★ Now-bottled 10 shows ripeness, with plum & malty overtones, slightly sweet finish, amenably firm tannins. Ready for drinking. **Chenin Blanc** ★★★ Full-of-body 12 full of flavour & character too: white & yellow peaches, grenadilla zing; viognier component adds weight, slipperiness. — CvZ

Hamilton Russell Vineyards

Location: Hermanus ▪ Map: Elgin, Walker Bay & Bot River ▪ WO: Hemel-en-Aarde Valley ▪ Est 1975 ▪ 1stB 1981 ▪ Tasting & sales Mon-Fri 9–5 Sat 9–1 ▪ Closed Easter Fri/Mon, Dec 26 & Jan 1 ▪ Tours by appt ▪ Fynbos reserve & 2 wetlands ▪ Owner(s) Anthony Hamilton Russell ▪ Winemaker(s) Hannes Storm (2004) ▪ Viticulturist(s) Johan Montgomery (2005) ▪ 170ha/52ha (pinot, chard) ▪ 9,352cs own label 50% red 50% white ▪ BWI Champion ▪ PO Box 158 Hermanus 7200 ▪ hrv@hermanus.co.za ▪ www.hamiltonrussellvineyards.com ▪ S 34° 23' 23.0" E 019° 14' 30.6" ▪ **T +27 (0)28-312-3595** ▪ F +27 (0)28-312-1797

Anthony Hamilton Russell has been at the helm of this Hemel-en-Aarde Valley pioneer for 21 years but, standing in the nature reserve above the estate and looking south over Walker Bay towards the Antarctic ('with nothing in-between') and north over the vineyards towards Babylonstoring Mountain, he admits to 'still being overwhelmed'. Hand axes from 1.5 million years ago can be found, 'as if dropped the day before', among the vines on the surface of 500-million-year-old Bokkeveld shale soils. Late Stone Age rubbing stones litter a site where the sandstone soil meets the clay. A Portuguese cross from the 15th century is carved into a rock overlooking the bay. 'Water once flowed here. What a place!' His pinot noir and chardonnay, now in their 30th vintages, reflect this unique location, and are appreciated around the world for the story of place they have to tell.

★★★★ **Pinot Noir** Compact 10 juxtaposes power & restraint: raspberry/cherry core well-wrapped in assertive & yet controlled tannins; augurs well for 5+ years. 09 (★★★★★) more silken, supple.

★★★★☆ **Chardonnay** Always among SA's best. Stately barrel-fermented 11 (★★★★★), 30th vintage, so tightly wound, precise & pure it almost defies description. Perfectly judged oak embraces citrus fruit & pinpoint acidity, extends the mineral finish. Only 13% alcohol, with 10+ years ahead, like fragrant 10. — CvZ

Hannay Wines

Location/WO: Elgin ▪ Map: Elgin, Walker Bay & Bot River ▪ Est/1stB 2011 ▪ Tasting & sales Mon-Fri 9-5 Sat/Sun/ after hours by appt only ▪ Fee R10 for groups of 10+ ▪ Closed Easter Fri-Mon & Dec 25 ▪ Cellar tours by appt ▪ BYO picnic ▪ Light/buffet lunches & picnics by appt ▪ Owner(s) Malcolm J Dicey ▪ Cellarmaster(s) Catherine Marshall (Jan 2011, consultant) ▪ Winemaker(s) Catherine Marshall (Jan 2011, consultant), with Shaun Fortuin (Jan 2011, consultant) ▪ Viticulturist(s) Johan Viljoen (Jan 2011, consultant) ▪ 72ha/20ha ▪ 150t mostly sold to other cellars, own label 50% red 50% white ▪ WIETA, IPW ▪ PO Box 36 Elgin 7680 ▪ info@valleygreen.co.za, elzaan@ valleygreen.co.za ▪ S 34° 12' 12.07" E 19° 02' 35.10" ▪ **T +27 (0)21-848-9770** ▪ F +27 (0)86-718-2203

Based at Elgin farm Valley Green (under which name it debuted in the last edition), owner Malcolm Dicey's wine venture is a radical jump from Hex River table grape farming, and a self-imposed challenge to grow vines in a cooler climate. Vineyard rejuvenation and sustainable techniques are focuses, and a biodynamic approach inspired by a visit to Burgundy is being phased in. The brand name Hannay honours Malcolm's mother, who passed away two days after lending it her name.

Cabernet Franc NEW 🌢 ★★★ Soundly crafted **11** has pleasant body & shape, but lacks varietal definition. Spicy berry juice with firm tannin cloak. **Sauvignon Blanc** 🍴 🌢 ★★★★ Promising 2nd release **12** still unsettled mid-2012 but showing substance & complexity, & a lingering finish. — GdB

■ **Harmony Tree** *see* United Nations of Wine

Harrison Hope

Location: Queenstown ▪ Est 2000 ▪ 1stB 2009 ▪ Tasting & tours by appt ▪ Accommodation ▪ Owner(s) Ronnie & Janet Vehorn ▪ Cellarmaster(s)/winemaker(s)/viticulturist(s) Ronnie Vehorn ▪ 2ha (merlot, ptage, chard) ▪ 1,000s own label ▪ PO Box 1394 Queenstown 5320 ▪ rvehorn@gmail.com ▪ www.harrisonhope.com ▪ S 32 10' 01.11" E 026 50' 28.28" ▪ **T +27 (0)40-842-9444/+27 (0)82-808-5284** ▪ F +27 (0)40-842-9200

No new wines to taste this edition, but Ronnie and Janet Vehorn of Harrison's Hope are still in business, and in June trekked down to the Eastern Cape coast to showcase their slowly but surely expanding public offering at The Wine Show Road Show event in Port Elizabeth.

Hartenberg Estate

Location/map/WO: Stellenbosch ▪ Est/1stB 1978 ▪ Tasting & sales Mon-Fri 9-5 (Nov-Easter 9-5.30) Sat 9-3 Sun (Dec-Easter only) 10-4 ▪ Closed Good Fri, Dec 25 & Jan 1 ▪ Tasting fee for groups, refunded with purchase ▪ Cellar tours by appt ▪ Picnics & lunches 12-2.15: daily seasonal blackboard menus, charcuterie, cheese platters ▪ Facilities for children ▪ Farm produce ▪ Conference facility by appt only ▪ Walking/hiking trail ▪ Bird watching ▪ Bottelary Renosterveld Conservancy ▪ Monthly tapas & jazz evenings in summer; monthly lazy Sunday lunches in winter ▪ Owner(s) Hartenberg Holdings ▪ Cellarmaster(s) Carl Schultz (Nov 1993) ▪ Winemaker(s) Patrick Ngamane (Jan 2001), with Oscar Robyn (Nov 2003) ▪ Viticulturist(s) Wilhelm Joubert (May 2006) ▪ 187ha/85ha (cab, merlot, shiraz, chard, riesling, sauv) ▪ 550t/30-40,000c own label 80% red 20% white ▪ BWI, IPW ▪ PO Box 12756 Die Boord 7613 ▪ info@hartenbergestate.com ▪ www.hartenbergestate.com ▪ S 33° 53'52.5" E 018° 47'30.4" ▪ **T +27 (0)21-865-2541** ▪ F +27 (0)21-865-2153

Eleanor Finlayson developed winemaking on this Bottelary Hills property (then known as Montagne) from the 1950s and her pioneering efforts are recognised in the top-end chardonnay, The Eleanor. Similarly, the labours of subsequent owners Ken Mackenzie and daughters Fiona and Tanya in building a culture of excellence are celebrated with The Stork Shiraz (Ken's air force call sign) and The Mackenzie red blend. Now at the respected zenith of Cape wine production, the current management team strives to maintain such distinction. A new entry-level shiraz — The Doorkeeper — extends the cellar's focus on the variety, while The Stork 2008 won France's prestigious 2012 Syrah du Monde to confirm its top-drawer status. Culinary developments include a full-time chef to upgrade the mealtime offerings as well as the tasting room food-and-wine-pairings. The annual Riesling Rocks and Shiraz & Charcuterie festivals are already industry benchmarks.

Ultra Premium range

★★★★☆ **Gravel Hill Shiraz** One of a quintet of very different shirazes. This is from estate's best site — dry, gravelly, strewn with koffieklip ('coffee stones') — yielding appropriately mineral, savoury, elegant shiraz. **08** is winemaking at its apogee; ethereal, spicy, very polished, with powerful fullness of flavour.

Super Premium range

★★★★☆ **The Stork Shiraz** An Aussie-style extrovert from heavier clay soil, in marked contrast to Gravel Hill: **09** is open — almost gulpable — but pimento-toned spice regiments the boisterous berry fruit & vanilla-oak (2 years all-new barrels) to retain elegance.

★★★★☆ **The Mackenzie** Previously listed with 'Cabernet Sauvignon-Merlot' suffix. **09** is mainly cab (85%), splashes merlot & petit verdot. The classic red Bordeaux associations — cigarbox, pencil lead, clean blackcurrant — all apply. Immense, yet understated in youth, like **08**.

★★★★☆ **The Eleanor Chardonnay** Stately restraint to wonderful depth of flavour, firm minerality & a year's all-new French oak give gravitas to enduring, viscous finish of **09**. Shows more as 'fine white wine of the world' than obvious New-World chardonnay.

Snuffbox Merlot Await new vintage.

CWG Auction Reserves

★★★★☆ **Loam Hill Merlot** NEW Serious but ready-to-play **09** has voluptuous floral/violet features & a savoury smoked meat depth. Deliciously drinkable at table now, should mature 4-7 years with great interest.

★★★★☆ **Shiraz** NEW Two best barrels of Gravel Hill melded with single best cask of The Stork to reach stupendous heights. The former's muscular body (2 years 100% new oak) is well apparelled with the berry fruit of the latter in brilliant **09**'s layered complexity.

Premium range

★★★★ **Cabernet Sauvignon** ✓ High-toned blackcurrant fruit in elegant framework (60% new oak), svelte **09** is fresh & accessible but will reward few years patience.

★★★★ **Shiraz** Textured but fruitier than shiraz siblings; **09** beautifully measured in athletic, carry-no-excess-baggage style. Still juicy though, with pliable tannins to boot.

★★★★ **Chardonnay** ✓ 🍸 The oak (French, 40% new) of **10** still obvious mid-2012, but its full yet elegant form is toned with lemon/lime flavours & given length by savoury complexity.

★★★★ **Riesling** ✓ 🍸 Respected track record of quality continues in **11**; delicate stonefruit flavours freshened by fresh acid grip, & dry finish satisfies mealtime partnerships.

Merlot New bottling not ready. **Doorkeeper Shiraz** NEW ✓ 🍸 ★★★★ Entry-level offering; **10** gentle, enough spice & sweet fruit for savoury frame, with tannins for a few years. **Cabernet Sauvignon-Shiraz** ✓ 🍸 ★★★★ Enduring favourite; **10** smoky plum aromas & sweet berry flavours with elegance. Delicious, it punches above its weight. **Sauvignon Blanc** ✓ 🍸 ★★★★ Bone-dry **11** gently tropical & less steely, like **10**. — DS

Hartswater Wine Cellar 🍷

Location: Hartswater ▪ Map: Northern Cape, Free State & North West ▪ WO: Northern Cape ▪ Tasting & sales Mon-Fri 8.30-1, 2-5 ▪ Sales also from outlet in Hartswater town; orders delivered to liquor stores in Northern Cape (350km radius), Free State & North West ▪ Cellar tours by appt ▪ Owner(s) Orange River Wine Cellars ▪ Winemaker(s) Deon Truter ▪ 1,200t ▪ PO Box 2335 Hartswater 8570 ▪ deon@wynkelder.co.za ▪ S 27° 55' 2.2" E 024° 49' 38.2" ▪ **T +27 (0)53-474-0700** ▪ F +27 (0)53-474-0975

Though recently acquired by Orange River Wine Cellars, this Northern Cape winery continues to operate independently. Winemaker Deon Truter, who moved here from ORWC some 6 years ago, is leaving no stone unturned in an effort to offer budget-conscious winelovers the best-quality products at affordable prices.

Elements range

Earth 🍸 ★★ Juicy, fruity, light-bodied off-dry ruby cab **NV** red. **Fire** 🍸 ★★ Fully sweet **NV** rosé ruby cab. **Wind** 🍸 ★★ Dry, lightish **NV** white from colombard is pleasant & undemanding. **Rain** 🍸 ★★ Easygoing sweet **NV** colombard, with modest 10.5% alcohol. **Thunder** 🍸 ★★ Sweet, lightish **NV** ruby cab. Discontinued: **Cabernet Sauvignon**, **Chenin Blanc**, **Chardonnay-Colombar**.

Overvaal range

Red Jerepico ★★★ Extremely sweet **NV** ruby cab fortified dessert is rescued by firm spirit grip. **White Jerepico** ⊕ 🍸 ★★ Fleshy raisin sweetness, **NV** fortified from fernão pires. — GdB

Haskell Vineyards

Location/map/WO: Stellenbosch ▪ Est 2002 ▪ 1stB 2008 ▪ Tasting & sales Tue-Fri 9-5 Sat/Sun 10-5 ▪ Fee R40 — only for tasting on weekends ▪ Closed Mon, Easter Fri-Mon, Dec 25 & Jan 1 ▪ Cellar tours on special request only ▪ The Long Table Restaurant & Café Tue-Sun 9-5; light dinners Fri (Sep-Mar) — booking essential ▪ Facilities for children ▪ Self-catering accommodation in 'The Residence' ▪ Owner(s) Preston Haskell ▪ Cellarmaster(s) Rianie Strydom (Jan 2005) ▪ Winemaker(s)/viticulturist(s) Wikus Pretorius (Dec 2005) ▪ 25ha/13.5ha (cabs s/f, merlot, shiraz, chard) ▪ ±80t/1,800cs own label 80% red 20% white ▪ PO Box 12766 Die Boord 7613 ▪ info@haskellvineyards.com ▪ www.haskellvineyards.com ▪ S 34° 0' 13.9" E 018° 51' 38.4" ▪ **T +27 (0)21-881-3895** ▪ F +27 (0)21-881-3986

American Preston Haskell bought this prime Helderberg property, located in Stellenbosch's renowned 'golden triangle', in 2002. It took six years before he and the team were happy that this premium range — sibling to separately listed Dombeya — produced the quality they envisioned. The Pillars Syrah burnished Haskell's already burgeoning reputation by being the first South African wine ever to trounce its Australian and New Zealand counterparts for top honours in the 2009 Tri-Nations Challenge. So how to ratchet quality up even further? GM/winemaker Wikus Pretorius and oeno-consultant Rianie Strydom believe that splitting the Pillars vineyard in two, farming one half organically and the other biodynamically will reap the results they seek. And all other wines in the range will benefit from the lessons learned.

★★★★★ **Pillars Syrah** Sensuous, textured & concentrated **10** (★★★★☆) follows brilliant **08** (no **09**). Intense, brooding yet silky & expressive refined black fruit. Perfumed & complex, with restraint in oaking evident. Glorious long finish.

★★★★☆ **Aeon Syrah** Expressive floral & spice abundance, **10** (★★★★) ample vibrant black fruit intensity & concentration but oak is tad prominent, needs time to knit. **08** more heady. **09** not made.

★★★★ **Haskell IV** Cab leads merlot, petit verdot & cab franc in sophisticated Bordeaux-style blend. **08** (★★★★☆) steps up from **07**. Rich, full, lithe & concentrated, with depth & intensity. Firm yet yielding structure.

★★★★☆ **Anvil Chardonnay** Powerful but effortlessly elegant **11** is smooth & silky yet fresh. Bright tangerine tang lifts marmalade on structured palate, oak is way down in the mix. Fine tannins & notable minerality.
Haskell II Occasional release. — FM

Hathersage

Location: Somerset West ▪ Map: Helderberg ▪ WO: Stellenbosch ▪ 1stB 2007 ▪ Tasting & sales by appt Mon-Fri 9-4 ▪ Closed all pub hols ▪ Tour groups ▪ Conference & wedding/function venue with catering (10-200 pax) ▪ Conservation area ▪ Owner(s) Stephan Holdings cc & Stephan Brothers (Pty) Ltd ▪ Winemaker(s) Michael Liedtke (Jan 2010, consultant) ▪ 40ha/12ha (cabs s/f, merlot, p verdot, shiraz, chard, sauv, sem) ▪ 52t/1,518cs own label 43% red 57% white ▪ PO Box 257 Somerset West 7129 ▪ info@hathersage.co.za ▪ www.hathersage.co.za ▪ S 34° 4'54.42" E 018° 51'55.32" ▪ **T +27 (0)21-851-1644/+27 (0)21-851-5076** ▪ F +27 (0)21-851-8382

A lot more than winegrowing happens here now (weddings, conferences, market days) on what cellarmaster Michael Liedtke describes as 'the last green belt almost in the centre of Somerset West'. But vines and wine go back the longest way, here on the banks of the Lourens River, with historic Schapenberg rising above.

★★★★ **Cabernet Sauvignon** ⓟ **09** barrel sample showed delicately herbal, with fine liquorice spice. Too restrained to be instantly attractive, but quietly seductive. More perfumed, less smoky than previous **07**.
Merlot Await next. **Special Edition Red Blend** ⓟ 🍴 ★★★★ Fine-textured old-oaked **08** merlot-cab made for spicy, delicious drinking when tasted a few years back. **Chardonnay** 🍴 ★★ Limy **11** previewed last year, now also some dank gamey notes. **Sauvignon Blanc** ✓ 🍴 ★★★★ **11** fulfills promise of last year's sample, with honeysuckle & tropical notes; a splash of semillon adds length & breadth. **Semillon** 🍴 ★★★ Partly oak-fermented **11** previewed last edition now with thatchy & soft earthy notes, leading to a firm finish. **White Reserve** 🍴 ★★★ **11** bone-dry blend of sauvignon & semillon, the former dominant. Zesty but insubstantial, as when previewed last year; not much in the way of charm. — MF

Haute Cabrière

Location/map: Franschhoek ▪ WO: Western Cape/Franschhoek ▪ Est 1982 ▪ 1stB 1984 ▪ Tasting & sales Mon-Fri 9–5 Sat & pub hols 10–4 Sun 11–4 ▪ Fee Classic Selection R30pp/5 wines, Premium Selection R40pp/6 wines, Exclusive Cap Classique R60pp/5 MCC ▪ Public cellar tour/tasting Mon-Fri 11 & 3 R50pp, Private tasting/tour (pre-booked) R60pp ▪ Cellarmasters tour/tasting Sat 11 R50pp ▪ Closed Good Fri, Dec 25 & Jan 1 ▪ Haute Cabrière Restaurant (see Restaurants section) ▪ Tour groups ▪ Conferences (max 120) ▪ Owner(s) Clos Cabrière Ltd ▪ Cellarmaster(s)/ winemaker(s) Achim von Arnim (1984), with Takuan von Arnim (2005) ▪ Viticulturist(s) Nikey van Zyl (Aug 2011) ▪ 30ha (pinot, chard) ▪ 40% red 60% white ▪ PO Box 245 Franschhoek 7690 ▪ marketing@cabriere.co.za ▪ www.cabriere.co.za ▪ S 33° 54′51.8″ E 019° 8′2.8″ ▪ **T +27 (0)21-876-8500** ▪ F +27 (0)21-876-8501

Note where the human element appears in the winery's motto: 'Sun, soil, vine, man' (you can see it mounted on a sundial-supporting pillar at the entrance to the tasting room). Then you can understand why owner Achim von Arnim says: 'We do not believe in winemaking or having a winemaker, but a cellarmaster who cares for the crop realising the full potential of the vintage.' Unsurprisingly, they are increasingly focusing on the vineyards (planted only with chardonnay and pinot noir). Nikey van Zyl, says Achim, is 'a dedicated viticulturist with green fingers and skin brown as a berry from being in the vineyards, working with the team.'

Haute Cabrière range

Pinot Noir ★★★ Russet-edged, soft berry notes, oak evident though integrated. **09** lacks purity, detail of cherry-like **08**. Franschhoek WO. **Unwooded Pinot Noir** 🍷 **★★★** Unwooded version unusual. Rounded, easy-drinking **11** (previewed last year) not completely dry; cherry fruit, slight spice. **Chardonnay-Pinot Noir ✓** 🍷 **★★★★** Salmon-pink **12** tank sample with bright aromas. Despite pleasing light viscosity finishes slightly bitter, tannic. Just off-dry.

Pierre Jourdan range

★★★★ Blanc de Blancs Classically styled MCC from chardonay, exuberant mousse dominating lime-fresh finely drawn biscuity notes mid-2012; subtle presence of oak & lees. **NV**.

★★★★ Cuvée Reserve Brilliant, luminous, pale green-gold **NV** MCC from chardonnay. Lengthy (60+ months) lees-ageing weaves rich brioche into mature fruit aromas. Subtle, persistent & steely.

Tranquille 🍷 **★★★** Simple, very pale chardonnay-pinot rosé, with sweet fruit aromas. **NV** is slight & just off-dry. **Cuvée Belle Rose ★★★** Coppery salmon pink **NV** MCC from pinot in unshowy style. Slightly aggressive mousse, brambly black cherry notes. **Brut ★★★** Frivolous & undemanding MCC with faint raspberry, citrus aromas. Current **NV** apple-fresh. **Brut Sauvage ★★★** Fine mousse, burnished, utterly dry. Latest **NV** bubbly developed & biscuity, but without hallmark freshness. Like most in range, from Franschhoek grapes but uncertified. **Ratafia ★★★★** Chardonnay fortified with house's own potstill chardonnay brandy. Insubstantial current **NV** lacks integration of previous release. — MF

Haut Espoir

Location/map: Franschhoek ▪ Est 1999 ▪ 1stB 2004 ▪ Tastings, sales & cellar tours by appt ▪ Closed all pub hols ▪ Fynbos walks ▪ Conservation area ▪ Owner(s) Armstrong family ▪ Cellarmaster(s)/winemaker(s)/viticulturist(s) Rob Armstrong ▪ ±23ha/12ha (cab, merlot, p verdot, shiraz) ▪ 70t/5,000cs own label 70% red 30% white ▪ BWI ▪ PO Box 681 Franschhoek 7690 ▪ wine@hautespoir.co.za ▪ www.hautespoir.co.za ▪ S 33° 56′23.6″ E 019° 6′20.9″ ▪ **T +27 (0)21-876-4000** ▪ F +27 (0)21-876-4038

Business as usual, reports gentle man-mountain Rob Armstrong from the family's perch on Scherpenheuwel, overlooking the Franschhoek mountains. Tonnages were down and no chardonnay was made last year but it's allowed him to focus on the proposed conservancy they and neighbouring Boekenhoutskloof are setting up in the area.

★★★★ Chardonnay ⓘ Wild yeast (40%), barrel fermented **08** broad, balanced & complex, spicy end when last tasted. Citrus gleamed through serious oaking (11 months Hungarian & French).

Cabernet Sauvignon ⓘ **★★★★** Previously **05**'s oak provided backbone for pure, ripe & rich black fruits. **Malbec** Await new vintage, as for **Petit Verdot, Syrah, Shiraz Rosé, Sauvignon Blanc. Shiraz** ⓘ **★★★★** Last-tasted **06** full bodied & concentrated compared with restrained **05** (**★★★**). Ripe berry & sweet spice flavours, part carbonic maceration. **Gentle Giant** ⓘ **★★★★** Improved **07** merlot-dominated combo previously showed bright sweet ripe berries, spicy oak, good intensity. **Semillon Reserve** ⓘ **★★★** Shy, crisp **07** last showed typical nolin & fynbos notes. Lightly oaked; modest 12.5% alcohol. **Viognier** ⊕ ★★★ Oak-fermented **08** previously roasted oak & spice; full body, with oily texture, warm finish from 14.3% alcohol. — FM

Havana Hills

Location: Philadelphia ▪ WO: Philadelphia/Coastal ▪ Est 1999 ▪ 1stB 2000 ▪ Closed to public ▪ Owner(s) Kobus du Plessis ▪ Winemaker(s) Piet Kleinhans (Sep 2008) & Joseph Gertse (Jan 2000) ▪ Viticulturist(s) Rudi Benn (Jan 2001) ▪ 260ha/60ha (barbera, cabs s/f, merlot, mourv, sangio, shiraz, sauv) ▪ 35,000cs own label 50% red 20% white 30% rosé ▪ Fairtrade, IPW, WIETA ▪ Postnet Suite #57 Private Bag X18 Milnerton 7435 ▪ sales@havanahills.co.za ▪ www.havanahills.co.za ▪ **T +27 (0)21-972-1110** ▪ F +27 (0)21-972-1105

Reaping the benefit of vineyard practices put in place over the past 10 years, winemaker Piet Kleinhans says the annual organic mulching has resulted in a dramatic reduction of diseases as well as need for irrigation, and the earthworm population is now so high that earth compaction is a thing of the past. Another benefit is access to varieties planted then, hence the release of two new wines this edition: petit verdot, and barbera in a blend with cabernet. Due for release shortly is a chardonnay/pinot. In the existing ranges, the highlights have been the continued success of chardonnay and phenomenal growth of rosé.

Kobus range

★★★★☆ **Red** ⊕ Flagship only in best vintages. Last-tasted **05** was majestic 4-way Bordeaux blend, seamless tannins cosseting sweet fruit.

★★★★ **Chardonnay** ⊕ Last was **10**, crushed hazelnuts & lemon preserve, satisfying palate weight from dab sugar, extended acid-brightened farewell.

Havana Hills range

★★★★ **Petit Verdot** NEW One of few single-variety bottlings, admirable typicity. Complex **09** shows dark fruit opulence with earthy, meaty nuances. Good oak backbone ensures ageability, dry savoury length.

★★★★ **Du Plessis Reserve** ⊕ Lovely mix plush berries, pepper & prosciutto reflects **07** blend shiraz, cab, merlot, with fruit deepening on palate. Silky seduction, already drinking well & will do till ±2018.

Cabernet Sauvignon √ 🍽 ★★★★ Mocha-toned dark plums, **09** is smoothly accessible, generous. Offers immediate enjoyment, few years ageing. **Merlot** ⊕ ★★★ Creamy berries with vanilla & spice infusion, **08** instantly appeals, has softly smooth drinkability. **Shiraz** ★★★ Juicy dark berries, touch of dried herbs, **10** is gentle, restrained & tasty. **Cabernet Sauvignon-Barbera** NEW √ ★★★★ This **09** blend shows something different, blackcurrants with a dusty, herbal note, a lively sleekness. **Sauvignon Blanc** √ 🍽 🧺 ★★★★ Gooseberries, fine & racy acidity, **12**'s dab of sugar adds balance, tangy finish. Lightish 12.5% alc but no lightweight in flavour.

Lime Road range

Shiraz ☺ ★★★ Luscious **10** does shiraz proud with its black plums, campfire smoke, nice fresh finish. **Cabernet Sauvignon-Merlot-Cabernet Franc** ☺ ★★★ Opulent berries, **09**'s soft luscious flavours are designed to please, & do. WO Coastal.

Merlot Rosé 🍽 Await new vintage. **Cabernet Sauvignon Rosé** 🍽 🧺 ★★ Glacé cherry-perfumed, off-dry **12** is ideal patio fare. **Sauvignon Blanc** 🍽 ★★★ Early drinking, zesty **12** preview is just off-dry, with nice lowish alc. — CR

Haven Point see Overhex Wines International

Hawksmoor at Matjieskuil

Location: Paarl ▪ Map: Paarl & Wellington ▪ WO: Paarl/Coastal ▪ Est 1692 ▪ 1stB 2005 ▪ Tasting by appt 10-4 daily; sales by appt Mon-Sat ▪ Fee R20, waived on purchase ▪ Closed Easter Fri-Sun, Dec 25/31 & Jan 1 ▪ Luxury guest house ▪ Owner(s) Brameld Haigh ▪ Winemaker(s) Various ▪ Viticulturist(s) Paul Wallace (2004) ▪ Farm manager Jan Lategan ▪ ±23ha (cab f, mourv, ptage, shiraz, chenin) ▪ ±130t/500cs own label 65% red 25% white 10% rosé ▪ PO Box 9 Elsenburg 7607 ▪ wines@hawksmoor.co.za ▪ www.hawksmoor.co.za ▪ S 33° 48' 27.4" E 018° 46' 14.1" ▪ **T +27 (0)21-884-4587** ▪ F +27 (0)21-884-4465

Grape farming started in the 18th century at Matjieskuil but the Hawksmoor branding is much more recent, the maiden bottling being 05. Word of mouth alone serves as marketing tool, sensibly leaving the production budget intact. Buildings have been returned to their former glory and serve as upscale accommodation with handcrafted wines reflecting the spirit of the place in their own special way

Limited Releases

★★★★ **Barrel 59** ⊕ 🍽 Just one (French) barrel of 08 shiraz. Fynbos & lavender, meaty-tarry core, black cherry juiciness. Intensely spicy, velvety tannins. All in this range tasted a few years back.

★★★★☆ **Barrel 69** ⊕ 🍽 Farm manager's Jan Lategan's best American oak barrel of shiraz, 08 ethereal fragrance, floral notes, intense black fruit centre. Noble & elegant, yet powerful.

★★★★ **Saint Alfege's** ⊕ 🍽 Mediterranean scrub, morello cherries on poised 08. Lightness with athletic substance. 85% shiraz, rest mourvèdre.

★★★★ **Algernon Stitch** ⊕ 🍽 08 shiraz/mourvèdre (90/10) was dark, intense & savoury. Robust, yet refined, with subtle aromatic lift.

Mourvèdre ⊕ 🍽 ★★★★ Appealing soft damson fruit, spicy aromas on 08, structure showed ripeness & poise. **Pinotage** 🍽 Await new. **Vanbrugh** ⊕ 🍽 ★★★ From pinotage, 07 was shy & restrained, with muted berry fruit encased by rigid tannins. **Shiraz** 🍽 Await new. **Rosé** ⊕ 🍽 ★★★ Pleasantly plump 0, from mourvèdre & sauvignon, restrained strawberry notes. WO Coastal. **Edward Goudge** ⊕ 🍽 ★★ Chenin from quarter-century-old bushvines, 09 was oaky & oxidative, lacking charm.

Classic range

> **Chenin Blanc** ☺ 🍽 ★★★ 12 adds floral honeysuckle finesse to delicate dried pear & stonefruit complexity. Light & dry, with crisp acidity.

Pinotage ⊕ 🍽 ★★★ Accessible 06 plummy, rich & earthy, lively tannins & judicious oaking. **Mourvèdre Rosé** 🍽 🉑 ★★★ Crafted with attention, previewed 12 has clean 'white-wine' entry with good berry richness & delicate lingering dry end. — JP

Hazendal 🍷 🥄 📷 🎿 &

Location/map/WO: Stellenbosch ▪ Est 1699 ▪ 1stB 1950 ▪ Tasting, sales & Hermitage Restaurant Tue-Sun 9–4.30 Fee R10/5 wines ▪ Closed Good Fri & Jan 1 ▪ Cellar tours Mon-Fri 11-3 ▪ Facilities for children ▪ Tour groups ▪ Gifts Cheese platters ▪ Conferences ▪ Mountain biking trail ▪ Russian Arts & Culture Museum ▪ Owner(s) Voloshin Schumacher families ▪ Winemaker(s) Ronell Wiid (Jan 1998) ▪ 140ha/48ha (cab, merlot, pinot, shiraz, chenin, sauv) ▪ 250t/19,000cs own label 40% red 60% white ▪ PO Box 336 Stellenbosch 7599 ▪ info@hazendal.co.za www.hazendal.co.za ▪ S 33° 54'2.7" E 018° 43'9.1" ▪ **T +27 (0)21-903-5035** ▪ F +27 (0)21-903-0057

Passion for the brand, the community and the country as a whole has kept the team at the 'Dale of Rabbits' estate in Stellenbosch's Bottelary wine ward positive in the face of challenges thrown up by the current economic tempest. So they've been batting down the hatches and trimming the sails (streamlining operations and product lines) in response to increasing costs and stagnating prices. While admitting change of this nature is never easy, they're confident it will provide an anchor for future growth.

Hazendal range

★★★★ **Shiraz** ⊕ Savoury core of red fruit, spicy dry tannins & bright acidity. Supple, juicy 08 (★★★★ shade off more structured 07.

★★★★☆ **The Last Straw** ⊕ Unbotrytised dessert from air-dried grapes. Massively sweet, viscous nectar 08 is pure delight, expressing chenin's typical dried apricot fruit in an embrace of honey.

Merlot ⊕ ★★★★ Satisfyingly full & intense, 09 improves on 07 (★★★★) with savoury hints & black fruit on substantial tannins. **Pinotage** Await next, as for **Marvol Pinotage** & **Shiraz-Cabernet Sauvignon**. **Reserve Red** ⊕ ★★★ 08 on review was sappy merlot-led blend with cab & shiraz. **Chenin Blanc Wooded** ⊕ ★★★★ Richly ripe tropical fruit shows through oaky mantle on old vine 09. **Bushvine Chenin Blanc** ⊕ ★★★★ Dense ripe 10 unwooded, from 30 year old vines. Over-delivers at price. **Sauvignon Blanc** ⊕ ★★★★ Previewed 1 lovely freshness, elegant structure, commendably gentle acidity. **White Nights Brut Cap Classique** ⊕ ★★★★ Champagne-method sparkling 07 (80% chard, with pinot) in classy livery.

De Haas range

Red ⊕ 🍽 ★★★ Base-level line of price-friendly quaffers. Meaty-spicy NV fresh & undemanding. **Rosé** ⊕ ★★★ Berry flavoured, salmon hued, semi-dry; NV with substance. **White** ⊕ 🍽 ★★★ NV white from chenin-sauvignon high on drinkability. — GdB

■ **HB Vineyards** *see Hout Bay Vineyards*
■ **Headbutt** *see D'Athis Wines SA Negociants*
■ **Heart & Soul** *see Anura Vineyards*
■ **Heeren van Oranje Nassau** *see De Villiers Wines*

Helderberg Wijnmakerij

Location: Somerset West ▪ WO: Stellenbosch ▪ Est 2010 ▪ 1stB 2009 ▪ Closed to public ▪ Owner(s) Boekenhoutskloof Winery (Pty) Ltd ▪ Winemaker(s) Heinrich Hugo (Sep 2010) ▪ 75% red 25% white ▪ BRC, IACCP ▪ PO Box 1037 Stellenbosch 7130 ▪ info@helderbergwijnmakerij.com ▪ www.helderbergwijnmakerij. com ▪ **T +27 (0)21-842-2371** ▪ F +27 (0)21-842-2373

The wood-etched, zebra-liveried offerings from Boekenhoutskloof's recently reinvented cellar on the Helderberg's Winery Road are beginning to make their mark. Stylistically quite distinct from their parent, and a far cry from the wines of yore, these are ones to watch.

■ **Sauvignon Blanc** ☺ 🍷 🖾 ★★★ **12** more expressive than previous, with tangy granadilla fruit & lemon-sherbert vibrancy. Eminently refreshing.

Cabernet Sauvignon 🍷 🖾 ★★★★ Fine varietal herbaceousness & leafy mulberry fruit on **11**, first release under new owners, far removed from previous. — GdB

Helpmekaar Wines

Location: Wellington ▪ Map: Paarl & Wellington ▪ Est 2007 ▪ 1stB 2008 ▪ Tasting, sales & tours by appt Mon-Fri 9-5 ▪ Closed all pub hols ▪ Function venue ▪ Owner(s) Hennie Lategan ▪ Winemaker(s) Hennie Lategan, Francois Louw & Daan Rossouw ▪ 25ha (cab, cinsaut, shiraz) ▪ 250t/150cs own label 100% red ▪ PO Box 2976 Paarl 7620 ▪ psycholat@telkomsa.net ▪ S 33°38'28.64" E 018°57'1.81" ▪ **T +27 (0)21-864-1041** ▪ F +27 (0)21-864-1041

Although psychologist Hennie Lategan and his wine-loving friends skipped their tradition of making a small amount of wine, and all the grapes from his Wellington farm were all sold off last harvest, they did get to bottle the cab in barrel.

■ **Hendrik Lodewyk** *see Du Preez Estate*
■ **Hercules Paragon** *see Simonsvlei International*

Hermanuspietersfontein Wynkelder

Location: Hermanus ▪ Map: Elgin, Walker Bay & Bot River ▪ WO: Sunday's Glen/Western Cape/Walker Bay ▪ Est 2005 ▪ 1stB 2006 ▪ Tasting & sales Mon-Fri 9-5 Sat 9-4 Sun (15 Dec-15 Jan) 10.30-3 ▪ Closed Easter Fri/Sun, Dec 25/26 & Jan 1 ▪ Cellar tours on request ▪ Food & wine market Sat 9-1 ▪ Self-catering cottages ▪ Owner(s) Johan & Mariette Pretorius, Bartho Eksteen, Gerard Scholtz & Gerrie Heyneke ▪ Winemaker(s) Bartho Eksteen, with Kim McFarlane (Feb 2006) ▪ Viticulturist(s) Ernst Bruwer (Oct 2009) ▪ 320ha/±61ha (cabs s/f, grenache, malbec, merlot, mourv, p verdot, shiraz, nouvelle, sauv, sem, viog) ▪ 250t/17,000cs own label 50% red 45% white 5% rosé ▪ WWI champion ▪ Hemel en Aarde Village, Suite 47, Private Bag X15, Hermanus 7200 ▪ kelder@hpf1855.co.za ▪ www.hpf1855.co.za ▪ S 34° 24'38.7" E 019° 11'51.7" ▪ **T +27 (0)28-316-1875** ▪ F +27 (0)28-316-1293

This Hermanus-based winery is headed by the indefatigable Bartho Eksteen, with support from his team and wife Suné. He is passionate about his wines, which are like family — hence the names. The shiraz-based Skoonma ('Mother-in-Law') is the latest addition. But sauvignon blanc remains Eksteen's primary love and he wishes he could convince winelovers that 'good sauvignon only comes into its own after two or three years in the bottle, and ages as well as most other white varieties'. A view borne out by the good but still unsettled 2012s and oaked 2011s. He believes the market for the oaked style is limited because of the difficulty of finding the right oaking regime. 'Chardonnay is much more forgiving than sauvignon with oak; with sauvignon you often get too much "oak juice" and unbalanced wines.'

Flagship Wines

★★★★ **Die Arnoldus** ✪ Cab-led Bordeaux quintet; **08** has lightness of touch, freshness as well as ripe fruit complexity. Polish of all-new oak lends final stamp to flagship status. This & next WO W Cape.

★★★★ **Die Martha** Appealing dark spice, meaty flavours developing on **09**. Richly textured, though with sound fresh backbone, this shiraz, mourvèdre, viognier blend ideal winter warmer with game dishes.

★★★★☆ **Die Bartho** 🏠 🍷 Regular blend of sauvignon (69%), semillon with splash nouvelle, which unusually prominent in **11**. Austere, quite aggressive in youth; richness from semillon & oaking will develop with time, though overall less concentrated than **10**. Will benefit from year or 2 in bottle.

Classic Wines

★★★★ **Swartskaap** 🍷 From cab franc. **10** (★★★☆) lighter in colour & in concentration than brooding **09**. Spicy, leafy notes, gentle flesh, rounded fine tannins & freshness balanced & readied for current drinking.

★★★★ **Kleinboet** ✓ Cab, merlot might head **09** (★★★★☆) Bordeaux quintet, but cab franc's (10%) perfumed spicy/leafy appeal with cedary oak set classy tone. Stern grip, fresh sweet flesh & dry finish suggest this built with ageing in mind. 'Little brother' in grown up mode! **08** was more approachable. WO W Cape.

★★★★ **Sauvignon Blanc No 5** 🏠 🍷 **11** continues in Bordeaux-like vein of **10** (★★★★☆) with slightly less intensity, breadth. Chalky, precise aromas, incisively clean, dry. Supportively oaked.

★★★★ **Sauvignon Blanc No 3 Bergblokke** 🏠 🍷 Adds Afrikaans for 'mountain blocks' to name. More assertive, less obviously fruity than No 7, though tasted just post-bottling, **12** should reveal more with time. Usual succulence, perkily dry finish. Nos 2, 3, 5, 7 all now 100% sauvignon.

★★★★ **Sauvignon Blanc No 7** 🏠 🍷 Billowing greengage, apple blossom scents introduce pure & intense **12**. Lightish, with delicious & prolonged fruity acids in lively but unaggressive mode.

★★★★☆ **Sauvignon Blanc No 2** NEW 🍷 Tantalising dessert sauvignon, **12** shows great balance c botrytis & varietal character. Full of long-lingering flavour, fruity acid tension; low 8% alcohol. 375ml bottles.

Skoonma NEW 🏠 ★★★★ Delicious, shiraz-based **11**. Full of lively spice, crushed velvet feel with refreshing savoury tail. Great drinkability. WO W Cape. **Bloos** 🏠 🍷 ★★★★ Pearly pink **12** rosé; distinctively aromatic plentiful, tangy berry flavours. Bled-off juice from the red wines, lightly oaked. Walker Bay WO.

Lifestyle Wines

1855 Posmeester 🏠 🍷 ★★★ Bordeaux varieties in **11** red blend. Happy, fruitily smooth, uncomplicate partnership. WO Walker Bay. Discontinued: **Sonner Nommer**. — AL

Hermit on the Hill Wines

Location: Durbanville ▪ WO: Coastal/Durbanville/Paarl/Stellenbosch/Wellington ▪ Est/1stB 2000 ▪ Tasting sales by appt ▪ Owner(s)/cellarmaster(s) Pieter de Waal ▪ Winemaker(s) Pieter de Waal & Lohra de Waal bastardo, cinsaut, gamay, grenache, malbec, mourv, shiraz, sauv ▪ 15t/800cs own label 60% red 40% white PO Box 995 Bellville 7535 ▪ pieter@dw.co.za ▪ www.hermitonthehill.co.za ▪ **T +27 (0)83-357-3864** ▪ F +2 (0)21-948-3441

Pieter de Waal is the ultimate wine geek — he's currently secretary of the produce body known as the Sauvignon Blanc Interest Group as well as a registered touris guide specialising in winelands visits. He also vinifies on the side and though h terms the results 'ludicrosities', they are often a lot more serious than that.

★★★★ **Aurora Grenache** NEW ✓ From Durbanville grapes, **10** is particularly pretty with red fruit & fynbo character. Medium bodied with fresh acidity.

★★★★ **Aurora Syrah** NEW ✓ Made by De Waal's wife Lohra from Durbanville grapes, **09** is medium bod ied with pure red fruit, spice & driving acidity. An elegant offering with great persistence on the finish.

★★★★ **The Second Crusade** ⊕ Shiraz, the Hermit's signature red grape, combo with third each grenache mourvèdre. Naturally fermented **08** shows red fruit, floral fragrance; fresh, with fine tannins.

★★★★ **Aurora Blanc** ⊕ De Waal's favoured white grape is sauvignon. This the tank-fermented versio aged older barrels 9 months. Durbanville grapes, **10** complex & unusual, broad structure, spicy but balanced.

★★★★ **The Infidel** ⊕ More traditional take on sauvignon: Stellenbosch grapes spontaneously fermented 'oxygen welcome' signs on the older barrels. Arresting **10** lime, green melon & peppery notes, bracing acidity

★★★★☆ **The White Knight** ✓ **11** (★★★★) blend of 90% sauvignon & semillon. Yellow fruit, creamy tex ture, gentle acidity. More commercial styling by winemaker's own admission after standout **09**. No **10**.

Wellington Grenache NEW ★★★ Dark cherry & mint on rustic **09**, finish is somewhat astringent. **Paa Syrah** ★★★★ **09** is shiraz & 8% mourvèdre; rich & broad with ultra-ripe fruit, moderate acidity & relative soft tannins. **Stellenbosch Syrah** Next awaited, as for **The Sauvignier**. **The Red Knight** ⊕ ★★★ Th family wild child: 85% shiraz, rest cinsaut, **09** earthy, meaty character to go with dark cherry, tart acidity, fir tannins. **Aurora GSM** NEW ★★★ **10** blend of 55% grenache & shiraz, made quirky by dash malbec, is rich broad with soft acidity, firm tannins. Durbanville grapes. — CE

Herold Wines

Location: George ▪ Map: Klein Karoo & Garden Route ▪ WO: Outeniqua ▪ Est 1999 ▪ 1stB 2003 ▪ Tasting, sales & cellar tours Mon-Sat 10-4 ▪ Fee R15, waived on purchase ▪ Closed Easter Sun, Dec 25 & Jan 1 ▪ Light refreshments/cheese platters during opening hours ▪ Picnic baskets/farm lunches with 2 days prior notice ▪ Facilities for children ▪ Tour groups ▪ Gifts ▪ Farm produce ▪ Walks/hikes ▪ Mountain biking ▪ Conservation area ▪ Self-catering Cottages ▪ Owner(s) Nico & Maureen Fourie ▪ Winemaker(s) Nico Fourie (Jul 2011) & Vivien Harpur (consultant) ▪ Viticulturist(s) Nico Fourie (Jul 2011) ▪ 324ha/6ha (cab, merlot, pinot, shiraz, chard, sauv) ▪ 30t/2,700cs own label 55% red 25% white 20% rosé ▪ PO Box 10 Herold 6615 ▪ info@heroldwines.co.za ▪ www.heroldwines.co.za ▪ S 33° 51'49.4" E 022° 28'9.9" ▪ **T +27 (0)72-833-8223** ▪ F +27 (0)86-698-6607

'Every day is like being at school, full of excitement and challenges,' say Nico and Maureen Fourie, the new owners of this farm in the Outeniqua Mountains. Determined to be hands-on, from sorting the grapes to bottling their own wines, they're finding winemaking to be 'as wonderful and complex as wine itself'.

Merlot NEW ☺ ★★★ Interesting meat, cumin & coriander savouriness in **10** (from older French oak?), genteel mealtime companion at just 13% alcohol. **Skaam Skaap** ☺ 🍷 ★★★ Characterful dry rosé from sauvignon, oaked chardonnay & pinot noir. **12** tank sample is salmon hued, billows apple & strawberry, ends with zesty flourish.

Cabernet Sauvignon NEW ★★★ Lovely balance on light-styled (±12% alcohol) **10** summer red, slight herbal hints to blackcurrant & dark plum. **Pinot Noir 'Screwcap'** ✓ 🍷 ★★★★ 2nd-label pinot noir (their flagship bottled under cork). Strawberry & smoke appeal on well-priced **10**, attractive meaty-spicy tealeaf complexity. **Pinot Noir** New vintage not available, as for **Gertrude**. **Red Men** ★★ Meaty **09** combo merlot, cab, shiraz with food-inviting acidic bite. **Sauvignon Blanc** 🍷 Sample **12** too unformed to rate. — WB/JP

Heron Ridge

Location: Somerset West ▪ Map: Helderberg ▪ WO: Stellenbosch ▪ Est 1997 ▪ 1stB 2001 ▪ Tasting, sales & cellar tours by appt ▪ Fee R20 ▪ Closed all pub hols ▪ Cheese lunches on Saturdays by appt ▪ Owner(s) Orpen family ▪ Cellarmaster(s)/winemaker(s) Pippa Orpen (May 2006) ▪ Viticulturist(s) Paul Wallace (Sep 1999, consultant) ▪ 4.29ha/2ha (cab, shiraz) ▪ 20t/150cs own label 100% red ▪ PO Box 5181 Helderberg 7135 ▪ orps@xsinet.co.za ▪ www.heronridge.co.za ▪ S 34° 2'45.6" E 018° 47'58.1" ▪ **T +27 (0)21-842-2501** ▪ F +27 (0)86-613-6960

The Orpens of Heron Ridge are very much a wine-loving family. Daughter Pippa makes the stuff here, while older brother Tom, national sales manager at Jordan Wine, and younger brother Harry, in his final year at agricultural college Elsenburg, are always ready with advice. Jane as mum loves the chat when they get together to taste and discuss every bottle opened.

Family Reserve range NEW

Shiraz ★★★★ **06** is full bodied, slightly rough around the edges but not without charm. Red & black fruit, vanilla, hint of spice. Contains 13% cab.

Heron Ridge range

Shiraz ⊕ ★★★★ **07** raised the bar on **06** (★★★★), showed attractive rusticity & real liveliness, interest when last tasted. 30% oak well integrated. **The Flight** ⊕ ★★★★ Spicy, well-built **06** shiraz/cab still selling. Peppery red fruit with slightly drying tannins but good savouriness. — CE

Het Vlock Casteel

Location: Riebeek-Kasteel ▪ Map/WO: Swartland ▪ Est/1stB 2005 ▪ Tasting & sales Mon-Fri 9-5 Sat 9-2 ▪ Closed Good Fri & Dec 25 ▪ Tour groups ▪ Gift shop ▪ Farm produce: olives, olive oil, jams, chutneys etc — sampling available ▪ Conferences ▪ Café Merlot functions: by appt only ▪ Owner(s) Johan Louw Vlok ▪ Winemaker(s) Alecia Boshoff ▪ Viticulturist(s) Johan Vlok snr & Johan Vlok jnr ▪ 100ha (cab, merlot, ptage, shiraz, chard) ▪ 1,300t/2,000cs own label 100% red ▪ PO Box 8 Riebeek-Kasteel 7307 ▪ info@hetvlockcasteel.co.za ▪ www.hetvlockcasteel.co.za ▪ S 33° 23'22.74" E 018° 53'40.75" ▪ **T +27 (0)82-567-9132** ▪ F +27 (0)86-720-6281

The Vlok family, wine and table-grape farmers near Riebeek-Kasteel since 1958, plan to bottle less, but better quality under their boutique brand, named after the Castle of Good Hope and vinified to spec by Riebeek Cellars. Wine is one of a cornucopia of products and amenities on offer at their castle-like visitor venue, including a fresh and preserved produce shop, conferences and functions at Café Merlot.

Cabernet Sauvignon ★★★ Accessible & juicy **09**, soft blackberry flavours, smooth savoury conclusion. **Merlot** ★★★ Similar mocha chocolate character to previous, **09** bit firmer, peppery, still a satisfying everyday red. **Shiraz** ★★★ Earthy, toasty & savoury notes balanced by juicy plums in **09** steakhouse wine. **Sauvignon Blanc** ✓ ★★★★ Step-up **12** hay & ripe melon combo, gentle acidity, clean pineappley aftertaste. — DB

■ **Hex River Crossing Private Cellar** *see Auction Crossing Private Cellar*

Hidden Valley Wines

Location/map/WO: Stellenbosch ▪ Est/1stB 1995 ▪ Tasting, sales & cellar tours Mon-Fri 9-6 (summer) & 9-5 (winter) Sat/Sun 9-5 ▪ Fee R30pp ▪ Closed Dec 25/26 & Jan 1 ▪ Overture Restaurant ▪ Cheese/chocolate platters ▪ Picnics, to be pre-booked ▪ Table olives & olive oil ▪ Tour groups ▪ Conferences ▪ Weddings/functions ▪ Walks/hikes ▪ Conservation area ▪ Owner(s) David Hidden ▪ Winemaker(s) Emma Moffat (May 2010) ▪ Viticulturist(s) Johan 'Grobbie' Grobbelaar (Feb 1999) ▪ STB: 28ha/15ha (cab, merlot, p verdot, shiraz, tannat, sauv, viog); ELIM: 56ha/13ha (cab, p verdot, shiraz, sauv, sem) ▪ 200t/6,000cs own label 60% red 40% white ▪ BWI ▪ PO Box 12577 Die Boord 7613 ▪ info@hiddenvalleywines.com ▪ www.hiddenvalleywines.com ▪ S 34° 1' 15. 3" E 018° 51' 13.9" ▪ **T** +27 (0)21-880-2646 ▪ F +27 (0)21-880-2645

'I am living my dream,' says David Hidden, owner, 'in a beautiful cellar, a beautiful farm in Stellenbosch with magnificent views and making great wines! Who can match that?' Increasing numbers of visitors are enjoying the amenities on offer at his Helderberg mountainside property, including wedding and function venues, awarded Overture restaurant, and various food-and-wine options. A partnership with Fairview breathes new life into the Land's End brand, now listed separately.

★★★★ **Pinotage** ✓ 🖩 No mistaking the variety. Smoky, meaty, bold **11** shows complex layers of spices, ripe fruit & preserves. Clean & precise fruit with a hint of dark chocolate on the finish. No **10**.

★★★★ **Hidden Gems** ⑨ 🖩 Overtly New World **08** (★★★★★), from cab & petit verdot, satisfies on many levels. Great depth & intensity, less oak clout than **07** improves balance.

★★★★ **Hidden Secret** ⑨ Dark, brooding **08** from shiraz & tannat bursts with black cherry fruit & Rhône-like spiciness. Rounded, smooth & satisfying.

★★★★ **Sauvignon Blanc** ✓ 🖩 ▨ Notch above last **10** (★★★☆), **12** is floral with honeysuckle & peach flavours from dash viognier. Broad bodied, with smooth acidity & mouthwatering citrus ending. **11** skipped.

Barbera Await new vintage. — WB

High Constantia Wine Cellar

Location: Constantia ▪ Map: Cape Peninsula ▪ WO: Constantia/Coastal ▪ Est 1693 ▪ 1stB 2000 ▪ Tasting, sales & cellar tours Mon-Fri 8–5 Sat 10-1 ▪ Fee R40 ▪ Closed Easter Sun, Dec 25 & Jan 1 ▪ BYO picnic ▪ Meals pre-arranged with private chef, Marc Wassung ▪ Owner(s) David van Niekerk ▪ Cellarmaster(s)/viticulturist(s) David van Niekerk (Jan 1999) ▪ Winemaker(s) David van Niekerk (Jan 1999) & Roger Arendse (Jan 2001) ▪ 14. 5ha (cabs s/f, malbec, merlot, pinot, chard, sauv) ▪ 70t/5,500cs own label 52% red 15% white 3% rosé 30% MCC + 1,900cs for clients ▪ Brands for clients: Terra Madre ▪ Groot Constantia Rd Constantia 7800 ▪ david@ highconstantia.co.za ▪ www.highconstantia.co.za ▪ S 34° 1' 31.3" E 018° 25' 36.1" ▪ **T** +27 (0)21-794-7171/+27 (0)83-300-2064 ▪ F +27 (0)21-794-7999

Two centuries ago, they were competing with their illustrious neighbours for the favour of Europe's royal courts, but this resurrection of the estate's name (and that of its founder, Sebastiaan van Renen) is based on leased vineyards, where David van Niekerk hopes to restore their former status.

High Constantia range

★★★★ **Cabernet Franc** ⑨ Lovely leafy aromatics & sweet fruit on **06** (★★★★), leaner than previous **04**.

★★★★ **Malbec** ⑨ Plush, aromatic, sweet-fruited **06** with big acid, dry tannins.

★★★★☆ **Sebastiaan** ⑨ **06** (★★★★) blend 5 Bordeaux red varieties well structured though shade les handsome than **04**.

★★★★☆ **Sauvignon Blanc** ⑨ 🖩 Creamy & fresh **10** tank sample had poise, balance & harmony previously.

★★★★ **Clos André MCC** ⑨ Last tasted bottle-fermented sparkling was dry but rich **07** (★★★★★). Lik **06**, 70% chard with pinot.

abernet Sauvignon ⑫ ★★★ Austere, simple **06** last tasted. **Merlot** 📖 Await next, as for **Rosé** & **iognier**.

ilverhurst range

Merlot 📖 New vintage not available, like **Rosé** & **Viognier**. **Sauvignon Blanc** ⑫ 📖 ★★★ Tasty **08** rassy-tropical melange. — TJ

Highgate Wine Estate

ocation: Howick ▪ Map/WO: KwaZulu-Natal ▪ Est/1stB 2010 ▪ Tasting & sales daily 8-5 ▪ Closed Dec 25 & Jan 1 ▪ Facilities for children ▪ Coffee shop (see www.pigglywiggly.co.za) ▪ Wine, ceramics, gifts, linen, etc ▪ Garden entre ▪ Farm stall ▪ Owner(s) Rudi & Cindy Kassier ▪ Winemaker(s) Rudi Kassier, with Wal Bornheimer ▪ Viti-ulturist(s) Rudi Kassier ▪ 57ha/3ha (cab, merlot, ptage, shiraz, chard) ▪ 2.5t/420cs own label 50% red 50% white ▪ PO Box 1025 Howick 3290 ▪ rudi@pigglywiggly.co.za ▪ www.highgatewineestate.co.za ▪ S 29° 27' 29. 2" E 030° 8' 8.66" ▪ **T** +27 (0)82-895-1667/+27 (0)33-234-2911 ▪ **F** +27 (0)86-535-3187

KZN-Natal Midlands fresh-produce grower Rudi Kassier took a bit of a 'gap year' in 2012. 'We skipped a vintage — too busy with the property development.' That included moving and rebuilding the cellar. But it's all systems go for 2013, with vineyards having established themselves nicely.

Highlands Road Estate

ocation/WO: Elgin ▪ Map: Elgin, Walker Bay & Bot River ▪ Est 2005 ▪ 1stB 2007 ▪ Tasting & cellar tours Wed-Sun 9-3 ▪ Sales daily 9-5 ▪ Closed Easter Sun/Mon, Jun 21, Jul 19, Dec 25 & Jan 1 ▪ Breakfast & light lunches ▪ Facilities for children ▪ Self-catering cottage (sleeps 4) ▪ Kayaking ▪ Fly fishing ▪ Boule ▪ Owner(s) Michael White, Justin & Mary Hoy ▪ Cellarmaster(s)/viticulturist(s) Justin Hoy (2007) ▪ Winemaker(s) Justin Hoy (2007), with Jacob September (2011) ▪ 28ha/10ha (pinot, chard, sauv, sem) ▪ 30t/2,250cs own label 35% red 65% white ▪ PO Box 94 Elgin 7180 ▪ info@highlandsroadestate.co.za ▪ www.highlandsroadestate.co.za ▪ S 34° 14' 4.4" E 019° 4' 14.3" ▪ **T** +27 (0)71-271-0161

The name 'Highlands' should give a clue as to the origin of some of those involved; the names Ruadh and Slainte confirm they hail from Scotland. With plans to expand the range as newly planted vines produce fruit, further Gaelic names will be required. The focus is firmly on pinot noir and sauvignon blanc, 'where we will strive to improve quality with "coolness" in mind'.

Pinot Noir 📖 ★★★ Deep-hued **10**, now bottled, very ripe, some grip, hot finish. **Ruadh** ⑫ 📖 ★★★ Straightforward **09** shiraz/merlot blend; juicy blackberry, smoky tones dimmed by roughish, dry tannins. **Rosé** ⑫ 📖 ★★★★ Fragrant, lightly spicy & dry **09** from merlot tasted few years back. **Sauvignon Blanc** 📖 Await next. **Sine Cera** 📖 ★★★ Light citrus, earthy aromas on otherwise straightforward, dry **11** semil-lon-sauvignon blend. **Slainte MCC Bubbly** ★★★ 'Oystershell' & lemony refreshment abounds on **08** (previously NV called just 'Slainte') from chardonnay; hint of developing creaminess to balance brisk bubble, brut/dry style. **Sauvignon Blanc Sweet** NEW ★★★★ Honeyed **11**, unheavy, nicely concentrated, with some length if a little soft. Discontinued: **Free Run Sauvignon Blanc**. — AL

Hildenbrand Wine, Olive & Art Estate

ocation/WO: Wellington ▪ Map: Paarl & Wellington ▪ Est 1991 ▪ 1stB 1999 ▪ Tasting & sales Mon-Sat 10-4 Sun 9-12 by appt ▪ Wine tasting R10pp/wine; olive & oil tasting R10pp ▪ Closed Easter Sat/Sun, Dec 24/25 & Jan 1 ▪ Restaurant ▪ Klein Rhebokskloof Country & Guest House ▪ Art by Adri Swart ▪ Owner(s)/cellarmaster(s) Reni Hildenbrand ▪ Winemaker(s) Reni Hildenbrand, with Marinus Bredell ▪ ±2,250cs ▪ PO Box 270 Wellington 7654 ▪ info@wine-estate-hildenbrand.co.za ▪ www.wine-estate-hildenbrand.co.za ▪ S 33° 39' 33.3" E 019° 1' 46.3" ▪ **T** +27 (0)82-656-6007

Reni Hildenbrand is a survivor and no mistake! Her road to winemaker/owner hasn't been easy but she has remained true to her commitment to putting personality in wine, and is delighted to be able to celebrate increasing export success with a 10 year anniversary bubbly (an 09, untasted by us), released last year.

★★★★ **Shiraz** ⑫ Big wine though not bold, more understated in last **07**. Cracked pepper, black cherry & warm spice meld in ripe palate.

Cabernet Sauvignon Barrique ⓟ ★★★★ Plush blueberry texture to **07**'s muscular frame noted previousl⌐ Savoury, ripe, dry tannins from 17 months French oak, just 25% new. **Cabernet Sauvignon Unwooded** ⓟ Await next. **Malbec** ⍉ ★★★ Earthy overtones of raisins, baked plums & prunes. **11** has savoury edge, swee⌐ black/red berries. **Shiraz Rosé** 🯄 ⍉ ★★★ Fresh raspberries on **12** tank sample, crisp quiet summer drin⌐ **Chardonnay Barrique** ⓟ ★★★★ **10** nutty tangerine vibrancy, creamy rich vanilla from older oak & lees-age⌐ ing. **Chardonnay Unwooded** ★★★ Floral highlights on **12** preview. Hints of honey & kerosene with soft ye⌐ low/green fruit. Individual & interesting wine. **Chenin Blanc** ⓟ ⍉ ★★★ Toasty apricot with ripe mouthfee⌐ structure & breadth on Hungarian-oaked **10**. **Semillon** ⓟ ★★★★ Last edition **08** continued tradition of lim⌐ zest & herbs on creamy, toasty palate from oak fermentation/ageing. **Lady Jemaima Cuvée** Next awaited⌐ **Emma & Asa** NEW ★★★ Named for farm's two goats, **09** blend of chenin, semillon & chardonnay. All barrel-fer⌐ mented in Hungarian oak, rich honey/muesli notes, fresh acidity, good match for goats' cheese! **Bonnie & Claire** Await new vintage. **Sleepless Nights Semillon Noble Late Harvest** ⓟ ★★★ **07** laudable effort, the nam⌐ tells it all! Less sweet, hint of estate's distinctive grassiness. — CM

Hill & Dale

Easy-drinking wines vinified from grapes off selected Stellenbosch vineyards a⌐ Stellenzicht (see that entry for tasting/sales information).

> **Shiraz** NEW ☺ ⍉ ★★★ Good typicity on **11**, with notes of black cherry, some floral fragrance & a hint of pepper. Medium body, fresh acidity. **Sauvignon Blanc** ☺ 🯄 ⍉ ★★★ Surprising complexity from **12** with pronounced yellow apple character before dry, almost saline finish.

Merlot ⍉ ★★ Dark fruit, distinct herbal edge to run-of-the-mill **11**. **Pinotage** ⍉ ★★ Fruit-driven **11** i⌐ soft & plummy. **Cabernet Sauvignon-Shiraz** ⍉ ★★★ Red fruit, mint & chocolate give Peppermint Cris⌐ quality to **10**. **Dry Rosé Merlot** 🯄 ⍉ ★★★ Appealing strawberry before pleasantly dry finish on neat &⌐ orderly **12**. Includes dashes cab & cab franc. **Chardonnay** 🯄 ⍉ **12** not ready for tasting. **Pinot Grigi⌐** NEW 🯄 ⍉ ★★★ White peach & pear, soft acidity on **12**. Not unappealing but entirely straightforward. Dis⌐ continued: **Kosher Vin Rouge, Kosher Vin Blanc.** — CE

Hillcrest Estate

Location/WO: Durbanville ▪ Map: Durbanville, Philadelphia & Darling ▪ Est/1stB 2002 ▪ Tasting & sales daily 9–5 ▪ Fee R10, waived on purchase ▪ Closed Good Fri, Dec 25 & Jan 1 ▪ Cellar tours by appt ▪ Restaurant (T +27 (0)21-975-2346) open daily for breakfast & lunch ▪ Wedding/function venue ▪ Farm produce ▪ Walking/hiking & moun-tain biking trails ▪ Conservation area ▪ Owner(s) PD Inglis, R Haw & G du Toit ▪ Winemaker(s) Graeme Read (Jan 2003) ▪ Viticulturist(s) G du Toit ▪ 25ha (cabs s/f, malbec, merlot, p verdot, chard, sauv) ▪ 60t/±3,000cs own labe⌐ 45% red 55% white ▪ Private Bag X3 Durbanville 7551 ▪ cellardoor@hillcrestfarm.co.za ▪ www.hillcrestfarm.co.za⌐ ▪ S 33° 49' 38.2" E 018° 35' 25.9" ▪ **T +27 (0)21-976-1110** ▪ F +27 (0)21-975-2195

The vineyards, their soils and management are paramount to Graeme Read, the self-taught, talented winemaker. He revels in the cool climate and specia⌐ terroir, which, together with his viticultural fine-tuning, have made the wines o⌐ this small-scale Durbanville winery so distinctively elegant. The Metamorphic Collection, featuring the Hornfels blend, alludes to the farm's interesting and ancient geology. Still enthusiastic and spry, Graeme will commemorate his first decade at Hillcrest by launching a white blend for this premier range.

Metamorphic Collection

★★★★ **Quarry** ⍉ **10** mostly merlot with dab petit verdot. Understated, but shade less gravitas than acclaimed **09** (★★★★★). Youthful, polished, with leafy blueberry tone. Deserves 3-5 years to shine.

★★★★ **Hornfels** Bordeaux quintet, named for the vineyard's geology, with savoury earthy tone & cab⌐ franc's perfume. Restrained & contemplative in **10**, deserves cellaring. Shade off **09** (★★★★★).

Hillcrest Estate range

> **Cabernet Sauvignon Rosé** ☺ 🯄 ★★★ Dapper & dry, **12** preview has appealing savoury & red berry flavours. Balanced & fresh, tailor-made for summer.

Cabernet Franc ✓ ★★★★ **11** shows elegant, 'feminine' styling. Richly fruited with scented nuance & firm chalky⌐ tannins. Future rewards in store. **Malbec** ★★★ Youthful & boisterous **11** needs time to harmonise. Dark & spicy⌐ fruit still jostling with firm dry tannins. **Petit Verdot** ✓ ★★★★ **11** blueberry & mineral-toned babe enveloped in⌐

fine powdery tannins. Good fruit purity & length, with potential to develop. **Cabernet Sauvignon-Merlot** ⊕ ★★★ **08** was a savoury, tight 5-way Bordeaux blend when tasted. **Sauvignon Blanc** ✓ 🏠 ★★★★ Vivacious **11** is fresh & tangy with a flinty nuance. Feisty structure & length for food pairing. — MW

Hillock Wines

Location: Ladismith ▪ Map: Klein Karoo & Garden Route ▪ WO: Klein Karoo ▪ Est 2010 ▪ 1stB 2011 ▪ Tasting, sales & cellar tours daily 10-5 ▪ Closed Dec 25 ▪ Light lunches & refreshments 10-5 daily; or BYO picnic ▪ Tour groups ▪ Gifts ▪ Farm produce ▪ Guided hikes & vineyard tours ▪ Mountain biking ▪ 4-star guest house (sleeps 14), Mymering Estate www.mymering.com ▪ Owner(s) Andy & Penny Hillock ▪ Winemaker(s) Duan Brits (Oct 2010) ▪ Viticulturist(s) Riaan Steyn ▪ 400ha/50ha (shiraz, chard, chenin) ▪ 20t/1,800cs own label 50% red 50% white ▪ PO Box 278 Ladismith 6655 ▪ penny@mymering.com ▪ www.hillockwines.com ▪ S 33° 29'55.24" E 021° 10' 18.65" ▪ **T +27 (0)21-551-1548** ▪ F +27 (0)28-551-1313

As a young man Andy Hillock held three ambitions: medicine, flying and winefarming. Fulfilment of the last has come late in life, in the shape of his and wife Penny's boutique winery on Mymering estate near Ladismith. The couple and winemaker Duan Brits are so pleased with their sauvignon block that they've opted to release two bottlings, one named after the farm manager's King Poodles.

Hillock range NEW

★★★★ **Black Poodle Reserve Sauvignon Blanc** ✓ 🏠 Top dog **12** is heady, intense; mouthfilling flavours of baked apple & passionfruit, poised acidity & enduring length make an elegant glassful. **Shiraz** 🏠 ★★★ Prune nuance on coconutty, oak-spiced easy-drinking **11. Mile High** 🏠 ★★★ We guess every pilot's wine range has to have one! **NV** dry red with roast beef & leafy tones, cheery berry fruit & gutsy tannins. **Chardonnay** 🏠 ★★★ Faint wax & toast on lightly oaked **12**, muted but classy citrus fruit, chalky finish. **Chenin Blanc** 🏠 ★ Soft & brief off-dry **12** has cooked apple tones. **Sauvignon Blanc** ✓ 🏠 ★★★★ **12** arresting grass & Karoo scrub, generous & balanced flavours, extended zesty aftertaste. **Barrel Roll** 🏠 ★★★ Blend of cask-fermented chenin/chardonnay & unwooded sauvignon showing appealing lees yeastiness & tropical fruit, with zippy acidity extending the tail of **12**. — GdB/CvZ

■ **Hilltop** see Rosendal Winery
■ **Hippo Creek** see PicardiRebel
■ **His Master's Choice** see Excelsior Vlakteplaas

Hofstraat Kelder

Location: Malmesbury ▪ Map: Swartland ▪ WO: Swartland/Darling ▪ Est 2002 ▪ 1stB 2003 ▪ Tasting, sales & tours by appt ▪ Owner(s)/cellarmaster(s)/winemaker(s) Wim Smit, Jack de Clercq & Jerry Finley ▪ 2.5t/125cs own label 100% red ▪ PO Box 1172 Malmesbury 7299 ▪ renosterbos@cornergate.com ▪ S 33° 26'56.1" E 018° 44'1.8" ▪ **T +27 (0)83-270-2352** ▪ F +27 (0)22-487-3202

'It is much better to work in a bigger area,' says co-owner/winemaker Wim Smit of the recently completed Malmesbury cellar, where he and Hofstraat partners Jack de Clercq and Jerry Finley produce tiny quantities — only 125 cases. They have joined the Swartland Independent and, in line with that movement's philosophy, all wines are now fermented naturally.

Renosterbos range

★★★★ **Barbera** ✓ Rare varietal bottling. Bold **11** is earthy, smooth & markedly dry with ripe intense black cherries, firm assertive tannins & spicy grip. **Cabernet Sauvignon** ★★★★ Ripe, bright blackcurrant & fynbos, good balance, ripe tannin structure & oaky finish on **11.** Like all reds following, needs 2-3 years to develop fully. **Merlot** ★★★★ Christmas cake fruit with soft ripe tannins, balanced by juicy acidity & sweet spicy ending on mouthfilling **11**, from Darling vines. **10** held back. **09** (★★★★) was a step up. **Pinotage** ★★★ Fresh & fruity **11** brims with bright plum, spicy fynbos & hint of coffee. Good acid balance with warm finish (16% alcohol). **Shiraz** ★★★ Bold & dark-fruited **11** with violet perfume, good structure but warming blackberry liqueur-like ending (±16% alcohol). — WB

Holden Manz Wine Estate

Location/map/WO: Franschhoek ▪ Est 2010 ▪ 1stB 2005 ▪ Tasting, sales & cellar tours daily 10-5 ▪ Fee R30 ▪ Franschhoek Kitchen (see Restaurants section) ▪ Spa ▪ Picnic area ▪ Holden Manz Country House (see Accommodation section) ▪ Owner(s) Gerard Holden & Migo Manz ▪ Winemaker(s) Schalk Opperman (Sep 2011) ▪ Viticulturist(s) Tertius Oosthuizen (Sep 2010) ▪ 20ha/16ha (cabs s/f, merlot, shiraz) ▪ 110t/6,666cs own label ▪ 85% red 3.85% white 6.65% rosé 4.5% port ▪ IPW ▪ PO Box 620 Franschhoek 7690 ▪ info@holdenmanz.com ▪ www.holdenmanz.com ▪ S 33° 56'6.3" E 019° 7'8.3" ▪ T +27 (0)21-876-2738 ▪ F +27 (0)21-876-4624

The main focus for Schalk Opperman, winemaker at this revived Franschhoek estate since 2011, is to ensure that the potential of the mature vineyards is achieved. No modern available technology will be ignored, from aerial photography to soil analysis. Vineyard blocks are vinified and matured separately to ensure that parcels are monitored and the best will be available for final blending. A maiden chardonnay is coming soon.

Holden Manz range

Cabernet Sauvignon 🌿 ★★★★ Dark brooding **10** has generous fruit concentration, with ultra-ripeness well contained. Textured & ready. **Merlot** Next awaited, as for **Shiraz**. **Big G** ★★★★ **09** equal parts cab & cab franc. Rich & confident, with fresh herbal lift. Integrated oak adds to plush impression. **Rosé** ✓ 🍴 ★★★★ Shy restrained red berry fruits waft off elegant & dry **12** blend of Bordeaux varieties & shiraz. Good weight, serious & lingering. **Good Sport Cape Vintage** ⊕ ★★★ **09** has serious port-style intention, but dense fruit, brandy spirit & obvious oak last year needed time to meld.

Klein Genot range

Discontinued: **Shiraz, Dry Cabernet Sauvignon Rosé**. — JP

■ **Honeypot** see Origin Wine

Hoopenburg Wines

Location/map: Stellenbosch ▪ WO: Stellenbosch/Coastal/Western Cape ▪ Est/1stB 1992 ▪ Tasting, sales & cellar tours Mon-Fri 8.30-4 ▪ Fee R20/6-8 wines ▪ Closed all pub hols ▪ BYO picnic ▪ Conferences ▪ Guest house T +27 (0)21-884-4534 ▪ Owner(s) Gregor Schmitz ▪ Cellarmaster(s) Anton Beukes (Aug 2009) ▪ Viticulturist(s) Gert Snyders ▪ 70ha/30ha (cab, merlot, shiraz, chard) ▪ 180t/20,000cs own label 80% red 18% white 2% MCC ▪ Transit Organic — Control Union (final organic audit Nov 2012) ▪ PO Box 1233 Stellenbosch 7599 ▪ info@hoopenburg.com ▪ www.hoopenburgwines.co.za ▪ S 33° 49'33.4" E 018° 49'9.3" ▪ T +27 (0)21-884-4221 ▪ F +27 (0)21-884-4904

For Hoopenburg winemaker/GM Anton Beukes, tough economic conditions aren't all bad; consumers are increasingly looking for value and therefore paying more attention to quality than brand. Staying with quality, Beukes challenges winemakers to spend more time between the rows getting to know their vines, instead of 'paying a visit just before harvest'. His own rows — bushvines only — are currently anticipating final 100% organic audit.

Integer range

★★★★☆ **Cabernet Sauvignon** Cab's classic blackcurrant shines through in savoury **09** (★★★★); given plenty grip from extracted tannins & oak, needing time to soften. More robust, less sleek than **08**.

★★★★ **Syrah-Mourvèdre-Carignan** ⊕ Not to be hurried, plenty in store, **09** (★★★★★) improves on **08** with layered dried herbs, spice, lush berries; firmly ripe tannins. Should keep well till ±2016. WO Coastal.

★★★★ **Chardonnay** Popular toasty styled **09** (★★★★) shows plenty sweet tangy ripe fruit intertwined with obvious vanilla oakiness at modest alcohol level. Less complexity than **08**.

★★★★ **Méthode Cap Classique Brut** Bone-dry chardonnay **NV** shows long lees maturation in classic toasty aromas. Partial oak ferment broadens mouthfeel, adds structure, complexity to focused lemon zest.

Syrah ★★★★ Aromatically complex, slightly wild **09** offers abundant spicy, heady red fruit flavours marred by heavy oaking. Discontinued: **White**.

Hoopenburg Bush Vine range

Chardonnay ☺ ★★★ A year on lees & touch of oak enlivens pleasantly tropical, charmingly light **11** quaffer. **Sauvignon Blanc** ☺ 🍴 ★★★ Characterful, harmonious **12** shows easy charm in lightly grassy yet boldly fruity style. WO Coastal.

Cabernet Sauvignon ✓ ★★★★ Cab's classic blackcurrant shines through in savoury **09**, given plenty grip from extracted tannins & oak needing time to soften. **Merlot** ★★★ Ingratiatingly sweet **10** preview offers ripe, baked dark fruit, checked by integrated savoury oak tannins. **Pinot Noir** 🍴 ★★★ Elgin fruit adds restraint to ripe, smooth **10**, gently supported by oak. Easy charm, balance; for early drinking. **Pinotage** NEW

★★★ Mocha **11** in popular easy-drinking Starbucks style; ample fruit offers pleasant dab sweetness. **Shiraz** Ⓟ ★★★★ Sleek & streamlined, **08** for pure drinking pleasure, smoky dark fruit capturing the essence of shiraz. WO Coastal. **Shiraz-Cabernet Sauvignon** NEW ★★ Savoury, simple, meaty **08** has funky dried fruit. WO Coastal, as next. **Rosé** NEW 🗒 ★★ Fruity, simple off-dry **11** from pinotage.

Guru range

Merlot ★★★ Friendly **09** in accessible, sweet & savoury style. WO W Cape. **Cabernet Sauvignon-Merlot** ★★ Very ripe baked fruit in **09** sufficiently checked by savoury oak. **Sauvignon Blanc** Await new vintage. Discontinued: Rosé.' — IM

Hornbill Garagiste Winery

Location: Hermanus ▪ Map: Elgin, Walker Bay & Bot River ▪ WO: Western Cape/Walker Bay ▪ Est 2004 ▪ 1stB 2005 ▪ Tasting, sales & tours Mon-Fri 9-5 Sat 9-2 ▪ Closed Easter Fri/Sun, Dec 25 & Jan 1 ▪ Gifts ▪ Art gallery & ceramic studio ▪ Restaurant ▪ Owner(s) John Dry ▪ Winemaker(s) John Dry (2004) ▪ 6t/400cs own label 100% red ▪ PO Box 4 Hermanus 7200 ▪ hornbill@intekom.co.za ▪ www.hornbillhouse.co.za ▪ S 34° 24'46.3" E 019° 11'54.4" ▪ **T** +27 (0)28-316-2696 ▪ F +27 (0)28-316-3794

For architect John Dry, 2012 marked a sea-change in his winemaking — it's the first year he's been able to hold the wines back before release allowing them time to show themselves properly. It's also the first vintage of his much-anticipated pinotage and he looks forward to releasing his first white wine later on in the year.

The Naked Vine Collection

★★★★ **Persuasion Pinotage** NEW Rich, individual & exciting **09**, bold & integrated plum pudding & savoury balanced with spiciness from well-managed oak. Upper Hemel-en-Aarde Valley grapes for this range. **Rapture Cabernet Sauvignon** NEW ★★★ Earthy, savoury tones in **09** with plum overlay, begs more time to fully integrate. **Mystique Merlot** Sold out, await new release. **Epiphany Cape Blend** NEW ★★★ Equal parts cab, merlot & pinotage give cranberry tang & crispness on **09**.

Hornbill range

Reinet Ⓟ ★★★ When last tasted, **08** showed plush fruit & a savoury conclusion. From merlot with splash cab. **Milan** Await new vintage. — DB

▪▪ **Horse Mountain** see Doran Vineyards
▪▪ **Houdamond** see Bellevue Estate Stellenbosch

House of Mandela

WO: Western Cape/Stellenbosch/Coastal/Elgin ▪ Est/1stB 2009 ▪ Closed to public ▪ Owner(s) Makaziwe Mandela & Tukwini Mandela ▪ Cellarmaster(s) Charles Back & Erlank Erasmus ▪ Winemaker(s)/viticulturist(s) Various ▪ 60% red 40% white ▪ info@houseofmandela.com ▪ www.houseofmandela.com

Ancestry is vital to this negociant business owned by South Africa's past president and Nobel laureate Nelson Mandela's children Tukwini and Makaziwe. Hence the new range's branding. 'Named for the Thembu tribe, the Thembu Collection honours our ancestors and the Mandela family's ties to Africa,' says Tukwini, 'while the sparkling wine [not ready at press time] is inspired by the Xhosa beads, which symbolically connect our present to the past.'

Royal Reserve range

★★★★☆ **Cabernet Sauvignon** Ⓟ Classic **08** from Stellenbosch fruit seductive nuances of cassis, lead pencil; silky precision, fine tannins, harmonious oak. These tasted a few years back.

★★★★ **Shiraz** Ⓟ From Paarl single-vineyard, **07**'s brooding black fruit wrapped in powerful, solid tannins. Rich, with savoury grip.

★★★★ **Chardonnay** Ⓟ Oaking on **09** ex Elgin gives vanilla glow to apple blossom & citrus; creamy core.

Thembu Collection NEW

Cabernet Sauvignon 🗒 🏵 ★★★ **12** most restrained in this line-up; smooth entry & pleasantly firm finish for unchallenging sipping. Labels for these inspired by colourful 'dashiki' shirt made famous by Nelson Mandela. **Shiraz** 🗒 🏵 ★★★ Coffee-infused **12** crisp & refreshing —like a shot of java. **Sauvignon Blanc** 🗒 🏵 ★★ Dusty liquorice & fennel notes, broad palate on lipsmacking **12**. WO W Cape, as all. — CvZ

Hout Bay Vineyards

Location: Hout Bay ▪ Map: Cape Peninsula ▪ WO: Hout Bay/Western Cape/Stellenbosch ▪ Est 2001 ▪ 1stB 2004 ▪ Tasting, sales & cellar tours by appt ▪ Fee R30, refunded when a case is purchased ▪ Facilities for children ▪ Owner(s) Peter & Catharine Roeloffze ▪ Cellarmaster(s)/winemaker(s)/viticulturist(s) Peter & Catharine Roeloffze (Jan 2004) ▪ 1.5ha/1.1ha (pinot meunier, pinot, chard) ▪ 7.2t/2,000cs own label 37% red 29% white 7% rosé 27% MCC ▪ Other export brand: HB Vineyards ▪ PO Box 26659 Hout Bay 7872 ▪ cathy@4mb.co.za ▪ www.houtbayvineyards.co. za ▪ S 34° 1'31.0" E 018° 22'31.0" ▪ **T** +27 (0)83-790-2372 ▪ **F** +27 (0)86-514-9861

A visit to the Roeloffze's precipitous Hout Bay vineyards leaves one mightily impressed at the toil of terracing these virgin slopes — and they've just moved more ground, excavating a maturation cellar beneath the tasting room. But, while they're leasing vines elsewhere in the area, they don't want to get much larger.

★★★★ **Petrus** Dense, youthful **10** cab-based 5-way Bordeaux blend with dark savoury fruit checked by firm tannins & balanced acidity. Best left in bottle another year or two to fully reveal charms.

Cabernet Sauvignon ★★★★ Youthful **10** seriously styled, tight tannins interwoven with seductively rich, spicy fruit in ripe cabernet mould. **Merlot** ★★★★ Deliciously ripe, baked plum **10** reined in by fine tannin structure & savoury acid thread. An opulent wine to be opened & enjoyed. This & above two WO W Cape. **Shiraz** ⓐ ★★★★ Preview of **09** revealed attractive if simple spicy fragrance, clean fresh flavours & comfortably cushioned tannins. **Blush** ★★★ Bone-dry **12** rosé from pinots noir & meunier & chardonnay appealing raspberry fruit & modest alcohol for satisfying summer sipping. **Sauvignon Blanc** ★★★★ More depth in **12** than quieter **11** (★★★☆); freshly vibrant & flavoursome, with vivacious juiciness. From own grapes. **Klasiek by Catherine** ★★★★ Rich, classically fine flavours in freshly disgorged, bone-dry **09** chardonnay, pinot MCC sparkling; harmonious & vibrant, with more character than **08** (★★★★) & a lingering finish. **Black Swan Vintage Port** ⓐ ★★★★ Five port varieties infuse fortified **10** with aromatic interest. Dry finish, good fruit; perhaps lacks grip for long ageing. WO Stellenbosch. — IM

Howard Booysen Boutique Wines

Location: Stellenbosch ▪ WO: Stellenbosch/Swartberg ▪ Est 2009 ▪ 1stB 2010 ▪ Sales by appt ▪ Owner(s) Howard Booysen ▪ Cellarmaster(s)/winemaker(s)/viticulturist(s) Howard Booysen (Nov 2009) ▪ (cinsaut, riesling) ▪ 3,500cs (6btl) own label 33.3% red 66.7% white ▪ howard@howardbooysenwines.com ▪ www. howardbooysenwines.com ▪ **T** +27 (0)72-414-5458

At premier Cape Town restaurant Aubergine, boutique winemaker Howard Booysen is gaining experience as a sommelier, and understands today's winelovers. They're adventurous, hence his decision to swim upstream with riesling and cinsaut. And curious. 'People demand a story — why this vineyard or that variety? I always use my own life journey as reference.'

Howard Booysen Wines range

★★★★☆ **Riesling** 🍷 Drops 'Weisser' from name. Mimics Germany's grand off-dry styles. **11** intensely aromatic, has pinpoint balance between 24g/l sugar, racy acidity & lingering nectarine, white peach end. 25+ year old Swartberg (Karoo) vines.

Cinsaut ⓐ 🍷 ★★★★ Premium-priced **11** a blueprint for the variety: creamy red berry & hint black olive; drinkability enhanced by light oaking, lowish alcohol, gentle sweetness.

Pegasus range NEW

Riesling ✓ 🍷 ★★★★ This version from Stellenbosch grapes virtually dry — and more wallet-friendly! Pineapple & spice, limy tang on **11**, satisfying flavour, intensity & length; enjoy well chilled. — CvZ

Hughes Family Wines

Location: Malmesbury ▪ Map/WO: Swartland ▪ Est 2000 ▪ 1stB 2004 ▪ Tasting by appt ▪ Owner(s) Billy & Penny Hughes ▪ Cellarmaster(s)/winemaker(s) Billy Hughes ▪ Viticulturist(s) Kevin Watt (Jul 2005, consultant) ▪ 52ha/27ha (grenache n/b, merlot, mourv, ptage, tempranillo, shiraz, chenin, rouss, viog) ▪ 180t total 25t/ 1,800cs own label 85% red 15% white ▪ 6 Riverstone Road Tierboskloof Hout Bay 7806 ▪ penny@nativo.co.za ▪ www.nativo.co.za ▪ S 33° 20'37.71" E 018° 43'45.09" ▪ **T** +27 (0)21-790-4824 ▪ **F** +27 (0)86-549-1080

Billy Hughes is surely the only Argentinian making wine here. The name Nativo loosely refers to Billy's complex journey to become a naturalised South African and his wish to produce wines that reflect their origins. From the 2013 vintage not only will the vineyards have formal organic accreditation, but winemaking will fully accord with the guidelines of the Swartland Independent movement — practices enhancing the reflection of 'that strong sense of belonging'.

Nativo range
★★★★ **Red Blend** Soft spice intro on shiraz-based blend — with mourvèdre, grenache, pinotage & merlot. Finely balanced **10** offers complexity, harmony & medium-bodied drinkability. Pure-fruited elegance.

★★★★ **White Blend** 🔳 **11** wooded viognier (60%) & chenin. Shy, then opens up to lovely peach aromas, followed on palate with composed richness & balanced acid. Just-off-dry, but good food partner. — JP

■ **Hugh Masekela** *see* Veenwouden Private Cellar

Huguenot Wine Farmers

Wellington ▪ Closed to public ▪ Owner(s) Kosie Botha ▪ Cellarmaster(s) Bill Matthee (1984) ▪ Trade enquiries Gert Brynard ▪ PO Box 275 Wellington 7654 ▪ jcb@mynet.co.za ▪ **T +27 (0)21-864-1293** ▪ F +27 (0)21-873-2075

Privately owned wholesalers, blending, marketing and distributing a wide range of wines, liqueurs and spirits. Own wine brands include Huguenot and Zellerhof.

Hunneyball Wines

Location: Stellenbosch ▪ WO: Western Cape ▪ Est 2012 ▪ 1stB 2011 ▪ Closed to public ▪ Winemaker(s) Jim & Marie Hunneyball ▪ 0.75t ▪ 100% red ▪ PO Box 6089 Stellenbosch 7612 ▪ jim.hunneyball@gmail.com ▪ **T +27 (0)76-284-6951**

'At present we are garagistes, but would love to make this our day job,' says IT specialist and business owner Jim Hunneyball. He and wife Marie left Sweden in 2007 and returned to South Africa, where their love of wine inspired them to try making it themselves. Initial efforts (excluding a batch made in a bathtub!) were encouraging, as was support from friends and neighbours, and they hope to follow this first release with a shiraz, port and méthode cap classique sparkling.

Cabernet Sauvignon ★★★ Unfettered by new oak, **11**'s walnutty blackcurrant comes powering through. Textbook cab, big, forthright, will have you reaching for braai tongs. Bonus low sulphur. Swartland vines. — HJ/JP

■ **Hunterspeak** *see* Niel Joubert Estate
■ **Hunting Family** *see* Slaley
■ **Hunting Owl** *see* African Terroir

Idiom Wines

Location: Sir Lowry's Pass ▪ Map: Helderberg ▪ WO: Stellenbosch ▪ Est 1999/1stB 2003 ▪ Tasting & sales: see website — new visitor centre to open in 2013; see also Whalehaven entry ▪ Vineyard tours by appt (Sir Lowry's Pass) ▪ Owner(s) Bottega family ▪ Winemaker(s) Reino Thiart ▪ Vineyard manager(s) Tim Clark ▪ 35ha (barbera, cabs s/f, merlot, mourv, nebbiolo, p verdot, ptage, sangio, shiraz, zin, sauv, sem, viog) ▪ 85% red 15% white ▪ PO Box 3802 Somerset West 7129 ▪ wine@idiom.co.za ▪ www.idiom.co.za, www.bottegafamilywine.co.za ▪ S 34° 6' 14.1" E 018° 56' 12.4" ▪ **T +27 (0)21-858-1088 (vyds), +27 (0)21-852-3590 (sales), +27 (0)28-316-1633 (tasting: Whalehaven)** ▪ F +27 (0)21-858-1089 (vyds), +27 (0)21-851-5891 (sales), +27 (0)28-316-1640 (winery)

The Bottega family are understandably proud of their Idiom Sangiovese and Idiom Zinfandel both being selected again for Team SA at the Five Nations Wine Challenge in Sydney. A tasting centre is nearing completion at their Da Capo Vineyards on the Hottentots Holland slopes, and will regale visitors with vistas of the Helderberg Basin and False Bay. The Italian-themed La Vendemmia harvest festival, held annually on the property, remains a firm favourite on the wine calendar.

Idiom range
★★★★ **Zinfandel** Wild strawberry, spice & dried herbs on elegant & varietally expressive **10**. Like **07**, firm acid & grippy savoury finish for mealtimes. No **08, 09**.

★★★★ **Merlot-Pinotage-Cabernet Sauvignon-Petit Verdot** ⊛ After accomplished 07 (★★★★), exuberant 08 wide array of aroma & flavour: plums, red cherry, fynbos & toasty oak. Rich & full, good intensity before savoury finish.

★★★★ **Viognier** Full-bodied yet still elegant 10 back to form after slight dip in 09 (★★★★) with rich floral, peach melba & subtle vanilla complexity.

900 Series Cabernet Franc ⊛ ★★★ Attractive red fruit on last 06; overwhelming oak may since have integrated. **900 Series Barbera** ⊛ ★★★★ Mid-2010, 08 showed concentrated red & black fruit, smooth tannins, soft acidity. **900 Series Mourvèdre** ⊛ ★★ Ultra-ripe, meaty 08 last appeared excessively weighty, tired. **900 Series Nebbiolo** Await next. **Sangiovese** ★★★★ 09 trumps previous with ripe, plush plummy fruit, robust body & firm tannin backbone; perfect for hearty Italian fare. **Cabernet Sauvignon-Merlot-Cabernet Franc-Petit Verdot** ⊛ ★★★ Fragrant, medium-bodied 08 pulls back from ultra-ripeness of previous but seems tad developed, not for further keeping. **Shiraz-Mourvèdre-Viognier** ⊛ ★★★★ Soft & accessible 08, juicy fruit compote & hints of flowers & spice. **900 Series SMV** ⊛ ★★★ 05 broad red-fruit flavour, some savouriness & lots of oak.

Enoteca Bottega range

Bianco di Stellenbosch NEW ☺ ★★★ Fresh & fruity 12 from pinot gris billows floral & ripe stonefruit perfume. Light, balanced & perfect for a summer seafood braai.

Super Rosso ⊛ 🍴 ★★★ Pizza-friendly 09 from 83% sangiovese, rest cab & merlot is fruit-driven yet not overly sweet. Follows powerful cab-led 05 (★★★★). **Rosso** ⊛ 🍴 ★★★ 10 from 4 Italian varieties not as interesting as might be hoped for. — WB

■ **Ikapa** *see* Handcrafted Wines
■ **Ilula Gepa** *see* Stellar Winery

Imbuko Wines

Location: Wellington ▪ Map: Paarl & Wellington ▪ WO: Western Cape ▪ Est/1stB 2004 ▪ Tasting Mon-Fri 9-4 Sat by appt ▪ Fee R15/5 wines ▪ Closed all pub hols; Dec 25-Jan 1 ▪ Sales 8-5 ▪ Meals/refreshments by appt (48hr notice) ▪ Olives, olive oil, pinotage/merlot/shiraz jams, pinotage relish ▪ Owner(s) Imbuko Wines (Pty) Ltd ▪ Cellarmaster(s) Theunis van Zyl (2004) ▪ Viticulturist(s) Jan-Louw du Plessis ▪ 60ha (cab, cinsaut, merlot, ptage, shiraz, chenin, sauv, viog) ▪ 570t/60,000cs own label 60% red 40% white ▪ Other export brands: Makulu, Releaf Organic & Rebourne Fairtrade, Van Zijls Family Vintners ▪ Fairtrade, IPW, ISO, Organic ▪ PO Box 810 Wellington 7654 ▪ crm@imbuko.co.za ▪ www.imbuko.co.za ▪ S 33 40′30.84″ E 019 01′18.87″ ▪ **T +27 (0)21-873-7350** ▪ F +27 (0)21-873-7351

The visitor-friendly Wellington wine farm of the Du Plessis family is also home to son-in-law Theunis van Zyl's wine export business (recently extended to the US). Aiding the intention of 'making Imbuko a household name', the new Shortwood range is being rolled out nationally, and Imbuko wines now fly with Comair.

Du Plevaux range

Pinotage ⊛ 📷 ★★★ Earthy mocha styling, berry-edged savoury twist on 10 preview. **Shiraz** ⊛ 📷 ★★★ Juicy 10 tank sample infused with chocolate & strawberries. **Sauvignon Blanc** ⊛ 📷 ★★★ 11 pungent herbal aromas, full body & nettly flavour.

Imbuko range

Cabernet Sauvignon 🍴 📷 ★★ 11 friendly braai mate with tannic hug, sweet-sour tang. **Iswithi Pinotage** NEW 🍴 📷 ★★ Strawberry jam flavour, 12 sweet & soft for spicy meals. **Chardonnay** 🍴 Await next. **Sauvignon Blanc** 🍴 📷 ★★★ Citronella & cut grass perfumes, 12 is easy to drink, with soft acidity, fruit-sweetness & fairly full body. Discontinued: **Pinotage Rosé**.

Shortwood range NEW

Red 🍴 ★★ NV from undisclosed varieties, sharpish raspberry taste, tad gruff. **White** 🍴 📷 ★★ Citrus blossom on 12 fragrant, crisp summer wine. **Rosé** 🍴 ★★ Spice, boiled sweets on leafy 12; enjoy well chilled. — CvZ

■ **Indaba** *see* Cape Classics
■ **Indalo** *see* Swartland Winery
■ **Infiniti** *see* Kumkani
■ **Infusino's** *see* Beau Joubert Vineyards & Winery

■ **Ingenuity** *see* Nederburg Wines
■ **Inglewood** *see* Neil Ellis Wines
■ **Inkará** *see* Bon Courage Estate
■ **Integer** *see* Hoopenburg Wines

Intellego Wines

Location: Malmesbury ▪ WO: Swartland ▪ Est/1stB 2009 ▪ Closed to public ▪ Owner(s)/winemaker(s) Jurgen Gouws ▪ 220cs own label 40% red 60% white ▪ jurgen@intellegowines.co.za ▪ **T +27 (0)82-392-3258**

Jurgen Gouws makes his wines at Lammershoek, where he works in the cellar. His operation is tiny, but he's now trebled the number of wines, with a typical Swartland red blend and — not tasted here because it sold out so quickly — a second chenin blanc, made with long skin contact (like a red wine). That inaugurates a new sub-brand, Elementis, allowing Jurgen 'to try shifting the boundaries as far as possible, to produce a wine in its "purest" form'.

★★★★ **Rooi** NEW 🖉 **11** adds mourvèdre to shiraz. Lovely clear, fresh fruit plus smoky savoury quality. Elegant but intense; strong tannins need few years (decant in youth) to soften, harmonise. Older oak.

Chenin Blanc 🖉 ★★★★ **11**'s pretty, floral perfumed quality leads to crisp greenish bite on the finish. Richness from a little sugar & time in old oak, but balanced by fresh acidity & moderate 13% alcohol. Should develop over few years. **10** sold out untasted by us. — TJ

■ **Interlude** *see* Nwanedi Estate
■ **Intulo** *see* Kumala

Iona Vineyards

Location/WO: Elgin ▪ Map: Elgin, Walker Bay & Bot River ▪ Est 1997 ▪ 1stB 2001 ▪ Tasting, sales & tours Mon-Fri 8-5 Sat by appt ▪ Closed all pub hols ▪ Walks/hikes ▪ Mountain biking ▪ Conservation area ▪ Owner(s) Andrew & Rozanne Gunn, Workers Trust ▪ Winemaker(s) Werner Muller (May 2011), with Thapelo Hlasa (Jun 1997) ▪ Viticulturist(s) Kevin Watt (Jan 2012, consultant) ▪ 100ha/40ha (cab, merlot, mourv, p verdot, pinot, shiraz, chard, sauv) ▪ 250t/12,000cs own label 25% red 75% white ▪ BWI ▪ PO Box 527 Grabouw 7160 ▪ orders@iona.co.za ▪ www.iona.co.za ▪ S 34° 16'42.2" E 019° 4'58.2" ▪ **T +27 (0)28-284-9678** ▪ F +27 (0)28-284-9078

Andrew Gunn, owner of this important Elgin estate, has become increasingly convinced of the relationship between unadulterated soils and the individuality of the resulting wines. With the vineyards well into conversion to organic, 2012 marked the first use of biodynamic preparations, while a new, cooler underground maturation cellar will prolong malolactic fermentation — all aimed at increasing Gunn's ability to reflect terroir. No time to contemplate retirement: 'We remain as inspired and dedicated as the day we started,' he says.

★★★★☆ **Pinot Noir Limited Release** NEW Tiny quantities (50 cases) of lithe, pale **10** display graceful silken charms of succulent, expressive, pure red berry fruit, underscored by subtle earthiness.

★★★★ **Syrah** 🕒 Convincing **06**, then classic **07** (★★★★★) tasted few years back. Fruit purity, boosted by splash mourvèdre. Supporting oak lets compact fruit & mineral core lead to long clean finish.

★★★★ **The Gunnar** 🕒 'Elgin too cool for cab' sceptics proved wrong in savoury **07** Bordeaux-style blend. Merlot, petit verdot add aromatic complexity & soften cab's youthfully austere edge.

★★★★☆ **One Man Band** NEW Impenetrable **08** an endeavour to bottle the property's best possible wine. Seamless eclectic blend comprises shiraz, merlot, cab franc, petit verdot & mourvèdre. Big, spicy tannins & fragrant sweet dark fruit in polished, booming balancing act.

★★★★☆ **Chardonnay** Charming **10** (★★★★) has usual mineral verve in harmonious, complex, elegant style with deftly integrated oak. Not quite as breathtakingly concentrated as **09** but engaging & delicious.

★★★★☆ **Sauvignon Blanc** ✓ 🖥 🖉 Ultra-fresh, vibrant, appetising **11** has cool-climate appeal, with layered pure fruit, incisive acid thread & area's signature ringing minerality. Still tightly bound: needs time.

Viognier Occasional release. — IM

■ **Isis** *see* Schalkenbosch Wines
■ **Island View** *see* Orange River Wine Cellars
■ **Ithemba** *see* Stellar Winery
■ **Ivy Du Toit** *see* Jason's Hill Private Cellar

■ **Iwayini** *see Maiden Wine Cellars*
■ **Ixia** *see Distell*

Izak van der Vyver Wines

Location/WO: Elgin ▪ 1stB 2002 ▪ Closed to public ▪ Owner(s) Izak van der Vyver ▪ Cellarmaster(s) Andries Burger (Paul Cluver Wines) ▪ Winemaker(s) Izak van der Vyver (Jan 2002) ▪ 1.4t/75cs own label ▪ PO Box 42 Grabouw 7160 ▪ drs@telkomsa.net ▪ **T** +27 (0)21-859-2508 ▪ **F** +27 (0)21-859-3607

2011 is the tenth release of this 'hobby' Elgin sauvignon by Grabouw general practitioner Dr Izak van der Vyver. He harvests rows 13 and 14 of Ryk Joubert's Smarag farm each year and makes two tanks in the Paul Cluver cellar with Andries Burger's help. It's as well, as the traditional press is "n gedoente!' (a business!).

Sauvignon Blanc ✓ 🍾 ★★★★ Powerful riverstone & gunflint notes energise the grapefruit profile of super **11**, fuller & better balanced than tense **10** (★★★★). — DS

Jacaranda Wine & Guest Farm

Location/WO: Wellington ▪ Map: Paarl & Wellington ▪ Est/1stB 2009 ▪ Tasting & sales Mon-Sat 10-5 ▪ Fee R20/4 wines, served with olives & bread ▪ Closed Easter Fri/Sun, Dec 25 & Jan 1 ▪ Mediterranean/cheese platters & picnic baskets by appt ▪ B&B: 2 cottage units (see Accommodation section) ▪ Owner(s) René & Birgit Reiser ▪ Cellarmaster(s)/winemaker(s)/viticulturist(s) René Reiser (Jun 2009) ▪ 4.5ha/4ha (cab, merlot, shiraz, chenin, viog) ▪ 9t/750cs own label 50% red 40% white 10% rosé ▪ PO Box 121 Wellington 7654 ▪ jacarandawines@gmail.com ▪ www.jacarandawines.co.za ▪ S 33° 36' 49.2" E 019° 0' 16.1" ▪ **T** +27 (0)21-864-1235

Restoration is ongoing at this Wellington farm as owners René and Birgit Reiser add a shady winetasting pergola to the stoep and continue to enhance their organic credentials with the introduction of a dozen chickens pottering amongst the vines. Extensions to the unique 'cellar ronda', ingeniously housed in a repurposed circular irrigation reservoir, are next.

Cuvée Rouge ☺ 🍾 ★★★ Bordeaux red with cab & merlot in charge, **11** preview minty mouthful with some dark chocolate & juicy black fruit, making for enjoyable quaffer.

SMV NEW 🍾 ★★★ **11** blend shiraz (75%), mourvèdre & viognier ex tank mid-2012 is closed, some whiffs of black fruit, spice. May well open up once bottled & settled. **Pinotage Rosé** 🍾 ★★★ **12** tank sample showing red cherries & strawberries with crisp dry finish. **Chenin Blanc** 🍾 ★★★ **12** preview offers fresh fruit salad flavours & aromas. Dashes of colombard & lightly oaked chardonnay add interest. — CM

■ **Jacksons** *see Stanford Hills Winery*

Jacobsdal

Location/map/WO: Stellenbosch ▪ Est 1916 ▪ 1stB 1974 ▪ Tasting & sales at Die Bergkelder (see entry) ▪ Owner(s) Dumas Ondernemings (Pty) Ltd ▪ Cellarmaster(s) Cornelis Dumas ▪ Winemaker(s)/viticulturist(s) Cornelis Dumas, with Hannes Dumas ▪ 100ha (cab, ptage, chenin, sauv) ▪ 600t/13,000cs own label 100% red ▪ PO Box 11 Kuils River 7579 ▪ info@jacobsdal.co.za ▪ www.jacobsdal.co.za ▪ S 33° 58' 4.9" E 018° 43' 34.6" ▪ **T** +27 (0)21-881-3336 ▪ **F** +27 (0)21-881-3337

It was 1966 when the 21-year-old Cornelis Dumas was compelled to abandon his oenology studies at University of Stellenbosch due to the death of his father and take over the management of this family farm — and he still heads it up today. Wines here really are made with minimal intervention — no commercial yeast has ever been used, leading researchers to believe a unique yeast strain has developed which imparts a particular set of flavour characteristics to the must.

Cabernet Sauvignon ★★☆ **08** less complex than previous, high-toned, medium bodied, rather pastoral. **Pinotage** ★★★ Two vintages tasted: **09** (★★★) already quite evolved. Red fruit & soft tannins provide some appeal but no great complexity. **10** jammy & even more straightforward. — CE

■ **Jacoline Haasbroek Wines** *see My Wyn*

Jacques Smit Wines

Location/WO: Wellington ▪ Map: Paarl & Wellington ▪ Est/1stB 2003 ▪ Tasting, sales & tours by appt ▪ Closed Easter Fri/Sun/Mon, Ascension Day, Dec 25/26 & Jan 1 ▪ Facilities for children ▪ Owner(s) Jacques & Marina Smit ▪ Cellarmaster(s)/winemaker(s)/viticulturist(s) Jacques Smit ▪ 60ha/32ha (cab, roobernet, shiraz, chenin, Cape riesling) ▪ 300t total 100% red ▪ Welvanpas PO Box 137 Wellington 7654 ▪ info@vines2wine.com ▪ www.vines2wine.com ▪ S 33° 39′ 2.2″ E 019° 1′ 9.0″ ▪ **T +27 (0)21-873-1265** ▪ F +27 (0)21-873-2143

Now offering visitors a tasting area under his garden oaks, artisanal winemaker Jacques Smit has put his vineyards, cellar and vine nursery on the tourist map — his spread is a stop on the popular Wellington Wine Walk as well as appearing on the Walk On Foot programme during the Wellington Wine Harvest Festival.

Limited Releases

Cabernet Sauvignon ⑨ ★★★★ Juicy & appealing **07** easygoing mealtime companion. **Shiraz** ⑨ ★★★★ Lively palate, intense palate hide **05**'s heavy 16% alcohol. **Vine Valley** ⑨ ★★★☆ Boldly fruited **06** blend cab (67%) & shiraz nicely integrated, pleasing firm handshake. **Chenin Blanc** Await next. **Cape Ruby Roobernet Port** ⑨ ★★★★ Exuberantly fruity **07** given ageability by firm tannins. Also in 375ml. — DB

Jakkalsvlei Private Cellar

Location: Herbertsdale ▪ Map: Klein Karoo & Garden Route ▪ Est 1987 ▪ 1stB 2008 ▪ Tasting & sales Mon-Fri 9.30-5 Sat 9.30-3 ▪ Closed Easter Fri & Dec 25 ▪ Cheese platters ▪ Deli ▪ BYO picnic ▪ Walks/hikes ▪ Mountain biking ▪ Owner(s)/cellarmaster(s)/viticulturist(s) JG Jonker ▪ 80ha/26ha (merlot, ptage, hanepoot) ▪ 280t/2,500cs own label 23% white 12% rosé 30% dessert + 125,000L bulk ▪ PO Box 79 Herbertsdale 6505 ▪ info@jakkalsvlei.co.za ▪ www.jakkalsvlei.co.za ▪ S 33° 59′ 15.31″ E 021° 43′ 9.33″ ▪ **T +27 (0)28-735-2061** ▪ F +27 (0)86-593-0123

Garden Route travellers should look out for Jantjie Jonker's wines in shops between Riversdale and Plettenberg Bay. They're made on Jakkalsvlei, a supplier of bulk wine to Distell since Jantjie's father Andrew planted vines in 1983. The 'one-man-show' also hosts winemaking and mountain biking events on the farm.

Jakob's Vineyards

Location: Hermanus ▪ WO: Walker Bay ▪ Est 2002 ▪ 1stB 2006 ▪ Tasting by appt ▪ Owner(s) André & Yvonne de Lange ▪ Winemaker(s) Peter-Allan Finlayson (2010, consultant) ▪ Viticulturist(s) Johan Pienaar (Jun 2003, consultant) ▪ Farm manager Peter Davison ▪ 5ha/2ha (cabs s/f, merlot) ▪ 10t/±500cs own label 100% red ▪ PO Box 15885 Vlaeberg 8018 ▪ wine@jakobsvineyards.co.za ▪ www.jakobsvineyards.co.za ▪ **T +27 (0)82-371-5686** ▪ F +27 (0)86-589-4619

André and Yvonne de Lange — he an attorney, she a scientist, then living in Johannesburg — bought this tiny farm in 2002 and now have two hectares of Hemel-en-Aarde vines producing their likeable blend. Their 'boutique approach' extends to marketing, where they 'target groupings of individual consumers'.

Bordeaux Blend ★★★★ Charming, fresh, very drinkable **08** from cab, cab franc & merlot aims at elegance not power. Lightish fruit, good firm balance. Discontinued: **Cabernet Sauvignon**. — TJ

Janeza Private Cellar

Location: Bonnievale ▪ Map: Robertson ▪ Est 2000 ▪ 1stB 2001 ▪ Tasting & sales by appt Mon-Sat ▪ Fee R5 pp for tour groups ▪ Owner(s) Jan & Eza Wentzel ▪ Winemaker(s) Jan Wentzel ▪ Viticulturist(s) Hennie Visser (consultant) ▪ 6ha (cab, merlot, shiraz) ▪ 3,200cs own label 100% red ▪ BWI ▪ PO Box 306 Bonnievale 6730 ▪ jan.eza@lando.co.za ▪ www.janeza.co.za ▪ S 33° 57′ 36.3″ E 020° 1′ 38.2″ ▪ **T +27 (0)23-616-3547** ▪ F +27 (0)23-616-3547

Jan and Eza Wentzel have suspended winemaking for the time being. All their grapes will go to nearby Langverwacht, and (aside from cellardoor tasting) they'll serve the last of their Tresuva and Dulcevida at private functions, including dramatic performances — the wine cellar being put to temporary use as a small theatre.

■ **Jardin** *see* Jordan Wine Estate
■ **Jason's Creek** *see* Jason's Hill Private Cellar

Jason's Hill Private Cellar

Location: Rawsonville ▪ Map: Breedekloof ▪ WO: Slanghoek/Breedekloof ▪ Est/1stB 2001 ▪ Tasting & sales Mon-Fri 8–5 Sat 10-3 (summer) & 10-1 (winter) ▪ Fee R10 ▪ Closed Easter Fri-Sun, Dec 25 & Jan 1 ▪ Cellar tours by appt ▪ Bistro Mon-Sat 10–3 ▪ Shop ▪ Facilities for children ▪ Weddings/functions ▪ 6.5km hiking trail ▪ Owner(s) Du Toit family ▪ Cellarmaster(s)/winemaker(s) Ivy du Toit (Jan 2001) ▪ Viticulturist(s) Alister Oates (Jan 2004) ▪ 100ha (shiraz, chenin) ▪ 800t 45% red 50% white 5% rosé ▪ Other export brands: Jason's Creek, Meme, Soet Izak, Stout Izak & Wolvenbosch ▪ PO Box 14 Rawsonville 6845 ▪ info@jasonshill.co.za ▪ www. jasonshill.com ▪ S 33° 39' 52.3" E 019° 13' 40.6" ▪ **T +27 (0)23-344-3256** ▪ F +27 (0)86-523-6655

Cellarmaster Ivy du Toit was born into wine — her ancestors have been making it here in Slanghoek Valley since 1844. Her curiosity about all things wine led her to make her first Shiraz in 2001. Awards followed — she was Diners Club Young Winemaker of the Year in 2003 and Woman Winemaker of the Year in 2004.

Jason's Hill range

Cabernet Sauvignon Await next, as for **Classic Red**, **Chenin Blanc**, **Sauvignon Blanc**, **Chardonnay**, **Viognier** & **Sparkling Rosé**. **Merlot** ⊕ ★★ Sweet berry notes on uncomplicated **09**. **Shiraz** ⊕ ★★★ **09** offers smoky-savoury notes with sweet berry fruit for easy quaffing. — JP

▪ **JC Kannemeyer** see Wolfkloof
▪ **JC le Roux** see The House of JC le Roux

Jean Daneel Wines

Location: Napier ▪ Map: Southern Cape ▪ WO: Western Cape ▪ Est/1stB 1997 ▪ Tasting & sales Tue-Sat 8-4 ▪ Closed Dec 25 & Jan 1 ▪ Cellar tours by appt ▪ Restaurant & deli ▪ Owner(s) Jean & René Daneel ▪ Winemaker(s) Jean-Pierre Daneel ▪ 30t 50% red 50% white ▪ PO Box 200 Napier 7270 ▪ info@jdwines.co.za ▪ www.jdwines. co.za ▪ S 34° 28' 38.11" E 019° 54' 15.47" ▪ **T +27 (0)28-423-3724** ▪ F +27 (0)28-423-3197

'Fortunately, we had growth volume-wise last year,' says Jean-Pierre Daneel, winemaking son of owners Jean and René, 'but the market's still very sensitive so we have to watch our pricing.' A recently appointed marketer should make a difference to sales, and, dare we say, another maximum star rating for their always exceptional Signature Chenin will do its bit, too.

Signature Series

★★★★ **Red** ⊕ Savoury mix cab, merlot & shiraz, lengthy (33 months) barrel maturation yields standout **08** (★★★★★), beautifully knit tannins & velvet texture. Follows more powerful **05**.

★★★★☆ **Chenin Blanc** Aromatic **11** (★★★★★) worthy successor to dry & savoury **10**, which triumphed over a tough vintage. Combines elegance & richness in stylish package adorned with perfectly judged oak (20% new barrels). Delicious now, & crafted for good few years cellaring.

Directors Signature Red Await new bottling, as for **Directors Signature Chenin Blanc**, **Brut**.

JD Initial Series

Red ★★★ Lightly oaked, herbaceous **11**, equal partnership cab & merlot, offers pleasant uncomplicated quaffing. **White** ★★★ Demure, light-bodied **11** from mainly chenin & colombard. **Port** Await next. — WB/GdB

▪ **Jemma** see Painted Wolf Wines

Jeu

NEW

Location/WO: Stellenbosch ▪ Est/1stB 2010 ▪ Closed to public ▪ Owner(s)/winemaker(s) Nadia Barnard ▪ jeuwines@gmail.com ▪ **T +27 (0)83-324-8466**

Nadia Barnard (wine marketer at showcase Helderberg winery Waterkloof) has released her first port, 'for my gran, from whom I've learnt to love fortified wines'. A handcrafted ruby style from tinta barocca, grapes from local Albert Bredell (from a port-making family), Jeu ('Game') may soon extend to a Chablis-style chardonnay and MCC sparkling, possibly a Natural Sweet. Friend Margaux Nel (of port champion Boplaas) and a two-year stint in Europe and Australasia also inspired.

eu **★★★ 10** port from tinta is delicious but not usual hail-fellow-well-met ruby style: chunky mouthful, lots f extracted dark chocolate & spicy plumcake, almost salty flavours, very low sugar; give time to blossom. — /B/IM

JH Meyer Signature Wines

ocation: Riebeek-Kasteel ▪ WO: Elgin/Walker Bay ▪ Est/1stB 2011 ▪ Private tastings on request ▪ Owner(s) ohan Meyer ▪ Cellarmaster(s)/winemaker(s)/viticulturist(s) Johan Meyer (2011) ▪ 3t/200cs own label 50% ed 50% white ▪ PO Box 396 Riebeek-Kasteel 7307 ▪ jhmeyerwines@gmail.com ▪ www.jhmeyerwines.co.za ▪ +27 (0)72-045-9592

After 'discovering Stellenbosch and the wine world' in 2002 and graduating from Elsenburg College, Johan Meyer criss-crossed the world's winelands, indulging his passion for pinot noir and chardonnay. Back home, in 2010 he won a Decanter World Wine Awards trophy for a wine from fruit sourced in Swartland. He's now based there, at Meerhof Family Vineyards, where he also makes 1,000 eponymous bottles from classic Burgundy varieties grown in Elgin and Walker Bay. Future plans include a reserve range from vineyards on the Cape south coast family farm.

★★★★ Chardonnay Old World styled, focusing on texture, minerality, though plenty of fruit (citrus & pear) in **11**, ably supported by older oak. Crisp, savoury undertone for mealtime compatibility. WO Walker Bay.
Pinot Noir ★★★★ From Elgin, lovely bouquet of strawberries, spice & earth, mirrored on 2011's palate with balanced oak, crisp food-friendly acidity. Everything in place, only needs more depth for higher rating. — WB/IM

▪ **JH Pacas & Co** see Bernheim Wines
▪ **JJ Handmade Wines** see StellenRust
▪ **Johan de Wet Wines** see Lorraine Private Cellar
▪ **John B** see Rietvallei Wine Estate

Jonkheer

ocation: Bonnievale ▪ Map: Robertson ▪ WO: Western Cape/Robertson ▪ Est 1912 ▪ 1stB 1956 ▪ Tasting & cellar tours by appt ▪ Wine sales Mon-Fri 8-5 at Jonkheer offices in Main Str ▪ Closed all pub hols ▪ 4 self-catering guest houses ▪ Lifestyle Centre ▪ Owner(s) Andries Jonker & Dirk Du Plessis Jonker ▪ Cellarmaster(s)/winemaker(s) Erhard Roothman (Feb 1971) ▪ Viticulturist(s) Andries Jonker (1984) ▪ 300ha/130ha (cab, merlot, muscadel r/w, ptage, chard, pinot grigio, sauv) ▪ 1,500t/17,000cs own label 25% red 65% white 10% rosé ▪ PO Box 13 Bonnievale 6730 ▪ info@jonkheer.co.za ▪ www.jonkheer.net ▪ S 33° 56′54.9″ E 020° 2′48.4″ T +27 (0)23-616-2137/8/9 ▪ F +27 (0)23-616-3146

The centenary of the Jonker family's ownership of this spread along the Breede River was marked by a wine made by youngest son, 13-year-old Johannes, which director Dirk says is 'our first fifth-generation wine, which will go on auction to benefit our local school'. Jonkheer has partnered with the Samora Biko Trust to form Jonkheer Africa, 'a new dynamic and black-owned entity that will drive responsible wine consumption and uptake in a largely virgin black market'.

Jonkheer range

★★★★ Muscatheer ⊛ From 30+ year old muscat de Frontignan bushvines. **05** (**★★★★**) first since maiden **00**, shade less elegant.
Pinotage ★ Rustic **10** dark fruited & high toned. **Shiraz Family Reserve ★★** Smoke & succulent fruit on oak & mocha **10**, juicy braai red. **Chardonnay Family Reserve** ⊛ **★★★** Zesty **09** had buttered pear flavours mid-2010. **Buccaneer Touriga Nacional** ⊛ **★★★★** Individual & attractive lighter styled fortified dessert, **04** shows a combination of port, sherry & jerepiko characters. Robertson WO. Last-tasted **02** **★★★★**) offered Xmas-cake flavours.

Bakenskop range

Cabernet Sauvignon 🍴 **★** Sour cherries & bold tannins on light-bodied **11**. **Merlot** 🍴 **★★** **11** has earthy hay notes, touch of chocolate in a lightish package. **Pinotage** ⊛ 🍴 🚫 **★★★★** Unapologetically pinotage, **11** fleshy banana & strawberry fruit, slippery as Teflon. **Shiraz** 🍴 **★** Smoky-savoury **11** for game dishes, reflects estate's moderate alcohol levels. **Chardonnay** 🍴 **★** Straightforward **12**, lemon/lime tones & brisk acidity. **Sauvignon Blanc** 🍴 **★★** Capsicum-tinged tropical fruit in light-textured **12**. **Es la Vida**

Blanca 🏠 ★★ **NV** off-dry party starter from muscadel, with honey & nut nuance, low alcohol & slight sparkle. **Es La Vida Rosa** 🏠 ★★ Pretty pink, off-dry **NV** with tingly bubbles for uncomplicated anytime sipping. **Red Muscadel** 🏠 ★★★ Tempting floral & grapey wafts, spirity bite on fortified **11** dessert. Follows last tasted perfumed & decadent **09** (★★★★). **White Muscadel** 🏠 ★★★ Savoury-sweet fortified **11** is star o line-up, ideal aperitif or nightcap. Robertson WO, as for Red version.

Beacon Hill range

Sauvignon Blanc ★★ Export only. Uncomplicated **12** greenpepper & tropical nuances, for early drinking.

Cape Auction range

Red ⓟ 🏠 ★★ Plummy **NV** crowd pleaser. **Rosé** ⓟ ★★ Muscatty **NV** rosé for the sweet-toothed. **Whit** ⓟ 🏠 ★★ **NV** with soft quaffability. **Late Harvest** ⓟ ★★ Affable chenin/semillon **NV** duo. — DB/JP

Joostenberg Wines

Location: Paarl ▪ Map: Paarl & Wellington ▪ WO: Paarl/Western Cape ▪ Est/1stB 1999 ▪ Tasting & sales daily 10–5 a the Deli on Klein Joostenberg Farm ▪ Cellar tours by appt ▪ Closed Dec 25 & Jan 1 ▪ Joostenberg Bistro (see Restaurants section) ▪ Facilities for children ▪ Tour groups ▪ Gifts ▪ Farm produce ▪ Honey shop ▪ Conferences ▪ Ludwig rose nursery & Van den Berg garden centre ▪ Owner(s) Philip & Tyrrel Myburgh ▪ Cellarmaster(s)/viticulturist(s Tyrrel Myburgh (1999) ▪ 31ha (cab, merlot, mourv, shiraz, touriga nacional, chenin, rouss, viog) ▪ 120t/8,000c own label 35% red 50% white 15% NLH ▪ PO Box 82 Elsenburg 7607 ▪ winery@joostenberg.co.za ▪ www. joostenberg.co.za ▪ S 33° 49'34.8" E 018° 47'45.5" ▪ **T +27 (0)21-884-4141** ▪ F +27 (0)21-884-4135

The Myburgh heritage is captured on the labels of the new Family Blend wine from their Paarl farm. A 1951 photograph features winemaker Tyrrel Myburgh' paternal grandparents, neighbour Raymond Starke and great-grandfathe Johannes Myburgh (plus greyhound Prince) at the front door of the manor house 'It portrays a time when people had time for family, friends and neighbours!' say Myburgh, explaining his choice. 'I want my customers to know that my wines an the people involved in making them are firmly rooted in this place.'

Joostenberg range

★★★★ **Syrah** 🏠 **10**, first since **07**, delights with floral/red fruit fragrance; more spicy flavour buzz born on supple, luscious mouthfeel. Too good not to drink now & in next few years.

★★★★ **Bakermat** 🏠 Cab-led blend with shiraz, merlot, touriga forged in dark-fruited, very fresh **1** (★★★★). Tastily savoury if rather straightforward & brief. **09** full bodied, great balance.

★★★★ **Fairhead** ⓟ 🏠 Chenin-based **10** joined by viognier & a little roussanne. More pronounced aro mas than **09**, still refined; gently creamy with purity, freshness. Natural ferment in barrel.

★★★★ **Family Blend White** **NEW** ✓ 🏠 🌿 Charming 1951 family photo depicted on label of unoake **11** chenin with viognier, roussanne. Pretty wildflower scents, creamy feel, gentle fruity tang on close make fo individual drinkability. **12** tank sample slightly drier, equally delightful. Certified as 'organic in conversion'.

★★★★☆ **Chenin Blanc Noble Late Harvest** Barrel-fermented sweet dessert from old-vine chenin. **1** regales with similar botrytis-laced lime marmalade features as **10** but more lively fruity acids, medium body & mellow sweetness.

Family Blend Red **NEW** ✓ ★★★★ Rich, spicy red fruit drama introduces shiraz-led **10**. Smooth, gently sup ple with roundly flavoursome lingering finish. Discontinued: **Shiraz-Merlot, Chenin Blanc-Viognier.**

Little J range

Shiraz ☺ 🏠 🌿 ★★★ Previously 'Red'. Fruit-driven **10**; fresh & smooth-tannined. Splashes cinsaut, mourvèdre, viognier increase spicy red berry interest. This range all WO W Cape. **Rosé** ☺ 🏠 🌿 ★★★ **11** basketful fresh ripe strawberries, with dusting of fruit-lifting sugar. **Chenin Blanc** ☺ 🏠 ★★★ Was 'White'. Splash viognier bit more evident aromatically in **11**, otherwise in usual fruitily dry, easy style. — AL

Jordan Wine Estate

Location/map/WO: Stellenbosch ▪ Est 1982 ▪ 1stB 1993 ▪ Tasting & sales daily 9.30–4.30 ▪ Fee R25pp, waived c purchase ▪ Closed Easter Fri-Mon, Dec 25 & Jan 1 ▪ Cellar tours by appt Mon-Fri 9.30–4.30 ▪ Jordan Restaurant Farm produce ▪ Conferences (60 pax) ▪ Walks/hikes ▪ Mountain biking ▪ Conservation area ▪ Visits to old prospec tor's mine shafts ▪ Fly fishing (catch & release) R100/adult & R50/child under 12, booking essential ▪ Owner(s) Jo dan family ▪ Cellarmaster(s) Gary & Kathy Jordan (1993) ▪ Winemaker(s) Sjaak Nelson (Jan 2002), with Brenda utler (Feb 2009) ▪ Viticulturist(s) Gary Jordan (1983) ▪ 146ha/105ha (cab, merlot, shiraz, chard, sauv) ▪ 850-50t/50,000cs own label 45% red 54% white 1% rosé ▪ Other export brand: Jardin ▪ Brands for clients: Pick's Pick, Woolworths ▪ BWI, HACCP ▪ PO Box 12592 Die Board Stellenbosch 7613 ▪ info@jordanwines.com ▪ www.rdanwines.com ▪ S 33° 56' 33.7"   E 018° 44' 41.3" ▪ **T +27 (0)21-881-3441** ▪ F +27 (0)21-881-3426

Having just celebrated their 20th vintage at Jordan, owner/winemaker team/usband and wife Gary and Kathy Jordan can feel justifiably proud. Never has the state had a richer year of awards than in 2012. They were all impressively nportant: Best Producer at the Top 100 Wine Awards with no less than 5 wines n the list; the Decanter World Wine Awards chardonnay trophy for Nine Yards; he American Express trophy for best cabernet at the Trophy Show; and a slew of 0+ ratings from Robert Parker, Stephen Tanzer, James Molesworth and other nternational critics. But there's no resting on their laurels, they've just com-leted the purchase of a section of a neighbouring farm, to further extend the pread of terroirs their estate can offer. The future looks assured.

ordan Estate range

★★★ **Cabernet Sauvignon** ✓ 🍽 09 is so immediately appealing with its berry-rich succulence & tobacco leaf nuance, it masks the underlying structure, the fine-grained tannins & good ageing potential.

★★★ **Merlot** ✓ 🍽 With complex nuances, herbs, cedar, dark chocolate layered through the lush berries, 10 is already drinking well, but years off its peak. Amenable tannins from 80% new oak back that up.

★★★★☆ **Cobblers Hill** Barrel-selected Bordeaux blend, aims for harmony & cracks it. Velvet-textured 09 offers supreme drinking pleasure, plush fruit interwoven with spice, dark chocolate, done with stylish elegance. New French barriques 2 years. Drink now till 2020.

★★★★☆ **Sophia** Blend of best Cobblers Hill barrels. Opening up in the glass, 09 offers dark fruit & exotic spices, fine Belgian chocolate, even hints of scrub. Misleadingly accessible, there's power under the sleekness, enough for an 8+ year future.

★★★ **Chardonnay Barrel Fermented** 🍽 🅶 With powerful peach & shortbread biscuit, 11 has heaps of character. Drinks very nicely too, zesty & long flavoured.

★★★★ **CWG Auction Reserve Chardonnay** 🅶 Grape selection from the Nine Yards vineyard, wild fer-ment & all new French barriques, 11 is a more elegant, sophisticated take on its stablemate. Offers hazelnuts & dried pears, yet with a delicacy, finesse that beguiles.

★★★★ **Nine Yards Chardonnay** 🍽 🅶 Single vineyard, always impressive & 11 (★★★★★) is excep-tionally so. Buttered toast & clementine preserve, kept fresh & focused by a seam of limy acidity, extending the flavours. Expertly balances concentration with verve, sinuous grace, as did sleekly curvaceous 10.

★★★ **The Outlier Sauvignon Blanc** 🍽 🅶 A different take on sauvignon, barrel fermented & with 3-4 years ageing potential. Savoury tones to 11's zesty fruit promise delicious drinking, a good food match.

★★★ **Sauvignon Blanc** ✓ 🍽 🅶 Elegant 12's leafy-nuanced minerality speaks an intensely focused & pure side of sauvignon, speaks of excellent vineyard management & cellar handling.

★★★ **Mellifera Noble Late Harvest** 🕘 🅶 11 (★★★★★), more intense than 10, shows riesling aro-mas with consummate style: floral notes & cardamom spicing, a perfume delicacy counterpoint to rich, intense pineapple flavours. Brightening acidity leaves a delicious tanginess.

he **Prospector Syrah** 🍽 ★★★☆ Plump hedgerow fruit lightly dusted with pepper, preview 10's silky ele-ance makes it a pleasure to drink. **Unoaked Chardonnay** 🍽 🅶 ★★★ Gentle white peach flavours in outhful 12, could reveal more with time in the bottle. Good acid balance keeps it lively. **Chenin Blanc Bar-el Fermented** ✓ 🍽 🅶 ★★★★ Name change from 'Chenin Blanc' for 11, & now bolder styling than 10 ★★★★). Hazelnuts & quince, with a fine acid thread carrying the flavours to a crisp conclusion. **The Real cCoy Riesling** ✓ 🍽 🅶 ★★★★ Aromatic & immediately appealing with its sliced pineapple & sweet ice aromas, off-dry 11 is a zesty anytime wine.

radgate range

Syrah 😊 🍽 🅶 ★★★ Smoky dark fruit & appealing succulence, 11 ticks all the easy-drinking shiraz boxes, as does 10. A bit riper, fuller, as delicious. Drink now till 2015. **Cabernet Sauvignon-Merlot** 😊 🍽 ★★★ Well spiced cassis & plums, 10 shows its oaking (17 months, half new) in the dry finish. Drink with rich food, can age a few years. **Sauvignon Blanc-Chenin Blanc** 😊 🍽 🅶 ★★★ Leafy note in 12's appley freshness shows sauvignon's effect, zesty & bright. Riper styling in 11 (★★★☆), apple & melon, a savoury thread from long lees-ageing, extra year in bottle.

Chameleon range

Cabernet Sauvignon-Merlot ☺ 🍽 ★★★ Lipsmacking cassis & nutmeg, **10** begs to be drunk, yet also has 3-4 years ageing potential. **Sauvignon Blanc-Chardonnay** ☺ 🍽 🌿 ★★★ Previewed **12** holds true to its drinkability aim with summer fruits, vibrant limy freshness.

Merlot No Added Sulphur NEW ✓ 🍽 🌿 ★★★★ **11** vivid & pure throughout, crimson coloured, black currant fruit & fresh-fruity succulence. No oak but good grape tannin. **Rosé** ⊕ 🍽 🌿 ★★★★ Admirab restraint in **11** from merlot & shiraz, exactly right for food, light enough for more than a glass. — CR

■ **Joseph Barry** *see Barrydale Cellar — SCV*
■ **Joubert Brothers** *see Beau Joubert Vineyards & Winery*

Joubert-Tradauw Wingerde & Kelder

Location: Barrydale ▪ Map: Klein Karoo & Garden Route ▪ WO: Tradouw ▪ Est/1stB 1999 ▪ Tasting, sales & cell tours Mon-Fri 9-5 Sat 10-2 ▪ Closed Easter Fri/Sun & Dec 25 ▪ R62 Deli Mon-Fri 9-3 Sat 10-1 breakfast lunches & Klein Karoo tapas ▪ Walks/hikes ▪ Mountain biking ▪ Conservation area ▪ Lentelus B&B (www lentelus.co.za) ▪ Owner(s) Lentelus Family Trust ▪ Cellarmaster(s)/winemaker(s)/viticulturist(s) Mey Joubert (1999) ▪ 1,100ha/30ha (cab, merlot, shiraz, chard) ▪ 2,500cs own label 70% red 30% white ▪ PO Bo 15 Barrydale 6750 ▪ info@joubert-tradauw.co.za ▪ www.joubert-tradauw.co.za ▪ S 33° 55' 26.4" E 020° 3 40.6" ▪ **T +27 (0)28-572-1619** ▪ F +27 (0)86-555-3558

The changed name (from 'Private Cellar' to 'Vineyards & Cellar') better describe the Joubert family's welcoming and visitor-friendly spread in the scen Tradouw Valley, believes co-owner and cellarmaster Meyer Joubert. Traffic o the Klein Karoo wine route is building up, he notes, as what was traditionall brandy and sweet wine territory adds lighter, crisper wines to its offerings.

★★★★ **Syrah** 🌿 **11** preview of one of region's most accomplished unfortified reds too unformed to ra though fine varietal black pepper & lily aromas promise well. **08** was last (no **09**, **10**).

R62 🌿 ★★★ Characterful '2nd red', recently 100% cab. **10** farmyard notes to pleasant leafy body; very dr drink soon with country fare. **Chardonnay Barrel Fermented** 🌿 ★★★ Name change (from 'Chardo nay') coincides with more obvious wood influence on **11**, masking orange & mandarin fruit mid-2012. Ma settle & harmonise in time. — GdB/CvZ

Journey's End Vineyards

Location: Sir Lowry's Pass ▪ Map: Helderberg ▪ WO: Stellenbosch/Coastal ▪ Est 1995 ▪ 1stB 2001 ▪ Tasting, sal & cellar tours by appt Mon-Fri 9-5 Sat 9-1 ▪ Fee R50pp (incl cellar tour) ▪ Closed Easter Fri-Mon, Dec 25 & Jan ▪ Cheese platters & snacks by appt; or BYO picnic ▪ Conferences (80 pax) ▪ Wedding venue (100 pax) ▪ Walk hikes ▪ Mountain biking ▪ Conservation area ▪ Peacock Cottage with private pool (min 2 nights) ▪ Owner Gabb family ▪ Cellarmaster(s)/winemaker(s) Leon Esterhuizen (Jun 2006) ▪ Viticulturist(s) Lodewyk Reti (Jun 2011) ▪ 50ha/32ha (cabs s/f, merlot, mourv, shiraz, chard, pinot gris, sauv, viog) ▪ 175t/15,000cs ov label 80% red 20% white ▪ IPW ▪ PO Box 3040 Somerset West 7129 ▪ info@journeysend.co.za ▪ www journeysend.co.za ▪ S 34° 6' 35.11" E 018° 54' 54.06" ▪ **T +27 (0)21-858-1929** ▪ F +27 (0)86-540-1929

Perched high on the Schapenberg above Somerset West, the Gabb family's pro erty not only enjoys spectacular views across False Bay, but the vineyard south-facing exposure allows for longer, slower ripening due to the coolin breezes flowing off the sea. Known for its chardonnay and cabernet, the farm now spreading its varietal wings: viognier, semillon, petit verdot and mourvèdr have been planted on recently acquired, adjacent land.

Reserve range

★★★★☆ **Cape Doctor Cabernet Sauvignon** ⊕ **07**'s sweet, fresh fruit shielded by fine-grained tanni Minty suggestion adds modern touch but savouriness is lasting memory. Well-judged oak reinforces status.

★★★★ **Destination Chardonnay** Bold mouthful of ripe fruit, oak, alcohol & sweetish finish, **11** not to taken lightly — & preferably taken with food. Drinkable now, can go few years.

The Cape Doctor Shiraz Await next.

ourney's End range

★★★ **Merlot** Typical minty profile accompanied by hint of earthy funk in **08** (★★★). Light fruit, slightly bitter, drying tannins. Less pleasing than **07**.

★★★ **Chardonnay** 🏠 Richer, more oaky version than Haystack. Ripe peachy fruit on **11** emphasised by softish core; gains form, length from freshness, dry firm finish.

abernet Sauvignon ⓟ ★★★★ Unshowy yet pure cab scents, flavours on **07**. Rounded tannins, some teresting savoury development. **06** (★★★★). **Shiraz** ★★★★ **07** several steps up from **06**. Generous dark ice, smoked meat attractions; supple & rich but with balanced mint-fresh lift.

ellar range

he Pastor's Blend ⓟ 🏠 ★★★ Minty hint on **09** lifts merlot's rich meaty tones. Smoothly accessible with avoury dry finish. Includes cab, shiraz. **Haystack Chardonnay** 🏠 ★★★★ Juicy, accessible style with sub-e oak enrichment. **11** medium bodied, peachy/oatmeal features balanced by gentle freshness. Like next, WO astal. **Weather Station Sauvignon Blanc** NEW 🏠 🈂 ★★★★ Chalky gooseberry fragrance, delicate t telling fruit on **11** lends quite European-like character. Pithy well-sustained conclusion. — AL

Joy *see Anura Vineyards*

JP Bredell Wines

cation: Somerset West ▪ Map: Helderberg ▪ 1stB 1991 ▪ Tasting & sales Mon-Fri 9-5 Sat by appt ▪ Owner(s) elderzicht Trust ▪ Cellarmaster(s)/viticulturist(s) Anton Bredell ▪ Winemaker(s) Denzil Tromp & Jacques edell ▪ 50ha/13ha (cab, merlot, ptage, pinot) ▪ 5,000cs own label 60% red 40% port ▪ PO Box 5266 elderberg 7135 ▪ info@bredellwines.co.za ▪ www.bredellwines.co.za ▪ S 34° 1'29.04" E 018° 46'18.72" ▪ **T 27 (0)21-842-2478** ▪ F +27 (0)21-842-3124

his winery was one of those responsible for the 1990s new wave of Portuguese-yle port. There have been no new releases for a few years (and clearly some big nanges), but young Jacques Bredell speaks enthusiastically about a new winery at is all about sustainability, and promises that there will soon be a new vintage.

redell's range

★★★ **De Rigueur** ⓟ **08** cab-led blend tasted a few years back.

★★★ **Late Bottled Vintage** ⓟ **04** port-style from tinta, souzão, tourigas last was still seductive.

★★★★ **Cape Vintage Reserve** ⓟ Last-tasted port-style **07** usual splendid blend tinta, touriga, souzão. ntriguing & complex; fiery in richly fruity-spicy & balanced style.

ape Vintage Await next, as for **Cape Tawny Port**. — TJ

JP le Hanie Wines *see Vredevol Private Wine Cellar*

ulien Schaal

cation: Elgin ▪ WO: Elgin/Hemel-en-Aarde Valley ▪ Est 2004 ▪ 1stB 2005 ▪ Sales from Paul Cluver Estate ▪ sting by appt only ▪ Owner(s)/winemaker(s) Julien Schaal ▪ 28t/2,000cs own label 15% red 85% white ▪ c/ ?O Box 48 Grabouw 7160 ▪ julien@vins-schaal.com ▪ www.vins-schaal.com ▪ **T +33 (0)6-10-89-72-14**

rom his first visit from Alsace to South Africa as a cellar hand in 2002, Julien Schaal anted to make his own wine here — and has done so since 2004, now based at Paul luver in Elgin. As a true Frenchman, his focus is on reflecting the origins of his gin chardonnay and Hemel-en-Aarde shiraz. This emphasis, he believes, 'is defi-itely the most significant trend here today'. As for the future: the first young chaal, Antoine (vintage 2011), will make his first trip here for the 2013 harvest.

★★★ **Syrah** 🈂 Tantalising echoes of northern Rhône syrah's delicacy & perfume in **11** (★★★★★). here's fruity substance & confident structure but its lithe, supple feel & freshness checks any sense of heaviness. ery good now, should mature well too. Like **10**, from Hemel-en-Aarde Valley.

★★★☆ **Chardonnay** 🈂 Retaining purity, minerality is Schaal's aim. Both evident in well-structured **11**. romatic lime, lees richness reined in, focused by palate's taut, energetic feel. Great persistence, potential. — AL

uno Wine Company

cation: Paarl ▪ Map: Paarl & Wellington ▪ WO: Western Cape ▪ Est/1stB 2004 ▪ Tasting & sales at 191 Main Str arl Mon-Fri 7.30-6.30 Sat 9-2 ▪ Open most pub hols ▪ Café Juno ▪ Winemaker(s) Anthony de Jager ▪ Viticultur-

ist(s) Thys Greeff ▪ ±50,000cs own label 70% red 30% white ▪ PO Box 68 Main Road Paarl 7622 ▪ info@junowine
com ▪ www.junowines.com ▪ S 33°44'36.9" E 018°57'46.1" ▪ **T +27 (0)21-872-0697** ▪ F +27 (0)21-872-18€

The Cape beauties paying tribute to Juno, Roman queen of the gods, in this funk
young Paarl-based brand are featured more prominently on the new wra₽
around labels — but no less buxomly! All the result of Fairview's Charles Back
savvy marketing input.

Cabernet Sauvignon ⊕ 🍴 🏺 ★★★★ Complex blackcurrant, spice & plum pudding combo, **10** te
tured, dry but concentrated, structure to last a few years. **Shiraz** ⊕ 🍴 🏺 ★★★★ Supple black fruit
cracked pepper on **10**, step up on previous. Dry, with firm tannic grip & density. **Shiraz-Mourvèdr€
Viognier** NEW ✓ 🍴 🏺 ★★★★ Fun & friendly blueberry spice, shiraz (80%) leads **11** with clove richness
depth. Sturdy but yielding. **Sauvignon Blanc** ⊕ 🍴 🏺 ★★ Lemon zest & grass on **11** from Darling grape
lively & fresh. — FM

▪ **Kaap Agri** see Breëland Winery
▪ **Kaapdal** see Robertson Wide River Export Company
▪ **Kaaps Geskenk** see Groupe CDV

Kaapzicht Wine Estate

Location/map/WO: Stellenbosch ▪ Est 1946 ▪ 1stB 1984 ▪ Tasting & sales Mon-Fri 9–4.30 Sat 9–12 ▪ F
R20pp, waived on purchase ▪ Closed Easter Fri/Sun, Dec 25 & Jan 1 ▪ Cellar tours by appt ▪ BYO picnic ▪ Confe
ence/function/wedding & braai venues ▪ Walks/hikes ▪ Mountain biking trail ▪ Conservation area ▪ 2 se
catering cottages ▪ Scenic wine tours with 4x4 overlander ▪ 'Booze-bus' (16 pax) with wine guide/winemak
on fun & informative tour, with option to braai & wine pair ▪ Owner(s) Steytdal Farm (Pty) Ltd/Steytler Fam
Trusts ▪ Cellarmaster(s) Danie Steytler snr (Jan 1979) ▪ Winemaker(s) Danie Steytler jnr (Feb 2009) ▪ Vitic
turist(s) George Steytler (Jan 1984) & Schalk du Toit (Jun 2003) ▪ 190ha/162ha (cabs s/f, cincaut, malb€
merlot, p verdot, ptage, shiraz, chard, chenin, hanepoot, rouss, sauv, sem, verdelho) ▪ 1,100t/30,000cs ow
label 70% red 30% white + 10,000cs for clients ▪ Other export brands: Cape View, Friesland ▪ Brands for c
ents: Escapades, Handmade, K&V Harmony ▪ IPW ▪ PO Box 35 Koelenhof 7605 ▪ kaapzicht@mweb.co.za
www.kaapzicht.co.za ▪ S 33°54'47.7" E 018°44'7.7" ▪ **T +27 (0)21-906-1620/1** ▪ F +27 (0)21-906-162

From the Bottelary Hills is the wonderful view over Cape Town and its mounta
that gives Kaapzicht its name. The large estate itself (only a third of the produ
tion is bottled here, the rest sold off) is a quintessentially family one, and h₂
been so since the Steytlers arrived in 1946. Brothers Danie and George own it ar
have overall responsibility for, respectively, the cellar and the vines. Wiv€
Yngvild and Mandy take care of export markets and look after the entertainme
and guest venues. Danie junior has been winemaker since 2009. The wines them
selves, mostly reds and off unirrigated vineyards (an increasingly rare thing
Stellenbosch), combine classic dryness (not all that common either) with mo
ern fruity flamboyance, power and flair.

Steytler range

★★★★☆ **Pinotage** ⊕ Intense, sweet-fruited (but bone-dry) **08**. A lock-forward of a wine, unasham€
old-fashioned, with big oak & big 14.6% alcohol. Brooding cab component adds middle & length.

★★★★★ **Pentagon** ⊕ **08** (★★★★) muscular & plush, lacking subtlety. Cab drives the cassis & ch€
character, with merlot in support, like **07**. Huge oak influence masks the powerful acidity & alcohol.

★★★★☆ **Vision** Classic Cape Blend, weaving cab (50%), pinotage & merlot into iconic cellar statement.
sweet fruited, showy, multi-layered — but less voluptuous, finer than **07**. All-new oak perfectly compacted

★★★★☆ **CWG Auction Cape Blend** NEW Sumptuously oaked but with plush fruit ascendant. **09** gain
harmony mid-2012. Redcurrant, plum notes, faint banana whiffs. Fine powdery tannins & bone-dry. Perfe
integrated blend of pinotage & cab; the former adds freshness & presence to the latter's brooding vinosity.

Kaapzicht range

★★★★ **Merlot** ⊕ **08** offers plum & mulberry notes, with tobacco & earthiness. The handsomely oa
ample sweet fruit is cut by a slightly clumsy dry, tannic finish.

★★★★ **Pinotage** ✓ Hallmark pinotage characteristically offering ripe strawberry & cherry notes. **09** inte
& vinous though with marked tannins layering a muscular, sinewy finish. Should develop over few years.

★★★★ **Shiraz** ✓ Cherry, raspberry aromas usually showy & forward, but **08** curiously restrained in you
the oak still repressing otherwise exuberant fruit. Needs time to integrate.

Combination ☺ 🍴 🧺 ★★★ Sauvignon & chenin involved as usual in lime-edged & tropical **12**, dry & crisp.

abernet Sauvignon ⏱ ★★★★ On **08** vanilla oak (2 years, half new) dominated fruit & vinosity at least in outh. **Bin-3** ✓ ★★★★ Stalwart value label, **09** from merlot, cab, pinotage. Intense red berry aromas, finely nanaged tannins, persistent sweet fruit. Juicier & better textured than less generous **08** (★★★). **Kaleido-cope** ⏱ 🍴 ★★★ Cab-based blend of 4 well-married grapes. **10** sweet-fruited & chunky. **Celebration** wait next. **Estate Red** ✓ 🧺 ★★★★ Bright red fruit on accessible **10** from shiraz & cab matured in older oak arrels, but lacks the integration of harmonious **09** (★★★★). **Shiraz Rosé** Await next. **Chardonnay** ⏱ ★★★★ Lightly oaked **09** caramel toffee whiffs, buttered toast, rich lime & tropical notes evident & evolving. **henin Blanc** ✓ 🍴 🧺 ★★★★ Peardrop & peach aromas on fresh & zesty. **12** more flamboyant than **11**. **auvignon Blanc** ✓ 🍴 🧺 ★★★★ Intensely tropical, overtly gooseberry, pineapple aromas, flavours on lush & exuberant **12**, after austere, herbaceous **11**. **Natural Sweet** ⏱ ★★★ Last tasted was succulent **07**. **lanepoot Jerepigo** ⏱ ★★★ Over-done **08**, gooey but spice still evident. **Tawny Cape Ruby** ⏱ ★★★★ resh **06** previewed some years ago as 'Tawny Port'. — GdB/MF/CR/CvZ

■ **Kakamas** *see* Orange River Wine Cellars
■ **Kango** *see* Oudtshoorn Cellar — SCV

Kanonkop Estate

ocation/map: Stellenbosch ▪ WO: Simonsberg–Stellenbosch/Stellenbosch ▪ Est 1910 ▪ 1stB 1973 ▪ Tasting & ales Mon-Fri 9–5 Sat 9–2 pub hols 10–4 ▪ Fee R10 ▪ Closed Good Fri, Dec 25 & Jan 1 ▪ Cheese platters in sum-ner; traditional snoek barbecues by appt (min 15 people); or BYO picnic ▪ Conservation area ▪ Art gallery ▪ wner(s) Johann & Paul Krige ▪ Cellarmaster(s) Abrie Beeslaar (Jan 2002) ▪ Winemaker(s) Abrie Beeslaar (Jan 002), with Jeremy Arries (2007) & Frikkie Elias (1992) ▪ Viticulturist(s) Koos du Toit (Jan 2004) ▪ 120ha/ 00ha (cabs s/f, merlot, ptage) ▪ 1,200t/85,000cs own label 98% red 2% rosé ▪ WIETA ▪ PO Box 19 Elsenburg 607 ▪ wine@kanonkop.co.za ▪ www.kanonkop.co.za ▪ S 33° 51′18.4″ E 018° 51′36.1″ ▪ **T +27 (0)21-884-656** ▪ F +27 (0)21-884-4719

o-owner Johann Krige's mission statement is simple: 'To ensure that Kanonkop continues to be regarded as South Africa's equivalent of a First Growth.' Towards his end, he says that the winemaking team is 'locked into a never-ending spiral f research and development'. Recently, the latest irrigation technology has een implemented in some of the very old pinotage blocks, satellite imaging is mployed during harvesting and state-of-the-art machine sorting equipment as been installed in the cellar. 'We need to change the perception that every-hing from Africa is secondary or cheap 'n cheerful. Our wines have shown that hey can compete with the best the world has to offer and the message needs to et out to those who matter.' Nobody's doing it more emphatically than Kanonkop.

★★★★☆ **Cabernet Sauvignon** One of SA's most celebrated examples, **09** (★★★★) will no doubt blos-som in years to come but currently serious oaking (23 months French, 50% new) makes it inscrutable, less approachable than **08**. Medium to full bodied, essentially savoury & classically styled.

★★★★☆ **Pinotage** 🧺 No other way to describe **10** (★★★★★) other than dead sexy. Great aromas of red & black cherry, a floral note, banana loaf. Medium bodied, with purity, freshness & fine-grained tannins. Worthy successor to showstopping **09**, also irresistible on release but many years from optimal drinking.

★★★★☆ **Paul Sauer** Cab-led (69%) Bordeaux red always in a restrained style, **09** (★★★★) comes across as particularly light, understated. Plums, cranberry & blueberry, some savoury notes. Medium bodied with well-judged oak. As with Cab, might unfurl, show better in time but mid-2012 lacks intricacy of **08** & previous.

adette Dry Red ★★★ Pinotage-led **10** is unpretentious, with ripe red fruit, bright acidity & fine tannins. VO Stellenbosch. **Kadette Pinotage Dry Rosé** ⏱ 🧺 ★★★★ **11** is substantial without being weighty, as great fruit purity, freshness. — CE

Kanu Private Cellar & Vineyards

ocation/map: Stellenbosch ▪ WO: Western Cape/Stellenbosch ▪ Est/1stB 1998 ▪ Tasting & sales Mon-Fri 9. 0–4.30 ▪ Fee R30/5 wines ▪ Closed all pub hols ▪ Owner(s) Ben Truter Trust ▪ Cellarmaster(s)/winemaker(s) han Grimbeek (Jan 2002) ▪ Viticulturist(s) Wynand Pienaar (2011) ▪ 48ha/26ha (cab, merlot, chard, sauv) ▪

200t/30,000cs own label 50% red 45% white 5% rosé + 4,000cs for clients ▪ BWI ▪ PO Box 548 Stellenbosc 7599 ▪ info@kanu.co.za ▪ www.kanu.co.za ▪ S 33° 53' 23.35" E 018°49' 8.44" ▪ T +27 (0)21-865-2488 F +27 (0)21-865-2351

The number of releases from the cellar of Johan Grimbeek calls to mind th mythical African bird, Kanu, present in the winery name and brand logo, whos appearance in the sky was said to promise a bountiful harvest. Operating fron the old Mulderbosch property on the R304 north of Stellenbosch, the Kanu team welcome visitors for tastings during the week (also by appointment) and plan t augment the cellardoor experience with a restaurant, deli and 'wine warehouse'

Premium range

★★★★ **KCB Chenin Blanc** ✓ Classic **09** delivers rich apple blossom, quince & honey, in fresh but sumptu ous off-dry style. Enriched by lees & oak, for drinking pleasure over the next 5 years.

★★★★ **Kia-Ora Noble Late Harvest** ⊕ **08** still selling. Previously showed vivaciously balanced oak & piquant kumquat & glacé pineapple flavours.

Cabernet Sauvignon ⊕ ★★★★ **08** is accessible, honest & appealing, with bright blackcurrant fruit & sup ple structure, for early enjoyment. **Merlot** ▨ ★★★ Less fruit-filled verve in **11**. Scented berry tone, warm rounded. **Shiraz** ★★★ Bold **07** is heartwarming, ripe & spicy, complementing hearty fare. **Keyston** ★★★★ Clean-cut Bordeaux-style red blend. **07**'s alluring minty cassis charm restrained by tighter structure oak. Like previous, needs time to shine. **GSM** NEW ★★★★ **10** grenache led blend, with shiraz & mourvèdre Supple, structured & youthful. Savoury red fruit just shining through spicy oak. **Chardonnay Barrel Fer mented** NEW ▨ ★★★★ Elegant **11** has lovely fruit purity & length. Deft oaking adds rich brioche ton zested with lemon/lime freshness. **Chardonnay Unwooded** NEW ▤ ★★★ Light & crisp, **11** is a gentle pear & lemon toned quaffer. **Sauvignon Blanc** ⊕ ▤ ★★★ Demure **11**, with a dab semillon, gently fruit & crisp. **Viognier** ▤ ▨ ★★★★ Step-up **11** is characterful & engaging. Tangy & aromatic, with feisty struc ture & leesy texture that complements food.

Prime range

Rockwood ⊕ ▤ ★★★ **08** shiraz spices up Bordeaux mix. Round, ripe & accessible quaffer. **Chenin Blan** ▤ ▨ ★★★ Plump apple-toned **12**, lacks aromatic verve of previous. Stellenbosch WO.

Méthode Cap Classique range

Giselle ★★★ Characterful traditional-method sparkling, unusually from 100% malbec in **09**. 'Brut' drynes but friendly, broad texture with savoury, earthy & biscuity nuances.

Pouring range

Rifle Range Red NEW ☺ ▤ ★★★ NV shiraz-led blend hits straight to the mark for supple, juicy fruited drinking pleasure. Enjoy solo or as a meal mate. **Semi-Sweet White** NEW ☺ ▤ ★★★ Vivacious, aro matic NV blend. Tangy & fresh, with a brush of oak & botrytis. Delightful quaffer & fusion food partner.

Merlot Rosé ⊕ ▤ ★★★ NV is crisply off-dry & plump, with cranberry savouriness. **Classic Dry Whit** NEW ▤ ★★★ NV chenin/sauvignon's crunchy acidity tempers warm tropical tone. **Natural Sweet Shira** NEW ▤ ▨ ★★ Warming, creamy **11** has sweetly spiced berry tone. — MW

■ **Kap Hase** see Migliarina Wines
■ **Karoo Classique** see Karusa Vineyards

Karusa Vineyards

Location: Oudtshoorn ▪ Map: Klein Karoo & Garden Route ▪ WO: Klein Karoo/Western Cape ▪ Est/1stB 2004 Tasting & sales Mon-Fri 9.30–4 Sat 10–2.30 ▪ Closed Good Fri & Dec 25 ▪ Karoo Tapas Restaurant & Deli Microbrewery ▪ Conferences (30-40 pax) ▪ Owner(s) Karusa Partnership ▪ Cellarmaster(s) Jacques Conrad (2004) ▪ 8ha (grenache, mourv, muscadel r, ptage, shiraz, touriga nacional, chard, sauv, viog) ▪ 50–70 2,500cs own label 30% red 50% white 5% rosé 15% other ▪ PO Box 1061 Oudtshoorn 6620 ▪ info@karusa.c za ▪ www.karusa.co.za ▪ S 33° 28'36.0" E 022° 14'33.2" ▪ T +27 (0)44-272-8717 ▪ F +27 (0)86-600-3167

The Conradie and Landman family owners push viticultural boundaries on th rocky slopes of the Swartberg range (also home to the famous Cango Caves). In competitive wine market, 'unhealthy when price reigns over quality and unique ness', the tourism-savvy partners believe in the 'character, personality, dynamisr nd presence' of handcrafted wines (and beers!) and business conducted, despite he e-commerce explosion, 'face to face, with a smile and a firm handshake'.

eserve Collection

he 5th Element Syrah-Viognier ★★★ Sweet wild berry, spice & violets on bright & clean **10**, 30% new ak well integrated, lovely black pepper dusting in tail. **Earth's Art Chardonnay-Viognier** 🗐 Await new.

erroir Specific Collection

ne Tree Hill Pinotage 🗐 **★★★** Improved **11** exudes dusty plums & chocolate, lightish & easy to drink. **erre Noire Syrah** 🗐 **★★★** Uncomplicated enjoyment & good typicity in savoury & firm **11**, honest & well ade. **Aloe Ridge Unwooded Chardonnay** ⊕ 🗐 **★★★** Promising **11** faint lemon/lime notes, slight reaminess; needs more oomph to take step up. **Southern Slope Sauvignon Blanc** ⊕ 🗐 🗷 **★★★★** ung up for **11**, unfolds in glass to (attractive) cat's pee aroma, lipsmacking freshness, stony finish. **tonerock Viognier** ⊕ 🗐 **★★★★ 11** restrained peach & apricot tones, well-handled oak gives structure gentle seasoning, zesty end. Range was 'Varietal Collection'.

ifestyle Collection

> **Muscat Rosé** ☺ 🗐 **★★★** Off-dry **12** candyfloss & ripe strawberries, zesty & refreshing. **Muscat Blanc** ☺ 🗐 **★★★** White muscadel's grapey perfume & spice suffuse charming **12**'s gently sweet apricot flavour.

hiraz-Cabernet Sauvignon 🗐 **★★★** Savoury plum pudding laced with pepper & spice, **11** is ripe & pleasntly light-hearted. WO W Cape. **Chenin Blanc-Sauvignon Blanc** 🗐 **★★★★** Chenin leads this time, provides **2**'s good ripe body, sauvignon adds pebbly minerality & complexity — more satisfying than previous.

aroo Classique Collection

inot Noir Rosé Brut ⊕ **★★★★** Dusky-hued **10** bottle-fermented sparkling not as delicately structured as ome but certainly well flavoured. **House Brut** Await new. Discontinued: **Prestige Cuvée Blanc de lancs**.

iqueur Collection [NEW]

oleil de Karusa Red Muscadel ★★★★ Solera-style NV fortified, standout in line-up. Marries spice & dcurrant with lovely tannin grip & ±17% alcohol. 375ml. **Soleil de Karusa Cape Vintage ★★★** Portyle **11** from touriga with chocolate-cherry nuances, taut grip & balanced fortification. Less sweetness & cohol (±16%) than most. 375ml. **Soleil de Karusa Cape White ★★** Unusual port-style fortified from ognier. **NV** lovely peaches & spice, smooth & very light for style. 375ml. — WB/JP

Katbakkies Wine

ocation/map/WO: Stellenbosch ▪ Est/1stB 1999 ▪ Tasting & sales Mon-Sat by appt ▪ Closed all pub hols ▪ wner(s) Andries van der Walt ▪ Cellarmaster(s) Andries van der Walt (1999) ▪ Winemaker(s) Teddy Hall 2002, consultant) & Andries van der Walt (1999) ▪ 29ha/10ha (cab, merlot, syrah) ▪ 500cs own label 40% red 0% white ▪ PO Box 305 Stellenbosch 7599 ▪ info@katbakkies.co.za ▪ www.katbakkies.co.za ▪ S 33° 55' 37.4" 018° 49' 14.6" ▪ **T +27 (0)21-886-5452** ▪ F +27 (0)21-557-0597

ome progress at this tiny Devon Valley property: though proprietor/cellarmaster ndries van der Walt says his house and cellar 'are still not complete', he's still nanaged to make his first pinot noir there from his neighbour's Cederberg vineards — 'all 40 litres of it'. You don't get more 'boutique' than that!

★★★★ Cabernet Sauvignon ⊕ Classic, understated character on mature **05** rather than overt fruitiness. Certainly pleasing, but on the austere side, with some drying tannins, through which the sweet fruit peeks.

★★★★ Syrah Reserve ⊕ Dense, complex **04** tasted few years back; firm structure, bold but balanced.

★★★★ Chenin Blanc ⊕ **09** (**★★★★**) more obviously off-dry than **08**; good depth of flavour, but the soft sweetness slightly awkwardly jostling some hard acidity. Pleasant enough, however.

★★★★ Viognier ⊕ **08** was elegant & fresh (despite 15.8% alcohol!) when tasted few years ago, with subtle, precise flavours. Off-dry sugar level giving richness; oak well absorbed. **07** was clumsy (**★★**).

yrah ⊕ **★★★★** Last was deliciously suave, spicy & unshowily fruity **08**. **Perpendiculum Viognier** ⊕ **★★** Quiet varietal character on **NV** blend of vintages 05 to 09, & quietly attractive, just off-dry. — AL

🖩 **KC** see Klein Constantia Estate

Keermont Vineyards

Location/map/WO: Stellenbosch ▪ Est 2005 ▪ 1stB 2007 ▪ Tasting, sales & cellar tours by appt ▪ Owner(s)
Wraith family ▪ Winemaker(s)/viticulturist(s) Alex Starey (Jan 2005) ▪ 156ha/27ha (cab, merlot, syrah, che
nin) ▪ 50t/1,000cs own label 65% red 33% white 2% sticky white ▪ BWI, IPW ▪ PO Box 713 Stellenbosch 759
▪ alex@keermont.co.za ▪ www.keermont.co.za ▪ S 34° 0'27.0" E 018° 53'39.0" ▪ **T +27 (0)21-880-0397** ▪
+27 (0)21-880-0566

It's exactly a decade since the Wraith family found beauty and a new challeng
on this patch of mountain land up the end of Stellenbosch's Blaauwklippen Roac
They took a chance on a young winemaker/viticulturist, Alex Starey, with hi
own dreams of making wine from unique and special sites, and together they'r
forging ahead, developing the vineyards, building a serious 'terroir-based' bran
in a standing-room-only market. 'We are young and small, with big dreams.'

★★★★ **Syrah** 🌱 Elegant spiciness in northern Rhône style. **10** from wind-reduced, concentrated cro
focused flavour but still a tad lighter than exhilarating **09** (★★★★).

★★★★ **Keermont** Premium Bordeaux/shiraz blend made in the naturally vinified, unfined/filtered hous
style. Super **09** (★★★★) ups the ante, polished fruit in ripe tannin cloak, measured & balanced. Serious, fc
the cellar. **08** also well-defined, with elegant spice & racy freshness.

★★★★ **Terrasse** 🌱 Barrel-fermented, chenin-driven, opulent white blend gets added steel from 149
sauvignon in **11**. **10** was noted as 'new' last edition, but maiden **09** since released; one barrel each chenin
viognier, the latter component now less rambunctious than at first, after time in bottle, more savoury & nutty

★★★★ **Fleurfontein** ⊕ 🌱 Admirable **10**, chenin & sauvignon desiccated on the vine, the 'syrup' the
oak-fermented for mere 580 half-bottles of decadent, not-too-sweet delight. — DS

Keets Wines

Location/WO: Stellenbosch ▪ Est 2008 ▪ 1stB 2010 ▪ Tasting by appt ▪ Owner(s) Christopher Keet ▪ Cella
master(s)/winemaker(s)/viticulturist(s) Christopher Keet (Oct 2008) ▪ 10t/500cs own label 100% red ▪ F
Box 5508 Helderberg 7135 ▪ chris@keetswines.co.za ▪ www.keetswines.co.za ▪ **T +27 (0)21-851-9844** ▪
+27 (0)86-544-3347

Chris Keet is keeping things flexible as he establishes his brand: sourcing grape
widely in Stellenbosch and vinifying them in rented space on the Polkadraa
Hills, from where he also works as a viticulture and winemaking consultan
Unsurprisingly the wine under his own name shows the understated elegance
he's become associated with (though there's no lack of power). He uses most
second-fill barrels; few top-level blends of this kind have no new-oak influenc
— but it's a part (a welcome one) of the unshowy Keet style.

★★★★☆ **First Verse** 🌱 Leafy fragrance & hint of cedar a lovely intro to unusually dry & restrained 5-wa
Bordeaux red **10** (★★★★). Light-stepping, balanced elegance belies powerful alcohol, but flavour leng
reveals subtle fruit intensity, untrammeled by oak. Drinks well but will mature, like maiden **09** (★★★★). — TJ

■ **Keimoes** *see* Orange River Wine Cellars

Keisseskraal Vineyards

Location: Bot River ▪ Map: Elgin, Walker Bay & Bot River ▪ WO: Western Cape ▪ Est 2004 ▪ 1stB 2005 ▪ Tastin
sales & cellar tours daily 10-5 ▪ Meals/refreshments by 24 hrs prior booking ▪ Facilities for children ▪ Farm pr
duce ▪ BYO picnic ▪ Walks/hikes ▪ 4x4 & mountain biking trails ▪ Owner(s) Johann & Ulrike Mendelsöhn
Cellarmaster(s) Johann Mendelsöhn (2004)4) ▪ Winemaker(s) Johann Mendelsöhn (1998)) ▪ Viticulturist
Johann Mendels (1998)98) ▪ 245h.6ha (shiraz) ▪ 4t/250cs own label 100% red + 100cs for clients ▪ PO B
85 Botrivier 185 ▪ galantskloof@gmail.com ▪ S 34° 10' 37.6" E 019° 13' 50.0" ▪ **T +27 (0)28-284-9219**

Ex-architect Johann   Mendelsöhn and wife Ulrike are committed to natur
winegrowing on their small Bot River farm along biodynamical principles.

Galantskloof Cabernet Sauvignon Await next. **Galantskloof Shiraz** ⊕ ★★★ Earthy, rustic **09** show
dark fruit & spice, but oak dominates. **Deep Red Shiraz** ⊕ ★★★ Ripe dark fruit on **09** but coffee, chocola
is over-riding impression. **Black & Red** ⊕ ★★ Mainly shiraz & cab, **08** lacks freshness, appears coarse. — IM

■ **Keizer's Creek** *see* Roodezandt Wines

Kellerprinz

...udget-priced white for the sweet-toothed, in 2L bag-in-box, by Distell.

...ate Harvest ★ Fresh & simple **NV**, semi-sweet party wine from chenin & colombard, widely sourced. —DB/HJ

■ **Kelvin Grove** *see* Simonsvlei International

Ken Forrester Wines

...ocation: Stellenbosch ▪ Map: Helderberg ▪ WO: Western Cape/Stellenbosch ▪ Est/1stB 1994 ▪ Tasting & sales on ...ome farm, cnr R44 & Winery Rd: Mon-Fri 9-5 Sat 9.30-3.30 (Sep-May) & 9.30-1.30 (Jun-Aug) ▪ Fee R40 KF & ...etit range/R50 Icon tasting/R80 entire range ▪ Closed Good Fri, Dec 25 & Jan 1 ▪ Sundays & after hours tasting ...vailable at 96 Winery Rd Restaurant (see Restaurants section) ▪ Cheese platters ▪ Self-catering 3-bedroom cot... ...ge ▪ Owner(s) Ken & Teresa Forrester ▪ Cellarmaster(s) Ken Forrester (1994) ▪ Winemaker(s) Ken Forrester ...994) & Martin Meinert ▪ Viticulturist(s) Pieter Rossouw (Oct 2009) ▪ 33ha/24ha (cab f, grenache, merlot, mourv, ...iraz, chenin, sauv) ▪ 200t/70,000cs own label 35% red 65% white + 30,000cs for clients ▪ Other export brands: ...nest, Workhorse (Marks & Spencer) ▪ Brands for clients: Woolworths ▪ ISO 9001:2000, BWI, HACCP, SEDEX, ...VIETA ▪ PO Box 1253 Stellenbosch 7599 ▪ info@kenforresterwines.com ▪ www.kenforresterwines.com ▪ S 34° 1' ...1.06" E 018° 49'05.92" ▪ **T +27 (0)21-855-2374** ▪ F +27 (0)21-855-2373

...mong the various efforts over the past 20 years aimed at getting Cape chenin ...lanc considered among the world's great wines, Ken Forrester Wines has played ... pivotal role. The top-end FMC is arguably one of South Africa's most famed ...ottlings, white or red, of the modern era but this winery makes versions of the ...rape that offer great quality relative to price at all market levels. 'The success of ...he chenin revival can be measured by the fact that the bulk price for grapes has ...ncreased for the last four years,' observes Ken. 'It's simple — better quality ...eans more demand.' The next challenge for him is to get Rhône varieties to find ...avour with the public. Wines like shiraz-grenache The Gypsy are a great start.

...on range

★★★★☆ **The Gypsy** 🗒 Classy, Old World-esque **09** (★★★★★) blend of near-equal shiraz & old-vine ...grenache from Piekenierskloof takes **08** to the next level. Pure red & black fruit, plenty of spice, great freshness & ...wonderfully fine-grained tannins. Possesses weightless intensity. Finish is extra long, savoury but not severe.

★★★★ **Three Halves** ⊕ 🗒 Mourvèdre (55%), grenache & shiraz interleaved in sultry **07**, complex but ...soft & ready for intimate dinners.

★★★★☆ **The FMC** 🗒 Always individualistic chenin, spontaneously fermented in all-new oak. **10** hugely ...omplex, with notes of beeswax, earth & spice to go with yellow fruit. Sweet on entry, smooth texture but then ...angy acidity kicks in, finishing long & dry. Home-farm grapes, as next.

★★★★ **FMC Première Sélection Moelleux** NEW 🗒 'Moelleux' meaning mellow, only made when ...weather permits. **10** chenin has real peaches & custard character about it. Sweet (sugar at 19g/l vs ±10 for ...MC), moderate acidity, creamy texture.

...' **Noble Late Harvest 10** not ready for tasting.

...en Forrester range

★★★★ **Reserve Chenin Blanc** 🗒 Substantial **11** has enticing honeysuckle aroma before palate of pure ...ruit, tangy acidity & well-judged oak. Subtle savoury note thanks to lees-ageing contributes to complexity. **...erlot** 🗒 🖉 ★★★★ Nicely judged, well-rounded **10** includes 15% cab franc. Good fruit concentration, ...esh acidity, fine tannins before long, dry finish. Accessible without being simple. Trumps **09** (★★★★). **Ren-...gade** 🗒 ★★★★ **08** is 47% grenache, shiraz & mourvèdre. Very expressive, with notes of red fruit & some ...oral fragrance. Medium bodied, soft & approachable. WO W Cape, others in this range Stellenbosch. **Sauvi-...non Blanc** 🗒 🖉 ★★★★ On preview, **12** is rich, with moderate acidity, notes of white peach & pear on ...ose and palate.

...etit range

...inotage 🗒 🖉 ★★★ Cheerful unwooded **11** abounds with plums & cherries, smooth, moderate acidity. **...abernet Sauvignon-Merlot** 🗒 🖉 ★★ **11** jammy, simple & soft. **Rosé** 🗒 🖉 ★★★ From grenache, ...2 is unassuming but more than sound. Upfront strawberry & well integrated acidity. WO Stellenbosch, oth-...s W Cape. **Chenin Blanc** 🗒 🖉 **12** unready. **Semi-Sweet** NEW 🗒 🖉 ★★ **12** from chenin, yellow ...ple flavour but overtly sweet, soft & simple. **Sauvignon Blanc** NEW 🗒 🖉 ★★ Previewed **12** slight lime ...aracter but rather basic. — CE

■ **Kevin Arnold** *see* Waterford Estate
■ **Kievits Kroon** *see* Glen Erskine Estate

Kingsriver Estate

Location/WO: McGregor ▪ Map: Robertson ▪ Est 2003 ▪ 1stB 2005 ▪ Tasting & sales Mon-Sat 8-9 Sun 8-5 ▪ Cellar tours daily 8-5 ▪ Tour groups ▪ Farm produce ▪ BYO picnic ▪ Hiking trails ▪ Conferences ▪ 4-star Kingsriver Country House & Restaurant ▪ Owner(s) De Clercq Family Trust ▪ Cellarmaster(s) Ruud de Clercq & Patrick Julius ▪ Winemaker(s) Ruud de Clercq (2005) ▪ Viticulturist(s) Patrick Julius (2005) ▪ 348ha/38ha (cab, ptage, ruby cab, shiraz, tannat, chard, chenin, cbard) ▪ 190t/5,000cs own label 80% red 20% white ▪ Other export label Mzansi ▪ PO Box 203 McGregor 6708 ▪ kingsriver-office@breede.co.za ▪ www.kingsriver-estate.com ▪ S 33° 55' 19.5" E 019° 49' 45.5" ▪ **T +27 (0)23-625-1040** ▪ F +27 (0)23-625-1045

Having completed the long process of implementing biodynamic farming, McGregor owner/cellarmaster Ruud de Clercq has two cows (Steak and Fillet) which supply manure, sheep which graze on winter weeds and chickens which eat the bad bugs. 'I'm surprised at how effective it is,' he adds.

Ruby Cabernet Await next. **Shiraz** ⊕ ★★★ Slightly warming 07 Aussie-style bluegum & charry oak, smoke & nutty nuances for added appeal. **Chardonnay** ⊕ ★★ Ripe tangerine fruit, vanilla highlights on crisp 10 crowd pleaser. **Sauvignon Blanc** New vintage not available. — JP/CvZ

Kirabo Private Cellar

Location: Rawsonville ▪ Map: Breedekloof ▪ Est 2002 ▪ 1stB 2003 ▪ Tasting, sales & cellar/vineyard tours Mon-Fri 30-5 Sat by appt ▪ Closed all pub hols ▪ Meals by appt only ▪ Facilities for children ▪ Tour groups ▪ Gift shop ▪ Farm produce ▪ BYO picnic ▪ Walking/hiking/4x4 trails ▪ Conservation area ▪ Owner(s) Pieter & Karen le Roux ▪ Cellarmaster(s) Pieter le Roux (2002) ▪ Winemaker(s) Pieter & Karen le Roux (2002) ▪ Viticulturist(s) Pieter le Roux ▪ 1,000t/6,000L total ▪ 10t own label 100% red ▪ IPW ▪ PO Box 96 Rawsonville 6845 ▪ info@kirabocellar.co.za ▪ www.kirabocellar.co.za ▪ S 33° 42' 36.68" E 019° 21' 27.55" ▪ **T +27 (0)23-349-6764** ▪ F +27 (0)23-349-6764

To matriarch Karen le Roux, the file of elephants tramping across Kirabo's label represent the succession of Le Roux generations — now up to six — inhabiting and tending the family's Rawsonville farm. Kirabo means 'a gift from God', gathered in and handed on in the bottles from this boutique reds-only cellar.

■ **Kiss My Springbok** *see* Anura Vineyards

Klawer Wine Cellars

Location: Klawer ▪ Map/WO: Olifants River ▪ Est 1956 ▪ Tasting & sales Mon-Fri 8-5 Sat 9-1 ▪ Fee R5 pp for groups of 5+ ▪ Closed all pub hols ▪ Facilities for children ▪ BYO picnic ▪ Conferences (office hours only) ▪ Owner(s) 92 members ▪ Cellarmaster(s) Pieter van Aarde (Nov 2011) ▪ Winemaker(s) Roelof van Schalkwyk, Cerina van Niekerk, with Christo Beukes & Richard Sewell ▪ Viticulturist(s) MG van der Westhuizen ▪ 2,095ha (cab, merlot, ptage, ruby cab, shiraz, chard, chenin, cbard, hanepoot, muscadel, sauv, viog) ▪ 43,000t, 30,000cs own label 40% red 40% white 5% rosé 15% other ▪ Other export brand: Travino ▪ ISO 22000:2000, Organic, DLG, IPW ▪ PO Box 8 Klawer 8145 ▪ klawerwyn@kingsley.co.za ▪ www.klawerwine.co.za ▪ S 31° 44' 34.9" E 018° 37' 36.1" ▪ **T +27 (0)27-216-1530** ▪ F +27 (0)27-216-1561

Revitalisation of this co-op-turned-company continues. New production manager/winemaker Pieter van Aarde (ex-Clairvaux in Robertson) now leads the team in establishing Klawer Wine Cellars as a bottled brand (gradually supplanting the Birdfield range). 'Intensive national and international marketing' and responding to demand for 'fruitier and lower-alcohol wines' is on the cards.

Grenache Blanc de Noir ☺ ▤ ★★★ Adds 'Grenache' to name in 12; off-dry, berry infused, lightish & tasty. Stock up for summer! **Sauvignon Blanc** ☺ ▤ ★★★ 12 in vein of step-up 11: satisfying vinosity & length, ample grass & tropical fruit flavour in a lightish body.

Cabernet Sauvignon ✓ ▤ ★★★★ 11 notch up from last-tasted 08 (★★★), leads the charge by reds from this producer away from excessive ripeness to restrained fruit. Dry & refreshing, with elegant tannins, smoky overtones. Enjoy in delicious youth. **Merlot** ▤ ★★★ 10 satisfyingly dry & food-friendly everyday red. **Pinotage** ✓ ▤ ★★★★ Strawberry- & chocolate-toned 11 confidently lifts the bar with generous flavo moderate alcohol & lipsmacking freshness. **Shiraz** Await new, as for **Shiraz-Merlot**. **Chardonnay** 🍷 📖 ★★★ **11** buttery & rich, nice solo sipper, though perhaps shade less lively than previous. **Chenin Blanc** 🍷 ★★★ Early picked **12** understated but well made, delivers persistent flavours at moderate 12.5% alcohol. **Viognier** 🍷 ★★★★ **11** different bottling to previous; this longer-matured version recognisable by restyled front label. A step up: perfumed ripeness lifted by lime/lemon zip. **Michelle Sparkling** Await new vintage, as for **Hanepoot**. **Red Muscadel** ⏱ ★★★★ Sweet fortified dessert **09** is complex, with tealeaf & dried apricot aromas, berry & molasses flavours. **White Muscadel** ⏱ ★★★★ **08** fortified dessert a real treat — perfect with crème brûlée. **Travino Matador** ★★ Port-style fortified dessert from ruby cab returns to guide, technically very sweet but well-judged spirit makes **09** seem dry. — DB/CvZ

Klein Constantia Estate

Location: Constantia ▪ Map: Cape Peninsula ▪ WO: Constantia/Western Cape ▪ Est 1823 ▪ 1stB 1824 ▪ Tasting & sales Mon-Fri 9-5 Sat 10–4.30 & 10-5 (Dec-Jan) ▪ Fee R30 ▪ Closed some pub hols ▪ Gift shop ▪ Estate honey for sale ▪ Collection of original Constantia bottles on display ▪ Owner(s) Zdenek Bakala, Charles Harman, Bruno Prats & Hubert de Boüard ▪ Winemaker(s) Matthew Day (2009) ▪ Viticulturist(s) Stiaan Cloete (Jul 2008) ▪ 146ha/82ha (cabs s/f, malbec, merlot, p verdot, shiraz, chard, muscat de F, riesling, sauv, sem) ▪ 500t/40,000cs own label 30% red 70% white ▪ BWI champion ▪ PO Box 375 Constantia 7848 ▪ info@kleinconstantia.com ▪ www.kleinconstantia. com ▪ S 34° 2' 19.0" E 018° 24' 46.5" ▪ **T +27 (0)21-794-5188** ▪ F +27 (0)21-794-2464

Respect for its rich cultural heritage is inherent in all the changes at this 'grande dame' of South Africa's vinous history. New MD Hans Astrom is determined, for example, that the already famous Vin de Constance, modelled on the great Constantia wines of the 18th and 19th centuries, will come to 'surpass even its own legacy'. Helping pursue such visions are Matthew Day, here since 2009 but now confirmed as winemaker, and, no doubt, the two Bordeaux eminences, Hubert de Boüard and Bruno Prats, who have become minor shareholders following Klein Constantia's amalgamation with Anwilka (the estates retain their identities). And, the team says, 'plans are already underway to improve and upgrade the cellar, tasting room, vineyards and manor house; all with special emphasis on retaining and preserving the history and spirit of the estate.'

Marlbrook range

★★★★☆ **Marlbrook** Flagship red honouring victorious military duke, now-bottled **09** equals the rank of **08**. Merlot-led, mostly Bordeaux blend shows focused red berry fruit in well tailored but firm structure. Youthful & ageworthy.

★★★★ **Mme Marlbrook** ⏱ Elegant **09** is the most balanced of all the whites. Mostly semillon with sauvignon & dab chardonnay, shows grapefruit tension leavened by subtle oak & rich lanolin & pear flavours.

Klein Constantia range

★★★★ **Cabernet Sauvignon** ⏱ **09** very restrained in youth & more unyielding than generous **08** (★★★★★). Cassis core tightly cosseted in supportive tannin structure. More classical styling, but needs cellaring to harmonise & show full potential.

★★★★ **Riesling** 🍷 Silk-textured **11** (★★★★), now in bottle, shows pine & floral nuance. A shade off **09** but has fruit pedigree & balance, just needs time.

★★★★☆ **Perdeblokke Sauvignon Blanc** 📖 **10** (★★★) is sleekly muscular, its quivering freshness & tight core of tangy fruit just starting to shine through steely minerality. Deserves cellaring, though in youth not showing elegance & concentration of **09** (★★★★★) or predecessor **07**.

★★★★ **Sauvignon Blanc** 🍷 **12** delicate yet focused, with bright stonefruit & some minerality. Dab of semillon adds waxy breadth. Returning to form after riper-styled **11** (★★★★).

★★★★ **Brut Méthode Cap Classique** Champagne-method sparkling gains extra vivacity from fine **09** (★★★★★) vintage after gentler **07** (★★★★). Back to all-chardonnay makeup, like **06**, 21 months on lees, showing delicate yet creamy fresh lemon & nutty brioche flavours. Elegant & appealing now & next 3-5 years.

★★★★☆ **Vin de Constance** Bottled decadence, **07** is the latest iconic dessert wine from unbotrytised muscat de Frontignan. New oak (65%) melts into unctuous glacé pineapple & barley sugar flavours. Rich & complex, but lacks the vibrant freshness of exceptional **06** (★★★★★).

KC range

Rosé ☺ 🍷 ★★★ **12** genteel, light & flavoursome, with cranberry/savoury tone & crisp balance.

Cabernet Sauvignon-Merlot ✓ 🏠 ★★★★ **10** dark berry fruit & mocha tone with creamy texture & fine supple tannins. Well crafted. WO W Cape, as for Sauvignon. **Sauvignon Blanc** ✓ 🏠 ★★★★ **12** widely sourced grapes give more fruit-filled style but retain crisp balance for refreshing summer enjoyment. —MW

■ **Kleindal** *see* Robertson Wide River Export Company

Klein DasBosch

Location/map: Stellenbosch ▪ Tasting by appt ▪ Owner(s) James Wellwood Basson ▪ Marketing director Nikki Basson-Herbst ▪ Viti/vini consultant Jan Coetzee (1997) ▪ Winemaker(s) Jan Coetzee (1994) ▪ 5.5ha ▪ 35t/ 3,200cs own label 90% red 10% white ▪ PO Box 12320 Stellenbosch 7613 ▪ dasbosch@telkomsa.net ▪ www. kleindasbosch.co.za ▪ S 33° 58'56.0" E 018° 51'44.5" ▪ **T +27 (0)21-880-0128, +27 (0)83-406-8836** ▪ F +27 (0)21-880-0999

Label vinified at Vriesenhof by Jan Coetzee for neighbour James 'Whitey' Basson, CEO of retailing empire Shoprite/Checkers. Current releases include 10/11 Merlot and 12 Chardonnay. Most are exported, though some do appear on selected local restaurant lists and wine shops. The wines can be tasted by appointment.

Kleine Draken

Location/WO: Paarl ▪ Map: Paarl & Wellington ▪ Est 1983 ▪ 1stB 1988 ▪ Tasting & sales Mon-Fri 8–4 ▪ Closed all pub hols & Jewish holy days ▪ Cellar tours by appt ▪ Pre-booked kosher picnics available ▪ Owner(s) Cape Gate (Pty) Ltd ▪ Winemaker(s) Jean van Rooyen (Dec 2007) ▪ Viticulturist(s) Frank Pietersen (1984) ▪ 12.5ha/5ha ▪ 55t/10,000cs own label 50% red 47% white 3% rosé ▪ IPW, OU certified ▪ PO Box 2674 Paarl 7620 ▪ zandwijk@capegate.co.za ▪ www.kosherwines.co.za ▪ S 33° 46'33.3" E 018° 56'50.4" ▪ **T +27 (0)21-863-2368** ▪ F +27 (0)21-863-1884

Orthodox Union certification potentially opens up new markets and opportunities for this kosher-only winery near Paarl. 'It's a globally recognised authentication that Jewish people know and trust,' winemaker Jean van Rooyen says. The logo appears alongside the Cape Town Beth Din seal on the bottles.

Cabernet Sauvignon 🏠 ★★★ **09** a notch up on last, fruity & light. **Merlot** ⓧ 🏠 🇿🇦 ★★ Pale, straightforward **11** sweetly oaky & fruity. **Dry Red** ⓧ ★★ Mature, merlot-led **06**, savoury, with bitter hint. **Rosé** ⓧ 🏠 🇿🇦 ★★ Light semi-sweet **10**, blend of red & white varieties. **Chardonnay** ⓧ 🏠 🇿🇦 ★★ Lightly oaked tropical **11**. **Sauvignon Blanc** ⓧ 🏠 🇿🇦 ★★ Uncomplicated dry **11** quaffer. **Vin Doux** ⓧ ★★ Carbonated **NV** version of Natural Sweet White. **Natural Sweet Red** 🏠 ★★ Low-alcohol **NV** cinsaut/merlot mix offers Fizz Pop-like sweet berry succulence, simple but nice. **Natural Sweet White** 🏠 ★ **NV** from riesling. Spicy pear drop in a light body (8% alcohol). **Kiddush** 🏠 ★★ Light (9% alcohol) **NV** wine for sacramental purposes. Ruby hued & syrupy sweet. Discontinued: **Pinotage, Shiraz.** —FM

■ **Kleine Parys** *see* Klein Parys Vineyards
■ **Kleine Rust** *see* StellenRust

Kleine Zalze Wines

Location/map: Stellenbosch ▪ WO: Coastal/Western Cape/Stellenbosch ▪ Est 1695 ▪ 1stB 1997 ▪ Tasting & sales Mon-Sat 9–6 Sun 11–6 ▪ R15/5 wines ▪ Closed Good Fri & Dec 25 ▪ Terroir Restaurant (see Restaurants section) ▪ Kleine Zalze Lodge ▪ De Zalze Golf Course ▪ Conference/function venue ▪ Owner(s) Kobus Basson & Rolf Schulz ▪ Winemaker(s) Johan Joubert (Nov 2002) ▪ Cellarmaster(s) Bertho van der Westhuizen (Dec 2004), with Zara Conradie (Feb 2008) ▪ Viticulturist(s) Henning Retief (May 2006) ▪ 90ha/84ha (cab, merlot, shiraz, chenin, sauv) ▪ 2,300t/200,000cs own label 40% red 50% white 10% rosé ▪ PO Box 12837 Die Boord 7613 ▪ quality@kleinezalze.co.za ▪ www.kleinezalze.co.za ▪ S 33° 58'14.1" E 018° 50'8.9" ▪ **T +27 (0)21-880-0717** ▪ F +27 (0)21-880-0716

The Kleine Zalze property near Stellenbosch has a history dating back 300 years, but it is in its latest incarnation, including a luxury housing estate, golf course and leading restaurant, Terroir, that it has come into its own. So has — emphatically — the eponymous winery on the premises, and trophies and awards continue to crowd the cabinet space. Ranges are clearly defined and offer good value at each level. Cellarmaster Johan Joubert is at the top of his game and must be a very busy man, but in addition to his daily duties he finds the time to produce something special for the Cape Winemakers Guild. A quiet sense of confidence about the project and these wines ensure an ever-growing challenge to the top ranks of commercially successful wineries in South Africa.

Family Reserve range

★★★★ **Cabernet Sauvignon** ⓣ Sweet-fruited **08** reflects vintage: less intense than multi-awarded **07** (★★★★★) with waves of flavour & interest in deep-piled structure. WO Stellenbosch.

★★★★ **Pinotage** ⓣ There's no doubting the variety: banana & plum fruit, hint of clove — but bold, out-the-blocks **09** has alluring sweet perfumes & a finely meshed structure to contain — just — its 15+% alc.

★★★★☆ **Shiraz** ⓣ 08 (★★★★) retains trademark swirling spice focus, as elegant but easier, fruitier than thrilling **07**, which mastered black berry fruits in firm tannic support. WO Stellenbosch.

★★★★★ **Sauvignon Blanc** ⃠ Previewed **11** (★★★★★) multi-layered, mouthfilling tropical fruit with weighty intensity, balanced by fine acidity; lingering send-off. Follows stellar **10**. WO W Cape.

Vineyard Selection

★★★★ **Cabernet Sauvignon Barrel Matured** Oaky gloss over tobacco, gravel, dark brooding cassis on ex-barrel **10**. Ripe & full bodied, with grippy tannin — a serious offering. WO Stellenbosch.

★★★★ **Chardonnay Barrel Fermented** ⃠ Rich **11** has 30% new oak in good support of yellow stonefruit & ripe apple, adds to rounded mouthfeel. Vibrant acidity keeps all composed. WO W Cape.

★★★★ **Chenin Blanc Barrel Fermented** ✓ ⃠ A buxom wine, full-flavoured, layered with tropical notes, cut by vibrant acidity. **11** has lovely detail & complexity, judicious oak lending gravitas. WO Stellenbosch.

Pinot Noir ⃠ ★★★★ Forest floor restraint to cherry perfume hints on balanced, generous **10**. Aromatic smoke & wood spice serve as good foil to juicy palate; chalky dry tannins. Step up on **09** (★★★★). **Shiraz Barrel Matured** ★★★★ Bold & seductively rich, aided by judicious oak & few grams sugar, yet **10** cask sample is fresh & vibrant. High 15.4% alcohol contained by red berry zippiness. Less gawky than **09** (★★★★). WO Stellenbosch. **Shiraz-Mourvèdre-Viognier** ▤ ⃠ ★★★★ Attractive spice & red berry lift combines with vibrant acidity in fruity & rich, off-dry **10**. 80% shiraz. WO W Cape.

Cellar Selection

> **Merlot** ☺ ▤ ★★★ **11** has clean plummy fruit balanced by pleasant oak, vibrant acidity; ends with charming sweetness. **Cabernet Sauvignon-Merlot** ☺ ▤ ★★★ Attractive freshness on just-dry **10**, nice tannic grip, with appealing medium body & finish. **Sauvignon Blanc** ⃠ ▤ ★★★ Clean tropical & upfront. **12** still very youthful mid-2012, but has good texture, fresh acidity, ending dry. WO W Cape.

Cabernet Sauvignon ▤ ★★★ Sour plums, smoky, with vanilla oak overlay. **10** is plush & fruity, ending on a sweetish soft note. **Gamay Noir** ▤ ★★★ Previewed **12** tart, with edgy tannin & raw acid despite being just off-dry & fruity. Needs to settle. **Pinotage** ⓣ ▤ ★★★★ Emphatic **10**, cinnamon & sweet-sour character in muscular frame. **Gamay Noir Rosé** ▤ ★★★ Previewed **12** shows like a white wine, with delicate, elegant fruit & a pleasant dry end. **Chardonnay** ▤ ⃠ ★★★ Unwooded, fruit-forward & ripe **12**. Bracing acid keeps the palate fresh, balancing off-dry sugar level. Needs to settle. WO W Cape. **Chenin Blanc Bush Vines** ✓ ▤ ★★★★ **12** will not disappoint its many fans, with botrytis component & few grams sugar adding to richness, balanced by zingy acid. WO Stellenbosch.

Foot of Africa range

Shiraz-Viognier ★★ Fresh, fruity & firm finish on off-dry **11**. These for export only; WO W Cape. **Chenin Blanc** ▤ ⃠ ★★★ Zippy acid lends nice cut to yummy fruit on **12**.

Zalze range

Pinotage ⓣ ▤ ★★★ **10** sweet fruited & ripe, usual light oak seasoning. **Shiraz-Mourvèdre-Viognier** ▤ ★★★ Bold fruit & meaty undertone, supported by subtle mocha notes from 14 months older oak on friendly **11**. WO W Cape. These for export only. **Shiraz-Grenache-Viognier** NEW ▤ ★★★ Shiraz-dominated blend has 'wet stone' earthiness, complemented by bright fruit. Off-dry **11** ends fresh & fruity. WO W Cape. **Cabernet Sauvignon-Shiraz Rosé** ▤ ⃠ ★★ Berried **12** dryish & short. **Bush Vine Chenin Blanc** ▤ ★★★ **12** not as well-knit as others across the ranges, its acidity somewhat apart. — JP

Kleinfontein

Location/WO: Wellington ▪ Est 1995 ▪ 1stB 2003 ▪ Closed to public ▪ Guesthouse ▪ Owner(s) Tim & Caroline Holdcroft ▪ Winemaker(s) Charles Stassen (May 2004, Nabygelegen) ▪ Viticulturist(s) Tim Holdcroft (Aug

1998) ▪ 12ha/1ha (cab, merlot) ▪ 5-8t/420cs own label 65% red 35% rosé ▪ IPW ▪ PO Box 578 Wellington 7654 ▪ kleinfon@iafrica.com ▪ www.kleinfontein.com ▪ **T +27 (0)21-864-1202** ▪ F +27 (0)86-587-2675

Named for the spring running through it, Tim and Caroline Holdcroft's Kleinfontein guest farm and vineyard offers relaxing home comforts in Wellington's beautiful Bovlei Valley. The bird-friendly indigenous garden attracts some 60 different species, while the organic vegetable garden provides seasonal produce for guests to enjoy with the house-brand wines.

★★★★ **Eminence** ⓘ Merlot & cab combo, **07** previously had meshed oak supporting mouthfilling red & black fruit.

Cabernet Sauvignon ⓘ ★★ Tad lean **09** shows red fruit, overt mint. **Merlot** ⓘ ★★★ Modest but likeable **07**, dark fruit, firm tannins before long, dry finish. **Rosé** ⓘ 🍴 ★★☆ **10** from merlot, refreshing & dry. — CM

■ **Klein Genot** *see Holden Manz Wine Estate*

Klein Gustrouw Estate

Location/WO: Stellenbosch ▪ Est 1817 ▪ 1stB 1993 ▪ Closed to public ▪ Owner(s) Klein Gustrouw (Pty) Ltd ▪ Winemaker(s) Warren Ellis (2006) ▪ Viticulturist(s) Pieter Smit (consultant) ▪ ±23ha/±14ha under vine ▪ 70% red 30% white ▪ PO Box 6168 Uniedal 7612 ▪ info@kleingustrouw.co.za ▪ **T +27 (0)21-882-8152** ▪ F +27 (0)86-609-7229

All the grapes in these wines came from the Jonkershoek valley, but not the home farm — yet. There was a first harvest in 2012 off the vines of the major replanting following Jannie Mouton's 2007 purchase of the farm (he also restored the historic manor house), but vinification must wait till they are more mature.

Reserve ★★★★ **10** blend of shiraz, cab & cab franc shows ripe upfront aromas cassis, espresso, vanilla. Sweet-fruited, densely packed & firm, with charming rustic element. **Sauvignon Blanc** 🍴 🌿 ★★★★ Previewed **12** with expressive tropical & grassy aromas. Mineral palate with vibrant acidity & tactile mouthfeel. **11** untasted, **09** (★★★★) more complex. — JPf

Kleinhoekkloof

Location: Ashton ▪ Map: Robertson ▪ Est 2004 ▪ 1stB 2006 ▪ Phone ahead for opening hours ▪ Owner(s) Raudan Trust ▪ Cellarmaster(s) Theunis de Jongh (2010) ▪ Winemaker(s) Theunis de Jongh (2011) ▪ Viticulturist(s) Loure van Zyl (Mar 2004, consultant) ▪ 114ha/11.8ha (merlot, p verdot, pinot, shiraz, sauv, viog) ▪ 110t/1,200cs own label 45% red 40% white 15% rosé ▪ Other export brand: Mountain Eye ▪ PO Box 95134 Waterkloof 0145 ▪ theunis@khk.co.za ▪ www.kleinhoekkloof.co.za ▪ S 33° 46' 51.87" E 020° 03' 17.30" ▪ **T +27 (0)23-615-2121** ▪ F +27 (0)86-677-5399

The De Jongh family farm high in the Wildepaardekloof near Ashton is so remote, you have to traverse two others to reach it. Water comes straight from a source even higher up in the mountains, and the location has a built-in 'vine cooler': the late-afternoon wind which blows without fail. These favourable conditions facilitate an organic approach to winegrowing.

■ **Klein Kasteelberg** *see Groupe CDV*
■ **Kleinood** *see Tamboerskloof Wine — Kleinood Farm*

Klein Optenhorst

Location/WO: Wellington ▪ Map: Paarl & Wellington ▪ Est/1stB 2001 ▪ Tasting & sales by appt ▪ Owner(s) Naas Ferreira ▪ Cellarmaster(s)/winemaker(s) Pieter Ferreira (2009, consultant) ▪ Viticulturist(s) Naas Ferreira (2001) ▪ 1ha/0.25ha (pinot) ▪ ±2t/82cs own label 100% rosé ▪ PO Box 681 Wellington 7654 ▪ kleinoptenhorstwines@gmail.com ▪ www.kleinoptenhorst.com ▪ S 33° 37' 48.60" E 019° 3' 19.54" ▪ **T +27 (0)21-864-1210**

Sparkling supremo and consultant winemaker Pieter Ferreira, who at Graham Beck oversees a total of 270,000 cases a year, and owner-viticulturist Naas Ferreira coaxed just 988 bottles of champagne-method bubbly from the 2010 crop of this tiny parcel of mature pinot noir in Wellington. Not unexpectedly, the focus is on increasing yield from the vineyard without compromising quality.

Pinot Noir Méthode Cap Classique ★★★★ **10** sparkling takes step up: tiny energetic bubbles, fresh strawberry & cream aromas, fine creamy persistence. More presence & joie de vivre than **09** (★★★★). —CvZ

Klein Parys Vineyards

Location: Paarl ▪ Map: Paarl & Wellington ▪ WO: Paarl/Western Cape ▪ Est 1692 ▪ 1stB 2002 ▪ Tasting, sales & cellar tours Mon-Fri 10–5 Sat 10–3 ▪ Fee R20/4 wines ▪ Closed Good Fri, Dec 25 & Jan 1 ▪ Facilities for children ▪ Conferences ▪ Weddings/functions ▪ Owner(s) Kosie Möller ▪ Cellarmaster(s)/winemaker(s) Kosie Möller (2002) ▪ Viticulturist(s) Jaco van Niekerk (Jan 2012) ▪ 56ha/45ha (cab, shiraz, chard, chenin) ▪ 1,800t/250,000cs own label 48% red 48% white 4% sparkling + 500,000cs for clients ▪ Brands for clients: Millers Mile, Tokolosh, Tooverberg ▪ PO Box 1362 Suider-Paarl 7624 ▪ sales@kparys.co.za ▪ www.kleinparysvineyards.co.za ▪ S 33° 45' 0.2" E 018° 58' 48.6" ▪ **T +27 (0)21-872-9848** ▪ F +27 (0)21-872-8527

'I regard blends as the best wines in the world,' says owner-cellarmaster Kosie Möller of this Paarl family winery (the Family Selection wines are named for Kosie's wife and sons). Abiding by the theory, even those of his wines with single-varietal names actually include a small percentage of another variety.

Family Selection
★★★★ **Jacob Selection** ⓐ Attractive **09** combo mainly pinotage, shiraz, cab franc & petit verdot. **Beatrix Selection** ⓐ ★★★ Last tasted was very ripe shiraz-dominated **07**. **Niclas Selection** Await new.

Kleine Parys Selection

Chenin Blanc ☺ 🍷 ★★★ Time on lees broadens dry but fruity tropical **12** sipper with modest alcohol.

Cabernet Sauvignon 🍷 ★★★ Earthy **11** unharmonious, needs to settle. **Merlot** Await next. **Pinotage** 🍷 ★★★ Elegantly floral, earthy aromas in **11** with nicely ripe, spicy, bright red fruit. **Pinotage Coffee Style** Await next. **Shiraz** 🍷 ★★ Spicy **11**'s fruit overwhelmed by firm acid & gruff tannins. **Chardonnay** 🍷 ★★★ Creamy oak textures to full-bodied **11**'s lemon flavours, needs touch more acidity to enliven. **Sauvignon Blanc** 🍷 ★★ Dollop viognier adds character to otherwise demure **12**. WO W Cape. **Méthode Cap Classique** ⓐ ★★★ Oak-fermented, buttery **09** sparkling from chardonnay in evolved though simple, dry style. **Cuvée Brut** Await next. **Red Muscadel** ⓐ ★★★ Last-tasted fortified **NV** dessert offered toffee richness.

Tooverberg range

Contour Merlot ☺ 🍷 ★★★ Smooth, easy **11** red with sufficient savoury grip from 15% cab. WO W Cape, as for rest in range. **Chenin Blanc** ☺ 🍷 ★★★ Drops 'Contour' from name. Tropical, sweetly fruity **12** has plenty of character & lovely balance.

Pinotage NEW 🍷 ★★★ Popular chocolate-mocha styled **12** more subtle than most. **Cabernet Sauvignon-Shiraz** NEW 🍷 ★★★ Fruity grip in decent, lightly oaked **12** blend. **Chenin Blanc-Chardonnay** NEW 🍷 ★★ **12** very simple easy-drinking quaffer. —IM

Klein Roosboom

Location/WO: Durbanville ▪ Map: Durbanville, Philadelphia & Darling ▪ Est 1984 ▪ 1stB 2007 ▪ Tasting, sales & cellar tours Tue-Fri 10–5 Sat/Sun 10–3 ▪ Fee R15, waived on purchase ▪ Closed Good Fri, Dec 25/26 & Jan 1 ▪ Cheese platters Sat/Sun; soup & bread in winter ▪ Café Ruby ▪ Facilities for children ▪ Tour groups ▪ Rubies & Roses: gifts, interior, deli & more ▪ BYO picnic ▪ Owner(s) Jean de Villiers Trust ▪ Cellarmaster(s)/winemaker(s) Karin de Villiers (2007) ▪ Viticulturist(s) Jean de Villiers (1984) ▪ 260ha/130ha (cab, merlot, shiraz, chard, sauv) ▪ 1,500cs own label 40% red 60% white ▪ Postnet Suite #3 Private Bag X19 Durbanville 7551 ▪ cellar@kleinroosboom.co.za ▪ www.kleinroosboom.co.za ▪ S 33°49'6.24" E 018° 34' 25.86" ▪ **T +27 (0)82-784-5102** ▪ F +27 (0)21-975-7417

This is a family-run boutique winery. Jean and Karin de Villiers handle the viticulture and winemaking, while daughter Marné runs the farm's craft shop and small restaurant, Café Ruby. Each wine is dedicated to a different family member, and octogenarian grandmother Janet is the next to be honoured with a shiraz.

Klein Roosboom range
★★★★ **Cabernet Sauvignon** Elegant, dark-berried **09** followed by somewhat more rustic **10** (★★★), with savoury flavours & a warming quality despite only ±12% alcohol.

Merlot Await new vintage, as for **Sauvignon Blanc** & **Marné Brut Méthode Cap Classique**.

Bandana range

Blanc 🍷 ★★ As previous, from 100% sauvignon, jauntily packaged **11** riper still, more tropical/melon end of the spectrum, rounded almost unctuous on the palate. — MW

■ **Klein Simonsvlei** *see* Niel Joubert Estate
■ **Klein Tulbagh** *see* Tulbagh Winery

Kling

Location: Hout Bay ▪ Map: Cape Peninsula ▪ Est 1984 ▪ Tasting & sales by appt but always welcome ▪ Owner(s) Gordon Kling ▪ Winemaker(s) Elena Corzana ▪ Viticulturist(s) Gawie Kriel (consultant, Jan 2005) ▪ 4ha/3.5ha (cab, merlot, shiraz, sauv, viog) ▪ 3t/70cs own label 70% red 30% white ▪ Constantia Nek Farm (Houtkapperspoort entrance) Hout Bay Main Road Constantia Nek ▪ wine@kling.co.za ▪ www.kling.co.za ▪ S 34°0'41.0" E 018° 24'3.7" ▪ **T +27 (0)21-794-3108** ▪ F +27 (0)21-794-0140

After Constantia's heights, where the road turns down to Hout Bay, are the vines that Gordon Kling started planting in 2005. They've already delivered fruit that speaks of cool conditions; as they mature they'll do so more eloquently. There's no winery — vinification since 2010 has been at Buitenverwachting.

Merlot ⊕ ★★★★ **09** has good fruit, but is restrained & light-footed, even a little lean, with a pleasant herbal note. No point in holding. **Shiraz** ⊕ ★★★★ Most attractive pure-fruited aromas & flavours on tactfully oaked, rather elegant **09**. A hint of green acidity on the unlingering finish. **Sauvignon Blanc** ⊕ ★★★★ **10** with an earthy-tropical succulence to its fleshy weight, finishing off with quite a green bite. **Viognier** ⊕ 🍷 ★★★ Rich **09** in youth showed excessive oakiness, but otherwise balanced. — JPf

■ **Kloof Street** *see* Mullineux Family Wines

Kloovenburg Wine & Olives

Location: Riebeek-Kasteel ▪ Map/WO: Swartland ▪ Est 1704 ▪ 1stB 1998 ▪ Tasting & sales Mon-Fri 9–4.30 Sat 9–2 Sun at Kloovenburg Pastorie Guesthouse 10.30-2 ▪ Fee R10 wine/olive tasting ▪ Closed Easter Fri-Mon, Dec 25/26 & Jan 1 ▪ Cellar tours during tasting hours ▪ Tour groups ▪ Gift shop ▪ Farm produce/olive products ▪ BYO picnic ▪ Walks/hikes ▪ Conservation area ▪ Christmas Market (Dec) ▪ Owner(s) Pieter du Toit ▪ Cellarmaster(s)/winemaker(s) Pieter du Toit (Jan 1998) ▪ Viticulturist(s) Kobus van Graan (Jan 1998, consultant) ▪ 300ha/130ha (cab, merlot, shiraz, chard, sauv) ▪ 229t/12,000cs own label 55% red 40% white 4% rosé 1% sparkling ▪ PO Box 2 Riebeek-Kasteel 7307 ▪ info@kloovenburg.com ▪ www.kloovenburg.com ▪ S 33° 23'36. 3" E 018° 53' 27.5" ▪ **T +27 (0)22-448-1635** ▪ F +27 (0)22-448-1035

Like his Swartland colleagues, Pieter du Toit is adopting a more natural winemaking approach. The new Naturally Fermented Chardonnay 'had no adjustments — not even acid, stopped fermenting of its own accord and was bottled unfiltered', says Pieter. From 2012 he's added a shiraz to the natural ferment list, while this year's chardonnay has fermented dry, unlike the previous. 'What makes naturally fermented wines unique is that they differ from year to year,' he notes.

★★★★ **Cabernet Sauvignon** 🍇 Classic-styled **10** best of these reds. Forthcoming cedary oak fragrance; firm & fresh, sound ripe fruit & dry finish. Best over next 2-3 years. **09** (★★★★) fairly simple.

★★★★ **Shiraz** 🍇 **10** (★★★★) very ripe, lacks fruit purity of **09**. Fruity & supple entry but rather gravelly, sweet close.

Merlot 🍇 ★★★ Full-bodied **10**; some plummy richness, tomato leaf lift. Smoothed & readied by few grams sugar — just off-dry. **Eight Feet** 🍇 ★★★★ Shiraz, cab equal partners in **10**, former's dark spicy notes, creamy mouthfeel to fore. Closing nip of tannin adds form, freshens. Good drinking now. **Barrel Fermented Chardonnay** 🍷 🍇 ★★★★ Quick 4 months in French oak (70% new) gives spicy interest to **12**'s lime purity. Otherwise nicely balanced, but oak-sweet finish needs time to meld. **Naturally Fermented Chardonnay** NEW 🍷 🍇 ★★★★ Complex oatmeal/earthy tones promise well on **11**. Lemon cream flavours, integrated new oak, let down by over-assertive acid (9g/l sugar). **Unwooded Chardonnay** 🍷 🍇 ★★★★ Good limy/oatmeal intensity on full-bodied, dry **12**; rich but uncloying creaminess complemented by firm finish. Food wine. **Sauvignon Blanc** 🍷 🍇 ★★★★ **12**'s fresh grassy vigour calmed, broadened by lees-padded palate. Roundly dry & persistent. Much improved on **11**. **White From Red Brut** ★★★ Coppery pink NV sparkling. Quiet spicy fruit lifted by vivacious bubble, off-dry tail. Discontinued: **Shiraz Rosé**. — AL

Knorhoek Wines

Location/map: Stellenbosch ▪ WO: Simonsberg-Stellenbosch ▪ Est 1827 ▪ 1stB 1997 ▪ Tasting, sales & cellar tours daily 10–5 ▪ Fee R20/5 wines ▪ Closed Easter Fri/Sun & Dec 25 ▪ Towerbosch Restaurant Wed-Sun 11.30-3.30 (Sat/Sun booking essential T +27 (0)21-865-2958) ▪ Facilities for children ▪ Tour groups ▪ Gift shop ▪ Weddings/conferences ▪ Hiking trail ▪ Horse riding ▪ Conservation area ▪ 3-star guesthouse & self-catering cottages ▪ Owner(s) Hansie & James van Niekerk ▪ Cellarmaster(s)/winemaker(s) Arno Albertyn (April 2005) ▪ Viticulturist(s) James van Niekerk (1977) ▪ ±80ha (cabs s/f, merlot, ptage, shiraz, chenin, sauv) ▪ 640t/ 12,000cs own label 51% red 42% white 4.65% rosé 2.35% sparkling & 184,500L bulk ▪ BWI ▪ PO Box 2 Koelenhof 7605 ▪ office@knorhoek.co.za, cellar@knorhoek.co.za, towerbosch@knorhoek.co.za ▪ www. knorhoek.co.za ▪ S 33° 52′ 44.8″ E 018° 52′ 19.1″ ▪ **T +27 (0)21-865-2114** ▪ F +27 (0)21-865-2627

Cellarmaster Arno Albertyn recalls as a child hearing from his father how much winemakers earned. He thought they had to be the richest people on earth. Wryly commenting that the salaries haven't changed much since, he says he's rich in other ways, such as the creativity of winemaking, being able to live his passion, in a beautiful environment, drinking great wines and working with the people on the farm and in the industry.

Knorhoek range

★★★★ **Cabernet Sauvignon** ✓ 🖾 Meaty, spicy, rich dark fruit, there's heaps to like in **10** (★★★★★), especially a superb balance. Tops **07**. Serious attention, 19 months all-new French oak, has paid off, drinks beautifully & could age 8+ years but doubt you'd wait. **08**, **09** sold out untasted.

★★★★ **Cabernet Franc** ✓ Plums & a typical herbal nuance, dash white pepper, **09** is a fine example of the variety. Textured tannins are amenable, perfectly judged. Enjoy now till ±2018. **07**, **08** sold out untasted.

★★★★ **Chenin Blanc Barrel Fermented** NEW ✓ 🖾 From dryland bushvines, **11** skillfully retains stonefruit flavours while basking in oak's savoury nutty richness. Sweetness (±19g/l) offset by acid & oak.

★★★★ **HVN Cape Ruby** NEW In tribute to the patriarch, Hannes van Niekerk. **NV** port from cab; mixed spice & fruitcake flavours, smooth, richly sweet. Enough acid grip to whet the appetite for a second glass. 375ml.

Konfetti Rosé Sparkling NEW ☺ ★★★ Fun in the name, packaging & in this **NV** bubbly. Abounds with red berry flavours, the sweetness & lowish 12% alc will get any party going.

Pinotage ⓘ ★★★ Dark tones in **09**, mulberries & smoked meat but palate is juicy, vibrant, all light & laughter. Good oak foundation. **Shiraz** ⓘ ★★★★ Ripe & fleshy, toned by 18 months in barrel, **09** is that irresistible force: classic shiraz appeal with a serious touch. **Pantére** ⓘ ★★★★ Cab-led Bordeaux blend, long skin contact & 22 months in French barrels, half new, invite you to take **07** seriously. Polished, dark fruited, delicious; long life ahead. Big jump from **06** (★★★). **Chenin Blanc** ✓ 🗒 🖾 ★★★★ Pre-bottled **12** retains house-style elegance. Ripe melon & passionfruit, lovely underlying minerality on palate, long finish. **Sauvignon Blanc** 🗒 🖾 ★★★ Tasted as sample, nice leafy/lemongrass freshness & purity in **12**, perky acidity extends the flavours. Good food partner. Discontinued: **Reserve**.

Two Cubs range

White Blend ☺ 🗒 🖾 ★★★ Ex-tank, light-textured **12** is spot on as a quaffer: crunchy summer fruits, tangy acidity, flavourful length. Sauvignon with chenin.

Red Blend 🗒 🖾 ★★★ Mainly cab in **10**, which explains the blackcurrant plumpness. Supported by firm tannins, finishes dry, ideal for food. **Rosé** 🗒 🖾 ★★ From pinotage in **12**, dry, lightish, restrained red fruit. — CR

▪ **Kobus** *see* Havana Hills
▪ **Koelenbosch** *see* Koelenhof Winery

Koelenhof Winery

Location/map/WO: Stellenbosch ▪ Est 1941 ▪ 1stB 1970's ▪ Tasting & sales Mon-Thu 9–5 Fri 9-4 Sat 10–2 ▪ Closed Easter Fri/Sun, Ascension day, Dec 25/26 & Jan 1 ▪ Cellar tours by appt ▪ Facilities for children ▪ Gift shop ▪ Farm produce ▪ BYO picnic ▪ Conference/function venue ▪ Owner(s) 67 shareholders ▪ Cellarmaster(s) Andrew de Vries (2006) ▪ Winemaker(s) Martin Stevens (Nov 2003) & Wilhelm de Vries (2002), with Erika van Zyl (Jun 2011) ▪ Viticulturist(s) Wilhelm de Vries (2010) ▪ 14,000t/11,000cs own label 45% red 45% white 8% rosé 2% fortified + 1,000cs for clients & 100,000 litres bulk ▪ Other export brand: Simonsbosch ▪ IPW ▪ PO

Box 1 Koelenhof 7605 ▪ koelwyn@mweb.co.za ▪ www.koelenhof.co.za ▪ S 33° 50' 5.2" E 018° 47' 52.7" ▪ T +27 (0)21-865-2020/1 ▪ F +27 (0)21-865-2796

This long-established grower-owned Stellenbosch cellar attributes steady growth over the past five years to the Chinese. One or another of the team visits four times a year, a special label has been developed for China, and winemaker Martin Stevens is on his way to becoming a Mandarin speaker.

Koelenbosch range

Sangiovese ☺ 📖 ★★★ **11** smoothly textured Italian variety with dried tomato flavours. Balanced & juicy for solo or antipasto pleasure.

Merlot ★★★ **09**'s bright, red fruit enrobes fine, supple tannins. Food friendly, with stamina for a few years. **Pinotage** 📖 ★★★ Barbecue mate **10** is robust, with smoky oak overlay to mulberry fruit. **Shiraz** ★★★ Tighter structure to **09**'s spicy, warm fruit. Dry food-friendly tannins still unfolding mid-2012. **Nineteenfortyone** ✓ 📖 ★★★★ Honours cellar's founding date. Mainly shiraz & cab in **10**. Smooth, flavoursome & accessible now & for 3-5 years. **Pinotage Rosé** ⊕ 🍴 📖 ★ Light-textured & dry **11**. **Chenin Blanc Wooded** ⊕ 📖 ★★ **10** undemanding, with gentle nutty texture. **Sauvignon Blanc** 🍴 📖 ★★ **12** light, fresh & tropical, tweaked by pithy citrus finish.

Koelenhof range

Koelenhoffer ☺ 🍴 📖 ★★★ Fruit-filled, gently crisp & friendly, **12** is a charming patio white from sauvignon.

Koelenberg ⊕ ★★★ Shiraz-led juicy anytime quaffer, briefly oaked. **09** still selling. **Pinotage Rosé** 📖 ★★ **12** candyfloss-light & semi-sweet. Frivolous summer fun. **Koelnektar** ⊕ 📖 ★★★ Sweetly crisp white, ideal for fusion food. **11** with gewürztraminer's rosepetal, riesling's spice, chenin's tropical flair. **Pinotage Rosé Vin-sec** ⊕ 📖 ★★★ **11** effervescent berry bonanza, fresh, light & inviting. **Sauvignon Blanc Vin-sec** ⊕ 🍴 📖 ★★★ Sweet but lively fizz, light & tropical-toned **11** a spring celebration. **Pino Porto** 📖 ★★★ **10** port from pinotage has spicy mulberry flavours in accessible ruby style. Warming fireside companion. — MW

Koelfontein

Location/WO: Ceres ▪ Map: Tulbagh ▪ Est 1832 ▪ 1stB 2002 ▪ Tasting & sales Mon-Fri 9-4 Sat 10-1 ▪ Closed all pub hols ▪ Farm produce ▪ BYO picnic ▪ Walks/hikes ▪ Conservation area ▪ Die Kloof self-catering historic house (sleeps 6) ▪ Die Snystoor function venue ▪ Owner(s) Handri Conradie ▪ Winemaker(s) Dewaldt Heyns (2004) ▪ Viticulturist(s) Hennie van Noordwyk ▪ 950ha/±6ha (shiraz, chard) ▪ ±24t/1,200cs own label 50% red 50% white ▪ BWI ▪ PO Box 4 Prince Alfred's Hamlet 6840 ▪ wine@koelfontein.co.za ▪ www.koelfontein.co.za ▪ S 33° 15'54.70" E 019° 19'29.28" ▪ T +27 (0)23-313-3304/+27 (0)23-313-3538 ▪ F +27 (0)23-313-3137

The Conradie clan in 2012 celebrated 180 years on this fruit and wine farm in the often snow-decked mountains along Ceres' Gydo Pass. Day and overnight visitors are equally welcome here: tourism and admin manager Isabel Swarts extols enjoying the award-winning wines (by Saronsberg's Dewaldt Heyns) and traditional 'witblits' grape distillate in renovated historic and conserved natural surrounds.

★★★★ **Chardonnay** Expressive **10** has lime, hazelnut & barrel-fermentation complexity, richness. Supple, with cool-climate minerality, but falls away tad more quickly than persistent & elegant **09** (★★★★★).
Shiraz ★★★★ Complex bouquet smoked meat, roasted nuts & hint truffle, **09** rich but unheavy, with integrated tannins. More elegant expression than dense yet well-judged **08** (★★★★), also tasted this edition. — WB/AL

■ **Kogmans Kloof** see Zandvliet Wine Estate & Thoroughbred Stud
■ **Koningshof** see Avondvrede

Koningsrivier Wines

Location: McGregor ▪ Map: Robertson ▪ Est/1stB 2002 ▪ Tasting, sales & tours by appt ▪ Owner(s) SW Colyn ▪ Cellarmaster(s)/winemaker(s) Niël Colyn ▪ Viticulturist(s) Briaan Stipp (consultant) ▪ 9ha (cab) ▪ 435cs own label 100% red ▪ PO Box 144 Robertson 6705 ▪ koningsrivier@barvallei.co.za ▪ S 33° 54'3.0" E 019° 51'45.9" ▪ T +27 (0)23-625-1748 ▪ F +27 (0)23-625-1748

Farmer Niël Colyn (winemaking's a hobby, he insists) reported a record 2012 harvest, both in yield and quality. He again made cab, merlot and shiraz, and finally found time to vinify some viognier. Most of his wine is exported to the UK but a small quantity is available at La Verne Wine Boutique in nearby Robertson.

Koopmanskloof Wingerde

Location/map: Stellenbosch ▪ WO: Stellenbosch/Western Cape ▪ Est 1801 ▪ 1stB 1970 ▪ Tasting & cellar tours by appt only Mon-Fri 9-4 ▪ Sales 8-5 ▪ Closed all pub hols ▪ Walks/hikes ▪ Mountain biking ▪ Private Nature Reserve with self-catering Berghuis, accommodate 35 people with overnight facilities for 16 ▪ Owner(s) Managed by Koopmanskloof Wingerde (Pty) Ltd ▪ Winemaker(s) Stephan Smit ▪ Viticulturist(s) Louwtjie Vlok ▪ 480ha (cab, carignan, merlot, ptage, roobernet, ruby cab, shiraz, chard, chenin, sauv, sem) 40% red 60% white ▪ ±3,700t/±2.5m litres ▪ Other brands: Vredehoek, One World ▪ BWI, Fairtrade, IPW, WIETA ▪ PO Box 19 Koelenhof 7605 ▪ info@koopmanskloof.co.za ▪ www.koopmanskloof.co.za ▪ S 33° 53'54.7" E 018° 45'36.7" ▪ **T +27 (0)21-865-2355** ▪ F +27 (0)21-876-2421

After two decades at the helm, Louwtjie Vlok retired, handing over to Stephan Smit but Louwtjie's still keeping an eye on things as the viticultural and environmental manager of this historic Bottelary Hills property. Harmony between commercial interests and nature is key, with their 100ha nature reserve as important as their vineyards.

Koopmanskloof range

Cabernet Sauvignon 🍷 🖤 ★★★ Cab for beginners. Step-up **11** is gentle & mild yet shows typical textured plummy flavours & mocha spice seasoning. **Motherblocks Carignan** NEW 🍷 🖤 ★★★ Dry but ripe **11**, sweet maraschino cherry & clove taste, lightish & fresh body. **Pinotage** ⓣ 🍷 🖤 ★★ Youthful **10** offers oaky sweet-fruited freshness. **Shiraz** 🍷 🖤 ★★★ Return to form in **11**, with soft plum fruit. **Cabernet Sauvignon-Shiraz** NEW 🍷 🖤 ★★★ Cab character leads **11** 60/40 mix, light smoky oak adds grip to plum taste. **Pinotage Rosé** 🍷 🖤 ★★ Fresh raspberry tang on easy **12** dry sipper. **Shiraz Rosé** NEW 🍷 ★★★ Cherry Fizz Pop vibrancy to flavourful **12**, with food-friendly weighty dry finish. **Chardonnay** 🍷 🖤 ★★★ Citrus freshness on unwooded **12**, lightish & uncomplicated. **Chenin Blanc** 🍷 🖤 ★★☆ Straightforward **12**, light & fresh quaffer. **Bushvine Chenin Blanc** NEW 🍷 🖤 ★★★ Ripe honeyed peach & apricot perfumes, **11** bit more depth & body than the other version but still light-footed & fresh. **Sauvignon Blanc** 🍷 🖤 ★★★ Grass & fig simplicity to **12**, easy-drinking summer white. **Sauvignon Blanc-Semillon** NEW 🍷 🖤 ★★★ Good start for inaugural **11** 70/30 blend, grapefruit crispness & honeyed undertone, pleasant structure & length. Discontinued: **Dry Red**.

Koffieklip range NEW

Pinotage 🍷 🖤 ★★★ Smoky mocha appeal to **10**, quite chunky in texture, for hearty country fare. — FM

Kranskop Wines

Location/map: Robertson ▪ WO: Klaasvoogds ▪ Est 2001 ▪ 1stB 2003 ▪ Tasting, sales & tours Mon-Fri 10-4.30 Sat & pub hols 10-2 ▪ Closed Easter Sun & Dec 25 ▪ BYO picnic ▪ Owner(s)/viticulturist(s) Newald Marais ▪ Cellarmaster(s)/winemaker(s) Newald Marais (2008) ▪ 43ha/30ha (cab, merlot, pinot, shiraz, tannat, chard, sauv, viog) ▪ 240t/1,500cs own label 75% red 25% white ▪ BWI, IPW ▪ PO Box 49 Klaasvoogds 6707 ▪ newald@kranskopwines.co.za ▪ www.kranskopwines.co.za ▪ S 33° 47'53.1" E 019° 59'56.6" ▪ **T +27 (0)23-626-3200** ▪ F +27 (0)23-626-3200

Softly spoken Newald Marais is where he's wanted to be since 14 (and after some 30 years as corporate cellarmaster): with hands in the soil 'where it all begins'; personally sharing his passion with people wanting a wine experience, not a brand; spending time and energy on handcrafted wines for 'perfect dishes'.

★★★★ **Viognier** ✓ 🖤 Now bottled, **11** impresses with dried pear & almond complexity, a savoury element that makes it food compatible, focused & full flavoured, well-judged oaking. Price worth raving about too. **Cabernet Sauvignon** ⓣ ★★★ **09** has dark berry & plum aromas, voluptuous terroir reined in by high acidity, firm but friendly tannins. **Merlot** ⓣ ★★★★ Opaque **09** chocolatey, smooth & sweet-fruited. Plush offering with creamy conclusion. **Shiraz** ⓣ ★★★★ Perfumed **09** quite soft & narrow shouldered for this variety, very sippable. **Chardonnay** 🖤 ★★★ **11** big, bold but balanced, buttery oak nicely synced with the burst of citrus flavour. More than a match for spicy food. **Sauvignon Blanc** ★★★ Unusual **11**, tobacco & spice aromas, savoury peach flavours, appetising acidity. — DB/JP

Krone *see* Twee Jonge Gezellen Estate-The House of Krone

Kronendal Boutique Winery

Location/WO: Durbanville ▪ Map: Durbanville, Philadelphia & Darling ▪ Est 2003 ▪ 1stB 2006 ▪ Tasting & sales
Mon-Fri by appt Sat 11-3 ▪ Fee R30/6 wines ▪ Closed Easter Fri/Sun, Ascension Day, Dec 25/26 & Jan 1 ▪ Cellar
tours by appt ▪ Cheese platters ▪ Conference facilities ▪ Art ▪ Seasonal 'langtafel' lunches ▪ Owner(s) Pieter &
Magdaleen Kroon ▪ Winemaker(s) Magdaleen Kroon ▪ 2ha/0.6ha (mourv, shiraz, tempranillo, viog) ▪ 4t/
260cs own label 100% red ▪ PO Box 4433 Durbanville 7551 ▪ info@kronendalwine.co.za ▪ http://kronendal
belmet.co.za ▪ S 33° 48' 30.78" E 018° 36' 50.82" ▪ **T +27 (0)82-499-0198** ▪ F +27 (0)086-603-1170

Durbanville garagistes Pieter and Magdaleen Kroon's wine journey began with
family and friends helping to bring in the harvest by hand and crush it by foot.
Equipment now handles the heavy tasks, but it remains a collaborative effort. 'The
complexity of wine, the fact that one never stops learning, and the search for that
wine that takes your breath away continues to fascinate me,' says Magdaleen.

★★★★☆ **Mirari** Tiny quantities of tempranillo & viognier join shiraz (75%), mourvèdre (20%) in convincing
09, with distinctive fynbos nuance, Rhône-like lily perfume & savoury persistence.
Impromptu Await new. These previously in 'Westerdale' range. — CvZ

Kumala

Location: Somerset West ▪ Map: Helderberg ▪ WO: Western Cape/Worcester ▪ Tasting, sales & cellar tours at
Flagstone Winery (see entry) ▪ Owner(s) Accolade Wines South Africa ▪ Winemaker(s) Ben Jordaan (Jul 2002),
Bruce Jack (Feb 2008) & Karen Bruwer (Oct 2008) ▪ 50% red 50% white ▪ PO Box 769 Stellenbosch 7599 ▪
hannelize.mouton@accolade-wines.com ▪ www.kumala.co.za ▪ S 34° 5' 26.38" E 018° 48' 30.04" ▪ **T +27
(0)21-852-5052** ▪ F +27 (0)21-852-5085

Until recently an export-only brand, several of the array of Kumala blends and
varieties have been released locally by the hugely successful label's owners, Accolade Wines South Africa. Local production is under the stewardship of Bruce Jack,
whose Flagstone and Fish Hoek labels are also part of the Accolade portfolio.

Zenith range

Chenin Blanc-Chardonnay ☺ 🍴 🄿 ★★★ Previewed **12**, for local release, promises gushes of fresh
fruit when settled. Riper, rounder than Core version.

Merlot-Cabernet Sauvignon-Shiraz ⊕ 🍴 🄿 ★★★ **11** preview has mulberry richness; soft & rounded,
with some depth & density; splash viognier adds interest. **Rosé** ⊕ 🍴 🄿 ★★★ Cherry Fizz Pop pleasure on
11, sampled from tank, light bodied, dry & fresh.

Reserve range

Shiraz 🍴 🄿 ★★★ Range returns to the guide after few years' break. Export-only **11** from Swartland
grapes, pleasing cherry fruit on spicy oak. **Chenin Blanc** NEW 🍴 🄿 ★★★ Lean, mildly fruity, light-bodied
11 has pinch of oak dust.

Core range

Chardonnay NEW ☺ 🍴 🄿 ★★★ Debut for **11** from Robertson/Ashton vines. Light but focused,
showing citrus fruit on waxy brush of oak.

Shiraz NEW 🍴 🄿 ★★★ **11**, from Robertson grapes, shows brisk fruit & spicy oak. **Merlot-Pinotage** 🍴
🄿 ★★★ 50/50 blend in **11** produces fruit-pop juicy freshness without pretension. Export-only; an auspicious intro to SA quaffing. **Pinotage-Shiraz** ⊕ 🄿 ★★★ Waxy berry blaze on ex-tank **11**, light bodied &
ripe. Exported. **Shiraz-Mourvèdre** 🍴 🄿 ★★★ **11** shows distinctive peppery spice with smoky oak notes
on light, juicy structure. Uncomplicated, easy drinking. **Cabernet Sauvignon-Shiraz** ⊕ 🍴 🄿 ★★★★
11 preview over-delivers. Typical cab with shiraz mocha spice lift; gentle body, firm core & concentration.
Long finish. **Merlot-Ruby Cabernet** ⊕ 🍴 🄿 ★★★ **11**, from tank, improves on previous. Ripe mulberry &
herb edge, textured density to medium aftertaste. **Dry Red** NEW 🍴 ★★ Very basic, light NV quaffing. **Rosé**
⊕ 🍴 🄿 ★★★ Dry berry/cherry mouthful on **11** preview, lively full body. **Chardonnay-Semillon** 🍴
🄿 ★★ **11** union of expedience for export. Drinkable but unexciting. **Colombard-Chardonnay** 🍴 🄿
★★★ Appealing mineral leanness of **11** lifted by lemon acidity. **Chenin Blanc-Chardonnay** 🍴 🄿 ★★

Waxy, woolly **11** tends to flabbiness, lacks fruit nuances. **Sauvignon Blanc-Colombard** 🗒 📰 ★★ Dry, fresh & zesty **11** offers unfussy refreshment. **Sauvignon Blanc-Semillon** 📰 ★★★ **11** shows pungent nettle tones on fresh, zippy acidity. **Chenin Blanc-Viognier** 🗒 📰 ★★★ Among best of the pack, **11** has some real body & fruit, with bright acidity bolstering ripe peaches. Export only. **Dry White** NEW 🗒 ★★ Light, just-dry & crisp NV local release with a candy-fruit lift. **Medium Sweet White** NEW ★★ Unassuming NV chenin has floral attraction from splash of muscat. **Medium Sweet Red** NEW ★★ Flippant, bland NV ruby cab & cinsaut blend for export.

Eternal range

Merlot-Cabernet Sauvignon-Shiraz ⊛ 📰 ★★★ Rich blackberry & cinnamon, **11** fleshy yet supple & gentle. Nuanced blend of merlot, cab, shiraz & dab viognier sampled from tank. **Chenin Blanc-Chardonnay-Semillon** 🗒 ★★★ Previewed **12** a permutation with no apparent direction. — GdB

Kumkani

A new 'queen' reigns over this well-established brand, 'Kumkani' derived from the Xhosa word for royalty. Allison Adams-Witbooi is now an equal partner with The Company of Wine People, and responsible for the winemaking. The Stellenbosch graduate has extensive local and international winemaking and marketing experience, and her aim is to increase sales by creating complex, elegant wines that appeal to both emerging and serious winelovers.

Infiniti Méthode Cap Classique range

Brut ⊛ ★★★★ Sparkling from mostly chardonnay with pinots noir & meunier. **07** step up on last-tasted **04** (★★★★). Rich & creamy, with ripe stonefruit, brioche & toasted nuts. WO W Cape.

Kumkani range

★★★★ **Sauvignon Blanc** 🗒 📰 Crisp & summery **11** (★★★★) preview from Darling has a grassy, stonefruit & lemony tone. Less fruit-filled verve than **10**. WO Coastal, as for Chardonnay.

Pinotage 🗒 ★★★ Riper, dark berry/plum flavours in more accessible **10**. Balanced structure, alcohol not intrusive. WO Stellenbosch, as for all reds. **Shiraz** 🗒 ★★★★ **11** ex barrel, riper & bolder than previous. Ample fruit & spice with smoother profile & earlier accessibility. **10** held back for further maturation. **Kumkani Reserve** NEW 🗒 📰 ★★★★ Promising debut, **10** from barrel is a generous & heartwarming Bordeaux blend. Characterful & spicy with supple structure. **Chardonnay** NEW 🗒 ★★★ Oak envelops succulent fruit in youthful **11**. Limy twist invites food. Time will harmonise & show true potential. Note: range previously listed as 'Kumkani Single Varietal'. Discontinued: **Chenin Blanc, Viognier**. — MW

Kupferberger Auslese

Liquid history, this 1952 Distell stalwart was among the first to benefit from cold and controlled fermentation of white wines.

Kupferberger Auslese ★★ Latest NV half notch down, uncomplicated semi-sweet sipper. — DB/HJ

◼ **K&V Harmony** *see* Kaapzicht Wine Estate

KWV

Location: Paarl ▪ Map: Paarl & Wellington ▪ KWV Wine Emporium: Kohler Street, T +27 (0)21-807-3007/8 F +27 (0)21-807-3119; moving to La Concorde Building, Main Street, Paarl in 2013 ▪ Tasting & sales Mon-Sat 9-4.30 Sun 11-4 ▪ Fee R20 for 5 products; R40 chocolate & brandy ▪ Cellar tour R30 ▪ Tours: Eng Mon-Sat 10, 10.30 & 2.15; Ger 10.15; Sun Eng 11 ▪ Tour groups by appt ▪ Closed Good Fri, Dec 25 & Jan 1 ▪ Owner(s) KWV (Pty) Ltd ▪ Cellarmaster(s) Richard Rowe ▪ Winemaker(s) Johann Fourie, Nomonde Kubeka, Anneke du Plessis, Izelle van Blerk & Christiaan Coetzee ▪ Viticulturist(s) Marco Ventrella & De Wet Hugo ▪ PO Box 528 Suider-Paarl 7624 ▪ customer@kwv.co.za ▪ www.kwv-wines.com, www.cafeculturewines.com, www.cathedralcellarwines.com, www.roodeberg.com, www.kwv.co.za ▪ S 33° 45′ 43.26″ E 018° 57′ 44.06″ ▪ **T +27 (0)21-807-3911 (Office)** ▪ F +27 (0)21-807-3000

This Paarl-based wine and spirits giant commands increased attention and respect; one of the latest accolades is being listed as one of the most recognised and admired wine brands by Drinks International. Innovation and stylistic awareness runs from the vineyard through to the bottle, with each brand having its own focus. These are the goals of cellarmaster Richard Rowe and his team. Other recent successes have included Best Producer at the 2011 Veritas Awards, and Most Successful Producer at the 2012 Trophy Show; these were complemented by frequent recognition on international shows. The company's major brands include (see listings) BerRaz, Bonne Esperance, Café Culture, KWV Wines (including Cathedral Cellar, previously listed separately), Laborie Pearly Bay and Roodeberg.

KWV Wines

Awards continue to be showered on KWV wines, including being named top producer at the 2012 Trophy Wine Show. But cellarmaster Richard Rowe and his team don't see any reason to rest on their laurels. 'We want to be better next year than this,' says Richard. 'Yes, it's about quality but also style, an aspect that's especially important in the flagship The Mentors range, where each variety is treated differently according to its strengths and weaknesses; there's no recipe winemaking.' Oaking has undergone a major change, he adds: 'Purchases are now a tenth of what they used to be. It all comes down to what I was told many years ago, the wines have to pass the drinkability test.'

The Mentors range

★★★★ **Pinotage** 🍷 🚫 Freshly ripe raspberry fragrance, lush juicy flavours & carefully managed tannins on modern **10**. Like Cab Franc & Shiraz, with around 15% alcohol. Styled for general appeal.

★★★★ **Shiraz** 🍷 🚫 Obviously oaked, ripe, **10** (★★★★); bold but carefully managed acid, tannin promote dark plum fruit. Hint of alcoholic glow on finish. **09** less oaky. WO W Cape, like all these unless noted.

★★★★ **Orchestra** 🍷 🚫 Modern in its freshly plush fruit, drinkability, **10** (★★★★★) clearly in style of classic cab-led Bordeaux red with its neat tailored frame, light texture & liveliness — as was **09**. More than the sum of its five parts, worthy of 4+ years ageing.

★★★★ **Canvas** 🍷 🚫 Careful selection determines final blend: **10** has 71% shiraz with 6 other Mediterranean varieties for a generous, dark-fruited, velvety & savoury mix. **09** untasted. WO Coastal.

★★★★ **Chardonnay** 🍷 🚫 Elgin's fresh structure reflected in **11**, with lemony purity, firm acid. Leesy rich undertones add dimension; good fruity length.

★★★★★ **Grenache Blanc** 🍷 🚫 **11** (★★★★★) expressive as **10** but an even more intriguing fresh hay, wet chalky soil & spice mélange, all refrained on the silky, elegant palate. In older oak 6 months. A fine mineral energy promises an excellent future for this delicious, savoury wine.

★★★★ **Sauvignon Blanc** 🍷 🚫 **11** with 15% semillon & oaked portion for more complexity & mouthfeel, with no loss of varietal vigour, minerality. Steely, lemongrass tones, bone-dry close. **10** untasted.

★★★★ **Semillon** 🍷 🚫 **11** strikes more sophisticated, less fruity note than **10**; driven by structure, texture but still within elegant frame & with freshening lemony thread. 30% fermented in older oak.

Cabernet Franc NEW 🍷 🚫 ★★★★ **10** in unusually bold, rich mode. Hints of leafy, spicy aromas are varietal indicators but dimmed by high alcohol & finishing glow. WO Coastal. **Petit Verdot** 🍷 Not tasted. **Chenin Blanc** 🍷 Not tasted. **Viognier** 🍷 🚫 ★★★★ Dry **11** ups interest on **10** (★★★★) with its elegance & polish. Very pretty peachy refinement, fresh lift lend unusual delicacy; oaked portion adds subtle dimension. WO Elgin. **Sauvignon Blanc-Semillon** 🍷 Not tasted.

Cathedral Cellar range

★★★★ **Cabernet Sauvignon** 🚫 Honest, straightforward **10** (★★★★) with well-judged oak, built to focus on ripe, blackberry juiciness. Readier, less depth than **09**.

★★★★ **Triptych** 🚫 Cab-based with shiraz, merlot, petit verdot in **10**. Ripely scented with good substance, freshness & rounded tannins to allow for current drinking.

★★★★★ **Chenin Blanc** NEW ✓ 🍷 🚫 Impressive debut in persuasive **11**. Chenin's haunting honey-kissed fragrance expanded by subtle earthy, spicy oak input. Concentration, rich texture refreshed, lengthened by bright lemon zest acidity, dry conclusion.

★★★★ **Sauvignon Blanc** 🍷 🚫 **11** more steely, pebbly than showy, but rich in viscosity with verve, concludes with flourish of tangy gooseberry & lemongrass.

★★★★ **MCC Brut** 🍾 Charming **09** sparkling from refreshing, lemony chardonnay with enriching 11% pinot noir. Fine, creamy mousse; properly dry. Potential to grow.

Merlot 🚫 ★★★★ **10** lighter vintage, takes small step back from ripely enticing **09** (★★★★). Pretty if rather simple flavours balanced by gentle grip. **Pinotage** 🚫 ★★★★ **10** leans towards pinot noir heritage with bright raspberry aromas, light texture & freshness. Concluding tannic tang more typical of pinotage. **Shiraz** 🚫 ★★★★

good crackle of black pepper on wholesome, straightforward **10**; closes smooth & savoury. **Chardonnay** ★★★★ **11** more subtle & elegant than **10** (★★★★) with a cool feel to its prominent citrus freshness (half fruit ex Elgin). Lovely supple, lees-enriched mouthfeel; roundly dry & long. These all WO W Cape or Coastal.

Reserve Collection

Cabernet Sauvignon ✓ ★★★★ Medium-bodied, fresh & flavoursome **10**. Plentiful blackberry flavours focused, lengthened by fine tannin grip. This range WO W Cape. **Merlot** ★★★ Uncomplicated bright red plum features on **10**. Balanced for current drinking. **Shiraz** ✓ ★★★★ Quiet yet satisfying spice, red berry fruits in velvety textured **10**. Good now & for few years. **Chardonnay** ★★★★ Fragrant lime, oatmeal, supple texture & balanced freshness add to **11**'s drinkability. Subtly oak enriched. **Sauvignon Blanc** ✓ ★★★★ **11** has discarded youthful assertiveness without loss of varietal vigour. Riper fruit style but figgy features composed, persuasive & well sustained by lively mineral core. **10** (★★★) simpler. Discontinued: **Shiraz-Tannat-Cabernet Franc**, **White Blend**, **Méthode Cap Classique Brut**.

Concordia range NEW

Concordia White ☺ ★★★ Happy sauvignon, chenin, chardonnay combo. Refreshing citrus scents, bouncy feel & fruity tail on off-dry **12**.

Concordia Red ★★ Cab-based, simple & off-dry **10**. WO W Cape for both.

Classic Collection

★★★★ **Cape Tawny** ✓ Latest **NV** more complex, seemingly less sweet than previous. Delicious mouthful spiced orange peel, nuts, dried fruit & spirity warmth.

Shiraz Rosé NEW ☺ ★★★ **12** juicy mouthful spice, wild strawberries; tangily fresh, just off-dry. **Chardonnay** ☺ ★★★ Gentle citrus, nutty tones, creaminess on lightly oaked, quaffable **11**. **Sauvignon Blanc** ☺ ★★★ Easy-drinking, characterful **12**; pure passionfruit, green pea flavours; unaggressively fresh. All these table wines off-dry. All WO W Cape.

Cabernet Sauvignon ★★★ Previewed **11** with easy-drinking smoothness, sweet red berry flavours. **Merlot** ★★★ Bright & crunchy red plum fruit, nip tannin in quaffable **11**. **Pinotage** ★★★ Initial ripe raspberry appeal on **11** dimmed by finishing alcoholic glow, sweetness. **Shiraz** ★★★ Ripe fruited **11** (ex-tank), gently fleshy, rounded finish. **Chenin Blanc** ★★★ **12** boasts luscious tropical features & bright fruity acids to balance sweetness. **Sparkling Rosé** ★★ Dullish fruit in semi-sweet **NV**. **Cuvée Brut** ★★ Off-dry **NV** sparkler from chenin; gentle fruit. **Sparkling Demi-Sec** ★★ Sweetish, fruity **NV** with lively fizz. From chenin. **Red Muscadel** ★★★ Expressive muscat scents, flavours. Smooth, sweet & lingering **NV**. These fortified desserts all moved from Dessert Range. **Cape Ruby** ★★★ Blended **NV** port; good ruby hue, plum jam richness; rather spirity grip to sweet tail. Discontinued: **Pinotage Rosé**, **Chêne**, **Vin Doux**, **Late Harvest**.

Contemporary Collection

Chenin Blanc-Chardonnay ☺ ★★★ Plentiful tropical juiciness in fresh & quaffable off-dry **11**.

Cabernet Sauvignon-Merlot ★★ Light fruit lifted by few grams sugar; rather gravelly tail on **11**. This & next 2 off-dry. All WO W Cape. **Cabernet Sauvignon-Shiraz** ★★ Name switch reflects blend. Light textured, fresh **11**; red berries, spice. **Chenin Blanc-Muscat de Alexandrie** ★★ Lightish **11** previewed last year as 'Chenin Blanc-Muscat'. Gentle grapey flavours, sweetness. — AL

Kyburg Wine Estate

Location/map: Stellenbosch ▪ WO: Devon Valley/Stellenbosch ▪ Est 1998 ▪ 1stB 2006 ▪ Tasting & sales by appt ▪ Closed Easter Sun, Dec 25/26 & Jan 1 ▪ Fully furnished self-catering guest house (exclusive, rental min 2 weeks) ▪ Owner(s) Fred & Rosmarie Ruest ▪ Cellarmaster(s)/winemaker(s) Jacques Fourie (Jan 2006, consultant) ▪ Viticulturist(s) Frans Snyman (Jul 2006, consultant) ▪ 28ha/18ha (cab, merlot, shiraz) ▪ 150-160t/ 1,750cs own label 100% red ▪ PO Box 12799 Die Boord 7613 ▪ info@kyburgwine.com ▪ www.kyburgwine. com ▪ S 33° 54' 59.3"   E 018° 49' 28.4" ▪ **T +27 (0)21-865-2876**

This Devon Valley property vinifies only one third of its crop. 'We sell the balance to other well-known private producers,' says owner Fred Ruest. Modern viticultural techniques, as well as infrared imagery ensure the fruit matches not only Ruest's standards but also those of the producers who buy from him.

Cabernet Sauvignon ⓟ ★★★☆ Bright, fresh cassis flavours, good fruit richness in balance with generous tannic base on **09**. With development potential, but **08** (★★★★) was more so. **Merlot** ⓟ ★★★★ **09** displays rich, ripe fruit with sweet length & firm tannin support. **Shiraz** ⓟ ★★★★ Spicy whiff livens up slightly jammy notes on **09**. Tasty, if simple; tannin requires time to soften. **08** (★★★★) more complex. **33 Latitude** ⓟ ★★★★ Fruity, savoury mix of cab with shiraz, merlot on **09**. Soft core with grippy tannin contrast. — AL

■ **La Bonne Vigne** *see Wonderfontein*

Laborie Wine Farm

Location: Paarl ▪ Map: Paarl & Wellington ▪ WO: Western Cape ▪ Est 1691 ▪ Tasting & sales Mon-Sat 9-5 Sun 11-5 ▪ Fee R20/5 wines R30/tour + tasting ▪ Chocolate & wine pairing ▪ Closed all Christian pub hols ▪ Tours for large groups by appt ▪ Harvest Restaurant T +27 (0)21-807-3095: lunch Tue–Sun 12-3 dinner Wed–Sun 6. 30-9 ▪ Lazy Day Markets (Sat) ▪ Carols by Candlelight ▪ Conferences ▪ Weddings/functions ▪ Accommodation ▪ Owner(s) KWV (Pty) Ltd ▪ Winemaker(s) Johan Fourie & Christiaan Coetzee ▪ Viticulturist(s) Marco Ventrella, with Hugo de Wet ▪ 59ha/23ha (ptage, pinots noir/meunier, shiraz, chard, chenin, sauv) ▪ 40,000cs ▪ BWI IPW, WIETA ▪ PO Box 528 Suider Paarl 7624 ▪ info@laboriewines.co.za ▪ www.laboriewines.co.za ▪ S 33° 45 55.2" E 018° 57' 27.6" ▪ **T +27 (0)21-807-3390** ▪ F +27 (0)21-863-1955

Refurbishing of this KWV-owned Paarl estate continues. Care is being taken to retain the atmosphere of the old buildings while giving them a more contemporary look. In the Harvest Restaurant, the old kitchen utensils and fireplace as well as tables and chairs recall the past, while Cecil Skotnes' modern art exhibition can be viewed here and at the Cellar Door and Manor House. The team hopes visitors will emotionally link the increasingly stylish wine with the farm.

★★★★ **Jean Taillefert** 🅟 For those who like their shiraz generously oak-spiced. Presently its sweet impression (abetted by high alcohol) dominates on rich, powerful **10**. Year/2 may bring greater harmony.

★★★★ **MCC Blanc de Blancs** ✓ Name change from 'Blanc de Blanc Brut' for **08** sparkling, showing expressive toasty notes of maturing chardonnay. Lively bubble, with emerging creamy texture. Long, unaggressive, dry. **07** (★★★★) was more oxidative. Like all these, WO W Cape.

★★★★ **Pineau de Laborie** NV dessert, previously vintaged, pinotage providing both fortifying spirit & base wine. Lifted varietal scent, smooth, flavoursome & not overly sweet.

Cabernet Sauvignon ✓ 🗒 🅟 ★★★★ **11** charms with unshowy yet pure fruit, suppleness & finishing grip of succulent grape tannin. Good now, further 2-3 years. **Merlot** 🗒 🅟 ★★★ Nicely balanced dark berry refinement with comfortable freshness on partially oaked **11** preview. **Shiraz** ✓ 🗒 🅟 ★★★★ Attractive breadth & spicy elegance in youthful **11**; cushioned feel with fresh core providing balance, length. **Limited Collection Shiraz** ⓟ ★★★★ **09** youthful, gawky tasted mid-2011. Perhaps now its pretty oak-laced spiced red fruits, gentle texture offering pleasure. **Merlot-Cabernet Sauvignon** ✓ 🗒 🅟 ★★★★ Previewed **11** unshowy yet characterful blend. Good substance, structure & freshness promise good early/medium-term drinking. **Chardonnay** ✓ 🗒 🅟 ★★★★ Easy-drinking satisfaction in step-up **11**'s zesty juicy flavours, bit of leesy bounce & oak spice. **Limited Collection Chardonnay** 🅟 ★★★★ Richer, bolder style, though moderate alcohol, on **11**. Forthcoming lemon butter scents, flavours, with balanced freshening acid. **Sauvignon Blanc** 🗒 🅟 ★★★★ Invigorating greengage & green apple notes on **12**, nicely fleshed out with some leesy padding. Fruitily dry. **MCC Brut Rosé** ★★★★ **09** bubbly from pinot noir. Well-sustained red fruit & biscuit tones complement creamy mousse & texture. Versatile food partner. **MCC Brut** ⓟ ★★★★ Elegant **08** sparkler, creamy yet invigorating. Gentle brioche scents, soupçon red fruit flavours. Very dry, persistent. Like **07** (★★★★) from pinot noir & chardonnay. — AL

La Bourgogne Farm

Location/map/WO: Franschhoek ▪ Est 1694 ▪ 1stB 1902 ▪ Tasting & sales Mon–Sun 10-3 ▪ Fee R30 ▪ Closed Easter Fri–Sun, Ascension day, Dec 25/26 & Jan 1 ▪ Facilities for children ▪ Farm produce ▪ Olive & olive oil tasting ▪ Walking/hiking trail ▪ Conservation area ▪ 6 self-catering riverside cottages ▪ Owner(s) La Bourgogne Farm (Pty) Ltd ▪ Winemaker(s) DP Burger (2008, consultant) ▪ Viticulturist(s) Gappie le Roux (2003, consultant) ▪ 22ha/4ha (malbec, shiraz, chard, sem, viog) ▪ PO Box 96 Franschhoek 7690 ▪ info@labourgogne.co.za ▪ www.labourgogne.co.za ▪ S 33° 55' 28.0" E 019° 7' 15.0" ▪ **T +27 (0)21-876-3245** ▪ F +27 (0)86-542-3615

The owners of historic Franschhoek farm La Bourgogne have added three new wines this year, each dedicated to one of their daughters, following the 'progeny theme. A new purchase is an olive press, used to make their own (and neighbours') olive oils, which are available for tasting on the farm.

Syrah NEW ★★★ 11 good varietal typicity (lots of black plums/cherries) & pleasing elegance, with whiffs of violets & spice. **Rosé** NEW 🖺 ★★★ 12 cheery dry flavours of cranberry & redcurrant for summer drinking. **Progeny Semillon** ★★★ Significantly lower yields in 10 (8.4t vs 20) make for more concentrated, honeyed, toasty mouthful, balanced by lively acidity & length. **Blossom White Blend** NEW 🖺 ★★ 11 semillon & sauvignon (80/20) in fruity, unwooded, citrussy style. Discontinued: **Progeny White Honey**. — CM

La Bri Estate

Location/map/WO: Franschhoek ▪ Est 1694 ▪ Tasting, sales & cellar tours Mon-Fri 10-5 Sat 10.30-4 ▪ Fee R20pp, waived on purchase ▪ Closed Easter Fri/Mon, Dec 25/26 & Jan 1 ▪ Chocolate & wine pairing ▪ Cheese platters ▪ BYO picnic ▪ Bicycle friendly ▪ Old wine cellar & tasting room open by appt ▪ Owner(s) Robin Hamilton ▪ Winemaker(s) Irene Waller (Oct 2010), with Glen Isaacs (Jun 2009) ▪ Viticulturist(s) Gerard Olivier (Oct 2010) ▪ ±24ha/±15ha (cabs s/f, merlot, p verdot, shiraz, chard, viog) ▪ 91t/3,500cs own label 80% red 20% white ▪ PO Box 180 Franschhoek 7690 ▪ info@labri.co.za ▪ www.labri.co.za ▪ S 33° 55′ 18.3″ E 019° 7′ 1.5″ ▪ **T +27 (0)21-876-2593** ▪ F +27 (0)86-275-9753

This is, says owner Robin Hamilton with simple eloquence, 'a small, quiet, very beautiful place'. It is also the name-bearing part of the first farm allocated to the refugee Huguenots who vitally helped establish the Franschhoek Valley as a prime wine producer. Could they have conceived of chocolate and wine pairing at La Bri? Or the 'pre-wedding functions and team-building events' planned 320 years later?

Cabernet Sauvignon ★★★★ Relatively soft 09, with attractive cassis & earthy note. Some warmth from big alcohol (as on all these reds) shows, as does oak (70% new). **Merlot** 🖾 ★★★ Ripe, dark-fruited 10's aromas mocha, chocolate & plums please, but the commendably dry palate a bit disjointed, short & warm. **Syrah** 🖾 ★★★★ 'Decadent & voluptuous' element from 6% viognier, notes winemaker. Like aromas of violets, lilies on 10. Loads of spice & fruit, but oak needs time to meld. **Affinity** ★★★★ 09 cab-led Bordeaux blend redolent of chocolate-coated raisins, plums & meat. Fine tannin & good oak integration, but lacks intensity. Follows savoury 06 (★★★★). **Chardonnay** 🖾 ★★★★ Softly tropical 11 with honeydew & ripe apple aromas framed by subtle oak. Not complex, but welcome acid uplift. **Viognier** 🖾 ★★ 11 rich ripe peach, oily texture, low acidity. — JPf

▪ **La Capra** see Fairview
▪ **La Cave** see Wellington Wines
▪ **Lace** see Almenkerk Wine Estate

La Chataigne

Location/map/WO: Franschhoek ▪ Est 1972 ▪ 1stB 2003 ▪ Tasting & sales Mon-Fri 10-4 Sat/Sun by appt ▪ Closed all pub hols ▪ 3 guest cottages ▪ Owner(s) Parkfelt family ▪ Winemaker(s) Gerda Willers (2003, consultant) ▪ 27ha/17ha (cab, merlot, ptage, shiraz, chenin, sauv, sem) ▪ 150t/2,000cs own label 25% red 65% white 10% rosé ▪ PO Box 7 La Motte 7691 ▪ office@lachat.co.za ▪ www.lachat.co.za ▪ S 33° 52′ 43.8″ E 019° 3′ 34.1″ ▪ **T +27 (0)21-876-3220** ▪ F +27 (0)86-545-1039

Many visitors regard this Franschhoek farm as a slice of heaven, the guest cottages surrounded by vine, river and mountain an ideal backdrop for wine appreciation. The chestnut, entwined in Parkfelt family history, lends its translated name to some of the wines — old-vine chenin being co-owner Richard's sister's favourite!

Marron ★★★★ Aromatic tarry notes blend attractively with stewed wild fruit on 09 mix merlot, cab & pinotage. Full-bodied, with meaty backdrop. **Rosé** 🖺 ★★★ Noted last year as discontinued; happily not. 11 merlot/shiraz, shy but perfumed, with a dollop of spice, ending dry. **Kastanje** ✓ 🖺 ★★★★ Old low-yielding chenin bushvines deliver lovely floral lift, with racy super-dry focus. Creamy 11 cut by freshening acid. **Sauvignon Blanc** 🖺 ★★★ Fresh 'seashore', hay & typical grassy aromas. 11 has assertive dry & refreshing zing. — JP

La Chaumiere Estate

Location/map/WO: Franschhoek ▪ Est 2001 ▪ 1stB 2003 ▪ Tasting & cellar tours by appt ▪ Sales from local outlets ▪ Owner(s) Michael Pawlowski ▪ Winemaker(s)/viticulturist(s) Wynand Pienaar (consultant) ▪ 3ha (cab,

pinot, chard) ▪ 18t/900cs own label ▪ PO Box 601 Franschhoek 7690 ▪ wynlprs@iafrica.com ▪ S 33° 54' 34.0"
E 019° 6' 54.9" ▪ **T +27 (0)21-876-4830/31** ▪ F +27 (0)21-876-2135

Owned by entrepreneur Michael Pawlowski, who came to Franschhoek on holiday and never really left, this small riverside estate's focus continues to be chardonnay and pinot noir. But '100% quality-driven' consultant winemaker Wynand
Pienaar is also excited about the new cab block: 'We've taken things to the next
level.'

★★★★ **Pinot Noir** NEW Beguiling floral & cherry perfumes lend an elegance, even delicacy to **11**, masking
the +15% alcohol. Firm, dry, very appealing but way too young still, really deserves more time.

Shiraz ★★★ Chunkier than sibling, but chalky tannins help keep **10**'s 15% alcohol amenable; pleasant cherry,
caramel & chocolate (from American oak) flavour combo. **MCC Chardonnay** NEW ★★★ **10** traditionally made
sparkler offers sweet apple fruit, racy freshness but limited complexity. Might perk up as it ages. — FM/GdB

La Couronne Wines

Location/map: Franschhoek ▪ WO: Franschhoek/Coastal/Calitzdorp ▪ Chocolate & wine tasting/sales Mon-
Sun 10–4 ▪ Open pub hols ▪ Weddings ▪ Conferences ▪ Le Chais Villa (6 en-suite rooms) ▪ Traditional braai &
picnics to be booked in advance ▪ Facilities for children ▪ Tour groups ▪ Winemaker(s) Rudi Zandberg ▪ 21h
(cabs s/f, malbec, merlot, p verdot, ptage, shiraz, chard, sauv, viog) ▪ 120t/±12,000cs own label 60% red
40% white ▪ eldorette@lacouronnewines.co.za ▪ www.lacouronnewines.co.za ▪ S 33° 55' 8.9" E 019° 6' 40.9
▪ **T +27 (0)21-876-3939/+27 (0)82-495-8579**

After a hiatus of two years, the tasting room at this welcoming winery has been
revamped and re-opened, part of a farm-wide revival which will include the re-
opening of the restaurant to complement the picnics and other visitor offerings.
A nautical theme is inspired by the link between indefatigable WW1 French war-
ship La Couronne and the estate's enduring presence in Franschhoek since 1866.

Merlot ⓟ ★★★★ Last-tasted **08** showed pure, focused aromas, smooth texture & sound structure. Satisfying
uncomplex. **Shiraz** ⓟ ★★★★ Fine-grained, elegant **06** noted few years back as one for long haul. Less showy
than **05** (★★★). **Portside Red** NEW 🍷 ★★ Unwooded **11** simple & sweet, from Bordeaux varietals. **Merlot
Rosé** NEW ✓ 🍷 ★★★★ Onionskin hue hints at shy berried nose on very dry, fresh, clean & finely balanced **11**.
Chardonnay Unwooded ⓟ 🍷 ★★★★ **09** showed creamy weight few years back, with limy distinction &
good length. **Sauvignon Blanc** 🍷 ★★★ Lightish, bone-dry **11** needs food to balance. For early drinking.
Muscadel ⓟ ★★★ Sun-bright **09** was luscious & grapey, with orange-peel twist in tail. Discontinued: **Caber-
net Sauvignon, Ménage à Trois, Chardonnay Wooded, MCC Chardonnay Brut.** — JP

Ladera Artisan Wines

Location: Wolseley ▪ Map: Breedekloof ▪ WO: Coastal/Robertson ▪ Est/1stB 2009 ▪ Tasting, sales & cellar tour
Mon-Sat by appt ▪ Picnics & longtable lunches in the fruit orchards by prior booking ▪ Owner(s) Charles Ochse ▪
Cellarmaster(s)/winemaker(s) Charles Ochse (2003) ▪ 115ha total ▪ 6-8t/400cs own label 51% red 33%
white 16% rosé ▪ PO Box 193 Wolseley 6830 ▪ charles@laderawines.co.za ▪ www.laderawines.co.za ▪ S 33°
28' 20.66" E 019° 11' 27.45" ▪ **T +27 (0)72-536-0055**

Charles Ochse recalls his schooldays running through vineyards 'chasing thiev-
ing birds away'. After 15 vintages plying his trade locally and abroad, he now
heads up the family's fruit farm in Wolseley and makes his artisanal Syrah
(showcased as a 'Future Star' at the London International Wine Fair) and Chardonnay after hours.

★★★★ **Zahir Syrah** ✓ Complex, ripe & rich mouthful of blue & black berries, naturally fermented, older
oak-aged **10** soft yet structured, layered & silky; lovely mouthfeel & long finish. Alcohol down from **09**'s 15%+.
Wild Child Chardonnay NEW 🍷 ★★★★ All creamy tangerine, luscious & smooth with good ripeness in
restrained oak frame. Elegant & poised **10** from native-yeast-fermented Robertson grapes. — FM

Ladismith Cellar — SCV

Location: Ladismith ▪ Map: Klein Karoo & Garden Route ▪ WO: Klein Karoo/Western Cape ▪ Est 1941 ▪ 1stB
1988 ▪ Tasting & sales Mon-Fri 9–5 Sat 9–3 ▪ Fee R25 for groups of 5 or more ▪ Closed Easter Fri-Mon, Dec 25,
26 & Jan 1 ▪ Book ahead for cellar tours ▪ Restaurant ▪ Owner(s) 75 members ▪ Cellarmaster(s) Hermia

Vollgraaff (2011) ▪ Winemaker(s) Hermias Vollgraaff (2010), with William Harvey (2011) ▪ Viticulturist(s) Hermias Vollgraaff (2009) ▪ 600ha/520ha (cab, merlot, ptage, ruby cab, shiraz, chard, chenin, cbard, viog) ▪ ±800t/10,000cs own label 20.25% red 79.75% white ▪ Other export brand: Decent ▪ PO Box 56 Ladismith 6655 ▪ info@scv.co.za ▪ www.ladismithwines.co.za ▪ S 33° 29'49.38" E 021° 15'59.40" ▪ **T +27 (0)28-551-1042** ▪ F +27 (0)28-551-1930

Riaan Marais is CEO, as he is at Barrydale and Oudtshoorn, the other cellars in the Southern Cape Vineyards group, and winemaker/viticulturist Hermias Vollgraaff is now also Ladismith production manager. 'Sales have doubled now that we have a venue on the Ladismith main road,' says Riaan, 'and we're boosting them with market days and our own Bastille Day, Klein Karoo style.'

Towerkop range

Shiraz ☺ ★★★ Spice, smoke & plum attractions on friendly unoaked **11**, fresh & charming anytime red. WO W Cape. **Rosé** ☺ 🖩 ★★★ Candyfloss **12**, off-dry shiraz, pleasant chilled summer sipping.

Cabernet Sauvignon ⓐ ★★★ **11** preview was characterful, with juicy & clean fruit flavour. **Merlot** ⓐ ★★★ Plummy **10** unfettered by oak, pleasant to sip. **Pinotage** ⓐ 🖩 ★★★ **11** laudably restrained aroma, unoaked to let pristine fruit shine through. **Ruby Cabernet** ⓐ 🖩 ★★ Unoaked **11** tank sample burst with berries; supple & juicy for effortless enjoyment. **Touriga Nacional** ⓐ ★★ (Unfortified) **09** slight malty overtone to jammy fruit. **Chardonnay** ⓐ 🖩 ★★ Unwooded **11** preview shy lemon/nut aromas, insubstantial flavours. **Chenin Blanc** ⓐ 🖩 ★★ Work-in-progress **11** Karoo scrub & nuts, bracing acidity from early picked grapes. **Sauvignon Blanc** ⓐ 🖩 ★★ Pre-bottling, **11** cool green varietal fruit, lowish 12% alcohol. **Chardonnay-Sauvignon Blanc** ⓐ 🖩 ★★★ Lipsmacking **10** in early-drinking style; chardonnay's citrus palate weight balanced by sauvignon's zestiness. **Aristaat** ⓐ 🖩 ★★ Sweetish white named for rare protea; drink-soon **10** featured dash muscadel. **Towersoet** ⓐ 🖩 ★★★★ Fortified dessert from muscat d'Alexandrie. **09** bottled sunshine: ripe & juicy grape flavours, lovely clean fresh finish, whereas **07** (★★★) was cloying. WO W Cape. **Amalienstein Muscadel** ⓐ 🖩 ★★★★ Delightful **10** fortified after-dinner treat again raises the bar. Bursts with enough lemon, lime, nutty complexity to brighten any dull winter's day. More depth & verve than last-tasted **06** (★★★). Discontinued: **Viognier**. — WB/JP

▪ **Lady Anne Barnard** see African Pride Wines
▪ **Lady Somerset** see Somerset Wines

La Ferme Derik

Location: Paarl ▪ Map: Paarl & Wellington ▪ WO: Paarl/Western Cape ▪ Est 1695 ▪ 1stB 1895 ▪ Tasting, sales & cellar tours by appt ▪ Function venue for 160 guests ▪ Guest house ▪ Owner(s) Hardus Otto ▪ Winemaker(s)/viticulturist(s) Eurica Scholtz ▪ 7ha (shiraz, grenache b/n, rouss, viog) + 45ha export table grapes & macadamia nuts ▪ 35t 10% red 90% white ▪ PO Box 2008 Windmeul 7630 ▪ functions@lafermederik.com ▪ www.lafermederik.com ▪ S 33° 40'33.348" E 18° 55'56.964" ▪ **T +27 (0)21-869-8380/+27 (0)82-953-0185** ▪ +27 (0)21-869-8433

Eurica Scholtz makes the wine on this Paarl property, where the main focus of activity is the farming of table grapes but conference, function and accommodation facilities are also available. She studied winemaking part-time, the small annual production intended to 'add to the package of what we offer'.

Adagio ★★★★ **10** is 88% shiraz, rest mourvèdre, viognier. Medium bodied with red fruit, some spice, zippy acidity. Flavourful & well balanced. WO W Cape. Previewed, as next. **Grenache Rosé** 🆕 ★★★★ More 'light red wine' than 'rosé', **12** nevertheless appeals with red cherries & spice, tangy acidity & a little tannic grip. **Vlinnay** Await next. **Chénine** ⓐ ★★★★ **09** a blend of old-vine chenin & viognier (80/20). Intense peach & apricot, rich & full with soft acidity. **Concerto 'les Quatre Saisons'** ⓐ ★★★★ 5-way white blend. **09** with sauvignon in lead (48%). Step up on **08** (★★★) with good fruit integrity, full body & balanced zesty acidity. **Vivace** ⓐ ★★★★ Blend of chenin (52%) & 4 other whites. **09** better concentration, more layers of flavour than maiden **08** (★★★). — CE

Laibach Vineyards

Location/map: Stellenbosch ▪ WO: Simonsberg-Stellenbosch/Western Cape/Stellenbosch ▪ Est 1994 ▪ 1stB 1997 ▪ Tasting & sales Mon-Fri 10–5 Sat 10–1 (Nov-Apr) pub hols 10–1 ▪ Fee R10/4 wines ▪ Closed Easter Fri/Sun, Dec 25/26 & Jan 1 ▪ Cellar tours by appt ▪ Laibach Vineyards Lodge (see Accommodation section) ▪

Owner(s) Petra Laibach-Kühner & Rudolf Kühner ▪ Cellarmaster(s)/winemaker(s) Francois van Zyl (Jan 2000)
▪ Viticulturist(s) /MD Michael Malherbe (Jun 1994) ▪ 50ha/37ha (cabs s/f, malbec, merlot, p verdot, ptage,
chard, chenin, viog) ▪ 300t/24,000cs own label 70% red 30% white + 4,500cs for Woolworths ▪ BWI, Organic
▪ PO Box 7109 Stellenbosch 7599 ▪ info@laibachwines.com ▪ www.laibachwines.com ▪ S 33°50'43.3" E 018°
51'44.2" ▪ **T +27 (0)21-884-4511** ▪ F +27 (0)21-884-4848

Farming without irrigation — even if you are one of the country's leading natural
and organic producers (since 2002/3) — is tough in dry years like 2012 when
200mm less rain fell than normal, admits the team behind German family-owned
Laibach. So, supplementary irrigation is on the cards, along with an organic pink
MCC Ladybird. The palate- and pocket-pleasing Ladybird in white and red guise
is set to become 80% of total production but famed London restaurant, Hakkasan,
still has first dibs on the top-notch Claypot Merlot, which sees winemaker
Francois van Zyl import special barrels to nurture his favourite grape.

★★★★ **Merlot** ✓ Stellar track record intact on **10** with grapes from Ceres again added. Deep, dark blue/
black berries yet lissome & silky too. Satisfyingly rich & full of elegant charm.

★★★★ **Claypot Merlot 10** (★★★★★) raises the bar on **09**. Deceptively mild, this wolf in sheep's garb
grows in power in the mouth. Leashed restraint evident in its plum & berry ripeness. Earthy cocoa is cloaked in
fine oak tannins. Seamlessly elegant.

★★★★ **Pinotage** ✓ Ripe red-fruit appeal on **11**. Savoury, with blueberry juiciness & light char from gentle
oak. Appealing & friendly, with long rich finish.

★★★★☆ **Friedrich Laibach** Bordeaux red blend toned down to two parts, with cab leading merlot in **09**.
No loss of class from 5-way **08**. Elegant, poised, cassis, cedar & spice resonate with ripeness & oak maturation,
superbly judged. Silky, harmonious, long tail.

★★★★ **Red Ladybird** 🍴 🍵 🌿 Cab, cab franc & merlot lead classy **11** 5-way Bordeaux blend. Elegant,
with layered complexity, ripeness & sleekly statuesque body. Velvety mouthfeel & long rewarding conclusion.
Cabernet Sauvignon ⓘ ★★★★ **08** vaults last tasted **05** (★★★★). Rich blackcurrant, spice & velvety
warm texture. Refined & elegant with good concentration. Just 10% new oak. Sadly, last bottling ever.
Widow's Block Cabernet Sauvignon Await new vintage. **Chenin Blanc** ⓘ 🍴 ★★★★ **11** ups the ante
on **10** (★★★). Rich apricot purity from old bushvines in Bottelary Hills. Lovely acid tang (all natural), full of
sunshine boldness yet rounded & stylish. **White Ladybird** 🍴 🍵 🌿 ★★★★ Smart tangerine tang cloaked
in oak sheen on **12**. Rich, ripe & mouthfilling, with lively zestiness. — FM

La Kavayan

Location/WO: Stellenbosch ▪ Est 1999 ▪ 1stB 2001 ▪ Closed to public ▪ Owner(s) Gabriël Kriel & Theo Beukes ▪
Winemaker(s) PG Slabbert (2001, consultant) ▪ Viticulturist(s) Gabriël Kriel ▪ 4ha (cab, shiraz) ▪ ±10,000cs
own label 100% red ▪ PO Box 321 Stellenbosch 7599 ▪ diana@lakavayan.co.za, theo@minpro.co.za ▪ **T +27
(0)21-881-3246/+27 (0)21-881-3289/+27 (0)83-601-9030** ▪ F +27 (0)21-881-3211

'Patience' and 'attention to detail' are the guidelines followed by friends and co-
owners Theo Beukes and Gabriël Kriel in their quest to produce wines of timeless
quality. The rest they leave to Mother Nature, content that her influence on
their tiny farm in Stellenbosch will help infuse each vintage with a unique
character.

Cabernet Sauvignon ⓘ ★★★★ Classic violet & blackcurrant scents, supple tannins on medium-bodied
09. **Cabernet Sauvignon-Shiraz** ⓘ ★★★★ Commendably savoury & dry **09** back on track with red/black
fruit complexity, more presence than **08**. — CvZ

■ LAM *see* Lammershoek Winery

Lammershoek Winery

Location: Malmesbury ▪ Map/WO: Swartland ▪ Est 1999 ▪ 1stB 2000 ▪ Tasting, sales & cellar tours by appt ▪
Light lunch platters by appt (R100pp incl wine tasting); or BYO picnic ▪ Owner(s) Paul & Anna Kretzel, Stephan
family ▪ Cellarmaster(s)/viticulturist(s) Craig Hawkins (Oct 2009) ▪ Winemaker(s) Craig Hawkins (Oct 2009,
with Jurgen Gouws (Jan 2010) ▪ 210ha/96ha (cab, carignan, grenache, merlot, mourv, ptage, shiraz, tinta
barocca, zin, chard, chenin, hárslevelü, sauv, viog) ▪ 150t/10,000cs own label 65% red 30% white 5% rosé ▪
PO Box 597 Malmesbury 7299 ▪ info@lammershoek.co.za ▪ www.lammershoek.co.za ▪ S 33°31'30.2" E 018°
48'21.1" ▪ **T +27 (0)22-482-2835** ▪ F +27 (0)22-487-2702

his large family-run farm is blessed with many old vines. The goal of Craig awkins' winemaking is to reflect the Perdeberg's naturalness and the essence those vines. 'Wines that are unpretentious, unassuming and pure, or basically mple. Wines that can capture the drinker, just like a glass of freshly squeezed ange juice would as opposed to a glass of commercial boxed stuff.' Merely sim- e they may seem until one comes to appreciate the unadulterated vitality. 'It's e hardest thing to capture,' Hawkins admits, 'but is achieved through farming d winemaking without chemicals, except for a little sulphur.' Both the LAM d Lammershoek wines are treated similarly, but the former are drawn from unger vineyards, the latter from the farm's top sites.

mmershoek range

★★★ **Syrah** 🌿 Delicacy, freshness & lightness of touch, flavour intensity define new-style **10**. Alluring pice, red earth perfume, more complex sanguine/iron flavours focused by supple yet lively structure. No **09**.

★★★★☆ **Roulette** ✓ 🌿 Complex mix game, red earth, dark fruits on generous **10**, headed by shiraz with renache, carignan, mourvèdre. Mouthfilling flavour, focusing mineral vitality & buzz of fine tannin forge fine wine that eloquently speaks of the Swartland. Only older oak used — vital part of new approach here. No **09**.

★★★★☆ **Chenin Blanc** 🌿 No additions except a little sulphur at bottling; 18 months in large old oak esponsible for 'old gold' tinge to **11**. No detriment to ethereal baked apple, nutty features. Delicious, creamy xidative texture, combined with natural vitality & near-endless length. Just 12% alcohol; a few grams sugar.

★★★★☆ **Roulette Blanc** ⑨ **10** Rhône-styled white continues on form of previous **09** (★★★★★) with ne oxidative styling. Mostly chenin & chardonnay with dash each viognier & clairette. Winemaking in natural dium produces layers of flavours with super-focused dry end; moderate 13% alcohol.

★★★★☆ **Straw Wine** ⑨ **10** (★★★★) tank sample from chenin less convincing than **09**. Exudes rich sun- ipened peaches, ultra-light with only 7.5% alcohol & lovely acid-balanced viscosity. Rating provisional.

M range

★★★ **Pinotage** ✓ 🌿 With hint of earth to its bright berry perfume, light texture & freshness from both atural acid & fine-tuned tannin, **11** reflects its pinot noir heritage. Best enjoyed slightly chilled.

★★★ **Syrah** ✓ 🌿 Wonderful contrast of substance, flavour without heaviness sets **11** apart from so many hirazes. Full of life, spice & savoury length. Like rest of range unfined, unfiltered.

rah Rosé ✓ 🌿 ★★★★ Adds variety to name with **11**. Natural ferment in older barrel & year on lees make s no ordinary rosé. More vinous than fruity, with delicious dry savoury close. **Chenin Blanc-Viognier** ✓ ★★★★ Was 'White'. Brims with verve & flavour, with lowish 12% alcohol, **11** wonderfully refreshing. tural ferment with extended lees-ageing add extra interest. — AL

.a Motte

🍴 🍷 📷 🎿 ♿

cation/map: Franschhoek • WO: Western Cape/Franschhoek/Walker Bay • Est 1969 • 1stB 1984 • Tasting & es Mon-Sat 9-5 • Fee R30 • Themed tastings R200pp — booking essential • Closed Easter Fri/Sun & Dec 25 • erneef à La Motte restaurant (see Restaurants section) • Facilities for children • Tour groups (max 16) book- g essential • Farm shop: lavender, vegetables, bread • Walking trail Mon-Sat 9-2 R50pp (duration 2-3hrs, t recommended for children under 10) • Historic walk Wed 10-11 R50pp • 35ha conservation area • useum Tue-Sun 9-5: Rupert family, history of La Motte, Cape Dutch architecture, life/art of JH Pierneef & her SA artists • Monthly classical music concerts • Owner(s) Hanneli Rupert-Koegelenberg • Cellarmaster(s) mund Terblanche (Dec 2000) • Winemaker(s) Michael Langenhoven (Dec 2006) • Viticulturist(s) Pietie le ux (May 1986) • 170ha/75ha (merlot, pinot, shiraz, chard, sauv) • 1,200t/60,000cs own label 30% red 69. 6 white 0.4% sparkling + 15,000cs for clients • Other export brand: Schoone Gevel • Brands for clients: polworths • ISO 14001:2003, BWI champion, EU & NOP organic certification, Farming for the Future: polworths • Global GAP, HACCP, IPW, WIETA • PO Box 685 Franschhoek 7690 • cellar@la-motte.co.za • www. motte.com • S 33° 52'49.9" E 019° 4'28.3" • **T +27 (0)21-876-8000** • F +27 (0)21-876-3446

ne recent renaissance at this Franschhoek showpiece included 'La Motte Rede- ned', an upgrading of visitor facilities — amongst them the restaurant named r famous local artist Pierneef, Shiraz Studio, Museum, Farm Shop and historic alking trail. Efforts were rewarded as the 2012 South African winner of Best of ine Tourism under the auspices of Great Wine Capitals of the World. The next ep, says the team led by owner Hanneli Rupert-Koegelenberg and CEO Hein egelenberg, is to market their unique amenities internationally. Of concern, ough, is the increasing view of wine as a commodity — homogenised products

at set price-points — where the variance and charm of a natural beverage is los
The response is to renew a focus on 'timeless elegance and the value of care'.

Pierneef Collection

★★★★★ **Shiraz-Viognier** Elegant & polished, a fresh & spicy flagship. **10** under wraps mid-2012, b
spicy pimento characters penetrate brooding blackberry fruit & promise luxurious pleasure in years to com
Standout **09** still evolving. Viognier (latest 12%) a subtle enhancement.

★★★★ **Shiraz-Grenache** ⊕ Earthy **08** had piquant spice & gamey tannin grip with a sweet liquorice
when last tasted. A 53/29 blend, dashes mourvèdre & carignan.

★★★★ **Sauvignon Blanc (Organically Grown)** 🔒 🌢 🈂 Fuller than cellarmate — and many pee
upholstered **12**'s nicely weighted gooseberry character is lifted by clean minerality. Walker Bay vineyards.

Classic Collection

★★★★ **Cabernet Sauvignon** 🈂 **10**'s rich blackcurrant fruit is layered within fine but still pliable tanni
fleshed out by tight-grained oak support. Yard off impressive, suave **09** (★★★★★) with lingering mineralit

★★★★☆ **Shiraz** 🈂 Consistent urbane house style. Spiced blueberry succulence the elegant trademark, b
10 (★★★★) in shadow of powerful, refined **09**.

★★★★ **Chardonnay** ✓ 🔒 🈂 **11**'s plush oak cut by twinkle-in-the-eye tangerine twist, its butterscot
breadth reined in by a fresh acid seam, ends with signature balance. Year 30% new wood. Franschhoek vine

★★★★ **Méthode Cap Classique** Broad, fresh-baked-bread luxury of **09** confirms up-tick since apple-l
maiden release, elegance still the watchword. 60% pinot noir & chardonnay, 2 years on lees. WO Franschhoek

La Motte Collection

★★★★ **Millennium** ✓ 🈂 Merlot/cab led Bordeaux quintet joined by 16% shiraz in **10** (★★★★). Smoc
& loaded with charming red berry fruit, but without gravitas of tighter, cellarworthy **09**.

Sauvignon Blanc ✓ 🔒 🈂 ★★★★ Grassy winter melon zip to dry **12**, its fresh acidity rejuvenating. —DS

Landau du Val

Location/map/WO: Franschhoek ▪ Tasting by appt ▪ Sales at La Cotte Wine Sales, Franschhoek ▪ Owner(s) Ba
& Jane Landau ▪ Winemaker(s) Wynand Grobler ▪ Viticulturist(s) Martin du Plessis ▪ 15ha under vine ▪ La B
Robertsvlei Road Franschhoek 7690 ▪ basillandau@mweb.co.za ▪ S 33° 55′ 34.3″ E 019° 6′ 34.1″ ▪ **T +**
(0)82-410-1130 ▪ F +27 (0)21-876-3369

As usual, the important news on Basil and Jane Landau's farm, La Brie, is that th
vineyard of ancient, unirrigated semillon is another year older and still holding
there — after 107 years, the vines are amongst the Cape's very oldest. As reflecte
below, in 2010 the tiny crop hung longer on the vines to make a sweeter wine.

★★★★☆ **Semillon Private Selection** ⊕ Always serene & lovely. Tasted a few years back **09** no exce
tion in its classic profile. Satisfying, easy drinking; the force of old vines shown in long-lingering subtlety.

★★★★ **Late Vintage Semillon Private Selection** NEW Richly honeyed **10** shows aromas of apric
vanilla, spice. Concentrated & intense, moderate sweetness (32g/l sugar) balanced by acid. Lengthy finish. —

◼ **Land of Hope** see The Winery of Good Hope

Land's End

A joint venture between Fairview and Hidden Valley sees Land's End wines no
made, marketed, distributed and sold by Fairview. Fairview is also responsib
for running the home farm near Elim, though ownership (land and bran
remains with Hidden Valley proprietor Dave Hidden. See Fairview for conta
details.

★★★★ **Syrah** Fynbos & a salty sea breeze note complement bright dark berries on cool-grown **09**. The p
ate is restrained, fruit mingling with smoky meat & an earthy touch. Will reward ageing year/2.

Rosé 🔒 Await next. **Sauvignon Blanc** ✓ 🔒 🈂 ★★★★ Bright green-gold **12**'s upfront tropical aroma
down a bit by fruit-shy palate & zingy acidity. Not the solid body of last **10** (★★★★). Elim grapes, as Syrah. —W

Landskroon Wines

Location: Paarl ▪ Map: Paarl & Wellington ▪ WO: Paarl/Western Cape ▪ Est 1874 ▪ 1stB 1974 ▪ Tasting & sales Mc
Fri 8.30-5 ▪ Closed Good Fri, Dec 25 & Jan 1 ▪ Cellar tours by appt Mon-Fri 8.30-5 ▪ Picnics in summer by appt

O picnic ▪ Play area for children ▪ Permanent display of Stone Age artefacts ▪ Self-catering cottage ▪ Owner(s) ul & Hugo de Villiers Family Trusts ▪ Cellarmaster(s) Paul de Villiers (Jan 1980) ▪ Winemaker(s) Abraham van erden (Sep 2007) ▪ Viticulturist(s) Hugo de Villiers jnr (1995) ▪ 330ha/200ha (cab, cinsaut, merlot, ptage, shiraz, uzão, tinta amerela, tinta barocca, touriga nacional, chenin, chard, sauv, viog) ▪ 1,200t 74% red 19% white 7% rt ▪ IPW ▪ PO Box 519 Suider-Paarl 7624 ▪ huguette@landskroonwines.com ▪ www.landskroonwines.com ▪ S ° 45′38.2″ E 018°55′0.8″ ▪ **T** +27 (0)21-863-1039 ▪ F +27 (0)21-863-2810

well-established Paarl family affair involving five members of the De Villiers clan. andskroon has been home to wine production since the 17th century and centre age is the beautiful old homestead of 1812, with expansive views of iconic Table ountain. But progress continues in the quest for better wine: the cellar has seen e purchase of new equipment, and vineyards have been replanted.

ul de Villiers range

★★★ **Cabernet Sauvignon** ✓ Good ripe regional expression. **10** exudes polished confidence with black erry opulence yet remains fresh & lively. 60% new French oak still apart, but will integrate.

★★★ **Reserve** ✓ Flagship blend shiraz & merlot plus a little cab & touriga. **10** has complex toasty cedar, lled earth & plummy fruit. Juicy core leads to cherry richness & balanced end.

iraz ★★★★ Rich & soft, with appealing dark berries, smoke & spice. **10** modern, with good long finish & teresting savoury edge.

ndskroon range

★★★ **Cape Vintage** Previously 'Port', fortified **08** from tintas barocca & amarella, souzão, touriga. Brood- g dark fruit complements chocolate & balanced savoury/sweetness. Will develop with time.

Pinotage ☺ 🖾 ★★★ Typical varietal banana loaf, dark berry support with attractive bright vinosity. **11** has firm tannin foil to ripeness. **Shiraz** ☺ ★★★ Spice lift balances **10**'s bold fruit, flowing to juicy, attrac- ive oak sweetness from year in older American oak. **Chenin Blanc Dry** ☺ 🍴 🖾 ★★★ Clean, easy, fruity welcome on nicely balanced **12**. Good combo peach & citrus notes for crisp refreshment. **Chenin Blanc Off-Dry** ☺ 🍴 🖾 ★★★ Riper than dry sibling above with well-balanced sweetness. **12** charming sipper for early drinking ends with clean acid zip. **Sauvignon Blanc** ☺ 🍴 🖾 ★★★ Easygoing **12** has soft, tropical, fruity appeal, nice dry finish. WO W Cape. **Paul Hugo White** ☺ 🍴 🖾 ★★★ **12** mostly chenin plus a little sauvignon for bite. Easy, crisp & summery. WO W Cape.

abernet Sauvignon ★★★ Previewed **11** still unsettled mid-2012 with oak particularly needing to integrate. ood vibrancy balances ripeness. Provisional rating. **Cinsaut** 🖾 ★★ Light, fruity unwooded **11**. **Merlot** 🖾 ★★ Sweet-fruited & easy **11**, with some oak support. **Cabernet Franc-Merlot** 🖾 ★★★ Wood spice & floral omas on appealing **11**, plus splash shiraz. Medium bodied & balanced. **Cinsaut-Shiraz** ★★★ Undemanding is soft & with staved oak sweetness. **Paul Hugo Red** 🍴 ★★ **11** a fruity, easy blend cab franc, shiraz & merlot. ush Camp Our Daily Red ⊕ ★★★ Red berry & spicy **09** is easy, soft & fruity. **Blanc de Noir Pinotage Off- y** 🍴 🖾 ★★ Pretty floral whiffs on simple **12** quaffer. **Bush Camp Blanc de Noir** ⊕ 🍴 ★★ Off-dry but sh **11**, with berry twist. **Chardonnay** ⊕ 🍴 🖾 ★★★ Ticks all the boxes with ripe fruit, delicious ripe ple. **11** has fresh zippy palate & juicy, yet dry end. **Bush Camp The Sundowner** ⊕ 🍴 🖾 ★★★ Pleasing weet-fruited chenin has good texture with cleansing acidity on well balanced **11**. — JP

.andzicht GWK Wines

cation: Jacobsdal ▪ Map: Northern Cape, Free State & North West ▪ Est 1976 ▪ 1stB ca 1980 ▪ Tasting & sales on-Fri 8-5 ▪ Fee R5 ▪ Closed all pub hols ▪ Tours — bottling plant ▪ Meals/refreshments by appt ▪ Owner(s) VK Ltd ▪ Winemaker(s) Ian Sieg ▪ Viticulturist(s) Johan Fourie ▪ Production: see under Douglas Wine Cellar ▪ Box 94 Jacobsdal 8710 ▪ landzicht@gwk.co.za ▪ www.landzicht.co.za ▪ S 29° 8′35.5″ E 024° 46′42.8″ ▪ **T** 27 (0)53-591-0164 ▪ F +27 (0)53-591-0145

cobsdal in north-western Free State since 1976 has been home to this winery, one the first to open outside the Cape. The first bottled vintages appeared in the rly 1980s. Currently, vinification of their signature low-alcohol table wines and rtified muscat desserts is done by colleagues at sibling Douglas Wine Cellar.

Langeberg Wineries see Wonderfontein
Langtafel see Mooiplaas Estate & Private Nature Reserve

Langverwacht Wynkelder

Location: Bonnievale ▪ Map/WO: Robertson ▪ Est 1954 ▪ Tasting, sales & tours Mon-Fri 8-5 ▪ Closed all pub h
▪ Owner(s) 25 members ▪ Cellarmaster(s) Johan Gerber (Dec 1986) ▪ Winemaker(s) Theunis Botha (Dec 20■
▪ Viticulturist(s) Hennie Visser (Jul 2008) ▪ 640ha (cab, ruby cab, shiraz, chenin, chard, cbard, sauv) ▪ 10,50■
4,000cs own label 64% red 36% white ▪ IPW ▪ PO Box 87 Bonnievale 6730 ▪ info@langverwachtwines.co.z■
S 33° 57' 32.8" E 020° 1' 35.3" ▪ **T +27 (0)23-616-2815** ▪ F +27 (0)23-616-3059

Cellarmaster Johan Gerber says his aim is to grow the winery's reputation as a co
sistent supplier of quality bulk wine to the trade — and adds for good measure th
flooding the overseas market with thousands of small labels will never reap t
industry the benefits of developing fewer but better recognised major brands.

Ruby Cabernet ☺ 🍴 🏷 ★★★ Unwooded **10** chocolate & raspberry toned pizza pal. **Chardonnay**
☺ 🍴 🏷 ★★★ Wallet-friendly & easygoing **12**, nice touch of lime marmalade & litchi complexity, delicious creamy conclusion.

Cabernet Sauvignon 🏵 🍴 🏷 ★★ **11** high-toned & sweet-fruited quick-quaff. **Shiraz** 🏵 🍴 ★★ ■
ing finish to **09**'s rich red fruit. **Chenin Blanc** 🍴 🏷 ★★★ Satisfying dry end to **12**'s parade of ripe gua■
melon & apricot, ideal solo or mealtime sipping. **Colombar** 🍴 🏷 ★★ **12** juicy tropical flavours for unco■
plicated anytime imbibing. **Sauvignon Blanc** ✓ 🍴 🏷 ★★★★ Raises the bar in **12** with more intense, p■
sistent & complex tropical fruit flavour — at only 12% alcohol. — DB/JP

Lanner Hill

Location/WO: Darling ▪ Est 1999 ▪ 1stB 2002 ▪ Sales Mon-Fri 9-3 via email/phone; from farm by appt on
Owner(s) David & Nicola Tullie ▪ Winemaker(s) Nicky Versfeld (2002) ▪ Viticulturist(s) David Tullie ▪ 91ha/5■
(cab, merlot, p verdot, shiraz, sauv, sem, viog) ▪ 450-500t/500cs own label ▪ PO Box 220 Darling 734■
tulliefamilyvineyards@gmail.com ▪ **T +27 (0)22-492-3662** ▪ F +27 (0)22-492-3664

This brand is a partnership between between seasoned winemaker and Ca
Winemakers Guild member, Nicky Versveld, and the Tullie family. It is also t
name of the family farm, situated in the cool Groenekloof ward that has beco■
synonymous with top-quality sauvignons.

★★★★ **The Yair** 🏵 Elegant **09** Bordeaux styled white (52% sauvignon, with semillon) exuded tropica
greenpepper flavours previously.
Sauvignon Blanc 🏵 🏷 ★★★★ Mouthfilling **11** preview trumpets Groenekloof's compatibility with ■
variety, no matter the vintage. Vivacious & racy, passionfruit & lime flavours & good length. — MW

Lanzerac

Location/map/WO: Stellenbosch ▪ Est 1692 ▪ 1stB 1957 ▪ Tasting & sales daily 9.30-5 ▪ Fee R20 ▪ Cellar tours a■
& 3 ▪ Closed Good Fri, Dec 25 & Jan 1 ▪ Cheese platters; wine & chocolate tasting ▪ 5-star Lanzerac Hotel, Spa & F■
taurant ▪ Conferences ▪ Weddings/functions ▪ Owner(s) Lanzerac Estate Investments ▪ Winemaker(s) Wyn■
Lategan (Jan 2005) ▪ Viticulturist(s) ▪ 150ha/46ha (cab, merlot, ptage, chard) ▪ 300t/12-13,000cs own label 5■
red 30% white 15% rosé ▪ BWI ▪ PO Box 6233 Uniedal 7612 ▪ winesales@lanzerac.co.za ▪ www.lanzeracwines■
za ▪ S 33° 56' 14.7" E 018° 53' 35.5" ▪ **T +27 (0)21-886-5641** ▪ F +27 (0)21-887-6998

The new owners of Lanzerac, stately Cape Dutch wine and hospitality estate
the entrance to Stellenbosch's Jonkershoek Valley, aim to restore the name to
former prominence. To this end a new marketing and brand manager has be■
appointed, and the decision made to undertake all aspects of production a
marketing directly from the property.

★★★★ **Cabernet Sauvignon** ✓ 🏷 Classic & restrained, **10** medley of bright black fruit, dark chocol■
Depth & complexity, fruit & fine tannin balance boding well for the future.
★★★★ **Merlot** ✓ 🏷 Black plums & savoury olives on vibrant **10**. Well integrated & complex, earthy nc
mingle with aromatic oak. Fine balance. Good varietal character.
★★★★ **Pinotage** ✓ 🏷 Juicy & fruity with bright red berries, dark chocolate notes. Elegant, stylish
understated, well balanced with a fragrant plum pudding conclusion.
★★★★ **Pionier Pinotage** ✓ **09** in recently more restrained style, sweet-sour black berry flavours, asser■
oaking & a perky acid on the finish. Good balance & structure. Will age well.

★★★☆ **Le Général** Understated 09 cab-led Cape Blend with shiraz, pinotage & malbec offers concentrated dark berry, vanilla & milk chocolate flavours. Well structured, complex with precise oaking & a delicious spicy lift. Built to last.

★★★ **Chardonnay** ✓ 📖 Citrus & buttered toast from barrel fermentation, 11 has delicate hints of vanilla oak, caramel with mouthfilling honeyed complexity; good structure & balance.

★★★☆ **Mrs English** NEW ✓ 📖 What a debut! 11 chardonnay from specially selected barrels has aromas of citrus peel, melon, white flowers & spice. Dense, with liquid silk texture, yet no excess weight. Unflagging vanilla cream on the finish.

★★★ **Sauvignon Blanc** ⊕ 📖 11 (★★★★) preview not the intensity of 10. More restrained gooseberry, grass & white peach fruitiness, perky lime twist.

Rosé ☺ 🍴 📖 ★★★ Off-dry 11 from shiraz & malbec, offers bright strawberry fruit, spicy grip, the perfect lunchtime wine. Serve well chilled. — WB

La Petite Ferme Winery

Location/map: Franschhoek • WO: Franschhoek/Western Cape • Est 1972 • 1stB 1996 • Tasting daily from 11 appt • Fee R50pp (complimentary if you book lunch) • Sales daily 8.30-5 • Cellar tours from 11-12.30 • Closed all pub hols • Restaurant & guest suites • Gift shop • Walking/hiking trails • Owner(s) Dendy Young family • Cellarmaster(s)/winemaker(s) Mark Dendy Young (1996) • Viticulturist(s) John Dendy Young • 16ha/ ha (cabs s/f, merlot, shiraz, chard, sauv, viog) • 60-70t/6,000cs own label 40% red 50% white 10% rosé • Box 55 Franschhoek 7690 • jomark@mweb.co.za • www.lapetiteferme.co.za • S 33° 55'6.43" E 019° 8'10. • **T** +27 (0)21-876-3016 • F +27 (0)86-720-6284

The younger chardonnay block has come of age, with the top row given over to the resident troop of baboons! 'This prevents them causing damage to the rest of the vineyards,' says co-owner and winemaker Mark Dendy Young. New at the popular Franschhoek winery-and-restaurant-with-a-view is a country-style tasting room.

Petite Ferme range

★★★ **Cabernet Franc** Youthful & lively 11 offers vibrant red berry fruit, leafy herbs & a smoky note. Concentrated fruit is offset by precise oaking & balanced tannins. Ideally kept year/2 before drinking.

★★★ **Barrel Fermented Chardonnay** 📖 Exotic & creamy 11 bursts with apple pie & lemon cream, toasted nuts highlights from well-judged oak & lees-ageing. Refreshing citrus finish. No 10.

Baboon Rock Unwooded Chardonnay Wild Yeast Fermented ☺ 📖 ★★★ Fresh floral perfumes on well-structured unoaked 12 version. For everyday drinking. WO W Cape.

Cabernet Sauvignon Await new vintage. **Merlot** ★★★★ 10 offers rich fruitcake, spice & dark mint chocolate. Balanced & structured, lingering, but misses the depth of 09 (★★★★). **Shiraz** ★★★★ 10 offers savoury olive, ripe mulberry & plum; vibrant, juicy & smooth oak influence. Dollop viognier adds floral lift. **The Verdict** ★★★★ Cabernet franc-based blend (with merlot & cabernet) 08 trumps 07 (★★★): smooth & harmonious with crème de cassis, spice & a light leafiness. Alcohol (15%) well integrated & hidden. **Sauvignon Blanc** ✓ 📖 ★★★★ Tropical aromas with green fruit streaks, 12 light bodied & tangy, with a lemony lustiness perfect for seafood.

Maison range

Rouge 📖 Await next release, as for **Blanc**. **Rosé** 📖 ★★★ Candyfloss & strawberries on fun summer sipper, 12 gentle & fruity with crisp acidity. — WB

La Petite Provence Wine Company

Location/WO: Franschhoek • Est 2001 • 1stB 2005 • Tasting & sales Mon-Sat by appt • Owner(s) La Petite Provence Wine Trust • Winemaker(s) Johan van Rensburg (2003, La Provence) • 3.5ha (cab, merlot) • 30t/450cs own label 90% red 10% rosé • 2 Cabernet Drive, La Petite Provence, Franschhoek 7690 • info@lapetiteprovence.co.za • www.lapetiteprovence.co.za • **T** +27 (0)21-876-4178 / +27 (0)21-876-3860

Satellite branches of this 'club' (for mainly seasonal international residents of Franschhoek's La Petite Provence Residential Estate, from whose vineyards these wines are made) have been established in Europe, says director Haydn Barry, and a foothold has been gained in the burgeoning Chinese wine market.

Cabernet Sauvignon ★★★ Very ripe, robust **10** needs time for tannins to integrate. **Merlot** ★★★ Swe plummy **10** structured by firm tannins. **Mélange** ★★★ Sternly-styled, ripe **10** cab, merlot blend. As for three, the high alcohol (15%) well tucked away. — IM

La Petite Vigne

Location/WO: Franschhoek ▪ 1stB 2012 ▪ Closed to public ▪ Owner(s) Kema Consulting (Kevin & Man Swart) ▪ Cellarmaster(s) Kevin Swart (Jan 2012) ▪ Winemaker(s) Kevin Swart (Jan 2012), with Gary Swar Jospeh Ratabana (both Jan 2012) ▪ Viticulturist(s) Jacques Wentzel (Jan 2012, consultant) ▪ 3.3ha/2.5 (cab) ▪ 4.5t/300cs own label 67% red 25% white 8% rosé ▪ PO Box 686 Franschhoek 7690 ▪ kevin lapetitevigne.co.za ▪ **T +27 (0)21-876-2903**

'A very steep learning curve!' is how Kevin Swart describes his first year makin wine at this small, newly acquired Franschhoek property. Gardener Jospe Ratabana came with him from Johannesburg to assist, and brother Gary and th team at The Amistad Wine Company also helped see the first vintage into bottle

La Petite Vigne range

Cabernet Sauvignon Not tasted. **Deep Red Rose** NEW ★★★ Full-bodied **12** from cab, satisfyingly su stantial. Bone-dry in fact, but high alcohol & bold fruitiness leave sweet impression.

Timothy White range NEW

The Sauvignon Blanc 🖷 ★★★ Water-white **12** attractively herbaceous with very brisk finish. — IM

- **La Place** *see Stellar Winery*
- **La Providence** *see Stony Brook*
- **Last Chance** *see Zoetendal Wines*
- **Lategan Family** *see Bergsig Estate*

Lateganskop Winery   🍷🍷🌿

Location: Wolseley ▪ Map/WO: Breedekloof ▪ Est 1969 ▪ 1stB 2004 ▪ Tasting & sales Mon-Fri 8–12 & 1– Closed Easter Fri-Mon, Dec 25/26 & Jan 1 ▪ Cellar tours by appt ▪ Owner(s) 5 members ▪ Cellarmaster(s) He rich Lategan (Oct 2008) ▪ Winemaker(s) Heinrich Lategan, with Kean Oosthuizen (May 2011) ▪ 238ha (c ptage, chard, chenin, sauv, sem) ▪ 2,900t/300cs own label 70% red 30% white & ±2m L bulk ▪ PO Box Breërivier 6858 ▪ lateganskop@breede.co.za ▪ S 33° 30'57.27" E 019° 11'13.65" ▪ **T +27 (0)23-355-171** F +27 (0)86-637-6603

The statistics — 300 cases own label vs ±2 million litres bulk wine — tell yo where the Lategan family winery's focus is, but as per the notes below, the hou bottlings are tasty and affordable (the 'Twins' are the sons of grandfather Wil Lategan), and the Zahir red will soon be joined by a chenin-based white siblin

Lateganskop Winery range

The Zahir 🌀 🖉 ★★★ Fresh & appealing Cape Blend, equal cab & pinotage, **10** chocolate & ripe berry fru

Twin's Peak range

Pinotage NEW ☺ 🖉 ★★★ Some caramel mingles with savoury & red berries on medium-bodied **10**.

Chenin Blanc Await next, as for **Chardonnay-Viognier** & **Hanepoot Jerepigo. Sauvignon Blanc** 🖉 ★★ Fresh & pleasant **12** summer tipple. — JP

La Terre La Mer

Location: East London ▪ WO: Swartland ▪ Est/1stB 2008 ▪ Closed to public ▪ Owner(s) Deon le Roux, Cha Benn, Mark Wiehahn, Stef Kriel & Adrian Toma ▪ Cellarmaster(s) Partners & Peter Turck (2008, consultan Winemaker(s) Peter Turck (2008, consultant), with Deon le Roux, Charles Benn, Mark Wiehahn, Stef & Fic Kriel, Adrian Toma (all Jan 2008) ▪ Viticulturist(s) Various ▪ 2.5t/150cs own label 100% red ▪ 6 Princess Dri Bonza Bay, East London 5241 ▪ dleroux@iafrica.com ▪ **T +27 (0)83-701-3148** ▪ F +27 (0)43-735-2494

Guided by winemaker Peter Turck and empowered by a Stellenbosch Universi garagiste course, five wine enthusiasts are vinifying from a facility overlooki East London's Quinera Lagoon. Their maiden shiraz, happily still available press time, is to be followed by a Swartland-sourced shiraz-mourvèdre blend.

Everything should be greener.
And everyone can drink to that.

If you are as passionate about wine as you are about the environment, youll be glad to know that Nedbank is committed to a sustainable future for the South African wine industry. We are actively involved in the Biodiversity & Wine Initiative, a Green Trust project, and have a 17-year partnership with the Cape Winemakers Guild. We are continually looking for ways to protect the environment by reducing our own carbon footprint as a bank and making banking greener for our clients through initiatives such as e-statements and our Green Affinity programme. These are just some of the ways we are helping to ensure a better future for generations to come. Heres to working for a greener Earth.

MAKE THINGS HAPPEN

In a stroke of PR genius, man of the cloth turned garage winemaker **Bertus van Niekerk**, artist wife **Selma Albasini** and son **Hendrik** launched their Revelation Red Horse Cinsaut (its name inspired by members of Van Niekerk's former flock, who were fascinated by the end of times and the apocalyptic events said to precede it) at a Somerset West naturist resort. The rather revealing event and resulting blaze of publicity were not only a fillip for their Osbloed brand but also possibly the catalyst for a rebirth of red-wine grape cinsaut, once a significant feature of the national vineyard and the parent, with pinot noir, of one of South Africa's flagship varieties, pinotage.

Elgin Ridge is the story of a foreign heart smitten by local beauty and a lifelong winegrowing dream fulfilled – the heart belonging to Briton **Marion Smith** and the dream being harboured by her husband **Brian**, pictured holding ducks taking a break from their pest-control duties in the vineyards. Marion fell in love with South Africa on a visit in 2001, so much so that she surprised her spouse with the impulse purchase of an apartment in Cape Town. The couple returned many times and finally, in 2007, with advice from a local vintner, bought an uprooted apple farm and began planting vines. 'You cannot grow wine organically in Elgin,' they were told. 'It's too wet.' Persevering, the Smiths developed their vineyards and recently completed cellar into an EU-certified fully organic operation, and are now also using biodynamic preparations. How did they do it? 'Maybe it was the guano we had imported from Namibia to use as fertiliser!'

A sophisticated turn-on

Sophistication is about refinement, perfection, ingenuity, taste and a little touch of style. Most importantly, sophistication is about meeting these high standards with absolutely no fuss.

When it comes to your wine, no words could ring more true, which is why Nampak Closures' range of screw caps are designed to give your wine a perfect sense of style that appeals to even the most sophisticated connoisseur.

Our screw cap closures are impermeable, eliminate the high risk of cork taint, experience no loss of resilience and have no finicky storage requirements. They are effortless to open and re-close, and offer beautiful high-end printing and finishes. With our screw caps, there are sure to be no unpleasant surprises, just a refined little twist to top off that perfect wine experience.

For more information, contact us on +27 21 507 8411 or email:
madene.koen@za.nampak.com
william.footman@za.nampak.com
barry.erasmus@za.nampak.com

N²
Nampak
Closures
packaging excellence

www.nampak.com

Having steeped himself in wine through study and numerous crushes locally and in cellars as far-flung as Mexico and Russia, in 2009 **Charles Ochse** was in charge of white-wine making at Franschhoek Cellar when a life-changing opportunity came calling: to take over the running of the family fruit farm in Wolseley. With precious little spare time and no vines on the property to draw from, he's keeping his dream alive by sourcing small parcels of quality grapes in Paarl, Robertson and Swartland for his boutique label, Ladera Artisan Wines.

vineyard hotel & spa
the perfect setting

diarise friday

Tastes of *2013*

eat, sip, savour

26th april	vineyard hotel's 5 wine partners
10th may	steenberg vineyards
24th may	de wetshof estate
07th june	shannon vineyards
21st june	tokara
05th july	the winery of good hope
19th july	buitenverwachting
02nd august	klein constantia estate
23rd august	strandveld wines
06th september	glen carlou
20th september	jordan wine estate
04th october	delaire graaf estate
25th october	constantia valley wines

Join us at the **square** and treat your tastebuds
to a dining experience created by our chef
to enhance the latest and greatest from
top estates and fêted winemakers.
Booking is essential for these popular events, so call us
on **021 657 4500** or e-mail us at **eat@vineyard.co.za**.

the SQUARE

In strong contrast to their ever-evolving Columella and Palladius blends, the Sadie Family Wines' more recent Die Ouwingerdreeks/Old Vine Series is the result of a project driven by winemaker/viticulturist **Eben Sadie** and aimed at showcasing South Africa's viticultural past through some of its most venerable vineyards. The wines in the series (depicted/represented by soils from the various vineyards) – including Eselshoek (muscat d' Alexandrie a.k.a. hanepoot), Mev. Kirsten and Skurferg (both chenin blanc), white blends Kokerboom and 'T Voetpad, and Pofadder (cinsaut) – are vinified, matured and packaged with absolute respect for tradition and exacting attention to detail, down to printing the labels on an ancient press.

Many friends talk over dinner about immersing themselves in wine. **Herman Nel** (left) and **Alan van Niekerk**, 40-somethings and lovers of 80s music, went beyond the usual well-intentioned banter by actually founding a boutique winery, Desert Rose, in the Olifants River Valley and vinifying their first wines. As envisioned, it's a hands-on operation with manual numbering of bottles, licking of labels, sealing of cases – and, unsurprisingly, plenty of tasting along the way.

● customs
● transport and logistics
● International trade
● media
● fishing and marine resources
● hedge funds
● insider trading
● human capital
● special projects
● litigation / dispute resolution
● IT law, technology and e-commerce
● public private partnerships
● swaps and derivatives
● transfer pricing
entertainment
● real estate / property
● intellectual property
● healthcare and pharmaceutical
● listed property funds
● insolvency, business rescue and debt recovery
● natural resources, oil and gas
● global mobility
● energy
● municipal
● franchising and licensing
● public private partnerships
● estates and estate planning
● restraint of trade
● forensics
● gaming / gambling
● telecommunications
● shipping and logistics
● integrated employment solutions
● employment
● anti-trust / competition
● trusts
● employee incentives
● private client
● pension and provident funds
● pro bono
● projects
● corporate governance
● employee benefits
● due diligence
● immigration
● aviation
● criminal matters
● insurance
● employee tax
● JSE / TRP / regulatory
● corporate commercial
● mergers and acquisitions
● mining
● environment
● construction and engineering
● retail
● black economic empowerment
● medical schemes
● sport
● advertising and ASA
● banking and finance
● tax
● constitutional
● capital markets

offering the full platter

of legal services

law | tax | forensics | IP | africa

johannesburg +2711 269 7600
cape town +2721 410 2500
durban +2731 301 9340
stellenbosch +2721 808 6620
edward nathan sonnenbergs

africa's largest
law firm
ens.co.za

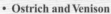

Shiraz Ⓢ ★★★ Step up **10** ripe red-fruit compote, leather & smoke, rounded, fuller, good length & texture. Swartland grapes, as for unrated preview **11**, light & juicy, still unformed. — IM

L'Auberge du Paysan

Location: Somerset West ▪ WO: Stellenbosch ▪ Closed to public ▪ Owner(s) Michael Kovensky ▪ PO Box 36825 Chempet 7442 ▪ kovensky@aroma.co.za ▪ **T +27 (0)21-529-3990** ▪ F +27 (0)21-555-3033

The auberge is closed but the vineyards on this small property on Winery Road near Somerset West are still producing: in fact, winemaker Tjuks Roos rates the 2012 'the best wine that's ever come off the farm'. It's pinotage and merlot only: 'That's our game and we're sticking to what we know.'

Merlot [NEW] ▨ ★★★ Bright minty tones, unyielding tannins over spicy red fruit on **10**. **Pinotage** ▨ ★★★ Aromatic, steely wild berries on **10** are appealingly ripe & generous, let down by bitter twist at finish. — GdB

L'Avenir Vineyards 🍷 🍴 🏠 🚸 ♿

Location/map: Stellenbosch ▪ WO: Stellenbosch/Western Cape ▪ Est/1stB 1992 ▪ Tasting & sales Mon-Fri 9–5 Sat 10–4 ▪ Fee R15 ▪ Closed Easter Fri/Sun, Dec 25 & Jan 1 ▪ Cellar tours by appt ▪ BYO picnic ▪ Child friendly ▪ Luxury 4-star Country Lodge ▪ Owner(s) Advini ▪ Cellarmaster(s) Tinus Els (Sep 2005) ▪ Winemaker(s) Tinus Els (Sep 2005), with Dirk Coetzee & Mattheus Thabo (Aug 2009/Jan 2007) ▪ Viticulturist(s) Leigh Diedericks, with Johan Pienaar ▪ 64.9ha/27.26ha (cabs s/f, merlot, ptage, chenin, sauv) ▪ 320t/18,000cs own label 50% red 40% white 10% rosé ▪ IPW ▪ PO Box 7267 Stellenbosch 7599 ▪ info@lavenir.co.za ▪ www.larochewines.com, www.lavenir-lodge.com ▪ S 33° 53' 18.7" E 018° 50' 59.1" ▪ F +27 (0)21-889-5258

While old vines are a benefit, their low yields are a financial negative especially in Stellenbosch. 'Our main challenge in the vineyard is to reach our goal of breaking even,' says Tinus Els, cellarmaster at this French wine business-owned cellar. 'Trellising all the bushvines for better yield is one solution.' Thankfully the farm's venerable 40-year-old chenin blanc vineyard does yield economic crops, the fruit going to the Grand Vin. The current vintage nods to the Loire, being aged mainly in Acacia barrels from France; this, Els suggests, 'lends it an elegant dimension'.

Icon range

★★★★☆ **Grand Vin Pinotage** Unusually, new oak initially dominant on **09**. Beneath lies plenty of ripe substance, harmonious tannins. Good now with decanting but also long-term potential. Fine match for game.

★★★★☆ **Grand Vin Chenin Blanc** ▤ ▨ Sophisticated, complex **11**; first since **08**. Glimpses of lees, minerals, chalk, lemon blossom & oak spice woven into creamy yet fresh mouthfeel. Dry & very long. An individual for contemplation & ageing.

Platinum range

★★★★ **Cabernet Sauvignon** ✓ ▨ Classic freshly ripe black-berry/-currant features on **11**; typically firm yet amiable tannin backing. Deliciousness increased by moderate alcohol. **10** sold out untasted.

★★★★ **Pinotage** ▨ **10** (★★★★) slightly more austere, densely tannic than **09**, which dims the underlying sweet raspberry & cherry fruit. May benefit from short-term ageing.

★★★★ **Stellenbosch Classic** ▤ ▨ Sternish cab-based **10** (★★★★); merlot & cab franc (25%/5%) add some flesh; but with noticeable acid & rigid tannins it lacks the charm of **08**; no **09**.

★★★★ **Chenin Blanc** ▤ ▨ **11** has usual unshowy refinement. Supple, lees-enriched base anchors gently persistent honey, floral features. Vibrant & dry; balanced to allow for delicious development. **10** untasted.

★★★★ **Brut Rosé Méthode Cap Classique** ✓ ▨ **10** switches from chenin to chardonnay as pinotage partner. Pretty colour, packaging. Subtle red fruits, biscuity tones, fine bead & refreshing brut dryness.

Merlot ▤ ▨ ★★★ Satisfyingly unpretentious **11**. Fragrant & flavoursome, with bright red plum features, tangily dry. **Chardonnay** ✓ ▤ ▨ ★★★★ Accent on peach fruit, with sprinkles hazelnut & oatmeal in **11**. Supple, juicy, with some leesy breadth. Fermented/aged in older oak only.

Classic range

Pinotage-Merlot [NEW] ☺ ▤ ▨ ★★★ Bright-fruited, succulent **11** with just squeeze of forming tannin. Plenty satisfaction if not great complexity.

Pinotage ▤ ▨ ★★★ Unoaked **12** (preview) a bowl of ripe crushed cherries freshened with a sprinkle of lemon zest: a tribute to grape's joyous fruit. This range WO W Cape. **Rosé de Pinotage** ▤ ▨ ★★★ Striking peach pink, redcurrant features on fruitily fresh, dry **12**. **Chenin Blanc** 🏠 🧆 ★★★★ Characterful ape style. **12** (ex-tank) expressive melon, wet wool purity; good flavour concentration, length. **Sauvigr Blanc** ✓ 🏠 🧆 ★★★★ Apple blossom, fresh Granny Smith apple scents appetising introduction on Medium bodied, juicily dry. Easy drinking. — AL

La Vierge Private Cellar

Location: Hermanus ▪ Map: Elgin, Walker Bay & Bot River ▪ WO: Hemel-en-Aarde Ridge/Hemel-en-Aarde \
ley ▪ Est 1997 ▪ 1stB 2006 ▪ Tasting & sales daily 10–5 ▪ Closed Good Fri & Dec 25 ▪ Cellar tours by appt ▪ Vierge Restaurant & Champagne Verandah (see Restaurants section) ▪ Tour groups by appt ▪ Owner(s) Vierge Wines (Pty) Ltd & Viking Pony Properties 355 (Pty) Ltd ▪ Winemaker(s) Marc van Halderen (Jun 200 with Jan Fortuin (Jun 2009) ▪ Viticulturist(s) Petrus Bothma (2008) ▪ 90ha/40ha (pinot, sangio, shiraz, cha riesling, sauv, sem) ▪ 75t 50% red 50% white ▪ PO Box 1580 Hermanus 7200 ▪ info@lavierge.co.za ▪ ww lavierge.co.za ▪ S 34° 22′ 22.3″ E 019° 14′ 29.4″ ▪ **T +27 (0)28-313-0130** ▪ F +27 (0)28-312-1388

With evocative names and labels to match, this range is an exotic journey throu history, myth and legend — but cleverly connected to and descriptive of the wi styles. They include biblical Original Sin, Last Temptation and Redemption; Anth lia, named 'from the ability to see angels'; Nymphomane, a reference to Gre mythology's nymphs or nature/water spirits; Satyricon, a 1st century satyri novel about wisdom found at the expense of innocence; and main focus Pinot Noi link to the Black Madonna, hence 'Noir'. And it all starts from La Vierge, 'the v gin', acknowledging that this was originally unplanted with vines.

La Vierge range

★★★★ **La Vierge Noir Pinot Noir** Nicely showcases this variety's split personality, vivid cherries in **11** p forest floor; admirable structural elegance, careful oaking, with flavours remaining to the very end.

La Vierge Collection

★★★★ **Original Sin Sauvignon Blanc** ✓ Classic styling in **11** thanks to cool growing conditions, g handling; minerality & earth, elegant & tight focus, with an extended finish. Some own H-&-A Valley grape **Nymphomane Cabernet Sauvignon-Malbec-Cabernet Franc** ★★★ Dark-fruited **10** shows lots of car attention; tannins are still youthfully firm without being edgy, enjoy now till 2018. **Anthelia Shiraz-Mourvè** ★★★★ Natural ferment, 30% whole bunch, 16 months small French oak for **10** gives intense dark berries, sup tannins, tasty succulence. **Satyricon Sangiovese-Nebbiolo-Barbera** ★★★★ Both serious & charming, bright cherry fruit, firm finish reminiscent of Italy where these varieties originated, & like there, food is the answ **Jezebelle Chardonnay** ★★★★ Citrus & oatmeal cookie scented/flavoured **11**'s elegant structure good for s enjoyment as well as with food. **The Last Temptation Riesling** Next awaited.

Special Vintage Releases

★★★★ **Redemption Sauvignon Blanc** ⓔ Previously reviewed **08** from shy-bearing single-viney available only from cellardoor & restaurant. Restrained yet complex & mouthfilling. **The Affair** Await new vintage. — CR

La Vigne Estate

Location/map: Franschhoek ▪ WO: Western Cape/Franschhoek ▪ Est 2004 ▪ 1stB 2005 ▪ Tasting, sales & cellar tc by appt ▪ Owner(s) Robert Joergensen ▪ Winemaker(s) Gerda Willers ▪ 6.7ha/4.7ha (cab, shiraz, sem) ▪ own la 100% red ▪ PO Box 69 Simondium 7670 ▪ wine@lavigne.co.za ▪ www.lavigne.co.za ▪ S 33° 53′ 28.0″ E 019° 5′0

Many studies, it seems, have shown that classical music enhances learning ar also (more bizarrely) shapes water molecules to form more balanced structure So winemaking and maturation receives a gentle, harmonising earful at sou engineer Robert Joergensen's tiny Franschhoek establishment.

★★★★ **Single Vineyard Shiraz** ⓔ Young vineyard provides amazing depth in **07**, mulberry viscosit tailored — yet refreshing — frame. Like below, tasted a few years back. **Owner's Selection Red** ⓔ ★★★★ **06** Bordeaux blend let berry fruit outshine oak in medium-bodied b ance. WO W Cape, as for next. **Edvard Grieg Edition** ⓔ ★★★ Cherry-fruited **06** harmonious & elega **Owner's Selection White** ⓔ ★★★ Broad **06** mainly semillion with 27% chardonnay, lightly oakec waxy. **Musical Edition** ⓔ ★★★★ **07** ex Citrusdal impressive melding of semillon (85%) & chard with bru new oak. — DS

Lazanou Organic Vineyards

Location/WO: Wellington ▪ Map: Paarl & Wellington ▪ Est 2002 ▪ 1stB 2006 ▪ Tasting & sales by appt ▪ Open days with wine & food pairing — booking required ▪ Tour groups ▪ Farm produce ▪ Owner(s) Josef Lazarus & Candice Stephanou ▪ Winemaker(s) Rolanie Lotz (Jan 2011, consultant) ▪ Viticulturist(s) Johan Wiese (Jan 2006, consultant) ▪ 8.48ha/5.54ha (mourv, shiraz, chard, chenin, viog) ▪ 50t/3,000cs own label 50% red 50% white ▪ Organic certification by SGS ▪ PO Box 834 Wellington 7654 ▪ wine@lazanou.co.za ▪ www.lazanou.co. za ▪ S 33° 35' 59.58" E 018° 59' 36.12" ▪ **T +27 (0)83-265-6341** ▪ F +27 (0)86-670-9213

Open days at Lazanou Organic Vineyards near Wellington have proved so popular, they will be offered more often. 'We live a relatively self-sustaining lifestyle, producing most food right here and sharing with employees and guests at open days,' says co-owner Josef Lazarus. 'Our mission is to make excellent wine naturally, striving towards a natural and healthy equilibrium and balanced eco system.'

Syrah ⊕ ☼ **★★★★** Fruit-driven style continues in single-vineyard **09**, with some spiciness, medium body, firm grip to finish. Attractive, but misses the complexity & minerality we admired in **08** (★★★★★). **Syrah-Mourvèdre** ⊕ ☼ **★★★** 10 shade off the pace of wow-factor **09** (★★★★★). Soft, sweet-ripe berries, medium body & an espresso lift. **Chardonnay** √ ☼ ▨ **★★★★** Floral tones mingle with Granny Smith apple aromas on **11**. Mouthfilling, with creamy vanilla oak flavours in harmony with the fruit. **Chenin Blanc** √ ☼ **★★★★** Subtle, understated **11**, tropical fruit & hint of vanilla oak, well structured with lees-ageing adding complexity. **Viognier** NEW ☼ **★★★★** Fragrant peach melba seduces on **11**, precise oaking balances the fruit well without intruding. Lipsmacking moreish finish. **Chenin Blanc-Chardonnay-Viognier** √ ☼ **★★★★** Aromatic peach & stonefruit perfume entices on unoaked **11**, fresh & harmonious with a long creamy farewell. Discontinued: **Wooded Chenin Blanc**. — WB

▪ **LB** see Anura Vineyards
▪ **Leatherwood** see Prospect1870
▪ **Le Bistro** see Zandvliet Wine Estate & Thoroughbred Stud

Le Bonheur Wine Estate

Location/map/WO: Stellenbosch ▪ Est 1790's ▪ 1stB 1972 ▪ Tasting & sales Mon-Fri 9–5 Sat/Sun 10–4 ▪ Fee R15/5 wines ▪ Closed Good Fri ▪ Conferences ▪ Foreign film festival, every last Fri of the month — booking essential ▪ Owner(s) Lusan Premium Wines ▪ Cellarmaster(s)/winemaker(s)/viticulturist(s) Sakkie Kotzé (Oct 1993) ▪ 163ha/75ha (cab, merlot, chard, sauv) ▪ 460t/20,000cs own label 30% red 65% white 5% rosé ▪ WIETA ▪ PO Box 104 Stellenbosch 7599 ▪ info@lebonheur.co.za ▪ www.lebonheur.co.za ▪ S 33° 50' 1.0" E 018° 52' 21.4" ▪ **T +27 (0)21-875-5478** ▪ F +27 (0)21-875-5624

Sakkie Kotzé celebrates 20 years at this old Stellenbosch estate in 2013. A highlight of his tenure is replanting the farm, matching variety to terroir. '90% complete,' he says. 'But the vineyards also provide the biggest challenges in water and canopy management and crop control.' And vineyards are where 'winemakers' footprints should be, rather than in the barrel'. The natural Le Bonheur style, says Sakkie, is 'wines with soft, ripe tannins that can age for years.'

★★★★ Cabernet Sauvignon 09 firmly built, soundly dry to please the classically inclined drinker. Lovely ripe & fresh cab fruit too, ending on a savoury note. 18 months in oak give a complementary polish.

★★★★ Prima ⊕ Unshowy, elegantly fresh **08** Bordeaux red. Merlot-led but shows cab's strong, informing tannins. Drinkable but should improve for good few years.

★★★★ Tricorne NEW Cab, cab franc, shiraz blend in slightly plusher mode for this winery. **09**'s bright, mint, spicy features enliven soft, fleshy core, add sweet-fruited length to dry finish. Tasty if fairly straightforward.

Pinot Noir Rosé NEW ▨ **★★★** Salmon-hued **11** with gently refreshing strawberries & cream flavours; unaggressively dry. **Chardonnay** ▨ **★★★★** Fruit-forward **11**; crisp lemony/oatmeal flavours augmented by balanced oak enrichment. Medium bodied, bone-dry & good drinking. **Sauvignon Blanc** ▤ ▨ **★★★** **11** slightly off usual pace; crisp, bone-dry but tame, tiring fruit. — AL

▪ **Leeumasker** see Maske Wines

Leeuwenberg

WO: Western Cape/Bot River/Coastal/Wellington ▪ Est/1stB 2010 ▪ Tasting only in Wiesbaden, Germany Mon-Fri 11-7 Sat 10-6 (T +49 (0)611-308-6778) ▪ Closed all pub hols ▪ Owner(s) Tanja Hilka ▪ Winemaker(s)

Frank Kastien & Kobie Viljoen ▪ 1,500cs own label 50% red 50% white ▪ PO Box 50723 West Beach 7449 ▪ sales@leeuwenbergwines.com ▪ www.leeuwenbergwines.com ▪ **T +27 (0)73-645-3284**

Germany continues to be the main focus for negociant Tanja Hilka, and her recent experience suggests that German consumers are looking for wines from lesser-known regions. There is also a growing enthusiasm for chenin and pinotage. Her export-only wines aim to satisfy some of these preferences.

Flagship range NEW

2 Barrels Shiraz ★★★★ Accomplished **10**, tasted pre-bottling shows great typicity. 15% cab adds to structure in support of fruit purity, whilst the all-new oak influence is well integrated. **Raphael Cape Blend** 🍷 ★★★★ Sampled **11** is half pinotage, blended with cab & shiraz & a few minor others. Floral lift to black cherry fruitiness impresses with poised ripeness. WO Coastal. **Sauvignon Blanc** 🍷 ★★★ **10** with 15% wooded semillon component is ready to enjoy, a weighty & bone-dry food partner.

De Kleine Leeuwen range

Shiraz NEW ☺ ★★★ Fresh aromas on **11** express lovely light spice, leading to vibrant fruity flavours & a dry finish. From Wellington grapes.

Cape Blend ★★★ Pinotage/cab combo on **11** sweet appeal, but dry. WO Wellington. **Chardonnay Unwooded** 🍷 Await next. Note: range last listed as 'Drie Kleine Leeuwen'. — JP

Leeuwenjacht

Location/WO: Paarl ▪ Est 1692 ▪ 1stB 1989 ▪ Closed to public ▪ Winemaker(s) Adele Dunbar ▪ 10,000cs own label + 2,500cs for clients ▪ Brands for clients: Cubana ▪ PO Box 583 Suider-Paarl 7624 ▪ info@fairview.co.za ▪ www.deleuwenjagtwines.co.za ▪ **T +27 (0)21-863-2450** ▪ F +27 (0)21-863-2591

The well-established De Leuwen Jagt brand (first bottling 1989) is now in the Fairview stable where the name has been contracted and simplified, and the wines given smart new labels reflecting Fairview's 'heritage and innovation' identity. Eventually it is hoped to incorporate winetasting and sales, with a farmstall located next to the vegetable garden on the historic property, granted in 1692.

Leeuwenrood ☺ 🍷 🎨 ★★★ **10**, now bottled, very palatable quaffing red with savoury, meaty nose, melange of black & red fruits. Chewy tannins, warm finish.

Rosé 🍷 🎨 ★★★ From muscadel, tank sample of **12** is a mouthful of Turkish Delight & lively grape flavours. Semi-sweet, characterful, charming. **Leeuwenblanc** 🍷✓🍷 🎨 ★★★★ **11** is all fig, gooseberry & herbs from sauvignon, chenin & nouvelle. Nice acid zip & structure. **Nuance** 🍷 🎨 ★★★ Delicate **12** from muscadel, sauvignon & riesling. Off-dry & refreshing for everyday drinking. Discontinued: **Cabernet Sauvignon, Pinotage, Shiraz, Muscadel**. — CM

Leeuwenkuil Family Vineyards

Location: Paarl/Swartland/Stellenbosch ▪ WO: Swartland/Coastal ▪ Est 2008 ▪ 1stB 2011 ▪ Closed to public ▪ Owner(s) Willie & Emma Dreyer ▪ MD Kobus de Kock ▪ Cellarmaster(s) Pieter Carstens (Aug 2008) ▪ Winemaker(s) Inge Terblanche (Nov 2010), Corrien Geleijnse & Sean Nieuwoudt (both Jan 2012), with Jehan de Jongh (Aug 2008) ▪ Viticulturist(s) Koos van der Merwe (Dec 2008) & Claude Uren (Jan 2012) ▪ 4,250ha ▪ 26,500t 10.5m L 70% red 30% white ▪ WIETA ▪ PO Box 249 Koelenhof 7605 ▪ kobus@leeuwenkuilfv.co.za ▪ **T +27 (0)21-865-2455** ▪ F +27 (0)21-865-2780

Grapes from Willie and Emma Dreyer's vast vineyard holdings in Swartland and Paarl have been channelled anonymously into many vaunted brands over the years but the couple have now launched a quartet of own-brand wines under the label Leeuwenkuil, the name of the historic farm on which they reside. The wines may represent but a drop in Leeuwenkuil Family Vineyards' production but it's clearly a thoughtfully made, rather tasty and even impressive drop.

Leeuwenkuil range NEW

★★★★ **Family Reserve White** 🍷 🎨 **11** 50% chenin with 4 supporters. Only seasoned oak so the focus stays on the (stone)fruit; a vanilla-tinged richness but also a ringing freshness for solo or seafood. WO Coastal.

Shiraz ☺ 🍴 📷 ★★★ Definitely a smiley-faced wine: **11** is juicy & dead easy to drink, with a light tannic grip that also makes it ideal for casual meals. **Chenin Blanc** ☺ 🍴 📷 ★★★ Another happy sipper from Swartland, perfumed apple & hint of blackcurrant, **12**'s modest alcohol makes it an all-day sipper, too.

Family Reserve Red 🍴 📷 ★★★★ Savoury, spicy Rhône blend mainly shiraz & 3 minors, WO Coastal. **11** deftly executed, & showing potential in the way older oak forms a supple framework on which to hang fresh, vibrant smoke-laced fruit. Stock up & watch this space. — JP/CvZ

Le Fût

Location/WO: Paarl ▪ Map: Paarl & Wellington ▪ Est 2004 ▪ 1stB 2005 ▪ Tasting by appt ▪ Conference/function/wedding venue ▪ Owner(s) Trevor & Joan Ernstzen ▪ Winemaker(s) Trevor Ernstzen ▪ Viticulturist(s) Joan Ernstzen (Nov 2004) ▪ ±17ha/9ha (shiraz, chenin, cbard, riesling) ▪ 80t/300cs own label 100% red ▪ PO Box 156 Paarl 7622 ▪ wine@lefut.co.za ▪ www.lefut.co.za ▪ S 33° 44′ 34.38″ E 019° 0′ 39.90″ ▪ **T +27 (0)83-561-1555** ▪ F +27 (0)86-675-5114

Trevor and Joan Ernstzen sell most of their grapes to other producers, but also vinify a limited quantity in their small Paarl cellar. Says winemaker Trevor: 'Spending time with a few winemakers of old confirmed my philosophy that good grapes will result in good wine and should never be rushed into the bottle.'

Shiraz Reserve 🊒 ★★★ Development shows on interesting **07**. Medium bodied (though big 15% alcohol), shy on fruit, with more savoury, smoky & earthy notes to follow. — JP

■ **Legends of the Labyrinth** *see* Doolhof Wine Estate

Le Grand Chasseur Wine Estate

Location/map: Robertson ▪ Est 1881 ▪ 1stB 1999 ▪ Tasting by appt ▪ Closed all pub hols ▪ Owner(s) Albertus de Wet ▪ Cellarmaster(s)/winemaker(s) Carel Botha (Jan 2011) ▪ Viticulturist(s) Francois Viljoen (Jan 1998, consultant) ▪ ±1,300ha/300ha (cab, merlot, ptage, ruby cab, shiraz, chard, chenin, cbard, muscadel w, nouvelle, sauv) ▪ ±4,500t ▪ IPW ▪ PO Box 439 Robertson 6705 ▪ cellar@lgc.co.za, sales@lgc.co.za ▪ www.lgc.co.za ▪ S 33° 48′ 26.8″ E 019° 52′ 40.1″ ▪ **T +27 (0)23-626-1048** ▪ F +27 (0)23-626-1048

A far longer than usual vintage delivered good quality grapes, which has filtered through to the wines, according to cellarmaster Carel Botha, now settled in at this Robertson cellar, where new plantings are in progress and exports have increased. 'Things are on track and looking positive!' No new vintages ready at press time.

■ **Leidersburg** *see* D'Athis Wines SA Negociants

Le Joubert

Location/WO: Paarl ▪ Map: Paarl & Wellington ▪ Est 1693 ▪ 1stB 2007 ▪ Tasting & sales by appt ▪ Owner(s) Dawie & Alison Joubert ▪ Cellarmaster(s)/winemaker(s) Dawie Joubert ▪ 25ha/4ha (cab, p verdot) ▪ 20t/1,000cs own label 90% red 10% white ▪ PO Box 2963 Paarl 7620 ▪ alison@lejoubert.com ▪ www.lejoubert. com, www.lejoubert.co.za ▪ S 33° 43′ 29.02″ E 018° 57′ 16.61″ ▪ **T +27 (0)21-870-1070/+27 (0)82-552-3671** ▪ F +27 (0)87-803-7886

Recognising what this farm on the slopes of Paarl mountain is capable of, and turning it into reality is what occupies the owners, Dawie and Alison Joubert. The traditional, robust reds have a loyal following and it's for their fans that a private tasting room is being created. The wines can also now be found in selected Paarl outlets and restaurants.

1070 ★★★★ Named for days between harvest & release. Cab-led **09** deft marriage showy cassis & new oak, good grip, ageworthy. **1070s** ★★★★ Shiraz-led with 4 Bordeaux varieties. **09** spice-laden rich fruitcake, mocha chocolate. Savoury foundation & length from new oak. **Brillianté** ✓ ★★★★ **09** same varieties, different blend to 1070's, dash viognier. Meaty, oodles of spice & dark fruit, new oak adds textured finish. **Viognier** ★★★ Pear & barley sugar, wooded **10** shows maturity, honeyed tones. Enjoy soon. — CR

Le Manoir de Brendel

Location/map/WO: Franschhoek ▪ Est/1stB 2003 ▪ Tasting daily 12-4 ▪ Fee R40pp, waived on purchase ▪ Sales daily 7.30-4.30 ▪ Closed Good Fri, Dec 25/26 & Jan 1; also closed when booked for weddings/conferences ▪ Group lunches on request, book ahead ▪ Facilities for children ▪ Gift shop ▪ Conferences: day package (60 pax)/overnight package incl 9 rooms ▪ Walks ▪ Weddings (up to 60 pax) with chapel & wooden terrace on the river ▪ 5-star guest house (10 suites) ▪ Spa, booking essential ▪ Owner(s) Christian & Maren Brendel ▪ Winemaker(s) Cerina de Jongh & André Bruyns ▪ Viticulturist(s) Paul Wallace (consultant) ▪ 30ha/±23ha (cab, merlot, ptage, shiraz, chard, chenin, sauv, sem) ▪ ±150t ▪ PO Box 117 La Motte Franschhoek 7691 ▪ lmb@brendel.co.za ▪ www.le-manoir-de-brendel.com ▪ S 33° 52'52.8" E 019° 3'42.2" ▪ **T +27 (0)21-876-4525** ▪ F +27 (0)21-876-4524

This Franschhoek luxury guest house and spa is celebrating its tenth vintage since German owners Christian and Maren Brendel bought it in 2003. To coincide with this milestone, they've launched a Brendel Collection, but production of all the wines stays small — mainly for guests and their many functions and events.

Le Manoir de Brendel Collection
Shiraz ★★★ 05's stewed fruit showing bottle-age nutty character, drink soon.

Brendel Collection NEW
Cabernet Sauvignon ★★★ Mature 07 drinks well now: rhubarb & prune notes, firm tannin structure for food pairing. **Merlot** ★★★ Tobacco, dried tomato & fruit-sweet edge to 06, nearing drink-by date. **Pinotage** ★★★ Sweet fruit, spicy aromas & typical acetone whiffs on ready 08; handles 15% alcohol with aplomb. **Shiraz** ★★★ Engaging sweet-sour ying-yang on meaty 06; soft textured, slips down easily. — FM/GdB

Lemberg Wine Estate

Location/map: Tulbagh ▪ WO: Tulbagh/Breedekloof ▪ Est 1978 ▪ Tasting, sales & cellar tours Mon-Fri 9-5 Sat/Sun 10-3 ▪ Fee R15 waived on purchase ▪ Closed Easter Fri/Sat/Mon, Dec 25 & Jan 1 ▪ Meals, cheese platters & picnics by appt — book prior to visit ▪ BYO picnic ▪ Table olives & olive oil ▪ Function venue (40-60 pax) ▪ 3 self-catering guest cottages (sleeps 2, 4 & 6 respectively) ▪ Fly fishing (equipment available) ▪ Sunset rowboat trips by prior arrangement ▪ Owner(s) Henk du Bruyn ▪ Winemaker(s) David Sadie (Feb 2011) ▪ Viticulturist(s) David Sadie (Feb 2011) & consultants ▪ 21ha/9ha (ptage, pinot, shiraz, hárslevelü, sauv, viog) ▪ 70t/4,200cs own label 60% red 30% white 9% rosé 1% sweet sauv ▪ IPW ▪ PO Box 221 Tulbagh 6820 ▪ suzette@lemberg.co.za ▪ www.lemberg.co.za ▪ S 33° 18'8.27" E 019° 6'23.06" ▪ **T +27 (0)21-300-1130** ▪ F +27 (0)21-300-1131

Owning Tulbagh boutique winery Lemberg is the realisation of Henk du Bruyn's dream of being a winegrower. With rising star David Sadie, he's rejuvenating the cellar and vineyards, in particular mature and once-celebrated sauvignon, establishing new blocks, and returning to the more natural approach espoused by former owner Janey Muller. Lower alcohol levels and 'greenness' are focuses (hence 'tree-free' paper for the labels), and portfolio tweaking sees an emphasis on reds, especially pinotage, and the launch (post our deadline) of a premium white blend.

★★★★☆ **Surin** NEW Distinctive & impressive 11 dessert from vine-dried sauvignon, older-oak fermented & aged. Elegant & beautifully balanced, spicy & pure stonefruit flavours so vibrant, you'll be reaching involuntarily for the wax-sealed 375ml bottle, adorned with acrylic by South African impressionist Derric van Rensburg.

Syrah Blanc de Noir ☺ 🍴 🖉 ★★★ Previewed 12 strawberry toned, dry & laudably light-textured (11%) yet quite serious — has more to say than most of this style.

Pinot Noir NEW ★★★ Natural fermentation (a hallmark of David Sadie's winemaking) for 11, slightly wild, more 'dry red' than varietal, oak obvious (though only older barrels). **Pinotage** ⓘ ★★★★ Restrained & integrated 10 had loads of body, showed potential last time. **Spencer** NEW ★★★ Second pinotage offering, more savoury, 10 malt & olive character, smooth & full, light wooding adds to charm. **Syrah** NEW ★★★ Oak-driven styling (though only 25% new barrels) for 11, more char & toast than cranberry fruit flavour mid-2012, might settle & integrate. **Cape Blend** NEW ★★★ 11 pairs pinotage with shiraz (66%) & splash pinot noir in easy-drinking country red. **Sauvignon Blanc** ✓ 🍴 🖉 ★★★★ Poised 12 tank sample different league to 11 (★★★), unusual & attractive blackcurrant note, bone-dry, good balance of lightness (12% alcohol) & texture thanks to oaked portion. 33 year old vines. **Viognier** ★★★★ Now bottled, apricot-perfumed 11 still understated but not frivolous, offers satisfying weight & length. Viognier for grownups. Breedekloof grapes. Discontinued: **Private Bin 13**. — CE/CvZ

Leopard Frog Vineyards

Location/WO: Stellenbosch ▪ Closed to public ▪ Owner(s) Dogwood Trust ▪ Cellarmaster(s)/winemaker(s) David John Bate (Jun 2005) ▪ 5,000cs own label 60% red 40% white ▪ 8 Royal Ascot Lane Sandown Sandton 2196 ▪ info@leopard-frog.com ▪ www.leopard-frog.com ▪ **T** +27 (0)11-884-3304 ▪ F +27 (0)11-883-0426

Canadian-born David Bate's wine production may be on the micro scale, but his creativity in crafting unusual and interesting blends (and labels) is boundless. Innovative in either their varietal or multi-vintage makeup, or lengthy oaking; not by artistic whim but by design, drawing on his Bordeaux Wine Institute training.

Proprietor's Limited Releases

Aphrodite Africa ⓟ ★★★☆ Cab franc 04 emerges after 60 months beauty sleep in oak paler but perfumed, with enough vitality for mealtime entertainment. **Tantra** ★★★ Cab franc's perfume & supple structure temper oak on Bordeaux blend. Lower-key 06 lacks gravitas & fruit of 05 (★★★★). **Tribe** ★★★ Bold, ripe-styled blend of pinotage (50%) & its parents, pinot noir & cinsaut. 06 robust, for hearty meals. **Kiss & Tell** ★★★ 06 ripe & savoury shiraz-led blend with shade less fruit-filled intrigue. For early drinking. **Tao** NEW ★★★☆ 09 quirky blend, mainly zinfandel with sangiovese & barbera. Supple, with bright savoury red fruit & lively drinkability. **Ingénue** NEW ⊘ ★★★ 11 savoury, tangy cab rosé. Feisty oak (all new) requires food. **Singularity** ⓟ ★★★★ Another unusual offering: viognier from vintages 2005-2009 (thus NV), retains freshness & drinkability. Refined & light, with lemon & starfruit. **Tryst MCC Blanc de Blancs Brut** NEW ★★★ Lengthy lees-aged 08 chardonnay méthode cap classique sparkling is contemplative, smooth & waxy. Note: range was Leopard Frog Vineyards'. Discontinued: **Midnight Maasai Shiraz**, **Spellbinding Chenin Blanc**. — MW

Leopard's Leap Wines

Location/map: Franschhoek ▪ WO: Western Cape ▪ Est 2000 ▪ Tasting & sales Mon-Sat 9-5 ▪ Fee R25/5 wines ▪ Culinary Studio: hands-on cooking classes & chef's tables by chef Liam Tomlin ▪ Culinary Store: cooking utensils, equipment, ingredients, culinary literature ▪ Meals/refreshments available ▪ Child friendly ▪ Owner(s) Hanneli Rupert-Koegelenberg & Hein Koegelenberg ▪ Cellarmaster(s) Eugene van Zyl (Nov 2002) ▪ 300,000cs own label 60% red 39% white 1% rosé ▪ PO Box 1 La Motte 7691 ▪ info@leopards-leap.com ▪ www.leopards-leap.com ▪ S 33° 52'58.8" E 19° 04'50" ▪ **T** +27 (0)21-876-8002 ▪ F +27 (0)21-876-4156

Launched in 2000 to serve the UK market, Leopard's Leap has been taken into some 40 countries by a philosophy that quality and affordability are not mutually exclusive. A recent partnership with Yangzhou Perfect sees a further near-3 million bottles a year pour into the burgeoning Chinese market alone. And the global brand now has a (stylish) local home: tasting facilities and the Liam Tomlin Food Culinary Studio & Store opened in Franschhoek last year.

Family Collection

Chenin Blanc NEW ☺ 🍴 ⊘ ★★★ Oak (50% in seasoned cask, 9 months) fills out orange blossom/apricot fruit core, aromatic 11 perfect partner for traditional spicy minced meat boboties.

Shiraz-Mourvèdre-Viognier ✓ 🍴 ★★★★ Exuberant tang of viognier explodes through brooding, sultry 09 to fill the flavour palette. Ample soft tannins, 20% new oak.

Classic range

Cabernet Sauvignon ☺ 🍴 ★★★ Appealing, open styling of cassis-laden 10 delicious in youth. **Merlot** ☺ 🍴 ★★★ 10 loaded with floral violet charm to plummy, meaty depth of flavour. **Shiraz** ☺ 🍴 ★★★ Smoky leather tones to red berry fruit profile, 10 tannins still tight, needs food. **Chenin Blanc** ☺ 🍴 ⊘ ★★★ Boisterous tropical fruit characters of 12 come to order in tasty dry tail. **Sauvignon Blanc** ☺ 🍴 ⊘ ★★★ Melon profile tightened by citric tang, 12 lipsmacking, dry.

Cabernet Sauvignon-Merlot ✓ 🍴 ★★★★ Velvet feel of 60/40 blend in 10, glossy red fruit & svelte, non-drying tannins. Like all reds, manageable 13.5% alcohol. **Chardonnay** 🍴 ★★ Unwooded 12 herbaceous rather than fruity.

Lookout range

Pinotage Rosé ☺ 🍴 ★★★ Lively strawberry bonbons jump out of glass of zippy, just-dry 12.

Cabernet Sauvignon-Shiraz-Cinsaut 🍴 ★★ Down-to-earth berry fruit in chunky **11**. **Chenin Blanc** **Semi Sweet** 🍴 🌿 ★★ **12** spun-sugar appeal balanced by fresh acid. **Chenin Blanc-Chardonnay** 🍴 🌿 ★★ Previewed not-quite-dry **12** lightly fruited. — DS

Le Pommier Wines

Location/map: Stellenbosch • WO: Stellenbosch/Banghoek ▪ Est/1stB 2003 ▪ Private tastings by appt; wine sales during restaurant hours ▪ Facilities for children ▪ Petting zoo ▪ Picnics ▪ Le Pommier Restaurant ▪ Spa ▪ Accommodation ▪ Owner(s) Marietjie van der Merwe ▪ Winemaker(s) Neil Moorhouse ▪ Viticulturist(s) Hannes Jansen van Vuuren ▪ 16ha/4.8ha (malbec, sauv) ▪ 2,000cs own label 45% red 55% white ▪ PO Box 916 Stellenbosch 7599 ▪ info@lepommier.co.za ▪ www.lepommierwineestate.co.za ▪ S 33° 55' 8.58" E 018° 55' 43.14" ▪ **T** +27 (0)21-885-1269/+27 (0)21-885-1561 ▪ **F** +27 (0)21-885-1274

With spa, wine lounge, country lodge, restaurant and even a petting zoo, this Banghoek property deserves to be called a destination. Owner Marietjie van der Merwe has welcomed Zorgvliet's two barrels of seriously styled Five-Thirty-Five — made by Neil Moorhouse in the Zorgvliet cellar — into the Le Pommier range.

★★★★☆ **Five-Three-Five** 🍴 Moves across from the Zorgvliet stable. From single-vineyard planted at altitude of 535m. Sweet tropical **11** (★★★★) lacks some of the verve of **10**, though natural ferment imparts lovely mouthfilling texture.

Cabernet Sauvignon Reserve Ⓐ 🍴 ★★★ Aromatic **08** shows serious intent but resolute tannin & firm acidity overwhelm fruit. **Jonathan's Malbec** Await new vintage. **Shiraz** Ⓐ ★★★ Bold, extracted **09** was overwhelmed by tannins, but plenty of mulberry fruit & spice. **Rosé** Ⓐ 🍴 ★★★ Dry, savoury **10** from cab franc delightfully fresh & vibrant as well as prettily pink. **Chenin Blanc** Ⓐ 🍴 ★★★☆ Flavoursome **10** tasted few years ago had frisky acidity enlivened by ripe tropical flavours. **Sauvignon Blanc** Ⓐ 🍴 ★★★ Easy, fresh, uncomplicated sample **11** has surely settled by now; less focus & vitality than previous vintages. **Natural Sweet Sauvignon Blanc** NEW ★★★ Lightly sweet & fresh **10** an attractive gold colour, with sufficient acidity to prevent cloying. — IM

Le Riche Wines

Location/map/WO: Stellenbosch ▪ Est 1996 ▪ 1stB 1997 ▪ Tasting & cellar tours by appt only ▪ Sales Mon-Fri 8. 30-4.30 ▪ Closed all pub hols ▪ Owner(s) Etienne le Riche ▪ Cellarmaster(s) Etienne le Riche (Jan 1997) ▪ Winemaker(s) Christo le Riche (Jan 2010), with Mark Daniels (Sep 2000) ▪ 70t/4,500cs own label 90% red 10% white ▪ PO Box 6295 Stellenbosch 7612 ▪ wine@leriche.co.za ▪ www.leriche.co.za ▪ S 33° 56' 26.5" E 018° 54' 14.3" ▪ **T** +27 (0)21-887-0789 ▪ **F** +27 (0)21-887-0789

What's been happening? What's coming up? we asked owner and cellarmaster Etienne le Riche. 'New vintage, new barrels', was the laconic reply. But he's also a veteran vinifier of cabernet sauvignon — one of the Cape's most renowned — and grows more loquacious on that subject. Stellenbosch (where he sources his grapes) is, he says, more than any other area, primarily 'cabernet country', worthy of the same international status as California's Napa Valley. When he muses that the days are gone when a producer can do everything, there's little doubt about the continued specialisation of this family winery. All this clearly doesn't imply conservatism, however. The house-style, perhaps nudged by winemaker son Christo, seems to be evolving in a more modern (Napa-style?) direction — fruit-rich wines, luxuriously oaked and ripely powerful expressions of their origins.

★★★★☆ **Cabernet Sauvignon Reserve** Grand **09** shows some return to elegance after **08** (★★★★), but also underlines rich fruit & ripe power, & shows much new oak in its youth — otherwise finely balanced. Full of good things that need 5+ years to unpack. The tannin structure is a marvel of succulent moreishness.

★★★★☆ **CWG Auction Reserve Cabernet Sauvignon** More alcohol & new oak than Cab Reserve, but **09** single vineyard selection has bright fruit, minty complexity, intensity & balance to cope brilliantly. Richly silky, it compels from enticing aromas to lingering & genuinely dry finish. Should improve for many years.

★★★★ **Cabernet Sauvignon** Easier-going than other cabs in range, but also serious, with firm structure supporting the full, ripe flavour. Go to the others for intensity, this **09** for earlier approachability.

★★★★ **Cabernet Sauvignon-Merlot** Merlot, dabs of cab franc & petit verdot, & avoidance of new oak all soften the 65% cab on **10**. Tasty & fresh, with bite enough to keep you alert, but enough charm to beguile.

★★★★ **Chardonnay** ⊕ **10** leads with great citrus & stonefruit purity, while judicious wooding (half in 50%-new oak, rest in tank) adds to wonderful composure & subtly textured, fine dry finish. — TJ

■ **Les Coteaux** *see Mont du Toit Kelder*
■ **Les Fleurs** *see Southern Sky Wines*
■ **Le Vin de François** *see Chateau Naudé Wine Creation*
■ **L'Huguenot** *see Leopard's Leap Wines*

Libby's Pride Wines

Location: Wellington ▪ WO: Western Cape/Wellington ▪ Tasting, sales & tours by appt ▪ Owner(s) Elizabeth Petersen ▪ Winemaker(s) Hennie Huskisson (Linton Park Wines) ▪ 750t/20,000cs own label 75% red 25% white ▪ info@libbyspridewines.com ▪ www.libbyspridewines.com ▪ **T +27 (0)82-745-5550** ▪ F +27 (0)86-215-1811

Elizabeth Petersen's motto is 'Never think your dream is beyond your reach'. With star sign Leo, which she associates with strength and pride, she's intent on developing Libby's Pride into South Africa's most successful black-woman-owned wine business. In this endeavour she's partnered by Linton Park Wines.

Shiraz ☺ 📝 ★★★ Unoaked off-dry **11**, spicy sweet fruit in an easy-drinking package. **Chardonnay** ☺ 📝 ★★★ Lively unwooded **11**, zesty lime & apple, unpretentious & seafood friendly.

Cabernet Sauvignon ⊕ ★★ Light, easy & noticeably dry, **10** is perfect for country fare. **Merlot** ⊕ ★★★ **10** is fun, fruit-forward & light-hearted, bursts with cherries & chocolate. **Signature Red** 📝 ★★ Merlot/shiraz combo from Wellington vines (as for Shiraz). Off-dry **11** is fruity, savoury & lightish. **Sauvignon Blanc** 📝 ★★ Shy, lightish **12**, faint grass & greenpepper, perky finish. — WB

■ **Libertas** *see Distell*

Lievland Estate

Location/map/WO: Stellenbosch ▪ Est/1stB 1982 ▪ Tasting, sales & cellar tours Mon-Fri 9-5 Sat/Sun 10-4 ▪ Closed Dec 25 ▪ Summer picnic baskets by arrangement ▪ B&B accommodation ▪ Owner(s) Susan Colley ▪ Winemaker(s) Kowie du Toit (2004) ▪ Viticulturist(s) Conrad Schutte (2010, Vinpro) ▪ 50ha (cab, merlot, shiraz) ▪ 250t/5,000cs own label 95% red 5% white ▪ PO Box 66 Klapmuts 7625 ▪ lievland@icon.co.za ▪ www.lievland.co.za ▪ S 33° 50′ 29.5″ E 018° 52′ 34.8″ ▪ **T +27 (0)21-875-5226** ▪ F +27 (0)21-875-5213

Lievland, on the highly prized foothills of Simonsberg, has been through several changes of late but dates back to 1715 — so it knows how to cope! The cellar was built in 1823 and the Cape Dutch manor house in 1828. Fine wines have emerged in the past, and more will surely come, but nothing new tasted this year.

Shiraz ⊕ ★★★★ Latest of three bottlings of **05** is soft, silky & savoury, with appealing dark-fruit flavours. For drinking now. **Lievlander** ⊕ 📖 ★★★★ Equal parts shiraz & cab with dash merlot, **08** is savoury, juicy & supple with loads of berry fruit. **Sauvignon Blanc** ⊕ 📖 ★★ **11** stonefruit flavours, for easy quaffing. — JP

■ **Like Father Like Son** *see Bon Courage Estate*

L'illa

Location: Hermanus ▪ WO: Eilandia ▪ Est/1stB 2006 ▪ Tasting & sales at Newton Johnson Vineyards ▪ Owner(s)/winemaker(s) Gordon & Nadia Newton Johnson ▪ Viticulturist(s) AA Cilliers (Jan 1973) ▪ (chenin) ▪ 110cs (12 x 375ml) own label 100% white ▪ PO Box 225 Hermanus 7200 ▪ gordon@newtonjohnson.com, nadia@newtonjohnson.com ▪ www.newtonjohnson.com ▪ **T +27 (0)28-312-3862** ▪ F +27 (0)86-638-9673

The name (pronounced leeya) means 'island' in Catalan, and alludes to the wine's origin in Robertson's Eilandia ward and to the farm there, also Eilandia, of the Cilliers family for six generations. Nadia Cilliers married into the Newton Johnson clan in the Hemel-en-Aarde and makes the wine in the eponymous cellar.

★★★★ **Noble Late Harvest** From chenin, **11** shows more raisiny notes among its range of flavours than botrytis ones, in its quiet but concentratedly intense way. Vibrant & silky, the sweetness balanced by alcohol & fine acid so as to avoid any cloy. **09** (★★★★★) showed more subtle botrytis. **10** sold out untasted. 375ml. — TJ

Limelight

Two years into the business, Limelight, a standalone brand from De Wetshof, is looking at growing its presence in restaurants, wine bars and supermarkets, with a drive into neighbouring countries and tentative steps into overseas markets.

Chardonnay-Pinot Noir ⊕ 🏠 📦 ★★★ Unpretentious 80/20 mix, **11** lightish alcohol, with just a smidgen of sugar, ideal chilled sunset sipper. — GdB/JPf

■ **Lime Road** *see* Havana Hills
■ **Lindenhof** *see* Boland Kelder

Lindhorst Wines

Location: Paarl ▪ Map: Paarl & Wellington ▪ WO: Paarl/Coastal/Durbanville ▪ Est 1996 ▪ 1stB 2002 ▪ Tasting, sales & cellar tours by appt 11–5 daily ▪ Closed Dec 25 ▪ Meals by special request only ▪ Self-catering cottage ▪ Owner(s) Mark & Belinda Lindhorst ▪ Winemaker(s) Mark Lindhorst, advised by Philip Costandius (Aug 2009, consultant) ▪ Viticulturist(s) Mark Lindhorst, advised by Kevin Watt (Jan 2001, consultant) ▪ 65ha/18ha (cab, merlot, mourv, ptage, pinot, shiraz, viog) ▪ 140t/4,000cs own label 100% red ▪ PO Box 1398 Southern Paarl 7624 ▪ mark@lindhorstwines.com ▪ www.lindhorstwines.com ▪ S 33° 47′ 46.0″ E 018° 56′ 59.0″ ▪ **T +27 (0)21-863-0990** ▪ F +27 (0)21-863-3694

Co-owner Mark Lindhorst was a chartered accountant for many years and financial statements were part of his daily life. When deciding on a name for his signature red blend 'Lindhorst Wines making a statement' was the obvious way to go. The vineyards are mostly shiraz and Statement is always shiraz dominated.

Cabernet Sauvignon ⊕ ★★★ Uncomplicated **07** shows dark fruit, fresh acidity, firm tannins; last year needed time to lose slightly hard edges. **Merlot** ⊕ ★★★ Rich & full **07** exhibits dark fruit & chocolate flavours; broad structured & smooth textured but lacks a little freshness. **Pinotage** ⊕ ★★★★ Succulent yet complex, **07** had liquorice, graphite nuances alongside brambleberry fruit when last tasted. **Shiraz** ★★★★ Big & bold **07** shows red & black fruit, some spice before long, savoury finish. Appears already quite evolved so drink up. **Partner's Choice** ⊕ ★★★★ **07** equal cab & shiraz, 2% pinotage. Red & black fruit, dusty oak on the nose, fresh acidity, fine tannins. **Max's Tribute** ★★★ **07** blend of 74% shiraz, rest mourvèdre, viognier. Rich & broad, already quite developed with lots of savoury character. WO Coastal. **Statement** ★★★ **07** a blend of 71% shiraz & merlot. Rich but somewhat unfocused. Sweet red & black fruit plus slight nutty, malty notes. Rung-up **06** (★★★★) was fleshy, had some cab. **Sauvignon Blanc** ✓ 🏠 ★★★★ From Durbanville grapes, **12** displays classic cool-climate grassiness, greenpepper. Fresh but not hard acidity. Discontinued: **Rosé**, **Viognier**. — CE

Lingen

Location: Stellenbosch ▪ WO: Jonkershoek Valley ▪ Est 2003 ▪ 1stB 2008 ▪ Tasting & sales at Stark-Condé Wines (see entry) ▪ Owner(s) JD Krige Family Trust ▪ Cellarmaster(s)/winemaker(s) José Conde (Jan 2003) ▪ Viticulturist(s) Pieter Smit (Jan 2003, consultant) ▪ 7ha/2ha (cab, p verdot, shiraz) ▪ 14t/200cs own label 100% red ▪ PO Box 389 Stellenbosch 7599 ▪ info@stark-conde.co.za ▪ www.stark-conde.co.za ▪ **T +27 (0)21-861-7700/+27 (0)21-887-3665** ▪ F +27 (0)21-887-4340

With the third vintage of this red blend in bottle, winemaker José Conde — of Jonkershoek Valley neighbour Stark-Condé Wines, where the wine is made, sold and offered for tasting — says it's a daily endeavour to better understand and improve it. From gravelly clay 'vilafonte' soils quite different to his own vineyards', it's softer, but no less classy.

★★★★ **Lingen** Cab/shiraz blend with 20% petit verdot, lithe & supple **10** has herb features, shade lighter than beautifully poised, brambly **09** (★★★★★). — DS

Linton Park Wines

Location: Wellington ▪ Map: Paarl & Wellington ▪ WO: Paarl/Wellington/Western Cape ▪ Est 1995 ▪ 1stB 1998 ▪ Tasting, sales & cellar tours between 9-4 by appt ▪ Fee R50pp ▪ Closed all pub hols ▪ BYO picnic ▪ Walks/hikes ▪ 4x4 & mountain biking trails ▪ Annual harvest festival Mar/Apr ▪ Owner(s) Camellia PLC UK ▪ Cellarmaster(s) Hennie Huskisson (2007) ▪ Winemaker(s) JG Auret (2007) ▪ Viticulturist(s) Vlok Hanekom (2006) ▪ 210ha/ 84ha (cab, merlot, pinot, shiraz, chard, sauv, viog) ▪ 650t/60,000cs own label 50% red 40% white 10% rosé ▪

Fairtrade ▪ PO Box 1234 Wellington 7654 ▪ sales@lintonparkwines.co.za, info@lintonparkwines.co.za ▪ www.
lintonparkwines.co.za ▪ S 33° 36' 40.1" E 019° 2' 15.0" ▪ **T** +27 (0)21-873-1625 ▪ F +27 (0)21-873-0851

The forebear of all Fouries in South Africa, Louis Fleurij, was the first to farm this
property in Wellington's Slangrivier Valley, granted in 1699 (the original act on
view in the manor house). As many descendants trace their roots to the UK-owned
and now Fairtrade certified estate, it's only fitting that a range is named for him.

Reserve range

★★★★ **Cabernet Sauvignon** ⓦ Rich & full-bodied 08 last was dominated by blackcurrant, dark cherry &
chocolate. Expressive fruit, firm centre of supple tannin, savoury tail.

★★★★ **Merlot** ⓦ When reviewed, 05 offered mint, liquorice & dark chocolate to vibrant wild-berry tone;
firm tannins should be accessible now.

★★★★ **Shiraz** ⓦ Oodles of violet, smoky, spicy plums in 07 last time. Juicy, full-bodied, firm tannins & a
savoury conclusion. Should be delicious now.

Linton Park range

Cabernet Sauvignon ⓦ ★★★★ Well-made, gluggable 08 is ripe & dark-fruited, hints of blackcurrant & firm
tannins. **Café Cabernet** NEW ⓥ ★★★ Fashionable coffee/mocha tone to 11, structure, texture & flavour all oak
derived. Mediumweight & pleasant. **Merlot** ⓦ ★★★★ Dark & ripe spicy fruitcake & plums, 09 juicy fruit mingles
with supple tannins, dry savoury conclusion. **Shiraz** ⓦ ★★★★ Juicy plum, mulberry & spice last edition, 08 full-
bodied, sweet fruit balanced by a refreshing acidity & smooth tannins. Paarl WO. **De Slange Rivier** NEW ⓥ
★★★★ Big & bold smoky entry for 10, concentrated deep dark fruit & liquorice. Ripe tannins add texture & length.
Wellington WO. **Chardonnay** ⓦ ★★★★ 09 a step up from 08 (★★★★), appeals with ripe pineapple & vanilla
biscuit. Round, fresh & creamy. **Private Bin 177 (Limited Release)** ⓦ ★★★ From sauvignon, off highest
vines on farm (±500m). Still-available 10 dry, food friendly, with firm acidity.

Louis Fourie 1699 range NEW

Cabernet Sauvignon ▤ ⓥ ★★★ Inky blackcurrant softness on maiden 11, rounded & medium bodied
with light chalky grip. **Merlot** ▤ ⓥ ★★★ Uncomplicated softness to 11 with hint of mint lurking on nose.
Enjoyable & easy to like for its gentle texture. **Shiraz** ▤ ⓥ ★★★ Olive tapenade smokiness on spicy 11.
Juicy but dry, with savoury nuance & medium structure. **Chardonnay** ▤ ⓥ ★★★ Uncomplicated 11
offers light green peach tang & oatmeal creaminess. **Chenin Blanc** ▤ ★★★ Green melon & light apricot on
11 undemanding quaffer. WO W Cape, as next. **Sauvignon Blanc** ▤ ⓥ ★★★ Shy fig leaf & granadilla on
light, zesty, easy-drinking 11. — FM

■ **Lion Creek** see Napier Winery
■ **Lion's Drift** see Silkbush Mountain Vineyards
■ **Liquor City** see Orange River Wine Cellars
■ **Lisha Nelson Signature Wines** see Nelson Wine Estate

Lismore Estate Vineyards

Location: Greyton ▪ Map: Southern Cape ▪ Est 2003 ▪ 1stB 2006 ▪ Tasting & sales by appt ▪ Facilities for children
▪ Tour groups ▪ Walking/hiking & mountain biking trails ▪ Owner(s)/winemaker(s) Samantha O'Keefe ▪ Viti-
culturist(s) Andrew Teubes (consultant) ▪ 235ha/12ha (shiraz, chard, sauv, viog) ▪ 40t/2,000cs own label
15% red 85% white ▪ PO Box 76 Greyton 7233 ▪ wine@lismore.co.za ▪ www.lismore.co.za ▪ S 34° 4' 25.23" E
19° 41' 16.83" ▪ **T** +27 (0)82-343-7913

Greyton boutique winemaker Samantha O'Keefe's country idyll includes vistas
of the Overberg, visits by leopards, secretary birds and baboons, and, unusually
for the area, vines, from which she produces a chardonnay, barrel-fermented
sauvignon blanc and viognier for a predominantly five-star restaurant and hotel
clientele that includes London's River Café.

■ **Little River** see De Meye Wines
■ **Live-A-Little** see Stellar Winery
■ **Living Rock** see Withington
■ **Lodewijkx** see Eerste Hoop Wine Cellar

L'Olivier Wine & Olive Estate

Location/map/WO: Stellenbosch ▪ Tasting & sales by appt only ▪ Fee R50 ▪ Conference & wedding venue ▪ Walks/hikes ▪ Mountain biking trail ▪ Horse riding ▪ Accommodation in manor house/villa & two cottages ▪ Owner(s) Theuns Kuhn ▪ Viticulturist(s) Leander Koekemoer ▪ 22ha (cab, chard, sauv) ▪ ±120t/1,457cs own label 30% red 70% white ▪ Stellenboschkloof Road Stellenbosch 7600 ▪ info@lolivierestate.com ▪ www.lolivierestate.com ▪ S 33° 55'37" E 018° 46'54" ▪ T +27 (0)21-794-1031 ▪ F +27 (0)21-794-1051

Grapes from this beautiful, multi-amenity Stellenboschkloof property are currently vinified in a nearby cellar but viticulturist Leander Koekemoer dreams of a purpose-built facility on the estate.

Non Pareil Boutique Wines
Cabernet Sauvignon Await new vintage. **Sauvignon Blanc** 📖 ★★★ Crunchy green apple & asparagus typicity, lively acidity adds lemony lift to **12**'s lightish palate. Flinty finish. — FM

■ **Lollapalooza** see Wine Concepts

Lomond

Location: Gansbaai ▪ WO: Cape Agulhas ▪ Est 1999 ▪ 1stB 2005 ▪ Tasting & sales at Farm 215 Mon-Sun 9-4 by appt ▪ Closed all pub hols ▪ Guest accommodation, restaurant, conferences, hiking trail, conservation area (www.farm215.co.za) ▪ Owner(s) Lomond Properties, Distell & workers trust ▪ Cellarmaster(s)/winemaker(s) Kobus Gerber (2004) ▪ Viticulturist(s) Wayne Gabb (1999) ▪ 1,100ha/120ha (merlot, syrah, nouvelle, sauv) ▪ 750t 40% red 60% white ▪ ISO 9002, BWI ▪ PO Box 184 Stellenbosch 7599 ▪ lomond@capelegends.co.za ▪ www.lomond.co.za ▪ S 34° 34'12" E 019° 26'24.00" ▪ T +27 (0)21-809-8330 ▪ F +27 (0)21-882-9575

Floral names reflect the commitment to sustainable farming on this large property: over 1,000ha in the Uilenkraal River Valley near fishing hamlet Gansbaai or Walker Bay. A member of the Biodiversity & Wine Initiative and the Walker Bay Fynbos Conservancy, the joint venture (involving Lomond Properties, Stellenbosch drinks giant Distell and a worker's trust) uses the cool coastal climate of the vaunted Cape Agulhas wine district and 120ha of vines (selectively established on previously virgin land marked by an array of soil types) for wines that show impressive, occasionally profound, site and varietal expression.

★★★★ **Syrah** Liquorice-nuanced **09** preview shade off delicately gripping & pure **08** (★★★★★). Complex & rich fruit (plums, cherries, damsons) cosseted by smooth tannins & well-judged oak (only 25% new).

★★★★☆ **Conebush Syrah** Previewed & provisionally rated last time, **09** has settled & meshed, & now reflects the star quality of its single-vineyard birthplace: prosciutto-wrapped dark fruit, lush berry flavours reined in by 50% new oak, giving a satin texture with a pinch of white pepper at the end. Impressive stuff.

★★★★ **Pincushion Sauvignon Blanc** 📖 📏 **11** (★★★★★) has blossomed into something special since previewed last time. Structured & balanced (more so than Sugarbush sibling), with deep, rounded varietal flavours of greenpepper & gooseberry that linger indefinitely. Same elegance as **10** but greater presence.

★★★★☆ **Sugarbush Sauvignon Blanc** 📖 📏 Now bottled, **11** (★★★★) is a delicious, juicy mouthful of greenpepper, asparagus & fig, with pinpoint acidity & excellent length. Finely crafted & elegant but still a half-star off **10** & previous.

★★★★☆ **SSV** NEW 📖 📏 Sauvignon (77%), semillon (18%) & viognier in **12**. Aromatic & generously flavoured with a notably rich, slightly smoky middle & dry apricot-tinged mineral end. Understatement & balance are the keys, viognier an important but subtle presence. Excellent food wine.

Merlot ★★★ Usual meaty whiffs, but riper **09** shows more fruit, substance & sophistication than previous release. **Cat's Tail Syrah** In abeyance. **Sauvignon Blanc** 📖 📏 ★★★☆ Tank sample **12** suggests this back on track after slight dip. Fairly light but flavoursome, balanced, more accessible in youth than the single-vineyard versions. **Snowbush** 📖 📏 ★★★★ Like engaging **10** (★★★★), step-up **11** pairs sauvignon with barrel-fermented semillon, nouvelle, smidgen viognier. Vanilla-tinged fruit cocktail flavours are deep & weighty, the whole more flamboyant than other blends from the area. — WB/GdB

Longbarn Winery

Location/WO: Wellington ▪ Map: Paarl & Wellington ▪ Est/1stB 2006 ▪ Cellar tours by appt ▪ Owner(s) David & Sue Power ▪ Winemaker(s) David Power (Feb 2006) ▪ Viticulturist(s) David Power (Sep 2003) ▪ 69ha/4ha

(pinot, sauv) ▪ 7t/140cs own label 100% white ▪ PO Box 1295 Wellington 7654 ▪ david@longbarn.co.za ▪ www.longbarn.co.za ▪ S 33° 34′ 13.6″ E 019° 3′ 53.6″ ▪ **T +27 (0)21-873-6396** ▪ F +27 (0)86-611-1534

Named for the Georgian barn which has been refurbished by owners David and Sue Power to serve as the cellar, this little vineyard in Wellington's Agtergroenberg has proudly announced its second production of pinot noir, still incubating at press time. Output is decidedly garagiste in scale, with most of the harvest sold off.

Pinot Noir 🍷 Not tasted. **Sauvignon Blanc** 🍷 ★★★☆ **12** preview has commendable body & vibrant fruit, bolstered by bracing acidity, showing this micro-vineyard's potential. — GdB

Long Beach

This attractively packaged brand by Robertson Winery for Vinimark is now for export only and winning fans in Europe, Asia and the rest of Africa.

■ **Longmarket** *see* Woolworths

Long Mountain Wine Company

Location: Stellenbosch ▪ Est/1stB 1994 ▪ Closed to public ▪ Owner(s) Pernod Ricard Sub Sahara (PR SSA) ▪ Cellarmaster(s)/winemaker(s)/viticulturist(s) Emile Gentis (Oct 2006) ▪ 100,000cs own label 50% red 48% white 1% rosé 1% MCC ▪ 2nd Floor, The Square, Cape Quarters, 27 Somerset Road, Cape Town 8005 ▪ emile. gentis@pernod-ricard.com ▪ www.longmountain.co.za ▪ **T +27 (0)21-405-8800** ▪ F +27 (0)86-504-2052

Africa looms large in the sights of global wine and spirits giant Pernod Ricard's newly formed Sub Sahara Wine Development Team. Tasked with building markets on the continent, while still maintaining their international presence, the team will use the two well-established South African wine labels in the P-R portfolio, Long Mountain and Gecko Ridge (both rebranded/redesigned, neither ready for tasting by us), to spearhead the drive. Once markets have been opened, international P-R brands such as Jacob's Creek, Campo Viejo, Brancott and Graffigna will follow. Says cellarmaster Emile Gentis: 'We've given our business a new structure and a fresh look to take to Africa during the year ahead.'

Longridge Wine Estate

Location: Somerset West ▪ Map: Helderberg ▪ WO: Stellenbosch/Western Cape ▪ Est 1841 ▪ 1stB 1992 ▪ Tasting & sales Mon-Sat 10-5 ▪ Closed Easter weekend & Dec 25 ▪ Cellar tours by appt ▪ Longridge Restaurant ▪ Conferences ▪ Owner(s) Aldo van der Laan ▪ Cellarmaster(s) Jasper Raats ▪ Winemaker(s) Jasper Raats, with Hendrien de Munck ▪ Viticulturist(s) Albert le Roux & Jasper Raats (consultant) ▪ 38ha (cab, merlot, pinot, chard, chenin) ▪ 255t/13,600cs 65% red 25% white 10% MCC ▪ PO Box 2023 Dennesig 7601 ▪ info@longridgewines.co.za ▪ www.longridgewines.co.za ▪ S 34° 0′ 55.2″ E 018° 49′ 60.0″ ▪ **T +27 (0)21-855-2005** ▪ F +27 (0)21-855-4083

A new team, headed by cellarmaster Jasper Raats, is being complemented by a focus on more natural farming and winemaking at this Stellenbosch family farm. Biodiversity in the form of Nguni cattle, sheep and ducks, as well as indigenous plants, is being increased. The end goal is biodynamic production. Similarly, the needs of the restaurant are being met by the organic vegetable and herb garden.

★★★★ **Cabernet Sauvignon** 🍷 **08** (★★★★) well-balanced with decent lightish cab fruit & well-judged tannins & oaking. Drink while waiting for elegant, complex **07** (★★★★).

★★★★ **Cabernet Franc** 🍷 Fragrant cranberries, minty nuance on **07**; firm tannins, lovely acidity when tasted a few years back. 1.5L magnum.

★★★★ **Pinotage** 🍷 Returned to form with **08** after less complex **07** (★★★). Individual spicy, fresh mushroom features. Sweet, juicy core to pinotage's often chainmail tannins.

★★★★ **Chardonnay** 🍷 Silky **08** (★★★★★) followed vibrant **07**. Last year, oak added toasty hazelnut, 5% viognier a perfumed nuance.

★★★★ **Chenin Blanc 11** (★★★★) full-bodied, seeming sweetness from oak vanilla, alcohol, but in fact bone-dry. Lacks concentration, potential of **10**.

★★★★ **Sauvignon Blanc** 🍷 Cool, clean lines focus attractive dried fig bouquet on **10**. Fresh acid is assimilated well with the rich flavours; most pleasurable drinking. **09** (★★★★) was less balanced.

★★★★ **Edelgoud** NEW A first in South Africa, Noble Late Harvest from verdelho? **11** a marriage of variety's spiced yellow peach & a deft brush of botrytis. Lightish body, crisply fresh & juicy. WO Stellenbosch, as all above. **Merlot** ⓦ ★★★ Light, simple fruit on **08** with a sweetish finish, for early drinking. **Shiraz** ⓦ ★★★★ Caressing crushed velvet feel highlights concentrated dark spice, salami & red fruits on well-structured, long **08**. Smart oak polish (52% new) rather than dryness of **07** (★★★★). **Rouge** ⓦ ★★★ Was 'HPG Red'. Unoaked merlot-shiraz blend. **10** just-cooked plum jam nose (but not jammy). Full bodied, rich & spicy with decent grip. **Blanc** 🗏 ★★★ Was 'HPG White'. **12** same interesting mix sauvignon, viognier, verdelho, chardonnay, chenin as last-made **10**, now with pinot blanc too. Harmonious & flavoursome but misses edge of previous. **Brut** ★★★★ Méthode cap classique sparkling. New disgorgement of **08**, year longer on lees. Touch more creamy & developed chardonnay toasty notes. Smoothly dry. Discontinued: **HPG Rosé**. — AL

■ **Lookout** *see* Leopard's Leap Wines
■ **Lord Somerset** *see* Somerset Wines

Lord's Wines

Location: McGregor ▪ Map: Robertson ▪ WO: McGregor/Robertson ▪ Est 2005 ▪ 1stB 2006 ▪ Cellar: Tasting, sales & cellar tours Mon-Fri 9-5 Sat/Sun by appt ▪ Lord's Wine Shop, Robertson: tasting & sales Mon-Fri 9-5 Sat/Sun 10-4, toffee & wine pairing R20, barrel tasting ▪ Closed Good Fri, Dec 25 & Jan 1 ▪ Tour groups by appt ▪ Farm produce ▪ Owner(s) 12 shareholders ▪ Cellarmaster(s)/winemaker(s) Ilse van Dijk (Nov 2010) ▪ Viticulturist(s) Jacie Oosthuizen (Jan 2003) ▪ 33ha/13ha (pinot, shiraz, chard, chenin, sauv) ▪ 90t/6,600cs own label 50% red 45% white 5% rosé ▪ PO Box 165 McGregor 6708 ▪ ilse@lordswinery.com, sales@lordswinery.com ▪ www. lordswinery.com ▪ S 33° 59' 20.98" E 019° 44' 28.39" ▪ **T +27 (0)23-625-1265 (Cellar)/+27 (0)23-626-3202 (Wine Shop)** ▪ F +27 (0)86-514-2512

Traffic on the Robertson Wine Route is increasing, says winemaker Ilse van Dijk, and now would-be buyers have something novel to experience at the Lord's Wines outpost in Robertson: tastings from barrel. Something new in the range too, when a MCC sparkling (which missed our deadline) is uncorked early this year.

Pinot Noir ★★★★ Elegant **10** similar earthy sour cherry & savoury notes to **09** (★★★) but oak laudably restrained. Serious attempt, hinting at these mountain vineyards' potential. **Shiraz** ✓ ★★★★ Smoky toast on **10** very appealing, soft & accessible with potential for few years keeping. Follows focused **09** (★★★★) from 50% Paarl grapes. **The Wicked Maiden Pinot Noir Rosé** 🗏 ★★★ Now identifies variety on label. **12** frisky, juicy & dry for summer party fun. WO Robertson, as for All Rounder, First Innings & Sauvignon. **Chardonnay Barrel Fermented** ★★★★ 100% new oak for **11**, giving bold vanilla/butter overlay to lime fruit, slight sweetness. Pulled back from the brink by freshening acidity. **All Rounder Chardonnay** 🗏 ★★★ Switches from 'Chardonnay Unwooded' to lightly oaked in **11**, shortbread & peaches, wood still slightly apart. **First Innings Chenin Blanc** NEW 🗏 ★★ 11's ripe herby fruit somewhat intimidated by aggressive bowling from the oak chip end. **Sauvignon Blanc** 🗏 ★★ Wild herb pungency padded with ripe melon; well chilled, **11** perfect for blue skies & picnics. **Nectar Natural Sweet** ⓦ ★★★ 11 sweetie from nouvelle deliveries whack of peachy flavour, crackling acidity. — DB/JP

■ **L'Ormarins** *see* Anthonij Rupert Wines
■ **Lorna Hughes** *see* Stonehill

Lorraine Private Cellar

Location: Rawsonville ▪ Map: Breedekloof ▪ WO: Goudini ▪ Est 1996 ▪ 1stB 2002 ▪ Tasting, sales & cellar tours Mon-Fri 8-1 ▪ Closed all pub hols ▪ Outdoor wine tasting & picnic by appt R200pp; or BYO picnic ▪ Tour groups ▪ Walks/hikes ▪ Conservation area ▪ Owner(s) Lorraine Trust (Johan & Lori Ann de Wet) ▪ Cellarmaster(s)/winemaker(s) Johan de Wet (Jan 2002) ▪ Viticulturist(s) Leon Dippenaar (2003, consultant) ▪ ±417ha/155ha (cab f, merlot, p verdot, ptage, ruby cab, shiraz, chard, chenin, nouvelle, sauv, viog) ▪ 2,000t total 50t/±4,200cs own label 45% red 50% white 5% rosé ▪ Fairtrade ▪ PO Box 2 Rawsonville 6845 ▪ info@lorraine.co.za ▪ www.lorraine.co.za ▪ S 33° 42' 43.14" E 019° 15' 40.83" ▪ **T +27 (0)23-349-1224** ▪ F +27 (0)86-664-2279

Cellarmaster Johan de Wet is deeply attached to this land, where his family has been making wine for five generations. Small wonder — the farm is situated in a fertile valley with crystal-clear rivers, diverse soils, late sunrises and long afternoon shadows cast by the Du Toitskloof Mountains towering overhead, creating perfect conditions for winegrowing.

★★★★ **Chardonnay** ⓣ 09 (★★★☆) in New World style, with lime, spicy vanilla oak & honeysuckle amongst its charms. Creamy mouthfeel, but perhaps not as much freshness as last-tasted 07.

★★★★ **Viognier** ⓣ Intensely scented 10 (★★★★) less Old Worldish than last-tried 08. Typical varietal character of apricot & orange blossom. Long-lingering flavours marked by high alcohol & ultra-ripeness.

> **Sauvignon Blanc** ☺ ★★★ Now bottled, 11 bright & tangy, gooseberry twist to gentle tropical flavours. Crisp & summery, solo or with a light meal.

Shiraz ⓣ ★★★★ When last tasted 04 was opulent, velvety & seductive. **Cape Harmony** ⓣ ★★★ 07 smooth & juicy blend pinotage, merlot & cab still selling. WO W Cape. **Love Of My Life Pinotage Rosé** ⓣ 🍶 ★★★ Fresh, off-dry & nicely balanced 10, on review offered easy summer fun. — MW

■ **Lorry** see Corder Family Wines
■ **Lo Splendore del Sole** see African Terroir

Lothian Vineyards

Location: Elgin ▪ Map: Elgin, Walker Bay & Bot River ▪ Est 2004 ▪ 1stB 2010 ▪ Tasting by appt only ▪ Honey ▪ Conferences/functions ▪ Conservation area ▪ Luxury guesthouse (7 double en-suite bedrooms) ▪ Owner(s) Wilson family ▪ Winemaker(s) Stefan Gerber, with Marco Benjamin (both 2010) ▪ Viticulturist(s) Kevin Watt (Mar 2009) ▪ 46ha/13ha (pinot, chard, riesling, sauv, viog) ▪ 60t 25% red 75% white ▪ IPW ▪ 68 Reservoir Rd Somerset West 7130 ▪ info@lothianvineyards.com ▪ www.lothianvineyards.com ▪ S 34° 11′31.49″ E 018° 58′ 57.78″ ▪ **T** +27 (0)21-859-9901 ▪ F +27 (0)86-718-1672

Lothian Vineyards is new to the guide, but its Wilson family owners are third-generation Cape winegrowers. Lothian takes its name from the Scottish-style stone walls on the Elgin estate, and its cool climate ideally suits the pinot noir and chardonnay grapes for the Burgundy-style wines Lothian aims to be known for. Certain parts of the property also suit the production of (dry) riesling, while a vine-dried viognier dessert wine rounds out the range.

Louiesenhof Wines

Location/map/WO: Stellenbosch ▪ Est/1stB 1992 ▪ Tasting & sales daily 9–5 (summer) Mon-Sat 10–3 (winter) ▪ Fee R10 ▪ Closed Christian holidays ▪ Louiesenhof B&B ▪ Light meals in summer ▪ Play area for children ▪ Function facilities ▪ Farm produce ▪ Owner(s) WS Smit Watergang Trust ▪ Cellarmaster(s) WS Smit ▪ Winemaker(s) Jos le Roux ▪ Viticulturist(s) Gawie Kriel (2000, consultant) ▪ 130ha (cab, merlot, ptage, shiraz, chard, chenin, pinot gris, sauv) ▪ 1,000t/2,000cs own label 70% red 28% white 2% rosé ▪ BWI ▪ PO Box 2013 Stellenbosch 7601 ▪ info@louiesenhof.co.za ▪ www.louiesenhof.co.za ▪ S 33° 53′34.7″ E 018° 49′35.3″ ▪ **T** +27 (0)21-865-2632/+27 (0)21-889-5550 **(JIR)** ▪ F +27 (0)21-865-2613

Stephan Smit, the prime mover here, learnt eco-values in his early studies in Germany, inspiring a 'bio-organic wine' way back in 1991. Respect for the environment persists, as evidenced by the fact that Louiesenhof supports the Bottelary Hills Conservancy and strives to make wines 'in harmony with nature'.

Premier Collection

Shiraz NEW 🍶 ★★★ Big tannins still evident on previewed 11. Riper in style, with baked pudding notes & bold palate (15% alcohol). **Cabernet Sauvignon-Cabernet Franc** 🍶 ★★★ Baked prune & Xmas cake pour from 11 barrel sample, fruity appeal continues to dry end. **Bordeaux Blend** Not tasted. Like some others, moves to this new range.

Louiesenhof Wines range

Pinotage 🍶 🍶 ★★★ Attractive smoke & flint harmonises with clean berry aromas & firm tannins on 10, good match for spicy food. **Cape Blend** 🍶 🍶 ★★★ Cab franc & pinotage combo on ultra-ripe, awkwardly balanced 10. **Perroquet Merlot Pétillant Rosé** ⓣ 🍶 ★★ 08 off-dry quaffer. **Chardonnay Sur-Lie** 🍶 ★★★ Charry wood cloaks peachy nose on 11 & really defines the wine with oaky sweetness (though dry). **Sauvignon Blanc** ⓣ 🍶 ★★★ 11 with unlingering tropical flavours. **Sweet Red** ⓣ ★★ Individual NV fortified dessert. **Perroquet Cape Tawny** ⓣ ★★★★ NV rustic glow-inducer from tinta, with savoury touches. **Roobernet Cape Ruby** ⓣ ★★★ Youthful 10 fortified has spicy, medicinal notes. Pleasantly dry, dusty, with typical sweetness. — JP

Louis

Location: Stellenbosch ▪ WO: Stellenbosch/Darling ▪ Est/1stB 2007 ▪ Closed to public ▪ Owner(s) Louis Nel ▪ Cellarmaster(s)/winemaker(s) Louis Nel (Jan 2007) ▪ 15t/1,500cs own label 50% red 50% white + 600cs for clients ▪ Brands for clients: Collaboration (Overture restaurant) ▪ 3 Chestnut Lane Stellenbosch 7600 ▪ louis@louiswines.com ▪ www.louiswines.com ▪ **T +27 (0)21-889-5555**

Louis Nel is a quietly spoken but talented negociant-style winemaker whose introduction to the vine was the red-wine icing on his first birthday cake. Colour and creativity have been a feature of his career ever since. Black Forest, with a chocolate nuance, serves the well-priced quality segment, while fun label Buckleberry alludes to Kate Middleton's home town, with eye-catching yellow packaging.

Louis range

★★★★ Cabernet Sauvignon ⊕ 08 (★★★★★) raises the bar on 07. Sweet reward from reprieved vineyard, the silky texture tempts earlier enjoyment but complexity & fruit depth deserve good few years cellaring.

★★★★ Sauvignon Blanc ✓ Flinty overlay to pungent tropical mix highlights Darling provenance in 12. Good fruit intensity, grip & length. Fine seafood partner. Debut 10 & 11 both missed deadline.

Cabernet Sauvignon-Merlot ⊕ **★★★★** Ripe & succulent 08 a step up on 07 (★★★). Well groomed & streamlined. Bottled yumminess that will grace both table & cellar.

Black Forest range NEW

Black Forest ✓ ★★★☆ 11 aptly named shiraz (85%) merlot blend. Ripe & juicy, with creamy textured savouriness that melts into subtle mocha flavours.

Buckleberry range NEW

Buckleberry ☺ 🍴 **★★★** Quintessential sauvignon, vivacious, tangy & fresh 12 has a melange of crisp tropical flavours. Balanced & friendly, ready to entertain. — MW

■ **Louis Fourie** *see* Linton Park Wines

Louisvale Wines

Location/map: Stellenbosch ▪ WO: Stellenbosch/Coastal ▪ Est/1stB 1989 ▪ Tasting, sales & cellar tours Mon-Fri 10-5 ▪ Fee R20 ▪ Closed all pub hols ▪ BYO picnic ▪ Owner(s) Louisvale Wines (Pty) Ltd ▪ Directors Altmann Allers, Hendrik Kluever, Johann Kirsten & Zane Meyer ▪ Winemaker(s)/viticulturist(s) Simon Smith (Jul 1997) ▪ 34ha/23ha (cab, merlot, chard) ▪ 220t/16,000cs (6btl) own label 50% red 50% white ▪ PO Box 542 Stellenbosch 7599 ▪ winery@louisvale.com ▪ www.louisvale.com ▪ S 33° 54′ 32.3″ E 018° 48′ 24.3″ ▪ **T +27 (0)21-865-2422** ▪ F +27 (0)21-865-2633

You realise this has been a long-time chardonnay specialist when told that those Devon Valley chardonnay vineyards are now considered too old (they date from the mid 1980s). Under the new owners ('four business friends' bought Louisvale in 2010) they are being replaced, a few hectares each year.

Stone Road Cabernet Sauvignon ★★★ Easy-drinking 11 is complicated by splash of cab franc; nicely firm. **Stone Road Merlot ★★★** Plush, dry-finishing 11 displays coffee & plums on its gentle, soft-tannined palate. **Dominique ★★★★** Cab-based 11 with merlot & cab franc in place of last 09's shiraz. Aromas of toasty oak with typical cassis, then a powerful palate needing time to integrate the oak. **Chardonnay** ⊕ **★★★★** 10 was the richest of the 3 chardonnays for last guide; 6 months half-new oak well integrated adding nutty complexity. **Chavant** ⊕ **★★★★** Crowd-pleasing 11 from chardonnay, lightly oaked & light-bodied; lemon, apricot & floral notes, elegant soft finish. **Chardonnay Unwooded ✓ ★★★★** Now bottled, 11 improved since previewed last year. Slightly more complex & precise; stonefruit & apple notes, lemon twist on finish. Wellington grapes. **Stone Road Sauvignon Blanc** 🍴 **★★★** Pleasant, fresh but unexciting 12 with delicate tropical notes. — JPf

Lourensford Wine Estate

Location: Somerset West ▪ Map: Helderberg ▪ WO: Stellenbosch/Western Cape ▪ Est 1999 ▪ 1stB 2003 ▪ Tasting, sales & cellar tours daily 9-5 ▪ Fee R30 ▪ Closed Good Fri & Dec 25 ▪ Millhouse Kitchen ▪ Tour groups ▪ Art exhibition ▪ Coffee roastery ▪ Cheesery ▪ Conferences ▪ Conservation area ▪ Owner(s) Christo Wiese ▪ Cellarmaster(s) Chris Joubert (Oct 2007) ▪ Winemaker(s) Hannes Nel (Nov 2002), with Timothy Witbooi (May 2005) ▪ Viticulturist(s) Francois Viljoen ▪ 4,000ha/217ha (cab, merlot, shiraz, chard, sauv, viog) ▪ 1,600t/120,000cs own label 40% red

58% white 2% rosé ▪ Brands for clients: Eden Crest (Checkers), Matumi (UK), Pracht Gaarden (Belgium), River Crossing (UK & Ireland) ▪ BRC, BWI champion, HACCP ▪ PO Box 16 Somerset West 7129 ▪ info@lourensford.co.za ▪ www.lourensford.com ▪ S 34° 4' 3.7" E 018° 53' 44.2" ▪ **T +27 (0)21-847-2300** ▪ F +27 (0)21-847-0910

It's enough to break a winelover's heart, but it had to be done. 'We took a brutal look at the economic sustainability of our vineyards,' says Koos Jordaan, general manager at leading businessman Christo Wiese's vast and scenic property on the Helderberg, 'and decided to uproot marginal blocks which did not deliver the volume or quality. A total of 118ha was uprooted. This "stop farming" practice has an enormous positive impact on our total cost structure.' Development of the diverse visitor facilities on the farm (art exhibit, coffee roastery, cheesery) continues with the complete revamp and enlargement of the restaurant. Looking ahead, Koos says Lourensford will continue to aim for 'cool-climate elegance'. The business will be leaner, focused on fewer markets, and have a 'very big presence in China'.

Winemaker's Selection range

★★★★ **Syrah** ⏺ Fruit-packed preview **09** (★★★★☆) followed oaky **07**. Mulberry & brambleberry with savoury/earthy nuances & dry tannic grip. Soupçons merlot, cab, viognier for complexity & panache.

★★★★☆ **Reserve Red Blend** NEW Excellent debut **09** shows plush berry fruit, wood spice & floral aromas from cab (64%), shiraz & smidgen viognier. Elegant, with a firm structure, beautiful balance & length. Decant to reveal all its charms or, better, wait a few years — built for the long haul.

★★★★ **Chardonnay** ▨ Captivating apple & floral nose on **11** (★★★★) a rich & textured expression of the variety. Creamy, rounded & seamless without being heavy. Lacks complexity of **09**. No **10**.

★★★★ **Sauvignon Blanc** ⏺ ▨ **11**'s cool, fragrant white peach, gooseberry, lime fruit provides good structure for elegant offering. Dry, full & complex. Deserves time to reach potential.

★★★★ **Viognier** ✓ Fine varietal character on dependable single-vineyard version. **11** no exception: spicy peach flavours enriched by creamy subtle vanilla oak. Vivacious, curvy & exotic.

★★★★☆ **Reserve White Blend** ▨ Was 'Lourensford 1700 White Blend'. **11** is back to form after lesser **10** (★★★★). A blend of best barrel-fermented (older wood) sauvignon, chardonnay & viognier. Rounded, with superb balance & poise, supported by subtle vanilla oak. Cellar or decant to reveal full potential.

★★★★☆ **Semillon Noble Late Harvest** ⏺ Unctuous botrytis dessert, **09** previously delighted with typical dried peach aroma, long juicy orange marmalade finish well balanced by fine acidity.

Lourensford range

★★★★ **Cabernet Sauvignon** ✓ ▨ **10** (★★★☆) blackcurrant & floral note, juicy, with soft oak influence, peppery aftertaste, lacks class of **09**.

★★★★ **Merlot** ⏺ ▤ ▨ Deep ruby **10** (★★★☆), trumped by **09**, offers plum pudding, pepper & smoke. Grainy finish needs food or time.

★★★★☆ **Shiraz** ✓ ▤ ▨ Medium-bodied **10** (★★★★) a shade off super **08**. Offers fragrant fruit, smoky & herbal notes, but lacks body. Needs time & food. **09** sold out untasted.

★★★★ **Shiraz-Mourvèdre-Viognier** ✓ ▨ **10** (★★★★) not same complexity as **09** or maiden **08** (★★★★★). Smoky, spicy notes & wild berry fruit, firm structure & earthy finish. Needs year/2. WO W Cape.

★★★★ **Chardonnay** ✓ ▤ ▨ **11** (★★★★) combines bright Granny Smith apple & lime fruit. Fresh, smooth & juicy, but misses body & complexity of **10** & **09** (★★★★☆).

★★★★ **Sauvignon Blanc** ⏺ ▤ ▨ **11** crammed with exuberant fruit: lime, gooseberry & nettle. Dry, with balance & depth — excellent food match. 10% semillon.

★★★★ **Méthode Cap Classique** Classy **08** (★★★★★) bottle-fermented sparkling from chardonnay a step up from **07**. Fine, lazy mousse blossoms in the mouth with crisp appley brioche flavour from 48 months lees-ageing. Fresh & smooth, with depth & texture.

River Garden range

★★★★ **Cabernet Sauvignon-Merlot** ⏺ ▤ Unexpectedly UN-tutti-frutti, **10** actually a fine glass of red with serious fruit concentration & a leafy pepper note previous editions.

Rosé ☺ ▤ ▨ ★★★ Off-dry **12** from shiraz, mourvèdre & merlot offers sweet strawberries & spice. Lively, light & friendly anytime rosé. **Chardonnay** ☺ ▤ ▨ ★★★ Slightly oaked **12** lifts the bar with lovely candied pineapple flavours, rounded & smooth. **Sauvignon Blanc** ☺ ▤ ▨ ★★★ **12** is toned with fresh greenpepper & greengage flavours. Dry & zingy for summer.

Shiraz-Cabernet Sauvignon ⊕ 🍴 📖 ★★★★ Last tasted **10** a Cinderella transformation after vin ordinaire **08** (★★★). Fragrant ripe plums, juicy berries heralding bold extrovert personality. **09** untasted. WO W Cape, as for Cab-Merlot. — WB

Lovane Boutique Wine Estate

Location/map/WO: Stellenbosch ▪ Est 2003 ▪ 1stB 2006 ▪ Tasting, sales & cellar tours Mon-Sun 10-5 ▪ Tasting fee R20, waived on purchase ▪ Closed all pub hols ▪ Conferences ▪ Guesthouse & cottage ▪ Owner(s)/viticulturist(s) Philip & Gail Gous ▪ Winemaker(s) Philip Gous (2006), with Gail Gous (2006) ▪ 3.6ha/2.5ha (cabs s/f, p verdot) ▪ 20t/1,400cs own label 90% red 5% white 5% rosé ▪ PO Box 91 Vlottenburg 7604 ▪ info@lovane.co.za ▪ www.lovane.co.za ▪ S 33° 57' 09.74" E 018° 48' 02.38" ▪ **T** +27 (0)21-881-3827 ▪ F +27 (0)21-881-3546

The Gous family planted this 2.5ha of then virgin earth between established Stellenbosch heavyweights Overgaauw and Neethlingshof ten years ago. Cabernet-led winemaking followed in 2006, along with a 4-star guest house and chic conference amenities. The rhythm is now set: from the 2007 vintage all reds are matured three years in oak, and from 2012 they're all bunch-pressed.

★★★★ **Cabernet Sauvignon Umbhidi Wholeberry** ⊕ Fine **07**, smoky oak depth to its juicy dark berries, buzz of supportive tannin when reviewed previously.

★★★★☆ **Isikhati** ⊕ Cab-led **07**, with tiny but telling input from petit verdot & cab franc, youthfully tight with a wealth of rich fruit promise when last tasted.

★★★★ **Sweet 77** NEW Voluptuous port-style dessert wine honours septuagenarian friend of the family; **11** drier than most (78g/l sugar), 18% alcohol. Super with cheese.

Cabernet Sauvignon Isivuno ⊕ ★★★★ Last tasted was mineral **06**. **Cabernet Sauvignon Iziko** NEW ★★ 'Fireplace' moniker suggests a warm hearth beside which to drink chunky **08**. **Cabernet Sauvignon Umgidi** NEW ★★★ Dense tannic structure of **07** calls for food accompaniment, as its name 'Feast' proposes. **Cabernet Sauvignon Tamkulu** NEW ★★★☆ 'Grandfather' dedicated to owner Gail Gous' parent. **08** filled with cassis character, but nicely within itself. **Cabernet Franc Iliwa** ★★★★ Meaning 'rock' or 'cliff', just 344 bottles from 500 vines. **08** packed with sappy fruit flavour — & 15% alc. Gear up on **06** (★★★★), no **07**. **Petit Verdot Umama** ★★★★ **08**'s pleasantly taut & lean profile will be appreciated New-World-weary palates. **Shiraz Lovane** New bottling not ready. **Cabernet Sauvignon-Petit Verdot Berries Only** NEW ★★★☆ **08** perfumed & more lissom than cellarmates, light feel belies 33 months in older oak & 14.8% alcohol. **Summer Mist** Next awaited. **Unfiltered Blanc de Noir** ★★★ **12** clean cherry fruit & fresh fillip in dry tail. **Méthode Cap Classique** ⊕ ★★★★ Dry **NV** (**09**) sparkler in pink form (from cab). Latest bone-dry & refreshing, albeit loose grained. — DS

▪ **Loyal Brothers** see Govert Wines
▪ **Luca & Ingrid Bein** see Bein Wine Cellar

Luddite Wines

Location: Bot River ▪ Map: Elgin, Walker Bay & Bot River ▪ WO: Western Cape/Cape South Coast ▪ Est/1stB 2000 ▪ Tasting & sales Mon-Fri 9-4 Sat/Sun by appt ▪ Closed Dec 25 & Jan 1 ▪ Cellar tours by appt ▪ Farm produce ▪ Walks/hikes ▪ Conservation area ▪ Owner(s) Niels Verburg & Hillie Meyer ▪ Cellarmaster(s)/winemaker(s) Niels Verburg (2000) ▪ Viticulturist(s) Penny Verburg (2000) ▪ 17ha/5.8ha (cab, mourv, shiraz, chenin) ▪ 30t/1,750cs own label 100% red + 2,000cs for clients ▪ Brands for clients: Elgin Vintners, Ridgelands ▪ PO Box 656 Bot River 7185 ▪ luddite@telkomsa.net ▪ www.luddite.co.za ▪ S 34° 12' 50.5" E 019° 12' 24.1" ▪ **T** +27 (0)28-284-9308/+27 (0)83-444-3537 ▪ F +27 (0)28-284-9045

Bot River (or Bot Riviera to those with tongue firmly in cheek) Spring Festival saw Luddite cellarmaster Niels Verburg flying solo at the artisanal winery, making bacon sandwiches from farm-reared pigs while viticulturist wife Penny was on rugby tour with son Kim. It was this budding Springbok who gave Niels' latest Cape Winemakers Guild offering its name. 'He plays rugby like a footballer and deserves an Oscar for his injury performances,' Verburg drolly observed.

★★★★☆ **Shiraz** Continuing track record of **07**, powerful yet elegant **08** packed with black & blue berries, seasoned with twist of pepper. Harmonious, sleek & sexy with nothing dominating. Serious & refined with long, gentle finish. Bot River & Stellenbosch grapes.

★★★★☆ **CWG Auction Reserve Oscar** NEW 09 adds dash (9%) of mourvèdre – & spicy clove lift – to shiraz. Cherry, plum & pecan interest on smoothly dense palate. Complex, layered, refined, elegant & with power lightly leashed. 15% alcohol blends in seamlessly. Cape South Coast WO. — FM

LuKa Wine Estate

ocation/WO: Plettenberg Bay ▪ Map: Klein Karoo & Garden Route ▪ Est 2008 ▪ 1stB 2011 ▪ Tasting in Dec, Mar/ pr or by appt ▪ Owner(s) Hennie & Anita Kritzinger ▪ Cellarmaster(s)/winemaker(s) Anton Smal (Bramon Vines) ▪ Viticulturist(s) Hennie Kritzinger ▪ ±7ha/1.5ha (sauv) ▪ ±3t/211cs own label 100% white ▪ PO Box 519 Plettenberg Bay 6600 ▪ henita@telkomsa.net ▪ www.lukawines.co.za ▪ S 34° 2' 28.14" E 023° 15' 57.56" **T** +27 (0)82-457-8110/+27 (0)82-332-3299 ▪ F +27 (0)44-533-6782

ittle wineries are popping up all over the Plettenberg Bay area, as pioneers ediscover the eastern frontier of the Cape. The Kritzingers, Hennie and Anita, lanted their tiny vineyard as a retirement venture, and they've just gone public vith an own on-site tasting venue.

auvignon Blanc ▦ ★★★ Vibrant, youthful **12** has delicately fragrant fruit flavour. Firm acidity undercores structure & finish. — GdB

Lula Wines

he Xhosa name of this Rudera export brand (previously reviewed with sibling lalala Afrika) means 'easy', and the wines are suitably effortless. The shiraz noved one UK fan to verse: 'A ripe and fruity body for when I unwind/ That's my ula, she's really such a find.'

hiraz ▦ ★★★ Plum, spice & hint of citrus on ripe, full-bodied **10** fireside sipper. **Chenin Blanc** ▦ ★★★ Flaoursome & mouthfilling **12** given weight & floral appeal by dollop viognier. Chill well for solo sipping. — CvZ

Lusan Premium Wines

losed to public ▪ clkirsten@distell.co.za ▪ **T** +27 (0)21-883-8988 ▪ F +27 (0)21-883-8941

Jmbrella organisation for Alto, Le Bonheur, Neethlingshof, Stellenzicht (and its value brand Hill & Dale) and Uitkyk (including Flat Roof Manor). See entries.

■ **Luscious Hippos** *see* United Nations of Wine

Lutzville Cape Diamond Vineyards

ocation/WO: Lutzville ▪ Map: Olifants River ▪ Est 1961 ▪ 1stB 1980 ▪ Tasting, sales & cellar tours Mon-Fri 9-5 Sat 0-2 ▪ Closed Sun, Easter Sat, Dec 25 & Jan 1 ▪ Coffee shop Mon-Fri 9-4 Sat 10-1 ▪ Function/conference venue ▪ Dwner(s) Lutzville Wingerde Beperk ▪ Cellarmaster(s) Gideon Theron (Nov 2005) ▪ Winemaker(s) Jaco van Niekerk (Sep 2009) & Brenda Thiart (Nov 2011) ▪ Viticulturist(s) Gideon Engelbrecht (Sep 2009) ▪ 2,100ha (cab, nerlot, ptage, pinot, ruby cab, shiraz, chard, chenin, cbard, nouvelle, sauv, sem, viog) ▪ ±42,000t/112,000cs own abel 11% red 89% white ▪ BRC ▪ PO Box 50 Lutzville 8165 ▪ info@lutzvillevineyards.com ▪ www. utzvillevineyards.com ▪ S 31° 33' 35.9" E 018° 21' 0.2" ▪ **T** +27 (0)27-217-1516 ▪ F +27 (0)27-217-1435

Vith a shift towards bulk sales and bottling in export markets, the quality and value-for-money of this very large (2,000+ hectares) Olifants River winery's bulk vines are among cellarmaster Gideon Theron's chief concerns. Vineyard block election and close attention to optimum ripeness feature, as expected, and ipgraded winery equipment carry the process through. The overseas focus has-'t eclipsed Lutzville's local roots though: a co-development has effectively urned the winery's tasting facilities into a new '19th hole' for the lucky (and hirsty) patrons of the Lutzville Golf Club.

he Diamond Collection

★★★★ **Chenin Blanc** NEW ✓ ▦ 🖾 Barrel-aged **11**, nut & cream appeal, rounded mouthfeel from unobtrusive grain sugar, endless softly dry finish. Clever! Drinks well, but will improve few years.

Cabernet Sauvignon ✓ ▦ ★★★★ **10** displays fine balance of oak & fruit, healthy tannins allow few years eeping. Fruit selection & barrel maturation (as opposed to oak staves) for reds & chardonnay distinguish this ange from Cape Diamond. **Shiraz** ✓ 🖾 ★★★★ Peppery notes to **10**'s cured meat & chocolate-mocha, commendably taut & savoury, structure to improve with 3+ years cellaring. **Ebenaezer** ✓ 🎍 ★★★★ Previewer 11 4-way blend, equal parts merlot, ruby cab, cab, 10% shiraz, plush fruit cosseted by 100% new oak. Unevolver mid-2012, deserves more time to unfold & fully express itself. **Chardonnay** 🏠 🎍 ★★★ 11 drops 'Wooder from name despite being barrel aged. Well made, oak/fruit are integrated, could do with tad more freshness. **Sau**vignon Blanc ✓ 🏠 🎍 ★★★★ Pungent tinned pea, grass & nettle, preview 12 flavourful & quite complex – a only 11% alcohol. Acidity a little assertive, needs a butter-grilled crayfish. **Semillon** ⓘ 🏠 ★★★★ Restraine 10 preview enticing honey, nougat, nectarine aromas. Early harvested & well crafted.

Cape Diamond range

> **Ruby Cabernet** ☺ 🏠 🎍 ★★★ Rejoins the range with 12, preview shows typical thatch & mulberry attractions. **Shiraz** ☺ 🏠 🎍 ★★★ Vanilla notes permeate nose & palate of juicy, unchallenging 11. **Chardonnay** ☺ 🎍 ★★★ Ex-tank 12, candied almond bouquet, citrus zing, savoury persistence. **Sauvignon Blanc** ☺ 🏠 🎍 ★★★ 12 preview food-friendly 'oystershell' minerality, balanced & easy.

Cabernet Sauvignon 🏠 🎍 ★★★ Smoke & spice to 11's dark sweet berries, smoother than stablemates All in this range fruity & early drinking, reds lightly oaked. **Merlot** 🏠 🎍 ★★ Chocolate-infused 11 ha some prune & sour cherry flavours. **Pinotage** 🏠 🎍 ★★★ Cranberry & mint appeal on 11 BBQ companion **Shiraz Rosé** ⓘ 🏠 🎍 ★★★ 11 lightish red berry sipper with candyfloss & cinnamon dusting. **Chenin Blanc** 🏠 🎍 ★★ Provisionally rated 12 preview, shows satisfying vinosity. **Muscadel** ⓘ ★★★★ Last edition 10 had benefited from extra time in bottle: rich & full but light-footed. Uncloying, delightful step up or last-tasted 07 (★★★).

Cape Elephant Natural Sweet range

Red 🏠 Not tasted. **Rosé** ⓘ 🏠 ★★ Dash muscat d'Alexandrie in low-alcohol (8%), unashamedly swee 11 preview. **White** ⓘ 🏠 ★★★ Tasted ex-tank last time, 11 tropical fruit melange from colombard & mus cat d'Alexandrie. — DB/CvZ

Lyngrove

Location: Somerset West ▪ Map: Helderberg ▪ WO: Stellenbosch ▪ Est/1stB 2000 ▪ Tasting & sales Mon-Fri by appr Sat-Sun 9-3 breakfast & wine tasting ▪ Guesthouse (see Accommodation section) ▪ Conferences (12 pax) ▪ Walk-ing/hiking trail (5km) ▪ Owner(s) Baarsma's Holdings B.V. ▪ Winemaker(s) Hannes Louw & Danielle le Roux (Ju 2006) ▪ Viticulturist(s) John Fullard ▪ 76ha (cab, merlot, p verdot, ptage, shiraz, chard, chenin, sauv) ▪ 50,000c own label 70% red 20% white 10% rosé ▪ WIETA ▪ PO Box 7275 Stellenbosch 7599 ▪ wine@lyngrove.co.za www.lyngrove.co.za ▪ S 34° 1'8.7" E 018° 48'10.2" ▪ **T +27 (0)21-880-1221** ▪ F +27 (0)21-880-0851

Early-bird weekenders can now enjoy breakfast with their tasting at the Lyngrove Country House, part of the Baarsma stable. Consumers should be encouraged to want wines made and bottled in South Africa, rather than bulk exports, believe the team, who focus on capturing 'character and soul' for the Lyngrove label.

Platinum range

★★★★ **Latitude** 🎍 Changing blend: equal parts cab & pinotage with dollop shiraz in shapely 1' (★★★★). Juicy fruitcake notes with light squeeze of tannin. Last 08 was mainly cab with merlot.

Pinotage ★★★★ 10 step up on 09 (★★★★). Smoky blueberry & spice appeal. Gentle, silky mouthfeel Depth & breadth without being brooding or charry. Lithe oak frame supports ripe fruit. **Shiraz** ★★★★ Plum concentration on 10, lightish yet integrated & harmonious. Nicely layered, oak supporting the fruit.

Reserve range

Shiraz-Pinotage ★★★★ Shiraz leads in 09, showing forward red fruit freshness & bold but toned oak. Suc culent & layered. Needs time to settle. **Chardonnay** ★★★★ 11 ticks the boxes of ripe peaches & cream wit rich oak backing. Integrated & approachable style.

Lyngrove Collection

Cabernet Sauvignon 🏠 🎍 ★★★★ Blackberry & cigarbox appeal on rung-up 11. Smooth & ripe ye structured, with light chalky grip. **Merlot** 🏠 🎍 ★★★ Gentle, appealing everything to plummy 11: length fruit, ripeness & structure. **Pinotage** ⓘ 🏠 🎍 ★★★ Dark, juicy, mocha-laced 10's ripeness pleasingly bal anced by savoury freshness. **Shiraz** 🏠 🎍 ★★★ 10 ratchets up a notch with textured mouthful of ripe blac cherry & spice. Balanced, with light intensity. **Chenin Blanc** 🏠 🎍 ★★★ Melon & stonefruit on fresh & lively 12. Tropical mouthful delights with rich lengthy aftertaste. **Sauvignon Blanc** 🏠 🎍 ★★★ Crisp tangy lime zest on vibrant 12. Pleasant mouthfeel & body, acidity kept in check allowing fruit to speak. — FM

Lynx Wines

Location/map/WO: Franschhoek • Est/1stB 2002 • Tasting, sales & cellar tours Mon-Fri 10–5 Sat/Sun & pub hols by appt • Fee R30 (tasting & tour) • BYO picnic • Owner(s) Vista Hermosa (Pty) Ltd • Cellarmaster(s) Dieter Sellmeyer (Jan 2002) • Winemaker(s) Dieter Sellmeyer (Jan 2002), with Helgard van Schalkwyk (Nov 2010) • Viticulturist(s) Theunis Brandt (Apr 2000) • 26ha/11ha (cabs s/f, grenache, merlot, shiraz, viog) • 90t/4,500cs own label 60% red 10% white 30% rosé • IPW • PO Box 566 Franschhoek 7690 • winemaker@lynxwines.co.za • www.lynxwines.co.za • S 33°51'46.1" E 019°2'14.6" • **T +27 (0)21-867-0406** • F +27 (0)21-867-0397

Former engineer Dieter Sellmeyer first made wine in 2002 with no greater ambition than having some for home consumption. 'We ended up with a wine but no name for it. We finally called it Xanache — after our three beautiful daughters Xan (Alexandra), Charlie and Anna who helped us make it.' Sellmeyer was hooked and soon started to take winemaking more seriously. Precisely ten years after that first effort the 'Xan' in 'Xanache' was married in front of their beautifully situated Franschhoek cellar.

Premium range

★★★★ **Cabernet Sauvignon** 🖺 **11** (★★★★) in a plusher style with softer tannins than **10**. Ultra-ripe dark fruit with a hint of tealeaf, vanilla. Very much in the easy modern idiom.

★★★★ **Cabernet Franc** 🖺 Understated **11** (★★★★) not as rich, complex as **10**. Red fruit, some herbal character, modest oaking make for appealing, if low-key, drinking.

★★★★ **Shiraz** 🖺 **11** (★★★★) is soft & accessible, lacks concentration, structure of **10**. Overtly fruity, for earlier drinking.

★★★★ **Xanache** 🖺 Bordeaux red blend **11** (★★★★) displays ultra-ripe fruit, soft acidity, smooth tannins. Not as convincing as **10**.

★★★★☆ **The Lynx** 🖺 Flagship **10** Bordeaux blend (equal cab & cab franc, 24% merlot) in another league. Red & black fruit, vanilla & cigarbox. Medium body with bright acidity & deft oaking; great composure & a pleasantly austere finish.

★★★★ **Viognier** 🖺🖺 **11** manages unusual subtlety for this variety, with notes of citrus, peach & pineapple plus hint of vanilla. Lipsmacking acidity the real hallmark.

Grenache 🕀🖺🖺 ★★★★ Vibrant ruby, with upfront soft red berries & spice, **10** light bodied yet serious, with a fresh oaky grip. **Merlot** 🖺 ★★★ Ripe dark fruit & soft tannins mark **11**. Medium bodied & easy to like although should probably be drunk young. **SMV** 🖺🖺 ★★★★ Mainly shiraz, seasonings of mourvèdre & viognier. Dark fruit, dried herbs on above-average **11**. Good fruit expression, fresh acidity & pleasantly firm tannic grip. **Sweet Lynx** Next awaited.

Classic range

Vino Tinto 🖺🖺 ★★★ 6-way red blend **11** displays red & black fruit, some spice but appears slightly tired. **Blanc de Noir** 🖺🖺 ★★★ From merlot, **12** has vague red fruit, bright acidity. **Viognier Tardio** 🖺 Await new vintage. Discontinued: **Rosado**.

French Connection range NEW

The French Connection 🖺🖺 ★★ Shiraz & dash viognier, **11** lacks concentration, toasty oak sits apart. —CE

▪ **Maankloof** *see* Mountain River Wines

Maastricht Estate

Location/WO: Durbanville • Est 1702 • 1stB 2009 • Closed to public • Owner(s) Wheaty Louw • Cellarmaster(s) Thys Louw (Jan 2009) & Mari van der Merwe (Jan 2009) • Viticulturist(s) Wheaty Louw (1986) • 105ha (cab, otage, shiraz, sauv) • ±1,100t/1,500cs own label 40% red 60% white • wine@maastricht.co.za • **T +27 (0)21-975-1995** • F +27 (0)21-976-7013

For years, grapes from Wheaty Louw's Durbanville farm were sold to producers in the area while the dream to launch an own label remained just that. Since 2009, however, a great deal of hard work and a vinification arrangement with Diemersdal turned it into a reality — and Wheaty is relishing every minute of it.

★★★★ **Pinotage** ✓ 🖺 **11** opens in glass to banana & curry leaf spicing found on **10**. Similarly serious but less dominated by oak; 14.8% alcohol well knit. Enjoyable now, should improve 3-5 years.

★★★★ **Shiraz** ✓ Choc-char oak highlights on **11**'s plump red fruit. Clean leather, fynbos whiffs; supple & very sippable despite 14.7% alcohol; overall savoury impression, like **10**.

Cabernet Sauvignon ★★★ Not-for-the-faint-hearted **11** dense black fruit, strong tannins, oak-sweet & warming finish from 14.7% alcohol. **Sauvignon Blanc** ✓ 🍴 ★★★★ Impressive mineral & grapefruit pith conclusion on grassy **12**, cleansing acidity softened by touch sugar. One to seek out. — CvZ

Maiden Wine Cellars

Location: Gordon's Bay ▪ Est 1995 ▪ 1stB 1999 ▪ Tasting/tours by appt; also tailor-made wine tours (max 6 people) ▪ Owner(s) Danie Hattingh ▪ 1,500cs 100% red ▪ PO Box 185 Gordon's Bay 7151 ▪ mwines@mweb.co.za ▪ www.maidenwines.co.za ▪ **T +27 (0)82-554-9395** ▪ F +27 (0)86-688-1177

Exporter Danie Hattingh is focusing on Malaysia and the US, where he has been shipping his Maiden wines for a dozen years, and on China, into which his Iwayini label has made inroads: 'The market in China is so enormous that we will spend the next 10 years developing that one!'

Main Street Winery

Location: Paarl ▪ WO: Swartland ▪ Est/1stB 1999 ▪ Tasting & tours by appt ▪ Owner(s)/winemaker(s) Marais de Villiers ▪ 100cs own label 100% red ▪ PO Box 2709 Paarl 7620 ▪ mainstreet@mweb.co.za ▪ **T +27 (0)21-872-3006** ▪ F +27 (0)21-872-3006

New under this occasional label, originating from wine production consultant and garagiste mentor Marais de Villiers' winery in Paarl is a southern Rhône style red blend from Koringberg in the heart of the Swartland.

Grenache-Shiraz NEW ★★ 50/40 ratio with viognier, pre-bottling **11** is cloaked with tannins, from under which peeps some very ripe fruit. Discontinued: **Main Street**. — GdB

Maison

Location/map/WO: Franschhoek ▪ Est 2005 ▪ 1stB 2008 ▪ Tasting & sales Wed-Sun 10-5 ▪ Closed Dec 25 ▪ The Kitchen @ Maison (fusion bistro, lunch 12-5) ▪ Owner(s) Chris Weylandt & Kim Smith ▪ Winemaker(s)/viticulturist(s) Antwan Bondesio ▪ 11ha/4.5ha (shiraz, chard, chenin, viog) ▪ 50% red 50% white ▪ PO Box 587 Franschhoek 7690 ▪ sales@maisonestate.co.za ▪ www.maisonestate.co.za ▪ S 33° 53'09.7" E 019° 4'39.80" ▪ **T +27 (0)21-876-2116** ▪ F +27 (0)21-876-2116

'Great wine, food and design in a magnificent setting' is the 'total experience' crafted by interior/homeware gurus Chris Weylandt and Kim Smith at their chic winery just off the road into Franschhoek. As more and more take up the invitation to 'make Maison home for the day', the wine offering has expanded to cover all the culinary style needs of its fusion bistro, The Kitchen.

Vin Maison range

★★★★ **Shiraz** ⏏ Modern **10** (★★★★) a tad jammy, with overt 15% alcohol, not as reined in as delicious spicy **09**, Young Wine Show class winner.

★★★★ **Straw Wine** NEW ✓ Stellar debut; **11** packed with lush, honeyed tropical fruit & warm-brioche richness, plump mouthful held in check by brisk acid. From chenin, fermented in older oak. 500ml.

Blanc de Noir NEW ★★★★ From shiraz; coral hues & delicacy in appealing dry **12**, filled out by fermentation in seasoned cask. **Chardonnay** NEW ★★★★ Creamy oak (7 months, 30% new) integrated with citrus fruit lavish **11** for table accompaniment. **Single Vineyard Chenin Blanc** ✓ ★★★★ 'Single vineyard' differentiation for deserving **11**, still in generous style of **10** (★★★★) but more mineral, more measured, better balanced, with penetrating length of flavour. **Viognier** NEW ★★★★ Emphatic dry example, with oak (25% new) and 14% alcohol to boot! **11** billows apricot kernel, perfect for fusion food. Just 100 cases. **Cape Ruby** NEW ★★★★ Shiraz-based port-style **11** proffers sweet spice & fruitcake. Wild, decadent, forest-floor earthiness & youthful spirit dictate some time in bottle. Elegant 500ml pack. — DS

■ **Maison De Cygne** *see* Oude Compagnies Post Private Cellar

Maison de Teijger

Location: Durbanville ▪ WO: Durbanville/Bottelary/Stellenbosch/Walker Bay/Paarl/Coastal ▪ Est/1stB 2004 ▪ Closed to public ▪ Owner(s)/cellarmaster(s) Charl van Teijlingen ▪ Winemaker(s) Charl van Teijlingen, with Danël, Matthew & Elda-Marie van Teijlingen (all 2004) ▪ 6-9t/325-400cs own label 100% red ▪ PO Box 2703 Durbanville 7550 ▪ charlvt@kingsley.co.za ▪ **T** +27 **(0)83-456-9410** ▪ F +27 (0)21-975-0806

These are handcrafted wines from the suburban Durbanville garage of anaesthetist Charl van Teijlingen. This Cape Wine Master annually takes four weeks out from his practice to make wine with his family, a passion since 2004. The six-bottle pinot noir edition below offers insight into the roles of regions and clones.

Pinot Noir range [NEW]

Walker Bay ★★★★ Part of 6-bottle tasting pack from 4 farms, culminating in Coastal blend below. Tealeaf, spice & herbal notes contrast with the fresh, fruity mid-palate. **11** has a tart bite to end but is most balanced of the range. PN 777B clone. **Durbanville Gold Screwcap ★★★** Easy-drinking **11** from BK5 clone, high-toned with green tea notes & sweetish follow-through. **Durbanville Gold Foil ★★★ 11** also BK5 clone, but different barrels; sweeter & less fresh than Gold Screwcap. **Durbanville Black Foil ★★★★** French clone mix, this version has richer body but a tighter structure, with more focus on fruit giving **11** a sweetish feel. **Paarl ★★☆** Darkest in colour, a ripe, soft & fruity **11** from PN 52C and PN 459B clones. **Coastal ★★★ 11** half Walker Bay plus combo of regions above, ditto for clones. Cherry mixed with spicy lift follows to sweetish rich palate.

Stellenbosch range

Cabernet Sauvignon ⓦ **★★★** Part of a tasting pack of components for Bordeaux-style red blend below sourced from selected Stellenbosch estates. **09** cab is from Cloetesdal; sweet blackcurrant, espresso & spice, tannic & charry. **Cabernet Franc** ⓦ **★★★☆** Darker fruit on well-structured **09**, full flavoured, solid vanilla oak & warm dustiness. From Bellevue, as for next. **Malbec** ⓦ **★★★ 09** full bodied & powerfully constructed, impressive berry aromas, mouthfilling bramble fruit & oak. **Merlot** ⓦ **★★★☆** Bursting with ripe berries, **09** is serious yet supple, balanced, lingering vanilla finish. From Bottelary Hills farm Mesco, as next. **Petit Verdot** ⓦ **★★★** Attractive spicy dark berries, **09** noticeable chunky oak & firm tail. **Voorhout Bordeaux Blend** ⓦ **★★★★** Malbec & merlot headline the blend from above Stellenbosch farms. Appropriately, **09** most complex of pack; dark berry fruit, firm structure & balance; promising but needs time to reveal charms.

Durbanville range

★★★★ Malbec Diemersdal ⓦ Pick of the pack is from Diemersdal. Fresh & complex **09**, good concentration of dark berries, rich spicy tobacco. Structured & balanced, excellent varietal expression bodes well.

Cabernet Sauvignon (Fermicru XL) ⓦ **★★★** Part of 9-bottle tasting pack from top Durbanville estates, culminating in Bordeaux-style red blend below. This from De Vallei/Morgenster, as next. Red fruit & blackcurrant, **09** fermented with Fermicru XL yeast. **Cabernet Sauvignon (NT 112)** ⓦ **★★★ 09** fermented with NT 112 yeast is darker, brooding, integrated vanilla oak & savoury finish. **Cabernet Franc** ⓦ **★★★☆** Bramble, tobacco & violet notes on big **09**. Rich & smooth, warm slightly astringent finish. From Groot Roosboom farm. **Malbec Bloemendal** ⓦ **★★★★ 09** oozes ripe plummy spice cake, creamy dark berry & chocolate. Full & rounded, firm finish. From Bloemendal. **Merlot Klein Roosboom** ⓦ **★★★** Very ripe minty plums on sweet & spirity **09** from Klein Roosboom farm. **Merlot Meerendal** ⓦ **★★** Porty & overripe **09**, not for the faint-hearted (16% alc). Meerendal grapes. **Petit Verdot** ⓦ **★★★** Green spicy notes, **09** solid dark-berry fruit & obvious oak influence. Uncomplicated red from De Grendel. **Voorhout Bordeaux Blend** ⓦ **★★★** The Van Teijlingens settled on blend fronted by merlot, petit verdot & malbec for their 7-farm Durbanville **09** flagship. It's big & warm, touch rustic, needs time or food. — JP

Makulu *see* Imbuko Wines
Malagas Wine Company *see* Sijnn
Malan de Versailles *see* Versailles

Malan Family Vintners

Export label of the Malan brothers from Simonsig, featuring wines produced and marketed specifically for distribution into East Africa.

Cape Rouge 🍶 **★★ NV** shiraz with splash petit verdot. Juicy & easy quaffer. This & next export only, WO Stellenbosch. **Cape Blanc** 🍶 **★★★** Pleasantly light **NV** sauvignon spiced with muscat. — GdB

Malanot Wines

Location/map: Stellenbosch ▪ WO: Stellenbosch/Western Cape/Swartland/Paarl/Elgin ▪ Est/1stB 2006 ▪ Tasting & sales Mon-Sat by appt ▪ Fee R25 ▪ Cellar tours by appt & during harvest only ▪ Owner(s) Malanot cc ▪ Cellarmaster(s)/winemaker(s)/viticulturist(s) Marius Malan (Jan 2006) ▪ 3ha/1.5ha (cab) ▪ 60t/5,000cs own label 50% red 50% white + 1,000cs for clients ▪ Brands for clients: Selma ▪ PO Box 22 Lynedoch 7603 ▪ info@malanotwines.co.za ▪ www.malanotwines.co.za ▪ S 33° 59'57.8" E 018° 49'55.2" ▪ **T +27 (0)72-124-7462**

Only 'one dissertation away' from becoming a Cape Wine Master, Marius Malan is relishing the freedom of working for himself. Sales in China continue to do well for his Chandos and Vior ranges, and the many clients he consults for are increasing volumes and targeting new markets in the US and Mauritius.

Malanot Wines range NEW

★★★★ **Family Reserve** From shiraz, aromatic nose of cinnamon, allspice & cloves, **10** is concentrated, elegant, with black cherries/cream balancing well-integrated oak (60% new French) & refreshing acidity.

★★★★ **Cherry Blossom** 🏠 Moves from Vior range. Confident 2nd release, **10** enticing nose of plums, tobacco & chocolate. Elegantly structured, lengthy finish with lingering pepper notes. WO Cape, as next.

Vino Café Pinotage 🏠 ★★★ Was 'Beanotage' in Vior range. Well-balanced **11** is a pleasant surprise: plenty of polished black fruit, leather & (only) some mocha. **Bush Pig** 🏠 ★★★ Natural barrel-fermented **11** from Swartland is a bit of an animal — fat & alcoholic with lavish yellow stonefruit & honey, plus tart acidity. Upgraded from Vior line-up. **Flower Pot** 🏠 Await new vintage.

Vior range

Cabernet Sauvignon Next awaited. **Pinot Noir** NEW ★★★★ Funky **10** mixes sweet red fruit (raspberries & strawberries) with perfumed tealeaves, rounding off with a caramelised finish. Elgin WO. **Pinotage** ★★★★ Sweet black fruit on the nose of **08** — cooked black cherries with some dried prunes. Big tannins & leathery palate. **Shiraz** ★★★ Pronounced aromas of black & white pepper on slightly muddy **08**. WO W Cape. **Red Blend** ⓘ 🏠 ★★★ Was 'Cabernet Sauvignon-Merlot'. Pretty, aromatic scents on **10**, with spicy oak condiment to ripe red fruit. **Chardonnay** NEW ★★★ **11** weighty oatmeal flavours with some oily citrus & cream. Paarl vines.

Chandos range NEW

Pinotage ★★★ **10** cheerful mouthful of red fruit with a hint of spice. **Red Blend** ★★ Soft rounded black fruit from **08** shiraz, merlot & pinotage. **Red Blend BIB** ★★ **10** confected, simple. 3L bag-in-boxes. WO W Cape.

Selma range

Shiraz Sold out, await new release. — CM

■ **Malgas** see Sijnn
■ **Mamre Vale** see Darling Cellars

Manley Private Cellar

Location/map: Tulbagh ▪ WO: Tulbagh/Coastal ▪ Est/1stB 2002 ▪ Tasting & sales Mon-Fri 9–5 Sat 10-3 ▪ Fee R25, waived on purchase ▪ Cellar tours by appt ▪ Closed Good Fri & Dec 25 ▪ Luxury B&B ▪ Restaurant ▪ Wedding & conference facilities ▪ Chapel ▪ Walks ▪ Owner(s) Manley Wine Lodge (Pty) Ltd ▪ Winemaker(s)/viticulturist(s) Stefan Hartmann ▪ 38ha/7ha (cab, merlot, ptage, shiraz) ▪ PO Box 318 Tulbagh 6820 ▪ bookings@manleywinelodge.co.za ▪ www.manleywinelodge.co.za ▪ S 33° 16' 15.8" E 019° 8' 43.8" ▪ **T +27 (0)23-230-0582** ▪ F +27 (0)23-230-0057

'Small but perfectly formed' has long described this Tulbagh winery, but continued export growth has prompted cellarmaster Stefan Hartmann to plant more pinotage to keep up with demand. 'We'll keep building volumes slowly to maintain quality,' he assures, adding that drinkability on release has become a key winemaking objective.

Cabernet Sauvignon ★★★★ Sense of restrained power about **09**, notch above **08** (★★★★). Rich blackfruit flavour, touches of cocoa & light char, well-judged tannic grip. **Merlot** ★★★★ **09** packed with vibrant red fruit, creamy spice, tannins obvious but amenable. Fresh & elegant wine. **Pinotage** ★★★ **10** no distinct pinotage character but crowd-pleasing chocolate & red-fruit flavour, slips down easily. **Shiraz** ★★★★ **09** mirrors big, spicy **08**. Vanilla oak highlights to plush black berry nose & palate, fresh acidity. **Thatch House Red** ⓘ 🏠 ★★★ Shiraz-led blend with cab & merlot, **09** interesting star anise fragrance, soft fruit-filled ody. **Semillon-Sauvignon Blanc ★★★★** Variation on **10** blend tasted last time. This has 64% semillon, tter balance & length, satisfying vinosity. Fine mealtime companion. WO Coastal. Discontinued: **Merlot-abernet Sauvignon, Thatch House White**. — CE/CvZ

Manor House *see* Nederburg Wines

MAN Vintners

cation: Stellenbosch/Paarl ▪ WO: Coastal/Paarl/Western Cape ▪ Est 2001 ▪ Tasting & sales by appt ▪ wner(s) MAN Vintners (Pty) Ltd ▪ Cellarmaster(s) Tyrrel Myburgh (2001) ▪ Winemaker(s) Francois ezuidenhout (Jul 2011) ▪ 175,000cs own label 60% red 39% white 1% rosé ▪ PO Box 389 Stellenbosch 7599 nfo@manvintners.co.za ▪ www.manvintners.co.za ▪ **T +27 (0)21-861-7759** ▪ F +27 (0)21-887-4340

AN Vintners is a collaboration between José Conde of Stark-Condé and Tyrrel and hilip Myburgh of Joostenberg, the name derived from the initials of their respec- ve wives, Marie, Anette and Nicky. Business is booming, with the reserve ormentoso label launched in 2011 already being exported to 10 countries, while ne accolades are also rolling in. All involved are busy outside of wine — last year ellarmaster Tyrrel swam from Robben Island to Blouberg, marketing manager Matthew Cooke ran the Jonkershoek Extreme Mountain Challenge, boss man José aught an owl in the office and winemaker Francois Bezuidenhout got married.

ormentoso range

★★★★ Cabernet Sauvignon 🍴 🌱 Ultra-ripe dark fruit on **10** (★★★★). Big & bold, sweet & soft, not as composed as **09**.

★★★★ Syrah-Mourvèdre 🍴 🌱 Dark fruit, toasty oak & some earthiness on rich, full **10** (★★★★). Lots of concentration & tannic grip but lacks charm of **08**.

★★★★ Old Vine Chenin Blanc 🍴 🌱 Prominent vanilla character on **11** (★★★★) despite only 5 months in oak, 40% new. Also peach, tangy acidity but not the same complexity as **09**.

Mourvèdre 🍴 🌱 **★★★** Red fruit, slight fynbos & spice on medium-bodied **10**, with 15% shiraz. Rustic in yle, ideal with country cooking. **Bush Vine Pinotage** 🍴 🌱 **★★★★** Cleverly conceived **10** includes 11% hiraz. Lighter bodied, with red cherry & attractive vanilla notes. Fruit driven, with fresh acidity & smooth tan- ns. WO Paarl for all these.

ssay range NEW

hiraz-Cinsault-Mourvèdre-Viognier 🍴 🌱 **★★★** Eminently likeable **10** is medium bodied, with red black fruit, hint of spice, bright acidity & fine tannins. Light the barbecue already. **Chenin Blanc-Viognier** 🍴 🌱 **★★★** Citrus, peach & slight leesy note on **11**, uncomplicated summer aperitif. WO W Cape for these.

MAN Vintners range

Cabernet Sauvignon ☺ 🍴 🌱 **★★★** Crowd-pleasing **11** is very fragrant, sweet on entry, gentle acid- ity, soft tannins. Includes 15% merlot. **Merlot** ☺ 🍴 🌱 **★★★** Pleasant, straightforward **10** has red & black fruit, hint of chocolate. A well-balanced pizza & pasta kind of wine.

inotage ⏲ 🍴 🌱 **★★★ 10** cranberry & rhubarb tang. Dab shiraz & American oak add spice, as it did in 9. Medium bodied & very accessible. **Shiraz** ⏲ 🍴 🌱 **★★★★** Bold blueberry & cocoa plum on spicy **10**, entle texture & savoury sweet/sour tang. Lengthy. **Rosé** 🍴 🌱 **★★** Was 'Old Vine Rosé'. Mainly from inotage, dash pinot noir, off-dry **12** lightly fruity with tart acidity. **Chardonnay** 🍴 🌱 **★★★ 11** is ripe & uicy with true-to-variety citrus flavour & relatively soft acidity. No great complexity but has appeal. **Chenin lanc** 🍴 🌱 **★★★ 12** slight guava & pear notes but generally lean, plain. **Cuvée V Chenin Blanc** 🍴 wait new vintage. **Sauvignon Blanc** ✓ 🍴 🌱 **★★★★ 12** is rich & full, has more concentrated fruit than 9 (★★★). Sweet & juicy on entry, plenty of yellow apple, tangy acidity lends balance. 10% semillon for extra mouthfeel. WO W Cape. — CE

Mapoggo *see* Druk My Niet Wine Estate
Marcel de Reuck *see* Crows Nest

Marianne Wine Estate

ocation: Paarl ▪ Map: Paarl & Wellington ▪ WO: Simonsberg-Paarl/Western Cape ▪ Est/1stB 2004 ▪ Tasting, ales & cellar tours Mon-Fri 9-6 Sat/Sun 9-5 ▪ Fee R20/5 wines, R45/9 wines ▪ Closed Good Fri, Dec 25 & Jan 1 Olivello Restaurant ▪ Tour groups ▪ Gift shop ▪ Conference facilities ▪ 1.5hr 'grape to wine' tour ▪ 4-star B&B

guest apartments ▪ Owner(s) Dauriac family ▪ Winemaker(s) Franco Lourens (2012) ▪ Viticulturist(s) André van den Berg (2004) ▪ 36ha/±18ha (cab, merlot, ptage, shiraz, sauv) ▪ 120t/10,000cs own label 90% red 5% white 5% rosé ▪ PO Box 7300 Stellenbosch 7599 ▪ info@mariannewinefarm.co.za ▪ www.mariannewinefarm.co.za ▪ S 33° 49′ 57.6″ E 018° 53′ 37.4″ ▪ **T +27 (0)21-875-5040** ▪ F +27 (0)21-875-5036

Change is in the air at the Simonsberg property owned by Bordeaux's Duriac family, with New York-trained lawyer Alex Brodbeck and wife Jana recently arriving from London to take over the management. The plan is to redesign and upgrade the tasting venue, adding a wine and coffee/deli bar. Red blends — flagship Floreal and entry-level Cape Blend — and wooded sauvignon blanc will be the wine focus.

Cabernet Sauvignon ⓦ ★★★★ Dramatic **09** shows plenty of fruit weight & power but also balance thanks to fresh acidity, firm tannins. Better assembled than **08** (★★). **Merlot** ⓦ ★★★★ Opulent but well-executed **09**, full structure & smooth texture, fresh acidity ensures whole package doesn't overwhelm. More complete than **08** (★★★★). **Pinotage** ⓦ ★★★ Rustic **09** shows jammy fruit, broad structure, slight bitterness. **Shiraz** ⓦ ★★★ Unrestrained **09**, huge dark fruit concentration but appears weighty, lacks poise before somewhat astringent finish. **Cape Blend** ⓦ ★★★ **09** approachable red including 30% pinotage is medium bodied, with juicy fruit, moderate acidity, soft tannins. **Floreal** ⓦ ★★★★ **09** equal cab & merlot, 20% shiraz. Full but balanced, relatively understated in context of big house style, not as oaky as **08** (★★★★). **Rosé** ▤ ★★ Red fruit, some dried herbs on **11**, admirably dry but straightforward. WO W Cape for this & next. **Sauvignon Blanc** ▤ ★★★ **11** is wooded, as previous, quite developed with noticeable leesy character. — CE

■ **Marimba** *see* Southern Sky Wines

Marklew Family Wines

Location/map: Stellenbosch ▪ WO: Simonsberg–Stellenbosch ▪ Est 1970 ▪ 1stB 2003 ▪ Tasting, sales & tours by appt ▪ Tour groups (max 20) ▪ Private/business functions for small groups ▪ Walks ▪ Mountain biking ▪ Conservation area ▪ Owner(s) Marklew family (Edward Dudley, Edward William, Lyn & Haidee) ▪ Winemaker(s) Henri Warren (Jan 2011) ▪ Viticulturist(s) Billy Marklew (Jun 2001), with Henri Warren (Jan 2011) ▪ 58ha/45ha (cabs s/f, merlot, ptage, shiraz, chard, sauv) ▪ ±300t/2,500cs own label 80% red 20% white ▪ BWI, IPW ▪ PO Box 17 Elsenburg 7607 ▪ wine@marklew.co.za ▪ www.marklew.co.za ▪ S 33° 50′ 35.7″ E 018° 51′ 50.3″ ▪ **T +27 (0)21-884-4412** ▪ F +27 (0)21-884-4412

It's ten years since siblings Bill and Haidee Marklew realised their dream of restarting the tradition of winemaking on the family farm, De Goede Sukses, in Stellenbosch's prime Simonsberg ward. Parents and grape farmers Dudley and Lyn having retired in 2001, their children renovated the 180-year-old cellar to accommodate boutique-scale production, and in 2003 vinified the maiden vintage. Their style, 'between classical/elegant and modern', remains unchanged today.

★★★★ **Cabernet Sauvignon** ✓ **08** sumptuous, with bearing, bolder than usual elegant house style. Spicy, predominantly American oak offers generous support for clean blackcurrant flavour, but retains poise.

★★★★ **Chardonnay** ✓ ▧ **11** bold but balanced. Expressive New-World fruit & ample oak — but with Old-World finesse. Broad & welcoming, a fine dining partner.

Merlot Await next, also for **Capensis Reserve**. **Cape Flora Pinotage** ✓ ▧ ★★★★ Evocative of leather & polish, **11** has fynbos scrub elements with plummy fruit, charmingly earthy. — DS

■ **Marlbrook** *see* Klein Constantia Estate
■ **Martinique** *see* Du Preez Estate

Mary Le Bow Trust

Location: Somerset West ▪ WO: Western Cape ▪ 1stB 2005 ▪ Wine sales Mon-Fri 8.30-4 ▪ Owner(s) Frater family ▪ Winemaker(s) Bruce Jack ▪ 258cs own label 100% red ▪ PO Box 3636 Somerset West 7129 ▪ catherine@terraceroad.com ▪ **T +27 (0)79-522-0597** ▪ F +27 (0)86-563-9533

Grapes for this wine come from a farm near Ashton owned by the Frater family and the winemaker is Bruce Jack of Flagstone fame — the late James Frater and Jack having been good friends. James's mother Angela has distant ancestors buried in the crypt of London's St Mary le Bow Church, giving rise to the name.

★★★★☆ **Mary le Bow** Blend of 44% shiraz & near-equal cab & cab franc in **09** (★★★★). Big & brooding, with lots of dark fruit, attractive oak though not quite the elegance of **07**. **08** sold out untasted. — CE

Maske Wines

Location: Wellington ▪ Map: Paarl & Wellington ▪ WO: Wellington/Coastal ▪ Est/1stB 2000 ▪ Tasting & sales Mon-Sun by appt ▪ Closed Ash Wed, Easter Fri/Sun & Dec 25 ▪ BYO picnic ▪ Owner(s) Erich Maske ▪ Winemaker(s)/viticulturist(s) Outsourced ▪ 7ha/5ha (cab, merlot, chenin) ▪ 80% red 20% white, blends outsourced ▪ Klein Waterval PO Box 206 Wellington 7654 ▪ laureat@iafrica.com ▪ www.maskewines.co.za ▪ S 33° 40'4.2" E 019° 2'37.3" ▪ **T +27 (0)21-873-3407** ▪ F +27 (0)21-873-3408

Easing off an international career, Erich Maske and lecturer wife Janine's increased involvement in their small Wellington winefarm includes 'going smaller on quantity, bigger on quality'; giving their Cape Blend an 'edge' with plantings of 'exotic' red varieties; new chenin vines; and planned tasting room renovations.

Leeumasker range

Cape Blend 🔲 ★★★★ Pinotage with cab, shiraz & minor others, previewed **11** offers flowers & black cherries, ripe but balanced fruity flavours.

Maske range

Cabernet Sauvignon 🄯 🔲 ★★ Preview **09** ripe-fruited, with chunky dry tannins, needed hearty fare last time. **Merlot** 🄯 🔲 ★★★ Lively pizza partner, still-selling **09** appealing cherry/red berry flavours. **Chenin Blanc** 🄯 🔲 ★★ Tangy freshness & gentle apple notes on **09**, sampled from tank last time. — MW

■ **Mason's Hill** *see* The Mason's Winery
■ **Maties** *see* Stellenbosch University Welgevallen Cellar
■ **Matumi** *see* Lourensford Wine Estate

Matzikama Organic Cellar

Location: Vredendal ▪ Map: Olifants River ▪ Est/1stB 2001 ▪ Tasting by appt ▪ Owner(s)/winemaker(s)/viticulturist(s) Klaas Coetzee ▪ 12ha/2.5ha (cab, shiraz) ▪ 24t 100% red ▪ PO Box 387 Vredendal 8160 ▪ klaas@matzikamawyn.co.za ▪ www.matzikamawyn.co.za ▪ S 31° 36'34.37" E 018° 44'11.32" ▪ **T +27 (0)82-801-3737**

Klaas Coetzee's own boutique label is still 'hibernating' while he works full time at organic giant Stellar Winery. 'Every year I plan to launch something commercially, but work keeps getting busier and busier so I never get the chance.' He hints that he may make a méthode cap classique bubbly for a celebratory comeback...

McGregor Wines

Location: McGregor ▪ Map: Robertson ▪ WO: McGregor/Western Cape ▪ Est 1948 ▪ 1stB 1978 ▪ Tasting & sales Mon-Fri 8-5 Sat 10-3 ▪ Closed Good Fri, Dec 25/26 & Jan 1 ▪ Cellar tours by appt ▪ BYO picnic ▪ Owner(s) 27 members ▪ Winemaker(s) Elmo du Plessis & Hugo Conradie ▪ 12,000t 22% red 78% white ▪ IPW ▪ PO Box 519 McGregor 6708 ▪ info@mcgregorwinery.co.za ▪ www.mcgregorwinery.co.za ▪ S 33° 56'5.4" E 019° 50'56.3" ▪ **T +27 (0)23-625-1741/1109** ▪ F +27 (0)23-625-1829

The backstory here is of a village and its eponymous winery, and the fact that McGregor is sited literally 'at the end of the road', so traffic is minimal and the life tempo famously slow. In fact, it's said harried parents in neighbour towns warned their children: 'Behave! Or you'll be sent to McGregor'. The winery has turned the rusticity into a marketing virtue, noting (tongue firmly in cheek): 'For years no-one believed McGregor could get any mellower. Then we started making wine.'

Winemaker's Reserve range

Cabernet Sauvignon 🄯 ★★★★ When last tasted, **08**'s dark fruit interwoven with leather & vanilla from year older oak worked well, though alcohol gave a slightly hot finish.

McGregor range

Chenin Blanc ☺ 🍴 🎍 ★★★ **12** billowing scents of melon, pineapple & yellow peach, limy tang, soft but dry finish. Stock up! **Sauvignon Blanc** ☺ 🍴 🎍 ★★★ **12** attractively understated, with ripe tropical layers alternating with cooler, greener ones. Like most whites in range, a notch up.

Pinotage 🍴 🎍 ★★★ Pinot noir ancestry evident in earthy hint to ripe plum fruit, **10** is eminently drinkable & commendably dry. **Ruby Cabernet** ⏱ 🍴 🎍 ★★ Untrammeled by oak, **10** is the template for a (tasty!) fru⸤ bomb. **Shiraz** 🍴 🎍 ★★★ Firm tannin base, plums & nutmeg spice combine to make **10** a good partner for re⸤ meats & game. **Cabernet Sauvignon-Merlot** 🍴 🎍 ★★★ Juicy & savoury **11** somewhat leaner than las⸤ time, easily remedied with a rich country stew. **Pinotage Rosé** ⏱ 🍴 🎍 ★★★ Appealing strawberries &⸤ candyfloss on light & not-too-dry **11** sunset sipper. **Chardonnay** ⏱ 🍴 🎍 ★★★★ Generous lime marmalad⸤ flavour, pithy tail adds interest to upfront (unoaked) fruit & bold 14% alcohol in **11** extrovert. **Colombard** ✓ 🍴 🎍 ★★★★ Step up for bright & breezy **12**, ripe guava flavour, soft & easy, modest 11.5% alcohol — this is wha⸤ summer afternoons were made for. **Red Muscadel** ✓ 🍴 🎍 ★★★★ **10** fortified dessert a rung up with bol⸤ aromas of raisins, marmalade & charry vanilla, persistent savoury flavours. Delicious. **White Muscadel** ⏱ ★★★⸤ **08** packed with flavour richness, like drinking liquidised sultanas. **Cape Ruby** ⏱ ★ **10** port-style from ruby ca⸤ not the characterful fireside sipper we enjoyed previous vintages. — DB/JP

MC Square

Location: Somerset West ▪ WO: Stellenbosch ▪ Est/1stB 1996 ▪ Closed to public ▪ Owner(s)/winemaker(s) viticulturist(s) Jean-Luc Sweerts ▪ 200cs (6btl) MCC Brut & 400cs (12btl) Sophiatown ▪ PO Box 436 Somerse⸤ West 7129 ▪ mcsquare@iafrica.com ▪ **T +27 (0)83·303·5467**

Maverick self-styled 'wine creator' Jean-Luc Sweerts is outspoken on many top⸤ ics, including the health warnings he's obliged to put on his fine wine. 'Wine i⸤ elegance, creativity, achievement, art!' he huffs, and a bonus to the contents o⸤ his MCC bubblies is the deliciously sly back label ridiculing the legislation.

★★★★ **Sophiatown** ⏱ Classically styled **05** cab; dry, elegant & serious, but not for keeping.

★★★★ **Red Square** ⏱ Deep, opulent cab-dominated Bordeaux blend, with merlot & cab franc. **0**⸤ showed dark tones, espresso, wild scrub, hedgerow fruit. Tasted a few years back, like all below.

★★★★ **Cuvée Chardonnay** ⏱ Traditionally vinified sparkling. **04** full & rich citrus flavours, attractiv⸤ toasty hint.

★★★★☆ **Cuvée Brut MCC** ⏱ Classic & expressive **06** sparkling from pinot noir, chardonnay, pino⸤ meunier. Persistent pinpoint bubbles & complex perfume; 3 years lees-ageing add richness & depth.

Isandlwana ⏱ ★★★★ Delicious **07**, sleek & supple, showcases pure shiraz fruit. — IM

■ **Meander** see uniWines Vineyards
■ **Meditation** see Nwanedi Estate

Meerendal Wine Estate   🍴 ☕ 🏛 📷 🎿 ♿

Location/WO: Durbanville ▪ Map: Durbanville, Philadelphia & Darling ▪ Est 1702 ▪ 1stB 1969 ▪ Tasting & sale⸤ Mon-Sun 9-6 ▪ Closed Good Fri, Dec 25 & Jan 1 ▪ Cellar tours by appt ▪ Meerendal Bistro Restaurant & Deli ope⸤ daily; closed Jan 1 ▪ Barn & Lawn function venue ▪ Facilities for children ▪ Tour groups ▪ Farm produce ▪ Confer⸤ ences ▪ Weddings/functions ▪ Walks/hikes ▪ Mountain biking ▪ Conservation area ▪ The Meerendal Boutiqu⸤ Hotel ▪ Owner(s) Coetze family ▪ Cellarmaster(s) Liza Goodwin (Sep 2006) ▪ Viticulturist(s) Victor Rossouw⸤ (Feb 2007) ▪ 220ha/70ha (merlot, ptage, pinot, shiraz, chard, sauv) ▪ 650t/25,000cs own label 75% red 20%⸤ white 5% rosé ▪ IPW ▪ Private Bag X1702 Durbanville 7551 ▪ info@meerendal.co.za ▪ www.meerendal.co.za ▪ S 33° 47′ 55.8″ E 018° 37′ 26.2″ ▪ **T +27 (0)21-975-1655** ▪ F +27 (0)21-975-1657

With fans like pop band Smokie and singing group Bony M signing the visitors⸤ book you'd be forgiven for thinking this revitalised Durbanville property was i⸤ the entertainment business. The team prefers the term 'lifestyle', and celebrate⸤ the culmination of years of hard work to realise the current owners' vision of ⸤ world-class food and accommodation retreat when the boutique hotel opened i⸤ 2012. But, with star-studded guests demanding star-studded wine, at least on⸤ eye remains on the vineyards where improved viticultural practices have uppe⸤ the quality of grapes arriving in the cellar.

Prestige range

★★★★ **Heritage Block Pinotage** Accomplished version from 1955-planted bushvines. Refined, elegant **10** (★★★★★) effortlessly pays homage to Old World restraint with fairly moderate alcohol & proper dryness, while offering vibrant strawberry fruit. No **08**, **09**. Flavours on **07** were muted by firm tannins.

★★★★ **Blanc de Blancs Méthode Cap Classique** ⑰ Well-structured **07** sparkling, typical yeast, brioche & green apple notes; 6 months lees-ageing for breadth.

★★★★★ **Natural Sweet** ⑰ From naturally fermented chenin, older oak. Previously, just enough acid to balance **09** (★★★★) overly ripe marzipan flavours. Medalled **06** was also from chenin.

Merlot Reserve ⑰ ★★★★ **07**'s porty ripeness (ex 14.7% alcohol) checked by big acid & tannin when last tasted. **Bin159 Shiraz** ⑰ ★★★★ Blockbuster style **07** also in ultra ripe **06** (★★★★); baked mulberry & fruitcake flavours, mouthfilling tannins. **Bin 242 Sauvignon Blanc** ⑰ ★★★★ Last tasted was subtle & rich **07**, more complex than **06** (★★★★).

Meerendal range

★★★★ **Pinotage** ⬚ Mulberries & cream on **10**; soft & juicy, well-executed 'older style'. Like other reds, savoury, not overworked; pliable tannins for early gratification.

Cabernet Sauvignon ⬚ ★★★ Olive notes to plummy **10**, supple tannins almost overwhelmed by plush & sweet fruit. **Merlot** ⬚ ★★★★ Turkish Delight, sugar plums & faint herbal whiffs, sour cherry acidity, lovely long tannin grip on smart, just-dry **10**. **Pinot Noir** ⬚ ★★★★ Too unformed to rate last edition, raspberry/cherry-infused **11** now yields refreshing acidity, meaty conclusion on fine tannin structure. **Shiraz** ⑰ ★★★★ Chocolate, leather, sour cherry & white pepper accents ensure **09** raises bar on jammy/tarry **06** (★★★). **Cabernet Sauvignon-Merlot** ⑰ ★★★★ **07**, with 65% cab, offers fresh blackcurrant, cedary spiciness. **Pinotage Rosé** ▱ ⬚ ★★★ **12** undemanding off-dry sipper, bright & refreshing, packs in the flavour. **Chardonnay Wooded** ⑰ ★★★ Half-oaked **08** had breadth courtesy lees-ageing, pronounced citrus-apple acidity. **Chardonnay Unwooded** ▱ ⬚ ★★★★ Engaging lime-lemon character, tang on nutty **12**. Flavoursome, focused & vibrant for solo sipping or mealtimes. **Sauvignon Blanc** ✓ ▱ ⬚ ★★★★ **12** nettle, grass & fig notes; bright, long finish. Discontinued: **Chenin Blanc**. — CvZ

Meerhof Family Vineyards

Location: Riebeek-Kasteel ▪ Map: Swartland ▪ WO: Western Cape/Coastal ▪ Est/1stB 2000 ▪ Tasting & sales by appt only ▪ Owner(s) Cobus Kotze ▪ Winemaker(s)/viticulturist(s) Johan Meyer ▪ 150ha/17ha (cab, merlot, ptage, shiraz, chenin) ▪ 1,200cs own label 55% red 45% white ▪ PO Box 1229 Malmesbury 7299 ▪ meerhof@ wcaccess.co.za ▪ www.meerhof.co.za ▪ S 33° 24′ 19.8″   E 018° 52′ 15.0″ ▪ **T +27 (0)87-230-7224/+27 (0)21-200-8521** ▪ F +27 (0)86-683-8132

There's much happening at this winery: 10 hectares of redundant vines have been uprooted while Rhône and Spanish varieties have been planted. With Meerhof a new member of the Swartland Independent group, all its wines are now naturally fermented, with no additives; and they use no new oak. A Chenin and Syrah under the Meerhof label, as well as Manifesto Pinotage and Antebellum Syrah, are due for release early 2013 but were unavailable for tasting for this edition.

★★★★ **Salomon** ⑰ Fragrant **08** has firm structure associated with cab-led Bordeaux-style blends, expressed with restraint, refinement. Focused, refreshing, with sweet-fruited persistence.

★★★★ **Drège** ⑰ Shiraz-headed **08** offers appealing spicy, truffly notes, savoury persistence. Light touch from deftly handled tannins, tangy mineral thread prolong drinking pleasure. Merlot & cab are other partners.

Syrah ⑰ ★★★★ Admirably delicate **08** presents full, pure dark spice, truffle flavours. Fresh core, comfortably padded tannins add to current enjoyment. Includes splashes mourvèdre, viognier. Previous was **06** (★★★★). **Antebellum Chenin Blanc** NEW ★★★★ **12** almost ethereal floral/earthy notes; daintily fresh with underlying lees-enriched breadth. Should develop well. Paarl grapes, natural ferment, mainly older oak. — AL

■ **Meerkat** *see* Welbedacht Wine Estate

Meerlust Estate

Location/map/WO: Stellenbosch ▪ Est 1693 ▪ 1stB 1975 ▪ Tasting & sales Mon-Fri 9–5 Sat 10–2 ▪ Fee R30 ▪ Closed all pub hols ▪ Cellar tours by appt ▪ Owner(s) Hannes Myburgh ▪ Cellarmaster(s) Chris Williams (Jan 2004) ▪ Winemaker(s) Altus Treurnicht (assistant, 2008) ▪ Viticulturist(s) Roelie Joubert (2001) ▪ 400ha/106ha (cabs s/f, merlot, p verdot, pinot, chard) ▪ 500t/25,000cs own label 90% red 10% white ▪ PO Box 7121

Stellenbosch 7599 ▪ info@meerlust.co.za ▪ www.meerlust.co.za ▪ S 34° 1′ 1.7″ E 018° 45′ 24.7″ ▪ **T +27 (0)21-843-3587** ▪ F +27 (0)21-843-3274

'It gets harder to find something new to say after 319 years!' jokes Meerlust's Chris Williams, although, naturally, fine-tuning in the vineyards continues on a daily basis. Most of the range has reached the quality benchmarks the winemaker set himself nine years ago, he says, with the merlot and chardonnay progressing well as mature plantings from new, virus-free clones come onstream. The cabernet franc is now excelling, Williams feels, and has made a measurable improvement to the Rubicon blend, as has the inclusion of petit verdot. An increase in the number of visitors to the estate's tasting centre has been gratifying. Atmospheric and quirky, it reflects owner Hannes Myburgh's eclectic taste in art and design, and affords a unique combination of traditional Cape hospitality and contemporary winemaking expertise.

★★★★☆ **Cabernet Sauvignon** 🍃 Impressive **10** in more austere style than last expressive vintage (now being released annually). Resolute, seamlessly integrated tannins conceal dense, nicely ripe blackcurrant fruit, patience will see it emerge to realise its full potential.

★★★★☆ **Merlot** Usual distinctive, classic styling in **09**, tightly structured but with lovely succulent dark plum & mineral core, embellished with dark chocolate & spice. Splash cab franc lifts, but best wait 2-3 years.

★★★★☆ **Pinot Noir** 🍃 Alluring, vibrant **11** envelops vivid wild red fruit & cherries in finely textured spicy tannins, shot through with property's trademark mineral thread. 25 year old vines deliver plenty of depth to a fine savoury finish. Also available screwcapped.

★★★★☆ **Rubicon** Signature restraint in classic **08** Cape cab-based Bordeaux benchmark, though more accessible & expressive than particularly tight **07** (★★★★). Boldly packed dense, dark fruit, seamlessly underpinned by lithe tannins, delivers harmonious, complete blend.

★★★★☆ **Chardonnay** 🍃 Engaging **10** gains rich textured creaminess from barrel ferment & year on lees. Complex oatmeal, citrus aromas precede structured layers of tropical & ripe stonefruit, balanced by stony minerality & vibrant thread of acidity. Back on track after unassuming **09** (★★★★). Also under screwcap. — IM

Meinert Wines

Location/map: Stellenbosch ▪ WO: Devon Valley/Elgin ▪ Est 1987 ▪ 1stB 1997 ▪ Tasting Mon-Sat strictly by appt only ▪ Closed all pub hols ▪ Owner(s) Martin Meinert ▪ Cellarmaster(s)/winemaker(s) Martin Meinert (Nov 1997) ▪ Viticulturist(s) Henk Marconi (Jan 1991) ▪ 16ha/12ha (cabs s/f, merlot, p verdot, ptage, sem) ▪ 90t/ 7,000cs own label 50% red 50% white ▪ PO Box 7221 Stellenbosch 7599 ▪ info@meinertwines.com ▪ www.meinertwines.com ▪ S 33° 54′ 1.8″ E 018° 48′ 50.2″ ▪ **T +27 (0)21-865-2363** ▪ F +27 (0)21-865-2414

Martin Meinert settles into his second quarter-century as owner of this family farm and boutique winery in Stellenbosch's Devon Valley. When he bought the first plot of land in 1987 it was known simply as 'Remainder of Farm 78'! Ten years later he gave up his prestigious security as Vergelegen winemaker (he'd helped plan both vineyards and cellar there) to realise, as he says, his 'dream of a small private vineyard and winery'. Wines which had been sold off in bulk now appeared under his own label. Sixteen years on, things are still developing (a chardonnay joins a new range also housing the established 'white merlot') but core values remain — including Martin's belief in 'the pleasure of wines that can age'.

Meinert Wines range

★★★★ **Cabernet Sauvignon** 🍾 Always a serious, strongly built & even powerful wine. **08** (★★★★) is on the sombre side, intense & rather heavy, while **09** has much more life, juicy bright fruit & general oomph. Well balanced & approachable, but will greatly benefit from a few years in some cool dark place.

★★★★ **Synchronicity** 08 (★★★★☆) shows the virtues of a classic approach to grapes from a warmer climate: power, yes, but also balance & drinkability; fruit & structure in partnership but neither overt. 65% cab, with merlot, pinotage, cab franc. Even grander than **07**. Deserves 5 years, will keep much longer.

Merlot 🍾 ★★★★ Easier, lighter drinking than the cab-based wines, but **09** still a serious prospect, with a good tannic grip, dry finish & ageability. **Printer's Ink Pinotage** 🍾 ★★★★ 08 a touch less aromatic a year later, now bottled, but some intriguing perfumed & sweet fruit notes, with the usual Meinert element of dry restraint. **La Barry Sauvignon Blanc** 🍾 ★★★★ Preview **12**'s exuberant, ripe aromas & flavour continue through a succulent mouthful to a lingering finish. **11** (★★★★) also tasted — nice enough but a touch aggressive in its bite, with more lean, green notes mixed in. These from Elgin. Discontinued: **Devon Crest**.

Family Collection

★★★★ **Chardonnay** NEW Oatmeal, citrus & some toasty oak the rather showy opening gambit on **11** ex Elgin. Balanced, fresh & very drinkable. Should acquire more complexity, depth over next year to justify rating.

The Italian Job ★★★ A merlot blanc de noir — well, a very pale coppery pink de noir in **11**. Puzzling wine, unfruity & indeterminate, but well structured; oaked but soft & just dry. — TJ

Melkboomsdrift Wines

Location: Lutzville • Map: Olifants River • Tasting & sales Mon-Fri 9-5 • Guesthouse B&B/self-catering • Dinner & picnic baskets on request • Conference venue (20 max) • Owner(s)/cellarmaster(s)/winemaker(s) Hilsa van Heerden • Viticulturist(s) Jeff Joubert • (cab, merlot, ptage, shiraz) • PO Box 1124 Vredendal 8160 • info@melkboomsdrift.co.za • www.melkboomsdrift.co.za • S 31°36'15.24" E 018°24'19.86" • **T +27 (0)27-217-2624** • F +27 (0)27-217-2535

For a more intimate encounter with the wines of the Olifants River area, usually associated with large wineries, visit Hilsa van Heerden on her farm, where she makes a limited range of mainly reds herself and serves them with dinner at her lodge (also offering weekday tastings and sales for non-residents).

Mellasat Vineyards

Location/WO: Paarl • Map: Paarl & Wellington • Est 1996 • 1stB 1999 • Tasting & sales Mon-Sat 9.30-5.30 Sun & pub hols 10-4 • Closed Easter Fri/Sun, Dec 25 & Jan 1 • Cellar tours by appt • Light lunches for groups/tours or private dinner functions by appt; also food-based events • Tour groups • Conferences • Paarl Ommiberg Festival • Owner(s) Stephen Richardson • Cellarmaster(s)/winemaker(s) Stephen Richardson (Jan 1999) • Viticulturist(s) Poena Malherbe (Sep 1996) • 13ha/8ha (cab, ptage, shiraz, tempranillo, chard, chenin, viog) • 50t/3,500cs own label 40% red 50% white 10% rosé • IPW • PO Box 7169 Paarl 7623 • mellasat@mweb.co.za • www.mellasat.com • S 33° 44'30.0" E 019° 2'31.0" • **T +27 (0)21-862-4525** • F +27 (0)21-862-4525

The tranquil setting of the Richardson farm belies a hive of activity and innovation: new tasting and function rooms with views of the mountain backdrop and Paarl Valley; first bottling of tempranillo; maiden crop of viognier; and a novel underground 'working museum', The Cemetery of Forgotten Wines, where the public can not only view but also swop old, one-off, unknown or overlooked wines.

Mellasat Premium range

'M' ✓ ★★★★ Equal cab/shiraz **07** is ripe, rich & spicy, with balance & fruity lift from dollop pinotage. Seriously oaked (30 months). **'Sigma' White Pinotage** ★★★★ Pinotage vinified in Romanian oak barrels as white wine, **11** is fruity & spicy, with structure & depth of flavour. Savoury tang to finish. **Chardonnay** ★★★★ Barrel-fermented **11**, creamy biscuit & toffee, citrus flavour & firm acidity, rounded & full. **Tuin Wyn** ⊕ 🍷 ★★★ Oak-matured **10** straw wine from air-dried chenin. Nutty nougat flavours & light feel despite substantial 17% alc.

Dekker's Valley range

Revelation ☺ 🍷 ★★★ Ex-tank cab, shiraz, pinotage **10** blend is fresh & vividly fruity, with bouncy tannins. Easy winter sipper. **Chenin Blanc** ☺ 🍷 ★★★ Apple, melon & guava toned preview **12** is juicy, with a brisk acidity.

Shiraz ⊕ 🍷 ★★★ Mulberry & mocha in **10** precede leather & fruit. **Shiraz Rosé** 🍷 ★★ Pre-bottling sample **12** is pale pink, crisp & fruity for summer fun. — WB

◼ **Meme** see Jason's Hill Private Cellar
◼ **Merchant's Mark** see Barrydale Cellar — SCV

Merwida Winery

Location: Rawsonville • Map/WO: Breedekloof • Est 1963 • 1stB 1975 • Tasting & sales Mon-Fri 8-12.30; 1. 30-5 Sat 9-1 • Closed Easter Fri-Mon, Dec 25-Jan 1 • Merwida Country Lodge T +27 (0)23-349-1435 • Owner(s) Schalk & Pierre van der Merwe • Cellarmaster(s)/viticulturist(s) Magnus Kriel • Winemaker(s) Magnus Kriel (Dec 2000), with Sarel van Staden (Aug 1982) & Jacques Geldenhuys (Jun 2011) • 630ha (cab, merlot, shiraz, chard, chenin, sauv, sem, viog) • 15,000t/20,000cs own label 40% red 60% white • ISO 22000, BWI, Fairtrade • PO Box 4 Rawsonville 6845 • wines@merwida.com • www.merwida.com • S 33° 41'24.9" E 019° 20'31.1" • **T +27 (0)23-349-1144** • F +27 (0)23-349-1953 / +27 (0)86-538-1953

This Breedekloof farm is named after the Merwede River in the Netherlands, where owners Schalk and Pierre van der Merwe's ancestors lived. But the brothers' focus is not so much on heritage as responding to modern demands. 'Increasingly health-conscious consumers want lower-alcohol wines,' says cellarmaster Magnus Kriel. 'Demand for our Fairtrade wines is also rising dramatically.'

★★★★ **Barbera** 🄡 Wild berry perfume with liquorice, dried herbs & tar. Unlike sweet-oaky **09** (★★★☆), fruit remains in driving seat in **10**, lifted by generous acidity. Great food wine.

★★★★ **Chardonnay** ⏣ 🍴 Partially wooded **11** vibrant lemon zest with sweet oak spiciness; full, creamy texture with potent lemon–butter flavours. **10** sold out untasted.

Sauvignon Blanc ☺ 🍴 🄡 ★★★ Super **12**, guava & gooseberry on nose, good fruit intensity & zippy acidity.

Cabernet Sauvignon 🄡 ★★★ Red-fruited **10**, elegant centre with leafy edges. Will benefit from short-term ageing. **Pinotage Limited Edition** ⏣ ★★★ **09** fleshy & succulent, toasty vanilla & dark ripe fruit with cedar trim. **Merlot Rosé** ⏣ 🍴 ★★★ Strawberry & white chocolate on off-dry **11** party sipper. **Cuvée Brut** New bottling not ready. **White Muscadel** ⏣ 🍴 ★★★ Utterly delicious fortified dessert, **11** lusciously sweet but balanced, lovely lemon & jasmine scents, lingering honeyed flavours. Even better than **09** (★★★☆). — HJ

■ **Metamorphic** *see Hillcrest Estate*

Metzer Wines

Location: Somerset West ▪ WO: Stellenbosch ▪ Est/1stB 2004 ▪ Tasting by appt ▪ Owner(s)/winemaker(s) Wade Metzer & Barry Holfeld ▪ 16t/1,200cs 100% red ▪ PO Box 35398 Northcliff 2115 ▪ metzerwines@gmail.com ▪ www.metzerwines.com, www.vitaminbwine.com ▪ **T +27 (0)82-774-4121**

Marketing gets ever harder, says owner/winemaker (and new father) Wade Metzer. He also sees a 'pretty bleak picture in terms of shelf space' for the many new local producers (like himself). So, while 'word of mouth is the next frontier', the innovative naming and packaging of his wines reveals a huge investment of energy and imagination. But as to winemaking, Wade is happy to cite a whisky advert suggesting that to be resolutely old-fashioned is to make real progress.

★★★★ **Vitamin B Syrah** ⏣ Clean black fruit with herbal & savoury notes, velvety **09** when tasted a few years back delivered mouthful of mulberry, white pepper & spice that lingered against refined tannins.

★★★★ **Syrah** ⏣ **09** (★★★★★) offers perfumes of dark berries, flowers & spice. Strikingly pure, vibrant & juicy fruit around a core of well-handled tannins. Helderberg grapes; **07** was from Swartland.

★★★★ **The Kitchen Sink Syrah** Renewed interest sees label revived. **10** (★★★★) big, ripe fruity aromas & some sweet flavours on firm base, but a little more awkward & oaky than maiden **05**, with drying tannins.

Vitamin B Blanc NEW 🄡 ★★★ Pleasingly gentle, easygoing charm on lightly, unobtrusively oaked **11** blend of chenin with chardonnay plus a touch of viognier to add a floral note. Fairly rich, with good texture. — TJ

M'hudi Wines

Location/map/WO: Stellenbosch ▪ Tasting & sales by appt ▪ Guest accommodation ▪ Owner(s) Rangaka family ▪ Winemaker(s) Outsourced ▪ 43ha total ▪ 35,000cs own label 70% red 30% white ▪ WIETA ▪ PO Box 30 Koelenhof 7605 ▪ malmsey@mhudi.com ▪ www.mhudi.com ▪ S 33° 50' 32.3" E 018° 45' 13.9" ▪ **T +27 (0)21-988-6960** ▪ F +27 (0)86-582-8974

The Rangaka family released their first M'hudi vintage in 2005. But if buying the derelict land and farming hadn't been challenge enough for these brave novices, they were now newcomers in a fiercely competitive market with wines to sell. Nothing daunted, matriarch and CEO Malmesy calmly asked Marks & Spencer for a listing, and today M'hudi wines are on sale in the US, Africa and Europe.

Merlot ☺ 🄡 ★★★ Lush ripeness of intriguingly spicy & aromatic **10** checked by tannic finish. Exclusively for Marks & Spencer, UK, like Sauvignon. **Chenin Blanc** ☺ 🄡 ★★★ Delightfully tropical **12** has earthy touch & appealing freshness, oaking provides breadth & texture.

Pinotage ★★★ Smoky, spicy, dark-fruited **10** structured by bold acidity with bitter almond finish. **Sauvignon Blanc** ✓ 🍴 ★★★★ Characterful **12** the customary mix of tropical & herbaceous flavours, zippily balanced by fresh acid thread. — IM

Micu Narunsky Wines

Location: Somerset West ▪ Map: Helderberg ▪ WO: Coastal/Stellenbosch ▪ Est 2005 ▪ 1stB 2006 ▪ Tasting by appt ▪ Owner(s)/cellarmaster(s)/viticulturist(s) Micu Narunsky ▪ Winemaker(s) Micu Narunsky, advised by Francois Naudé ▪ 4.8t/225cs own label 85% red 15% white ▪ PO Box 427 Somerset Mall 7137 ▪ micunarunsky@gmail.com ▪ www.micunarunsky.com ▪ S 34° 1′ 52.20″ E 018° 50′ 46.73″ ▪ **T +27 (0)73-600-3031 / +27 (0)21-855-2520**

Micu Narunsky, musician and winemaker, exercises the latter art for Anatu Wines and his own label out of the old Cordoba winery on the Helderberg. Micu has 'discovered' colombard, he announces. 'An experiment with this unassuming variety, from a single vineyard, manicured to perfection, has produced an interesting result, one that I am keen to pursue.' For the reds, he continues working with the Portuguese varieties he admires so much.

★★★★ **Iemanjá** ⓟ Ever-improving touriga-led red (with 30% tinta), among handful such (unfortified) blends in SA. **09** brooding, sweet/spicy berries, robust, skilfully oaked — a food wine with ageing potential. **Olodum** ⓟ ★★★★ Mirror image of above red blend: tinta leading, 17% touriga in **09**. Softer, juicy & spicy, medium bodied with well-judged oak. Delicious. **La Complicité** ★★★★ Fresh & friendly **11** reaches higher than usual for colombard. Last tasted under this name was **06** (★★★) from muscat. Quince, melon & herbal notes, oak well integrated; the palate full but fresh. Mixed oak/tank fermentation. WO Stellenbosch. — JPf

Middelvlei Estate

Location/map: Stellenbosch ▪ WO: Devon Valley ▪ Est 1941 ▪ 1stB 1973 ▪ Tasting & sales daily 10–4.30 ▪ Fee R15pp ▪ Closed Good Fri, Dec 25 & Jan 1 ▪ Cellar tours by appt ▪ Traditional lunchtime braai on Sat & Sun; by prior arrangement for groups of 15+ on any other day ▪ Facilities for children ▪ Conferences ▪ Walking/hiking & mountain biking trails ▪ Cottage (2 pax) ▪ Owner(s) Momberg family ▪ Cellarmaster(s)/winemaker(s)/viticulturist(s) Tinnie Momberg (Feb 1992) ▪ 160ha/110ha (cab, merlot, ptage, shiraz, chard, sauv) ▪ 650t/30,000cs own label 95% red 5% white ▪ Other export brand: Hagelsberg ▪ IPW, WIETA ▪ PO Box 66 Stellenbosch 7599 ▪ info@middelvlei.co.za ▪ www.middelvlei.co.za ▪ S 33° 55′41.2″ E 018° 49′55.9″ ▪ **T +27 (0)21-883-2565** ▪ F +27 (0)21-883-9546

Any visitor looking for an authentic South African experience should consider joining the Momberg family on their Stellenbosch farm every Saturday or Sunday lunchtime for their open-house 'boerebraai' (BBQ). An expert is on hand to show you how (using old vines for firewood) to cook the perfect chop, all helped along by a glass of the preferred Middelvlei Pinotage.

★★★★ **Shiraz** ✓ Satisfyingly dry, savoury **10** appeals with succulent fruit flavours, checked by spicy tannins. Usual quality, harmony & complexity from reliable shiraz producer.

★★★★☆ **Momberg** Intensely aromatic, handsomely plush & polished **10** (★★★★) shiraz-led Cape Blend shows tad less depth than last-tasted **07**. Solidly ripe red fruit; savoury, spicy tannins from all-new oak. **Cabernet Sauvignon** ★★★★ Elegant feel to **10** despite alcohol near 15% — bone-dry, balanced & food friendly. Rich red fruits meld well with textured tannins. **Merlot** NEW 🍴 ★★★ Well-made **11** in bold, alcoholic, popular mocha style; succulence & sweet richness will appeal, as will smooth tannins. **Pinotage** ⓟ ★★★★ 'Free Run' on **09** label, so expect fruit focus; vivid blueberries, supple tannins. Part of sale goes to Endangered Wildlife Trust. **Pinotage-Merlot** 🍴 ★★★ Intended for juicy enjoyment. Equal blend **11** doesn't disappoint, with smooth savouriness & easy drinkability. **Chardonnay** ⓟ 🍴 ★★★ Unwooded **11** the answer for those disliking oaked whites. Nothing but tasty tropical fruit, fresh & tangy. — IM

Migliarina Wines

Location: Stellenbosch ▪ WO: Stellenbosch/Western Cape ▪ Est 2001 ▪ 1stB 2002 ▪ Closed to public ▪ Owner(s)/winemaker(s) Carsten Migliarina ▪ 1,200cs own label 65% red 35% white + 160cs for clients ▪ Brands for clients: Kap Hase, Fridham Gaard ▪ PO Box 673 Stellenbosch 7599 ▪ carsten@migliarina.co.za ▪ www.migliarina.co.za ▪ **T +27 (0)72-233-4138**

Carsten Migliarina's wine business grows apace. He created two individual ranges for overseas customers, one in Germany, the other in Sweden, while his local lineup grew by one, with the addition of a chardonnay. He has other projects up his sleeve, and made a minuscule quantity of barrel-fermented chardonnay bubbly 'just for fun' which might or might not be released, he hasn't yet decided.

★★★★ **Shiraz** With dark plums at core, **09** reflects quite savoury styling, scrub & black pepper, further confirmed by the oak-influenced dry palate, finish. Drink now till 2017.

Chardonnay NEW ★★★☆ Singular peach pip savouriness on the nose but elegant **11**'s palate opens up to the fleshed version, livened by acidity. WO W Cape. — CR

■ **Migration** see D'Athis Wines SA Negociants
■ **Miko** see Mont Rochelle Hotel & Mountain Vineyards

Miles Mossop Wines

Location: Stellenbosch ▪ WO: Stellenbosch/Coastal ▪ Est/1stB 2004 ▪ Closed to public ▪ Owner(s)/winemaker(s)/viticulturist(s) Miles Mossop ▪ 15t/1,000cs own label 47% red 48% white 5% NLH ▪ PO Box 7339 Stellenbosch 7599 ▪ miles@milesmossopwines.com ▪ www.milesmossopwines.com ▪ **T +27 (0)82-413-4335** ▪ F +27 (0)21-808-5911

Miles Mossop is now established as one of the top winemakers in South Africa. It's evident in the wines he makes at Tokara and in his own range — named for his three children. The late Tony Mossop was a famous wine judge and journalist and the same vinous element flows in the blood of Miles, his son. What makes the latter's winemaking so acute is his reliance on his gut-feel and his ability to take what nature offers and deliver wines of great polish as well as integrity.

★★★★☆ **Max 09** continues excellent track record. Blend of half cab with petit verdot, merlot % malbec. Like **08** (★★★★★), modern & plush in the best possible sense. Textured, with silky tannins & fine dry end. Deserves time before broaching.

★★★★☆ **Saskia** 🌿 Stunning new-generation blend from chenin, viognier & splashes clairette & verdelho. **11** (★★★★★), with attractive toasty intro, yet more voluptuous opulence than **10**, delivers promised richness with great finesse (despite 15% alcohol), ending drier than previous. Stellenbosch, Swartland & Paarl fruit.

★★★★☆ **Kika** 🌿 Noble Late Harvest from chenin, **11** has typical sweet/sour apricot & tinned peach richness. The ultra-sweet palate offers viscous pleasure cleaned out by tangy, vibrant acid, with balanced lowish alcohol. Extremely rich, with just the right amount of botrytis complexity. — JP

■ **Millberg** see Tulbagh Winery
■ **Millers Mile** see Klein Parys Vineyards
■ **Millstone** see Stettyn Cellar

Millstream

Established range by DGB chiefly for the UK, Ireland and the Netherlands.

Cinsaut-Ruby Cabernet 🍴🌿 ★★☆ Juicy, smooth & quaffable **11**, light cherry/smoky tone. **Rosé** 🍴🌿 ★★ Semi-sweet **12** is crisply balanced, berry fruit for sipping with a summer's breeze in your hair. **Chenin Blanc** 🍴🌿 ★★★ **12** attractive easy-drinker with tangy peach & granadilla flavours. WO W Cape for all. — MW

Mimosa Boutique Wines

Location: Montagu ▪ Map: Klein Karoo & Garden Route ▪ WO: Robertson ▪ Est 2004 ▪ 1stB 2003 ▪ Tasting & sales daily 9-5 ▪ Facilities for children ▪ Tour groups ▪ Conservation area ▪ 4-star Mimosa Lodge: 23 rooms, conference centre, pool, boules pitch, wine cellar, tasting room & Ma Cuisine restaurant (see Restaurants section) ▪ Owner(s) Bernhard Hess ▪ Cellarmaster(s)/winemaker(s)/viticulturist(s) Lourens van der Westhuizen (consultant) ▪ 5ha/3ha (cab, shiraz, chard, sauv) ▪ 20t/1,240cs own label 70% red 30% white ▪ PO Box 323 Montagu 6720 ▪ bernhard@mimosa.co.za ▪ www.mimosawines.co.za ▪ S 33° 47' 27.59" E 020° 6' 44.55" ▪ **T +27 (0)23-614-2351** ▪ F +27 (0)86-535-0720

What began for Mimosa Lodge owner and chef Bernhard Hess as a 'hobby' — offering his guests wine made to be paired with his food — in the past six years has evolved into a standalone wine brand. It's still relatively small — some 25,000 bottles annually — but it's exported (to Switzerland, Germany and others) and growing (an untasted Natural Sweet the latest addition).

★★★★ **Chardonnay** Brisk acidity, generous citrus & yellow apple, buttery vanilla on barrel-fermented **11** (★★★★), flavours more open than taut & youthful-on-release **09**, probably best enjoyed early. No **10**.

Cabernet Sauvignon Await new, as for **Shiraz** & **Sauvignon Blanc**. **Hess Reserve** ★★★★ Elegant Bordeaux blend **10** from Somerset West vines, harmonious & fresh marriage of sweet fruit & oak. — JP/CvZ

Miravel

Location: Somerset West ▪ Map: Helderberg ▪ WO: Stellenbosch ▪ Est 2002 ▪ 1stB 2005 ▪ Tasting & sales Mon-Sat & pub hols by appt ▪ Closed Ash Wed, Easter Fri-Mon, Ascension day, Pentecost, Dec 25/26 & Jan 1 ▪ Meals & cheese platters by prior arrangement ▪ Self-catering Fynbos Cottage ▪ Owner(s) Maarten van Beuningen ▪ Winemaker(s) Gerda Willers, Wynand Lategan & André Liebenberg (consultants) ▪ Viticulturist(s) Paul Wallace (Jun 2004, consultant) ▪ 39ha/27ha (cab, merlot, p verdot, ptage, chenin, sauv) ▪ 125t/750cs (sauv) & 1,500L (cab, p verdot) own label 25% red 75% white ▪ PO Box 5144 Helderberg 7135 ▪ maarten@miravel.co.za ▪ www.miravel.co.za ▪ S 34° 1′58.7″ E 018° 46′46.9″ ▪ **T +27 (0)21-842-3154** ▪ F +27 (0)21-842-3154

'If we don't change, we won't survive,' says owner Maarten van Beuningen who, with wife Janine, was forced by circumstance to swap ostrich farming for wine ten years ago. Now a quality grape producer in the Helderberg basin, steadily more of the sought-after crop is going to market under their own handcrafted Miravel label. Which they're about to redesign...

Cabernet Sauvignon ⓘ ★★★★ **08** previously showed generous fresh fruit & firm tannins. **Ella Family Reserve** ⓘ ★★★★ Streamlined **08** from cab has pure fresh blackcurrant appeal. Gentle grip & modest oaking (no new barrels) allow for uncomplicated yet satisfying drinking. **Merlot** ⓘ ★★★★ Last tasted was **06** with iron & spice aromas, bouncy grip. **Sauvignon Blanc** 🏠 ★★★ Generous rather than steely, **11** offers peach & pine characters in gentle mouthful. — DS

Mischa Estate

Location/WO: Wellington ▪ Map: Paarl & Wellington ▪ Est/1stB 1999 ▪ Tasting, sales & tours (vine nursery in winter & cellar in summer) by appt ▪ Fee R250, waived if purchase equals/exceed it ▪ Closed all pub hols ▪ Snacks & meals by appt ▪ Walks ▪ Mountain biking ▪ Dunedin Manor House & Oak Tree cottage; Talana Hill cottage & garden room ▪ Owner(s) JA & GH Barns ▪ Cellarmaster(s)/winemaker(s) Andrew Barns (Jan 1999) ▪ Viticulturist(s) Ruiter Smit (Jun 1960) & Eben Archer ▪ 40ha (cab, merlot, shiraz, sauv, viog) ▪ 97t/4,000cs own label 75% red 25% white ▪ PO Box 163 Wellington 7654 ▪ info@mischaestate.com ▪ www.mischaestate.com, www.mischawines.blogspot.com ▪ S 33° 36′13.1″ E 019° 0′46.8″ ▪ **T +27 (0)21-864-1016/19/20** ▪ F +27 (0)21-864-2312/+27 (0)86-514-9818

Mischa Estate in Wellington is first and foremost the site of a successful vine nursery. 'We graft in excess of two million vines a year and have over 300 clients, but quality rather than size is our real focus,' says Andrew Barns, current proprietor. He's also a self-taught vintner, having made wine since 1999. 'I put on my Nikes and just did it.'

Mischa Estate range

★★★★ **Cabernet Sauvignon** ⓘ Exuberant **08** (★★★★) is full & intense, sweet dark fruit & smooth tannins; includes dashes cab franc, merlot. More powerful than balanced **07**.

★★★★ **Roussanne** 🔎 **11** (★★★★★) even more impressive than maiden **10**. Not for the uninitiated, but very expressive: generally savoury but also slight citrus & peach notes. Good palate weight before a long, almost saline finish. 'Will reward those with patience,' says Andrew Barns.

Merlot ⓘ ★★★ **09** red fruit but lacked freshness, appeared simple, short when last tasted. **Shiraz** ⓘ ★★★ **08** sweet dark fruit & toasty oak make for appealing if rather obvious result.

Eventide Cellar range

★★★★ **Shiraz** ⓘ 🏠 **08** fragrant aromas of red berries & fynbos; medium to full body with pure fruit, spice, fresh acidity & unobtrusive oak.

Sauvignon Blanc 🏠 ★★ Unexpressive **10** shows slight lime character, tart acidity. **Viognier** ⓘ 🏠 ★★★ Elegant **09** peach flavour, smooth texture, gentle acidity. Includes 15% roussanne, barrel matured. — CE

■ **Mischief Maker** *see* Valley Vineyards Wine Company
■ **Miss Molly** *see* Môreson
■ **Misty Kloof's** *see* Goedverwacht Wine Estate

Misty Mountains Estate

Location: Stanford ▪ Map: Elgin, Walker Bay & Bot River ▪ WO: Walker Bay ▪ Est 2004 ▪ 1stB 2008 ▪ Tasting & sales Mon-Fri 10-5 Sat 10-2 ▪ Closed Good Fri & Dec 25 ▪ Barrel tasting on request ▪ Cellar tours by appt ▪ Cheese platters ▪ Conferences (±60 pax) ▪ Owner(s) Misty Mountains Estates (directors LL le Roux & A van Vuuren) ▪ Winemaker(s) Philip Costandius ▪ Vineyard manager(s) Robert Davis ▪ 46ha/16ha (mourv, shiraz, sauv, sem) ▪ PO Box 1874 Hermanus 7200 ▪ info@mistymountains.co.za ▪ www.mistymountains.co.za ▪ S 34° 25'04" E 019° 25'35" ▪ **T +27 (0)28-341-0486** ▪ F +27 (0)28-341-0561

Strangely perhaps, it was water — the discovery of a natural spring — that led to once neglected land between Hermanus and Stanford now bearing vineyards, winery and tasting room. Not to mention grand views (which were always there), a restaurant and other facilities and, of course, 'world class water'.

Single Vineyard range

Shiraz ⊕ ★★★ 09 sweet-fruited, savoury, with rich meaty notes. 60% new oak hides 15% alc. **Sauvignon Blanc** ⊕ ★★★ Herbal, capsicum notes, pungent green fig on last-tasted **10**.

Misty Mountains range

Wooded Sauvignon Blanc ⊕ ★★★★ **10**'s seductive fruitiness integrating with butterscotch whiffs. **Sauvignon Blanc Reserve** ⊕ ★★★★ Herbaceous, quince notes showed on grippy-textured grassy **10** a few years back. Ripe, but moderate intensity & concentration.

Misty Mountains Vineyards range

Pinotage ⊕ 🖵 ★★★★ Step up on previous bottling of **09**: ripe red fruit, fragrant & spicy. Off-dry plushness masks firm finish, but oak evident. — MF

Mitre's Edge

Location: Paarl ▪ Map: Stellenbosch ▪ WO: Simonsberg-Paarl ▪ Est 1999 ▪ 1stB 2004 ▪ Tasting & sales by appt Mon-Fri 9-5 Sat 9-1 ▪ Cellar tours by appt ▪ Guest house B&B ▪ Olive oil ▪ Owner(s) Bernard & Lola Nicholls ▪ Winemaker(s) Lola Nicholls (2004), with Bernard Nicholls ▪ Viticulturist(s) Danie Kritzinger (consultant) ▪ Vineyard manager Bertus de Clerk ▪ 28ha/18ha (cabs s/f, malbec, merlot, p verdot, shiraz) ▪ 150t/1,000cs own label 95% red 5% rosé ▪ PO Box 12290 Die Boord 7613 ▪ info@mitres-edge.co.za ▪ www.mitres-edge.co.za ▪ S 33° 49'47.3" E 018° 52'34.4" ▪ **T +27 (0)21-875-5960** ▪ F +27 (0)21-875-5965

As members of resurgent Paarl Wine Route, boosted by publicity surrounding reality TV series Masterchef South Africa, staged at Nederburg, boutique vintners Bernard and Lola Nicholls are planning to make themselves more visible (via official signage) and available (by opening at set hours vs by appointment currently).

Flagship range

Cabernet Sauvignon ⊕ ★★★★ Vigorous tannin surrounded by cushion of sweetness (sugar & fruit) in appealing, well-composed **08**. **Merlot** Await next.

Mitre's Edge range

Shiraz ⊕ ★★★ 08 plush fruit flavours but tad spiritous from very big alcohol. **Rosé** Not tasted. — CvZ

Mofam Wines

Location/WO: Elgin ▪ Map: Elgin, Walker Bay & Bot River ▪ Est 2005 ▪ 1stB 2010 ▪ Tasting daily 8-5 ▪ Closed Dec 25 ▪ Flavours Restaurant — full à la carte menu ▪ Facilities for children ▪ Tour groups ▪ Conferences ▪ Walks/ hikes ▪ Mountain biking trail ▪ Conservation area ▪ Mofam River Lodge 4-star B&B & self-catering chalets ▪ Owner(s) Derek & Sharon Moore ▪ Cellarmaster(s) Justin Hoy (Dec 2009, consultant) ▪ Winemaker(s) Justin Hoy (Dec 2009, consultant), with Paul Lötter (Mar 2012) ▪ Viticulturist(s) Johan Wiese & Paul Wallace (Jan 2005, consultants) ▪ 260ha/20ha (pinot, shiraz, sauv, viog) ▪ 80t/1,872cs x 6btls own label 25% red 56% white 19% rosé ▪ Global Gap ▪ PO Box 192 Elgin 7180 ▪ paul@mofam.co.za ▪ www.mofam.co.za ▪ S 34° 13'42. 06" E 018° 59'18.30" ▪ **T +27 (0)21-846-8345** ▪ F +27 (0)86-295-0084

Derek and Sharon Moore, after years of nurturing their Elgin vineyards, have finally bottled an own range with the help of winemaker Justin Hoy who, they say, 'carefully sculpted these wines, making Mofam a wine producer not to be under-estimated'. Each wine is named for a family member (Shaz for Sharon, Zar for Zaren), and they have started to make small inroads into the UK and Namibia. They're ardent about protecting their flora and fauna, and guests at Mofam River Lodge can enjoy it all with waterskiing, quad biking, fishing and hiking available.

Zar Pinot Noir ▤ ★★★ Food-styled **11** is dark hued & funky, beefy alcohol noticeable in very firm finish. **Shaz Sauvignon Blanc** ▤ ★★★★ **11** Elgin's green-spectrum notes of nettle, fig & apple; broad & balanced, not too crisp. Bottle-age honey appearing — think about drinking up, or keep & see what happens. — HJ/JP

MolenVliet Wine & Guest Estate

Location/map/WO: Stellenbosch ▪ Est/1stB 2005 ▪ Tasting & sales by appt ▪ Fee R50 ▪ Wedding/conference venue ▪ Self-catering accommodation/B&B ▪ Owner(s) Ockie & Susan Oosthuizen ▪ Winemaker(s) Jan Coetzee (2007, consultant) ▪ Viticulturist(s) Calvin Booysen (2005) ▪ 14ha/8ha (cab, merlot, shiraz) ▪ 13t/±1,250cs own label 100% red ▪ PO Box 6288 Uniedal 7612 ▪ info@molenvliet.co.za ▪ www.molenvliet.co.za ▪ S 33° 54' 52.9" E 018° 56' 30.6" ▪ **T +27 (0)21-885-1597** ▪ F +27 (0)21-885-1684

Wine aside, the main attraction at this winelands lifestyle venue is the wedding and conference facility, which consumes a significant portion of the production. Owners Ockie and Susan Oosthuizen have fashioned a beautiful place in Banhoek Valley to complement their Limpopo lodge and central Stellenbosch guest house.

★★★★ **Cabernet Sauvignon** ⓦ Despite 16% alcohol, **07** achieved elegance & fine balance previously. Full bodied & rounded.

★★★★ **Shiraz** ⓦ **07** last was rich, bold & complex. Silky texture & lingering vanilla chocolate flavours, savoury conclusion.

★★★★ **Proprietors Blend** ⓦ **05** classy Bordeaux blend with enticing blackcurrant/plum & mineral bouquet, tasted for **10** edition.

★★★★ **Diagonal Reserve** ⓦ Full-bodied, elegant shiraz/cab-led **07** offered upfront perfumed black fruit last time.

★★★★ **Meraz** ⓦ Merlot & shiraz in equal proportion, finely structured **07** debut tasted for 2011 guide.

Proprietors Selection ⓦ ★★★ **05** on review offered fresh herbal hints, plum & mulberry flavours. — WB

▪ **Moments Collection** *see* Teddy Hall Wines
▪ **Monfort** *see* Ultra Liquors

Monis Wines

Location: Paarl ▪ WO: Breede River Valley/Calitzdorp ▪ Est 1906 ▪ Closed to public ▪ Owner(s) Distell ▪ Cellarmaster(s)/winemaker(s) Dirkie Christowitz ▪ PO Box 266 Paarl 7620 ▪ dchristowitz@distell.co.za ▪ www.moniswines.co.za ▪ **T +27 (0)21-860-1601** ▪ F +27 (0)21-872-2790

This fortifieds-only cellar is based in Paarl, but draws fruit from areas renowned for each style. Muscadel grapes come from the Breede River, while Calitzdorp supplies traditional Portuguese varieties for the Vintage Port, with the fortifying brandy spirit coming from Monis' own distilleries.

★★★★★ **Wood Matured Muscadel** ⓦ Flame-licked **04** 500ml of irresistible dried orange zest, spice, muscat complexity. Rich, silky sweetness disciplined by 5 years older oak, tangy acid. Breede River fruit.

★★★★ **Tawny Port** ⓦ Gorgeous **96** ex Paarlberg tinta & cinsaut still selling.

Vintage Port ⓦ ★★★★ From Calitzdorp fruit. Dried fruit, leather with touriga's fragrance enhance **06** with its warming spirity tail. Slightly more concentration could lead to higher rating. — AL

Mon Rêve Estate

Location: Paarl ▪ Map: Paarl & Wellington ▪ WO: Simonsberg-Paarl ▪ Est 2009 ▪ 1stB 2011 ▪ Tasting, sales & cellar tours by appt ▪ Fee R15pp, waived on purchase ▪ Closed Easter Fri/Sun, May 1, Dec 25 & Jan 1 ▪ Facilities for children ▪ BYO picnic ▪ Owner(s) Guillaume & Heidi Masson ▪ Cellarmaster(s)/winemaker(s)/viticulturist(s) Marius Malan (Jan 2012) ▪ 12ha/±6ha (cab, merlot, shiraz, muscat d'A) ▪ 8,000L own label 94% red 6% white

+ 12,000L for clients ▪ PO Box 438 Paarden Eiland 7420 ▪ heidim@naturalstonewarehouse.com ▪ S 33° 49'4.98" E 018° 54'47.21" ▪ **T +27 (0)82-379-9937** ▪ F +27 (0)21-511-0880

'We live the dream on our farm outside Paarl: ride horses, grow grapes, make wine,' Heidi Masson modestly says — but she and husband Guillaume also run a thriving Cape Town tiling business 9-5! Marius Malan has signed on as winemaker and future plans include an MCC bubbly — from cabernet.

Cabernet Sauvignon ⊕ ★★★ Youthful **10** is ripe & bold, sweet red-fruit flavours still masked by firm oaking. Needs time. **Single Vineyard Merlot** ⊕ ★★★ Very ripe **10** oozes dark fruit flavours with hint of cured meat smokiness & warm finish. **Appaloosa** ⊕ ★★★ **10** from merlot, cab & splash of shiraz is bold with rich meaty red-berry fruit & firm finish. **Muscat D'Alexandrie** ⊕ ★★★★ Grapey **10** fortified dessert is pretty & unctuous, slightly cloying, needs bit more zing in tail. — FM

Mons Ruber Estate

Location: Oudtshoorn ▪ Map: Klein Karoo & Garden Route ▪ Est ca 1850 ▪ Tasting & sales Mon-Fri 9-5 Sat 9-1 ▪ Closed Easter Sun & Dec 25 ▪ Self-catering accommodation ▪ Farm produce ▪ Hiking trail in proclaimed conservation area ▪ Owner(s) Radé & Erhard Meyer ▪ Winemaker(s) Radé Meyer ▪ Viticulturist(s) Johannes Mellet (consultant) ▪ 38ha (cab, muscadel r/w, chard, chenin, hanepoot, palomino) ▪ ±500t/10,000cs own label 50% red 50% white ▪ PO Box 1585 Oudtshoorn 6620 ▪ monsruber@gmail.com ▪ S 33° 32'1.0" E 022° 28'38.9" ▪ **T +27 (0)44-251-6550** ▪ F +27 (0)86-566-6550

The ever-philosophical Meyer brothers' quaint Klein Karoo outpost, renowned for its traditional distilled and fortified wines (muscadels, jerepigos, ports and brandies), has survived two 'very difficult seasons' (including extreme weather conditions and the demise of a wholesaler partner in business since the 1970s). But 2012's 'abundant winter rain' gave hope for 'regaining lost ground'.

Montagu Wine & Spirits Co

Location: Montagu ▪ Map: Klein Karoo & Garden Route ▪ WO: Klein Karoo/Montagu/Upper Langkloof ▪ Est 1941 ▪ Tasting & sales Mon-Fri 9-5 Sat 9-1 ▪ Owner(s) 79 shareholders ▪ Winemaker(s) Christiaan van Tonder (Rietrivier) & Chris Crafford (Uitvlucht) ▪ 553ha ▪ 10,000t/15,000cs 28% red 22% white 50% muscadel ▪ PO Box 332 Montagu 6720 ▪ admin@mwsc.co.za ▪ www.mwsc.co.za ▪ S 33° 46'59.8" E 020° 7'53.6" ▪ **T +27 (0)23-614-1340** ▪ F +27 (0)86-556-1340

Christiaan van Tonder, master of one of two cellars that vinify for the close to 80 shareholders, had 25% more to work with last year, given the bumper harvest. He reports that MW&SC's recently launched line-up in recyclable 1L plastic bottles — a red, a white and a jerepico — is taking off.

Uitvlucht Wines range
Cabernet Sauvignon ⊕ ★★★ **08** offered honest fruit mid-2009, firm tannins may since have softened. Upper Langkloof WO. **Shiraz** ⊕ ★★★★ **08** deep, dark & voluptuous, more serious than **07** (★★★). **Sauvignon Blanc** 🏠 Not tasted.

Montagu Wine & Spirits Co range

> **Pinotage** ☺ ★★★ Step-up **09** freshest of the red bunch: mulberry & vanilla appeal, deepening tar nuance. **Jerepico Reserve** NEW ☺ ★★★ Fortified NV from red muscadel. Strawberries & a nice nibble of tannin which neutralises the sweetness, gives better balance than range mates. **Jerepico White** ☺ 🏠 ★★★ Latest fortified sweetie from muscadel is NV (previously vintage dated), goes up a notch with rich but uncloying raisin sweetness, hint of apricot in firm moreish conclusion. **Cape Ruby Port** ☺ 🏠 ★★★ Preserved fruit & dates, lively fresh spirit & tannin bite on step-up NV from touriga. Pin-up for the style.

Merlot Await new, as for **Viognier**, **Rietrivier Red Muscadel**, **Muscat de Frontignan**, **Port**. **Rouge** NEW 🏠 ★★ Oak spice & plum on easy-drinking NV equal merlot/pinotage mix. **Chardonnay** 🏠 ★★ Tank sample **12** is lightish, with understated tangy lemon taste. **Chenin Blanc** 🏠 ★★ Thatch-toned **12's** bracing freshness calls for butter-basted braai snoek. **Sauvignon Blanc** NEW 🏠 ⌀ ★★ Demure **12**, faint blackcurrant taste, acidic bite. **Red Muscadel** ⊕ ★★★ **11** fortified sweetie boasts red sultanas & fiery spirit. **White Muscadel** ⊕ ⌀ ★★ Shy fortified dessert **11** has Golden Syrup sweetness & warm tail. **Rietrivier Muscadel White** ⊕ ★★★★ Gorgeous peach & nectarine on fortified **07**, very sweet yet not cloying, well-judged alcohol lends buoyancy, verve. **Jerepico Red** ★★★ Fortified dessert from muscadel, now **NV** & improved: fragrant tealeaf, candyfloss & strawberry complexity, warming spirit glow. **Vintage Port Revolution** ★★★ Fireside sipper **08** from touriga, plum & clean leather, raisin character is more 'fortified dessert' than 'port'. — CvZ/GdB

Montagu Wine Cellar

Location/WO: Montagu ▪ Map: Klein Karoo & Garden Route ▪ Est 1941 ▪ 1stB 1975 ▪ Tasting & sales Mon-Fri 8-5 Sat 9–12 ▪ Closed all pub hols ▪ Cellar tours by appt during harvest 10-4 ▪ Farm produce ▪ Owner(s) 62 members ▪ Cellarmaster(s) Eben Rademeyer (2006) ▪ Winemaker(s) Aldert Nieuwoudt (Nov 2011) ▪ Viticulturist(s) Johannes Mellet (2005, consultant) ▪660ha (11 varieties r/w) ▪ 15,257t/5,500cs own label 12% red 82% white 6% muscadel ▪ IPW ▪ PO Box 29 Montagu 6720 ▪ sales@montaguwines.co.za ▪ www. montaguwines.co.za ▪ S 33° 46′ 37.3″ E 020° 7′ 58.4″ ▪ **T +27 (0)23-614-1125** ▪ F +27 (0)23-614-1793

It was a record harvest last year — almost 25% up — as it was throughout the Breede River region: 'I'm still suffering,' complained cellarmaster Eben Rademeyer several months later, while admitting to being satisfied all round. Once recovered, he plans to supervise a sprucing up of the cellar's public areas.

Colombard ☺ 🍴 🎨 ★★★ Tank sample **12** fresh & pleasantly fruity, light & refreshing. **Late Harvest** ☺ ★★★ Step-up **12** preview offers some pineapple & melon complexity, lipsmacking crisp balance.

Cabernet Sauvignon ⨁ 🍴 ★★★ Straightforward **08** was tad oaky mid-2009. Still selling. **Merlot-Ruby Cabernet** 🍴 Await new vintage. **Chenin Blanc** 🍴 🎨 ★★ **12** stonefruit & hint of flint, fair flavour on lightish body. **Red Muscadel** ⨁ 🍴 🎨 ★★ **10** fortified dessert previewed previously was sweet & warming. **White Muscadel** ⨁ 🍴 ★★★ Tank sample **11** fortified dessert, lovely grapey flavour, light lime lift, long fresh finish. Discontinued: **Montagu Lover's Walk**, **Hanepoot**. — GdB/CvZ

■ **Montagu Wine Company** see Montagu Wine & Spirits Co

Mont Destin

Location/WO: Paarl ▪ Map: Paarl & Wellington ▪ Est/1stB 1998 ▪ Tasting, sales & cellar tours by appt ▪ Closed all pub hols ▪ Open air wine bath ▪ Owner(s) Ernest & Samantha Bürgin ▪ Winemaker(s) Samantha Bürgin (May 1996) ▪ Viticulturist(s) Bertus de Clerk (2006, consultant) ▪ 10ha/7ha (cab, cinsaut, grenache, mourv, shiraz, viog) ▪ 15t/1,000cs own label 100% red ▪ IPW ▪ PO Box 1237 Stellenbosch 7599 ▪ info@montdestin.co.za ▪ www.montdestin.co.za ▪ S 33° 49′ 58.9″ E 018° 53′ 27.8″ ▪ **T +27 (0)21-875-5870** ▪ F +27 (0)21-875-5870

Winemaker and co-owner Samantha Bürgin says they are 'catering for a growing demand for high-end wines with a personal touch, fabulous quality and packaging to match'. No idle boast, proof is found in the fact that flagship Destiny Shiraz is a 2-3 barrel selection, although demand far outstrips supply. Giving new meaning to the term handcrafted, each bottle is hand-labelled, numbered and waxed, the waxing with the participation of 7-year-old son Destin and his grandparents!

★★★★☆ **Destiny Shiraz** ⨁ Stepping up from **06**, elegant & serious **07** (★★★★★) shows exhilarating pristine fruit expression, excellent weight, velvety texture & balance. Lengthy blackberry & black pepper finish bodes well for the future.

★★★★☆ **Passioné** ⨁ Generous & clever blend led by shiraz, cinsaut & mourvèdre. **09**'s rich & earthy, blackberry fruit concentration balanced by firm ripe tannins, moreish conclusion. **08** sold out untasted.

11 Barrels 🍴 🎨 ★★★★ Changing blend, **11** lightly oaked cinsaut & 3 other southern French varieties. Dark fruit, luscious & full-bodied, celebrates ripeness. — CR

Mont du Toit Kelder

Location: Wellington ▪ Map: Paarl & Wellington ▪ WO: Paarl ▪ Est 1996 ▪ 1stB 1998 ▪ Tasting, sales & cellar tours Mon-Fri 9-4.30 Sat by appt ▪ Fee R15/R35 ▪ Closed all pub hols ▪ Walking/hiking trails ▪ BYO picnic, picnic area by arrangement ▪ Guest cottages ▪ Owner(s) Stephan du Toit ▪ Cellarmaster(s) Bernd Philippi & Loftie Ellis (1997, consultants) ▪ Winemaker(s) Chris Roux (2012), with Abraham Cloete (Jan 2005) ▪ Viticulturist(s) Ettienne Barnard (Oct 2010) ▪ ±40ha/±28ha (alicante bouschet, cabs s/f, merlot, mourv, p verdot, shiraz, tinta barocca) ▪ ±165t/±8,000cs own label 100% red; ±1,000cs for clients ▪ IPW ▪ PO Box 704 Wellington

7654 ▪ kelder@montdutoit.co.za ▪ www.montdutoit.co.za ▪ S 33° 39′27.72″ E 019° 1′45.81″ ▪ **T +27 (0)21 873-7745** ▪ F +27 (0)21-864-2737

Owner Stephan du Toit speaks gloomily of wineries having to learn 'the art of survival in an overstocked world' — high taxes not helping. But progress in his corner of Wellington continues. Cabernet franc, for example, joins the range of single-cultivar reds introduced a few years back. There's been a turnover of winemakers recently (welcome Chris Roux!), but two eminent long-time consultants — local Loftie Ellis and German Bernd Philippi — ensure continuity.

Mont du Toit Kelder range

★★★★ **Mont du Toit 07** red has 6 varieties supporting cab — even more than brooding **06** (★★★★★). An interesting, if chunky, package of ripe richness, sweet dark fruit; austere dryness a little awkward.

★★★★☆ **Le Sommet** ⊛ Ambitious blend. Last-tasted **03**'s (★★★★) composition was a secret, like **02**. **Hawequas** ⊛ ★★★ Cab-based combo destined for export markets. **07** had dark fruit, dry oaky end.

Les Coteaux range

★★★★☆ **Cabernet Sauvignon** ⊛ **10** (★★★★) built to last in classic style, as was **09**. Handsome & serious — with even some elegant austerity which should start mellowing in a few years, given the good fruit.

★★★★☆ **Sélection** ⊛ **07** cab-based with merlot + 4 minor contributions. Drier, more elegant than other in range, but no less charming, & with bottle age augmenting classic, delicate fragrance of fruit & cedar. Lots of structure, subtly intense flavours.

Cabernet Franc NEW ★★★★ Attractive herbal fragrance marks the **11**, tasted pre-bottling. Forceful & flavourful though fruit quite light; finish is notably dry; should benefit from few years in bottle. **Merlot** ★★★ Appealing, friendly **11** preview. Light-fruited & modest, but with drily tannic finish. **Shiraz** ★★★★ A serious-minded **11** pre-bottling sample, though sweet ripe fruit lacks intensity to match the big dry tannins. — TJ

■ **Montebello** see Wine-of-the-Month Club

Monterosso Estate

Location/map: Stellenbosch ▪ WO: Stellenbosch/Western Cape ▪ Est/1stB 2000 ▪ Tasting, sales & cellar tour Mon-Fri 9-4 Sat/Sun & pub hols by appt ▪ Fee R10pp ▪ Owner(s) Francesco, Socrate & Orneglio De Franchi ▪ Cellarmaster(s)/winemaker(s) Orneglio De Franchi (Jan 2000) ▪ Viticulturist(s) Francesco De Franchi & Orneglio De Franchi (both Jan 2000) ▪ 83ha/60ha (cab, merlot, ptage, sangio, shiraz, chard, chenin, riesling sauv, sem) ▪ 540t/380cs own label 60% red 40% white ▪ PO Box 5 Stellenbosch 7599 ▪ defranchivin@mweb co.za, monterosso@mweb.co.za ▪ www.monterosso.co.za ▪ S 33° 54′6.8″ E 018° 50′10.4″ ▪ **T +27 (0)21 889-7081/+27 (0)21-889-5021** ▪ F +27 (0)21-889-7081/+27 (0)21-889-5021

'I forgot where I'd parked!' Orneglio 'Meaty' De Franchi candidly admits. That's just one of the consequences of an extremely convivial group tasting (by appointment only) at this Italianate Stellenbosch property. The De Franchi family, including patriarch and Second World War Partisan Socrate, born in Monterosso Al Mare, Liguria, may have lost a few hours fraternising with the customers but sales were brisk...

Sauvignon Blanc ☺ 🍴 🚫 ★★★ Back to quaffable form in **12**, bright, crisp & grassy for easy drinking.

Sangiovese Socrate 🚫 ★★★ Gentle fruitcake & cherry spice simplicity to **10**. Light dry tannins & lithe body. **Cabernet Sauvignon-Merlot** 🚫 ★★★★ Steady as she goes for **10**'s 55/45 mix. Chewy earthiness & tobacco on firm, textured body. Nice long-lasting finish. **Chenin Blanc Old Bush Vine** 🍴 🚫 ★★★ **12** matches previous for ease of access. Light, fresh & fruity. — FM

■ **Montestell** see Boland Kelder

Montpellier

Location/map/WO: Tulbagh ▪ Est 1714 ▪ Tasting, sales & tours Mon-Fri 9-12 & 2-5 Sat 9-12 ▪ Closed all pub hols ▪ Pre-booked cheese platters & light meals available during tasting hours ▪ Tour groups — gazebo with pizza oven ▪ Olives ▪ Walking/hiking trails ▪ Conservation area: Renosterbos ▪ Guesthouse/B&B/self-catering ▪ Weddings ▪ Owner(s) Lucas J van Tonder ▪ Cellarmaster(s) Theo Brink (Jan 2008) ▪ Winemaker(s)/viticulturist(s) Theo Brink (Jan 2008), with Niël Russouw (Dec 2011) ▪ 482ha/60ha (cab, merlot, p verdot, pinot, shiraz hard, chenin, gewürz, viog) ▪ 300t/2,200cs own label 48% red 27% white 25% MCC + 150,000 litres in bulk ▪ PO Box 79 Tulbagh 6820 ▪ montpellier@montpellier.co.za ▪ www.montpellier.co.za ▪ S 33° 16'30.4" E 019° 5'40.0" ▪ **T** +27 (0)23-230-0656 ▪ **F** +27 (0)23-230-1574

Heritage and modernity meet at this verdant old Tulbagh property, where the eco-friendly hay bale insulation for the barrel hall has been such a success that it is being extended to the méthode cap classique bubbly cellar. A young vineyard has come into full production, prompting cellarmaster Theo Brink and team to release the farm's first oak-fermented viognier.

Cabernet Sauvignon ★★★ Touch mint, dark berries on sweet-fruited **10** early drinker. **Shiraz** Await next. **Spyseniersberg** NEW ★★★ Spicy black fruit & brisk acidity on **10** Bordeaux blend cab, merlot & petit verdot; leaner than other reds but more refreshing. **Chardonnay** ★★ Briefly oaked in older barrels, now-bottled **11** is delicately flavoured, doesn't linger. **Chenin Blanc** 🍷 ★★ Brisk **11**, revisited as bottled wine, has faint thatch aroma, equally light flavour. **Gewürztraminer** NEW ★★ Litchi, rosepetal, Turkish Delight – textbook varietal aromas on **10**; year older oak appears to accentuate grape's bitter lift. **Sauvignon Blanc** 🍷 ★ Unrated preview last edition, bottled **11** fresh & light in body, taste. **Viognier** NEW ★★★ Promising **11** pre-view, unblowsy, oak aromas/flavours from 15 months older French wood, convincing apricot entry & conclusion. **Theo's Synchrony** 🍷 ★★★ 50/50 gewürztraminer & chenin. **11**, now bottled, appealing rosepetal-infused summer sipper with well-disguised sweetness. **Méthode Cap Classique** ⓟ ★★★ Traditional-method sparkling NV from pinot noir; apple & strawberry flavours, lively mousse. **Port** ⓟ ★★ Dusty plum-budding NV fireside fortifier from shiraz. — CE/CvZ

Mont Rochelle Hotel & Mountain Vineyards

Location/map: Franschhoek ▪ WO: Franschhoek/Western Cape ▪ Est 1994 ▪ 1stB 1996 ▪ Tasting & sales 10–7 daily ▪ Fee R20 ▪ Closed Dec 25 ▪ Cellar tours Mon-Fri 11, 12.30 & 3 Sat/Sun/pub hols 11 & 3 ▪ Mange Tout & Country Kitchen restaurants (see Restaurants section) ▪ Mont Rochelle Hotel (see Accommodation section) ▪ Conferences/functions ▪ Picnics ▪ Walking/hiking trails ▪ 'Tasting 101' quarterly educational wine tastings ▪ Full moon hikes in summer ▪ Annual harvest festival ▪ Owner(s) Erwin Schnitzler & Rwayitare family ▪ Cellarmaster(s)/winemaker(s)/viticulturist(s) Darran Stone (Jun 2011) ▪ 33ha/16ha (cab, merlot, shiraz, chard, sauv, sem) ▪ 100t/6,000cs own label 60% red 35% white 5% rosé ▪ PO Box 334 Franschhoek 7690 ▪ wine@montrochelle.co.za ▪ www.montrochelle.co.za ▪ S 33° 54'52.1" E 019° 6'21.9" ▪ **T** +27 (0)21-876-2770 ▪ **F** +27 (0)21-876-2362

This is not just a winery, it is a luxurious destination overlooking the Franschhoek Valley and part of the legacy of the late Miko Rwayitare, who made South African history in 2001, in being the first black South African to become the sole owner of a wine estate. Sadly, he passed away before he could enjoy the special oaked chardonnay made in his honour. Cellarmaster Darren Stone will continue to make this wine, fittingly, only in the best vintages.

Miko Premier range

★★★★☆ **Chardonnay Sur Lie** ⓟ Flagship white honours late owner. Cooler **09** (★★★★) when last tasted was intense, youthful, needed time. Shade off previous elegant **06**.

Cabernet Sauvignon Await new vintage.

Mont Rochelle range

★★★★ **Barrel Fermented Chardonnay** ✓ Vivacious **10** is elegantly balanced, with a good marriage of oak, pear, butterscotch & lime. Natural ferment adds richness to lively clean-cut citrus tone. No **09** made.

> **Unwooded Chardonnay** ☺ 🍷 ★★★ **11** delightfully fresh summer quaffer. Gentle pear/melon flavours given a zesty citrus tweak. Walker Bay grapes.

Cabernet Sauvignon ★★★ Richly textured **07** retains supple elegance, with alcohol integrated into juicy fruit & structure. **Merlot** ★★★ Character change in **06** to minty & leafy. Creamy oak pacifies edginess, but best with a meal. **Syrah** ★★★★ Robust **07** is concentrated & juicy. Generous savoury fruit & firm structure absorb alcohol. **Artemis** ★★★ **08** is mostly a Bordeaux blend, splashes shiraz & mourvèdre. Fruit-filled, supple structure for satisfying food-friendly enjoyment. **Rosé** 🍷 ★★ Shiraz-based **11** is savoury & light. Pithy dry exit invites food. **Sauvignon Blanc** 🍷 ★★★ **11** shade off previous (labelled 'Reserve') but still satisfying balance of herbaceous fruit & acid. Dab of oak & semillon add palate weight. — MW

■ **Moody Lagoon** see Benguela Cove

Mooi Bly Winery

Location/WO: Paarl ▪ Map: Paarl & Wellington ▪ Est/1stB 2005 ▪ Tasting, sales & cellar tours by appt ▪ Fee R50pp ▪ Closed Dec 25 & Jan 1 ▪ BYO picnic ▪ Walks ▪ 6 self-catering cottages (see Accommodation section) ▪ Owner(s) Wouters family ▪ Cellarmaster(s)/winemaker(s) Erik Schouteden (Jan 2005) ▪ Viticulturist(s) Erik Schouteden (Feb 2001) ▪ 32ha/18ha (cab, malbec, shiraz, tannat, chard, chenin) ▪ 70t/3,000cs own label 50% red 50% white ▪ PO Box 801 Huguenot 7645 ▪ wine@mooibly.com ▪ www.mooibly.com ▪ S 33° 41' 7.0" E 019° 1' 21.9" ▪ **T +27 (0)21-868-2808** ▪ F +27 (0)21-868-2808

Explaining how rare-in-South-Africa tannat came to be planted here, cellarmaster Erik Schouteden says he first tasted it on home turf Madiran in southwest France, liked it, and that impression was strengthened by a tasting Fairview's Charles Back did some years ago. Wanting something 'unique for the farm', Erik made enquiries, learnt Mooi Bly had the right soils and climate, and the rest, as they say, is history.

Selection range

★★★★ **Malbec** ⓐ Hedgerow fruit, intriguing wax polish note, **08** keeps in dark-toned character. Tasty accessibility via elegant oak-seamed succulence. Drink now till ±2015.

Tannat ⓐ ★★★★ One of only few on market, **08** has earthy, green olive notes, smoky dark fruit. Dry finish from firm but ripe tannins.

Cultivar range

Cabernet Sauvignon Not tasted. **Shiraz** ★★★ **09**'s ripe plums, mulberries backed by grippy dry tannins. Needs rich dishes or some ageing. **Chardonnay** ★★ Muted minerality, light nuttiness, **11** drinks crisply dry. **Chenin Blanc** ✓ ★★★★ Old vines add weight, complexity to **11**. Melon & peach tones, some thatch, textured & long despite admirably moderate 12.5% alc. — CR

Mooiplaas Estate & Private Nature Reserve

Location/map/WO: Stellenbosch ▪ Est 1806 ▪ 1stB 1995 ▪ Tasting & sales Mon-Fri 9-4 Sat 10-2 ▪ Fee R10 ▪ Closed Easter Fri/Sun/Mon, Dec 25/26 & Jan 1 ▪ BYO picnic ▪ Walks/hikes ▪ Mountain biking ▪ 16ha private nature reserve ▪ Langtafel (30 seater) luncheons or dinners every 6-8 weeks in the manor house (a National Monument); Taste Experience presented by Dirk Roos in the 'voorkamer' (10-16 guests); booking essential ▪ Owner(s) Mooiplaas Trust ▪ Cellarmaster(s) Louis Roos (1983) ▪ Winemaker(s) Louis Roos (1983), with Mathilda Viljoen (Jan 2011) ▪ Viticulturist(s) Tielman Roos (1981) ▪ 250ha/100ha (cab, ptage, chenin, sauv) ▪ 750t/8,000cs own label 57% red 41% white 2% rosé ▪ Other export brand: The Collection ▪ BWI, IPW ▪ PO Box 104 Koelenhof 7605 ▪ info@mooiplaas.co.za ▪ www.mooiplaas.co.za ▪ S 33° 55' 16.3" E 018° 44' 21.4" ▪ **T +27 (0)21-903-6273/4** ▪ F +27 (0)21-903-3474

In some instances, more is more. Like when you grow your export market with double digits. But in other cases, less is... well, more. Like when you decrease your range to ensure you remain focused on quality. The team at this family-owned Stellenbosch property achieved both in the past 12 months, and doing so again is what they'll be striving for in those ahead.

The Mercia Collection

★★★★ **Watershed Shiraz** ⓐ Impressive **08** earthy bouquet, unevolved dark-fruit centre & rather firm tannins. Fruit intensity & acid balance show fine potential.

★★★★ **Rosalind** ⓐ Cab-led blend with cab franc & merlot. **07** balanced & lingering, no sharp edges, just an enjoyable — maybe old-fashioned — classic glass of SA red. **06** was more muscular.

★★★★ **Houmoed Chenin Blanc** ⓐ Estate's first barrel-fermented/aged (9 months) chenin. Intriguing fennel, anise, salty interplay on **09**; well-judged oak, knife-like acidity to cut richness of apricot fruit.

Duel Méthode Cap Classique ⓐ ★★★★ **NV** champagne-method sparkling from pinot noir & chardonnay has strawberry sherbet appeal, creamy but dry finish.

Classic range

★★★★ **Chenin Blanc Bush Vine** Old-vine, lees-aged treasure. Regal **11** in different style to voluptuous **10**, but as good. Virtually no botrytis (versus **10**'s 15%) yields fresher aromas, steelier core.

Cabernet Sauvignon ★★★★ Classic cab markers on **06**: cassis, pencil shavings & old leather; taut tannins & properly dry mineral conclusion. Better balanced than **05** (★★★★) when oak slightly out of sync. **Cabernet Franc** ⓐ ★★★ **07**'s ripe black fruit seamed with variety's leafy tones for refreshing mouthfeel. **Merlot** ⓐ

★★★★ Supple but showy **08** boasted morello cherry, plum & smoke. **Pinotage** ⦾ ★★★★ Estate's mainstay grape unoaked for early access, gained some heft from 10% oaked cab in **08** yet retained easy-drinking appeal. **Shiraz** ⦾ ★★★★ Blueberry fruited **05**'s firm tannic structure abetted by 40% new French oak. **Sauvignon Blanc** ⦾ ★★★ **10** had white asparagus & herbaceous bottle-age notes, tangy grapefruit acidity.

Langtafel range

> **White** ☺ 🍷 📖 ★★★ Sample **12** fresh & grassy; satisfying weight & length, cleansing acidity.

Red ⦾ ★★ Creamy blend, mostly merlot in **10**, uncomplicated & enjoyable. **Rosé** ⦾ 📖 ★★★ Leafy **11** pink from cab, a touch sweeter than previous. — CvZ

Mooiuitsig Wine Cellars

Location: Bonnievale ▪ Map: Robertson ▪ Est 1947 ▪ Sales Mon-Thu 8-5 Fri 8-1.30 ▪ Tours by appt ▪ Stay-overs at De Rust Lodge info@outdoorarena.co.za; T +27 (0)23-616-2444 ▪ Owner(s) Jonker & Claassen families ▪ Winemaker(s) Nico van der Westhuizen & Jean Aubrey, with Lazarus Kholomba ▪ Viticulturist(s) Casper Matthee ▪ 150ha total ▪ 2,900t ▪ PO Box 15 Bonnievale 6730 ▪ info@mooiuitsig.co.za ▪ www.mooiuitsig.co.za ▪ S 33° 56'59.0" E 020° 2'36.1" ▪ **T +27 (0)23-616-2143** ▪ F +27 (0)23-616-2675

This family-owned Bonnievale drinks enterprise has its own distribution network and even retail outlets and caters unabashedly to South Africa's enduring off-dry palate, but founder Adolph Jonker's motto 'We strongly believe that the success of our product lies in the consistent production of high-quality grapes', still hangs, metaphorically at least, over the chairman's desk.

■ **Mooiuitzicht** see Mooiuitsig Wine Cellars
■ **Moonlight Organics** see Stellar Winery

Moordenaarskop

Location: Sir Lowry's Pass ▪ Map: Helderberg ▪ WO: Stellenbosch ▪ Est 1999 ▪ 1stB 2002 ▪ Tasting, sales & cellar tours by appt ▪ Owner(s)/cellarmaster(s)/winemaker(s)/viticulturist(s) Graham Smith ▪ 0.33ha (cab) ▪ 2t/ 120cs own label 100% red ▪ PO Box 2889 Somerset West 7129 ▪ mwsmiths@mweb.co.za ▪ S 34° 5'55.3" E 018° 54'53.7" ▪ **T +27 (0)21-858-1202** ▪ F +27 (0)86-672-6797

The breezy 'Cape doctor' (plus a hot 2012 January and lack of rain) was unkind to owner-winemaker Graham Smith, knocking his yield down from 2t to 200kg. But he's in the game for the love of wine and the lifestyle, and maintains his eye on the goal of making small quantities of good, easy-drinking cab.

Cabernet Sauvignon Reserve Occasional release. **Cabernet Sauvignon** ⦾ ★★★ Earthy & savoury **09** quite firm, needs time bottle to soften & show its potential. — IM

Môreson

Location/map: Franschhoek ▪ WO: Coastal/Franschhoek ▪ Est 1983 ▪ 1stB 1994 ▪ Tasting, sales & cellar tours daily 9.30-5 ▪ Fee R30 ▪ Closed Dec 25 ▪ Bread & Wine Restaurant daily 12-3 & The Farm Grocer (for lighter meals) daily 9.30-4.30 ▪ Charcuterie produced by Neil Jewell ▪ Exotic Plant Company ▪ Wine blending & breadmaking ▪ Owner(s) Richard Friedman ▪ Winemaker(s) Clayton Reabow (May 2007), with Marozanne Grobbelaar (Nov 2008) ▪ Viticulturist(s) James McNaught Davis ▪ 35ha/±18ha (chard, chenin) ▪ ±120t 30% red 45% white 25% MCC ▪ Euro Gap, IPW ▪ PO Box 114 Franschhoek 7690 ▪ sales@moreson.co.za ▪ www.moreson.co.za ▪ S 33° 53'11.9" E 019° 3'30.6" ▪ **T +27 (0)21-876-3055** ▪ F +27 (0)21-876-2348

Owner Richard Friedman fulfilled his personal dream by making the first wine on this Franschhoek Valley farm in 1993. It has since become a thriving family business, having been joined by daughter Nikki, as general manager, and her two children. The main focus, with 85% of vines, is chardonnay, made in both still and champagne-method sparkling styles by Clayton Reabow. A super-premium version is next. Named Foxtrot Yankee Mike, it alludes to Richard's other love, flying.

Môreson range

★★★★ **Pinotage** 📖 **11** barrel sample from 18 year old Stellenbosch vineyard too youthful to rate. **10** showed lavish dark fruit, with streamlined, supple structure.

★★★★ **Mata Mata** Merlot & cab franc-led Bordeaux quartet retains elegance & lower alcohol in warm **10** vintage. Good fruit weight, supple oak & tannin framework, but likely earlier maturing than **09**.

★★★★ **Premium Chardonnay** 🖫 Rich & complex **11** (★★★★☆) raises the bar on riper **10**. Four clones of this flagship cultivar show tangy lime & nectarine infused with creamy toasted nut flavours. Will reward cellaring 4-6 years. WO Franschhoek, as for all whites below.

Cabernet Franc ★★★★ **10** shows lovely fruit purity, perfume & length. Balanced & youthful, with development potential. **Magia** Not tasted, as for **Chenin Blanc**, **Pink Brut Rosé**, **Gala Cuvée Cape** & **One** **Méthode Cap Classique**. **Sauvignon Blanc** 🖫 🖫 ★★★★ Vivacious, bright & tropical **12** given extra-crisp verve from splash of nouvelle. Enjoy solo or with a meal. **Solitaire Blanc de Blancs Méthode Cap** **Classique** ★★★★ New NV brightened but restrained by one-third portion 2009 vintage, giving tart lemon & green apple tone. Less harmonious in youth than previous. Time's smoothing hand should restore balance & higher rating. Discontinued: **Petit Verdot**.

Miss Molly range

In My Bed Cabernet Sauvignon-Merlot 🖫 Await new vintage, as for **Hoity Toity Chenin Blanc**, **Kitchen Thief Sauvignon Blanc** & **Méthode Cap Classique**. — MW

■ **Môrewag** see Blomendahl Vineyards

Morgenhof Wine Estate 🍴🍷☕🏠📷✕♿

Location/map: Stellenbosch • WO: Simonsberg–Stellenbosch/Stellenbosch • Est 1692 • 1stB 1984 • Tasting & sales Mon-Fri 9–5.30 (Nov-Apr) & 9-4.30 (May-Oct); Sat/Sun 10-5 (Nov-Apr) & 10-3 (May-Oct) • Fee R20/ Morgenhof, R10/Fantail • Closed Good Fri, Dec 25 & Jan 1 • Cellar tours/viewing of underground barrel cellar on request • Cheese platters • Morgenhof Restaurant (see Restaurants section) • Facilities for children • Gift shop • Conferences • Weddings/functions • Heli-pad • Conservation area • Morgenhof Manor House (see Accommodation section) • Owner(s) Anne Cointreau • Winemaker(s) Andries de Klerk (Jan 2012) • Viticulturist(s) Pieter Haasbroek (Apr 1998) • 212ha/74ha (cabs s/f, malbec, merlot, chenin) • 410t/35,000cs own label • 60% red 38% white 2% rosé • BWI, IPW • PO Box 365 Stellenbosch 7599 • info@morgenhof.com • www. morgenhof.com • S 33° 53'38.5" E 018° 51'39.2" • **T +27 (0)21-889-5510** • F +27 (0)21-889-5266

It's two decades since this winery on the Simonsberg slopes came under French ownership (Anne Cointreau is from the famous cognac and liqueurs family): three centuries earlier the land was granted for farming. More recently, Andries de Klerk arrived as winemaker — just in time for the 'fantastic' 2012 harvest. Another year they like to recall here is 1995, when they decided to pull out a vineyard of chenin blanc. This wasn't done for some reason, and its 1996 crop went into in older French oak barrels for the first time. Awards followed, the vineyard was saved, and still produces lovely wine at the handsome age of 43.

Morgenhof Estate range

★★★★ **The Morgenhof Estate** Cab-driven Bordeaux blend, **06** offers delicious aromas cassis, espresso & Asian spice, with floral note. Firm & well structured, but acid dominant; with some complexity & length.

★★★★ **Chardonnay** **11** (★★★★) preview shows melon, butterscotch, nutty aromas. Creamy & balanced palate supported by poised acidity & subtle oak. Needs time to harmonise; might well gain quality of **09**.

★★★★ **Chenin Blanc** 🖫 🖫 Lightly oaked **11** naturally fermented off 43-year-old vines; plush & packed but still elegant, with fairly modest 13% alcohol, some depth & a lingering finish.

★★★★ **Brut Reserve** Attractive nutty, dried apple & brioche notes on **07** sample from chardonnay & pinot noir. Steely & fresh, an almost severe acidity finely balanced; just enough weight to the elegance.

Cabernet Sauvignon ★★★★ Powerful & concentrated **09** first tasted by us since **06** (★★★★). Densely packed, rich & well structured, but needs a year or 2 to shed some tannin. **Merlot** ★★★★ Beautiful **09** with house's restraint, offers aromas blackberry, dark chocolate & scorched earth. Elegant & classic, with lots of energy; fine tannin & a dry finish. No **08**. **07** (★★★★) more rugged. **Merlot-Cabernet Franc** ★★★ Food-friendly **08** with herbaceous, meaty aromas. In classic style, but slightly acidic, rustic finish. **Sauvignon Blanc** 🖫 🖫 ★★★★ **12** straightforward herbal & tropical flavour mix. Beautiful mouthfeel & palate weight. A preview sample, rating provisional. **Noble Late Harvest** Occasional release. **Cape Vintage** 🕲 ★★★★ Last-tasted **03** had delicacy & power. Dry finish, like previous **00** (★★★★).

Fantail range

Cabernet Franc-Cabernet Sauvignon ☺ ★★★ Switch in name to reflect 85% cab franc on no-problems **09**; redcurrant, cherry & herbaceous notes; juicy but firm.

Pinotage 🍴🖼 ★★★ Juicy & easy drinking as usual, lightly oaked **11** preview has soft & pleasing texture. **Pinotage Rosé** ⊕🍴🖼 ★★★ Delicious, gluggable **11** fresh & nearly dry, with a zesty strawberry finish. This, Pinotage & white blend in this range WO Stellenbosch. **Chenin Blanc-Sauvignon Blanc** ⊕🍴🖼 ★★ Off-dry **11** simple & soft. Discontinued: **Merlot**, **Chardonnay**, **Sauvignon Blanc**, **Semi-Sweet**. —JPf

Morgenster Estate

Location: Somerset West ▪ Map: Helderberg ▪ WO: Stellenbosch ▪ Est 1993 ▪ 1stB 1998 ▪ Tasting & sales Mon-Fri 10-5 Sat/Sun 10-4 ▪ Tasting fee R25 wine/R20 olive oil & olive products ▪ Closed Good Fri & Dec 25 ▪ Sofia's at Morgenster restaurant ▪ Owner(s) Giulio Bertrand ▪ Cellarmaster(s)/winemaker(s) Henry Kotzé (Oct 2009) ▪ Viti-culturist(s) Bob Hobson (Aug 2008) ▪ 200ha/30ha (cabs s/f, merlot, nebbiolo, p verdot, sangio) ▪ ±200t own label 90% red 5% white 5% rosé ▪ BWI, IPW ▪ PO Box 1616 Somerset West 7129 ▪ info@morgenster.co.za ▪ www. morgenster.co.za ▪ S 34° 5'2.9" E 018° 53'7.8" ▪ **T +27 (0)21-852-1738** ▪ F +27 (0)21-852-1141

When Giulio Bertrand purchased this historic Stellenbosch farm, it was with the idea of retiring rather than producing the wine and olive oil Morgenster is now renowned for. It was the hills behind the homestead, reminding him of Tuscany, that changed his mind. Although the main focus is on the Bordeaux varieties, Giulio also introduced the Tuscan sangiovese and Piedmontese nebbiolo, special to him from the wines he grew up with. Winemaker Henry Kotzé admits these Italian classics offer a challenge: 'I'll never be able to reproduce Chianti or Barolo; rather I focus on what I can do, which is to incorporate our style and quality, and emulate the philosophy behind the wines to produce something unique.'

Morgenster Estate range

★★★★☆ **Morgenster** 🖼 Carefully judged merlot (48%), with cab, cab franc & petit verdot blend brings out best in lighter **10**. Less plush than usual, with lively freshness & a fine, succulent grip. Oak subtle enhancement. As drinkable as a good young wine should be; has room to improve in medium term.

★★★★☆ **Lourens River Valley** 🖼 **10** from half cab franc with merlot, cab & petit verdot. Elegant & charming; shows restrained dark berry, spice fragrance, complexity. Sweet flesh contained by natural freshness, fine polished tannins. Balanced to age.

White 🖼 ★★★★ Unrated barrel sample (as 'Sauvignon Blanc-Semillon') last year; partner to red flagship. Aromatic waxy semillon (45%) notes on oaked maiden **11**; palate lighter, less interesting than nose suggests; may grow over short term.

Italian Collection

Tosca 🖼 ★★★★ Initial sour cherry, savoury appeal ex 65% sangiovese in **10** rather diminished by riper, fleshy feel from splashes of merlot & cab. Some finishing punch but early drinking suggested. **Nabucco** 🖼 ★★★★ True-to-type tarry, violet aromas & flavours on light-textured, fresh **10**; buzz of tannin, though more accessible than usual in young nebbiolo. **Caruso** 🖼 ★★★★ **12** rosé from pure sangiovese; plentiful sour cherry attractions, roundly dry, long. Food-friendly. More distinctive than **11**. — AL

▪ **Mori Wines** see Casa Mori
▪ **Morkel** see Bellevue Estate Stellenbosch

Mostertsdrift Noble Wines

Location/map/WO: Stellenbosch ▪ Est/1stB 2001 ▪ Tasting, sales & cellar tours by appt ▪ Fee R10pp for groups ▪ Meals for groups by prior arrangement ▪ Facilities for children ▪ Conference venue ▪ Owner(s) André Mostert & Anna-Mareè Uys (Mostert) ▪ Cellarmaster(s)/winemaker(s) Anna-Mareè Uys (Jan 2001) ▪ Viticulturist(s) Nico Mostert (Jan 2001) ▪ 13ha/±8ha (cab, merlot, pinot, chard, hanepoot) ▪ ±80-100t/1,993cs own label 70% red 10% white 20% rosé + 15,000L bulk ▪ PO Box 2061 Dennesig Stellenbosch 7601 ▪ winemaker@ mostertsdrift.co.za ▪ www.mostertsdrift.co.za ▪ S 33° 53'31.7" E 018° 50'17.6" ▪ **T +27 (0)21-889-5344** ▪ F +27 (0)86-516-1730

Just beyond the northern edge of Stellenbosch town, first turn to your right after Cloetesville, you'll find the easygoing Mosterts plying their trade with little fuss or bother. Winemaker Anna-Mareé's emphasis remains on the light, uncompli cated style for early drinking. No new releases this edition.

Cabernet Sauvignon ⊕ ★★★ Previously, 07 was more accessible than preceding vintage, with nutt complexity & creamy mouthfeel. **AnéRouge** ⊕ ★★★ Mainly cab, rest merlot. Last-tasted 07's well man aged ripe fruit delivered balance & soft appeal. **Cape Blend** ⊕ 🍴 ★★★ Overtly fruity 08 shows som development, good ripeness. Mainly merlot & pinotage (50/30), rest cab. **Merlot Rosé** ⊕ 🍴 ★★ Off-dr 10 preview had tutti-frutti styling when last reviewed. **Chardonnay** ⊕ 🍴 ★★★ 10 charmed previousl with peach & white flower aromas, was tasted pre-bottling. **White Muscadel** Await next. — GdB

Mount Abora Vineyards

Location: Riebeek-Kasteel ▪ Map/WO: Swartland ▪ Est/1stB 2012 ▪ Tasting & sales by appt ▪ Owner(s) Herma Redelinghuys & Krige Visser ▪ Winemaker(s)/viticulturist(s) Johan Meyer ▪ 90ha/10ha (cinsaut, grenache, shi raz, tempranillo, chenin, rouss) ▪ 1,200cs own label 70% red 30% white ▪ PO Box 148 Riebeek Kasteel 7303 ▪ wine@abora.co.za ▪ www.abora.co.za, www.cinsaut.co.za ▪ S 33° 24' 19.8" E 018° 52' 15.0" ▪ **T +27 (0)87 230-7224/+27 (0)82-413-6719/+27 (0)76-474-6349** ▪ F +27 (0)86-683-8132

Named after the imaginary landmark in Coleridge's poem Kubla Khan and based at the Meerhof cellar in the Swartland, Mount Abora aims to make 'luminous wines inspired by the Loire and northern Rhône. Their (untasted) Saffraan is a bid to create 'the pinot noir of the Swartland' using traditional Cape variety cinsaut. Saffronne is a 'delightful spinoff rosé', while Koggelbos Chenin is the result of 'extreme natural winemaking', including mostly hot fermentation and bunch pressing. Their own vineyards are newly planted on ancient south-facing shale and schist sites with exotic Rhône and Spanish varieties. Watch for The Abyssinian, a mourvèdre, shiraz and cinsaut blend due this year.

Mount Abora range

★★★★ **Koggelbos Chenin Blanc** Epitomises serious new-generation Swartland chenin; lovely lees/oa complexity on rich-yet-fresh 11, flavours are fruity (lemon, lime & tangerine) but retain a vibrant mineral core. **Saffronne Cinsaut Blanc de Noir** ★★★ Seriously conceived & priced but gregarious & fun too. Pale blushing 12 tangy & spicy, acidity hovers appetisingly between food & solo. — JP/CvZ

■ **Mountain Eye** see Kleinhoekkloof

Mountain Oaks Organic Winery

Location: Rawsonville ▪ Map: Breedekloof ▪ WO: Slanghoek ▪ Est/1stB 2003 ▪ Tasting, sales & cellar tours by appt ▪ Farm tours & talks on organic farming by appt ▪ Farm produce ▪ Owner(s) Stevens family ▪ Cellar master(s)/winemaker(s) Christine Stevens (2003) ▪ Viticulturist(s) Christine & Mark Stevens (2000) ▪ 200ha, 16ha (cabs s/f, ptage, shiraz, chard, chenin) ▪ 20-30t own label 70% red 20% white 10% rosé ▪ SGS organi certification ▪ PO Box 68 Rawsonville 6845 ▪ christine@mountainoaks.co.za, eikenbosch@iafrica.com ▪ S 33° 38' 16.1" E 019° 13' 36.0" ▪ **T +27 (0)23-344-3107** ▪ F +27 (0)86-613-6687

Local demand for organic wines is picking up, according to co-owner-winemaker Christine Stevens, though exports still count for the majority of her sales. The Slanghoek Valley farm is self-sustaining and, Christine says, 'the whole family is deeply involved, as are the animals who make the farm complete and produce such wonderful fertiliser for our vineyards.'

★★★★ **Pinotage** 🌿 After juicy 10, pre-bottling sample 11 (★★★★) has ripe raspberry scent & deliciou flavours, but perhaps not the depth for its ambitious structure. Drying tannin might resolve in a few years. **Cabernet Sauvignon-Cabernet Franc** 🌿 Await next vintage, as for **Le Jardin Rosé, Chardonnay Reserve, Chenin Blanc Barrel Reserve, Chenin Blanc Reserve, Eikenbosch White** & **Le Jardin Eikenbosch Red** 🌿 ★★★ Lively, pleasant 10 cab/cab franc blend balances ripe flavours with more spicy savoury character. Firmly structured. **Le Jardin Rouge** NEW 🌿 ★★ Pleasant aromas, but porty 11 blend ex tank has more structure than fruit. **Chenin Blanc**✓ 🌿 ★★★★ Returns to the guide with full flavours on 12 preview, but just 12.5% alcohol in overall good balance. A light richness, good texture & pleasant herbal appley finish. — TJ

Mountain Range Products

ocation: Cape Town ▪ Closed to public ▪ Owner(s) Belinda Traverso, Paul Finlayson & Paul de Waal ▪ 1,000cs ▪ 1 Product Street Maitland 7405 ▪ info@mountainrange.co.za ▪ www.mountainrange.co.za ▪ **T +27 (0)21-510-2700** ▪ F +27 (0)21-511-4772

I have no idea what people do with our bottles after drinking the wine!' laughs marketing manager Janet Benn from this tourism-focused business. The Table Mountain-shaped bottles are an unusual souvenir available at outlets around Cape Town, and popular as corporate gifts both at home and overseas.

Table Mountain Red ⓧ ▤ ★★★ Fresh & juicy multi-variety NV combo. **Table Mountain White** ⓧ ▤ ★★★ Granny Smith apple acidity in sauvignon-semillon NV summer sipper. — DB

Mountain Ridge Wines

ocation: Wolseley ▪ Map: Breedekloof ▪ WO: Western Cape ▪ Est 1949 ▪ 1stB 1976 ▪ Tasting & sales Mon-Fri 8–5 ▪ Closed all pub hols ▪ BYO picnic ▪ Owner(s) 20 members ▪ Cellarmaster(s) Paul Malan (Oct 2010) ▪ Winemaker(s) Christo Stemmet (Jan 2010) ▪ Viticulturist(s) Pierre Snyman (consultant) ▪ 477ha (cab, shiraz, henin, cbard) ▪ 6,600t/2,500cs own label 48% red 37% white 15% rosé ▪ IPW ▪ PO Box 108 Wolseley 6830 ▪ ales@mountainridge.co.za ▪ www.mountainridge.co.za ▪ S 33° 28' 42.8" E 019° 12' 16.2" ▪ **T +27 (0)23-231-1070** ▪ F +27 (0)23-231-1102

A programme initiated in 2010 to transform this Wolseley winery from a bulk-wine house into a leading, quality-driven producer of bottled (and bulk) wine is bearing fruit — witness the appearance of red type below. New to the range are the (untasted) De Liefde red and white, available at cellardoor and local retail outlets.

★★★★ **Shiraz Reserve** ⊘ Big, dramatic 10 continues improved form of 09, integrates rich dark berries with elegant tannins, French oak adds boldness. From Hemel-en-Aarde vines.

Cabernet Sauvignon Reserve ⊘ ★★★★ 10, from Stellenbosch grapes, firm tannins supporting ripe blackberry flavours. Could age elegantly. **Shiraz Rosé** ⓧ ▤ ⊘ ★★★ 11 delicate off-dry charmer with strawberry & rosepetal nuances. **Sauvignon Blanc** ▤ ⊘ ★★★ Lightish 12, easy-drinking style, grassy greenpepper & some ripe melon notes. — DB

Mountain River Wines

ocation: Paarl ▪ WO: Western Cape ▪ Est 1993 ▪ 1stB 1998 ▪ Closed to public ▪ Owner(s) De Villiers Brits ▪ Cellarmaster(s) De Villiers Brits, with consultants ▪ 1.2ha (shiraz) ▪ 30,000cs own label 60% red 40% white ▪ 46 Main Road Paarl 7646 ▪ dev@mountainriverwines.co.za, mattie@mountainriverwines.co.za ▪ www.mountainriverwines.co.za ▪ **T +27 (0)21-872-3245/6/7** ▪ F +27 (0)21-872-3255

Owner and winemaker De Villiers Brits wanted to honour the giraffe and his country when it came to naming his Zaràfa range. Using ZA, the international code for South Africa, and a little flair he arrived at a name that should be easy to pronounce in Russia, destination for large export quantities!

Mountain River range

Pinotage New vintages of this & **Pinotage-Shiraz** not ready at print time.

Maankloof range

Chenin Blanc ☺ ▤ ⊘ ★★★ Tank sample 12 is zingy, better balanced than sauvignon; attractive thatch/hay characters, satisfying dryness. And just 12% alcohol.

Cabernet Sauvignon ▤ Not tasted. **Pinotage** ★★ Crushed sage, dark berry 11 slips down easily, leaves sweet impression. **Shiraz** Not reviewed. **Sauvignon Blanc** ⊘ ★★ Racy acidity on nettly, very dry 12 slimmer's friend.

Jkuzala range

Dry Red ⓧ ★★ 11 merlot-led combo previewed last edition. Supple & fresh, lightish for youthful enjoyment. **Dry White** ⓧ ★★ Lemon & thatch tones on 11, from chenin & colombard.

Zaràfa range

Cabernet Sauvignon 🗺 ★★ Now bottled, **11** fruit-filled quick-sip with good grip, moderate 13.5% alcohol. **Pinotage** 🗺 ★★ No rough edges on strawberry-infused **11**, light textured despite 14% alcohol. **Shiraz** 🗺 ★★ **12** faint red fruits, fresh acidity, gruff end. **Sauvignon Blanc** 🗄 🗺 ★★ Lipsmacking acidity on grassy **12**. Discontinued: **Pinotage Rosé**. — CvZ

■ **Mountain Shadows** see Wineways Marketing
■ **Mountain Stream** see Ashton Wynkelder
■ **Mountain View** see Farm 1120

Mount Babylon Vineyards

Location: Hermanus ▪ Map: Elgin, Walker Bay & Bot River ▪ Est 2002 ▪ 1stB 2007 ▪ Tasting, sales & cellar tours by appt ▪ Cheese platters ▪ Owner(s) Johan Holtzhausen ▪ Winemaker(s) Jean-Claude Martin (2008, consultant) ▪ Viticulturist(s) Johan Pienaar (2002, consultant) ▪ 65ha/6ha (malbec, shiraz, viog) ▪ ±38t/±200cs own label 90% red 10% white ▪ PO Box 7370 Stellenbosch 7599 ▪ info@mountbabylon.co.za ▪ www.mountbabylon.co.za ▪ S 34° 19'44.0" E 019° 19'34.3" ▪ **T +27 (0)21-855-2768/+27 (0)84-511-8180** ▪ F +27 (0)21-855-2768

Johan Holtzhausen owns this small family business, the most inland of the Hemelen-Aarde wine-farms. As a corporate financier, he says, winemaking was 'a dream realised when I bought our own little "Heaven on Earth"' of vines, fynbos and birdsong. Since then (is he surprised?), 'passion has often ruled common sense!'

★★★★ **SMV** ⊛ Bright & refreshing **07** (★★★★) last showed mocha, chocolate aromas; harmonious but lacking complexity & concentration of maiden **06** (from 87% shiraz, with malbec, viognier).

★★★★ **Pioneer Brut Reserve** ⊛ Polished **07** tasted last year, a rare 100% shiraz blanc de noir MCC sparkling. Apricot-tinged, with berry hints, intriguing nuttiness & herbal persistence. — MF

Mount Pleasant Vineyards [NEW]

Location: Darling ▪ Est 2009 ▪ 1stB 2011 ▪ Closed to public ▪ Owner(s) Pascale Palmer & the Legner family ▪ Winemaker(s) Wim Smit (Dec 2010, Hofstraat) ▪ Viticulturist(s) Alfred Legner (Jun 2006) ▪ 0.2ha/0.1ha (shiraz) ▪ 2t/ha 33cs own label 100% red ▪ 11 High Street, Darling 7345 ▪ info@darlingmusic.org ▪ **T +27 (0)72-015-1653**

Former London banker Alfred Legner, arts patron of the creative West Coast community of Darling, views 'fine wine, like good food and classical music', as 'an expression of culture'. When not managing the classical/contemporary Darling Music Experience (conceived in 2006 with leading SA conductor David Tidboald and composer Hendrik Hofmeyr, and featuring local and international musicians), Alfred tends vines on his 0.2ha property. Darling Pascale's Shiraz (after Mount Pleasant partner Pascale Palmer) is made by Hofstraat Kelder.

Mount Rozier Estate

Location: Sir Lowry's Pass ▪ Map: Helderberg ▪ WO: Stellenbosch ▪ Est/1stB 2011 ▪ Tasting & cellar tours by appt only ▪ Wine sales Mon-Fri ▪ The Peacock Cottage; Mount Rozier wedding & conference venue (T +27 (0)73-338-7032/shelleyr@journeysend.co.za) ▪ Owner(s) Gabb family ▪ WIETA ▪ PO Box 3040 Somerset West 7129 ▪ wines@mountrozier.co.za ▪ www.mountrozier.co.za ▪ S 34° 6'21.22" E 018° 54'35.80" ▪ **T +27 (0)21-858-1929** ▪ F +27 (0)86-540-1929

This scenic Sir Lowry's Pass property in the Helderberg Bowl continues the revitalisation begun when it was acquired by the Gabb family of Journey's End. 'The label,' says Rollo Gabb, 'is classical with a twist, and mirrors styles of the early 20th century when the original Mount Rozier homestead was built.' He adds: 'This is also reflected in our winemaking — traditional with a contemporary twist.'

Myrtle Grove Cabernet Sauvignon [NEW] 🗄 🗺 ★★★ **10** most reticent of the line-up: just-discernible cassis & lead pencil, austere tannins. Very tight, needs time or food. **The Beekeeper Merlot** [NEW] 🗄 ★★★ Olive & meaty savouriness in **10**, light textured, touch sweetness helps smooth tad lean tannins. **Tobacco Street Shiraz** [NEW] ★★★★ Cardamom & fennel infused **10**, light textured with well-judged oak (±15 months in small French barrels, as for all reds). **Cabernet-Merlot-Cabernet Franc-Petit Verdot** [NEW] 🗄 ★★★ Mixed berry compote, liquorice & cigarbox notes on juicy & uncomplex easy-sipping **10** 4-way Bordeaux blend. **Peacock Chardonnay** NEW ★★★ **11** forthcoming lemon-lime notes, zesty acidity & reined-in alcohol, light oaking (6 months) for early enjoyment. **The Garland Sauvignon Blanc** NEW ✓ 🍴 ★★★★ Tropical-toned **11** packed with flavour, has brisk acidity, composure & good length. Very drinkable, nudges next level. — CvZ

Mount Vernon Estate

Location: Paarl ▪ Map: Paarl & Wellington ▪ WO: Simonsberg-Paarl/Western Cape ▪ Est 1996 ▪ 1stB 2005 ▪ Tasting, sales & cellar tours Mon-Fri 9-4 Sat 10-3 ▪ Light snacks available ▪ Picnics (booking essential) ▪ Owner(s) David & Debbie Hooper ▪ Cellarmaster(s) Debbie Hooper (Jan 2003) ▪ Winemaker(s) Debbie Hooper (Jan 2003), with Philip du Toit (Jan 2005) ▪ Viticulturist(s) Philip du Toit (Jun 1997) ▪ 110ha/27.5ha (cab, malbec, merlot, p verdot, ptage, shiraz, chard) ▪ 210-225t/1,800cs own label 80% red 15% white 5% rosé ▪ PO Box 348 Klapmuts 7625 ▪ john@mountvernon.co.za ▪ www.mountvernon.co.za ▪ S 33° 48′ 57.8″ E 018° 52′ 51.9″ ▪ **T +27 (0)21-875-5073** ▪ F +27 (0)86-618-9821

The Hoopers, who run liquor distributors E Snell, have taken a family seat in Klapmuts north of Stellenbosch. For the past six generations, every male Hooper child has been given the middle name Vernon, so it was a small, logical leap to name their farm after US president George Washington's spread on the Potomac River. New buildings and additions have been springing up all over the estate: barrel cellar extensions, bulk store, offices and a tasting room.

Mount Vernon range

★★★★ **Cabernet Sauvignon** Soft & plush, with a deep, dark side, impressive **09** shows subtle glimpses of liquorice & blackcurrants through satin tannins. Easily upstages less ripe **08** (★★★★).

★★★★ **Malbec 09** is darker, more brooding than previous, seasoned with sweet oak spiciness. Characterful, with substance & presence, promising improvement with some age.

Chardonnay Single Vineyard 🍴 ★★★ Gains 'Single Vineyard' suffix this edition. As in **10**, oaky **11** drowns out brave attempt by ripe & willing citrus fruit. May integrate better with time.

Three Peaks range

Pinotage ☺ 🍴 🎨 ★★★ Toasty oak dominates, but spicy berries show through on **11**, big improvement on previous. **Jean Pierre's Lunchtime Rosé** ☺ 🍴 🎨 ★★★ **12** blend, now merlot-led, retains dry strawberry-juice style.

Cantata ✓ 🍴 🎨 ★★★★ Vibrant, appealing up-front dark cherry fruit on **10**, now shiraz-led 6-way blend, with commendable body & finish. **Sauvignon Blanc** ⓣ 🍴 🎨 ★★★ Fresh & sprightly **11** shows promise. Light, likeable & unpretentious fruit-driven quaffer. WO W Cape. — GdB

Mulderbosch Vineyards

Location/map: Stellenbosch ▪ WO: Stellenbosch/Western Cape ▪ Est 1989 ▪ 1stB 1991 ▪ Tasting & sales Tue-Sun & pub hols 10-6 ▪ Fee R35 ▪ Closed Mon, Easter Fri-Mon, Dec 25 & Jan 1 ▪ Pizzas & cheese boards, cappuccinos, artisanal beer, juice ▪ Gift shop ▪ Olive oil ▪ Bocce ball courts (Italian boules) ▪ Conservation area ▪ Owner(s) Terroir Capital ▪ Winemaker(s) Adam Mason (Dec 2011), with Annalie van Dyk (Jan 2009) ▪ Viticulturist(s) Lucinda Heyns (Jun 2011) ▪ 80ha/45.2ha (cabs s/f, merlot, p verdot, shiraz, chenin, nouvelle, sauv, viog) ▪ BWI ▪ PO Box 12817 Die Boord Stellenbosch 7613 ▪ info@mulderbosch.co.za ▪ www.mulderbosch.co.za ▪ S 33° 53′ 22.8″ E 018° 49′ 8.3″ ▪ **T +27 (0)21-881-8140** ▪ F +27 (0)21-881-3514

Terroir Capital, the California-based investment group focused on wine-related hospitality, purchased Mulderbosch in late 2010, with the intention of taking this brand to the next level, and one of the most significant developments has been the appointment of Adam Mason (previously at Klein Constantia) as winemaker at the end of 2011. Mulderbosch currently has a good foothold in the US, with around 35% of its annual production exported there, and one of Mason's key tasks will be to build on this. Chenin blanc is set to feature prominently, volumes of the ever-reliable Steen op Hout to be increased as well as more premium offerings due to come on line. 'Mulderbosch deservedly enjoys much goodwill amongst its loyal consumer base globally, and we dare not disappoint,' says Mason.

★★★★☆ **Faithful Hound** Complex & complete Bordeaux-style red **10** shows cassis, violets, cigarbox, hir of coffee, basically everything you could wish for. Pure, perfectly delineated fruit, fresh acidity, fine tannins Long, dry finish. Big & bold but balanced.

★★★★ **Chardonnay** 🎨 Impeccably constructed **11** shows citrus, white blossom & subtle vanilla aromas Great fruit purity, snappy acidity, unobtrusive oak (30% new) on palate. Should keep until at least 2016. No **10**.

★★★★☆ **Chardonnay Barrel Fermented** 🎨 **10** all about reined-in power. Very expressive, with note of ripe citrus, burnt matchstick & intriguing leesy wet wool. Huge concentration, layers of flavour, scintillating acidity. Spontaneous ferment, nine months in French oak, 100% new.

★★★★ **Small Change Chenin Blanc** ⏱ **09** (★★★★) even more extravagant than **08**, with high suga (±15 g/l), 10% botrytised sauvignon. Rich, dense, with wide array of flavours including citrus, peach & apricot.

★★★★ **Sauvignon Blanc Noble Late Harvest** ⏱ Still-selling **09** is relatively light & fresh, with notes c honey, slight pepperiness, botrytis character not very much in evidence; 6 months in oak, 100% new.

Cabernet Sauvignon Rosé 🍴 🎨 ★★★ Shocking pink in colour, **12** is well balanced, with juicy red fruit lively acidity. Serve with cold crayfish salad. Coastal WO. **Chenin Blanc** 🍴 🎨 ★★★★ Aka 'Steen op Hout **11** (★★★★) is fruit-driven, medium bodied, clean & fresh. Juicy white peach flavour before dry finish. Pre viewed **12** is step up, more concentrated & complex — apricot, yellow peach, some leesy character. Rich & fu with tangy acidity. W Cape WO, like next. **Sauvignon Blanc** 🍴 🎨 ★★★★ Tank sample **12** rather lean & tight with apparently high acidity. Hint of gunpowder, lime & some paprika on the finish. — CE

Mullineux Family Wines

Location: Riebeek-Kasteel ▪ Map/WO: Swartland ▪ Est 2007 ▪ 1stB 2008 ▪ Tasting, sales & tours Mon–Fri & Su by appt Sat 10–3 ▪ Closed Easter Sun, Dec 25 & Jan 1 ▪ Owner(s) Mullineux Family Wines (Pty) Ltd ▪ Cella master(s)/winemaker(s)/viticulturist(s) Chris & Andrea Mullineux (May 2007) ▪ 18ha (carignan, cinsau mourv, shiraz, chenin, clairette, viog) ▪ 90t/4,500cs own label 50% red 40% white 10% dessert ▪ PO Box 36 Riebeek-Kasteel 7307 ▪ info@mullineuxwines.com ▪ www.mullineuxwines.com ▪ S 33° 23′1.16″ E 18°53′4(65″ ▪ **T +27 (0)22-448-1183** ▪ F +27 (0)86-720-1541

Wife Andrea, raised with wine in an American Italian family, really wanted to b an astronaut, but went straight to UC Davis to study oenology. Husband Chris, o the other hand, switched from accounting to wine at Stellenbosch at the age o 21, in a fortuitous epiphany. Their paths first crossed on an overseas workin experience in southern France, and again at Tulbagh Mountain Vineyards which they left in 2007 to set up Mullineux Family Wines. They have been at th forefront of the Swartland's terroir-focused resurgence, which defines their sty listic aspirations. Their scale and pretensions are modest, but their status is soar ing. In their first three listings in this guide, they garnered an impressive four star ratings, to which they now add another three, plus Red Wine of the Year fo their Syrah 10. No wonder Mail & Guardian listed them in the Top 20 Sout African wineries.

Terroir Specific range [NEW]

★★★★☆ **Granite Syrah** 🎨 This & Schist Syrah a seminal study in terroir. Near identical viticulture & win making show soil's effect to great advantage. **10** granite produces ethereal Rhône-like violets & pepper spice couched in supple 'feminine' form.

★★★★★ **Schist Syrah** 🎨 Second, more 'masculine' sibling of **10** terroir twins is bolder, richer, but retair beguiling floral fragrance, with a touch more muscle on the supple body. Hints of fruitcake & tobacco, same sill texture.

Mullineux Family Wines range

★★★★★ **Syrah** 🎨 Restraint & moderation triumph over excess in impressive **10**, our Red Wine of the Yea Understated elegance, faultless composition & balance, mystifying complexity from back-to-basics treatme of special vineyard blocks. An icon in the making.

★★★★☆ **White Blend** 🎨 Captivatingly subtle blend of very special blocks of Swartland chenin, clairette viognier, expertly handcrafted into a Cape benchmark. **11** follows impeccable class of **10** (★★★★★) & prev ous; nuanced & balanced with a gracious peacock's tail finish.

★★★★★ **Straw Wine** 🎨 Mesmerising tobacco-like aromas, intense spiciness & unctuous honey sweetness elevate benchmark vin de paille above rivals in **11**. Air-dried chenin, fermented for 6 months in old oak, retains all the variety's charm.

Kloof Street range

★★★★ **Swartland Rouge** 📖 Unassuming 2nd-tier range still gets the full house-style treatment. **11** is mostly shiraz, but still echoes Côtes du Rhône-style juiciness with peppery spices. **10** sold out untasted.

★★★★ **Chenin Blanc** 🍴 📖 Enviable second label from old Swartland vines, **12** combines rich, lees/mineral structure with vibrant tropical fruit. Elegant & complex, yet exuberantly youthful. — GdB

Muratie Wine Estate 23-12-12   🍴🍵⛰️📷

Location/map: Stellenbosch • WO: Stellenbosch/Simonsberg–Stellenbosch/Western Cape • Est 1685 • 1stB ca 1920 • Tasting & sales daily 10–5 • Fee R20/5 wines R30/port & chocolate • Closed Good Fri, Dec 25/26 & Jan 1 • Cellar tours by appt • Light lunches daily 12–3 • Cheese platters • Conference/function venue • Art gallery • Guest cottage • Harvest festival with live music • Owner(s) Melck Family Trust • Cellarmaster(s) Francois Conradie (Dec 2005) • Winemaker(s) Francois Conradie (Dec 2005) & Simon Zeeman (2005) • Viticulturist(s) Francois Conradie (1995), assisted by Paul Wallace • 110ha/42ha (cab, merlot, pinot, shiraz, chard, hanepoot, port) • 300t/15,000cs own label 60% red 14% white 6% rosé 20% other • BWI, IPW, IPW • PO Box 133 Koelenhof 7605 • info@muratie.co.za • www.muratie.co.za • S 33° 52' 14.8" E 018° 52' 35.1" • **T +27 (0)21-865-2330/2336** • F +27 (0)21-865-2790

They take history seriously at Muratie, with wines named after important figures from the estate's past, like young German soldier Laurens Campher (1685-1735), the first owner, who fell in love with and married slave girl Ansela van de Caab. MCC 1763 commemorates the date the first Melck bought the farm, while later owner/painter George Paul Canitz planted the country's first pinot noir. He also created Amber in the 1940s, so named for the colour and the novel Forever Amber. His daughter Alberta Annemarie inherited the farm, and her talented wine- and port-maker Ben Prins was renowned for always wearing shorts and no shoes. Then famous wine personality Ronnie Melck bought the estate in 1987, realising a long-held dream. Coming full circle, Rijk, his son and CEO, has a daughter, Isabella.

Apex range

★★★★ **Ronnie Melck Shiraz Family Selection** ⊕ Premium low-yielding grapes for this. Last time **08** (★★★★★) showed greater complexity & structure than **07**. Bold intense aromas, core of cassis & mulberry.

Flagship range

★★★★☆ **Ansela van de Caab** Cab-led Bordeaux blend a handsome figure: opulent fruitcake perfume jumps out of the glass, gutsy & vibrant **09** is packed with flavour. Well oaked but no hard edges.

★★★★ **Laurens Campher** 📖 Changing oaked blend, chenin-led in **11** with 3 others; exotic mix of melon preserve, dried peach, lime pickle freshness. Each variety plays its part, the result is delicious. Stellenbosch WO.

Premium range

★★★★ **George Paul Canitz Pinot Noir** 📖 Red berries & forest floor notes vie for attention in **10** as pinot reveals its multiple personalities. Good oak adds seasoning & a firm base for some ageing.

★★★★☆ **Ronnie Melck Shiraz** 📖 Renamed from 'Shiraz' to honour family patriarch & industry luminary who loved shiraz. Dense & dark toned, **10** is a force to be reckoned with (as was its namesake), seriously made to develop over next 10 years. Start drinking after year or 2.

★★★★ **Isabella Chardonnay** 📖 Clementine preserve, honeycomb & roasted nuts, **11** isn't shy, struts its stuff, will make many conquests. Rich, full-flavoured with lemon zest livening freshness.

★★★★ **1763 Methode Cap Classique** Fennel & green apple perfumed **09** has piercing freshness, perfect as an aperitif. The biscuit thread from 26 months bottle ferment doesn't detract from the essential character.

Alberta Annemarie Merlot ★★★★ Was 'Merlot'. Succulent cherries & blackcurrants in **09**, oak fully integrated, adding white pepper spicing. Stellenbosch WO for all except MCC. Discontinued: **Cabernet Sauvignon**.

Fortified Wines range

★★★★ **Cape Ruby** Deep rich fruitcake & brandy, this port-style **NV**'s perfume is already seductive & the flavours don't disappoint either. Nutty, a savoury underpin, finishing with a livening alcohol grip. WO Stellenbosch.

★★★★ **Ben Prins Cape Vintage** Name change from 'Cape Vintage'. Cocoa dusting on **09**'s deep fruitcake richness, with spirit adding grip to the sweetness. Classic styling, from Portuguese port varieties, as LBV.

★★★★ **Late Bottled Vintage** With its prune-rich black toffee flavours, **07** is the ideal fireside companion, mellow, warming & delicious. Perfectly judged 5-year barrel ageing.

Amber Forever ★★★★ Fortified dessert mainly muscat d'Alexandrie. Notch up on **09** (★★★★), showing expected sultana richness, **10**'s surprise is a very tasty spicy ginger pudding tone throughout. WO W Cape.

Melck's range

> **Shiraz-Cabernet Sauvignon** ☺ 🍽 ★★★ Name change from 'Red', but our Superquaffer of the Year remains a model of lively drinkability. Juicy black plums with a spice infusion, **11**'s partial oaking well managed, leaving a curvaceous smoothness.

Cabernet Franc Rosé 🍽 🖼 ★★★ Cranberries, sprinkle of herbs, dry **12** showcases the variety. **Sauvignon Blanc** 🍽 🖼 ★★★ Previously 'White'. Minerality & gooseberry, light-textured **12** drinks easily. WO Western Cape, as rest. — CR

Mvemve Raats

Location/map/WO: Stellenbosch ▪ Est/1stB 2004 ▪ Tasting & sales by appt ▪ Fee R200 (up to 20 pax per tasting) ▪ Closed all pub hols ▪ Owner(s) Bruwer Raats & Mzokhona Mvemve ▪ Cellarmaster(s)/viticulturist(s) Bruwer Raats & Mzokhona Mvemve (both Jan 2004) ▪ Winemaker(s) Bruwer Raats & Mzokhona Mvemve (both Jan 2004), with Gavin Bruwer Slabbert (Feb 2010) ▪ 5t/ha ▪ 450cs (6btl) own label 100% red ▪ PO Box 2068 Stellenbosch 7601 ▪ braats@mweb.co.za ▪ www.raats.co.za ▪ S 33° 58' 16.6" E 018° 44' 55.3" ▪ **T +27 (0)21-881-3078** ▪ F +27 (0)21-881-3078

Bruwer Raats and Mzokhona Mvemve reckon that every bottle of this, their joint venture, should be hand-sold. Which is not a problem for either of these two likeable, voluble enthusiasts — both have plenty to say, particularly about their favourite cabernet franc. Export orders and overseas accolades continue to fall their way but Bruwer (of Raats Family Wines) and Mzokhona count themselves most fortunate to be working for themselves, doing what they love.

★★★★★ **MR De Compostella** Breakaway from cab franc dominance in 09 (★★★★★) makes absorbing, complex mouthful (& step up from **08**). Alternates between powerful & elegant, intense cherry/berry notes supported by seamless tannins & hints of spice. Equal malbec & cabs franc & sauvignon, dashes petit verdot & merlot, made to last. — CM

■ **Mwitu** see African Terroir
■ **My Best Friend** see Zandvliet Wine Estate & Thoroughbred Stud

My Wyn

Location/map/WO: Franschhoek ▪ Est/1stB 2001 ▪ Tasting, sales & cellar tours Mon-Fri 10-1 Oct-Apr; after hours weekends & pub hols by appt or as indicated on the gate ▪ Fee R50pp, waived on purchase ▪ Sunset MCC tastings on koppie (15min walk, weather permitting) by appt only ▪ Cheese platters by prior booking ▪ Owner(s) Jacoline Haasbroek ▪ Winemaker(s) Jacoline Haasbroek (2001) ▪ 1,250cs (6btl) own label 40% red 20% white 20% port 20% MCC ▪ IPW ▪ PO Box 112 Franschhoek 7690 ▪ tastewine@telkomsa.net ▪ www.mywynfranschhoek.co.za ▪ S 33° 53' 29.3" E 019° 8' 3.6" ▪ **T +27 (0)21-876-2518, +27 (0)83-302-5556** ▪ F +27 (0)86-608-0233

Never one for high heels and makeup, Franschhoek garagiste Jacoline Haasbroek also believes in 'working with the best of what nature provides' when it comes to winemaking. But her Wine Thief Semillon was a case of zero intervention: a barrel made by never-identified pranksters attending her mid-harvest braai for local vintners! 'It developed into a little gem — worthy of a separate bottling.'

My Wyn range

★★★★ **Petit Verdot** 🖼 Excellent but brashly youthful **10** takes no prisoners: opaque & brooding, vibrant blackberry fruit, bracing tannins & mouthwatering acidity. Don't broach until 2015.

★★★★ **Semillon** NEW 🖼 Only older oak for layered **11** offering: stonefruit, cream & vanilla contrast with slight grass & dust. Velvety, slips down easily now but has structure to improve few years.

Cabernet Franc 🖼 ★★★★ Balanced **10** boasts bright berry fruit, engaging herbal edge, handles 15% alcohol with aplomb. A regular on Franschhoek's renowned Le Quartier Français' tasting menu. **Merlot** Not ready at press time, like **Amber**. **Shiraz** ★★★ High 15.5% alcohol & strong tannins detract from ripe mulberry fruit on **09**. Might soften & meld given time. **Chardonnay** NEW 🖼 ★★★★ New oak fermented **10** is sweet fruited & smooth, with attractive yellow-gold hue; just-out-the-oven apple pie, cinnamon & clove deliciousness. **Viognier** 🖼 ★★★ **11** exudes honey, pears & peaches; touch sugar sweetness & gentle pétillance

Sauvriognier ★★★★ Equal partnership older-barrel-fermented sauvignon & viognier (what else!) yields all the richness of the Rhône variety & briskness of the Loire. Sip **11** solo or with elegant fare. **Méthode Cap Classique** ★★★★ Lean & savoury **09** 56/44 chardonnay/pinot noir sparkling is perfect for oysters. **Robyn** ★★★ Shiraz fortified with 3 year old potstill brandy for pleasant fireside sipping. **09** Xmas pud & dark chocolate; lighter than most port-styles.

The Wine Thief range [NEW]

★★★★☆ **Semillon** Barrel-fermented version **10** opulently fruited, dusted with vanilla, well integrated & very persistent, turns savoury in the farewell. Superb! Will steal your heart. — WB/IM

Mzanzi *see Kingsriver Estate*

Mzoli's Wines

Location: Cape Town ▪ Map: Cape Peninsula ▪ WO: Darling ▪ Meals & tasting daily 11-8 ▪ Owner(s) Mzoli Ngcawuzele ▪ NY 115 Shop No 3 Gugulethu 7750 ▪ mzoli@darlingwine.co.za ▪ www.mzoliwine.co.za ▪ S 33° 58'34.9" E 018° 34'11.1" ▪ **T +27 (0)21-638-1355/+27 (0)82-487-0980**

The shisa nyama ('buy and barbecue') offered at Mzoli's Place in Gugulethu is a 'must do' attraction for tourists to Cape Town. The larger-than-life man behind it, Mzoli Ngcawuzele, now has a red wine called Madala, fittingly bottled in magnum. He also oversaw an expanded Gugulethu Wine Festival, and presented his wines in Johannesburg for the first time.

Mandisi Merlot ☺ ★★★ Light smoke & mulberry, **11** medium depth but attractively soft, approachable.

Madala [NEW] ★★★★ 'The Elder' also the most serious wine in meat-friendly range. Cab & merlot in **11**, layers of black berry, spice & liquorice. Good grip; long, velvety finish. **Unathi** ★★★ Herbal fynbos edge to black cherry succulence of **09**, different blend to version tasted last edition. **One One Five Rosé** Await next. — FM

Nabygelegen Private Cellar

Location: Wellington ▪ Map: Paarl & Wellington ▪ WO: Wellington/Western Cape ▪ Est 2001 ▪ 1stB 2002 ▪ Tasting, sales & cellar tours Mon-Fri 10-5 Sat 10-1 ▪ Closed all pub hols ▪ Picnics (booking essential) ▪ Tour groups ▪ Conferences/functions ▪ Small weddings ▪ Walks/hikes ▪ Mountain biking trail ▪ Self-catering luxury accommodation & rustic river cabin ▪ Owner(s) James McKenzie ▪ Cellarmaster(s) James McKenzie (Jan 2002) ▪ Winemaker(s) Charles Stassen (consultant), with Maria Bosman (Jan 2002) ▪ Viticulturist(s) Johan Wiese (May 2001, consultant) ▪ 35ha/17ha (cab, merlot, p verdot, tempranillo, chenin, sauv) ▪ 180t/12,000cs own label 50% red 50% white ▪ PO Box 302 Wellington 7654 ▪ marketing@nabygelegen.co.za ▪ www.nabygelegen.co.za ▪ S 33° 37'54.7" E 019° 3'51.2" ▪ **T +27 (0)21-873-7534** ▪ F +27 (0)86-561-7761

Two wines from this Wellington farm were the only ones chosen last year for a Jubilee banquet for Commonwealth leaders — the fact that other guests included Australians and New Zealanders merely enhancing owner James McKenzie's pleasure at the achievement. A new tasting room in the old stables and forge welcomes all, while a new website does the same online.

Nabygelegen Private Cellar range

★★★★☆ **1712** ⚘ **07** roughly equal merlot & cab, soupçon petit verdot shows concentrated dark fruit, fresh acidity, firm but fine tannins. 30% new oak a subtle presence. More like **05** than lighter **06** (★★★★).
Merlot ★★★★ **11** a big step up on **07** (★★★) (**08** to **10** not made). Excellent varietal character (polished black plums & more than a hint of mint), elegant tannins & supportive charry oak. **Petit Verdot** ⚘ ★★★★ **08** spice & earthiness in addition to red fruit, bright acidity, fine tannins when reviewed. **Scaramanga** ★★★★ Cab, merlot, malbec & tempranillo combine in **11** for a glassful of sweet black fruit surrounded by darkly lurking tannins. **Chenin Blanc** ▤ ★★★★ **11** back on track with rich baked grapefruit, hints of lavender & herbs, oily/warm finish. Good food partner. **Sauvignon Blanc** ▤ ★★☆ Acceptable quaffer **12** with aromas of lemongrass, fresh hay & limes. **Lady Anna** ✓ ▤ ★★★★ Over-delivering chenin-led blend **11** a really lovely mouthful of yellow fruit, blossoms, spiced hazelnuts & lemon meringue.

Snow Mountain range

★★★★ **Syrah** Elegant cool-grown example. **10** with cranberry fruit given definition by spicy, peppery tannins with some whiffs of baked meats & liquorice. WO W Cape, as rest of range.

Pinot Noir ★★★ A good summer red, **11** soft crushed berries & floral notes, hint of spice & easy tannins. **Merlot Rosé ⓘ ★★★☆** Strawberry & some herbal notes, **09** medium body, fresh acidity & drink last time. **Chardonnay 🍴 ★★★★ 11** confident combination of integrated oak, citrus fruit & tangy acidity. — CM

■ **Naked Truth** see PicardiRebel
■ **Naked Vine Collection** see Hornbill Garagiste Winery

Namaqua Wines

Location: Vredendal ▪ Map: Olifants River ▪ WO: Olifants River/Koekenaap ▪ Est/1stB 2002 ▪ Tasting & sales Mon-Fri 8-5 Sat 9-3 ▪ Closed Easter Fri-Mon, Ascension day & Dec 25/26 ▪ Cellar tours Mon-Fri 10 & 3, book ahead ▪ Die Keldery Restaurant Mon-Fri 8-5 Sat 9-3 Sun buffet 11-3 booking required ▪ Facilities for children ▪ Conferences ▪ Owner(s) 200 members ▪ Cellarmaster(s) Pieter Verwey & Koos Thiart ▪ Winemaker(s) Driaan van der Merwe, Dewald Huisamen, Roelf Retief, Koos Thiart, Johan Weideman, Reinier van Greunen & Jaco Theron ▪ Viticulturist(s) Marina Cornellisen, Heine Janse van Rensburg & Nicholas Bruyns ▪ 4,990ha ▪ 112,500t/9.3m cs 20% red 80% white ▪ PO Box 75 Vredendal 8160 ▪ info@namaquawines.com ▪ www.namaquawines.com ▪ S 31° 42'34.9" E 018° 30'15.6" ▪ **T +27 (0)27-213-1080** ▪ F +27 (0)27-213-3476

Everybody knows Namaqua's 5L boxes, which are everywhere, but if you consider that this Vredendal grower-owned winery's range includes a pinotage awarded gold by Decanter — a first for the region — it's worth taking a fresh look. Quite simply, the winemakers here know all about mass production but have their 'boutique' side too, and they're building on it by, among others, installing new technology for extracting high-quality juice. It's not all work and no play, however. If fact, the production team say one of their goals is to see their CEO spending less time on his mountain bike. More seriously, they believe that without large-scale consolidation, South Africa's wine industry will cease to exist.

Spencer Bay Winemakers Reserve range

★★★★ Cabernet Sauvignon ✓ Smoky **09** maintains pace set by warm-hearted **08**; firm tannic grip & bright acidity rein in intense fruit.

★★★★ Pinotage ✓ Last edition, **08** raised the bar few notches. This improved form equalled by **09** & Decanter gold-winning **10**. Both structured for 3+ years cellaring, with mulberry centre & acetone hint.

Shiraz ✓ ★★★★ 09 powerful (14.8% alcohol) without being warming; satisfying weight & length, lipsmacking appeal. Step up on smooth **08** (★★★☆). **The Blend ★★★★** Cab dominates confident **09** 5-way Bordeaux-style red. Commendably dry, unheavy (13.7% alcohol), amenably firm. Improves on ripe, plummy **08** (★★★☆). Discontinued: **Chardonnay, Sauvignon Blanc**.

Cellar Door range [NEW]

Merlot ☺ ★★★ Inviting sugar plum & dark chocolate on juicy **10** easy-drinker.

Namaqua range

★★★★ Noble Late Harvest [NEW] 10 older-oak-matured botrytis dessert from semillon. Unctuous & sweet (265g/l sugar) but as elegant & attractive as the bottle it's presented in.

★★★★☆ Red Muscadel [NEW] Burnished copper hue, Indian spices & warm honey appeal on much awarded fortified winter warmer. **NV**. Full-sweet (253g/l) but lively, moreish.

Merlot ☺ 🍴 ★★★ Friendly **11** ruby hued, plum toned, gently tannic. **Sauvignon Blanc ☺ 🍴 🎐 ★★★** Concentration & freshness on improved **12**, summer enjoyment from Koekenaap grapes.

Cabernet Sauvignon 🍴 ★★ Peppery **11** has gentle acidic bite, light oaking for youthful imbibing, as all these reds. **Pinotage ⓘ 🍴 ★★** Old-style **10** fleeting earth & plum flavours. **Shiraz 🍴 ★★★** Clove- & mulberry infused **11** big on taste, structure. **Guinevere Méthode Cap Classique ⓘ ★★★** Lively **06** brut sparkling. Savoury notes from pinot noir (60%), appley flavours ex chardonnay. **Hanepoot Jerepigo [NEW] ★★★** Slightl funky **NV**, with hints of papaya & fynbos. **White Muscadel [NEW] ★★★** Tasty **NV**, honeyed almonds, pithy apricots & integrated spirit. Perfect solo, over ice or ice-cream, as all the Namaqua fortifieds. — DB/CvZ

Napier Winery

Location: Wellington ▪ Map: Paarl & Wellington ▪ WO: Wellington/Coastal ▪ Est 1989 ▪ Tasting, sales & cella tours Mon-Fri 8-5 Sat 10-3 ▪ Fee R10 ▪ Closed Easter Fri-Sun, Dec 25/26 & Jan 1 ▪ Tapas platters, preferab

pre-booked ▪ Conferences ▪ Owner(s) Michael & Catherine Loubser ▪ Cellarmaster(s)/winemaker(s)/viticulturist(s) Leon Bester (Apr 2000) ▪ 60ha/±38ha under vine ▪ 70% red 30% white ▪ Other export brand: Sir George ▪ PO Box 638 Wellington 7654 ▪ info@napierwinery.co.za ▪ www.napierwinery.co.za ▪ S 33° 38'37.0" E 019° 2'24.8" ▪ **T +27 (0)21-873-7829** ▪ F +27 (0)21-864-2728

International successes for family-owned Napier in Wellington include Emirates Airline serving Sir George Quintas (untasted this edition) in First Class and extensive distribution throughout Asia. That includes a wine-by-the-glass listing at 5 star Shangri-La in Hong Kong for St Catherine and Lion Creek Cabernet. Nor has local focus been neglected: registration of the Bainskloof Educational Trust, designed to aid previously disadvantaged children, is in process.

Napier range

★★★★ **Red Medallion** Ⓣ Cedar & red berries, some violets, **07** still tightly held mid-2011. 5-part Bordeaux blend, built for ageing but tannins accessible if you don't want to wait; best paired with rich dishes.

★★★★ **St Catherine** Single-vineyard chardonnay. Different styling in **10**, with peach pip & citrus peel piquancy, a creamy oatmeal flavour effect from oaking. Nicely dry, it will add interest to any meal.

Greenstone ★★★★ Single-vineyard chenin, **11** is seamed with minerality, has restrained peach pip, melon top notes. Individual, pure & elegant.

Lion Creek range

> **Cabernet Sauvignon** ☺ 🍽 ★★★ Exuberant fruity **10** offers crushed blackcurrants & juicy drinkability, the supple tannns a hidden support. **Sauvignon Blanc-Chenin Blanc** ☺ 🍽 ★★★ Summer fruits in **12** preview, tangy & vibrant, awaken the taste buds. Nice leafy note from sauvignon. WO Coastal.

Cabernet Sauvignon-Shiraz [NEW] 🍽 ★★★ Mulberry & smoky toned **10** has just enough grip for food pairing. **Chenin Blanc** Ⓣ 🍽 ★★ **11** thatch & melon, nicely rounded despite lowish 12.5% alcohol. — CR

▪ **Natalie** see The Butcher Shop & Grill
▪ **Nativo** see Hughes Family Wines

Natte Valleij Wines

Location/map: Stellenbosch ▪ WO: Simonsberg-Paarl/Coastal ▪ Est 1715 ▪ Tasting, sales & cellar tours Mon-Fri 10-4 Sat 10-3 ▪ Closed all pub hols ▪ Facilities for children ▪ Conference/indaba venue ▪ Art gallery & art classes ▪ Artifacts & various paintings ▪ Natte Valleij B&B/self-catering cottages (see Accommodation section) ▪ Owner(s) Milner family ▪ Winemaker(s) Alexander Milner (2005), with Marcus Milner (2010) ▪ 28ha total ▪ 15t/1,000cs own label 100% red ▪ PO Box 4 Klapmuts 7625 ▪ alex@boerandbrit.com ▪ www.nattevalleij.co.za ▪ S 33° 50'3.6" E 018° 52'43.2" ▪ **T +27 (0)21-875-5171**

This venerable Cape farmstead was bought by the Milner family in 1969 and operated as a thoroughbred racehorse stud. The current generation, brothers Alexander and Marcus (also winemaker at De Meye Wines) have reinstated the vineyards. Each bottle they produce bears a seal proclaiming proudly: Picked, pressed, bottled, sealed, labelled, drunk BY HAND.

Natte Valleij range [NEW]

P.O.W. ★★★★ Bordeaux-style red blend, majority cab, **09** shows impressive poise & purity of fruit, with darker notes of liquorice & toasted oak.

Swallow range

The Blend ★★★ Listed as 'Swallow' last time. Barrel sample of **12** merlot-led 5-way blend is unsettled, with funky notes. Substantial body & sweet fruit should prevail in time. WO Coastal. — GdB

▪ **Natural Star** see Stellar Winery

Naughton's Flight

Location: Constantia ▪ WO: Stellenbosch/Paarl/Coastal ▪ 1stB 2003 ▪ Closed to public ▪ Owner(s) Francis Naughton ▪ Winemaker(s) Ronell Wiid (consultant) ▪ (carignan, mourv, shiraz, viog) ▪ ±15,000 btls ▪ 25 Willow Rd Constantia 7806 ▪ naughts@mweb.co.za ▪ **T +27 (0)21-794-3928** ▪ F +27 (0)21-794-3928

Francis Naughton, after many years with SFW (now Distell) following his 'flight' from his native Ireland (he brought his accent and a bit of blarney with him), this year can celebrate ten years of his own venture. With him from the start has been Ronell Wiid in the cellar.

Shiraz ⓟ ★★★★ Broad, savoury **07** ex Paarl, some stalkiness & cherry flavours. Like all, tasted previously. **Tribua** ⓟ ★★★★ Step-up **09** from shiraz & mourvèdre, viognier for fragrance. Engaging, ripe flavours: sweet fruit in modestly oaked, dry, firm package. WO Coastal. **Viognier** Next awaited. **Délice** ⓟ ★★★ **09**, from rack-dried shiraz, deliciously grapey. Sweet, clean & fresh; only 11% alcohol. — TJ

Nederburg Wines   23-12-12   🍷🍴☕📷🦪

Location: Paarl • Map: Paarl & Wellington • WO: Western Cape/Paarl/Coastal/Groenekloof/Philadelphia/Darling/Stellenbosch • Est 1791 • 1stB ca 1940 • Tasting & sales Mon-Fri 8–5; Sat 10–2 (Apr-Oct) & 10–4 (Nov-Mar); Sun 11–4 (Nov-Mar) • Various tasting fees, waived on purchase of R100+ • Closed Good Fri, Dec 25 & Jan 1 • Cellar tours Mon-Fri 10.30 & 3; Sat 11; Sun 11 (Nov-Mar) • Large groups/foreign language tours by appt only • Visitors' centre: foundation platters in summer; soup & ciabatta in winter • Historic Manor House (national monument): breakfast, lunch & dinner for groups by appt • Picnic lunches by appt (Nov-Mar) • Tour groups • Gifts • Conferences • Museum • Conservation area • Owner(s) Distell • Cellarmaster(s) Razvan Macici (2001) • Winemaker(s) Wilhelm Pienaar (reds, 2009) & Wim Truter (whites, 2012), with Samuel Viljoen (reds) & Danie Morkel (whites) • Viticulturist(s) Henk van Graan & Hannes van Rensburg • 1,100ha (cab, carignan, grenache, malbec, merlot, p verdot, ptage, shiraz, tannat, tempranillo, chard, riesling, sauv, sem) • 18,000t/1.4m cs own label • ISO 0001:2008, ISO 14001:2004, BWI, HACCP, IPW, BRC, SGS organic certification • Private Bag X3006 Paarl 7620 • nedwines@distell.co.za • www.nederburg.co.za • S 33° 43′ 15.4″ E 019° 0′9.4″ • **T +27 (0)21-862-3104** • F +27 (0)21-862-4887

With its unrivalled award-winning track record plus a large, carefully constructed range, you'd think Nederburg had all bases covered. Until the release of the Heritage Anthology range, that is, which fits neatly into a personal, nostalgic, handcrafted gap. Honouring the major personalities who played a part in building Nederburg into what it is today, the wines are quite different to anything else in the lineup. There's 'Anchorman' Phillipus Wolvaart, the first owner in 1791; 'Brew Master' Johann Graue, brewery owner in Germany and trained viticulturist, who after buying the farm in 1937, meticulously managed the vineyards; 'Young Airhawk', his talented son Arnold tragically killed in a light aircraft crash at 29; and 'Motorcycle Marvel' Günter Brözel, cellarmaster 1956-1989 who took Nederburg to new heights. He'd drive around on a 250cc BSA motorbike at dawn, to check on work progress.

Ingenuity range

★★★★☆ **Red** Equal sangiovese & barbera, dab nebbiolo, a local version of the best of Italy. Deep, richly fruited **09** boasts black cherries & truffles, cigarbox, underpinned by polished tannins to keep it in prime condition for 8+ years to come.

★★★★★ **White** 🍷 Impressive 8-part sauvignon-led blend which includes aromatic varieties, some oaking. Following superb **10**, playing with your senses, **11** offers floral & fruity notes, a touch of spice & resonating freshness that acts as their perfect foil.

Heritage Heroes range [NEW]

★★★★ **The Brew Master** ✓ Cab-led classic 4-way Bordeaux blend, **09** has a meaty blackcurrant ripeness that gives pleasure, but this is no pushover. The tannin is firm but ripe, designed for the longer haul.

★★★★☆ **The Motorcycle Marvel** ✓ Near equal grenache, carignan & shiraz gives **09** hedgerow fruit, black pepper & cloves, a cocoa dusting, transporting you to a wild & rocky land of venison & game birds. Individual & very impressive.

★★★★ **The Anchorman** ✓ 🍷 Combo oak & tank, capturing **11**'s chenin character. Thatch & just-ripe melon, a light almond dusting; nothing overt, just admirable restraint & focused purity. Coastal WO.

★★★★☆ **The Young Airhawk** ✓ 🍷 Pungent & arresting, oaking adds savoury element to **11**'s 'green' sauvignon flavours, deepening them to something rich & distinctive, that stays long after the glass is empty.

Manor House range

★★★★ **Cabernet Sauvignon** Previewed **10**, succulent ripeness & enough lush blackcurrant & plummy fruit to more than match the assured oaking. Made to drink on release, & to cellar 3/4 years. Paarl WO.

★★★★ **Shiraz** Scrub & hedgerow fruit in pre-bottled **10**, the youthful, peppery oak a strong presence, without edginess, just needs time to meld. Promises well. WO Philadelphia.

★★★★ **Shiraz-Mourvèdre** NEW 🔲 Attractive seasoning in **10**'s red berries from a mix of different barrels: Provençal herbs, allspice, cardamom. Delicious to drink & an adventurous food match. Groenekloof WO.

★★★★ **Sauvignon Blanc** 🔲 Gooseberries with whiffs of greenpepper, fynbos, the **12** tank sample manages its appealing 'ripe but green' styling with verve, assurance.

Two Centuries range

★★★★ **Cabernet Sauvignon** Flagship cab available cellardoor only. Selection best Paarl vineyards, 2 years new French barriques. Improves on **07**, showing great fruit concentration, layered complexity, **08** (★★★★☆) is one to keep, watch unfold, but already drinks well.

★★★★ **Sauvignon Blanc** ⊕ Subtle interplay of melon & granite minerality in **09**, the age & year oaking adding to the complexity. Not showy, can underestimate it, but there's finesse, lots of class here. Coastal WO.

Private Bin range for Nederburg Auction

★★★★ **Cabernet Sauvignon Private Bin R163** Opulent **09**'s blackcurrant fruit easily handles 18 months new oak, getting extra spicing, dried herb notes from the oak mix. Layered complexity. WO Paarl.

★★★★ **Grenache Private Bin** NEW Piquant red berries & white pepper, **09** charms & seduces from the outset. Fleshy but ultra-smooth; layers of interest, underbrush, dried herbs, suggestion of wildness. WO Paarl.

★★★★ **Merlot Private Bin R181** Always a serious version, **09** has plush berries with a herbaceous thread, supported by well-padded tannins courtesy of 2 years all new oak. Drink now till 2020. WO Groenekloof.

★★★★ **Petit Verdot Private Bin R104** ⊕ Last was **07**, black plums & beef extract, fruit good match for the firm tannins but wine still in infancy. Would reveal its true potential over time.

★★★★☆ **Pinotage Private Bin R172** ⊕ Previously, dark-toned **07** had the polished elegance the variety can deliver in careful hands; deep muscle strength from all-new barrels ensured 8+ year rewarding future.

★★★★☆ **Shiraz Private Bin R121** Intensely perfumed, red berries with tobacco leaf & smoky spice, **09**'s 2 years new oak has smoothed all edges, leaving luscious drinkability & structure for a good future. WO Paarl.

★★★★ **Cabernet Sauvignon-Merlot Private Bin R109** A proven partnership, in **09** reveals creamy berries, chocolate, deft oaking that doesn't upset fruit balance, fleshy appeal. Despite amenability, will age well.

★★★★ **Cabernet Sauvignon-Shiraz Private Bin R103** Prosciutto & sweet spice combine with dark berries to give **09** a rich, savoury appeal, opulently ripe & flavourful, with enough oak backing to stay in shape for years to come. No **08**. Paarl WO.

★★★★ **Chardonnay Private Bin D270** 🔲 Expertly combining oak & fruit, **11** has presence & style. Offers toasted brioche & citrus, an intriguing beeswax note, & streamlined zesty elegance. Coastal WO.

★★★★ **Sauvignon Blanc Private Bin D215** 🔲 The more tropical partner to D234, **12** offers crunchy gooseberries with a whiff of fynbos, coming together with a lively freshness that gives instant gratification.

★★★★☆ **Sauvignon Blanc Private Bin D234** 🔲 Showing grapefruit & slatey minerality, **12** has an admirable focus, refinement that is more Old World than New. The long, lingering ultra-fresh flavours are perfect for seafood. WO Darling.

★★★★ **Semillon Private Bin D266** 🔲 Riveting intensity in **12**, fennel & greengage laced with racy acidity, keeping it focused & vibrantly fresh. Still youthful but structured to age well. No **11**. Philadelphia WO.

★★★★ **Viognier Private Bin D212** NEW 🔲 Melon & ginger-perfumed **11** takes a different tack; the flavours are restrained, have an attractive delicacy, savoury peach pip edge makes it food compatible. WO Darling.

★★★★★ **Sauvignon Blanc-Chardonnay Private Bin D253** ⊕ 🔲 The longer **10** (★★★★★) is in the glass, the greater the sauvignon (70%) & chardonnay interplay; white peach, crushed almonds, but lime there throughout. Elegant & pure, less complex than **09**, but an acid seam will keep it youthful for years. Coastal WO.

★★★★☆ **Sauvignon Blanc-Semillon Private Bin D252** 🔲 Lots of layers in **12** (★★★★★), fynbos & fennel, litchi, it keeps on unfolding in the glass, but the final say goes to a sleek, salty minerality that lasts & lasts. Complex & involving wine, as was step-up **11** with more appetite appeal than previous.

★★★★ **Gewürztraminer Special Late Harvest Private Bin S354** NEW Always looking for something special, the cellar picked this **11** gem. Turkish Delight in a stylishly elegant form, with a livening acidity that takes one back to fruit at the end. Stellenbosch WO.

★★★★☆ **Eminence** 🔲 Natural Sweet white from Paarl muscat de Frontignan. Richest of the trio, **11** has candied pineapple & ginger flavours, luscious & satin-textured, tangy-sweet & very long. High sugar offset by racy acidity, but lacks the finesse of **10** (★★★★★).

★★★★★ **Edelkeur** ⊕ The first Cape NLH, always chenin. Melon & apricot preserve, overlaid with savoury botrytis in **11** (★★★★★). Limy acidity seams the sweetness, converts it into delicious nectar & extends the flavours. Follows superb **10**. All these NLHs unoaked, 375ml only.

Winemaster's Reserve range

★★★★ **Edelrood (Cabernet Sauvignon-Merlot)** ✓ On track after earlier-drinking 09 (★★★★), the class of **10** is found in perfume layers, silk texture, perfectly judged oaking. Can age but already drinking well.

★★★★ **Special Late Harvest** ✓ Improving on **11**, ex-tank **12** (★★★★★) seduces with apricot & pine-apple richness, an intriguing floral note & wonderful tangy intensity that stays long after the glass is empty.

★★★★★ **Noble Late Harvest** Cellar's expertise demonstrated here, its only botrytis dessert freely available. Following very slightly lesser **10** (★★★★★), chenin/muscat's golden-hued **11** is like drinking apricot & pineapple essence, a dash of ginger; tangy, richly mouthfilling.

Cabernet Sauvignon ✓ ★★★★ Richly fruited **11** showcases cab's blackcurrants & oak's spice array, smooth-textured tannins are a hidden support. All these WO Western Cape unless noted. **Merlot** ✓ ★★★★ Chocolate notes & violets in **11** vie with the red berries, but the fruit holds sway on the palate, vibrant & delicious. **Pinotage** ✓ ★★★★ Dark berries, plums & mocha chocolate, **10** is succulent & appealing, with ripe tannins as a pliable backbone. **Shiraz** ✓ ★★★★ A template for shiraz, with hedgerow fruit & heaps of smoky spice, now-bottled **10** is supple & smooth, destined for early enjoyment. **Baronne (Cabernet Sauvignon-Shiraz)** ✓ ★★★★ Well-matched varieties, **11**'s lush berries also reflect a spicy note, all backed by harmonious tannins for current enjoyment. **Cabernet Sauvignon Rosé** ★★★★ 'Rosé' last time. For export only. Dayglo pink with red berries & a herbaceous note, **12** is hard to ignore. Crisply dry, drink solo or with food. **Chardonnay** ✓ ★★★★ Citrus with tropical fruit padding, **11** goes for flavour & light-textured drinkability & succeeds on both counts. **Chenin Blanc** ⊕ ★★★★ Limy spark to **10**, while retaining taut fruit, zesty appetite appeal. From bushvines. WO Coastal. **Pinot Grigio** ✓ ★★★★ Made in an off-dry style, **12** shows pear-rich fruit salad flavours, appealing soft-textured elegance (12.5% alcohol). **Riesling** ✓ ★★★★ Pre-bottling, **12** offers ginger & pineapple, some floral notes, with a refined delicacy, lovely off-dry appeal. **Sauvignon Blanc** ✓ ★★★★ Appealing combo of litchi & greenpepper, **12** offers best of both worlds: ripe flavour, heaps of freshness.

Foundation range

Duet (Shiraz-Pinotage) ☺ ★★★ With 61% dominance, shiraz dictates in **11**, showing mocha-rich dark fruit, but pinotage supplies the fresh juicy texture. Sold in SA. **Stein** NEW ☺ ★★★ Back after a name change to 'Chenin' in **11**, this **12** chenin semi-sweet is like drinking the essence of summer fruits. Sold in SA. **Lyric (Sauvignon Blanc-Chenin Blanc-Chardonnay)** ☺ ☺ ★★★ Sauvignon leads in **12** with leafy tones but the tangy off-dry tropical palate comes from the blend partners, & nicely so. Sold in SA. **Première Cuvée Brut** ☺ ★★★ NV sparkling from sauvignon, dab chenin, with first-mentioned variety giving the expected lift & freshness. Ideal aperitif. Sold in SA.

Cabernet Sauvignon ★★★ Vanilla-spiced **11**'s plush blackcurrants show just-picked freshness, integrated tannins give support, allow ready drinking. Export only, as rest unless specified. **Merlot** ★★★ Violets & red berries, **11**'s deft oak handling allows them centre stage, contributes a savoury note, smooth tannins. **Pinotage** ★★★ Mocha-toned blueberries but **11** isn't a pushover, there's good tannin structure under the juiciness, can age a few years. **Shiraz** ★★★ With scrub & pulpy red berries, **11** shows tasty accessibility, has a softly curvaceous smooth texture. **Shiraz-Viognier** Await new vintage. **Cabernet Sauvignon-Shiraz** ★★★ Light oaking keeps **11**'s fruit intact, gives gentle grip to the finish. **Rosé** ★★★ Nicely packaged **12** charms with semi-sweet cranberry flavours. Sold in SA. **Chardonnay** ★★★ Peach & buttered toast in previewed **12**, but retaining a core of freshness that makes drinking a pleasure, will match food. **Chenin Blanc** ★★★ Just off-dry **12** sample offers vibrant appley freshness in a sleek body. Friendly 12.5% alcohol. **Sauvignon Blanc** ★★★ Litchi & lime throughout, laced with bright acidity, tasty **12** has admirable intensity, focus. **Chardonnay-Viognier** ★★★ Blend emphasises the peachiness of gently appealing **12** tank sample. **Sauvignon Blanc-Chardonnay** ★★★ Proven combo, **12** ex-tank already showing the citrus flavours, crisp acidity each variety contributes. Discontinued: **Cape Riesling**, **Premier Grand Cru**. — CR

Neethlingshof Estate

Location/map/WO: Stellenbosch ▪ Est 1692 ▪ 1stB 1880 ▪ Tasting & sales Mon-Fri 9–5 (Dec/Jan 9-7); Sat/Sun 10-4 (Dec/Jan 10-6) ▪ Fee R30pp ▪ Closed Good Fri & Dec 25 ▪ Cellar tours by appt ▪ 'Flash Food & Slow Wine' pairing R95pp — booking required ▪ Jungle gym ▪ Tour groups ▪ Conferences ▪ Conservation area ▪ Annual 'Slenterfees' (Mar) & Christmas concerts (Dec) ▪ Lord Neethling Restaurant & Palm Terrace ▪ Owner(s) Lusan Premium Wines ▪ Cellarmaster(s) De Wet Viljoen (Jun 2003) ▪ Winemaker(s) Lauren Snyman (Sep 2006) ▪ Viticulturist(s) Hannes van Zyl (Jun 2002) ▪ 284ha/120ha (cabs s/f, malbec, merlot, p verdot, ptage, shiraz, chard, chenin, gewürz, riesling, sauv, viog) ▪ 1,400t/50,000cs own label 55% red 45% white ▪ BWI Champion,

WIETA ▪ PO Box 104 Stellenbosch 7599 ▪ info@neethlingshof.co.za ▪ www.neethlingshof.co.za ▪ S 33° 56'28. 2" E 018° 48'6.7" ▪ **T** +27 (0)21-883-8988 ▪ F +27 (0)21-883-8941

The past and present are commemorated at this historic Stellenbosch estate in the wines of the Short Story Collection. An active biodiversity program has re-established indigenous vegetation, encouraging the return of natural predators such as owls and caracal. They reduce vineyard pests on the property, originally called Wolwedans. Maria Marais, who helped establish the farm and was one of the Cape's first woman winemakers, is also honoured with a delicious dessert wine.

Short Story Collection

★★★★ **Owl Post Pinotage** 🉐 Less fruit concentration in warmer **10** (★★★★) than **09**. Dark & savoury, tobacco & leather impression with youthfully firm tannins that will reward ageing.

★★★★☆ **Caracal** 🉐 **10** (★★★★) Bordeaux trio cab, merlot & petit verdot shows warmth, with riper & smoother tone to cassis & cedar flavours. Balanced & satisfying, but shade less impressive than classical **09**.

★★★★☆ **Maria** 🉐 Tangy return to form in **12** of one of Cape's few botrytised rieslings, after softer **11** (★★★★). Unctuously rich layers of glacé pineapple, barley sugar & lime flavour from low (3t) yield, balanced by a splash of sauvignon.

Six Flowers NEW 🍴🉐 ★★★★ **12** preview of engaging chardonnay & chenin-led sextet, with sauvignon & aromatic understudies. Supple structure & creamy oak platform for a harmonious & entertaining performance.

Neethlingshof range

> **Sauvignon Blanc** 😊🍴🉐 ★★★ **12** bright-faced & lively, ripe tropical tone for fresh summer quaffing.

Cabernet Sauvignon ★★★ Fresher **07** regains charm, dark fruit pastille flavours clothing fine tannins. Balanced, juicy & satisfying. **Malbec** 🍴 ★★★ **11** tad brusque & denser than previous, with wild berry, savoury tone. Time will harmonise. **Merlot** ★★★ Cooler vintage shows in leaner **09**'s edgy minty/green tone. **Pinotage** 🉐 ★★★ Brisk, lighter **10** lacks depth & harmony of last-tasted **07**. **Shiraz** ★★★ **07** continues in powerful, dark & savoury mode. Structured & muscular, needs time to mellow. **Cabernet Sauvignon-Merlot** 🉐 ★★★★ **10** good weight & freshness with firm but supple tannins. Less complex, but potential for 3-5 years. **Chardonnay Unwooded** 🍴🉐 ★★★ **12** gentle pear & stonefruit, understated, with creamy texture & crisp finish. **Chenin Blanc** NEW 🍴🉐 ★★ Demure **12** debut for waxy & gentle apple-toned quaffer. **Gewürztraminer** 🍴🉐 ★★★ **12** shows niche variety's perfume & incense. Just off-dry, smooth, not as fresh as previous but still pleasant aperitif or fusion food partner. **Sauvignon Blanc Single Vineyard** 🍴 🉐 ★★★★ Fine **12** vintage raises bar on **11** (★★★). Richer & more structured than sibling, crisp stonefruit & flintiness. Balanced lunch partner. — MW

Neil Ellis Meyer-Näkel

Location: Stellenbosch ▪ WO: Stellenbosch/Jonkershoek Valley ▪ Est/1stB 1998 ▪ Tasting & sales at Neil Ellis Wines ▪ Owner(s) Neil Ellis Meyer-Näkel (Pty) Ltd ▪ Winemaker(s) Neil Ellis, Werner Näkel & Warren Ellis (2006) ▪ Viticulturist(s) Pieter Smit & Warren Ellis ▪ 3,500cs own label 100% red ▪ PO Box 917 Stellenbosch 7599 ▪ tasting@neilellis.com ▪ www.neilellis.com ▪ **T** +27 (0)21-887-0649 ▪ F +27 (0)21-887-0647

Zwalu, 'new beginning' in Sotho, is an apt name for the first wine of this partnership between friends and renowned winemakers Neil Ellis and Werner Näkel, Germany's 'king of red wine', at a time when South Africa was emerging from the apartheid era. Appropriate, too, that the father of South Africa's new democracy, Nelson Mandela, was presented with a magnum of the wine.

★★★★ **Zwalu** 🍴🉐 Equal blend of Jonkershoek grapes (cab, cab franc & shiraz) achieves elegance even in warmer **10** vintage. More open textured & earlier maturing than **09**, still supple & satisfying.

Z 🉐🍴🉐 ★★★★ The junior version of Zwalu, previewed **10** cab shows bright blackcurrant fruit & a brush of cedar. Toned & supple, with underlying seriousness. Stellenbosch WO. — MW

Neil Ellis Wines

Location/map: Stellenbosch ▪ WO: Stellenbosch/Elgin/Jonkershoek Valley/Groenekloof/Western Cape/ Piekenierskloof/Coastal ▪ Est 1986 ▪ 1stB 1984 ▪ Tasting & sales Mon-Fri 9.30-4.30 Sat & pub hols 10-5 ▪ Fee R25 Premium range/R35 Vineyard Selection range ▪ Closed Good Fri, Dec 25/26 & Jan 1 ▪ Antipasto platters ▪ Tour groups ▪ Owner(s) Neil Ellis Wines (Pty) Ltd ▪ Winemaker(s)/viticulturist(s) Warren Ellis (2006) ▪

50,000cs own label 50% red 50% white ▪ Brands for clients: Woolworths ▪ WIETA ▪ PO Box 917 Stellenbosch 7599 ▪ info@neilellis.com ▪ www.neilellis.com ▪ S 33°55'34.92" E 018°53'32.46" ▪ **T +27 (0)21-887-0649** ▪ F +27 (0)21-887-0647

'Is Neil Ellis a real person?' many visitors ask of the man behind this brand, renowned for its quality and elegance. Doubters could be excused, as despite his success Neil remains self-effacing. Yes he is real, a rock-solid gentle giant at that, and he has made an immeasurable contribution to South African wine, charting new cooler vinegrowing territory as our first negociant winemaker. Neil's response to his queried existence was to create a brand, Aenigma, using the Greek spelling, meaning riddle or puzzle. It now comprises an unusual muscat-clone chardonnay and a variable red blend. After 30 years he concedes getting the basics right but his personal 'enigma' is understanding vineyard sites and their potential. Resolution will come with time and input from son Warren, armed with a viticulture MSc.

Vineyard Selections

★★★★☆ **Cabernet Sauvignon 09** more classically styled than **07**. Firmly tailored tannins envelop cassis & blueberry flavours, new oak (26 months) in harmony, showing elegance, power & finesse. Deserves 6-10 years. No **08**. From single-vineyard (as most in this range) in Jonkershoek Valley.

★★★★☆ **Grenache** 🗹 Rare gem from old block in Piekenierskloof always elegantly understated. Deserves decanting & contemplation, to reveal depth, complexity & rewarding drinking pleasure. **10** more expressive in youth than **09** (★★★★), both distinguished & ageworthy.

★★★★ **Pinotage** 🗹 **10** exudes pinotage's spicy tobacco & mulberry appeal, silkier texture in warmer year, but with fine structure & length. Youthful & cellarable wine from Jonkershoek.

★★★★☆ **Syrah** 🗹 Groenekloof vines reveal benefits of cooler area in **10** (★★★★). Sleek structure & integration of savoury fruit & oak tempt enjoyment, but can go 5-8 years. Shade off more complex last-bottled **07**.

★★★★☆ **Sauvignon Blanc** 🗹🗹 **11** (★★★★) more understated & herbaceous despite riper aromas. Retains poise & structure. 8 months oak adds succulence, but needs year/2 to show fruit evident in **10**. Jonkershoek, Stellenbosch & Groenekloof vines.

Aenigma White NEW 🗹🗹 ★★★★ **11** preview from muscat clone of chardonnay has beguiling aromatic nuance woven into silky texture & lingering farewell. Graceful fusion food partner from Elgin.

Premium range

★★★★ **Cabernet Sauvignon** 🗹🗹 **10** retains cool cassis & elegance despite vintage's heat, with chalky tannins tempering fruit ripeness. Less austere & ageable than **09**, best in 3-5 years. Stellenbosch WO.

★★★★ **Shiraz** 🗹🗹 **10** (★★★★) good varietal fruit & spice, supple & creamy. Shade off & less long-lived than structured **09**. WO Elgin.

★★★★ **Cabernet Sauvignon-Merlot** 🗹🗹 **10** better balance & more accessible in youth than firmly structured & ageworthy **09**. Still shows hallmark elegance to grace a table over 3-5 years. Stellenbosch grapes.

★★★★ **Aenigma Red** 🗹🗹 Cab-led Bordeaux blend with dusting of shiraz's white pepper, showcases Elgin area's elegance & fruit. Flavoursome & supple, **09** is both engaging & worth ageing.

★★★★☆ **Stellenbosch Chardonnay** ✓ 🗹 **12** unrated work-in-progress (as **11**) has rich cream-textured butterscotch threaded with zesty lime. **10**, also ex-tank, showed exhilarating vitality.

★★★★☆ **Groenekloof Sauvignon Blanc** 🗹🗹 **12** (★★★★) tank sample shows glimpses of Groenekloof's hallmark minerality & fruit intensity. Herbaceous, with clean-cut flinty tone but tad closed when tasted. Time in bottle should restore **10**'s higher rating. **11** was an unrated preview.

Pinotage NEW 🗹🗹 ★★★★ **09** sweet-fruited elegance with supple structure & balance. Streamlined for satisfying drinkability. Stellenbosch WO.

Inglewood range

Red NEW 🗹🗹 ★★★★ Established range returns to guide with generously fruited **10** shiraz/grenache duo, anchored by savouriness & supple tannins. Dapper & enjoyable over 3-5 years. **White** NEW 🗹🗹 ★★★★ Delicious **11** from sauvignon. Vivacious & tangy, passionfruit & green fig flavours. WO W Cape for both. — MW

Location/WO: Paarl ▪ Map: Paarl & Wellington ▪ Tasting, sales & cellar tours by appt only ▪ Closed all pub hols ▪ Facilities for children ▪ Tour groups ▪ Conferences ▪ Weddings ▪ Walks/hikes ▪ Mountain biking trails ▪ Guest accommodation ▪ Owner(s) Alan Nelson ▪ Cellarmaster(s) Lisha Nelson (Nov 2007) ▪ Winemaker(s) Lisha Nelson (Nov 2007), with Solly Hendriks (Apr 2011) ▪ Viticulturist(s) Daniel Nelson ▪ 142ha/46ha (cabs s/f, merlot, p verdot, ptage, shiraz, chard, chenin, sauv, sem) ▪ 210t/4,670cs own label 30% red 60% white 10% rosé ▪ IPW ▪ PO Box 2009 Windmeul 7630 ▪ lisha@nelsonscreek.co.za ▪ www.nelsonscreek.co.za ▪ S 33° 39′31.2″ E 018° 56′17.3″ ▪ **T +27 (0)21-869-8453** ▪ F +27 (0)21-869-8424

It was another active year at home for the Nelson family, with weddings and other functions on the increase at their Paarl estate, whilst head of the family Alan still enjoys getting out and about on his motorbike. Animal lovers of note, they have extended their charitable activities to include fundraisers for the SPCA as well as other local community projects.

Lisha Nelson Signature Wines

★★★★☆ **Cabernet Franc** ⓐ Last time we admired **08**'s delicious ripe black fruit & herbal minerality, succulence. Grip & backbone apparent on long finish. Well-judged oak — all new French for 21 months.

★★★★ **Dad's Blend** ⓐ Floral blackberry & violets previously on **08** 4-way cab franc-led blend. Spicy plum & cassis in smooth, juicy mouthful, leading to complex long finish.

Nelson Estate range

Sauvignon Blanc ☺ 🍷 ⍉ ★★★ Cheery quaffer **12** is flinty & fresh with lemon fruit & just a touch of sweetness to fill out the palate.

Shiraz ⓐ ★★★★ Spicy coconut & juicy plum, **08** smoky hint, firm dry tannin from 18 months new oak. **Cabernet Sauvignon-Merlot** ⓐ ★★★★ When tasted, deliciously lithe **08** had berry compote & cigarbox tones, was velvety, genteel & lingering. **Rosé** ⓐ 🍷 ⍉ ★★★ Rhubarb tartness on dry **11**, nice taut body & zippy vitality. **Chardonnay** 🍷 ⍉ ★★★★ Lots of toasty butterscotch on nose of **11** with some lemons, limes & naartjies. Oak dominating at present but sufficient fruit to justify keeping a while. **Noble Late Harvest** Await next.

Nelson's Creek range

Shiraz 🍷 ⍉ ★★★★ Stewed plums & black cherries, step-up **11** with plenty of rustic appeal. Supportive oak, well integrated, & charry finish. **Pinotage Rosé** ⓐ 🍷 ⍉ ★★ Natural Sweet-style **11** with candyfloss flavour keeps up the standard. **Chenin Blanc** 🍷 ⍉ ★★★ Whiffs of pineapple & tropical fruit, **12** off-dry, with tinned grapefruit conclusion. — CM

New Beginnings Wines

Location: Cape Town ▪ WO: Paarl/Swartland ▪ Est 1996 ▪ 1stB 1999 ▪ Closed to public ▪ Owner(s) Klein Begin Farming Association ▪ Brand manager FMS Food & Beverages SA cc ▪ 13ha/10ha (cab, ptage, shiraz, chard, chenin) ▪ 10,000cs own label 70% red 25% white 5% rosé ▪ PO Box 51869 Waterfront 8002 ▪ info@fms-wine-marketing. co.za ▪ www.fms-wine-marketing.co.za ▪ **T +27 (0)21-426-5037** ▪ F +27 (0)21-413-0825

Vineyard workers empowerment cooperative New Beginnings now has just five committed members, and is hopefully in line for an injection of Department of Rural Development seed capital soon. In the meantime CEO Anton Blignault has been away marketing in 'hard-working, but relaxed and hospitable' Warsaw, an export destination already showing double-digit growth.

Shiraz Rosé NEW ☺ 🍷 ⍉ ★★★ **11** crisp & tangy quaffer with savoury cranberry tone.

Cabernet Sauvignon ⓐ ★★★ Blackcurrant succulence on **09**, combination juicy & ripe fruit & good vintage; pleasing & easy. **Pinotage** Await new vintage. **Shiraz** ⍉ ★★★ Anytime sipping delivered by quince & blackberry toned, lightish **11**. **Pinotage Rosé** 🍷 Not tasted. **Chardonnay** ⓐ 🍷 ⍉ ★★★ Tasted as bottled wine last time, **10** from Swartland showed good development: delicious, balanced & crisply ripe. **Chenin Blanc** NEW 🍷 ★★★ Plump & easy-drinking **10** has waxy apple & almond flavours. — MW

▪ **New Cape Wines** *see* Eagle's Cliff Wines-New Cape Wines
▪ **New Gate** *see* Ernst Gouws & Co Wines
▪ **New Mountain View Partnership** *see* Farm 1120, Santa Cecilia

Newstead Lund Family Vineyards

Location/WO: Plettenberg Bay ▪ Map: Klein Karoo & Garden Route ▪ Est 2008 ▪ 1stB 2012 ▪ Tasting & sales by appt ▪ Closed Dec 25 ▪ Cheese platters, deli, home bakes by arrangement ▪ Tour groups ▪ Gift shop ▪ Farm produce ▪ Walks ▪ Mountain biking trail ▪ Owner(s) Doug & Sue Lund ▪ Cellarmaster(s)/winemaker(s) Anton Smal

(Jan 2011, consultant) ▪ Viticulturist(s) Doug Lund & Gift Lwazi ▪ 11ha/5ha (pinot, chard, sauv) ▪ 24t/2,250cs own label 80% white 20% MCC ▪ PO Box 295 The Crags 6602 ▪ info@newsteadwines.com ▪ www.newsteadwines.com ▪ S 33° 57'7.24" E 023° 28'18.66" ▪ **T +27 (0)84-586-1600** ▪ F +27 (0)44-534-8387

Doug and Sue Lund last year celebrated their first harvest from young vines, and report that the cool Garden Route climate and 'meticulous attention to detail' have gone into their first bottling of Newstead wines (vinification by seasoned Anton Smal). They deliver wines countrywide, but of special interest to Plettenberg Bay holidaymakers are their special wine events in December.

Chardonnay 🖫 ★★★ Confident start: **12** pleasantly light & fruity, unfettered by oak, with brisk acidity & salty overlay; ideal with sushi. **Sauvignon Blanc** 🖫 ★★★★ Passionfruit-nuanced **12** shows focused minerality & purity; sense of gravitas; 1st harvest so expect greater depth, complexity as vines mature. — FM/GdB

Newton Johnson Vineyards   🏠🍷☕♿

Location: Hermanus ▪ Map: Elgin, Walker Bay & Bot River ▪ WO: Upper Hemel-en-Aarde Valley/Cape South Coast/Elgin/Walker Bay ▪ Est 1996 ▪ 1stB 1997 ▪ Tasting & sales Mon-Fri 9–4 Sat 10–2 ▪ Closed all pub hols ▪ Heaven Restaurant Tue-Sun 11-4 ▪ Owner(s) Dave & Felicity Johnson ▪ Cellarmaster(s)/viticulturist(s) Gordon Newton Johnson (Jan 2001) ▪ Winemaker(s) Gordon Newton Johnson (Jan 2001) & Nadia Newton Johnson (Aug 2006) ▪ 140ha/18ha (grenache, mourv, pinot, shiraz, chard, sauv) ▪ 240t/10,000cs own label 50% red 50% white ▪ PO Box 225 Hermanus 7200 ▪ wine@newtonjohnson.com ▪ www.newtonjohnson.com ▪ S 34° 22'9.7" E 019° 15'33.3" ▪ **T +27 (0)28-312-3862** ▪ F +27 (0)86-638-9673

'More of the same!' reports Bevan Newton Johnson, managing director and marketer at this increasingly famous Hemel-en-Aarde winery (two generations of the family are involved, and an infantile third has a destiny written in the stars the wines receive). 'We are still learning what our vineyards can do. 2012 (a stellar vintage) was our first substantial harvest from our pinot noir and chardonnay vineyard on the south-facing slopes with a much cooler climate than our current north-facing ones. In the cellar it is refining our wood management, our fermentations, extractions, etc. This is all pushing here and pulling there to find our limitations and paths forward.' They have, though, planted albariño, amongst the first local vineyards of this Spanish grape. 'But all in all — more of the same.'

★★★★ **Elgin Pinot Noir** Name invokes origin with **11**. Lovely, fresh-fruited & perfumed aromas lead to slightly less substantial, lighter palate. But well balanced, with understated firm structure.

★★★★★ **Family Vineyards Pinot Noir** 🎕 Was 'Domaine'. Pure-fruited **11** more depth, complexity than Elgin version (& brick rather than crimson). Vital structure so harmonious as to be near-invisible, but allows flavours to linger long. Delicious now, but few years will add profundity, smooth edges.

★★★★☆ **Full Stop Rock** Shiraz with drops mourvèdre & grenache. **09** (★★★★) a touch less generous & harmonious than **08** but savoury & juicy, with a gentle grip — slips down easily. From 2 H-en-A wards.

★★★★ **Grenache Blend** 🕐 Working name for a 2nd Rhône-inspired blend, **10** with 68% grenache + mourvèdre, syrah. Sweet, generous fruit less dense than other version in **08**; supple, silky, fresh.

★★★★ **Chardonnay** **11** from H-en-A vineyards rather than Kaaimansgat (like untasted **10**), & maybe less showy — though balancing elegance & modern fruitiness. Not much length, but a penetrating, vivifying acidity.

★★★★☆ **Family Vineyards Chardonnay** Previously 'Domaine'. **11** back on form after tough-vintage **10** (★★★★). Spice & some oak aromas, but the palate brings in the lime-lemon power of fruit intensity. Rich, with delectable creaminess, but a fine integrated acidity ensures balance, guiding to a good finish.

★★★★ **Sauvignon Blanc** ✓ 🖫 🎕 Elgin contributes 5% oaked semillon to **12**. Less green/flinty than **11** — here a full, interesting range of ripe flavours. Silky, some weight & a pleasing, unaggressive bite.

★★★★ **Resonance** 🎕 Home organic sauvignon plus 13% oaked Elgin semillon adding breadth & depth to **11**. Vibrant, elegant & charming; perhaps even more succulently incisive than current Sauvignon. — TJ

■ **Nicholas L Jonker** *see* Jonkheer

Nick & Forti's Wines   🍷

Location: Tulbagh ▪ WO: Coastal ▪ Est/1stB 2004 ▪ Tasting at Saronsberg Cellar (see entry) ▪ Owner(s) Fortunato Mazzone & Saronsberg ▪ Winemaker(s) Dewaldt Heyns (2004) ▪ 2,000cs own label 85% red 15% white ▪ Box 25032 Monument Park Pretoria 0105 ▪ ritrovo@mweb.co.za ▪ www.saronsberg.com ▪ **T +27 (0)12-460-4367** ▪ F +27 (0)12-460-5173

A venture born of friendship, that between Pretoria restaurateur Fortunato (Forti) Mazzone and Saronsberg winery owner Nick van Huyssteen, continues to flourish. There is now a fourth wine in the range (untasted by us), a white blend which is a best-seller in Forti's restaurant, Ritrovo, his stores and the selected outlets and restaurants he supplies.

★★★★ **Epicentre** Perfumed **10** (★★★★) 5-way Bordeaux blend is firmly structured, cab tannins framing succulent core of fruit. Shade quieter than **07** (★★★★★) & earlier vintages. (**08** & **09** sold out untasted.) **Shiraz** 🔲 ★★★★ Supple & concentrated **10** unfolds in glass to reveal red fruit & chocolate, satisfying if tad pedestrian. **Viognier** ⊛ ★★★★ Peach pip & shortbread, rich consistency & resonating savoury length on **09**. Rung up on **08** (★★★★), with peach & pinenut opulence. — WB/AL

Nico van der Merwe Wines

Location/map: Stellenbosch ▪ WO: Stellenbosch/Western Cape ▪ Est/1stB 1999 ▪ Tasting & sales by appt only ▪ Owner(s) Nico & Petra van der Merwe ▪ Cellarmaster(s)/winemaker(s) Nico van der Merwe ▪ 50t/2,000cs own label 80% red 20% white ▪ PO Box 12200 Stellenbosch 7613 ▪ nvdmwines@vodamail.co.za ▪ S 33° 57'48.2" E 018° 43'51.8" ▪ **T +27 (0)21-881-3063** ▪ F +27 (0)21-881-3063

This is long-time, much-decorated Saxenburg cellarmaster Nico van der Merwe's own boutique wine venture, with wife Petra, on Stellenbosch's Polkadraai Hills. In 14 years of bottling, the couple have built their brand carefully and patiently, and they now have their own land and cellar and soon, they excitedly hope, a visitor venue (and half-hectare of riesling) too. The five star wine below affirms that Nico's philosophy of 'quality, and only consistent quality' is not mere marketing spiel. In fact, he believes the troubled and unpredictable state of world wine markets means that South African producers generally must maintain an image of quality at all costs. To focus on the mass market, he cautions, is a sure way to get lost and disappear.

Nico van der Merwe Wines range

★★★★☆ **Mas Nicolas Cape** Cab & shiraz (54/46) from same vineyards since maiden **99**. Elegant **07** (★★★★★) has great depth & noble structure. Layers of black berry & plum fruit with great intensity, concentration & finesse. Perfectly judged oak is precise & supportive, as for equal cab/shiraz **06**.

Nicolas van der Merwe range

★★★★ **Red** ✓ Rich & smooth Bordeaux-style **07** (★★★★★) trumps **06**, billowing pure red berry & spice aromas. Elegant, with a plush silky mouthfeel, intense fruit concentration & super balance. Finishes with a lovely vanilla spice grip. ★★★★ **White** ✓ Vibrant aromas of green apple, dusty citrus & candied ginger on **11**, from sauvignon & semillon. Dense & powerfully structured, creamy mouthfeel with a fine minerality on the finish. WO W Cape. **Syrah** ⊛ ★★★★★ Big, muscular (15.5% alcohol) **07** set new standard for label last edition. Larger-than-life fruit demanded attention, needed time — contrast with open-textured **06** (★★★★).

Cape Elements range

Shiraz-Cinsaut-Grenache ⊛ ★★★★ New-wave blend of warm-climate varieties, **09** has malty whiff, but unfurls delightfully juicy berry flavours.

Robert Alexander range

Merlot ⊛ ★★★★ Opulently concentrated fruit on **09** reflects good vintage after softer **08** (★★★★). Dense & finely textured, with enduring finish, belies modest pitch of range. **Shiraz** ✓ ★★★★ Improving on **08** (★★★★), **09** shows ripe black fruits, richness & depth. Lush, harmonious & moreish, with good balance & length. Excellent value. **Méthode Cap Classique Brut** ⊛ ★★★★ **08** chardonnay sparkling was extroverted, expressively leesy last time, with an attractive shortcake finish. — WB

Nico Vermeulen Wines

Location: Paarl ▪ WO: Coastal ▪ Est/1stB 2003 ▪ Closed to public ▪ Owner(s)/viticulturist(s) Nico Vermeulen ▪ Winemaker(s) Nico Vermeulen, with Judy & Izelle Vermeulen ▪ 1,500cs own label & 240,000L bulk export ▪ 3 Pieter Hugo Str Courtrai Suider-Paarl 7646 ▪ nicovermeulen@webmail.co.za ▪ **T +27 (0)21-863-2048/+27 (0)82-553-2024** ▪ F +27 (0)21-863-2048

While his latest vintages were not ready for tasting in this guide, Nico Vermeulen remained busy with other projects, like a bulk-wine business for the UK. He comments (like many), that trading conditions are tough, but he's experienced enough to plan for the future. Look out for a pinot noir and light sangiovese to come.

★★★★☆ **The Right Red** ⓅⓉ 08 (★★★★) ticks all the shiraz boxes: luscious fruit, a spice array, some scrub notes. For earlier drinking (no hardship). Less concentration than **06**. **07** skipped.

★★★★ **The Right White** 🍷 Sauvignon minerality & nettles on **11** (★★★★), gentle pear flavours crisp dry end. Less expressive than **10**.

The Right Two Reds ⓉⓉ ★★★ Last tasted was sleek **05** merlot/cab blend with refreshing acidity & friendly tannins. **The Right Two Whites** 🍷 Await next. — CR

Niel Joubert Estate

Location/WO: Paarl ▪ Map: Paarl & Wellington ▪ Est 1898 ▪ 1stB 1996 ▪ Tasting & sales Mon–Fri 9–4 by appt ▪ Closed all pub hols ▪ Owner(s) Joubert family ▪ Cellarmaster(s) Ernst Leicht ▪ Winemaker(s) Ernst Leicht with Niel Joubert jnr (May 2011) ▪ Viticulturist(s) Daan Joubert ▪ 1,000ha/300ha (cab, merlot, ptage, shiraz, chard chenin, sauv) ▪ 1,953t/±80,000cs own label 49% red 50% white 1% rosé ▪ Other export brand: Hunterspeak ▪ Global Gap, IPW ▪ PO Box 17 Klapmuts 7625 ▪ wine@nieljoubert.co.za ▪ www.nieljoubert.co.za ▪ S 33° 49'54.7" E 018° 54'3.2" ▪ **T** +27 (0)21-875-5936 ▪ F +27 (0)86-599-0725

Klein Simonsvlei, on the Simonsberg near Paarl, has been the Joubert family seat since 1898, producing wine continuously since the earliest days under three successive generations of Daniels, known as 'Daniel', 'Niel' and 'Daan'. The new generation — Mari, Corne and another Niel — is now being groomed into the business.

Christine-Marié range

Cabernet Sauvignon ⓅⓉ 🍷 ★★★★ Elegant **09**, blackcurrant, violet & cigarbox refinement on pre-bottling sample. Step up from last-tasted **06** (★★★★). Firm body & length, harmonious & complex. **Merlot** ⓅⓉ 🍷 ★★★★ Bold cherry & brambles, **06** dark earthy grip & concentration, big alc (15%) but soft appeal. **Shiraz** 🍷 ★★★★ Seriously conceived premium label, **08**'s herbaceous, spicy seasoning adds appeal to super-ripe fruit. Alcohol reined in a bit, oak less dominant than **06** (★★★★). No **07**. **Chardonnay** ⓅⓉ 🍷 ★★★★ Tangerine blast on smoky vanilla **08**, lavishly oaked (18 months 2nd fill), rich & delicious. **Viognier** ⓅⓉ 🍷 ★★★★ **08** is redolent of peaches & cream. Rounded & full, restrained but firm toasty oak from (older) barrels. **Méthode Cap Classique** ★★★★ Opulent & appealing **09** brut bubbly from chardonnay, harbours powerful yeasty influence. Rich, creamy & persistently dry, with chalky lime finish. Improves on **08** (★★★★). **First Kiss Fortified Chenin Blanc** ⓅⓉ 🍷 ★★★★ Waxy honey & apricot, **07** last edition was sweet but balanced by limy freshness. 2 years oak, 100% new.

Niel Joubert Estate range

Chardonnay ☺ 🍷 ★★★ Previewed **12** has better body than previous. Tiny whisper of oak with ripe citrus flavour & fresh acidity.

Cabernet Sauvignon 🍷 ★★★ **10** tad less attractive than previous, with stewed prune flavour, hard tannins. **Merlot** 🍷 ★★★ **10** straightforward, with adequate berry fruit & oaky spice. **Pinotage** 🍷 ★★★ Lively with berry fruit on **10**, an improvement on previous. Supple & juicy. **Shiraz** 🍷 ★★★ First tasted since **06**, new **09** repeats liquorice & cherry profile on slender body. Sappy, with stiff tannins. **Rosé** ⓅⓉ 🍷 ★★★ Dry **11** from pinotage, with variety's cranberry tang. **Chenin Blanc** 🍷 ★★★ Fresh & dry, **12** expresses the variety in enjoyable light-bodied, fruit-driven style. **Sauvignon Blanc** 🍷 ★★★ Previewed **12**, with dash nouvelle, shows promising weight & ripe fruit, soft acid. Discontinued: **Voice**. — GdB

■ **Niels Verburg** see Luddite Wines

Nietgegund   NEW

Location/WO: Stellenbosch ▪ Est 2004 ▪ 1stB 2008 ▪ Closed to public ▪ Owner(s) Nietgegund Boerdery (Edms) Bpk ▪ Cellarmaster(s)/winemaker(s) Marius Malan (May 2007, consultant) ▪ Viticulturist(s) Francois Hanekom (Sep 2006, consultant) ▪ 3.4ha/1ha (merlot, shiraz) ▪ 4t/50cs own label 100% red ▪ IPW ▪ PO Box 12684 Die Boord 7613 ▪ jan@dreyer.za.net ▪ **T** +27 (0)21-880-0738

When in 2001 Stellenbosch lawyer Jan Dreyer bought a Blaauwklippen property amidst red-wine luminaries Waterford, Stellenzicht and Dornier, he couldn't not plant a hectare of merlot and shiraz (adding cab in his childrens' former horse paddock). Tapping into experience — viticultural adviser Paul Wallace, viticulturist Francois Hanekom, consultant winemaker Marius Malan — he's focusing on niche wines, ensuring that 'the friend you enjoy them with remains your friend!'

Pro Amico ★★★★ Merlot spiced by 10% shiraz; serious intent evident in firm structure & judicious oaking (30% new). **10** provisionally rated preview still very youthful, needs time to settle & integrate. — WB/IM

Nietvoorbij Wine Cellar

Location/map: Stellenbosch ▪ Est 1963 ▪ 1stB 1992 ▪ Tasting & sales Mon-Fri 9–4; phone ahead on Sat ▪ Fee R5/wine ▪ Cellar tours Fri by appt T +27 (0)21-809-3140 ▪ Closed all pub hols ▪ Conferences ▪ Owner(s) Agricultural Research Council ▪ Winemaker(s) Kajo Malek ▪ Vineyard manager(s) Guillaume Kotzè (Apr 2002) ▪ 32ha (cabs s/f, malbec, merlot, ptage, shiraz, chard, sauv, viog) ▪ 75t/3,000cs own label 56% red 40% white 4% port ▪ Private Bag X5026 Stellenbosch 7599 ▪ cellar@arc.agric.za ▪ www.arc.agric.za ▪ S 33° 54' 43.5" E 018° 51' 48.9" ▪ **T +27 (0)21-809-3084/3140** ▪ F +27 (0)86-623-4014

The Agricultural Research Council-Infruitec/Nietvoorbij is a Stellenbosch-based research institute where the Nietvoorbij wine-production arm sees its biggest challenge as balancing the making of 1,300 experimental wines for their clients with that for commercial wines, with limited financial resources. They've sharpened their focus on research, and winemaker Kajo Malek sees a trend for young, fruity and market-ready wines.

Cabernet Sauvignon ⊕ ★★★ Previously tasted **05** was dark-fruited, with toasty vanilla highlights. **Merlot** Await new, as for **Pinotage**, **Shiraz** & **Pinotage Rosé**. **Kwartet** ⊕ ★★★ Last-tasted **07** a cab-led 4-way Bordeaux blend; had pencil shaving notes from French oak. **Theart Reserve** ⊕ ★★★ Second **05** Bordeaux blend tad leafier & more tannic than sibling a while ago. **Chardonnay** ⊕ ★★★ Lightly oaked **10** had soft pear nuance, slightly sweet farewell on review. **Cape Ruby** ⊕ 🏺 ★ Port-style **08** from pinotage, big alcohol (21%) & medicinal hint some time back. — JP

Nieuwedrift Vineyards

Location: Piketberg ▪ Map/WO: Swartland ▪ Est/1stB 2002 ▪ Tasting, sales & cellar tours Mon-Fri 9–1 & 2–6 Sat 9–2 ▪ Closed Easter Fri/Sun, Dec 25/26 & Jan 1 ▪ Meals on request; or BYO picnic ▪ Facilities for children ▪ Tour groups ▪ Conferences ▪ Owner(s)/viticulturist(s) Johan Mostert ▪ Cellarmaster(s) Johan Mostert (Jan 2002) ▪ 151ha/31ha (shiraz, chard, chenin, cbard) ▪ 410t total 10t/658cs own label 28% red 40% white 16% rosé 16% MCC ▪ PO Box 492 Piketberg 7320 ▪ nieuwedrift@patat.za.net ▪ S 32° 58'28.1" E 018° 45'10.6" ▪ **T +27 (0)22-913-1966/+27 (0)82-824-8104** ▪ F +27 (0)88-022-913-1966

Johan Mostert made the leap from growing grapes for others to making his own small quantity of wine in 2002, with help from mentor Marais de Villiers of Main Street Winery. Johan's vineyards near Piketberg, on the banks of the Berg River, won Vinpro's Best Practice Awards for the Swartland in 2003, 2004 and 2006.

Shiraz ★★★★ Juicy, generous **10**, baked red berry flavour with spicy notes; ripe, full bodied & jovial. Tiny portion spent 2 years in old oak. **Blanc de Noir** 🍷 ★★★ Dry **12** from shiraz offers a gush of primary strawberry juice. **Chenin Blanc** 🍷 ★★★★ Mineral, lees-driven style of **12** shows promise. Unsettled mid-2012, but balance & structure should prevail. **Méthode Cap Classique** ★★★ Longer lees-ageing for 2nd disgorgement of **10** sparkling brings added body & texture. Resolutely dry, with oaky nuttiness. — GdB

Nitida Cellars

Location: Durbanville ▪ Map: Durbanville, Philadelphia & Darling ▪ WO: Durbanville/Coastal ▪ Est/1stB 1995 ▪ Tasting & sales Mon-Fri 9–5 Sat 9.30–3 Sun 11–3 ▪ Closed Good Fri, Dec 25 & Jan 1 ▪ Cassia Restaurant (see Restaurants section) ▪ Tables at Nitida T +27 (0)21-975-9537, www.tablesatnitida.co.za ▪ Conference & function venue at Cassia T +27 (0)21-976-0640 ▪ Facilities for children ▪ Mountain biking: Vellerdrome track for novice riders; part of Hillcrest/Majik forest trail (www.tygerbergmtb.co.za) ▪ Conservation area ▪ Annual festivals: Season of Sauvignon (Oct); Feast of the Grape (Mar); Soup, Sip & Bread (June) ▪ Owner(s) Bernhard & Peta Veller ▪ Cellarmaster(s) Bernhard Veller ▪ Winemaker(s) RJ Botha (2007) ▪ Viticulturist(s) Bernhard Veller & RJ

Botha ▪ 35ha/16ha (cabs s/f, p verdot, riesling, sauv, sem) ▪ 150t/9,000cs own label 30% red 70% white +
1,500cs for clients ▪ Brands for clients: Woolworths ▪ PO Box 1423 Durbanville 7551 ▪ info@nitida.co.za
www.nitida.co.za ▪ S 33° 50' 3.8" E 018° 35' 37.0" ▪ **T** +27 (0)21-976-1467 ▪ F +27 (0)21-976-5631

Co-owner Bernhard Veller explains that the secret behind the quality here is 'no
producing wines to win awards but rather wines that we love to drink'. Well, he'
got excellent taste, because white blend Coronata Integration has just earne
Nitida their first 5 stars. Back after a 3 year gap is the Semillon Noble Late Harvest
renamed Modjadji after the Rain Queen of the Balobedu tribe in Limpopo, becaus
of the crucial role moisture plays in the formation of the fungus that creates nobl
rot. There is also an intended link back to the theme of women, as reflected in th
two Matriarch bubblies.

★★★★ **Cabernet Sauvignon** ✓ 🈂 Offering plum compote & loads of spice, **10**'s tailored tannins give
lovely savoury effect, already accessible but with a 6-year future mapped out.

★★★★☆ **Calligraphy** ⏱ 🈂 Bordeaux blend **10** shows merlot predominance, with third cab: cassis, blac
cherry perfume & fleshy ripeness lead you in, but as befits a flagship, the structure is serious; savoury tannins wi
keep it in perfect health for years to come.

★★★★ **Riesling** ✓ 🗄 🈂 Previously 'Weisser Riesling'. With singular delicacy & finesse, dry **12** is floral
fruity, has Old World elegance (12% alcohol) & a racy acidity to aid its development till ±2020.

★★★★ **Sauvignon Blanc** ✓ 🗄 🈂 Expressive & complex, showing the signature 'green but ripe' characte
of the area, **12** has the sleek muscle tone of a racehorse, vibrating with health.

★★★★ **Club Select Sauvignon Blanc** 🗄 🈂 Special selection to highlight cool terroir, elegant **1**.
expresses minerality with a green edge; acid brightened to extend the lovely flavours, giving good potential.

★★★★☆ **Semillon** ✓ 🗄 🈂 Greengage with a distinctive fynbos presence in previewed **12**, the 50% bar
rel-fermented portion deftly combined to give more weight, a gentle savoury thread, without detracting fror
the lovely purity. **11** sold out untasted.

★★★★☆ **Coronata Integration** ✓ 🗄 🈂 Name promises perfect partnership sauvignon/semillon & i
merging with oak, expertly done in **11** (★★★★★). Extra year adds to the magic; lime & ginger biscuit, ye
minerality seamed throughout, an ultra-long tangy finish. Like **10**, will be even better over time.

★★★★☆ **Modjadji Semillon Noble Late Harvest** 🈂 Previously 'Semillon NLH'. Worth the wait sinc
08 preview, **11**'s lime marmalade & barley sugar sweetness tempered by the acidity, remaining rich, impres
sively long. 375ml.

Pinotage 🗄 🈂 ★★★ Blueberry-toned, fleshy & exuberant **11** is tasty, showcasing the friendly side c
pinotage. **Shiraz** ✓ 🗄 🈂 ★★★★ Lovely drinkability in **10**, smooth-textured, pepper & nutmeg-spiced plum
fruit & ready accessibility. **Chardonnay** ✓ 🗄 ★★★★ Lightly oaked **12** combines peach & citrus flavours, it
appeal further enhanced by the streamlined body, palate freshness. **Matriarch in Red** ⏱ ★★★ Rare tradi
tional-method sparkling from shiraz. Plums & berries, nice fruit purity in **10**'s perfume; flavours show mor
fruitcake, slight smokiness. **Matriarch Méthode Cap Classique** ⏱ 🈂 ★★★ Champagne-method spar
kling; mainly chardonnay, 30% pinot noir's influence seen in **10**'s berry aromas, hint of pink. Dry & fresh wit
lively mousse, an aperitif style. WO Coastal. — CR

▪ **Nixan Wines** *see* Blue Crane Vineyards

Noble Hill Wine Estate   🍽 🍷 📷 🎿 ♿

Location: Paarl ▪ Map: Paarl & Wellington ▪ WO: Simonsberg-Paarl/Paarl/Western Cape/Overberg/Coastal
Est/1stB 2001 ▪ Tasting & sales daily 10–5 ▪ Fee R30, waived on purchase ▪ Cellar tours by appt during tasting
hours ▪ cosecha Restaurant (see Restaurants section) ▪ Picnic baskets ▪ Facilities for children ▪ Farm-produce
extra-virgin olive oil ▪ Conservation area ▪ Owner(s) Noble Hill Trust ▪ Winemaker(s) Bernard le Roux (Ma
2010), with Rodney Zimba (2001) ▪ Viticulturist(s) Etienne Southey (2006) & Johan Viljoen (consultant)
50ha/30ha (cabs s/f, merlot, mourv, p verdot, shiraz, sauv, viog) ▪ PO Box 111 Simondium 7670 ▪ info@
noblehill.com ▪ www.noblehill.com ▪ S 33° 49' 38.0" E 018° 56' 12.1" ▪ **T** +27 (0)21-874-3844

A 'problem' block of over-vigorous mourvèdre required drastic intervention bacF
in 2008: every second vine was sacrificed and now it's in balance and producing a
delicious new rosé. Viticulture aside, investment in this American family owne
estate in the Simonsberg foothills is not only financial but also environmenta
(mulching, composting and recycling, among others). Feedback from their first US
clients has been positive, much like the local response to their new Bloem brand.

Noble Hill range

★★★★ **Cabernet Sauvignon** ⑨ Delicious pristine blackberry fruit, forest floor, cedar highlights to understated & elegant **08**. Firm & mouthfilling, vanilla oaky finish. A keeper.

★★★★ **Merlot** ✓ Plum & black cherry appeal, **09** luscious & soft but with power & cocoa depth, yielding yet firm tannin backbone. Good harmony & elegance.

★★★★ **Syrah** ⑨ Very fruit-forward & bold **08** (★★★), sweet, spicy dark berry fruit & a warm savoury ending. Touch overripe compared with last-tasted maiden **05**, listed as 'Shiraz'.

★★★★ **1674** 3-way mix of cab, merlot & petit verdot. Rich chocolate & plum attraction on **09** reflects prime vintage. Range of flavour on stratified palate. Wood's prominent mid-2012 but will marry beautifully.

★★★★ **Syrah-Mourvèdre-Viognier** ⑨ Intense aromas of black fruit, Rhône-style **08** is rich & deep, with delicate spice & toast. Enjoy with robust & hearty food.

★★★★ **Sauvignon Blanc** 🏠 Tropical toned with granadilla primacy, **12** (★★★★) zesty flint & gravel add interest, length, to lively mouthful. Less acidity than **09**. Some Elgin & Durbanville grapes.

★★★★☆ **The Longest Day Sauvignon Blanc** 🏠 'Sauvignon Blanc Reserve' last time. Intricate vinification of hand-selected grapes ex Elandskloof vineyard. **11**, now bottled, fresh, juicy & balanced. Lime, fig & granadilla zip. Good depth & complexity.

★★★★ **Viognier** Natural ferment in old oak adds creamy feel to **11** (★★★★), buttery stonefruit on lively, full palate. Last-made **09** was seductive & peachy. Coastal WO.

Bloem White NEW ☺ 🏠 🏠 ★★★ Tangy entry on **12** chenin/viognier mix, nectarine & peach simplicity & light acid make an ideal quaffer. WO Paarl, as for Red.

Bloem Red NEW ✓ 🏠 🏠 ★★★★ Instant blueberry love affair on **11** shiraz & mourvèdre blend. Cocoa depth & density. Firm, toned frame. A delight. **Mourvèdre Rosé** NEW 🏠 🏠 ★★★★ Tasty cranberry zing on **12**, lovely candyfloss blush & spicy charm. Succulent dry body, good structure. **Chardonnay** NEW 🏠 ★★★★ **11** ample lemon curd, marmalade & toasty appeal. Nutty flavour & rounded mouthfeel from toned oak. Structured & long.

Austin range
Cabernet Sauvignon-Merlot Occasional release. — FM

Noble Savage

This standalone brand from Bartinney Private Cellar epitomises much of the style, chic and joie de vivre of co-owner Rose Jordaan, but it's neither frivolous nor trivial — under the guidance of consultant Ronell Wiid, it's a feisty, fun range of serious wines with real character.

★★★★ **Cabernet Sauvignon-Merlot** ✓ 🏠 Was 'Noble Savage'. Sweet jammy black fruit on **10** edged with some meaty savouriness, liquorice/anise & elegant length. Stellenbosch WO, as all.

Cabernet Sauvignon Rosé 🏠 🏠 ★★★ **12** shows plenty of pomegranate pungency & slight medicinal note, but appealing, cherry menthol fruit & fresh finish. Previewed, as next. **Sauvignon Blanc** NEW 🏠 🏠 ★★★ Lots of pink grapefruit on **12** with spoons of lemon curd & lime marmalade, & well-managed acidity. — CM

Nomada Wines

Location/WO: Durbanville ▪ Est/1stB 2007 ▪ Tasting on the farm Sat 10-3 or by appt ▪ Owner(s) Riaan & Gina Oosthuizen ▪ Winemaker(s)/viticulturist(s) Riaan Oosthuizen (2007) ▪ 66ha/7ha (cabs s/f, merlot, chenin, sauv) ▪ 55t total 10t/1,000cs own label 40% red 60% white + 3,000cs for clients ▪ Brands for clients: Klein Roosboom Wines, Red White Pink Wines, Schaap Wines (Netherlands), Signal Gun Wines ▪ PO Box 5145 Tygervalley 7536 ▪ nomadawines@gmail.com ▪ **T +27 (0)83-280-7690**

The winery name reflects owners Riaan and Gina Oosthuizen's wish to make wines from many different terroirs, although they were fairly nomadic themselves before settling on a farm in Durbanville. Ironically, it is the 1,000 ostriches on the property that should be on the move to allow the building of a winetasting venue, but for now are confined there by bird flu restrictions.

Georgina ★★★★ Bordeaux-style red blend is robust in youth but more balanced & riper in **10**, with firm tannin structure. Ageworthy table mate. **Sauvignon Blanc** 🏠 Await next. **Rustica** 🏠 Missed our deadline. — MW

■ **Non Pareil** *see* L'Olivier Wine & Olive Estate

■ **Nordic Wines** *see* Wedgewood Wines
■ **Nuwehoop** *see* uniWines Vineyards

Nuweland Wynkelder

Location: Malmesbury ▪ WO: Swartland/Coastal ▪ Est 2007 ▪ 1stB 2008 ▪ Vygevallei farm stall & Nuweland wine house (R27): Tasting & sales Mon-Sat 10-6 Sun 10-4 ▪ Closed Dec 25 & Jan 1 ▪ Restaurant ▪ Facilities for children ▪ Tour groups ▪ Gifts ▪ Art ▪ Farm produce ▪ Conferences ▪ Cellar tours by appt only ▪ Owner(s) Juan Louw ▪ Winemaker(s)/viticulturist(s) Juan Louw (Jan 2007) ▪ 300ha/96ha ▪ 560t/470cs own label 50% red 40% white 10% dessert + 2,700L bulk ▪ PO Box 283 Malmesbury 7299 ▪ juan@nuweland.za.net ▪ www.nuweland.za.net ▪ S 33° 24'03.87" E 018° 16'41.73" ▪ **T +27 (0)78-111-7913**

Hugely enthusiastic, Juan Louw would love to teach you more about wine. He believes in creating interesting blends and in the alchemy of food and wine. His dream of making wine off his family's vineyards was realised in 2008 when an old chicken coop was turned into a cellar. His passion for old vines and improving dryland vineyards is relentless, and as a member of the Swartland Independent movement he is set to celebrate these visions.

★★★★ **Straw Wine** Now settled in bottle. From muscat d'Alexandrie with rum & raisin charm. Composed **08** has lovely richness ending dryish & long. 4 years oak maturation adds to complexity.

★★★★ **Muscat de Alexandrie** Now bottled, **09** fortified dessert wine from air-dried grapes, the juice fortified then oak-aged 3 years. Rich & very sweet but seductive & silky liquid decadence, harmonised by fine acid.

★★★★ **Muscat de Frontignan** Red & white muscadel mix in gorgeous **09**, previously previewed fortified dessert. Honey nuance, typical raisiny nose, with lovely integrated old oak maturation. Some Worcester fruit.

Rooipad Cabernet Sauvignon NEW ★★★ From ultra-low yielding vineyards. Older-oaked **11** has ripe fruit profile following to juicy & generous palate. **18 Mei Grenache Noir** ★★★ **10** delivers on preview promise last year. Picked 18 May, very late for Swartland harvest. Ripe & smoky notes with firm & savoury support. **Makstok Pinotage** ★★★ High-toned **11** has lovely pure sweet fruit & dry food-friendly tannins. Only older oak. Off ungrafted bushvines. **Haasbek Tinta Barocca** ★★★ **11** seems very young & unformed mid-2012, but interesting ripe nose. Prominent acidity would be good foil for richer foods. **Juan II** ✓ ★★★★ Interesting blend of Bordeaux varieties plus pinotage & tinta. **10**, now bottled, has vibrant fruit, attractive tarry oak & dry end. **Bosstok Steen Chenin Blanc** ▦ ★★★ Now bottled. From 30 year old bushvines; **11** distinctly different, off-dry & rich. **Gesuierde Sauvignon Blanc** Not tasted. **Sauvignon Blanc** NEW ✓ ▦ ★★★★ Wonderful food wine ('Snoek braai' says winemaker). **11** especially given maximum sun exposure to ensure concentrated tropical fruit richness; both soft & dry. WO Coastal. Discontinued: **Sauvignon Blanc-Chenin Blanc-Semillon**. — JP

Nuy Wine Cellar

Location/map: Worcester ▪ WO: Nuy/Breedekloof/Worcester/Western Cape ▪ Est 1964 ▪ 1stB 1966 ▪ Tasting & sales Mon-Fri 8.30-4.30 Sat 8.30-12.30 ▪ Closed Dec 25/26 & Jan 1 ▪ BYO picnic ▪ Mountain biking ▪ Owner(s) 19 members ▪ Cellarmaster(s) Christo Pienaar (Sep 2003) ▪ Winemaker(s) Louwritz Louw (Dec 2008) ▪ Viticulturist(s) Pierre Snyman (Vinpro) ▪ 580ha (cab, merlot, muscadel, ptage, shiraz, chard, chenin, cbard, nouvelle, sauv) ▪ 16,000t/5,000cs own label ▪ PO Box 5225 Worcester 6849 ▪ wines@nuywinery.co.za ▪ www.nuywinery.co.za ▪ S 33° 39'8.7" E 019° 38'30.9" ▪ **T +27 (0)23-347-0272** ▪ F +27 (0)23-347-4994

Embracing change, Nuy Winery is now on Facebook 'to connect more with consumers' and has handed a two-hectare Muscadel vineyard to its workers in an empowerment deal. 'They work on it after hours and the wine gets bottled separately,' explains winemaker Louwritz Louw. 'What won't change is Nuy's wines of excellent quality at affordable prices.'

★★★★ **Barrel Selection Cabernet Sauvignon** ✓ After **08** (★★★★★) trumped **07** (★★★), elegant **10** affirms improved form of this reserve label. Gentle spice & cedar from 2 years in oak, intense blackcurrant flavour, dry & savoury aftertaste. Modest 13.2% alc adds to appeal. **09** unready.

★★★★ **Barrel Selection Syrah** ✓ Bright & poised **10**, well crafted to showcase succulent fruit, judiciously oaked (2 years). More powerful (14.5% alc) than **08** but no less elegant. **09** missed our deadline.

★★★★ **Red Muscadel** ▦ **12** fortified dessert on track after slight wobble in **11** (★★★★). Full-sweet but uncloying, spiced raisin richness & uplifting conclusion. Delicious on release, these age beautifully too. Stock up!

★★★★ **White Muscadel** ▦ Classic South African fortified dessert, worth cellaring. **10** irresistible honeyed raisins buoyed by tangy acidity & integrated spirit. Same intriguing ginger nuance as **07**. **08** & **09** skipped.

Cabernet Sauvignon ⓘ 🍾 ★★ Cranberry fruit, oak grip on early-drinking, lightish (12% alc) **10**. **Rouge de Nuy** ⓘ 🍾 ★★★ Lightly oaked cherry & liquorice **10** easy-sipper punches above its price point. **Chardonnay** 🍾 ★★★ Attractive interplay of citrus & vanilla oak on buttery & smooth **11**. **Chenin Blanc** ⓘ 🍾 ★★★ **11** early picked for cool green-apple crispness & lowish 12% alc. **Colombar Dry** 🍾 ★★ Modestly flavoured **12** slimmer's friend, with low sugar & alcohol. **Colombar Semi-Sweet** ⓘ 🍾 ★★★ Slightly sweet **11**, gentle guava taste, rounded mouthfeel. **Sauvignon Blanc** 🍾 ★★ **12** faintly grassy & lean, bracing acidity. **Chant de Nuit** ⓘ 🍾 ★★ Tropical-toned NV unchallenging sipper. **Sauvignon Blanc Sparkling Vin Sec** ⓘ ★★★ NV vibrant any-occasion sparkling with burst of bubbly passionfruit on the tongue. Discontinued: **Shiraz, Reserve Chenin Blanc**. — HJ/CvZ

Nwanedi Estate

Location: Paarl ▪ Map: Paarl & Wellington ▪ Est 1997 ▪ 1stB 2005 ▪ Tasting & sales Mon-Sat 10-4.30 Sun by appt & for events ▪ Closed Easter Fri/Sun, Dec 25/26 & Jan 1 ▪ Fee R15 ▪ Cellar & vineyard tours by appt ▪ 12-suite Nwanedi Country Hotel ▪ Conference/wedding/function venue ▪ Restaurant ▪ Owner(s) Gavin & Jean Stork ▪ Cellarmaster(s) Gavin Stork (Apr 2004) ▪ Winemaker(s)/viticulturist(s) Nico Vermeulen (2010) ▪ 17ha (cab, mourv, shiraz, viog) ▪ 188t/2,500cs own label 100% red ▪ PO Box 955 Wellington 7654 ▪ info@nwanedi.com ▪ www.nwanedi.com ▪ S 33° 40' 46.3" E 018° 58' 8.1" ▪ **T** +27 (0)21-872-8723/+27 (0)73-967-3790/+27 (0)83-407-4246 ▪ F +27 (0)86-618-5251/+27 (0)86-618-5275

Named after the game reserve in Limpopo where they married many years ago, Gavin and Jean Stork's estate north of Paarl was conceived as a retirement playground to indulge their passion for trains of all kinds and sizes. A couple of detours and sidetracks later, they're running a luxury guest house and purveying their own-brand wines, vinified on site by seasoned consultant Nico Vermeulen.

First Dawn range
Classic Shiraz (Reserved Private Bin) ⓘ ★★★★ Previously tasted, velvety **07** packed with cinnamon, clove & chocolate raisins; had firm oak grip. **Shiraz** ⓘ ★★★ Last tasted **08**'s chocolate & liquorice fruit balanced by dry roasted nuts & tannin from oak (85% new).

Interlude range
Chenin Blanc 🍾 New bottling not ready.

Meditation range
Cabernet Sauvignon ⓘ ★★★ **08** last had ample fruit, juice & spice from 85% new wood. — FM

■ **Oak Lane** *see Beau Joubert Vineyards & Winery*

Oak Valley Wines

Location/WO: Elgin ▪ Map: Elgin, Walker Bay & Bot River ▪ Est 1898 ▪ 1stB 2003 ▪ Tasting & sales Mon-Fri 9-5 Sat/Sun 10-4 ▪ Closed Sat/Sun Jun 15-Aug 15, Easter Fri-Sun, Dec 25/26 & Jan 1 ▪ The Pool Room @ Oak Valley (see Restaurants section) ▪ Deli (artisanal breads, homegrown free-range meats & charcuterie) ▪ Self-catering 1-bedroom cottage ▪ Walks/hikes ▪ Mountain biking trail ▪ Greenhouse flower tours every Fri 10.30-12 (book ahead) ▪ Conservation area ▪ Owner(s) AG Rawbone-Viljoen Trust ▪ Winemaker(s) Pieter Visser ▪ Viticulturist(s) Pieter Visser, assisted by Kevin Watt ▪ 37ha (cabs s/f, merlot, p verdot, pinot, shiraz, chard, sauv, sém) ▪ ±200-250t/±15,000cs own label 45% red 50% white 5% rosé ▪ BWI champion, GlobalGap, IPW, WIETA ▪ PO Box 30 Elgin 7180 ▪ wines@oak-valley.co.za ▪ www.oakvalley.co.za ▪ S 34° 9' 24.4" E 019° 2' 55.5" ▪ **T** +27 (0)21-859-4110 ▪ F +27 (0)21-859-3405

One can believe Anthony Rawbone-Viljoen's pride in the Australian academic achievements of son Christopher but is it really 'time for a father to move over as my local qualifications cannot compete'? Those qualifications promise well (and Christopher has already introduced a tourism-driven business model — a restaurant/deli and wine-tasting centre opened in 2012), but the old man's achievement of adding a great wine reputation to this huge Elgin family farm (with flowers, cattle, pigs, etc) is not easily matched. Pinot noir has been one of the many success stories, and father and son (not to mention winemaker/ viticulturist Pieter Visser) 'eagerly await the new vintages which will include grapes from our high density vineyard. A wild ferment made from these grapes shows exceptional promise and could provide inspiration.'

★★★★☆ **Pinot Noir** ⓲ ⓜ Black cherry & gamey notes on **11** (★★★★); savoury at first but finishing a touch ungenerous. More chunky, less satiny than **09** (★★★★★) or **08**; no **10**. Might develop over year or two.

★★★★ **Shiraz** NEW ⓜ Intense cerise, almost opaque barrel sample **11**. Raspberry, red fruit whiffs, plus tannins, full yet unflamboyant. Lovely wood integration, fine peppery hints on finish.

★★★★ **The Oak Valley Blend** ⓲ Ripe, sweet merlot spiced with cab & cab franc & whiff of French oak combine in polished **07**. Firm but not harsh or inaccessible so enjoy over next 5 or so years.

★★★★★ **Chardonnay** ✓ ▤ ⓜ **11** apricot & grapefruit aromas lead to plush & multi-layered, textured palate with honeyed notes belying dry, lingering finish. Developed & biscuity, the oak (some new) perfectly concealed

★★★★★ **The OV** ⓲ ▤ **09** bounded back after **08** (★★★★). Persuasive citrus, honey-rich complexity with precise mineral lines. Distinctive 81/19% sauvignon/semillon blend, compatibly oaked. Lovely prospects.

Sauvignon Blanc ✓ ▤ ⓜ ★★★★ Nettly, gunflint & burnt match whiffs on **11** with tiny semillon compo nent; austere & lacking generosity, but with bright zesty finish. Discontinued: Rawbones range. — MF

Obikwa

Distell good-value brand named for the indigenous Obikwa people and sold in more than 40 countries. Widely sourced, and made for early enjoyment.

Chenin Blanc ☺ ▤ ⓜ ★★★ Soft, cheerful **12**, wide spectrum of flavour — crushed leaves, fruit salad, ripe quince — charming & easy to drink. **Moscato** ☺ ▤ ⓜ ★★☆ Delicious, oh-so-quaffable **12** preview from chenin, colombard & muscat is sweet, perfumed & low in alcohol (7.5%).

Cabernet Sauvignon ▤ ⓜ ★★★ Two vintages tasted: pre-bottling sample of well-made **12**, solid structure of tannin with a light red-fruit centre, ideal food partner. **11** (★★★★) is similar, red berries & undaunting tannins, shows benefit of extra year in bottle. **Merlot** ▤ ⓜ **11** (★★), now bottled, needs to be enjoyed soon with hearty fare. Ex-tank **12** too unformed to rate but looks more like the soft easy-drinker we encountered last time. **Pinotage** ▤ ⓜ ★★★ Two vintages reviewed: **12** tank sample punchy in a good way, controlled tannins, ripe & balanced banana-laced mulberry flavours. Clever wine. **11** (★★★) similar, bit firmer, fruit not quite as bright. **Shiraz** ▤ ⓜ ★★★ Previewed **12** spicy, fruit-driven Glühwein-in-a-glass styling, broadened by a grain of sugar (like most Obikwas), clean, tasty. **Pinotage-Cabernet Sauvignon** ▤ ⓜ ★★ Name change prompted by pinotage (51%) leading **11** blend. Casual sipper with creamy & light red fruit, sprinkled with milk chocolate. **Pinotage Rosé** ▤ ⓜ ★★ Lightish **12**'s seductive strawberries and-cream intro leads to sweetish palate & surprisingly brisk, food-styled finish. **Chardonnay** ▤ ★★ Unwooded **12** lime cordial flavour with evident sweetness, best served well chilled. Tasted pre-bottling & provisionally rated. **Pinot Grigio** ▤ ★★ 'Pinot Gris' last time. From tank, lightish **12** lemon blossoms & boiled sweets character, casual semi-dry sipping. **Sauvignon Blanc** ▤ ⓜ ★★ Uncomplicated fun **12** friendly summer fruit salad flavours with lunchtime-lowish 12% alcohol. **Classic Dry White** ▤ Not tasted **Cuvée Brut** ▤ ★★★ Happy & lively **12**, just-dry, simple but nice party bubbly. **Natural Sweet Red** ★★ Straightforward low-alcohol sweet red with boiled sweet flavour. This & Natural Sweet White previously vin tage dated, now NV. **Natural Sweet White** ★★ NV sweet, low-alcohol picnic wine from chenin, colombard & muscat. W Cape WO for all the above. — DB/HJ

■ **Ocean Basket** *see* Simonsvlei International
■ **Oddbins** *see* Shoprite Checkers

Oewerzicht Private Cellar   🍴 ⛺ 📷

Location: Greyton ▪ Map: Southern Cape ▪ WO: Overberg ▪ Est/1stB 2002 ▪ Tasting & sales daily by appt ▪ Guest cot tages & tents ▪ Wedding, conference & function facilities ▪ Mountain biking/hiking trails ▪ Owner(s) winemaker(s)/viticulturist(s) Kootjie Viljoen ▪ 0.5ha (cab) ▪ 1,000cs own label 100% red ▪ PO Box 18 Greyton 7233 ▪ info@oewerzicht.com ▪ S 34° 6′ 14.6″   E 019° 40′ 7.9″ ▪ **T +27 (0)28-254-9831** ▪ F +27 (0)28-254-9968

'I'm passionate about good wine but making it is a hobby,' says Kootjie Vijoen explaining the sporadic releases from his apple, pear, sheep, cattle and wheat (and sometimes wine) farm in Sonderend River Valley near Greyton. He's looking for ward to featuring a new bottling next edition. We'll take that as a definite maybe.

Cabernet Sauvignon ⓲ ★★★ Juicy **06** last was an exotically spiced diamond-in-the-rough. — MW/CvZ

■ **Oggendau** *see* Eerste Hoop Wine Cellar

Old Bridge Wines

St Francis Bay ▪ Closed to public ▪ Owner(s) Paulinas Dal Mountain Vineyards (Pty) Ltd ▪ 20,000cs 60% red 40% white ▪ PO Box 557 St Francis Bay 6312 ▪ rickety@iafrica.com ▪ **T +27 (0)82-777-1519**

Export-focused producer and negociant sourcing wines for various brands, including private labels for specialised corporate clients. The wines include limited-edition African Gold Collection mainly for US, Europe and Asia; Big Six Collection, boxed sets for local game lodges/retreats and export; and Old Bridge.

■ **Old Brown** see Sedgwick's Old Brown

Oldenburg Vineyards

Location/map: Stellenbosch ▪ WO: Stellenbosch/Banghoek ▪ Est 1960s ▪ 1stB 2007 ▪ Tasting & sales Mon-Fri 10-4.30; Sat & pub hols 10-3 (Nov-Apr) & by appt (May-Oct) ▪ Fee R25 ▪ Closed Sun, Easter Fri, Dec 25/26 & Jan 1 ▪ Refreshments for sale (cheese platters, biltong, etc.) ▪ Owner(s) Adrian Vanderspuy ▪ Winemaker(s) Simon Thompson (May 2004) ▪ Viticulturist(s) Simon Thompson (May 2004), with Paul Wallace (consultant) ▪ 50ha/30ha (cabs s/f, merlot, shiraz, chard, chenin) ▪ 198t/3,750cs own label 66% red 34% white ▪ PO Box 2246 Dennesig 7601 ▪ cellardoor@oldenburgvineyards.com ▪ www.oldenburgvineyards.com ▪ S 33° 55' 7. 61" E 018° 56'8.75" ▪ **T +27 (0)21-885-1618** ▪ F +27 (0)21-885-2665

Adrian Vanderspuy was born in the lovely Banhoek Valley and after a long sojourn overseas bought Oldenburg farm there in 2003: 'It was a real chance to participate in two very positive stories, the rise of South Africa and its wine industry's renaissance.' The vineyards were in 'a sorry state', however, and replanting began. As the vines mature, the fruits of optimism may be tasted in vinified form — and are receiving plaudits not only from us.

★★★★ **Cabernet Sauvignon** ⊕ Restrained, detailed **09** offers black fruit, almond & lead pencil aromas. With savoury fine tannins, the wine is elegant & spare, despite ripeness & the big 14.5% alcohol.

★★★★☆ **Merlot** NEW Plum-rich but not plush, fragrantly savoury **10** off young vines showing Bordeaux-like fruit. Subtle mulberry whiffs without silicone-implant showiness. Oak (50% new French barrels) integrated to the point of invisibility. Altogether silken & restrained. WO Banghoek, as for Chenin & Chardonnay.

★★★★ **Chenin Blanc** ✓ 🍴 Intense but restrained **11** (★★★★☆), with oak, apricot & mineral notes interwoven. Finer, more intense & densely textured than **10**, offering palate weight & food-friendliness before flamboyance. Fairly modest 13% alcohol. Half-new oak well concealed. Great persistence.

Cabernet Franc ⊕ ★★★★ **09** more about fine texture than taste; the fruit is faintly green-edged, with spice & oak harmoniously interwoven. **Syrah** ⊕ ★★★ Raspberry & allspice notes on **09**, with opulent tannins, dollops of sweet fruit; slightly hot finish from big alcohol. **Chardonnay** 🍴 ★★★★ Funky lime citrus aromas. Some pineapple whiffs on **11** lurking behind well managed charry oak. Easy though uncomplex. — MF

Old Vines Cellars

Location: Cape Town ▪ WO: Stellenbosch/Coastal ▪ Est/1stB 1995 ▪ Closed to public ▪ Owner(s) Irina von Holdt & Françoise Botha ▪ Winemaker(s) Irina von Holdt ▪ 12,000cs own label 40% red 60% white + 4,000cs for clients ▪ 50 Liesbeek Rd Rosebank 7700 ▪ info@oldvines.co.za ▪ www.oldvines.co.za ▪ **T +27 (0)21-685-6428** ▪ F +27 (0)21-685-6446

Irina von Holdt's love of chenin blanc is almost as deep as the roots of the gnarled old vines she harvests. Fittingly so, as she was one of the earliest advocates of their quality and continued survival. The boutique winemaker takes an almost matriarchal pride in being able to showcase her wines amongst our finest chenins. She has received 'royal' recognition for her efforts, hers being the only SA white wine to sail with Cunard's Queen Mary 2, Queen Elizabeth and Queen Victoria.

Old Vines range

★★★★ **Barrel Reserve Chenin Blanc** 🍷 Tiny yield from 63 year old vines, now-bottled **10** layered complexity & genteel Old World restraint. Contemplative food wine with silky texture & dried peach/almond tone.

★★★★ **Chenin Blanc** ✓ 🍷 Unoaked tank sample **11** shows rich leesy support for bright dried peach/pineapple flavours. Older vines reward with depth & balance.

★★★★ **Vintage Brut** ⊕ Unusual variety for méthode cap classique sparkling, but natural choice for chenin devotee. **04** from bushvines, still selling. Creamy, with mineral finish when last tasted.

Baron von Holdt Await new vintage.

Spring Valley range

Chenin Blanc-Sauvignon Blanc ☺ 🍴🏺 ★★★ Ex-tank **12** a crisp 60/40 duo with yellow peach flavours & bright acidity. Juicy & fresh picnic quaffer.

Merlot 🏺 ★★★ **11** preview a ripe winter-warming fruit compote. **Shiraz-Merlot** 🏺 ★★ Taste out of vintage sequence, **10** is ripe, brusque & savoury, for robust fare. Coastal WOs for these. — MW

Olifantsberg Family Vineyards

Location: Worcester ▪ Map/WO: Breedekloof ▪ Est 2003 ▪ 1stB 2005 ▪ Tasting & sales Mon-Fri by appt ▪ Owner(s) Paul J Leeuwerik ▪ Cellarmaster(s)/winemaker(s)/viticulturist(s) Jacques du Plessis (Nov 2009) ▪ 95ha/8ha (carignan, grenache n/b, mourv, ptage, shiraz, chard, chenin, rouss) ▪ 25t/700cs own label 75% red 25% white ▪ PO Box 942 Worcester 6849 ▪ duplessis.je@gmail.com ▪ www.olifantsberg.com ▪ S 33° 35'42 76" E 019° 21'42.39" ▪ **T +27 (0)23-342-0401** ▪ F +27 (0)23-342-8734

Biodynamic experimentation is on the cards at this small Breedekloof farm or the slopes of the Brandwacht Mountains, where, cellarmaster Jacques du Plessis says, elevation, shale soils, constant winds and big diurnal temperature differences provide unique conditions. 'We aim to put this location in a bottle and let the wines tell our story.'

Cabernet Sauvignon ⚛ ★★★ When last tasted, **09** was shy & herbaceous, its subtle blackcurrant fruit hidden by taut oak tannins which may since have softened. **Pinotage** NEW ✓ ★★★ Approachable **11** exudes plummy mulberry varietal charm. Firm but supple structure with sweet-fruited length. **Syrah** ⚛ ★★★ Name change from 'Shiraz' in **10**, more robust, with Rhône-like pepperiness. **Chardonnay** In abeyance. **Chardonnay-Chenin Blanc** NEW ★★ **11** plump & waxy, with gentle baked apple/almond nuance. — MW

Olsen Wines

Location/WO: Paarl ▪ Map: Paarl & Wellington ▪ Est/1stB 2002 ▪ Tasting by appt only ▪ Fee R25pp ▪ Light meals for groups of ±10 by appt ▪ Farm-style jams ▪ Owner(s) Greg & Kimberly Olsen ▪ Cellarmaster(s)/viticulturist(s) Armand Botha (2000) & Kimberly Olsen ▪ Winemaker(s) Armand Botha (2007) & Loftie Ellis ▪ 30ha ▪ 500cs own label 90% red 10% white ▪ Europgap registered ▪ PO Box 9052 Huguenot 7645 ▪ olsenwines@ mweb.co.za ▪ S 33° 44'4.7" E 019° 3'5.0" ▪ **T +27 (0)21-862-3653** ▪ F +27 (0)21-862-2589

During his nine-month astronaut training in Kazakhstan, winemaker, entrepreneur and third-private-citizen-in-space Greg Olsen provided the wines to accompany the evening meal. 'I became very popular,' he says. He even took some of his beloved pinotage into space with him. US-based Olsen spends every harvest on his Paarl farm and has also planted pinotage on his land in Montana.

Pinotage ★★★ Owner's favourite variety in ripe spicy style, **09** nicely structured by half new oak — slightly bitter finish, though marginally less so than also-tasted **08**. **Chardonnay** 🏺 ★★★ Butterscotch & marzipan on oak-fermented (all new) **11**; pleasantly light yet mouthfilling. **Chenin Blanc** ★★★ Fresh **10** has chenin's trademark savoury acidity to lift & carry tropical flavours. — IM

Onderkloof

Location: Somerset West ▪ Map: Helderberg ▪ WO: Western Cape/Walker Bay/Stellenbosch ▪ Est 1998 ▪ 1stB 1999 ▪ Tasting, sales & cellar tours by appt ▪ Conservation area ▪ Self-catering cottages ▪ Owner(s) Beat Musfeld ▪ Winemaker(s) Yves Musfeld (Jan 2012) ▪ Viticulturist(s) Botha Marais (Aug 2012) ▪ 64ha/12ha (ptage, shiraz, chenin, muscat d'A, sauv) ▪ 35t ▪ PO Box 90 Sir Lowry's Pass 7133 ▪ info@onderkloof.com ▪ www.onderkloof.com ▪ S 34° 6'37.9" E 018° 53'49.2" ▪ **T +27 (0)21-858-1538** ▪ F +27 (0)21-858-1536

Change is afoot at this now Swiss-owned Helderberg property. Owner Beat Musfeld has entrusted general management and winemaking to son Yves who, armed with knowledge attained at Geisenheim University in Germany, is looking forward to the challenge. Much is planned, including revitalising the vineyards with new viticulturist, Botha Marais, and enhancing the tourism appeal of recently renovated self-catering cottages with other attractions in situ.

Cabernet Sauvignon ⓟ ★★★☆ Violet-toned **06** wild berry fruit, unknit tannins when tasted a few years back. **Pinotage** ⓟ ★★★★ From low-cropped bushvines, **07** black plum & cherry flavours when last tasted. **Shiraz** Await next. **Chardonnay** 🔲 ★★★★ Ripe yellow stonefruit aromas lead to rounded soft-styled **12** with elegant dry finish. Light oak nicely harmonises whole. WO Walker Bay. **Sauvignon Blanc** 🔲 ★★★ **12** s fruity & floral with vibrant & dry finish. Stellenbosch WO. **Floreal Blanc de Blanc** 🔲 ★★★ Lovely floral & grape aromas introduce hanepoot-led medley **12** plus chard & chenin. Bright freshness ends just off-dry. — JP

Ondine *see* Ormonde Private Cellar

Oneiric Wines

Location: Elgin ▪ Map: Elgin, Walker Bay & Bot River ▪ WO: Western Cape ▪ Est 2007 ▪ 1stB 2009 ▪ Tasting & sales by appt only Mon-Sat 10-5 Sun 10-3 ▪ Closed Ash Wednesday, Mar 21, Easter Fri-Mon, Ascension Day, Dec 16/25/26 & Jan 1 ▪ BYO picnic ▪ Walks/hikes ▪ Conservation area ▪ Owner(s) Matt & Jennifer Pascall ▪ Winemaker(s) Niels Verburg (2009, consultant) & Werner Muller (May 2011, consultant) ▪ Viticulturist(s) Paul Wallis (Aug 2007, consultant) ▪ 64ha/8ha (cab, merlot, syrah, chard, sauv) ▪ ±90t/2,500cs own label 65% red 35% white ▪ shan.pascall@oneiric.co.za ▪ www.oneiric.co.za ▪ S 34° 14'31.0" E 019° 03'05.8" ▪ **T +27 (0)71-481-9560**

Oneiric, 'of or pertaining to dreams', describes Matt and Jennifer Pascall and family's aspiration to bottle wines from their Elgin property under an own brand. Vinification to date has taken place offsite, but at press time production and bottling were being moved to an own cellar. Situated on the border of the Kogelberg Biosphere, the property's fynbos and dams attract wildlife, and birdwatching and picnic areas are being developed. Visitors are welcome to stroll along the boardwalk to admire some 2,000 indigenous trees planted to offset the carbon footprint.

Cabernet Sauvignon 🔲 ★★★ **09** bright blackcurrant fruit but also very firm tannins & mouthwatering acidity, inviting further maturation or hearty food. **Shiraz** ★★★ Vibrant berry fruit & spice, savoury edge to chunky **09** everyday glassful. **Cabernet Sauvignon-Merlot** 🔲 ★★★ Equal partnership in **09** offers light fruit, zesty acidity for uncomplicated sipping. **Chardonnay** ★★★ Year in French oak evident in **09**'s butterscotch & toffee notes to bruised apple flavour, to be enjoyed soon. **Sauvignon Blanc** 🔲 ★★★★ Food-friendly **10** shows layers of green grass, hay & guava in a commendably lean structure with mineral seam, gravelly finish. — WB/IM

One World *see* Koopmanskloof Wingerde

Oom Tas

Distell big-volume brand depicts winefarmer 'Uncle Tas' beaming from retro label.

Oom Tas 🔲 ★ NV's amber hue implies sweetness but simple fruity white is bone-dry. 1,2, 5L bottles. — DB/HJ

Opener's *see* Waterstone Wines

Opstal Estate

Location: Rawsonville ▪ Map: Breedekloof ▪ WO: Breedekloof/Slanghoek ▪ Est 1847 ▪ 1stB 1978 ▪ Tasting, sales & cellar tours Mon-Fri 9-5 Sat 10-2 Sun by appt ▪ Closed Easter Fri-Mon, Dec 25/26 & Jan 1 ▪ Restaurant Wed-Sun 9-5 ▪ Facilities for children ▪ Tour groups ▪ Gift shop ▪ Farm produce ▪ Conferences ▪ Conservation area ▪ Mountain biking trail ▪ Monthly music/theatre shows with dinner (Jul-Nov) ▪ Quarterly farmers market ▪ Owner(s) Stanley Louw ▪ Winemaker(s) Attie Louw (Sep 2010), with Donovan Ackermann (Jan 2012) ▪ Viticulturist(s) Gerhard Theron (Jan 2002) ▪ 419ha/101ha (cab, ptage, shiraz, chard, chenin, muscat d'A, sauv, sem, viog) ▪ 1,500t/6,000cs own label 20% red 65% white 10% rosé 5% dessert ▪ Other export brand: Attie's Long Shadow ▪ BWI, IPW ▪ PO Box 27 Rawsonville 6845 ▪ wine@opstal.co.za ▪ www.opstal.co.za ▪ S 33° 38' 19.8" E 019° 13'40.8" ▪ **T +27 (0)23-344-3001** ▪ F +27 (0)23-344-3002

No shortage of history here, as 6th and 7th generation Louws are currently involved on the family farm. Attie Louw is a vibrant young winemaker eager to share knowledge and adapt to current trends. The last two years have seen more focus on viticulture, leading to cleaner, better expression of the Slanghoek Valley terroir. Look out for their forthcoming top-end chenin blanc.

Opstal Estate range

★★★★ **Hanepoot** ✓ 🅺 Engaging **11** fortified dessert shows fragrant typicity, bright lively spice a goo counterweight to pure ripeness. Composed intensity from 30 year old vines, further enlivened by fine acidity.

Sauvignon Blanc ☺ 🍴 🅺 ★★☆ **12** offers easy tropical appeal, hint of oak adds weight. WO Slanghoek, as for next 3.

Cabernet Sauvignon ✓ 🍴 🅺 ★★★★ Taut, structured **11** has fresh lift to bright cherry. Red-fruited wit light juicy appeal & dry firm end. **Syrah-Viognier Blush** ✓ 🍴 🅺 ★★★★ Vibrant colour on **12** from co-fe mented shiraz/viognier (plus a few minorities). Light & dry, with serious intent & fine length. **The Mill Iro** NEW 🍴 🅺 ★★ **12** perfumed, litchi-toned, fresh off-dry sipper from viognier, muscat d'Alexandrie colombard. **Sauvignon Blanc Sparkling Sec** ⓟ ★★★ Enjoy happy celebrations with fresh yeasty tones carbonated **NV. Chardonnay Barrel Dessert** 🅺 ★★★★ Fruity green fig intro to charming **11** fortifie dessert, oak in judicious support of viscous freshness. Discontinued: **Chenin Blanc.**

Sixpence range

Cabernet Sauvignon-Merlot ☺ 🍴 🅺 ★★★ Perfumed cherry bounce adds lively start to bright & confident **11**. Clean & focused for quality everyday drinking. **Sauvignon Blanc-Semillon** ☺ 🍴 🅺 ★★★ **12** pure fruit appeal with dryish end. Wonderfully clean, light styled for easy summer drinking. — JP

■ **Oracle** *see* Distell

Orangerie Wines

Location: Malmesbury ▪ Map/WO: Swartland ▪ Est 1707 ▪ 1stB 2009 ▪ Tasting, sales & cellar tours by appt only Paardeberg Conservation Area ▪ Owner(s)/viticulturist(s) Loffie & Pieter Euvrard ▪ Winemaker(s) Pieter Euvrar (2009) ▪ 200ha/70ha (cab, malbec, merlot, mourv, ptage, shiraz, chard, chenin, rouss, sauv, verdelho, viog) ▪ 15 300cs own label 60% red 40% white ▪ PO Box 92 Malmesbury 7299 ▪ orangeriewines@yahoo.com ▪ www orangeriewines.co.za ▪ S 33° 32' 20.8" E 018° 49' 55.6" ▪ **T +27 (0)22-482-2169** ▪ F +27 (0)22-487-3046

As well as supplying grapes to others from this historic Perdeberg farm, Piete Euvrard makes some wines in his own tiny cellar that meet the radical 'natura wine' standards of the Swartland Independent organisation. New plantings c scarce varieties destined for his blends (and for some clamorous grape buyers include roussanne, verdelho and mourvèdre. Others are to follow.

★★★★ **White** ⓟ **10** chenin-led, with dabs semillon, viognier, chardonnay. In fairly oxidative, un-fruity bu flavourful style popular in the area. Rich & satiny, serenely balanced.

Red ⓟ ★★★★ Sample **10** typical of new-wave Swartland reds in blend (shiraz + 17% mourvèdre) & deli cious, not obviously fruity flavours; firm & fresh. **09** (★★★★) included grenache. — TJ

Orange River Wine Cellars

Location: Upington ▪ Map: Northern Cape, Free State & North West ▪ WO: Northern Cape/Central Orange Rive ▪ Est 1965 ▪ 1stB 1968 ▪ Tasting & sales Mon-Fri 8–4.30 Sat 8.30–12 ▪ Fee R10/5 wines ▪ Closed all pub hols Cellar tours Mon-Fri 9, 11 & 3 (Jan-Mar) ▪ Owner(s) ±890 shareholders ▪ Cellarmaster(s) Gert Visser ▪ Cella managers Bolla Louw (Kakamas), Chris Venter (Keimoes), Johan Esterhuizen (Upington), Johan Dippenaa (Grootdrink), Riaan Liebenberg (Groblershoop), with winemakers (in same cellar order) George Kruger/Heir rich Coetzee/Andre Smit; Rianco van Rooyen/Cobus Viviers/Mariken Jordaan; Jopie Faul/Ferdinan Laubscher/Philane Gumede; Jim de Kock/Tinus Kotze; Marco Pentz ▪ Viticulturist(s) Henning Burger (viticul tural services manager), with (in same cellar order) Stoney Steenkamp, Louwna Viviers, Dirk Sutherland Tharien Hansen ▪ 4,200ha (ptage, ruby cab, shiraz, chard, chenin, cbard, Muscat varieties) ▪ 122,000t/20m own label 20% red 40% white 20% rosé 20% other + 30m L for clients/bulk ▪ Other export labels: Islan View, Gilysipao, Star Tree ▪ Ranges for customers: Country Cellars & Carnival (Spar); Seasons Collection (Liquo City) ▪ ISO 9001:2008 & 2011; PAS 220:2010; FSSC 20 000; PAS 220:2008; BRC; IPW; HACCP; WIETA ▪ P Box 544 Upington 8800 ▪ info@orangeriverwines.com ▪ www.orangeriverwines.com ▪ S 28° 26' 33.0" E 021 12' 30.6" ▪ **T +27 (0)54-337-8800** ▪ F +27 (0)54-332-4408

Kakamas is known for its peaches, especially the sweet sun-dried kind, but it' also the source of Orange River Wine Cellars' first ever sauvignon blanc. The vineyard of origin may be young, and small (less than 1ha), but it's vigorous yielding a bountiful 20 tons! It's part of a massive five-cellar, 120,000+ tons-a year operation spanning@roughly 400km along the Orange River — from Groblershoop in the east to Grootdrink, Upington, Keimoes and Kakamas in the west. Their Reserve wines are showing potential (see the new unfiltered Bordeaux blend debuting this edition), while the ORWC range is the epitome of value and quaffability (with numerous Best Value Wine Awards). The marketing team rack up airmiles trading their wares as far afield as China but, they say, nothing beats returning home to a braaied Kalahari lamb chop or skilpadjie, a succulent liver parcel wrapped with caul fat.

Reserve range

Lyra NEW ★★★ Equal parts merlot & petit verdot, dollop cab in **09**. Chunky grip matches ripe black fruit. Needs time to knit. **Chenin Blanc de Barrique** ⊕ ★★★ Serious oaking for **10** shows in vanilla perfume; ripe fig flavour gets limy twist from tiny portion unoaked chardonnay. Central Orange River WO. **Straw Wine** Await new vintage.

Orange River Wine Cellars range

★★★★ **White Muscadel** 🍷 🔲 Seductive wealth of mango, litchi & jasmine, **11** mouthfillingly bold & powerful yet not overwhelming. Restrained & elegant, in fact, with lingering rich aftertaste.

Pinotage NEW ☺ ★★★ Uncomplicated ripe plum & cherry fruit, **11** dark density from light oak provides balance. Easy drinking. **Shiraz** ☺ 🔲 ★★★ **11** again improves on previous. Cherry ripeness with structure & nutty oak sheen at end. Nice quaffer. **Rosé** ☺ 🍷 🔲 ★★★ Floral litchi vibrancy on sweetly off-dry **12**, good acid ensures sprightly mouthful. **Chenin Blanc** ☺ 🍷 🔲 ★★★ Big step up, **12** better concentration of lively pear drop fruit. Juicy & refreshing. **Colombard** ☺ 🍷 🔲 ★★★ Tangy crunchy green melon on uncomplicated off-dry **12**. **Sauvignon Blanc** NEW ☺ ★★★ **12** shows typical crisp melon & lemon freshness. **Sparkling Rosé** ☺ ★★★ Sweet cranberry & Turkish delight appeal to lively NV (**12**) chenin/pinotage mix.

Cabernet Sauvignon 🔲 ★★★ Uncomplicated **11** displays good varietal typicity allied with succulence. Some smoky grip on lightish, structured body. **Ruby Cabernet** 🔲 ★★★ Appealing fynbos & blueberry rivalry on fruitcake-rich palate of **11**, gentle squeeze of tannin adds structure & interest. **Shiraz-Cabernet Sauvignon** 🍷 Not tasted. **Chardonnay** 🔲 ★★★ Improved **11**, good body & length, vanilla sheen of oak gently framing light citrus fruit. **Sparkling Brut** 🔲 ★★★ NV (**12**) offers up light melon & pear in uncomplicated dry sparkler. **Soet Hanepoot** 🍷 ★★★★ 'Sweet Hanepoot' last time. **NV** continues upward trend. (Previous bottling was vintage dated.) Fortification harmonises with sweet raisin & barley sugar abundance. Rich, dry-seeming end. **Red Muscadel** 🍷 🔲 ★★★★ Builds on upward trajectory of previous **10** (★★★). **11** cornucopia of glacé fruit, powerfully rich & sweet yet balanced, with muscat typicity evident throughout. Finishes beautifully clean. **Red Jerepigo** 🍷 ★★★ Previously vintage dated; now **NV**. Ripe Christmas pudding abundance but balanced & broad, sweetness held in check. **White Jerepigo** 🍷 ★★★ Mix of chenin & sultana for latest bottling, now **NV** (previous was **10**). Blend works well, poached peach & raisined nectar notes, maintains equilibrium to end. — FM

■ **Oranjerivier Wynkelders** see Orange River Wine Cellars

Org de Rac

Location: Piketberg ▪ Map/WO: Swartland ▪ Est 2001 ▪ 1stB 2005 ▪ Tasting, sales & tours Mon-Fri 9–5 Sat 9–1 ▪ Closed Good Fri, Dec 25 & Jan 1 ▪ Meals/refreshments/cheese platters by prior arrangement; or BYO picnic ▪ Tour groups ▪ Weddings/functions/conferences ▪ Walks/hikes ▪ Mountain biking ▪ Conservation area ▪ Game viewing ▪ Owner(s) Nico Bacon ▪ Winemaker(s) Gilmar Boshoff (Jan 2011) ▪ Viticulturist(s) Wesley du Plessis (Jun 2010) ▪ 47ha (cab, merlot, shiraz, chard) ▪ 260t/20,000cs own label 87% red 8% white 5% rosé + 8,500cs for clients ▪ Other export brand: Abbotsville ▪ Brands for clients: Imbuko Wines ▪ SGS (Organic) ▪ PO Box 268 Piketberg 7320 ▪ wine@orgderac.co.za ▪ www.orgderac.co.za ▪ S 32° 57′ 44.3″   E 018° 44′ 57.4″ ▪ **T +27 (0)22-913-2397/3924** ▪ F +27 (0)22-913-3923

Piketberg organic producer Org de Rac, the self-styled 'green heartbeat' of the Swartland, has introduced a new easy-drinking label, the whimsically named Green Shebeen, along with a house vinegar, range of essential oils (rosemary, lavender), conference facilities and a cheese board to be ordered when winetasting here. Sustainability in all its forms, from organic vinegrowing and vinification to recycling and composting, is a central concern for this regional eco-pioneer.

Reserve range

Cabernet Sauvignon ★★★★ Previewed **11**, big ripe blackberries with cinnamon & cedar. Elegant, with well-managed tannins & ageability. Balanced & food friendly. **Merlot** ★★★★ Smooth **11** barrel sample shows good balance between savoury intro & juicy berry flavours. **Shiraz** ★★★★ Fruit-forward & rounded **11**, ex cask dark berry flavours supported by ripe spicy tannins. This range listed as 'Family Reserve' last time.

Org de Rac range

★★★★ **Merlot** Spicy, easy-drinking **11** (★★★★), from cask not as complex as **10** but still plenty of soft mocha/fruit taste.

Cabernet Sauvignon ★★★ Previewed **11** continues fruitier styling of previous, tannins are firm but friendly, conclusion is savoury. **Shiraz** ★★★ Variety-true **11** barrel sample, clove & cinnamon notes, clean cranberry freshness. **Merlot Rosé** ★★ Now bottled & renamed (from simply 'Merlot'), lightish **12** perky picnic pink with dry cranberry charm. **Wooded Chardonnay** ★★★ Gets 'Wooded' prefix in pre-bottling **12**, light oak adds buttery note to peachy comfortable quaffer.

Green Shebeen range NEW

Merlot ☺ ★★★ Preview **11** a spicy treat packed with dark berries & firm but undaunting tannins.

Cabernet Sauvignon ★★ Easy-drinking **11**, ex-cask offers mix of black berries & spice. **The Blend** ★★★ NV amiable cab/merlot packed with juicy fruit & easy tannins. **Rosé** ★ Fetching pink **12** from undisclosed varieties, dry faintly berried flavour. **Chardonnay** ★ **12** unoaked poolside dry white. — DB

***

Origin Wine

Location/map: Stellenbosch ▪ WO: Western Cape/Stellenbosch ▪ Est/1stB 2002 ▪ Tasting strictly by appt ▪ Owner(s) Bernard Fontannaz ▪ Cellarmaster(s) Hermias Hugo (2011) ▪ Production manager Ferdi Coetzee (2012) ▪ Winemaker(s) Seugnét Rossouw (2007), with Monique Fourie, Siphiso Mbele, Terence Capes & Ernst van der Merwe ▪ 5 million cs ▪ 50% red 40% white 10% rosé ▪ BRC, DLG, Fairtrade, HACCP, IFS, WIETA ▪ PO Box 7177 Stellenbosch 7599 ▪ info@originwine.co.za ▪ www.originwine.co.za, www.fairhills.co.za, www.stormhoek.co.za, www.streetart.co.za ▪ S 33° 52′ 39.01″ E 018° 48′ 35.50″ ▪ **T +27 (0)861-ORIGIN/+27 (0)21-865-8100** ▪ F +27 (0)21-865-2348

This mainly export winery has over 1,200 reasons to do well in the market, says CEO Bernard Fontannaz, namely the 1,200 beneficiaries of Origin's Fairhills Project, funded through sales of Fairhills wines, one of the largest global Fairtrade brands. Through this initiative, Origin most recently opened an adult literacy and computer learning centre to enable its winery staff to improve their skills. It also awarded an apprenticeship to Siphiso Mbele, who is making wine in The Apprentice range, created the Unsung Heroes range to honour vineyard and winery staff, and fund improvements to their living and working conditions.

The Apprentice range NEW

Cabernet Sauvignon-Petit Verdot ★★★ Mellow black fruit, some char on slightly astringent **11** cab-led tank sample. This range made by Origin Apprentice winner, Siphiso Mbele. **Shiraz-Cabernet Sauvignon** ★★★ Red berry, black pepper on unchallenging **11** 60/40 preview. Soft & slightly sweet palate ex American oak fermented portion. **Chenin Blanc** ★★★ Al fresco dining companion **12**, nut & peach aromas, satisfying vinosity from modest 12.5% alcohol. Previewed.

Commonwealth range NEW

Pinotage-Mourvèdre-Petit Verdot ☺ ★★★ Pinotage's strawberry/cherry aromas, flavours, & slight bitterness evident in pliable **12** ex tank. Most fruit-filled, well knit in red line-up. Some American oak.

Semillon ★★★ Demure **12**, shy cut grass & thatch notes, lemony farewell.

Sustainable range NEW

Chardonnay-Viognier ★★ **12** preview is floral, with suggestion of musky sweetness, slips down easily.

Fairhills Unsung Hero range

Shiraz NEW ★★★ Lightly flavoured summer red **11** tank sample, faint cherry fruit, toffee from American oak, brief finish. **Shiraz-Cabernet Sauvignon** ★★★ Sweet-fruited **11** preview has savoury black olive notes, soft tannins & brush of bitterness for interest. **Chenin Blanc** NEW 🗔 🅺 ★★★ Attractive floral notes on refreshing **12** preview; nutty persistence ex 40% barrel ferment portion.

Fairhills range

1962 Vineyards Selection Shiraz 🅺 Not tasted, as for **Shiraz-Merlot, Rosé, Rosé Moscato, 1962 Vineyards Selection Chenin Blanc, Moscato, Sauvignon Blanc, Sparkling Rosé Brut** & **Sparkling Chardonnay Brut. Cabernet Sauvignon-Petit Verdot** 🗔 🅺 ★★★ Preview **11** unassuming cab-led quaffer, lightly oaked. **Semillon-Sauvignon Blanc** 🗔 🅺 ★★ Brief but balanced **12** tank sample has Granny Smith apple bite, lowish 12% alcohol for lunchtime refreshment.

Stellenbosch Drive Reserve range NEW

Cabernet Sauvignon-Merlot 🅺 ★★★ Intense toasty oak (60% American), red fruit & savoury highlights on **11** 70/30 combo from Stellenbosch grapes, tasted ex-barrel. One of the best from this producer. **Chardonnay-Viognier** 🅺 ★★★ Preview **12** floral & nutty from 70% barrel-fermented portion; brisk lemon acidity for easy drinkability. WO Stellenbosch.

Stellenbosch Drive range

Merlot-Cabernet Sauvignon 🗔 🅺 Not reviewed, like **Chardonnay, Oaked Chenin Blanc** & **Sauvignon Blanc**.

Greenfields Organic range

Shiraz-Cabernet Sauvignon 🗔 🌸 🅺 ★★★ Lightly oaked (American) **12** ex tank is unforced, offers lightly fruity supple enjoyment. **Chardonnay-Viognier** 🅺 Not reviewed.

Cape Original Organic range

Shiraz-Cabernet Sauvignon 🌸 Not tasted, as **Rosé**.

Fair Exchange range NEW

Merlot-Malbec 🗔 ★★★ Everyday companion **11** attractive plum, spice & tar; sweet-fruit finish. Tasted from barrel, 15% American oak. **Colombard-Sauvignon Blanc** 🗔 🅺 ★★ Guava appeal, no sharp edges on **12** 60/40 tank sample.

South Atlantic range NEW

Shiraz-Cabernet Sauvignon 🅺 ★★ **11** offers cherry flavours to get the party started. 3L bag-in-box.

Stormhoek Reserve range NEW

Shiraz-Cabernet Sauvignon 🅺 ★★★ Pre-bottling, **11**'s dark fruit sprinkled with oak spice, plushness reined in by firm tannins. Slightly warm tail (14% alcohol). Portion fermented in American oak. **Chardonnay** ✓ 🅺 ★★★★ Enticing nuts & lemon cream aromas/flavours, well-judged oak & commendable richness on refreshing **12** preview. Just needs a little more concentration to take next step up.

Stormhoek range

> **Petillant White Moscato** NEW ☺ 🅺 ★★★ **12** sweet lemon & grape flavour, with a smack of sea breeze freshness. Only 5.5% alcohol. **Moscato Grigio** NEW ☺ 🗔 🅺 ★★★ Sweet but crisp **12** tank sample has faint pink blush, good flavour & weight at low 5.5% alcohol.

Cabernet Sauvignon 🗔 🅺 Not tasted, as for **Organic Merlot, Pinotage, Cap'occino Coffee Pinotage, Rosé, Organic Chardonnay** & **Rosé Moscato Sparkling. Moscato** NEW 🗔 🅺 ★★★ Grapey, low 8.5% alcohol **12** preview is sweet but not cloying, perfect for spicy/picnic fare. **Pinot Grigio** 🗔 🅺 ★★★ White peach **12** pre-bottling promises much on the nose, delivers good flavour, acidity & length. **Sauvignon Blanc** 🗔 🅺 ★★ Zesty **12** tank sample water-white, delicately flavoured for uncomplicated enjoyment. **Petillant Rosé Moscato** NEW 🗔 🅺 ★★★ **12** strawberry toned, drier than 5.5% alcohol version; more weight at 11.5%. **Low Alcohol Petillant Rosé Moscato** NEW 🗔 🅺 ★★★ **12** blush hue, frothy bubbles & grapey sunshine; good weight/flavour for 5.5% alcohol.

Honeypot range

Moscato Not tasted, as for **Sweet Shiraz**.

Bundustar range NEW

Shiraz-Petit Verdot-Viognier 🅺 ★★ Bubblegum & slight grip on **11**, in 3L bag-in-box. — CvZ

Ormonde Private Cellar

Location: Darling ▪ Map: Durbanville, Philadelphia & Darling ▪ WO: Darling/Coastal ▪ 1stB 1999 ▪ Tasting & sales Mon-Fri 9–4 Sat & pub hols 9–3 ▪ Closed Good Fri, Dec 25/26 & Jan 1 ▪ Vineyard tours by appt ▪ Cheese & wine tasting R55pp by appt — tasting fee applies to Ormonde range only ▪ Picnic baskets by appt or BYO ▪ Facilities for children ▪ Walks ▪ Owner(s) Basson family ▪ Winemaker(s) Michiel du Toit ▪ Viticulturist(s) The Basson ▪ ±300ha (cabs s/f, merlot, mourv, p verdot, pinot, shiraz, chard, chenin, sauv, sem) ▪ 1,000t/35,000c own label 40% red 60% white ▪ BWI ▪ PO Box 201 Darling 7345 ▪ info@ormonde.co.za ▪ www.ormonde.co.za ▪ S 33° 22' 20.2" E 018° 21' 23.6" ▪ **T +27 (0)22-492-3540** ▪ F +27 (0)22-492-3470

A pioneer in Darling, this was the first farm planted to classic grapes, when the area was supplying Malmesbury Co-operative with KWV distilling wine. Nico Basson, father of current MD Theo, was helped in the 1970s with finance and technical expertise by SFW, and thus started the area's quality transformation. Later, Neil Ellis's Groenekloof label further confirmed its credentials. Aware of his heritage, Theo remains focused on quality and also looks forward: an Ormonde pinot noir and sauvignon blanc were due at press time.

Ormonde range

★★★★☆ **Vernon Basson** ⊕ Last tasted 07 (★★★★) blend, cab franc's leafiness accentuated by lighter vintage, cab ensuring class & balance. Follows richer debut 06, with dash merlot.

★★★★ **Chardonnay** ⊕ Lime & oatmeal are 09's primary flavours but there are many nuances, including orange peel, honeycomb. Elegant, complex but unshowy, still in the prime of youth.

★★★★ **Proprietor's Blend** ⊕ Top-end 09 blend sauvignon, semillon & chenin. Bellpepper & tinned pea notes, firm acidity. Creamy texture from oak & lees influence.

Theodore Eksteen ⊕ ★★★★ Nothing shy about 08 shiraz & grenache blend; ripe (15.5% alc), fruit driven, spice rich, especially aniseed, & all-new oak.

Ondine range

Cabernet Sauvignon ⊕ ★★★ When last tasted, angular 08 offered peppers & herbs, cedar & flint. Lean & bone-dry, it demanded time. **Cabernet Franc** ⊕ ★★★☆ Previously, 08 offered velvety ripe tannins, opulent plum & cherry fruit with variety's typical leafy notes. **Merlot** ⊕ ★★★ Last reviewed 08 was dusty & lean, showed hints of strawberry & prunes. Somewhat sharp & dry. **Shiraz** ⊕ ★★★ Previously, angular 08 showed sweet spice & toasty notes, blackcurrants & tarry smoke. Dry tannic finish. Heady 15.5% alc. **Chardonnay** ⊕ 🎘 ★★★★ Richly flavoured 10 offers butterscotch & melon preserve, smoothly rounded appeal. Becomes more savoury on finish. **Chenin Blanc** ⊕ 🎘 ★★★ Melon & white peach in attractive 10, enlivened by brisk acidity. Good food match. **Sauvignon Blanc** ✓ 🎘 ★★★★ Minerality interwoven with fig leaf, lemongrass, there's purity & focus in 11; intensity backed by taut acidity. Ageworthy. **Semillon** ⊕ 🎘 ★★★★ Freshness is the key in 10, grassy, quite sauvignon-like, with fine acidity.

Alexanderfontein range

Merlot ☺ 🍴 🎘 ★★★ Previewed 10 has light & fruity red-berry-packed appeal, juicy & accessible. **Shiraz** ☺ 🍴 🎘 ★★★ Mulberries & black plums, no shortage of fruit in 10, also shows in palate succulence. Nice dry finish from oak. WO Darling. **Chenin Blanc** ☺ 🍴 ★★★ Perfumed with green apples, hint of passionfruit, 12's crispness makes it a good food wine.

Cabernet Sauvignon ✓ 🍴 ★★★★ Cassis & dusty cedar, herbaceous nuance adds interest. 09's soft ripe tannins cushion the fruit, provide balance. Coastal WO for this range unless noted. **Chardonnay** 🍴 🎘 ★★★★ Light-textured peach styling in 12, perked by fresh finish. **Sauvignon Blanc** ✓ 🍴 🎘 ★★★★ Previewed 12 zings with litchi, lime freshness, fynbos underpin adds interest. Steely bite should settle, ensure ageing. — CR

Osbloed Wines

Location: Somerset West ▪ Map: Helderberg ▪ WO: Paarl ▪ Est 2009 ▪ 1stB 2010 ▪ Tasting, sales & cellar tours daily — please call ahead ▪ Tasting fee R20, waived on purchase ▪ Owner(s) Bertus van Niekerk & Selma Albasini ▪ Cellarmaster(s) Bertus van Niekerk (Jan 2010) ▪ Winemaker(s) Bertus van Niekerk (Jan 2010), with Selma Albasini (2010) & Hendrik van Niekerk (2011) ▪ 300cs own label 75% red 25% white ▪ 33 Eagle Crescent Somerset West 7130 ▪ bertus@osbloed.com ▪ www.osbloed.com ▪ S 34° 5' 26.22" E 018° 51' 55.87" ▪ **T +27 (0)83-400-2999**

It was a revelation when garagiste winemaker (and former clergyman) Bertus van Niekerk and his artist wife Selma Albasini launched their Horses of the

Apocalypse wines at a nudist retreat last year. Clothing was optional and all was revealed by a Godiva-like woman on horseback... Production has tripled, son Hendrik has begun oenology studies at Stellenbosch and there are some interesting projects in the pipeline — including a pinotage, cinsaut and pinot noir blend.

Horses of the Apocalypse

Black Horse Cabernet Sauvignon ★★★ 2nd release **11** again uses Helderberg grapes for its cassis vibrancy & juicy appeal. Lead pencil dryness & good frame. **Red Horse Cinsaut** ★★★★ Exotic perfume & vibrant strawberry on now-bottled **11**. Sweetly appealing unadorned simplicity from 40 year old bushvines. **White Horse Chardonnay** ★★★★ Gutsy & big **11** is packed with citrus. Lively & yet also restrained, with not overplayed oak. Good mouthfeel throughout. **Pale Horse Riesling** ★★★ Individual styled tropicality & bold oxidative notes on wooded **11**. Good body & length. Note: all above uncertified, listed previously under Revelation range.

Osbloed range

Osbloed ★★★★ Mourvèdre joins shiraz in juicy **10**, pomegranate & spice succulence on a light frame courtesy of older oak. — FM

Oubenheim Estate

Location: Vredendal ▪ Est/1stB 2002 ▪ Closed to public ▪ Owner(s) DW Viljoen & Philip Viljoen ▪ Winemaker(s) Philip Viljoen ▪ 800cs 100% red ▪ PO Box 52 Vredendal 8160 ▪ info@oubenheim.com ▪ **T +27 (0)27-213-5624/+27 (0)83-509-9885** ▪ F +27 (0)27-213-5624

Third-generation grape grower and supplier to big Olifants River wineries, Philip Viljoen has been making and bottling own-label wines from selected single vineyards for a decade, but decided not to vinify in 2012 given extremely competitive market conditions. 'But my little cellar's still standing... so maybe this season?'

Oude Compagnies Post Private Cellar

Location/map/WO: Tulbagh ▪ Est 1996 ▪ 1stB 2003 ▪ Tasting, sales & cellar tours by appt ▪ Walking trail (flower season Sep-Oct) ▪ Hiking trail 1-2 days (sleepover on Obiqua mountain in own tent) ▪ Mountain bike (difficult) & 15km off-road motorbike trails ▪ Owner(s) Jerry Swanepoel Family Trust ▪ Cellarmaster(s) Jerry Swanepoel ▪ Winemaker(s) Jerry Swanepoel, with Ervin Koen (Jul 2011) ▪ Viticulturist(s) Marius Robert (consultant) ▪ 235ha/18ha (cab, grenache, merlot, mourv, ptage, shiraz) ▪ 70t/5,000cs own label 90% red 10% rosé + 20,000L bulk ▪ Other export brand: Maison De Cygne ▪ Fairtrade ▪ PO Box 11 Tulbagh 6820 ▪ swanepoel@ intekom.co.za ▪ S 33° 14' 56.9" E 019° 6' 49.1" ▪ **T +27 (0)23-230-1578** ▪ F +27 (0)23-230-0840

At their Tulbagh mountainside farm, Jerry and Henriette Swanepoel have completed preparations to make méthode cap classique bubbly from their own grapes in 2015 (those under their label to date were made elsewhere). Chardonnay and pinot noir previously planted, the old fruit packing shed was converted to house riddling racks and provide space for bottle storage.

Compagnies Wijn range

Cabernet Sauvignon ★★ Sweet fruit & contrasting herbaceous element, **09** best enjoyed while still in balance. **Merlot** Await new vintage, as for **Pinotage Grand Reserve**, **Shiraz** & **Ruby Blanc**. **Mourvèdre** ★★★ **10** cherry cola flavour & hint of spice, amiable get-together-with-friends wine. **Pinotage** ★★ **09** plump & juicy with some funky notes. **Caap Ensemble** ⓦ ★★★ Cape Blend of merlot, cab & dash pinotage; **09** oak still integrating when last tasted. **Cabernet Sauvignon-Merlot** ★★★ Name change from 'Duet'. **10** 50/50 combo, quite stern, with savoury plum tones. **Merlot-Mourvèdre** NEW ★★ Equal partnership **08** has warm fruit & vanilla charm, needs enjoying soon. — CE/CvZ

Oude Denneboom

Location: Paarl ▪ Map: Paarl & Wellington ▪ WO: Voor Paardeberg ▪ 1stB 2003 ▪ Tasting by appt ▪ 4-star self-catering cottage ▪ Private game reserve ▪ Owner(s) Niel de Waal ▪ Cellarmaster(s)/viticulturist(s) Willem de Waal ▪ 194ha/±45ha (cab, mourv, ptage, shiraz, chenin, nouvelle, viog) ▪ 400t/500cs own label 70% red 30% white ▪ Global GAP ▪ PO Box 2087 Windmeul 7630 ▪ info@oudedenneboom.co.za ▪ www.oudedenneboom.co.za ▪ S 33°37'47.28" E 018°51'55.08" ▪ **T +27 (0)21-869-8072** ▪ F +27 (0)86-552-2695

Niel de Waal feels less like the owner of this Voor Paardeberg estate than its custodian. 'We have to leave the place in better condition than we found it,' he says.

Some families on the farm have been working there for seven generations, and Niel sees its healthy state as a tribute to their loyalty and dedication.

Black Harrier Shiraz ⚡ ★★★★ 08 higher flier than 07 (★★★★). Fleshy plum, blueberry & nutmeg spice on lissome, velvety frame. Succulent & ripe. Like next, tasted a few years back. **Eland** ⚡ ★★★★ Shoulder above maiden 07 (★★★), 08 blend of shiraz, mourvèdre, grenache full of cherry, blackberry & pepper. Velvet texture, superb wood integration. **Grysbok Chenin Blanc** 🔖 Await next, as for **Steenbok**. — FM

Oude Kaap

High-volume range by DGB mainly for Holland, Scandinavia and Germany.

Reserve Collection

Cabernet Sauvignon 🔖 ★★★☆ 11 raises the bar with balanced juicy dark fruit & creamy texture, in supportive, supple structure. **Pinotage** 🔖 ★★★ Sweet spicy oak envelops plum flavours on 11. **Shiraz** 🔖 ★★★ Savoury, dark & spicy 11 is balanced but robustly structured, for hearty fare. **Chardonnay** 🔖 🔖 ★★★ 11 ripe pear/cider flavours with creamy, warm & toasty nuance. **Chenin Blanc** ⚡ 🔖 ★★★ Youthful 11 preview shows creamy apple texture. **Sauvignon Blanc** 🔖 🔖 ★★★ 11 more dried than fresh fruit character. Still crisp, with pithy almond nuance.

Oude Kaap range

Cabernet Sauvignon-Merlot 🔖 ★★★ Smooth 11 berried blend is an easy, balanced quaffer. **Klassiek Rood** 🔖 🔖 ★★★ 12 ripe compote of cinsaut & ruby cab. Genial, smooth & tasty. **Cinsault-Ruby Cabernet** 🔖 ★★★ Smoky berry jam & thatchy nuance on 11. Smooth warm & spicy. **Blanc de Noir** 🔖 🔖 ★★★ 12 off-dry, tangy, crisp & light blush from pinotage & shiraz. **Chenin Blanc** 🔖 🔖 ★★★ Fresh & crunchy Golden Delicious apple on 12 beach party sipper. **Klassiek Wit** 🔖 🔖 ★★★ 12 demure chenin/sauvignon duo shows clean elegance & dry finish. **Elegant Wit** ⚡ 🔖 ★★ Bouquet of fragrant white varieties in light, crisp semi-sweet 11. WO W Cape for both ranges. — MW

■ **Oude Rust** *see* Mooiuitsig Wine Cellars

Oudtshoorn Cellar — SCV

Location: Oudtshoorn ▪ Map: Klein Karoo & Garden Route ▪ WO: Klein Karoo ▪ Est/1stB 1975 ▪ Tasting & sales at Kango Wijnhuis Mon–Fri 9–5 Sat 9–3 ▪ Fee R25 for groups of 5 or more ▪ Closed Easter Fri-Mon, Dec 25/26 & Jan 1 ▪ Book ahead for cellar tours ▪ Tour groups ▪ BYO picnic ▪ Conferences ▪ Owner(s) 35 members ▪ Cellarmaster(s)/winemaker(s)/viticulturist(s) Emile Schoch (2011) ▪ 200ha (merlot, muscadel, chard, cbard) ▪ 1,016t/5,000cs own label 16% red 84% white ▪ Other export brand: Van Hunks ▪ PO Box 46 Oudtshoorn 6620 ▪ oudtshoorn@scv.co.za ▪ www.oudtshoornwines.co.za ▪ S 33°36'50.0" E 022°12'1.1" ▪ **T +27 (0)44-272-8660** ▪ F +27 (0)44-279-1038

As one of three Southern Cape Vineyards cellars (with Barrydale and Ladismith), this Klein Karoo winery is benefiting from the group's expanded product portfolio as well as shared management and distribution systems. The biggest challenge, according to CEO Riaan Marais, is to create a wine and brandy experience along Route 62, the scenic road that links the sibling operations.

Rijckshof range

Hanepoot Untasted, as **Gold Jerepigo**, **Red Muscadel** & **Red Jerepigo**. **White Muscadel** 🔖 ★★★ Fortified NV (12) dessert from muscat d'Frontignan, with oodles of grapey succulence for the sweet-toothed. **Cape Ruby** ★★ Was 'Ruby Port'. Step-up NV (12) gentle & charming, with toffee, nut & chocolate flavours.

Kango range

> **Cabernet Sauvignon-Merlot-Shiraz** 😊 🔖 ★★★ Unoaked equal three-way combo, 11 layered with black fruit pastilles & chocolate, very affable & tasty. **Sauvignon Blanc** 😊 🔖 ★★★ Takes another step up with zestier acidity & fuller tropical flavours in 12. Stock up for summer.

Merlot 🔖 🔖 ★★★ Herby & spicy 11 is unfettered by oak, drinks easily.

Baroness range

Sparkling Sweet Rosé ★★ NV (12) sweet frothy fun from shiraz. — WB/JP

■ **Out of Africa** *see* African Terroir

Overgaauw Wine Estate ♟☂◎&

Location/map/WO: Stellenbosch ▪ Est 1905 ▪ 1stB 1970 ▪ Tasting & sales Mon-Fri 9–5 Sat 10–3.30 (Oct-Apr) & 10-2 (May-Sep) ▪ Fee R10pp for groups of 6+ ▪ Closed Easter Fri-Mon, Dec 25/26 & Jan 1 ▪ Port & snack pairing R35pp, 48-hr advance booking essential ▪ BYO picnic ▪ Owner(s) Braam van Velden ▪ Winemaker(s) David van Velden (Jan 2003) ▪ Viticulturist(s) Braam & David van Velden; Vinpro ▪ 100ha/60ha (cabs s/f, merlot, ptage, touriga, chard, chenin, sauv, sylvaner) ▪ 60% red 40% white ▪ Other export brand: Sandrivier ▪ HACCP ▪ PO Box 3 Vlottenburg 7604 ▪ info@overgaauw.co.za ▪ www.overgaauw.co.za ▪ S 33° 56' 52.1" E 018° 47'33.4" ▪ T +27 (0)21-881-3815 ▪ F +27 (0)21-881-3436

David van Velden, winemaker at this established and pioneering Stellenbosch family farm, believes the challenges that he faces, as the fourth generation of his wine-farming family, are the same as his great grandfather faced: 'It's just the nature and circumstances which have changed,' he says. 'As custodian, rather than landowner, my generation needs to diversify, create a permaculture where all activities on the farm are sustainably interrelated and interdependent to produce top quality distinctive wine and, in addition, produce natural bio-logic food. Past generations converted from polyculture to monoculture. This needs to change.'

Overgaauw Estate range

★★★★ **Cabernet Sauvignon** 🖹 Great modern appeal in **10**'s dark berry fragrance; reverts to more classic mode with its succulent grape tannins, freshness, savoury edge & potential.

★★★★ **Tria Corda** ✓ 09 (★★★★★) the first since **06**. Most classic, elegant of reds with evident cab bias (60%, with merlot & cab franc); glimpses of fragrant, fresh fruit yet to fully emerge from finely honed structure. Lovely maturation potential.

★★★★ **Cape Vintage** ✓ The oldest new release in the winelands? **93** from sextet port varieties, smooth, warmingly ready with mature polished bouquet & fruity richness.

Merlot 🖹 ★★★★ **10** dark plum fruit tipping over-ripeness but balanced tannins & judiciously used oak promote good drinking with hearty fare. **Touriga Nacional-Cabernet Sauvignon** ⊕ 🖹 ★★★★ Just-dry **10** country-style blend, with extra violet, sweet dark berry attractions from 87% touriga (75% previously). **Chardonnay** 🖹 ★★★★ **11** step up on **10**; nuanced mix citrusy freshness, subtle oak spice. Juicy & plump with clean, dryish finish. **Sauvignon Blanc** 🗄 🖹 ★★★ **12** crisp & dry, with plentiful, sustained ripe fig features, but modest 12.5% alcohol. Tasted ex tank. **Sylvaner** 🗄 🖹 ★★★ Unusually expressive spicy baked apple aromas, flavours on pre-bottling **12**; long, fruitily dry. Aperitif style 12.5% alcohol. Discontinued: **Chenin Blanc**.

Shepherd's Cottage range

Cabernet Sauvignon-Merlot ⊕ 🗄 ★★★ Plentiful ripe fleshy dark berries on tasty, lightly oaked **10**. Accessible but with good forming grip. **Chenin Blanc-Chardonnay** 🗄 🖹 ★★★ Ex-tank **12** offers refreshing citrusy flavours; zestily dry. Discontinued: **Pinotage Rosé**. — AL

Overhex Wines International ♟🍷◎✗&

Location/map: Worcester ▪ WO: Western Cape/Coastal ▪ Est/1stB 2006 ▪ Tasting & sales Mon-Fri 8–5 Sat/Sun 10–4 ▪ Closed Easter Fri-Sun, Dec 25 & Jan 1 ▪ Cellar tours by appt ▪ Bistro Wed-Sun 10-4 ▪ Facilities for children ▪ Tour groups ▪ Conferences ▪ Owner(s) G van der Wath & JC Martin ▪ Cellarmaster(s) Jandre Human (Aug 2009) ▪ Winemaker(s) Willie Malan (2002) & Ben Snyman (Dec 2010), with Dirk Rust (Jan 2012) ▪ Viticulturist(s) Pierre Snyman (Vinpro) ▪ 9,000t ▪ 45% red 50% white 5% rosé ▪ ISO 22000, Fairtrade, WIETA ▪ PO Box 139 Worcester 6849 ▪ marketing@overhex.com ▪ www.overhex.com ▪ S 33° 39' 28.6" E 019° 30' 55.8" ▪ T +27 (0)23-347-5012 ▪ F +27 (0)23-347-1057

The image of a jovial elephant perched on a tiny stool is the playful representation of the balance sought in these amenable, well-priced wines from thoroughly modern, social-media-savvy Overhex, whose visitor attractions include a Friday evening wine bar and a family bistro with jungle gym, now also open on Sunday afternoons. New in this edition are Fairtrade-sanctioned Haven Point and sweeter, lower-alcohol Balance Buddy ranges.

Balance Winemaker's Selection

Merlot ☺ 🗄 🖹 ★★★ Our pick of the red bunch: nicely composed **11** offers sugar-coated plums, friendly tannin grip. **Chardonnay** ☺ 🗄 🖹 ★★★ Creamy barrel-fermented version, **12** soft & lemony.

Pinotage 🍴 📖 ★★★ **11** more 'dry red' than 'pinotage', but not without charm & commendable dryness. **Shiraz** 🍴 📖 ★★★ Spice & vanilla toned **11** shows more oak than other reds in range, still makes for pleasant sipping. **Chenin Blanc** 🍴 📖 ★★★ Dry this time, less tutti-frutti, tad more aromatic in **12**. **Sauvignon Blanc** ✓ 🍴 📖 ★★★★ **12** raises the bar with Granny Smith apple/asparagus typicity, brisk acidity, mineral conclusion. Ideal summer white.

Balance Classics

> **Shiraz-Merlot** ☺ 🍴 📖 ★★★ **11** 50/50 combo, ripe & plump easy-drinker with food-friendly leafy & savoury overtones. **Muscat d'Alexandrie** ☺ 🍴 📖 ★★★ Among handful of unfortified versions of aromatic white variety. Improved **12** rosepetal & grape aromas, attractive sweet flavours. Enjoy chilled. **Sauvignon Blanc-Semillon** ☺ 🍴 ★★★ Upping the quality, **12** offers intense tropical & crisp apple refreshment at moderate 12.5% alcohol.

Cabernet Sauvignon-Merlot 🍴 📖 ★★ Vanilla & berry scented **11** tad gawky, with sweet ending. **Pinotage-Shiraz** ⊕ 🍴 ★★ **10** nicely rounded sipper. Like other reds, lightly oak-staved. **Shiraz Rosé** 🍴 📖 ★★ Boiled sweet & candyfloss charm on softly dry **12**. **Pinot Gris-Sauvignon Blanc** ⊕ 🍴 📖 ★★ **11** pleasant if somewhat neutral quaffer. **Chenin Blanc-Colombar** 🍴 ★★ **12** light, modestly flavoured seafood companion. Discontinued: **Reserve Cabernet Sauvignon**, **Sauvignon Blanc**.

Balance Sparklings

Sweet Temptation Sparkling ⊕ ★★ Sweet NV rosé bubbly, just 8% alcohol. **Boldly Brut Sparkling** ⊕ ★★★ Lean NV sparkler bursts with bubbles & joi de vivre. **Lusciously Fruity Sparkling** ⊕ ★★ Aromatic NV party fizz is gently sweet, with hint of litchi.

Balance Buddy range NEW

Natural Sweet White 🍴 ★★★ Chenin & hanepoot deliver perlé enjoyment in softly sweet NV. **Natural Sweet Rosé** 🍴 ★★★ Pinotage strawberry & chenin tang combine in slightly petillant, not-too-sweet NV. **Semi Sweet Red** 🍴 📖 ★★ Sweet entry, but surprisingly dry conclusion on unabashedly fruity **10**.

Haven Point Fairtrade range NEW

Shiraz 🍴 📖 ★★★ Combo New/Old World styling on **11**: savoury & spicy facets to sweet-fruit flavours, contrasting gruff tannins call for food. **Viognier-Shiraz** 🍴 📖 ★★ Unusual varietal pairing for a rosé, but fun. 20% shiraz supplies the faint pink tinge in (dry) **12**. WO Coastal, as for all in this range. **Pinot Gris** 🍴 📖 ★★★ Super drinkability from lime- & pineapple-infused **12**. — HJ/CvZ

Overmeer Cellars

Since 1996, no-frills range by Distell. Modest alcohol levels and 3/5L packs for all.

Selected Red ★★ Warm hay & sour cherry combo, lightish NV has some character, nice dry tannic finish. **Rosé** NEW ★ Copper-hued NV, straightforward, overtly sweet strawberry flavour. **Premier Grand Cru** ★★ Previously without 'Premier' prefix. Uncomplicated NV dry white with zingy, bone-dry peach & grass flavours. **Stein** ★★ Green apple taste, NV is bit simpler than PGC sibling but nice & crisp. **Late Harvest** ★★ Pack aptly says 'fresh fruity', NV well rounded & balanced, sunny sweetness ends clean, brisk. — DB/HJ

◼ **Overvaal** *see Hartswater Wine Cellar*

Paardebosch Wines

Location: Malmesbury ▪ Map/WO: Swartland ▪ Est/1stB 2011 ▪ Tasting & cellar tours Mon-Sat by appt ▪ Sales Wed & Fri 10-4 ▪ Closed all pub hols ▪ BYO picnic ▪ Walks/hikes ▪ Owner(s) Wiggo Anderson & Des Kruger ▪ Cellarmaster(s)/winemaker(s) Marius Malan (2011, consultant) ▪ Viticulturist(s) Christopher Lawak (2005) ▪ 45ha/22ha (malbec, ptage, chenin, sem) ▪ 25t/1,250cs own label 15% red 85% white + 2,200cs for clients ▪ redlex@cybersmart.co.za ▪ S 33°32'41.41" E 018°49'36.14" ▪ **T +27 (0)82-565-4218, +27 (0)23-626-1413**

Des Kruger and co-owner Wiggo Anderson were inspired by 'enthusiastic and enigmatic' consultant winemaker Marius Malan, raised on Perdeberg, to 'embrace the ethos of the Swartland Revolution' on their 18th-century Siebritskloof farm. Their 22ha include 65-year-old chenin and semillon, 20-year-old pinotage and local rarity malbec. Harvesting small quantities of fruit off mostly dryland vines, and vinifying this without additives in older oak barrels in the area's oldest cellar (re-commissioned after a century), they're having 'fun' reviving tradition.

★★★★ **Phoenix White Blend** Impressive fusion semillon (60%), chenin, both barrel fermented. **11** similar nutty oxidative notes to Shani but greater focus, textural qualities. Worth seeking out if you enjoy the style.
Shani Chenin Blanc  ★★★★ Barrel-fermented **11**'s sweet baked apple, caramel & toffee oxidative bouquet belies its tangy-dry, sherry-like palate. Quirky & individual meal companion. — WB/IM

PaardenKloof

Location/WO: Bot River ▪ Map: Elgin, Walker Bay & Bot River ▪ Est 2003 ▪ 1stB 2007 ▪ Tasting & tours by appt ▪ Sales Mon-Fri 9-12 ▪ Winemaker(s) Kobie Viljoen (cab & shiraz), Stefan Gerber (sauv) & Kevin Grant (pinot) ▪ Vineyard manager Michael Edon ▪ Viticulturist(s) Kevin Watt (Dec 2006) ▪ 23.6ha (cab, pinot, shiraz, sauv) ▪ BWI, IPW ▪ PO Box 381 Bot River 7185 ▪ info@paardenkloof.co.za ▪ www.paardenkloof.co.za ▪ S 34° 17'44.1" E 019° 14'5.4" ▪ **T +27 (0)28-284-9824** ▪ F +27 (0)28-284-9419

PaardenKloof is the Bot River property of leading businessman Mohseen V Moosa and his wife Daphne Neethling. More than 80% of the 1,430ha of fynbos-rich land is actively conserved but ±23ha of vineyard were established from 2004 and now the resulting wines are coming to market. Labels bear renditions of the work of Peter E Clarke, one of South Africa's great artists who found inspiration in Tesselaarsdal, a little village near the farm, and a portion of sales will go towards the establishment of a foundation to assist young artists from under-privileged communities.

Peter Clarke Collection Gaiety Sauvignon Blanc NEW ★★★ Just-bottled **12**, from young vines, is light & delicate, with gravelly minerality, slight gunsmoke whiff. Good potential, deserves time. — GdB/CR/CvZ

Paarl Wine Company

Closed to public ▪ Owner(s) Izak Visagie ▪ 9 Zuidmeer Str Huguenot Paarl 7646 ▪ izak.v@pwcwines.co.za ▪ **T +27 (0)21-862-2100** ▪ F +27 (0)21-862-6400

Wine wholesalers and owners of the Cape Style bag-in-box/Purepack range.

Packwood Wines

Location: Knysna ▪ Map: Klein Karoo & Garden Route ▪ WO: Plettenberg Bay ▪ Est 2006 ▪ 1stB 2009 ▪ Tasting & sales Mon-Fri 11-3 ▪ Fee R15, waived if case is purchased ▪ Closed all pub hols ▪ Cheese lunch — book ahead ▪ Tour groups by appt ▪ Farm produce ▪ Walks/hikes ▪ Mountain biking trail ▪ 4-star country house & self-catering cottages (see Accommodation section) ▪ Owner(s) Peter & Vicky Gent ▪ Winemaker(s) Teddy Hall (Mar 2009, consultant) ▪ Viticulturist(s) Vicky Gent (Jan 2006) ▪ 380ha/3.5ha (pinot, chard, sauv) ▪ 5t/5,000cs own label 80% white 20% rosé ▪ PO Box 622 Knysna 6570 ▪ vicky@packwood.co.za ▪ www.packwood.co.za ▪ S 34° 0'18.77" E 023° 13'43.33" ▪ **T +27 (0)44-532-7614** ▪ F +27 (0)86-510-0741

Most farms face some kind of loss of crop from birds and animals but Packwood on the outskirts of the Knysna forest has it particularly bad. 'Vervet monkeys, bush pigs, baboons, bushbuck and Cape White-eyes hammer the grapes every year and we've learnt the real meaning of blood, sweat and tears,' says co-owner and viticulturist Vicky Gent.

Sauvignon Blanc ★★★★ **11** impresses with better fruit expression than **10** (★★★★). Intense fruit punch flavour, good richness & weight, tangy acidity. Moderate ±12% alcohol means you can drink it all day long. **Gent Méthode Cap Classique** NEW ★★★ NV rosé sparkling from pinot noir rather rustic, with earthy & spicy notes to go with red fruit. — CE

■ **Paddagang** see Tulbagh Winery

Painted Wolf Wines

Location: Paarl ▪ Map: Paarl & Wellington ▪ WO: Swartland/Paarl/Western Cape/Stellenbosch/Coastal ▪ Est/1stB 2007 ▪ Tasting & sales by appt Mon-Sun 10-5 ▪ Fee R25 ▪ Closed Easter Fri-Mon, Dec 25 & Jan 1 ▪ Lunch by appt (parties of 6 or less) ▪ Owner(s) Jeremy & Emma Borg, & 16 'pack members' ▪ Cellarmaster(s) Rolanie Lotz, Inge Terreblanche & Trizanne Barnard (consultants) ▪ Winemaker(s) Jeremy Borg ▪ ±65ha/40ha (grenache, merlot, mourv, ptage, shiraz, chenin, sauv, viog) ▪ 65t/8,000cs own label 70% red 20% white 10%

rosé ▪ Other export brand: Jemma ▪ PO Box 1489 Suider Paarl 7624 ▪ sales@paintedwolfwines.com ▪ www.
paintedwolfwines.com ▪ S 33° 46' 14.8" E 018° 57' 14.6" ▪ **T +27 (0)21-863-2492**

Continued growth in sales for this Paarl-based enterprise mirrors developments in
label design, innovative wine ranges and efforts to develop conservation projects.
Work on raising quality has also brought competition recognition for Jeremy Borg
and his team. It's possible to draw parallels between the wines (some aligned in
new ranges below) and the African wild dogs that inspire their brand name. They —
the dogs, certainly — are highly social and committed to community, remarkably
persistent and energetic. Not to mention having unique and beautiful markings!

The Black Pack range

★★★★ **Shiraz 10**, now bottled, delivers ample plum softness; juicy but dry ripe palate, with light tannic grip
from combo French/American oak. Savoury undertone lends balance to finish. WO Coastal.

Merlot ✓ ★★★★ Attractive fresh lift on plummy, poised & ripe **11**; soft silky tannins with a dry bite to end. These
all previously listed under 'Our Pack'. **Stellenbosch Pinotage** ✓ ★★★★ Drops 'Juergen' from name. Previewed
last edition, **10** now more settled showing banana loaf/savoury combo, with integrated oak. **Pictus Red** ★★★★
Shiraz-led **10** plus splashes pinotage & grenache. More ambition than **09** (★★★★). Complex & multi-faceted, it
will reward cellaring which will allow new oak to meld. Only just dry. **Wild Yeast Barrel Fermented Chenin
Blanc** ★★★★ **11** now bottled shows broad melange of sweet peach & pear notes. Rich & off-dry. Older French
oak provides toasty platform. WO Swartland. **Roussanne** ★★★★ Nectarine freshness vies with spicy vibrancy on
now-bottled **11**. Creamy texture & flavour follows to rich, scarcely dry end. WO Paarl.

The Pack range

> **Rosalind Paarl Pinotage Rosé** ☺ 🍴 ★★★ Delicate pink, with primary red fruit flavours. **12** has dry
> elegance, with clean acid freshness.

Guillermo Swartland Pinotage 🍴 ★★★★ Now-bottled **10** manages richness with bright fruit expression. Savoury element adds extra dimension. Includes dashes mourvèdre & grenache, step up on **09** (★★★).
Penny Swartland Viognier 🍴 ★★★★ Pretty peach & spice on now-bottled **11**; has concentrated viscous
palate weight, but remains 'cool' despite hefty 15% alcohol. These 3 previously listed under 'Our Pack'.

Cape 'Hunting' Blends range

★★★★ **Lekanyane** ⊕ 🍴 Aka Jemma White. **11** vibrant chenin, viognier, verdelho (40/30/20) blend.
Tropical pineapple & elderflower, breadth on palate from oaking (older barrels & staves).
Madach ⊕ 🍴 ★★★★ Aka Jemma Red. Shiraz/pinotage blend in **10**. Smoky prune, liquorice & smooth
body from 50/50 barrel/stave oaking.

The Den Comfort Wines range

Cabernet Sauvignon 🍴 ★★★ **11** previewed last year, still approachable & sweet-fruited, but oak staving still
obvious. **Pinotage** ⊕ 🍴 ★★★ Raspberry & fruitcake on **11**. Rich cocoa depth & intensity. Dry texture from
oaking, long spicy finish. **Chenin Blanc** 🍴 ★★★★ Lightly oaked **12** tasted ex barrel shows regional typicity,
from old Swartland & Paarl vines. Youthful fruit purity; just-dry but good acidity. **Sauvignon Blanc** NEW ✓ 🍴
★★★★ Gentle & refreshing **12** has layers of tropical fruit co-mingled with greengage. Dry. WO Paarl. — JP

- ▪ **Palesa** see uniWines Vineyards
- ▪ **Papillon** see Van Loveren Family Vineyards
- ▪ **Paradyskloof** see Vriesenhof Vineyards
- ▪ **Parker Family** see Altydgedacht Estate
- ▪ **Parlotones** see Woolworths

Passages Wine

WO: Stellenbosch/Coastal/Swartland ▪ 1stB 2006 ▪ Closed to public ▪ Owner(s) Ronald T Gault & Charlayne
Hunter-Gault ▪ Cellarmaster(s)/winemaker(s) Ernst Gouws (2007, consultant) ▪ (cab, merlot, ptage, chard) ▪
±5,000cs own label 70% red 30% white ▪ gaultronald@gmail.com ▪ www.passageswine.com

Former banker Ron Gault and journalist wife Charlayne Hunter-Gault (former SA
bureau chief of CNN) arrived at the birth of the democratic era — and put down
permanent roots. Passages kicked off in 2005 and is winning fans in the United
States with its growing range, made by Ernst Gouws of Ernst Gouws & Co Wines.

Merlot ★★★☆ Cocoa & mulberry fruit appeal on **11**. Displays length, depth & breadth. Light chalk texture & mouthfeel add interest. **Pinotage** NEW ★★★ Tail-waggingly friendly new offering of **11** has chocolate blueberry instant appeal. Good depth, body & juicy length. **Cabernet Sauvignon-Merlot** ★★★ Black cherry succulence vies with cocoa depth on **09**. Medium body & length, with light tannic grip. **Chardonnay** ★★★★ Rich creamy peach & citrus fruit of **11** cloaked in light oak sheen. Soft & approachable yet juicy & fresh. Long tail. —FM

Paul Cluver Estate Wines

Location/WO: Elgin ▪ Map: Elgin, Walker Bay & Bot River ▪ Est 1896 ▪ 1stB 1997 ▪ Tasting & sales Mon-Fri 9–4 Sat 9–2 ▪ Fee R50 for groups — limited to 10 pax per group ▪ Closed Easter weekend, Dec 25/26 & Jan 1 ▪ Restaurant 'Fresh' Tue-Sat 9-3 (closed Jun-Aug) ▪ Conservation area (part of UNESCO Heritage Site Kogelberg Biosphere) ▪ Mountain biking track open to public, fee payable ▪ Open air amphitheatre hosting concerts Dec-Mar ▪ Owner(s) Cluver family ▪ Cellarmaster(s)/winemaker(s) Andries Burger (Nov 1996) ▪ Viticulturist(s) Craig Harris (Jan 2010) & Kevin Watt (Mar 2005, consultant) ▪ 2,400ha/90ha (pinot, chard, gewürz, riesling, sauv) ▪ 300t/20,000cs own label 20% red 80% white ▪ Brands for clients: Woolworths, Scrucap ▪ BWI Champion ▪ PO Box 48 Grabouw 7160 ▪ info@cluver.com ▪ www.cluver.com ▪ S 34° 10' 6.2" E 019° 5' 8.1" ▪ **T +27 (0)21-844-0605** ▪ F +27 (0)21-844-0150

While this Elgin spread could rest on its laurels — it's a diverse, mixed-farming operation with family roots going back to 1896, recognised amongst South Africa's wine elite — there's no thought of that. 'We are constantly re-assessing and improving what we do,' says managing director Paul Cluver junior. That includes technological innovation, but not at the expense of sustainable production. A conservation pioneer, the family team recently added the Nedbank Green Award and Woolworths Farming for the Future status to the eco-cabinet. And there's some interesting intercontinental cooperation in a 'closer working relationship' with Martin Prieur of Burgundy heavyweight Domaine Jacques Prieur.

★★★★ **Pinot Noir** ⓘ 🍴 Refined & serious, radiant **10** has medium-weight mineral centre with succulent cherry fruit, & a tangy, structured texture. 11 months 20% new wood fully absorbed into the edifice.

★★★★☆ **Seven Flags Pinot Noir** Stellar barrel selection of single clone from farm's best site; a fine, measured, polished, elegant package. **10** quiet in youth, a step behind super **09** which is power in the gentlest, most beguiling, form. 'Burgundian everything' — clones, yeasts, oak (11 months, 30% new).

★★★★☆ **CWG Auction Reserve Pinot Noir** ⓘ 2nd lot (24 cases) of **10** for 2012 auction. Selected grapes of 3 clones ex highest vineyard. Leaps from the glass with alluring cherry & spice from 11 months oak, 20% new. Follows with astounding texture, bold fruit & full grip of powdery tannins. Very fine layered finish.

★★★★☆ **CWG Auction Reserve Wagon Trail Chardonnay** From farm's oldest chardonnay vineyard (23 years), **10** the complete package, delivered with restraint. Full flavoured, with generous texture, a fine mineral base ensures balance, power, & elegance.

★★★★☆ **Chardonnay** 🍴 A keeper: toned citrus fruit, cosseted by fine oak in youth, unfurls splendidly given year or two. **11** (★★★★) tad quieter than super **10**. Wild yeast ferment in French cask, 40% new.

★★★★ **Gewürztraminer** ✓ 🍴 Semi-dry rendition, a Cape benchmark. Taut **11** has delicate litchi notes with a super sugar/acid balance & grip for food.

★★★★ **Riesling** ✓ 🍴 Delicate orange-peel features & white pepper facet to 'wet pebble' minerality are hallmarks. **11** drier (8.9g/l sugar) than previous & 'Close Encounter' cellarmate, a penetrating mouthful.

★★★★ **Close Encounter Riesling** 🍴 Sweeter than cellar sibling (32.6g/l sugar; 9.7% alcohol), in 'German Auslese' style. **11** offers floral ginger & lime fruit in a lovely fresh finish; it yearns for food partners.

★★★★ **Sauvignon Blanc** ✓ 🍴 Neither tart nor tropical, **11** just beautifully elegant with all in its ordered place. Like **10**, edgy capsicum & minerality leavened by leesy width & plump 8% wooded semillon.

★★★★☆ **Noble Late Harvest** Elegantly packaged botrytised riesling dessert that takes the breath away. Our White Wine of the Year, **11** (★★★★★) shimmering old-gold, succulent apricot ripeness emphatically cut by tangy lime, leaving a stony minerality in long electric finish. Brilliant balance, a thing of beauty. —DS

▪ **Paul de Villiers** *see* Landskroon Wines
▪ **Paulina's Reserve** *see* Rickety Bridge Winery

Paul Wallace Wines

Location/WO: Elgin ▪ Est/1stB 2004 ▪ Closed to public ▪ Owner(s)/viticulturist(s) Paul Wallace ▪ Winemaker(s) Paul Wallace, with Justin Hoy ▪ 25ha/10.5ha (malbec, pinot, sauv) ▪ 80t/330cs own label 100% red ▪ BWI,

IPW ▪ PO Box 141 Elgin 7180 ▪ wallovale@mweb.co.za ▪ www.wallovale.co.za ▪ **T +27 (0)21-848-9744/ +27 (0)83-255-1884/+27 (0)82-572-1406** ▪ F +27 (0)86-646-3694

'Dark in colour, well muscled, intense and full of character.' Thus Elgin-based Paul Wallace sums up both his wine and Jake, his canine shadow after whom it is now named. Malbec was a chance choice for Wallace's single wine: as a viticultural consultant he knew of an excellent vineyard with a fine crop that wasn't going to be harvested. Believing the variety is underrated, he 'gave it a bash'.

★★★★ **Black Dog Malbec** ✓ Was 'Malbec'. Dark-hued 09 more closed, concentrated than 08. Has all basics in place; ripe, mineral-laced black cherry fruit, rich texture, freshness & French oak for great future. — AL

Pax Verbatim Vineyards

Location: Somerset West ▪ WO: Western Cape ▪ Est 2003 ▪ Closed to public ▪ Owner(s) Richard Hilton ▪ Cellarmaster(s)/winemaker(s) Richard Hilton (2003) ▪ Viticulturist(s) Tjuks Roos & Richard Rose (consultants) ▪ (shiraz, viog) ▪ 12-14t/800cs own label 35% red 65% white ▪ richard@paxverbatim.co.za ▪ www.paxverbatim.co.za ▪ **T +27 (0)21-855-5244** ▪ F +27 (0)86-618-4089

For any winemaker, there is nothing more satisfying than reaching the milestone of a decade of vintages. For Richard Hilton, owner and boutique vintner, it is an opportunity to fine-tune the current range while looking at new wines and new markets — a 'super-cuvée' is in the near future...

★★★★ **Blazing Hill Syrah** ⓟ From Helderberg vineyard, 09 in riper, more dark-fruited mould than restrained 08. Dense palate expresses richer style with complex savoury undertone. Nicely dry to end.

★★★★ **Rockwater Fountain Viognier** 🗎 Plenty of varietal appeal here, 11 fresh apricots, peaches, limes & overtones of perfumed lily of the valley. Tiny amount of oak (5%) adds spice & richness. — CM

▪ **Peacock Ridge** see False Bay Vineyards
▪ **Pearlstone** see Rhebokskloof Wine Estate

Pearly Bay

Named for a pearly white beach on the Southern Cape coast, this KWV range is unpretentious, modestly priced and styled to encourage novices to enjoy wine.

Dry Red 🗎 ★★ Like many of these, drops 'Cape' from the name. **NV** with bright fruit, clip of finishing tannin. **Sweet Rosé** 🗎 ★★ Easy **NV** summer sipper with luscious sweet muscat fruit, low alcohol. **Rosé** 🗎 ★★ Appealing wild strawberries & cream flavours; **NV** semi-sweet & quaffable. **Sweet White** 🗎 ★★ Grapey, light & not cloyingly sweet **NV**. **Dry White** 🗎 ★★ Herby tang adds refreshing edge to **NV**'s fruity (note: off-dry) charm. **Celebration Sparkling Rosé** ★★ Gently fizzing, fresh grapey **NV** party wine. Low alcohol & sweet, like next wine. **Celebration White** ★★ Perfumed muscat fruit on fresh **NV** sparkler. **Sweet Red** **NEW** 🗎 ★★ Seems very sweet in fact, **NV** with hint of bitterness. These widely sourced. — AL

▪ **Pecan Stream** see Waterford Estate
▪ **Pegalle** see Bonview Wines
▪ **Pella** see Super Single Vineyards
▪ **Pepin Condé** see Stark-Condé Wines

Perdeberg Winery

Location/WO: Paarl ▪ Map: Paarl & Wellington ▪ Est 1941 ▪ 1stB 1942 ▪ Tasting & sales Mon-Fri 8–5 Sat 9.30–2 ▪ Closed Easter Fri-Mon, Dec 25/26 & Jan 1 ▪ Cellar tours Mon-Fri by appt ▪ Meals, pre-booked week in advance, for groups of 10+ ▪ BYO picnic ▪ Annual October festival ▪ Owner(s) 30 members ▪ Cellarmaster(s) Albertus Louw (Oct 2008) ▪ Winemaker(s) Riaan Möller (Dec 2006) & Carla Herbst (Jun 2008) ▪ Viticulturist(s) Jaco Engelbrecht (Nov 2011) ▪ 6,000ha/2,564ha (cab, cincaut, merlot, ptage, shiraz, chard, chenin, sauv) ▪ 18,000t/150,000cs own label 63% red 37% white ▪ BWI, HACCP, IPW, WIETA ▪ PO Box 214 Paarl 7620 ▪ info@perdeberg.co.za ▪ www.perdeberg.co.za ▪ S 33° 39' 30.00" E 018° 49' 37.00" ▪ **T +27 (0)21-869-8244** ▪ F +27 (0)21-869-8245

Joseph Huskisson, long-serving winemaker at what was then Perdeberg Co-operative, from 1956 until his retirement in 1994 was a staunch supporter of chenin and pinotage, shunning the 'new' varieties like cabernet and sauvignon blanc. Current trends in this region would seem to bear out his views! Founded in 1941, the winery as produced standout chenin since the earliest days. Lately, the emphasis has been on lower alcohol levels in the wines and social upliftment of farm employees.

Reserve range

★★★★ **Pinotage** From old bushvines. Fruit just one of **10**'s attractions: crushed berry vibrancy supported by balanced oaking.

★★★★ **Chenin Blanc** ✓ **11** remains a price-point benchmark for purity of fruit, balance & refinement. Elevated & broadened by gentle brush of oak, trace of sugar.

★★★★ **Sauvignon Blanc** ✓ Bold & forthright **11** delivers strident aromatic whiff followed up by robust ripe fruit & sustained finish. A perennial over-performer at the price.

★★★★ **Chardonnay-Viognier** Heavily oaked **11** (★★★★) 70/30 blend from Agter Paarl vines has rich ripe fruit struggling to emerge. Needs time to settle. **10** bolder, smoother.

★★★★ **Méthode Cap Classique Brut** Classy bottle-fermented bubbly from chardonnay, **09** made an admirable debut last year.

★★★★☆ **Weisser Riesling** Natural Sweet with a touch of oak, gorgeous **10** is a powerhouse of flavours. Pure pineapple essence, tangy & irresistible. From Durbanville grapes.

Cabernet Sauvignon NEW ✓ ★★★★ Generously big-bodied, plush **10** belies modest price, with refined texture & aristocratic dark fruit. **Shiraz** ✓ ★★★★ Smoky, aromatic **10** offers generous body & structure, but remains supple & approachable. Unpretentious but carefully shaped.

Simply Delicious range

Merlot ☺ ★★★ Pure berry fruit borne on soft tannins, **11** offers uncomplicated, immediate enjoyment. **Chenin Blanc** ☺ ★★★ **12** is pleasantly approachable, with ripe freshness & bracing acidity. Light-hearted & refreshing. **Sparkling Chenin Blanc** NEW ☺ ★★★ Happy new **12** bubbly is just-dry, with lively fruit.

Cabernet Sauvignon ★★★ Juicy, lively **10** packed with berries, oak savouriness. Enjoy rather than age. **Pinotage** ★★★ Trademark blueberries in a juicy package, **10** firm backbone, dry finish good match for rich dishes. **Shiraz** ★★★ Smoky hedgerow berries, soft luscious texture, **10** is oh so easy to drink. **Cabernet Sauvignon-Merlot** ★★ **11** rather austere, chalky, but shows hints of savoury berries. **Rosé** ★★★ Last was strawberry-scented **09**, crisp & dry. **Sauvignon Blanc** ★★★ Minerality abounds in **11**, clean & focused, no pretensions. **Sparkling Rosé** NEW ★★ Cheerfully frothy sweet carbonated NV, based on chenin. **Soft Smooth Red** ★★★ **11** shiraz, cinsaut, cab mix with a dash of sweetness. Note: Flagship Collection discontinued. — GdB

Peter Bayly Wines

Location/WO: Calitzdorp ▪ Map: Klein Karoo & Garden Route ▪ Est 2002 ▪ 1stB 2004 ▪ Tasting, sales & tours by appt ▪ Owner(s) Peter Bayly Wines (Pty) Ltd ▪ Winemaker(s)/viticulturist(s) Peter Bayly ▪ 6.6ha/1.2ha (tinta, touriga, souzão) ▪ ±8t/±660cs own label ▪ PO Box 187 Calitzdorp 6660 ▪ info@baylys.co.za ▪ www.peterbayly.co.za ▪ S 33° 26' 54.62" E 021° 47' 33.92" ▪ **T +27 (0)44-213-3702** ▪ F +27 (0)86-513-2727

Deep in the secluded Groenfontein Valley near Calitzdorp, its hillsides covered with Karoo succulents, is Peter and Yvonne Bayly's meticulously tended vineyard of Portuguese varieties planted in ancient red soils. Here the couple are fulfilling their dream of 'living free range', handcrafting port-style wines and a country red, whose volumes are steadily rising to meet demand.

★★★★ **Cape Vintage** Port-style **09** mostly touriga (45%), roughly equal tinta & souzão. Choc/savoury flavours, balanced fortification & sugar; tad firmer than **07**, inviting cellaring — though hard to resist. No **08**.

★★ **Rustic red, 11** older-oak-matured touriga with dashes tinta & souzão. **Cape Late Bottled Vintage** NEW ★★★ Ripe plum & malty berry compote, **08** chiefly souzão (58%) & tinta, dash touriga. Soft & accessible, as per style. **Cape White** ★★ NV port-style from chenin, with sherry-like nutty marzipan tone. Versatile: sip solo or over ice, or mix things up! — GdB/CvZ

Peter Falke Wines

Location/map: Stellenbosch ▪ WO: Stellenbosch/Coastal ▪ 1stB 2003 ▪ Tasting & sales Tue-Sun 11-7 Mon by appt ▪ Fee R40 ▪ Closed Good Fri, Dec 25/26 & Jan 1 ▪ Cellar tours by appt 11-4 ▪ Cheese platters & refreshments ▪ Owner(s) Franz-Peter Falke ▪ Winemaker(s) Rianie Strydom (2012, consultant) ▪ Viticulturist(s) /GM

Werner Schrenk (Jan 2009) ▪ 20ha/±6ha (cab, shiraz) ▪ 100t/6,000cs own label 65% red 25% white 10% rosé ▪ PO Box 12605 Stellenbosch 7599 ▪ info@peterfalkewines.co.za ▪ www.peterfalkewines.com ▪ S 34° 0' 2.1" E 018° 50' 19.3" ▪ **T** +27 (0)21-881-3677 ▪ F +27 (0)21-881-3667

Continuing the focus 'to make small quantities of terroir-driven wines', the line-up has changed to capitalise on the strengths of this predominantly red-wine area (Stellenbosch's vaunted 'golden triangle'), with the discontinuation of the sauvignon from the signature range. The addition of a pinot noir to the PF range was an experiment that worked; pinot was originally bought in for the MCC bubbly (untasted), available cellardoor only.

Signature range

★★★★ **Signature Blend** Listed as 'The Blend' last time. Cab franc dominant, with merlot, cab, **09** (★★★★) improves on **08** with its ripeness manifest in molten berries, plums, fruitcake spicing. Delicious drinkability is ensured by a fleshy palate, polished tannins.

Syrah ★★★★ Admirable fruit focus in **09** masks the 15.2% alc. Tannins are integrated, the wine ready to enjoy, drink now till ±2016. Discontinued: **Sauvignon Blanc.**

PF range

Pinot Noir NEW ★★★★ Bright & pure 2011 vibrantly juicy, the variety given full fruit expression, with oak subservient. **Blanc de Noir** ★★★ Pale salmon-hued & bone-dry **12** reflects merlot/pinotage restrained fruitiness with food in mind. **Sauvignon Blanc** ✓ ★★★★ Fynbos note from portion Durbanville fruit, **12**'s limy freshness extends the flavours, intense & vital. WO Coastal. Discontinued: **Cabernet Sauvignon.** — CR

▪ **Petit** see Ken Forrester Wines

Pfeifer's Boutique Wines

Location: Somerset West ▪ Map: Helderberg ▪ Est 2000 ▪ 1stB 2003 ▪ Tasting & sales by appt ▪ Closed Easter Fri/Sun, Dec 25 & Jan 1 ▪ Owner(s) René Hans & Maya Pfeifer ▪ Winemaker(s)/viticulturist(s) Pascal Pfeifer (Jun 2006) ▪ 1.675ha/1.4ha (shiraz) ▪ 14-16t/±75cs own label 100% red ▪ IPW member ▪ PO Box 5238 Helderberg 7135 ▪ enquiries@pfeifersvineyard.co.za ▪ www.pfeifersvineyard.co.za ▪ S 34° 01' 10.98" E 018° 47' 17.06" ▪ **T** +27 (0)21-842-3396 ▪ F +27 (0)86-616-8850

The Pfeifers' expansive Helderberg farm becomes boutique when it comes to wine. Pascal Pfeifer advises that vintages from 2005 to 2007, the last made, are still available from the cellar. What's more: 'We haven't raised prices in the last three years, even with mounting cost increases.'

▪ **Phambili** see Wellington Wines
▪ **Philip Jonker** see Weltevrede Estate

Philip Jordaan Wines

WO: Western Cape ▪ Est/1stB 1998 ▪ For wine orders call T +27 (0)82-573-0620 ▪ Owner(s)/cellarmaster(s)/winemaker(s) Philip Jordaan ▪ Viticulturist(s) Leon Dippenaar ▪ P/Bag X15 Hermanus 7640 ▪ jordaanphilip1@telkomsa.net ▪ **T** +27 (0)82-573-0620

The eponymous cellarmaster-owner of this venture was also cellarmaster for 26 years at a somewhat larger venture — Du Toitskloof. There he acquired his taste for cabernet franc. With talk of more vintages of it in barrel, we are hopeful.

Limited Edition Cabernet Franc ⊛ ★★★★ Elegant, supple & mature **06** with savoury, lean red fruit. Frequent Wine of the Month Club 'Most unusual red' choice. — IM

Phizante Kraal

Location/WO: Durbanville ▪ Map: Durbanville, Philadelphia & Darling ▪ 1stB 2005 ▪ Tasting & sales Mon-Fri 9-4 Sat 10-2 ▪ Fee R15 ▪ Owner(s) André & Ronelle Brink ▪ Winemaker(s) Thys Louw (Jan 2005, Diemersdal) ▪ Viticulturist(s) André Brink ▪ 50ha (cab, shiraz, chenin, sauv) ▪ 1,000cs own label ▪ PO Box 8 Durbanville 7551 ▪ info@phesantekraal.co.za ▪ www.phizantekraal.co.za ▪ S 33° 47' 7.66" E 018° 40' 15.6" ▪ **T** +27 (0)21-976-2114 ▪ F +27 (0)21-976-2113

It's baby steps at this Durbanville boutique winery for owners André and Ronelle Brink, but all in the right direction! Slowly but surely they are increasing production under their own label and now, in hopes of attracting more visitors to the farm, renovation of a function space and tasting centre (built in 1698) is underway.

★★★★ **Sauvignon Blanc** 🍴 🍷 **12** (★★★★★) an 'in-your-face' wine, step up from **11**, with pungent aromas of peas/asparagus followed by mouthwatering pink grapefruit, lemons & lime zest. Intense & powerful, deserves time to show all its charms.

Cabernet Sauvignon ★★★ **09** sweet black & red fruit, a little coarse on the finish. **Shiraz** ★★★ Spiced plum cake & dark chocolate notes on **09** give way to sour black cherries with chewy, supportive tannins. **Chenin Blanc** NEW 🍴 🍷 ★★★★ Very pleasant mouthful of pineapple & baked honeyed fruit shows promise in maiden **12**. Warm alcohol asserts at finish. — CM

PicardiRebel

Est 1994 ▪ PO Box 1868 Cape Town 8000 ▪ **T** +27 (0)21-469-3300 ▪ **F** +27 (0)21-469-3434

The PicardiRebel nationwide chain of drinks stores offers budget wine shoppers a number of good-value options under its house brand Coast (and occasional labels Hippo Creek, Naked Truth and Simply Red/White).

Pick 'n Pay

WO: Robertson ▪ Enquiries Neil Cooke ▪ Pick 'n Pay Corporate Brands PO Box 908 Bedfordview 2008 ▪ ncooke@pnp.co.za ▪ www.picknpay.co.za ▪ **T** +27 (0)11-856-7000 ▪ **F** +27 (0)86-616-5949

Senior wine buyer Neil Cooke is pleased with initial customer response to full-colour Pick n Pay branding for what was formerly the blue-and-white No Name boxed wine range, sourced from Robertson Winery. He's not planning any changes to the bottled house wines from Swartland Winery (not reviewed by us this edition), but some bubbly from Orange River Wine Cellars should hit shelves soon.

Smooth Dry Red ★★ Budget-priced (as all) NV with crisp black fruit flavours. All these wines variously available in 500ml, 3L & 5L packs. **Natural Sweet Rosé** ★★ Gently sweet party fun, NV tastes like strawberries & cream. **Rosé** NEW ★★★ Fresh cranberries & raspberries, NV is sweet but not cloying. Chill & enjoy. **Dry White** ★★ Guava-toned NV is an anywhere, anytime kind of wine. **Extra Light Dry White** ★ Apple & citrus refreshment, NV with bonus of low alcohol. **Stein** NV quick-sip for the sweet-toothed. **Johannisberger Sweet White** ★ Latest NV's sweetness comes with a twist of lemon. **Late Harvest** ★ Light, semi-sweet, no-complications picnic white. NV. **Johannisberger Sweet Red** ★ NV braai wine with a sweet-gamey contrast. — CE/HJ/CvZ

Place in the Sun

Location/WO: Stellenbosch ▪ Est/1stB 2010 ▪ Closed to public ▪ Owner(s) Distell ▪ Cellarmaster(s)/winemaker(s) Deon Boshoff (2010) ▪ Viticulturist(s) Annelie Viljoen (2010) ▪ 1,000t ▪ ISO 9001 & ISO 14001 (pending), Fairtrade, IPW ▪ PO Box 184 Stellenbosch 7599 ▪ dboshoff@distell.co.za ▪ www.placeinthesun.co.za ▪ **T** +27 (0)21-809-7000

This Distell-owned wine range is Fairtrade accredited and its grapes are sourced from FLO-CERT/Fair Label Organisation-certified vineyards, a proportion of their purchase price being directed towards workers' social development. Winemaker Deon Boshoff, also Distell's Adam Tas cellarmaster in Stellenbosch, is himself the son of farmworkers and learned his trade on a bursary open to the community.

Cabernet Sauvignon 🍴 🍷 ★★★ **11** bright blackberry fruit & pleasant tannic bite, good with hearty stews. **Merlot** 🍴 🍷 ★★★ Cappucino on the nose, ripe blackberry flavour, slathering of mocha oak makes improved **11** delicious. **Shiraz** 🍴 🍷 ★★★ Dusty thatch & some leathery spice introduce **11**'s brooding black cherry flavour, slight astringency in the farewell. **Sauvignon Blanc** 🖩 📖 **12** preview too unformed to rate, shows tangy green pineapple notes, big tropical fruit salad flavours. — DB/HJ

Plaisir de Merle

Location: Paarl ▪ Map: Franschhoek ▪ WO: Simonsberg-Paarl/Western Cape/Coastal ▪ Est 1993 ▪ 1stB 1994 ▪ Tasting, sales & cellar tours Mon-Fri 9–5 Sat 10–4 (Nov–Mar) & 10–2 (Apr–Oct) Sun by special request for groups of 15+ ▪ Fee R25 standard tasting/R40 sweet sensation tasting/R60 flavour & exclusive tasting ▪ Closed Easter Fri/Sun & Dec 25 ▪ Cheese platter R70, available during trading hours ▪ Facilities for children ▪ Gifts ▪ Conservation area ▪ Manor House (sleeps 8) can be booked for functions, conferences & weddings ▪ Owner(s) Distell ▪ Cellarmaster(s) Niel Bester (1993) ▪ Viticulturist(s) Hannes van Rensburg & Freddie le Roux (both 1993) ▪ 974ha/400ha (cabs s/f, malbec, merlot, p verdot, shiraz, chard, sauv) ▪ 800t/40,000cs own label 80% red 20% white ▪ ISO 9001:2008, ISO 14001:2004, BRC, BWI, SGS ▪ PO Box 121 Simondium 7670 ▪ plaisirdemerle@capelegends.co.za ▪ www.plaisirdemerle.co.za ▪ S 33° 51'0.0" E 018° 56'36.2" ▪ **T** +27 (0)21-874-1071 ▪ F +27 (0)21-874-1689

In 2012 Niel Bester celebrated 20 years as winemaker at this Distell flagship winery in Paarl, and recalled some highlights: 'Working at Château Margaux with Paul Pontallier changed my view about extraction of colour, flavour and tannin during fermentation.' And challenges: 'Creating a Plaisir style and using oak to support rather than overpower fruit.' And lessons about the farm's terroir: 'Dryland vineyards on higher slopes can produce quality red grapes, even in dry years; lower-lying, sandy soils need irrigation to avoid the fruit ripening too quickly.'

★★★★ **Cabernet Sauvignon** ✓ **09** typically temptingly drinkable in youth. Replete with gently fresh ripe fruit, hint of dusty oak & succulent tannins. Dabs malbec, cab franc, petit verdot increase ageworthiness.

★★★★☆ **Cabernet Franc** ⊛ From a single vineyard, spicy, fragrant & leafy **07** is supple & rich. No **09**.

★★★★ **Malbec** Forthcoming yet not overly showy. **10** well oaked, with underlying sweet mulberry fruit, tangy lift, soft dry tannins. No **09**.

★★★★ **Shiraz** ⊛ Oak (some American) more evident than usual on **09**, otherwise usual affable light touch, spice, red fruit purity with poised savoury length.

★★★★ **Grand Plaisir** Cab-based Bordeaux sextet with shiraz. Maturing savoury features already evident on **08**; charry oak hints too. Good flavour concentration, rounded tannins & fresh core allow for current drinking.

★★★★ **Chardonnay** Sprightly, fresh citrus notes introduce **11** (★★★★), with oak in subtle support. Crisp & flavoursome but lacks substance of **10**. May grow with short time in bottle. Some Robertson grapes.

★★★★ **Sauvignon Blanc** ✓ 🖩 📖 **12** notable for striking yet refined aromatic purity: greengage & sweet Golden Delicious apple. Refreshing, full of vitality; supple, mouthfilling & persistent. Includes Darling fruit.

Merlot ★★★ **10** slighter & more austere than previous. Pleasant if simple sweet fruit dwarfed by gravelly acid & unusually aggressive tannins. **Petit Plaisir** NEW ★★★★ **10** sweet-fruited shiraz, cab & splash merlot. Flavoursome, balanced freshness, rounded tannins. Offers more than the 'little pleasure' of its name. WO W Cape. — AL

Plettenvale Wines

NEW

Location/WO: Plettenberg Bay ▪ Map: Klein Karoo & Garden Route ▪ Est 2008 ▪ 1stB 2011 ▪ Tasting & sales by appt ▪ Self-catering cottages ▪ Owner(s) Gloria Strack van Schyndel ▪ Winemaker(s) Anton Smal (2011 MCC, consultant) & Lourens van der Westhuizen (2012 MCC & rosé, consultant) ▪ Viticulturist(s) Paul Wallace (Nov 2007, consultant) ▪ 5.3ha/2.3ha (pinot, shiraz, chard) ▪ 7t/±325cs (6btl) own label 33% rosé 67% MCC ▪ PO Box 2103 Plettenberg Bay 6600 ▪ plettenvalewines@gmail.com ▪ www.plettenvalewines.co.za ▪ **T** +27 (0)44-533-9146 ▪ F +27 (0)44-533-9146

Gloria Strack van Schyndel was inspired on a 2007 Tuscan walking and cooking tour by small vineyards producing 'super wines' to follow suit on her Plettenberg Bay estate. Despite the area's trained-staff shortage, the worst drought in over 130 years and birds wreaking havoc, 2011's minute crop produced the first bottle-fermented bubbly by nearby Bramon's Anton Smal. Better weather and bird nets ensured a bigger 2012 harvest, handled by Arendsig's Lourens van der Westhuizen.

Dry Rosé 🖩 ★★ Chardonnay (60%) combines with pinot noir in made-for-food **12**, with mouthwatering acidity, bone-dry finish. — WB/IM

▪ **Poetry** see Flagstone Winery
▪ **Poker Hill** see Somerbosch Wines

■ **Polkadraai Road** *see Beau Joubert Vineyards & Winery*
■ **Polo Club** *see Val de Vie Wines*

Pongrácz

This méthode cap classique bubbly label of Distell pays homage to aristocratic Hungarian refugee Desiderius Pongrácz's contribution to the local wine industry. The prestige cuvée comes in a handsome fluted bottle — 100 of them were fashioned by a Skills Development Centre into a huge chandelier for a charity auction.

Rosé ★★★★ Lightly pink **NV** dry bubbly has lovely freshness & more complexity this bottling; creamy mousse offers lively dimension. **Desiderius ⓟ ★★★★** Persistent, harmonious & fresh **03** sparkling step-up from **02** (**★★★★**), showing yeasty complexity & creamy texture. 60:40 blend chardonnay, pinot noir; other 2 reverse these proportions. **Brut ★★★** Enormously popular **NV** sparkler shows admirable consistency; lees adds some weight to apple flavours. This & Rosé also in 375ml bottles. — IM

■ **Porcelain Mountain** *see Porseleinberg*
■ **Porcupine Ridge** *see Boekenhoutskloof Winery*

Porseleinberg

Location: Malmesbury ▪ WO: Swartland ▪ Est 2009 ▪ 1stB 2011 ▪ Closed to public ▪ Owner(s) Boekenhoutskloof Winery Pty Ltd ▪ Winemaker(s)/viticulturist(s) Callie Louw (Jun 2009) ▪ 85ha/15ha (shiraz) ▪ 6t/300cs own label 100% red ▪ Organic EU Control Union ▪ PO Box 433 Franschhoek 7690 ▪ callie@porseleinberg.com ▪ www.porseleinberg.com ▪ **T +27 (0)79-884-2309** ▪ F +27 (0)86-566-9332

Things are happening on this Swartland farm owned by Boekenhoutskloof — which will take the majority of the organically grown fruit off, eventually, 50ha of vines. Certain blocks, though, go into the ambitious wine made here by Callie Louw, who also takes care of the vines (nothing new tasted as they're holding back the 2011). Callie's cellar has been upgraded and 2013 sees the first crops off the vineyards he planted. The chickens and Nguni cattle are doing well, he says (it's all very holistic farming here), 'and pigs and sheep are next on the list'.

★★★★ Porseleinberg ⓟ ☙ 100% shiraz, superb **10** mid-2011 was a velvet hand in an iron glove: beautifully ripe, lavender fruit tightly gripped by fine dry tannin, demanding patience or vigorous aeration. — TJ

■ **Porter Mill Station** *see Tulbagh Winery*
■ **Porterville Cellars** *see Tulbagh Winery*

Post House Vineyards

Location: Somerset West ▪ Map: Helderberg ▪ WO: Stellenbosch ▪ Est/1stB 1997 ▪ Tasting, sales & cellar tours Mon-Fri 9-5 Sat by appt ▪ Fee R30 ▪ Closed all pub hols ▪ BYO picnic ▪ Guest house ▪ Owner(s) Nicholas Gebers ▪ Cellarmaster(s) Nick Gebers ▪ Winemaker(s) Nick Gebers, with Pippa Orpen ▪ 70ha/39ha (cab, merlot, p verdot, ptage, shiraz, chenin, sauv) ▪ 200t/8,000cs own label 65% red 35% white ▪ PO Box 5635 Helderberg 7135 ▪ info@posthousewines.co.za ▪ www.posthousewines.co.za ▪ S 34° 1' 8.1" E 018° 48' 41.6" ▪ **T +27 (0)21-842-2409** ▪ F +27 (0)21-842-2409

The wines from this unpretentious, quality-driven Helderberg boutique winery come with back-label stories. Having set up home in an old post office building next to the village of Raithby, owner/winemaker Nick Gebers chose a philatelic theme for his range of blockbusters. From the literally black Penny Black to the whimsical Missing Virgin, each carries a historical explanation and a yarn to entertain you while you sip the wares.

★★★★☆ Cabernet Sauvignon Some wild notes intrude on super-ripe **09** (**★★★**) heavyweight. Follows impressive **08**.

★★★★ Merlot After elegant **08**, high-toned aromas a detraction on otherwise full & rich **09** (**★★★**).

★★★★ Shiraz Heavy, intensely dark & brooding, yet showing delicate floral scents & sweet black cherry fruit, **09** is brusquely masculine. Hot & dense, with thick tannins. Needs time.

★★★★ Missing Virgin Overstated **10** pinotage & petit verdot blend labours under huge (15.7%) alcohol, unyielding tannins & dense, spicy berry concentrate. For the deepest part of the cellar.

★★★★☆ **Penny Black** Impossibly concentrated **09** takes colour extraction to new levels. Earthy, sombre black Bordeaux-style blend with dash of chenin, big & bold in every way, yet retaining focus. Inky sanguine & floral hints on chalky tannin texture.

★★★★☆ **Stamp Of Chenin** ✓ Listed as 'Chenin Blanc' previously. Delightful showboat, barrel-matured **11** shows the full spectrum of tropical fruit, waxy honeyed lees, with marmalade twist at finish. Cocksure & extroverted, showing good ageing potential.

★★★★☆ **Treskilling Yellow 10** (★★★★) barrel-fermented botrytised chenin, showing oxidative sherry-like nuttiness. Exotically complex tobacco aromas with charming honeyed finish. Misses fruity richness of **08**.

Blueish Black ✓ ★★★★ Well-judged **10** shiraz-led Cape Blend improves on **09** (★★★★), gushing with ripe black berries. Light oaking leaves prominent vibrant fruit to make the statement. **Sauvignon Blanc** ⊕ ★★★★ **09** pungent green fruit & gooseberry, good acid structure, mineral undertone. **Blueish White** ★★★★ Mostly sauvignon blend with chenin, **11** is lean, minerally & restrained, threaded with wisps of tropical fruit. — GdB

■ **Post Tree** see Valley Vineyards Wine Company
■ **Pracht Gaarden** see Lourensford Wine Estate
■ **Princess** see Alluvia Winery & Private Residence Club
■ **Private Collection** see Saxenburg Wine Farm
■ **Prohibition** see Camberley Wines

Prospect1870

Location: Ashton ▪ WO: Western Cape ▪ Est 1990 ▪ 1stB 1998 ▪ Closed to public (tasting at The Wine Boutique, Main Rd, Ashton) ▪ Owner(s) De Wet Family ▪ Winemaker(s) Chris de Wet ▪ 35ha (cab, merlot, ptage, shiraz, chard, sauv, viog) ▪ 500cs ▪ PO Box 141 Ashton 6715 ▪ chris@prospectvineyards.co.za ▪ www.prospectwines. com ▪ T +27 (0)82-878-2884 ▪ F +27 (0)86-513-1999

Chris de Wet vinifies small quantities from grapes grown on the family's Ashton farm. New are a Viognier (unready at press time) in the Leatherwood good-value line-up, and a decision to join the trend to screwcaps for the same range.

Prospect1870 range
Prospect ★★★ Smoky, savoury **10**, big & bold cab-shiraz (60/40) blend shows serious intent. At 15% alcohol, not for the faint hearted!

Leatherwood range
Cabernet Sauvignon ▦ ★★ **10**'s sweet fruit has food-friendly herbal & savoury twist. **Shiraz** ▦ ★★ Listed as 'Shiraz-Viognier' last time. Pine-needle top notes on ready-to-drink **10**. — DB/JP

■ **Protea** see Anthonij Rupert Wines
■ **Provenance** see Saronsberg
■ **Provoyeur** see Devonvale Golf & Wine Estate

Pulpit Rock Winery

Location: Riebeek West ▪ Map/WO: Swartland ▪ Est 2003 ▪ 1stB 2004 ▪ Tasting & sales Mon-Fri 8.30–5 Sat 10–2 ▪ Closed Easter Fri-Sun, Dec 25/26 & Jan 1 ▪ Cellar tours by appt ▪ BYO picnic ▪ Walks/hikes ▪ Mountain biking trail ▪ Annual olive festival (May) ▪ Restaurant T +27 (0)22-461-2030 ▪ Self-catering accommodation ▪ Owner(s) Brinkshof Wines (Pty) Ltd ▪ Winemaker(s) Riaan van der Spuy (Dec 2011) ▪ Viticulturist(s) Marco Roux (Dec 2008, consultant) ▪ 600ha/450ha (ptage, shiraz, chard, chenin) ▪ 650t/15,000cs own label 70% red 29% white 1% rosé + 200,000L bulk ▪ Other export brand: Cape Tranquility ▪ PO Box 1 Riebeek West 7306 ▪ info@pulpitrock.co.za ▪ www.pulpitrock.co.za ▪ S 33° 20' 47.4" E 018° 51' 14.1" ▪ **T +27 (0)22-461-2025** ▪ F +27 (0)22-461-2028

Riaan van der Spuy took over as winemaker in late 2011 after six years making bulk wine in Uruguay. He's generally happy to abide by owner Ernst Brink's simple motto of 'good quality for a good price' but feels his challenge is to make an outstanding red wine which can sell at more of a premium.

Reserve range
★★★★ **Pinotage** ▨ Sturdy **10** displays dark fruit, hint of vanilla. Rich & full, balanced by bright acidity, while the finish is long & pleasantly dry.

★★★★ **Chardonnay** ⊕ Pure & focused **09**, citrus, peach, vanilla & spice; medium body with good fruit definition, well-judged oak, bright acidity.

Cabernet Sauvignon ⚑ ★★★ Pleasant, undemanding **09** is medium bodied with plenty of red & black fruit, fine tannins. **Merlot** ⚑ ★★★ **09** juicy dark fruit, fresh acidity, pleasing tannic grip makes for well-balanced, appealing proposition. **Shiraz** ⚑ ★★★ **09** has dark fruit, fresh acidity, fine tannins but doesn't shout the variety.

Brink Family range

Chenin Blanc ☺ 🍴 🌿 ★★★ Honest-to-goodness **12** is bursting with white peach & pear. Bright acidity, 2 months lees-ageing for extra palate weight. Uncomplicated but utterly charming.

Cabernet Sauvignon 🌿 ★★★★ Modern in style, **10** is big & bold. Ultra-dark fruit, smooth tannins, arguably lacking a degree of freshness but will have its fans. **Merlot** ⚑ 🌿 ★★ **10** is earthy, tart, puckering. **Pinotage** 🌿 ★★★ Straightforward **10** has black cherry fruit, bright acidity, firm tannins. **Shiraz** 🌿 ★★★★ **10** impresses with concentration of dark fruit but also fynbos & pepper notes. Perhaps too sweet but lots to like otherwise. **Pinotage Rosé** 🍴 🌿 ★ Was 'Rosé'. Off-putting dustiness on NV (**12**). **Chardonnay** 🍴 🌿 ★★★ Honest **12** is well balanced, with upfront citrus & bright acidity. No great complexity but easily likeable. — CE

■ **Pure African** see Bellevue Estate Stellenbosch

Quando Vineyards & Winery

Location: Bonnievale ▪ Map/WO: Robertson ▪ Est/1stB 2001 ▪ Tasting & sales by appt ▪ Closed all pub hols ▪ Owner(s) F M Bruwer cc ▪ Cellarmaster(s)/winemaker(s) Fanus Bruwer (Jan 1991) ▪ Viticulturist(s) Martin Bruwer (Jan 1991) ▪ 190ha/80ha (mourv, chenin, sauv) ▪ 3,000cs own label 10% red 90% white ▪ PO Box 82 Bonnievale 6730 ▪ info@quando.co.za ▪ www.quando.co.za ▪ S 33° 56'9.6" E 020° 1'28.8" ▪ **T +27 (0)23-616-2752** ▪ F +27 (0)23-616-2752

Winemaker Fanus Bruwer had enough in production last year to 'play around', so left some sauvignon blanc grapes on the vine for a month longer. Voila! A Natural Sweet wine. Also new from the Bonnievale brothers (Martin is the viti man) is a mourvèdre rosé à la Provence.

★★★★ **Chenin Blanc-Viognier** ⚑ 🍴 🌿 Creative & delicious unwooded **11** gets pineapple, thatch & vibrant freshness from chenin (ex 30 year old vines), opulence from 23% viognier, & weight from lees-ageing. **Pinot Noir** 🍴 ★★ From high-lying vineyard in Langeberg, **11** makes for clean & fragrant summer sipping. **Mourvèdre Rosé** NEW 🍴 ★★ **12** spicy little number with crisp dry tail. **Sauvignon Blanc** 🍴 🌿 ★★★★ **12** back on track with crushed nettle, tropical fruit & lime complexity, satisfies at modest 13% alcohol. **Natural Sweet Sauvignon Blanc** NEW ★★★ All raisins & ripe peaches, **12** an attractively balanced sweetie with bonus of light alcohol. Chill well & enjoy anytime. — DB/JP

■ **Quay 5** see Two Oceans
■ **Queen** see Alluvia Winery & Private Residence Club

Quest Wines

Location: Worcester ▪ WO: Western Cape ▪ Est 2006 ▪ 1stB 2010 ▪ Closed to public ▪ Owner(s) Anja van Rijswijk & Hendrik Myburgh ▪ Cellarmaster(s)/winemaker(s) Hendrik Myburgh (2006) ▪ 1,000cs own label 100% red ▪ 12 Otto du Plessis Street Worcester 6850 ▪ admin@questwines.co.za ▪ www.questwines.co.za ▪ **T +27 (0)23-342-5856** ▪ F +27 (0)23-342-5856

'Looking at a photograph of my grandfather working in the vineyards, as I do, I'm reminded of how what we do influences those who come after us,' muses Hendrik Myburgh. He's the winemaker on the Worcester family farm, while co-owner Anja van Rijswijk attends to marketing.

Cape Roots range
Cabernet Sauvignon 🍴 ★★ **11** more 'dry red' than 'cab' but soft & juicy. **Merlot** ⚑ 🍴 ★★★ Cheerful, light, well-formed **10** picnic sipper with hint of liquorice. — CM

Quinta do Sul

Location: Calitzdorp ▪ Map: Klein Karoo & Garden Route ▪ WO: Klein Karoo ▪ Est 2005 ▪ 1stB 2008 ▪ Visits by appt ▪ Owner(s) Alwyn & Louw Liebenberg, Beulah Grobbelaar ▪ Cellarmaster(s)/winemaker(s) Alwyn Liebenberg (Jun 2005) ▪ 10ha/2.5ha (tannat, tinta amerela/barocca/roriz, tourigal, shiraz, souzão) ▪ 5t/290cs own label ▪ 54 Siffie Crescent Vermont 7201 ▪ alwyn@thegoosewines.com ▪ www.quintadosul.co.za ▪ **T +27 (0)82-610-2279**

No wine was made in 2012 for this award-winning port, traditionally crafted by Alwyn Liebenberg (also cellar chief at The Goose Wines). His port expertise comes from stints in the Douro and at top Cape port cellar Boplaas; the grapes from his small vineyard in Calitzdorp.

★★★★ **Vintage Port** ⊕ Traditional port grapes plus shiraz, tannat. Very ripe & fruit-sweet **09** is plump & pliable, more Ruby in style, with less spirit attack & tannic grip than Vintage. — CvZ

Quoin Rock Winery

Location/map: Stellenbosch • WO: Simonsberg-Stellenbosch/Cape Agulhas/Cape South Coast • Est 1998 • 1stB 2001 • Tasting & sales daily 9–5 (summer) & 10-4 (winter) • Fee R20 • Closed Easter Fri/Sun, Dec 25/26 & Jan 1 • Cheese platters • Owner(s) Ukrainian businessman • Winemaker(s) Narina Cloete (Jun 2010) • Viticulturist(s) Louis Buys (Dec 2007) • 193ha/45ha (cabs s/f, merlot, mourv, shiraz, sauv, viog) • 200t/11,000cs own label 55% red 35% white 7% MCC 3% dessert • PO Box 1193 Stellenbosch 7599 • tasting@quoinrock.co.za • www.quoinrock.com • S 33° 52′ 42.5″ E 018° 52′ 2.3″ • **T +27 (0)21-888-4740** • F +27 (0)21-888-4744

Over the past year there has been a great deal of widely publicised controversy over ownership of this prime property, but that has at last been put to rest. Breaking news at time of this guide going to press is that, after buying its Cape Agulhas vineyard parcel earlier, a Ukranian businessman successfully tendered for the Stellenbosch winery. A winelover who has been searching for his ideal winefarm, his vision is to make it one of the best in the country. Fans will be reassured to learn that the next year will be one of consolidation while plans are put in place to achieve that goal, all within the context of sustainable farming practices.

★★★★☆ **Simonsberg Syrah** ⬚ Meaty dark-fruited **10** has all the ripe shiraz tones one expects from Stellenbosch, without going to excess. There's focus & a fine-boned structure for ±5 years rewarding cellaring. With a dash of mourvèdre. No **09**.

★★★★ **The Centaur** ⊕ Great care in shiraz-led **09**: whole-berry natural ferment, long skin contact, new oak maturation, result is crimson-hued brambleberries & black pepper, fine-grained tannins. Drink till ±2020.

★★★★ **The Mendi** ⊕ Cab & shiraz comprise 80%. Opulent dark fruit in **07**, offset by firm dry tannins, which add a savoury seam to the flavours. One to age 7+ years.

★★★★ **Chardonnay** ✓ ⬚ Was 'Cape Agulhas', now cross-regional, **11** loses nothing in the process. Peach & almond from portion Stellenbosch fruit & barrel wild-ferment, it remains elegantly silky, poised. No **09**, **10**.

★★★★★ **The Nicobar Reserve Sauvignon Blanc** ⬚ Distinctive sauvignon only in best years. Not quite a match for standout **09**, but with minerality at core, **11** (★★★★★) offers complexity, opens up in the glass, wafts of lime, savoury oak. Subtle, refined & splendid. Wild ferment in 225L French oak. No **10**.

★★★★☆ **Cape Agulhas Sauvignon Blanc** ⬚ Vintage-influenced **11** shows appealing gooseberry ripeness but there's no mistaking the cool-climate terroir in the racy lime-acidity. Crackles with tension & vitality, giving a long exit to the flavours. No **10**.

★★★★ **Simonsberg Oculus** ⬚ Sauvignon with a twist, wild ferment & ageing in French oak, portion viognier. Savoury peach overlay to **10**'s leafy minerality adds intrigue, creativity, heaps of flavour. No **08**, **09**.

★★★★ **Cape South Coast Cap Classique** Origin change from Cape Agulhas. With a touch of pinotage to pinot noir & chardonnay, latest **NV** gains more red berry profile but the elegance, finely crafted bubbles & refined palate remain intact, memorable.

★★★★☆ **Simonsberg Vine Dried Sauvignon Blanc** ⬚ In a word, sumptuous. From the first sniff of preserved pineapple & quince to **11**'s ample curves, heady marmalade flavours, it will enthral. And the racy acidity gives definition, length, 8+ years ageing. No **10**.

Simonsberg Merlot ⬚ ★★★★ Listed as 'Merlot' last time. With 14% cab for structure & complexity, **10** has sturdy 'masculine' lines, is tightly knit, needs time to show its full potential. — CR

Raats Family Wines

Location/map: Stellenbosch • WO: Coastal/Stellenbosch • Est/1stB 2000 • Tasting & sales by appt only • Fee R200 (up to 20 pax per tasting) • Closed all pub hols • Owner(s) Bruwer Raats • Cellarmaster(s)/viticulturist(s) Bruwer Raats (Jan 2000) • Winemaker(s) Bruwer Raats (Jan 2000), with Gavin Bruwer Slabbert (Feb 2010) • 25ha (cab f, chenin) • 120t/9,000cs own label 15% red 85% white • PO Box 2068 Stellenbosch 7601 • braats@mweb.co.za • www.raats.co.za • S 33° 58′ 16.6″ E 018° 44′ 55.3″ • **T +27 (0)21-881-3078** • F +27 (0)21-881-3078

New wines joined the stable last year, as cabernet franc expert Bruwer Raats consolidated his position as a leading New World maker of this often overlooked variety. He hopes that an 'entry level' version will introduce new audiences to his favourite grape variety, in particular to his handcrafted, soil-specific wines. Cab franc also features heavily in his new blend, a homage to his father, Jasper senior, the family viticulturist for many years, whose legacy includes two winemaking sons (junior at Longridge), both with a strong belief in sustainable farming.

Raats Family Wines range

★★★★☆ **Cabernet Franc** ⊘ Aromatic floral hints of violets giving way to classic aromas of furry green leaves, black fruit, liquorice & tobacco on **10**. A mouthful of elegance, as black cherries & blackcurrants take turns with subtly spiced oak. Vanilla/chocolate in lengthy finish. Stellenbosch WO.

★★★★ **Dolomite Cabernet Franc** NEW 🗟 ⊘ Some 'entry level'! **10** absolutely typical flavours of cherries, black plums, sweet spice. Powdery tannins & freshening acidity sweep through to long finish. 10% malbec.

★★★★ **Red Jasper** NEW ⊘ Distinctive cab franc (80%) nose on **10** Bordeaux blend, liquorice & herbaceousness. Generous dollops sweet black fruit weigh in with pleasing oak/tannin integration, good length.

★★★★☆ **Old Vine Chenin Blanc** 🗟 ⊘ Add's 'Old Vine' prefix in **11** (★★★★). Creamy, toasty nose with dabs of nuts, herbs & butter. Well integrated oak adds a touch of sweet caramel on palate, all freshened by crisp acidity & a clean finish. **10** 'declassified'. **09** showed quietly magical finesse. Stellenbosch WO.

Original range

Chenin Blanc 🗟 ⊘ ★★★★ Quiet **12** tank sample offers concentrated flavours of crunchy yellow & green apples. Weighty mouthfeel augurs well for future development. Discontinued: **Red Blend**. — CM

- **Racetrack** *see* Damarakloof
- **Radford Dale** *see* The Winery of Good Hope
- **Radisson Blu** *see* Wines of Cape Town

Rainbow's End Wine Estate ⏐ 🎋 📷

Location/map: Stellenbosch ▪ WO: Banghoek ▪ Est 1978 ▪ 1stB 2002 ▪ Tasting, sales & tours by appt ▪ Fee R25, waived on purchase of 4+ btls ▪ Closed Dec 25 & Jan 1 ▪ Sales also via website, delivery free of charge ▪ BYO picnic ▪ Conservation area ▪ 4x4 trail ▪ Owner(s) Malan family ▪ Cellarmaster(s) Anton Malan (Nov 2000) ▪ Winemaker(s) Anton Malan (Nov 2000) & Francois Malan (Jan 2005) ▪ Viticulturist(s) Francois Malan (Jan 2005) ▪ 52ha/21.6ha (cabs s/f, malbec, merlot, p verdot, shiraz) ▪ 120t/4,100cs own label 90% red 10% rosé ▪ ♦PW, GlobalGap (CMI) ▪ PO Box 2253 Dennesig 7601 ▪ info@rainbowsend.co.za ▪ www.rainbowsend.co.za ▪ S 33° 56' 25.8" E 018° 56' 42.6" ▪ **T +27 (0)21-885-1719/+27 (0)83-411-0170/+27 (0)82-404-1085** ▪ F +27 (0)21-885-1722

Patriarch Jacques Malan, civil engineer by training and descendant of French Huguenots, was born with a passion for farming. The original 'fruit salad of fruits' on the family property overlooking Banhoek was steadily replaced with vines as sons Anton (winemaker) and Francois (viticulturist) became involved. Today fashion-immune terroir wines are the focus, and they're found (most recently) in Kenya and The Netherlands, and at luxury game reserve Singita.

★★★★ **Cabernet Sauvignon** ✓ ⊘ **10**'s deep cassis & earthy herbal notes mingle with sweet oak flavours, leading to a lively firm finish. Good balance & structure for future enjoyment.

★★★★ **Cabernet Franc** ⊘ **10** shows full ripeness & a fine array of earthy, peppery, cassis & mint chocolate elements. Full body, firm oaky grip & blackberry tang. Excellent expression of the variety.

★★★★ **Limited Release Cabernet Franc** Milk chocolate & dark cherries in a firmly structured mouthful of fruit, lingering spicy herbal conclusion. **10** drinking well now.

★★★★ **Merlot** ✓ ⊘ **10** is full-bodied with earthy rich plumcake & spice. Ripe & serious with a silky mouthfeel & firm grip as the flavours linger on & on. Still lots of life.

★★★★ **Shiraz Single Vineyard** ✓ ⊘ Was 'Shiraz'. **10** offers spicy plum & mulberry compote, elegant & fresh with a firm finish. A keeper.

> **Rosé** NEW ☺ 🗟 ★★★ Perky pink from all varieties on farm, **11** bone-dry but balanced, bright berries in a light body — just the ticket for summer.

Mystical Corner NEW ✓ 🗟 ★★★★ 4-way Bordeaux-style red blend **11** is well upholstered with juicy black fruit, supple tannins in support. Rounded & harmonious — a sure crowd puller. — WB

Raka

Location: Stanford ▪ Map: Elgin, Walker Bay & Bot River ▪ WO: Klein River/Western Cape/Coastal ▪ Est/1stB 2002 ▪ Tasting & sales Mon-Fri 9–5 Sat 10–3 ▪ Tasting fee: 4 wines on daily tasting list free, other wines R10/wine ▪ Closed Sun, Good Fri & Dec 25 ▪ Cellar tours & large groups by appt ▪ BYO picnic ▪ Conservation area ▪ Owner(s) Piet Dreyer ▪ Winemaker(s) Josef Dreyer (Jan 2007) ▪ Viticulturist(s) Pieter Dreyer (Jan 2007) ▪ 760ha/62ha (5 Bdx, mourv, ptage, sangio, shiraz, sauv, viog) ▪ 350t/15,000cs own label 75% red 17% white 8% rosé ▪ BWI, IPW ▪ PO Box 124 Caledon 7230 ▪ info@rakawine.co.za ▪ www.rakawine.co.za ▪ S 34° 23'56.1" E 019° 37' 26.7" ▪ **T +27 (0)28-341-0676** ▪ F +27 (0)86-606-5462

Piet Dreyer's life took an unexpected turn when his father was seriously injured in a motorcycle accident, prompting the 16 year old to begin catching fish over weekends and crewing on a friend's fishing boat after school to support the family. Impassioned by the sea and fishing, Piet progressed from ski-boat operator to owner of a freezer vessel. After the umpteenth repaint necessitated by squirting squid ink, the ebullient 'kaalvoet' (barefoot) skipper decided to have a black vessel built, which he duly christened Raka after the dark-skinned central character in the NP van Wyk Louw epic. His dream of an own wine brand was realised in 2002, and last year Piet and his family marked the 10th anniversary of winegrowing on their vast Stanford property with a special Bordeaux blend, set for release in 2013.

★★★★ **Cabernet Sauvignon** ✓ 10 has trademark ripe dark berry fruit, concentrated flavours & gentle oak spice. Elegant, with a super balance, freshness & structure.

★★★★ **Cabernet Franc** ✓ Stellar 09 (★★★★★) shows more class & presence than 08, with elegant perfume, concentrated berry flavours, herbal edge & dusty tannins. The fresh & intense fruit is in perfect harmony with the oak, & balanced by a fine acid structure.

★★★★ **Malbec** ⊛ 09 starts very shy (some cellar time wanted?). Fine lavender & sea breeze notes lead to firm but fine tannin structure & good mouthfeel.

★★★★ **Mourvèdre** ⊛ Varietal meaty, coriander spice intro on fine debut 09. Palate continues with savoury rather than fruity flavours. Good acidity rounds out complex food-friendly composition.

★★★★ **Petit Verdot** ✓ Deep ruby-hued 10 offers intense dark cherry & blackcurrant with great fruit purity. Rich, complex savoury support & refreshing acidity. Will reward ageing.

★★★★★ **Biography Shiraz** ✓ Flagship offers a kaleidoscope of black berry, violet, vanilla & white pepper aromas & flavours in 10 (★★★★★). The lush texture, seamless & complex structure adds to elegance & refinement. Excellent expression of the variety, like more delicate 09.

★★★★ **Figurehead Cape Blend** ✓ Five Bordeaux varieties & a dollop of pinotage, 09 (★★★★) is big & bold, with upfront lively spicy fruit. Balanced, but doesn't have the soul of 08.

> **Spliced** ☺ 🍴 ★★★ Friendly all-sorts red blend from Robertson grapes, 10 is juicy, spicy with a moreish dry & savoury grip. Ticks every drinkability box. WO W Cape. **Rosé** ☺ 🍴 🍾 ★★★ Tank sample 12 (merlot, shiraz-led) is fragrant & juicy, with juicy strawberry flavours & dry finish. Good balance for easy drinking.

Barrel Select Merlot ★★★★ Spicy sweet plum fruit on improved 10 is tightly wound around firm tannin core, needs time to reveal charm. **Pinotage** ⊛ ★★★★ Good oak balance supports ripe perfumed fruit concentration. 10 is slow to open up to compact layers & savoury edge. With some Franschhoek grapes **Sangiovese** ★★★ Ripe & sweet 10 shows fragrant mulberry compote, earthy tones with firm dry tannins & warm finish. **Quinary** ✓ ★★★★ Five-way Bordeaux style red shows smooth, harmonious berry & vanilla flavours in 08. Good balance, with mouthfilling savoury fruit & silky tannins, a step up on 07 (★★★★). Drinking well now. **Chenin Blanc** ✓ 🍴 🍾 ★★★★ Ex-tank 12 is fresh with apple pie & light vanilla flavours. Mouthfilling, rounded, with a good zesty finish. Coastal WO. **Sauvignon Blanc** ✓ 🍴 🍾 ★★★★ Preview 12 offers ripe tropical fruit flavours, concentrated & juicy with a smooth mouthfeel. Well structured, ending on a perfumed lemon zest note. **Shannonea** ✓ 🍴 ★★★★ 12 preview from sauvignon & viognier, flirts with the senses: heady fruit & floral perfume, to the rounded mouthfeel & textured food friendly end. — WB

Rall Wines

Location: Stellenbosch ▪ WO: Swartland/Coastal ▪ Est/1stB 2008 ▪ Tasting, sales & cellar tours by appt ▪ Owner(s)/winemaker(s)/viticulturist(s) Donovan Rall ▪ 10t/500cs own label 50% red 50% white ▪ info@rallwines.co.za ▪ www.rallwines.co.za ▪ **T +27 (0)72-182-7571**

With one winemaking foot in the Swartland and one in Stellenbosch, and a mind attuned to the 'natural' principles of the Swartland new wave, Donovan Rall's passion is for 'ever purer site expression' of particular vineyards — never to produce more than 10 barrels of each. His enthusiasm for the 2011 and 2012 vintages means a single-vineyard grenache noir to look forward to.

★★★★ **Rall Red 10** (★★★★★) more depth & complexity than 09; soft in style, with trademark lily perfume, plush but active tannins. Blend of shiraz & 15% grenache, to be labelled a 'Swartland Independent' wine. Excellent exposition of low-intervention winemaking.

★★★★★ **Rall White 11** possibly the best yet. Excellent vintage conditions produced fine balance of opulent stonefruit with a vibrant acidity to keep it focused. Swartland-Stellenbosch selection of chenin, verdelho, chardonnay & viognier form a layered whole. Only older oak used. **10** (★★★★★) similar combo. — JP

- **Ralph Parker** *see* Altydgedacht Estate
- **Raoul's** *see* Beaumont Wines
- **Ready Steady** *see* Southern Sky Wines
- **Rebourne Fairtrade** *see* Imbuko Wines
- **Red Gold** *see* Bushmanspad Estate

Red Tape

Location: Somerset West ▪ WO: Elgin ▪ Est 2007 ▪ 1stB 2010 ▪ Sales by prior arrangement ▪ Owner(s) Tanja Beutler ▪ 250cs own label 100% red ▪ PO Box 804 Somerset Mall 7137 ▪ tanja@hiddengems.co.za ▪ **T +27 (0)21-855-4275** ▪ F +27 (0)86-612-6118

Two weeks is all it took for consumers to vote with their cash and snap up the meagre 4,000 bottles of inaugural Red Tape Merlot. The (untasted) 2010 is expected soon and the quirky label pokes yet more fun at the bureaucracy surrounding wine, promises dynamic marketer and brand mama Tanja Beutler.

★★★★☆ **Merlot** ⓘ Savoury 09 classically styled with intense heart of red berries, fine integrated tannin structure. Perfect for food (& easing bureaucratic headaches). — GdB/IM

- **Red White Pink** *see* Nomada Wines

Reginald James

Location/WO: Durbanville ▪ Est/1stB 2011 ▪ Closed to public ▪ Owner(s) RJ Botha & Bernhard Veller ▪ Winemaker(s)/viticulturist(s) RJ Botha (Feb 2011) ▪ 3t/140cs own label 100% white ▪ rj@nitida.co.za ▪ **T +27 (0)83-560-3419** ▪ F +27 (0)21-976-1467

Winning Diners Club Young Winemaker of the Year in 2010 was a turning point for Nitida winemaker RJ Botha. It spurred him on — with the generous support of Nitida owner Bernhard Veller — to take what will hopefully be the first step on the ladder to solo success by launching his own wine label.

★★★★ **Sublime** ⓘ 🍴 Excellent Bordeaux-inspired white blend, **11** unwooded sauvignon (70%) with heft from oaked semillon. Fresh & mouthwatering now, sublimer pleasures promised with time. — GdB/IM

Reiersvlei   **NEW**

Location: Prince Albert ▪ Map: Klein Karoo & Garden Route ▪ WO: Prince Albert Valley ▪ Est 1999 ▪ 1stB 2010 ▪ Tasting, sales & cellar tours Tue-Fri 10-3 Sat 10-2; or by arrangement ▪ Closed Sun-Mon, Easter Fri-Mon, Dec 25/26 & Jan 1 ▪ Light refreshments for group tastings — booking essential ▪ Owner(s) Reiersvlei Investments CC (Russell & Elize Inggs) ▪ Cellarmaster(s)/winemaker(s)/viticulturist(s) Russell Inggs (Sep 2007) ▪ 113ha/9ha (cab, p verdot, ptage, red muscadel, shiraz, tinta, touriga, sauv) ▪ 70t/1,800cs own label 90% red 10% white ▪ PO Box 33 Prince Albert 6930 ▪ reier@absamail.co.za ▪ S 33° 16′ 50″ E 022° 14′ 38″ ▪ **T +27 (0)23-541-1983/556** ▪ F +27 (0)23-541-1983

Five years ago, property company CEO Russell Inggs was living in Johannesburg with his wife Elize; today they're in Prince Albert Valley, on a farm in the folds of the Great Swartberg named after resident grey herons. Convinced that the Groot Karoo can produce quality wine, winemaker/viticulturist Russell has added port and dessert-wine varieties as well as cabernet to the existing pinotage, shiraz and sauvignon blanc, and is helping to establish a Groot Karoo Wine Route.

Pinotage 11 barrel sample too unformed to rate, as for **Shiraz, Tinta Barocca, Touriga Nacional, Sauvignon Blanc** & **Red Muscadel Jerepigo. Cape Blend Reserve** ★★ Shiraz & pinotage mix (60/40) in **10** notes of meat & beef stock, warming 14.8% alcohol & modest fruit; savouriness makes it a natural partner for venison & tomato bredies. **Cape Vintage Port** ★★ Charming cherry notes on rustic **10** from shiraz. — FM/GdB

■ **Releaf Organic** see Imbuko Wines

Remhoogte Wine Estate

Location/map: Stellenbosch ▪ WO: Simonsberg-Stellenbosch ▪ Est 1994 ▪ 1stB 1995 ▪ Tasting & sales Mon-Fri 9–4.30 Sat 10–4 ▪ Closed Easter Fri-Sun, Dec 25/26 & Jan 1 ▪ Cellar tours by appt ▪ Picnic baskets — booking required ▪ Functions ▪ Walking/hiking trails ▪ Game ▪ Guest cottage ▪ Owner(s) Murray Boustred Trust ▪ Cellarmaster(s) Chris Boustred (Jan 2011) ▪ Winemaker(s)/viticulturist(s) Chris Boustred (Jan 2007) ▪ 55ha/30ha (cab, merlot, ptage, shiraz, chenin) ▪ 170t/8,000cs own label 80% red 20% white ▪ BWI, IPW ▪ PO Box 2032 Dennesig 7601 ▪ info@remhoogte.co.za ▪ www.remhoogte.co.za ▪ S 33° 53' 4.2" E 018° 51' 4.6" ▪ **T** +27 **(0)21-889-5005** ▪ F +27 (0)21-889-6907

Into its third century (founded 1812), this mainly red-wine estate in the Simonsberg now employs the talents of both Boustred sons, as sales and marketing chief Rob joins cellarmaster Chris on the estate. Father and owner, Murray Boustred, continues to look forward, adding new attractions to the property with function facilities and picnic venues augmenting the charms of the game camp, with its springbok, wildebeest and zebra.

★★★★☆ **Merlot Reserve** ⑨ When last tasted, **07** impressed with huge concentration while remaining balanced & fresh.

★★★★ **Bonne Nouvelle** ⑨ Red blend including pinotage. Cab-led **03** & more impressive **04** (★★★★★) both still available; **04** displayed a chocolate-mocha sheen to plush tannins, fresh finish when last tasted.

★★★★ **Estate Blend** ⑨ Powerful **07** (★★★★) even more demanding than bold **06**. Merlot, shiraz, cab, pinotage deliver plush black fruit concentration, well-rounded mouthfeel; tannins a satisfyingly dry conclusion.

★★★★☆ **Honeybunch Reserve Chenin Blanc** ⃝ Much-lauded flagship white from oldest single-vineyard (26 years). Barrel fermented & year aged, **11** is subtle not showy, with apricots, limes, spiced hazelnuts & honey. Zesty acidity keeps it fresh, should improve over 3-5 years.

Cabernet Sauvignon Await new vintage. **Merlot** ⑨ ★★★★ Plush **09** is rich & full with ripe red fruit, smooth texture before slightly 'hot' finish. **Pinotage** ⃝ ★★★★ Polished **10** from very low-yielding vines (3t) shows concentration of black cherry fruit with hints of cinnamon & cloves. Supportive tannins, long charry finish all impress more than softer **09** (★★★). **Valentino Syrah** ⃝ ★★★★ Was 'Valentino Shiraz'. Attractive meaty sweetness on nose of **10** offset by classic hints of violets, pepper & dark plums. Doesn't linger, but steps up on previous. **Aigle Noir** ✓ ⃝ ★★★★ Reliable Cape Blend from merlot, shiraz, cab & pinotage, **10** is pleasing mouthful of blackberry crumble with creamy, spicy finish. **Wood brook Cabernet Sauvignon-Shiraz** NEW ⃝ ★★★ Easy-drinking blend (60/40) with dark fruit, liquorice. **11** less exuberant than expected for stated 'New World' style. **Chenin Blanc** ✓ ▤ ⃝ ★★★★ **11** notably drier than **10** (★★★★) & all the better for it. Lively, zippy aromas & flavours of citrus, muesli & some tropical fruit. Additional richness & depth from oaked portion & lees-ageing. — CM

Re'Mogo Wines

Location/map: Stellenbosch ▪ WO: Bottelary ▪ Est 2004 ▪ Tasting & sales Mon-Fri & pub hols 9-3 Sat 9-12 ▪ Owner(s) Re'Mogo Holdings (Pty) Ltd ▪ Winemaker(s) Klaas Coetzee (Stellar Winery) ▪ 50% red 50% white ▪ Khayamandi Tourism Centre PO Box 7462 Stellenbosch 7599 ▪ remogo.holdings@gmail.com ▪ www.remogo.co.za ▪ S 33°55'9.47" E 018°51'7.90" ▪ **T +27 (0)82-638-6774, +27 (0)82-253-5126, +27 (0)72-030-5317** ▪ F +27 (0)86-610-7047

The name means 'standing together', points out Thamsanqa Hombana, international business manager of this Stellenbosch empowerment venture which now sources from organic Stellar Winery. He says that, with exports slow, they're concentrating on the local market — 'with the 2,000-member Soweto Wine Club showing much potential as a partner'.

Cabernet Sauvignon ⑨ ▤ ★★★ Fruity, dark cherry **09** had fresh acidity to cut tarry oak. All except Chenin were previewed mid-2010, none re-tasted this edition. **Pinotage** ⑨ ▤ ★★★ Vibrant red fruit combined with soft vanilla in **09**, juicy yet firm. **Pinotage Rosé** ⑨ ▤ ★★ Red-fruited dry **10** needed time to settle. **Chenin Blanc** ⊕ 🏠 ★★★ Attractive combo honey & ripe apple, **10** was soft, fleshy & balanced. **Sauvignon Blanc** ⊕ 🏠 ★★★ **10** fruity & light, with herbal edge. —IM

■ **Renosterbos** *see Hofstraat Kelder*

Restless River

Location: Hermanus ▪ Map: Elgin, Walker Bay & Bot River ▪ WO: Upper Hemel-en-Aarde Valley/Western Cape ▪ Est 1999 ▪ 1stB 2005 ▪ Tasting, sales & tours daily by appt ▪ Closed all pub hols ▪ Charcuterie, cheese platters & refreshments — booking essential ▪ BYO picnic ▪ Owner(s) Craig & Anne Wessels ▪ Winemaker(s) Craig Wessels (Jan 2005) ▪ Viticulturist(s) Anne Wessels (Nov 2004) & Craig Wessels ▪ 20ha/6ha (cab, chard) ▪ 10t/500cs own label 55% red 45% white ▪ PO Box 1739 Hermanus 7200 ▪ anne@restlessriver.com ▪ www.restlessriver.com ▪ S 34° 21′ 26.11″ E 19° 16′ 32.80″ ▪ **T +27 (0)28-313-2881, +27 (0)82-650-3544** ▪ F +27 (0)21-448-7487

Craig and Anne Wessels, with obvious passion for their work on their little patch of the Hemel-en-Aarde, speak convincingly about the story their wine can tell: 'about the marginal conditions in which it grew, and how each block underwent an entirely different, hands-off and natural vinification process... What the wine can't tell you about is the struggle and sacrifice behind the scenes, handcrafting vines and wines, without much machinery, just to turn this dream into a reality.'

★★★★ **Chardonnay** Power, personality on **09**; bold aromas dried apple, bread, vanilla. Acid/alcohol balance gives intrigue, delight — but the rich flavour intensity is not for the faint-hearted. Some Elgin grapes.

Cabernet Sauvignon ★★★★★ Tasted out of sequence, beautiful & juicy **07** impresses with precise & fresh aromas of blackcurrant, blackberry liqueur & earthy undertones. Much more impressive than **08** (★★★★), the energetic & vibrant palate with a soft tannin structure & well managed 13.5% alcohol. This is serious fun! —JPf

Retief Wines

Location/WO: Paarl ▪ Map: Paarl & Wellington ▪ Est 1747 ▪ 1stB 2004 ▪ Tasting & sales by appt ▪ Closed all pub hols ▪ Owner(s) Pearl Mountain Wines (Pty) Ltd ▪ Winemaker(s) Robert Frater (2004, De Zoete Inval) ▪ Viticulturist(s) Graham Retief ▪ 10.08ha (cab, merlot, shiraz, chard) ▪ 67t/7,500L 100% red ▪ PO Box 709 Northern Paarl 7623 ▪ retief@new.co.za ▪ S 33° 41′ 44.4″ E 018° 57′ 11.1″ ▪ **T 021-872-9088** ▪ F 021-872-9983

The 4th and 5th generation of Retiefs, Graham and David, are expanding the wine concerns of this mainly table-grape Paarl farm by adding chardonnay, sauvignon and chenin to the current all-red line-up. Also planned are private functions.

Above the Mist range

Cabernet Sauvignon ⊕ ★★★ Honest, well-oaked **07**, cassis & cedar. **Merlot** ⊕ ★★★ Whiffs coffee & chocolate on fleshy **07**.

Retief range

Wagon Trail Await new, as for **Above the Mist** & **Yes It's Red**. —CvZ

■ **Revelation** *see Osbloed Wines*

Reyneke Wines

Location/map: Stellenbosch ▪ WO: Stellenbosch/Coastal ▪ Est 1863 ▪ 1stB 1998 ▪ Tasting, sales & cellar tours Mon-Fri 10-5 Sat & pub hols by appt ▪ Paintings by Mila Posthumus on display ▪ Owner(s) Reyneke Wines (Pty) Ltd ▪ Cellarmaster(s) Rudiger Gretschel ▪ Winemaker(s) Rudiger Gretschel & Ryan Mostert (Jan 2011) ▪ Viticulturist(s) Johan Reyneke ▪ 40ha/32ha (cabs s/f, merlot, ptage, shiraz, chenin, sauv) ▪ 160t/15,000cs own label 70% red 30% white + 1,000cs for clients ▪ Brands for clients: Woolworths ▪ CERES (organic), Demeter (biodynamic), FFF (Woolworths), IPW, WIETA ▪ PO Box 61 Vlottenburg 7604 ▪ wine@reynekewines.co.za ▪ www.reynekewines.co.za ▪ S 33° 57′ 27.7″ E 018° 45′ 7.0″ ▪ **T +27 (0)21-881-3517/3451** ▪ F +27 (0)21-881-3285

Johan Reyneke likes to quote American ecologist Aldo Leopold's view that 'when we see land as a commodity to which we belong', rather than the other way round, 'we may begin to use it with love and respect'. But people are also respected at this family farm — among the first registered biodynamic Cape winefarms. Its workers, Johan says, are its cornerstone, hence the name of a wine whose profits go to a project benefitting them and their families. It meant that in 2012, Lizanne Wagenaar, daughter of cellar-assistant George Wagenaar, was able to enrol in university.

'Quality with integrity' is the Reyneke mantra, and there's a purity and freshness allied with growing finesse in the wines that speaks volumes for both.

Biodynamic range

★★★★ **Pinotage** ⓐ ⓒ 🖾 Latest **10** has perfume abundance, lavender whiffs over sweet fruit promise. Brooding rich palate follows with fine acid & tannin balance for bright & fresh end. **09** skipped.

★★★★ **Syrah** NEW ⓒ 🖾 Warm, generous aromas on **10** lead to rich, pleasingly rounded, firm palate. All integrated & harmonious, with an edge of gratifying sweetness. Much readier for drinking than Cornerstone.

★★★★ **Cornerstone** ✓ ⓒ 🖾 Cab-based **10** with merlot & cab franc aims not at youthful display but balance & longevity. Yet powerful; strong, savoury tannins support sweet fruit. More pleasure in a few years.

★★★★☆ **Reserve Red** ⓐ ⓒ **09** has a stunning nose of coriander, pepper & dry spices. Bold palate shows plush shiraz spice & vibrant fruit; dash cab adds fine structure. Harmoniously poised to evolve over 10 years.

★★★★ **Chenin Blanc** ⓒ 🖾 Unshowy but confident **11** (★★★★☆) a far cry from brash, oaky, sweet blockbusterdom. Subtle, supple & serenely harmonious, with a good grip & bright acidity lifting the fruit. Earthy notes, but a delicious kernel of sweet apricot lingers on the dry finish. Like **10**, from old, low-yielding vines.

★★★★☆ **Reserve White** ⓐ ⓒ 🖾 Subtle oak aromas, lime & fynbos introduce fresh & pure **10**. Classy palate precise & focused, lingering to a perfectly dry conclusion. Excellent example of balance. Undisclosed variety/ies; **09** was 100% sauvignon.

★★★★☆ **Sauvignon Blanc** ⓐ ⓒ 🖾 **10** (★★★★) had softer palate texture with prominent acid, while fine **11** is all about balanced tension between fruit weight, taut acid & fine lingering minerality. Both barrel-fermented in older oak adding nuance to structure.

Organic range

★★★★ **Chenin Blanc-Chardonnay-Sauvignon Blanc** ✓ 🖺 🌣 🖾 **11** (★★★★) perhaps less intense than **10** & not complex — but really well balanced & pleasant, with restrained fruitiness & mineral fresh elegance. Light oak influence. WO Coastal.

Shiraz-Cabernet Sauvignon NEW 🖺 🌣 ★★★★ Just a splash of cab on ripe, spicy, lively **11**, the fruit untrammelled by modest oaking. Untrivial, good drinking for 3-5 years. WO Coastal. Discontinued: **Shiraz**. — TJ

Rhebokskloof Wine Estate

Location: Paarl ▪ Map: Paarl & Wellington ▪ WO: Paarl/Coastal ▪ 1stB 1975 ▪ Tasting & sales Mon-Fri 9-5 Sat/Sun 10-3 ▪ Fee R15/5 wines ▪ Cellar tours by appt ▪ Rhebokskloof Restaurant open daily for b'fast & lunch, dinner Tue-Sat ▪ Facilities for children ▪ Tour groups ▪ Gifts ▪ Weddings, functions & conferences ▪ Walks/hikes ▪ Live concerts ▪ Owner(s) Siebrits & Albie Laker, ASLA Group ▪ Cellarmaster(s)/winemaker(s) Rolanie Lotz (Jan 2007) ▪ Viticulturist(s) Karin Louw (Jan 2007) ▪ 180ha/30ha (grenache, mourv, ptage, shiraz, chard, viog) ▪ 250t/20,000cs own label 80% red 15% white 5% rosé + 1,500cs for clients ▪ PO Box 2637 Paarl 7620 ▪ info@rhebokskloof.co.za ▪ www.rhebokskloof.co.za ▪ S 33° 41' 6.1" E 018° 55' 56.6" ▪ **T +27 (0)21-869-8386** ▪ F +27 (0)21-869-8386

'Clean sheet' is the word from this Paarl winery, referring to the new packaging introduced in 2012 (that for the Black Marble Hill Syrah is exceptional — an ebony bottle with the initials etched in white) and to the fact that the farm was replanted to a new varietal mix. The goal is nothing less than recognition as a Top 10 winery in South Africa. 'There's a lot to be done to attain that, but with the dedicated people and terroir we have, it is possible,' says marketer Anton du Toit.

Mountain Vineyards Reserve range

★★★★ **Black Marble Hill Syrah** 🖾 Limited-production flagship in striking etched black glass bottle. Smoky **10** concentrated yet unheavy; controlled tannins & only faint suggestion of 15% alcohol. **09** untasted.

Sandstone Grove Chardonnay Await new.

Rhebokskloof range

Pinotage ⓐ 🖾 ★★★★ **10** more affable & fruity, less reliant on wood than several other reds from this stable. **Shiraz** 🖾 ★★★★ **10** with dollops grenache, mourvèdre. Integrated & long, with old leather & savoury notes; a little residual sugar; deserves year/2 to gain complexity. **Mourvèdre-Grenache-Shiraz** ✓ 🖾 ★★★★ Varieties shuffled in name to reflect proportions in **10**. Smidgen US oak adds sweetness to mulberry/cranberry fruit. Melded, with intense spicy nose & finish. **Chardonnay** 🖾 ★★★ **11** smooth & rich, slippery feel ex dash viognier. Oak still a tad unknit on finish. **Viognier** Await new. **Chardonnay Méthode Cap Classique** ⓐ ★★★★ Inviting toffee apple & toasty brioche, fine mousse & creamy finish lifted the bar in **07** champagne-method celebration bubbly. **Tamay Sparkling** ⓐ ★★ Chardonnay-led with viognier in **08**, softly sweet & frothy sparkler.

Pearlstone range

Chenin Blanc ☺ 🍴 📖 ★★★ Forthcoming thatch & floral attractions on brisk **12** summer tipple from Perdeberg grapes.

Pinotage 📖 📖 ★★ **10** has resiny oak & bitter lift. WO Coastal, as all unless noted. **Shiraz** ⊕ 📖 ★★ Medicinal scent on **09** muted red berry/plum fruit. **Cabernet Sauvignon-Merlot** ⊕ 📖 ★★★ Generous fruit, fair grip in well-knit **09** cab-led dinner companion. **Rosé** 📖 📖 ★★ Drops 'Merlot' in name, now shiraz-based; **11** undemanding off-dry pink sipper. **Sauvignon Blanc** ⊕ 📖 ★★★ Green apple & grass-nuanced **11** cheerful pick-me-up. **Sparkling Rosé** ⊕ ★★★ Drop shiraz provides rosy hue to viognier-led carbonated **NV** fizz. — CvZ

■ **Rhino** *see* The Rhino of Linton Park
■ **Rhinofields Reserve** *see* Durbanville Hills

Richard Kershaw Wines

Location: Elgin ▪ Est/1stB 2012 ▪ Tasting by appt ▪ Owner(s) Richard Kershaw ▪ Cellarmaster(s) Richard Kershaw (2012) ▪ 20t/±1,250cs own label 52% red 48% white ▪ PO Box 77 Grabouw 7160 ▪ richard@rikipedia.co ▪ www.rikipedia.co ▪ **T +27 (0)21-300-1629 (VOIP)** ▪ F +27 (0)86-637-6202

A sterling start to a solo career saw Richard Kershaw celebrate completion of his Master of Wine last year. It's a journey that started in UK chef school, before he completed a winemaking diploma and arrived in Africa after working vintages around the world. Plus points for chosen home-base Elgin include the cool climate and excellent soils, which he intends planting with carefully selected clones. Marketing wise, he plans to harness the power of the internet combined with a very personal, face-to-face approach.

Rickety Bridge Winery

Location/map: Franschhoek ▪ WO: Franschhoek/Western Cape/Coastal/Paarl ▪ Est 1990 ▪ Tasting, sales & cellar tours Mon-Sat 9-7 (Dec-Mar) & 9-5 (Apr-Nov) Sun 10-5 ▪ Closed Dec 25 & Jan 1 ▪ Fee R20, waived on purchase ▪ Rickety Bridge Restaurant in the Vines (see Restaurants section) ▪ Facilities for children ▪ Gift shop ▪ Conferences ▪ Weddings ▪ Rickety Bridge Manor House (see Accommodation section) ▪ Owner(s) DS Sarnia (Pty) Ltd ▪ Cellarmaster(s) Wynand Grobler (Nov 2007) ▪ Winemaker(s) Wynand Grobler (Nov 2007), with Danie de Bruyn (Jan 2011) ▪ 91ha/39ha (cab, merlot, shiraz, chard, chenin, sauv, sem) ▪ 160t/10,000cs own label 45% red 45% white 10% rosé ▪ PO Box 455 Franschhoek 7690 ▪ info@ricketybridge.com ▪ www.ricketybridge.com ▪ S 33° 53' 58.5" E 019° 5' 27.6" ▪ **T +27 (0)21-876-2129** ▪ F +27 (0)21-876-3486

Granted to the widow Paulina de Villiers in 1797 and now in the hands of Briton Duncan Spence, this Franschhoek spread recently launched its 'Tasting room in the vines'. A three-sided glazed facade and 'floating terraces' in the vineyards bring visitors closer to the source of the wines. Of modern monochromatic design, the new facility hasn't compromised the rustic charm of the old; the tasting counter was once a feeding trough on the Argentinian pampas!

Icon Wines

★★★★☆ **The Bridge** ⊕ 100% cab in tasteful — & tasty — package, from own bushvine single-vineyard. Elegant **08** last showed integration of cool blackcurrant fruit & fine wood tannin.

Paulina's Reserve range

★★★★ **Cabernet Sauvignon** Stellar **09** (★★★★★) rises to new heights; cool minty edge to lissom cassis fruit very elegantly knitted into lacy but firm tannins, layers of complex flavours in fresh acid finish. Unflashy, very fine. Like more approachable in youth **08**, plenty in store for those who wait. WO Paarl.

★★★★ **Sauvignon Blanc** ✓ 📖 Serious, & antithetical to prevailing styles. **11** broad, wooded (30% barrel-fermented, 1/4 new) & oxidative — far from green & spiky. Satisfying at table. WO W Cape, as next.

Chenin Blanc ✓ 📖 ★★★★ Vanilla patina (6 months in cask, 20% new) gilds soft apple pie & custard flavours of **11**, firmed by fresh acidity. **Semillon** ★★★★ Broad-of-beam **09** replete with lanolin texture & subtle oak (9 months, 25% new); relative age adds to laidback allure.

Rickety Bridge range

★★★★ **Shiraz** Perfumed **10** admirable successor to lauded **09**; piles of juicy mulberries spliced with supple tannins, sweet-fruited long finish. WO W Cape.

Chenin Blanc ☺ 🍴 ★★★ Fruit ex 40-year-old bushvines gives oatmeal gloss & breadth to generous **12**.

Merlot ✓ ★★★★ Less obvious perhaps than cellarmates, but with striking balance. **09** svelte smoked meat profile seamed with fine tannins. Delicious! Floral **08** (★★★★) less penetrating. **Pinotage** ★★★ Rustic **11** has darkly fruited plum features tucked into brawny tannins. WO Coastal. **The Foundation Stone** ⓟ ★★★ Shiraz & 4 other mainly southern Mediterranean varieties; previewed **10** sunny fruit flavours but rather severe youthful tannins, needing time. WO Coastal. **Rosé** ⓟ 🍴 ★★★ **11** ex-tank bursts with strawberries, really tangy dry tail. WO W Cape. **Chardonnay** ✓ ★★★★ Upholstered **11**'s ripe hazelnut & caramel tones (9 months in cask) tempered by delicate orange blossom, invigorated by crisp citrus fruit. **Sauvignon Blanc** 🍴 ★★★ Direct **12** is clean & dry in tropical style. WO W Cape. **Brut Rosé** NEW ★★★★ Smouldering magnetism to **10**; onion skin hue, languid bubble & smooth, yeasty mousse. Oaked 6 months then 18 months on lees in bottle. Own grapes. **Natural Sweet Chenin Blanc** ⓟ 🍴 ★★★ Near-ochre-hued **10** has a swashbuckling full-sweet finish. Only seasoned oak. — DS

Rico Suter Private Cellar

Location: Worcester ▪ Map/WO: Breedekloof ▪ Est/1stB 2004 ▪ Tasting, sales & tours by appt ▪ Cheese platters & homemade bread ▪ Tour groups ▪ Olive oil & table olives ▪ BYO picnic ▪ Walking/hiking & mountain biking trails ▪ Bird watching ▪ Guesthouse (bookings: erika@ricosuterwines.com) ▪ Owner(s) Suter Family Trust ▪ Cellarmaster(s) Rico Suter, advised by Carlo Suter ▪ Winemaker(s) Rico Suter ▪ Viticulturist(s) Bruno Suter (2004) ▪ 750ha/45ha (cab, cinsaut, p verdot, ptage, shiraz, sauv, viog) ▪ 8-15t/ha 8,850L own label 95% red 5% white ▪ PO Box 38 Breerivier 6858 ▪ ricosuterwines@breede.co.za ▪ S 33° 31′39.00″ E 019° 15′13.00″ ▪ T +27 (0)23-355-1822 ▪ F +27 (0)86-642-6591

Now assisted by a cellar-hand team, son Carlo having moved to Switzerland to study, co-owner/cellarmaster Rico Suter reports that Angola may well join Denmark, Canada and Switzerland on his list of export markets. 'I could never afford a winemaker,' he says wryly, but it's clear he's happy working more or less solo.

★★★★ **L'Amitié** ⓟ Individual & complex **06** combo cinsaut, shiraz, petit verdot, viognier. Silky mouthfeel, floral notes, emphatic dry exit.

★★★★ **Cabernet Sauvignon-Syrah** ⓟ **06** earthy wafts, ripe black berries, soft & seductively juicy centre contrasts with elegant dry end.

Cabernet Sauvignon ⓟ ★★★ **05** succulent & plummy, with savoury flavours. **Petit Verdot** ⓟ ★★★★ Broad shouldered **04**, savoury tones & chocolate/mocha overlay. Good tannic support, provides backbone for ageing. **Pinotage** ▨ ★★★ Youthful **12** preview (first since **08**) exudes scented fruit pastille charm. Smooth textured & supple. **Syrah** Await next, as for **Cabernet Sauvignon-Petit Verdot**, **Sauvignon Blanc**, **Viognier-Chenin Blanc**. — MW

Ridgeback

Location: Paarl ▪ Map: Paarl & Wellington ▪ WO: Paarl/Western Cape ▪ Est 1997 ▪ 1stB 2001 ▪ Tasting & sales Mon-Sat 10-5 (summer) & 10-4 (winter) Sun 10-4 ▪ Fee R15/5 wines, R25/10 wines ▪ Closed Good Fri, Dec 25 & Jan 1 ▪ Cellar tours by appt ▪ The Deck Restaurant Tue-Sun 9.30-3 ▪ 4-star/5-room Ridgeback Guest House ▪ Hiking trails ▪ Children's play area ▪ Owner(s) Kilimanjaro Investments ▪ Cellarmaster(s)/winemaker(s) Toit Wessels (Jan 2007) ▪ Viticulturist(s) Toit Wessels (Mar 2000) ▪ 65ha/35ha (cabs s/f, grenache, merlot, mourv, p verdot, shiraz, sauv, viog) ▪ 225t/15,000cs own label 60% red 35% white 5% rosé ▪ BWI ▪ PO Box 2076 Windmeul Paarl 7630 ▪ tasting@ridgeback.co.za ▪ www.ridgebackwines.co.za ▪ S 33° 40′24.9″ E 018° 54′53.5″ ▪ T +27 (0)21-869-8068 ▪ F +27 (0)21-869-8146

Toit Wessels has come a long way since arriving as a viticulture student in 2000. He's now winemaker, farm manager and viticulturalist. 'Of the 2012 vintage, the stand-out is sauvignon blanc,' Toit reports, 'now bearing the fruits of a viticulture plan put in place in 2004.' The current trend towards fruit expression continues, with new oak reserved for only the very top wines. Always environmentally aware, Ridgeback is now a proud Biodiversity & Wine Initiative member.

Ridgeback Wines range

★★★★ **Cabernet Franc** Ⓟ Pepper spice & leafiness accentuate herbal edge in elegant **08** blend. Savoury acidity & well-judged oaking enhance satisfyingly ripe, succulent core of pure red fruit.

★★★★ **Shiraz** Perfumed **08** in elegant, serious style. Well-ripened fruit restrained by oak (60% new), offers ample flavour & savoury spiciness. Admirably, genuinely dry, like other reds.

★★★★ **Journey** ⓅMerlot, cab franc blend, splash cab in fine **06** tasted mid-2010. Plenty fruit lurking in slightly sombre, vinous & oaky shell, needed few years. Smooth tannic firmness, lovely light elegance.

★★★★ **Chenin Blanc** 🅿 Off-dry, rich **12** in robust barrel-fermented style. Small portion Natural Sweet chenin added for complexity, could do with a touch more acidity to balance.

Vansha Red ☺ 🍴 🅿 ★★★ Was 'Cabernet Sauvignon-Merlot'. Savoury, juicily accessible cab-led **11** blend with other Bordeaux varieties. **Vansha SGMV** ☺ 🍴 🅿 ★★★ Spicily perfumed 4-way shiraz-based **11** blend offers all you could want in plush, easy, everyday style. **Vansha White** ☺ 🍴 🅿 ★★★ Fresh sauvignon in harmonious, just-dry **12** blend with tropical chenin & barrel-fermented viognier promises gorgeous summer drinking. WO W Cape.

Cabernet Sauvignon ★★★★ Classic, elegant charm & succulence in pure-fruited **09**, structured by accessible tannins. Compact flavours offer delicious drinkability & greater depth than **08** (★★★★). **Merlot** ★★★★ Restrained, elegant **09** shows more depth than **08** (★★★★). Harmoniously oaked with pleasing balance of ripe fruit & tannins, held by fine thread of acidity. **His Master's Choice** ★★★★ **06** tasted mid-2009, ripe shiraz & Coastal mourvèdre; floral hints to sweet fruit, but elegance nudged tannic leanness. **Shiraz Rosé** Ⓟ 🍴 ★★ Fresh appeal in simple, earthy **11** with splash viognier. **Sauvignon Blanc** ✓ 🍴 🅿 ★★★★ Staggered pickings in **12** ensure delightful mix of flavours, from fully ripe tropical fruit flavours to fresh, zingy herbaceousness & flinty backbone. **Viognier** ✓ 🅿 ★★★★ Dry, earthy **11** more restrained & harmonious than **10** (★★★★), with well-absorbed oak adding breadth to ripe fruit, in turn focused by pithy textured finish. **Natural Sweet Viognier** 🅿 ★★★★ Delicately sweet, fresh **11** has markedly light 9.5% alcohol with tad less intensity, complexity than **10** (★★★★) though delightful to drink. **Cape Ruby** Occasional release. — IM

Riebeek Cellars   🍴🌲

Location: Riebeek-Kasteel ▪ Map/WO: Swartland ▪ Est 1941 ▪ Tasting & sales Mon-Fri 9-5 Sat 9-4 Sun 10.30-4 (wine boutique) ▪ Closed Good Fri, Dec 25 & Jan 1 ▪ Cellar tours by appt ▪ BYO picnic ▪ Owner(s) ±40 shareholders ▪ Cellarmaster(s) Zakkie Bester (Dec 1999) ▪ Winemaker(s) Eric Saayman & Alecia Boshoff (Jan 1997/Dec 2004), with JM Crafford (Dec 2009) ▪ Viticulturist(s) Hanno van Schalkwyk (Sep 2000) ▪ 1,200ha (cab, carignan, merlot, mourv, ptage, shiraz, tinta amerela, chard, chenin, sauv, viog) ▪ 17,000t/150,000cs own label 50% red 40% white 10% rosé & ±40,000cs for clients ▪ Brands for clients: Broken Rock, Rocheburg, Royal, Steenbok ▪ BWI, Fairtrade, HACCP, WIETA ▪ PO Box 13 Riebeek Kasteel 7307 ▪ info@riebeekcellars.co.za ▪ www.riebeekcellars.com ▪ S 33° 22' 58.0" E 018° 54' 54.5" ▪ **T +27 (0)22-448-1213** ▪ F +27 (0)22-448-1281

While tiny producers in this part of the Swartland take the headlines, large wineries play a vital part in the scheme of things — not only in supplying grapes to some well-known Cape brands, but also in offering affordable good value, with easygoing, often rather sweet and simply fruity wines. Not that ambition is lacking, as shown in the more serious-minded Few Good Men wines and the Kasteelberg range, which, the winemakers say, 'gives us the opportunity to slow down the process'. Unsurprisingly perhaps — given that this is the Swartland — shiraz and chenin respond particularly well to that slower approach.

A Few Good Men range

Cabernet Sauvignon 🍴 ★★★ Classic, pleasing fruit profile on **11**. Drier, more structure than standard version. Ready now, but could keep a few years. **Merlot** Ⓟ 🍴 ★★★ Attractive berry & toasty notes on fruity **09**. **Pinotage** ★★★ Spicy, smoky oak notes add complexity to heavy-textured **11**, but tannins are too much for the modest sweet fruit. **Shiraz** ✓ 🍴 ★★★★ Less oak (& power) than Kasteelberg version means lovely berry fruit shows more. Satisfying grip takes **10**'s charm to a decent dry finish. **Chardonnay** Ⓟ ★★★★ Sumptuous **09** tasted a few years back.

Kasteelberg range

Shiraz 🆕 🅿 ★★★★ Ripely powerful & showy **10**, but high alcohol balanced by rich fruit & savoury tannins. Generous oaking adds spicy tobacco notes. **Chenin Blanc** 🆕 ✓ 🅿 ★★★★ Good fruit flavour on **10** with vanilla & nut from well-integrated oak. Not intense, but a fresh dry elegance & charm. **Viognier** Await next.

Kasteelberg MCC ✪ ★★★ NV sparkler tasted some years back, from pinots blanc & noir, apple zip & baked bread richness. **Soet Steen** NEW ★★★★ From brandy-fortified chenin, NV (**10**) jerepigo celebrates settler 'discovery' of Riebeek Valley in 1661. Very sweet but piercingly balanced, good flavour. 18 months older oak. 500ml.

Riebeek Collection

Cabernet Sauvignon ☺ 🍴 🚾 ★★☆ Fruit pastille sweetness & flavour on **11**; just about dry & a little tannic grip. **Pinotage** ☺ 🍴 🚾 ★★☆ Gently boisterous aromas followed by a juicy, flavourful mouthful on appealing **11**; ripe but not gushing thanks to good balance. **Shiraz** ☺ 🍴 🚾 ★★☆ Soft, smooth **11**. Easy come (cheap), easy go (gluggable). **Cabernet Sauvignon-Merlot** ☺ 🍴 ★★☆ Successful **11** blend, the pretty, sweet fruitiness well contained. **Chardonnay** ☺ 🍴 ★★☆ Expressive **11** has much to offer: fresh citrus flavour, well balanced & dry. Not for keeping but for much pleasure now. **Chenin Blanc** ☺ 🍴 🚾 ★★☆ Bubblegummy, easy tropicality on light-feeling **12**.

Merlot 🍴 🚾 ★★☆ **11** slips down easily, with sweet-fruited richness & herbal note. **Shiraz-Cinsaut** ✪ 🍴 ★★ **09** red-fruited unwooded sipper tasted few years back. **Pinotage Rosé** 🍴 ★★ Lightly fruity, nearly dry **12**. No problems! **Sauvignon Blanc** 🍴 🚾 ★★ Lightish, slightly insipid but vaguely pleasant & modest **12**. **Viognier** ✪ 🍴 ★★ **09** simple & fruity, tasted a few years back. **Montino Petillant Light** ✪ 🍴 ★★ Semi-sweet, grapey NV white fizz. **Montino Petillant Natural Sweet Rosé** ✪ 🍴 ★★ NV fizz — perfumed, sweet & light. **Pieter Cruythoff Brut** ✪ ★★★ Fruity & crisp NV sparkling from chard & pinot. **Cape Ruby Port** ✪ ★★★ Friendly, fruity NV has gentle toffee notes leading to lingering, fiery end. Mostly touriga. Discontinued: **Cape Vintage Port**. — TJ

■ **Rietrivier** see Montagu Wine & Spirits Co

Rietvallei Wine Estate

Location/map: Robertson ▪ WO: Robertson/Western Cape ▪ Est 1864 ▪ 1stB 1975 ▪ Tasting & sales Mon-Fri 8. 30-5 Sat 10–2 ▪ R20pp for groups of 15+ ▪ Closed Easter Fri/Sun, Dec 25 & Jan 1 ▪ Cellar tours by appt ▪ Cheese platters, book ahead for groups of 6+ ▪ Farm produce ▪ Conservation area ▪ Owner(s)/viticulturist(s) Johnny Burger ▪ Cellarmaster(s)/winemaker(s) Kobus Burger (2003) ▪ 215ha/130ha (cab, red muscadel, shiraz, chard, sauv) ▪ 2,500t/50,000cs own label 40% red 45% white 10% rosé 5% fortified + 1,000,000L bulk ▪ Other brands: Stonedale ▪ PO Box 386 Robertson 6705 ▪ info@rietvallei.co.za ▪ www.rietvallei.co.za ▪ S 33° 49' 25.7" E 019° 58' 39.4" ▪ **T +27 (0)23-626-3596** ▪ F +27 (0)23-626-4514

Robertson cellarmaster Kobus Burger for some years now has been working on a white blend, a partner to the flagship red Estéanna, named after his and wife Elizabeth's daughters Esté and Annie. He finally deemed the 2011 vintage worthy of carrying their names. Also new is a joint-venture label, The Innings, which seals legendary South African cricket teammates Mark Boucher, who retired after an eye injury, and Jacques Kallis' friendship off the field. Note: good-value John B range available but not tasted.

Special Select range

★★★★ **Estéanna Red** Bordeaux blend cab & cab franc (49/48), petit verdot in **09**. Cool fruited & elegant, judicious 3rd fill oak seasoning; seamless & fresh despite 14.7% alcohol. Will reward cellaring a few years.

★★★★ **Estéanna White** NEW 🚾 Flagship barrel fermented white led by sauvignon & chardonnay (56/31), dashes chenin & viognier. **11** creamy, lemony, very flavoursome at just 13% alcohol. Deserves ageing.

★★★★☆ **Muscadel 1908** 🚾 Gorgeous fortified dessert from 105 year old red muscat de Frontignan. **11** amazingly nuanced perfume — tealeaf, cranberry, lime, strawberry — all in a light almost delicate body that endures forever. Special wine for special occasions. **08** more unctuous but still brilliantly balanced. No **09**, **10**.

Shiraz 🚾 ★★★★ Welcoming spice & red berries on concentrated & generous yet still refreshing **10**, plush fruit laps up 100% new oak. **Chardonnay** 🍴 Await next. **Sauvignon Blanc** 🍴 ★★★★ Brings in 50% Durbanville fruit in **12**, tank sample tropical aromas & flavours; brisk, balanced & persistent. Nudges next level. Discontinued: **Juanita Cabernet Sauvignon Rosé**.

Classic Estate range

Cabernet Sauvignon ★★★ Takes time to open in glass to classic blackcurrant, slight mint/herbal edge (from 5% cab franc). **10** fresh & cool, from highest vineyards on the estate. **Pinot Noir** NEW 🚾 ★★☆ Cherry perfumed **10** tad brusque & very dry. Allow time to settle & develop. **Shiraz-Petit Verdot-Viognier** 🚾 ★★★ **10** very ripe berry compote, rather astringent tannins & fruit-sweet finish. **Natural Chardonnay** 🍴 ★★★ Lovely lime-lemon freshness on unwooded **12**, gets extra weight & depth from 4 months lees-ageing. **Chenin Blanc**

▤ **★★★** Concentrated sipper from venerable vineyard. Improved **12** thatch & stewed apple, tangy quince flavour & lightish 13% alcohol. **Sauvignon Blanc** ▤ ▨ **★★★** Picked at three different ripeness levels for added interest. **12** youthful & bit introverted on review, should perk up by summer. **Red Muscadel ★★★★** Raisin & orange marmalade on focused & pure **11** winter warmer. Delicious though sweeter than old-vine '1908'.

The Innings range NEW

Cabernet Sauvignon ✓ ▤ **★★★★** These a joint venture with cricketers Jacques Kallis & Mark Boucher. No dropped catches in **10**, creamy black fruit pastilles, perfect for summer (lightly chilled, if preferred). **Sauvignon Blanc** ▤ **★★★** If we had to pick a Protea to match with **12**, it would be more Dale Steyn than Kallis or Bouch: lean (early picked), flinty & ultra-brisk, with no padding of sugar to cushion the attack. — CvZ/MW

■   **Rijckholt** *see* Zandvliet Wine Estate & Thoroughbred Stud
■   **Rijckshof** *see* Oudtshoorn Cellar — SCV

Rijk's

Location/map: Tulbagh ▪ WO: Tulbagh/Coastal ▪ Est 1996 ▪ 1stB 2000 ▪ Tasting & sales Mon-Fri 10–4 Sat 10–2 ▪ Fee R10/wine, waived on purchase ▪ Closed Easter Fri-Mon, Dec 25 & Jan 1 ▪ Cellar tours by appt ▪ Rijk's Guest House ▪ Conferences ▪ Owner(s) Neville Dorrington ▪ Winemaker(s) Pierre Wahl (Jan 2002), with Lukas van Loggerenberg (Jan 2010) ▪ Viticulturist(s) Boet Eddy (Jun 1996) ▪ 135ha/36ha (carignan, grenache noir, mourv, ptage, shiraz, tinta amarela, chenin, viog) ▪ 210t/12,000cs own label 75% red 25% white ▪ IPW ▪ PO Box 400 Tulbagh 6820 ▪ wine@rijks.co.za ▪ www.rijks.co.za ▪ S 33° 16' 1.5" E 019° 8' 42.0" ▪ **T +27 (0)23-230-1622** ▪ F +27 (0)23-230-1650

Continuing consolidation sees the amalgamation of the two separate Tulbagh Valley sites under one brand, simply called Rijk's. Cellarmaster Pierre Wahl (doting new dad to Lienke) finds varying expressions of the same three varieties within distinct ranges: accessible, lightly wooded Touch of Oak; more structured, food-friendly Private Cellar; and intense Reserve barrel selection. Larger and older oak, lower alcohol (the latter 'difficult' in the valley's summer heat) are current refinements amid consistent acclaim, growing exports and an expanding database 'keeping our consumers in touch'. All belie initial 1990s scepticism among 'experts' when Rijk's pioneered the traditionally white-wine area's fine red reputation.

Estate range

★★★★ Shiraz ⊕ Despite baked fruit hints, very ripe **07** retains elegance thanks to crisp acidity, savoury oak & dash viognier; ±15% alc not a detraction.

★★★★ The Master ⊕ **07** shiraz-led (50%) with dashes mourvèdre, pinotage. Dark fruited & opulent but new oak hides ±15% alc. Firm tannin previously noted may have relaxed now.

Reserve range

★★★★☆ Pinotage Distinguished from Private Cellar & Touch of Oak ranges by greater new-oak portion, this version typically big, bold & unashamedly pinotage. **08** fits the mould, is also juicy & well composed, with enough tannin to reward extended cellaring. Ups the ante on espresso-spiked **07** (**★★★★**).

★★★★ Shiraz NEW **09** another well-crafted & satisfying offering from the maestro of the riper end of the spectrum. Harmonious & silky, handles 66% new French oak very well.

★★★★☆ Chardonnay ⊕ When last tasted, sumptuous **07** exuded apple & citrus complexity, delivered depth & richness. Despite its intensity, showed assured balance.

★★★★ Chenin Blanc ⊕ **08**'s (**★★★★★**) fine expression of Tulbagh fruit raises bar on **07**. Mouthcoating honey, candied lime & butterscotch, creamy persistence.

Private Cellar range

★★★★ Pinotage ✓ Much-awarded **08** (**★★★★★**) sleek & elegant, finely balanced with silky tannins, fruit-filled persistence for solo enjoyment. Less powerful than Reserve, but still 'proudly pinotage'. Lingering savoury highlights, like **07**.

★★★★ Shiraz Fruit-packed **07** has mulberry & vanilla dusting, is refreshing & vibrant, deliciously dry with supple tannins. Excellent, but like **06** lacks presence of showstopping **05** (**★★★★★**).

★★★★ Bravado 05 (**★★★**) shiraz/merlot-led combo dominated by oak, showing some development; not as compelling as **04** shiraz/pinotage version, for earlier drinking.

★★★★ **Chenin Blanc** Serious, consistently excellent barrel fermented/aged chenin, from **09** off own vines; extravagantly flavoured, lemony & slightly sweet from 14.6% alc, 4.7g/l sugar. Well-structured **08** (WO Coastal) was more tropical.

The Crossing ⊕ ★★★★ Slick & smooth early-drinking **06** trumps **05** (★★★★), shows warm spice, floral lift, leathery/peppery shiraz & mourvèdre fruit. **Chardonnay** ⊕ ★★★★ Rich, bold & engaging barrel-fermented **07** big improvement on **06** (★★★), concentrated candied lemon & butter flavours, lush vanilla oak. **Fascination** ★★★★ Sauvignon's (51%) green pea & asparagus trumps on the nose of **09**; barrel-fermented semillon's weight & slipperiness lead the palate. Tasty, but not as harmonious as **08** (★★★★). WO Coastal.

Touch of Oak range

★★★★ **Pinotage** ⊕ **10** gently oaked to let the berry fruit shine. These all for early enjoyment.
★★★★★ **Chenin Blanc** ⊕ ▨ **10** (★★★★) touch off flamboyant **09**, crisp apple & citrus flavours.
Shiraz ★★★ Deft dab of oak, medium body & olive-like savoury flavours in **10**. — CE/CvZ

■ **Rijk's Estate** see Rijk's

Rivendell

Location: Bot River ▪ Map: Elgin, Walker Bay & Bot River ▪ WO: Walker Bay ▪ Est 2008 ▪ 1stB 2011 ▪ Tasting & sales daily 8-5 ▪ Closed Jan 1 ▪ Bistro open daily 8-5; Fri eve by prior booking; cater for functions of various sizes ▪ Facilities for children ▪ Tour groups ▪ Venue for weddings & conferences with fully equipped kitchen (100-120 pax inside) ▪ Walks/hikes ▪ Owner(s) Whales & Castle Investments (Pty) Ltd, with shareholders Heimo & Maria Thalhammer ▪ Winemaker(s) Kobie Viljoen (Mar 2010, Gabriëlskloof) ▪ Viticulturist(s) Schalk du Toit (Mar 2008, consultant) ▪ ±8ha/±4ha (shiraz, sauv) ▪ 32t/500cs own label 33% red 67% white ▪ PO Box 181 Onrusrivier 7201 ▪ office@rivendell-estate.co.za ▪ www.rivendell-estate.co.za ▪ S 34°18'5.22" E 019° 8' 32. 23" ▪ **T +27 (0)28-284-9185/+27 (0)28-284-9597** ▪ F +27 (0)28-284-9597

A busy year at this boutique winery near Bot River has seen, first, the Bistro go from strength to strength and, second, the arrival of a life-sized wire rhino named Wetsi, mascot of Rivendell's Whale Coast Save the Rhino initiative. Two new wines (Syrah and Rosé), by Gabriëlskloof winemaker Kobie Viljoen, await release.

Sauvignon Blanc ▤ ▨ ★★★★ **12** preview continuing promise shown in **11** (★★★★) & delivering pronounced gooseberry nose with figs, apples, taut acidity & appealing mineral finish. — CM

■ **River Crossing** see Lourensford Wine Estate
■ **River Garden** see Lourensford Wine Estate
■ **River Grandeur** see Viljoensdrift Wines & Cruises
■ **Riverscape** see Viljoensdrift Wines & Cruises
■ **River's Edge** see Weltevrede Estate
■ **Robert Alexander** see Nico van der Merwe Wines

Robertson Wide River Export Company

See Vinimark for contact details

Joint venture between Robertson Winery and Vinimark, handling all Robertson Winery exports under brand names such as Robertson Winery, Kaapdal, Kleindal, Silversands and Veldt.

Robertson Winery

Location/map/WO: Robertson ▪ Est 1941 ▪ 1stB 1987 ▪ Tasting & sales Mon-Thu 8–5 Fri 8–5.30 Sat/Sun 9–3 ▪ Closed Good Fri, Dec 25 & Jan 1 ▪ Cellar tours by appt ▪ Conferences ▪ Small wine museum ▪ Owner(s) 43 members ▪ Cellarmaster(s) Bowen Botha (Jan 1982) ▪ Winemaker(s) Francois Weich (Sep 1997), Jacques Roux (Jan 2001), Thys Loubser & Olivia Poonah (both Jan 2012) ▪ Viticulturist(s) Briaan Stipp (May 2005) ▪ 2,200ha (cab, shiraz, chard, chenin, sauv) ▪ 35,000t ±25m L for clients ▪ ISO 22000, WIETA ▪ PO Box 37 Robertson 6705 ▪ info@robertsonwine.co.za ▪ www.robertsonwinery.co.za ▪ S 33° 48' 36.8" E 019° 52' 51.4" ▪ **T +27 (0)23-626-3059** ▪ F +27 (0)23-626-2926

Identifying a market shift towards more elegant wines, 'we're paying attention to balance: between natural acidity and residual sugar, alcohol and oak maturation/extraction,' say the team at one of South Africa's largest wineries. Led by Bowen Botha (now into his third decade here), that team now comprises four dedicated winemakers, including the first woman since the grower-owned winery was established in 1941. It's challenging turning out ever-increasing quantities (up some 5,000 tons in bountiful 2012) yet 'RW' retains a balance between volume, consistency of quality, innovation — varieties (still rare-in-Cape pinot gris); styles ('light' merlot); packaging (varietally labelled and vintaged cartons and slimline bag-in-boxes) — and progressive employee economic empowerment.

Constitution Road range

★★★★ **No. 1 Constitution Road Shiraz** Serious flagship from single-vineyard, cosseted by 100% new oak. **09** unashamedly 'New World', with obvious wood, great concentration, spice & balance (even at 15.4% alcohol) though perhaps shade less finesse than **08** (★★★★★).

Vineyard Selection range

★★★★ **Prospect Hill Cabernet Sauvignon 08** (★★★★), previewed last edition, could now be in 'dumb' phase: seems less layered & complex, still mouthfilling & enduring though, & as curvy as **07**.

★★★★ **Kings River Chardonnay** ✓ 🗐 Forward, lavish oak treatment results in textured, creamy **11**, tasted pre-bottling. Lovely butterscotch, lemon & lime marmalade complexity. Barrel fermented, 50% new.

★★★★ **Retreat Sauvignon Blanc** ✓ 🗐 **12** preview too unformed to rate; heady & intense but unknit. Racy **10** was similar to well-defined **09**, while **11** (previewed last edition) was heading in same direction.

Wolfkloof Shiraz ✓ ★★★★ Tank sample last year, **08** now in drinking well. Bold & ripe, generous sprinkles pepper & spice.

Winery range

★★★★☆ **Red Muscadel** NEW Fortified style not noted for elegance but this **NV** bottling shows great refinement & delicacy. Red fruit, some raisin, spice & nuts in a medium body, with fresh acidity & well-handled fortification; subtle & poised conclusion.

> **Ruby Cabernet** ☺ 🗐 ★★★ Good typicity on improved **12** tank sample: black fruit pastilles & fennel, gentle fruity tannins. **Cabernet Sauvignon-Shiraz** ☺ 🗐 🖾 ★★★ Harmonious marriage cab's dark fruit & cedar, shiraz's breadth in **11**. Lovely weight, length. American oak well judged. **Chardonnay** ☺ 🗐 🖾 ★★★ Oak & lees influence noticeable on fruit-filled **12**, generously padded with yellow stonefruit, lime & vanilla. **Chenin Blanc** ☺ 🗐 🖾 ★★★ **12** over-delivers at the price — all 1.6m litres of it! Quince & breakfast fruit punch, few grams sugar nice counter to fresh acidity. **Beaukett** ☺ 🗐 🖾 ★★★ **12** is sweet but vibrant thanks to clever mix muscat (70%) & colombard, delightful aromas of litchis & flowers.

Cabernet Sauvignon 🗐 🖾 ★★★ **11** perfect mealtime companion: sufficient fruit, dry impression. Like most reds in range, oak-staved in tank for flavour, mouthfeel. **Merlot** 🗐 ★★ Light-bodied & fresh **12**, pleasant & slightly leafy. **Pinot Noir** 🗐 ★★★ Unoaked **12** preview showcases appealing strawberry aromas/flavours; gentle spice; commendably moderate ±13% alcohol, savoury finish. **Pinotage** 🗐 🖾 ★★☆ American oak cradles sour cherry fruit in medium-bodied **11**. Chill lightly in summer. **Shiraz** 🗐 🖾 ★★☆ Firm tannin enlivens juicy **11** easy-drinker, brushed with combo French/American oak. **Pinot Grigio** 🗐 🖾 ★★ Last a preview **11**, now bottled & ready to drink; zesty lemon & typical (attractive) peach pip character. **Sauvignon Blanc** 🗐 🖾 ★★★ Some grass & nettle whiffs on crisp **12** summer tipple. **Viognier** 🗐 🖾 ★★★ No mistaking the variety: **12** floral perfumes & spice, some grip on palate, slightly warm finish (14.8% alcohol). **Méthode Cap Classique** NEW ★★★ **07** dry sparkling from chardonnay & pinot noir is subtle & fresh, with a savoury conclusion. **Gewürztraminer Special Late Harvest** 🗐 🖾 ★★★★ **11** raises the bar with charming pot-pourri scents, sun-kissed raisins & long, balanced finish. Like last-tasted **09** (★★★★), light bodied but rich, delicious. **White Muscadel** Was listed as 'Muscadel'. New vintage unready. **Cape Ruby** Was 'Port'. Await new release.

Chapel range

Red ★ Smoky **NV** (**12**) braai buddy. **White** ★★ Drink-soon **NV** (**12**) colombard/chenin mix more savoury than fruity. **Semi-Sweet** ★★★ Semi-sweet **NV** (**12**) lifted by zesty acidity, appealing baked fruit aromas. **Natural Sweet** ★★ Was 'Rosé'. **NV** (**12**) hits the spot with soft, sweet red fruit. Drink ice cold, poolside.

Natural Sweet range

Red ★★ Light, fresh **NV**'s sweetness balanced by tealeaf tang, which takes it up notch. **Rosé** ★★ Crowd-pleasing pink **NV** with strawberries-&-cream appeal. **White** ★★ Tangy acidity lifts the full-sweetness in moreish **NV**.

Two-Litre Certified Cultivar Cask range

Merlot ☺ ▨ ★★★ Satisfying everyday **12**, sour cherry taste, bright acidity. **Ruby Cabernet** ☺ ★★★ Raising the bar, **12** preview brings cherries & boiled sweets to the party, with zippy acidity & firm handshake. **Shiraz** ☺ ▨ ★★★ **11** uncomplex but true to variety; noticeable coconut & spice from brief oaking

Cabernet Sauvignon ▨ ★★ Leafy herbal notes on crisp **11**, fattened by touch sugar. **Chardonnay** ▨ ★★★ Oak-touched **12**, quite lush blood orange & peach flavours, glides down easily. **Chenin Blanc** ▨ ★★★ **12** pleasant anytime sipping at modest ±13% alcohol. **Sauvignon Blanc** ▨ ★★★ Pungent & tropical **12**, grain sugar adds body without sweetening, lightish alcohol ideal for lunchtime sipping.

Three-Litre Cultivar Slimline range

Merlot ☺ ▨ ★★★ After sullen version last edition, **12** is engaging & fruity, nice grip from deft oaking.

Cabernet Sauvignon **11** of this & **Shiraz** selling but not tasted. **Chardonnay** ▨ ★★★ Citrus & bready notes on mouthfilling **12**, brushed with oak. **Sauvignon Blanc** ▨ ★★★ **12** back on track with tropical fruit & crunchy Granny Smith apple balancing a little bit of sugar. **Sauvignon Blanc Extra Light** ▨ ★★ Green apple **12** has tart end.

Three-Litre Blended range

Smooth Dry Red ★★ Black fruit, vibrant acidity, terse grip on **NV** wallet pleaser. **Crisp Dry White** ★★ **NV** guava-toned, refreshing glassful. **Extra Light** ★ Apple & citrus tang on low-alcohol **NV**. **Johannisberger Semi-Sweet White** ★★ Frangipani redolence, sweet-sour flavour in drink-soonest **NV**. **Natural Sweet Red (Slimline Packed)** ★★ Latest **NV** ups ante, is more drinkable & balanced. **Natural Sweet Rosé (Slimline Packed)** ★★ Fragrant **NV** offers strawberry-toned low-alcohol fun. **Johannisberger Semi-Sweet Red** ★ Funky accent on meaty **NV**.

Combibloc range

Smooth Dry Red ★★ Very dry but balanced **NV** sipper. **Crisp Dry White** ★★ Guava appeal on lightly fruity, just-dry **NV**. **Crisp Extra Light** ★ Zesty **NV** with lightish alcohol for uncomplicated sipping. **Selected Stein** ★ Sweet & simple white **NV**. **Fruity Late Harvest** ★★ Perfumed & spicy (rather than fruity) semi-sweet **NV**. **Natural Sweet Rosé** ★ Fascinating strawberry/balsamic jus contrast in latest **NV**. Sip well chilled. Low ±8% alcohol, as next two. **Natural Sweet White** ★★ **NV** with grapey aroma, drinkability from brisk acidity. **Smooth Sweet Red** ★★ Improved **NV** not as sweet as expected; tealeaf & cranberry charm.

Light Cultivar range

Extra Light Merlot ▤ ▨ ★ Was 'Merlot'. **11** lean & astringent, begs food. **Pinotage Rosé** ▤ ▨ ★ Vague strawberry tone in light, dryish & lean **12**. **Light Chenin Blanc** ▤ ▨ ★★ As advertised: **12** light & breezy summer companion. **Extra Light Sauvignon Blanc** ▤ ▨ ★★ **12** Granny Smith apple in slimmer's delight, low-alcohol of ±9% (as for all in this range). — CE/HJ

Robert Stanford Estate

Location: Stanford ▪ Map: Elgin, Walker Bay & Bot River ▪ WO: Walker Bay ▪ Est 1855 ▪ 1stB 2008 ▪ Tasting & sales Fri-Mon 10-3.30 ▪ Closed Dec 25 & Jan 1 ▪ Madre's Kitchen Thu-Mon 8-4 ▪ Facilities for children ▪ Gift shop ▪ Farm produce ▪ Conservation area ▪ Distillery (grappa, brandy & fruit spirits) ▪ Art studio ▪ Tractor tours/ vineyard walks by appt ▪ Owner(s) Kleinrivier Beleggings (Pty) Ltd ▪ Cellarmaster(s)/winemaker(s) Johan Joubert (Sep 2007, Kleine Zalze) ▪ Viticulturist(s) Jan Malan (Jan 2003) ▪ 176ha/68ha (pinot, shiraz, chard, sauv, sem) ▪ 370t/1,200cs own label 40% red 30% white 15% rosé 15% MCC ▪ BWI champion ▪ wines@ robertstanfordestate.co.za ▪ www.robertstanfordestate.co.za ▪ S 34° 25′ 49.41″E 019° 27′ 49.98″ ▪ **T +27 (0)28-341-0441** ▪ F +27 (0)86-655-6944

A process of rejuvenation has seen much of the energy and entrepreneurship displayed by 19th century owner Robert Stanford restored to one of Walker Bay's most historic properties. The new spirit is reflected in the varied visitor offering, which includes a country-style restaurant, distillery, art studio and the Klein River

Conservancy. There's also a new wine range, named after the bay from which sea-faring farmer Robert Stanford set sail to deliver his fresh produce to Cape Town.

Sir Robert Stanford Estate range

★★★★ **Shiraz** [NEW] Potentially boisterous blackberry fruit of **10** cajoled into order by layers of warm spice; lovely composure & unwavering length of flavour swaddle 14.9% alcohol.

★★★★☆ **The Hansom** Bold cab-led **10** (★★★★) is piled high with bramble fruit, but derailed by weighty 15.3% alcohol. Understated **09** offered concentrated blackcurrant fruit, & its notable alcohol & smidgen sugar didn't jar.

★★★★ **Sauvignon Blanc** Natural acidity of cooler clime enlivens **12**'s riper fig profile; great persistence, like **10**. No **11**.

Rosé ★★★ Strawberry freshness in brisk dry **12**. **Chenin Blanc** Not tasted.

Cutters Cove [NEW]

Shiraz-Viognier ☺ ★★★ **09** brims with succulent cherry/mulberry fruit only just hemmed in by cedar spice, all bursting to be enjoyed. Lipsmacking & delicious.

Chenin Blanc 🖩 ★★ Crisp tropical tones to gluggable **12**. — DS

■ **Robin Hood Legendary Wine Series** *see* Arumdale Cool Climate Wines
■ **Rocheburg** *see* Riebeek Cellars
■ **Rockfield** *see* Du Preez Estate

Romond Vineyards

Location: Somerset West ▪ Map: Helderberg ▪ WO: Stellenbosch ▪ Est 1993 ▪ 1stB 2003 ▪ Tasting, sales & tours by appt Mon-Sat 10-5.30 Sun 11-5.30 ▪ Fee R30, waived on purchase ▪ Closed Easter Fri-Sun, Dec 25/26 & Jan 1 ▪ Olive oil ▪ The Vintner's Loft self-catering apartment ▪ Owner(s) André & Rhona Liebenberg ▪ Winemaker(s) André Liebenberg ▪ Viticulturist(s) Francois Hanekom (May 2007) ▪ 11.5ha/9.5ha (cabs s/f, merlot, ptage) ▪ PO Box 5634 Helderberg 7135 ▪ info@romond.co.za ▪ www.romond.co.za ▪ S 34° 1' 52.61" E 018° 49' 59.67" ▪ **T +27 (0)21-855-4566** ▪ F +27 (0)21-855-0428

'Nothing's changed, it's business as usual; just constant beavering away at making natural wines that are the best expression of our vineyards beneath Helderberg's West Peak,' says André Liebenberg, long in the film industry before throwing himself and his 'sometimes bewildered' family into this boutique venture.

★★★★ **Rebus** ✓ Fragrant **09** (★★★★☆) best yet; complex, classic cab franc leads blend with cab, merlot. Savoury fruit balances firmly structured tannins, great for food. Step up from **07**; no **08**.

Pinotage ⊕ ★★★★ **09** fruity but serious, with pure ripe dark berries, plums & leafy notes. Balanced & juicy, with delicious grip to finish. **Impromptu** ⊕ ★★★★ Dry rosé from merlot. **10** more complex & vibrant than previous, with mouthfilling ripe cherries, rosepetal & spice. — IM

Roodeberg

With a new wine, this famous KWV brand now pays tribute to Charles Niehaus, who developed Roodeberg back in 1949. 'Dr Charles', as he was known, experimented with many varieties before determining that shiraz was an ideal component for his new wine; it still plays an important role in today's blend.

Dr Charles Niehaus [NEW] 🍾 ★★★★ **10** shiraz-based with cab, merlot. Bright, oak-assisted spiciness; modest sweet fruit trimmed by dry tannins. **Roodeberg Red** 🍾 ★★★★ Cab-based blend offers satisfaction without stopping the conversation. **11** good dark-berried substance, rounded grip. WO W Cape for both. — AL

Roodezandt Wines

Location/map/WO: Robertson ▪ Est 1953 ▪ Tasting & sales Mon-Fri 8-5 ▪ Cellar tours by appt Mon-Fri 8-12 & 2-5 ▪ Closed all pub hols ▪ Sales (at cellar price) also from La Verne Wine Boutique Mon-Fri 9-5.30 Sat 9-5 ▪ Facilities for children ▪ Owner(s) 60 members ▪ Cellarmaster(s) Christie Steytler (May 1980) ▪ Winemaker(s) Ferdi Coetzee (2009), with Tiaan Blom (Oct 2005) ▪ Viticulturist(s) Jaco Lategan (Dec 2006) ▪ 1,800ha (cab, merlot, ptage, ruby cab, shiraz, chard, chenin, cbard, muscadel w, sauv) ▪ 30,000t/23m L bulk ▪ BSCI, HACCP, IPW ▪ PO Box 164 Robertson 6705 ▪ info@roodezandt.co.za ▪ www.roodezandt.co.za ▪ S 33° 48'33.2" E 019° 52'47.3" ▪ **T +27 (0)23-626-1160** ▪ F +27 (0)23-626-5074

According to Roodezandt's Mynhardt Marais, marketing and sales manager for bulk exports, 'The more things change, the more they stay the same'. Pressed for details, he says Roodezandt aims simply to remain a preferred supplier of specialist bulk wine to the bigger brand owners, adding that the trending shift in supply 'over the mountain' from Paarl and Stellenbosch can only help.

Balthazar range

★★★★ **Chardonnay Brut Méthode Cap Classique** Elegant top-label sparkling. Vintage-dated **09** maintains standard set by **NV (07)**, with appealing marzipan notes, toned yet generous body, nutty conclusion.
Classic Cabernet Sauvignon ⊛ ★★★★ Soft & integrated **05** dates & fynbos scents, should be ready now.

Roodezandt range

Cabernet Sauvignon ▨ ★★★ BBQ companion **11**, leafy mulberries on offer, tad four-square but friendly. **Shiraz** ★★★ Spicy tomato & pepper-dusted red berries on plump & juicy **11**. **Chenin Blanc** NEW ▤ ★★★ Fresh & affable **12** offers ripe tropical fruit, tingly acidity & bracingly crisp farewell. **Sauvignon Blanc** ▤ ★★ Intense herby aromas, standout acidity on **12**. **Special Late Harvest** ⊛ ▤ ★★★ From chenin & hanepoot: floral **11** lively & fruity; good match for spicy food. **Red Muscadel** ⊛ ▤ ★★★★ Seductive apricot-toned **10**'s grapey sweetness well balanced by firm acidity; for fireside conversations.

Keizer's Creek range

The Red ★★ Undemanding **NV** quick-sip from mainly cab, light & brief. — GdB

Rooiberg Winery   🍴🍷🎡📷🏃♿

Location/map/WO: Robertson ▪ Est 1964 ▪ 1stB 1974 ▪ Tasting & sales Mon-Fri 8–5.30 Sat 8–4 ▪ Fee R10pp for tour groups ▪ Closed Good Fri, Dec 25 & Jan 1 ▪ Bodega de Vinho restaurant & bakery Mon-Fri 8–5.30 Sat 8–4 ▪ BYO picnic ▪ Facilities for children ▪ Tour groups ▪ Gift shop ▪ Rooiberg Conservancy ▪ Owner(s) 30 members ▪ Cellarmaster(s) André van Dyk (Oct 2002) ▪ Winemaker(s) André Scriven (Jan 2008), with Johan Gerber (Jun 2011) ▪ Viticulturist(s) Hennie Visser (2007, Vinpro consultant) ▪ 667ha (cab, merlot, ptage, ruby cab, shiraz, chard, chenin, cbard, sauv) ▪ 12,000t/200,000cs own cellar 40% red 60% white ▪ Export brands: African Dawn, Amandalia, Cape Avocet, Goeie Tye, Table View, Tembana Valley, Zebra Collection ▪ Brands for clients: AlexKia, Cape Dreams, Ferling Noble, Woolworths ▪ ISO 9001:2000, BWI, HACCP, IPW, SGS Organic ▪ PO Box 358 Robertson 6705 ▪ info@rooiberg.co.za ▪ www.rooiberg.co.za ▪ S 33° 46′ 35.3″ E 019° 45′ 42.9″ ▪ **T +27 (0)23-626-1663** ▪ F +27 (0)23-626-3295

Although the past year has seen this enterprising Robertson winery make the successful transition from cooperative to private company, CEO Johan du Preez insists Rooiberg's vision remains the same, and in fact is even more focused: 'To harness nature into excellent wines for the global market.' Actively involved in several conservation projects, including the Landmark Foundation's Leopard & Predator Project, the Rooiberg team is 'quietly proud' of its grape farmers, who have set aside almost 60% of their land for conservation.

Reserve range

★★★★ **Pinotage** ✓ ▨ Opulent & seductive **11** handles its 100% new French oak & big 14.5% alcohol with aplomb, shows as silky smooth with a clean dry end. 'Try with chocolate dessert' say winemakers.
Cabernet Sauvignon ✓ ▨ ★★★★ Vibrant **11**'s dense core of fruit soaks up 100% new oak, shows satisfying vinosity & lovely freshness at commendably moderate 13.5% alcohol. Appealing now & for few years. **Merlot** ▨ ★★★ **11** exudes ripe plum & coconut/spice nuances from 100% new oak, lipsmacking dryness, but oak-dominated finish. **Shiraz** ⊛ ▨ ★★★★ **10** brooding savoury bacon aromas, vibrant, refreshing, despite intense fruit concentration. Raised the bar on admirable **09** (★★★★). **Cape Blend** NEW ▨ ★★★★ Impressive debut showing that less (oak) can be more: **11** only older barrels provide supportive backbone, subtle spice. Strawberry tone supplied by 50% pinotage, supple tannins & freshness by shiraz (30%) & cab. **Chardonnay** ✓ ▨ ★★★★ Step-up **11** is a smart wine: lots of layers, doesn't rely on on oak (though all-new) for definition or identity. Beefy alcohol well handled, shows only as slight sweetness on finish.

Rooiberg range

Pinotage ☺ ▨ ★★★ Lovely varietal typicity on **11** preview: strawberry, banana, sweet fruit appeal, plus lovely dry finish. **Mountain Red** ☺ ▤ ▨ ★★★ Smoky **11** 'anything goes' blend now bottled; unwooded for immediate enjoyment; drink soon. **Pinotage Rosé** ☺ ▤ ▨ ★★★ Salmon-hued **12** is a candyfloss-toned, just off-dry picnic basket staple. **Blanc Natural Sweet** ☺ ▤ ▨ ★★★ Peachy **12** pre-bottling big step up: clean, bright, exudes joie de vivre. Rating provisional.

Cabernet Sauvignon ★★★ **11** notch up: gently spicy, fresh & vibrant, just the right amount of oak, thanks to clever combo older barrels & staves, like all single-variety reds in this range. **Merlot** ★★ Gentle spicy notes & stalky grip on plummy **11**. **Shiraz** ★★★ Lightly oaked, red-berried **11** preview drinks easily, helped by sweetness from 14.5% alcohol. **Cabernet Sauvignon-Merlot (Roodewyn)** ★★ Cellar's stalwart is cab with merlot, petit verdot. Very ripe in **11**, tad sweet-sour but still friendly, gluggable. **Chardonnay** ★★★ Lemony **12** tank sample, fresh & zesty anytime companion. **Chenin Blanc** ★★★ **12** fresh & floral with thatch, lemon highlights for summer enjoyment. **Colombar** ★★★ Was 'Cape White'. Shy floral **12** has hint of spice, balanced sweetness in tail. Notch up. **Sauvignon Blanc** ★★ Subdued **12** faintly aromatic, frisky. **Chenin Blanc-Sauvignon Blanc** ★★ Quiet 51/49 **12** combo tropical & just off-dry summer staple. **Flamingo Sparkling** ★★ Candied apples & honey on gently sweet & frothy **NV**. **Brut Sparkling** ★★ Tangy wallet-friendly **NV** bubbly. **Vin Doux Sparkling** ★★ NV sparkler is grapey & sweet. **Red Natural Sweet** Lovely texture on **12** preview but too young to rate conclusively. **Rosé Natural Sweet** ★★★ Turkish Delight appeal on **12** genteel sweetie. **Red Muscadel** ★★★★ Preview **11** raises bar by some measure! Complex rooibos & lavender aromas, seamless fortification make for flavourful & elegant winter warmer. **Cape Vintage** Await new vintage. —JP/CvZ

■ **Rooi Kalahari** see Die Mas van Kakamas

Rosendal Winery

Location/map: Robertson ▪ WO: Western Cape ▪ 1stB 2003 ▪ Tasting, sales & cellar tours Mon-Sat 8-5 Sun 9-1 ▪ Fee only charged for groups of 10+ ▪ Wine & Lindt chocolate tastings ▪ Restaurant & Guesthouse (see Restaurants & Accommodation sections) ▪ Spa & wellness centre ▪ Conferences ▪ Owner(s) Geir Tellefsen & Sissel Anderssen ▪ Cellarmaster(s)/winemaker(s) Therese de Beer (Jan 2012) ▪ 18ha ▪ 80% red 15% white 5% rosé ▪ PO Box 3 Suite 128 Roggebaai 8012 ▪ info@rosendalwinery.com ▪ www.rosendalwinery.com ▪ S 33° 48'7.8" E 019° 59'19.0" ▪ **T +27 (0)21-424-4498 (sales)/+27 (0)23-626-1570 (farm)** ▪ F +27 (0)21-424-1570

Accomplished Therese de Beer (Doolhof, Bartinney) took over as winemaker at this luxury Robertson winery, guest house, spa and restaurant last year, as small changes to the tasting venue were introduced along with innovations like wine-and-Lindt-chocolate tastings. Therese will be getting feedback via Rosendal's telesales team about client preferences, and tweaking the portfolio accordingly.

Reserve Limited range

★★★★ **Black Eagle** First since **04**, Stellenbosch-sourced **07** (★★★★) is shiraz (40%) & 3 Bordeaux reds. Savoury & earthy flavours in more Old than New World style, with juicy balance.

Merlot This & **Red Rock** occasional releases. **Blue Mountain** NEW ★★★ Stellenbosch merlot (68%) & cab franc combo, **09** reflects structured vintage with firm tannins, good concentration. **Cape Francolin** NEW ★★★ **09** cab-led Bordeaux blend from Durbanville grapes flies above siblings. Light texture, touch leafy but juicy & satisfying. **Classic Cuvée** ★★★ Merlot & cab, supported by 3 other Bordeaux reds from Stellenbosch. Spicy oak (50% new vs 30% for other reds here) adds exotic nuance to **09**'s savoury appeal. Discontinued: **Wild Blue Yonder**.

Rosendal range

Chardonnay ★★ Smoky spice pervades lightly oaked, delicately flavoured **11**. **Riesling** NEW ★★★ Semi-dry **11** from Hermanus is balanced & round, terpene notes & deep straw colour invite early drinking. **Sauvignon Blanc** ★★★ **11** attractively un-fruity & food friendly, fresh acidity, pebbly minerality & silk texture from extended ageing on lees.

Barony range

Candelabra Shiraz Await next, as for **Sophie**. **Cecile Sauvignon Blanc** ★★★ Intense asparagus & tinned pea bouquet, soft acidity & creamy texture on balanced **11** from Hermanus vineyards.

Hilltop range

Cabernet Sauvignon Reserve ★★★ **10** is a food wine showing cab's firm structure & tightly packed fruit, crisp lemon-like acidity. Simonsberg grapes. **Merlot** Await new, as for **Sauvignon Blanc**. — CvZ

Ross Gower Wines

Location/WO: Elgin ▪ Map: Elgin, Walker Bay & Bot River ▪ Est 2003 ▪ 1stB 2004 ▪ Tasting & sales by appt ▪ Glen Stuart self-catering cottages ▪ Conservation area ▪ Owner(s) Gower family ▪ Winemaker(s) James Gower (2007), assisted by Mike Dobrovic ▪ Viticulturist(s) James Gower ▪ 83ha/±7ha (shiraz, sauv) ▪ 10,000cs own

label 20% red 25% white 55% MCC ▪ PO Box 161 Elgin 7180 ▪ info@rossgowerwines.co.za ▪ www.
rossgowerwines.co.za ▪ S 34° 14′17.7″ E 019° 7′3.7″ ▪ **T +27 (0)21-844-0197** ▪ F +27 (0)86-611-2179

Late patriarch Ross Gower's optimistic and tenacious spirit lives on at the Elgin
family farm, where son James now makes the wines, assisted by the very experienced Mike Dobrovic. They have weathered the storm of a difficult few years, and
are now ready to move on. MCC sparkling production has risen and hopefully there will be more cause for celebration in the future.

★★★★ **Sauvignon Blanc** ⓟ 🍷 Previously tasted **09** (★★★★) was pleasingly textured & elegant but
shade off **08**.

Cabernet Sauvignon ⓟ 🍷 ★★★★ **07** when last tasted showed brooding cassis & liquorice with a tinge of
greenpepper & firm structure. **Merlot** Await new release. **Shiraz** ⓟ 🍷 ★★★★ **08** combines savoury white
pepper nuance & red berry juiciness in supple & accessible styling. **Rosé** ⓟ 🍷 ★★★ **11** is savoury with lowish
alcohol, from cab/shiraz. Tart tannic twist suits al fresco fare. **Rhine Riesling** ⓟ 🍷 ★★★★ Perfumed **10**
crisply off-dry, genteel, shows varietal's delicate sweet/sour balance & potential to develop. **Pinot Noir Brut** ⓟ
★★★★ Fruity champagne-method sparkling **08** is dapper & appealing aperitif or food partner. — MW

■ **Rouana** see Simonsig Landgoed
■ **Roulou** see Boutique Baratok
■ **Rowlands** see Southern Sky Wines
■ **Royal** see Riebeek Cellars
■ **Royle** see Arra Vineyards
■ **Ruby Ridge** see Govert Wines

Rudera Wines

Location: Paarl ▪ Map: Paarl & Wellington ▪ WO: Stellenbosch/Western Cape/Elgin ▪ Est 1999 ▪ 1stB 2000 ▪
Tasting, sales & cellar tours Mon-Fri 11–4 Sat/Sun by appt ▪ Fee R30 ▪ Closed all pub hols ▪ Conferences ▪
Owner(s) Rudera Wines CC ▪ Winemaker(s) Adele Swart ▪ Viticulturist(s) Andre Roux ▪ Mentor/consultant
Chris Keet ▪ 15ha/10ha (cab, shiraz, chenin) ▪ ±100t/5,000cs own label 40% red 60% ▪ IPW ▪ 14 Napier Street
Paarl 7646 ▪ info@rudera.co.za ▪ www.rudera.co.za ▪ S 33° 43′25.67″ E 018° 57′27.51″ ▪ **T +27 (0)21-852-
1380 (office), +27 (0)21-871-1749 (cellar)** ▪ F +27 (0)21-852-1380

Adele Swart is not shy to get her hands dirty: 'I still wear my purple post-harvest
hands with pride,' she says. As a young cellar hand at Rudera back in 2001 (then
Stellenbosch based, now with a Paarl home), she started to gain experience and
now finds herself the winemaker. She speaks proudly and passionately about the
'steadfast' wine quality she aims for. This constant ultimately comes from team-
work, she thinks. The plan is that this label will continue to develop from its
garagiste beginnings and leap into the future. There seems no reason to doubt it.

★★★★☆ **Cabernet Sauvignon 09** now bottled, delivers on preview last time. Brooding dark fruit & dense
compact palate has 'masculine' tannins now more integrated. Combo Stellenbosch & Bot River fruit. This a serious offering with fine dry end. Shows less super-ripeness than **08** (★★★★).

★★★★☆ **Platinum Cabernet Sauvignon** ⓟ Last tasted was intense & concentrated **07** with finely
managed velvety tannins & persistent spicy finish.

★★★★ **Syrah 10** in opulent mould. Dark fruited with palate to match, generous & ripe — with a few extra
grams sugar. Ready to enjoy. Grapes mostly from Paarl home-farm, rest Bot River.

★★★★ **De Tradisie Chenin Blanc 10**'s ripe yellow stonefruit & crisp apple lead to textured mouthfeel
with good weight — only just dry but balanced by clean freshness. Obvious oak should integrate.

★★★★☆ **Robusto Chenin Blanc** ⓟ **09** (★★★★) displays citrus combo with toasty oak aromas. In drier
style than **08**, with bright cleansing acid cutting barrel fatness in support of balanced clear fruit.

★★★★☆ **Noble Late Harvest** Drops 'Chenin' from name with fine oak-matured **10**, which has smatterings
chardonnay, viognier & sauvignon. Excellently balanced & finely crafted, with right hint of honeyed botrytis adding complexity to luscious ripe peach & tart apricot. Pristine conclusion.

Platinum Chenin Blanc ⓟ ★★★★ Tasted few years back, **09** from Elgin had smoky lime-apricot notes,
taut flinty palate & good length. — JP

Rudi Schultz Wines

Location/WO: Stellenbosch ▪ Est 2002 ▪ Tasting by appt ▪ Closed all pub hols ▪ Owner(s) Rudi Schultz ▪ Cellarmaster(s)/ winemaker(s) Rudi Schultz (Jan 2002) ▪ Viticulturist(s) Dirkie Morkel (consultant) ▪ 10t/670cs own label 100% red ▪ 8 Fraser Road Somerset West 7130 ▪ rudi@thelema.co.za ▪ **T +27 (0)82-928-1841** ▪ F +27 (0)21-885-1800

Rudi Schultz, with his successful and even illustrious 'day job' making wine at Thelema, has a little time to shape his small own-label venture. He's dropped the Viognier, and the Reserve is something only for great years but, he says tantalisingly, 'a new red blend will be released in 2013'. Furthermore, 'finally' some long-term markets have been established.

★★★★ **Syrah** 'Masculine' style **10** has savoury tones of black pepper & fresh earth, well supported by dark fruit & savoury olive note. Weighty palate, good lingering finish. Should keep.

Reserve Syrah Occasional release. Discontinued: **Viognier**. — JPf

■ **Runner Duck** see Vergenoegd Wine Estate
■ **Running Duck** see Stellar Winery

Rupert & Rothschild Vignerons

Location: Paarl ▪ Map: Paarl & Wellington ▪ WO: Western Cape ▪ Est 1997 ▪ 1stB 1998 ▪ Tasting, sales & cellar tours Mon-Fri 9-4.30 Sat (Nov-Feb) 9-4.30 ▪ Fee R5/wine ▪ Closed Ash Wed, Easter Fri-Mon, Dec 25 & Jan 1 ▪ Owner(s) Rupert family & Baron Benjamin de Rothschild ▪ Cellarmaster(s) Schalk-Willem Joubert (Jun 1997) ▪ Winemaker(s) Yvonne Lester (Sep 2001), with Clive Radloff (Jun 1997) ▪ 90ha (cabs s/f, merlot, p verdot) ▪ 900t/71,000cs own label 93% red 7% white ▪ ISO 14001, HACCP, IPW ▪ PO Box 412 Franschhoek Valley 7690 ▪ info@rupert-rothschildvignerons.com ▪ www.rupert-rothschildvignerons.com ▪ S 33° 50' 14.5" E 018° 56' 51.1" ▪ **T +27 (0)21-874-1648** ▪ F +27 (0)21-874-1802

Schalk-Willem Joubert, cellarmaster here since the first harvest, has some considered thoughts about his 15 years incumbency. He particularly values 'being part of a team that has established an international brand selling in more than 50 countries, with each vintage being a sell-out.' That enviable situation has its challenges: 'Striving for perfection with wine that is consistent in quality, balance and elegance.' Joubert adds that, to achieve consistency, 'one mustn't follow trends or mind critics' opinions.' He might also mention the many vineyards from which he draws fruit; most of the red grape vineyards have been more or less the same since the start; as far as consistency in the chardonnay is concerned, he has a well-established vinification regime for each region involved.

★★★★★ **Baron Edmond** Excellent cab-led **10** gains extra perfumed complexity & finesse from increased cab franc input (20%); merlot 35%. Pure-fruited intensity, freshness & fine insistent tannins ensure great presence & potential. Stellenbosch & Darling grapes, as for Classique.

★★★★ **Classique** Usual fresh cassis features in cab-merlot blend; hint smoky oak scents, sweet fruit, gentle flesh & fine, forming tannins preserve classic style, even in less concentrated **10**.

★★★★ **Baroness Nadine** 🖉 From Elgin, Barrydale & Robertson chardonnay; familiar roast hazelnut enlivened by lime attractions, **10** fresh-fruity feel in lighter vintage, but lovely balance for now, few years. — AL

■ **Rupert Wines** see Anthonij Rupert Wines

Russo Family Vintners

Location: Durbanville ▪ Map: Durbanville, Philadelphia & Darling ▪ Est 2004 ▪ 1stB 2007 ▪ Tasting, sales & tours Mon-Fri 9-4 Sat by appt ▪ Closed all pub hols ▪ Owner(s) Henk & Terèsa Rossouw ▪ Winemaker(s) Terèsa Rossouw (2007) ▪ 6.5ha/4ha (cabs s/f, malbec, merlot, p verdot) ▪ 35t/400cs own label 100% red ▪ PO Box 4402 Tyger Valley 7536 ▪ teresa@russowines.co.za ▪ www.russowines.co.za ▪ S 33° 48'37.9" E 018° 37'04.3" ▪ **T +27 (0)21-979-1960** ▪ F +27 (0)21-979-1996

Terèsa and Henk Rossouw bought this Durbanville smallholding in 2004, and feel inspired by one of the Cape's first winemakers — Pierre Rousseau, who arrived in 1688. The potential for fine red wine from Bordeaux varieties was early identified. Now the whole family (including dog) is involved, and caught up in the dream.

★★★★ **Russo** ⑨ Opulent but elegant & well structured **07** still selling; tasted a few years back. — JP

Rustenberg Wines

Location/map: Stellenbosch ▪ WO: Simonsberg-Stellenbosch/Stellenbosch/Coastal/Western Cape ▪ Est 1682 ▪ 1stB 1892 ▪ Tasting & sales Mon-Fri 9-4.30 Sat 10-4 Sun 10-3 ▪ Closed Good Fri, Dec 25 & Jan 1 ▪ Garden ▪ Weddings ▪ Owner(s) Simon Barlow ▪ Cellarmaster(s) Murray Barlow (Nov 2011) ▪ Winemaker(s) Randolph Christians (Nov 1995), with Gareth le Grange (2003) ▪ Viticulturist(s) Nico Walters (1999) ▪ 1,200ha/±154ha (cabs s/f, grenache n/b, malbec, merlot, mourv, p verdot, shiraz, chard, rouss, sauv, sem, viog) ▪ ±1,050t/77,000cs own label 51% red 47% white 2% other ▪ BWI, IPW ▪ PO Box 33 Stellenbosch 7599 ▪ wine@rustenberg.co.za ▪ www.rustenberg.co.za ▪ S 33° 53' 44.8" E 018° 53' 33.6" ▪ **T +27 (0)21-809-1200** ▪ F +27 (0)21-809-1219

There's no resting on laurels at this historic Cape wine estate: Rustenberg is open longer on the weekends, with a wedding venue and picnics in the picture-perfect gardens swelling the service offering. The broadening market appeal includes excellent new entry-level wines — the Ida's red and white blends, named after a lady rumoured to be more than a close friend of the Cape's first governor, Simon van der Stel. While catering to visitors to the beautiful property, the Rustenberg team (now vitally including Murray Barlow, the next generation of the owning family) is also looking further afield, and sees South Africa's BRICSA partners becoming ever more important. Markets are growing familiar, relationships are forming, trade barriers will be coming down.

Site Specific range

★★★★☆ **Peter Barlow** ✪ 100% cab from Rustenberg's finest red vineyard. Cassis- & herb-laden **08** with restrained power & regal bearing. Gorgeous fruit still masked by polished oak. Should reward 5+ years ageing.

★★★★☆ **Syrah** Impenetrably youthful, opaque **10** will need time to show its full potential. Constructed for the long haul: seamless integration, dense fruit currently masked by tannins. Powerful but neatly contained.

★★★★☆ **Five Soldiers** 🍴 🄽 Majestic, convincingly classy **10** chardonnay has quietly powerful presence. Multi-layered, intense citrus fruit tightly wound in finely integrated oak persists throughout, imparting an astonishingly long, harmonious finish.

Regional range

★★★★☆ **John X Merriman** 🍴 🄽 Classic, austerely structured **10** (★★★★) blend 5 Bordeaux red varieties has youthful tannins with lurking complexity, though not as exceptional as **09**. Best kept a few years.

★★★★ **RM Nicholson** ✪ 🍴 Ex-barrel **10**'s blackcurrant spiced by dried herbs & fynbos. Cab/shiraz/merlot-led blend with pure fruit & hint of oaky vanilla. Balanced, firm & rich. Stellenbosch WO, as next.

★★★★ **Chardonnay** 🍴 🄽 Gregarious sweet fruit in charming **11** held by vibrantly fresh acidity & cloaked in creamily integrated oak. Staggered picking allows appealing combo ripeness & freshness.

★★★★ **Roussanne** ✪ 🍴 🄽 **11** preview back on form after **10** (★★★★). Balanced sweet peach, white flowers & apple flavours, creamy vanilla overtones. Simonsberg-Stellenbosch WO.

★★★★ **Sauvignon Blanc** ✪ 🍴 🄽 **11** preview showed lemongrass, pear & herbal aromas. Bright & focused, full flavoured with a grassy, lemony bite; drop semillon adds weight; portion Elgin fruit.

★★★★☆ **Straw Wine** ✪ Pure melon, ripe peach & white flowers on **10** from air-dried viognier, chenin, crouchen. Bright, rich & elegant fruit with ample streaks of fresh lemon acidity. Coastal WO.

Merlot ✪ 🍴 🄽 ★★★★ **10** preview with bright red fruit, lavender & vanilla wafts. Poised & well-structured, with a delicious concluding fruit acid grip. Stellenbosch WO. **Unwooded Chardonnay** ✪ 🍴 🄽 ★★★★ Well-balanced **11** preview showed fresh citrus & apple notes, lemon cream finish. Coastal WO. Discontinued: **Schoongezicht White**.

Ida's / Est.1682 range NEW

Red 🍴 🄽 ★★★★ Bordeaux varieties & shiraz intended for easy accessibility, but **11** over-delivers in more serious style; tight tannins underpin wealth of fruit. **White** ✓ 🍴 🄽 ★★★★ Also seriously styled; sauvignon-led 6-way **11** blend has overtly aromatic passionfruit; fresh, steely acidity to focus rich flavours. Both WO Stellenbosch. — IM

Rust en Vrede Estate

Location/map/WO: Stellenbosch ▪ Est 1694 ▪ 1stB 1979 ▪ Tasting, sales & cellar tours Mon-Sat 9-5 ▪ Fee R40/4 wines & R70/6 wines, waived on purchase ▪ Closed Easter Fri/Sun, Dec 25 & Jan 1 ▪ Rust en Vrede Restaurant (see Restaurants section) ▪ Gift shop ▪ Owner(s) Jean Engelbrecht ▪ Cellarmaster(s) Coenie Snyman (Dec 2006) ▪ Winemaker(s) Coenie Snyman (Dec 2006), with Roelof Lotriet (Nov 2011) ▪ Viticulturist(s) Dirkie

Mouton (Jun 2010) ▪ 50ha/45ha (cab, merlot, shiraz) ▪ ±300t/20,000cs own label 100% red ▪ IPW ▪ PO Box 473 Stellenbosch 7599 ▪ info@rustenvrede.com ▪ www.rustenvrede.com ▪ S 33° 59′ 54.0″ E 018° 51′ 22.5″ ▪ T **+27 (0)21-881-3881** ▪ F +27 (0)21-881-3000

Owner Jean Engelbrecht is cognisant of Rust en Vrede's position within the South African wine fraternity — and is unyielding in his demand for maintaining the grand Stellenbosch estate's reputation for top quality. The reaction its sleek gentility elicits from awed first-time visitors is reward enough. Engelbrecht has worked hard at making it one of the country's most admired properties, not least because of its perennially top-rated restaurant. His piloting has been steady, and transitions have been handled with nary a ripple of change in wine style. Incumbent winemaker Coenie Snyman, a Diners Club Winemaker of the Year, is tasked with ensuring the signature elegance and restraint, coupled with power and abundant fruit, remains.

★★★★ **Merlot** Elegant & refined **11** shows sleek grip knit with powerful, abundant cocoa & black berry flavours. Tarry note adds an edge.

★★★★ **Shiraz** Return to form for **09** & **10**, both reviewed. Violet perfume with chunky, brambly plum generosity. Alcohol of 15.2% on latter doesn't trouble but oak needs some time to knit harmoniously.

★★★★☆ **Single Vineyard Syrah** Rich & sexy **10** ramps up a notch on previous **09** (★★★★). Ultra-ripe (alcohol 15.2%) but gracious & silky, with a light spice sheen over muscular prune & chocolate fruit. Concentrated & poised, oak is well absorbed.

★★★★☆ **1694 Classification** ⊕ Pricey shiraz-cab blend honouring date property was granted. Massive & unabashed **09**, with dense raisiny fruit, weighty & plush. Tobacco & wood-shaving whiffs (customary new oak, mostly French here), sumptuous textures, fruit & generous alcohol.

★★★★☆ **Estate** 3-way combo of cab, shiraz & merlot, **09** epitomises the house style: long, deep & glossy with ample heft & persistence. Deep-piled hedgerow fruit is tempered by savoury oak, the underlying structure is firm yet toned. Needs time.

Cabernet Sauvignon ★★★★ Two vintages tasted: **09** (★★★★) is smart, shows poised typicity. It edges out **10**, still a tad gawky, ample cassis & earthy grip but needs time. — FM

■ **Rusthof** see Mooiuitsig Wine Cellars
■ **Rustler** see Flagstone Winery

Saam Mountain Vineyards

Location/WO: Paarl ▪ Est/1stB 2007 ▪ Tasting at Perdeberg Winery ▪ Owner(s) Bibendum Wine Limited & Perdeberg Winery ▪ Cellarmaster(s) Albertus Louw (Oct 2008) ▪ Winemaker(s) Riaan Möller (Dec 2006) & Carla Herbst (Jun 2008) ▪ Viticulturist(s) Jaco Engelbrecht (Nov 2011) ▪ 6,000t/50,000cs own label 80% red 20% white ▪ PO Box 214 Paarl 7620 ▪ info@saam-mountain.cm ▪ www.saam-mountain.com ▪ T **+27 (0)21-869-8244** ▪ F +27 (0)21-869-8245

Describing itself as 'the home of ethical winemaking', Saam ('Together') is a joint venture between leading UK wine merchants Bibendum and Perdeberg Winery to source exclusive wines from selected growers stretching from Paarl across the Swartland to Durbanville. Saam are now headquartered on Eenzaamheid farm near Paarl in SA's oldest registered building (1688), now under restoration.

Saam Single Vineyard Selection

★★★★☆ **Middelburg Chenin Blanc** ⊕ 🍷 🖉 From Perdeberg vineyard. Savoury **10** (★★★★) comes down a notch from impressive **09**, oaking still a dominant factor, needs time to meld with fruit.

Koopmanskraal Shiraz Await new, as for **Heldersig Shiraz-Viognier** & **Phisantekraal Sauvignon**.

Saam Quality range

Cabernet Sauvignon ⊕ 🍷 🖉 ★★★ Luscious berries in **10**, light oak giving savoury seam, palate grip. **Pinotage** ⊕ 🍷 🖉 ★★★ Juicy blueberries lightly oaked, **10** finishes dry enough for food compatibility. **Shiraz** ⊕ 🍷 🖉 ★★★ Savoury, smoky overlay to **10**'s piquant berries, appealing fruity plumpness. **Chenin Blanc** ⊕ 🍷 🖉 ★★★★ Distinctive thatch & red-apple styling in **10**, brightened by racy acidity. Has ability to age a few years. **Sauvignon Blanc** ⊕ 🍷 🖉 ★★ **10** asparagus flavours, lightish & ultra-fresh. — CR

■ **Sabi Sabi** see StellenRust

Sadie Family Wines

Location: Malmesbury ▪ Map: Swartland ▪ WO: Swartland/Stellenbosch/Olifants River ▪ Est 1999 ▪ 1stB 2000 ▪ Tasting by appt ▪ Owner(s) The Sadie Family (Pty) Ltd ▪ Winemaker(s)/viticulturist(s) Eben Sadie (1999) ▪ 25ha (cinsaut, grenache n/b, mourv, syrah, tinta barocca, chenin, clairette, palomino, rouss, sem, verdelho, viog) ▪ 60t/4,000cs own label 50% red 50% white ▪ PO Box 1019 Malmesbury 7299 ▪ office@thesadiefamily com ▪ S 33° 31'31.0" E 018° 48'18.1" ▪ **T +27 (0)76-151-7131** ▪ F +27 (0)86-692-2852

The range has expanded to include Old Vine wines which might appear in this guide for the first time, but were previously released in small volumes, after many years in development. For these are precious old vineyards from unirrigated bushvines, many found neglected and thereafter rehabilitated, but all a reflection of a particular terroir. Respecting this, Eben Sadie used minimal interference in the winemaking, kept it as natural as possible so that the wines could mirror the personalities of the vineyards. The range includes 9 wines but the 5 below are the main focus. Situated in different places, each wine is named for its vineyard, the oldest of which are 'T Voetpad, planted 1900-1928 on the vines' own roots, ungrafted, and Mev. Kirsten from the 1920s, the oldest chenin vineyard in the country. This is more than wine, it's history.

Signature Series

★★★★★ **Columella** Shiraz-led with mourvèdre & grenache. Crammed with luscious berries, **10** tannins provide sleek musculature, but seamed throughout are violets, scrub, graphite, complex notes setting this wine apart.

★★★★★ **Palladius** ⓦ Unfined/filtered, 18 months lees-ageing. **10** (★★★★★) blend 8 mainly Rhône whites, unspecified combo but who cares? It's what's in the glass that counts & that's masterly. Melon & kumquat, crushed almonds, a mineral core. Smooth, curvaceous & a very long finish. Follows stellar **09**.

Old Vine Series NEW

★★★★☆ **Pofadder** Honouring cinsaut, the out-of-favour workhorse of earlier times. From 42 year old vines, minimally handled, unfined/filtered **11** shows how it's done: from plump ripe fruit, violet whiffs, to velvety tannins & mouthfilling succulence. Gorgeous.

★★★★☆ **Treinspoor** Tinta barocca from 38 year old vines. Very aromatic & forthcoming, there are juicy red berries & spice in **11**, some attractive wildness & as for the previous wine, masterly palate appeal; svelte tannins & very long finish, ending dry.

★★★★☆ **Mev. Kirsten** With such a provenance, one has to approach this **11** with some reverence; 1T harvested off ancient chenin Stellenbosch vineyard a mere hectare in size. Quince with earthy, almost waxy notes balanced by lovely fresh elegance. Expect a 15 year lifespan.

★★★★★ **Skurfberg** Tiny yield off 80 year old dryland chenin vines, expect something noteworthy: peach pip, hints of melon preserve, **11** is underpinned by savoury minerality. Minimally handled, natural ferment, this is old-vine terroir; noteworthy indeed. WO Olifants River.

★★★★☆ **'T Voetpad** Semillon, chenin, palomino & muscat d'Alexandrie all from a tiny 105-year old vineyard, fermented together. Hovers between fruity, earthy & savoury, challenging the senses, but **11**'s appeal is beyond dispute, smoothly rounded, balanced, ultra long. — CR

■ **Safari** see De Zoete Inval Estate

Saltare

Location: Stellenbosch ▪ WO: Western Cape/Swartland/Paarl ▪ 1stB 2005 ▪ Closed to public ▪ Wines available for tasting & sales every Saturday at the Stellenbosch Fresh Goods Market, Oude Libertas ▪ Owner(s) Christof & Carla Pauw ▪ Cellarmaster(s)/winemaker(s) Carla Pauw (2005) ▪ 12t/900cs own label 15% red 15% white 70% MCC ▪ PO Box 2290 Dennesig Stellenbosch 7601 ▪ info@saltare.co.za ▪ www.saltare.co.za ▪ **T +27 (0)21-883-9568** ▪ F +27 (0)88-021-883-9568

At the heart of some of Carla Pauw's beloved traditional-method bubblies lies a chardonnay block farmed by a veteran Robertson grower who switched to natural practices after realising the harm done by chemical sprays. The health of the vines shows in the flavour and purity of her wines, and she has expanded her range with a Rosé and a Blanc de Blancs (untasted by us), making up a sparkling foursome.

★★★★ **Méthode Cap Classique Brut Rosé** NEW Fine, stylish NV from Stellenbosch pinot noir. Delicate, complex & bone-dry. Partial oaking structures creamy persistence. As for all, label gives disgorgement date.

★★★★ **Méthode Cap Classique Brut Nature** Aiming for freshness & steely mineral style. Lean, bone-dry, focused, lightly oaked chardonnay-pinot blend NV a step up. Robertson, Stellenbosch grapes, as Reserve. **Syrah** ★★★★ Robust 09 from organic Swartland fruit, with carignan. Ripe but not overly sweet, with savoury spiciness & bright acidity. **Specialis** ★★★★ Perfumed 08 blend merlot & cab plus a little cab franc. Juicy ripe fruit firmly underpinned by fresh, brisk acidity. WO Paarl. Previous was lavish 06 (★★★★). **Chenin Blanc** ★★★☆ Slightly quirky, just-off-dry 10 from Swartland naturally fermented in oak. Vigorous acidity needs to harmonise with the ripe fruit. **Méthode Cap Cassique Brut Reserve** ★★★★ More mature of MCC trio, 3-4 years on lees, still nicely fresh. Chardonnay-led NV (was vintaged), pinot noir & light oaking provide backbone. — IM

■ **Sandrivier** see Overgaauw Wine Estate

Santa Cecilia

Location: Riebeek-Kasteel ▪ Map: Swartland ▪ Est/1stB 2008 ▪ Tasting facility in The Wine Kollective: Mon-Sat 10-5 Sun 10-3 ▪ Closed Good Fri, Dec 25 & Jan 1 ▪ Gifts ▪ Farm produce ▪ Adjacent Bar Bar Black Sheep Restaurant ▪ Overnight facility 'The Santa Cecilia Boudoir' ▪ Owner(s) Anton Espost & Thys Greeff ▪ Winemaker(s) Anton Espost, Thys Greeff & Hugo Basson (2008, Annex Kloof) ▪ Viticulturist(s) Thys Greeff (Feb 2008), Outback Viticulture ▪ 1,000cs own label 30% red 70% white ▪ PO Box 61 Riebeek-Kasteel 7307 ▪ espost@telkomsa.net ▪ S 33° 23' 1.48" E 018° 53' 46.54" ▪ **T +27 (0)22-448-1008/+27 (0)82-776-9366**

Having first secured some top Swartland vineyards, Riebeek-Kasteel wine partners Anton Espost and Thys Greeff believe location is everything for winemaking too. 'Our new cellar is 20.323m from the Royal Hotel's bar, and there are six restaurants within 20m. We believe the happiness of the winemaker reflects in the wine. The more fun we have, the better our wine gets.'

Sarah's Creek

Location: Robertson ▪ Closed to public ▪ Owner(s) Dirk C Malherbe ▪ Winemaker(s) Marga Malherbe ▪ 20ha (cab, merlot, sauv) ▪ PO Box 6531 Welgemoed 7538 ▪ info@sarahscreek.co.za ▪ www.sarahscreek.co.za ▪ **T +27 (0)76-838-6507**

The name of this Robertson Valley winery hinges on a family legend of a young girl distracted on her way to school by the beauties of her surroundings, which serves in the present day to inspire a winemaking ethos based on simplicity, love of nature and dedication to life.

Saronsberg

Location/map: Tulbagh ▪ WO: Tulbagh/Coastal ▪ Est 2002 ▪ 1stB 2004 ▪ Tasting & sales Mon-Fri 8–5 Sat 10–2 ▪ Fee R25pp ▪ Closed Easter Fri/Sun, Ascension day, Dec 25 & Jan 1 ▪ Cellar tours by appt ▪ Olive oil ▪ BYO picnic ▪ Art works & sculptures on display ▪ Christmas in Winter Tulbagh festival (Jun) ▪ Owner(s) Saronsberg Cellar (Pty) Ltd ▪ Cellarmaster(s) Dewaldt Heyns (2003) ▪ Winemaker(s) Dewaldt Heyns (2002), with Jolandie van der Westhuizen (2011) ▪ Viticulturist(s) Chris Immelman ▪ 500ha/50ha (shiraz) ▪ 320t own label 70% red 30% white ▪ WIETA ▪ PO Box 361 Tulbagh 6820 ▪ info@saronsberg.com ▪ www.saronsberg.com ▪ S 33° 14'48. 2" E 019° 7' 2.0" ▪ **T +27 (0)23-230-0707** ▪ F +27 (0)23-230-0709

Dewaldt Heyns and his Tulbagh team are relishing the start of their second decade of winemaking buoyed by a slew of awards (and first five star rating). 'It's been interesting to see the subtle changes in the wines as the vines have attained more maturity,' says Dewaldt. 'I am most pleased with the resulting finesse.' They are 'slowly but surely' extending their vineyards, and plan to enlarge the cellar fermentation and barrel maturation capacity. Finally, after many years of 'undetermined delays', Dewaldt reveals, 'it seems our 2006 sauvignon blanc straw wine might actually be allowed to leave the nest'.

Saronsberg range

★★★★ **Shiraz** 🍷 Acclaimed label enters a higher league in 10 (★★★★★), supple & silky, with intricate flavour spectrum red/black fruits, dark spices, roasted nuts & smoked meats. Like 09, shows leashed power but greater depth, concentration; firm tannin structure to reward many years cellaring.

★★★★☆ **Seismic** ⊕ Starry **08** cab (72%) with merlot, petit verdot & malbec. Ripe blueberry & fruitcake with earthy density. Muscle from 20 months French oak, 100% new. Fine tannin for ageing. WO Coastal.

★★★★☆ **Full Circle** Shiraz-led Rhône blend with grenache, mourvèdre, viognier. Rich, bold & tannic **10** (★★★★) slightly porty compared with **09**'s elegance, spice & integrated wood. As usual, drinks well now & can go for years.

★★★★ **Viognier** 🎐 Plenty of honeysuckle-fragrant fruit on **11** to harmonise with still evident oak (14 mths mix new/older). Fresher style than **10**, but as good, satisfying. 30% naturally fermented.

★★★★ **Sauvignon Blanc Straw Wine** ⊕ **06** had molten pineapple & honeycomb, rich sweetness; shortbread seasoning, hidden strength from 22 months barrel fermentation/ageing.

Brut Méthode Cap Classique ★★★★ Classy **09** champagne-method sparkling from pinot noir & chardonnay ups the ante on all-chardonnay **07** (★★★★). Elegant; true 'brut' dryness, yeasty complexity from 36 months lees-ageing. **08** sold out untasted.

Provenance range

★★★★ **Shiraz** 🎐 House's modern take on variety. **10** satisfying & spicy with plump fruit; as plush as **09** & **08**, supple tannins courtesy 20 months in French oak, third new. WO Coastal, like next.

★★★★ **Rooi** ⊕ Bordeaux red blend consistently punches above its weight. **10**'s plush texture masks brooding intensity. Smoothly compelling, beautifully integrated & supple. Like **09**, will improve.

Shiraz Rosé ⊕ ★★★ Light & fresh **11**, zesty dry pomegranate flavours, amiable quaffing. **Sauvignon Blanc** ✓ 🏠 🎐 ★★★★ Always flavoursome, typically fattened by dollop semillon. **12** still sweaty but focused & 'cool', with superb precision, broad fantail finish. 3 months bottle-aged vs 6 months on lees for **11** (★★★★). — WB/AL

Sauvignon.com

Location: Durbanville ▪ WO: Western Cape ▪ Est/1stB 2010 ▪ Closed to public ▪ Owner(s) Thys & Tienie Louw ▪ Winemaker(s) Thys Louw & Mari Branders (both Jan 2010) ▪ Viticulturist(s) Div van Niekerk (Jan 2010) ▪ 200t/ 10,000cs own label 40% red 60% white ▪ PO Box 27 Durbanville 7551 ▪ info@sauvignon.com ▪ www.sauvignon.com ▪ **T +27 (0)82-442-1317** ▪ F +27 (0)21-979-1802

Diemersdal's Thys Louw cannily conceived this as a 'digital' label (the striking logo is a vine leaf fragmenting (coalescing?) into a myriad pixels; the website and social media presence integral to the brand), so no surprise to see a post on Sauvignon.com's Facebook page during London 2012: 'If the Olympics had wine-tasting, I'd be a gold medal winner'. Spoken like a true millennial.

Sauvignon Blanc ☺ 🏠 🎐 ★★★ Unashamedly 'sauvignon', **12** mixes cool & grassy with warm & tropical, & throws in a little more pungency than usual (& a hint of sweat). Chill & enjoy.

Cabernet Sauvignon NEW 🏠 🎐 ★★★ Contrast with fruit-driven sibling, **11** overpowers with intense almost resinous wood-derived character, very firm & lacking the playfulness at heart of this brand. — CvZ

Savage Wines NEW

Location: Cape Town ▪ Est 2006 ▪ 1stB 2011 ▪ Closed to public ▪ Owner(s) Duncan Savage ▪ Cellarmaster(s)/ winemaker(s)/viticulturist(s) Duncan Savage (Jan 2006) ▪ 11-15t/600cs own label 50% red 50% white ▪ somethingsavage@live.co.za ▪ **T +27 (0)21-785-4019**

Cape Point Vineyards winemaker Duncan Savage vowed to make his own-brand wine before he was 35. He's cut it fine (January 2013 was D-day) but thanks to plenty of support from his family, he made it in the nick of time with a 2011 Red and White. His goal is elegant wines which are truly South African, with an international feel. Key words are terroir, whole-bunch ferments, minimal intervention and seasoned, subtle wood. 'I can't afford new oak anyway!'

Savanha

The team at Spier, Stellenbosch-based brand owner, say the Savanha wines have an important purpose: to share the vibrancy of South Africa's sun, sky and soil with cultures around the world. While most are for export, recently repackaged Savanha Sun wines are now available in their country of origin. See Spier entry.

Naledi range

★★★★ **Cabernet Sauvignon** Showing restraint in a warm vintage, **10** has black olive, leather & spice highlights to red fruit compote, charry oak finish. Like **09**, drinks well young. WO Coastal, as all these.

★★★★ **Pinotage** Exceptionally ripe **10** manages to show restraint, beautiful pinotage strawberry, hint smoke & slight acetone lift. Not at all heavy; handles big alcohol better than **09** (★★★★).

Merlot ★★★★ Soft & rounded **10** has mulberries, plum & iodine notes, slight green astringency. Shade off taut & zesty **09** (★★★★). **Chardonnay** ★★★★ Barrel-fermented **11** takes step up with fresh, tangy lemon & lime, subtle & precise oak detail; shows more varietal fruit than butterscotch & toffee infused **10** (★★★★).

Special Reserve range

Cabernet Sauvignon ★★★ Ripe red fruit, meat & leather on firm **11**; powerful 14.7% alcohol but not the fruit to match. These all for export, WO Coastal. **Merlot** ★★★ Brooding **11** could rate higher once austere tannins have settled. **Shiraz** ★★★ Pepper & spice notes to **11**'s deep red fruit, satisfying freshness & tannic grip. **Sauvignon Blanc** ★★★★ Forthcoming grass & fig aromas, passionfruit flavours on zesty **12**; interesting pithy texture & length; finishes somewhat lean. **Special Noble Late Harvest** ★★★★ Lusciously botrytised chenin from Durbanville. **09** preview shows apricot, almond & marzipan complexity; orange rind & zippy acidity to lift sweetness.

Winemakers Selection

Cabernet Sauvignon ★★★ Black fruit, wood spice & lipsmacking acidity do the job on **11**. Brush of oak & a few grams sugar for this export-only range; all WO W Cape. **Merlot** ★★★ **11** quite intense mulberry & plum notes, slightly green tannin, finishes dry despite the few grains of sugar. **Shiraz** ★★★★ Faint pepper & lily whiffs on **11**, still booting up mid-2012; supple tannins, silky texture bode well for when it comes online. **Chardonnay** ★★★ **12** (tank sample) won't disappoint fans: spice & vanilla aromas, bright lemon palate, slight sweetness make an appealing glassful.

Savanha Sun range

Merlot ☺ ★★★ **12** is plummy, friendly & well priced, equally good with food as without. **Chardonnay** ☺ ★★★ **12** preview has surprising lemon butter & floral intensity; limy freshness neutralises dab sugar.

Cabernet Sauvignon ★★ Lively **11** leafy & light-bodied summer red. **Shiraz** ★★ No real varietal character on businesslike **11**. **Pinotage-Shiraz** NEW ★★ **11** light-bodied everyday red with amenable tannins. **Pinotage Rosé** ★★★ Previewed **12** just-dry, savoury-tinged berry styling that welcomes food; chill & bring on the tapas. **Chenin Blanc** NEW ★★★ **12** tank sample still finding its feet, should perk up & reveal more of its sunny apricot character once bottled. **Sauvignon Blanc** ★★★ Tank sample **12** shows herbaceous aromas, passionfruit flavours & gentle pithy bite. Range was 'Savanha'. All WO W Cape.

Frieda's Vine NEW

Shiraz-Mourvèdre ★★★ Vanilla & berry-laden **10**, sweetish everyday red with enough grip for food. Fairtrade certified & for export, like next. **Chenin Blanc-Viognier** ★★★ Aromatic & balanced **12**, medium bodied, semi-dry but lively. Both WO W Cape. — CvZ

Saxenburg Wine Farm

Location: Kuils River ▪ Map/WO: Stellenbosch ▪ Est 1693 ▪ 1stB 1990 ▪ Tasting & sales Mon-Fri 9-5 Sat/Sun 10-5 ▪ Fee R20 ▪ Closed Good Fri, Dec 25 & Jan 1 ▪ Cheese platters ▪ Gifts ▪ BYO picnic ▪ Conservation area ▪ Game park ▪ The Guinea Fowl Restaurant T +27 (0)21-906-5232 ▪ Saxenburg guest cottages (see Accommodation section) ▪ Owner(s) Adrian & Birgit Bührer ▪ Cellarmaster(s) Nico van der Merwe (Nov 1990) ▪ Winemaker(s) Nico van der Merwe (Nov 1990), with Edwin Grace (Jan 2005) ▪ Viticulturist(s) Donovan Diedericks (Apr 2008) ▪ 195ha/85ha (cabs s/f, malbec, merlot, ptage, shiraz, chard, chenin, sauv, viog) ▪ 650t/50,000cs own label 78% red 20% white 2% rosé ▪ Other export brands: Bosman's Hill, Gwendolyn ▪ PO Box 171 Kuils River 7580 ▪ info@saxenburg.co.za ▪ www.saxenburg.co.za ▪ S 33° 56' 47.9" E 018° 43' 9.4" ▪ **T +27 (0)21-903-6113**

Given the downturn-induced focus on cost cutting, budget pricing and down trading in the wine industry, here's a fascinating insight into the longer-term role and importance of quality-orientated producers, specifically in Stellenbosch, by Nico van der Merwe, awarded cellarmaster at this Swiss-family-owned Polkadraai Hills winery for over two decades: 'Because of enforced mass production due to market pressure, most vineyards will reach production fatigue in the next 5-10 years. This will result in our stagnation in the lower end of the market, and higher production costs driving up the prices again. With this scenario, South Africa will no longer be competitive in the international market. By contrast, producers aiming for quality, who continually renew their vineyards, will be able to maintain their prices as quality grapes will be scarce.'

Saxenburg Limited Release

★★★★★ **Shiraz Select** Stunning depth & complexity of **09** (★★★★★) excites. Beautifully judged weight & structure underscore rich, complex fruit in a dry, concentrated package. Seamless, complete & integrated now, but shows great ageing potential. A class act. Just a shade off magnificent **07**. No **08**.

Private Collection

★★★★☆ **Cabernet Sauvignon 09** maintains superior standard of range. Supple, plush & stately, showing fine craftsmanship. Precision & remarkable balance, black fruit with herbal flecks, in classic Bordeaux style. Excellent expression of a superior vintage.

★★★★☆ **Merlot ✓ 09** Plush spicy complexity on **09** offers layers of succulent black fruit, dark chocolate with real backbone, & expansive & long finish. Good balance of depth, freshness & varietal expression.

★★★★☆ **Shiraz ✓** Bright, vibrant & smooth **09** maintains the pattern. Bold & concentrated wild berry fruit & charming floral scents, wild scrub & peppery spices. Finely crafted & complex, with thickly textured tannins, promises years of development in bottle.

★★★★☆ **Chardonnay ✓** Opulent heavyweight **11**, yet noble & elegant. Offers many intense layers of buttery citrus, crushed stone, vanilla & flowers; bold judicious oaking (10 months French, only 10% new). A keeper.

★★★★ **Sauvignon Blanc ✓** ▤ **12** only just misses the complexity of standout **11** (★★★★★). Concentrated grapefruit & lime flavours, clean & brisk with a good finishing thrust. Just off-dry.

★★★★ **Méthode Cap Classique** NEW Green-tinged **NV** sparkling from chardonnay tastes extra-dry, vibrant & youthful with creamy fine mousse. The intense pure flavours of lemon curd & pie crust are unflagging.

Pinotage ★★★ **09** a tad off previous. Full-bodied, loads of fruit, but finishes a bit short. For early drinking. **Le Phantom Brut Cap Classique** ⚘ ★★★★ Mainly chardonnay, **NV** (**08**) sparkler was focused, lean & refreshing when tasted.

Guinea Fowl range

White ☺ ▤ ★★★ Ripe fruit appeal on unwooded **12** chenin/viognier blend. Tank sample is juicy & bouncy with loads of flavour. Will please the many fans.

Red ✓ ▤ ★★★★ 2nd-tier merlot, cab & shiraz blend, **10** is juicy & fruity with oaky vanilla to add to weight & body. Delicious anytime wine! **Rosé** ⚘ ▤ ★★★ Sweetly spicy, **11** with tart strawberry fruit, tiny hint of sugar.

Concept range

Grand Vin Rouge ☺ ▤ ★★★ **NV** Bordeaux-style red ticks all easy-drinking boxes — effortless & fruity. **Grand Vin Blanc** ☺ ▤ ★★★ Fun entry-level **NV** from sauvignon & chenin, bursts with ripe fruit & a balancing acidity. Delicious! — WB

Scali
🍷 🏠

Location: Paarl ▪ Map: Paarl & Wellington ▪ WO: Voor Paardeberg ▪ Est/1stB 1999 ▪ Tasting, sales & cellar tours Mon-Sat by appt ▪ Closed all pub hols ▪ B&B ▪ Owner(s) Willie & Tania de Waal ▪ Cellarmaster(s)/winemaker(s) Willie & Tania de Waal (Aug 1999) ▪ Viticulturist(s) Willie de Waal (Feb 1991) ▪ 270ha/70ha (cab, merlot, ptage, shiraz, chard, chenin, rouss, sauv, viog) ▪ 30t/2,000cs own label 67% red 33% white ▪ CERES Cert (vyds certified organic) ▪ PO Box 7143 Paarl 7620 ▪ info@scali.co.za ▪ www.scali.co.za ▪ S 33° 36 70.6 ″ E 018° 51′49.5 ″ ▪ **T +27 (0)21-869-8340** ▪ F +27 (0)21-869-8383

The De Waals of Scali aspire to make authentic wine more than most and towards that end were recently certified organic. 'Excessive use of chemicals makes it very difficult for a wine to express its sense of belonging to a certain place,' says vigneron Willie. They also recently made their first méthode ancestrale sparkling wine from chenin blanc (a single fermentation completed in bottle rather than the two for cap classique). Only 500 bottles were made, so sadly not tasted by us.

★★★★ **Pinotage** ⚘ Engaging **08** shows red cherry, some earthiness; good fruit concentration, fresh acidity & densely packed tannins; year French oak, 20% new, an unobtrusive scaffolding.

★★★★ **Syrah** ⓘ Noble **08** (★★★★★) has real sense of place; only 20% new oak (2 years French) attuned to De Waals' goal of fruit (not wood) expression, as was slightly higher 30% for **07**.

★★★★★ **Blanc** ⓘ Super-dry **09** 50% chenin, 20% chardonnay with roussanne, sauvignon, viognier; year older oak. Intellectually demanding, hugely complex with great breadth, depth of flavour, intensity. — CE

■ **Scarlett Organic** *see* Seven Sisters
■ **Schalk Burger & Sons** *see* Welbedacht Wine Estate

Schalkenbosch Wines

Location/map: Tulbagh ▪ WO: Tulbagh/Western Cape ▪ Est 1792 ▪ 1stB 2002 ▪ Tasting, sales & tours by appt ▪ Closed all pub hols ▪ Tour groups ▪ Walking/hiking & mountain biking trails ▪ Conservation area ▪ Self-catering cottages ▪ Owner(s) Platinum Mile Investments ▪ Cellarmaster(s)/winemaker(s) Gielie Beukes (Jun 2010) ▪ Viticulturist(s) Johan Wiese & Andrew Teubes ▪ 1,800ha/37ha (cab, shiraz) ▪ 140t/10,000cs own label 80% red 18% white 2% rosé ▪ BWI champion ▪ PO Box 95 Tulbagh 6820 ▪ info@schalkenbosch.co.za ▪ www.schalkenbosch.co.za ▪ S 33° 18'49.7" E 019° 11'59.9" ▪ **T +27 (0)23-230-0654/1488** ▪ F +27 (0)86-519-2605/+27 (0)86-654-8209

A cool 2012 growing season and slow ripening at this Tulbagh estate resulted in some of the most promising wines to date, according to winemaker Gielie Beukes. A new Bordeaux-style blend, Cumulus, joined Stratus as a flagship under the hand-crafted Schalkenbosch label as the guide went to press. Sustainability remains a top priority for this Biodiversity & Wine Initiative Champion property.

Schalkenbosch range

★★★★ **Stratus** ⓘ Elegant flagship a characterful shiraz blend. Silky **07** offers intense, complex berry fruit; underlines estate's affinity with Rhône style. WO W Cape.

Cuvée Brut Cap Classique ⓘ ★★★★ Limited-release traditional-method sparkling (pinot noir & chardonnay). **07** resolutely dry, austere & refreshing.

Edenhof range

Cabernet Sauvignon ⓘ ★★★★ Carefully crafted, great value, as for rest of this range. From classic vintage, **09** dry, lithe & elegant. **Pinotage** ⓘ ★★★ Generous body & plummy fruit on tad rustic **09**. **Shiraz** ⓘ ★★★ Middleweight **09** offers dry, dark, fruity core with hints of spiciness. **Cabernet Sauvignon-Merlot** ⓘ ★★★ Ripe, softly fruity **09** over-delivers. **Bin 409** ⓘ ★★★★ A worthy understudy to Stratus, **09** shows similar fruit & structure. Charming, affordable everyday quaffing. **Chardonnay** 🍴 🥂 ★★★ **12** unwooded, as previous, creamy, & a shade more attractive. **Sauvignon Blanc** 🍴 🥂 ★★★ **12** achieves a good balance between ripe tropical fruit flavour & zesty acidity. **Viognier** 🍴 🥂 ★★ Gently perfumed **12**, shade off the mark, acerbic bite a slight detraction. **Blanc de Blanc** ⓘ 🍴 🥂 ★★ Previewed **11** less fruity than previous, tartly acidic. Discontinued: **Glen Rosa**.

Isis range

Dry Red ⓘ 🍴 🥂 ★★★ Entry-level pocket pleaser, previewed **10** a bit gawky, mid-2011 needed time to settle. **Rosé** 🍴 🥂 ★★★★ Savoury, leafy & dry **12** quite stylish, bright with tight structure, good length & juice. **Dry White** ⓘ 🍴 🥂 ★★ Pungent & fruity tank sample **11**, pleasant quaffer. 1L bottle, as for Red. — WB/AL

■ **Scholtzenhof** *see* Ken Forrester Wines
■ **Schoone Gevel** *see* La Motte
■ **Schultz Family** *see* Rudi Schultz Wines

Scrucap Wines

NEW

WO: Elgin/Western Cape/Stellenbosch/Swartland/Coastal/Durbanville ▪ Est 2011 ▪ Closed to public ▪ Cellarmaster(s) Andries Burger (Paul Cluver Estate Wines), Chris & Andrea Mullineux (Mullineux Family Wines), JD Pretorius (Steenberg Vineyards), Charles Hopkins (De Grendel Wines) & Edouard Labeye (Winery of Good Hope) ▪ 10,000cs own label 40% red 40% white 10% rosé 10% MCC ▪ ksconsult@mweb.co.za ▪ www.luxislandresorts.com ▪ **T +27 (0)83-484-8781**

Guests of LUX* Resorts on Indian Ocean islands Mauritius, Réunion and the Maldives are being invited to 'say farewell to corks and Old World wines and say hi to Scrucap, a collection of exclusive South African wines specially selected' for the hotel group. Consultant Kent Scheermeyer says the aim is to offer 'fresh, sexy' wines that combine quality and value — a goal that should be met, considering the elite Cape wine sources: Paul Cluver, De Grendel, Steenberg, Winery of Good Hope and Mullineux Family.

★★★★ **Swartland Blend** 🍷 **10** vintage of Mullineux Family Wines' Kloof Street shiraz-based rouge 'hijacked' for export. Stylish, with character, focus & length.

★★★★☆ **Sauvignon Blanc** 🍷 Edgy **11** is somewhat unusual but utterly compelling. Along with typical herbal note, there's also bruised apple, tropical fruit. Rich & ripe, balanced by snappy acidity. Made by De Grendel's Charles Hopkins. 70% Witzenberg grapes, rest Darling.

★★★★ **Popcap** 🥂 Deliciously fine, harmonious **10** MCC sparkling by Steenberg from Robertson chardonnay, offers plenty of flavour & dimension from more than year on lees & addition of reserve wine.

Pinot Noir 🍷 ★★★ Red fruit, typical varietal perfume on lighter-bodied, pretty **10**. Moderate acidity, soft tannins make it readily accessible. By De Grendel. **Shiraz** 🍷 ★★★ **10** polished peppery spice in lightly styled Paul Cluver bottling. **Stellenbosch Blend** ✓ 🍷 🥂 ★★★☆ Clever balance in **11** between respectable restraint & a burly friendliness & generosity. Cab/merlot blend ready for early but untrivial drinking. By the Winery of Good Hope. **3 Valleys Blend** 🍷 🥂 ★★★★ Name refers to Constantia, Robertson & Darling valleys, each adding their stamp to savoury, fresh & accessible cab-led **10** blend, with merlot & cab franc. By Steenberg. **Rosé** 🍷 ★★★ Red fruit, some tannic grip on coral pink **11** from mainly pinotage, dash cab, by De Grendel. **Chardonnay** 🍷 ★★★ Light, clean citrus profile geared up by partial oaking & lees-ageing in tasty **11** by Paul Cluver. **Chenin Blanc** ✓ 🍷 ★★★★ Bursting with aromas & flavour (everything from melon to peach); **11** balanced, fresh & entirely delightful. Notably good value. By The Winery of Good Hope. **Sauvignon Blanc** 🍷 ★★★★ Neither tart nor tropical **11**, elegant, greenpepper features plumped by 6% wooded semillon. Ex Paul Cluver. — GdB/CE/IM/TJ/DS

Seal Breeze Wines

Location: Lutzville ▪ Map: Olifants River ▪ WO: Lutzville Valley ▪ Est 2004 ▪ 1stB 2005 ▪ Tasting, sales & cellar tours Mon-Fri 9-4 Sat 9-12 ▪ Closed Easter Fri-Mon, Ascension Day, Dec 25 & Jan 1 ▪ Meals/refreshments by prior arrangement ▪ Facilities for children ▪ Tour groups ▪ BYO picnic ▪ Owner(s) John & Joan Wiggins ▪ Cellarmaster(s) Joan Wiggins (Feb 2004) ▪ Winemaker(s) Joan Wiggins (Feb 2004), with Toy Brand (Feb 2006) ▪ Viticulturist(s) Joan Wiggins ▪ ±92ha/±70ha (cab, merlot, shiraz, chenin, cbard, hanepoot, sauv) ▪ 1,200t/780cs own label ▪ PO Box 33 Lutzville 8165 ▪ jwiggins@kingsley.co.za ▪ www.sealbreezewine.co.za ▪ S 31° 34' 50.1" E 018° 19' 9.8" ▪ **T +27 (0)84-505-1991** ▪ F +27 (0)27-217-1458

Joan Wiggins, whose winery is the most north-westerly in South Africa, annually produces only 2,000 bottles of each variety for her own label. Of these, 50 are magnums, each containing a diamond. Last year, a delighted buyer reported that the bottle she'd bought contained a sparkler worth 26 times what she'd paid!

Cabernet Sauvignon 🕐 🥂 **10** too young & unknit to rate. **09** (★★★★) went up a notch mid-2010; had generous but balanced alcohol, fine tannin structure. **Merlot** 🕐 🥂 ★★★ Charry oak seasoning to prune & date aromas, pre-bottling **10** lovely if unconcentrated milk chocolate flavours, warm afterglow. **Shiraz** 🕐 ★★★ Appealing meaty aroma & dusty overlay, **10** tannins still quite gruff when last tasted, may since have softened. **Sauvignon Blanc** 🕐 ★★★ **11** ripe lemon & passionfruit, engaging if unlingering fruity mouthful. Very youthful (we noted last edition), could score higher given time, as for all these. — DB/MW

◼ **Season's Collection** *see* Orange River Wine Cellars
◼ **Secateurs** *see* AA Badenhorst Family Wines
◼ **Secret Cellar** *see* Ultra Liquors

Sedgwick's Old Brown

Venerable Distell brand, blend of jerepiko and dry sherry, in 750ml, 1L and 2L.

Sedgwick's Old Brown 😊 🍷 ★★★ Fortified winter warmer since 1916. Latest **NV** a step up, lovely gold-edged brown hue, liquid raisins, very ripe & sweet, delicious. — DB/HJ

◼ **Selma** *see* Malanot Wines
◼ **Semara** *see* Wine-of-the-Month Club

Sequillo Cellars

Location: Malmesbury ▪ Map/WO: Swartland ▪ Est/1stB 2003 ▪ Tasting & sales Mon-Fri by appt ▪ Closed all pub hols ▪ Owner(s) Eben Sadie Trust & Cornel Spies Trust ▪ Cellarmaster(s)/winemaker(s) Eben Sadie (Jan 2003) ▪ 20ha (carignan, grenache, mourv, syrah, chenin, clairette, rouss, viog) ▪ 45t/3,000cs own label 50% red 50% white ▪ PO Box 1019 Malmesbury 7299 ▪ info@sequillo.com ▪ www.sequillo.com ▪ S 33° 31'31.0" E 018° 48'18.1" ▪ **T +27 (0)76-151-7131** ▪ F +27 (0)86-692-2852

Eben Sadie (Sadie Family Wines) and Australia-based wine partner Cornel Spies started this range to honestly reflect the Swartland's terroir or, as Sadie puts it, 'truth in a bottle will always do better than a story with lots of cosmetics'. Therein lies part of the approach: the grapes are hand picked and naturally fermented; there's no fining, filtration, new wood nor additives, and the varieties are Rhône/Mediterranean because they're considered the most terroir-compatible. The line-drawing label designs change each year and even the white's and red's differ. At first glance there's a tranquil vineyard, but on the curve is a broken machine, overgrown by vines. This year's message: mechanisation is bad. And Nature triumphs.

★★★★☆ **Sequillo Red** A blend of 5 Rhône varieties. Reflecting the intense wildberry fruit of an excellent vintage, **10**'s approachable, cigarbox perfumed tannins offer immediate enjoyment but this is a wine designed to age, unfold, reveal more complexity over time.

★★★★☆ **Sequillo White** A 7-part blend, selected to showcase the area. There's beeswax & melon but **11** is difficult to pin down, too complex. Best just to enjoy the experience as it opens up in the glass, offers lovely textured freshness, mouthfilling & complete. — CR

■ **Sereia** *see* Anatu Wines

Ses'Fikile

Location: Wellington ▪ Est 2004 ▪ 1stB 2006 ▪ Closed to public ▪ Owner(s) Ses'Fikile Wine Services ▪ Winemaker(s) Hugo Truter (Wellington Wines) ▪ 5,500cs own label 70% red 30% white ▪ PO Box 38055 Pinelands 7430 ▪ sesfikile@gmail.com

Now solo, brand owner and ex-teacher Nondumiso Pikashe has teamed up with Wellington Wines to continue production of her good-value wines. (Ses'Fikile translates as 'we have arrived, in style'.) Exports continue, but local markets occupy most of her time, notably the Cape townships which offer 'huge potential'.

■ **7even** *see* Zevenwacht

Seven Oaks

Location: Worcester ▪ Map: Breedekloof ▪ WO: Breedekloof/Western Cape/Robertson ▪ Est 2003 ▪ 1stB 2004 ▪ Tasting by appt ▪ Owner(s) Patrick & Jacqui Pols ▪ Cellarmaster(s) Bennie Wannenburg (May 2010, Waboomsrivier) ▪ Winemaker(s) Bennie Wannenburg, with Wim Viljoen (both May 2010, Waboomsrivier) ▪ Viticulturist(s) Pierre Snyman (2003, consultant) ▪ 62ha/42ha (cinsaut, ptage, ruby cab, shiraz, chard, chenin, cbard, sauv) ▪ 345t/2,000cs own label 50% red 45% white 5% rosé ▪ Customer brand: Villa Verde ▪ PO Box 11 Breerivier 6858 ▪ jacqui@sevenoaks.co.za ▪ www.sevenoaks.co.za ▪ S 33° 31' 48.59" E 019° 13' 40.46" ▪ **T +27 (0)83-639-0405** ▪ F +27 (0)86-617-8102

A second appearance at the Nederburg Auction in 2012, two years on from its debut at the prestigious event, saw the last 60 bottles of 2005 6+1 Cabernet Sauvignon-Shiraz, the private stock of owners Patrick and Jacqui Pols, raided. All in a good cause, the Breedekloof winefarmers agreed.

Padre Rednose Merlot-Cabernet-Sauvignon ⊕ ❀ ★★★ Blueberry & caramel toffee galore, **06** soft & approachable, with warm feel. Robertson WO. **Cabernet Sauvignon-Shiraz** 🍴 🍷 ★★★ Smoky **11** picks up where **09** left off. 65/35 blend mingles plum & spice with toned oaking. Long finish. **6+1 Cabernet Sauvignon-Shiraz** Await new vintage. **Pinotage Rosé** ⊕ 🍴 🍷 ★★★ **10** semi-sweet cherry, berry quaffer with light acid lift. WO W Cape. **Chenin Blanc** 🍴 🍷 ★★★ **12** returns to form. Easy, crisp & tangy poolside white. Melon & granadilla zip to end. **Sauvignon Blanc** 🍴 🍷 ★★★ Grapefruit tang & fig leaf on lightish **12**, not as flinty as previous. Discontinued: **Chenin Blanc Semi Sweet**. — FM

Seven Sisters

Location/map: Stellenbosch ▪ WO: Western Cape/Swartland ▪ Tasting & sales at Seven Sisters Farm, Welmoed Rd, Stellenbosch — phone ahead ▪ Owner(s) African Roots Wine ▪ Winemaker(s) Andries Blake ▪ PO Box 4560 Tygervalley 7536 ▪ vivian@africanrootswines.com ▪ www.sevensisters.co.za ▪ S 33° 59' 23.41" E 018° 46' 34.35" ▪ T +27 (0)71-049-4109/+27 (0)83-624-0391 ▪ F +27 (0)86-514-5569

The seven Brutus sisters from Paternoster, a West Coast holiday and fishing village, are ready to share their celebration of life. They are now open to the public in Stellenbosch, with wines named after each of them. They are also now exported to 42 states in America! Certainly worth celebrating.

Pinotage-Shiraz Dawn ☺ ⓥ ★★★ 55% pinotage on **11**, still shy, with attractive dark cherry & oak aromas. Lovely texture follows with dry perfumed tail. **Chenin Blanc Yolanda** ☺ 🍷 ⓥ ★★★ **12** upfront & tropical; pineapple/melon follows to soft palate, with white stonefruit & nice fruit sweetness.

Cabernet Sauvignon Carol 🍷 ⓥ ★★★ **11** very young herbal & cherry combo. Astringent end. **Merlot June** ⓥ ★★★ Earthy & shy **11**, a bit awkward still, for light quaffing. WO Swartland. **Bukettraube Odelia** 🍷 ⓥ ★★ **12** easy Natural Sweet curry partner. **Sauvignon Blanc Vivian** ✓ 🍷 ⓥ ★★★★ Forthcoming khaki bush, grassy, white pepper & spice. Light **12** has brisk acidity, grapefruit, passionfruit appeal. Ultra-dry. **Sweet Rosé Twena** ① 🍷 ★★★ Happy, vibrant & fruity **11** offers satisfying semi-sweet profile, with perfume & tasty end. Light rose in colour. — JP

Seven Springs Vineyards

Location: Hermanus ▪ WO: Overberg ▪ Est 2007 ▪ 1stB 2010 ▪ Closed to public ▪ Owner(s) Tim & Vaughan Pearson ▪ Winemaker(s) Riana van der Merwe (Nov 2009) ▪ Viticulturist(s) Peter Davison (Jul 2007, consultant) ▪ 12ha/±8ha (pinot, syrah, chard, sauv) ▪ ±56t/4,000cs own label 50% red 50% white ▪ Private Bag X15 Suite 162 Hermanus 7200 ▪ info@7springs.co.za ▪ www.7springs.co.za ▪ T +27 (0)82-487-7572; UK +44 1789740502 ▪ F +27 (0)86-571-0623

Harvest had a few red-letter days in 2012: pinot noir came in on Valentine's Day, while the chardonnay almost came a cropper en route to the cellar... UK co-owner and active social media user Tim Pearson reports that plantings continue to gain maturity and new markets were established in Europe and America.

Pinot Noir NEW 🍷 ⓥ ★★★★ Light but brooding intensity lurking on **11** from young vines. Typical bright fruit & commendable silky texture, classy oak sheen. **Syrah** 🍷 ⓥ ★★★★ Savoury olive tapenade appeal to light, chalky **10**, fresh in bottle. Fresh, with buoyant spice & earthy tail. **Oaked Chardonnay** 🍷 ⓥ ★★★★ **11** maintains track record of previous with rich orange brûlée appeal framed by stylish oak. Smooth finish. **Unoaked Chardonnay** 🍷 ⓥ ★★★ Vibrant light citrus typical of the variety on now-bottled **11**. Ripe but fresh, creamy lees fullness fleshing out the finish. **Sauvignon Blanc** 🍷 ★★★★ Rounded palate on gooseberry & pineapple richness of now-bottled, tropical-styled **11**. Good texture & richness. — FM

Seven Steps Wines

Location: Cape Town ▪ WO: Western Cape/Elgin ▪ Est/1stB 2009 ▪ Tasting by appt only ▪ Owner(s) Travis Braithwaite & Pragasen Ramiah ▪ Cellarmaster(s)/winemaker(s) Travis Braithwaite ▪ (shiraz, sauv) ▪ 800cs own label 30% red 70% white ▪ PO Box 981 Sea Point Cape Town 8060 ▪ info@sevenstepswines.com ▪ www.sevenstepswines.com ▪ T +27 (0)82-368-5270 ▪ F +27 (0)86-625-0109

This community-conscious brand, named for the last remaining concrete evidence of the old District Six in Cape Town, is looking at ways of investing in its revival. Other projects include sponsorship of local pro surfer Stacey Guy. With wines selling out, awaiting new vintages, there are plans for a few single-vineyard bottlings.

Syrah ① ★★★★ Last **08** rose geranium scent, meaty hint, charry oak smoothed by few grams sugar. WO W Cape. **Sauvignon Blanc** ① ★★★★ Passionfruit with leafy nuance, **10** tangy appetite appeal. WO Elgin. — CR

■ **Sgt Pepper** see Teddy Hall Wines

Shannon Vineyards

Location/WO: Elgin ▪ Map: Elgin, Walker Bay & Bot River ▪ Est 2000 ▪ 1stB 2003 ▪ Tasting, sales & vineyard tour first weekend of each month, or by appt ▪ Owner(s) Stuart & James Downes ▪ Winemaker(s) Gordon Newton Johnson & Nadia Newton Johnson ▪ Viticulturist(s) Kevin Watt (consultant) ▪ 75ha/15.5ha (merlot, pinot, sauv, sem, viog) ▪ 100t/3,000cs own label 66% red 34% white ▪ BWI, Global GAP, IPW, Tesco's Natures Choice ▪ PO Box 20 Elgin 7180 ▪ james@shannonwines.com ▪ www.shannonwines.com ▪ S 34° 11'3.9" E 018° 59'3. 6" ▪ **T +27 (0)21-859-2491** ▪ F +27 (0)21-859-5389

'It's not always what you know, but who you know,' laughs James Downes, part-owner of this rising Elgin star. Viticulturist Rosa Kruger helped with the Mount Bullet merlot vineyard, which they were about to pull out after long struggle. Three years later, the 2008 was hugely acclaimed! They now enjoy the more permanent viticultural support of Kevin Watt. But the meticulous attention of Downes himself and his team ensures there's not a tendril out of place in the 15ha of vines. Visitors can see for themselves, now that the farm is open to the public once a month, with vineyard tours as well as tastings and sales on offer.

★★★★☆ **Mount Bullet** 🏅 Among South Africa's most highly regarded merlots. **10** lacks immediate appeal of previous vintages in its sterner build, noticeable acidity. Patience should reveal underlying suavely textured ripe fruit, framed by classic dry finish.

★★★★☆ **Rockview Ridge Pinot Noir** 🏅 Difficult year, **10** has bigger profile than earlier vintages, but agreeably fresh, supple — & less oaky. **11** best to date: delicate yet convincing, with haunting black/red fruit perfume, complexity supported by enlivening minerality & subtly important tannin frame.

★★★★☆ **Sanctuary Peak Sauvignon Blanc** 🍾 🏅 **11** cool, sleek with evident oaked semillon portion adding breadth but still maintains great energy. Clean, sweet-fruited (& with a few grams sugar) conclusion.
Macushla Pinot Noir Noble Late Harvest Await next. — AL

■ **Shepherd's Cottage** *see* Overgaauw Wine Estate

Ship Sherry

Another piece of Distell-owned South African wine patrimony, launched in 1929.
Ship Sherry 🍾 ★★ Misnamed **NV** actually sweet, spirity (17%) jerepiko-style fireside comforter. — DB/HJ

Shoprite Checkers

Enquiries: Stephanus Eksteen ▪ 80,000cs own label 50% red 40% white 10% rosé ▪ PO Box 215 Brackenfell 7561 ▪ sekseen@shoprite.co.za ▪ www.shoprite.co.za ▪ **T +27 (0)21-980-4000** ▪ F +27 (0)21-980-4421

This national supermarket chain's in-house Oddbins brand is now the second largest seller in the group after a big-name private label, 'which of course shall remain anonymous here', quips wine buyer Stephanus Eksteen. Oddbins is a constantly replenished cornucopia of value-for-money all-sorts and its ongoing success reflects consumers' taste for pocket pleasers of reliable source.

■ **Short Story** *see* Neethlingshof Estate
■ **Shortwood** *see* Imbuko Wines
■ **Signal Cannon** *see* Vondeling

Signal Gun Wines

Location/WO: Durbanville ▪ Map: Durbanville, Philadelphia & Darling ▪ Est/1stB 2006 ▪ Tasting & sales Mon-Thu by appt Fri-Sat 10-5 Sun 10-4 ▪ Fee R15 ▪ Closed Good Fri, Dec 25 & Jan 1 ▪ Ke-Monate Wine Bar & Bistro (see Restaurants section) ▪ Conferences ▪ Conservation area ▪ Owner(s) WRM de Wit ▪ Cellarmaster(s)/winemaker(s) MJ de Wit (Jan 2006) ▪ Viticulturist(s) MJ de Wit (Jan 2001) ▪ 210ha/100ha (cab, merlot, ptage, shiraz, chard, sauv) ▪ 12t/ 400cs own label 50% red 50% white ▪ PO Box 2359 Durbanville 7551 ▪ info@signalgun.co.za ▪ www.signalgun. co.za ▪ S 33° 49'13.26" E 018° 36'40.32" ▪ **T +27 (0)21-976-7343** ▪ F +27 (0)86-611-8747

The range of wines — launched in 2006 by MJ de Wit as a mere 'hobby' with grapes off the old Hooggelegen family farm in Durbanville — soon developed into 'project Ke-Monate'. Its Sotho name appropriately meaning 'that's nice!', the project includes tasting room and restaurant. And it looks like more wines are on the way.

★★★★ **Shiraz 09** (★★★★) in restrained mode, as was **07** (**08** not sampled by us). Herbal & savoury. Nicely silky, sensitively oaked & all in balance. Moderate alcohol, but a shade lean & ungenerous.

Chardonnay NEW 🍷 ★★★★ Pale yet flavourful **12** with tropicality commoner in sauvignon but also variety's citrus. Very light oaking; bone-dry; chalky texture. **Sauvignon Blanc** 🍷 ★★★★ Flavourful but not too fruity **12**, not intense, but crisply balanced & with a streak of stony elegance. — TJ

Signal Hill Wines

Location: Cape Town ▪ Map: Cape Peninsula ▪ WO: Stellenbosch/Coastal/Piekenierskloof/Constantia ▪ 1stB 1997 ▪ Tasting, sales & cellar tours Mon-Fri 11-6 Sat 12-4 in season ▪ Closed all pub hols ▪ Cheese platters, sushi, sirloin & tapas during open hours ▪ Owner(s) Signal Hill Wines cc ▪ Cellarmaster(s)/winemaker(s)/viticulturist(s) Laurence Buthelezi ▪ 4ha (cab f, mourv, pinot, shiraz) ▪ 75% red 20% white 5% rosé ▪ Heritage Square, 100 Shortmarket Street, Cape Town 8001 ▪ info@winery.co.za ▪ www.winery.co.za ▪ S 33° 55′ 15.06″ E 018° 25′ 5.54″ ▪ **T** +27 (0)21-424-5820 ▪ F +27 (0)21-422-5238

Signal Hill's Jean-Vincent Ridon is a tireless experimenter and explorer of wine styles. He has coaxed 20 bottles of wine from the 'oldest known fruit-bearing vine in the southern hemisphere', namely a chenin planted here in 1711 — and cuttings have gone back to France, from where this clone had disappeared. His latest offering is a masterly take on Pineau des Charentes. Ridon does this in the Heritage Square winery in Cape Town's city centre, where he and winery partner Laurence Buthelezi stock 'the best wines in the world' for tasting and sale. They are in the process of trimming the extensive Signal Hill range so that all offerings are grown and vinified within the city limits.

Single Barrel range NEW

★★★★ **Pinot Noir 10** lighter-footed style than **08** standard bottling, also from Stellenbosch fruit, with more appetising acidity & cranberry flavours imparting an elegant cool-climate feel.

★★★★ **1771 Heritage Vine** One 240 year-old chenin vine in city centre (a 'national monument') bore 20 bottles of this intriguing **11** curiosity: full of flavour, with a sweet impression despite low alcohol & sugar.

★★★★☆ **Pineau de Ludovic** Contemplative **NV** aperitif in Pineau des Charentes style; chenin-colombard blend spent a decade in (a single) barrel. 200g/l sugar & 16% alcohol fit snugly into astonishingly complex & delicious fortified wine — reminiscent of oloroso sherry more than modern Pineau. Stellenbosch/Paarl fruit.

Signal Hill range

★★★★ **Petit Verdot** ⓘ Sharp **04** (★★★★) needed food to show best. **03** more seductive.

★★★★☆ **Clos d'Oranje** Evocatively perfumed, individual **07** is bold but quite beautifully fresh, from tiny, apparently vineyard-shy shiraz vineyard in central Cape Town. **06** (★★★★★) more finely structured.

★★★★ **Grenache Blanc** ⓘ Scintillating **08**; subtle scents; silky, & savoury mineral core. Used oak. Piekenierskloof grapes.

★★★★ **MCC Pinot Noir** ⓘ **06** disgorged on demand at winery. Quiet mousse, but lovely mature aromas. Shows benefit of long time on lees, dryness of no dosage. No sulphur added.

★★★★☆ **Empereur Rouge** ⓘ Delicious, ultra-sweet, warm & raisiny **06** from cab.

★★★★ **Crème de Tête Muscat d'Alexandrie NLH** ⓘ Last tasted was hedonistic **03**.

★★★★★ **Eszencia** ⓘ Magnificent **NV** (**02**), probably a one-off, sweet & rich, electrified by nervy acidity.

★★★★ **Mathilde Aszú 6 Puttonyos** ⓘ Last **02** Tokaji lookalike from botrytised furmint & sauvignon.

★★★★ **Vin de l'Empereur** ⓘ Vivid **05** last-tasted botrytised dessert from muscat d'Alexandrie.

★★★★☆ **Vin de l'Empereur Solera** NEW Unctuous, golden **NV** from 8 year-old solera of Constantia muscat d'Alexandrie. Layered complexity with no shortage of concentration; sweetness (115g/l) balanced by perfectly integrated acidity to finish dry, long & gracefully. Quite delicious!

Olympia Cabernet Franc ⓘ ★★★ Attractive aromas on mature-looking **08**. Light-centred, with just a little fruit concentration & a rather uneasy structure. **Grenache Noir** In abeyance, as for **Malbec**, **Rosé de Saignée** & **The Threesome**. **Camps Bay Vineyard** Await next. **Pinot Noir** ★★★★ Fragrant, enticing **08** made in traditional earthy style with sure-footed presence & at same time a silky complex lightness from Stellenbosch fruit, a step-up from **07** (★★★★). **Syrah** ⓘ ★★★★ Fresh & fleshy **06**. **Straw Wine** ⓘ ★★★★ None since **01**.

Buthelezi range

Tutuka Syrah Occasional release. — IM

■ **Signatures of Doolhof** *see* Doolhof Wine Estate

Sijnn

Location: Stellenbosch/Malgas • WO: Malgas • Est 2003 • 1stB 2007 • Tasting & sales at De Trafford Wines Fri & Sat 10-1 • Closed all pub hols • Owner(s) David & Rita Trafford, Simon Farr, Quentin Hurt • Winemaker(s) David Trafford, with Waldo van Zyl (May 2011) • Viticulturist(s) Schalk du Toit (2002, consultant) • 125ha/16ha (cab, mourv, shiraz, touriga nacional, trincadeira, chenin, rouss, viog) • 36t/1,900cs own label 83% red 10% white 7% rosé • PO Box 495 Stellenbosch 7599 • info@sijnn.co.za • www.sijnn.co.za • **T +27 (0)21-880-1611** • F +27 (0)21-880-1611

Nothing that co-owner and winemaker David Trafford does is without careful thought, as befits his architectural training. Sijnn (rhymes with 'sane') might look like an almost hobbyist project because of his holiday home there, but planting warm varieties in a cool climate like Malgas, which he has, makes sense when one considers inevitable global warming. Establishing an independent cellar is on the cards (wines are currently made at De Trafford in Stellenbosch), when the economic conditions are right, all part of the 'search for excellence outside the traditional areas' because he believes in future 'that's where real interest lies'.

★★★★ **Sijnn** All-sorts blend with shiraz, touriga playing important roles, **10** is individualistic. Scrub & coffee, wild berries, it's hard to pin down but very easy to enjoy. The savoury oak grip makes it the ideal food wine.

★★★★ **White** Improving on **10**, chenin upped to 73%, rest viognier in **11** (★★★★★), natural ferment in barrel, bottled unfiltered. Melon & quince, dry but tastes off-dry due to ripeness, fruit expression. Oak shows as crushed almonds, adds savoury richness.

Saignée ★★★★ Previously 'Rosé', which style it remains. Oaked blend of mourvèdre with shiraz, trincadeira, **11** has scrub, cherry piquancy, savoury dryness. — CR

Silkbush Mountain Vineyards

Location: Wolseley • WO: Breedekloof • Est 2000 • 1stB 2007 • Closed to public • Kingsbury Cottage — self-catering accommodation — www.silkbush.com/kingsbury • Owner(s) Silkbush Holdings LP • Winemaker(s) Bennie Wannenburg (2007, consultant) • Viticulturist(s) Anton Roos (2000) • 143ha/87ha (cabs s/f, malbec, merlot, mourv, p verdot, ptage, shiraz, sauv, sem, viog) • 1,200t/5,000cs own label 100% red • Other export brand: Lion's Drift • PO Box 91 Breërivier 6858 • anton@silkbush.net • www.silkbush.net • **T +27 (0)83-629-1735** • F +27 (0)86-520-3261

New to the guide but well-established and -reputed as a supplier of top-quality grapes to some of the Cape's majors, this California-owned spread below the towering Sybasberg (Silkbush Mountain) exports its own-brand wine to the US but has plans to enter the local arena and markets elsewhere in Africa as demand grows. Winemaker Bennie Wannenburg tries 'to catch the spirit and uniqueness of Silkbush' in the wines, and says 'we are big enough to supply greater volumes of specific products, yet specialised enough to deliver what markets expect'. Also on the scenic property is the luxury self-catering Kingsbury Cottage.

Pinotage ▦ ★★★ Aromatic **09** preview mixes sweet strawberry fruit & vanilla from new US & French oak in a satisfying, lengthy body; refreshing tingly acidity perfect for food partnering. **Shiraz** ▦ ★★★ Barrel sample **10** is ripe & generous, with sweet stewed fruit, firm acidity & tannin, gutsy 15% alcohol. — FM/GdB

■   **Silverhurst** see High Constantia Wine Cellar

Silvermist Vineyards

Location: Constantia • WO: Constantia/Coastal • Est 1984 • 1stB 2010 • Closed to public • Silvermist Mountain Lodge, offering accommodation, conferences & weddings • Conservation area • Owner(s) Constantia Ridge Estates (Pty) Ltd • Cellarmaster(s)/winemaker(s)/viticulturist(s) Gregory Brink Louw (Jan 2005) • 22ha/3ha (cab, shiraz, sauv) • 5.2t/290cs own label 30% red 70% white • Certified organic (BDOCA) • PO Box 608 Constantia 7848 • gm. silmist@mweb.co.za • www.silvermistvineyards.co.za • **T +27 (0)21-794-7601** • F +27 (0)21-794-7602

It's taken seven years to release the first wines, but winemaker Gregory Louw hasn't been idle at this guest house and conference centre high above Constantia. Most of his efforts have been bent towards clearing alien vegetation and planting new vineyards, all of which are farmed organically (they are the only farm in Constantia to be certified organic). Following in illustrious neighbours', Eagles' Nest's, footsteps, they have high hopes for their cool-climate shiraz.

★★★★ **Cabernet Sauvignon** A liqueur richness, blackcurrant, cedar — youthful **10** ticks all the cab boxes but needs time for new oak to integrate. Serious effort, with a savoury undertone bridling the fruit. WO Coastal.

Sauvignon Blanc ✿ ★★★★ Promising debut for **11**, blending a herbal touch with concentrated flavours of tinned pea & creamy white asparagus. Acidity is bright, & there's minerality in the extended conclusion. — JP/CvZ

■ **Silver Myn** *see Zorgvliet Wines*
■ **Silversands** *see Robertson Wide River Export Company*

Silverthorn Wines

Location/WO: Robertson ▪ Est 1998 ▪ 1stB 2004 ▪ Closed to public ▪ Owner(s) Silverthorn Wines (Pty) Ltd ▪ Cellarmaster(s)/winemaker(s)/viticulturist(s) John Loubser (1998) ▪ 10.5ha/4ha (cab, shiraz, chard) ▪ 50t/ 1,500cs own label 66% white 34% rosé ▪ IPW ▪ PO Box 381 Robertson 6705 ▪ john@silverthornwines.co.za ▪ www.silverthornwines.co.za ▪ **T +27 (0)21-712-7239** ▪ F +27 (0)21-712-7239

'Come quickly, I am drinking the stars!' said Dom Perignon reputedly. Inspiration here for the new bubbly from this small Robertson outfit owned by Karen and John Loubser (he of Steenberg fame). Hidden within the Southern Cross constellation is a cluster of vibrant stars nicknamed Jewel Box — 'a casket of variously coloured precious stones', said astronomer John Herschel, plotting the southern skies on a visit to Cape Town in the 1830s. Now brought down to earth, and bottled for us.

★★★★ **Genie Rosé Brut** ✪ MCC from shiraz; **NV** but 2010 (previously vintaged). Dry, pink & frivolous with inviting crisp, bright red fruits & a little spice, & a touch of attractive yeastiness on the finish.

★★★★ **The Green Man Blanc de Blancs** ✪ **09** (★★★★★) sparkling from chardonnay has typical linear feel. Aromas brioche, apple & yeast — all very elegantly displayed. Fresh & vibrant, with fine mousse & good length. **08** also in leesy style.

★★★★★ **Jewel Box** NEW A very smart debut. **09** chardonnay-driven sparkler with 20% pinot noir spent 36 months on its lees (6 more than Green Man), which gives fantastic aromas of fresh bread, ripe apple & white flowers. Rich & creamy, great texture; intense flavour. — JPf

■ **Simonay** *see Simonsvlei International*
■ **Simonsbosch** *see Koelenhof Winery*

Simonsig Landgoed

Location/map: Stellenbosch ▪ WO: Stellenbosch/Stellenbosch/Darling ▪ Est 1953 ▪ 1stB 1968 ▪ Tasting & sales Mon-Fri 8.30-5 Sat 8.30-4 Sun 11-3 ▪ Fee R25pp (incl glass) ▪ Closed Easter Fri/Sun, Dec 25 & Jan 1 ▪ Cellar tours daily at 11 & 3 (booking advised) ▪ Cuvée restaurant (see Restaurants section) ▪ Facilities for children ▪ Tour groups ▪ Gifts ▪ Farm produce ▪ Conferences ▪ 4x4 Landrover experience ▪ Labyrinth vineyard ▪ Owner(s) Pieter, Francois & Johan Malan ▪ Cellarmaster(s) Johan Malan (1981) ▪ Winemaker(s) Debbie Thompson (Nov 1999) & Hannes Meyer (Jul 2009), with Juan Carstens (Jan 2011) ▪ Viticulturist(s) Francois Malan (Jan 1981) & Tommie Corbett (Nov 2008), with Conrad Schutte (Vinpro) ▪ 300ha/210ha (cab, merlot, ptage, pinot, shiraz, chard, chenin, sauv) ▪ 2,720t/163,000cs own label 33% red 47% white 2% rosé 18% MCC & ±18,500cs for clients ▪ Brands for clients: Champany Inn, Malan Reeks, Rouana, The Warhorse, Wine of the Month Club, Woolworths ▪ HACCP 2009, BWI, SANAS ▪ PO Box 6 Koelenhof 7605 ▪ wine@simonsig.co.za ▪ www.simonsig. co.za ▪ S 33° 52'12.1" E 018° 49'31.7" ▪ **T +27 (0)21-888-4900** ▪ F +27 (0)21-888-4909

Large in scale and status, the Malan family's estate on Kromme Rhee Road near Koelenhof has been at the innovative forefront of the wine industry throughout the modern era. Frans Malan, visionary elder statesman of the Cape wine industry, who bought the farm in 1964, produced South Africa's first méthode champenoise bubbly over 40 years ago. A newly opened photo exhibit in their degorging cellar commemorates the event. Around the same time, Frans was teaming up with likeminded trail-blazers like Spatz Sperling (Delheim) and Niel Joubert (Spier) to create the Stellenbosch Wine Route. Frans' sons Francois, Johan and Pieter have run the estate since his retirement. Laurels this year include Kaapse Vonkel served to Commonwealth heads of state at the royal Jubilee banquet in London.

★★★★☆ **Redhill Pinotage** ✪ **09** (★★★★) lovely fruit flavour underpinning the all-new oak. Powerful, thickly textured & well-built with noticeable fruit sweetness. Less suave than **08**.

★★★★☆ **Merindol Syrah** 🅿 Dense, brooding fist in a velvet glove, muscular **10** (★★★★★) flagship surpasses 08's lofty standard. Complex layered fruit unfolds graciously, revealing sweet & peppery spices, wild scrub & black maraschino cherries. No **09**.

★★★★☆ **CWG Auction Reserve Heirloom Shiraz** NEW 🅿 Very special reserve bottling, **10** has impeccable structure, balance & length, with tight flavour core, years away from unfurling. Big, exuberant & muscular, with complex, finely detailed spiciness & vibrant black cherry fruit.

★★★★☆ **Tiara** Return to classical form for flagship Bordeaux-style 5-way blend after 08 (★★★★). Exceptional **09** vintage offers heady tobacco aromas with focused minerality, sombre black fruit with finely etched tannins, all neatly bound in spicy oak.

★★★★ **Frans Malan Cape Blend** Perennial Cape Blend standard bearer, **09** is pinotage-led (71%) with cab & a splash of merlot. Smoky oak spices up solid, reliable fruit profile.

★★★★ **Aurum Chardonnay** Prime vintage **09** (★★★★) swamped by potent oak, buttery/yeasty lees notes. Weighty, rich & ripe, may emerge in time, like last-tasted **07**.

★★★★ **Chenin Avec Chêne** 🅿 **10** belies difficult vintage with focus, elegance & healthy ripeness. Restrained oak emphasises creamy lees body without intruding on concentrated summer fruit core.

★★★★ **Kaapse Vonkel Brut Rosé** 🅿 Strawberry sherbet **11** features pinots noir & meunier with pinotage, in seductively dry, floral come-hither charmer. Uncomplicated but more refined & balanced than **09** (★★★★). **10** sold out untasted.

★★★★☆ **Cuvée Royale** Special occasion méthode cap classique sparkling from unwooded chardonnay, **07** is remarkably fresh & generously fruity but showing mineral breadth on palate. Classy, understated & precisely focused, with delightfully taut, salty finish.

★★★★ **Kaapse Vonkel Brut** 🅿 Respected pioneer champagne-method bubbly from pinot & chardonnay. More recent, richer style repeated in **10**, generous brioche aromas with lean, elegant baked apple fruit.

★★★★☆ **CWG Auction Reserve Cuvée Chêne Blanc de Blancs Méthode Cap Classique** NEW Chardonnay with 18 months in old oak produces rich, intensely nutty **07** sparkling. Long, broad & deep, yet elegantly focused, with creamy layers of brioche & baked apples on persistent mousse. Irresistible.

★★★★ **Vin de Liza** ⓣ 🅿 Noble Late Harvest from sauvignon & semillon. After simple **09** (★★★★), **10** satisfies with silky, gently unctuous charm.

★★★★ **Cape Vintage Reserve** First recorded since **94** (LBV), all-shiraz port-style **09** is liquid Christmas pudding, complete with brandy! Dense, spicy & rich, made for cold winter nights.

Cabernet Sauvignon-Shiraz ☺ 🍴 🅿 ★★★ Youthful, vibrantly fresh **11** delivers generous sweet-edged berry fruit on soft tannins. **Chenin Blanc** ☺ 🍴 🅿 ★★★ Charming expression of dry, unwooded Stellenbosch chenin (widely sourced) shows ripe tropical fruit salad on previewed **12**.

Labyrinth Cabernet Sauvignon ⓣ ★★★ Ripe, flavoursome barrel sample **08** rather more light-centred than previous. **Pinotage** ★★ Unoaked to emphasise berry fruit, **09** dominated by wild, funky aromas. **Mr Borio's Shiraz** 🅿 ★★★ Pleasantly plump **10** belies difficult vintage, showing healthy ripe fruit & firm tannins. Rather brief finish. **Adelberg Cabernet Sauvignon-Merlot** 🍴 🅿 ★★★ Was 'Adelberg'. Reliable, generously fruity **11** blend for everyday drinking. **The SMV** ⓣ 🍴 ★★★ Just a smidgen viognier with the shiraz & mourvèdre of **09**. Continues soft, off-dry, coffee-redolent style of previous. **Chardonnay** 🍴 🅿 ★★★ Robust body & elegant finish suggest toasty oak on **11** should give way to underlying ripe citrus fruit in time. **Gewürztraminer** 🍴 🅿 ★★★★ Distinctively fragrant **12** bolstered by dash of morio muscat. Elegantly sweet partner for spicy foods. **Sunbird Sauvignon Blanc** 🍴 🅿 ★★★★ **12** tank sample still unsettled but pleasantly full. Well-modulated acidity, ripe fruit & rounded body auger well. Some Darling grapes. **Adelberg Sauvignon Blanc** 🍴 🅿 ★★★ Was 'Adelblanc'. **12** quaffable but unassuming. Sweet edge, rather unintense. **Straw Wine** 🅿 ★★★★ Boldly aromatic **11** sun-dried muscat ottonel is rich, sweet & ripe, with honeyed raisin fruit & clean, tight finish. Discontinued: **Encore Vin Sec**. — GdB

Simonsvlei International

Location: Paarl ▪ Map: Paarl & Wellington ▪ WO: Western Cape/Coastal ▪ Est/1stB 1945 ▪ Tasting & sales Mon-Fri 8–5 Sat 8.30–4.30 Sun 11–3 ▪ Fee R20pp ▪ Cellar tours by prior arrangement ▪ Closed Dec 25 ▪ Eat@ Simonsvlei restaurant serving hot meals, snacks & refreshments ▪ BYO picnic ▪ Playground for children ▪ Gift shop ▪ Conference/function venue (80 pax) incl. equipment, break-away areas, lunches, etc. ▪ Conservation area ▪ Owner(s) 65 shareholders ▪ Winemaker(s) Ryan Puttick (Nov 2010), with Mari de Jager (Jan 2012) ▪ Viticulturist(s) Ryan Puttick (Nov 2010) & Francois van Zyl ▪ 1,158ha (shiraz, chenin) ▪ 7,400t ▪ 48.5% red 48.5% white 2% rosé 1% other ▪ Brands for clients: Kelvin Grove, Ocean Basket, Woolworths ▪ ISO 9001:2008, BWI, Fairtrade, HACCP, IPW, WIETA ▪ PO Box 584 Suider-Paarl 7624 ▪ info@simonsvlei.co.za ▪ www.simonsvlei.com ▪ S 33° 47' 24.9" E 018° 55' 49.1" ▪ **T +27 (0)21-863-3040** ▪ F +27 (0)21-863-1240

Constituted in the aftermath of World War II to grow quality wines on a larger and sustainable scale, Simonsvlei took its name from the father of the South African wine industry, Simon van der Stel, and this Paarl area's vlei (wetlands) landscape. Co-founder Sonny le Roux in 1945 expressed a vision of 'quality wines at affordable prices' and that's still the mantra today, as evidenced by the many good-value offerings. Innovation is another constant, witness the upcoming Vanilla Pod Chardonnay and traditional-method sparkling slotting into the line-up.

Hercules Paragon range

★★★★ **Méthode Cap Classique** NEW Super debut of **NV** champagne-method sparkling from chardonnay & pinot. Creamy lemon mousse in balance with apple & brioche notes through to a refreshing dry finish. **Cabernet Sauvignon** ⓕ ★★★★ Flagship of range, featuring occasional bottlings. **08**, first tasted since **05** (★★★★), elegant fruit profile & big oak vanilla which may since have settled & integrated. **Shiraz** ✓ ★★★★ Upfront mulberry & spice on full-bodied yet unheavy **08**, rich & smooth but shade off friendly, charming **05** (★★★★). **SMCV** Await new vintage. **Sauvignon Blanc** ✓ 🖩 ★★★★ Pungent upfront aromas, fresh **12** packed with juicy flavour of lemon, lime & gooseberry, lifted finish.

South Atlantic range

Shiraz ⓕ ★★★★ Range again not revisited this edition. Maiden **08** smoky mantle, with meaty pepper-spicy fruit. Coastal WO, as for all following. **Shiraz-Cabernet Sauvignon** ⓕ ★★★★ Stylish **08** solid fruit core & silky tannins, with dark berry, damson & sour cherry. **Chardonnay** ⓕ 🖩 ★★ Wooded **09** rather bland & spirity. **Sauvignon Blanc** ⓕ 🖩 ★★★ **10**, from Durbanville fruit, pear drop & apple flavours with grassy finish.

New Generation range

Ja-Mocha Pinotage ✓ ★★★★ Bright ripe red berry fruit with strong whiffs of espresso on **11**, smooth & rounded crowd pleaser. **Toffee Chunk Syrah** ✓ ★★★★ Name now identifies this as shiraz/syrah. Robust & bold **11** vanilla, plum & mulberry flavours. Spicy & well built, with chunky tannins & smoky oak finish.

Premier range

> **Cabernet Sauvignon** ☺ 🖩 ★★★ Succulent dark berries on **10**, big, soft, ripe tannins with a rounded balance & smooth ending. **Pinotage** ☺ 🖩 ★★★ Sweet ripe plum aromas, everyday **11** bursts with berry & spicy coffee flavours. Try with biltong. **Cabernet Sauvignon-Merlot** ☺ 🖩 ★★★ **09**, tasted out of vintage sequence, trumps previous with deliciously smooth, vibrant herb-dusted blackberry fruit, seamless tannins. **Bukettraube** ☺ 🖾 ★★★ Rare white grape in curvaceous bottle. Soft & fragrant floral aromas on light-textured off-dry **11**. **Chardonnay** ☺ 🖩 ★★★ Vibrant lemon cream flavours mingle with soft vanilla oak on harmonious & refreshing **11**. **Sauvignon Blanc** ☺ 🖩 ★★★ **12** offers greenpepper, grassy flavours, soft & fresh.

Shiraz ✓ 🖩 ★★★★ Super-spicy mulberry thrills on fresh & fruity **10**. Fynbos & white pepper add to savoury tail. You'll want to buy several cases of this. **Chenin Blanc** ✓ 🖩 ★★★★ Ripe tropical fruit & zingy pineapple & kiwi, **12** balanced by a mouthwatering fresh conclusion. Delicious! **Humbro Hanepoot** 🖩 ★★★ Ever-reliable **NV** fortified dessert offers plump raisin, muscat & spice. Very sweet, with a spirity farewell. Just add a campfire. **Humbro Red Jerepiko** 🖩 ★★★ Bold, full-sweet **NV** winter warmer vibrates with Christmas cake & spice flavours & a delicious spirit grip to end. Discontinued: **Shiraz Rosé**, **Rosé**.

Lifestyle range

> **Cabernet Sauvignon** ☺ 🖩 ★★★ Soft berry-fruited & friendly **10** is for unpretentious sipping. Unoaked, as for the next five. **Pinotage** ☺ 🖩 ★★★ Fruity & juicy, with dark chocolate on smooth & easy-drinking **10**. **Shiraz** ☺ 🖩 ★★★ **10** rich brambleberry fruit, peppery spices with a delicious savoury juiciness. Over-achieves at the price.

Merlot 🖩 ★★★ **11** appeals with juicy fruit, slips down easy on few grains sugar. **Charming Red** 🖩 ★★ Fruity cinsaut-led **NV** blend is semi-sweet & uncomplicated. **Simonsrood** 🖩 ★★★ 4-way **NV** blend is fruity, but dry, with a hint of oak spice for easy sipping. **Blanc de Blanc** 🖩 ★★ **NV** from chenin, for lightish, dry fruity summer fun. **Sweet Chenin Blanc** 🖩 ★★ Semi-sweet **12** is floral & light, with honey & litchi hints. **Stein** 🖩 ★★ Light, easy-drinking, off-dry fruity **NV** from chenin. **Simonsblanc** 🖩 ★★★ Semi-dry **NV** quaffer from chenin is fresh fruited, balanced & rounded with a zingy aftertaste. **Natural Sweet Rosé** 🖩 ★★ Extra-light **NV**, sweet & spicy from chenin & pinotage. Serve chilled at picnics. **Sweet Shiraz** 🖩 ★★ Sweet, light & nutty **11**. Serve chilled.

Eco Glass Lifestyle range
Cabernet Sauvignon ⑬ 🍴 ★★ Entry-level, fresh & off-dry **09**. Anytime quaffer in PET (plastic) packaging. **Chenin Blanc** ⑬ 🍴 ★★ Light & fruity **11** ideal picnic wine in shatterproof PET bottle.

Simonay range
Classic Red ★★ Soft berry flavour, smooth **NV** party wine. 5L bag-in-box, as all in this range. **Blanc de Blanc** ★★ Fragrant, fruity & fresh **NV** with zippy end. Lightish 12% alcohol. **Stein** ★★ Perfumed, soft & fragrant semi-sweet **NV** sipper. **Late Harvest** ★ Mild **NV** for casual sweet quaffing. **Natural Sweet Rosé** ★ Extra-light pink **NV** sweetie. — WB

■ **Simply Red/White** *see* PicardiRebel
■ **Sir George** *see* Napier Winery

Sir Lambert Wines

Location/WO: Lamberts Bay ▪ Map: Olifants River ▪ Est 2004 ▪ 1stB 2007 ▪ Tasting Mon-Fri 9-5 Sat 9-3 at Diemersdal or by appt in Lamberts Bay ▪ Closed Easter Fri/Sun, Dec 25 & Jan 1 ▪ BYO picnic ▪ Xamarin Guest House & Restaurant ▪ Conference & function venue (up to 250 people) ▪ Game drives ▪ Golf course ▪ Tour groups ▪ Conservation area ▪ 4x4 trail ▪ Facilities for children ▪ Owner(s) John Hayes, Johan Teubes & Thys Louw ▪ Winemaker(s) Thys Louw & Mari Branders ▪ Viticulturist(s) Johan Teubes (2004) ▪ 10ha (shiraz, sauv) ▪ 60t/3,000cs own label 10% red 90% white ▪ PO Box 27 Durbanville 7551 ▪ info@sirlambert.co.za ▪ www.sirlambert.co.za ▪ S 32°5'52.40" E 018° 18'19.50" ▪ **T +27 (0)21-976-3361** ▪ F +27 (0)21-979-1802

Winemaker Thys Louw takes a three-hour drive (one-way) up the West Coast when he checks on the Lamberts Bay vines owned by this joint venture between his Diemersdal family estate and local partners. But he doesn't begrudge it. 'The vineyards are just three kilometres from the sea and inspire me each time I visit.'

★★★★ **Sauvignon Blanc** ✓ 🍴 🖾 Consistently proves wisdom of planting in this maritime-influenced region. Like **11**, **12** 'oystershell' minerality, fruity acidity, measured weight & body.
The Admiral's Shiraz Await new. — CvZ

■ **Sir Robert Stanford Estate** *see* Robert Stanford Estate

---

Six Hats

Location: Citrusdal ▪ WO: Western Cape ▪ Est/1stB 2007 ▪ Closed to public ▪ Owner(s) Charles Back, Mike Paul & other grape farm owners ▪ Cellarmaster(s) Jaco Brand (Nov 2009) ▪ Winemaker(s) Jaco Brand, with Andries de Klerk (both Nov 2009) ▪ Viticulturist(s) Charl du Plessis (Nov 2009) ▪ 550ha (cab, grenache, ptage, shiraz, chard, chenin, pinot grigio, sauv, viog) ▪ 5,000t/25,000cs own label 50% red 45% white 5% rosé + 100,000cs for clients ▪ Brands for clients: Co-op, Fairtrade Original, M&S, Sainsbury's ▪ Fairtrade, HACCP 2004, WIETA ▪ PO Box 41 Citrusdal 7340 ▪ info@citrusdalwines.co.za ▪ www.citrusdalwines.co.za ▪ **T +27 (0)22-921-2233** ▪ F +27 (0)22-921-3937

The 'six hats' of this young Fairtrade brand are the principles (partnership, change, potential, equity, dignity and sustainability) which guide the collaboration between Fairview's Charles Back, Citrusdal Wines and participating farms in Malmesbury and Piekenierskloof. Firm demand for South African Fairtrade wines in Europe is bolstering resolve, and keeping the associated social and empowerment benefits flowing.

Six Hats Fairtrade range

Cabernet Sauvignon ☺ 🍴 🖾 ★★★ Easy-drinking **10** crammed with lively fruit, savoury dark chocolate & cedar from combo French/American oak. **Viognier** ☺ 🍴 🖾 ★★★ Packed with healthy pear & green apple fruit, pre-bottling **12**'s lack of oak adds to charm.

Pinotage 🍴 ★★★ Ex-tank **11** honest & juicy everyday quaffer with scented plum flavours. **Shiraz** 🍴 🖾 ★★★ Well-balanced **10** leads with succulent dark berries, follows with black pepper & plum notes. **Pinotage Rosé** 🍴 🖾 ★★ Dusty & savoury **12**, straightforward dry sipper. **Chardonnay** 🍴 🖾 ★★★ Clean, focused lemon freshness on **12** tank sample. **Chenin Blanc** 🍴 🖾 ★★ Uncomplicated green apple crunch on **12**, piquant dry finish. **Sauvignon Blanc** 🍴 🖾 ★★★ Pleasing tangy pineapple & green herbs, **12** preview shows good varietal character. Discontinued: **Grenache**. — DB

■ **Sixpence** *see* Opstal Estate
■ **1685** *see* Boschendal Wines

■ **Sixty 40** *see Boland Kelder*

Skaap Wines   🍷🍽🏛📷👣 NEW

Location: Sir Lowry's Pass ▪ Map: Helderberg ▪ WO: Durbanville/Coastal ▪ Est/1stB 2011 ▪ Tasting by appt only ▪ Wine sales Mon-Fri 9-5.30 Sat/Sun 10-3 ▪ Closed all pub hols ▪ Private functions (lunch/dinner) by appt ▪ Swimming pool ▪ Tour groups ▪ Local art on display & for sale ▪ Olive oil ▪ Conferences (up to 18 pax) ▪ Walks/hikes ▪ Mountain biking trail ▪ Conservation area ▪ 5-bedroom guesthouse, dining room with chef & 2 self-catering lodges ▪ Owner(s) Thierry Schaap ▪ Cellarmaster(s)/winemaker(s) Riaan Oosthuizen (Jan 2011) ▪ Vineyard manager(s) Jaco Mouton ▪ 17ha/4ha (shiraz, sauv) ▪ 550cs own label 30% red 70% white ▪ BWI, IPW ▪ PO Box 75 Sir Lowry's Pass 7130 ▪ info@skaapwines.com ▪ www.skaapwines.com ▪ S 34°06'11.35" E 018°55'05.87" ▪ **T +27 (0)21-858-1982/+27 (0)83-452-2083** ▪ F +27 (0)21-858-1983

Dutch banker Thierry Schaap has planted 4ha of high-density dryland vines on his prime 17ha Schapenberg site (Schaap and Schapen, meaning 'sheep'; pure coincidence; 'Skaap' the Afrikaans version). Supported by sister Marie-Hélène of nearby Wedderwill Estate, and experienced winemaker Riaan Oosthuizen and viticulturist Jaco Mouton, Thierry is committed to sustainable farming, including local Sir Lowry's Pass village community involvement with a soup kitchen, children's foundation and amateur artists (whose beadwork is featured on the label).

★★★★ **Skaap 40 Sauvignon Blanc** 🏠 Has a rock star personality (spice, flint, lime, herb — you name it, the whole performance) but **11** is serious too, respectful of cool Durbanville provenance.

Shiraz 🏠 ★★★★ Old & New World fans will come together (around a braai) over **11**, attractive spread of pepper-zested dark fruit, oak char & freshness. WO Durbanville, as next. **MCC Brut** ★★★ Bottle-fermented sparkling from pinot noir & chardonnay; **11** is lightish, savoury & dry, refreshing glassful with your sushi. — HJ/JP

Skilpadvlei Wines   🍷🍽🏛📷👣♿

Location/map/WO: Stellenbosch ▪ Est 2004 ▪ 1stB 2001 ▪ Tasting & sales Mon-Sat 8-5 Sun 8-4 ▪ Fee R15 ▪ Closed Dec 25/26 & Jan 1 ▪ Restaurant Mon-Sat 8-late Sun 8-4 ▪ Facilities for children ▪ Gift/décor shop ▪ Conferences ▪ Weddings & functions ▪ B&B guesthouse & self-catering cottages ▪ Owner(s) WD Joubert ▪ Cellarmaster(s) Koewie du Toit (consultant) ▪ Viticulturist(s) Johan Pienaar & Eben Archer (consultants) ▪ 78ha/55ha (cab, merlot, ptage, shiraz, chenin, sauv) ▪ 652t/6,000cs own label 80% red 20% white ▪ PO Box 17 Vlottenburg 7604 ▪ info@skilpadvlei.co.za ▪ www.skilpadvlei.co.za ▪ S 33°57'31.5" E 018°45'52.4" ▪ **T +27 (0)21-881-3237** ▪ F +27 (0)21-881-3538

No deviation from the 'affordable quality' mantra at the Joubert family's welcoming spot on the M12 into Stellenbosch. Fourth-generation Willie Joubert oversees yet more expansion and recognises that families need room to grow and children to play, so he's providing the leisure facilities and parking to accommodate them.

Skilpaddop Dry Red 🕒 🏠 ★ Previously, **09** was a herbal near-equal mix merlot & pinotage. **ML Joubert** ★★★ Shiraz, cab & merlot in **08**. Clove spice & juicy black fruit but wood still prominent mid-2012, needs time to harmonise. **Cabernet Sauvignon-Shiraz** ★★ Cab leads shiraz in **10**, with spicy oak yet to knit with berry fruit on review. **Chenin Blanc** 🕒 🏠 ★★ Figgy **11** a light & crisp quaffer. **Sauvignon Blanc** 🕒 🏠 ★★ Gooseberry lightness to **11**, tangy summertime sipper. — FM

■ **Skoon Vallei** *see Eerste Hoop Wine Cellar*

Slaley   🍷🍽🏛📷

Location/map: Stellenbosch ▪ WO: Simonsberg–Stellenbosch ▪ Est 1957 ▪ 1stB 1997 ▪ Tasting & sales Mon-Sat 10-4 ▪ Fee R20, waived on purchase ▪ Closed Good Fri, Dec 25/26 & Jan 1 ▪ Cellar tours by appt ▪ Light meals during tasting hours ▪ Farm produce ▪ Venue & conference facility with AV capacity ▪ Owner(s) Hunting family ▪ Winemaker(s) Consulting ▪ Viticulturist(s) Sean Burgoyne ▪ 240ha/51ha (cab, merlot, ptage, shiraz, chard, sauv) ▪ 320t/12-15,000cs own label 90% red 9% white 1% rosé ▪ IPW ▪ PO Box 119 Koelenhof 7605 ▪ info@slaley.co.za ▪ www.slaley.co.za ▪ S 33°51'53.7" E 18°50'51.1" ▪ **T +27 (0)21-865-2123** ▪ F +27 (0)86-529-2347

Slaley reports one of its 'best years ever', in part due to the fire that caused the tasting room to be rebuilt last year and 'turned our lives around'. Visitors stream in and phone friends to join them on the newly created deck. That in turn has led to an increase in functions and attendance at the monthly Social Sundays. And

environmental issues are receiving renewed attention through their membership of the Simonsberg Conservancy.

Hunting Family range

★★★★ **Merlot** ✓ Back on form after edgy **04** (★★★★), **06** shows elegance, refinement, layered black-currants, cedar, savoury dark chocolate. Drinks beautifully. No **05**.

★★★★ **Shiraz** Luscious berries & spice array, touch of wintergreen, doesn't quite cloak **06**'s (★★★★) dry tannins, less seductive than **04**. No **05**.

★★★★ **Reserve Noble Late Harvest Chardonnay** ⓣ Last was **07**, decadent & irresistible, concentrated honey/raisin character (from vine-dried grapes) perfect match for strong cheeses.

Pinotage ★★★★ Loads of dark fruit & opulent smoky tones, **07**'s freshening acidity keeps it juicy, lively. **Cabernet Sauvignon-Merlot** ⓣ ★★★ When tasted, **07** equal blend had ripe fruit with tar, liquorice & nettle hints. Heady 15% alc needed time to integrate. **Chardonnay** ⓣ ▨ ★★★★ Lacking the fruit of **09** (★★★★), barrel-fermented **10** has an attractive citrus & mineral profile, restrained slate-dry finish.

Broken Stone range

★★★★ **Pinotage** ✓ Vanilla from 70% American barrels enriches **06**'s mulberry fruit while leaving the supple juiciness intact. Admirable intensity yet elegant (13% alc), polished. No **05**.

Cabernet Sauvignon ✓ ★★★★ Lots going on in **06**, brambleberries, meaty notes, firm but ripe tannin, succulent drinkability. Enjoy now or keep a few years. **Shiraz** ★★★ Dark plum/prune ripeness with savoury spice, sturdily built **07** has a food-friendly firm grip. Could still age. **Cabernet Sauvignon-Shiraz-Pinotage** ✓ ★★★★ 'Cabernet Sauvignon-Shiraz' last time. Ripe & expressive, **07**'s cedar-dusted cassis nicely presented in a succulent, smoothly rounded body. Drinks well. **Sauvignon Blanc** ★★★ **11** gooseberries & litchi, sprinkle wild herbs, fresh & light.

Social range

Lindsay's Whimsy Cape Blend ⓣ ▤ ▨ ★★★ Smoky hedgerow fruit, **10** charms with its gutsy rusticity. Equal pinotage & merlot, splash cab. **Lindsay's Whimsy Rosé** ⓣ ▤ ▨ ★★★ Dry **10** from shiraz is light-hearted (12.9% alc) summer fare. — CR

Slanghoek Winery

Location: Rawsonville ▪ Map: Breedekloof ▪ WO: Slanghoek ▪ Est 1951 ▪ 1stB 1970 ▪ Tasting & sales Mon-Fri 8-5 Sat 10-1 ▪ Closed Easter Fri/Sun, Dec 25 & Jan 1 ▪ Cellar tours by appt ▪ Picnic baskets, booking required ▪ Slanghoek MTB Route, fee R20: 13km ride with optional extra, more challenging 4km ▪ Owner(s) 25 producers ▪ Cellarmaster(s) Pieter Carstens (Aug 2002) ▪ Winemaker(s) Nico Grundling & Paul Burger (Dec 2002/Dec 2008), with Jacques de Goede & Jaco Theron (Dec 2001/Oct 2007) ▪ Viticulturist(s) Callie Coetzee (Nov 2010) ▪ 1,830ha ▪ 30,000t/40,000cs own label 25% red 50% rosé 10% fortified ▪ Other export brand: Zonneweelde ▪ ISO 22000, BWI, IPW ▪ PO Box 75 Rawsonville 6845 ▪ info@slanghoek.co.za ▪ www. slanghoek.co.za ▪ S 33° 39' 1.1" E 019° 13' 49.0" ▪ **T** +27 (0)23-344-3026 ▪ F +27 (0)23-344-3157

This value-for-money grower-owned winery is all but surrounded by the majestic Slanghoek Mountains from which it derives its name. So when the winemakers claim they take their inspiration from the diversity of their environment, think soaring peaks, tumbling gorges and undulating valleys... and then believe them!

Private Selection

★★★★ **Noble Late Harvest** ⓣ Honey & nougat nuanced **07** complex, well-knit, though lacks weight, vibrancy of previous. Mainly chenin, dash muscat d'Alexandrie; 9 months French oak.

Merlot ☺ ▤ ▨ ★★★ **10** more cherry flavour than merlot plum & savoury; a fraction drier than Cab. **Pinotage** ☺ ▤ ▨ ★★★ **10** leads the pack; though alcohol nudges 14%, it's unobtrusive; decent spice & fruit compote, grip on finish. **Shiraz** ☺ ★★★ **09** the whopper in the line-up: generously fruited, off-dry & 14.5% alcohol well handled. **Camerca** ☺ ▤ ★★★ **10** Bordeaux red blend characterful, supple, & comparatively light bodied. **Sauvignon Blanc** ☺ ▤ ▨ ★★★ Demure **12** has good vinosity, fair green grass distinction; easy-sipping & off-dry. **Red Jerepiko** ☺ ▨ ★★★ Fortified sweetie from pinotage. **12** packed with berries & plump raisins; sweeter than the white offering but delicious.

Cabernet Sauvignon ▨ ★★★ Raspberry-toned, off-dry **10** has fair structure, spice from some new French oak. At just 13% alcohol (as for all reds unless noted), slips down easily. **Chardonnay** ▤ ▨ ★★★ Barrel-aged portion adds breadth, toast to lemon-toned **12**; noticeably off-dry. **Chenin Blanc** ▤ ▨ ★★★ Guava & apple, thatch on fruitful, crisp **12** sipper. **Crème de Chenin** ⓣ ★★★★ **10** Natural Sweet has dried apricots

& bitter almond notes from small portion botrytis, gentle sweetness enlivened by lime tang. Nudges higher rating, worth seeking out. **Cuvée Brut** ★★ Like following, **NV** tank-fermented sparkling; this from chardonnay & chenin. Fresh & appley. **Vin Doux** ★★★ Frothy & grapey **NV** sweet party starter; chill well. **Special Late Harvest** 🔲 📠 ★★★ Muscat d'Alexandrie provides white blossom bouquet & grapey palate on gently sweet **12**. Uncloying & pleasant. **Hanepoot Jerepigo** ✓ 📠 ★★★★ Was 'Sweet Hanepoot'. Integrated spirit, creamy texture & nutty profile on seamless **12**. Not as full-sweet as some versions, invigorating cleansing melon finish. **Red Muscadel** ⊕ 📠 ★★★★ Cherry-toned **11** has spirity succulence, but less complex than last-tasted **09** (★★★★). **Cape Ruby** ★★★ **11** balanced port-style fortified, now bottled, showing jam & almond; sweeter than many local ports but drinks easily.

Vinay range

> **Crispy White** ☺ ★★★ Decent vinosity from 11% alcohol, off-dry **NV** combo sauvignon, chenin, colombard. Chill well for extra verve.

Red ★★ Latest **NV** blend is berry infused & moreish. **Rosé** ★★★ Latest sweet, low-alcohol, floral **NV** from red muscadel, delightful enough. — CvZ

■ **Slent** see Ayama Wines

Slowine

Location/map: Villiersdorp ▪ WO: Western Cape/Overberg ▪ Est/1stB 2005 ▪ Tasting & sales at Villiersdorp Cellar (see entry) ▪ Owner(s) Villiersdorp Cellar ▪ Shareholders Beaumont Wines & Luddite Wines ▪ Technical team: Sebastian Beaumont, Niels Verburg & Flip Smith ▪ Production Flip Smith, with André Bruyns (Dec 2009) ▪ Cellarmaster(s) Flip Smith (Jan 2011) ▪ Viticulturist(s) André Bruyns (Dec 2009) ▪ 300ha (merlot, chenin, sauv) ▪ 3,600t/20,000cs own label 40% red 40% white 20% rosé ▪ BWI, IPW, PO Box 14 Villiersdorp 6848 ▪ marketing@slowine.co.za ▪ www.slowine.co.za ▪ S 33° 59'11.2" E 019° 17'48.5" ▪ **T +27 (0)28-840-1120** ▪ F +27 (0)28-840-1833

Slowine is a collaboration between owner Villiersdorp Cellar and shareholder wineries Luddite and Beaumont. Their motto urges us to slow down and relax... with slow food, slow wine and slow living. A portion of the sales in Japan aids the preservation of the Geometric Tortoise, the emblem on the label.

> **Cabernet Sauvignon** ☺ 🔲 📠 ★★★ **10**, different bottling, same cheery balanced quaffability. Sweet vanilla permeates chunky plum fruit. **Merlot** ☺ 🔲 📠 ★★★ Though medium bodied, **10** more substance & enjoyment than previous. Bright juicy berries & good chewy tannins for everyday tipple. **Chenin Blanc** ☺ 🔲 📠 ★★★ Now bottled, **11** is vibrant, brims with white peach & crisp apple, floral nuance in aftertaste. **Sauvignon Blanc** ☺ 🔲 📠 ★★★ **12** zings with bright lemon, grapefruit & Granny Smith apple flavours. **Chenin Blanc-Sauvignon Blanc** ☺ 🔲 📠 ★★★ **11**, now bottled, hints of blossom & grass, seamless zesty lemon conclusion. Lipsmacking!

Shiraz ⊕ 🔲 ★★★ When tasted, easy sipper **09** upstaged previous with brooding dark berries & white pepper spicing. **Rosé** ⊕ 🔲 📠 ★★★ Dry charmer from pinotage. **11** candyfloss & punnet of ripe red berries. — WB

■ **Smokey Mountain** see Wandsbeck Wyne Koöp Bpk
■ **Smook Wines** see Anthony Smook Wines
■ **Snow Mountain** see Nabygelegen Private Cellar
■ **Social** see Slaley
■ **Soek Die Geluk** see Goedverwacht Wine Estate
■ **Soet Izak** see Jason's Hill Private Cellar

SoetKaroo Wine Estate

Location: Prince Albert ▪ Map: Klein Karoo & Garden Route ▪ WO: Western Cape ▪ Est 2000 ▪ 1stB 2004 ▪ Tasting & sales Mon-Sat 9-1; afternoons by appt ▪ Closed Dec 25 ▪ Owner(s) Herman & Susan Perold ▪ Cellarmaster(s)/winemaker(s) Susan Perold (Jan 2007) ▪ Vineyard manager(s) Herman Perold ▪ 2t ▪ 56 Church Str Prince Albert 6930 ▪ perold@netactive.co.za ▪ www.soetkaroo.co.za ▪ S 33° 13'21.9" E 022° 1'48.0" ▪ **T +27 (0)23-541-1768** ▪ F +27 (0)86-524-3801

Winemaking at this tiny Prince Albert boutique 'became much easier when my little water press entered the cellar to replace the muscle-straining manual basket press', Susan Perold says. Her and husband Herman's maturing touriga vines are producing more body, so instead of 'dessert wine', the 2011 is the first 'Cape Ruby'.

★★★★ **Cape Ruby Touriga Nacional** Classic port grape previously lighter styled; cinnamon-dusted **11** now touted as port-style, offers plum & redcurrant, firm tannin for fireside sipping. **10** (★★) tad sugary.

Red Muscat d'Alexandrie ★★★★ Delicious fortified dessert from unusual red hanepoot, smidgen (red) muscadel. **11** back on track: characterful & appealing red berry/savoury combo. **Petit Verdot** Await new.

Petit Verdot Dessert Wine NEW ★★★★ One-of-a-kind NV (**11**) is intense & succulent, satisfying depth & savoury length, structured for ageing. 'Tried to make elegant wine' says Susan Perold. Mission accomplished. — WB/JP

■ **Solms-Astor** see Solms-Delta

Solms-Delta

Location/map: Franschhoek ▪ WO: Western Cape/Coastal ▪ Est 1690 ▪ 1stB 2004 ▪ Tasting & sales daily 9-5 ▪ Fee R20pp ▪ Closed Dec 25 & Jan 1 ▪ Cellar tours by appt ▪ Fyndraai Restaurant (see Restaurants section) ▪ Walking farm tours ▪ Dik Delta fynbos culinary garden ▪ Museum van de Caab & archaeological sites ▪ Harvest festival (Mar) ▪ Summer music concerts ▪ Delta draf/trap (Apr) ▪ Owner(s) Solms & Astor Family Trusts and Wijn de Caab Workers' Trust ▪ Winemaker(s) Hilko Hegewisch (Mar 2003-Aug 2012) & Maria Botha (May 2011) ▪ Viticulturist(s) Rosa Kruger (Jul 2011) ▪ 78ha/30ha (grenache n/b, mourv, shiraz, chenin, muscat d'A, muscat de F, rouss, sem, viog) ▪ 220t/25,000cs own label 63% red 33% white 4% rosé ▪ BWI, IPW ▪ PO Box 123 Groot Drakenstein 7680 ▪ info@solms-delta.co.za ▪ www.solms-delta.co.za ▪ S 33° 51'51.0" E 018° 59' 23.8" ▪ **T** +27 (0)21-874-3937 ▪ F +27 (0)21-874-1852

Working alongside academics excavating a site inhabited by people who lived here 7,000 years ago, Bennie Pietersen, a long-time resident on this Franschhoek farm, held up an artefact to co-owner Mark Solms and said: 'Jy sien, Prof, my mense was hier voor jou!' (See, Prof, my people were here before yours!') The shared process of digging up the past and honestly confronting it brings an understanding of, and pride in, a shared heritage. It's reflected all around this remarkable place — from the museum to the rural music programme, social history tourism, traditional cuisine, indigenous culinary garden and, of course, wine. Says Mark: 'South African wines with integrity must perforce be more than chocolate box wines. An honest confrontation with our past is what defines our future.'

Solms-Delta range

★★★★☆ **Africana** 🌿 From desiccated shiraz — a style specialised in here. Cassis-infused **10** concentrated, has great presence at only 13.5% alcohol. Ends dry despite few grams sugar. No **09**. WO Coastal.

★★★★ **Hiervandaan** 🌿 Vine-dried blend shiraz, mourvèdre, grenache, carignan, fermented on viognier skins. Piquant **10** has grippy persistence, salty farewell; from Paarl/Swartland fruit. Last was feisty **07**.

★★★★ **Lekkerwijn** 🌿 'Nice Wine' indeed, but for 'nice' read 'lipsmacking': multi-region **11** lightly wooded & fruity mourvèdre, grenache & viognier; just-dry. Previous included shiraz.

★★★★★ **Amalie** 🌿 Barrel-fermented/aged grenache blanc, roussanne, viognier. Sample **11** too unknit to rate. **10** was seductive, rich & rounded. WO Coastal.

★★★★ **Koloni** 🌿 Muscat d'Alexandrie & vine-dried muscat de Frontignan fermented/aged in oak. **11** unrated sample preview off-dry, as was perfumed, zingy **10**. Previous was **07** (★★★★★).

★★★★☆ **Gemoedsrus** 🌿 Unique take on port: vine-dried shiraz fortified with husk spirit. **10** (★★★★) spiced with cigarbox & cloves; viscous, with lively acidity but still ends very sweet. Less successful than **09**.

Solms-Astor

Langarm ☺ 🌿 ★★★ Quirky blend pinotage, touriga, shiraz, mourvèdre. **11** fresh & fruit-filled; unwooded & just-dry. **Vastrap** ☺ 🍴 🌿 ★★★ Older oak matured chenin with semillon, riesling. **11** rich & satisfying, but still brisk & dry for al fresco dining/quaffing.

Cape Jazz Shiraz ★★★ Unusual semi-sweet red sparkling explodes with berries; tannin touch & very light oaking mask the sugar. NV under 10% alcohol. Enjoy chilled. — CvZ

Solo Wines

Location: Stellenbosch ▪ WO: Western Cape ▪ Est/1stB 2009 ▪ Closed to public ▪ Wine sales by appt or telephonically ▪ Owner(s)/winemaker(s) Philip Costandius ▪ 50% red 50% white ▪ PO Box 241 Stellenbosch 7599 ▪ wine@solowines.com ▪ www.solowines.com ▪ **T +27 (0)21-881-3200** ▪ F +27 (0)21-881-3200

Multi-talented and artistic Philip Costandius is turning into a tandem act rather than a solo one. The long-standing Cape Winemakers Guild member has taken over the reins at the Bot River winery, Eerste Hoop, he consulted to. His Solo wines rest in barrel, awaiting the next consignment of bottles and corks before release.

Syrah ⓐ ★★★★ 09's spicy, ripe black fruit balance chalky texture & dry tannin from 18 months oak. **Viognier** ⓐ ★★★★ Spicy restraint, elegance on lightly oaked 10. Juicy honey & quince tang, not overblown. — FM

Somerbosch Wines

Location: Stellenbosch ▪ Map: Helderberg ▪ WO: Stellenbosch/Western Cape ▪ Est 1950 ▪ 1stB 1995 ▪ Tasting & sales daily 9-5 ▪ Fee R20/6 wines, waived on purchase of any 3 btls; R40pp/ice cream & red wine tasting ▪ Closed Dec 25 & Jan 1 ▪ Cellar tours by appt ▪ Somerbosch Bistro: b'fast & lunch daily ▪ Facilities for children ▪ Farm produce ▪ Conferences ▪ Owner(s) Somerbosch Wines cc ▪ Cellarmaster(s)/winemaker(s)/viticulturist(s) Marius & Japie Roux (both 1995) ▪ 55ha/43ha (cab, merlot, shiraz, sauv) ▪ 350t 55% red 45% white ▪ PO Box 12181 Die Boord 7613 ▪ enquiries@somerbosch.co.za, sales@somerbosch.co.za ▪ www.somerbosch.co.za ▪ S 34° 01' 28.6" E 018° 49' 6.9" ▪ **T +27 (0)21-855-3615** ▪ F +27 (0)21-855-4457

Named for home-farm Die Fonteine's location midway between Somerset West and Stellenbosch, this brand by the brothers Le Roux (Marius, Japie and Wrensch) hopes to give a taste of their kind of wine lifestyle: fun, relaxed and affordable. They're spreading the love: more restaurant space here, Asian market explorations abroad.

Somerbosch range

★★★★ **Kylix** ⓐ 🍽 Amply bottle-aged red blend, 04 from cab, shiraz, merlot. Vivid fruit & minerals, solid oaking structures ripe flavours, as does ample freshness.

Shiraz-Merlot NEW ☺ 🍽 ★★★ Accessible, spicy 11 blend cheerfully youthful with plenty red fruit & spice. Only lightly oaked, like most of these reds. **Chenin Blanc** ☺ 🍽 ★★★ Zippily fresh pineapple 12 perfect for summer picnics. WO W Cape. **Sauvignon Blanc** ☺ 🍽 ★★★ Zesty 12 in refreshing herbaceous, easy-drinking style.

Cabernet Sauvignon 🍽 ★★★ Dry, well-structured 10 has lean, simple fruit. **Merlot** 🍽 ★★★ Savoury, herbal 08 in fresh, straightforward but structured style. **Pinotage** ⓐ 🍽 ★★★ Uncomplicated meaty, vanilla 09 for everyday drinking. **Shiraz** 🍽 ★★★ Spicy, mocha-laced, just-dry 09 fresh & easily drinkable. Structure & charm of good vintage apparent. **Chardonnay** ⓐ 🍽 ★★★ Last-tasted 10 with melon & sweet baked-apple flavours. **Méthode Cap Classique Brut** Await new. **Late Bottled Vintage Port** ⓐ ★★★ 06 from cab; warming fireside sipper tasted a few years back. Discontinued: **Chenin Blanc Natural Sweet Limited Release**.

Poker Hill range
Shiraz-Merlot 🍽 Await next, as for **Semillon-Chenin Blanc**. — IM

Somerset Wines

Location: Somerset West ▪ Map: Helderberg ▪ WO: Western Cape ▪ Est 2010 ▪ 1stB 2011 ▪ Tasting & sales Mon-Fri 8.30-5 Sat 9-1 ▪ Closed all pub hols ▪ Tour groups ▪ Wine shop ▪ Owner(s) Boetie Rietoff ▪ Cellarmaster(s) Nicky Versfeld, Hennie Huskisson & JG Auret ▪ 100,000cs 80% red 20% white ▪ PO Box 2240 Somerset West 7129 ▪ info@somersetbeverages.co.za ▪ www.somersetwines.com ▪ **T +27 (0)21-851-8188** ▪ F +27 (0)21-852-9563

Owner Boetie Rietoff has been in the wine industry for over 40 years and with his passion for it undimmed, says he's now 'giving back'. Socially aware and involved, he gives a portion of his wine sales to local charities and communities in need. The release of very competitively priced new range Lady Somerset shows he hasn't lost his marketing touch either.

Lord Somerset range

Chenin Blanc Bushvine ☺ 🖬 🗟 ★★★ With pear & melon, **12** is a tasty, lightish (12.5% alc) freshly dry quaffer.

Cabernet Sauvignon ⑨ 🖬 🗟 ★★★ Dark fruit, well supported by oak, **10** could age a few years. **Shiraz Reserve** ⑨ ★★★ Ripe plums threaded through with savoury spice, **08** has enough succulent accessibility for everyday enjoyment. **Merlot-Cabernet Sauvignon** 🖬 🗟 ★★★ Unwooded but backed by grape tannin, supports **11**'s red fruit. **Sauvignon Blanc** 🖬 🗟 ★★★ Summer fruits, herb nuance in **12**'s fresh & clean dryness. **Soft Smooth Red** 🖬 ★★ Light & juicy **11** has a plum sweetness that goes down easily.

Lady Somerset range NEW

Natural Sweet White ☺ 🖬 ★★★ Intriguing peppermint & lime cordial notes in light-textured **NV**'s fruity flavours add appeal. Has a delicious sweet/sour finish.

Stylish Elegant Red 🖬 ★★★ Unwooded, fruity **NV**'s dry grape tannin good for food pairing. **Crisp Dry White** 🖬 ★★★ Peach tones in **NV** from chardonnay, crisp dryness from sauvignon. **Natural Sweet Red** 🖬 ★★★ Smoky dark fruit from shiraz portion, **NV** berry-rich, low-alcohol sweet quaffer. **Natural Sweet Rosé** 🖬 ★★★ 'Flirtatious' on the label says it; light-bodied **NV** with red berry tangy sweetness. — CR

Somfula Wines ⚑ NEW

Location: Malmesbury ▪ Est/1stB 2009 ▪ Tasting by appt ▪ Closed Easter Fri/Sun/Mon, Dec 25/26 & Jan 1 ▪ Owner(s) Nokubonga Somfula ▪ 60% red 20% white 20% rosé ▪ 5698 Chris Hani Street Malmesbury 7300 ▪ bongis86@gmail.com ▪ **T +27 (0)79-464-0204** ▪ F +27 (0)86-293-3443

Malmesbury-based Nokubonga Somfula developed a love of wine while working as a wine label designer in Cape Town, where 'we used to taste it every Friday'. Working hand in hand with Pulpit Rock Winery near Riebeek-West, her intention is to market good quality, fruit-driven wines for fellow wine enthusiasts, and learn as much about the wine industry as she can in the process. Current line-up includes Cabernet Sauvignon 09, Merlot 10, Pinotage Rosé 11 and Chardonnay 11 .

▪ **Sonata** see Waterstone Wines
▪ **Songloed** see Groupe CDV

Sonklip Wine ⚑⚑ NEW

Location/map: Stellenbosch ▪ 1stB 2009 ▪ Tasting & cellar tours for groups only, by appt ▪ Owner(s)/ winemaker(s) Frik Kirsten ▪ 100cs own label 100% red ▪ PO Box 6198 Uniedal 7612 ▪ sonklip@gmail.com ▪ S 33° 56'3.55" E 018° 53'44.95" ▪ **T +27 (0)21-887-5869** ▪ F +27 (0)21-887-5869

Engineer Frik Kirsten's later-in-life winemaking was inspired by a 2008 garagiste course and the 'thinking-out-the-box' approach of top Cape vintner Eben Sadie (whose vaunted Mev. Kirsten old-vine chenin comes from Frik's family farm Westridge). Frik's 'no-nonsense' Sonklip reds are vinified in the farm's cellar from grapes bought in mainly from nearby Jonkershoek Valley properties, hand bottled and gradually increased in quantity each year (50 cases in 2012, 100 cases in 2013). Available are a mourvèdre and cab-based blend, with a cabernet, malbec and shiraz-viognier still in barrel at press time.

▪ **Sonop Organic** see African Terroir

Sophie ⚑

Location/WO: Elgin ▪ Est/1stB 2009 ▪ Closed to public ▪ Owner(s) Andrew Gunn ▪ Cellarmaster(s) Werner Muller (May 2011) ▪ (cab, merlot, shiraz, sauv) ▪ 150t/10,000cs own label 10% red 85% white 5% rosé ▪ PO Box 527 Grabouw 7160 ▪ orders@sophie.co.za ▪ www.sophie.co.za ▪ **T +27 (0)28-284-9678** ▪ F +27 (0)28-284-9078

Raised on grapes from Elgin, Sophie Te'blanche is a good-time girl, and her sisters Le Rouge and Rose too. Demand for their attendance last year exceeded supply, but their guardians assure us that over-exposure will never be allowed to prejudice their fresh character and natural tartness.

Le Rouge ✓ 🖿 ★★★★ Accessible plummy, spicy **10** Bordeaux-shiraz blend has seamlessly integrated tannins & welcome freshness. **Rose** ⊕ 🖿 ★★★★ **10** rosé from cab is dry & well structured, lipsmacking red-fruit flavours & lingering berry finish. **Te'blanche** ✓ 🖿 ★★★★ 'Sophie Te'blanche' vernacular name for sauvignon blanc. Vibrant **12**, abundant fresh fruit flavours in delightfully appetising mineral style. Over-delivers. — IM

- **Sopiensklip** see Springfontein Wine Estate
- **South Africa** see Wineways Marketing
- **South African Soul** see Belbon Hills Private Cellar
- **South Atlantic** see Simonsvlei International
- **Southern Cape Vineyards** see Barrydale, Ladismith & Oudtshoorn Cellar

Southern Right

Location: Hermanus ▪ Map: Elgin, Walker Bay & Bot River ▪ WO: Hemel-en-Aarde Valley/Walker Bay ▪ Est 1994 ▪ 1stB 1995 ▪ Tasting, sales & cellar tours Mon-Fri 9-5 Sat 9-1 ▪ Closed Easter Fri/Mon, Dec 25/26 & Jan 1 ▪ Fynbos reserve, renosterveld reserve & 3 wetlands ▪ Quad bike route ▪ Owner(s) Mark Willcox, Mikki Xayiya & Anthony Hamilton Russell ▪ Winemaker(s) Hannes Storm (2004) ▪ Viticulturist(s) Johan Montgomery (2005) ▪ 447ha/±36ha (ptage, sauv) ▪ 225-280t/15-20,000cs own label 20% red 80% white ▪ PO Box 158 Hermanus 7200 ▪ hrv@hermanus.co.za ▪ S 34° 24'3.2" E 019° 13'0.4" ▪ **T +27 (0)28-312-3595** ▪ F +27 (0)28-312-1797

We're preempting a milestone, but next edition Anthony Hamilton Russell and his Southern Right partners mark 20 years of focusing on just two wines — Pinotage and Sauvignon — a laudable achievement given the temptation to diversify and expand. And, after two decades, their enthusiasm is undimmed. Asked about recent achievements, Anthony says: 'We harvested the first grapes from a new sauvignon vineyard. We also launched the Southern Right Conservation Award to recognise an individual who significantly develops and protects the Hermanus area as an eco-tourist destination. And we staged a fun comparative tasting of a magnum of Pinotage that went to the Antarctic and back — being the Southern Right's annual migratory route — against a magnum of the same wine that stayed home. The latter was significantly less developed!'

★★★★☆ **Pinotage** ⊕ Poised & precise expression of the variety, with well-judged oak. Measured & finely textured **10** has, despite dashes of 5 other varieties, quintessential strawberry & earth tones.

★★★★☆ **Sauvignon Blanc** ✓ **12** less flamboyant & intense than **11** but as striking & accomplished. Subdued nettle/khaki bush aromas, ruby grapefruit flavour & mineral length. Will reward cellaring few years. — CvZ

Southern Sky Wines

Location: Paarl ▪ Map: Paarl & Wellington ▪ WO: Western Cape ▪ Est/1stB 2002 ▪ Tasting & sales by appt ▪ Owner(s) Andrew Milne ▪ Winemaker(s) Andrew Milne (Jan 2003) ▪ 10,000cs own label 95% red 5% white ▪ Other export brands: Les Fleurs, Rowlands ▪ PO Box 1312 Paarl 7624 ▪ andrew@ssw.co.za ▪ www.ssw.co.za ▪ S 33° 45'8.78" E 018° 57'42.55" ▪ **T +27 (0)21-863-4440** ▪ F +27 (0)21-863-0444

International markets are responding well to visits from Paarl-based brand owner Andrew Milne, while wife Elizma helps look after the expanding local market. Ink-blots on the labels of the new Imagine wines reflect the Milnes' desire to demystify wine. 'Just as we might see different things in an ink-blot, we all have different wine personalities and there are no incorrect answers. "Imagine" what you like!'

Signature Selection NEW

Tara Hill ★★★☆ Cab (88%) & petit verdot blend from Stellenbosch & Paarl. Serious effort, ably executed. **09** noble fruit on nose, pleasing earthy notes on palate. Quite fresh but well formed, smooth & concentrated.

Imagine range NEW

Cabernet Sauvignon 🖿 ★★★ **08** shows some maturity but sweet berry fruit tastily intact for now & another year/2. **Shiraz** 🖿 ★★★ Ideal braai bro, ready-to-drink **08** has meaty charred oak notes already embedded. Just add T-bone steak.

Marimba range
Cabernet Sauvignon ★★ A savoury version, **09** concentrated black cherry fruit, ends with a dried-fruit tang.

Almara range
Cabernet Sauvignon ★★ Medium-weight **10** cab offering typical blackcurrant flavour & crisp acidity.

Ready Steady range
Red ★★ Lightish, juicy & pleasant **NV**, chiefly cinsaut & 3 others, mostly unwooded. — GdB/HJ

South Hill Vineyards

Location/WO: Elgin ▪ Map: Elgin, Walker Bay & Bot River ▪ Est 2001 ▪ 1stB 2006 ▪ Tasting Mon-Fri 9-5 Sat/Sun 10-4 ▪ Original artworks (Red Gallery) ▪ The Guest House @ South Hill (see Accommodation section) ▪ Function venue for conferences & weddings ▪ Gordon Manuel @ The Venue (see Restaurants section) ▪ Conservation area ▪ Owner(s) South Hill Vineyards (Pty) Ltd ▪ Winemaker(s) Sean Skibbe (Jun 2005) ▪ Viticulturist(s) Andrew Teubes (Mar 2006, consultant) ▪ 57ha/28ha (cab, pinot, shiraz, chard, riesling, sauv, sem, viog) ▪ 130t/3,500cs own label 20% red 80% white ▪ PO Box 120 Elgin 7180 ▪ info@southhill.co.za ▪ www.southhill.co.za ▪ S 34° 13'59.5" E 019° 6'44.3" ▪ **T +27 (0)21-844-0888** ▪ F +27 (0)21-844-0959

In 2012 Sean Skibbe, winemaker of this small Elgin farm, was thankfully working in a new local cellar, at last able to do such things as bunch and berry sorting on all varieties. He also made experimental batches of pinot, shiraz, mourvèdre and barbera off the home farm — 'so watch this space in the coming year or two!'.

★★★★☆ Cabernet Sauvignon 🍷 Elegant 10's (★★★★) shy aromas explode on the palate with intense sour black cherry, dark choc & a touch of vanilla. Modest oaking. Lingering & fresh but not quite at level of 09.

★★★★ Sauvignon Blanc 🍷 Intriguing, juicy 12 in more generous style than the nettly 09, with a medley of tropical fruit & a fine, lively acidity. Year/2 will add complexity. 10 (★★★★) less expressive. 11 untasted.

Cabernet Sauvignon Rosé 🍷 **★★★★** Beautiful redcurrant & cherry on lightish, lively & fresh 12. Intriguing mineral feel; bone-dry. **Blanc de Blancs Méthode Cap Classique** **NEW** **★★★★** Rich 08 sparkling from chardonnay has a very 'winey' feel. Forward aromas of ripe apple & melon lead to a generous mouthful & a slight sweetness to conclude. — JPf

■ **Spencer Bay** *see Namaqua Wines*

Spice Route Winery

Location: Malmesbury/Paarl ▪ Map: Paarl & Wellington ▪ WO: Swartland/Western Cape/Darling ▪ Est/1stB 1998 ▪ Tasting & sales daily 9-5, last tasting 30min before closing ▪ Closed Good Fri, Dec 25 & Jan 1 ▪ Spice Route Restaurant (see Restaurants section) ▪ Tour groups by appt ▪ Glass blowing studio ▪ Chocolate studio & visual factory ▪ Micro beer brewery ▪ Owner(s) Charles Back ▪ Winemaker(s) Charl du Plessis (Dec 2001), with Licia Solomons (Jan 2006) & Adele Dunbar (Jun 2012) ▪ 400ha/115ha (cab, grenache, merlot, mourv, ptage, shiraz, chenin, sauv, viog) ▪ 900t 60% red 40% white ▪ IPW, WIETA ▪ PO Box 583 Suider-Paarl 7624 ▪ spiceroute@iafrica.com ▪ www.spiceroutewines.co.za ▪ S 33° 45'50.5" E 018° 55'9.7" ▪ **T +27 (0)21-863-5200** ▪ F +27 (0)21-863-3797

Maximum rating for their chenin this edition is yet another salute to Spice Route (and Fairview) visionary Charles Back, whose acquisition of Swartland farm Klein Amoskuil in the late 1990s set in motion an extraordinary revival that's recently crystallised under the banner of the non-interventionist movement, Swartland Revolution. Spice Route fans who long missed a brand home now have one right next door to Fairview — a new tasting room and restaurant, glass-blowing studio Red Hot Glass, chocolate-and-wine paring by DV Artisan Chocolates and, watch this space, a micro brewery — making up for lost time.

★★★★ Pinotage 🍷 Consistent & appealing — 09 with usual seductive logan/blackberry note, firm but unobtrusive structure, subtle oaking, leaving pure, fresh fruit. Few years in bottle will do only good.

★★★★ Flagship Syrah 10 has knockout aromas of wild berries, dry herbs, fynbos & lavender, & is ripe, sumptuous & powerful. Oaky, but balanced by fruit with a savoury clean finish.

★★★★ Shiraz 🍷 Sweet-fruited, ripe, full-flavoured, full-throttle... 09 has full everything, really — it's a big, rich, oaky, assertive wine, with its own sort of balance & successful within its chosen style.

★★★★ **Malabar 09** is opulent & ripe but more restrained than **07** (★★★★). Bold & richly structured with a berry liqueur character, supported by smooth tannins. Neither up to lofty standard of **06** (★★★★★). No **08**.

★★★★★ **Chenin Blanc** ✓ 🍴 🌿 Exceptional expression of the variety, **11** (★★★★★) is lush & silky, with kaleidoscopic crème brûlée, lemon, honey & vanilla. Freshness permeating the pure fruit ensures the whole remains vibrant while restrained oak & lees-age complexity raise it above **10** & all previous. WO W Cape.

★★★★☆ **Sauvignon Blanc** ⑨ 🍴 🌿 **11** (★★★★) from Darling vineyards as always, but less flamboyant in its attractive mix of green & tropical styles than **10**. Restrained acidity, refined & very enjoyable.

Mourvèdre 🌿 ★★★★ Preview **10** is fruity & balanced, with an earthy, dusty finish. Medium bodied, juicy & delicious. **Chakalaka** ✓ ★★★★ Easy & delicious 6-way shiraz-led blend with dash tannat. Loads of sweet fruit & spice, **10** harmonious, groomed & well built. **Viognier** Next awaited. — WB

Spier

Location/map: Stellenbosch ▪ WO: Western Cape/Coastal/Stellenbosch/Paarl ▪ Est 1692 ▪ 1stB 1770 ▪ Tasting 10–4.30 & sales 9–5 daily ▪ Tasting from R35 ▪ Facilities for children ▪ Tour groups ▪ Gift shop ▪ Farm produce ▪ Conferences ▪ Manor House museum & The Heritage Walk ▪ Conservation area ▪ 4-star Spier Hotel & Spa (see Accommodation section) ▪ Eight Restaurant (see Restaurants section) & Spier Hotel Restaurant ▪ Owner(s) Spier ▪ Cellarmaster(s) Frans Smit (Dec 1995) ▪ Winemaker(s) Johan Jordaan (reds, Jul 2007) & Jacques Erasmus (whites, Apr 2007), with Tania Kleintjies, Godfrey Singo & Anthony Kock (2007/2008/2009) ▪ Viticulturist(s) Johann Smit (Dec 1999) ▪ 850ha/193ha (barbera, cabs s/f, malbec, merlot, mourv, p verdot, ptage, shiraz, chard, chenin, sauv, sem, viog) ▪ 3,340t/±1.1m cs own label 65% red 31% white 3% rosé 1% MCC ▪ ISO 22000:2007, BWI, Fairtrade, IPW, Organic, WIETA ▪ PO Box 99 Lynedoch 7603 ▪ info@spier.co.za ▪ www.spier.co.za ▪ S 33° 58' 24.63" E 018° 47' 2.23" ▪ **T +27 (0)21-809-1143 (wine retail)** ▪ F +27 (0)21-809-1930

At this hugely popular, visitor-welcoming Stellenbosch property, where wine-as-a-lifestyle is communicated through tasting and restaurant facilities that emphasise provenance and heritage, chenin blanc enjoys a special status. 'We believe chenin is South Africa's best-kept secret and will, in the years to come, become the country's flagship variety,' says cellarmaster Frans Smit. They celebrate this grape in many wines across the portfolio, including the top-tier 21 Gables range. The other wine in this line-up, pinotage, is another nod to the country's winemaking history. Fitting, then, that both are made on the farm with, apparently, the country's oldest dated cellar: 1767. In addition to the wines available both locally and abroad, two ranges are destined solely for export — the Vintage and Private Collections, not reviewed here.

Frans K. Smit range

★★★★★ **Frans K. Smit** ⑨ Lavishly oaked (30 months 100% new) flagship. **07** (★★★★★) loses shiraz, ups cab & malbec. Fruit-filled yet savoury & well composed. Like **06**, should develop for 5+ years. Coastal WO.

21 Gables range

★★★★ **Pinotage** ✓ Coffee, orange-rind highlights on plum & mulberry toned **10** (★★★★★) from Stellenbosch grapes. Concentrated but not heavy, balanced 14.7% alcohol, dry conclusion. Ups ante on lush **09**.

★★★★☆ **Chenin Blanc** 🍴 🌿 Barrel fermented/aged **11** rich & well-composed; off-dry 7.7g/l sugar enhancing silky finish. Oak less obvious than on previous. From Tygerberg grapes.

Creative Block range

★★★★ **5** Merlot & cab lead **10** 5-way Bordeaux blend. Plum fruit unfettered by obvious oak; warmer vintage, late picking showing in 14.8% alcohol sweetness. **09** had tauter structure. WO Coastal, as next 2.

★★★★ **3** ✓ Shiraz with mourvèdre, viognier seasoning; mainly French oak, some American. Like polished **09**, **10** is sleek & smooth, with savoury farewell. Less concentrated than red stablemate, as good.

★★★★ **2** ✓ 🍴 🌿 From widely sourced fruit; step up **12** (★★★★★) mostly sauvignon. Like **10**, small portion of semillon barrel fermented (**11** was unoaked). Mineral, satisfying grip ex 5 months lees-ageing.

8 ⑨ 🌿 ★★★★ Pinotage & 6 other red varieties, drop viognier in **10**. Dried grass, fynbos & smoked meat notes, very dry 'woody' tannins, big alcohol. From Paarl Fairtrade farm.

Methodé Cap Classique range

★★★★ **Méthode Cap Classique** ✓ Accomplished dry sparkler from chardonnay & pinot noir. **10** youthful apple character, tight mineral finish; deserves some bottle-ageing to gain complexity. WO Stellenbosch.

ignature range

Cabernet Sauvignon ☺ 🏠 🖾 ★★★ Slight herby nuance on widely-sourced **11**; dark fruited, lightly oaked & refreshing for uncomplicated sipping. **Pinotage** ☺ 🏠 🖾 ★★★ Quintessential strawberry & acetone appeal, herb & floral notes on improved **11**; juicy & supple, commendably dry. **Chardonnay** ☺ 🏠 🖾 ★★★ Faint lemon & lime nuances on brushed-with-oak **12**; crowd-pleasing fruit sweetness bolstered by sugar — only just dry, like other whites in range. **Chenin Blanc** ☺ 🏠 🖾 ★★★ Thatch & white peach **12**, packed with flavour, exhibits fair concentration & depth. Nudges next level. **Sauvignon Blanc** ☺ 🏠 🖾 ★★★ Summer sipper **12** wafts nettles, mint & grass; zesty acidity & grapefruit pith end.

Merlot 🏠 🖾 ★★★ Plum & mulberry **11** is smooth, with sweet impression, slight bitter lift on finish. **Shiraz** ✓ 🏠 🖾 ★★★★ Dark & brooding **11** dinner companion most successful oak integration in line-up; avoury, with black pepper freshness & dry tail. Discontinued: **Rosé**. — CvZ

Spioenkop Wines

Location: Elgin ▪ Map: Elgin, Walker Bay & Bot River▪ WO: Western Cape/Elgin ▪ Est 2008 ▪ 1stB 2010 ▪ Tasting, ales & cellar tours by appt only ▪ Fee R20, waived on purchase (case of wine) ▪ Closed all pub hols ▪ Facilities or children ▪ BYO picnic ▪ Walking/hiking trails ▪ Conservation area ▪ Weddings/functions ▪ Self-catering cottage ▪ Owner(s) Valuline 119 (Pty) Ltd, 5 shareholders ▪ Cellarmaster(s)/winemaker(s)/viticulturist(s) Koen Roose-Vandenbroucke (2008) ▪ ±47ha/10ha (ptage, pinot, chenin, riesling, sauv) ▪ 40t/2,500cs own label 0% red 80% white ▪ PO Box 340 Grabouw 7160 ▪ info@spioenkopwines.co.za ▪ www.spioenkopwines.co.za S 34° 14' 14" E 019° 3' 50" ▪ **T +27 (0)21-859-1458**

This property is located on a hill in Elgin similar to the one in KwaZulu-Natal vere the Battle of Spioenkop was fought during the Anglo-Boer War, hence the ame. It is co-owned by Belgian couple Koen and Lore Roose, whose intention to produce wines where 'terroir overtakes technology'.

900 range

★★★★☆ **Pinotage** Unusual but rewarding **11** (★★★★) shows plums, red cherries but also overt spicy note. Dense despite relatively moderate 13% alcohol. Lacks purity, freshness of **10**.

★★★★ **Chenin Blanc** NEW Understated, subtle **11** shows citrus, peach & a leesy wet wool note. Medium bodied, with a long, nearly saline finish. Spontaneous ferment, 30% matured in old barrels. WO W Cape, as next.

★★★★ **Sauvignon Blanc** Serious expression of the variety. **11**, with 8% semillon, previewed last time, now starting to come into its own. White & yellow fruit, some pepper on finish. Good weight, gentle acidity.

Sauvignon Blanc Barrel Selection In abeyance.

Spioenkop Wines range

★★★★ **Riesling** Now bottled, **11** only just beginning to reveal potential. Intense lime & green apple flavour, good texture, riveting acidity, bone-dry finish.

★★★★☆ **Sauvignon Blanc** **11**, now bottled, demonstrates great purity & focus. Notes of lime, Granny Smith apple & pear. Good concentration, really vivid acidity, persistent finish. Should age extremely well. Better balanced, less austere than **10** (★★★★). — CE

▪ **Splattered Toad** see Cape Point Vineyards
▪ **Splendour** see Villiersdorp Cellar

Spookfontein Wines

Location: Hermanus ▪ Map: Elgin, Walker Bay & Bot River ▪ WO: Upper Hemel-en-Aarde Valley ▪ Est 2000 ▪ 1stB 2004 ▪ Tasting, sales & cellar tours by appt ▪ Two self-catering guest cottages ▪ Conservation area ▪ Owner(s) Spookfontein Wines cc (Mike Davis) ▪ Winemaker(s) Craig Sheard (Feb 2006) ▪ Viticulturist(s) Andries Gotze (Jan 2000) ▪ 313ha/±12ha (cabs s/f, merlot, pinot) ▪ 50t/1,000cs own label 100% red ▪ PO Box 12031 Mill Street Cape Town 8010 ▪ cjswine@hotmail.com ▪ S 34° 21' 19.5" E 019° 17' 20.8" ▪ **T +27 (0)82-265-1071**

The 2013 harvest should be a milestone in many respects for this Upper Hemel-en-Aarde Valley property. Owner Mike Davis and winemaker Craig Sheard anticipate celebrating its organic certification, the first in the Overberg; the first application of its first farm-made biodynamic preparation ('Cowpat pit!'); and its young block of pinot noir reaching the cordon wire.

Cabernet Sauvignon ★★★★ One of the Cape's leaner versions. Naturally fermented **08**'s mulberries & cream stretched over taut cab backbone. **Cabernet Franc ★★★★ 08**, while tending to the lean (unlike **07**), has plenty of sweet fruit flesh, easygoing tannins but sufficient tug for structure & interest. **Merlot ★★★★** Sugarplum note to step-up **08**'s mulberry & prune complexity. Only slightly herbal, very persistent & wonderfully dry (like most of these reds). **Pinot Noir ⓐ ★★★** Fresh raspberry, earthy allure on **08** ex young single-vineyard. **Phantom ✓ ★★★★** Merlot-led (with cab & cab franc) **08** raises the bar on **07** (**★★★★**). Poised & lengthy, but greater grip & just the right amount of flavour without seeming worked. Textbook stuff. Discontinued: **Rosé**. — CvZ

Spotswood Wines   🍷 NEW

Location/map/WO: Stellenbosch ▪ Est 2007 ▪ 1stB 2008 ▪ Tasting & sales by appt ▪ Owner(s) Spotswood family ▪ Cellarmaster(s)/winemaker(s) Guy Webber (Jan 2012, consultant) ▪ Viticulturist(s) Bill Spotswood (Sep 2007) ▪ 7.05ha/3ha (durif, shiraz, chard, viog) ▪ 28t/1,100cs own label 92% red 2% white 6% rosé ▪ Suite 200 Private Bag X4 Die Boord 7613 ▪ nick@limpro.co.za ▪ S 33° 59' 2.0" E 018° 51' 35.0" ▪ **T +27 (0)21-880-2893** ▪ F +27 (0)21-880-2893

In 2007, father and son Bill and Nick Spotswood, the former retired from the international confectionery business and the latter a civil engineer from Polokwane, bought a Blaauwklippen Road property in Stellenbosch's 'golden triangle' named Down The Road Farm. They inherited youngish vines — shiraz, whose first crop was in 2008, and rare-in-South-Africa red-wine variety durif, which came onstream in 2011. 'It's our flagship,' says Nick, 'because it's unusual and a divine wine, drinkable with anything.'

Durif ⌀ ★★★★ Variety, also known as petite sirah, shares its typical dark plum/prune fruit & juicy tannins in **11**. Still tight, brooding, deserves year/2 to unfurl & reveal all its charms. **Shiraz ⌀ ★★★** A giant at 15% alcohol, but a gentle one; **11** spicy/savoury red berry flavours are smooth, affable, lead on to a dry herbal conclusion. **Shiraz Reserve ⌀ ★★** More concentrated than sibling, **11** also more tannic & dry, with alcohol quite overt. **Dry Rosé ⌀ ★★★** Demure **11** from shiraz. Savoury, dry; enjoy well chilled. — JP/CvZ

Springfield Estate   🍴🍷🎋

Location/map/WO: Robertson ▪ Est/1stB 1995 ▪ Tasting & sales Mon-Fri 8-5 Sat 9-4 ▪ Closed Easter Fri/Sun, Dec 25 & Jan 1 ▪ Cellar tours by appt ▪ BYO picnic ▪ Owner(s) Bruwer family ▪ Cellarmaster(s)/viticulturist(s) Abrie Bruwer ▪ Winemaker(s) Abrie Bruwer, with Johan van Zyl ▪ 150ha (cabs s/f, merlot, p verdot, chard, sauv) ▪ IPW ▪ PO Box 770 Robertson 6705 ▪ admin@springfieldestate.com ▪ www.springfieldestate.com ▪ S 33° 50' 12.1" E 019° 54' 54.0" ▪ **T +27 (0)23-626-3661** ▪ F +27 (0)23-626-3664

What's new at this eminent Robertson estate of the Bruwer family ('Bruère' is how Huguenot ancestors who arrived in the Cape in 1688 would have had it)? 'It's all old news,' sighs winemaker Abrie. 'Every year we plant vines, do something to the cellar, buy some new equipment...' And no new tricks to explain the rare quality of especially his white wines in these warm parts. 'No tricks — just making the choices that lead to quality, the hundreds of little choices made each day'. Abrie agrees, though, that the lovely winter of 2012 was a boon. But news? No. Then he remembers to add that 'every year I do the same — but try to do it better!'

★★★★☆ Méthode Ancienne Cabernet Sauvignon ⓐ Naturally fermented, unfined & unfiltered as usual, **04** tasted few years back was alive & intense; fresh cedary cassis notes; fine, insistent dry grip.

★★★★ The Work of Time Time has softened the big tannins on **06** blend & added savoury complexity; herbaceous note part of the liveliness. Previous **04** (**★★★★★**) led by cab franc, this by cab & merlot.

★★★★☆ Méthode Ancienne Chardonnay ⓐ Something lively & exciting (&, wonderfully, a touch funky) on naturally made **09**. Full, ripe flavours absorb the new oak; rich, substantial, balanced.

★★★★ Wild Yeast Chardonnay ⓐ Earthy & oatmeal touches to ripe, flavourful **09** — more obvious sweet fruit, & a little less light-footed though with good acidity, than Méthode Ancienne. To seriously enjoy.

★★★★ Life From Stone Sauvignon Blanc 🎋 12 bursts with sweaty, grenadilla, tinned pea aromas & flavours. A stylistic choice, good of its type. Crisp, bone-dry, drinking well now. **11** (**★★★★**) a touch less fresh.

★★★★ Special Cuvée Sauvignon Blanc 🎋 As usual, **12** subtler than Life from Stone version, with citrus as well as ripe tropical tones. Some depth of flavour & weight — less aggressive than many Cape sauvignons.

Whole Berry Cabernet Sauvignon ⌀ ★★★★ Appealing ripe character on deft **10**, well built, with a finish that some might find too herbal but goes with the light-fruited freshness. **Pinot Noir** Await next. — TJ

Springfontein Wine Estate

ocation: Stanford ▪ Map: Elgin, Walker Bay & Bot River ▪ WO: Walker Bay ▪ Est 1996 ▪ 1stB 2004 ▪ Tasting, ales & cellar tours Mon–Fri 10–4 Sat by appt 10–2 ▪ Closed Easter Fri/Sun, Dec 25/26 & Jan 1 ▪ Tour groups ▪ arm produce ▪ BYO picnic ▪ Walking/hiking trail ▪ 3 self-catering cottages ▪ Owner(s) Johst & Jennifer Packard Veber, Jürgen & Susanne Schneider, with family & friends ▪ Cellarmaster(s) Christo Versfeld (Dec 2006) ▪ Winemaker(s) Christo Versfeld (Dec 2006), with Charlton Pietersen (Oct 2009) ▪ Viticulturist(s) Christo ersfeld (Dec 2006), with Johannes Janse (Mar 2009) ▪ 500ha/25ha (cab, p verdot, ptage, chenin) ▪ 145t/ 0,000cs own label 80% red 18% white 2% rosé ▪ PO Box 71 Stanford 7210 ▪ info@springfontein.co.za ▪ www.springfontein.co.za ▪ S 34° 25' 38.5" E 019° 24' 32.7" ▪ **T +27 (0)28-341-0651/+27 (0)72-371-**546 ▪ F +27 (0)28-341-0112

ver since seeing this unique sea site and its limestone soils in 1994, co-owner, winelover and collector Johst Weber understood its potential. His dream of nvolving friends and family in a 'unique combination of nature and human raftsmanship' has been so realised that both sets of owners, the Webers and chneiders, are relocating to Stanford from Germany. With the increasing erroir experience of winemaker Christo Versfeld, the range is being adapted, ines were regrafted and the process of organic conversion has commenced.

Single Vineyard range

★★★★ **Jonathan's Ridge Pinotage** ⓣ Refined pinot noir-like grace to sweetly fruited **09**, generous (mostly new) wooding unobtrusive. For winter log fires & oxtail.

★★★★ **Jonathan's Ridge Mendocino Pinotage** NEW Smooth & supple **09** is very nicely put together. Mulberry & spice perfume & flavours, succulently presented, oak perfectly judged. For drinking now till ±2016.

★★★★ **Jil's Dune Chenin Blanc** 🕸 Back on form after **10** (★★★★), flaunting butterscotch & stonefruit, **11**'s sexy face hides a serious side — silky elegance, perfect fruit/acid balance & ageablity.

Estate Wines

★★★★ **Red** ⓣ Stylish **07** showed refinement last year, the substantial new oak well melded.

★★★★ **Ikhalezi Noble Late Harvest** From chenin. Amber-hued raisiny, **07** (★★★★★) is one of a kind. Astonishingly rich at 372g/l sugar, it is so refreshed by racy acidity that it drinks beautifully; syrupy, tangy apricot with an added savoury roasted almond tone from new oak. 375ml. Even better than gorgeous **06** preview.

Special Red NEW ★★★★ Cab-strong Bordeaux blend packed with blackcurrants, **07**'s firm but ripe tannins providing structural support. **Ulumbaza** ⓣ ★★★★ Shiraz led mourvèdre in **07**'s spicy pears-in-red-wine styling previously. **White** ⓣ ★★★★ Sauvignon's penetrating intensity was leavened in **09** by pithy semillon fruit & just enough wood when last reviewed.

Terroir Selection

★★★★ **Cabernet Sauvignon** ✓ Blackcurrants & cappuccino & a scrub nuance, **09**'s attractions don't stop there. The supple body hints at underlying muscle tone, offers immediate drinking pleasure. Nudges next level.

★★★★ **Chardonnay Wild Yeast** NEW ✓ 🕸 Attractively perfumed **11**'s orange rind & hazelnuts get a tighter, racier focus on the palate, more lemon/lime, finishing on a vibrant high note.

Pinotage ⓣ ★★★★ Trenchant **08** offers sweet plum flavour; no longer new wood, but with a 15% alcohol bang! **Chardonnay** 🕸 ★★★ Was 'CY01 Chardonnay'. Restrained peach & buttered toast, **10** drinks well but enjoy now, not for keeping. **Chenin Blanc** 🕸 ★★★★ Some oaking gives **11**'s thatch richness an almond seam, increases the appealing fresh drinkability. Borders next level. **Sauvignon Blanc** 🕸 ★★★ With its gentle melon flavours & freshening acidity, **11** is easy to drink, on its own or with food.

Sopiensklip range

Red ☺ 🍷 ★★★ An easy-drinker & **09** does it with panache. Cab/merlot's fleshy plums given spicing & a pliable backbone from oak. **White** ☺ 🍷 🕸 ★★★ Unoaked semillon/chardonnay shows leafy intensity in **11**, appealing bruised apple fullness, finishing crisply dry. Friendly 12% alcohol.

Pink 🍷 🕸 ★★★ Bone-dry **11** from mourvèdre offers piquant red berry flavours. — CR

Spring Grove Wines

Location/map/WO: Stellenbosch ▪ 1stB 2005 ▪ Tasting & sales by appt ▪ Owner(s) Parodi family ▪ Winemaker(s) Neil Moorhouse (2005) ▪ Viticulturist(s) Hannes Jansen van Vuuren (Mar 2008) ▪ 10ha/6.4ha sangio, shiraz, pinot gris, sauv, viog) ▪ 41t/25,200L bulk ▪ PO Box 670 Vereeniging 1930 ▪ hannes@zorgvliet. om ▪ S 33° 54' 46.50" E 018° 56' 13.6" ▪ **T +27 (0)82-856-8717** ▪ F +27 (0)86-697-3938

No significant developments over the past year, says Hannes Jansen van Vuuren, who nurtures the vineyards on this Banhoek farm, its wines still made at neighbour Zorgvliet by Neil Moorhouse. Italian varieties will play an increasingly starring role, as one might hope given the Genovese roots of co-owner David Parodi.

★★★★ **Sauvignon Blanc** ✪ 🍽 Harmonious sample 11 (★★★★) fresh & enticing with lovely zesty mineral finish, though not as gutsy as 10.

Sangiovese NEW 🍽 ★★★★ Berries almost leap from the glass in delightfully fresh & youthful 10, sweet fruit flavours tailored by ageing in older barrels. **Shiraz** ✪ 🍽 ★★★★ Barrel sample 09's succulent fruitiness underlined by savoury, spicy tannins; pleasing balance & some seriousness. **Pinot Grigio** NEW 🍽 ★★★ nice change from sauvignon for fresh summer drinking. Preview 12 offers satisfying mouthful from this fashionable variety. **Viognier** ✪ ★★ Bold 10 tasted few years back. — IM

- ■ **Spring Valley** see Old Vines Cellars
- ■ **Spruitdrift** see Namaqua Wines
- ■ **Stablemate** see Excelsior Estate

Stanford Hills Winery

Location: Stanford ▪ Map: Elgin, Walker Bay & Bot River ▪ WO: Walker Bay ▪ Est 1856 ▪ 1stB 2002 ▪ Tasting, sales & tours Mon-Fri 8-5 by appt; Sat 10-1 ▪ Closed all pub hols ▪ Grappa, olive oil, preserves ▪ BYO picnic ▪ Cellar dinner (±20-30 guests), pairing food & wine ▪ Hiking/mountain biking trails ▪ Horse riding ▪ Fishing ▪ Whale watching flights from own airfield ▪ 5 self-catering cottages ▪ Owner(s) Stanford Hills Estate (Pty) Ltd ▪ Cellarmaster(s), winemaker(s) Peter Kastner (Apr 2005) ▪ Viticulturist(s) Peter Kastner ▪ 131ha/12ha (ptage, shiraz, chard, sauv) ▪ 60t/2,000cs own label 66% red 34% white ▪ PO Box 1052 Stanford 7210 ▪ info@stanfordhills.co.za ▪ www.stanfordhills.co.za ▪ S 34° 25' 21.4" E 019° 28' 25.7" ▪ **T +27 (0)28-341-0841** ▪ F +27 (0)28-341-0286

Stanford Hills farms indigenous flowers as well as grapes and now there's a link between the two with a new red wine — named Veldfire, after a protea natura hybrid which emerged on these hills some 30 years back. A white wine is to follow but they're not sure which flower to name it after, says Peter Kastner ('director winemaker, viticulturist and flower farmer' — who's the bottle-washer, then?).

★★★★ **Jacksons Pinotage** Two vintages tasted. Current 11 has usual prettily perfumed pure fruit aroma & flavours; fresh & well balanced despite weighty alcohol, with unobtrusively firm structure in support. Lighter-fruited 10 (★★★★) a slightly less convincing version, with over-emphatic dry tannins.

Veldfire NEW 🍽 ★★★ 11 pinotage a little dusty from the oak staves used, a little fiery from the massive alcohol (15.7%), with lighter, sweeter fruit than the senior Pinotage — yet undeniably appealing. **Jacksons Chardonnay** ★★★★ Oxidative element on modestly oaked 11 much better controlled than in some earlier vintages, adding to complexity & not reducing vibrancy. Powerful but harmonious & elegant, with good limy/nutty finish. 10 (★★★★) attractive but a little too big & rough. **Jacksons Sauvignon Blanc** 🍽 Await next. — TJ

Star Hill

Location: Montagu ▪ Map: Klein Karoo & Garden Route ▪ WO: Tradouw Highlands ▪ Est 2005 ▪ 1stB 2009 ▪ Tasting & sales Mon-Fri 9-4 Sat/Sun 9-3 ▪ Closed Dec 25 ▪ Cellar tours by appt ▪ Akkerboom Farm Stall & Restaurant ▪ Facilities for children ▪ Gifts ▪ Farm produce ▪ Conference facilities on Killarney farm ▪ Walks/hikes ▪ Mountain biking ▪ Akkerboom self-catering cottages (www.akkerboomcountrycottages.com) ▪ Owner(s) Grant Hatch & Christopher Palmer Tomkinson ▪ Winemaker(s) Lourens van der Westhuizen (consultant) ▪ Viticulturist(s) Lourens van der Westhuizen & Leander Gagiano (consultants) ▪ 15ha (shiraz, chenin, sauv, viog) ▪ 500cs own label 60% red 40% white ▪ PO Box 342 Montagu 6720 ▪ starhill@tradouw.co.za ▪ www.starhillwines.com ▪ S 33° 54' 46.86" E 020° 29' 32.31" ▪ **T +27 (0)28-572-1610** ▪ F +27 (0)28-572-1644

'Tradouw Highlands' is not a Wine of Origin you see much on labels, so these wines should immediately pique the curiosity. They're from vineyards on a plain 723m up the Langeberg Mountains where the conditions, though harsh and dry, are perfect for vines, say owners Grant Hatch and Christopher Palmer Tomkinson. Vinification is by Robertson single-vineyard specialist Lourens van der Westhuizen.

★★★★ **Shiraz** ✪ Single-vineyard 09 pepper/spice highlights to blackberry, rounded mouthfeel; elegant expression of the variety.

Chenin Blanc Wild Yeast ⓟ ★★★★ Older oak matured **10** engaging & persistent, with fresh acidity well balanced by juicy green/yellow apple fruit. **Viognier** ⓟ ★★★★ Substantial alcohol, softening dab sugar well disguised by **09**'s energetic lime freshness courtesy different picking dates. — CE/JP

Stark-Condé Wines

Location/map: Stellenbosch ▪ WO: Stellenbosch/Jonkershoek Valley/Elgin ▪ Est/1stB 1998 ▪ Tasting & sales Mon–Sun 10–4 ▪ Fee R30pp ▪ Closed Good Fri, Dec 25 & Jan 1 ▪ Postcard Café Tue–Sun 9.30–4 for light meals, coffee & cake ▪ Owner(s) Jonkershoek Cellars (Pty) Ltd ▪ Cellarmaster(s)/winemaker(s) José Conde (1998) ▪ Viticulturist(s) Andrew Klinck & Pieter Smit (1998, consultant) ▪ 250ha/40ha (cabs s/f, merlot, p verdot, shiraz) ▪ 100t/6,000cs own label 80% red 20% white ▪ PO Box 389 Stellenbosch 7599 ▪ info@stark-conde.co.za ▪ www.stark-conde.co.za, www.postcardcafe.co.za ▪ S 33° 57' 15.81" E 018° 54' 34.96" ▪ **T +27 (0)21-861-7700/+27 (0)21-887-3665** ▪ F +27 (0)21-887-4340

The 'unexpected popularity' of Marie Conde's Postcard Café — where the tables are filled thrice a day in summer — has left husband and cellarmaster José wondering if they're wine producers or restaurateurs. And more than a bit surprised when a wine show patron asks him if the winery is 'attached to that wonderful café'! As the young team injects new energy into an established wine business, they recognise its roots, Oude Nektar (the Jonkershoek home farm, which Marie's father Hans-Peter Schröder bought in the late 1980s, and its original wine brand, discontinued in the early 1990s), in the naming of a one-off wine from the sole 2008 crop of a high-lying organic vineyard ravaged by fire in March 2009.

Three Pines range

★★★★☆ **Cabernet Sauvignon** Extraordinary grace — a reflection the fine single-vineyard soil of origin — defines house-style. **10** has floral nuance to pristine bramble fruit in a pampering structure. Like standout **09** (★★★★★), a rare combination of delicacy & power. Unfined/filtered; dabs merlot & petit verdot.

★★★★☆ **Syrah** From lofty home-vineyard revered for elegance; alluring **10** ethereal spiciness & loads of berry flesh in a pliable parcel. Complex vinification: cold soak, portion whole-berry ferment, combo wild & commercial yeasts (local & Rhône), 40% new oak 2 years. Not to be hurried: **05** tasted sensational mid-2012.

Stark-Condé range

★★★★☆ **Oude Nektar** NEW One-off cab from the only harvest of a young high-lying (600m) organic vineyard, destroyed by fire in March 2009. **08** more muscular, less athletic than Three Pines stars, but retains stamp of elegance. Mere 45 cases. Vineyard in rehab, next due only 2017. WO Jonkershoek Valley, as for Three Pines.

★★★★ **Cabernet Sauvignon** Home-farm's four best cab blocks, with dashes finest merlot & cab franc, soupçon petit verdot; **10** epitomises the stylish red berry refinement of Jonkershoek.

★★★★ **Syrah** Striking pepper spice & ripe, full mulberry fruit grounded by tannin, **10** denser & gutsier than Three Pines version, no less enjoyable.

Pepin Condé range

★★★★ **Rowey Vineyards Pinot Noir** NEW 🍷 In Pepin range as grapes not home grown, but with Stark-Condé finery & gravitas. **11**'s plush texture embeds bright red berry fruit, deeply layered. WO Elgin.

★★★★ **Chenin Blanc** ✓ 🏠 🍷 Voluptuous but balanced **11** offers generous fruit & a lovely (not-quite-dry) roundness without being blowsy. Wild yeasts & 40% barrel fermented, 5% new.

Cabernet Sauvignon ⓟ 🏠 ★★★★ **09**'s rich dark fruit guided by firm yet yielding tannic structure. Gear up on **08** (★★★★), attractive onvext few years. **Pinot Noir** ✓ 🏠 🍷 ★★★★ Elegant cherry charm with earthy grip, **11** delicate but not superficial. Enjoyable young, it will reward patience. Production ave to 500 cases. WO Elgin. **Sauvignon Blanc** ✓ 🏠 🍷 ★★★★ Soft & supple, the converse of 'green' styling. Natural acidity of **11** fleshed out with oak richness (20%, old cask). Like **10**, shade less compelling than previous. WO Elgin. — DS

▪ **Starlette** *see* Allée Bleue Wines
▪ **Star Tree** *see* Orange River Wine Cellars

Steenberg Vineyards

Location: Constantia ▪ Map: Cape Peninsula ▪ WO: Constantia/Western Cape/Coastal ▪ Est 1990 ▪ 1stB 1996 ▪ Tasting & sales Mon–Fri 9–6 Sat/Sun 10–6 ▪ Fee R50 for flagship range, waived on purchase ▪ Closed Good Fri & Dec 25 ▪ Cellar tours 11 & 3 daily ▪ Bistro Sixteen82 (see Restaurants section); Catharina's at Steenberg ▪ Steenberg Hotel & Spa (see Accommodation section); conferences; world-class golf course, walking trail ▪

Extensive merchandising area ▪ Annual festivals: Constantia Fresh (Feb), Spring it on Constantia (end Oct) ▪ Conservation area ▪ Owner(s) Graham Beck Enterprises ▪ Winemaker(s) JD Pretorius (Mar 2009) ▪ Vineyard manager(s) Johann de Swardt ▪ 90ha/60ha (merlot, sauv) ▪ 312t/35,000cs own label 40% red 60% white ▪ WIETA ▪ PO Box 224 Steenberg 7947 ▪ info@steenbrg.co.za ▪ www.steenberg-vineyards.co.za ▪ S 34° 4'17.0" E 018° 25'31.1" ▪ T +27 (0)21-713-2211 ▪ F +27 (0)21-713-2201

Steenberg are bidding sad farewell to their top reserve sauvignon bottling, as their oldest vineyard, no longer considered viable, undergoes replanting. Just one of the many changes wrought since the late Graham Beck bought the estate in 2005, and yet another is planned: 'We're in the process of changing the whole concept of the restaurant at Steenberg Hotel,' reports GM John Loubser, 'and it's not just a tweak — it's going to be a quantum leap.' From cellardoor experience to social and traditional media, the drive to improve is relentless, the team under Loubser determined to secure the winery a place in South Africa's top five.

Steenberg Vineyards range

★★★★ **Merlot** ⊘ Property's signature fresh herbal character & spicy oak a foil for ripe **10**'s damson fruit, masking richness & providing elegance with incisive acidity & firm oak tannins. Includes 14% cab.

★★★★☆ **Nebbiolo** ⊘ **10** needed time once opened to blossom & show itself to be every bit as excellent as **09**; perfectly ripe & savoury sour cherry flavours given definition by robust tannins & acidity associated with variety. Decant in youth, before enjoying with food.

★★★★☆ **CWG Auction Reserve Garibaldi Nebbiolo** NEW Reserve **09** bottling is excellent rendition of noble Italian variety. Judicious use of older barrels allows pure expression of richly savoury & lithe dark cherry fruit, framed by firm grape tannins. As with standard bottling, needs decanting to show its many charms.

★★★★ **Shiraz** ⊘ Beguilingly rich **10** elegant & expressive, with plenty of spice & earthiness to appeal. Smoky oak char more obvious, not as convincing & vivid as **09** (★★★★★).

★★★★☆ **Catharina** Barrel selection best of **09** vintage; exhibits vineyard's trademark perfumed eucalypt in powerful yet graceful cab-led Bordeaux blend, with ripe, compact fruit lifted by elegance of cab franc, softened by merlot & underpinned by all-new oak. No **08**.

★★★★ **Sauvignon Blanc** ▤ ⊘ Fabulously vibrant, concentrated **12** a delightful combination of fresh minerality & rich weightiness, derived from lees-ageing & barrel-fermented component. Stylish & harmonious.

★★★★☆ **Sauvignon Blanc Reserve** ⊘ Majestic **11** a fitting farewell for last bottling from property's oldest vineyard with its pitifully low, concentrated yields. Layer upon layer of intense flavours provide extraordinary depth & complexity, complemented by flinty minerality & pithy texture.

★★★★☆ **Semillon** ⊘ Usual richness & texture in **11** ensures perfectly satisfying mouthful of complex, weighty, harmoniously oaked wine. Extended time on lees in barrel provides dimension, breadth, while minerality & savoury acidity keep the focus throughout.

★★★★★ **Magna Carta** ⊕ Fine **10** (★★★★★) barrel-fermented sauvignon-semillon. Pristine (like **09**), layered herbaceous fruit with semillon's weighty, textured richness to match steely acidity & stony minerality.

★★★★☆ **Sauvignon Blanc-Semillon** ⊕ **08** with 66% new-oaked semillon mid-2009 showed complex flavours & creamy oak. Delicious but needed touch more verve. Occasional bottling.

★★★★ **1682 Pinot Noir** Fragrant **09** MCC rosé sparkling pleasingly firm; 3 years on lees for breadth & complexity. Firm all-pinot backbone masks fruit at present in lean, serious style. These MCCs WO W Cape.

★★★★ **1682 Chardonnay** ⊘ MCC **11** blanc de blancs sparkler in richly creamy, drily voluptuous style. Fresh & balanced apple, citrus flavours broadened by 18 months on lees & carried by deliciously frothy mousse.

HMS Echo ▤ ⊘ ★★★★ Cab-led **10** blend, adds Stellenbosch, Darling & Robertson grapes to home fruit. Accessible & fresh, perfect for decent everyday drinking. **HMS Sphynx Chardonnay** ▤ ⊘ ★★★ Lightly oaked, tropical **12** harmonious & appealing, more charming than serious. With brought-in grapes, like other HMS wines. **HMS Rattlesnake Sauvignon Blanc** ▤ ⊘ ★★★ Barrel-ferment portion & dash semillon add dimension to pleasingly balanced **12**, acidity focuses brisk finish.

Klein Steenberg range

Cabernet Sauvignon ⊕ ★★★ Accessible **10**'s juicy fruit makes easy everyday quaffing. **Sauvignon Blanc** ▤ ⊘ ★★★ Crisp & light **12**, simple multi-regional quaffer. — IM

▪ **Steenbok** see Riebeek Cellars
▪ **Steenhuis** see Wine-of-the-Month Club
▪ **Steenrust** see StellenRust
▪ **STELL** see StellenRust

Stellar Winery

Location: Klawer ▪ Map: Olifants River ▪ WO: Western Cape ▪ Est 2000 ▪ 1stB 2001 ▪ Tasting & sales Mon-Fri 8–5 ▪ Closed all pub hols ▪ Cellar tours by appt ▪ BYO picnic ▪ Owner(s) Rossouw family, Stellar Empowerment Trust & others ▪ Cellarmaster(s) Berty Jones (Oct 2008) ▪ Winemaker(s) Klaas Coetzee (Aug 2010) & Mauritius Naude ▪ Viticulturist(s) Elizabeth Cloete (2011) ▪ ±68ha/Stellar Farming & ±149ha/Independent organic producers (cab, merlot, ptage, ruby cab, shiraz, chenin, chard, muscat d'A, sauv) ▪ 11,900t ▪ Other export brands: African Star, Firefly, Ithemba, Moonlight Organics, Natural Star, Running Duck, Sunshine Organics, Ubuntu ▪ Brands for clients: Ilula Gepa, La Place, Usapho ▪ Control Union (organic certification), Fair for Life (fairtrade) ▪ PO Box 4 Klawer 8145 ▪ info@stellarorganics.com ▪ www.stellarorganics.com ▪ S 31° 53' 13.7" E 018° 37' 53.0" ▪ **T +27 (0)27-216-1310** ▪ F +27 (0)86-635-1968

'The Stellar Organics brand appeared on the market in 2002 with not a customer in sight and backed purely by optimism, faith and a lot of chutzpah,' recalls marketer Shelagh de Rosenwerth of a venture that started out with one cellar sans a roof over the tanks, dubbed 'The Cellar beneath the Stars', and 'an awful lot of organic wine to sell'. Fast-forward a decade to a transformed environment that encompasses a multi-estate operation with a solid reputation for ethical production and trading; two fully operational cellars at Trawal and Vredendal, easing capacity pressures and enhancing the quality of the 2012 wines; and a 2.5-million bottles-per-year global market for their products. They are also the largest producer of no-added-sulphur wines in the world. Remarkable achievements to raise a glass of organic wine to!

Stellar Organic Reserve range NEW

Pinot Noir 🍷 ☼ 🖾 ★★ 'Forest floor' earthiness on austere **11** food wine. **Cabernet Sauvignon-Pinotage** 🖾 ☼ 🖾 ★★★ Cab-led (70%) **11** a tad rough around the edges, packed with fruit but also strong tannins. **Semillon-Sauvignon Blanc** 🖾 ☼ 🖾 ★★★ Previewed **12** lightish bone-dry sipper, with interesting combo blackcurrant, khaki bush & red apple.

Stellar Organics range

Cabernet Sauvignon ☺ 🖾 ☼ 🖾 ★★★ **12** offers juicy anytime enjoyment. Drinkability enhanced here & throughout range by moderate alcohol (±13%), lively acidity &, for reds, restrained oaking. **Merlot** ☺ 🖾 ☼ 🖾 ★★★ Mulberry-infused **12** supple, soft, slips down easily. **Rosé** ☺ 🖾 ☼ 🖾 ★★★ **12** marries mostly chenin with pinotage for satisfyingly dry, lightish, wallet-friendly enjoyment. **Chenin Blanc** ☺ 🖾 ☼ 🖾 ★★★ Preview **12** thatch & pear aromas, lipsmacking acidity, emphatic dry tail. **Chenin Blanc-Sauvignon Blanc** ☺ 🖾 ☼ ★★★ Appley **12** is a 70/30 blend, soupçon sugar softens finish.

Pinotage 🖾 ☼ 🖾 ★★★ Slight acetone hint on fruit-sweet **12** preview. **Shiraz** 🖾 ☼ 🖾 ★★ Dip in **12**, one-dimensional & brief. **Chardonnay** 🖾 ☼ 🖾 ★★★ Noticeable sweetness on gently oaked, lemony **12**. **Sauvignon Blanc** 🖾 ☼ 🖾 ★★★ **12** grassy & brisk seafood companion. **Sparkling Extra Dry** NEW ☼ 🖾 ★★ Frothy, pleasant **12**, good partner (winemakers say) for oysters or strawberries. Discontinued: **Sauvignon Blanc Reserve, Semillon Reserve, Colombard-Sauvignon Blanc**.

Stellar Organics No-Sulphur-Added

Cabernet Sauvignon 🖾 ☼ 🖾 ★★★ Interesting warm hay aroma on improved **12** lightish juicy sipper. **Merlot** 🖾 ☼ 🖾 ★★★ **12** summer red with firm tannins & refreshing acidity. **Pinotage** NEW 🖾 ☼ 🖾 ★★ Slight funk, rubber notes on juicy **12**. **Shiraz** 🖾 ☼ 🖾 ★★★ Vibrant **12**, leap up in quality, quintessential shiraz red berries, plush tannins. **Rosé** NEW 🖾 ☼ 🖾 ★★★ Another standout in this improved lineup, **12** pretty pink, strawberry infused & dry. Try with pizza. **White** NEW 🖾 ☼ 🖾 ★★ **12** from colombard, casual dry quaffing.

Live-A-Little range

Really Ravishing Red 🖾 ☼ ★★★ From pinotage, with cranberry aroma, acidic flick. **NV**, as for all these carefree quaffers. **Rather Revealing Rosé** 🖾 ☼ ★★ Delicate off-dry quick sip from ruby cab. **Wildly Wicked White** 🖾 ☼ ★★★ Easygoing just-dry picnic partner from chenin & sauvignon. **Slightly Sweet & Shameless** 🖾 ☼ ★★ Aromatic, not-too-sweet curry companion with litchi fragrance.

Heaven on Earth range

Natural Sweet ✓ ☼ ★★★ Honey-sweet dessert from sun-dried muscat d'Alexandrie, usually fermented in older oak but latest **NV** is unwooded. A lime marmalade indulgence, if tad less complex than previous. — DB/CvZ

Stellekaya Winery

Location/map: Stellenbosch ▪ WO: Stellenbosch/Western Cape ▪ Est 1998 ▪1stB 1999 ▪ Tasting, sales & cellar tours Mon-Fri 10–4 ▪ Closed all pub hols; Dec 16 to Jan 2/3 ▪ Private luncheon & wine tasting with winemaker by arrangement (up to 6 pax) ▪ Owner(s) Dave & Jane Lello ▪ Winemaker(s) Ntsiki Biyela (Feb 2004) ▪ Viticulturist(s) Paul Wallace (Jan 2005, consultant) ▪ 23ha/15ha under vine ▪ 6,000cs own label 100% red ▪ Brands for clients: Exact Africa, The Grand Beach Café ▪ IPW ▪ PO Box 12426 Die Boord Stellenbosch 7613 ▪ info@stellekaya.co.za ▪ www.stellekaya.co.za ▪ S 33° 56′ 27.6″ E 018° 50′ 47.3″ ▪ **T +27 (0)21-883-3873** ▪ F +27 (0)21-883-2536

With sangiovese an important component in the red-wine lineup, winemaker Ntsiki Biyela spent the 2011 vintage at Petra Winery in Tuscany, immersing herself in viticulture, winemaking and the culture (including learning to make focaccia!). She proudly reports that Stellekaya is on track with the variety. Looking to the future, work is starting on a tasting venue and underground cellar at the Stellekaya estate on the edge of Stellenbosch.

Premium range

★★★★ Merlot ⊛ Such power in the berry, mint crisp flavours, one almost forgets how well made **08** is. Oak is in careful support, mainly older barrels, to retain the supple sleekness, fruit focus.

★★★★ Shiraz ⊛ Luscious red berries are **08**'s platform for spice array, vanilla, black pepper, cinnamon, but a wilder scrub note creeps into the palate, adding to the complexity. Ripe & ready.

★★★★ Orion Flagship cab-led Bordeaux blend. Heaps of concentration in **08**, intense blackcurrants & cigarbox, yet the palate remains juicy, streamlined, with supple tannins.

Cabernet Sauvignon ⊛ ★★★★ Cappuccino & ripe plums, **08** captures your attention but best is still to come — has 7+ year future, needs year or 2 to meld. **Pinotage** ✓ 🍸 🖾 ★★★★ Only partial barrel ageing, which accounts for **10**'s ebullient fruitiness, youthfully vibrant palate appeal. WO Western Cape. **Aquarius** NEW ★★★★ Equal cab, merlot, cab franc in **11** shows succulent plums, peppery underbrush tones that add interest; firm but ripe tannins. **Cape Cross** ⊛ ★★★★ Cab domination shows in **08**'s lush blackcurrant, matches dry tannins but even better in a year. **Hercules** ★★★★ Mainly sangiovese, dash cab gives **09** black cherry richness dusted with white pepper & the variety's renowned dry tannins. Bring on the food!

Boschetto range

Red ⊛ 🍸 ★★★ Mainly cab in appealing **09** with 3 partners; vibrant blackcurrants juicy counterpoint to oaking. **White** 🍸 🖾 ★★★★ White peach & fresh pear on exuberant **12**; brisk & breezy for summer enjoyment. — GdB/CR/CvZ

■ **Stellenbosch Drive** *see Origin Wine*

Stellenbosch Hills Wines

Location/map: Stellenbosch ▪ WO: Stellenbosch/Polkadraai Hills ▪ Est 1945 ▪ 1stB 1972 ▪ Tasting & sales Mon-Fri 8–5 Sat/pub hols 10–3 ▪ Fee R10; R40 wine, biltong & droëwors tasting ▪ Closed Good Fri, Dec 25 & Jan 1 ▪ The Tank art gallery ▪ Owner(s) 16 members ▪ Cellarmaster(s) PG Slabbert (Jan 1997) ▪ Winemaker(s) Juan Slabbert (Jan 2009) ▪ Viticulturist(s) Johan Pienaar & Eben Archer (consultants) ▪ 715ha (cab, merlot, ptage, shiraz, chard, chenin, muscat de Hambourg, sauv) ▪ 8,000t/10,000cs own label 68% red 30% white 2% other ▪ IPW ▪ PO Box 40 Vlottenburg 7604 ▪ info@stellenbosch-hills.co.za ▪ www.stellenbosch-hills.co.za ▪ S 33° 57′ 38.2″ E 018° 48′ 1.8″ ▪ **T +27 (0)21-881-3828** ▪ F +27 (0)21-881-3357

Stellenbosch Hills is now more at the heart of the local community than ever, thanks to its annual Polkakids sponsorship of Vlottenburg Primary School, involving a percentage of sales from the popular Polkadraai range. At the cellar, the focus is increasingly on wines that complement food. 'Lower alcohol is also important,' says marketing manager Tanja Fourie, 'given SA's strict drinking and driving laws.'

Stellenbosch Hills range

★★★★ 1707 Reserve Red ⊛ **08** (**★★★★**) from shiraz plus Bordeaux grapes. When last tasted, cranberry fruit was dominated by sweet toasty oak, fine tannins added to soft mouthfeel. **07** was more harmonious.

Cabernet Sauvignon ☺ 🍸 🖾 ★★★ Easy, appealing **10**, lots to like: blackcurrant, berry, meaty notes & peppery spices. Robust & dry for mealtime partnering.

Merlot ⊛ 🍸 ★★★ Food-friendly **08** displaying mocha & blackberry notes. Fresh & pleasant, if straightforward. **Pinotage** 🍸 🖾 ★★★ Tobacco & cedar perfumes, **10** rich dark berries & variety's firm tannins. **Shiraz** 🍸

Await next. **Chenin Blanc** 🍴 🏵 ★★ Honest, unpretentious **12**, shows apple crispness. **Sauvignon Blanc** 🍴 🏵 ★★ Understated **12**, hint of asparagus, marked dryness good match for richer seafood. **1707 Reserve White** ⚡ ★★★ Opulent **09** chardonnay with semillon & viognier. All-new oak drives intensely flavoured, ultra-rich but dry palate. **Muscat de Hambourg** ✓ 🏵 ★★★★ Now vintage-dated, **10** takes this unique-in-SA jerepiko-style fortified dessert to a new level: fragrant sweet-raspberry & clove, broad but lively flavours, vibrant freshness. Bargain price & a great future, too. Eclipses pedestrian **NV (★★)** bottling. Discontinued: **Chardonnay**.

Polkadraai range

> **Pinotage-Merlot** ☺ 🍴 🏵 ★★★ Friendly **10** offers juicy plum pudding & spice. WO Polkadraai Hills, as for all these. **Sauvignon Blanc** NEW ☺ 🏵 ★★★ **12**, in 3L box, bursts with balanced greenpepper & pineapple appeal.

Merlot-Shiraz NEW 🏵 ★★ **10** cranberry braai buddy in 3L box. **Chenin Blanc-Sauvignon Blanc** 🍴 🏵 ★★★ Easy **12**, tropical fruit & bellpepper combo, softly dry. **Pinot Noir Rosé Sparkling** 🏵 ★★★ Party pleaser **12**, strawberry sweetness on a big, bouncy bed of bubbles. — DB

Stellenbosch Ridge

Location/map/WO: Stellenbosch ▪ Est 2004 ▪ 1stB 2005 ▪ Tasting & sales at Guardian Peak (see entry) ▪ Owner(s) Jean Engelbrecht ▪ Winemaker(s) Coenie Snyman (Jan 2005) ▪ Viticulturist(s) Dirkie Mouton (Jan 2010) ▪ 7t/750cs own label 100% red ▪ IPW ▪ PO Box 473 Stellenbosch 7599 ▪ info@rustenvrede.com ▪ www.stellenboschridge. com ▪ S 34° 0′ 40.19″ E 018° 50′ 31.99″ ▪ **T +27 (0)21-881-3881** ▪ F +27 (0)21-881-3000

Production is up to 750 cases from 600 of this Bordeaux-style blend, a niche project by Rust en Vrede owner Jean Engelbrecht and winemaker Coenie Snyman. The idea is for Stellenbosch Ridge to utilise top-notch fruit from beyond the estate's Helderberg confines. Plans are also afoot to expand the portfolio.

★★★★ **Stellenbosch Ridge** Elegant & refined **10** hides its power beneath a velvety black fruit sheen. Cab (71%) ramped up in 4-way Bordeaux-style blend. Layers of plum, chocolate & cassis mingle superbly with restrained oak (50% new). Structured for the long haul. — FM

Stellenbosch University Welgevallen Cellar

Location/map/WO: Stellenbosch ▪ Est 2001 ▪ 1stB 2009 ▪ Tasting Mon-Fri 9-4 Sat by appt ▪ Fee R10pp ▪ Closed all pub hols, Dec 25-Jan 10 ▪ Owner(s) Stellenbosch University ▪ Cellarmaster(s)/winemaker(s) Riaan Wassüng (Jan 2004) ▪ Viticulturist(s) Vaatjie Jacobs (Jan 1973) ▪ 11ha/10ha (cab, ptage, shiraz, chard, sauv) ▪ 2,300cs own label 68% red 32% white ▪ Department of Viticulture & Oenology Private Bag X1 Matieland 7602 ▪ winesales@sun.ac.za, rfw@sun.ac.za ▪ http://academic.sun.ac.za/viti_oenol/ ▪ S 33° 56′ 22.38″ E 018° 52′ 1.92″ ▪ **T +27 (0)21-808-2925** ▪ F +27 (0)21-808-4781

In the premises where where Abraham Perold crossed pinot noir and hermitage (cinsaut) to create pinotage in the 1920s, Stellenbosch University oenology students today still learn their winecraft. While respect for tradition is an important part of their ethos, so too is creating value for money wines in the current climate.

Die Laan range

Rector's Reserve Occasional release. **Pinotage** ✓ ★★★★ Pleasingly styled **10** has bright fruit & fine acid backbone throughout. Oaking, almost half new, lends seriousness. **Cape Blend** ✓ ★★★★ Well-constructed, ripe **10** cab & pinotage blend with splash petit verdot is as appetisingly fresh & savoury as previous. **Sauvignon Blanc** NEW 🍴 ★★★ **12** tank sample bit unsettled but shows typical crisp herbaceousness. **Viognier** 🍴 Await new.

Maties range

Rooiplein ☺ ★★★ Was 'Dry Red'. Latest **NV** shiraz smoky mocha quaffer in easy-drinking style. — IM

Stellendrift — SHZ Cilliers/Kuün Wyne

Location/map/WO: Stellenbosch ▪ Est 1995 ▪ 1stB 1996 ▪ Tasting & cellar tours by appt ▪ Owner(s) Fanie Cilliers (SHZ Cilliers/Kuün Wines) ▪ Cellarmaster(s)/winemaker(s)/viticulturist(s) Fanie Cilliers (Nov 1995) ▪ 5,800cs own label 90% red 10% white ▪ PO Box 6340 Uniedal 7612 ▪ fcilliers@vodamail.co.za ▪ www. stellendrift.co.za ▪ S 33° 58′ 54.92″ E 018° 46′ 15.91″ ▪ **T +27 (0)21-887-6561** ▪ F +27 (0)21-887-6561

Wine's in his blood — Stellenbosch-based owner Fanie Cilliers' ancestors were French vignerons before they fled to the Cape in 1700; by 1709 they had 8,000 vines under cultivation. Their descendant is now exporting to Germany and the UK, and his stock-in-trade is 'more mature, softer wines, competitively priced'.

Stellendrift range

Reserve Cabernet Sauvignon Not tasted. **Merlot** 🍴 ★★ Green austerity in **08**, bone-dry, medium-bodied food wine. **Kruispad Pinotage** ⊕ 🍴 ★★★ When last tasted, **05** earthy & herbal, with integrated alcohol & firm tannins which should have softened by now. **VOC Syrah** 🍴 ★★★★ White pepper & violets on improved **09**, 15% alcohol held in check by perfumed fruit, fresh acid & sweet oak aroma. **Merlot-Cabernet Sauvignon Blitz** Await new release. **Cape Huguenot Merlot-Pinotage** ⊕ ★★★ Merlot-led **05**, pasta partner with mocha & plum flavours when reviewed. **Giant Sauvignon Blanc** 🍴 Await next. **Cape White Savour** Temporarily out of stock.

Cilliers Cellars range

De Reijgersdaal Cabernet Sauvignon Not tasted. **Elizabeth Couvret Merlot** New bottling missed our deadline. **Jacko's Pinotage-Cabernet Sauvignon** ⊕ ★★ 05 no spring chicken yet still juicy & accessible, toffee scent & sweet berry taste.

De Oude Opstal range

Cabernet Sauvignon Reserve ⊕ ★★★ Blackberry & dried fruit on earthy **05**, oak was still obvious mid-2010. **Merlot-Cabernet Sauvignon** ⊕ ★★★ When last we tried, **04** was leaner, with herbal notes, best enjoyed soon. — HJ

StellenRust

Location/map/WO: Stellenbosch ▪ Est/1stB 1928 ▪ Tasting & sales Mon-Fri 10–5 Sat 10–3 ▪ Fee R20 incl appetisers ▪ Bottelary property: tasting by appt only ▪ Closed Ash Wed, Easter Fri-Mon, Ascension Day, Dec 25/26 & Jan 1 ▪ Cellar tours by appt ▪ Farm-style platters & pre-arranged lunches/dinners ▪ BYO picnic ▪ Tour groups ▪ Grape 'stompings' ▪ Gifts ▪ Conferences ▪ Weddings/functions (300+ pax) ▪ Walking/hiking & mountain biking trails ▪ Art exhibition ▪ Owner(s) StellenRust Family Trust ▪ Cellarmaster(s) Tertius Boshoff (Jan 2004) ▪ Winemaker(s) Tertius Boshoff (Jan 2004), with Christo van Rooyen (Feb 2012) ▪ Viticulturist(s) Kobie van der Westhuizen (Jan 2000) ▪ 500ha/250ha (cab, cinsaut, merlot, ptage, shiraz, chard, chenin, muscat d'A, sauv) ▪ 1,700t/150,000cs own label 69% red 30% white 1% rosé + 20,000cs for clients ▪ Other export brands: Steenrust, STELL, Steynsrust ▪ Brands for clients: Amera, Embrace, Sabi Sabi private game lodge ▪ HACCP 2005, Fairtrade ▪ PO Box 26 Koelenhof 7605 ▪ info@stellenrust.co.za ▪ www.stellenrust.co.za ▪ S 33° 59' 18.0" E 018° 50' 57.9" (Hberg) S 33° 51' 44.41" E 018° 46' 34.11" (Btlry) ▪ **T** +27 (0)21-880-2283 ▪ F +27 (0)21-880-2284

StellenRust was once part of the farm bought in 1692 by master stonemason Douwe Steyn who built the Castle of Good Hope. There is now a young but equally rock-solid duo who run this large family farm. They have a healthy respect for both their venerable bushvines as well as their modern clients, having quadrupled sales in South Africa and had the singular honour of suppling four different cultivar wines for the London Olympic Games.

Super Premium range

★★★★ **Peppergrinder's Shiraz** Complex & elegant **09** (★★★★★) from revived 67 year old single-vineyard, raises the bar on **08** (★★★★) & **07**. Pepper dominates, as advertised, with aromatic lift & wild berry tone from dabs viognier & mourvèdre. New oak (22 months) & supple structure all in harmony.

★★★★ **Timeless** Brighter & more harmonious in classic vintage, **09** (★★★★★) shows more fruit intensity than **08**, with a tight core of cool cassis & cedar. Complex & firmly structured to reward handsomely after cellaring for 6-8 years.

★★★★ **Barrel Fermented Chardonnay** 🎖 Tightly woven **11** tad less expressive in youth than **10** (★★★★★). Still shows fruit purity & mineral nuance with creaminess from natural fermentation & oak. Elegant & ageworthy.

★★★★☆ **'47' Barrel Fermented Chenin Blanc** 🎖 Tiny (2t) crop from 47 year old single-vineyard has less botrytis in drier **11** vintage. Not as flamboyantly rich as **10**, showing toasty caramel, quince flavours, but more tangy acidity, for lively ageability.

★★★★ **Chenin d'Muscat Noble Late Harvest** ⊕ Old chenin & muscat vineyards yield a light & vivacious elixir in **09** from mere 1t of grapes. Gentle apricot, almond & hint of perfume, subtly oaked. Delightful!

Cornerstone Pinotage ★★★★ **09** concentrated plum & spicy tobacco flavours from low-yield (2t) old vines, tightly focused in vintage's classic structure & integrated new oak. Youthful & cellarworthy step up on **08** (★★★★). **JJ Handmade Reserve** ★★★★ **09** pinotage-led Cape Blend is more complex & structured than **08** (★★★★). Handsomely crafted with new oak integrated into richly spiced fruit. Supple & ageworthy.

Premium range

Cabernet Sauvignon 🍴 🖄 ★★★ Riper **10** more approachable than previous, with warm berry fruit & dry food-friendly finish. **Merlot** 🍴 🖄 ★★★★ **10** shows better balance of minty blueberry fruit & tannins in warmer year. Greater potential with time. **Pinotage** 🍴 🖄 ★★★ Brighter **11** is balanced, with clean juicy fruited appeal. Food friendly & good for 3-5 years. **Shiraz** 🍴 🖄 ★★★★ More harmonious nod to the Rhône in **10**. White pepper, fynbos & red berry flavours streamlined by firm chalky tannins. **Simplicity** ✓ 🍴 🖄 ★★★★ Shiraz's spicy drinkability given structural support by merlot & cab on riper **10** blend. Well crafted & satisfying. **Chardonnay** ✓ 🍴 🖄 ★★★★ Elegant & understated **12** has creamy pear & lime flavours with bright food-friendly acidity & a brush of oak. **Chenin Blanc** 🍴 🖄 ★★★ Old vines show good fruit/acid balance, brushed with botrytis on **12**. Succulent, rich & satisfying. **Sauvignon Blanc** 🍴 🖄 ★★★ Bright & racy **12** has tangy passionfruit & herbaceous flavours that complement food.

Kleine Rust range

Pinotage Rosé ☺ 🍴 🖄 ★★★ **12** tangy & light tipple with bright cranberry/savoury tone. **White** ☺ 🍴 🖄 ★★★ **12** chenin/sauvignon with crisp & crunchy ripe apple flavours. **Semi-Sweet** ☺ 🍴 🖄 ★★★ **12** scented muscat lift to tropical-toned chenin/sauvignon quaffer.

Red 🍴 🖄 ★★★ **11** is juicy, plump & savoury for outdoors/barbeque quaffing. — MW

Stellenzicht Vineyards

Location/map/WO: Stellenbosch ▪ Est 1982 ▪ 1stB 1989 ▪ Tasting & sales Mon-Fri 9–5 Sat/Sun 10–4 ▪ Fee R25, waived on purchase ▪ Closed Good Fri, Dec 25 & Jan 1 ▪ Cellar tours by appt ▪ Owner(s) Lusan Premium Wines ▪ Winemaker(s) Guy Webber (Oct 1998), with Nataleé Botha (Aug 2010) ▪ Viticulturist(s) Quintus van Wyk ▪ 228ha/99ha (cab, merlot, ptage, shiraz) ▪ 795t/20,000cs own label 85% red 15% white ▪ BRC, HACCP ▪ PO Box 104 Stellenbosch 7599 ▪ info@stellenzicht.co.za ▪ www.stellenzicht.co.za ▪ S 33° 59' 50.0" E 018° 51' 59.8" ▪ **T +27 (0)21-880-1103** ▪ F +27 (0)21-880-1107

Over the years, Stellenzicht's reputation has been founded primarily on shiraz, the maiden 1994 vintage of the flagship Syrah famously rating better than the 1990 of the iconic Grange Hermitage (as it was then known) in the watershed SAA Shield tasting of 1995. However, winemaker Guy Webber, who joined in 1998, has no qualms about admitting that pinotage is his favourite variety and he has been very much part of its 'gentrification' in recent times. A pinotage from Stellenzicht placed among the winners at the annual Absa Pinotage Top Ten every year from 2003 to 2009, while more recently the 2010 Golden Triangle Pinotage was awarded gold at last year's Old Mutual Trophy Wine Show.

Stellenzicht Specialities range

★★★★★ **Syrah** Old-school **06** (★★★★) is rich & full with plenty of savoury character to go with ripe dark fruit but perhaps shade less convincing than **05**.

★★★★ **Semillon Reserve** ⓐ Boldly envisioned **09** (★★★★★) is complex, rich & full; big but perfectly balanced, oak apparent but an embellishment rather than a distraction & a long, savoury finish. Better than **08**.

Rhapsody ★★★★ Ambitious **09** from pinotage & shiraz, like last **07** (★★★★). Prominent oak (31 months in barrel, 100% new) but also plums & spice. Rich & broad, drying on finish. **08** sold out untasted.

Cellarmaster's Release range

Petit Verdot (No Added Sulphites) ★★★ Noble rusticity about **09**. Concentrated dark fruit plus iodine note, slightly tart acidity, firm tannins. **Pinotage (No Added Sulphites)** ★★★ Intense black cherry, malty note on **09**. Rich & full, soft tannins, apparent sweetness due to over 16% alcohol. **Chardonnay (No Added Sulphites)** ⓐ 🖄 ★★★ Fascinating **10** has hint of citrus alongside yeasty, almost malty tones; fresh acidity lends verve. Discontinued: **Cabernet Sauvignon, Shiraz**.

Golden Triangle range

★★★★★ **Pinotage** 🖄 **10** (★★★★) bigger, less polished than **09**. Concentrated black cherry, bright acidity, firm tannins. Very young — needs a good few years to settle, unfurl.

Cabernet Sauvignon 🍴 ★★★ Herbal note along with dark fruit, malty note to awkward **10**. Medium bodied, drying on finish. **Shiraz** ★★★ Straightforward **09** shows red fruit, slight herbal note, vanilla. Medium body, with somewhat tart acidity. **Sauvignon Blanc** 🍴 ⌸ ★★★ **12** has broad appeal with subtle citrus, some texture thanks to 2 months on the lees, moderate acidity. Discontinued: **Merlot, Chardonnay**. — CE

Sterhuis

Location/map: Stellenbosch ▪ WO: Bottelary ▪ Est 1980 ▪ 1stB 2002 ▪ Tasting, sales & cellar tours by appt ▪ Closed Christian holidays ▪ Facilities for children ▪ Conservation area ▪ Owner(s) Kruger family ▪ Winemaker(s) Johan Kruger ▪ Vineyard manager(s) Christo Crous ▪ 100ha/40ha under vine ▪ 300t/6,000cs own label 25% red 75% white ▪ PO Box 131 Koelenhof 7605 ▪ johan@sterhuis.co.za ▪ www.sterhuis.co.za ▪ S 33°54'43.1" E 018°46'4.2" ▪ **T +27 (0)83-411-0757** ▪ F +27 (0)21-906-1195

Ten years years of winemaking at this Bottelary family farm was celebrated in 2012 with sold-out signs for the first time on three of their wines. The introduction of recession-proof entry-level wines, as an added 'sales-engine', enticed more happy consumers to try their top-tier wines, says winemaker Johan Kruger. A hardworking ethos, with further sustainable focus, continues to work for Johan and father André on this chardonnay-focused estate.

★★★★ **Cabernet Sauvignon** 🕭 Good varietal character, pure freshness & quiet authority on last-tasted **07**. Gently sweet-fruited, but with strong, lean muscularity & earthy tang. All in balance.

★★★★☆ **Sterhuis Astra Red** 🕭 Tasted few years back, **06** (★★★★) from 70/30 cab & merlot had more herbaceous tones than plummy **05**, on lean side, with moderate fruit, but pleasing notes cedar, tobacco.

★★★★ **Chardonnay Barrel Selection** ✓ A consistently serious offering, **10** (★★★★★) goes up a notch with white stonefruit enveloped in fine oak, leading to medium-bodied creamy palate. Cleansing acid keeps richer elements in check. Lingering finish. Follows well-balanced, piquant **09**.

★★★★ **Chenin Blanc** 🕭 From 41 year old vines, **09** (★★★☆) rather subdued, but round & richly textured. Tasted few years back, it looked as though it might offer more with time. Like **08**, only older oak used.

★★★★ **Sauvignon Blanc** Like other whites in range more palate-driven than aromatic. **11** has some citrus & quince notes, with a focused long & dry palate. 15% barrel component adds to complexity & length.

★★★★☆ **Astra White** 🕭 **08**'s aromas tasted mid-2010 suggested peachy viognier as well as oak — but no, equal blend sauvignon, chardonnay, chenin. Lime, lemongrass on balanced, lingering fresh palate.

★★★★ **Blanc de Blancs Méthode Cap Classique** **09** sparkling from chardonnay. Ultra-dry, with fine mousse, rounded mouthfeel & integrated oak; continues to an almond/apple finish. Will evolve a few years.

Merlot 🕭 ★★★★ **08** in serious, even austerely elegant style, properly dry, with a slight herbal note to its red fruit. **Merlot-Cabernet Sauvignon** 🕭 🍴 ★★★ Easygoing, approachable but untrivial **08**, its ripe fruit unobscured by modest oaking. **Unwooded Chardonnay** ✓ 🍴 ★★★★ Shy to start, **12** proffers green apple & gunpowder aromas; dry light entry with fuller end. Unshowy & food friendly. **Chenin Blanc-Viognier** 🕭 🍴 ★★★ Subtle, attractive aromas on **11** advertise the 30% viognier component. Gentle, soft & dry, with a finishing hard bite. Discontinued: **Viognier**. — JP

Stettyn Cellar

Location/map: Worcester ▪ WO: Western Cape/Worcester ▪ Est 1964 ▪ 1stB 1984 ▪ Tasting & sales Mon-Thu 8–5 Fri 8-4.30 Sat (Oct-Mar) 10-1 ▪ Closed all pub hols ▪ Cellar tours from 1.30–4 by appt ▪ Lunch by arrangement (24 hrs in advance); or BYO picnic ▪ Facilities for children ▪ Vineyard tours R200pp ▪ Stettyn music evenings (±Oct) ▪ Owner(s) 4 major producers (3 family owned) ▪ Cellarmaster(s) Albie Treurnicht (Nov 2000) ▪ Winemaker(s) Albie Treurnicht (Nov 2000), with Jean-Prieur du Plessis (Oct 2007) ▪ Viticulturist(s) Pierre Snyman (Vinpro) ▪ 365ha (cab, merlot, ptage, shiraz, chard, chenin, sauv) ▪ 7,500t/9,000cs own label 25% red 75% white + 5.1m L bulk ▪ Brands for clients: FirstCape; Felicité ▪ ARA, BEE, HACCP, IPW ▪ PO Box 1520 Worcester 6849 ▪ info@stettyncellar.co.za ▪ www.stettyncellar.co.za ▪ S 33°52'14.8" E 019°22'2.3" ▪ **T +27 (0)23-340-4220** ▪ F +27 (0)23-340-4220

No longer a co-operative but a company with a new chairman in the person of Hendrik Griessel, this winery between Villiersdorp and Worcester has recently joint-ventured with Newton Johnson Vineyards, vinifying some of their Felicité labels. Stettyn has also ventured into the Chinese market, notching up two successful transactions so far.

Signature Reserve range

Shiraz-Cabernet Sauvignon ① ★★★★ Highly drinkable **09** opaque & brooding, with cab's leafy notes, shiraz's supple mouthfeel. WO W Cape.

Millstone range

Stone Red ☺ 🍴 ★★★ Well-priced & creative cab blend with splashes merlot, souzão & viognier. **NV** fresh & friendly easy-sipper with lightly spiced berry flavours, good dry conclusion. **Chenin Blanc** ☺ 🍴 🗑 ★★★ Floral & lemon appeal on **12**, satisfying weight from 15% semillon & some lees-ageing. **Sauvignon Blanc** ☺ 🍴 🗑 ★★★ Attractive khaki bush, green fig & white asparagus aromas on **12** summer charmer, touch sugar fluffs out tail.

Discontinued: **Shiraz Rosé**. — HJ/CvZ

■ **Steynsrust** see StellenRust

■ **Steytler** see Kaapzicht Wine Estate

St Francis Point Vineyards NEW

Location: St Francis Bay ▪ Est 2009 ▪ Tasting by appt ▪ Five Elements restaurant: www.five-elements.co.za ▪ Owner(s) Jean Fynn ▪ Viticulturist(s) Ryan Fynn (2009) ▪ 3.5ha (chard, sauv, sem) ▪ PO Box 355 St Francis Bay 6312 ▪ rjsfynn@yahoo.com ▪ **T +27 (0)42-294-1638**

What was virgin land is now olive groves and vineyards interspersed with indigenous forest in the delightful resort of St Francis Bay. Caracal, porcupines and a bush pig add a touch of the wild, and a restaurant provides a sophisticated counterpoint. In 2009, the Fynn family planted mostly sauvignon blanc with a little semillon and chardonnay: 'Everyone pitches in,' says owner Jean Fynn's nephew and viticulturist Ryan. He hopes their maiden vintage will be launched this year.

■ **Stilfontein** see Eerste Hoop Wine Cellar

Stoep

Est/1stB 2001 ▪ Tasting, sales & tours by appt ▪ Owner(s) Zelpy 1023 (Pty) Ltd: 3 shareholders Gerrit Mars (SA), Sven Haefner (Swiss) & Daniel Hofer (Swiss) ▪ Cellarmaster(s)/winemaker(s) André Liebenberg (Romond) & Gerrit Mars ▪ 50% red 50% white ▪ gerritmars@mweb.co.za ▪ **T +27 (0)82-352-5583**

Frequent flyer Gerrit Mars' envisaged slower pace didn't materialise, but the brand co-owner last year did find time to bottle a quantity of red, made by Romond Vineyards, under the Stoep label. Gerrit plans to select other Romond-vinified reds and, time permitting, a chardonnay by Joubert-Tradauw for future bottling.

■ **Stonedale** see Rietvallei Wine Estate

Stonehill

Location/map/WO: Stellenbosch ▪ Est 1990 ▪ 1stB 2003 ▪ Tasting by appt ▪ Owner(s)/vineyard manager(s) Lorna Hughes ▪ Winemaker(s) Mark Carmichael-Green ▪ 4ha/3.2ha (cab, shiraz) ▪ 70% red 30% white ▪ PO Box 612 Stellenbosch 7599 ▪ llhughes@telkomsa.net, lorna@stonehillwines.co.za ▪ www.stonehillwines.co.za ▪ S 33° 54′4.8″ E 018° 48′56.4″ ▪ **T +27 (0)73-420-3300** ▪ F +27 (0)21-865-2740

Lorna Hughes, wife of respected winelands sage Dave (both dog lovers of note), confesses to neglecting business matters somewhat while working on rehabilitation at Animal Welfare. The 'Bristle' branding of her wines refers to the furry family member of dubious parentage that runs their little Devon Valley property.

Bristle Red ① ★★★ Modestly oaked, juicy **08** nicely structured & balanced cab-shiraz blend. **Dry Cabernet Sauvignon Rosé** ① 🍴 ★★★ Appetisingly fresh, oaked **09** noted last time as better for extra year in bottle. Satisfyingly dry, & weighty. **Bristle White**✓ 🍴 🗑 ★★★★ Solid, ripe, wooded viognier, **11**'s peachy fruit prevails over lees creaminess & oak spices. Generous & appealing. — GdB

Stone Ridge Wines

Location/WO: Paarl ▪ Map: Paarl & Wellington ▪ Est 2002 ▪ 1stB 2003 ▪ Tasting by appt only ▪ Winemaker(s) Bertus Fourie (Jan 2010, consultant) ▪ Viticulturist(s) Jan Eksteen (2002) ▪ 300ha (cab, ptage, shiraz, chard, chenin, sauv) ▪ 20t/1,200cs own label 50% red 50% white ▪ PO Box 7046 Northern Paarl 7623 ▪ stoneridge@uitkijk.co.za ▪ S 33° 34′ 19.72″ E 018° 52′ 45.48″ ▪ **T +27 (0)82-324-8372** ▪ F +27 (0)21-869-8071

It's all systems go for an enlarged offering from this Voor Paardeberg property, where the Eksteens have been growing wine grapes for six generations. With a passion for people, wine 'and everything in-between', viticulturist Jan Eksteen dreams of the day when his hard work pays off and Stone Ridge is a household name for quality and value.

Eksteen Family Vineyards Reserve range

★★★★☆ **Chenin Blanc 'Bush Vine 1977'** ⓘ 🏠 Tropical notes & some pear on previously tasted **10** from bushvines. Lees-ageing & sensitive oaking added complexity & depth to candied orange conclusion. **Shiraz** ⓘ ★★★★ Barrel sample **10** from Paarl single-vineyard is ripe & smooth, with well-hidden 14.5% alcohol, integrated tannins. Black plum & pepper appeal.

Stone Ridge range

Cabernet Sauvignon NEW This, **Merlot** & **Chardonnay** additions to range missed our deadline. **Shiraz** As for **Sauvignon Blanc**, await next. — CvZ

▪ **Stone Road** see Louisvale Wines

Stonewall Wines

Location: Somerset West ▪ Map: Helderberg ▪ WO: Stellenbosch ▪ Est 1828 ▪ 1stB 1997 ▪ Tasting & sales by appt Mon-Fri 10-5 Sat 10-1 ▪ Closed Easter Fri-Sun, Dec 25/26 & Jan 1 ▪ Refreshments by appt ▪ Helderberg wine festival ▪ Owner(s) De Waal Koch ▪ Cellarmaster(s) Ronell Wiid (Jan 2000, consultant) ▪ Winemaker(s) De Waal Koch (Jan 2000) ▪ Viticulturist(s) De Waal Koch (Jun 1984) ▪ 90ha/70ha (cabs s/f, merlot, ptage, shiraz, chard, pinot gris, sauv) ▪ 300t/2,000cs own label 80% red 20% white ▪ PO Box 5145 Helderberg 7135 ▪ stonewall@mweb.co.za ▪ S 34° 1′59.0″ E 018°49′14.6″ ▪ **T +27 (0)21-855-3675** ▪ F +27 (0)21-855-2206

The cellar behind the white perimeter wall of this Helderberg property was built in 1828. 'With its thick walls and cement vats, the 'olden times' atmosphere of loving care is still evident in our products,' believes owner-winemaker De Waal Koch. 'We'll never increase production at the cost of quality'.

Cabernet Sauvignon ✓ 🖉 ★★★★ Appealing upfront dark berry fruit & milk chocolate in **10** concealed by oak mid-2012. Good, firm structure needs time to reveal full charm. **Rubér** ✓ 🖉 ★★★★ Merlot, cabernet blend **10** displays bright juicy black fruit with firm dusty tannins in balance. A food wine. **Chardonnay** ✓ 🖉 ★★★★ Buttery cinnamon-dusted apple pie flavours, **11** generous & rounded with a zingy citrus end. Value over-delivers. **Valle Felice** ★★★ Barrel-aged fortified sweetie from merlot. **09** is light, fruity with a spirity grip. Serve well chilled with soft cheese. — WB

StoneyCroft

Location/map/WO: Stellenbosch ▪ Est 2000 ▪ 1stB 2001 ▪ Tasting by appt ▪ Owner(s) John Stone ▪ Winemaker(s) Danie Steytler (2001), with Danie Steytler jnr (both Kaapzicht) ▪ Viticulturist(s) Gary Probert (Jan 2010, consultant) ▪ 4ha/3.5ha (cab, shiraz) ▪ 20t/1,500cs own label 100% red ▪ PO Box 239 Koelenhof 7605 ▪ john@stoneycroft.co.za ▪ www.stoneycroft.co.za ▪ S 33° 53′ 24.41″ E 018° 48′ 19.78″ ▪ **T +27 (0)21-865-2301/+27 (0)82-801-1804** ▪ F +27 (0)21-865-2360

Respecting an 'increasingly discerning SA market wanting out-of-the-ordinary, good-value boutique wines', John Stone opted not to release his 2008 shiraz, deeming it 'not of suitable standard'. But the variety on which he and late wife Margie had been focusing on their Bottelary Hills farm should soon be supported by some cabernet planted in 2011.

Stony Brook

Location/map: Franschhoek ▪ WO: Franschhoek/Elgin/Western Cape/Coastal ▪ Est 1995 ▪ 1stB 1996 ▪ Tasting & sales Mon-Fri 10-5 (Oct-Apr) & 10-4 (May-Sep); Sat 10-1 ▪ Fee R35 ▪ Closed all pub hols ▪ Self-catering cottages ▪ Owner(s) Nigel & Joy McNaught ▪ Cellarmaster(s) Nigel McNaught (1995) ▪ Winemaker(s) Nigel McNaught (1995) & Craig McNaught (2011), with Michael Blaauw (Jan 2008) ▪ Viticulturist(s) Paul Wallace (consultant) ▪ 23ha/14ha (cab, malbec, merlot, mourv, p verdot, pinot, shiraz, tempranillo, chard, sem, viog) ▪ 80t/5,000cs own label 56% red 40% white 4% rosé + 700cs for clients ▪ Brands for clients: Elgin Grove, La Providence ▪ ISO 14001:2003 ▪ PO Box 22 Franschhoek 7690 ▪ info@stonybrook.co.za ▪ www.stonybrook.co.za ▪ S 33° 56′ 28.7″ E 019° 7′ 4.1″ ▪ T +27 (0)21-876-2182 ▪ F +27 (0)86-664-2794

It's been a year of changes at this Franschhoek family winery. The McNaughts' son Craig joined his father Nigel and Michael Blaauw in the cellar, after assisting for the 2011 harvest. New also is much of the cellar equipment, including the possibility of photovoltaic electricity generation for both cellar and tasting room. And not forgetting the vineyards, where tempranillo and marsanne have been identified as suited to meet the effects of climate change.

★★★★ Syrah ✓ In more serious, traditional style; 09 well-fleshed, savoury, with flashes of white spice extended by fresh core. Lovely drinking now, but can benefit from further 3-5 years. First since 06.

★★★★☆ Ghost Gum ⓐ Mainly cab from single vineyard; splash merlot for extra breadth. 07 still oak veiled. Suggestion of sweet fruit, clipped by alcohol glow in tail. Lacks depth of 06 (★★★★★).

★★★★ The Max ✓ Both fine blackcurrant fragrance & fortress tannins indicate that cab leads 09 4-way Bordeaux-style blend. Needs time to round out, & to harmonise with the hints of fleshy merlot.

★★★★ SMV ✓ Shiraz-based with effective drops mourvèdre, viognier in appetising 08. Comfortably fleshy with well-sustained game, spice features.

★★★★ Snow Gum Individual 50/50 mourvèdre/malbec blend, the latter lifting former's earthy, gamey features on 09. Broad & flavoursome, with a good rumble of chunky tannins. First since 07.

★★★★ Semillon Reserve ⓐ Last-tasted aromatic 08 (★★★★★) finer than 06; needing time to show best.

★★★★ The 'J' ▤ Harmonious blend viognier, semillon, sauvignon (from Elgin); 10 (★★★☆) developing honeyed tones, but with light & fleeting flavours. Not in league of 09 (★★★★☆) or 08.

★★★★ The Lyle Golden-hued 07 (★★★☆) MCC sparkling from chardonnay & pinot noir. Pleasant leesy, biscuity nose; aggressive spritz, quite simple flavours. Less elegant than 06. WO Coastal.

★★★★ V on A Barrel-fermented dessert from viognier. 10 subtly fragrant, luscious; sweetness tempered by tangy, cleansing acid. Tad less exciting than 09 (★★★★☆).

Shiraz ▤ ★★★★ The name, versus 'Syrah', as well as a hint of sweet oak vanilla reflects modern style of 08. Big but balanced, with rounded grip, straightforward spicy pizzazz. Camissa ⓐ ▤ ★★★★ Almost liqueur-like perfume on 08 (no 07). Sweet fruit too from cab/merlot mix held by frisson of dry tannin. Rosé ▤ ★★★ Pearly pink 12 from merlot. Smooth, dry & savoury, with inviting wild strawberry tang. Heart Of The Lees Sauvignon Blanc ⓐ ★★★★ Unshowy 09 shows cool lines of Elgin; lees, natural ferment in barrel add to textural interest, restrained complexity, lengthy finish. Up on 08 (★★★★). Sauvignon Blanc ▤ ★★☆ Brisk, just-dry 11 with modest tropical fruit. WO Elgin. Ghost Gum White NEW ★★★☆ Semillon's sleek silkiness sets tone on 10. Sauvignon (33%; from Elgin) lifts simple, quiet, waxy honeyed notes with subtle toasty oak extras. Discontinued: Merlot, Mourvèdre, Rose de Vert. — AL

▪ **Stormhoek** see Origin Wine
▪ **Stormy Cape** see uniWines Vineyards

Stoumann's Wines

Location: Vredendal ▪ Map: Olifants River ▪ WO: Olifants River/Lamberts Bay ▪ Est 1998 ▪ 1stB 2008 ▪ Tasting, sales & cellar tours Mon-Fri 8-5 Sat by appt ▪ Closed all pub hols ▪ Cheese platters/meals/braai available on request ▪ Tour groups ▪ Farm produce ▪ Conferences ▪ Owner(s) Napoleon Stoumann ▪ Cellarmaster(s)/winemaker(s) Napoleon Stoumann & Kobus Rossouw (Aug 2012, consultant) ▪ Viticulturist(s) CG Stoumann (Jan 2010) ▪ 100ha (cab, merlot, muscadel r/w, ptage, ruby cab, shiraz, chard, chenin, cbard, hanepoot) ▪ 1,040t/2,000cs own label 50% red 40% white 10% rosé + 800,000L bulk ▪ IPW ▪ PO Box 307 Vredendal 8160 ▪ stoumanns@cybersmart.co.za ▪ www.stoumanns.co.za ▪ S 31° 41′ 20.5″ E 018° 30′ 23.3″ ▪ T +27 (0)27-213-2323/+27 (0)83-236-2794 ▪ F +27 (0)27-213-1448

Kobus Rossouw, ex cellarmaster at Slanghoek Winery in Breedekloof, is now consulting winemaker at the Olifants River Valley's smallest cellar. The range of reds, whites and jerepigos is branded with the endangered Geometric Tortoise, endemic to the southwestern Cape, as part of the Stoumann family's conservation efforts.

Cabernet Sauvignon ⚃ ★★ Blackcurrant-infused **10**, nice & supple, slips down easily. **Shiraz** ⚃ ★★★ Winter-warming **10**'s tannins are feisty, need time or a meaty accompaniment. **Vin de la Tortue** ⚃ ★★★ **10** cab/shiraz combo has fruitcake appeal, is easy to drink. **Rosé Perlé Wine** Not ready. **Chardonnay** Await next. **Chenin Blanc** ⚃ ★★★ Wallet-pleasing **12** preview satisfyingly dry & tangy, with yellow peach fragrance. **Sauvignon Blanc** ⚃ ★★★ Cool-grown Lamberts Bay vines deliver bright acidity, fair flavour & complexity at moderate alcohol in pre-bottling **12**. **Hanepoot Jerepigo** ⚀ ★★★ **08** sun-ripe fortified sweetie offers honeyed ripe apricot, zippy lime acidity. **Red Jerepigo** ★ Fortified **NV** dessert from red muscadel, some tealeaf character but lacks the style's sweet succulence. — DB/CvZ

■ **Stout Izak** see Jason's Hill Private Cellar

Strandveld Wines

Location/WO: Elim ▪ Map: Southern Cape ▪ Est 2002 ▪ 1stB 2003 ▪ Tasting, sales & cellar tours Mon-Thu 8–5 Fri 8-4 Sat 10-3 ▪ Closed Good Fri & Dec 25 ▪ Farm produce ▪ BYO picnic ▪ Walks/hikes ▪ Mountain biking ▪ Conservation area ▪ Two self-catering cottages ▪ Owner(s) Strandveld Vineyards & Rietfontein Trust ▪ Winemaker(s) Conrad Vlok (Dec 2004) ▪ Viticulturist(s) Tienie Wentzel (Oct 2009) ▪ 850ha/70ha (pinot, shiraz, sauv, sem) ▪ 246t/12,000cs own label 43% red 57% white ▪ BWI ▪ PO Box 1020 Bredasdorp 7280 ▪ info@strandveld.co.za ▪ www.strandveld.co.za ▪ S 34°39'59.2" E 019°47'26.8" ▪ **T** +27 (0)28-482-1902/+27 (0)28-482-1906 ▪ F +27 (0)28-482-1902/+27 (0)28-482-1906

'Tough market conditions are making selling your wine more and more difficult, even if you over-deliver at a price point,' says winemaker Conrad Vlok. 'Consumers are either trading up or down, so budget and super-premium are where the action is.' But Strandveld has a plan: first, a stellar new top-line Rhône blend, second, a charming entry-level rosé and, third, a plant-and-supply agreement with first-rank winery La Motte for 10ha of sauvignon and shiraz grapes.

Strandveld range

★★★★ **Anders Sparrman Pinot Noir** ⚀ Limited release (221 cases) **09**, less immediately showy than First Sighting version, though greater oak influence (40% new) & richer fruit. Fine potential.

★★★★☆ **Syrah** ⚀ ✓ Dashes grenache & viognier, longer period in higher proportion new oak than junior bottling. **09** quiet but not sombre, taut but not ungenerous despite the cooler vintage.

★★★★☆ **The Navigator** NEW ✓ ⚃ Rhône-style blend paying homage to Henry the Navigator, patron of early Portuguese explorers. Mainly shiraz, grenache (58/24) with mourvèdre, viognier, 10% brush new oak in superb **10**, beautifully upholstered with spicy berries, liqueur-like satin finish.

★★★★☆ **Sauvignon Blanc Pofadderbos** ✓ ⚃ Frequent vineyard encounters with puff adders prompts name change for standout (in region & SA) bottling. **11** hallmark cool green fruit with asparagus whiffs, stony mineral undertones, rich & long finish. **10** (★★★★★) had exceptional weight & freshness. Both for keeping.

★★★★☆ **Adamastor** ✓ ⚃ Stately Bordeaux-style white flagship, slightly more sauvignon (51%) in steely, lean & appealingly austere **11**. As in semillon-led **10** (57%), judicious partly new oak seasoning. Should improve good few years.

First Sighting range

Shiraz Rosé NEW ☺ 🍴 ⚃ ★★★ Strawberry & rosepetal aromas on youthful **12**, satisfying dry, spicy conclusion.

Pinot Noir 🍴 ⚃ ★★★★ **10** floral & meaty notes, light build but commendable long tail. Drink while big brother matures. **Shiraz** 🍴 ⚃ ★★★ Rhubarb & spicy cherry fruit, **11** tank sample very ripe & tad unformed; rating provisional. **Sauvignon Blanc** 🍴 ⚃ ★★★ Bold & approachable **11** has tinned pea, asparagus whiffs, crisp acidity. Very appealing summer sipper. — WB/GdB

■ **Street Art** see Origin Wine
■ **Strelizia** see Blue Crane Vineyards
■ **String of Pearls** see Francois La Garde

Strydom Vintners   NEW

Location/WO: Stellenbosch ▪ Est 2012 ▪ 1stB 2009 ▪ Closed to public ▪ Owner(s) Louis & Rianie Strydom ▪ Cellarmaster(s) Rianie Strydom ▪ 8.5ha/6.5ha (cab, merlot, shiraz, sauv, sem) ▪ ±30t/500cs own label 50% red 50% white ▪ IPW ▪ PO Box 1290 Stellenbosch 7599 ▪ rianie.strydomvineyards@gmail.com ▪ **T** +27 (0)21-889-8553 his is an own label by leading husband-and-wife winemakers Louis and Rianie trydom (both involved independently with two prime Helderberg properties). Grapes grown on their Stellenbosch-Simonsberg smallholding have gone into stablished brands to date, and will continue to do so until they're ready to bottle their entire crop. 'It takes patience,' says Rianie, to create 'hopefully something great'. The energetic mom of three also sees the family venture as 'offering opportunities to our children'.

The Freshman ☺ 🎨 ★★★ Aptly named **12** is youthful & upbeat, appealing greenpepper & riper passionfruit in a lightish, slightly saline body. 95% sauvignon, rest semillon, to enjoy chilled.

Retro ★★★☆ Big guns behind shiraz (90%), mourvèdre partnership, so you expect a booming cannon. Refreshingly, **09** an unflamboyant everyday companion with savoury berries & supple tannin for solo or food. — JP/CvZ

■ **Stumble Vineyards** *see Flagstone Winery*
■ **Suikerbosch** *see Zidela Wines*
■ **Suikerbossie Ek Wil Jou Hê** *see Boer & Brit*

Sumaridge Wines

Location: Hermanus ▪ Map: Elgin, Walker Bay & Bot River ▪ WO: Upper Hemel-en-Aarde Valley ▪ Est 1997 ▪ 1stB 2000 ▪ Tasting & sales daily 10–3 ▪ Fee R25 for groups of 6+, waived on purchase ▪ Closed Easter Fri/Sun, Dec 25/26 & Jan 1 ▪ Seasonal tasting platter options plus kiddies platter, also available (Aug-May) as picnic ▪ Facilities for children ▪ Tour groups ▪ Conferences ▪ Weddings/functions ▪ Luxury self-catering guesthouse ▪ Conservation area ▪ Extensive nature trails ▪ Mountain biking ▪ Bass & fly fishing by arrangement ▪ Owner(s) Simon & Holly Turner-Bellingham ▪ Cellarmaster(s)/vineyard manager(s) Gavin Patterson (Jun 2005) ▪ Winemaker(s) Gavin Patterson (Jun 2005), with Reginald Maphumulo (Jun 2000) ▪ 210ha/42ha (cab f, malbec, merlot, ptage, pinot, shiraz, chard, sauv, sem, viog) ▪ 150t/10,000cs own label 45% red 50% white 5% rosé ▪ IPW ▪ PO Box 1413 Hermanus 7200 ▪ info@sumaridge.co.za ▪ www.sumaridge.co.za ▪ S 34° 22'1.6" E 019° 15'18.6" ▪ **T +27 (0)28-312-1097** ▪ F +27 (0)86-623-4248

Zimbabwean Gavin Patterson has been with this Hemel-en-Aarde producer since 2005, learning 'the peculiarities of this region – the land, the climate and its people'. He has been shifting things, he says, towards wines of individuality, expressive of the Cape (hence wine names like Epitome and Maritimus), and also towards sustainable farming. Incidentally, he offered a rare, admirable 'news item': 'An intensive labour audit gave us an opportunity to address numerous areas to ensure a safe, secure and content working environment for all our staff.' WIETA accreditation should follow soon.

★★★★ **Pinot Noir** ⏱ 🎨 Elegant, perfumed **10** already drinkable mid-2011. Great freshness but also supple & silky with charming, poised cherry, forest floor features.

★★★★ **Epitome** Dark-fruited, savoury **09** from pinotage & shiraz (**08** also some merlot). Concentrated & flavourful, with soft tannins & good palate weight, but acidity needs a little time to integrate.

★★★★ **Sauvignon Blanc** 🎨 🎨 Refreshing, thirst-quenching **11**, tending to citrus, nettle & green tropical aromas & flavours. Finishes with mouthwatering delicacy. **10** (★★★★) rather too bracing.

Merlot ★★★★ Precise & fresh **09** now bottled, showing real poise & delicacy – though not lacking intensity & cool-climate acidity on the soft palate. Step up on **08** (★★★★). **Rosé** 🎨 🎨 ★★★★ Intensely coloured, joyously aromatic **12** drops 'Merlot' from name to allow for malbec & cab franc. Just off-dry yet refreshing: a great thirst-quencher; not complex, but fun. **Chardonnay** 🎨 ★★★★☆ Previewed last year, **10** showing even better. Restrained aromas lime, apple, hazelnut. Energetic, taut palate with mineral undertones & creamy texture uplifted by vibrant, mouthwatering acidity. Like **09** (★★★★), fermented/aged in 30% new oak. **Maritimus** 🎨 ★★★★ Previewed last year, **10** 65% sauvignon, with oaked chardonnay, semillon & drop viognier now shows beautiful restrained aromas, but full palate bit disjointed. Follows step-up **09** (★★★★). — JPf

Summerhill Wines

Location/map/WO: Stellenbosch ▪ 1stB 2008 ▪ Tasting & sales Mon-Thu 9-4.30 Fri 9-2 ▪ Closed all pub hols ▪ Dorpstraat Restaurant Theatre open for lunch & dinner Tue-Sat 11-10; live performances evenings 8.30-10 (bookings T +27 (0)21-889-9158 or info@dorpstraat.co.za) ▪ Tour groups (120 pax) ▪ Owner(s) Summerhill Wines cc, Charles R Hunting ▪ Winemaker(s) Hannes Meyer (whites, Simonsig) & Marius Malan (reds, Malanot

Wines) ▪ Viticulturist(s) Paul Wallace (consultant) ▪ 15ha/3.5ha (merlot, shiraz, chenin) ▪ 24t/1,250cs ow label 40% red 60% white ▪ PO Box 12448 Die Boord 7613 ▪ charles@summerhillwines.co.za, manager@ summerhillwines.co.za, reception@summerhillwines.co.za ▪ www.summerhillwines.co.za ▪ S 33° 52′ 57.71 E 018° 50′ 49.39" ▪ **T +27 (0)21-889-5015** ▪ F +27 (0)86-621-8047

One of several Stellenbosch properties in the post-WWII portfolio of Huntin patriarch Gerald Lindsay, Summerhill is home to the Dorpstraat Restauran Theatre, amplifying Charles Hunting and team's increasingly popular estate offering: winetasting, meals and an array of novel dinnertime shows.

Chenin Blanc ☺ 🍴 🎨 ★★★ Bang for your buck, **12** is sunshine in a bottle, exuding tropical fruit.

Shiraz-Merlot 🥂 🍴 ★★ Chunky, berried **09** had a spicy overlay from oak staving when last tasted. —DS

Sumsaré Wines

Location/map/WO: Robertson ▪ Est 2008 ▪ 1stB 2007 ▪ Tasting, sales & tours by appt Mon-Fri 9–5 Sat 9–1 ▪ Close Easter Fri-Mon, May 13, Pentecost, Dec 25/26 & Jan 1 ▪ Tour groups ▪ Facilities for children ▪ Farm produce ▪ BY picnic ▪ Weddings ▪ Owner(s) Francèl Rabie, Daniël Johannes Erasmus, Danielle Jackson & Janine Joubert Winemaker(s) Lourens van der Westhuizen (Arendsig) ▪ Viticulturist(s) Briaan Stipp (Robertson Winery) ▪ 450ha 40ha (cab, ruby cab, shiraz, chard, chenin, cbard, muscadel w) ▪ 700t/±130cs own label 40% red 60% white ▪ P Box 402 Robertson 6705 ▪ sumsare.wines@barvallei.co.za ▪ www.sumsarewines.co.za ▪ S 33° 54′ 14.66" E 019 40′4.75" ▪ **T +27 (0)23-626-2152, +27 (0)82-221-6653** ▪ F +27 (0)86-505-8590

Sumsaré's five-year-old potstill brandy will be released this year. A double celebra tion, as the Erasmus family will be toasting their first five years as wine producer too. While the brand may be relatively new, the beautifully restored 1830 tasting room on the Robertson farm is steeped in seven generations of family history.

Limited Release Shiraz Await next. **Wild Yeast Limited Release Chardonnay** NEW ★★★ Single vineyard **11** offers friendly apricot flavour, sweet buttery vanilla from sojourn in older French oak. **Sauvignon Blanc 12** missed our deadline. — DB/JP

▪ **Sunshine Organics** *see* Stellar Winery

Super Single Vineyards

Location/map: Stellenbosch ▪ WO: Stellenbosch/Sutherland-Karoo ▪ Est/1stB 2004 ▪ Tasting Mon-Sat 9–5 Owner(s)/viticulturist(s) Daniël de Waal ▪ Winemaker(s) Daniël de Waal, with Kyle Zulch ▪ 60ha Canettevallei farm ▪ (cab, nebbiolo, p verdot, pinot, shiraz, tempranillo, riesling) ▪ 1,000cs own label 80% red 20% white ▪ PO Box 89 Vlottenburg 7604 ▪ marketing@ssvineyards.co.za ▪ www.supersinglevineyards.co.za ▪ S 33° 56′ 29.73" E 018° 45 15.20" ▪ **T +27 (0)72-200-5552 (Daniël)/+27 (0)82-556-0205 (Kyle)** ▪ F +27 (0)21-881-3026

When the De Waal family of Uiterwyk decided to go their separate ways, brother Daniël turned his attention to wines that expressed their provenance. He decided on small volumes produced from very special sites, rather than the estate-specific family tradition, which stretches back to 1682. This preoccupation with terroir led among other interesting directions, to the first-ever WO Sutherland-Karoo, in an effort to find the most extreme continental climate in South Africa.

Pella Coastal Wines range

★★★★ **Cabernet Sauvignon** After focused **08** (★★★★★), 3rd edition **09** has noble, dark & earthy Bor deaux overtones with rich ripeness & lovely dry finish. Slightly gawky oak spices should integrate with time.

★★★★ **Thomas Se Dolland Pinotage** Solid, meaty **09** (★★★★) from 50-year-old bushvines, with dashes malbec & shiraz. Hefty tannins. Notch down from seriously conceived & handled maiden **08**.

★★★★ **The Vanilla** Mainly chenin, dollops semillon & viognier. Whereas **10**'s eponymous vanilla notes were deftly integrated, awkward **11** (★★★) is dominated & unbalanced by potent spicy American oak.

Sutherland Continental Wines

★★★★ **Mount Sutherland Syrah** 🥂 Maiden crop off Sutherland vines, explores cool-climate potential. Revisited last time, still-available **09** had improved, showed Rhône-like pepperiness, elegance & length. —GdB

▪ **Sustainable** *see* Origin Wine
▪ **Sutherland** *see* Thelema Mountain Vineyards

Sutherland Continental *see* Super Single Vineyards
Swallow *see* Natte Valleij Wines

Swartland Winery

ocation: Malmesbury ▪ Map/WO: Swartland ▪ Est/1stB 1948 ▪ Tasting & sales Mon-Fri 8–5 Sat 9–2 ▪ Closed Mar 1, Easter Fri/Sun, Dec 25/26 & Jan 1 ▪ Facilities for children ▪ Tour groups ▪ Farm produce ▪ Owner(s) 60 producers ▪ Cellarmaster(s) Andries Blake (Dec 1995) ▪ Viticulturist(s) Claude Uren (Nov 2010) ▪ 2,689ha (cab, malbec, merlot, ptage, shiraz, chard, chenin, sauv) ▪ 20,000t 55% white 38% red 5% rosé 2% sparkling ▪ Brands for clients: ■ick 'n Pay, Woolworths ▪ BRC, IFS, IPW, WIETA ▪ PO Box 95 Malmesbury 7299 ▪ suzanne@swwines.co.za ▪ www.▪wwines.co.za ▪ S 33° 27' 12.7" E 018° 45' 17.7" ▪ **T +27 (0)22-482-1134** ▪ F +27 (0)22-482-1750

One of the ubiquitous giant co-ops that dominated the Cape wine industry several decades ago, this Malmesbury operation was one of the first to reinvent itself as a quality producer of regionally specific brands. Now, swept up in the waves of change washing over the region, they've restructured into three business units: the company repositions itself as a marketing instrument, concentrating on building brands and expanding exports; the winemaking facilities east of Malmesbury are leased to bulk-wine producers Leeuwenkuil (who vinify the core ranges for them); while the laboratory and bottling plant service outside customers. This arrangement allows each segment to operate profitably and effectively, concentrating on their core specialisations.

Swartland Bushvine range

★★★★ **Shiraz** 🌿 **10** revisited as bottled wine, lives up to expectations, with solid black fruit core cloaked in silky tannins. Substantial, ripe & full-bodied, but showing restraint.

★★★★ **Idelia** ⊕ The blend make-up for **08** a cellar secret. Attractive upfront dark fruited charm, balanced, ripe & rich.

Cabernet Sauvignon 🌿 ★★★☆ Now tasted as finished wine, **10** shows distinctive green leaf herbaceousness on taut, smoothly textured structure. **Pinotage** 🌿 ★★★★ Sweetly spicy **10** shows improvement since last edition's preview. Vibrant, fruity enjoyment with satisfying weight & complexity. Follows last-tasted, lusciously fruity **08** (★★★★). **Chenin Blanc** Await new vintage, as for **Sauvignon Blanc**.

Swartland range

★★★★ **Red Jerepigo** ✓ 🍴 Remarkably complex flavour mix on fortified **NV** from pinotage: dark toffee & molasses, raisins & cocoa, all winding down to appealing nutty finish.

> **Cabernet Sauvignon** ☺ 🍴 🌿 ★★★ Lively, medium-bodied **11** is fresh & youthful, showing leafy-tarry aromatic nose & well-defined berry fruit. **Pinotage** ☺ 🍴 🌿 ★★★ Effusive bright wild berry fruit on **11** produces fun-times quaffer with appeal. Unpretentious, unwooded crowd pleaser. **Bukettraube** ☺ 🍴 🌿 ★★★ **12** shows sweetness tempered with crisp acidity, peachy fruit. **Chardonnay** ☺ 🍴 🌿 ★★★ Bright, fresh & fruity **12** faintly brushed with oak.

Merlot 🍴 🌿 ★★ Savoury **11** leaner, less jammy than previous. **Shiraz** 🍴 🌿 ★★★ Decently full **11** has real ripe-berry appeal, varietal character. Vibrant & youthful with firm tannic texture. **Tinta Barocca** 🍴 🌿 ★★★ Nutty oak notes on light-bodied **11** lead onto wild berry fruit. **Dry Red** 🍴 ★★★ Uncomplicated, light & juicy **NV** entry-level braai wine. **Blanc de Noir** ⊕ 🍴 🌿 ★★★ Delicate strawberry perfume on **11** in light & fruity style. **Chenin Blanc** 🍴 🌿 ★★★ Light tropical fruit on **12**, less expressive than previous. **Sauvignon Blanc** 🍴 🌿 ★★ Touch of sugar on **12** shows in sweet/sour granadilla fruit. **Cuvée Brut** ★★★ Dry carbonated **NV** sparkling from sauvignon blanc. Frothy & fun. **Demi Sec** ★★ Peachy-floral, cheerful, sweetish **NV** bubbly from bukettraube. **Hanepoot** ✓ 🍴 ★★★★ Enticing muscat fragrance & long, clean finish add charm to intensely sweet (200g/l) **NV** fortified winter warmer. **White Jerepigo** 🍴 ★★★ Edgy, spicy fortified chenin **NV** with syr-upy raisin fruit. **Cape Ruby** 🍴 ★★★ Listed as 'Port' last time. Wild notes & unyielding tannins mar rich chocolate fruit on **NV**. **Vintage Port** ⊕ ★★★★ **07** greater complexity than **06** (★★★★), layered flavours & nutty rich texture, harnessed by well-judged oak & fortification. Discontinued: **Merlot-Shiraz**.

D' Vine range

Cabernet Sauvignon-Merlot 🍴 ★★ Off-dry **NV** fruit cordial. **Rosé** 🍴 ★★ Sweet low-alcohol pinotage **NV**. **Chenin Blanc-Sauvignon Blanc** 🍴 ★★ Off-dry **NV**, lightish & brief. — GdB

Sweet Darling *see* Darling Cellars

SylvanVale Vineyards

Location/map: Stellenbosch • WO: Stellenbosch/Devon Valley • Est 1997 • 1stB 1998 • Tasting & sales daily 11–7 • Fee R25 • Open pub hols • Flavours Restaurant: 120 seater (see Restaurants section); Vineyard Terrace Cedarwood Bar & Lounge • The Devon Valley Hotel: 50 rooms (see Accommodation section) • Facilities for children • Tour groups • Conferences • 6 banqueting venues (max capacity 98 pax) • Walking/hiking trails • Owner(s) Louis Group Hotels, Spas & Vineyards • Winemaker(s) Mark Carmichael-Green (Sep 2003, consultant) • Viticulturist(s) Lorna Hughes (1997, consultant) • 8ha/4.3ha (cab, ptage, chenin) • 6t/525cs own label 100% rosé • PO Box 68 Stellenbosch 7599 • info@sylvanvale.com • www.sylvanvale.com • S 33° 54' 12.5" E 018° 48' 57.7" • **T +27 (0)21-865-2012** • F +27 (0)21-865-2610

Upmarket Louis Group Hotels are in the happy situation of owning an own wine brand but also own vineyards: the Sylvanvale wines are vinified to spec by seasoned consultant Mark Carmichael-Green, while the (recently replanted) vines share the scenic Stellenbosch premises of Devon Valley Hotel.

★★★★ **Pinotage Reserve** ⏺ Suitably mature, sweetish, violet-scented **05**, bold flavours ready to be enjoyed now. Oak maturation structures richly lush fruit flavours.

Dry Cabernet Sauvignon Rosé ☺ 🍴 ★★★ Characterful **11** is dry, crisp & appetising. Light oaking adds breadth.

Cabernet Sauvignon ⏺ ★★★★ Accessible, refreshing **05** offers juicy fruit & sufficient structure (from mostly new oak) for seriousness in style & ageability. **Ghost Tree Pinotage** Occasional release. **Shiraz** Await next. **Family Reserve** ⏺ ★★★★ Firm cab & spicy shiraz harmonise well with pinotage juiciness, **05** steps up from **04** (★★★★). Ready to drink. Oak, mostly new, complements sweet black cherry flavours. **Old Vine Chenin Blanc** 🍴 Await next. **Ghost Tree Sauvignon Blanc** NEW 🍴 ★★★ Delightfully fresh **11**, attractively light for summer lunchtime enjoyment. Koelenhof grapes. Discontinued: **Devon Valley Red.** — IM

▪ **Table Bay** see Ultra Liquors
▪ **Table Mountain** see Distell
▪ **Table View** see Rooiberg Winery

Tall Horse

Cheery labels and easy, fruit-forward style of this giraffe-themed DGB brand have clearly captured consumer tastes locally and overseas, where volumes are growing. Website www.tallhorsewines.com continues the quirky brand persona.

Tamboerskloof Wine — Kleinood Farm

Location/map/WO: Stellenbosch • Est 2000 • 1stB 2002 • Tasting, sales & cellar tours Mon-Fri 9-4.30 • Fee R20, waived on purchase • Closed all pub hols • Owner(s) Gerard de Villiers • Winemaker(s) Gunter Schultz (Sep 2007), with Julio Engelbrecht (Jan 2008) • Viticulturist(s) Gunter Schultz (Sep 2007) • 22ha/10ha (mourv, shiraz, rouss, viog) • 70t/5,000cs own label 87% red 8% white 5% rosé • BWI, IPW • PO Box 12584 Die Board 7613 • admin@kleinood.com • www.kleinood.com • S 33° 59' 42.6" E 018° 52' 14.8" • **T +27 (0)21-880-2527** • F +27 (0)21-880-2884

Last year it was olive oil, this year's addition to the focused Helderberg boutique winery's offerings is an elegant pink charmer, named for owner Gerard de Villiers' daughter. The accompanying neck tag sketch is by Katharien's grand — art being the link to their sponsorship of a culture centre at a nearby Jamestown primary school. Syrah will always be the calling card — top notch, small volumes.

★★★★☆ **Syrah** Elegant textured mouthful of silky black fruit, livened with splashes mourvèdre & viognier **08** well-judged ripeness & oak which adds backbone to generous fruit. Trademark pepper still present — & will be for years to come.
Katharien Syrah Rosé NEW 🍴 🖉 ★★★★ Deceptively simple pink shiraz. **12** light spice & blueberry nose but ample juicy appeal. Structured, elegant & lingering. **Viognier** 🖉 Not tasted. — FM

Tanagra Private Cellar

Location/WO: McGregor • Map: Robertson • Est/1stB 2003 • Tasting (wine/grappa), sales & cellar/distillery tours daily by appt • Farm produce • Boutique distillery (European style grappa & eau de vie) • Luxury farm accommodation in 5 cottages (self-catering/B&B) • Adjoining Vrolijkheid Nature Reserve • Owner(s) Robert &

nette Rosenbach ▪ Cellarmaster(s)/winemaker(s) Robert Rosenbach & Lourens van der Westhuizen ▪ Viticul-urist(s) Jaco Lategan (McGregor Winery) & Lourens van der Westhuizen ▪ 78ha/12.5ha (cabs s/f, merlot, tage, shiraz, cbard) ▪ 120t/300cs own label 90% red 10% rosé/blanc de noir ▪ IPW ▪ PO Box 92 McGregor 708 ▪ tanagra@tanagra-wines.co.za ▪ www.tanagra-wines.co.za ▪ S 33° 55′ 29.6″ E 019° 52′ 15.9″ ▪ **T +27 (0)23-625-1780** ▪ F +27 (0)23-625-1847

After consolidating the myriad wines, labels, stories and people behind this mall wine farm since settling here in 2009 (though avid SA visitors since 1996), German owners Robert and Anette Rosenbach are delighted to welcome new vinemaker/viticulturist Lourens van der Westhuizen, increase production, and ntroduce a new-look label and a focus on single-vineyard cab and shiraz.

Cabernet Sauvignon ⓘ ★★★ 07 big & bold, with earthy dark-berried tones, firm tannin base. **Merlot** Await ew, as for **Shiraz** & **Felicity**. **John's Medley** ⓘ ★★★ 07 merlot (80%) & cab franc duo offer dark chocolate & pe plum. **Heavenly Chaos** ⊘ ★ Bordeaux red, **11** showing some dried fruit character, should be enjoyed soon. **arah** ⊘ ★★★ Early drinking **11** cab & shiraz combo has rustic charm, firm & savoury taste. — CvZ/MW

▪ **Tangled Tree** *see Van Loveren Family Vineyards*

Tanzanite Wines

ocation: Worcester ▪ WO: Western Cape ▪ Est 2006 ▪ Tasting Mon-Sat by appt ▪ Owner(s) Wentzel & Melanie an der Merwe ▪ Cellarmaster(s) Melanie van der Merwe (Apr 2006) ▪ 400cs own label ▪ PO Box 5102 Worces-er 6850 ▪ melanie@tanzanitewines.co.za ▪ www.tanzanitewines.co.za ▪ **T +27 (0)23-347-0018** ▪ F +27 (0)86-694-0654

Melanie van der Merwe, the champagne-method sparkling guru who swapped giant Distell's JC le Roux for her own boutique bubbly winery in 2006, is inextri-ably tied to nature, the source of her product. She now donates a portion of ales to the Thanda Foundation, for rhino preservation. While the promised nagnums and vintaged bottles develop, mature...

★★★★ **Méthode Cap Classique Brut Rosé** More delicate, less opulent, than white cellarmate, grip of 60% pinot noir adds texture to penetrating finish. **NV**, degorged 11th of the 11th of 2011. At 11 perhaps? ★★★★ **Méthode Cap Classique** ✓ Luxurious, hand-nurtured sparkler from 80% chardonnay, with ele-gance in the vanguard. Latest **NV**, now 40 months on lees, for both contemplation and celebration. — DS

▪ **Tara Hill** *see Southern Sky Wines*

Tassenberg

Enduring light dry red affectionately known as 'Tassies'. Launched 1936, blend has varied over the years but not the affable persona. 750ml, 2L & 5L. By Distell.

Tassenberg ▤ ★★★ Lightish quaffing red, latest **NV** same spicy plum & gentle herbal grip as before. — DB/HJ

Taverna Rouge

Big-selling budget-priced red blend by Distell; available in 750ml and 2L.

Taverna Rouge ▤ ★★ Dusty, sweet-spicy **NV** tapas wine with a firm tannin finish. — DB/HJ

TCB Wines

ocation: Rawsonville ▪ Map: Breedekloof ▪ WO: Western Cape ▪ Est 2002 ▪ 1stB 2008 ▪ Tasting, sales & cellar ours Mon-Fri 8-5 ▪ Fee R10pp ▪ Closed all pub hols ▪ Tour groups ▪ BYO picnic ▪ Conferences ▪ Self-catering units ▪ Owner(s) TC Botha ▪ Cellarmaster(s) TC Botha & Christo Basson ▪ Winemaker(s) Christo Basson (Oct 2008) ▪ Viticulturist(s) Johan Slabber (Feb 1999) ▪ 190ha (cab, merlot, ptage, ruby cab, shiraz, chenin cbard, nouvelle, sauv, sem) ▪ 1,800t/300cs own label 50% red 50% white + 100cs for clients ▪ IPW ▪ PO Box 56 Rawsonville 6845 ▪ basson.christo8@gmail.com ▪ S 33° 42′ 5.63″ E 019° 18′ 21.92″ ▪ **T +27 (0)23-349-1748** ▪ F +27 (0)23-349-1325

This picturesque Rawsonville property is in the hands of the sixth TC Botha farming here. His cellar chief Christo Basson is celebrating ten years in the wine industry, and the completion of a journey from general cellar worker to cellar assistant, assistant winemaker to cellarmaster.

Cape Sparrow Selection

Classic Red ☺ 🖾 ★★★ Cheerful **11** is lighter than previous, soft & fruity 5-way blend for early pleasure.
Sauvignon Blanc ☺ 🏠 🖾 ★★★ Light-bodied, crisp & fruity **12** anytime sipper. — WB

Teddy Hall Wines

Location/WO: Stellenbosch ▪ Closed to public ▪ Owner(s)/cellarmaster(s)/winemaker(s)/viticulturist(s)
Teddy Hall ▪ PO Box 2868 Somerset West 7129 ▪ teddy@teddyhallwines.com ▪ www.teddyhallwines.com ▪
+27 (0)83-461-8111 ▪ F +27 (0)86-504-8178

Teddy Hall started out as a financial whizz in Gauteng, but chucked it all in to study
winemaking in 1992. He soon made a name for himself, becoming Diners Club
Winemaker of the Year in 2001 where the featured category was chenin blanc, and
he won the annual Chenin Blanc Challenge run by the now defunct Wine magazine
four times. Teddy Hall Wines was born in 2006, and Teddy has slowly but surely
gone about extending the range since then — his premium wines are named after
individuals associated with the early Cape, described as 'special characters but not
the type of people which usually receives any honour' (see website for full details).
Inevitably Dr Jan Cats Chenin Reserve is the 'jewel in the crown'.

Premium range

★★★★☆ **Hercùles van Loon Cabernet Sauvignon** ⓐ **08** is everything cab should be: aromas of cassis
& cedar before a palate which shows concentrated, optimally ripe fruit, fresh acidity & firm but fine tannins.

★★★★ **Syrah Reserve** ⓐ Plump & succulent, bright red fruit, fine pepper & clove spice on attractive
ageworthy **08** when last tasted.

★★★★☆ **Dr Jan Cats Chenin Blanc Reserve** ⓐ At cutting edge of what can be done with chenin, **1**
perfectly proportioned, pure & focused with great line of acidity. Will benefit from time in bottle.

Sybrand Mankadan Chenin Blanc 🏠 🖾 ★★★★ No mess, no fuss **11** is well balanced with notes of peach
& dried apricot, hint of vanilla thanks to 20% matured in older barrels. **Jan Blanx Super White Cuvée** ⓐ 🏠
★★★ **NV** is sauvignon-led but includes dashes semillon, chenin. Super-grassy but also hint of lime, bracing acidity. **Blanc de Blancs Méthode Cap Classique** ⓐ ★★★★ Champagne-method sparkling from chardonnay,
retasted **05** is rich & full with developed character; baked bread, yeasty notes, creamy mousse, gentle acidity.

Moments Collection

Winter Moments Shiraz-Cabernet Sauvignon ☺ 🏠 🖾 ★★★ Clean, uncomplicated **10** is medium-
bodied with red & black fruit, brush of vanilla, bright acidity.

Summer Moments Chenin Blanc ✓ 🏠 🖾 ★★★★ **11** punches above its weight, displaying great complexity. Notes of citrus, apple, peach & some waxiness, great acidity. Altogether more stylish than **10** (★★★).

Sgt Pepper range

Sgt Pepper ⓐ 🏠 ★★★ Shiraz-led **09** shows ripe berry fruit, not nearly as piquant as name implies. — CE

■ **Tembana Valley** see Rooiberg Winery

Tempel Wines

Location/WO: Paarl ▪ Map: Paarl & Wellington ▪ Est 2000 ▪ 1stB 2003 ▪ Tasting, sales & cellar tours by appt ▪ Fee
R25 ▪ Guest lodge (B&B), with 5 cottages ▪ Owner(s)/winemaker(s) Alf Ljungqvist ▪ 6ha/4.2ha (ptage) ▪ 24t/
850cs own label 85% red 15% white ▪ PO Box 7295 Noorder-Paarl 7623 ▪ sales@tempelwines.co.za ▪ www.
tempelwines.co.za ▪ S 33° 40' 34.0" E 018° 58' 32.2" ▪ **T +27 (0)21-872-4065** ▪ F +27 (0)21-872-3883

Paarl-based owner-winemaker Alf Ljungqvist says he knows the 'magic formula'
for his bushvines, so the resulting red and rare white pinotage receive a very satisfying reception among his mainly Scandinavian buyers. 'Expectations among
our clientele have risen to a level where we can't allow ourselves to slip or stumble,' he reports. 'A little fine-tuning, but mainly we're just trying to stay focused.'

Evidence Pinotage ★★★★ Was 'Pinotage Bush Vine Reserve'. Smooth & genteel **10**; variety's strawberries
& a fleeting hint of leather on offer, the charry oak is cushioned by plush fruit. **Innocence Blanc de Noir**
★★★ Unusual & distinctive barrel-fermented pinotage, **11** is white, not the expected blush, with almond,
stonefruit & light vanilla packed into rich & rounded palate. 'Great with curries' says its creator. — JP/CvZ

■ **Terra Del Capo** *see* Anthonij Rupert Wines
■ **Terra Madre** *see* High Constantia Wine Cellar

Teubes Family Wines

Location: Vredendal ▪ Map: Olifants River ▪ WO: Western Cape ▪ Est 2010 ▪ 1stB 2011 ▪ Tasting & sales Mon-Fri 8-5 Sat 9.30-5 ▪ Fee R20 ▪ Closed Easter Sat/Sun, Dec 25 & Jan 1 ▪ Cellar tours by appt ▪ Tour groups (up to 40 pax) ▪ Farm produce ▪ BYO picnic ▪ Conferences ▪ Walks/hikes ▪ Bergkraal 4x4 trail ▪ Mountain biking ▪ Conservation area ▪ Guest cottages ▪ Owner(s) Johan & Ella Teubes ▪ Cellarmaster(s) Sybrand Teubes ▪ Winemaker(s) Sybrand Teubes, with Alta Stone ▪ Viticulturist(s) Johan Teubes ▪ (cab, ptage, shiraz, chard, sauv) ▪ 300t ▪ PO Box 791 Vredendal 8160 ▪ sybrand@teubeswines.co.za ▪ www.teubeswines.co.za ▪ S 31° 43' 49.1" E 018° 30' 14.5" ▪ **T** +27 (0)27-213-2377 ▪ F +27 (0)27-213-3773

The Teubes family of Vredendal covered all bases last year. They made good a long-standing deficit and transformed an old tannery into their very own cellar, while embracing modern marketing philosophy with market research and product differentiation in mind. An uptick in volume testifies to their rising confidence.

> **Malkopbaai Pinotage** NEW ☺ ▤ **★★★** Pleasing **11** strawberry scented & flavoured, supple tannins for easy sipping.

> **Cabernet Sauvignon Private Selection** ▤ ▨ **★★★★** 'Cabernet Sauvignon' last edition. **10**'s silkiness enhanced by sweet vanilla from 2 years in French oak, pliable tannins. Nudges next level; allow few years in bottle to show full potential. **Pinotage** New vintage not ready, as for **Shiraz**, **Chardonnay**. **Malkopbaai Sauvignon Blanc** ▤ **★★★** Early-drinking **12** is packed with gooseberry & kiwi fruit flavours — at laudably moderate 12.5% alcohol — but fades rather quickly. — DB/CvZ

Thabani Wines

Location: Cape Town ▪ Closed to public ▪ Owner(s) Jabulani Ntshangase ▪ PO Box 1381 Stellenbosch 7599 ▪ abspice@iafrica.com ▪ www.thabani.co.za ▪ **T** +27 (0)82-734-9409 ▪ F +27 (0)86-648-3676

From his upmarket World of Wine shop at the Westin Hotel on Cape Town's Foreshore, Jabulani Ntshangase is planning to enter new wines under his Thabani 'Joyful') label in next year's guide. 'Something fresh,' promises the veteran wine-man, whose bottlings are mainly made to spec for the restaurant industry.

Thandi Wines

Location: Elgin ▪ Map: Elgin, Walker Bay & Bot River ▪ WO: Western Cape/Elgin/Stellenbosch ▪ Est 1995 ▪ Tasting & sales daily 7.30-5 ▪ Fee R20pp ▪ Closed Dec 25 & Jan 1 ▪ Restaurant: T +27 (0)21-844-0343 open daily 7.30-5 ▪ Facilities for children ▪ Tour groups ▪ BYO picnic ▪ Hiking/mountain biking trails ▪ Owner(s) Thandi Wines (Pty) Ltd ▪ Cellarmaster(s)/winemaker(s) Nicky Versfeld (Oct 2009, consultant) ▪ Fairtrade ▪ PO Box 597 Stellenbosch 7599 ▪ vernon@thandiwines.co.za ▪ www.thandiwines.co.za ▪ S 34° 11'7.08" E 019° 5'53.91" ▪ **T** +27 (0)21-844-0247/+27 (0)21-844-0041 ▪ F +27 (0)86-561-0152

This empowerment company, more than half-owned by 250 farmworker families, produced the world's first Fairtrade-accredited wine label. Profits go towards upliftment initiatives but we've often noted that the wines need no political 'feelgood' gloss to make them appeal. And most of them really good value too.

Thandi Single Varietal range

Cabernet Sauvignon ⊕ ▤ **★★★** Overt, ripe, sweet fruitiness on **08**, but firm & dry. All the still wines in his range tasted two or more years ago. **Pinot Noir** ⊕ **★★★★** 07's cherry fruit & balanced freshness promised charming early drinking. WO Elgin. **Shiraz Rosé** ⊕ ▤ ▨ **★★** Just-dry & just-fruity **10**. **Chardonnay** ⊕ ▤ ▨ **★★★★** Quiet, attractive citrus aromas & flavours on easygoing but serious **10**. **Sauvignon Blanc** ⊕ ▤ ▨ **★★★★** 10's showy aromas led to mouthful of succulence & tropical flavour. **Shiraz Rosé Sparkling** ⊕ ▨ **★★** Sweet **11** with light fruit & spice amongst the bubbles.

Thandi Dual Varietal range

Cabernet Sauvignon-Merlot ⊕ ▤ ▨ **★★★** Unpretentious & thoroughly tasty **10**, unoaked to keep the flavours pure, a little structure to hold them in place. **Shiraz-Cabernet Sauvignon** ⊕ ▤ ▨ **★★★** This **10** perhaps the more exciting of the two reds, packed with flavour. Neither one is bone-dry, but this adds to the fruit impact. **Chardonnay-Chenin Blanc** ⓑ 🍴 🐾 ★★★ Inviting, attractive **11** is deft, fresh & easy-drinking. The chardonnay was oak-aged. These whites have welcome modest alcohol levels. **Sauvignon Blanc-Semillon** ⓑ 🍴 🐾 ★★☆ Less seductive than previous vintage but pleasant, **11** has light flavours, shows some sweetness. Most Thandi wines ex-Stellenbosch, but WO W Cape. — TJ

The Amistad Wine Company   🍴 ⛲ 🏠 📷 NEW

Location/map: Franschhoek ▪ WO: Western Cape/Franschhoek ▪ Est 2011 ▪ 1stB 2008 ▪ Tasting, sales & cellar tours Mon-Sat by appt ▪ Closed all pub hols ▪ BYO picnic ▪ Walks/hikes ▪ B&B Bo La Motte Guest Farm & Self-Catering Cottages ▪ Owner(s) Jacques Wentzel & Ossie Sauermann ▪ Cellarmaster(s)/viticulturist(s) Jacques Wentzel & Ossie Sauermann (both Sep 2011) ▪ 66t/4,000cs own label 80% red 20% white + 3,000cs for clients ▪ PO Box 51 Simondium 7670 ▪ jacques@amistadwine.co.za, ossie@amistadwine.co.za, peter@amistadwine.co.za ▪ www.amistadwine.co.za ▪ S 33° 55' 15.6" E 019° 7' 39.9" ▪ **T +27 (0)21-876-2454**

In an artful backstory, friends and awarded winemakers Jacques Wentzel and Ossie Sauermann are invoking the tale of the mutiny on the misnamed 19th-century slave ship Amistad ('Friendship') to liken their release from a previous life as 'cellar-rats, pump-over jockeys, pipe draggers and barrel fillers' for other brands to the freedom of vinifying for their own label in Franschhoek's Bo La Motte cellar.

Amistad range

> **The Back Roads** ☺ ★★★ Appetising combo shiraz (85%) with double the cab to merlot. Dark berry **10** nicely spiced, reined in by dry tannins. Swartland & Wellington grapes; attractively packaged.

Syrah ★★★ Complex vinification — natural/inoculated ferments, some whole bunches, open/closed vessels, 2 years older oak — for **08**. Rich, super-ripe blackberry fruit & vanilla ready for drinking now. WO W Cape for the reds. **Sauvignon Blanc** 🍴 ★★★ Friendly **12**, soft tropical fruit with fresh grip, tiny barrel-fermented portion adds to appeal of this summer sipper. — HJ/JP

> ▪ **The Apprentice** see Origin Wine
> ▪ **The Auction Crossing** see Auction Crossing Private Cellar
> ▪ **The Belief** see Thembi & Co
> ▪ **The Bernard Series** see Bellingham

The Berrio Wines   🍴

Location: Elim ▪ Map: Southern Cape ▪ WO: Elim/Western Cape ▪ Est 1997 ▪ 1stB 2002 ▪ Tasting & sales Mon-Fri 9-4.30 Sat 10-3 (booking essential) ▪ Closed Sun, Easter Fri/Sun, Dec 25/26 & Jan 1 ▪ Snack/lunch platters by prior booking; or BYO picnic ▪ Owner(s) Francis Pratt ▪ Cellarmaster(s)/winemaker(s) Francis Pratt (Feb 2009) ▪ Viticulturist(s) Andrew Teubes (Jan 2006, consultant) ▪ 2,276ha/35ha (cabs s/f, malbec, merlot, p verdot, pinot, syrah, sauv, sem, viog) ▪ ±40t/17,170cs own label 20% red 80% white ▪ Fairtrade ▪ PO Box 622 Bredasdorp 7280 ▪ wine@theberrio.co.za ▪ www.theberrio.co.za ▪ S 34° 37' 17.0" E 019° 48' 32.3" ▪ **T +27 (0)28-482-1880** ▪ F +27 (0)86-603-2894

Owner and winemaker Francis Pratt has his eye on green matters as well as producing wines that will stand the test of time. He and fellow Elim vinegrowers subscribe to the Nuwejaars Wetland Special Management Area initiative, which strives to bring sustainable conservation in line with farming in the region. The object is to preserve the unique fauna and flora of the Agulhas coastal area. Francis, who believes packaging should be as eco-friendly as possible, sees his style as balanced, with alcohol levels not too high.

★★★★ **Cabernet Sauvignon** ⓑ 🍴 First since **06**, **09** (★★★★) surprisingly succulent for cool vintage. Tad herby, but plumped by fruit, sweet vanilla from some American oak. Portion Stellenbosch grapes.

★★★★ **Sauvignon Blanc** ✓ 🍴 🐾 Bold yet refined **11** shows great intensity, salty mineral persistence & a riper passionfruit nuance. Same coiled tautness as **10** & previous, similar longer-term cellaring prospects.

★★★★☆ **The Weathergirl** ✓ 🍴 🐾 Unlike Elim's weather, unwooded blend sauvignon (59%), semillon a paragon of consistency. **11** exudes confidence, pinpoint balance, silky persistence. Asparagus & greenpepper rather than **10**'s grass (70% sauvignon), but both will impress even more given time. — WB/GdB

The Butcher Shop & Grill

Location: Sandton ▪ WO: Stellenbosch/Western Cape/Durbanville/Elgin/Elim/Coastal ▪ Owner(s) Alan Pick ▪ Shop 30 Nelson Mandela Square Sandton 2196 ▪ thebutchershop@mweb.co.za ▪ T +27 (0)11-784-8676/7 ▪ F +27 (0)11-784-8674

Sandton's Butcher Shop & Grill proprietor Alan Pick has long been a prolific, high-profile Cape Winemakers Guild customer, and has built good relationships with its members. Some (as well as other estates) provide exclusive bottlings for his impressive top range, to complement his mostly carnivorous menu.

Limited Editions

★★★★☆ **Teddy Hall Cabernet Sauvignon** NEW Delicious **07** offers compelling, pure, ripe cassis fruit in a show of superb balance & integration; sufficient structure from cedary oak to underpin ripeness.

★★★★ **Hartenberg The Snuffbox Merlot** Austere **06** bold but classic, from prime single-vineyard. Oak (mostly new) seasons sour plum flavours & adds evolved but still firm tannins.

★★★★ **Niels Verburg Shiraz** NEW Powerful **08** has dense, darkly complex fruit & spices, with lithe, integrated tannins. WO W Cape.

★★★★ **Le Riche The Natalie** ⓣ Sister to Le Riche Cabernet-Merlot, with cab franc & petit verdot. **09** in similar style with dark fruits, slightly more prominent oaking & firm long finish. Very dry.

★★★★★ **Morgenster** ⓣ Old-World-style flagship with noble bearing & sense of seamless completeness. **05** 85% merlot with cab, awesome integration of fruit, savoury oak & tannic grip.

★★★★ **Vergelegen The Dani** NEW Labelled for the restaurant, **04** a fully mature, meaty & firm, ready to drink Bordeaux-styled red blend from this famous Stellenbosch estate.

★★★★☆ **Ernie Els Cabernet Sauvignon-Merlot** NEW Lushly ripe, opaque bold **06** offers hugely dense, dark fruit enveloped by ripe tannins. Great for restaurant's meaty fare, but caution if driving home: 15% alcohol.

★★★★ **Rust en Vrede The Sara** Opulently ripe **07** shiraz-cab blend makes a big statement. Showily oaked, developed '1694 Classification' has reached peak, had muscular tannins which have softened. Drink up.

★★★★★ **Reyneke Reserve Red** ⓣ Exceptional **07** adds 35% cab to shiraz. Delicate red fruit leads to smooth palate with fine chalky tannins. Doesn't show high alcohol, or 22 months 85% new oak.

★★★★ **Catherine Marshall SMG** ⓣ Individual, youthful shiraz-led **08** blend, with mourvèdre & juicy organic Swartland grenache; dried herbs & spicy red fruit threaded by fine acidity. WO Coastal.

★★★★ **Vergelegen The Carine** NEW Ingratiatingly fruity **11** sauvignon blanc is softer, less steely & bracing than the property's usual style.

First Sighting Pinot Noir ⓣ ★★★ **07** from Elim delivers appealing cherry/earth aromas & flavours but beefy tannins out of kilter with overall early-drinking persona. **Dombeya Heritage Ridge** NEW ★★★★ Accessible **05** cab-merlot blend with malbec in ripe & showy style.

Pick's Pick range

★★★★ **Cabernet Sauvignon** Sweet-fruited, charming **11** from Diemersdal in Durbanville; modest oak seasoning a perfect fit for succulent fruit, very moreish & delicious.

★★★★ **Cabernet Sauvignon-Shiraz-Merlot** ⓣ 🍴 By Guardian Peak, **10**'s savoury tone inherently food compatible. Easy solo drinker, too, thanks to not-quite-dry styling. WO W Cape.

★★★★ **Sauvignon Blanc** ⓣ 🍴 🌿 Lemongrass & fig, Jordan's **11** tank sample has less vibrancy, tension than thrilling **10** (★★★★★) but remains sleekly delicious.

★★★★ **Late Bottled Vintage** ⓣ Last **02** from JP Bredell had ripe fruit, measured structure, long finish.

Cabernet Sauvignon ⓣ ★★★★ Red berries & a grassy note, befitting Paul Cluver's Elgin terroir, nicely rounded **09** has a serious side, enough tannin to age. **Merlot** 🍴 ★★★★ Made for accessible drinking; Jordan's plummy, sweet **09** fruit has sufficient structure to cope with establishment's steaks. **Protea Merlot** ★★★★ Friendly choc-mint quaffer **11** with soft, sweet black plums & cherries mid-palate & dry finish. Ex Anthonij Rupert. **Shiraz** 🍴 ★★★★ Vibrant **11**, sweet ripe fruit & fine tannin, good body & tasty spice-laden length. From Guardian Peak. WO W Cape. **Shiraz** ⓣ 🍴 ★★★ **07**, with dash mourvèdre, juicy red & black fruit, a grind of pepper, fresh & soft mouthful. By Zevenwacht. **Syrah-Mourvèdre-Viognier** ⓣ 🍴 ★★★★ Fruit the hero in last-tasted **08** from Boekenhoutskloof. Plum coulis intensity, depth & succulence, smoky, spicy notes. **The Blend** ⓣ 🍴 ★★★★ Neil Ellis' **09** cab/shiraz blend (dash other varieties) is smoky, tasty & generous, with smoothly succulent dark fruit. WO W Cape. **Rosé** ⓣ 🍴 🌿 Merlot blend ex Jordan, **11** preview was cranberry scented, light textured & zesty. Works both as an aperitif & with food. **Chardonnay** ⓣ 🍴 ★★★ Lees-ageing adds richness to white peach, citrus flavours on stylish **10** from The Winery of Good Hope. Zesty acidity, minerality. WO W Cape. **Protea Sauvignon Blanc** ⓣ ★★★★ Last tasted **09** from Anthonij Rupert had zesty tropical & gooseberry tones & a

mineral flick in its tail. **Cape White Blend** ⏱ 🗄 ★★★★ Last-tasted **09** chenin-viognier-chardonnay by Tedd‐
Hall had intriguing perfume, flavours. Portion oaked. More delicious than **06** (★★★★). **Bubbly** NEW ★★★
Vivacious **NV** MCC from traditional varieties & dollop pinotage, from bubbly specialists Villiera. Creamy mouss‐
enlivens & textures flavourful mouthful. — IM

■ **The Cirrus Wine Company** *see* Cirrus Wines
■ **The Collection** *see* Mooiplaas Estate & Private Nature Reserve

The Company of Wine People

Location/map: Stellenbosch ▪ Est 2004 ▪ Tasting & sales Mon–Fri 9–5.30 Sat 9–5 Sun 10–4 ▪ Fee R10pp ▪ Closed
Good Fri, Dec 25 & Jan 1 ▪ The Duck Pond Restaurant (www.duckpond.co.za) ▪ Facilities for children ▪ Wed‐
dings/functions ▪ Owner(s) 200+ shareholders ▪ Winemaker(s) Abraham de Villiers (Dec 2004), Bernard
Claassen (Feb 2005), with Rudi Adams (2009), Justice Balula (May 2002) & Felicity Seholoba (Jan 1993) ▪ Viti‐
culturist(s) Francois de Villiers (1998) ▪ 500t ▪ 45% red 45% white 10% rosé ▪ ISO 22000, IPW, WIETA ▪ PO Box
465 Stellenbosch 7599 ▪ info@thecompanyofwinepeople.co.za ▪ www.thecompanyofwinepeople.co.za ▪ S
33° 59′ 26.06″ E 018° 46′ 2.21″ ▪ **T +27 (0)21-881-3870** ▪ F +27 (0)21-881-3102

A busy 2012 for this large Stellenbosch-based winery: all the brands within their
stable (Arniston Bay, Versus, Welmoed) gained either new lines or labels, whilst
their long-running Kumkani brand became a joint empowerment venture with
local businesswoman, Allison Witbooi-Adams, and the ultra-premium Credo range
last seen in our 2006 guide, was revived. (See separate listings for all.) Marketing
focus is on seeking new customers for their good-value accessible wines through
online channels, as well as keeping in touch with existing buyers via Facebook
Twitter and other social networks. Clean, modern packaging — including novel
green options — keeps them in the front line, and their attentions are turning East
as they identify and target new markets for their multi-faceted business.

■ **The Den** *see* Painted Wolf Wines
■ **The Diamond Collection** *see* Lutzville Cape Diamond Vineyards

The Drift Farm

Location: Napier ▪ WO: Western Cape ▪ 1stB 2005 ▪ Wine sales Mon–Fri 8.30-4 ▪ Owner(s) Jack family ▪
Winemaker(s) Bruce Jack & Trizanne Barnard ▪ Viticulturist(s) Chris Keet (consultant) ▪ 204ha/12ha (barbera, mal‐
bec, pinot, shiraz, tannat, tinta barocca, touriga franca, touriga nacional, chard) ▪ WIETA ▪ PO Box 55 Napier 7270 ▪
farmmanager@thedrift.co.za ▪ www.thedrift.co.za ▪ **T +27 (0)86-150-2025** ▪ F +27 (0)86-563-9533

Bruce Jack (also awarded maker of Flagstone, Kumala etc wines) loves to play
whether it's creating interesting blends and packaging or writing label copy you
enjoy reading. So expect surprises from his family farm near Napier. A case in
point is Year of the Rooster Rosé, so named because it's his and wife Penny's
birth year in the Chinese calender; she designed the pretty graphic on the bottle
and it's made from touriga franca (well, the Portuguese know about dry rosé,
right?). To come is MCC bubbly, port still in barrel and a red blend called 'There
Are Still Mysteries'. As we said!

★★★★ **Bowwood Cabernet Sauvignon-Merlot** ⏱ Classic Bordeaux style, **05** sumptuous blackcurrant
& leafy tobacco; well developed, drinking very well now. Agter Paarl grapes.

★★★★ **Riesling** ⏱ 🗄 Off cool Swartberg vines, **08** shows some development though still lively, fruity & a
good expression of the variety. Lightish alc (±11%) perfect for lunchtime.

Year of the Rooster Rosé ✓ 🗄 🚫 ★★★★ Previewed last time, now (attractively) bottled, **11** bone-dry
yet flavourful, tangy cranberries, crackling freshness. From port grape touriga franca. — CR

The Fledge & Co

Location: Calitzdorp ▪ WO: Stellenbosch/Western Cape ▪ Est 2007 ▪ 1stB 2010 ▪ Tasting & sales by appt at
Boplaas ▪ Closed all pub hols ▪ Owner(s) Margaux Nel & Leon Coetzee ▪ Winemaker(s) Margaux Nel & Leon
Coetzee (both Jan 2007) ▪ Viticulturist(s) Margaux Nel (Jan 2007) ▪ 3t/65cs (x 6) own label 40% red 60%
white ▪ IPW ▪ winemaker@boplaas.co.za, leon.mrfoo@gmail.com ▪ www.thefledge.co.za ▪ **T +27 (0)82-
828-8416/+27 (0)72-385-6503**

Impassioned 'terroirists' Margaux Nel (of the Boplaas Nels) and Leon Coetzee are fledglings who as students dreamed of producing 'individual, small batch lots of old-school wines'. The 'Co' is the licence plate prefix for Calitzdorp, where they vinify in 'gifted' cellar space from special blocks of chenin and viognier (touriga nacional, souzão and muscat de Frontignan 'still in the planning phase'). Leon's 'wine moment' came the first time he tasted touriga: 'It was as though a door to the wonderful world of wine opened and I walked through it'.

★★★★ **HoekSteen** ✓ Aka 'Cornerstone'. Chenin ('steen') ex veteran Stellenbosch bushvines, lees-aged 6 months (no oak); **11** understatedly impressive; bone-dry, svelte & finely tuned. Delightful retro label.

Vagabond ✓ ★★★★ Barrel-fermented viognier from single Klein Karoo vineyard; **10** only 160 bottles — we tasted No. 29. Characterful, gutsy, a white for red-wine lovers. Deserves time to fully integrate. —GdB/CvZ

The Foundry

Location/map: Stellenbosch ▪ WO: Stellenbosch/Voor Paardeberg ▪ Est 2000 ▪ 1stB 2001 ▪ Tasting, sales & cellar tours by appt ▪ Closed all pub hols ▪ Owner(s) Chris Williams & James Reid ▪ Cellarmaster(s)/winemaker(s) Chris Williams (Nov 2000) ▪ Viticulturist(s) Chris Williams (Nov 2000), with growers ▪ 11ha (grenache, shiraz, rouss, viog) ▪ ±30t/2,000cs own label 40% red 60% white ▪ PO Box 12423 Die Boord 7613 ▪ thefoundry@mweb.co.za ▪ www.thefoundry.co.za ▪ S 34° 1' 1.7" E 018° 45' 24.7" ▪ **T +27 (0)82·972·1360** ▪ F +27 (0)21-843-3274

'Regionalism, and adapting grape varieties to specific geographies and climates' are current trends that co-owner/winemaker (and Meerlust cellarmaster) Chris Williams highlights and, indeed, ones which gave impetus when establishing The Foundry over ten years ago. Partnered by Voor Paardeberg vinegrower James Reid, they have refined their vineyard sources there and in Stellenbosch, choosing Rhône varieties suited to the Mediterranean climate and granite soils. Williams talks of 'wines of purity, focus and distinction,' which is the imprint that all in this portfolio bear.

★★★★★ **Syrah** Classy Cape interpretation of the northern Rhône, smooth & polished **08** bridges the spicy/fruity style divide, melds best of both in harmonious whole.

★★★★★ **Grenache Blanc** ✓ Generous, fleshy lemon-cream & pear braced by clean minerality in elegant, honeyed — but dry — **11**. As with just-dry **10**, a step behind thrilling **09** (★★★★★) debut. Older cask fermentation, like all whites. Latest WO Voor Paardeberg.

★★★★ **Viognier** ✓ Unequivocal but balanced peachy, apricot pip ripeness, **10** more restrained than most New World examples, ends with stony grip. Like **09**, flavourful without big alcohol or cloying sweetness.

Roussanne ★★★★ Delicate perfumed/floral allure to **11**'s 'pebbly' minerality & stonefruit flavours. Silky, bone-dry finish gears up on just-dry **10** (★★★★). —DS

The Giant Periwinkle   🍷 [NEW]

Location: Bredasdorp ▪ Map: Southern Cape ▪ Est 2009 ▪ 1stB 2012 ▪ Tasting by appt only ▪ Owner(s) PJ Rabie snr & PJ Rabie jnr ▪ Cellarmaster(s) Johan de Kock (2011, consultant) ▪ Winemaker(s) Johan de Kock (2011, consultant) & Pierre Jacques Rabie jnr ▪ 0.06ha (sauv, pinot) ▪ 250kg own label 50% red 50% white ▪ PO Box 415 Bredasdorp 7280 ▪ pjrabie@capebar.co.za ▪ **T +27 (0)21-426-2653** ▪ F +27 (0)21-422-2142

Great wine is 'a living work of art' expound enthusiastic Bredasdorp father-son duo Pierre Jacques Rabie senior and junior. They're making small quantities of sauvignon blanc, shiraz and pinot noir sourced from the Elim ward in Cape Agulhas (hence the maritime brand name), but also nurturing their own 'special' vines (310 pinot, 306 sauvignon): 'Who doesn't dare, doesn't win!' Much-appreciated assistance comes from Zoetendal's Johan de Kock, The Berrio's Francis Pratt and Diemersdal's Mari Branders.

■ **The Goats do Roam Wine Company** see Goats do Roam Wine Company

The Goose Wines

Location: George ▪ Map: Klein Karoo & Garden Route ▪ WO: Upper Langkloof/Western Cape ▪ Est 2005 ▪ Tasting & sales by appt ▪ Meals/refreshments by appt ▪ Guest house ▪ Owner(s) Retief Goosen & Werner Roux ▪ Cellarmaster(s)/winemaker(s) Alwyn Liebenberg (Jan 2007) ▪ Viticulturist(s) Bennie Botha (Jan 2009) ▪ 500ha/21ha (cab, shiraz, sauv) ▪ 120t/9,333cs own label 66% red 34% white + 70cs for clients ▪ Brands for clients: Reuben's (Franschhoek & Robertson) ▪ HACCP ▪ PO Box 10 Oudtshoorn 6620 ▪ info@thegoosewines.com ▪ www.thegoosewines.com ▪ S 33° 48' 53.5" E 022° 34' 23.4" ▪ **T +27 (0)83-787-3000** ▪ F +27 (0)86-540-8077

'Our wines are always made with great focus on reflecting the full potential of our amazing terroir,' says Giuam de Korte, sales and marketing man at this farm in the Outeniqua mountains near George, co-owned by golfer Retief Goosen. The Gander range, previously blended with grapes from warmer areas, is now proudly certified as WO Upper Langkloof. And the single-vineyard The Goose wines are increasingly 'individualistic': 'We listen to nature for what works and what does not work', says Giuam. 'The natural biodiversity is always our highest priority.'

The Goose range

★★★★ **Expression** Plush ripe-styled **09** from cab & shiraz. Dark plummy fruit has vibrant acid support, soft supple tannins. 30% new French oak. WO W Cape.

★★★★ **T-Box Sauvignon Blanc** NEW The weightiest of the 3 sauvignons, **11** spent 9 months in new oak. Citrus peel, spice & pure fruit in fine balance with oak, acid & alcohol. Dry & soft with apple-fresh finale.

Sauvignon Blanc ★★★★ Shy bruised apple, lime & white pepper spice waft off delicate **11**. Lovely core of fruit follows to ultra-dry but soft end.

The Gander range

Shiraz 🗔 ★★★ Perfumed spicy lift on oaky **10**, with attractive fruity palate & pleasant sweetish send-off. **Sauvignon Blanc** ✓ 🗔 📖 ★★★★ Bone-dry, with lingering fresh & vibrant zing, **12** a step up from previous. — JP

■ **The Grand Beach Café** *see* Stellekaya Winery

The Grape Grinder

Location: Paarl ▪ WO: Coastal/Western Cape ▪ Est/1stB 2010 ▪ Closed to public ▪ Owner(s) Oliver Kirsten & Johan du Toit ▪ Cellarmaster(s)/winemaker(s) Pieter Carstens & Richard Rowe (both Dec 2010, consultants) ▪ 24,000cs own label 80% red 20% white ▪ ISO 2009, BRC, WIETA ▪ PO Box 606 Paarl 7624 ▪ oliver@grapegrinder.com ▪ www.grapegrinder.com ▪ **T +27 (0)21-863-3943** ▪ F +27 (0)86-588-4338

Pinotage remains the focus and driving force of this vibey Paarl wine business, along with the core belief of delivering what the customer wants. With no time for pinotage purists, they believe their style of winemaking is appealing and accessible, and hope their new wines will further enhance these values and strengths.

The Grape Grinder range

The Grinder Pinotage ☺ 🗔 📖 ★★★ Well-named **11** delivers big 'cuppa Joe' aromas giving way to smoky salami notes, pepper & plums. Cheerful & well-balanced. WO W Cape.

The Milkwood range NEW
Shiraz-Viognier 🗔 ★★★ Pleasantly perfumed nose on **09** with hints of cardamom & cumin spice. Oak prominent on entry leading to sweet black fruit finish. Paarl & Durbanville vines.

The Wild Olive range NEW
Old Vines Chenin Blanc 🗔 📖 ★★★ **12** from 30 year old Swartland vines. A little unbalanced but charming fruit. — CM

■ **The Greenhouse** *see* Bon Cap Organic Winery

The High Road

Location/map/WO: Stellenbosch ▪ Est/1stB 2003 ▪ Tasting & sales at Pane E Vino Food & Wine Bar Mon-Fri 10-6 Sat 10-5 ▪ Closed all pub hols ▪ Boardroom facilities ▪ Owner(s) Les Sweidan & Mike Church ▪ Winemaker(s) Mark Carmichael-Green (2004, consultant) ▪ Viticulturist(s) Paul Wallace (2004, consultant) ▪ 26t/2,000cs own label 100% red ▪ PO Box 4721 Cape Town 8000 ▪ wine@thehighroad.co.za ▪ www.thehighroad.co.za ▪ S 33° 56' 27.1" E 018° 50' 49.1" ▪ **T +27 (0)21-425-4209** ▪ F +27 (0)21-886-4288

Nadine Roets, GM of this small Stellenbosch Bordeaux-blend specialist, gives an interesting gloss to its name: 'Our wine is a tribute to the peaceful transition achieved when our country took the high road in 1994.' She adds that they use

The source of our wines is top secret.

The awards they win are breaking news.

At the 2012 Old Mutual Trophy Wine Show, Secret Cellar did it again. Secret Cellar Sauvignon Blanc 2011 captured the Old Mutual Discovery of the Show Award, for the best value Gold Medal wine. It also came third in the "Top 10 Best Value Whites", where our Table Bay Chenin Blanc 2011 came second. Proof once again that Ultra Liquors is not just the lowest-cost wine and liquor retailer in SA, but comes first for value for money.

FOLLOW US ON

www.facebook.com/ultraliquors and twitter – @ultraliquors

0800 004 414
www.ultraliquors.co.za

ULTRA Liquors

Not for sale to persons under the age of 18

The Township Winery is the tale of housing developer **Kate Jambela's** journey into wine, demystifying it and using it as a tool for empowering the women of Langa, Gugulethu and Philippi. Facilitated by wine entrepreneur **Graham Knox**, this urban winery project seeks to bridge the wide but also very deep divide between land owners who can afford to plant grapes for wine and the majority of the population. Grapes are currently sourced from various regions, but planting of vineyards within and adjacent to the townships has already begun.

J.

Joostenberg

Family traditions, good food & wine,
happy times & lots of laughter.
Some things never change...

Tel: 021 8844 141 | bistro@joostenberg.co.za
Joostenberg Bistro, Deli, Events Venue, Wines & Pork Butchery
Klein Joostenberg R304 Muldersvlei 7606
www.joostenberg.co.za

Among the Cape winelands' true characters, **Niels Verburg** and his wife
Penny have built a brand and a lifestyle on their shared aversion to
technology. The couple met at Elsenburg Agricultural College, where he
was vinifying his first shiraz and she was studying animal husbandry.
With children Daisy, Alice and Kim, they now live their dream of making
wine on their farm near Bot River, Niels vinifying wine that's 'as natural as
possible, with little or no intervention' and Penny caring for the vineyards,
growing vegetables and rearing 'happy pigs' for home-cured sausages
and charcuterie, also sold from the property.

crane
crystal

Distributed by Crystal DIRECT

021 887 2173
www.crystaldirect.co.za

Legend has it that well-established winemakers **Ossie Sauermann** (left) from Namibia and **Jacques Wentzel**, who was born on Robben Island, were kidnapped from their homes and forced to labour as wine slaves in several South African and international wineries. Their experiences as cellar rats, pump-over jockeys, pipe draggers and barrel fillers, combined with secret samplings of the fruits of their labour, kindled a passion for wine – and the stirrings of a revolt against their 'masters'. Finally, on a beautiful spring day in 2011, the pair launched their rebellion, ultimately winning the right to vinify for their own account. Thus was Amistad Wine Company born, with a vow by the rebels to never 'let the wine of friendship run dry'.

After dabbling in what he calls 'the dark arts of economics' and attaining an MBA at the University of Stellenbosch, **Pieter de Waal** found enlightenment in wine: first as a retailer and distributor, and latterly as co-owner/winemaker (with wife and Pilates instructor **Lohra**) of garagiste winery Hermit on the Hill. The metal statuettes they're holding reflect his fascination with the crusades – his wines pay tribute to medieval monk Peter the Hermit – and Arthurian legend. The granite outcrop alluded to in the branding, which represents the heart of the storied French appellation of Hermitage and the spiritual home of the syrah (shiraz) grape, reflects Pieter's acknowledgement that 'the Rhône is in my blood'. (Quite literally: one of his ancestors is credited with planting the first syrah vines at the Cape.) No surprise, then, that Hermit was launched with a syrah, or that grenache, cinsaut, mourvèdre and other Rhône varieties form part of the Hermit's playbook.

Riedel recognises that the bouquet, taste, balance and finish of a wine is affected by the shape of the glass from which it is drunk. Over forty years ago Claus Riedel began his pioneering work to create stemware that would match and complement different wines and spirits.

"The Finest glasses for both technical and hedonistic purposes are those made by RIEDEL. The effect of these glasses on fine wine is profound.

I cannot emphasize enough what a difference they make."
Robert M.Parker Jr – The Wine Advocate.

RIEDEL
THE WINE GLASS COMPANY
GRAPE ● VARIETAL SPECIFIC®

In giving up a successful career upcountry in the financial sector, moving to the winelands to study Viticulture and Oenology, and going on to become one of South Africa's star winemakers, **Teddy Hall** created his own backstory. Now he's linking his eponymously named wines with a ragbag of anti-heroes from the early history of the Cape settlement – a rebellious soldier, a bibulous theologian (Sybrand Mankadan, recalled in the kerbstone in Stellenbosch's Mancadan Street he's sitting atop), a doctor whose surgery was all too close to the mortuary – and thereby injecting an edginess into the Teddy Hall brand while bringing to life some of the winelands' most characterful and largely forgotten personalities.

-26.191125

28.007714

BELONG

IF YOU THINK GOOD FOOD IS BEST
ACCOMPANIED BY FINE WINE, YOU BELONG

DINERS CLUB WINELIST 2012 AWARDS

SOME THINGS JUST GO TOGETHER NATURALLY. LIKE
GOOD FOOD AND FINE WINE. IF YOU'RE PLANNING
TO DINE OUT, WE SUGGEST YOU CHOOSE FROM OUR
2012 DINERS CLUB WINELIST AWARD WINNERS AT
CONNOISSEURS.DINERSCLUB.CO.ZA, WHERE YOU
WILL FIND A LIST OF THOSE RESTAURANTS THAT GO
THE EXTRA MILE TO PAIR OUTSTANDING FOOD FARE
WITH MEMORABLY MATCHING WINES.

OliverM^cIntyre 17132/R

THE VINEYARD
CONNECTION

021 884 4360
info@vineyardconnection.co.za

EXPORTERS OF WINES FROM THE CAPE

TO
CAPE
TOWN

TO P

R44

exit 47

N1

R101

KLAPN

KLAPMUTSKOP

LIEVL

MULDERSVLEI ROAD

THE VINEYA
CONNECTI
AT DELVE

R44

KANONKOP

BOTTELARY
ROAD

SIMONSIG TO STELLENBOSCH

KROMME
RHEE ROAD

Wine Business
AWARDS

FM

wine
shop.co.za

Best Independent Wine Retailer • Best Logistics

ɪgh road practices', employing 'experienced professionals to oversee our wine-
ɑaking from start to finish, in a state-of-the-art winemaking facility'.

★★★ **Director's Reserve** ⓔ Classic **08** from 60% cab plus equal merlot, cab franc. Plush & luminous, its
ɒright blackcurrant fruit interwoven with vanilla spice from the all-new oak. Evenly, richly textured.
ɑassique ★★★☆ Dark-fruited, savoury **09** cab-led, with merlot & cab franc. Follows through well to inter-
ɛsting palate: firm, tannic & a touch rustic. **Reserve** ⓔ ★★★☆ Same varieties, with more cab. Robust & firm
ᴃ, tannic & savoury, showing evidence of all-new oak (but well integrated). — JPf

The Hills

ᴑcation/WO: Stellenbosch ▪ Est/1stB 2006 ▪ Tasting & sales by appt ▪ Owner(s) The Victor Hills Family Trust ▪
ᴠinemaker(s) Martin Meinert (Feb 2006, consultant) ▪ Viticulturist(s) Vic Hills (Jan 1998) ▪ 6ha/5ha (cab,
ɱnot, shiraz, chenin) ▪ 40t/300cs own label 80% red 20% white ▪ PO Box 12012 Die Boord Stellenbosch 7613
ᴠwhills@iafrica.com ▪ S 33°55'04.1" E 018°48'47.1" ▪ **T +27 (0)21-865-2939** ▪ F +27 (0)21-865-2939

ɦimanimani is a smallholding in prime Stellenbosch wine ward Devon Valley,
ᴠhere Vic Hills, whose family has owned the property since 1964, oversees 5ha
ᴏf noble reds and a block of nearly 40-year-old chenin. The harvest mostly goes
ᴑ local merchants but since 2006 a soupçon trundles over the river and up the
ɦill for vinification by celebrated wine man Martin Meinert.

ɑbernet Sauvignon ★★★ Classic cedar-dusted blackcurrant, **08** satisfying herby taste, bright almost zingy
ᴇshness throughout. Loves strong cheese. Modest ±13% alcohol, as all here. **Pinot Noir ★★★** Variety-true **10**,
ɑrthy cherries & hint of mint, light textured but generous, zesty & commendably dry. Ready now & good for few
ᴇars. **Shiraz ★★★** Meal mate **08**, acidic verve to spicy-smoky plum flavour, friendly hug of tannin. **Ensemble**
★★★ **08** 60/40 cab & shiraz blend is at peak, its bone-dry herby berry flavours ready to be enjoyed now (with
ᴏod, ideally). **Chenin Blanc** 🛢 ★★ **11** crisp for summer sipping. Serve well chilled. — JP/CvZ

The House of GM&Ahrens

ᴑcation/map: Franschhoek ▪ WO: Western Cape ▪ Est 2007 ▪ 1stB 2008 ▪ Tasting, sales & cellar tours by appt ▪
ᴄlosed all pub hols ▪ Meals/refreshments by appt ▪ Owner(s) Albert Ahrens & Gerrit Maritz ▪ Cellarmaster(s)/
ᴠiticulturists Albert Ahrens (Jan 2007) ▪ 7t/350cs own label 100% MCC ▪ P O Box 5619 Helderberg 7135 ▪
ɪnfo@gmahrens.co.za ▪ www.gmahrens.co.za ▪ S 33°54'14" E 019°07'08" ▪ **T +27 (0)79-196-6887**

ɦe méthode cap classique maturing in the cellars of this boutique bubbly house
ɪn Franschhoek is launched at a special breakfast every Spring Day. Most 'joyous
ᴄcasion' to date was 1 September 2011, when the maiden 2008 took flight in a
ɦot air balloon: a 'dream come true' for lawyer Gerrit Maritz and winemaking
ɒartner Albert Ahrens.

★★★★ **Vintage Cuvée** NEW Almost year barrel maturation for base wine & 2½ bottle attest to serious
ɪntent of rich, weighty & delicious **08** traditional-method sparkling from widely sourced chardonnay (71%),
pinot noir. White pepper, spice & obvious oak, latter not detracting from overall focus & fine acidity. — HJ/JP

The House of JC le Roux

ᴑcation/map: Stellenbosch ▪ WO: Western Cape ▪ 1stB 1983 ▪ Tasting & sales Mon-Fri 8-5 Sat 10-4 Sun 10-3 ▪
ᴇe R35-R75 ▪ Self tour available during opening hrs ▪ Closed Good Fri & Dec 25 ▪ Tour groups ▪ Gifts ▪ Seasons res-
ɑurant ▪ Owner(s) Distell ▪ Cellarmaster(s) Elunda Basson ▪ Winemaker(s) Elunda Basson (2007), with Hentie
ɦermishuys (Oct 2002) ▪ Farm manager Willem Laubscher ▪ Viticulturist(s) Bennie Liebenberg (Jan 2000) ▪ 27ha
ᴑwn vyds ▪ 20% red 80% white ▪ ISO 9200 ▪ PO Box 184 Stellenbosch 7599 ▪ info@jcleroux.co.za ▪ www.jcleroux.
ᴄo.za ▪ S 33°54'16.6" E 018°48'37.4" ▪ **T +27 (0)21-865-8200** ▪ F +27 (0)21-865-2585

Affection for this popular brand remains high among consumers, the House of JC
ɛ Roux having being voted the country's top wine brand for the second consecu-
ɪve year in the 2012 TGI ICON Brand Survey. The winery is dedicated exclusively
ɑo sparkling wine, and has increased tasting capacity and upgraded the tasting
ᴑom with a more vibrant colour scheme. Phase Two of the upgrade, culminating
ɪn late 2012, involved a facelift for the restaurant and a new tasting deck outside
ɦe new La Fleurette room on the ground floor.

Méthode Cap Classique range

★★★★ **Scintilla** Well-constructed, bone-dry, earthy **03** still youthfully fresh a decade after harvest. Seriously structured, complex citrus flavours in chardonnay-led blend, with pinot noir.

Pinot Noir Rosé ⊕ ★★★ Delicate pink **08** has developed, yeasty aromas. Fresh & subtly fruity, with decent structure, breadth & focus. **La Vallée Rosé** ⊕ ★★★★ Pretty onion-skin **NV**. Raspberry fruitiness in off-dry but refreshing style. **Pinot Noir** ⊕ ★★★★ Steely **08** vinified pale & notably dry. Fresh, lean & steely style with enduring finish. **Brut** ★★★ Pinot noir dominated **NV**, not as much character or complexity as previous bottling, but nevertheless pleasingly harmonious. **La Vallée** ★★★ Off-dry **NV** for those who prefer their MCC a little softer & sweeter. Mostly pinot noir. Charmingly drinkable, fruity & refreshing.

Sparkling range

La Chanson ★★ Pleasingly sweet red **NV** bubbly, mostly pinotage. **La Fleurette** ★★ Sweet **NV**, more red than pink, mostly sauvignon. As for most of these, low 7.5% alcohol. **Sauvignon Blanc** ⊕ ★★★ Fresh carbonated **11** sparkler delivers plenty appeal & cheer. Although dry, abundant fruit gives sweet impression. **Le Domaine** ★★ Sweet celebration **NV** fizz, grapey muscat softens sauvignon. — IM

- ■ **The House of Krone** *see* Twee Jonge Gezellen Estate-The House of Krone
- ■ **The House of Mandela** *see* House of Mandela
- ■ **The Hughes Family** *see* Hughes Family Wines
- ■ **The Innings** *see* Rietvallei Wine Estate
- ■ **The Juno Wine Company** *see* Juno Wine Company
- ■ **The Legends** *see* Bellingham

Thelema Mountain Vineyards   🍷🍴🎋🚻♿

Location/map: Stellenbosch ▪ WO: Stellenbosch/Elgin/Western Cape ▪ Est 1983 ▪ 1stB 1988 ▪ Tasting & sales Mon-Fri 9-5 Sat 10-3 ▪ Fee R25/6 wines, waived on purchase ▪ BYO picnic ▪ Owner(s) McLean & Webb Family Trusts ▪ Cellarmaster(s) Gyles Webb (1983) ▪ Winemaker(s) Rudi Schultz (Dec 2000), with Duncan Clarke (Jan 2009) ▪ Viticulturist(s) Talitha Venter (Jan 2010) ▪ 250ha/95ha (cab, grenache, merlot, p verdot, pinot, shiraz, chard, muscat d'F, riesling, rouss, sauv, viog) ▪ 850t/50,000cs own label 40% red 60% white ▪ PO Box 2234 Dennesig Stellenbosch 7601 ▪ wines@thelema.co.za ▪ www.thelema.co.za ▪ S 33° 54'30.0" E 018° 55'23.4" ▪ **T** +27 (0)21-885-1924 ▪ **F** +27 (0)21-885-1800

While the younger vineyards on Thelema's Elgin outpost are maturing to produce ever-finer wine, some back home in Stellenbosch are showing their age — a reminder that it is now exactly 30 years since the old fruit farm was bought by the McLeans and Webbs and the conversion to vines began (what a great idea that was!). Two of the oldest cabernet blocks are being replanted — but the parcel producing the muscatty chardonnay for Ed's Reserve remains to honour the memory of Thelema matriarch Edna McLean. 'Ed worked in the tasting room and is still very fondly missed by visitors,' says manager (and her grandson) Thomas Webb. As for Sutherland, says Tom: 'The leaner, more minerally styles we get from there seem to suit customers looking for more balance and concentration at the expense of big fruit and weight.' Though in fact there's plenty of weight in some of them — and great balance in the Stellenbosch versions too.

Thelema range

★★★★☆ **Cabernet Sauvignon 09** tight (needs decanting) in youth, but the full fruit will expand in a few years & the hints of dusty tobacco oak be harmonised — it should keep a decade at least. Already fine, supple, with focused flavours, & the power expertly managed & balanced.

★★★★☆ **The Mint Cabernet Sauvignon** ▨ The herbal element behind the name shows pleasingly as ever on **10**. Big & forceful, all in balance — maybe a touch more severe & less graceful than the Cab Sauv (but that's a year older), though alcohol 0.5% lower, at 13.8%. Surely 10+ years ahead, satisfying all the way!

★★★★☆ **Merlot Reserve** ▨ **10** again shows this to be one of the Cape's best merlots, delicious enough in youth but will harmonise & gain complexity over 5 or more years. Subtly powerful, with strong tannins & fresh acidity big but balanced, the all-new oak well constrained by fruit.

★★★★ **Shiraz** Handsome & forthright, firmly built & rather virile **09** — less perfumed than Sutherland version. Poised, but should benefit in terms of harmony with a few years in bottle.

★★★★☆ **Rabelais** Rich, expressive **08** even finer than maiden **07**. Mostly cab, to give its strong structure, with petit verdot & merlot — both adding fragrance & charm. Tasty, unabashed dark fruits triumphantly carried by tannin & acid; despite the power, a liveliness prevails. Silky texture, brilliantly dry long finish. A great future.

★★★★ **Chardonnay** 🗔 🏵 As usual, **11** shows winning combo of lipsmacking structure & flavour (touched by butterscotch from effective oaking) & serious restraint. Dry, not over-powerful; ready for drinking.

★★★★ **Ed's Reserve Chardonnay** 🏵 **11** from single-clone block giving muscat/face-powdery notes. Poised acidity, but richer, prettier, sweeter-fruited than standard Chardonnay. Great texture, good dry finish.

★★★★ **Sauvignon Blanc** 🗔 🏵 Tasted pre-bottling as usual, crisply fresh **12** offers lots of green & citrus notes, with a little weight to it & a grapefruity bite on the finish.

Mountain Red ☺ 🗔 ★★★ **09** blends cab, shiraz, grenache & petit verdot for characterful, lightly spicy fruitiness. Easygoing but no pushover — well oaked, succulently firm. WO W Cape.

Merlot 🏵 ★★★★ Bright, ripe & flavoursome but unfrivolous **10**; attractive aromas lead to a solid, chewy, slightly tannic mouthful. **Muscat de Frontignan** 🗔 ★★★ Pre-bottling, **12** seems drier than usual, exposing some insipidity on grapey, scented charm. Fresh, pleasant. **Riesling** ⊕ 🗔 🏵 ★★★ **10** not quite usual standard: pleasant, with balanced sweet touch & limy freshness, but early terpene notes & a bit insipid. **Rhine Riesling Late Harvest** ★★★★ **09** in customary light style; easily gratifying but neither very sweet nor very acidic. Satisfying & even dryish feel as it lingers. 375 ml. **Vin de Hel Muscat Late Harvest** ★★★★ Showy, grapey & floral scents on **09**; sweeter than Riesling version, but one-dimensional in its shallowly assertive charm. 375 ml.

Sutherland range

★★★★ **Chardonnay** ⊕ 🗔 🏵 Drops 'Wooded' from name with **10** (★★★★). Paler colour than the Stellenbosch versions, & generally paler flavours, aromas too; green liminess thinner than in **09**.

★★★★ **Sauvignon Blanc** 🗔 **12** preview has more lyrical, floral charm than greener Stellenbosch version, without forgoing the focus. Very satisfying.

★★★★ **Viognier-Roussanne** 🗔 Was 'Roussanne-Viognier'. Herbal, peachy complexity on lovely aromas & lingering flavours of **10** (★★★★★) — even finer than **09**. Despite ripeness, viognier subtle rather than over-blown presence in effective, restrainedly rich, modestly oaked blend. Should only gain with few years in bottle.

Pinot Noir ★★★★ Good varietal character on fresh, lightly perfumed **11**, with clearer fruit expression & more integrated oak than on previous. **Syrah** ★★★★ Renamed from 'Shiraz'. **09** especially attractive to sniff. Notably ripe flavours with sweet fruit; firm build, well-balanced oak. **Cabernet Sauvignon-Petit Verdot** ★★★★ Big, ripe, rather solid & chunky **09** packed with fruit & savoury flavours. More forceful than previous vintage. **Riesling** 🗔 ★★★ **11** drops 'Rhine' from name. Elegantly steely, even austere — but technically only just dry, with a few grams sugar for richness. Dried peach & citrus notes. Great with food. — TJ

■ **The Light** *see* Arniston Bay
■ **The Marais Family** *see* Wonderfontein

The Mason's Winery

Location/WO: Paarl ▪ Map: Paarl & Wellington ▪ Est/1stB 2001 ▪ Tasting & sales by appt at Proviant Restaurant — adjacent to cellar ▪ Owner(s) JA Clift (Pty) Ltd — Clift family ▪ Cellarmaster(s)/winemaker(s) Derek Clift (2001) ▪ Viticulturist(s) Derek Clift ▪ 47ha/4ha (shiraz) ▪ 30t/1,000cs own label 100% red ▪ Main Street Suider-Paarl 7646 ▪ masons@cliftgranite.co.za ▪ www.cliftgranite.co.za ▪ S 33° 45' 20.5" E 018° 57' 42.6" ▪ T +27 (0)83-228-7855 ▪ F +27 (0)21-863-1601

If you love red wine but it doesn't love you the next morning, chances are you imbibed too much or are allergic to sulphur. If the latter, Paarl-based shiraz specialist Derek Clift's offerings may be just what the doctor ordered, as his own sulphur intolerance has led him to make wines with minimal levels of it.

Mason's Shiraz ★★★ Robust **07** has abundant rich & ripe fruit. Huge 16.4% alcohol on these reds is remarkably well contained. **Voëltjiegat Shiraz** NEW ★★★★ Single-vineyard **07** not for the faint-hearted. Warm glow on big, bold fruit. Both reds will have enthusiasts & detractors. **Klipkapper Chenin Blanc** Await next. — IM

Thembi & Co

Location: Paarl ▪ Est/1stB 2009 ▪ Tasting by appt ▪ Owner(s) Thembi Tobie ▪ Winemaker(s) Jaco Brand (Citrusdal Cellars) ▪ Fairtrade ▪ thembi@thembiwines.co.za ▪ www.thembiwines.co.za ▪ T +27 (0)22-921-2235/+27 (0)83-277-5117

Owner of this eponymous brand, Thembi Tobie is a woman filled with self-belief, hence the name of the new range below. Now fully Fairtrade accredited, Thembi's wines are made at Citrusdal Cellars, and though currently she operates from an office in Paarl, Thembi dreams of a permanent brand home.

The Belief range NEW

Pinotage ☺ ★★★ Uncomplicated & friendly **11** offers up blueberry & raspberry succulence & light spice.

Shiraz 🗒 ★★★ Fruit pastille appeal on soft & gentle **11** charmer. Christmassy spice & plum notes. Medium body & length. **Chardonnay** ★★☆ Approachable tangy mouthful of citrus with touch of honey on **11**. **Chenin Blanc** Await new vintage.

Thembi range

Pinotage NEW Next awaited, as for **Shiraz**, **Chardonnay** & **Chenin Blanc**. —FM

- ■ **Thembu** *see* House of Mandela
- ■ **The Naked Vine** *see* Hornbill Garagiste Winery
- ■ **The Old Man's Blend** *see* Groote Post Vineyards
- ■ **The Pavillion** *see* Boschendal Wines

The Rhino of Linton Park   🍷 NEW

Location: Wellington ▪ WO: Western Cape ▪ Tasting & sales by appt at Linton Park (see entry) ▪ Owner(s) Camellia PLC UK ▪ Cellarmaster(s) Hennie Huskisson (2007) ▪ Winemaker(s) JG Auret (2007) ▪ Viticulturist(s) Rudolf Jansen van Vuuren (2012) ▪ PO Box 1234 Wellington 7654 ▪ sales@lintonparkwines.co.za ▪ www.rhinowines.com ▪ **T +27 (0)21-873-1625** ▪ F +27 (0)21-873-0851

Once a plentiful fynbos type in the Cape, renosterveld today is highly endangered — much like the rhinos which share the name. Wellington producer Linton Park has merged a variety of interests in establishing The Rhino label, in that it is Fairtrade accredited, forms part of the farm's employee empowerment scheme, and benefits Save The Rhino through the donation of a portion of profits.

Red Rhino range

Pinotage ☺ 🗒 ★★★ Candyfloss whiffs lead to raspberry simplicity on **11**. Juicy, light & unchallenging. Good length & depth. **Cape Red** ☺ 🗒 🕸 ★★★ Quaffable seriousness from **11**'s 50/50 merlot/pinotage mix. Firm & full-bodied with ample dark fruit, spice & cocoa allure.

Cabernet Sauvignon 🗒 🕸 ★★★☆ **11** offers fruitcake appeal, serious savoury dryness & depth. Firm yet lithe structure allows for few years ageing. **Merlot** 🗒 🕸 ★★★☆ Bold entry on inky **11**, soft-textured chocolate palate holds interest to long, layered finish. Dinner party contender. **Shiraz** 🗒 🕸 ★★★☆ Cushioning effect of layered blue & black berries on **11**'s dryness is instant, fleshing out the squeeze of tannins in firm frame.

Pink Rhino range

Rosé ☺ 🗒 🕸 ★★★☆ Lightish & fresh **12**, tangy fynbos on off-dry pink from chardonnay & cab.

White Rhino range

Chardonnay ☺ 🗒 🕸 ★★★ Dab of citrus marmalade on crisp, juicy & light **11**. **Chenin Blanc** ☺ 🗒 ★★★ Passionfruit zip & succulent piquancy, **12** light but with rich honeyed note on a medium-length finish. **Sauvignon Blanc** ☺ 🗒 🕸 ★★★ Green citrus zing & gooseberry on **12**, zesty & fresh. **Cape White** ☺ 🗒 🕸 ★★★☆ Sauvignon/chardonnay mix on **12**, exuding juicy lemon vibrancy. —FM

- ■ **The Royal** *see* Valley Vineyards Wine Company
- ■ **The Ruins** *see* Bon Cap Organic Winery
- ■ **The Sadie Family** *see* Sadie Family Wines
- ■ **The Shore** *see* Arniston Bay
- ■ **The Spice Route Winery** *see* Spice Route Winery

The Three Foxes

Location: Riebeek-Kasteel ▪ WO: Groenekloof/Swartland/Voor Paardeberg ▪ Est/1stB 2004 ▪ Tasting by appt at Mullineux Wines ▪ Owner(s) Pascal Schildt, Olivier Schildt & Chris Mullineux ▪ Winemaker(s)/viticulturist(s) Chris Mullineux (Jan 2004) ▪ 1.2ha (syrah, chenin, clairette) ▪ 6t/400cs own label 80% red 20% white ▪ PO Box 369 Riebeek-Kasteel 7307 ▪ info@the-three-foxes.com ▪ www.the-three-foxes.com ▪ **T +27 (0)82-333-6888** ▪ F +27 (0)82-121-333-6888

Outside his day job of making precisely focused wine for Mullineux Family Wines, Chris Mullineux collaborates with brothers Pascal and Olivier Schildt on these unfettered projects, to produce wines entirely free of constraints like marketability, replication, volumes or even general stylistic direction. Rather like improvised jazz music, the end results are mostly very satisfying. This year's offering is an intriguing riff on oxidative processes and sherry yeasts.

★★★★ **Sangiovese** ⑧ From Groenekloof single-vineyard, **08** when last tasted showed Xmas cake, ginger & iodine nuances. Judiciously oaked, supple yet structured.

★★★★ **Castillo Syrah** ⑧ Fragrantly herbaceous **09** from Swartland vines not retasted, was elegantly weighted, juicy & complex. Unshowy but focused, unfurling over time in glass.

★★★★☆ **Roussanne** NEW Another exercise in radical winemaking sees this Rhône white variety emulating Jura's classic sherry-like (but unfortified) style. **09** fermented & 3 years in old oak barrels under flor yeast. Dry, oozing character & complex style; prepare to be amazed. Voor Paardeberg WO. — GdB

■ **The Tin Mine** *see Zevenwacht*

The Township Winery

Location: Philippi ▪ WO: Western Cape ▪ Est 2009 ▪ 1stB 2010 ▪ Closed to public ▪ Owner(s) The Township Winery cc ▪ Cellarmaster(s) Wilhelm van Rooyen (Oct 2009, consultant) ▪ 400cs own label 100% white ▪ PO Box 63 Philippi 7781 ▪ kate@jambela.co.za ▪ **T +27 (0)21-371-6083** ▪ F +27 (0)21-371-6083

Entrepreneurial developer Kate Jambela builds 'RDP' houses for lower-income families. In the course of this day job, she became aware of the viticultural land-use opportunities in the depressed neighbourhoods of the Cape Flats, as well as the unique soil profiles churned up by cement factories around Philippi, over many years. She's combining these values with a community involvement winemaking project to bridge the social and economic chasms that isolate the townships.

The Township Winery range

Philippi Sauvignon Blanc 🍸 🎴 ★★★☆ Asparagus, grassy character beginning to dominate **10** on retaste. Roasted nuts & nettles spice up full, nicely balanced palate. Drink now.

Dido range

★★★★ **Cabernet Sauvignon** ⑧ Drink-now **04** impressed previously with brooding black fruit & tealeaf herbaceousness. Wellington grapes, as all unless noted.

Hamilcar Merlot Await new vintage. **Pinotage** ⑧ 🍸 ★★★ When last tasted, **09** was fresh, youthful, with vibrant berry fruit, restrained tannins. Some Darling vines. **Shiraz** Untasted. **The Storm Mourvèdre-Shiraz** ⑧ 🍸 Light-bodied **09** last time showed feisty cherry fruit, hints of pepper & spices. **Pinot Grigio** ⑧ 🍸 🎴 ★★★☆ Charming, smoothly rounded body, **10** couches beeswax & stonefruit notes. Forthright & elegant. WO W Cape. **Sauvignon Blanc** ⑧ 🍸 ★★★ **09** from Durbanville grapes was lean & steely on review, with restrained gooseberry flavour. — GdB

Theuniskraal

Location/map/WO: Tulbagh ▪ Est 1705 ▪ 1stB 1947 ▪ Tasting & sales Mon-Fri 9–12 & 1–4 Sat 10–1 ▪ Closed Easter Sat/Sun, Dec 25 & Jan 1 ▪ Owner(s)/viticulturist(s) Jordaan family ▪ Cellarmaster(s) Andries Jordaan (1991) ▪ Winemaker(s) Andries Jordaan (1991) & Wagner Jordaan ▪ 140ha total ▪ BWI ▪ PO Box 34 Tulbagh 6820 ▪ tkraal@lando.co.za ▪ www.theuniskraal.co.za ▪ S 33° 13' 41.3" E 019° 8' 7.1" ▪ **T +27 (0)23-230-0687/89** ▪ F +27 (0)23-230-2284

A venerable Tulbagh label and South Africa's first white-wine estate, Theuniskraal has been farmed by the Jordaan family since 1927. The current team are fourth-generation winemaker Andries and viticulturist/winemaker cousin Wagner, whose goals include encouraging people to enjoy wine in moderation every day.

Prestige ⊕ 🗅 **★★★** Ripe & bright **10**, uncomplicated ruby cab-based red. **Rosé** 🗅 **★★** Sweet berry flavours in **11**, from shiraz, duo of muscats & ruby cab. **Cape Riesling** 🗅 **★★★** Cape institution since 1948, from grape also known as crouchen. Characteristic Granny Smith apple bite on light, fruity **12** picnic basket staple. **Semillon-Chardonnay** ⊕ 🗅 **★★★** **11** near-equal unwooded combo lingers pleasantly, gives fruity satisfaction. **Bouquet Blanc** 🗅 **★★★** Natural Sweet from gewürztraminer, chenin & muscat de Frontignan. Now bottled, **11** light rosepetal & cantaloupe prettiness, overtly sweet conclusion. — CE/CvZ

■ **The Village Walk** *see Franschhoek Cellar*
■ **The Warhorse** *see Simonsig Landgoed*

The Wine Fusion

Location: Wellington ▪ WO: Western Cape ▪ Est 2007 ▪ Closed to public ▪ Cellarmaster(s) Graham Knox (Dec 2007) ▪ Winemaker(s) Various ▪ 1.5m litres bulk 60% red 40% white ▪ c/o Wine Masterpieces (Pty) Ltd PO Box 1209 Wellington 7654; TWF 90 London Rd London SE16LN UK T +44 2077171569 ▪ graham@thewinefusion. com ▪ **T +27 (0)21-447-4476/+27 (0)76-900-0717 (Wilhelm)/+27 (0)83-625-2865 (Graham)** ▪ F +27 (0)21-447-4476

In an innovative take on entrepreneurial wine-selling, Wellington-based Graham Knox gathers a team of winemakers (Nico Vermeulen and Linley Schultz for this edition) to produce singular and evocatively named wines, bottled in the UK. So far, they're not available to local consumers.

The Wine Fusion range NEW

★★★★ **Linley's Pure Chardonnay-Viognier** 🗅 Peach, tangerine, zesty citrus lead to soft creamy palate. **11**'s off-dry appeal balanced by crisp acid, giving a rounded richness. Only a splash viognier.

The Director's Cut Merlot 🗅 **★★★** Fruity & tangy **11**, with wood spice & zingy freshness. **Highwire Summit Pinot Noir** 🗅 **★★★** Austere **10** from Elgin, with lifted tealeaf aroma, dry & light with acidic bite. **Desert & Dunes Shiraz** 🗅 **★★★** Spice route allusions in wine's name echoed in white/black pepper aromas of **11**, tight-coiled Swartland & Durbanville fruit cushioned by gram sugar. **Red Ocean Chardonnay** 🗅 **★★★** Soft & easy style has lovely balance but **11** lacks verve. **The Puddingstone** 🗅 **★★★★** Rhône-inspired white. **11** from marsanne, grenache blanc & roussanne, with typical broad stonefruit softness. Ready to enjoy. — JP

The Winery of Good Hope

Location: Somerset West ▪ Map: Helderberg ▪ WO: Stellenbosch/Swartland/Western Cape/Elgin/Stellenbosch ▪ Est/1stB 1998 ▪ Tasting & sales Mon-Fri 9-5 by appt ▪ Closed all pub hols ▪ Owner(s) Alex Dale, Andrew Openshaw, Yalumba, Edouard Labeye, Cliff Roberson, Ben Radford, Heather Whitman ▪ Cellarmaster(s) Edouard Labeye (1998) ▪ Winemaker(s) Jacques de Klerk (Oct 2009), with Tubby May (2002) ▪ Viticulturist(s) Edouard Labeye & Jacques de Klerk ▪ ±100ha (cab, merlot, pinot, shiraz, chard, chenin, viog) ▪ 500t/40,000cs own label 50% red 50% white ▪ Brands for clients: Pick's Pick ▪ BEE, IPW, WIETA ▪ Postnet Suite 124 Private Bag X15 Somerset West 7129 ▪ thewineryofgoodhope@thewineryofgoodhope.co.za ▪ www.thewineryofgoodhope.com ▪ S 34° 0'57.5" E 018° 49'2.6" ▪ **T +27 (0)21-855-5528** ▪ F +27 (0)21-855-5529

This year marks the 15th vintage for this winery which has, possibly, the most owner nationalities of any in the Cape (Brits, Frogs, Ozzies, not to mention locals). Within the diverse wine range, there's a developing focus on chenin blanc and pinot noir — at last count there were four distinctive versions of each. Says co-owner and MD Alex Dale: 'Our sustained swing to natural wine production guides all our decisions for both these varieties and everything else we do. This is far more than a vogue, it is a return to basic values, away from the botox and plastic-surgery winemaking of the points- and medal-driven, winemaker-idolising, contrived wines and styles of the past decade.' That's telling us. And it seems to be working well in all ways.

Radford Dale range

★★★★☆ **Merlot** 🗅 🗅 Good, ripe aromas & flavours on **10** (**★★★★**), with herbal twist to sweet fruit; forceful, dense-textured & big, but perhaps less intensity than **09** so slightly drying oak tannins less harmonised.

★★★★☆ **Freedom Pinot Noir** 🗅 🗅 Dark, pure-fruited fragrance on **11** from Elgin, but not simply so: an intriguing edge of earthy funkiness too. Deeply flavoured, supple, with a good deal of structure — lovely fresh acidity; tannins more forceful than in some pinots. Deserves a few years in bottle, or decanting in youth.

★★★★☆ **Pinot Noir AD** NEW 🍴 🅿 Name invokes part-owner Alex Dale & puns on date. Selection released after 3 years, more ageing intended. **10** from Elgin just starting to flaunt cherry perfume, with savoury forest-floor undertones. A little more complex & deep than Freedom version, tannic but richly delicate.

★★★★ **Frankenstein Pinotage** NEW 🍴 🅿 **11** most un-monstrous, though remarkably perfumed — almost tarty in its charm. Ripe, sweet fruit well controlled by firm acidity, modest tannins & bone-dry finish.

★★★★☆ **Shiraz** 🍴 🅿 Appealing, complex mix of spice & tobacco with berries on **10** (★★★★), flavour-some like **09**. Powerful, but the sweet fruit restrained; unlingering finish with dry tannic touch.

★★★★ **Shiraz-Viognier** 🍴 Notably floral aromas announce the viognier in **09**, first since **06**. Charming, balanced & elegantly light-feeling rather than dense or intense (13% alc less than most in range).

★★★★ **Shiraz-Merlot** 🍴 🅿 **10** fairly stern, but less intimidating tannins than **09** (★★★★). Nicely combines spicy, firm shiraz with lusher fruitcake notes, soft texture of merlot. Big alcohol glows on finish.

★★★★ **Black Rock** 🍴 Was 'Red Blend' in now shelved Black Rock range. Pleasant shiraz-based Swartland blend; very firm tannic grip a little at odds with unsubstantial sweet ripeness of **09** — but might yet harmonise.

★★★★☆ **Gravity** 🍴 Expressive **09** from usual merlot, cab, shiraz with forward but not too overt ripe berry appeal, in restrained modern style. Succulently fresh but warmly rich & sweet-fruited, with firm but understated structure & masterly supportive oaking. All unforcedly harmonious & generous.

★★★★☆ **Chardonnay** 🍴 🅿 Fresh floral aromas & citrus on elegant & subtle **11**. Fine balance, brilliant acidity attuned to stony mineral notes. Despite a knife-edged & delicate intensity rather than the rich, oaky broadness more common in Cape, it's far from austere. Should develop well for a good few years.

★★★★☆ **Renaissance Chenin Blanc** 🍴 🅿 The elegant intensity on **11** derives from old, unirrigated bushvines & is untrammelled by the mostly older oak used for fermentation & maturation. Good fruit flavour with stony notes; penetrating intensity, any richness well balanced by fresh acidity. Harmonious & lingering.

★★★★ **Viognier** 🍴 🅿 **11** as usual in less showily perfumed, drier & less alcoholic style than most locals. Possibly the fruit even too muted, allowing the modest oaking to show too much. Lovely succulence.

★★★★☆ **Vine Dried Viognier** 🍴 🅿 Intense but not overdone aromas and flavours in **11** dessert wine supported by subtle oaking, fresh acidity & modest 12% alcohol. These all in excellent balance with rich texture & fine mineral tension.

Land of Hope range

★★★★☆ **Cabernet Sauvignon** 🍴 🅿 **11** (★★★★) preview still very young (dense, plush **09**, then **10** not tasted by us). Solid ripe fruit & long finish hint at future complexity, but now too dominated by oak & drying tannin. Might gain grace, harmony with time.

★★★★ **Reserve Pinot Noir** NEW ✓ 🍴 🅿 Enticing red-fruit & savoury scents on **11** from Elgin & Stellenbosch. Less intensity than Radford Dales, but lovely cherry fruit, savoury elegance & light but firm grip.

★★★★ **Chenin Blanc Reserve** 🍴 🅿 Drier & bit less charming than **10**, **11** (★★★★) shows good fruit richness & complexity, but oak dominates (though only 20% new), adds roughness. Year/2 should help.

Vinum range

★★★★ **Cabernet Sauvignon** ✓ 🍴 🅿 Delicious, bright, savoury flavours lurk behind the youthful tannic austerity of **11**, with greater harmony to come after a few years in bottle.

★★★★ **Chenin Blanc** ✓ 🍴 🅿 Most flamboyant of all the fine chenins from this cellar, with an obvious deliciousness & confidence. Satisfying freshness wrapping up **11**'s full flavour, with well integrated oak.

The Winery of Good Hope range

★★★★ **Granite Ridge Reserve** ✓ 🍴 **09** from shiraz the most serious in this range, but still combines fairly easy drinkability with character & interest. Less powerful than lithe; ripe but not pushy; clean & fresh.

Pinot Noir Reserve 🍴 🅿 ★★★★ Red fruit fragrance & flavours on **11**. Readier for drinking than other pinots from this cellar (less structure & intensity); promising rare pleasure & integrity for this variety at a decent price. **Bush Vine Pinotage** ✓ 🍴 🅿 ★★★★ Clean, dark-frutied aromas on easy-going **11**, though with strong tannic grip. Sweet, jammy notes, though bone-dry & quite restrained. **Mountainside Shiraz** 🍴 🅿 ★★★ Full-flavoured, solid, even sinewy **11**; strong structure not quite suited to sweetish finish. **The Beautiful Game Shiraz** 🍴 Occasional release. **Oceanside Cabernet Sauvignon-Merlot** ✓ 🍴 🅿 ★★★★ Clever balance in **11** between respectable restraint & burly friendliness. Ready for early but untrivial drinking. WO W Cape. **Unoaked Chardonnay** ⊕ 🍴 🅿 ★★★ Charming, easy-drinking but classy **11**. Lees-ageing adds richness & breadth. WO W Cape. **Bush Vine Chenin Blanc** ✓ 🍴 🅿 ★★★★ Herbs, melon & peach among the mouthfilling flavours of vivacious & delicious **12**; balanced & fresh for easy but deeply satisfying pleasure. — TJ

■ **The Wolftrap** *see Boekenhoutskloof Winery*
■ **Thierry & Guy** *see Fat Bastard*

Thokozani Wines

Location/WO: Wellington • Map: Paarl & Wellington • Est/1stB 2005 • Tasting & sales daily 10-5 • Closed Dec 25 • Cellar tours by appt • Seasons Restaurant • Tour groups • Conferences • Walks/hikes • Mountain biking trail • 4-star Thokozani Cottages • Owner(s) Diemersfontein employees, external investors & Diemersfontein Wines • Cellarmaster(s) Francois Roode (Sep 2003) • Winemaker(s) Francois Roode (Sep 2003), with Lauren Hulsman (2011) • Viticulturist(s) Waldo Kellerman (Aug 2007) • 180ha/60ha (cabs s/f, grenache, malbec, moury, p verdot, ptage, roobernet, shiraz, chenin, viog) • 60t/4,000cs own label 40% red 40% white 20% rosé • WIETA • PO Box 41 Wellington 7654 • info@thokozani.co.za • www.thokozani.co.za • S 33° 39'41.1" E 019° 0'31.1" • **T +27 (0)21-864-5050** • F +27 (0)21-864-2095

'The focus is development of our skills base,' says business development director Denise Stubbs. She's encouraged by increasing confidence and ability in both the cellar and markets, locally and abroad, of the Diemersfontein Wines employees who are at the heart of this black economic empowerment venture in Wellington. It's aptly named for the 'celebration' of its people.

★★★★ **CCV** ⊕ 🖳 Named according to blend proportions: delicious **10** mainly chenin, dollops chard, viognier, unwooded; citrus aromas, round & creamy body from lees-ageing, lingering floral aftertaste.

SMV ✓ ★★★★ Shiraz, mourvèdre & viognier. **11** bold black berry fruit & glossy choc-mocha layered on robust oak foundation. For early drinking, with food. **Rosé** ⊕ 🖳 Await new vintage. — DS

- **Thorntree Wines** *see* Doran Vineyards
- **Three Peaks** *see* Mount Vernon Estate
- **Three Pines** *see* Stark-Condé Wines
- **Three Rivers** *see* Bon Courage Estate

Thunderchild

Location/WO: Robertson • Est 2003 • 1stB 2008 • Wines available from Rooiberg Winery, Ashton Cellar, Robertson Winery, Ashton Wine Boutique, Affie Plaas Farmstall, Platform 62, Tanagra Winery, De Wetshof Winery & La Verne Wine Boutique — see individual cellars for opening times • Owner(s) Thunderchild Wingerd Trust • Cellarmaster(s) Various Robertson winegrowers • 5ha (cabs s/f, merlot) • PO Box 770 Robertson 6705 • info@thunderchild.co.za • www.thunderchild.co.za • **T +27 (0)23-626-3661** • F +27 (0)23-626-3664

In 2003, the Robertson community came together in support of Die Herberg Children's Home and planted 5ha of vines with entirely donated materials, labour and expertise. That vineyard now produces Thunderchild, made for free in sympathetic local cellars and sold in their tasting rooms. After audited costs, all revenue is ploughed back into the education of Die Herberg's young charges.

Thunderchild ⊕ ★★★★ Boldly flavoured Bordeaux blend, 37% each cab franc & merlot, rest cab. **08** mulberry compote, chocolate swirl, pepper twist & amenable tannins to enjoy with hearty fare. — DB/WB

Tierhoek

Location: Citrusdal • Map: Olifants River • WO: Piekenierskloof • Est 2001 • 1stB 2003 • Tasting, sales & cellar tours on the farm Mon-Fri 8.30-4.30 Sat by appt; alternatively tasting & sales in Sandveld Huisie cnr Church & Muller Str Citrusdal Mon-Fri 8.30-4.30 Sat 8.30-1.30, light meals & beverages • Fee R20, waived on purchase • Closed all pub hols • BYO picnic • Walks/hikes • Conservation area • Guest house (sleeps 9) • Owner(s) Shelley Sandell • Cellarmaster(s) Roger Burton (Oct 2006) • Winemaker(s) Basie Snyers (assistant, Oct 2006) • Viticulturist(s) Ryno Kellerman (Aug 2006), advised by Johan Viljoen • 700ha/16ha (grenache, shiraz, chenin, sauv) • 60t/3,000cs own label 30% red 70% white • PO Box 53372 Kenilworth 7745 • admin@tierhoek.com • www.tierhoek.com • S 32°23'27.49" E 018°51'24.14" • **T +27 (0)21-674-3041** • F +27 (0)86-731-6351

Set amidst the wonderful landscapes of the Piekenierskloof, this must be one of the most remote wineries in the Cape. There are old vineyards here, but the more recently planted ones are starting to mature, says winemaker Roger Burton, who can see the results showing in the sauvignon and the wines with shiraz. The 2011 Guide reported tastings and sales at the Sandveld Huisie in Citrusdal — but it seems that getting the licence took three years; we repeat it now, with more confidence.

Tierhoek range

★★★★ **Grenache** 🍇 Blackberry liqueur, cassis & allspice notes on softly structured **10**, with 10% shiraz. Only older oak used, so fruit not hidden, only broadened. Slightly warm finish suits generous style.

★★★★ **Syrah-Grenache-Mourvèdre** 🍇 Name change from 'Grenache-Syrah' reflects shiraz dominance in **11**; inviting aromas of black pepper & plum purée with floral overtones. Luscious flavours, with delightfully silky tannin & low acidity. Drinking well now, but no hurry.

★★★★ **Chardonnay** NEW 🍇 Vigorous, fresh & clean **11** shows restrained aromas of lime blossom & crushed stones, unobscured by the older oak used. Fairly intense, though light-feeling (just 13% alcohol).

★★★★ **Chenin Blanc** 🍇 Delicious off-dry, lightly oaked **11** with complex notes of ripe melon, pear & beeswax. Nicely balanced palate with subtle fruity sweetness but a satisfying dry finish.

★★★★ **Sauvignon Blanc** **12** has intense gooseberry, grassy aromas. Very crisp, clean & flavourful, with flinty mineral finish. Tank sample, rating provisional; could grow to level of complex **11** (★★★★★).

★★★★ **Straw Wine** Intense, viscous **07** (★★★★★) from air-dried chenin displaying complex aromas/flavours dried apricot, honey, nuts. Wild ferment; matured in older oak 5 years! Acid balances unctuous sweetness, as in **06**. Richly textured, with a long fantail finish.

Discontinued: **Shiraz**.

Piekeniers range

Sauvignon Blanc Await next. **White** 🍽 🍇 ★★★★ **11** is pure sauvignon, with granadilla & melon notes. Good but not too complex drinking, with bone-dry finish. Discontinued: **Red**. — JPf

■ **Timbili** *see* Ernst Gouws & Co Wines
■ **Timothy White** *see* La Petite Vigne
■ **Tin Mine** *see* Zevenwacht
■ **Title Deed** *see* Croydon Vineyard Residential Estate

TMV Wines

WO: Swartland/Western Cape/Coastal ▪ Est 1999 ▪ 1stB 2004 ▪ Closed to public ▪ Owner(s) Jason Scott & George Austin ▪ ±500cs own label 50% red 45% white 5% sweet wine + 800cs for Woolworths ▪ PO Box 190 Tulbagh 6820 ▪ tmvwines@gmail.com ▪ **T +27 (0)82-897-2272** ▪ F +27 (0)82-897-2272

When Tulbagh Mountain Vineyards estate (now Fable) was sold, a non-compete clause was included. 'Once this period has expired we intend to blend and make available new cuvées,' says part-owner Jason Scott. Meanwhile, 'the remaining stock of the TMV brand of bought-in wines continues to be sold.'

★★★★☆ **Swartland Syrah** 🍷 🍽 Delicious **07**, with fleshy succulence; subtle tannin & oaking.

★★★★ **Mourvèdre-Cinsault** 🍷 **06** one-off; iron & spice tones, warmingly long. W Cape.

★★★★☆ **White** 🍷 Earth & minerals with riper spicy flavours on oaked **09** chenin-led quintet. Natural ferment lessens varietal dominance, adds intricacy. Soft but well structured, persistent. WO Coastal.

★★★★☆ **Vin Pi Three** 🍷 Gorgeous **NV** sticky from air-dried Swartland chenin, solera-aged. 3rd edition, with lifted honey, lingering toffee, apricot. Fine acidity prevents cloy (despite 300g/l sugar!). — AL

Tokara

Location/map: Stellenbosch ▪ WO: Stellenbosch/Walker Bay/Western Cape/Elgin ▪ 1stB 2001 ▪ Tasting & sales Mon-Fri 9-5 Sat/Sun 10-3 ▪ Closed Easter Fri/Mon & Dec 25 ▪ Tokara Restaurant Tue-Sun lunch 12.30-2.30 & dinner 7-9.30 ▪ Delicatessen Tue-Sun 10-4 ▪ Facilities for children ▪ Gift shop ▪ Art exhibitions ▪ Owner(s) GT & Anne-Marie Ferreira ▪ Winemaker(s) Miles Mossop (Jan 2000), with Dumisani Mathonsi (Jan 2004) ▪ Viticulturist(s) Aidan Morton (Nov 2000) ▪ 104ha (cabs s/f, grenache, malbec, merlot, mourv, p verdot, ptage, shiraz, chard, chenin, sauv, sem) ▪ 705t/50,000cs own label 40% red 59% white 1% rosé ▪ PO Box 662 Stellenbosch 7599 ▪ wine@tokara.com ▪ www.tokara.com ▪ S 33° 55' 2.9" E 018° 55' 13.7" ▪ **T +27 (0)21-808-5900** ▪ F +27 (0)21-808-5911

Great wine is made in the vineyard rather than the cellar — a principle more often quoted than put into practice. At Tokara it's more than a matter of words. Viticulturist Aidan Morton is working with the boffins at Stellenbosch University to implement new techniques in vineyard management in order to achieve the flavour profile wanted from Tokara's cool-climate sauvignon blanc vineyards in Elgin and Walker Bay. And at the home farm in Stellenbosch they're working on some red-wine vineyards, wanting 'to achieve wines of balance and ripeness with lower alcohols'. Great grapes are not quite enough, of course — it helps to have the Miles Mossop touch in the cellar. Altogether, Tokara's combination of classicism and modernity seems, quite simply, to give finer results each year.

Reserve Collection

★★★★☆ **Pinotage 10** (★★★★) perfumed & rather showy & oaky by Tokara standards; opulent like **08**. But better disciplined tannins than many versions & a dry, almost elegant finish. **09** untasted.

★★★★☆ **Director's Reserve Red** Cab with dollops petit verdot, merlot & malbec in **09** superbly balancing seductive ripe fruit with oak, depth with charm, firm structure with easy appeal, the obvious & the subtle, the classic & modern virtues. Irresistible now, it can only gain with good few years in bottle.

★★★★ **Stellenbosch Chardonnay** 🖾 Impeccably bred, slightly aloof, restrained & elegant **11**. All components in balance, including modest oak & juicy acidity. Drinks well now, should improve a few years.

★★★★ **Walker Bay Chardonnay** As usual **11** more expressive than Stellenbosch version, with similarly quiet complexity, but its balanced & harmonious charm retains a particularly elegant delicacy.

★★★★☆ **Walker Bay Sauvignon Blanc** 🍋 **12** (★★★★★) the mostly calmly composed of the 3 Tokara versions — as forceful, but subtler & less exuberant, with a wider spread of flavour notes, including dried peach & pear on the lingering finish, plus a stony minerality. **11** untasted by us; **10** (★★★★) was lighter, leaner.

★★★★☆ **Elgin Sauvignon Blanc** 🍋 **12** both grassier & more tropical than Walker Bay version — like it, should benefit from a few years in bottle, though delightful now. Penetrating freshness gives extra bite & mouthwatering juiciness. Good long citrus-tinged finish. **11** sold out before we could try it.

★★★★★ **Director's Reserve White** 🍋 🖾 Usual 70/30 sauvignon/semillon blend in **11**; with lemon-cream aromas from latter, blackcurrant & tropical notes from former. Oak integrated & supportive. Precise & elegant, yet with full flavour & a kind of luxurious languidness. Keep 5+ years for more depth & harmony. ℗

★★★★☆ **Noble Late Harvest** 🖾 Very rich, very sweet, gorgeously delicious but not overpowering **11** from oaked sauvignon. As usual, clean & fresh, with a fine vein of acidity enlivening the whole. WO W Cape.

Discontinued: **Cabernet Sauvignon**.

Tokara range

★★★★ **Shiraz** 🍋 🖾 **10** (★★★★) perhaps less complex than **09** but balancing bright red fruit with savoury element; affable, elegant & lightly gripping.

★★★★ **Sauvignon Blanc** 🍋 🖾 Hugely flavourful ripe tropical aromas & flavours, edged with grassiness, on penetratingly powerful **12**, leading to long lemon-drop conclusion. **11** sold out untasted by us. WO W Cape.

Cabernet Sauvignon 🍋 🖾 ★★★★ **10** a lighter, paler reflection of the Reserve Red, modestly but seriously oaked for early, easy & very satisfactory drinking. **Grenache Rosé** 🍋 🖾 ★★★ Palely gleaming **12** from Walker Bay with pleasantly forward pastille fruit. Bright, fresh & bone-dry. **Chardonnay** ✓ 🍋 🖾 ★★★★ Easygoing but firm **11**, restrained, elegant & balanced; invisibly supportive oak. Some chenin & verdelho. WO W Cape. **Noble Late Harvest** Occasional release. — TJ

■ **Tokolosh** *see* Klein Parys Vineyards
■ **Tooverberg** *see* Klein Parys Vineyards

Topaz Wine

Location/map: Stellenbosch ▪ WO: Elgin/Stellenbosch ▪ Est 2000 ▪ 1stB 2001 ▪ Tasting & sales by prior arrangement ▪ Owner(s) Topaz Wine Company (Pty) Ltd, shareholders Clive Torr, Tanja Beutler, Anthony Hill & Christopher Cosgrove ▪ Cellarmaster(s) Clive Torr (May 2000) ▪ Winemaker(s) Clive Torr, with Tanja Beutler (both May 2000) ▪ 600cs own label 80% red 20% white ▪ IPW ▪ PO Box 804 Somerset Mall 7137 ▪ tanja@topazwines.co.za ▪ www.topazwines.co.za ▪ S 33°50'55.67" E 018°51'26.19" ▪ **T +27 (0)21-855-4275** ▪ F +27 (0)86-612-6118

Clive Torr and Tanja Beutler were pioneering local garagistes, adding bought-in grapes to the crop from their 'garden'. Now aspiring small-scale winemakers can learn from their experience every February at Delvera in Stellenbosch. Equally enthusiastic about wine appreciation, they are also promising to launch an online introductory wine course.

★★★★ **Pinot Noir** ℗ **08** tasted a few years back was elegant yet lively, with concentrated varietal farmyard character. Firm structure & minerality suggested a promising future. Elgin vines.

★★★★ **Custom Crush** ℗ Fresh, complex, herbal **08** blend cab & cab franc, with well integrated oaking. Joyful & inviting, a wine to tuck into at the price, delivering the smile promised on the label.

Syrah Await next, as for **Viognier**. — IM

Topiary Wines

Location/map/WO: Franschhoek ▪ Est 2005 ▪ 1stB 2006 ▪ Tasting, sales & tours Mon-Sat by appt ▪ Closed Easter Sun, Dec 25/26 & Jan 1 ▪ Meals/refreshments on special request; or BYO picnic ▪ Small tour groups ▪ 1. 7km Fynbos hiking trail ▪ Conservation area ▪ Owner(s) Roy & Hilary Andrews ▪ Cellarmaster(s)/winemaker(s) Mark Carmichael-Green (Nov 2010, consultant) ▪ Viticulturist(s) Malcolm Pemberton (Jan 2005), with Paul Wallace (consultant) ▪ 63ha/20ha (cab, shiraz, chard, chenin) ▪ 60t/3,500cs own label 72% red 15% rosé 13% MCC + 25,000L bulk ▪ IPW ▪ PO Box 108 La Motte 7691 ▪ topiarysales@telkomsa.net ▪ www. topiarywines.com ▪ S 33° 51'52.2" E 019° 2'39.0" ▪ **T** +27 (0)21-867-0258 ▪ **F** +27 (0)86-750-1742

There are at least three reasons to visit this Franschhoek property: the beautiful setting in the foothills of the Wemmershoek Mountains, surrounded by fauna and flora and with a wetland nearby; the 30 different topiary designs in the garden, a unique setting for functions such as weddings; and of course the wines. They are all from own grapes, and the accolades, especially for the chardonnay-based MCC sparkling, twice awarded 5 stars by this guide, speak volumes about the quality of fruit and winemaking care.

★★★★ **Cabernet Sauvignon** ⓘ Seductive perfume array — black plum, scrub, sweet spice — but the palate is the main attraction: fruit rich, lush, smooth textured. **08** ready now, can keep a few years.

★★★★ **Shiraz** ⓘ Tar & wild berries in **08**, follows in **07**'s footsteps with its succulence & silky smooth body. Drinking so well, hard to resist or cellar.

Cabernet Sauvignon-Shiraz ⓘ ★★★★ Despite 54% cab, **07** has the dark fruit, gamey profile of shiraz. Underpinned by firm tannins, will keep 3-5 years. **Rosé** ✓ 🍷 📒 ★★★★ Fresh berry & rosewater perfume, flavour brightens up **11**'s just-dry cerise-hued shiraz/cab mix. Good focus, intensity. **Blanc de Blancs Brut** Not tasted. — CR

▪ **Tormentoso** see MAN Vintners
▪ **Torres Claude** see Crows Nest
▪ **Totus** see Trajan Wines
▪ **Touch of Oak** see Rijk's
▪ **Towerkop** see Ladismith Cellar — SCV
▪ **Township Winery** see The Township Winery

Trajan Wines

Location: Stellenbosch ▪ WO: Coastal/Western Cape ▪ Est 2005 ▪ 1stB 2008 ▪ Closed to public ▪ Owner(s) Shareholders ▪ Winemaker(s) Mark van Schalkwyk (Sep 2005) ▪ Viticulturist(s) Outback Viticulture ▪ 6,000cs own label 70% red 30% white ▪ Fairtrade ▪ PO Box 1498 Stellenbosch 7599 ▪ info@trajanwines.co.za ▪ www. trajanwines.co.za ▪ **T** +27 (0)83-505-2681 ▪ **F** +27 (0)86-299-4281

Established in 2005 by 'wine enthusiasts' with dreams of an own brand and community service, Trajan started out in bulk wine exporting but since 2008 focused increasingly on premium range Totus ('Complete'). Fairtrade accredited for 6 years, the brand funds a crèche/daycare school and donates R3 for every bottle of Totus sold to Missing Children South Africa.

Totus range

Cabernet Sauvignon 🍷 ★★★★ Ripe, fruity **09**'s sweet berries are still dominated by oak spices. Good structure & balance should prevail, given time. **Pinotage** 🍷 ★★★ High-toned & piercing, with opulent fruit & easygoing body, **09** displays balanced ripeness. Riebeek & Stellenbosch grapes. **Shiraz** NEW 🍷 ★★★★ Riebeek & Paarl grapes for debut **09**, made in super-ripe, big-bodied style, expressing red fruit jam & confectionery. **Shiraz-Mourvèdre** ⓘ 🍷 ★★★★ Appealing **08** partnership mid-2010 was full of spicy warmth, gamey red fruit extras. Well structured without heaviness. **Chenin Blanc** ⓘ 🍷 📒 ★★★★ Appealing **10** shows sunny ripeness, deftly handled oak lends body & form without dominating. **Sauvignon Blanc** ⓘ 🍷 📒 ★★★★ Classy, nicely balanced **11**, typical Durbanville fruit character, ripe & supple, with leesy weight & crisp acidity. — GdB

▪ **Transkaroo-Bring My Huis Toe/Take Me Home** see Boer & Brit
▪ **Travino** see Klawer Wine Cellars

Tread Lightly by Backsberg

Location: Paarl ▪ WO: Western Cape ▪ Est/1stB 2010 ▪ Tasting, sales & cellar tours at Backsberg Estate (see entry) ▪ Owner(s) Michael Back ▪ Winemaker(s) Alicia Rechner (Jun 2012) ▪ Viticulturist(s) Clive Trent (Jul 1992) ▪ PO Box 537 Suider-Paarl 7624 ▪ info@treadlightly.co.za ▪ www.treadlightly.co.za ▪ S33° 49′ 42.9″ E018° 54′ 56.9″ ▪ T +27 (0)21-875-5141 ▪ F +27 (0)21-875-5144

A field of 500 trod lightly on mountain bike tracks around family-owned and -run Backsberg in the inaugural women's only Tread Lightly MTB race last year. Carbon footprint reduction is what the Paarl estate aimed for in pioneering certified wine in shatterproof and lightweight PET (plastic) bottles, but the convenience factor has also caught on locally and abroad, and export orders are rising.

PET range
Merlot 🏠 🚫 ★★★★ Chocolate & fynbos edge to mulberry fruit of **10**, flexing a good body, ripeness & length. **Chenin Blanc** 🏠 🚫 ★★★ Crisp & zesty **12** tank sample as light as its PET container. **Sauvignon Blanc** 🏠 🚫 ★★★ **12** preview is tangy & lemon fresh but misses some of the body of previous. — FM

▪ **Tribal** see African Terroir

Trizanne Signature Wines

Location: Somerset West ▪ WO: Elim/Swartland ▪ Est 2008 ▪ 1stB 2009 ▪ Closed to public ▪ Wine sales via website ▪ Owner(s)/winemaker(s) Trizanne Barnard ▪ 12t/650cs own label 40% red 60% white ▪ Postnet Suite 407 Private Bag X15 Somerset West 7129 ▪ info@trizanne.co.za ▪ www.trizanne.co.za ▪ T +27 (0)21-789-2185/+27 (0)82-383-6664 ▪ F +27 (0)86-669-0913

While boutique winemaker Trizanne Barnard's loyal local customers have been eagerly awaiting the next result of her terroir-quest endeavours, she's been busy making wine for customers in the US, UK and Belgium, the latter a cool-climate semillon. What's planned is the local release shortly of an Elim shiraz and two further sauvignons. Collective sigh of relief: all is well on this winemaking front.

★★★★ **Syrah** ⊕ 09 is 86% shiraz, plus splashes mourvèdre, grenache & carignan, which Trizanne B's careful touch converts to a sleek, scrub-toned thing of beauty, full of interest. WO Swartland.

★★★★ **Sauvignon Blanc** NEW 🏠 🚫 Capturing the Elim terroir, **11** seamlessly combines salty minerality with green notes, creating yet another memorable wine in this range, deliciously individual.

★★★★ **Sauvignon Blanc-Semillon** ⊕ 🏠 🚫 Passionfruit attests to ripeness of Elim grapes but no mistaking **10**'s taut intensity, limy minerality. Slight oak infusion from barrelled semillon. Few years ahead. — CR

Truter Family Wines

Location: Wellington ▪ WO: Western Cape ▪ Est 2008 ▪ 1stB 2010 ▪ Closed to public ▪ Owner(s) Hugo & Celeste Truter ▪ Winemaker(s) Hugo Truter ▪ 500cs own label 50% red 50% white ▪ hugo@truterfamilywines.co.za ▪ www.truterfamilywines.co.za ▪ T +27 (0)83-639-6288

Hugo and Celeste Truter, both trained winemakers, believe in pursuing dreams. Theirs are manifested in these handcrafted wines — and the wine industry is ultimately quilted together with such dreams. Here the focus remains on blends rather than the 'boring' single-cultivar wines populating the wine shelves.

Agaat range
★★★★ **Christina** ✓ 🏠 🚫 'Agaat' moves to range name. Sauvignon plus nouvelle, chenin & viognier in finely crafted **12**; crisp & clean, with good palate-weight. Tasted ex-tank, should have settled by early 2013.
John David NEW ✓ 🏠 ★★★★ Cape Blend cab, pinotage & shiraz, **10** bursts with dark berry fruit. Juicy cherry cola palate has long-lingering dry end. — JP

TTT Cellar Calitzdorp

Location/WO: Calitzdorp ▪ Map: Klein Karoo & Garden Route ▪ 1stB 2003 ▪ Tasting, sales & tours Mon-Fri 8-4 Sat 8-2 Sun by appt ▪ Closed Easter Fri-Mon, Apr 27, May 1, Dec 25 & Jan 1 ▪ Honey & olive oil ▪ BYO picnic ▪ Owner(s) Ashley & Pat Mason ▪ Cellarmaster(s)/viticulturist(s) Ashley Mason ▪ Winemaker(s) Ashley Mason, with Johan Julies ▪ 0.5ha (souzão, tinta, touriga, hanepoot) ▪ 4t/300cs own label 100% red ▪ PO Box 7067 Newton Park 6055 ▪ tttcellars@iafrica.com ▪ S 33° 31′ 50.94″ E 021° 41′ 44.88″ ▪ T +27 (0)44-213-3114 ▪ F +27 (0)44-213-3114

Ashley Mason is wistful about retiring to Calitzdorp — 'Maybe next year'. In the interim, he occasionally takes time off from his peripatetic life as an electrical contractor and makes for the family cellar in the Klein Karoo. This year he's bottling a new red blend, made from port grapes.

Hanepoot ☺ ★★★ Odd but pleasant combo ginger beer & warm honey on **11** sweetie, low fortification (15.5%) makes for silky sipping.

Cabernet Sauvignon Misreported as discontinued last time. **11** a tad wild & funky, will have its fans. **LTD** ⓛ ★★ From petit verdot, **10** needs drinking soon. **Shiraz** Await new vintage. **Dry Red** NEW ★★ Shiraz & splash cab, cloves & some berries on high-toned, brief **NV**. **Hilltop Blend** ★★ Touriga leads two other port grapes in very dry & savoury **10**. **Rosé** Await next. **Chenin Blanc** ⓛ ★★★ **11** fairly neutral, doesn't linger. **Muscat d'Brigne** ⓛ **11** unfortified mix mainly chenin & white muscadel, too unformed to rate. **Red Muscadel** ⓛ ★★ Red-berry-infused **10** fortified dessert in lighter style, with low (15%) alcohol. **Cape Ruby** ★★ Port-style **NV** from 50/50 touriga & tinta. Brimstone whiffs & fiery grip. **Cape Vintage** ✓ ★★★★ Honest campfire compadre, **10** half touriga with tinta & souzão. Spicy mouthful of dried dates & brandy-doused Christmas cake. **Cape White** ⓛ Port-style **NV** fortified from chenin past best. — GdB/CvZ

Tukulu

Location: Darling ▪ WO: Groenekloof ▪ Est 1998 ▪ 1stB 1999 ▪ Tasting by appt at Trinity Lodge in Darling ▪ Owner(s) Distell, Leopont 98 Properties, Maluti Groenekloof Community Trust, a group of Gauteng based black businessmen ▪ Winemaker(s) Samuel Viljoen (Sep 2007) ▪ Viticulturist(s) Hannes van Rensburg (1998) ▪ 975ha/373.36ha under vine ▪ 73% red 27% white ▪ BWI, Fairtrade, SGS Lacon, WIETA ▪ PO Box 184 Stellenbosch 7599 ▪ tukulu@ capelegends.co.za ▪ www.tukulu.co.za ▪ **T +27 (0)21-809-8330** ▪ F +27 (0)21-882-9575

Established as an empowerment project in 1998, Tukulu, based near Darling, is a joint venture between Distell, a consortium of black taverners from Gauteng, and a local community trust. The most notable focus from the outset has been on the transfer of skills, from farming to marketing, to ensure the project's sustainability. As a Fairtrade-accredited winery, the farm's workers are paid a premium, deciding among themselves how to allocate funds for community initiatives; converting an old school building for a rest area is a current undertaking.

Fairtrade Cabernet Sauvignon ▦ 🌿 ★★★ **11** something of a raw youth, with simple sweetish fruit grasped by forceful tannins. May harmonise with year or so. **Papkuilsfontein Pinotage** ⓛ ★★★★ Pure ripe raspberry notes on modern **09**. Juicy, smooth & fresh with nip of framing tannin. **Fairtrade Unwooded Syrah** ⓛ ▦ 🌿 ★★★ Smoky, dark-berry aromatic intensity; contrasting juicy easygoing flavours, supple tannins on **10**. **Organic Chardonnay** ▦ 🌿 🌿 ★★★★ Different, & less fruity than suggested in last year's preview, **11** shows slight oxidative intrigue with earthy citrus notes. Medium bodied, fresh & just lightly oak-spiced. **Fairtrade Chenin Blanc** ✓ ▦ 🌿 ★★★★ Uncluttered purity of freshly ripe grapes in eminently quaffable, bone-dry & satisfying **12**. Memorably long. **Fairtrade Sauvignon Blanc** ▦ 🌿 ★★★ **12** refreshingly crisp & dry with quiet 'sauvage' fruit. — AL

Tulbagh Winery

Location: Tulbagh/Porterville ▪ Map: Tulbagh ▪ WO: Tulbagh/Western Cape/Coastal ▪ Est 1906/2006 ▪ 1stB 1910 ▪ Tulbagh Cellar: Tasting & sales Mon-Fri 8–5 Sat & pub hols 9–1 Sun at Paddagang Wine Shop 11–3 ▪ Porterville Cellar: Tasting & sales Mon-Fri 8–5 ▪ Closed Easter Fri-Sun & Dec 25/26 ▪ Cellar tours by appt ▪ Gifts ▪ Farm produce ▪ BYO picnic ▪ Conferences ▪ Walks/hikes ▪ Mountain biking in the area ▪ Owner(s) 86 members ▪ Cellarmaster(s) /Production manager Naude Bruwer (Jan 2010) ▪ Winemaker(s) Porterville: Paul Jordaan (Apr 2010); Tulbagh: Helena Neethling (Jun 2010) ▪ Viticulturist(s) /Winemaker Hugo Lambrechts (Oct 2007) ▪ 1,230ha (cab, merlot, ptage, shiraz, chenin, chard, sauv) ▪ 11,823t/50,000cs own label 60% red 35% white 5% rosé & 8m L bulk + 20,000cs for clients ▪ Brands for clients: Grimont (Germany), Millberg (UK/France) ▪ PW ▪ PO Box 85 Tulbagh 6820; PO Box 52 Porterville 6810 ▪ info@tulbaghwine.co.za ▪ www.tulbaghwine.co. za ▪ S 33° 15' 8.8" E 019° 8' 36.5" ▪ **T +27 (0)23-230-1001 (Tulbagh); +27 (0)22-931-2170 (Porterville)** ▪ F +27 (0)23-230-1358; +27 (0)22-931-2171

Marketer Quintus Basson and the team at this grower-owned winery, with cellars and tasting venues in Tulbagh and Porterville, found themselves in an enviable position last year. They bucked the slowdown in exports to the UK, showing instead positive growth of 36%. Their Tulbagh range has been flying off the shelves — the Shiraz-Pinotage in particular — so fast that their biggest 'problem' was moving on to the next vintage sooner than anticipated.

Klein Tulbagh Reserve range

Cabernet Sauvignon ⚗ ★★★ Mid-2011, **10** preview promised oak-driven choc-mocha notes with ripe cherry support, was richer than previous **05**. **Merlot** ★★★ Step up **11** has good fruit intensity, harmonious tannins, minty undertone. **Pinotage** ★★★ Fynbos-nuanced **11** unknit mid-2011, sweet fruit in grip of firm oak tannin; would benefit from year/2 in bottle. WO W Cape. **Shiraz** ⚗ 🖷 ★★★ Jump from **04** to **10** pre-view, with bold fruit, 15.4% alc, obvious oak in modern idiom. Discontinued: **Vintage Port**.

Porter Mill Station range

> **Sauvignon Blanc** ☺ 🍴 🖷 ★★★ Improved **11** for those who don't like their sauvignon too fruity; mineral, dry & pithy.

Reserve Cabernet Sauvignon 🍴 🖷 ★★★ Back-on-track **11** (with 'Reserve' now in name) mixes dark berries & vanilla oak, medium body & slight tannic touch from wood staves. WO W Cape, as for all in this range. **Pinotage** 🍴 🖷 ★★★ Mulberry & coffee enticement on decently dry **11**. **Shiraz** Not tasted. **Chenin Blanc** 🍴 🖷 ★★ Engaging spring meadow aromas on lightish **11**, flavours fading, drink up.

Tulbagh range

> **Pinotage** ☺ 🍴 🖷 ★★★ **12** raises the bar with ample raspberry taste, friendly tannin; chill for summer fun. **Chardonnay** ☺ 🍴 🖷 ★★★ Invigorating citrus freshness & flavour on easy-drinking, creamy **12**. **Chenin Blanc** ☺ 🍴 🖷 ★★★ Light floral & tropical **12** lifted by touch of sweetness. **Colombard-Chenin Blanc** ☺ 🍴 🖷 ★★★ Up a notch, off-dry **12** has green apple & blossom appeal, upbeat finish for food partnering.

Cabernet Sauvignon ⚗ 🍴 🖷 ★★ Slight herbal astringency on **10**. **Merlot** 🍴 🖷 ★★ Mid-2012, tentatively rated **12** needs time for plummy fruit to emerge from tannin cocoon. **Shiraz** 🍴 🖷 ★★★ Now bottled, **10** smoky, savoury & balanced despite firm oak & tannin. **Shiraz-Pinotage** ⚗ 🍴 🖷 ★★ Coffee aromas, juicy fruit-sweetness on off-dry **11**. WO Coastal. **Rosé** 🍴 🖷 ★★ Modest strawberry tones on tad cloying **NV** (previously vintage-dated). **Sauvignon Blanc** 🍴 🖷 ★★ **12** easygoing appley sipper. **Sparkling Pinotage Doux** 🖷 ★★★ Cheerful **11** ruby red sparkler, bright & not over-sweet. WO Coastal. **Sauvignon Blanc Brut** NEW 🖷 ★★ **11** frothy & uncomplicated dry sparkling. Serve well-chilled. **Sauvignon** 🍴 ★★ Cabernet sauvignon & sauvignon blanc give their name to this fruity, sweetish quaffing red, previously vintage dated, now **NV**. **Port** ⚗ ★★ **07** oxidative, with toffee sweetness.

Paddagang range

Brulpadda Port ⚗ ★★★ Named changed from just 'Brulpadda' but same bottling of **NV** sweet fortified from pinotage & ruby cab still selling. Discontinued: **Paddapoot Hanepoot**. — WB/AL

■ **Tullie Family Vineyards** *see Lanner Hill*

Twee Jonge Gezellen Estate-The House of Krone

Location/map: Tulbagh ▪ WO: Western Cape ▪ Est 1710 ▪ 1stB 1937 ▪ Tasting & sales Mon-Fri 9-4 Sat & selected pub hols 10-2 ▪ Cellar tours Mon-Fri 11 & 3; Sat & selected pub hols 11 ▪ Annual festivals: Christmas in Winter (Jun) & Summer Elegance (Dec) ▪ Owner(s) TJG Estate (Pty) Ltd ▪ Cellarmaster(s) Nicky Krone ▪ Winemaker(s) Matthew Krone ▪ Viticulturist(s) Rosa Kruger ▪ PO Box 16 Tulbagh 6820 ▪ tjg@mweb.co.za, info@tjg.co.za ▪ www. houseofkrone.co.za ▪ S 33° 14' 18.1" E 019° 6' 51.8" ▪ **T +27 (0)23-230-0680** ▪ F +27 (0)23-230-0686

One of SA's historic estates, established in 1710, 'TJ' has the latest generation of twee jonge gezellen (two young companions), brothers Matthew and Luke, respectively making and promoting its wines. Grandfather NC was a pioneer of cold fermentation in the southern hemisphere; father Nicky was the first to introduce night harvesting and help establish bottle-fermented sparkling wine in the Cape (in which the estate now specialises). And, like many Champagne houses, Krone has its grande dame: the boys' mother, Mary, instrumental in the brand's trailblazing work on achieving healthier wines without added preservatives.

Krone range

★★★★ **Rosé Cuvée Brut** ✓ Pearly pink **08** (★★★★) sparkling, delicate raspberry aromas, creamy mousse; harmonious 60/40 pinot/chardonnay marriage. Pretty aperitif glassful though less complex than **05**.

★★★★ **Borealis Cuvée Brut** ✓ Always an elegant sipper from pinot noir & chardonnay; 55/45 in engaging & uplifting **09**. Bruised apple, clean yeasty notes & truly 'brut' dry conclusion.

★★★★☆ **Nicolas Charles Krone Marque 1** ✓ Exceptional **NV** multi-vintage (**01**, **02**, **03**) sparkling from 50/50 pinot noir/chardonnay, most recent degorgement 7 years on lees. Restrained, with pinot richness, chardonnay freshness on palate, indefinite bone-dry farewell. Worth seeking out. — WB/AL

24 Rivers *see* Valley Vineyards Wine Company

Twin's Peak *see* Lateganskop Winery

Two Centuries *see* Nederburg Wines

Two Cubs *see* Knorhoek Wines

Two Oceans

Location: Stellenbosch ▪ WO: Western Cape ▪ Tasting & sales at Bergkelder ▪ Owner(s) Distell ▪ Cellarmaster(s) Deon Boshoff & Andrea Freeborough ▪ Winemaker(s) Justin Corrans, Pieter Badenhorst, Bonny van Niekerk, Elize Coetzee ▪ Viticulturist(s) Bennie Liebenberg, Annelie Viljoen ▪ Distell PO Box 184 Stellenbosch 7599 ▪ info@distell.co.za ▪ www.twooceanswines.co.za ▪ **T +27 (0)21-809-7000**

'Light' is the keyword for this successful Distell brand, selling in over 80 countries. For starters, each wine is packaged in a recyclable 350g bottle, 110g lighter than its predecessor (saving 120kg in equivalent carbon emissions for every 1,000 bottles produced). And, as the guide went to press, the brand launched a 5.5% alcohol by volume range, Quay 5, targeting 'urbanites' desire for beverages to suit a more responsible lifestyle — without being a 'party-pooper'.

Shiraz-Cabernet Sauvignon ☺ 🍷 ★★★ **11** happy combo spice, savouriness & ripe red fruit, light & appetising everyday red. **Sauvignon Blanc** ☺ 🍴 🍷 ★★★ **12** well-expressed & balanced mix of tropical & greener varietal flavours, pleasant light-textured mouthfeel, definite notch up.

Pinot Noir ✓ ★★★★ Improving by the vintage! Variety-true **12** preview, more 'above ground' strawberry fruit flavours, less undergrowth/forest floor than **11** (★★★★). Generous, spicy, very long. Great value. **Pinotage** ★★★ **12** tank sample packed with fragrant berry flavours, good tannins hold them together. Also-tasted **11** (★★) more reserved, less succulent, firmer. **Shiraz** ★★★ Pre-bottling, **12** shows quite serious savoury dark fruit, well-handled spicy vanilla oak overlay. **11** (★★) less sombre, lighter quaffing style with pinch white pepper. **Cabernet Sauvignon-Merlot** ★★★★ **12** light footed & attractively lean, bit firmer than previous but still slips down easily. **Soft & Fruity Red** 🍴 ★★★ **12** ex tank is true to name, charming berry flavours. **11**, also reviewed, equally appealing, clove-dusted plum in balanced, accessible palate. **Shiraz Rosé** 🍴 ★★★ Pretty **12** boiled sweets & plums, dryish & creamy, hard to resist. **Chardonnay** ★★★ **12**, tasted pre-bottling, is (citrus) fruit focused, zesty, well supported by oak. **11** (★★) shade more wood driven, buttery vanilla centre stage, fruit in orchestra pit. **Pinot Grigio** 🍴 ★★ Fashionable white grape in **12** yields lightish, semi-dry, citrussy summer quaffer. **Semillon-Chardonnay** 🍴 ★★★ Previewed **12** shows some varietal character & complexity, vibrant herbaceous flavour, ideal pool/patio fare. **Chenin Blanc-Sauvignon Blanc** 🍴 ★★ Sauvignon's grassy character in the lead this time, **12** light & fresh, if tad undefined. **Fresh & Fruity White** 🍴 🍷 ★★ **12** fresh & fruity as advertised, lightish, 20% riesling & half-spoon sugar make it extra drinkable. — DB/HJ

Two Tunns *see* Valley Vineyards Wine Company

Tygerberg *see* Altydgedacht Estate

Ubuntu *see* Stellar Winery

Uiterwyk Estate *see* DeWaal Wines

Uitkyk Estate

Location/map: Stellenbosch ▪ WO: Stellenbosch/Simonsberg-Stellenbosch ▪ Est 1712 ▪ 1stB 1957 ▪ Tasting, sales & cellar tours Mon-Fri 9–5 Sat/Sun 10–4 ▪ Fee R15/5 wines ▪ Closed Good Fri & Dec 25 ▪ Facilities for children ▪ Tour groups ▪ BYO picnic; or order 24hrs in advance ▪ Conferences ▪ Conservation area ▪ 4x4 trail ▪ Manor House museum ▪ Owner(s) Lusan Premium Wines ▪ Cellarmaster(s) Estelle Lourens (Oct 2000) ▪ Winemaker(s) Estelle Lourens (Oct 2000), with Ian Wolmarans (Jul 2011) ▪ Viticulturist(s) Rudi Buys ▪ 591ha/

140ha (cab, shiraz, chard, pinot grigio, sauv) ▪ 772t/9,200cs 55% red 45% white (Uitkyk) & 35,500cs 53% re﹖ 45% white 2% rosé (Flat Roof Manor) ▪ BWI champion ▪ PO Box 104 Stellenbosch 7599 ▪ info@uitkyk.co.za▪ www.uitkyk.co.za ▪ S 33° 51′ 24.8″ E 018° 51′ 50.7″ ▪ **T +27 (0)21-884-4416** ▪ F +27 (0)21-884-4717

This historic property at the foot of Simonsberg has a colourful history. Now, 300 years after its establishment, the wines show some modern tweaking — suiting the slogan: 'where trends and history meet'. Similarly, the tasting room is reso﹒ lutely modern, in balanced contrast to the fine neoclassical homestead.

★★★★ **Carlonet** Oak aromas dominate on charming & modern-styled cab-based **09**. Dark berry fruit wit﹢ herbal tinge sees return of this historic label to riper, richer form after **08** (★★★★).

Shiraz Reserve Not tasted. **Shiraz** NEW ⌀ ★★★★ **10**, with 13% cab, in ripe dark-berried idiom. Obviou﹖ oaking adds to full-bodied palate, but lacks freshness & balance for higher rating, ends sweetish. **Caberne﹖ Sauvignon-Shiraz** ✦ ★★★★ Soft & satisfying **07** had expressive liquorice & coffee notes a few years back﹒ **Chardonnay** ⌀ ★★★★ **11** continues in established vein with attractive lemon pie whiffs. Medium bodied﹢ wooded, with pleasant weight & a dry end. **Sauvignon Blanc** ▤ ⌀ ★★★ **12** fresh & vibrant, with appeal﹒ ing fruit sweetness on juicy white peach palate. — JP

▪ **Uitvlucht** see Montagu Wine & Spirits Co
▪ **Ukuzala** see Mountain River Wines

Ultra Liquors

Location: Cape Town ▪ WO: Western Cape/Coastal/Robertson/Paarl/Darling ▪ Owner(s) Colin Robinson ▪ Winemaker(s) Various ▪ 426 Main Rd Wynberg Cape Town 7824 ▪ marknorrish@ultraliquors.co.za, dale@ tablebayinternational.co.za ▪ **T +27 (0)21-797-4341** ▪ F +27 (0)21-797-4351

Liquor retail chain turned specialist wine merchants, Ultra have taken note o﹖ the public's craving for a bargain and have morphed into full-blown, card-carry﹒ ing negociants, buying stock from reputable producers for their own labels. The common thread running through their in-house ranges is amazing quality a﹖ rock-bottom prices. 'Chief broker' Mark Norrish is currently trawling foreign producers for equivalent bargains, and they already sell a sub-R200 champagne.

Table Bay range

Chenin Blanc ☺ ▤ ⌀ ★★★ **12** has layers of dried apricots & honey melon, borne on light, breezy body. Charmingly honest.

Cabernet Sauvignon ✓ ★★★★ Brooding & dark, with seaweed/iodine notes, **09** offers real characte﹖ Shows elegance way above its station. WO Coastal, as for all in this range unless noted. **Merlot** ⌀ ★★★ Generous body & plummy ripe fruit with savoury edge on previewed **10**. Unsettled, but showing potentia﹖ WO Coastal. **Shiraz** ✦ ★★★ **08** upped the quality last year with spicy leather nuance, ripe berries, lingerin﹢ juicy finish. **Starboard Red** ✦ ★★ Lean, nutty **NV** 4-way blend with hint of jammy red berries. WO W Cape **Spinnaker White** ✦ ★★★ **NV** sauvignon-chenin blend with waxy-nutty oxidative notes. WO W Cape **Sauvignon Blanc** ★★★ Tank sample **12** is unsettled, but offers wholesome passionfruit on bracing acidity﹒ **Méthode Cap Classique** ✓ ★★★★ Traditional-method bubbly, mostly chardonnay from Robertson, **NV** repeats previous fresh crispness, apple fruitiness. Perfect breakfast tipple.

Monfort range

Cape Tawny ★★★ Typical fisherman's friend for icy pre-dawn quaffing. Fortified **NV** from Bonnievale ha﹖ muscat-like raisin fruitiness.

Secret Cellar range

Share The Secret Merlot NEW ☺ ★★★ Baked fruit with chocolate notes on **11**, backed up with ripe tannins. Juicy & quaffable. WO Robertson. **Shiraz** NEW ☺ ★★★ **07** from Paarl, augmented by splash of Rhône components, is meaty & bold, with sweet berries & seaweed. Enticingly dark. **Share The Secret Red Blend** NEW ☺ ★★★ Evolved, substantial **NV** Bordeaux-style blend with savoury tarry notes & appealing leafy, liquorice spicing. WO Coastal.

Cabernet Sauvignon Selection 633 Occasional release. **Cabernet Sauvignon Reserve** ✦ ★★★ Com﹒ petent, middleweight **07** shows evolution, elegant blackcurrant fruit beginning decline. For current enjoy﹒ ment. **Merlot Reserve** NEW ✓ ★★★★ Leafy & (attractively) lean, with hint of mint, **09** presents healthy ripe fruit on elegant structure. WO W Cape. **Shiraz Selection 480** ⊕ ★★★ 04 was more sedate than '275' stablemate, meaty edge to luscious berry fruit. **Shiraz Selection 275** ⊕ ★★★ When last tasted, 05 was big & warming with mulberry & black pepper heart. **Shiraz Reserve** ⊕ ★★★ 07 shows development, but also finesse. Stately oak a tad rich for juicy berry fruit. Drink-now bargain. **Cabernet Sauvignon-Merlot** NEW ★★ Rather tired 06 ex Paarl vines doesn't ring any bells. **Cabernet Franc-Petit Verdot Selection 299** Await new vintage. **Sauvignon Blanc** NEW ✓ ⍉ ★★★★ Pungent, wild 11 from Darling demands attention. Trophy Show Discovery Award winner has presence & character. **Méthode Cap Classique Blanc de Blanc** NEW ✓ ★★★★ Pocket-friendly champagne-method sparkling. 07, from chardonnay, is fuller, more expressive than Brut, with toasty yeast notes. WO W Cape, as for Brut. **Méthode Cap Classique Brut** NEW ★★★ 08 bottle-fermented sparkling from chardonnay/pinot belies age, shows fresh but brief fruit on foamy mousse. Discontinued: **Classic Red Selection 220**. — GdB

■ **Umfiki** *see* Goudini Wines

Umkhulu Wines

Location: Franschhoek ▪ Est/1stB 2000 ▪ Closed to public ▪ Owner(s) Fiona Phillips ▪ Winemaker(s) Wilhelm Kritzinger ▪ 10,000cs own label 100% red ▪ PO Box 132 Simondium 7670 ▪ fiona@cybercellar.com ▪ www.cybercellar.com ▪ **T +27 (0)21-876-2649** ▪ F +27 (0)21-876-2649

'Umkhulu', in both Xhosa and Zulu, means 'the big one' and therefore an apt moniker for the bold red wines under this label. Owned by Fiona Phillips of online retailer Cybercellar, it remains solely an export brand.

★★★★☆ **Pinotage** ⊕ Firmish tannins previously added texture to modern 04's slightly sweet fruit.

★★★★ **Tian** ⊕ Cab-led Bordeaux blend. Last 03 (★★★★) shy, light textured; 02 was dense & extracted.

Malbec ⊕ ★★★★ 05's exuberant mulberry fruit curtailed by tannins which should since have softened. **Shiraz** ⊕ ★★★★ Last 04 was straightforward & rich. **Ubuntu** ⊕ ★★★★ Cape Blend pinotage, merlot, petit verdot in pliable 05 last time. **Akira** ⊕ ★★★★ 03 mixed cab, petit verdot & pinotage for generous sipping a while back. **Njalo** ⊕ ★★★ Few years ago 05's tannins needed time or food. Combo merlot, shiraz, pinotage. — CvZ

United Nations of Wine

Location: Sandton ▪ WO: Western Cape ▪ Est/1stB 2005 ▪ Closed to public ▪ Owner(s) Dogwood Trust ▪ Cellarmaster(s)/winemaker(s) David John Bate (Jun 2005) ▪ 20,000cs own label 30% red 70% white ▪ 8 Royal Ascot Lane Sandown Sandton 2196 ▪ info@unitednationsofwine.com ▪ www.unitednationsofwine.com ▪ **T +27 (0)11-884-3304** ▪ F +27 (0)11-883-0426

David John Bate, 'secretary general' of this playful portfolio, says UNOW is now 'certified carbon neutral', and Frisky Zebras are 'the first accredited carbon neutral delivered wines in SA'. David is equally pleased with local and international best buy/value awards, and expanded exports to Baltic states.

Frisky Zebras range

Captivating Cabernet Sauvignon ☺ 🍴 ★★★ Cassis-laden **NV**, flavoursome & approachable. **Sublime Chardonnay** ☺ 🍴 ★★★ Name changed from 'Succulent Chardonnay' but engaging & friendly **NV** remains succulent, butterscotch & melon fullness tweaked by lime. **Sultry Chenin Blanc** ☺ 🍴 ★★★ Fruit-filled **NV** quaffer exudes joie de vivre. Best value chenin locally & lauded in US & Canada.

Mystic Merlot 🍴 ★★ Shy & firm **NV**, needs hearty fare. **Seductive Shiraz** 🍴 ★★ Savoury & smoky but a touch rustic **NV**. **Sensuous Sauvignon Blanc** 🍴 ★★★ Crisp, ripe melon flavours for easy **NV** drinking pleasure. Note: Luscious Hippos, Harmony Tree, G Spot & Dusty Rhino ranges in abeyance. — MW

uniWines Vineyards

Location: Rawsonville ▪ Map/WO: Breedekloof ▪ Est/1stB 2007 ▪ Tasting & sales Mon-Thu 8–5 Fri 8-4 Sat & pub ols 10–2 ▪ Closed Easter Fri-Mon, Dec 25/26 & Jan 1 ▪ Cellar tours Mon-Fri & by appt Sat/during harvest ▪ our groups ▪ BYO picnic ▪ Conferences ▪ Soetes & Soup festival (Jul) ▪ Breedekloof outdoor festival (Oct) ▪ wner(s) 50 shareholders ▪ Cellarmaster(s) Nicolaas Rust (Oct 2008) ▪ Winemaker(s) WS Visagie (Nov 2010), attingh de Villiers (Sep 2010), Charl Myburgh (Dec 2007), Schalk van der Merwe (Dec 2007), Christo Smit an 2001) & Marie Stofberg (Nov 2008) ▪ Viticulturist(s) Gert Engelbrecht (Aug 2009) ▪ 6,000+ha/2,050ha (cab, cinsaut, merlot, ptage, shiraz, chard, chenin, cbard, sauv) ▪ 45,000t/100,000cs own label 50% red 50% white + 50,000cs for clients ▪ Brands for clients: Cape Nelson, Cape Promise, Fairtrade Original, Stormy Cape ▪ ISO 22000:2008, BWI, Fairtrade, IPW, WIETA ▪ PO Box 174 Rawsonville 6845 ▪ info@uniwines.co.za ▪ www.uniwines.co.za ▪ S 33° 43′ 16.7″ E 019° 21′ 0.0″ ▪ **T** +27 (0)23-349-1110 ▪ F +27 (0)86-529-1392

Fifty producer-shareholders contribute to this extensive, widely-accredited winery, operating from three large Breedekloof cellars: Groot Eiland, Nuwehoop and Daschbosch. They vinify 45,000 tons of grapes annually into over 25 million litres of wine. Mostly bulk, the production also includes the premium Daschbosch range (debut this year for the Bordeaux-style red, Procavia), the Palesa Fairtrade range and what's believed to be the world's first Fairtrade grappa.

Daschbosch range
Procavia Cabernet Sauvignon-Merlot NEW ★★★☆ Commendable debut for premium-label Bordeaux-style red, **09** ably combines overt oakiness with lean, honest fruit.

Ankerman range
★★★★ **Nectar de Provision White** ✓ Colombard grapes find their soul-mate (brandy) in this distinctly individual & appealing fortified **NV**. Plenty of sweetness from 180+ g/l sugar. **Cabernet Sauvignon-Merlot** 🍷 🌀 ★★★ **11** juicy-fruity, unassuming light-bodied 50-50 blend. **Chenin Blanc-Chardonnay** 🍷 🌀 ★★★ Hint of almond creeping into **11**, revisited this edition as bottled wine. Drink now. **Nectar de Provision Red** ★★★ Less successful version of Cognac's classic aperitif, Pineau des Charentes, than white sibling. Merlot sits awkwardly on all this sugar. **NV**.

Groot Eiland range
Sauvignon Blanc ☺ 🍷 🌀 ★★★ Well-focused **12** delivers uncomplicated fruitiness on bracing acidity. Punches above its weight.

Cabernet Sauvignon 🍷 ★★★ **09** shows promising black fruit, but lean body fades quickly. **Merlot** 🍷 ★★★ Sweet, minty fruit with softly textured tannins, **09** fades to lean, brief finish. **Pinotage** 🍷 ★★★ Juicy & ripe **09** had supple tannins when last tasted, ideal for pasta partnering. **Shiraz** 🍷 ★★★ **09** is nutty, light, juicy. Pleasant everyday tipple. **Shiraz-Pinotage** ✓ 🌀 ★★★ Spicy & aromatic cooked fruit on **11** shows dominance of pinotage in this Cape blend. Substantial & satisfying. **Shiraz Rosé** 🍷 🍷 ★★★ Strawberry delight, **11** presents sweet fruit parfait in a glass. Ripe & appealing accompaniment to frivolous fun days. **Chardonnay** 🍷 ★★ Understated fruit previously on **09**. **Chenin Blanc** 🍷 🌀 ★★★ Quite pungent sauvignon-type flavours show on **12**. Discontinued: **Brut Sparkling Rosé**.

Meander range
Chenin Blanc-Colombar ☺ 🍷 🌀 ★★★ **12** crisply dry, light & cheerful 50/50 blend.

Merlot-Shiraz 🍷 🌀 ★★★ **11** offers juicy-sweet fruit in lightweight package. **Moscato** NEW ★★ Seriously sweet & aromatic **12** is lightly sparkling, has low 7.6% alcohol.

Palesa Fairtrade range
Merlot 🍷 🍷 ★★★ Firmer tannin grip on **10**, with pleasant juicy berry fruit. Ripe & friendly quaffer. **Pinotage** 🍷 Not tasted. **Chenin Blanc** 🍷 🍷 ★★★ Fresh & enticingly tropical **11** brims with fruit. Rounded body, gentle acid. Summer delight. **Moscato** NEW 🍷 🌀 ★★ Screwcap version of Meander, above. **12** light, sweet & slightly sparkling. **Sauvignon Blanc** 🍷 ★★★ Tangy & flavoursome **12** shows well, but fades quickly. — GdB

▪ **Unplugged 62** see Joubert-Tradauw Wingerde & Kelder
▪ **Unsung Hero** see Origin Wine
▪ **Upington** see Orange River Wine Cellars

Upland Organic Estate   🍷 ⚲ 📷

Location/WO: Wellington ▪ Map: Paarl & Wellington ▪ Est 1990 ▪ 1stB 1996 ▪ Tasting, sales & tours by appt ▪ Self-catering cottages ▪ Distillery: brandy & grappa ▪ Organic olives, olive oil, dried fruit & nuts ▪ Craft workshop ▪ Owner(s) Edmund & Elsie Oettlé ▪ Cellarmaster(s)/winemaker(s)/viticulturist(s) Edmund Oettlé ▪ 46ha/10ha (cab, chenin, cbard, crouchen) ▪ 10t/600cs own label 100% red ▪ QCS organic certification ▪ PO Box 152 Wellington 7654 ▪ info@organicwine.co.za ▪ www.organicwine.co.za ▪ S 33° 40′ 19.9″ E 019° 2′ 40.0″ ▪ **T** +27 (0)82-731-4774 ▪ F +27 (0)21-873-5724

Upland's Edmund Oettlé is taking his natural approach a step further with vegan wines, which he says are not only organic and sulphur-free, but animal product free as well. 'Reminiscent of how wines might have tasted in ages past, before the addition of sulphur and animal products became commonplace.'

Cabernet Sauvignon ☀ ★★★ Core of dark savoury fruit on **09** bridled by firm structure. Needs time & good hearty fare. Organic, & claimed sulphite free, as is the port. **Tandem Cape Ruby** ☀ ★★★ Listed as 'Guinevere Cape Ruby' previously. **07** fortified dessert from cab. Pleasant liquorice tone but quite stern for ruby style. —MW

Usana

Location/map: Stellenbosch • WO: Stellenbosch/Western Cape • Est/1stB 2003 • Tasting & sales by appt • Owner(s) JP & Pierre Winshaw • Winemaker(s) Jasper Raats (2012, consultant), with Hendrien de Munck (2010, consultant) • Viticulturist(s) Deon Joubert, Nikki Joubert & Henry Kotzé (consultant) • 300ha/60ha (cabs s/f, merlot, chard, pinot gris, sauv) • 29t/2,000cs own label 15% red 85% white • PO Box 68 Lynedoch 7603 • jp@usanawines.co.za, pierre@usanawines.co.za • www.usanawines.co.za • S 33° 56' 29.7" E 018° 46' 16.3" • **T +27 (0)83-650-9528**

While many diversify from husbandry and fruit into wine, the Winshaw brothers move in the other direction on their Stellenbosch farm. Last year grass-fed beef was added to their offering; this year it's lamb, and eggs from free-range chickens. All to be available from a tasting room in... a renovated sheep shed.

★★★★ **The Fox Cabernet Sauvignon** ✓ Judiciously oaked **09** on track after **07** (★★★) shifted stylistic gear to 100% cab (previously a blend). Intense sweet plum & cassis aromas/flavours, subtle tannic underpin.

★★★★ **Sauvignon Blanc** 🍴 Retiring grass & hay, creamy lees notes on gravelly **12** mealtime companion from Stellenbosch; less brisk than **11** which included Elgin fruit.

Pinot Gris 🍴 ★★★ **12**, with a drop of pinot blanc, shows restrained aromas, faint dried pear flavours & a satisfying vinosity. — CvZ

■ **Usapho** see Stellar Winery

Uva Mira Vineyards

Location/map/WO: Stellenbosch • Est 1997 • 1stB 1998 • Tasting & sales Mon-Fri 9-5 Sat/Sun 10-4 • Fee R20-R40 • Closed Good Fri, Dec 25 & Jan 1 • Cheese platters & savoury meat platters • Tour groups • Farm produce • Conservation area • Owner(s) Denise Weedon • Winemaker(s) Matthew van Heerden (May 2003), with Desmond Solomons (Nov 2004) • Viticulturist(s) Matthew van Heerden (May 2003) • 140ha/30ha (cabs s/f, merlot, shiraz, chard, sauv) • 100t/7,000cs own label 60% red 40% white • IPW • PO Box 1511 Stellenbosch 7599 • info@uvamira.co.za • www.uvamira.co.za • S 34° 1' 31.3" E 018° 51' 26.1" • **T +27 (0)21-880-1683** • F +27 (0)21-880-1682

Winemaker Matthew van Heerden celebrates ten years at this tiny winery high on the Helderberg. This experience allows him to refine the in-depth analyses of each of the site-specific vineyards and helps to ensure the character of each is reflected in the bottle. Attention to sustainable viticultural practices also promotes purer fruit expression. This, in turn, leads to greater consistency while taking into account vintage variations. Another reward came when Matthew was named Diners Club Young Winemaker of the Year.

Vineyard Selection

★★★★ **Syrah** ⓟ Vivid spice, minerals on last-tasted **08**, but opulent red fruit, ripe tannins.

★★★★☆ **Red Blend** ⓟ Layered brilliance, complex aromas & classy oak attractions on **07**. Fresh, deep flavours beautifully balanced with cab-focused structure. Merlot, cab franc, shiraz add savoury conclusion.

★★★★☆ **Single Vineyard Chardonnay** Modern accessible style combined with traditional maturation potential. **11** displays much besides usual expressive, oak-spiced lime/oatmeal features; creamy texture harnessed by tense minerality with hint of sweetness calming the conclusion.

Cellar Selection

★★★★ **Sauvignon Blanc** 🍴 These usually tasted ex-tank, so ratings provisional. **12** sample in usual bracing, tangily dry style; still taut, yet to exhibit full flavour, lees-enriched dimension. **11** sold out untasted.

Merlot-Cabernet Sauvignon ★★★★ Maturing savoury edge to previewed **08**'s dark plum, berry fruit adds to complexity. Opulent yet fresh, for delicious current drinking. Step up on **07** (★★★★). — AL

Vaalvlei Wines

Location: Stanford ▪ Map: Elgin, Walker Bay & Bot River ▪ WO: Walker Bay ▪ Est 2005 ▪ 1stB 2008 ▪ Tasting & sales Mon-Sat 11-5 by appt ▪ Closed Good Fri & Dec 25 ▪ Self-catering cottages ▪ Fly-fishing ▪ Owner(s) Terblanche family ▪ Cellarmaster(s)/viticulturist(s) Naas Terblanche (Mar 2005) ▪ Winemaker(s) Naas Terblanche (Mar 2005) & Josef Dreyer (Aug 2005, Raka), advised by Charl van Teijlingen CWM (Mar 2008) ▪ 50ha/3ha (shiraz, sauv) ▪ 19t/ 325cs own label 40% red 60% white ▪ PO Box 92 Stanford 7210 ▪ info@vaalvlei.co.za ▪ www.vaalvlei.co.za ▪ S 34° 26'56.11" E 019° 33'07.05" ▪ **T +27 (0)28-341-0170/+27 (0)72-782-3431**

'Looking after our environment is as important to us as selling our wines,' say the Terblanche family owners, whose special concern is the frogs of the area, especially the endangered Western Leopard Toad, featured in the logo on their bottles and a very welcome resident on their Stanford farm, which is a great getaway for nature lovers and keen fishermen.

Shiraz Reserve ⑫ ★★★ Big & bold, sweet-fruited, spicy **10** ends with a warm hug of vanilla. **Shiraz** ⑫ ★★★ Concentrated spicy black fruit, **10**'s 16% alc not for the faint of heart. **Sauvignon Blanc** ▤ ★★★ Ex-tank, **12** promising nose of lime sweets & marmalade, fresher than previous vintages, with chalky dryness. — HJ

Val de Vie Wines

Location: Paarl ▪ Map: Paarl & Wellington ▪ WO: Western Cape/Coastal ▪ Est 2003 ▪ 1stB 2004 ▪ Tasting & sales Mon-Fri 8-5 Sat/Sun & pub hols 10-4 ▪ Cellar tours by appt ▪ Closed Good Fri, Dec 25 & Jan 1 ▪ Platters by prior arrangement ▪ Polo Club Restaurant (see Restaurants section) ▪ Conservation area ▪ Owner(s) Val de Vie Wines (Pty) Ltd ▪ Winemaker(s) Harold Versfeld ▪ Vineyard manager(s) Heinie Nel ▪ 14ha (carignan, cinsaut, grenache n/b, mourv, petite sirah, shiraz, clairette, marsanne, rouss, viog) ▪ 75t/4,250cs own label 60% red 40% white ▪ PO Box 6223 Paarl 7620 ▪ wine@valdevie.co.za ▪ www.valdevie.co.za ▪ S 33° 48'15.0" E 018° 58'4.0" ▪ **T +27 (0)21-863-6143** ▪ F +27 (0)21-863-2741

'Elegant and voluptuous' wine is the aim here, and all the varieties chosen for the job are originally from one region: the Rhône. In fact, Val de Vie wine, polo and lifestyle estate near Paarl prides itself on being one of the world's most extensive producers of Rhône cultivars, with 11 of the French wine valley's 22 permitted grape types planted and onstream. Vinification is in a facility dating from 1825, upgraded and modernised but with 'foundations and traditions standing strong'. The tasting room now conveniently situated next to the restaurant, general manager Nikki Van Aardt can justly claim this as 'the place to visit for an out-of-the-norm wine and culinary experience.'

Val de Vie range

★★★★ **Shiraz** ⑫ **08**'s smoky mulberry & plum appeal follows similar **07**. Rounded yet muscled & firm. Dark char depth & density. Oak shows restraint, 70% new for 11 months. Long finish.

★★★★ **Ryk Neethling** Pepper & spice abound on taut & toned **10** from shiraz, mourvèdre, carignan, grenache & cinsaut. Rich & savoury, with restrained black fruit wrapped around a firm body of tannin.

★★★★☆ **Val de Vie** ⑫ Premium-priced flagship, mainly mourvèdre (50%), shiraz & dabs grenache, carignan & cinsaut. **07** last time was ripe & concentrated yet elegant, 80% new wood already assimilated.

★★★★ **GVC** ⑫ ▤ Graceful **08** blend of grenache blanc (50%), viognier & clairette blanche. Vanilla (from 100% new oak, 7 months on lees) layered with citrus & stonefruit freshness. Not revisited.

Polo Club range

Cabernet Franc NEW ✓ ▤ ★★★★ Lighter styled, with precise oaking for balance & structure, **10** offers harmonious fynbos & dried herb flavours. WO Coastal. **Craftsman** ✓ ▤ ★★★★ Was 'Red'. **08** five-way Rhône-style blend is earthy & spicy, with succulent black fruit. Semi-dry with a refreshing acid counterweight. **Chardonnay** ▤ Next awaited. **Sauvignon Blanc** NEW ▤ ★★★ Upfront grassy & greenpepper aromas, **11** fresh & tightly wound, ends with refreshing lemon lift. **Polo White** ✓ ▤ ★★★★ Misreported as discontinued last time. Lightish, unoaked **11** viognier blend is fresh & bouncy, with floral appeal. Discontinued: **Filly**. — WB

Val du Charron

Location: Wellington ▪ Map: Paarl & Wellington ▪ WO: Western Cape ▪ Est 2007 ▪ 1stB 2009 ▪ Tasting daily 10-4 ▪ Sales Mon-Fri 8-5 ▪ Cellar tours during tasting hours ▪ Breakfast & lunch daily; dinner by appt ▪ Tour groups ▪ Conferences/functions (100 pax) ▪ Walks/hikes ▪ Mountain biking trail ▪ 4-star guesthouse (stay@vdcwines.

com) ▪ Owner(s) Val du Charron Wines (Pty) Ltd ▪ Winemaker(s) Bertus Fourie (Apr 2010, consultant) ▪ Viti-culturist(s) Heinie Nel (Apr 2010, consultant) ▪ 43ha/21ha (cab, ptage, shiraz, chard, chenin) ▪ 200t ▪ Other export brands: Girlfriends ▪ IPW ▪ PO Box 890 Wellington 7654 ▪ ce@vdcwines.com ▪ www.vdcwines.com ▪ S 33° 37' 28.14" E 019° 2' 55.32" ▪ **T +27 (0)21-873-1256** ▪ F +27 (0)86-509-4865

Speaking of how it all started, Catherine Entwistle says they went into buying the neglected Wellington fruit farm 'with our eyes wide shut'. It had no fruit future, so they replaced the trees with 18 different grape varieties, always intending to be a producer of blends. Available cellardoor is their successful Five Girlfriends range, made from bought-in wine and exported to America.

★★★★ **Four White Legs** ✓ Previewed last edition, **11**'s 4-way blend mainly chenin, sauvignon, has unfolded into a beauty. Stonefruit & melon, enriched by deft oaking; poised, balanced, delicious.
Erasmus ★★★★ Mainly merlot, pinotage, cab gives **11** mixed berries, sprinkle of herbs. Mocha nose & palate reveals oak, ends nicely dry. **Black Countess** ★★★★ Blend shiraz, pinotage, Rhône varieties, **11**'s plush ber-ries underpinned by youthful oak. Age extra year or match to rich dishes. — CR

■ **Valley Green** *see* Hannay Wines
■ **Valley Road Vintners** *see* Ross Gower Wines

Valley Vineyards Wine Company

Location: Riebeek-Kasteel ▪ WO: Swartland ▪ Est/1stB 2009 ▪ Closed to public ▪ Owner(s) Richard Addison & Richard James ▪ ±50,000cs own label 40% red 40% white 15% rosé 5% other ▪ Other export brand: Two Tunns ▪ PO Box 2175 Riebeek-Kasteel 7307 ▪ raddison@valleyvineyardswine.com ▪ www. valleyvineyardswine.com ▪ **T +27 (0)79-174-2801**

The main calling cards in the US and UK markets remain the Post Tree and Royal ranges, reports Richard Addison, partner in this UK merchant house with Richard James. They have looked eastwards and established a toehold in China, while conti-nental Europe is showing a thirst for the Swartland-sourced and -made wines.

24 Rivers range
Merlot ⊛ 🍷 ★★★ Understated **10** is juicy & light with fresh acidity. **Chardonnay** ⊛ 🍷 ★★ Light lemon fruit on straightforward unwooded **10**. **Chenin Blanc** ⊛ 🍷 ★★★ Tropical toned **10** ripe but crisp. **Sauvignon Blanc** ⊛ 🍷 ★★ Light-hearted **10** is nicely tart with hints of greengage.

Mischief Maker range
Cabernet Sauvignon ⊛ 🍷 ★★★ Leafy, spicy **10** with appealing varietal character on light, compact body. **Merlot** ⊛ 🍷 ★★★ Raspberry cordial on juicy **10**; brief but racy end. **Pinotage** ⊛ 🍷 ★★★ Ribena & cherry, **10** sweet, pleasant sipping. **Chardonnay** ⊛ 🍷 ★★ Cheerful & plump **10**, ripe pear & lemon unfettered by oak. **Chenin Blanc** ⊛ 🍷 ★★★ **10** ripe apple & almond, warm farewell. **Sauvignon Blanc** ⊛ 🍷 🥂 ★★ **10** quaffer is light in alcohol (±11%) for summer fun.

Post Tree range
Shiraz-Cinsaut ⊛ 🍷 🥂 ★★★ With coffee aroma, sweet smoky berry flavours, **10** a friendly BBQ com-panion. **Chenin Blanc** ⊛ 🍷 ★★★ Fresh **10**, flowers & green fruit for anytime enjoyment.

The Royal range
Shiraz-Cabernet Sauvignon 🍷 Await new. **Chenin Blanc** ⊛ 🍷 ★★★ Hint whites nuts on fresh & fruity, light & limber **09**. — GbB/MW

■ **Van Hunks** *see* Oudtshoorn Cellar — SCV

Van Loveren Family Vineyards

Location/map: Robertson ▪ WO: Robertson/Western Cape ▪ Est 1937 ▪ 1stB 1980 ▪ Tasting & sales Mon-Fri 8.30-5 Sat 9.30-3 Sun 11-2 ▪ Closed Easter Fri/Sun, Dec 25 & Jan 1 ▪ Cellar tours ▪ Food & wine tasting plat-ters ▪ Walking/hiking & mountain biking trails ▪ Self-catering farm cottage ▪ Christina's @ Van Loveren restaurant ▪ Owner(s) Nico, Wynand, Phillip, Hennie, Bussell & Neil Retief ▪ Cellarmaster(s) Bussell Retief ▪ Winemaker(s) Danelle van Rensburg (Jan 2007), with Malcolm Human (Jan 2012) ▪ Viticulturist(s) Neil & Hennie Retief ▪ 400ha (cab, merlot, mourv, muscadel r/w, ptage, pinot noir/gris, ruby cab, shiraz, touriga nacional, chard, chenin, cbard, gewürz, morio muscat, nouvelle, sauv, sem, viog) ▪ 6,700t/1,000,000cs own label 33% red 33% white 34% rosé ▪

Brands for clients: Woolworths ▪ BWI, Fairtrade, IPW ▪ PO Box 19 Klaasvoogds 6707 ▪ info@vanloveren.co.za ▪ www.vanloveren.co.za ▪ S 33° 52' 31.3"   E 020° 0' 9.1" ▪ **T +27 (0)23-615-1505** ▪ F +27 (0)23-615-1336

Visitors to the new tasting venue, which flows into the famous garden, can see two intertwined Karee trees planted by first-generation owners Hennie and Jean Retief. This tangled tree doesn't only symbolise their love for each other, it is now also the name of a range of wines in fully recyclable PET bottles with Treefree labels — summing up the eco-friendly approach of a farm built on family values, yet in touch with a rapidly changing market. 'From social media to innovative packaging, from lower alcohol to sweeter styles, we'll continue thinking outside the box.'

Christina Van Loveren Limited Releases

★★★★ **Shiraz 10** (★★★) not up to form of iron fist/velvet glove **09**. Well-judged oak detail (100% new, 10% American), nicely dry but ±15% alc slightly warming & hollow on palate. WO W Cape.

★★★★ **Sauvignon Blanc** ⦿ 🍴 🌀 Darling grapes in melon & pineapple-nuanced **11**. Intensely flavoured & smooth, with lipsmacking acidity. Like lime & herb **10**, has great persistence. WO W Cape.

★★★★ **Noble Late Harvest Rhine Riesling 09** (★★★) barley sugar & apricots; softer acidity, creamier than zingy **08**. Lacks wonderful presence of previous examples at less than 11% alcohol.

Cabernet Sauvignon ★★★★ Milk chocolate infused, smooth **10** (now bottled) nicely savoury, fairly complex with good structure for few years ageing. **Chardonnay** 🌀 ★★★★ Vanilla & oak tannins currently dominate citrus, creamy lees notes on barrel-fermented **11**. Like **10**, delivers elegant drinkability without overt sweetness or big alcohol. **Méthode Cap Classique Brut** ★★★★ Traditional-method sparkling from chardonnay (86%) & pinot, 9 months on lees. Latest **NV** subtle citrus & brioche, good weight, intensity & length. Nudges next level.

Van Loveren range

★★★★ **Red Muscadel** 🌀 **12** (★★★★) signature red fruit pastille character, delightfully clean & uncloying, but misses the complexity & enduring length of **11**.

> **Neil's Pick Colombar** ☺ 🍴 🌀 ★★★ Bears name of viticulturist Neil Retief. **12** vibrant & attractive guava-toned picnic pal. **Special Late Harvest Gewürztraminer** ☺ 🍴 🌀 ★★★ Genteel **12**, all rosepetals & delicate sweetness, perfect for spicy foods.

Merlot ⦿ 🌀 ★★★ **11** bursts with sour cherries & plums, affable tannins for quaffing fun. **African Java Pinotage** 🌀 ★★ Expected coffee aroma **12**, albeit muted, crowd-pleasing touch sweetness. **Cramond Cabernet Sauvignon-Merlot** 🍴 ★★★ Black fruit compote **10**, medium body, smart oaking (older barrels only). Unpretentious outdoorsy red. **River Red** ⦿ 🍴 🌀 ★★★ Delightful sipper **11** unwooded combo ruby cab (60%), merlot, shiraz. **Blackberry Cabernet Sauvignon-Shiraz** 🌀 ★★★ Gains 'Blackberry' moniker in **11**, appropriately dark fruited & friendly, lightly oaked. **Blanc de Noir Shiraz** 🍴 🌀 ★★ Dry & savoury **12** lends itself to food partnering. **Blanc de Noir Red Muscadel Blush** 🍴 🌀 ★★ Juicy **12** pink has appealing rosepetal bouquet, sweet aromatic flavours. **Cape Riesling** 🍴 🌀 ★★ Fresh & tangy **12**, slender body lightly brushed with oak. **Chardonnay** 🍴 🌀 ★★ Vanilla nuance, light pear & melon fruit on briefly oaked **12**. **Chenin No. 5** NEW 🍴 🌀 ★★ White peach & soft acidity, moderate ±12% alcohol for easy sippability in **12**. **Pinot Grigio** 🍴 🌀 ★★ Tad less excitement in **12**, with fleeting pear nuance. **Sauvignon Blanc** 🍴 🌀 ★★ Faintly aromatic **12**, zesty, 12.5% alcohol for easy drinkability. **Cramond Sauvignon Blanc-Chardonnay** 🍴 🌀 ★★ Lightly oaked **12**, sauvignon's grassiness meets chardonnay's vanilla-tinged stonefruit. **Blanc de Blanc** 🍴 🌀 ★★ Delicate & light **12**, inoffensive colombard & sauvignon combo. **Cape Ruby** 🔥 ★★★ NV fortified port-style from touriga shows commendable dryness, seamless spirit integration for winter warmth. Savoury tones, firm tannic goodbye. Discontinued: **Vino Blanc**.

Four Cousins range

Dry Red ★★ Cherry, thatch & good grip in ruby cab/merlot NV (**12**) braai companion. **Dry White** 🍴 ★★★ Balanced drinkability in grassy & fresh **NV** colombard/sauvignon combo. **Extra Light White** 🍴 ★ NV slimmer's friend, feather-light & racy. **Natural Sweet Red** ★★ NV (**12**) sweet & light in alcohol (9.5%). **Sweet Rosé** ★★ 'Natural Sweet Rosé' last time. Latest **NV** (**12**) shows cranberry-tinged sweetness. **Light Natural Sweet Rosé** 🍴 ★★ Strawberry notes on **NV** summer delight. **Natural Sweet White** 🍴 ★★ Low alcohol (8.5%) & grapey appeal in **NV** for the sweet toothed. Note: above variously available in 500ml, 750ml & 1.5L.

Five's Reserve range

Cabernet Sauvignon 🌀 ★★ **12** unfettered by oak, packed with juicy blackcurrant. **Pinotage** 🌀 ★★ Rustically charming **12**, pure black cherry flavour uncluttered by wood. **Merlot Rosé** 🍴 Await new vintage. **Chenin Blanc** 🍴 🌀 ★★ Guava & peach appeal, **12** not as markedly dry as previous.

Tangled Tree range NEW

Tropical Sauvignon Blanc ☺ 🍴 🌿 ★★★ Lives up to name: papaya/pineapple on bright, breezy **12**.

Chocolate Cabernet Sauvignon 🍴 🌿 ★★ 11 smooth, but has us wondering: where's the chocolate? **Spicy Shiraz** 🍴 🌿 ★ 11 with savoury biltong whiffs, touch ungenerous. **Moscato Rosé** 🍴 🌿 ★★ Strawberry-toned **12** for casual sweet sipping. **Butterscotch Chardonnay** 🍴 🌿 ★★ Creamy vanilla **12** slips down easily.

Papillon Sparkling range

Vin Doux ★★ NV sparkling from red muscadel offering lots of frothy sweetness. **Brut** ★★★ Latest NV uncomplex but easy & charming bubbly. **Demi-Sec** ★★ Foamy pink semi-sweet NV from red muscadel, uncomplicated party fun.

Four Cousins Sparkling range

Red ★★ NV from ruby cab tad plain but cheery. **Blush** ★★ Cranberries lifted by lively acidity in NV semi-sweet sparkler. **Sauvignon Blanc Brut** ★★ Carbonated NV dry, brisk for seaside sipping. **White** ★★ Sweet end on fragrant NV bubbly. — CE/MW

■ **Vansha** *see* Ridgeback
■ **Van Zijls Family Vintners** *see* Imbuko Wines

Van Zylshof Estate 🍷

Location: Bonnievale ▪ Map/WO: Robertson ▪ Est 1940 ▪ 1stB 1994 ▪ Tasting & sales Mon–Fri 9–5 Sat 9–1 ▪ Closed Good Fri, Ascension day, Dec 25 & Jan 1 ▪ Cellar tours by appt ▪ Owner(s) Van Zylshof Trust ▪ Cellarmaster(s)/winemaker(s)/viticulturist(s) Andri van Zyl (Mar 1993) ▪ 37ha/32ha under vine ▪ 450t/±4,000cs own label 15% red 80% white 5% rosé ▪ PO Box 64 Bonnievale 6730 ▪ vanzylshof@lando.co.za ▪ www.vanzylshof.co.za ▪ S 33° 56′ 18.5″ E 020° 6′ 23.4″ ▪ **T +27 (0)23-616-2401** ▪ F +27 (0)23-616-3503

Andri van Zyl, in his 20th year as winemaker, is looking forward to son Dirk linking up with him and his father on the Bonnievale family farm. The youngster at the time of writing was completing his Stellenbosch studies and will gradually become more involved with wine-making and -marketing, eventually moving to the farm. 'We will then have the privilege of working together as three generations.'

★★★★ **Chardonnay Unwooded Riverain** 🍴 Addition of 'Unwooded' to name helps emphasise untrammelled peach fruit purity of **12**, provisionally rated preview is concentrated yet light-hearted, summery.

Chenin Blanc ☺ 🍴 ★★★ Smooth & peachy **12** slides down easily for everyday refreshment.

Cabernet Sauvignon-Merlot 🍴 ★★★ 11 on track with fragrant dark cherries & berries, uncomplicatedly pleasant toasty flavours. **Rosé** 🌗 🍴 ★★★ Cheerful 11 pink from merlot; food-friendly, dry & spicy. **Chardonnay** 🌗 🍴 ★★★ 10 melds citrus fruit, vanilla & 'pine needle' oak notes. **Sauvignon Blanc** 🍴 ★★★★ **12** good concentration of greenpepper flavour, refreshing despite rounder body & softer acidity. — DB/JP

Vaughan Johnson's Wine & Cigar Shop

Location: Cape Town ▪ Map: Cape Peninsula ▪ WO: Paarl ▪ Est/1stB 1985 ▪ Sales Mon–Fri 9–6 Sat 9–5 Sun 10–5 ▪ Open pub hols ▪ Gifts, souvenirs, spirits & beer available ▪ Owner(s) Vaughan Johnson ▪ PO Box 50012 Waterfront 8002 ▪ vjohnson@mweb.co.za ▪ www.vaughanjohnson.co.za ▪ S 33° 54′ 19.15″ E 018° 25′ 10.68″ ▪ **T +27 (0)21-419-2121** ▪ F +27 (0)86-509-6401

No new wines to review, but a producer has been sourced to ensure that the canny wine drinker will be well served. Value for money is always a concern for Vaughan Johnson, proprietor of this landmark Cape Town Waterfront wine shop. Wines below R100 make up 90% of his sales and he warns of a growing sensitivity towards greedy wine pricing: three times the price is not always three times the quality.

Vaughan Johnson range

Good Everyday Cape Red 🌗 🍴 ★★★ Juicy berry fruit with hint of smokiness on likeable NV. This & next 3 from Paarl, not retasted. **Good Everyday Cape White** 🌗 🍴 ★★ Fresh & fruity NV quintessential quaffer.

Waterfront Collection

Captain's Claret ① 🍷 ★★★ Ripe, spicy plum fruit & good body on **09**. **Great White** ① 🍷 ★★☆ **11** dependable easy-priced, easy-drinking blend. — JP

Veenwouden Private Cellar

Location: Paarl ▪ Map: Paarl & Wellington ▪ WO: Paarl/Coastal ▪ Est 1989 ▪ 1stB 1993 ▪ Tasting, sales & cellar tours by appt ▪ Fee R100, waived on purchase ▪ Owner(s) The Van Der Walt Trust ▪ Cellarmaster(s) Marcel van der Walt ▪ Winemaker(s) Marcel van der Walt, with Faried Williams ▪ Viticulturist(s) Marcel van der Walt, with Sias Louw ▪ 14ha/12.5ha (cabs s/f, malbec, merlot, p verdot) ▪ ±100t/5,500cs own label 90% red 10% white ▪ PO Box 7086 Northern Paarl 7623 ▪ admin@veenwouden.com ▪ www.veenwouden.com ▪ S 33° 41'7.0" E 018° 57'52.4" ▪ **T** +27 (0)21-872-6806 ▪ F +27 (0)21-872-1384

Music runs through the veins of the Van der Walt family, owners of this boutique Paarl winery; the cellar can even double as a concert hall! Now there's a joint venture wine with South African trumpeter extraordinare Hugh Masekela, with his name and photo on the label. Winemaker Marcel van der Walt explains: 'I've been involved with the Paarl Youth Initiative, sponsoring local children to better themselves. With the idea of taking this further we teamed up with Hugh Masekela to produce a special blend under his name. Proceeds will help rural children with autism, and a music scholarship for a student from a disadvantaged background.'

Premium Collection
Chardonnay Await next.

Hugh Masekela Collection NEW

★★★★ **Hugh Masekela** Harmonious merlot-based **10** blend with cab, shiraz. Invitingly rich, savoury with caressing velvet feel, gentle grip. Easy as 'listening to Hugh's soul soothing sounds of Jazz,' as per back label.

Reserve Collection

★★★★ **Merlot** 🍷 Recently shows more supple, fleshy texture, softer integrated tannins & less oak. **11** in that vein with fresh core harnessing ripe, dark plum fruit. Good medium-term potential. **10** untasted.

★★★★ **Syrah** Modern, bright-fruited style in **11** (**09** sold out, no **10**); attractive lilies, spicy features; fresh, with firm yet unaggressive tannins, sweet-fruited tail. Will benefit from year/2.

★★★★ **Classic** Quintet Bordeaux varieties, cab-led in **09**. Ripe fruit profile, richly textured with balancing fresh core, lively, succulent grape tannins. Oak a subtle extra. Drink now or keep 5+ years. **08** sold out untasted.

Chardonnay NEW ★★★★ Fruit-driven **11**, just 5% oaked for extra flesh. **11** is accessible, with attractive citrus vitality, gently rounded, dry.

Vivat Bacchus Collection

Red ★★★★ Velvety, approachable merlot-based **11** with a little shiraz; fresh red plums, spicy flavours polished with French oak, 20% new. WO Coastal. **Chenin Blanc** ① 🍷 ★★★ **11** easy but not simple; attractive tropical flavours, plump & juicy with tangy fruity acid tail. — AL

Vendôme

Location/WO: Paarl ▪ Map: Paarl & Wellington ▪ Est 1692 ▪ 1stB 1999 ▪ Tasting & sales by appt ▪ Closed all pub hols ▪ Conferences/functions (up to 150 pax) ▪ Owner(s)/winemaker(s)/viticulturist(s) Jannie le Roux ▪ 40ha (cabs s/f, merlot, shiraz, chard, chenin, cbard, sauv, sem) ▪ 5t/300cs own label 50% red 50% white ▪ PO Box 36 Paarl 7645 ▪ lerouxjg@icon.co.za ▪ www.vendome.co.za ▪ S 33° 45'27.8" E 018° 58'42.4" ▪ **T** +27 (0)21-863-3905 ▪ F +27 (0)21-863-0094

On their Berg riverside property in Paarl, Jannie le Roux senior and junior focus on blends, possibly to reflect the fusion of France and Africa in their history. Farmed by the Le Roux family for 10 generations, Vendôme was named to honour their Huguenot heritage and ancestral home in central France.

Classique Await next, as for **Merlot-Cabernet Sauvignon**. **Sans Barrique** ① ★★★★ **09** unoaked semillon/sauvignon blend (61/39) raises the bar on last-tasted **06** (★★★★). Rounded & rich courtesy 6 months lees-ageing, buoyed by freshening acidity. — CvZ

■ **Vera Cruz Estate** see Delheim Wines

Vergelegen Wines

Location: Somerset West ▪ Map: Helderberg ▪ WO: Stellenbosch/Western Cape ▪ Est 1987 ▪ 1stB 1991 ▪ Tasting & sales daily 9.30–4.30 (gate closes at 4) ▪ Cellar tours daily at 10.30, 11.30 & 3 (Nov–Apr); 11.30 & 3 (May–Oct) ▪ Tasting R30/6 wines (excl Vergelegen Red and White), R10 each for flagship wines; Cellar tour R20pp incl. tasting of 4 premium range wines ▪ Closed Good Fri, May 1 & Dec 25 ▪ Vergelegen Restaurant, Stables Bistro & Camphor Forest Picnic (see Restaurants section) ▪ Facilities for children ▪ Gift shop ▪ Historic Cape Dutch homestead; library; exhibition corridor ▪ 300 year old camphor trees (proclaimed as National Monuments in 1942) ▪ Conservation area ▪ 17 exquisite gardens including the Camellia Garden of Excellence; programme of events on website ▪ Owner(s) Anglo American plc ▪ Winemaker(s) André van Rensburg (Jan 1998) ▪ Viticulturist(s) Niel Rossouw (Apr 1995) & Dwayne Lottering (Nov 2003) ▪ 3,000ha/158ha (cab, merlot, sauv) ▪ 680t/63,000cs own label 58% red 42% white ▪ ISO 9001, ISO 14001, OSHAS 18000, BWI champion, WIETA ▪ PO Box 17 Somerset West 7129 ▪ info@vergelegen.co.za ▪ www.vergelegen.co.za ▪ S 34° 4′37.0″ E 018° 53′30.6″ ▪ **T +27 (0)21-847-1334** ▪ F +27 (0)21-847-1608

Is 'DNA' too modern and clinical a moniker for a wine from this historic (and internationally celebrated) Helderberg estate? Disinformation is the word on its naming. 'A team-building exercise gone awry,' is managing director Don Tooth's spin. 'When the name was suggested, we liked it because it lends itself to different interpretations, such as the balance between soil, climate and the winemaker's skill, each with their own unique attributes.' Others suggest its origins lie in the go-ahead-nod from (D)on a(N)d a wink from irrepressible winemaker (A)ndré van Rensburg. Whichever interpretation you accept, DNA is only available from selected retailers and the estate, now with a stylishly made-over tasting venue, new family-friendly bistro The Stables, and refurbished fine-dining restaurant.

Flagship range

★★★★☆ **Vergelegen Red** Ⓣ Accomplished flagship **06**, mainly cab (90%), merlot, cab franc; measured tannic grip cossets plush fruit, fine & dry. Like handsome **05** (★★★★★), should improve good few years.

★★★★☆ **Vergelegen V** Ⓣ Mainly cab with merlot, cab franc. **07** classically structured, with authoritative tannins, lush fruit, firm acidity; will reward cellaring 5+ years.

★★★★☆ **Vergelegen White** Ⓣ 🌿 Pioneering barrel fermented/aged semillon-sauvignon blend. **10** (59% semillon) flint overlay to white peach, delicate 'wet stone' minerality. Introverted **09** had more sauvignon.

Reserve range

★★★★☆ **Cabernet Sauvignon** Ⓣ Poised **07** (★★★★) seductive savoury richness, firm tannins; not as concentrated as **06**, vintage possibly playing a role. Dashes petit verdot, cab franc, merlot.

★★★★☆ **Merlot** Ⓣ Ripe & lavishly oaked but so very well judged & accomplished, **08** a study in finessed fruit & complexity: plum, blackberry, fenugreek & dust; mimics distinguished, dark-berried **07**.

★★★★ **Shiraz** Ⓣ **07** riper style but gently handled/oaked maximised bright red fruit & spice, supple texture. Shade off silky **06** (★★★★★).

★★★★☆ **DNA** Ⓣ New name for 'Cabernet Franc-Merlot'. **06** (★★★★☆) sold out; bold **05** still selling.

★★★★☆ **Chardonnay Reserve** Ⓣ 🌿 Magnificent **10** signature citrus grip/creamy tension, fennel notes to oatmeal & nut base, refined savoury conclusion. Like riveting **09**, worth ageing 5+ years.

★★★★☆ **Sauvignon Blanc Reserve** Ⓣ 🌿 Aficionados know this as 'Schaapenberg', a reference to its 23 year old hillside vineyard. **11** reserved, taut with 'oystershell' minerality & greengage vivacity.

★★★★ **MMV** [NEW] Individual **08** MCC sparkler from chardonnay & pinot noir fermented & aged 6 months sur lie in old chardonnay barrels; 3 years on lees in bottle; every 6 months 'shaken not stirred' says winemaker. As a result, biscuity, savoury & austere; not as creamy as many others. WO W Cape.

Semillon Await new.

Premium range

★★★★ **Shiraz** Peppery notes on **09**'s lily/red fruit; supple & light textured yet with sufficient body for winter warming; lovely dry tail & tannic tug, only 30% new oak.

★★★★ **Cabernet Sauvignon-Merlot-Cabernet Franc** Name now recognises cab franc's 25% role in cab-led **09** (28% merlot, some from Elgin), adding to complexity. 'Old-style' Bordeaux leafiness, balanced & integrated with fine tannins.

★★★★ **Chardonnay** 🍴 🌿 Masterly lemon-vanilla touches on partially oaked **11**. Like lemongrass-toned **10**, satisfying vinosity for food or solo. Includes fruit from widespread vineyards.

★★★★ **Sauvignon Blanc** ✓ 🍷 🌿 **11** sedate but distinctly sauvignon fruit with grass/green pea hints, balanced acidity, plus some weight from 6 months lees-ageing.
Discontinued: **Vin de Florence**. — CvZ

Vergenoegd Wine Estate

Location/map: Stellenbosch ▪ WO: Stellenbosch/Western Cape ▪ Est 1696 ▪ 1stB 1972 ▪ Tasting & sales Mon-Fri 9–5 Sat/Sun 9.30–4 ▪ Fee R15 ▪ Closed Good Fri, Dec 25 & Jan 1 ▪ Cellar tours by appt ▪ Facilities for children ▪ Tour groups ▪ Wine-related gifts ▪ Fresh duck eggs in spring ▪ 6 boule courts ▪ Guided historical walks & duck tours by appt ▪ Conservation area ▪ Pomegranate Restaurant open for lunch Tue-Sun, dinner by appt ▪ Owner(s) Vergenoegd Trust ▪ Cellarmaster(s) John Faure (Nov 1983) ▪ Winemaker(s) Marlize Jacobs (Dec 2007) ▪ Viticulturist(s) Marlize Jacobs (Dec 2007), advised by Drikus van der Westhuizen (2004) ▪ 300ha/ ±68ha (cabs s/f, malbec, merlot, p verdot, shiraz, tinta, touriga) ▪ 500t ▪ 94% red 3% white 3% rosé ▪ BWI, IPW ▪ PO Box 1 Faure 7131 ▪ info@vergenoegd.co.za ▪ www.vergenoegd.co.za ▪ S 34° 2'2.8" E 018°44'20.1" ▪ **T +27 (0)21-843-3248** ▪ F +27 (0)21-843-3118

This is one of Stellenbosch's oldest farms, and owned by the Faure family since 1820. Current cellarmaster John Faure led a vertical tasting in 2012 celebrating the history of the estate Cabernet Sauvignon. Few wineries in the New World could offer 40 vintages of which not a single one was undrinkable — and most were much more than that. The 1972 was not only alive, but deliciously mature. Most of the wines currently on offer are well off their brash youth, many replete with classic (even slightly old-fashioned) virtues. The Vergenoegd philosophy, says John, is that: 'If a wine is not ready to be consumed, then it is not ready to be released.'

Vintage Collection

★★★★ **Cabernet Sauvignon** ⓣ **04** had estate's signature restraint, with cedar spice.

★★★★ **Shiraz** ⓣ **04** sappy red fruit with house's savoury finish. All in range tasted a few years back.

★★★★☆ **Vergenoegd** ⓣ Bordeaux blend **04** succulent, accessible yet cellarworthy.

Merlot ⓣ ★★★★ Blackcurrant & leafy notes to food-friendly & firm **04**. **Terrace Bay** ⓣ ★★★★ Blend of 5 red varieties. **04** less serious than previous, but big 14.5% alcohol in balance.

Standard range

★★★★ **Cabernet Sauvignon** **06** includes a good dollop cab franc, all matured in mostly older oak. Ripe black-berried fruit aromas, earthy undertones. Full bodied; firm, fine tannins, good acidity, lingering finish.

★★★★ **Merlot** In usual house style, **07** has classic shaping. Ripe earthy plums & sushi wrapper notes. Fresh palate with fine tannin structure & intelligent oaking. Drops of malbec, cab franc aid complexity.

★★★★ **Shiraz** Ripe **06** with 8% touriga. Beautiful gamy, truffle & leather undertones; attractively rustic palate shows decent intensity & weight, with a nice warming finish. Harmonious, ready to drink.

★★★★ **Vergenoegd** Classic Cape Bordeaux blend, rewarding the patient. **06** has usual firm structure & earthy tones, uplifted by fresh red currant, tar & spicy plum. Mostly new oak now happily integrated.

Terrace Bay ★★★★ **06** a slightly earthy, easygoing & food-friendly 5-way red blend with enough intensity, length & interest. **Old Cape Colony Vintage Port** ★★★★☆ **05** entices with deep aromas of chocolate, spices, ripe plums & black fruits. The palate balanced & intensely flavoured, packed with blackberry liqueur, chocolate & cassis, leading to long fantail finish. From tinta & touriga, like less-impressing **04** (★★★★).

Runner Duck range

Red ✓ 🍷 🌿 ★★★★ Intensely aromatic, spicy **10** from touriga, cab franc, malbec. Rich, soft, powerful but approachable, with an attractive rusticity. **Rosé** 🍷 🌿 ★★★ Notably soft, full bodied malbec-led **12** shows plums, blood orange & earthy tones. Previewed, as next. **White** 🍷 🌿 ★★★ Tropical **12** from mostly sauvignon shows forward ripe granadilla & lemon fruit. WO W Cape.

Limited Edition range

Cabernet Franc ⓣ ★★★★ Heady, super-ripe **09** made in tiny volumes, with notes of tobacco, leather, spiced plums. Light oaking. Warming 15% alcohol. **Malbec** [NEW] ★★★★ **10** invitingly offers spice box, floral & blackberry liqueur notes, leading to a soft & approachable but concentrated palate, with bright acidity. **Tawny Port** ⓣ ★★★ Sweetly rich & rustic once-off **99** from tinta barocca. — JPf

Verlieft Wines

Location: Stellenbosch ▪ Est 2010 ▪ Tasting & sales by appt ▪ Closed Easter Fri-Mon, Dec 25/26 & Jan 1 ▪ Owner(s) Roos & Co. Wines ▪ Cellarmaster(s) Dirk Roos ▪ PO Box 104 Koelenhof 7605 ▪ dirk@verlieftwines.com ▪ www.verlieftwines.com ▪ T +27 (0)82-904-6886

Taking a bite out of the Big Apple, the focus of their exports, Verlieft won a blind tasting against Bordeaux's Château Cheval Blanc, Tuscany's La Macchiole Paleo and other wines at an event hosted by JP Morgan. Now owner and cellarmaster Dirk Roos, with his wife Kirsten handling finances and exports, is setting his mind to a white blend and a possible méthode cap classique sparkling.

Versailles

Location/WO: Wellington ▪ Map: Paarl & Wellington ▪ Est/1stB 2004 ▪ Tasting, sales & tours by appt ▪ Conservation area ▪ Owner(s) Annareen de Reuck (Malan) ▪ Vineyard manager(s) M Joseph ▪ 100ha (cab, cinsaut, merlot, shiraz, chenin, cbard, riesling) ▪ ±1,200t ▪ PO Box 597 Wellington 7654 ▪ adereuck@ezinet.co.za, orders@versailleswines.co.za ▪ www.versailles.co.za ▪ S 33° 37' 34.98" E 018° 59' 37.11" ▪ T +27 (0)21-873-2618/+27 (0)82-898-9314 ▪ F +27 (0)86-502-1482

Exactly 150 years ago the Malan family gave the town of Wellington a parcel of land to build a train station, with the proviso that all trains would stop to allow passengers to alight, thereby guaranteeing local shop owners a predictable number of customers. To celebrate their shared history, boutique vintner Annareen de Reuck (née Malan) this year is inviting local dignitaries to high tea — and, if they tarry, a glass of her finest...

Merlot NEW ★★★ Sweet plummy fragrance & flavours, unoaked **11** is delicate, soft & smooth. **Shiraz** Await next, as for **Cabernet-Merlot** & **Chenin Blanc**. **Sauvignon Blanc** ★★★ Goes up a notch in **11**, greenpepper & grenadilla briskness, flavoursome yet lightish for lunchtime sipping. — CvZ

Versus

'Serv us Versus, we deserv it' is the website strapline for this easy-drinking range from The Company of Wine People (www.servusversus.com). 'Connecting to younger audiences' is what it's all about, says communications manager Maryke Visagie, with blog, Facebook and Twitter updates featuring anything from Versus jelly wine shots to win-a-party competitions.

Versus Original range

Red ★★★ **11** smooth & savoury, with balanced gentle structure. Unwooded. W Cape WO, as for both ranges. **Rosé** ★★ **12** muscat-scented preview lightish, tart & crisp for snacks. **White** ★★ **12** mainly chenin & colombard is lightish, aromatic, with crunchy apple tone.

Versus Naturally Sweet range

Sweet Red ★ Sweetly spicy, light & genial quaffing wine. **NV. Sweet Rosé** ★★ **NV** sweet & crisp tipple with spice & light alcohol. **Sweet White** ★★ Crisply tropical, low-alcohol **NV** charmer. — MW

▪ **Vertex Reserve** see Bonnievale Cellar
▪ **Victoria Bay** see Darling Cellars

Vilafonté

Location/map: Stellenbosch ▪ WO: Paarl ▪ Est 1996 ▪ 1stB 2003 ▪ Tasting, sales & tours by appt ▪ Owner(s) Mike Ratcliffe, Zelma Long & Phil Freese ▪ Winemaker(s) Zelma Long & Martin Smith (May 2010) ▪ Viticulturist(s) Phil Freese (1996) & Edward Pietersen (2006) ▪ 17ha (cabs s/f, malbec, merlot) ▪ 60t/2,000cs own label 100% red ▪ Unit 7C Lower Dorp Street Bosman's Crossing Stellenbosch 7600 ▪ info@vilafonte.com ▪ www.vilafonte.com ▪ S 33° 56' 26.8" E 018° 50' 49.8" ▪ T +27 (0)21-886-4083 ▪ F +27 (0)21-883-8231

Celebrating a decade since Vilafonté's first release off their Paarl vineyards (the winery itself is in Stellenbosch town), managing partner Mike Ratcliffe talks happily of the 'unexpected rise' of malbec as a component in the two Bordeaux-style blends, especially the M Series where it plays an increasingly pivotal role (M used to be for merlot). 'This is a refreshing and exciting development to us', he says. 'Us' being Ratcliffe and, first and foremost, the two eminent Americans who paid the Cape an immense compliment by investing and working here from the mid 1990s: winemaker Zelma Long and viticulturist Phil Freese. As for the wine in general: 'It's all about balance,' says resident winemaker Martin Smith. 'And making sure that quality is never compromised at any point.'

★★★★☆ **Series C** Intense black fruit aromas, cassis & almond notes on plush & concentrated **10** — cab-dominated as always, with 25% cab franc, merlot, malbec. Opulent, brocaded textures & real mid-palate weight are defining features of this iconically styled wine, a near clone to super-rich, finely balanced **09**.

★★★★☆ **Series M** M is still for merlot (49%) in **10**, with malbec & cab. Profound & vinous, rendered approachable by sweet redcurrant aromas, juicy accessibility. Light caramel notes, dryish tannins confirm substantial oaking. Elegance, spice remain hallmarks in **10** — finer, less intense than **09**. — MF

Viljoensdrift Wines & Cruises

Location/map/WO: Robertson ▪ Est/1stB 1998 ▪ Tasting & sales at Riverside venue Mon-Fri 9-5 Sat & 1st Sun/mnth 10-3 ▪ Closed Good Fri, Dec 25, Jan 1 ▪ Deli — create your own picnic ▪ Facilities for children ▪ Tour groups ▪ Gift shop ▪ Conferences ▪ Robertson Wacky Wine/Wine on River/Slow weekend ▪ Owner(s) Fred & Manie Viljoen ▪ Cellarmaster(s) Fred Viljoen (1998) ▪ Winemaker(s) Fred Viljoen, with Zonia Lategan ▪ Viticulturist(s) Manie Viljoen (1998) ▪ 240ha/120ha (cab, ptage, shiraz, chard, chenin, sauv) ▪ 200t/±80,000cs own label 55% red 40% white 4% rosé 1% port + 15,000L for clients ▪ Other export brands: Elandsberg, Riverscape, Vuurgloed ▪ BWI, IPW, WIETA ▪ PO Box 653 Robertson 6705 ▪ wines@viljoensdrift.co.za ▪ www.viljoensdrift.co.za ▪ S 33°52'8.4" E 019°59'13.6" ▪ **T** +27 (0)23-615-1901 (cellar); +27 (0)23-615-1017 (tasting/cruises) ▪ F +27 (0)23-615-3417

The brothers Viljoen, winemaker Fred and viticulturist Manie, are pleased to have seen 2012 export volumes increase, with bulk wine now going to the Netherlands as well as Scandinavia. Holland is their biggest market and destination for two export brands, Vuurgloed and Elandsberg, the latter named for the mountain range across the river from their substantial Robertson farm, docking point for many a tourist cruise.

River Grandeur range
Cabernet Sauvignon ⑳ ★★★★ Savoury & long **09**, nudges next level with 'oystershell & graphite' minerality, nice herbaceous lift. **Merlot** ⑳ ★★★★ When last tasted, **09**'s smoky oak veneer & bright acidity tweaked 15% alcohol into harmony. **Pinotage** 🖼 ★★★ Fresh & bold **11**'s sweet fruit enhanced by clever combo French/American oak. Ideal match for Springbok bobotie, Viljoens say. **Shiraz** 🖼 ★★★ Rusticity part of the charm of supple & savoury **11**. **Cape Blend** ✓ 🖼 🖼 ★★★★ Well-crafted & affable merlot-led **11**, succulent & smooth, thread of lively acidity keeps the pastille-like flavours light & buoyant. **Chardonnay** ⑳ 🖼 🖼 ★★★ **11** commendable example of variety; acacia & nuts, balanced lemon & lime palate. **Sauvignon Blanc** 🖼 🖼 ★★ Khaki bush & musk sweets on zesty **12** swigger, misses complexity of previous. Discontinued: **Chenin Blanc**.

Viljoensdrift range
Serenity Await new. **Rosé** ⑳ 🖼 ★★★ **11** delicately perfumed, vinous but lightly flavoured & dry. **Villion** ⑳ ★★★ NV méthode cap classique sparkling showing deepish yellow hue, nutty/honeyed bottle-age. **Muskapino Sweet Sparkling Rosé** NEW 🖼 ★★ Splash pinotage adds colour to muscat de Frontignan in sweet & frothy party-starting **12**. **Cape Vintage Reserve** ★★ Port-style fortified from tinta with souzão, **09** Christmas mince pie character & still-integrating spirit mid-2012. — CvZ/MW

■ **Villa San Giovanni** see Zandvliet Wine Estate & Thoroughbred Stud
■ **Villa Verde** see Seven Oaks

Villiera Wines

Location/map/WO: Stellenbosch ▪ Est/1stB 1983 ▪ Tasting, sales & cellar tours Mon-Fri 9-5 Sat 9-3 ▪ Closed Good Fri, Dec 25 & Jan 1 ▪ Dalewood cheese platters & soft drinks; or BYO picnic ▪ Conferences (up to 40 pax) ▪ Wildlife sanctuary ▪ Game drives & birding R150pp (R75 for children under 15) incl tasting & self-guided tour of cellar, book ahead ▪ Owner(s) Grier family ▪ Cellarmaster(s) Jeff Grier (1983) ▪ Winemaker(s) Christiaan Visser (Dec 2008) ▪ Viticulturist(s) Simon Grier ▪ 400ha/210ha (cab, merlot, ptage, pinot, shiraz, chard, chenin, sauv) ▪ 1,800t/60,000cs own label 24% red 37% white 3% rosé 36% MCC; 14,000cs for Marks & Spencer; 21,000cs for Woolworths ▪ Other export brand: Groot Geluk (Belgium) ▪ HACCP, WIETA ▪ PO Box 66 Koelenhof

7605 ▪ wine@villiera.com ▪ www.villiera.com ▪ S 33°50'14.4" E 018°47'34.4" ▪ **T +27 (0)21-865-2002/3** ▪ F +27 (0)21-865-2314

In the South African wine world, this Stellenbosch family estate is practically a byword for social, business and environmental ethics — not to mention good value. A méthode cap classique pioneer, Villiera remains a premier producer, and maintains a reputation for innovation with sulphur-free MCC and riesling, and the release of a moscato and other light wines for Woolworths in response to current trends. The estate's new Fizzytherapy ad campaign ties the bubbly in with the upgraded, contemporary 'Wine Sanctuary' tasting room — in its turn a reference to the farm's popular game sanctuary. 'These days, electronic contact with your customer base is pivotal,' says Jeff Grier, 'but it will never supplant direct contact with consumers on the farm and at shows.'

Villiera Wines range

★★★★ **Monro** Complex herbal **07** a vintage reflecting elegance in harmonious merlot-led blend, with both cabs. Well structured to age, though succulent savoury fruit makes it accessible now.

★★★★ **Traditional Barrel Fermented Chenin Blanc** 📷 Richly tropical **11** (★★★★) appeals with full flavours, a few grams sugar, & oaky breadth — though less layered depth than **10**.

★★★★ **Traditional Bush Vine Sauvignon Blanc** 📷 Great depth & richness in **12** despite early picking, after lesser **11** (★★★★). Careful viticulture gives fresh acidity, modest alcohol, strong herbaceous element.

★★★★☆ **Reserve Brut Rosé** 🕐 **00** tasted a few years back 'a unique one-off' bubbly in magnum, 52% pinotage & pinot-led, nine years sur lie! Rich texture with black-grape weight, was amazingly fresh.

★★★★ **Brut Natural** Quietly-spoken charm in whistle-clean, delicate **09** sparkler. Bone-dry, no dosage yet manages soft, refined edge. Persistent mousse carries bright pure-fruited citrus flavours. No sulphur used.

★★★★★ **Monro Brut** ✓ Showing same class as **05**, ultra-elegant, creamy **07** MCC sparkling reflects cool vintage's remarkable freshness & ageing potential. 4 years on lees imparts great dimension & complexity to blend of barrel-fermented chardonnay (50%) & both pinots. **06** (★★★★★) only marginally less fine.

★★★★☆ **Inspiration** 🕐 📷 Botrytised chenin, riesling dessert style. Bronze **10** shows unctuous dried fruit flavours with citrus twist. Delightful fresh acidity ably controls richness.

Merlot ☺ 📷 ★★★ Plummy, ripe **10** for pleasurable drinking rather than impressing. Lively acidity & tannins add structure. **Pinotage** ☺ 📷 ★★★ Aromatic, mocha-laced **10** is smooth & lively for simple, early enjoyment. **Gewürztraminer** ☺ 📷 ★★★ Plenty of Turkish Delight on **12** with touch honeyed botrytis, delightfully off-dry with light touch for lunchtime enjoyment.

Cabernet Sauvignon ✓ 📷 ★★★★ Classic varietal expression in chiselled **10**; attractively fruity & well oaked, though tad less complex than last-tasted **08** (★★★★). **Shiraz** Not tasted. **Chenin Blanc** ✓ 📷 ★★★★ Step-up **12** brims with bold fruit flavours (apples galore) & refreshing acidity. Careful oaking adds breadth & creamy richness to mouthfilling style. **Rhine Riesling** 🕐 ★★★★ Last tasted was ethereal, spicy, off-dry **09**. **Sauvignon Blanc** ✓ 🍴 ★★★★ Perfectly balanced **12** offers more seriousness than **11** (★★★) with layered flavours bound by fine acidity. Neither overtly herbaceous nor tropical in style. **Tradition Rosé Brut** ★★★ Pinotage-led **NV** sparkling has simple, earthy appeal, though there's a touch of bitterness on the firm finish. **Brut Special Dosage** 🕐 ★★★★ Attractive **NV** sparkler slightly sweeter than Tradition, softens & adds richness, for those who find Brut a little too dry. **Tradition Brut** ★★★★ Reliable, popular **NV** MCC bubbles from chardonnay & both pinots. Exuberantly fresh, crafted for affordable drinkability at posher end of the market. **Fired Earth** 🕐 ★★★★ LBV-style port. Last tasted was harder spiritous but flavourful **04** from touriga, shiraz & pinotage.

Down to Earth range

Red ☺ 📷 ★★★ Temptingly spicy **11** touriga-shiraz blend. Exotic, deliciously smooth & drinkable right now. **White** ☺ 🍴 📷 ★★★ **12** sauvignon-semillon blend intended for affordable, easy drinking delivers on promise with plenty of flavour. — IM

Villiersdorp Cellar

Location/map: Villiersdorp ▪ WO: Western Cape ▪ Est 1922 ▪ 1stB 1974 ▪ Tasting & sales Mon-Fri 8-5 Sat 9-1 ▪ Fee R10 for groups of 7+ ▪ Closed Easter Fri-Mon & Dec 25/26 ▪ Kelkiewyn restaurant/farm stall T +27 (0)28-840-0900 Mon-Fri 9-4 Sat/Sun & pub hols 8-3 ▪ Farm produce ▪ Walks/hikes ▪ Mountain biking & 4x4 trails ▪ Tractor museum open on request ▪ Owner(s) 40 growers ▪ Cellarmaster(s) Flip Smith (Jan 2011) ▪ Winemaker(s) Flip Smith (Jan 2011), with André Bruyns (Dec 2009) ▪ Viticulturist(s) André Bruyns (Dec 2009)

▪ 300ha (merlot, chenin, sauv) ▪ 3,600t/9,500cs own label 30% red 30% white 30% rosé 10% fortified ▪ BW IPW ▪ PO Box 14 Villiersdorp 6848 ▪ marketing@slowine.co.za ▪ www.villiersdorpcellar.co.za ▪ S 33° 59' 11.2 E 019° 17' 48.5" ▪ **T +27 (0)28-840-1120** ▪ F +27 (0)28-840-1833

'Valley of splendour' is not mere marketing speak: Villiersdorp Cellar and its 4 vinegrower owners truly are blessed with immense scenic beauty including th viticulturally important Theewaterskloof Dam, whose name echoes in the good value unfortified range. The multi-attraction tasting venue in Villiersdorp tow has been revamped to accommodate a Slowmarket, natural habitat for their Geo metric-Tortoise-emblazoned (and separately listed) Slowine brand.

Dam Good range

Red ☺ 🍷 🌿 ★★★ Now bottled, **10** merlot/shiraz perfect cheer for cold, rainy days. Dark fruit, soft spice, pleasant grip of tannin.

White ⏰ 🍷 🌿 ★★★ Thai-food-friendly **11**, ex tank cheerful fragrant fruit (mainly chenin), ends with lemo flick. **Rosé** ⏰ 🍷 🌿 ★★★ Pretty pink Natural Sweet **11** with silky texture, pinotage's strawberry tones.

Villiersdorp Cellar range

Treintjiewyn Hanepoot Jerepiko ✓ ★★★★ 'Little Tractor' fortified dessert is now **NV**, oozes orange rind watermelon & sunshine. Slippery, luscious, long, with balanced alcohol. **Cape Ruby** ★★ Unwooded **NV** (pre viously vintaged) more 'high-alcohol red' than traditional port style. Light hearted & sweet. — WB

■ **Vinay** *see* Slanghoek Winery

Vinimark

Stellenbosch ▪ Closed to public ▪ Directors Tim Rands, Cindy Jordaan, Geoff Harvey & Gys Naudé ▪ Export Geoff Harvey ▪ geoff@vinimark.co.za ▪ PO Box 441 Stellenbosch 7599 ▪ www.vinimark.co.za ▪ **T +27 (0)21 883-8043/4** ▪ F +27 (0)21-886-4708

Wine merchants marketing, selling and distributing various ranges with loca partners, including Robertson Winery, Kleindal, Long Beach and Silversands some listed separately.

■ **Vin Maison** *see* Maison

Vins d'Orrance

Location: Constantia ▪ WO: Western Cape ▪ Est/1stB 2000 ▪ Tastings by appt ▪ Owner(s) Christophe & Sabrin Durand ▪ Cellarmaster(s)/winemaker(s) Christophe Durand ▪ 11ha ▪ 30t/4,000cs (6btl) own label ▪ PO Bo 23923 Claremont 7735 ▪ christophe@vinsdorrance.co.za ▪ www.vinsdorrance.co.za ▪ **T +27 (0)21-683 7479** ▪ F +27 (0)21-683-7489

Born in France to a family of Calvados producers, Christophe Durand moved t Cape Town 18 years ago to set himself up as a barrel importer. Seduced by ran dom parcels of 'irresistible' grapes and with the encouragement of friends in th business, he was inexorably drawn into producing his current trio of fine wines.

★★★★☆ **Syrah Cuvée Ameena** Flawless **10** illustrates the joy of vividly pure sweet fruit underpinned b spicy, supple tannins. Combo Perdeberg, Elgin shiraz grapes creates accessible but elegantly restrained style offering appetising nod to northern Rhône.

★★★★ **Chardonnay Cuvée Anaïs** Exquisitely formed **11** (★★★★★) a rousing step up from stylish **10** also from top-quality Elgin & Franschhoek fruit. Perfectly integrated, fine oak binds multi-layered, expressiv flavours in harmonious, deliciously complex whole. Ultra-long, fresh & steely finish.

★★★★☆ **Kama Chenin Blanc** Barrel-fermented **11** from old Perdeberg vines again fulfils meaning Sanskrit name ('sensual pleasure'). **10** (★★★★★) showed more exceptional concentration & complexity though no shortage here of richness (just dry) & purity, held by fine acidity & textured pithiness. — IM

■ **Vinum** *see* The Winery of Good Hope
■ **Vior** *see* Malanot Wines

Virgin Earth

Location: Riversdale ▪ WO: Langeberg-Garcia/Philadelphia/Coastal/Overberg ▪ Est 2002 ▪ 1stB 2003 ▪ Closed to public ▪ Owner(s) Kobus du Plessis ▪ Winemaker(s) Piet Kleinhans (Sep 2008) & Joseph Gertse (Jan 2000) ▪ Viticulturist(s) Rudi Benn (Jan 2001) & Hendrik Otto (2004) ▪ 13,000ha/21ha (cabs s/f, merlot, p verdot, shiraz, sauv, sem, verdelho, viog) ▪ 35,000cs own label 40% red 45% white 15% rosé ▪ Fairtrade, organic in conversion, WIETA ▪ Postnet Suite #57 Private Bag X18 Milnerton 7435 ▪ sales@havanahills.co.za ▪ www. havanahills.co.za ▪ **T +27 (0)21-972-1110** ▪ F +27 (0)21-972-1105

Being remote (the nearest big town, Riversdale, is 60km away) and in the setting of a 14,000 ha game farm, the team here have a closer understanding of nature. Hence the process of organic conversion is seen not just for the grapes but also for the animals' improved environment. Additionally, the wines' lees, rich in micronutrients, has been found to be an excellent fertiliser for the poorer pastures.

★★★★ **Pinot Noir** ⊕ Red berries & undergrowth nuances, **09** is tightly focused reflection of cool-climate terroir. Pure, elegant & classic. WO Philadelphia.

★★★★ **High Five** ✓ Merlot-led Bordeaux blend, dash shiraz, **08** has weight, gravitas, plenty more to show over time. Seamless red fruit, serious but non-intrusive tannins, still tightly held. Drink over 6+ years.

★★★★ **Noble Late Harvest** ⊕ From semillon, last **08** ticked all the boxes: deeply rich & full flavoured; apricot, pineapple, good length. Deliciously easy to drink. 30% in seasoned barrels. 500ml.

Pinotage ✓ ★★★★ Huge step up from **08** (★★), showing more concentration & complexity. **09** intense bueberries, layers of spice & lipsmacking succulence. Delicious quintessential pinotage. **Lost Barrel Shiraz** ⊕ ★★★ Last was **07**, with smoky dark fruit, plump, & nice tannin grip. Designed to please now & next few years. Overberg WO. **Chenin Blanc** ⊕ 🏛 ★★★★ Thatch & bruised apple in last-tasted **10**, off-dry but acidity provided balance, touch of oak complexity. Coastal WO. **Pepper Tree Sauvignon Blanc** ✓ 🏛 🖉 ★★★★ Touch sugar tames **12**'s zesty acidity, wild herb & lemongrass intensity, leaving a vibrant tang, long tail. **Succulent** ⊕ ★★★★ Wooded off-dry semillon, viognier blend. When last tasted **10** had waxy melon styling, full-bodied yet retained freshness. Delicious on release, could age few years. Improved on aptly named **08** (★★★★). **Viognier MCC** ⊕ ★★★ Bubbles enhancing peachiness, **08** previously was not your usual méthode cap classique style. Flavourful enough for creative food pairing. — CR

Virginia

For over 40 years, a consistent semi-sweet white, widely sourced, by Distell.

Virginia 🏛 ★ Usual chenin/colombard mix ends clean & crisp in latest **NV**, doesn't cloy. 2 & 5L. — DB/HJ

■ **Vivat Bacchus** *see* Veenwouden Private Cellar

Vleiland Wines

Location: Vredendal ▪ Map/WO: Olifants River ▪ Est 2004 ▪ 1stB 2005 ▪ Tasting & sales by appt Mon-Fri 8-5 Sat 8-12 ▪ Closed Easter Fri-Mon, Dec 25 & Jan 1 ▪ BYO picnic ▪ Farm produce ▪ Walks/hikes ▪ 4x4 & mountain bike trails ▪ Owner(s) Nico Laubscher snr, Alette Laubscher, Nico Laubscher jnr ▪ Winemaker(s)/viticulturist(s) Nico Laubscher ▪ 60ha (cab, ptage, shiraz, chenin, cbard, sauv) ▪ 790t/280cs own label 100% red ▪ PO Box 627 Vredendal 8160 ▪ alzanne@nashuaisp.co.za ▪ S 31° 44'42.24" E 018° 32'8.16" ▪ **T +27 (0)27-213-2525/ +27 (0)82-905-1640** ▪ F +27 (0)27-213-2825

The purchase of additional vineyards has pushed plantings up by 25% at this laid-back Olifants River farm, still supplying most of its grapes to Namaqua Wines. But the Laubschers are most proud of the Cab-Shiraz blend they make in partnership with their long-term farming partners, the Afrikaners: 'Two of the best families combined with two of the best varieties.'

Cabernet Sauvignon-Shiraz ☺ 🏛 ★★★ Previously 'Two of the Best'. Step-up **11** is a value-for-money 55/45 combo with blackberry flavour. 'Lekker now, but will also age well' says winemaker. — DB/CvZ

Vondeling

Location: Paarl ▪ Map: Paarl & Wellington ▪ WO: Voor Paardeberg ▪ Est 2001 ▪ 1stB 2005 ▪ Tasting, sales & tours by appt ▪ Owner(s) Richard Gower, Julian Johnsen & Anthony Ward ▪ Cellarmaster(s) Matthew Copeland (Jul 2007) ▪ Winemaker(s) Emile van der Merwe (Dec 2011), with William Mofokeng (Jan 2005) ▪ Viticulturist(s)

Julian Johnsen (Aug 2000) ▪ 100ha (cabs s/f, carignan, grenache r/w, malbec, merlot, mourv, p verdot, shiraz, chard, chenin, Muscat de F, sauv, viog) ▪ 450t/30,000cs own label 40% red 55% white 5% rosé ▪ Other export brand: Signal Cannon ▪ PO Box 57 Wellington 7654 ▪ admin@vondelingwines.co.za ▪ www.vondelingwines. co.za ▪ S 33° 35′ 45.7″ ▪ E 018° 51′ 6.4″ ▪ **T +27 (0)21-869-8595** ▪ F +27 (0)21-869-8219

This progressive and eco-conscious winery pays more than mere lip service to sustainability and environmental conservation by having a full-time botanist on the payroll, actively geo-tagging, DNA fingerprinting and cataloguing the endangered fynbos on its biodiverse Voor Paardeberg property. Julian Johnsen and his British partners bought the erstwhile David Frost cellar across the road to boost diversity even more, establishing visitor and conference facilities which they previously did not have.

★★★★ **Erica Shiraz** ✓ With touches grenache, carignan & mourvèdre, rich black berry concentration of **09** matches **08**. Supple dark intensity balanced by fruit purity & third new oak.

★★★★ **Sauvignon Blanc** 🍴 🍷 Flinty lemon leaf vibrancy on **12** (★★★☆) pre-bottling sample. Fresh acidity & lots of life on long palate but not quite the intensity of **11**.

★★★★ **Babiana** 🌱🍴 Well-crafted 4-way chenin-led blend, naturally fermented & no added acid. Complex **09** lime marmalade fullness, body & breadth yet dances lightly on oak stage.

★★★★ **Sweet Carolyn** Ambrosial straw wine from muscat de Frontignan. 'Labour-intensive endeavour' yields **09**, first tasted since stellar **06** (★★★★☆). Heady muscat fragrance with apricot tang. Light, clean, dry & vibrant finish. **08** not made. **07** sold out unreviewed.

Cabernet Sauvignon NEW 🍷 ★★★★ Natural ferment on **11** makes for elegant blueberry charmer. Serious yet softly balanced & genteel, with firm chalky grip from third new oak. Barrel sample deserves time to knit. **Baldrick Shiraz** 🍴 🍷 ★★★★ With contributions from dabs mourvèdre & viognier, **11** improves on previous with lipsmacking earthy chocolate & plum flavour. Chunky but toned. **Cabernet Sauvignon-Merlot** 🍴 ★★★★ **07** a notch up on **06** (★★★★). More rounded, nuanced black fruit & cigar spice. Svelte & sexy. **Petit Rouge** 🍴 🍷 ★★★ Blue & youngberry life from merlot & cab mix, soft & approachable yet lengthy. **11** upholds the standard. **Chardonnay** 🍴 🍷 ★★★★ **10** ratchets quality up a notch on **09** (★★★★). Smoky oatmeal & marmalade nuances add appeal in spades. Poised, classy & elegant with balance & concentration. Lovely oak platform. **Petit Blanc** 🍴 🍷 ★★★ **12** granadilla & fig flavours on chenin-led viognier & chardonnay blend. Uncomplicated, fresh & animated. — FM

Von Ortloff

Location/map: Franschhoek ▪ WO: Stellenbosch/Franschhoek ▪ Est 1992 ▪ 1stB 1994 ▪ Tasting, sales & cellar tours by appt only ▪ Owner(s) Evi & Georg Schlichtmann ▪ Cellarmaster(s)/winemaker(s)/viticulturist(s) Evi & Georg Schlichtmann (1992) ▪ 34.5ha/8ha (shiraz, chard, sauv) ▪ 50t/2,000cs own label 70% red 30% white ▪ PO Box 341 Franschhoek 7690 ▪ vonortloff@mweb.co.za ▪ **T +27 (0)21-876-3432** ▪ F +27 (0)21-876-4313

Sticking to existing markets rather than expanding elsewhere in the current economic climate, Franschhoek-based Georg and Evi Schlichtmann neverless still have plans. One is to extend plantings higher up the Dassenberg slope than their shiraz vineyard. The planned blocks will be unirrigated, and soil samples taken bode very well for quality. The other plan is to release a riesling using the No 3 label that is reserved for experimental wines.

★★★★☆ **Quintessence** Flagship which gets serious attention, 2 years all new French oak, but cab franc **08** (★★★★★) laps it up. Belgian chocolate, dusty berries, underbrush & velvety tannins, gives immediate pleasure but there's an 8+ year future here. Last was **05**, seriously oaked blend cab & merlot.

★★★★ **No. 1 Syrah** Lush dark berries & scrub, **09** becomes more savoury on the palate, liquorice & tar. But there's a fleshy body, giving dark-toned drinkability, solo or with venison, rich casseroles.

★★★★ **Cabernet Sauvignon-Merlot** From barrel, **09** has fruitcake richness in its perfume, a minty note that deepens on the palate. The firm backbone will hold it in prime condition till 2018. Last tasted was **05**.

★★★★ **Chardonnay** ✓ Toned down since last-tasted **08**, now shows lovely balance, **11**'s fruit & oak well meshed, leaving seductive clementine & almond flavours, smooth textured & long.

No. 7 Merlot ★★★★ Blackcurrants & dark chocolate, **09** shows perfect ripeness in its fleshy succulence, a good foil for the tailored tannins. Finishes dry & savoury. Notch up from last **05** (★★★★). **No. 5 Sauvignon Blanc** ✓ 🍴 ★★★★ Elegant & fresh-styled **12** green apple & leafy tones, finishing crisply dry. Lovely food wine. — CR

Vrede en Lust Wine Farm

Location: Paarl ▪ Map: Paarl & Wellington ▪ Est 1688 ▪ 1stB 2002 ▪ Tasting & sales daily 10–5 (tasting room closed on Mon from 1 Jun to 31 Aug) ▪ Closed Good Fri & Dec 25 ▪ Tours 10–4 by appt ▪ Cotage Fromage Deli & Restaurant ▪ Guest accommodation in three deluxe suites & Manor House ▪ Tour groups by appt ▪ Conferences & functions ▪ Play area for children ▪ Petanque courts ▪ Owner(s) Buys family ▪ Winemaker(s) Susan Erasmus (2006), with Ansoné Fourie (2009) ▪ Viticulturist(s) Etienne Buys (Jun 1998) ▪ 340ha total ▪ Vrede en Lust: 66ha (cab, grenache, malbec, merlot, p verdot, shiraz, chard, viog); Casey's Ridge, Elgin: 88.9ha (cabs s/f, merlot, shiraz, chard, chenin, pinots g/n, riesling, sauv, sem, viog); Ricton: 122ha (cab, cinsaut, ptage, shiraz, chard) ▪ 680t/20,000cs own label ▪ WIETA ▪ PO Box 171 Groot Drakenstein 7680 ▪ info@vnl.co.za ▪ www.vnl. co.za ▪ S 33° 50′ 15.9″   E 018° 57′ 13.4″ ▪ **T +27 (0)21-874-1611** ▪ F +27 (0)21-874-1859

Partly filmed here, popular local movie Semi-Soet generated amazing awareness of this Simonsberg-Paarl property and its wines, according to marketing manager Nicola Momberg. 'We've opened a proper Vryersvoetpad, complete with black pig, due to popular demand,' she says of the hiking trail portrayed in the movie. Labels have been re-designed to clearly differentiate between the three tiers of wine. En route to carbon neutral status, they have installed a 212kWp solar plant to power the entire winery.

▪ **Vredehoek** *see Koopmanskloof Wingerde*

Vredenheim Wines

Location/map/WO: Stellenbosch ▪ Tasting & sales Mon-Sat 9-4.45 ▪ Closed Good Fri, Dec 25 & Jan 1 ▪ Restaurant Barrique T +27 (0)21-881-3001 (see Restaurants section) ▪ Hudson's Coffee Shop T +27 (0)21-881-3590 ▪ Conferences/functions ▪ Vredenheim Angus Stud ▪ Big Cats Park ▪ Jaguar cars for hire ▪ Curio shop ▪ Guesthouse ▪ Owner(s) Bezuidenhout family ▪ Winemaker(s) Kowie du Toit ▪ Viticulturist(s) Kalie Kirsten ▪ 80ha under vine ▪ 10,000cs own label 60% red 40% white ▪ PO Box 369 Stellenbosch 7599 ▪ wine@vredenheim.co.za ▪ www. vredenheim.co.za ▪ S 33° 57′ 38.2″   E 018° 48′ 29.4″ ▪ **T +27 (0)21-881-3637** ▪ F +27 (0)21-881-3296

Love for wild animals has prompted the Bezuidenhout family owners to open a Big Cats Park at their Stellenbosch farm so visitors can closely observe lion, leopard, cheetah and lynx while enjoying Vredenheim wines. Gardens, food, curios, a nursery and in-cellar conferencing broaden an unusually diverse visitor experience.

Cabernet Sauvignon 🏠 ★★★ Not discontinued, as reported last time. Ripe berry & chocolate flavours, **10** good structure & grip, easy drinking. **Merlot** 🏠 ★★★ Fruity ripe plums & dark chocolate on smooth **10** quaffer. **Pinotage** 🏠 New bottling not ready. **Shiraz** 🏠 ★★★ Improved **09** more structure than previous, with vibrant dark fruit & punchy spice for satisfying sipping. **Reserve** ⓘ 🏠 ★★★★ **08**, from shiraz & cab, is juicy, smooth & spicy, sweet fruit & soft tannins, lovely balance. **Rosé** ★★ Step-up **NV** from sauvignon & splash shiraz, semi-sweet, soft & piquant. Serve well chilled. **Sauvignon Blanc** 🏠 ★★★ Fresh, zesty **12**, tropical fruit flavours for pleasant everyday drinking. **Vredenvonkel** ★★★ Light-bodied, fruity, off-dry **NV** pink sparkler to start the fun. Discontinued: **Angel's Natural Sweet**. — WB

Vredevol Private Wine Cellar

Location: Klawer ▪ Est 2010 ▪ 1stB 2008 ▪ Closed to public ▪ Owner(s) Johan & Anne-Mari le Hanie ▪ Cellarmaster(s)/winemaker(s) Johan van Wyk (Jul 2010) ▪ 30ha ▪ 500cs own label 50% red 50% white ▪ PO Box 12695 Die Boord 7613 ▪ vredevol.wines@vodamail.co.za ▪ **T +27 (0)21-887-1277** ▪ F +27 (0)21-887-1288

Johan and Anne-Mari le Hanie are overseeing the building of a new barrel maturation cellar at Klawer in the Olifants River Valley for an Out of Region range, to be sourced in Stellenbosch. A cab/merlot blend is first in the pipeline for this line-up.

Vriesenhof Vineyards

Location/map: Stellenbosch ▪ WO: Stellenbosch/Piekenierskloof ▪ Est 1980 ▪ 1stB 1981 ▪ Tasting & sales Mon-Thu 10–4 Fri 10–3.30 Sat by appt ▪ Fee R25 ▪ Closed all pub hols ▪ Cellar tours by appt ▪ Owner(s) Landgoed Vriesenhof (Pty) Ltd ▪ Cellarmaster(s) Jan Coetzee ▪ Winemaker(s) Nicky Claasens (2008), with Richard Phillips (2001) ▪ Viticulturist(s) Coetzee Ehlers ▪ 60ha/45ha (cabs s/f, grenache, merlot, pinot, ptage, chard) ▪

300t/17,000cs own label 90% red 10% white ▪ PO Box 155 Stellenbosch 7599 ▪ info@vriesenhof.co.za ▪ www.vriesenhof.co.za ▪ S 33° 58'16.7" E 018° 52'2.8" ▪ **T +27 (0)21-880-0284** ▪ F +27 (0)21-880-1503

Vriesenhof makes wines to age, says winemaker Nicky Claasens, who works with cellarmaster/co-owner Jan Coetzee. Nicky claims inspiration from a bottle of 1973 Kanonkop Cabernet — made by Jan, of course. 'In the past the focus was on wines of character and longevity. People have forgotten the pleasure of drinking older wines, the joy of tasting the evolution of character.' And let grenache represent innovation. The Piekenierskloof Grenache was introduced a few vintages back and the plan is for it to be bottled only in magnums (ideal for ageing) and the version from newly planted Stellenbosch vines in standard bottles.

Vriesenhof range

★★★★ **Cabernet Sauvignon** ⑱ Traditional in its dryness, lack of upfront fruitiness, & strong build. **06** (no **05**) a touch austere, with slightly drying tannic finish, but satisfying & ready. Only in magnums.

★★★★ **Grenache 10** (★★★★★) happily combines succulent deliciousness with firm, savoury structure, leading to a lingering, properly dry finish. More oak influence than many from this variety, but all in balance. Like **09**, from Piekenierskloof grapes, but this one not only in magnums. Should age a good few years.

★★★★ **Pinot Noir** Good varietal character on **10** with lovely, albeit uncomplex cherry fruit & some oak spice. Fresh acidity but less tannic than promising **08** (★★★★★) last tasted (**09** being held back).

★★★★ **Kallista** ⑱ Last-tasted **05** blend merlot, cab, cab franc had big tannins & moderate substance.

★★★★ **Chardonnay** Lime, spice & nut work well with a hint of honeyed 'sweetness' on **11** (though bone-dry). Usual steely & elegant style; silky texture shot through with fine, freshening acidity. Only older oak.

Pinotage ⑱ ★★★☆ **07** with sweet fruit intensity but a rather heavy feeling to it. House-style dry finish.

Paradyskloof range

> **Chardonnay** ☺ ★★★ As usual, in same classic mould as Vriesenhof version, but **11** a little lighter fruited & easier. Balanced & fresh, attractive weight & texture.

Cabernet Sauvignon ★★ Modest-fruited **10**; dry, rather austerely dull & fleeting. **Pinot Noir** ★★★ **11** more pleasant, easy 'dry red' than varietal. Quietly fruity, a touch jammy, with good acidity & a little tannic grip. **Pinotage** ★★★ **11** light-hearted & friendly with a firm handshake. Sweet fruit controlled by variety's strong tannins & a bone-dry finish. **Grenache-Malbec-Shiraz** NEW ★★★ **11** more dully lean & light than usual with this varietal blend; plenty of structure plus a brief sweet fruitiness. **Muscat d'Alexandrie** ⑱ ★★★ Light, bright & not too sweet **08** from rather rare red hanepoot — 50 year old vines. Tawny-coloured; just 15% alc. — TJ

Vruchtbaar Boutique Winery

Location/map/WO: Robertson ▪ Est/1stB 2001 ▪ Tasting, sales & cellar tours Mon-Sat by appt ▪ Closed all pub hols ▪ Owner(s) Alwyn & Francois Bruwer ▪ Cellarmaster(s)/winemaker(s) Francois Bruwer ▪ Viticulturist(s) Briaan Stipp (consultant) ▪ 35ha (cab, merlot, ptage, ruby cab, chard, chenin, sauv) ▪ 400t/±437cs own label 62% red 38% white ▪ PO Box 872 Robertson 6705 ▪ vruchtbaar@mweb.co.za ▪ S 33° 48'17.7" E 019° 51'43.6" ▪ **T +27 (0)82-739-5553/+27 (0)82-335-1152** ▪ F +27 (0)23-626-2334

At his family's boutique winery near Robertson, cellarmaster Francois Bruwer continues to eschew machinery, preferring to follow a very hands-on traditional approach to winemaking. Last crush they enjoyed their biggest harvest to date but the extra work was well worth it: 'I must say the wine quality is exceptional!'

★★★★ **Cabernet Sauvignon** ⑱ Concentrated **08** preview fruit-filled sipper with modern styling. Dense & lingering, with tannins giving form. Rating provisional. Last **06** was integrated, polished & harmonious.

★★★★ **Chenin Blanc Limited Edition** ⑱ In contrast to sinuous **08**, bold **09** (★★★★) not for the faint-hearted: ripe tropical tones lashed with buttery oak, warming 15% alcohol.

Pinotage ⑱ ★★★ Quintessential banana & strawberry on **09**. Dense, delivers power but with noticeable sweetness. **Island Red** ⑱ ★★★ Happy **NV** combo cab & pinotage, bright & refreshing, light tannin for everyday sipping. **Chardonnay** Await new vintage, as for **Chenin Blanc Unwooded** & **Noble Late Harvest**. — CvZ

Vukani Wines

Location: Plettenberg Bay ▪ WO: Durbanville/Robertson/Stellenbosch ▪ Est 2005 ▪ Tasting & sales daily 9-5.30 ▪ Fee varies per wine ▪ Owner(s) Peter & Caroline Thorpe ▪ Cellarmaster(s)/winemaker(s) Anton Smal ▪ Viticulturist(s) Peter Thorpe ▪ ±1,400cs own label 56% red 44% white ▪ PO Box 1606 Plettenberg Bay 6600 ▪ peter@vukaniwines.com, danny@bramonwines.co.za ▪ www.bramonwines.co.za ▪ S 33° 57' 25.0" E 023° 28' 50.8" ▪ T +27 (0)44-534-8007 ▪ F +27 (0)44-534-8007

Vukani ('Wake Up') is a 2005 empowerment project established by the owners of Bramon farm in Plettenberg Bay specialising in training previously disadvantaged farmers in the area in viticulture and winemaking. Wines are listed in restaurants, guest houses and hotels locally, with some exported.

Cabernet Sauvignon ★★★ Tough, grippy **10** needs food to ameliorate the tannins. **Pinotage** ★★★ Ripe, sweet-fruited & oak-staved **11** from Robertson grapes. **Chenin Blanc** ★★★ Easygoing tropical quaffer **11** perfect for summer lunches. WO Stellenbosch. Discontinued: **Shiraz Rosé**, **Sauvignon Blanc**. — IM

Vuurberg

Location/map: Stellenbosch ▪ WO: Stellenbosch/Western Cape ▪ Tasting, sales & cellar tours by appt ▪ Closed all pub hols ▪ Owner(s)/cellarmaster(s) Sebastiaan Klaassen ▪ Winemaker(s) Donovan Rall (Oct 2010) ▪ 8ha (cabs s/f, malbec, merlot, p verdot, chenin, viog) ▪ 2,000cs own label 50% red 50% white ▪ PO Box 449 Stellenbosch 7599 ▪ info@vuurberg.com ▪ www.vuurberg.com ▪ S 33° 54' 28.9" E 018° 56' 52.7" ▪ T +27 (0)82-387-6235

Donovan Rall had already made a name for himself with his own-label white blend when he joined this Banhoek Valley boutique cellar as winemaker in mid-2010, so no surprise when he says 'I think white blends are a big part of our future and will eventually become South Africa's most recognised category'.

Vuurberg Reserve ⓘ ★★★★ 09 from half petit verdot plus cab, merlot, malbec — a really tasty ensemble. Bit less woody than **08**, but also big, bold. **White** ★★★★ 11 is now 7-way blend with chenin to the fore at 39%. Yellow fruit, spice (from a third new oak), firm line of acidity. Needs time to open up. WO W Cape. — CE

■ **Vuurgloed** *see* Viljoensdrift Wines & Cruises
■ **W** *see* Whalehaven Wines

Waboomsrivier Wine Cellar

Location: Worcester ▪ Map/WO: Breedekloof ▪ Est 1949 ▪ Tasting & sales Mon-Fri 8-5 ▪ Closed all pub hols ▪ Cellar tours by appt during harvest ▪ Soetes & Soup festival ▪ Cellarmaster(s) Bennie Wannenburg (Sep 2005) ▪ Winemaker(s) Wim Viljoen (Sep 1991), with Gustav Fouché (Jan 2011) ▪ Viticulturist(s) Pierre Snyman (Vinpro) ▪ ±1,106ha (cab, ptage, chenin, cbard) ▪ 15,799t/6,000L 5% red 95% white ▪ ISO 22000:2011 ▪ PO Box 24 Breërivier 6858 ▪ sales@wabooms.co.za ▪ www.waboomsrivier.com ▪ S 33° 31' 43.08" E 019° 12' 35. 24" ▪ T +27 (0)23-355-1730 ▪ F +27 (0)23-355-1731

From home-grown 'Cloete separators' and open fermenters to state-of-the-art combi-tanks and centrifuges, this grower-owned Breede River winery the past 64 years has kept pace with new technology (while its general manager has changed only three times). Another milestone on the path of progress came last year, when nostalic but costly-to-maintain cement storage tanks made way for stainless steel.

Wagenboom range

Arborea NEW ☺ 🏷 ★★★ Elegantly fruity Cape Blend, equal pinotage & shiraz with cab, **10** offers great value & easy enjoyment.

Pinotage In abeyance. **Chenin Blanc** 🏷 ★★ **12** made in appealing fresh, dry & fruity style. **Sauvignon Blanc** 🏷 ★★ Light, cheerful & unpretentious **12**. **Hanepoot** ⓘ ★★★ Fortified **08** is grapey & fresh with pleasant alcohol bite in the conclusion. Serve well chilled. — GdB

■ **Wagenboom** *see* Waboomsrivier Wine Cellar

Waka Waka Wines

Location/WO: Paarl ▪ Est 2011 ▪ 1stB 2010 ▪ Tasting & sales at Perdeberg Winery ▪ Owner(s) REH Kendermann & Perdeberg Winery ▪ Cellarmaster(s) Albertus Louw (Oct 2008) ▪ Winemaker(s) Riaan Möller (Dec 2006) & Carla Herbst (Jun 2008) ▪ Viticulturist(s) Jaco Engelbrecht (Nov 2011) ▪ PO Box 214 Paarl 7620 ▪ info@perdeberg.co.za ▪ www.perdeberg.co.za ▪ **T** +27 (0)21-869-8244 ▪ F +27 (0)21-869-8245

Anybody who had even a passing interest in the 2010 FIFA World Cup would smile at the mention of this US-bound, export-only label from Perdeberg Winery, in partnership with German REH Kendermann. Awards are reportedly beginning to flow in from both Germany and California.

Sauvignon Blanc NEW ☺ 🗏 🖉 ★★★ Vibrantly fresh, youthful **12** debutant. Light bodied, with commendably moderate alcohol.

Discontinued: **Shiraz-Cabernet Sauvignon**, **Sauvignon Blanc-Chenin Blanc**. — GdB

Walker Bay Vineyards

Location: Stanford ▪ Map: Elgin, Walker Bay & Bot River ▪ WO: Walker Bay ▪ Est 1997 ▪ 1stB 2007 ▪ Tasting & sales Mon-Sat 10-5 Sun 11-4 ▪ Fee R20 wine/beer ▪ Closed Good Fri & Dec 25/26 ▪ Cellar tours by appt ▪ Micro brewery ▪ Restaurant ▪ BYO picnic ▪ Facilities for children ▪ Tour groups ▪ Owner(s) Birkenhead Holdings Ltd (Isle of Man) ▪ GM Reinhard Odendaal ▪ Winemaker(s)/viticulturist(s) Reinhard Odendaal ▪ 300ha/22ha (cab, merlot, p verdot, pinot, shiraz, chard, sauv, sem) ▪ 72t/6,000cs own label 40% red 60% white ▪ PO Box 530 Stanford 7210 ▪ info@birkenhead.co.za ▪ www.birkenhead.co.za ▪ S 34°26'30.5" E 019°27'40.5" ▪ **T** +27 (0)28-341-0183 ▪ F +27 (0)28-341-0196

Many changes at this scenic 'home of fine food, wine and beer' in Stanford — previously listed as Birkenhead Estate & Brewery. Reinhard Odendaal has taken up the reins as GM and winemaker in a new cellar where, for the first time, wine was made on-site. His pal, an adopted Siberian Husky, co-hosts the cellar tours.

Cabernet Sauvignon ⓧ ★★★★ Bright, spicy, red-fruited **10** deliciously accessible. Integrated tannins gently restrain appetisingly ripe flavours. **Amesteca** ★★★ Petit verdot-led (unusually) Bordeaux red. Smoothly integrated **10** offers simple fresh ripe fruit, structured by agreeably firm tannins. **Rosé** Tank sample **12** too unsettled to rate. **Chardonnay** 🗏 ★★ **11** a fruity, lightly oaked quaffer. **Chardonnay** ⓧ 🗏 ★★★ Unwooded version. Sample **11**'s tropical flavours cheerful & unpretentious. **Sauvignon Blanc** 🗏 ★★ Freshly herbaceous **11** unusually flat & hollow. — IM

Wandsbeck Wyne Koöp Bpk

Location/map/WO: Robertson ▪ Est 1965 ▪ 1stB 1986 ▪ Tasting & sales Mon-Fri 8-5 Sat/Sun by appt ▪ Closed all pub hols ▪ Cellar tours by appt ▪ Owner(s) 21 members ▪ Cellarmaster(s) Jacques du Toit (Jun 2008) ▪ Winemaker(s) Adriaan Foot (Jan 2009) ▪ Viticulturist(s) Hennie Visser ▪ 8,777ha/516ha (cab, cinsaut, merlot, ruby cab, shiraz, chenin, chard, cbard, sauv) ▪ 8,000t/2,000cs own label 43% red 29% white 14% rosé 14% other + 6,000,000 L bulk ▪ Brands for clients: Grysberg, Smokey Mountain ▪ IPW ▪ PO Box 267 Robertson 6705 ▪ wandsbeck@breede.co.za ▪ www.wandsbeckwyne.co.za ▪ S 33° 55'60.0" E 019° 36'34.4" ▪ **T** +27 (0)23-626-1103 ▪ F +27 (0)23-626-3329

This Robertson co-operative winery is growing apace. Two new growers have joined the 19 members whose vineyards are now overseen by dedicated viticulturist Hennie Visser. Tonnage has increased to 8,000 and bulk wine to 6 million litres, keeping marketer Lara Varney (winemaker Adriaan Foot's wife) on her toes!

Revelation Red NEW ☺ 🗏 🖉 ★★★ Soft & plump easy-drinker from merlot, **12** bright raspberry core.

Cabernet Sauvignon ⓧ ★★★ Nutty/vanilla overlay on sweet plums of friendly **09**. **Shiraz** Await new. **Sauvignon Blanc** 🗏 🖉 ★★★ Nettles & greenpepper on fresh, chill-and-enjoy **12**. **Revelation White** ⓧ 🗏 🖉 ★★★ Pineapple, lemon, thatch on crisp & lightish **11** chenin/chard combo, bursts with character. **Symphony of Rosé** ⓧ 🗏 🖉 ★★ Natural Sweet-style perlé pink from shiraz, **10** cranberry-toned party starter. **Muscadel** 🖉 ★★★ Fortified dessert loses 'Red' from the label. **10** all sunshine & raisins, well-knit fortification. Discontinued: **Merlot**, **Ruby Cabernet-Shiraz**. — CvZ/MW

Warwick Estate

Location/map: Stellenbosch ▪ WO: Simonsberg-Stellenbosch/Western Cape/Stellenbosch ▪ Est 1964 ▪ 1stB 1983 ▪ Tasting & sales daily 10-5 ▪ Cellar tours by appt ▪ 'Big 5' vineyard safari on horseback ▪ Gourmet picnics in summer; tapas inspired winter menu ▪ Facilities for children ▪ Gifts ▪ Conferences ▪ Conservation area ▪ Owner(s) Ratcliffe family ▪ Winemaker(s) Nic van Aarde (May 2011) ▪ Viticulturist(s) Ronald Spies (Nov 2001) ▪ 110ha/70ha (cabs s/f, merlot, ptage, shiraz, chard, sauv) ▪ 300t/40,000cs own label 60% red 40% white ▪ BWI, WIETA ▪ PO Box 2 Elsenburg 7607 ▪ info@warwickwine.com ▪ www.warwickwine.com ▪ S 33° 50′27″ E 018° 51′54.0″ ▪ **T +27 (0)21-884-4410** ▪ F +27 (0)21-884-4025

Ever mindful of consumer trends — MD/co-owner Mike Ratcliffe is a savvy marketer — unoaked First Lady Chardonnay was introduced to capitalise on growing demand for chardonnay. The interaction with customers is wide ranging, and includes the Warwick Wine Family wine club, now up to almost 1,000 members, plus an innovative iPad app in the tasting room to allow foreign visitors to buy wine in their own currency for later international delivery. And in planning stage is an annual charity wine auction at Warwick inspired by the highly successful Napa Wine Valley one. Sales are up, but there's a great deal of hard work behind the success of this estate; Mike says it took him 7 years to build the business in China, focusing on restaurants and hotels only. It now accounts for 21% of Warwick's sales.

★★★★ **The First Lady Cabernet Sauvignon** ✓ Starts with vibrant blackcurrant perfume, **10** sustains the fruit focus into a silky, juicy, oak-balanced appeal that's hard to resist. Earlier drinking than rest. WO W Cape.

★★★★★ **Cabernet Franc** Following **08**, varietal-pure **09** again confirms the terroir match here. Mulberries, white pepper & a distinctive herb/scrub nuance are bolstered by firm but ripe tannins. A great future, 10+ years, for those who can wait.

★★★★ **Old Bush Vines Pinotage** ✓ 🖥 🈂 Plush blueberries & good oaking, **10** demands your attention with its smoky, savoury tones, textured body, dry finish. Well made, serious, with 5+ years' ageing potential.

★★★★☆ **Trilogy** Bordeaux-style red blend & flagship, **09** shows bright ripe fruit without losing its serious, ageworthy side. Immediate pleasures include a spice array, hint of meat extract & lovely savoury dryness.

★★★★ **Three Cape Ladies** Cape Blend with cab, shiraz, pinotage each bringing its part to **10**. Smoky notes in the dark berries, supple juiciness backed by ripe tannin to hold it in perfect shape till 2016+. **09** untasted.

★★★★ **Chardonnay** 🈂 With house-style citrus flavours, **11** deftly combines oak-influenced nuttiness with a lively acidity that will keep this wine fresh & delicious till ±2016.

★★★★ **The First Lady Unoaked Chardonnay** NEW ✓ 🖥 🈂 A citrus mix & preserved melon, **11** doesn't lack flavour, body or richness. Admirable example of how good chardonnay can stand on its own, unadorned. WO W Cape, as for Three Cape Ladies.

★★★★☆ **Professor Black Sauvignon Blanc** ✓ 🖥 🈂 Individually styled **11** takes sauvignon to a different place, stonefruit & quince, drawing to a pinpointed flavour intensity laced with bright, toned acidity.

The Black Lady Syrah Not tasted. — CR

Waterford Estate 21-12-12

Location/map: Stellenbosch ▪ WO: Stellenbosch/Elgin/Western Cape ▪ Est/1stB 1998 ▪ Tasting, sales & cellar tours Mon-Fri 9-5 Sat 10-5 ▪ Tasting fees: R40/standard; R65/chocolate; R50/The Jem (current vintage only); R120/romantic (bubbly & chocolate); R200/reserve; R550/wine drive; pre-booking essential ▪ Closed Good Fri, Dec 25 & Jan 1 ▪ Tea/coffee/soft drinks & chocolates ▪ 14ha BWI conserved land ▪ Owner(s) Jeremy & Leigh Ord, Kevin Arnold ▪ Cellarmaster(s) Kevin Arnold (1998) ▪ Winemaker(s) Francois Haasbroek (2005), with Mark le Roux (Jul 2009) ▪ Viticulturist(s) Tollie van der Spuy (Jun 2012) ▪ 120ha/60ha (barbera, cab, sangio, shiraz, tempranillo, chard, sauv) ▪ 503t/40,000cs own label 51% red 45% white 3% rosé 1% other ▪ PO Box 535 Stellenbosch 7599 ▪ info@waterfordestate.co.za ▪ www.waterfordestate.co.za ▪ S 33° 59′54.6″ E 018° 52′12.7″ ▪ **T +27 (0)21-880-0496** ▪ F +27 (0)21-880-1007

This family-owned and very stylish Helderberg estate won the 2012 international Best in Wine Tourism Services Award from the Great Wine Capitals organisation. Quite a mouthful — but so is the wine and chocolate tasting put on for visitors. Who could rather (or also) choose a 'wine drive safari' around the farm's 120 hectares, including the conservation areas; or just concentrate on the wines. The flagship Jem returns this year, after not being made in the 2008 vintage, as part-owner and cellarmaster Kevin Arnold felt the quality was not adequate. Including seven of the farm's 11 grape varieties makes this an unusually comprehensive reflection of Waterford soils, aspects and climates — but it remains something of a work-in-progress in looking for the perfect expressive blend.

Waterford Estate range

★★★★☆ **Cabernet Sauvignon** Sleekly muscular **09** very youthful & tight — surely needs 5 years to express its fruit (as revealed in flavour persistence) in complex harmony with forceful tannins. Undoubtedly impressive, but still a touch forbidding.

★★★★☆ **Reserve Chardonnay** Single-vineyard, natural ferment **11** less forthcoming in youth than standard version, but subtly exudes quality. Restrained but forceful, with oaky note over the citrus & fruit intensity veined by insistent acidity — really well balanced. Drinking now, but will benefit from ageing.

★★★★☆ **CWG Auction Reserve BB** NEW The 25% merlot blended with cab in this fine, rich **09** both adds fruitcake notes to the intriguing aromas, & makes it suppler, readier for drinking than the straight Cab — though tannins really need 5+ years to soften. A notably pleasing texture. Good dry finish.

★★★★☆ **The Jem** Cab & shiraz plus 5 other varieties in rich & grand **09** (no **08** made). Supple & silky, refined but generous & modern in its fruit insistence — all superbly balanced on quite a big scale. Will develop further complexity & harmony with good few years but readier to drink now than the cab and cab-heavy blends.

★★★★ **Chardonnay** Unshowy, elegant **11** drinking well already (though no hurry, should develop 5+ years); lightly rich & creamy, with sweet limy fruit & fine thread of acidity.

★★★★ **Sauvignon Blanc** Ripe grenadilla & citrus (tangerine rather than grapefruit) in restrained mode on balanced, fresh & not too intense **11**. Tasty, but a little less impressive than **10** (★★★★★).

Rose Mary 🖷 ★★★★ The palest of pale-gold pinks, with a delicately fruity character to match on **11**. Beautifully poised, dry & elegant.

Library Collection

★★★★ **Edition SBS** ⊕ **07** blend sauvignon, semillon — the latter's lanolin & lemon prominent, but the flavours showing maturity. Soft, lingering, well balanced. For pleasurable drinking soonish.

★★★★ **Edition CSMCF** NEW **09** half cab, with merlot & cab franc — which adds a leafy-spicy character. The lightest-feeling & liveliest of the cab-based wines; dry tannins but a good fruit sweetness. Will develop.

★★★★ **Edition CSS** ⊕ Combo cabernet, sangiovese, shiraz works oddly & interestingly well! Youthful **08** dry & succulently savoury; fresh red fruit packed on firm structure. Italianesque finish of sour cherries.

Edition MB ⊕ ★★★★ Shiraz-based 'Mediterranean blend'. **04** shows marked ripeness on aromas, flavours — tasty, but slightly unharmonious with dry tannic presence.

Waterford range   *purchased*

✓ ★★★★☆ **Kevin Arnold Shiraz** Lovely dark notes on **09** (berries, olive) along with cedary element (but no new barrels used) that should integrate with the few years needed for this powerful, assertive wine to relax. Strong tannins now slightly drying, beneath sweet fruit & rich but fine-grained texture. Has 10% mourvèdre.

★★★★ **Heatherleigh Family Reserve** Lightly oaked muscat-based **NV** dessert (up to 5 vintages); chenin, chardonnay, viognier in latest. Fragrant, charmingly delicate & not too sweet. Some Swartland grapes.

Elgin Pinot Noir ★★★★ Adds origin to name with **11**. Good varietal character; insubstantial, but some charm, nicely dry. Less toasty than previous. **Elgin Sauvignon Blanc** 🖷 ★★★★ Adds origin to name with **12** — tasted as usual pre-bottling. More overt tropical flavours than Estate version, but simpler. Crisp green succulence.

Pecan Stream range

Chenin Blanc ✓ 🖷 ★★★★ **12** ripe, full & gently fruity. Dollop oaked viognier (ex Elgin & from previous vintage) adds a touch of peach. Refreshing & totally pleasing. **Pebble Hill** ⊕ 🖷 ★★★ Blend shiraz & 4 others. Chunkily built but not too powerful **09** preview is ripely fruity, with easy appeal. **Sauvignon Blanc** 🖷 ★★★ Fresh, ripe, easy-going & deftly delivered **12**, from home & Elgin grapes. Straightforward & unlingering. — TJ

■ **Waterfront Collection** *see* Vaughan Johnson's Wine & Cigar Shop
■ **Waterhof** *see* Waterstone Wines

Waterkloof

Location: Somerset West ■ Map: Helderberg ■ WO: Stellenbosch ■ Est 2004 ■ 1stB 2005 ■ Tasting & sales daily 10-5 ■ Fee R30/6 wines ■ Closed Good Fri, Dec 25 & Jan 1 ■ Cellar tours by appt ■ The Restaurant at Waterkloof (see Restaurants section) ■ Walking/hiking trails ■ Conservation area ■ Art collection on display ■ Tutored horse riding tours with ploughman's platter & wine tasting ■ Owner(s) Paul Boutinot ■ Cellarmaster(s) Werner

Engelbrecht (Jun 2004) ▪ Winemaker(s) Werner Engelbrecht (Jun 2004), with Jacques van der Vyver (Jan 2012) ▪ Viticulturist(s) Christiaan Loots (Jan 2010), advised by Werner Engelbrecht ▪ 120ha/52ha (cabs s/f, grenache, merlot, mourv, shiraz, chard, chenin, sauv, sem, viog) ▪ 450t/10,000cs own label 50% red 45% white 5% rosé ▪ BWI champion ▪ PO Box 2093 Somerset West 7129 ▪ info@waterkloofwines.co.za ▪ www. waterkloofwines.co.za ▪ S 34° 5′55.4″ E 018° 53′22.8″ ▪ **T +27 (0)21-858-1292** ▪ F +27 (0)21-858-1293

British wine merchant Paul Boutinot moved significantly towards realising his vision of a 'sustainable, eco-conscious wine farm' in Stellenbosch, when the estate's formal certification process as a biodynamic producer was started in 2012. There's much involved in their farming practices that is more earthbound than the cosmos and esoteric mysticism: like two percheron horses joining the team that replaces heavy equipment in ploughing, spraying and harvesting. Along with the cows, sheep ('nature's weed-eaters') and chickens they play their part — as do the denizens of the earthworm farm. And showing that elegance in bricks and mortar is not ignored, Waterkloof also won the Best Architecture and Landscape award in the local section of the Great Wine Capitals competition in 2012.

Waterkloof range

★★★★ **Circle of Life Red** 🍽 🍷 **10** from merlot (for accessibility), shiraz (fragrance & spice) & tiny dollops of 3 others (added interest, no doubt). Balanced for easy & early but not trivial drinking. Delightful.

★★★★☆ **Sauvignon Blanc** ⓐ 🍷 **10** open & expressive, with flavours expanding & proliferating as they linger. Some invisible sugar softens acidity, adds breadth. Takes Circumstance version to higher level.

★★★★ **Circle of Life White** 🍽 🍷 Harmonious, flavourful **11** mix sauvignon & chenin with touches of a few others, sensitively oaked. Silkily rich (clearly not bone-dry), stressing personality rather than simple fruit.

Circumstance range

★★★★☆ **Syrah** 🍽 🍷 **10** as usual the star of the range, flaunting its floral-spicy charm, yet serious — & modest in the best sense of the word. Quietly assertive, succulent & satisfying, with a sweet edge to its juicy fruit & dry finish. Approachable, but should respond well to ±5 years in bottle.

★★★★ **Chardonnay** 🍽 🍷 Attractive, rather simple **10** (★★★★) has same light-feeling moderate alcohol (12.5%) & restraint in **09**. New-oak fermentation & maturation shows, but blends with lemony fruit.

★★★★ **Sauvignon Blanc** 🍽 🍷 Always a characterful, slightly different version. Intense fruit character & some weight on **12**, but not flamboyant, with a savoury element & a big structuring acidity.

Cabernet Sauvignon 🍽 🍷 ★★★★ **10** the most successful yet, nudging higher rating. Carries its big alcohol lightly & lithely. Good sweet fruit but dry finish. **Merlot** 🍽 🍷 ★★★★ **10** far from plump varietal stereotype — a bit lean & tannic rather, but herbal element restrained. Respectable rather than exciting. **Cape Coral Mourvèdre** ⓐ 🍽 ★★★ Dry, unfruity, understated **11** rosé. Round & balanced with a little finishing bite. **Chenin Blanc** 🍽 🍷 ★★★★ The usual overt oakiness on **11** partly obscures the fruit's depth & character, but much still to enjoy: creamy texture, fresh vitality, flavour intensity. **Viognier** 🍽 🍷 ★★★★ **11** as usual with good but comparatively restrained floral peachy character, though less successfully balanced than **10** (★★★★). Big alcohol, a little sugar & a lot of oak produce a somewhat hot & clumsy finish. Note: Peacock Ridge range now listed under False Bay Vineyards. — TJ

Waterstone Wines

Location: Somerset West ▪ Map: Helderberg ▪ WO: Western Cape/Stellenbosch/Coastal ▪ Est/1stB 2007 ▪ Tasting, sales & cellar tours by appt ▪ Closed all pub hols & Dec 15-Jan 3 ▪ Tour groups ▪ Self-catering accommodation ▪ Owner(s) Pim de Lijster & Reino Kruger ▪ Cellarmaster(s)/winemaker(s) Clinton le Sueur (Jan 2011) ▪ 41ha (cab, merlot, ptage, shiraz, chard, merlot, sauv) ▪ 40,000cs own label 65% red 35% white ▪ Other export brand: Compadre ▪ PO Box 1560 Somerset West 7129 ▪ info@waterstonewines.co.za ▪ www. waterstonewines.co.za ▪ S 34° 2′0.3″ E 018° 48′34.8″ ▪ **T +27 (0)21-842-2942** ▪ F +27 (0)86-505-8691

Owners Pim de Lijster and Reino Kruger chose the name 'Waterstone' for their substantial brand because it joins two natural elements — a symbol of foundational strength and a vital condition for life. It also speaks to the partnership between nature and man, working together to create something of pleasure and enjoyment. Proof of the successful liaison lies in the accolades their wines have achieved over the years, including 16 wines in South Africa's 2013 Best Value Guide.

Waterhof range

Cabernet Sauvignon Reserve ⓟ ★★★ Sweet fruit & vanilla oak notes on **08**, bitter cherry astringency, may have mellowed. **Shiraz Reserve** ⓟ ★★★ **07** harked back to Old Cape with sweet-sour flavours, but had good length & balance. **Chardonnay Reserve** ★★★ Creamy, faint lemon & lime flavours on **11**; tad dilute finish. **Sauvignon Blanc Reserve** ⓟ ★★★★ Showing best varietal character & balance at commendably moderate alcohol, **10** was stand-out in range. These mostly WO Stellenbosch.

Africa range

Bomvu ☺ 🍴 ★★★ Easy-drinking, refreshing **11** cab/shiraz, bright red fruit & friendly grip. **Ifula** ☺ 🍴 ★★★ Was 'Infulu'. Grass & thatch **11** mainly sauvignon with dollop chenin; quiet but good vinosity. This range WO Coastal.

Africa Five range

Pinotage ☺ ★★★ Lovely strawberry, faint acetone varietal character on **11**. Sleek & light-footed. **Cape Premier Red** ☺ ★★★ Now **NV**. Good cassis attack on latest, lipsmacking follow through; characterful campfire sipper. All reds in range lightly oaked.

Cabernet Sauvignon ★★ Sherbety foursquare **11**. **Merlot** ★★★ Lightly oaked **11** for youthful sipping; juicy & brisk. **Shiraz** 🍴 ★★ **11** woody, with juicy sweet tail. **Cabernet Sauvignon-Shiraz** Not tasted. **Chardonnay** ★★★ Lemon tones, some creaminess on evanescent **11**. **Chenin Blanc** ⓟ ★★ Thatch & pear drop nuances, **11** soft pithy grip. WO Stellenbosch. **Sauvignon Blanc** ⓟ 🍴 ★★★ **11** standout white in range, uncomplex but unmistakably sauvignon.

African Lizard

Cabernet Sauvignon In abeyance, as are **Shiraz**, **Cape Premier Red Blend**, **Chardonnay** & **Chenin Blanc**.

Cape Discovery range

Pinotage NEW ☺ ★★★ **NV** glugger with strawberries, juicy centre, slight bitter lift.

Cabernet Sauvignon ⓟ ★★ Solid fruit centre, firm tannin on **10** quick-quaff. **Chardonnay** ★★ Faint peachy hint on **NV** (previously vintage dated). **Sauvignon Blanc** NEW ★★ Asparagus & cream burst on off-dry **NV**.

Golden Vine

Shiraz ⓟ ★★ Red-fruited **09** leathery & meaty. WO Stellenbosch. **Cape Premier Red** NEW ★★★ Gruff but likeable **11** led by merlot, offers pleasant light fruit.

Opener's range

Rosé ☺ 🍴 ★★★ Easy-drinking **11** from sauvignon with dollop merlot, thus more grassy than berry but still lots of off-dry fun. **Chenin Blanc** ☺ 🍴 ★★★ **11** leading the bunch with thatch, stonefruit & pear; satisfying vinosity; moderate alcohol for lunchtime enjoyment. WO Stellenbosch, like Rosé & Sauvignon.

Cabernet Sauvignon 🍴 ★★★ Vibrant raspberry appeal, spice & herb notes on plump **10**. **Merlot** 🍴 ★★ **11** plums & cream, soft & brief. These reds lightly oak-staved. **Dry Red** 🍴 Not tasted. **Sauvignon Blanc** NEW ★★ Drink-soon **11** has fig, slight funky notes.

Sonata range

Cabernet Sauvignon 🍴 ★★★ Improved **10** raspberry & clean leather wafts, rounded tannins; neat dinner companion. **The Ludwig** ⓟ 🍴 ★★ Gruff **04** blend; raisiny, dominated by merlot. **Chenin Blanc** 🍴 ★★★ Reticent floral & thatch nose on fresh **11**; chill for maximum enjoyment. **Sauvignon Blanc** 🍴 ★★★ Now bottled, **11** offers nettles, fresh hay; palate-cleansing sweet-sour acidity. — CvZ

Waverley Hills Organic Wines & Olives   🍷🍴🎋📷☕👜

Location/map/WO: Tulbagh ▪ Est 2006 ▪ 1stB 2004 ▪ Tasting, sales & cellar tours Mon-Fri 8-5 Sat 10-4 Sun 11-3 ▪ Closed Easter Fri/Mon & Dec 25 ▪ Restaurant Tue-Fri 9-4 Sat 10-4 Sun 11-3 & Wed evenings ▪ Picnic baskets by appt; or BYO picnic ▪ Facilities for children ▪ Tour groups ▪ Farm produce ▪ Conferences ▪ Wedding venue & chapel ▪ Walks/hikes ▪ Mountain biking ▪ Conservation area ▪ Fynbos nursery & eco-centre ▪ Owner(s) Brenn-O-Kem (Pty) Ltd ▪ Cellarmaster(s) Johan Delport (Oct 2008) ▪ Winemaker(s) Albert Viljoen, with Andre Ewerts (Dec 2006/Jul 2008) ▪ Viticulturist(s) Johan Greeff (May 2012) ▪ 80ha/30ha (cab, grenache, merlot, mourv, shiraz, chard, pinot gris, sauv, sem, viog) ▪ 230t/10,000cs own label 75% red 15% white 5% rosé 5% MCC ▪ Other export brand: Dixon's Peak ▪ BWI Champion, WIETA ▪ PO Box 71 Wolseley 6830 ▪ info@waverleyhills.co.za ▪ www.waverleyhills. co.za ▪ S 33° 24' 21.2" E 019° 14' 19.6" ▪ **T +27 (0)23-231-0002** ▪ F +27 (0)23-231-0004

Success for this Tulbagh eco-minded farm and visitor destination, with a second-year-running Great Wine Capitals Sustainable Tourism award and local recognition for environmental officer Johann van Biljon, while the Shiraz 2009 took gold at Veritas 2011 and the 2009 Shiraz-Mourvèdre-Viognier was voted Best Southern Hemisphere Organic Wine at the Bordeaux Challenge International du Vin.

Cabernet Sauvignon ⊕ ✿ ⬚ ★★★ Modern, plush **10** (with drop merlot) has toffee-sweet impression from oak. **Cabernet Sauvignon No Added Sulphites** NEW 🍴 ✿ ⬚ ★★★ Pre-bottling, **12**'s ripe blackberry flavour lifted by 100% new American oak. Attractively styled, for early enjoyment. **Shiraz** ✿ ⬚ ★★★ Ultra-ripe **10** has port-like aroma & strong tannins, notch down on previous, which was soft & rounded. **CW Reserve Shiraz** NEW ✿ ⬚ ★★★☆ Limited-release (only 960 bottles), premium-priced bottling from tiny parcel within existing vineyard, minuscule 2t yield. **10** tentatively rated preview still cloaked in oak (100% new French) mid-2012, needs time to meld, show its true potential. **Cabernet Sauvignon-Merlot** ⊕ ✿ ★★★ Sweetish **09** 50/50 blend, warming alcohol showing on finish. **Shiraz-Mourvèdre-Viognier** ✿ ⬚ ★★★ **10** full-bodied (15.4% alc) & flavoursome, needs hearty food to cushion the very dry tannins. **Cabernet Sauvignon-Shiraz** ⊕ ✿ ⬚ ★★★ Juicy & spicy **10** preview, dash merlot gives herbal lift. **Rosé** 🍴 ✿ ⬚ ★★ Strawberries-&-cream appeal, tangy acidity on improved **11** make for easy summer dry sipping. **Pinot Grigio** NEW 🍴 ✿ ⬚ ★★ Crisp acidity softened by touch sugar on earthy **12** tank sample. **Sauvignon Blanc-Semillon** 🍴 ✿ ⬚ ★★★ 'Semillon-Sauvignon Blanc' previously. **12**, sampled from tank, led by sauvignon (60%) this time, light & bright for summer enjoyment. **Viognier-Semillon-Chardonnay** NEW 🍴 ✿ ⬚ ★★★ Ex tank, **11** shows promise with interleaving of spicy oak, apricot & white peach, generous body & pleasant dry finish. **Méthode Cap Classique Brut** ✿ ⬚ ★★★ 'Brut' added to name in **10** from chardonnay/semillon. Notch up; expressive gingerbread bouquet, brisk creamy mousse. — WB/AL/IM

▪ **Weathered Hands** *see Dewaldt Heyns Family Wines*

Webersburg Wines   🍴☕🏠📷♿

Location/map/WO: Stellenbosch ▪ Est 1995 ▪ 1stB 1996 ▪ Tasting, sales & cellar tours Mon-Fri 10-5 Sat 10-4 ▪ Fee R5/wine ▪ Closed Ash Wed, Easter Fri-Mon, Dec 25/26 & Jan 1 ▪ Seasonal menu's ▪ Tour groups ▪ Historic buildings: Manor House 1786; cellar & Jonkershuis 1796 ▪ 5-star Cape Dutch Guesthouse ▪ Conferences ▪ Weddings/functions ▪ Owner(s) Fred Weber ▪ Winemaker(s) Giorgio Dalla Cia & Matthew van Heerden (both consultants) ▪ Viticulturist(s) Johan Pienaar (consultant) ▪ 20ha/5ha (cab) ▪ 30t/2,000cs own label 80% red 20% white ▪ PO Box 3428 Somerset West 7129 ▪ info@webersburg.co.za ▪ www.webersburg.co.za ▪ S 34° 0' 22.1" E 018° 50' 34.5" ▪ **T +27 (0)21-881-3636** ▪ F +27 (0)21-881-3217

With the beautifully restored Cape Dutch buildings in the Helderberg foothills available for accommodation and functions like weddings — for which two méthode cap classique sparklings (untasted by us) have been produced — one can understand the steady stream of visitors here. However, owner Fred Weber does not believe in pandering to fashion, which is evident in the wines, elegant and ageable, and his long association with estimable winemaker Giorgio Dalla Cia.

★★★★ **Cabernet Sauvignon** Always released after sufficient oak & bottle age to ensure market readiness, **07** (★★★★★) gives even greater pleasure than **06**. Complex, involving & harmonious, with great finesse.

★★★★ **Sauvignon Blanc** ✓ 🍴 Shows an individual style. Melon & apple is the main fruit profile of **11**, cloaking a seam of minerality that keeps it pure & tightly focused.

Webersburg Await new vintage. — CR

Wedderwill Wine Estate   🍴🍷🏛🏠📷♿

Location: Sir Lowry's Pass ▪ Map: Helderberg ▪ WO: Stellenbosch ▪ Est 1992 ▪ 1stB 1997 ▪ Tasting, sales & tours by appt Mon-Fri 9-5 Sat 9-12 ▪ R200 for the first 6 people, R30pp for over 6 people ▪ Closed all pub hols ▪ Farm produce ▪ BYO picnic ▪ Guided walks/mountain bike tours T +27 (0)82-462-3624 Di Marais ▪ Game reserve ▪ Conservation area ▪ Conference/function facilities ▪ Lalapanzi Lodge T +27 (0)21-858-1982 & Cape Country Living T +27 (0)21-858-1607 ▪ Owner(s) Neil Ian Jowell & Cecil Jowell ▪ Cellarmaster(s) Nico Vermeulen ▪ Winemaker(s) Nico Vermeulen (Jun 2004) ▪ Viticulturist(s) Wolfgang von Loeper (Apr 2004) ▪ 400ha/41ha (cab, merlot, shiraz, sauv) ▪ 80-100t/15,000cs own label 60% red 40% white ▪ BWI champion, Carbon Neutral, Control Union Organic,

Demeter Biodynamic, IPW ▪ PO Box 75 Sir Lowry's Pass 7133 ▪ sales@wedderwill.co.za ▪ www.wedderwill.co.za ▪
S 34° 5'55.0" E 018° 56'42.0" ▪ **T** +27 (0)21-858-1558 ▪ F +27 (0)21-858-1461

The name, 'Will of the Weather', encapsulates this Hottentots Holland Mountain
farm's strong relationship with nature. Besides biodynamic farming, sustainability
is key here, with recycling, waste management, energy and water conservation
projects successfully implemented and fully supported by the staff. As a BWI Champion, they've cleared 180ha of alien vegetation, set aside a 27ha reserve for
endemic game, and are rehabilitating 4ha of wetlands and another 4km of river
beds. A special site, and they're taking the responsibility seriously.

★★★★ **Shiraz** Return to form for vibrantly youthful, late-released **07**. Peppery spices laced with maraschino
cherries, all very Rhône-like. Classy, well-judged oak & supple body. Improves on **06** (★★★★).

★★★★☆ **Sauvignon Blanc** Elegant, sophisticated **11** (★★★★) maintains a high standard with rip
understated fruit on mineral lees-rich body. Modest 12.5% alcohol. Just a shade less intense than **10**.

Wedderwill Await next, as for **17degreeC** & **12degreeC**. — GdB

Wederom Boutique Winery

Location/map: Robertson ▪ WO: Western Cape/Robertson ▪ Est 2002 ▪ 1stB 2003 ▪ Tasting, sales & cellar tour
by appt ▪ Fee R20pp tasting/tour ▪ Closed Good Fri & Dec 25 ▪ Meals by appt ▪ Tour groups ▪ Gifts ▪ Farm produce ▪ Conferences ▪ Weddings/functions ▪ Hikes ▪ Conservation area ▪ Italian prisoner of war museum ▪
Hanepoot Huisies guesthouse ▪ Owner(s) Philip & Almien du Toit ▪ Cellarmaster(s)/winemaker(s)/viticulturist(s) Philip du Toit ▪ 111ha/±17ha (cinsaut, merlot, shiraz) ▪ ±130t/419cs own label 100% red + 42t grapes
for clients ▪ IPW ▪ PO Box 60 Robertson 6705 ▪ wederom@myisp.co.za ▪ www.wederom.co.za ▪ S 33° 49'5.5
E 019° 47' 15.8" ▪ **T** +27 (0)23-626-4139 ▪ F +27 (0)23-626-3306

A barn gable at this Italian-toned Robertson winery features a mural in the naif
style depicting Italian prisoners of war, captured in Abyssinia (Ethiopia) in 1943
working in the Wederom vineyards. Featured prominently is the cook Salvadori
memorialised a second time on the label of the Du Toit family's shiraz.

Shiraz ★★☆ Smoked meat & red fruit, **10**'s savouriness & firm flavours perfect for Du Toits' suggested oxtail
game birds & strong cheeses. **Salvadori Vino Rosso Shiraz** ★★☆ Exuberant, charry **10** as advertised
'whole day, everyday drinking wine'. — CvZ/MW

Wedgewood Wines

Location: Robertson ▪ WO: Stellenbosch/Swartland ▪ Est 2007 ▪ 1stB 2010 ▪ Closed to public ▪ Wine order
Mon-Sat 9-5 from export offices: Nordic Wines, Robertson ▪ Owner(s) Wiggo Andersen & Peter Tillman
Winemaker(s)/viticulturist(s) Marius Malan (Nov 2010, consultant) ▪ Other export brand: Selma ▪ PO Box 89
Robertson 6705 ▪ nordicwines@xpoint.co.za, wedgewoodwines@xpoint.co.za ▪ www.nordicwines.co.za
T +27 (0)23-626-1413/+27 (0)83-283-5354 ▪ F +27 (0)23-626-1031

This main brand of Nordic Wines, whose focus is Norway, Sweden and Finland a
well as the hotel, restaurant and catering markets, is sourced from producer
meeting integrity as well as quality criteria. 'Increased preference for organic
and Fairtrade wines in the overseas market is promoting social responsibility in
South Africa,' observes co-owner Peter Tillman.

Director's Choice range
Cabernet Sauvignon-Merlot ⊕ 🍴 ★★★ Understated **09** appealing combo of cedar & savoury rip
berry. **Malbec-Pinotage** 🍴 Await next. **Chenin Blanc** ⊕ 🍴 ★★★ Thatch & peach nuances, tang
lime-apricot tail on juicy **10** from venerable Malmesbury vines. — DB

Welbedacht Wine Estate

Location/WO: Wellington ▪ Map: Paarl & Wellington ▪ Est/1stB 2005 ▪ Tasting, sales & cellar tours Mon-Fri 9-
Sat 9-2 ▪ Fee R15 ▪ Closed Dec 25 & Jan 1 ▪ No. 6 @ Welbedacht (see Restaurants section) ▪ Facilities for children ▪ Tour groups ▪ Gifts ▪ BYO picnic ▪ Conferences ▪ Welbedacht Cricket Oval ▪ Bradgate Manor House (see
Accommodation section) ▪ Owner(s) Schalk Burger Family Trust ▪ Winemaker(s) Hein Hesebeck & Rob Gowe
(both Jan 2012) ▪ Viticulturist(s) Tony Julies (Jan 2007, consultant) ▪ 140ha/130ha (19 varieties r/w) ▪ 1,300
75% red 20% white 5% rosé ▪ IPW ▪ PO Box 51 Wellington 7654 ▪ tiaan@welbedacht.co.za ▪ www

meerkatwines.co.za, www.schalkburgerandsons.co.za ▪ S 33° 34'39.8" E 019° 1'12.8" ▪ **T +27 (0)21-873-1877** ▪ F +27 (0)86-669-5641

Both new wines from this established family farm in Wellington have stories to tell. Mon René, the MCC named after Schalk and Moira Burger's daughter, was served at her January 2012 wedding. Copious bottles were also at hand to toast Schalk Burger junior at his wedding the previous month and later in the year at the arrival of the first Burger grandchild. The Patriot has a less obvious association with Welbedacht. It takes its name (and Gothic script) from the first Afrikaans newspaper, Die Afrikaanse Patriot, published in the Cape in the 1870s. The editor, CP Hoogenhout, taught for many years at the Groenberg school on the farm.

Schalk Burger & Sons Proprietors Reserve range

★★★★ **No. 6** ⊕ Striking shiraz-led 6-way mix. **06** (★★★★☆) plush fruitcake & plum spice, big & bold but harmonious, lithe as a flank brushing off a tackler. 2 years older French oak. Step up on **05**.

★★★★ **Myra** ⊕ Last tasted was **07** viognier, chenin, chardonnay blend. Oxidative styling, rich & satiny.

Mon René NEW ★★★★ Extra-dry MCC sparkling from chardonnay, named for Burger daughter. **NV** with emerging & well-sustained toasty, creamy notes; fine, lively bubble adds to overall elegance.

Welbedacht Estate range

★★★★ **Cabernet Sauvignon Barrique Select** ⊕ Stylish **08**, structured & concentrated from 2 years 50% new oak, offers ample cranberry & fynbos in rich, dry body. Maintains refined & supple standard of **07**.

★★★★ **Merlot Barrique Select** ⊕ **08** matches **07**'s promise. Ripe mulberry & cocoa depth. Soft texture yet firm structure from 2 years French oak, 15% new. Stylish & refined. Lengthy too.

★★★★ **Syrah** ⊕ 🍷 Plush fruit vies with fresh acid in **08**, made for long haul. Nuanced, deep, smoky & spicy with dry tannin & solid centre. Follows improved **07** in terms of concentration, length.

★★★★ **Cricket Pitch** ⊕ **08** hit for 4! Striking cassis & cigar spice on rich, soft palate. Harmony of fruit, acid & wood. Gentle but structured blend of cab, merlot & cab franc. Lesser **07** (★★★★) preview needed time.

★★★★ **Hat Trick** ⊕ Textured length previously on three-way Cape Blend, pinotage (50%) with shiraz, merlot. **07** had blueberry, plum & nutmeg spice. Juicy & rounded.

Pinotage ★★★★ Refined, just-dry **10** charms with hint of pinot parentage in its dark cherry features, supple mouthfeel. Carefully managed & integrated tannins add form, freshness. Good now, 3-4 years. **09** (★★★★) dense with dry tannin. **Patriot** NEW ★★★★ Merlot-led Bordeaux quartet in showy (for this producer) style. Ready **08** fronted by spicy oak, with ripe fruit spread smoothly to sweetish conclusion. **Chardonnay Barrel Fermented** ⊕ 🍷 ★★★★ **09** keeps the standard. Creamy orange blossom on broad palate. Juicy & fresh from natural fermentation. **Chenin Blanc Barrel Fermented** ⊕ 🍷 ★★★ Rich tarte tatin on previewed **09**, ample width on palate & finish. Wood a bit prominent, needing time to settle. **Sauvignon Blanc** 🍷 ★★★ For those who like some perkiness but unshowy fruit in sauvignon, **12** fits the bill. Medium-bodied summer sipping.

Meerkat range

Pinotage 🍷 ⊘ ★★★ Friendly & forthcoming raspberry juiciness on **11**; straightforward but with good substance. Fruitily sweet close balances bold alcohol. **Burrow Blend** 🍷 ★★★ Velvety merlot lifted by splashes spicy cab franc, petit verdot. Just-dry — few grams sugar increases easy drinkability on **09**. **Pinotage Rosé** 🍷 ★★ Wild strawberries & cream flavours in gently fresh, sweetish **12**. **Sun Angel Semi-Sweet** 🍷 ★★ Juicy, soft but uncloying **NV** semi-sweet from chardonnay. Previously vintaged. **Chenin Blanc** 🍷 ⊘ ★★★ Tropical fruits with apricot whiff from dollop viognier on smoothly dry **12**. Plump but unheavy. **Sauvignon Blanc** NEW 🍷 ★★☆ **12** showing restraint in its figgy notes; gently fresh, fruitily dry. — AL

Welgegund Wines

Location: Wellington ▪ Map: Paarl & Wellington ▪ WO: Wellington/Western Cape/Paarl ▪ Est 1800 ▪ 1stB 1997 ▪ Tasting & sales by appt at Welgegund farm ▪ B&B cottage with pool & tennis court ▪ Walks ▪ Wine sales & cellar tours at Boutique Baratok (see entry) ▪ Owner(s) Alex & Sheila Camerer ▪ Cellarmaster(s)/winemaker(s)/viticulturist(s) Daniël Langenhoven (Jun 2008) ▪ 35ha/15ha (carignan, cinsaut, ptage, chenin) ▪ 84t/320cs own label 62% red 38% white ▪ PO Box 683 Wellington 7654 ▪ sales@welgegund.co.za ▪ www.welgegund.co.za ▪ S 33° 39'38.3" E 019° 2'13.6" ▪ **T +27 (0)21-873-2123** ▪ F +27 (0)21-873-2683

Alex and Sheila Camerer's boutique-sized Wellington winery shares winemaking facilities with other small producers in Boutique Baratok cellar at Zomerlust Guest House in Paarl. The range may also be tasted there. On a wider scale, exports to China and Eastern Europe are being explored.

★★★★ **Pinotage** ⊕ Bright hue, buchu & cherry aromas mark **10**. Silkiness clipped by fine, freshening tannins; long savoury, liquorice tail. Mostly new oak a subtle enrichment.

★★★★☆ **Chiara** ⊕ 🍽 Grenache blanc joins chenin, chardonnay, sauvignon & viognier in **10**. Haunting complexity on aromas & suave, smooth-textured palate. Oaked portion highlights pure vinosity. WO Paarl.

Ricco ★★★★ Ripe & rich fruitcake, spice bouquet on retasted **09** shiraz-led blend with splash barbera. Soft core, smooth, with 15.2% alcohol glow, sweetness. WO W Cape. **Divina Carignan-Pinotage Rosé** ⊕ 🍽 ★★★ Uncomplicated plum, straw hints were noted few years back on **09**. — AL

Welgeleë Boutique Wedding & Wine Farm

Location: Paarl ▪ Map: Paarl & Wellington ▪ Est 1999 ▪ 1stB 2003 ▪ Tasting & sales daily 9–5 ▪ Picnics by appt ▪ Function venues (±45 & 160 pax) ▪ Owner(s) Liris Trust (Chris & Lidea Meyer) ▪ Winemaker(s) Chris Meyer ▪ Viticulturist(s) Chris & Lidea Meyer ▪ 26ha/3ha (shiraz) ▪ 300cs 100% red ▪ PO Box 439 Klapmuts 7625 ▪ chris@welgelee.com ▪ www.welgelee.com ▪ S 33°47′45.3″ E 018°53′35.4″ ▪ **T +27 (0)21-875-5726** ▪ F +27 (0)21-875-5726

Chris and Lidea Meyer ceased circumnavigating the world's oceans to settle on this small wine estate near Paarl, tapping into the growing market for winelands weddings and country conferences. Contributing to the farm's charm — it's home to the couple's two children, pack of dogs and field full of horses — is a handmade shiraz.

Welgemeend Estate

Location/WO: Paarl ▪ Map: Paarl & Wellington ▪ Est 1974 ▪ 1stB 1979 ▪ Tasting, sales & cellar tours Mon-Fri 10–4 Sat 10–2 ▪ Closed all pub hols ▪ Owner(s) Welgemeend Estate (Pty) Ltd ▪ Winemaker(s) Lizette Steyn-James (Mar 2007), with Abraham Suse (Jan 2008) ▪ Viticulturist(s) Lizette Steyn-James (Mar 2007) ▪ 16ha/11ha (cabs s/f, grenache, malbec, merlot, ptage, shiraz) ▪ 19t own label 100% red ▪ PO Box 1408 Suider-Paarl 7624 ▪ welgemeend@worldonline.co.za ▪ www.welgemeend.co.za ▪ S 33° 47′50.8″ E 018° 53′8.5″ ▪ **T +27 (0)21-875-5210** ▪ F +27 (0)86-654-3806

A strategy of reverting to its classic Billy Hofmeyr roots is unfolding (Hofmeyr was the francophile founder/winemaker of this in many ways pioneering Paarl boutique estate). Earlier release of the reds is in process, the new label is based on the original, and plans have been approved to upgrade the homestead for function use. And another classic is on its way: a white Bordeaux blend.

Estate Reserve ★★★★ First commercial Cape Bordeaux red blend in 1979. Merlot-led **06** appeals with cassis, violets, backed by firm dry tannin, 2 years oaking. **Douelle** ★★★★ Mainly malbec & cab, giving **06**'s fruit a tarry, liquorice character. Well structured, enough flesh to handle the dry tannins. **Soopjeshoogte** ★★★ Simpler blend than stablemates, in **06** cab/merlot. Dark plums & violets, noteworthy elegance (12.5% alc) & grippy dry finish. **Amadé** ⊕ ★★★ Individual blend, shiraz with grenache, pinotage, gives **05** enough brambleberry fruit to balance the sturdy tannins. — CR

■ **Welgevallen Cellar-Stellenbosch University** *see* Stellenbosch University Welgevallen Cellar

Welgevallen Wines

Location/map/WO: Stellenbosch ▪ Est/1stB 2000 ▪ Visits Mon-Fri 10–2 ▪ Closed pub & school hols ▪ Owner(s) Paul Roos Gymnasium Old Boys Union ▪ Winemaker(s)/viticulturist(s) Wouter Pienaar & Tinnie Momberg (consultants) ▪ 400cs own label 75% red 25% white ▪ c/o Paul Roos Gymnasium Old Boys Union Suidwal Stellenbosch 7600 ▪ oldboys@prg.wcape.school.za ▪ www.paulroos.co.za ▪ S 33° 56′31.2″ E 018° 51′41.1″ ▪ **T +27 (0)21-883-8627** ▪ F +27 (0)21-883-8627

Funds from the sale of Welgevallen wines assist talented boys from economically disadvantaged families attend one of Stellenbosch's most prestigious institutions Paul Roos Gymnasium. Welgevallen, the farm on which the school was built, translates loosely as 'well received', and that's exactly what is hoped for the latest offerings, Jolla Bolla Rouge and Blanc. The wines below also available at press time.

Pinotage ⊕ ★★★★ **09** succulent & smooth, worth seeking out as much for palate appeal as for noble (fund-raising) intentions. **Cabernet Sauvignon-Merlot** ⊕ ★★★ Good expression of the varieties in **09**, plum/violet merlot aromas, firm cab tannins, zesty acidity. **Sauvignon Blanc** ⊕ 🍽 ★★★ **11** delivers gravelly texture & weight absent in previous, though still tad closed mid-2011, may show better given time. — CvZ

Wellington Wines

Location/WO: Wellington ▪ Map: Paarl & Wellington ▪ Est 1941 ▪ Tasting & sales Mon-Fri 8–5 Sat 8.30–12.30 ▪ Closed all pub hols ▪ Cellar tours by appt ▪ Owner(s) 70 shareholders ▪ Production manager Gert Boerssen (Oct 1980) ▪ Winemaker(s) Pieter-Niel Rossouw (Jun 2009), Chris Smit (Nov 2005), Hugo Truter (Oct 2005) & Fritz Smit (Jan 2009) ▪ Viticulturist(s) Marko Roux (Nov 2008) ▪ 2,400ha ▪ 27,000t ▪ 60% red 40% white ▪ BWI, BRC, Fairtrade, IPW, WIETA ▪ PO Box 509 Wellington 7654 ▪ sales@wellingtonwines.com ▪ www.wellingtonwines.com ▪ S 33° 38' 17.7" E 018° 59' 20.6" ▪ **T +27 (0)21-873-1582** ▪ F +27 (0)21-873-3194

Wellington Wines was formed in 2011 after the merging of business and production interests of long-time neighbour cellars Wamakersvallei and Wellington. MD Johan Truter relishes the challenge of making the merged entity 'bigger and better' while delivering on the promise to consumers of making handcrafted wines. Their grower base has access to hundreds of hectares of old bushvine chenin in the greater Wellington area, and one of Wellington Wines' goals is to ensure that this vinous heritage is not lost but rather celebrated and acknowledged.

La Cave range

★★★★ **Pinotage** 🧉 **10** maintains the standard of **09** with its raspberry spice vibrancy. Oak regimen well handled, frames the ripe fruit beautifully.

★★★★ **Cape Blend** [NEW] 🧉 Maiden **10** a 3-way pinotage, shiraz, cab mix. Layered black fruit melange that, while succulent & fresh, glides silkily to an intense, long finish.

Cabernet Sauvignon 🧉 ★★★★ Boldly fruited **10** a step up on lighter **09** (★★★☆). Chalky tannic squeeze adds structure while whole remains lithe & elegant. Savoury, supple & long. **Shiraz** ★★★★ Lovely tug between ripe black fruit & earthy char on **10**'s rounded palate. Medium body, fine tannin & length. **VCC** ⊕ 🍽 ★★★★ Barrel-fermented viognier, chenin & chardonnay. Debut **08** tangy & fresh previously, richer peach, pineapple & lemon overlay. Oak restrained: year new French.

Wellington Wines range

Cabernet Sauvignon ⊕ ★★★ Spice & red fruit on maiden **10**, bit short & light bodied. **Pinotage** ⊕ 🍽 🧉 ★★★ Unpretentious berry spice & vanilla, **10** soft consistency with chocolate richness. Previewed, as for all reds. **Shiraz** ⊕ 🍽 🧉 ★★★ **10** displays black cherry spice & some smoky meat. Light, chalky tannin grip. High 15.4% alcohol but still accessible. **Chardonnay** 🍽 🧉 ★★☆ **12** tank sample light, apple-fresh & tangy. **Chenin Blanc** 🍽 🧉 ★★☆ Pear drop & melon life to uncomplicated **12**.

Fortified dessert range

Fishermans Jerepigo In abeyance.

Bain's Way range

Viognier ☺ 🍽 🧉 ★★★ Forward peach & nectarine on lightly textured **11**, oodles of drinking pleasure with ripeness not overplayed.

Merlot 🍽 ★★★ Rich mulberry & cocoa on **09**, structured & firm with light grip & long fruited finish. **Sauvignon Blanc** 🍽 🧉 ★★ Simple lemon/lime tang on uncomplicated **11** quaffer. **Jagters Port** ★★★☆ Last listed under Fortified Desserts. Unpretentious raisined spice on fruity **NV** (**11**) fortified. — FM

Welmoed

This well-priced, easy-drinking range takes its name from the venerable Stellenbosch property Welmoed, once owned by rebel-with-a-cause Jacobus van der Heyden, and nowadays the home of brand owner The Company of Wine People. Achieving wider representation in China and elsewhere in Asia is a brand objective, along with connecting to younger audiences through Twitter tastings, alternative packaging and lightweight bottles.

Shiraz ☺ 🍽 🧉 ★★★ **11** is balanced & bright, with unpretentious pepper & spice. Food friendly quaffer. WO Stellenbosch, as for all reds below. **Rosé** ☺ 🍽 🧉 ★★★ Fruitful & crisp **12**, is a cranberry-toned summer quaffer. WO Western Cape, as for most whites below. **Chardonnay** ☺ 🍽 🧉 ★★★ Appealing **12** is ripe & tangy. Creamy pear & melon flavours have brush of oak & zesty lime thread. Friendly meal mate. **Heyden's Courage White** ☺ 🍽 🧉 ★★★ Preview of **11** is a sauvignon-led, satisfying & flavoursome quaffer. Plump & juicy 6-way blend. WO Coastal. **Sparkling Brut** ☺ ★★★ **NV** delightfully fresh, creamy-textured summer sparkler. Balanced & light, for carefree summer aperitif /picnic.

Cabernet Sauvignon 🍷 🏵 ★★★ More herbaceous, leaner style in **11**, best with food. **Merlot** 🍷 🏵 ★★ Cool & leafy **11** is light, with tart red berry tone. **Pinotage** 🍷 🏵 ★★ Leaner **11** a tad rustic, with touch of spice. **Heyden's Courage Red** ✓ 🍷 🏵 ★★★★ Sample of bold & flavoursome **10** Bordeaux blend, has creamy texture & firm, supple structure. Enjoy over next few years. **Chenin Blanc** 🍷 🏵 ★★★ **12** Bright, crunchy green apple flavours, perfect for a picnic. **Sauvignon Blanc** 🍷 🏵 ★★★★ **12** vivacious & crisp, with melange of tropical & herbaceous flavours & good fruit/acid balance. For solo or mealtime pleasure. **Viognier** NEW 🍷 🏵 ★★★ Light & fresh **12** has spicy, dried apricot tone with pithy twist. — MW

Weltevrede Estate

Location: Bonnievale ▪ Map: Robertson ▪ WO: Robertson/Western Cape ▪ Est 1912 ▪ 1stB 1945 ▪ Tasting & sales Mon-Fri 8–5 Sat 9–3.30 ▪ Closed Easter Fri/Sun, Dec 25/26 & Jan 1 ▪ Cellar tours & underground tasting by appt ▪ Weltevrede Bistro Tue-Sat 9–3.30 ▪ Walks/hikes ▪ Conservation area ▪ Conferences ▪ Weddings/functions ▪ 4 self-catering guest cottages ▪ Owner(s) Lourens Jonker ▪ Cellarmaster(s) Philip Jonker (Jan 1997) ▪ Winemaker(s) Neil Strydom (2009) ▪ Viticulturist(s) Francois Viljoen (consultant) ▪ 360ha/106ha (cab, merlot, pinot, shiraz, chard, cbard, gewürz, sauv) ▪ 1,300t/25,000cs own label 15% red 75% white 10% other ▪ Brands for clients: Woolworths ▪ BWI ▪ PO Box 6 Bonnievale 6730 ▪ info@weltevrede.com ▪ www.weltevrede. com ▪ S 33° 56'30.9" E 020° 3'4.4" ▪ **T +27 (0)23-616-2141** ▪ F +27 (0)23-616-2460

2012 brought dual celebrations for the Jonkers: a century of winemaking on the family farm and the first harvest from a parcel of venerable white-wine vines found in a neglected state on Robben Island at the site where Nelson Mandela buried the manuscript for his famous Long Walk to Freedom. The vines' rejuvenation was entrusted to the Weltevrede Aansporingstrust, an empowerment association whose members for generations have worked the vines on the Bonnievale estate. The revival involved many early morning trips, coping with rough seas and birds that devoured two harvests. Finally, after three challenging years, 2012 yielded a crop, and the first bottle of the resulting wine was proudly presented to South Africa's first democratic president on his 94th birthday.

Estate range

★★★★☆ **Poet's Prayer Chardonnay** 🕐 Developed **07** (★★★★), like oak-rich **06**, from limestone/shale soils. Rich texture, cleansing mineral core & warming alcohol.

★★★★ **The Travelling Stone Sauvignon Blanc** 🕐 Bone-dry & grassy **10** (★★★★) lively, tasty; first reviewed since racy **07**.

Bedrock Black Syrah 🏵 ★★★★ Back-on-track **11** cosseted by restrained oak; has brooding fruit, black pepper complexity & fresh conclusion. **Place of Rocks Chardonnay** 🍷 🏵 ★★★ Fresher, fruitier styling takes **11** up a rung, engaging yellow peach & sweet pear notes, 100% new oak is deferential, no impediment to current enjoyment. **Gewürztraminer** 🕐 🏵 ★★★★ Unshowy but typical rosepetal fragrance in **10**, fruity sweetness lifted by brisk acidity. Discontinued: **Rusted Soil Chardonnay**.

Philip Jonker Brut Cap Classique Collection

★★★★ **Entheos** 🕐 'Energy of spontaneous laughter' apt name for sparkling wine. This NV chardonnay (60%) & pinot noir MCC in more serious vein; brioche nuance, lingering appley refreshment.

Lindelize 🕐 ★★★★ Rosé bottle-fermented bubbly for Philip J's wife; current **NV** is 100% pinot noir, hence the meaty/savoury element, fine firm structure. **The Ring** 🕐 ★★★★ Fresh mineral 'rockpool' highlights, invigorating bubble on **07** bone-dry bubbly from chardonnay. **Aletheia** 🕐 ★★★ **07** richer & sweeter than stablemate sparklings. Oak-daubed pinot noir/chardonnay combo.

Simplicity range

Cherrychoc Merlot NEW 🍷 🏵 ★★★ Appropriately named **11** has milk chocolate & sweet cherry appeal, like Chardonnay kissed by new oak & smoothed by grain sugar to boost crowd appeal. **Vanilla Chardonnay** 🍷 🏵 ★★★ Was 'Chardonnay' in 'Vanilla' range, now rechristened. **11** as advertised: vanilla permeated, moderate 12.5% alcohol for anytime sipping. **Trop!co Sauvignon Blanc** NEW 🍷 🏵 ★★★ Breezy **12**'s tropical appeal spiced up with whiff white pepper. WO W Cape.

Heritage range

Oupa se Wyn 🏵 ★★★★ Sundried raisins, honey & hay complexity on **11** fortified dessert from muscats Hamburg & de Frontignan. Delightful sweet fireside treat. **Ouma se Wyn** ★★★★ 'Granny's Wine' rises to standard of 'Grandpa's's' in **10**, from muscat de Frontignan: raisins, subtle spice & uncloying sweetness in delicious mouthful. — DB/JP

Welvanpas

Location/WO: Wellington ▪ Map: Paarl & Wellington ▪ Est 1704 ▪ 1stB 1994 ▪ Tasting & sales Tue–Fri 8–5 Sat/Sun 8–3 ▪ Fee R10pp ▪ Closed Easter Fri-Mon, Dec 16-Jan 2 ▪ Die Ou Meul coffee shop open daily ▪ Facilities for children ▪ Tour groups ▪ History package incl lunch & talk on Piet Retief family ▪ Farm produce ▪ BYO picnic (day permit R20pp) ▪ Walks/hikes ▪ Bains mountain bike trails ▪ Owner(s)/viticulturist(s) Dan Retief ▪ Cellarmaster(s) Dan Retief (Jan 1993) ▪ Winemaker(s) Dan Retief (Jan 1990), with Neels Kruger (Jan 1999) ▪ 260ha/50ha (11 varieties r/w) ▪ 25t own label 80% red 15% white 5% rosé ▪ PO Box 75 Wellington 7654 ▪ welvanpas@gmail.com ▪ S 33° 37'59.9" E 019° 4'12.5" ▪ **T +27 (0)21-864-1239** ▪ F +27 (0)21-864-1239

When the family is descended from Groot Trekker Piet Retief and there are Thomas Bains trails on the farm, you know there's a lot of history going on. The farm was once called Krakeelhoek (Argument Corner) after a feud between Retief's grandfather and a neighbour, and their Krakeelhoek Rood still reflects that sour bit of history. The kinder, gentler present day includes plans for a function and reception area in the cellar, and overnight facilities.

Cabernet Sauvignon ⏀ 🍷 ★★★ **10** cranberry & dark cherry notes, savoury end. **Shiraz** ⏀ 🍷 ★★★ Bold & robust **09** toasty tobacco & liquorice aromas; needs year/2 to knit. **Revival Red** 🍷 Await next, also for **Chardonnay** & **Sauvignon Blanc**. **De Krakeelhoek Rood** ⏀ 🍷 ★★★ Attractive merlot & shiraz **NV** combo; smoky & dry for easy everyday drinking. **Suzanne Rosé** ⏀ 🍷 ★★★ Crisp **10** from pinotage, cranberry fruitiness takes edge off dry palate. **Amity** ⏀ 🍷 ★★★ Unwooded chardonnay/chenin summer sipper; earthy & herbal **10** crisped by green-apple acidity. — DB

■ **Weskus** see Winkelshoek Wine Cellar

Westbridge Vineyards

Location/map: Stellenbosch ▪ Est 1998 ▪ 1stB 1999 ▪ Tasting & sales by appt only (T 083-631-2229) ▪ Muldersvlei Stables B&B ▪ Chapel/wedding/conference venue ▪ Sunday lunch (booking required) ▪ Owner(s) JC Starke & Muldersvlei Estates ▪ Winemaker(s) Ian Starke ▪ Viticulturist(s) Julian Starke ▪ 3ha cab (chenin & sauv bought in) ▪ 40t/3,000cs own label 50% red 50% white ▪ PO Box 66 Muldersvlei 7607 ▪ wine@muldersvlei.co.za ▪ www.muldersvlei.co.za ▪ S 33° 49'30.2" E 018° 50'17.6" ▪ **T +27 (0)21-884-4433** ▪ F +27 (0)86-624-7446

It seems that Ian Starke's Westbridge wines are no sooner released than they're sold out (and hence not tasted by us) from the family farm Muldersvlei, with its guest house accommodation and conference-and-wedding venue. They planned to open a pub and grill by late summer, which would no doubt grow the market for the wines, available exclusively at the historic Stellenbosch property.

■ **Westerdale** see Kronendal Boutique Winery

Whalehaven Wines

Location: Hermanus ▪ Map: Elgin, Walker Bay & Bot River ▪ WO: Coastal/Elgin ▪ Est/1stB 1995 ▪ Tasting & sales Mon–Fri 9.30–5 Sat/Sun 10.30–4.30 ▪ Fee R10pp for groups of 5+ ▪ Tours by appt ▪ Owner(s) Bottega family ▪ Winemaker(s) Reino Thiart ▪ Vineyard manager(s) Tim Clark ▪ 120t capacity ▪ Private Bag X14 Hermanus 7200 ▪ wine@whalehaven.co.za, info@bottegafamilywine.co.za ▪ www.whalehaven.co.za, www.bottegafamilywine.co.za ▪ S 34° 24'36.9" E 019° 11'60.0" ▪ **T +27 (0)28-316-1633** ▪ F +27 (0)28-316-1640

Owned by the Bottega family of Idiom Wines, this Hemel-en-Aarde winery says it's getting good feedback about the new 'W' labels (depicting a mother whale and calf, linking the brand to its home, Hermanus, world famous for whale spotting). In addition, the tasting room is about to undergo a major remodelling and will feature a shop, 'sensorium' and function venue to enhance the visitor experience.

Whalehaven range

★★★★ **Pinot Noir** ⏀ **09** (★★★), from Elgin grapes, medium bodied with fresh acidity, fine tannins; lacks complexity, concentration of **08**.

Viognier-Chardonnay ☺ 🍷 ★★★ 2 vintages reviewed. Floral-toned **10** mouthfilling richness balanced by crisp acidity. **12** same flavour profile with more zingy appeal, less breadth. Both perfect for summer enjoyment.

Cabernet Franc ④ ★★★ Dark fruit, some herbs & toasty oak on rich & full-bodied **08. Merlot** ④ ★★★ **09** good fruit concentration but very dry, resinous finish when reviewed. **Pinotage** ④ ★★★★ **09** red & black fruit, prominent but not unattractive oak, nicely tart. **Chardonnay** ④ ★★★ Evolved **08** last showed sherrylike notes, some citrus. **Sauvignon Blanc** 🛢 ★★★ Hay & floral wafts on light-bodied, uncomplicated **11. Sauvignon Blanc-Semillon** NEW ★★★ Light & tangy **10**, crisp green-fruit flavours; creamy vanilla from oaked semillon portion. Harmonious, but does not linger.

W range

Old Harbour Red 🛢 ★★ Gluggable merlot-driven **10** more appealing than previous. **Pinotage Rosé** 🛢 🌿 ★★☆ Strawberry & spice on easy dry **12** sipper. — WB

■ **Whispering Jack** see Flagstone Winery
■ **White River** see Bergsig Estate

Wildehurst Wines

Location: Koringberg • Map/WO: Swartland • Est 2006 • 1stB 2009 • Tasting & sales daily at The Wine Kollective & Bar Bar Black Sheep Restaurant, Riebeek-Kasteel • Closed Dec 25 & Jan 1 • Cellar tours by appt at 1 Main Road, Koringberg • Owner(s) Chris & Joanne Hurst • Winemaker(s) Marais de Villiers (Nov 2008, consultant) • Viticulturist(s) John Loxton (2006, consultant) • 0.5ha/±0.3ha (shiraz, viog) • 1.8t/211cs own label 35% red 53% white 12% rosé • PO Box 103 Koringberg 7312 • joanne@wildehurst.co.za • www.wildehurst co.za • S 33° 01'10.10" E 018° 40' 26.42" • **T +27 (0)21-872-3006 (Marais)** • F +27 (0)86-657-8251

It wouldn't be unreasonable to expect something interesting and characterful from a tiny, isolated shiraz-viognier vineyard (other varieties are brought in) and winery at the foot of the Koringberg, in the heart of the vast Swartland Especially when the wine is made with all the naturalness and passion proper to a member of the radical Swartland Independent organisation. Expectations met.

★★★★ **Shiraz-Mourvèdre** Was 'Red'. Sample pure-flavoured **10** has viognier touch for added fragrance Characterful & fruit-filled, controlled by smooth tannins. Only older oak. Maybe best young & delicious.

★★★★ **Chenin Blanc** Was 'White'. **12** preview from Perdeberg grapes, with 5% viognier. Rich, silky, dry & only subtly fruity — but a lovely sweet, apricotty centre. Fermented in older oak barrels. Good for a few years.

Grenache-Shiraz NEW ★★ Some charm on pre-bottling **11**, but weak, overripe fruit outgunned by tannins **Rosé** ★★★★ Previously 'Blush'. Sophisticated, savoury, bone-dry **12** tasted pre-bottling — not simply fruity rather packed with flavour & personality. Great with food. From grenache, shiraz, mourvèdre. — TJ

Wildekrans Wine Estate

Location/WO: Bot River • Map: Elgin, Walker Bay & Bot River • Est/1stB 1993 • Tasting, sales & cellar tours Mon-Fri 8.30–5 Sat/Sun 11-3 • Fee R15 • Closed Dec 25 • Tour groups • Picnics to order • Conferences/functions • Walks/hikes • Mountain biking • Birding • Conservation area • Self-catering Cottages • Owner(s) Wildekrans Trust • Winemaker(s) William Wilkinson (2006) • Viticulturist(s) Braam Gericke (2008) • 1,015ha, 70ha (ptage, pinot, chard, chenin) • 350t own label 55% red 40% white 5% rosé; ±6,600cs for clients • WIETA • PO Box 31 Botriver 7185 • wines@wildekrans.com • www.wildekrans.com • S 34° 9'42.6" E 019° 0'36.0" • **T +27 (0)28-284-9902** • F +27 (0)21-413-0967

While this Bot River farm focuses on the future — planting bushvines to maximise micro-climatic control and hopefully minimise the effect of climate change — the past is not forgotten. The original 1930 cellar has been restored and is being used from harvest 2013 for vinifying the premium pinotage. Meanwhile, the farm's oldest building, a barn, has been converted into a function venue overlooking the river and the new polo field. Another part of all this re-thinking is a big reduction in the number of wines made and tweaking the names of the remainder.

Reserve range

★★★★ **Pinotage Barrel Select** 🌿 Modern, fruit-forward **10** with pinot slant to its ripe raspberry flavours. Smooth, sweetish edge clipped by firm but smartly polished tannins. Good now to around 2016.

★★★★ **Shiraz Barrel Select** 🌿 **10** (★★★) much riper & sturdier than **09**, which had a nice lightness of touch. Jammy, with sweet effect from big alcohol & a few grams sugar.

★★★★ **Cape Blend Barrel Select** NEW 🌿 Harmonious mix equal parts pinotage & shiraz plus 15% cab **10** ripe but with plenty of dimension to its floral, raspberry appeal. Rich & creamy, with succulent tannins.

Chenin Blanc Barrel Select ★★★★ Rich, full-bodied **11** with its honeyed fruit augmented by noticeable oak vanillins & with a sweetish finish. **Sauvignon Blanc Barrel Select** ★★★★ Creamy **11**, previewed last ed; oak, balanced freshness spice up very quiet tropical features. Good food partner. **Méthode Cap Classique** ★★★ Rather sombre fruit cheered by bright, breezy bubble, sweetish lift on **09** from chenin. Note: This range previously listed as Osiris. Jake White Selection, & Caresse Marine & Wildekrans Estate ranges discontinued. — AL

William Everson Wines

Location: Grabouw ▪ Map: Elgin, Walker Bay & Bot River ▪ WO: Elgin/Stellenbosch/Paarl ▪ Est/1stB 2001 ▪ Tasting, sales & tours by appt ▪ Self-catering accommodation (www.mentmor.co.za) ▪ Owner(s)/winemaker(s) William Everson ▪ 4t/400cs own label 60% red 40% white ▪ 2281 Essenhout Avenue Klipkop Grabouw 7160 ▪ william@eversonwine.co.za, william@eversoncider.com ▪ www.eversonwine.co.za, www.eversoncider.com ▪ S 34° 8′ 44.01″ E 019° 1′ 1.21″ ▪ **T +27 (0)82-554-6357** ▪ F +27 (0)86-662-4045

Grabouw-based William Everson produces small quantities of wine which he markets 'on a very personal level'. Currently he's working on a shiraz-mourvèdre blend from Elgin and Overberg vines, and a wooded chardonnay, the barrels for which will be reused to store and mature his artisanal cider.

Stellenbosch Cabernet Sauvignon ⊕ ★★★ **09** earthy tones mixed with sour cherry flavours, when last tasted needed more time to fill out. **Stone's End Pinot Noir** ⊕ ★★★ Textured **10**, lovely balance between earthy notes & mulberry fruit, crisp & dry. WO Stellenbosch. **Paarl Shiraz** ⊕ ★★★★ Fruity & rounded **08** abounds with dark ripe berries & warm plums. **Elgin Shiraz** ⊕ ★★★ Smoky/leathery **09** more elegant, subtle & crisp than previous. **One Barrel Chardonnay** ★★★★ Now bottled & renamed (from simply 'Chardonnay'), **10** full of character: cinnamon notes, creamy texture & gentle acidity make for pleasant drinking. Very individual style, improves on understated **09** (★★★). **Sauvignon Blanc** Await next. **Sauvignon Blanc-Chardonnay** ⊕ ★★★ Early picked freshness on **10**, light bodied, leafy, hints of greenpepper & lime. — DB

◼ **Willowbrook** *see* Wine-of-the-Month Club

Windfall Wine Farm

Location/map/WO: Robertson ▪ Est 1998 ▪ 1stB 2006 ▪ Tasting, sales & tours by appt ▪ Closed all pub hols ▪ BYO picnic ▪ Owner(s) Bianca Weingartz, Sarah Alexander & Jaco de Wet ▪ Cellarmaster(s) Kobus van der Merwe (Jan 2006, consultant) & Jaco de Wet ▪ Winemaker(s) Kobus van der Merwe (Jan 2006, consultant), with Van Zyl de Wet (Jan 2009, consultant) ▪ Viticulturist(s) Jaco de Wet (Jan 2003) ▪ ±288ha/30ha (cab, merlot, pinot, ruby cab, chard, chenin, sauv) ▪ 534t/275cs own label 75% red 25% white ▪ PO Box 22 Robertson 6705 ▪ info@windfallwine.co.za ▪ www.windfallwine.co.za ▪ S 33° 56′ 33.37″ E 019° 38′ 42.98″ ▪ **T +27 (0)83-320-8473** ▪ F +27 (0)86-743-4162

Termites. 'You could almost hear them working behind the plaster of the walls,' says co-owner Bianca Weingartz. Fearing the old farmhouse would collapse, a rebuild commenced and the 'beautiful new Windfall' in Agterkliphoogte Valley, once owned by cricket legend Eddie Barlow, now has a tasting room, visitor venue and indigenous garden, with paths leading through the gum trees to a new boma.

Cabernet Sauvignon ⊕ ★★ **08** infused with mint & vanilla, tad green & leafy. **Pinot Noir** Await new. **Shiraz** ⊕ ★★★ **08** herbaceous tones to ripe fruit, firm tannic grip & spicy-sweet tail. **Barrel 41** ⊕ ★★ Sweet-sour fruit on easy-drinking **09** shiraz/cabernet (50/50). **Sauvignon Blanc** 🖩 ★★★ **12** still showing bubblegum ferment character mid-2012 but pleasantly crisp & bright, should be at least as good as elegant **11**. **Mendola** NEW ★★★ Long-gestated méthode cap classique sparkling from chardonnay, **07** genteel caramelised apple aroma & creamy bubbles, perfect now. — CvZ/MW

Windmeul Cooperative Cellar

Location: Paarl ▪ Map: Paarl & Wellington ▪ WO: Paarl/Coastal ▪ Est 1944 ▪ 1stB 1945 ▪ Tasting & sales Mon-Fri 8–5 Sat 9–3 ▪ Closed all pub hols ▪ Cellar tours by appt ▪ Farmers' market every 1st Sat of each month, with fresh produce & meals ▪ Owner(s) 42 members ▪ Cellarmaster(s) Danie Marais (Oct 1999) ▪ Winemaker(s) Francois van Niekerk (Dec 2004), with Liani Theunissen & Pieter Rossouw (Dec 2010/Jan 2011) ▪ Viticulturist(s) Anton Laas (Oct 2007) ▪ 1,700ha ▪ 13,500t/6,000cs own label 54% red 44% white 1% rosé 1% fortified + 400cs for clients ▪ PO Box 2013 Windmeul 7630 ▪ windmeul@iafrica.com ▪ www.windmeulwinery.co.za ▪ S 33° 40′18.1″ E 018° 54′ 30.6″ ▪ **T +27 (0)21-869-8100/8043** ▪ F +27 (0)21-869-8614

Monthly farmers' markets are a feature at this Paarl winery, and the team are now using the popular events to showcase their Reserve wines during winemaker-conducted tastings. These limited-release bottlings are key to Windmeul's aspiration of rising above the perception that grower-owned wineries can make only 'good-value' wines — an ambition the solid block of red text below (and a steady stream of competition awards) should help achieve. A key focus is lower alcohol levels 'without sacrificing the characteristic fullness and complexity in our wines'.

Reserve range

★★★★☆ **Pinotage** ✓ **11** back to form of medalled **09**. Oozes succulent cocoa dusted blueberries, fynbos & cinnamon spice from 18 months new French barrels (as for most other reds). Generous, with a polished tannin structure built for 8+ years, like firmer **10** (★★★★).

★★★★ **Shiraz** ⏱ A serious wine, **10** needs time. Ripe (15% alcohol) but masked by fruit & oak. Organic notes in awarded **09** add to the complexity, supple tannins supply definition. Both improve on **08** (★★★★).

★★★★ **Cape Blend** ⏱ Ripeness seen in black plums, fleshy body, **10** is mainly pinotage (60%) & it shows; cab's role is to aid structure, which it does with style & serious intent. Enjoy now till ±2018. No **09**.

★★★★ **Chardonnay** ✓ Concentrated citrus curd & buttered toast, **11** though mouthfilling & rich has enough acid to balance the overall structure. Will reward ageing for few years.

★★★★ **Chenin Blanc** ✓ Serious intent evident in knockout citrus & tropical aromas mingled with sweet vanilla oak. **11** concentrated & focused, with a delicious freshness. Over-delivers on price. Stock up!

Cabernet Sauvignon ⏱ ★★★★ Heaps of potential in **10**, ups the ante, molten berries counter the tannins, give a smoothly textured effect. Drink now till ±2018. Meatier **09** (★★★★) has similar palate appeal. **The Legend** Await new vintage.

Windmeul range

★★★★ **White Muscadel** [NEW] Fragrant vibrant orange peel on fresh **10** fortified dessert. Slippery, dense & concentrated, with a delicious alcohol grip balancing sweetness. Great debut! WO Coastal.

Cabernet Sauvignon ☺ ★★★ **09** trumps previous with more complexity, bright plums & spice. **Merlot** ☺ ★★★ Juicy ripe plum flavours, sprinkle of spice on easygoing **10**. **Pinotage** ☺ ★★★ Vibrant spicy plum & blueberry fruit on well-made **10**, firm body is good for a few years. **Shiraz** ☺ ★★★ Plump & lush **10** is juicy & fruity with a delicious spicy edge. Ticks all quaffing boxes. **Chenin Blanc** ☺ ★★★ Crunchy apple flavours on crisp, dry **12** summer sipper. **Sauvignon Blanc** ☺ ★★★ Zesty & light **12** with zippy green leafy notes.

Cabernet Sauvignon-Merlot ★★★ Crowd-pleasing **10** up a notch with spicy plum fruit & smooth end. **Chardonnay** Await new. **Port** ★★★ Lightish & juicy sweet-berry fruit, touch of spice on **09**. WO Coastal. — WB

■ **Winds of Change** *see* African Terroir

Wine Concepts

Location: Cape Town ▪ Tasting & sales Mon-Fri 9–7 Sat 9.30-4.30 ▪ Owner(s) Michael Bampfield-Duggan, Derick Henstra, Peter Fehrsen, Neil & Sue Proudfoot, Corlien Morris ▪ Winemaker(s) Derick Henstra & Peter Fehrsen ▪ Cardiff Castle cnr Kildare & Main St Newlands 7700 ▪ newlandshop@wineconcepts.co.za ▪ www. wineconcepts.co.za ▪ **T +27 (0)21-671-9030 (Newlands), +27 (0)21-426-4401 (Gardens)** ▪ F +27 (0)21-671-9031, +27 (0)88-021-426-4401

After a dry spell when Wine Concepts speciality stores produced no wines under their Lollapalooza house label, partners Derick Henstra and Peter Fehrsen jointly vinified two barrels of 2012 pinot noir which, co-owner Michael Bampfield-Duggan says, will be released this year and available only in Wine Concepts stores.

Winegro Marketing

Location: Bellville ▪ Est/1stB 2004 ▪ Closed to public ▪ Winemaker(s) Johan Pietersen ▪ Barinor's Vineyard, South Building A, Ground Floor, The Vineyards, 99 Jip de Jager Drive, Bellville 7530 ▪ matubawine@gmail.com ▪ www.matuba.co.za ▪ **T +27 (0)21-913-8950** ▪ F +27 (0)21-913-8954

Winegro Marketing owns the well-established Matuba and Kleinbosch value brands, blended for easy, early enjoyment.

■ **Wine Lover's Collection** *see* Anura Vineyards

Wine-of-the-Month Club

Location: Cape Town ▪ Est 1986 ▪ MD Tai Collard ▪ Private Bag X2 Glosderry 7702 ▪ wineclub@wineofthemonth.co.za ▪ www.wineofthemonth.co.za ▪ **T +27 (0)21-709-6300** ▪ F +27 (0)86-674-4690

Wine-of-the-Month Club, South Africa's original and still leading wine mail-order business, distributes third-party wines selected by its expert panel as well as own-label brands such as Berg en Dal, Giant's Peak, Montebello, Semara, Steenhuis and Willowbrook.

■ **Winery of Good Hope** *see* The Winery of Good Hope

Wines of Cape Town

Location: Durbanville ▪ Map: Durbanville, Philadelphia & Darling ▪ WO: Western Cape ▪ Est 2007 ▪ Tasting by appt ▪ Sales Mon-Fri 8-4.30 ▪ Owner(s) DS Sarnia (Pty) Ltd ▪ 80% red 20% white ▪ Other export brand: Dolphin Sands ▪ Brands for clients: Diamond Creek, Radisson Blu ▪ 11 La Med Crescent, Elishua Villas, Sonstraal Heights, Langeberg Rd, Durbanville 7550 ▪ sales@winesofcapetown.com ▪ www.winesofcapetown.com ▪ **T +27 (0)21-987-0079** ▪ F +27 (0)86-513-7643

This negociant business run by long-time manager Christine Brand and newcomer Debbie Roberts (Lana Greeff having moved on to pastures new) has relocated to Durbanville, from where it continues to source 'good-value, well-made wines' from around the winelands for a local and overseas clientele.

Bushman's Creek range

Sauvignon Blanc ☺ 🍴 🚫 ★★★ Youthful & lightish **12** bursts with tropical fruit & tangy acidity.

Cabernet Sauvignon 🍴 🚫 ★★★ Easy & accessible **10**, now bottled, offers pine-needle freshness & light red berries. **Merlot** ★★★ Dark mocha chocolate & dry blackberry flavours on a firm tannin base in **10**. **Shiraz** ★★★ Rounded & easy **11**, savoury toast followed by big, juicy oak-brushed berries. **Chardonnay** 🍴 ★★★ Now bottled, **10**'s marzipan & pineapple are best enjoyed soon. Discontinued: **Cabernet Sauvignon-Merlot, Chenin Blanc**.

Dolphin Bay range

Sparkling Vin Doux ☺ ★★★ Big fruit salad of flavours in **11**'s sweet, bouncy, bubbly mouthful.

Sparkling Brut ★★ Appley & biscuity **12** adds fizz to parties. From chenin, like Vin Doux. Discontinued: **Cabernet Sauvignon, Chenin Blanc, Semi-Sweet**. — DB

Wine Village-Hermanus

Location: Hermanus ▪ Map: Elgin, Walker Bay & Bot River ▪ WO: Western Cape ▪ Est 1998 ▪ 1stB 2004 ▪ Open Mon-Fri 9-6 Sat 9-5 Sun 10-3 ▪ Closed Good Fri & Dec 25 ▪ Owner(s) Paul & Cathy du Toit ▪ ±1,000cs 50% red 50% white ▪ PO Box 465 Hermanus 7200 ▪ wine@hermanus.co.za ▪ www.wine-village.co.za ▪ S 34° 24' 40.7" E 019° 12' 1.9" ▪ **T +27 (0)28-316-3988** ▪ F +27 (0)86-509-4931

'We're a merry group at the Wine Village and wanted an uncomplicated label that reflects wine's enjoyment,' is how Cathy du Toit of this wine shop in Hermanus explains the brand name. They also enjoy designing a new label every year. As for selection: 'We see what spine-tingling wines are available that meet our criteria of good quality for value and easy on the palate, then usually buy a whole tank.'

Are We Having Fun Yet range

Semillon NEW ☺ 🍴 ★★★ Charming **11** from Durbanville; lilting lime, waxy features in soft-as-down feel, contrasting with mineral, fresh finish. 50% oaked. Lots of easy-drinking appeal.

Merlot ✓ 🍴 ★★★★ No more waiting required on **05**; subtly oaked to focus merlot's meaty, blood, iron maturity. Fleshy yet fresh, with sound, roundly dry finish. An absolute bargain from the Hemel-en-Aarde. Previous **09**

(★★) had dusty tannins. **Shiraz** ⊕ 🍴 ★★★ Delicate fruit, brush of spicy oak & warm afterglow on **07**. **Shiraz-Cabernet Sauvignon-Merlot** ⊕ 🍴 ★★★ Ripe & juicy **09**, tad rustic but characterful. **Chardonnay** ⊕ 🍴 ★★★ **09** summer quaffer with lemon & toasty notes appeal. **Sauvignon Blanc** ⊕ 🍴 ★★ Zesty tail to gently tropical, ripe **09**. **Viognier** ⊕ 🍴 ★★ Soft, rounded **09** with 14.5% alcohol glow in tail. — AL

Wineways Marketing

Location: Kuils River ▪ WO: Western Cape/Swartland/Stellenbosch ▪ Est 2000 ▪ Closed to public ▪ Owner(s) Carl Schmidt, Stephen Vermeulen & Fanie Marais ▪ Winemaker(s) Andries Blake (Swarland) & Morné van Rooyen (The Company of Wine People) ▪ 200,000cs own label 60% red 40% white ▪ Plot 689, Zinfandel Street, Saxenburg Park 2, Blackheath 7580 ▪ info@wine-ways.co.za ▪ www.wine-ways.co.za ▪ T +27 (0)21-905-7713/6/9 ▪ F +27 (0)86-509-9587

'You have to be innovative if you want to stand out, especially in the current economic circumstances,' says Carl Schmidt, a co-owner of this negociant business. A first for the local market is a four-litre bag-in-a-box offering, the (untasted) Coral Reef Crispy White and Smooth Red. They've also had a gratifyingly good response to their relaunched-by-popular-demand Tin Cups range.

Mountain Shadows range

Merlot ☺ 🍴 🔲 ★★★ Smooth & well-rounded **11**, with hints of mocha & blackberry.

Cabernet Sauvignon ⊕ 🔲 ★★ **10** juicy drinkability with dark chocolate & red berry aromas. Unwooded, as for all wines/ranges. **Merlot** ★★ **NV** softly dry braai buddy in 3L pack. **Pinotage** ⊕ 🔲 ★★ Dusty plum wafts on outgoing & eager-to-please **10**. **Shiraz** 🍴 🔲 ★★ Good mix of fruit & savoury notes in **11** meal mate. Stellenbosch WO. **Merlot-Cabernet Sauvignon** ★★★ Ripe, medium-bodied **NV** party pleaser with gentle tannic touch. 3L pack. **Chenin Blanc** ⊕ 🔲 ★★ **11** fresh & fruity, with lime & green apple notes. **Sauvignon Blanc** ⊕ 🔲 ★★ Light-bodied **11**, grassy & herbal, easy-drinking style.

Coral Reef range

Cabernet Sauvignon 🔲 ★★★ Nutty dark berries, **11** savoury tinge, for early enjoyment, like all wines & ranges. Swartland WO. **Merlot** ⊕ ★★ **10** chocolate & raspberry quick-quaff. **Pinotage** NEW ★★★★ **08** good advertisement for the variety; rounded, spicy ripe fruit & savouriness that invites meaty pasta. **Merlot-Cabernet Sauvignon** 🔲 ★★ Dry & packed with supple berry flavours, **11** is easy to like. **Sauvignon Blanc** 🍴 🔲 ★★ Pleasing tropical fruit & greenpepper combo, **12** light-textured sundowner. **Shiraz Natural Sweet** ⊕ ★★ **10** dusty & fruit-filled glugger.

Tin Cups range

Merlot-Cabernet Sauvignon 🍴 🔲 ★★ Piquant dry berries, **11** ideal for quaffing around the braai. **Sweet Rosé** 🍴 ★★ Coral pink, sweet & juicy **NV** from Swartland grapes. **Sauvignon Blanc** 🍴 🔲 ★ Lightish **11**, pungent greenpepper, tangy freshness. **Smooth Red** 🍴 ★★ Succulent semi-sweet **NV** ex Swartland. Budget priced, as all these.

Black Box range

Merlot ★★ Bright fruit & dark chocolate in **NV** easy-drinker. 5L bag-in-box, as for all these. **Pinotage** ★ Chocolate-dusted red berries in latest semi-dry **NV**. **Shiraz** ★★ Spicy plum notes on friendly just-dry **NV**. **Merlot-Cabernet Sauvignon** ★★ Cranberry freshness on earthy, food-styled **NV**. Grapes from Swartland.

Black Tie range

Pinotage NEW ☺ 🔲 ★★★ Light-bodied **11**, packed with lush fruit, finishes fresh.

Cabernet Sauvignon 🔲 ★★ Soft & accessible **11**, with spicy ripe blackberry fruit. **Merlot** 🔲 ★★ Medium-bodied **11** savoury pizza wine. **Merlot-Cabernet Sauvignon** 🔲 ★★ Everyday red with clean red berry taste in **11**. **Sauvignon Blanc** 🍴 🔲 ★★ **12** uncomplicated but bright tropical & greenpepper flavours. **Shiraz Natural Sweet** ★★ **11** spicy/fruity fireside tipple for the sweet toothed.

South Africa range

Cabernet Sauvignon 🍴 New release unready, as for **Merlot**, **Merlot-Cabernet Sauvignon** & **Shiraz Natural Sweet**. — DB

Winkelshoek Wine Cellar

Location: Piketberg ▪ Map: Swartland ▪ Tasting & sales Mon-Fri 9–4 Sat 9–12 ▪ Gifts ▪ Owner(s) Hennie Hanekom & Jurgens Brand ▪ Cellarmaster(s) Hennie Hanekom ▪ Winemaker(s) Hennie Hanekom (1984) ▪ PO Box 395 Piketberg 7320 ▪ info@winkelshoek.co.za ▪ S 32° 54'22.4" E 018° 46'2.0" ▪ **T +27 (0)22-913-1092** ▪ F +27 (0)22-913-1095

This cellar's easy-drinkers are available for tasting and sale from the visitor centre near the intersection of the N7 and R44 roads outside Piketberg. The wines, untasted this edition, include Weskus Dry Red, Sweet Rosé, Grand Cru, Blanc de Blanc and Late Harvest; and the Cap Vino Red (unwooded) and White (chenin).

Winters Drift

Location/WO: Elgin ▪ Map: Elgin, Walker Bay & Bot River ▪ Est 2004 ▪ 1stB 2010 ▪ Tasting by appt ▪ Conservation area ▪ Owner(s) Molteno Brothers (Pty) Ltd ▪ Cellarmaster(s) Kobie Viljoen (Gabriëlskloof) & Koen Roose (Spioenkop) ▪ Viticulturist(s) Christiaan Cloete (Jan 2011) & Francois Viljoen (Vinpro) ▪ 1,600ha/±54ha (grenache, merlot, mourv, pinot, shiraz, chard, sauv, sem, viog) ▪ 206t/3,000cs own label 17% red 66% white 17% rosé ▪ PO Box 128 Elgin 7180 ▪ gerhard@wintersdrift.com ▪ www.wintersdrift.com ▪ S 34° 08'59.42" E 019° 02'22.61" ▪ **T +27 (0)21-859-2527** ▪ F +27 (0)21-859-4893

'Elegantly Elgin', showcasing subtlety and lower alcohols, is how marketing and sales manager Gerhard Bruwer describes the style of wines made for the Molteno Brothers fruit farming business by nearby Kobie Viljoen (Gabriëlskloof) and Koen Roose (Spioenkop). The old Elgin train station is being restored as a tasting room.

Rosé 🍷 🖾 ★★★ Merlot grapes give red fruit & meaty tones in **11**, lightish body & flavour, ends dry. **Chardonnay** ✓ 🍷 🖾 ★★★★ Equal wooded & unwooded components result in broad but balanced **11**, with integrated oak, juicy fruit & good drinkability. **Sauvignon Blanc** 🍷 🖾 ★★★ Revisited as bottled wine, **11** reveals ripeness in baked apple & toffee flavours, classic Elgin flint in dry finish. — HJ

Withington

Location: Darling ▪ Map: Durbanville, Philadelphia & Darling ▪ WO: Darling/Coastal/Paarl ▪ Est 2001 ▪ 1stB 2003 ▪ Tasting & sales at Darling Wine Shop Mon-Sat 10-6 (10-7 in summer) Sun 11-2 ▪ Closed Mar 21, Easter Fri/Sun & Dec 25/26 ▪ Fresh West Coast oysters served when available ▪ Owner(s) Withington family ▪ 3,000cs own label 70% red 30% white ▪ 4,000cs for clients ▪ Brands for clients: Cape Diversity, Greendale ▪ PO Box 236 Darling 7345 ▪ mail@withington.co.za ▪ www.withington.co.za ▪ S 33° 22'28" E 018° 22'38" ▪ **T +27 (0)22-492-3971/+27 (0)74-194-1711** ▪ F +27 (0)86-516-4010

Good friend and renowned UK wine merchant John Avery, sadly now deceased, not only set negociant Charles Withington on his wine course but also mooted the idea of a shiraz/cabernet blend. Invariably apron-clad, Charles reports that it's a top seller in his now well-established Darling wine shop and tasting venue.

Withington range

Carignan 🍷 🖾 ★★★ Overtly plummy, ripe **10** similar to previous. Cheerful, sunny & appealing take on variety. WO Coastal. **Shiraz-Cabernet Sauvignon** 🍷 🖾 ★★★ Likeable, easy-drinking **09** shows vintage's ripeness, with sweet cherry & plum fruit, soft tannins. Paarl fruit. **Chardonnay** 🖾 ★★★ **11** a step up; honeyed citrus marmalade with rich palate. Medium body, good ripeness & length. **Semillon** 🍷 ★★★ Unwooded **10** follows form, striking nettle & greenpepper notes backed by fullish, lanolin-oily body. Discontinued: **Merlot**.

Darlington range

Malbec NEW ☺ 🖾 🖾 ★★★ Tangy blueberry pastille appeal to succulent **11**, light structure to easy-drinking palate.

Pinotage 🍷 🖾 ★★★ Fresh & zesty wild berry fruit on **09** lends quaffing appeal. Light & undemanding.

Greendale range

Chenin Blanc-Chardonnay 🖾 Await new vintage. Discontinued: **Pinotage**.

Living Rock range
Cinsaut-Ruby Cabernet ⊛ 🍷 ★★ Drink-now soft & juicy **10** shows vibrant berries unfettered by oak.
Chenin Blanc-Chardonnay 🍷 New bottling not ready. —FM

Withoek

Location/WO: Calitzdorp ▪ Map: Klein Karoo & Garden Route ▪ Est/1stB 1996 ▪ Tasting, sales & cellar tours by appt ▪ Self-catering cottages ▪ Farm produce ▪ Walks ▪ Conservation area ▪ Owner(s) Geyser family ▪ Winemaker(s) Fanie Geyser ▪ Viticulturist(s) Johannes Mellet ▪ 454ha/28ha (cab, p verdot, ruby cab, shiraz, tinta, touriga, chenin, cbard, hanepoot, muscadel) ▪ ±300t/400cs own label 50% red 50% white ▪ PO Box 181 Calitzdorp 6660 ▪ withoek@telkomsa.net ▪ www.withoek.blogspot.com ▪ S 33° 32'24.1" E 021° 40'59.8" ▪ T +27 (0)44-213-3639 ▪ F +27 (0)86-628-7853

A very good harvest, and one of the biggest he can remember, was sold off as Fanie Geyser was left with no time to make his own-label wines. Fortunately previous vintages are still available for tasting and sale at the Calitzdorp family farm.

Cabernet Sauvignon ⊛ Artisanal **10** slightly spritzy. **Shiraz** ⊛ ★★ Tasted mid-2010, **09** had beefy alcohol & dry tannin from 11 months oak. **Sauvignon Blanc** ⊛ ★★ Amiable **11** is grassy & fresh, with satisfying vinosity. **Kairos Muscadel** ⊛ ★★★ Fortified dessert from mainly white muscadel, dash red for pinkish hue. **10**'s watermelon & honeyed notes appeal but fade fast. **Fick's Ruby Port** ⊛ ★★ Raisin & dusty spices on uncomplex **NV**. **Geyser Cape Ruby** ⊛ ★★ Rustic **NV** port-style fortified fireside sipper. **Geyser Cape Vintage** ⊛ ★★★ House's 3rd port-style offering; cranberry & tealeaf-toned **10** makes up for lack of tannin grip with a fiery tail. — CE/JP

▪ **Witklip** *see Eerste Hoop Wine Cellar*

Wolfkloof

Location/map: Robertson ▪ Est 1883 ▪ 1stB 2004 ▪ Tasting, sales & cellar tours by appt ▪ Meals by appt; or BYO picnic ▪ Tour groups ▪ Conferences (40 pax) ▪ Weddings/functions (100 pax) ▪ Hiking trail ▪ Art & craftwork ▪ Owner(s) JC Kannemeyer ▪ Cellarmaster(s)/winemaker(s) Jan Kannemeyer ▪ Viticulturist(s) Hennie Visser (consultant) ▪ 360ha/4ha (merlot, chard) ▪ 10t/500cs own label 40% red 40% white 20% rosé ▪ 90cs for clients ▪ PO Box 40 Robertson 6705 ▪ info@wolfkloof.co.za ▪ www.wolfkloof.co.za ▪ S 33° 47'28.1" E 019° 52'1.4" ▪ T +27 (0)74-339-5008 ▪ F +27 (0)86-554-4894

Jan Kannemeyer's boutique vintning story began in 2004 when he concluded he couldn't call himself a vinegrower and not make wine. Merlot — all of one barrel — was his first attempt and the variety is still his pride and joy. Production has steadily climbed to 10t, all made as naturally as possible 'so when people taste it they'll know it comes from Wolfkloof in Robertson Valley'. His long-time mentor is Springfield's Abrie Bruwer. 'He'll say when my wine is %$#@'.

JC Kannemeyer range
Child's Dream Merlot Available but not tasted, like **Child's Dream Private Blend**, **Wolfkloof Merlot Rosé** & **Wolfkloof Tribute Chardonnay**.

▪ **Wolvenbosch** *see Jason's Hill Private Cellar*

Wolvendrift Private Cellar

Location/map: Robertson ▪ Est 1903 ▪ Tasting & sales Mon-Fri 8.30–4.30 Sat 10–1 ▪ Closed Easter Fri-Mon, May 1, Dec 25/26 & Jan 1 ▪ Cellar tours by appt ▪ Refreshments/meals by pre-booking ▪ Facilities for children ▪ Tour groups ▪ Walking/hiking trails ▪ Conservation area ▪ Weddings & functions ▪ Owner(s) Michael Klue ▪ Winemaker(s) Jan Klue (Jan 2003) ▪ Viticulturist(s) Jan Swart (Jan 2000) ▪ 120ha (cab, merlot, chard, chenin, cbard, sauv) ▪ 45% red 45% white 10% fortified ▪ PO Box 24 Robertson 6705 ▪ info@wolvendriftwines.co.za ▪ www.wolvendriftwines. co.za ▪ S 33° 55'0.1" E 020° 0'9.0" ▪ T +27 (0)23-616-2890 ▪ F +27 (0)23-616-2396

Highlight of an exceptional year was the wedding of owner Michael Klue's daughter Carlin at the function venue on the Robertson family farm overlooking the Breede River. Three-course meals combined with wine tastings, and cheese-and-wine tastings on the cellar deck are attracting many more feet through the door.

Cabernet Sauvignon-Merlot 🍷 Selling but not reviewed, as **Sauvignon Blanc** & **Red Muscadel**.

Women in Wine

Location: Stellenbosch ▪ WO: Western Cape ▪ Closed to public ▪ PO Box 12869 Die Boord Stellenbosch 7613 ▪ info@womeninwine.co.za ▪ www.womeninwine.co.za ▪ **T +27 (0)21-872-8967** ▪ F +27 (0)21-872-8967

This wine-producing collective of 20 professional black women at the Cape special-ises in export, yet they have their hearts set on advancing women in the Cape winelands, particularly giving farmworkers a stake in the industry. At Prowein in Düsseldorf, Germany, in 2012 they released the last of the three wines in their Three Graces range, named for the trio of goddesses in Greek mythology. For now there are no new labels planned. Rather, 'the shift is towards brand building'.

Three Graces Reserves NEW!

Euphrosyne Cabernet Sauvignon ★★★ Striking & graceful labels a feature throughout. **08** commands attention with its substance & grip, ideally kept year/2 or matched with full-flavoured food. **Thalia Merlot** ★★★ 09 takes SA merlot's sometimes herbaceous quality to the max: leafy, minty, very dry & lean. A love/hate wine, but we urge: try! **Aglaia Chardonnay** ★★★ Opulent & mouthfilling, **09**'s sweet-seeming hon-eyed lemon-cream character is surprisingly assertive, needs rich food or thorough chilling for solo. — JP/CvZ

Wonderfontein

Location/map/WO: Robertson ▪ Est ca 1884 ▪ Tasting by appt only ▪ Sales Mon-Fri 8.30-6 Sat 8.30-1 ▪ Tour groups ▪ Conferences/events (40-80 guests) & picnic facilities, 4×4 trail & other attractions ▪ Owner(s) Paul René Marais ▪ Winemaker(s) Stefan Bruwer ▪ Viticulturist(s) Gert Visser, Gerald Stemmet & Bennie Stemmet, advised by Brian Stipp ▪ 270ha (cab, merlot, ptage, pinot, ruby cab, shiraz, chard, chenin, sauv) ▪ 5,500t/3,000cs own label 10% red 80% white 1% rosé 9% fortified ▪ PO Box 4 Robertson 6705 ▪ henk@wonderfonteinestate.co.za ▪ www.wonderfonteinestate.co.za ▪ S 33° 49'3.5" E 019° 52'2.1" ▪ **T +27 (0)23-626-2212** ▪ F +27 (0)23-626-2669

Happy days at this fifth-generation family-owned Robertson property: they've acquired two neighbour farms, and the long-gestated maiden méthode cap classique bubbly rewarded the team's patience by selling out fast. Even legend-ary Dalmation Suzy is wagging her tail as she has a new companion, English Pointer Gina, to roam the gardens with.

★★★★ **Paul René MCC Brut** NEW! Lipsmacking debut for strikingly packaged NV (**09**) bottle-fermented sparkling from chardonnay. Vibrant mousse, apricot & green apple freshness, emphatic & persistent dry finish.

La Bonne Vigne Rosé ☺ ▦ ★★★ Friendly NV (**12**) ups the quaffability level with strawberry aromas & flavours, dollop sugar enlivened by zesty acidity. From colombard, colour by merlot.

The Marais Family Merlot ⓥ ▦ ★★★ Spice-dusted **10** ideal for early enjoyment: juicy plum gently wrapped with tannin. **La Bonne Vigne Merlot** Not tasted. **La Bonne Vigne Shiraz** ▦ ★★★ Smoky **09** rich & full, slightly sweet tail. **La Bonne Vigne Sauvignon Blanc** ✓ ▦ ★★★ Green fig & tropical appeal on **12**, lightish & softly dry for effortless sipping. **Wonderfontein Red Muscadel** Not tasted. — DB/HJ

Woolworths

WO: Various ▪ Selector Allan Mullins T +27 (0)21-407-2777 AllanMullins@woolworths.co.za ▪ Buying man-ager Ivan Oertle T +27 (0)21-407-2762 IvanOertle@woolworths.co.za ▪ Owner(s) Woolworths Holdings ▪ Woolworths House 93 Longmarket Street Cape Town 8000 ▪ www.woolworths.co.za ▪ **T +27 (0)21-407-9111** ▪ F +27 (0)21-407-3958

More than twenty years of bespoke wine-buying and -blending has given upmarket retailing group Woolworths' Allan Mullins an unparalleled network of connec-tions, tasting notes and memories. Finally (and fittingly) he has brought it all together into a new, eponymous pair of wines — the Allan Mullins 'My Song' range. Long-term partner-in-wine and buying manager, Ivan Oertle, continues to expand the Woolworths stocks of overseas wines as well as the increasingly popular Light and No Added Sulphur ranges, and proudly notes that for all their innovation, they haven't lost sight of their quality standards as the MCC Trophy at last year's Old Mutual Trophy Wine Show can attest. And plans for the future include sourcing more wines from hardy Mediterranean cultivars, enabling them to help reduce water usage in line with their continuing Good Business Journey goals.

Cabernet Sauvignon range

★★★★☆ **Exclusive Cabernet** Unshowy 08 (★★★★) from Grangehurst, carefully judged to allow for lighter fruit. Already shows maturity of colour, more savoury flavours, these fleshed out by 13% merlot. Smooth tannins, shortish finish suggest best enjoyed early. 07 richer, longer lived.

★★★★ **Founder's Reserve Cabernet Sauvignon** Full & rich 10, measured cassis woven into soft, ripe tannin. Understated tobacco & herbal notes, with the firm grip of its Diemersfontein origin.

★★★★ **Cabernet Sauvignon Reserve** (🖾) Mocha-toned 10 similar to 09, showing dense fruit centre & firm oak structure. Both from Spier, both should be kept few years to allow tannins to mellow.

> **Tell It Like It Is Cabernet Sauvignon** 😊 🍴 🖾 ★★★ Unoaked juicy red berries, slight grip on smooth, lightish & easy 11 by Bergsig.

The Hutton Cabernet Sauvignon (🍐) ★★★★ Named for dominant soil type from which grapes are sourced. Cassis mingles with milk chocolate, vanilla courtesy Spier's oaking on 09. **NSA Organic Running Duck Cabernet Sauvignon** 🍴 🔥 🖾 ★★★ 12 fresh & taut, to match boldly flavoured meat dishes. From Stellar Winery. **Cabernet Sauvignon** (🖾) ★★★★ Chiselled 10 in classic blackcurrant varietal expression; from Villiera. Judicious oaking lends grip & seriousness. **Longmarket Cabernet Sauvignon** (🖾) ★★★ 11 cherry tobacco nuances, coffee highlights on unlingering plummy palate. From Bergsig.

Merlot range

★★★★ **Merlot Reserve** Firmly structured 09 from Morgenhof shows dark cherries, blackberries, & slight herbaceous note. Powerful, with integrated acidity but warmish finish ex 14.8% alcohol.

★★★★ **Exclusive Merlot** From Jordan. With its succulent blackcurrants, dark chocolate & spices woven through the fruit, 10 is lovely to drink now & for the next ±4 years.

> **Breath Merlot** (NEW) 😊 🍴 ★★★ Ripe, vibrant berry fruit on 10 from Wellington Wines ex Paarl vines, in PET (plastic) bottles. Pleasantly plump & generous.

Koffie Klip Merlot ★★★★ By Spier; named for dominant soil type in the vineyard. Bold 10's plum fruit cosseted by 60% new French oak, slightly spiritous farewell (14.7% alcohol). **NSA Organic Swooping Falcon Merlot** 🍴 🔥 🖾 ★★★ Ex Stellar Winery. Peppery highlights to 12's mulberry fruit. **Merlot** (🖾) ★★★ Cedar, tar & black plum imprints on La Motte's 11; juicy, with just enough grip for food. **Merlot** (🖾) ★★★ Plummy, ripe 10 from Villiera, for drinking rather than impressing. Lively acidity & tannin add structure. **Longmarket Merlot** 🍴 ★★★ Easy, fresh & round 11 shows succulent red berries. From Simonsvlei. **Tell It Like It Is Merlot** 🍴 ★★★ Wellington Wines-sourced, barrel-matured 11 is light & basic. **Organic Merlot** ✓ 🔥 🖾 ★★★★ 11, by Laibach, has tangy blue & black berry fruit with earthy nuance. Smooth & lissom, it has a firm frame but is still friendly. **Light Merlot** (🍐) ★★ Plummy 11 has decent grip & fruit, slight metallic edge; from Spier. Discontinued: **What Merlot**.

Pinot Noir range

★★★★ **Pinot Noir Reserve** (🍐) (🖾) 10's red berries give flesh to underbrush & farmyard features, elegant but a smidgen light. 20% new oak for 11 months, from Paul Cluver.

★★★★☆ **Limited Release CM Pinot Noir** (🖾) 11 (★★★★) more slender than impressive 10, though highlights Cathy Marshall's tender touch. Built on pinot's essential freshness, smoothed by gentle silky feel & judiciously buffed with oak (10% new).

Limited Release Pinot Noir Not tasted. **Cabrière Pinot Noir** (🍐) ★★★★ 08's softly savoury, fresh cherry flavours underlined by pliable tannins & firm thread of acidity. From Haute Cabrière. **DMZ Pinot Noir** (NEW) 🍴 🖾 ★★★★ Expressive red strawberry features on easy but not simple 10 from DeMorgenzon. Fresh & supple with nip of forming tannin. **Longmarket Pinot Noir** (NEW) 🍴 ★★★ Wet earth & cherry aromas/flavours, stalky grip on (relatively) wallet-friendly 12 from Robertson Winery.

Pinotage range

★★★★ **Simonsig Pinotage** (🖾) Deft handling shows in well-mannered, appealingly juicy 10 with no rough edges. Berry compote fruit cosseted in smoothly textured tannin.

DF Coffee Pinotage (NEW) 🍴 🖾 ★★ Close your eyes & 11 tastes of, well, coffee, with light tannins for an easy glide. From Diemersfontein. **NSA Organic Glowing Firefly Pinotage** 🍴 🔥 🖾 ★★ Food-friendly grip of tannin, not unattractive 'wild' note on juicy 12. **Pinotage** (🖾) ★★★ From M'hudi, 10 exudes smoke & spice, has refreshing palate courtesy zesty acidity & slightly bitter lift. **Tell It Like It Is Pinotage** 🍴 🖾

★★★ Fruit-driven, no hard tannins on **11**. Ex Ken Forrester. **Longmarket Pinotage** 🍷 ★★★ **11** lipsmackingly dry with soft strawberry tones. Try with smoked meats selection. By Rooiberg. **Bellevue Exclusive Selection Pinotage** NEW 🍷 ★★ **11** is lean & less than generous. **Diemersfontein Pinotage Reserve** NEW ★★★★ Charming & demure **11**, plummy interest without brash tannins. Discontinued: **Pinotage Reserve, Limited Release Pinotage**.

Shiraz range

★★★★ **Shiraz Reserve** ⑨ Distinctive & forceful **09** ex Groenekloof vines has delightful cocoa & pepper fragrance, coupled to silky black cherry fruit. Finely balanced offering from Darling Cellars.

Exclusive Shiraz ✓ 🍷 ★★★★ Bearing Diemersfontein's generous plummy stamp, **11** brims with bonhomie. Food-friendly oak tannins, for early enjoyment. **Organic Hunting Owl Shiraz** ⑨ 🌿 🍷 ★★★ Succulent red berry fruit pads out tad stalky grape tannins on unoaked **11**. For early quaffing, ex African Terroir. **Hercules Paragon Shiraz** ⑨ ★★★★ Smoky, intense **08** from Simonsvlei brims with black cherry fruit cloaked in chalky tannins. Pleasing spicy aromas. **Pumphouse Shiraz** ★★★★ Floral delicacy to European-styled **08** by Backsberg. Improvement on **07** (★★★). Powerful & restrained. Fine tannins, ample black fruit. Textured palate with lovely weight & length. **Longmarket Redstone Shiraz** ⑨ 🍷 ★★★ Honest & upfront, **10** charms with juicy red fruit, dusty oak & floral highlights. Ex Rooiberg. **Longmarket Shiraz** 🍶 🍷 ★★★ **10** from Swartland Winery is earthy with baked plum pudding fruit. **Light Shiraz** ⑨ 🍶 ★ Low alc & sweetness on Spier's dilute **11**. **Arendsig Shiraz** NEW ★★★★ Single-vineyard offering. Tar & meat, **11** full bodied & ripe with appealing spicy black cherry overlay.

Niche Red Cultivars range

★★★★ **Cabernet Franc Reserve** ✓ 🍷 Showcases variety's sappiness, but **10** (★★★★) a touch lean, not as succulent & plump as red berry fruited **09**. Elgin wine by Paul Cluver.

★★★★ **Nederburg Grenache** NEW ✓ 🍷 Sweetly perfumed with red berries, scrub & nutmeg, **10** takes you to the south of France with its 'drink me' fruity exuberance. Harmonious & smoothly accessible.

★★★★ **Limited Release Malbec** ⑨ Straightforward **09** (★★★) from Bellevue: shows red fruit, vanilla, noticeable herbal character. Not as accomplished as juicy, vivacious **08**.

★★★★ **DF Malbec Reserve** NEW 🍷 Nutmeg & roasted nut profile of **11** contrasted & balanced by lissom tannin. Needs few years to unfurl. By Diemersfontein.

★★★★ **Granite Blocks Cabernet Franc** NEW 🍷 **10** powerful & concentrated mouthful of black fruit & some truffle notes. Ripe berries lent a savoury edge with fragrant herbs of lavender & rosemary. By Raats Family.

Red Blends range

★★★★ **Cabernet Sauvignon-Merlot Reserve** 🍷 Neil Ellis's **10** shows dense fruit core, still restrained by firm structure, from Elgin. All components in place. Ageworthy 3-5 years, but maturing earlier than **09**.

★★★★☆ **Cobblers Hill** Bordeaux blend, best barrel selection, from Jordan. **08** has depth & layers of interest, savoury meat extract, chocolate, a herbal nuance, & an impressively svelte body despite 2 years new French barriques. Drink now till ±2018.

★★★★ **The Ladybird Red** ⑨ 🌿 **10** from Laibach follows in **09**'s footsteps. 5-way Bordeaux combo. Ripe but still refreshing, tobacco leaf & earth nuances to firm body & slight chunky texture.

★★★★☆ **Allan Mullins Red 'My Song'** NEW Class act in honour of the man who pioneered Woolworths' wine business. **09** 50/43 merlot/cab blend with cab franc, from Coastal vineyards. Plush fruit soaks up serious oaking (100% new French, 16 months), sculpting & providing support for good few years ageing. By Spier.

★★★★ **Warwick Cape Lady** NEW Shiraz-led with pinotage, dash cab, **10**'s dark-toned opulence & savoury juiciness is the ideal match for venison, rich casseroles. Drink now till ±2016.

★★★★☆ **The W (Syrah-Mourvèdre)** ⑨ 🌿 'W' recognises sustainability. Last-tasted **07** ex TMV (now Fable) was mainly shiraz, some mourvèdre, tightly held & complete, but all in fine moderation.

★★★★ **Exclusive Selection Shiraz-Grenache** Pretty **08** is 55:45 blend matured in older oak, 12 months. Red fruit, some floral fragrance. Medium body with fresh acidity, fine tannins. By Ken Forrester.

★★★★ **Shiraz-Cabernet Sauvignon** ✓ 🍷 Mocha-toned **10**'s (★★★★) tannins cloak the fruit mid-2012, so there's not the complexity we admired in spicy, juicy **08**. **09** sold out untasted. Ex Diemersfontein.

★★★★ **Cabernet Sauvignon-Shiraz Reserve** 🍷 La Motte stalwart. **10** (★★★) decidedly softer, easier, for earlier enjoyment than taut **09**, which had sufficient tannins for 2-3 years.

Grand Rouge ☺ 🍷 ★★★ Amply fruited & suffused with spice, La Motte's cab-led **10** Bordeaux blend veritably glides down. **One Off Red** ☺ 🍶 ★★★ 6-way eclectic **NV** blend from Wellington Wines is light-bodied, juicy & likeable.

Limited Release Cabernet Sauvignon-Merlot ★★★★ Step up **10** from De Wetshof offers dark berry, chocolate complexity, satisfying grip & savoury end for food. **Cabernet Sauvignon-Merlot** ★★★★ Compote of dark berries on riper **10** from Delheim. Structured & juicy table mate, but less gravitas & elegance than **09** (★★★★). **Parlotones Giant Mistake** NEW 📖 ★★ **09** from Wellington Wines; 5-way cab/merlot-led blend with trendy burst of mocha. Real ripe fruit, body & substance. **Capstone Shiraz-Cabernet Sauvignon** ⊚ ★★★★ Ripe-fruited, savoury & serious **09** from biodynamic producer Reyneke more interesting than **08** (★★★★). Spicy, floral aromas, then a supple but grippy palate needing year or two to flesh out. **Longmarket Shiraz-Pinotage** 📖 📖 ★★★ Light-toned, easy-sipping, lipsmacking **11** perfect for summer evenings. From Spier. **Goshawk's Chant** ⊕ 📖 ★★★★ Bordeaux base with rare red grape roobernet, in **10** preview ex Diemersfontein shows nice black fruit purity, herby overlay, lingering oaky grip. **The Portuguese Connection** ★★★★ Marries Portuguese grapes touriga & tinta with cab in spicy, juicy **11**. Quite robust, enjoy with hearty food now or age few years to soften. From Boplaas. **Juicy Red** ★★ Suitably succulent (but dry) cinsaut & shiraz-based **NV**, by Wellington Wines. **The Spaniard** NEW 📖 ★★★ **11** Mediterranean 4-way blend ex Paarl is juicy but somewhat dilute. Less convincing than original BLANKbottle version. **Natural Sweet Red** 📖 📖 ★★ Faintly berry-toned, cab-led low-alcohol **12** quaffer from Spier. **Juicy Sweet** ★★ 'Bel Rosso Sweet Red' previous editions. Dusty plums & spice on lightish sweet red, best served chilled. **NV** by Bergsig. Discontinued: **Longmarket Merlot-Cabernet Franc**, **House Red**, **Racy Red**.

Rosé Wines range

Longmarket Blanc de Noir ☺ 📖 📖 ★★★ Cheerful rosepetal **12** from pinotage. Off-dry, lightish, easygoing summertime wine with personality by Swartland Winery. **Pinotage-Shiraz Rosé** ☺ 📖 ★★★ **12** tangy, light & savoury, with hint of muscat, in refreshing just off-dry style. Picnic & aperitif-perfect pink from Delheim.

NSA Organic Diving Hawk Rosé 📖 ♻ 📖 ★★★ **12** your Italian food companion; frisky, dry & sippable. By Stellar Winery. **Longmarket Rosé** 📖 ★★★ Undemanding blush quaffer in light, off-dry style. **12** ex Villiera. **Chenin Blanc-Pinotage** ⊕ 📖 📖 ★★★ A tinge of pink in the gold, a little pinotage berry flavour in fruity, easy & charming, nearly-dry **11**. Ex Simonsig. **Zesty Rosé** ★★ Name change from 'Perky Pink', but character stays same. Off-dry perfumed fruity berries, zippy acid on very light **NV** from Bergsig. **Pierre Jourdan Tranquille Blush** ★★★ Simple, very pale chardonnay-pinot rosé, **NV** with sweet fruit whiffs, light & just off-dry. **Light Pinot Noir Rosé** NEW 📖 📖 ★★ **12** just off-dry, under 10% alcohol from Villiera. Chill for summer. **Parlotones We Call this Dancing** NEW 📖 ★★★ Characterful dry 27-way (!) blend, **12** generous strawberry fruit. Fresh semi-dry fun-times quaffing from Wellington Wines. **Natural Sweet Rosé** 📖 📖 ★★ By Spier, **12** low-alcohol sweet red berry sipper needs chilling.

Chardonnay range

★★★★☆ **Chardonnay Reserve** De Wetshof's bold, ripe & curvaceous **10** (★★★) shows serious intent but oak outpaces lime fruit mid-2012, so seems less fresh & integrated than **09**. Might yet settle down.

★★★★ **Abacus Chardonnay** ⊕ 📖 Lemon-toned **10** composed & considered, with 60% new oak supporting, not dominating. Taut & dry, wet clay & 'oyster shell' mineral notes, enjoyable now & for next year/2. From Spier.

★★★★ **Chardonnay Lightly Wooded** 📖 Peach & roasted almonds, Jordan's **11** gives immediate pleasure, leaps out of the glass. Crisply dry, it has the added plus of friendly 13% alc.

★★★★ **Elgin Chardonnay** 📖 📖 Though no longer named, Neil Ellis the maker of streamlined **11** (★★★★★), elegant step up on **10**. Focused lime marmalade & toasted hazelnut flavours seamlessly interwoven, shows deft oaking. Succulent, balanced & complex, long.

★★★★ **Exclusive Chardonnay** ⊕ 📖 Tropical fruit is part of Jordan's **11** (★★★★) appeal, rounded body, fresh drinkability the rest. Simpler than **09**.

★★★★ **Wild Yeast Chardonnay** ⊕ Earthy & oatmeal touches to ripe, flavourful **09** from Springfield. Sweet, delicious fruit untrammelled by oak, with weight balanced by good acidity. To seriously enjoy.

Longmarket Chardonnay ☺ 📖 ★★★ Happy summer refresher from Robertson Winery. **12** pops with appetising citrus & peach flavour, well rounded, brightened by acidity.

Organic Feeding Duck Chardonnay 📖 ♻ 📖 ★★★ Plump, lemon-buttery **12** a good partner (Stellar Winery winemakers say) for pasta, pork or chicken. **The Ladybird Chardonnay** 📖 ♻ 📖 ★★★★ Rich citrus flavour burst but restraint evident in oak sheen on zesty organic **11** ex Laibach. Vibrant & integrated. **Limestone Hill Chardonnay** ★★★ **11** from De Wetshof, creamy & mouthfilling easy-sipper with lemon/lime nuance. **Tell It Like It Is Chardonnay** 📖 📖 ★★ Buttery vanilla biscuit, dried fruit & moderate alcohol in drink-soon **11** by Weltevrede. **Light Chardonnay** ⊕ 🍴 🖬 ★ **11** faintly lemon-toned; ex Spier. Discontinued: **Limited Release Chardonnay**, **Chardonnay**, **What Chardonnay**.

Chenin Blanc range

★★★★☆ **The W (Chenin Blanc)** ◎ 🖬 **10** (★★★★) from biodynamic producer Reyneke more fruity (supported by a little sugar) than savoury **09**. Firmly structured & quite serious, with a mineral core.

★★★★ **Exclusive Selection Barrel Matured Chenin Blanc** 'Limited Release Chenin Blanc' previously. Restraint in oaking regime shows in opulently ripe tropical fruit on **10** from Simonsig. Mouthwatering acidity complements lees richness, forming & rounding body appealingly.

★★★★☆ **Chenin Blanc** 🍴 🖬 Lovely butter & toast on fruit-filled **11** (★★★★). Flavoursome & rich, balanced 14.7% alcohol but obvious sweetness (8g/l RS) makes you wish for a bite of acidity. Shade off hedonistic **10** & **09**, which showed variety's characteristic crisp freshness. From Spier.

★★★★ **Noble Late Harvest Chenin Blanc** ⊕ Barrel-fermented/aged **08** by Ken Forrester tasted some years back; tangerine & pine nuts, mouthwatering tangy-sweetness packed with lingering botrytis flavours. **Chenin Blanc Reserve** 🍴 ★★★ Slight peach note, bright acidity on straightforward **11**. Could do with more concentration but pleasant drinking, even so. By Ken Forrester. **Tell It Like It Is Chenin Blanc** 🍴 🖬 ★★★ **11** a reliable quaffer with lime through peach, good line of acidity, dry finish. By Ken Forrester. **Longmarket Chenin Blanc** 🍴 🖬 ★★★ **12** gentle peach & thatch on brief summer sipper from Rooiberg. **M'hudi Chenin Blanc** ⊕ 🍴 🖬 ★★★ Full-flavoured **11** blends tropical & light herbaceousness in engagingly rich fruitiness, balanced by zesty acidity. **Light Chenin Blanc** ⊕ 🍴 ★ Reticent **11** from Spier lacks varietal character.

Sauvignon Blanc range

★★★★ **Sauvignon Blanc Reserve** 🖬 Gooseberry, ripe apple greets you, there's richness in **11** but cool Groote Post terroir never lets go. Seam of minerality throughout, deepening on the finish.

★★★★☆ **Exclusive Selection Sauvignon Blanc** 🖬 **11** (★★★★) ex Cape Point & Walker Bay vines, sleek & elegant restraint with flinty, green-fruited tone. Unoaked, with creamy richness, but shade off **10**. By Cape Point Vineyards.

★★★★ **Exclusive Selection Nitida Sauvignon Blanc** 🍴 Consistently delicious example from Nitida Cellars. Some Darling fruit in **12**, gooseberries, with a fynbos edge adding focus, individuality.

★★★★ **Lonely Blue Gum Sauvignon Blanc** 🍴 🖬 Restrained grass & herb notes, creamy lees on **12** from Spier. In footsteps of elegant **11**, brisk acidity, pithy grapefruit texture, persistent steely end for oysters.

★★★★ **Elgin Sauvignon Blanc** ⊕ 🖬 Riper **11** (★★★) vintage shows melon & grenadilla flavours in earlier-drinking, plump & succulent style, by Neil Ellis. Shade off mineral, focused **10**.

★★★★ **La Motte Sauvignon Blanc Organically Grown** 🍴 🌱 🖬 Fuller than many of its peers; upholstered **12** has nicely weighted gooseberry character lifted by clean minerality. WO Walker Bay.

> **Breath Sauvignon Blanc** NEW ☺ 🍴 🖬 ★★★ Pungent nettle herbaceousness, **11** real charm & character at the price. By Wellington Wines, in PET (plastic) bottle.

Organic Swooping Swallow Sauvignon Blanc 🍴 🌱 🖬 ★★★ Brisk, lightish **12** by Stellar Winery has dried grass & nut nuances, unusual pineapple aftertaste. **Sauvignon Blanc Bush Vine** ⊕ ★★★ Typical Swartland dusty-grassy aromas on **11** follow to bracingly fresh crispness & lean mineral finish. From Darling Cellars. **Longmarket Sauvignon Blanc** ★★★ **12** by Robertson Winery; fresh, packed with cut grass & capsicum, zesty & youthful. Enjoy chilled, soon. **Wet Rocks Sauvignon Blanc** ⊕ 🖬 ★★★ Mineral **11** is crisp & moderately flavoured, 12% alc; perfect lunchtime companion. This, Tell It Like It Is ex Bergsig. **Light Sauvignon Blanc** 🍴 🖬 ★ **12** is light in all respects, including 9.5% alcohol. By Spier. **Tell It Like It Is Sauvignon Blanc** ⊕ 🍴 🖬 ★★★ Dried grass, hay aromas/flavours on **11**, lovely pithy farewell grip. Discontinued: **What Sauvignon Blanc**.

Niche White Cultivars range

★★★★ **NSA Rhine Riesling** 🖬 Absolutely charming, lively, dry **11**'s layers of pure fruit perfectly balanced by focused line of acidity, with underlying earthiness. No sulphur added by Villiera.

★★★★ **Ferricrete Riesling** ⊕ Named for ironstone soils yielding low alcohol (10%), semi-sweet (19 g/l sugar) **11**, with Germanic touch. Gloss to 'riverstone' minerality, lime & ginger in fresh finish. By Paul Cluver. **Pinot Grigio** 🍴 🖬 ★★ Pear toned **12** barely there, brief. Ex Van Loveren. **Limited Release Semillon** Not tasted. **Moscato Light** NEW 🍴 🖬 ★★ **12** a spicy, spritzy, sweet & low-alcohol charmer from Villiera. Discontinued: **Limited Release Gewürztraminer**.

White Blends range

★★★★☆ **DMZ White** ✓ 🍷 🍇 Was 'Garden Vineyards White'. Pure yet subtle, intriguing fresh earth, spice, dried peaches mix introduces complex, savoury **11**. Rich yet unheavy, with firm tangy conclusion. Whole greater than viognier, roussanne, chardonnay & chenin parts. Older oak fermented. By DeMorgenzon.

★★★★ **Nitida Cellars Sauvignon Blanc-Semillon Reserve** NEW 🍷 🍇 Gooseberry & leafy-toned white Bordeaux blend, **12** has nervy elegance; fresh & focused. Portion oak fermented.

★★★★★ **Spectrum White** ⓣ 🍷 From TMV, chenin-based blend. A mellow earthiness to 09 (★★★★★) distinguished it when tasted a few years back. Cellar-worthy, as for standout **08**.

One Off White ☺ 🍷 ★★★ NV from chenin & sauvignon, dash nouvelle. Dry, with spicy fruit. By Wellington Wines. **Longmarket Sauvignon Blanc-Chenin Blanc** ☺ 🍇 ★★★ Dry **12** Villiera blend more serious than flighty, over-delivers on flavour, with positive, pithy finish.

NSA Organic Fluttering Butterfly White 🍷 🌿 🍇 ★★ Now from colombard, **12** dry & light in body/flavour. By Stellar Winery. **Allan Mullins White My Song** NEW Not tasted. **Longmarket Chardonnay-Viognier** 🍷 🍇 ★★★ Uncomplicated everyday enjoyment from Spier. Lightly oaked **11** has chardonnay's lemon flavour, viognier's floral lift. **Nederburg Sauvignon Blanc-Chardonnay** NEW Missed our deadline. **Longmarket Sauvignon Blanc-Semillon** ⓣ ★★★ Zesty passionfruit flavours, satisfying weight & vinosity on **11** from Spier. **Zesty White** ★★ Fresh, if rather unconcentrated, NV chenin from Wellington Wines. **Bianca Light** ⓣ 🍇 ★★ **11** off-dry, low-alcohol blend from Delheim. **Zesty Sweet** ★★ 'Sassy Sweet' previously. Uncomplicated, lightish NV white by Bergsig, quaffable tropical fruit salad flavours. **Parlotones Push Me To The Floor** NEW 🍷 ★★★★ Aromatic, oxidative chenin-based 4-way blend by Wellington Wines, **10** shows body & complexity. Marzipan notes on spicy fragrance. Enjoy soon. **Chardonnay-Pinot Noir** ★★★ Faint blush in pretty, just off-dry **11** light lunchtime sipper, slips down easily. **Natural Sweet White** 🍷 🍇 ★★ Sauvignon leads colombard & viognier in **12** low-alcohol sweet delight from Spier. Discontinued: **Wild White**, **Chardonnay-Semillon**, **House White**, **House Sweet**.

Méthode Cap Classique Sparkling range

★★★★☆ **Exclusive Selection Pinot Noir Rosé NSA** 🍇 'Limited Release' previously. Pretty pale-blush **11** by Simonsig is persistently dry, with dense, creamy texture. Refined, understated, with delightful layers of baked berries & shortbread. More developed than vintage would suggest.

★★★★ **Blanc de Blancs Brut** Voluptuous NV from Villiera, for those who enjoy generously styled MCC; dry but plenty flavour & richness delivered on wave of fresh creamy mousse.

★★★★ **Brut Natural** ✓ Great charm in whistle-clean, delicate chardonnay **09** from Villiera. Bone-dry, yet a soft, refined edge. Persistent mousse carries pure-fruited citrus flavours. No added sulphur.

★★★★☆ **Vintage Reserve Brut** Ultra-elegant, creamy **07** from Villiera shows cool vintage's remarkable freshness & ageing potential. 5 years on lees imparts dimension & complexity to blend of pinot & barrel-fermented chardonnay.

★★★★ **Krone Borealis Cuvée Brut** ✓ From MCC specialist The House of Krone. **09** in style: bruised apple, creamy mousse, emphatic dryness. 55/45 chardonnay, pinot blend. As engaging as elegant **08**.

Brut Rosé ★★★ Pinotage-led MCC NV from Villiera offers simple flavours with a touch of bitterness. **Krone Rosé Cuvée Brut** NEW ✓ ★★★★ 60/40 pinot/chardonnay **08** perfect aperitif or chocolate dessert partner: delicate, creamy & persistent bottle-fermented bubbly from The House of Krone. **Brut** ★★★★ Reliable, popular Villiera NV MCC from chardonnay & both pinots. Exuberantly fresh.

Sparkling Wines range

Spumante Rosé ★★ Frothy strawberry & peach on NV sweet sparkler. By Rooiberg, as all these. **Spumante Brut** ★★ Lively NV bubbles with appley bite, tangy dry lemon finish. **Organic Sauvignon Blanc Brut** 🌿 ★★★ Fresh, dry & brisk NV, perfect for lazy brunches. **Spumante Doux** ★★ For the sweet toothed, NV light sparkler with candied almond flavour.

1L Box range

Dry Red ★★ All-sorts NV for easy sipping. By Simonsvlei, as all following. **Off-Dry Rosé** ★★ Bright, juicy berry-fruited NV with spice from shiraz. Serve chilled for summer. **Crisp White** ★★ NV from chenin with understated apple flavours. **Light White** NEW ★ NV from chenin, dry, light in all departments. **Semi-Sweet** ★★ Soft easy NV sipper from chenin.

2L Box range

Longmarket Merlot ★★ Light plummy fruit on **11** quaffer. By Simonsvlei, like Cab-Merlot. **Longmarket Cabernet Sauvignon-Merlot** ★★ Ripe berry tones on easy **11** picnic companion. **Longmarket Chardonnay**

★★★ Flavoursome **12** for easy sipping with refreshing blood orange & peach flavours, gentle brush of oak. By Robertson Winery. **Longmarket Pinot Grigio** NEW Not tasted. **Longmarket Sauvignon Blanc** ★★★ From Robertson Winery, **12**, boasts fresh grass & fig notes, is light & gently sweet for lunchtime enjoyment.

3L Box range

Light Red NEW ★★ Off-dry NV party starter, mainly shiraz, low ±10% alcohol. By Simonsvlei, as for all. **Dry Red** ★★ Soft, easy NV berry-flavoured sipper. **Light Rosé** ★★ Low-alcohol light-berried NV from shiraz. **Light White** ★ Dry, light NV al fresco tipple. **Crisp White** ★★ Off-dry NV from chenin, bright & zippy.

5L Box range

Dry Red ★★ Undemanding smooth & spicy NV quaffer. By Simonsvlei, as all these. **Blanc de Blanc** ★★ Lightish, friendly & dry NV from chenin. **Stein** ★★ Off-dry NV from chenin, light but quite zingy apple taste. — DB/WB/GdB/CE/MF/HJ/TJ/AL/CM/FM/IM/JP/Jpf/DS/CR/CvZ/MW

■ **Workhorse (Marks & Spencer)** see Ken Forrester Wines
■ **Wyma Vineyards** see Cape Hutton
■ **Xenna** see Annex Kloof Wines
■ **Y** see Yonder Hill

Yardstick Wines

Location/map: Stellenbosch ▪ WO: Elgin/Stellenbosch/Western Cape ▪ Est/1stB 2009 ▪ Tasting by appt ▪ Owner(s) Peter Tempelhoff & Adam Mason ▪ Winemaker(s) Adam Mason ▪ 171cs own label 50% red 50% white ▪ adam@mulderbosch.co.za, peter@collectionmcgrath.com ▪ www.yardstickwines.com ▪ S 33° 53′ 22. 8″ E 018° 49′ 8.3″ ▪ **T +27 (0)82-924-3286 (Adam)/+27 (0)82-578-5320 (Peter)** ▪ F +27 (0)86-528-6463 (Adam)/+27 (0)86-216-7271 (Peter)

Collaborations between chefs and winemakers usually focus on food preparation — not the other way around. Mulderbosch winemaker Adam Mason partners Cellars-Hohenort chef Peter Tempelhoff to make this funky-named range of wines. New fruit sources added excitement this year, along with a move to Mulderbosch cellar space. Due to 'overwhelmingly positive' response, the Marvellous range has been upgraded from a 'cheeky once-off to a more permanent fixture'.

Yardstick range

★★★★ **Pinot Noir** 🌿 **11** is food friendly & light yet still abundantly fruity. Smoky red & black berries with firm tannin backing & structured intensity. An example of leashed power & length.

★★★★ **Chardonnay** NEW 🌿 Stellar debut for **11**. Elgin fruit makes for a vibrant, zesty, tangerine-filled mouthful. Creamy oak provides structure & length. Elegant, but with a mischievous glint lurking.

Marvellous range

Kaboom! ✓ 🌿 ★★★★ Cab-led Bordeaux blend, previewed **10** fynbos edge to vibrant berry fruit, chalky texture to medium body, long ripe aftertaste. WO W Cape. **Shazam!** NEW ✓ 🌿 ★★★★ Ex-tank **11**, from shiraz & dab viognier, shows plum richness & succulence. WO Stellenbosch, as next. **Ka-Pow!** NEW 🌿 ★★★ 3-way blend of chenin with chardonnay & viognier in pre-bottling **12**. Leesy pomelo balanced by toned acid. Nice freshness & length. — FM

Yonder Hill

Location: Somerset West ▪ Map: Helderberg ▪ WO: Stellenbosch/Western Cape ▪ Est 1989 ▪ 1stB 1993 ▪ Tasting & sales Mon-Fri 9-4 Sat (Oct-Mar) 10-2 ▪ Closed all pub hols ▪ Tour groups ▪ Gift shop ▪ Olives & olive oil tasting ▪ Cheese platters ▪ 'Winemakers Friday' includes tasting & snacks prepared by winemaker ▪ Owner(s) Naudé family ▪ Cellarmaster(s) Bennie Avenant (2008) ▪ Winemaker(s)/viticulturist(s) Bennie Avenant ▪ 14ha/10ha (cabs s/f, merlot, p verdot) ▪ 80t/10,000cs own label 95% red 5% white ▪ PO Box 914 Stellenbosch 7599 ▪ wines@yonderhill.co.za ▪ www.yonderhill.co.za ▪ S 34° 2′ 22.5″ E 018° 49′ 40.2″ ▪ **T +27 (0)21-855-1008** ▪ F +27 (0)21-855-1006

They specialise in red Bordeaux varieties on what winemaker/viticulturist Bennie Avenant calls the 'micro-terroirs' of this Helderberg farm (a little sauvignon and shiraz is brought in). And a lot of fine-tuning goes on. So the new vineyards (2013 sees their first harvest) are planted with different clones, with different rootstocks and irrigation, plus new pruning and trellising methods.

'This will definitely make for some interesting and complex terroir blends,' says Bennie happily.

Yonder Hill range

★★★★☆ **Merlot** ⊕ Statuesque, aristocratic bearing of **09** enhanced by opulent ripeness. Great concentration & complexity. Deep, dry, focused black fruit.

★★★★ **Inanda** 🍱 Cab in a rather sombre style dominates **09** blend with merlot & cab franc. Extracted & powerful, with dense & chewy fruit. Subtle elegance is not the point here!

★★★★☆ **Nicola** ⊕ Previously 'Estate'. **08** Bordeaux-style blend still in infancy a few years back, but showed enticing herbaceous notes, ripe blackcurrant fruit. Real thoroughbred focus & agility.

Discontinued: **Cabernet Sauvignon**, **Shiraz-Merlot**.

Y range

Merlot ⊕ 🍱 ★★★ Enticing juicy fruit on easy-drinking **09** tasted few years ago. **Shiraz** ⊕ 🍱 ★★★ Last tasted was loud & spicy **09**, with varietal character, leathery finish. WO W Cape for these. **Sauvignon Blanc** 🍱 ★★★ **12** doesn't linger, but fruitily friendly while it's there, & leaves with a touch of acid-drop sweetness. — TJ

ZAHarmonie Wine Cellar

Location: Sutherland ▪ Est 2012 ▪ 1stB 2011 ▪ Tasting, sales & cellar tours Mon-Sat by appt ▪ Fee R30pp, waived on purchase ▪ Closed Easter Fri/Sun & Dec 25 ▪ Meals/refreshments by appt ▪ BYO picnic ▪ Owner(s) Bi-Anne du Toit ▪ Winemaker(s) Bi-Anne du Toit (Aug 2008) ▪ (mourv) ▪ 1t/59cs own label 42% red 58% port ▪ PO Box 154 Sutherland 6920 ▪ harmoniekelder@gmail.com ▪ **T +27 (0)23-571-1137/+27 (0)78-165-8429** ▪ F +27 (0)23-571-1137

Things are done a little differently at the 'coldest winery in South Africa', the first in Sutherland, by pioneering winemaker Bi-Anne du Toit, who traded the Swartland for this starry-skied plateau when she married the love of her life. Malolactic fermentation, for example, proved a challenge and was completed on the 2012 wines only in August: 'After heating the barrels, I kept them covered with blankets and duvets!' Grapes are being sourced from the Boland until her mourvèdre comes into production. Wines (Anti-Freeze Cape Ruby NV and The Maiden Cabernet Sauvignon 11) missed our deadline.

▪ **Zalze** *see* Kleine Zalze Wines

Zanddrift Vineyards

Location/WO: Paarl ▪ Map: Paarl & Wellington ▪ Est 1995 ▪ 1stB 2006 ▪ Tasting & sales Mon-Fri 9-1 & 2-5 ▪ Function venue: contact +27 (0)72-181-1780 (Marco)/+27 (0)71-580-6767 (Jackie) ▪ Owner(s) Windshare Trading 23 (Singapore) ▪ Winemaker(s)/vineyard manager(s) Christo Jacobs ▪ 48ha/6.6ha (cab, shiraz) ▪ PO Box 1302 Suider-Paarl 7624 ▪ zanddrift@telkomsa.net ▪ http://zanddrift.webs.com/ ▪ S 33° 45'39.20" E 018° 59'11.41" ▪ **T +27 (0)21-863-2076/+27 (0)82-256-5006** ▪ F +27 (0)86-530-1892

No excuses for glasses to run dry at this Singapore-owned boutique winery near Paarl: the chapel-like visitor locale has been remodelled and now trebles as a tasting, function and wedding venue — a festive-sounding arrangement the Italian POWs confined here in the 1940s doubtless would have raised a toast to.

Chapel Cellar range

Cabernet Sauvignon ⊕ 🍱 ★★★ With supple tannins & chalky fruit, **07** slipped down easily last time despite 14.7% alcohol. **Shiraz** ⊕ 🍱 ★★★ Step-up **07** high-toned red fruit, zesty acidity. — CvZ

Zandfontein

Location: Napier ▪ WO: Cape Agulhas/Western Cape ▪ Tasting & sales by appt ▪ Owner(s) Hennie & Annatjie Andrews ▪ Cellarmaster(s)/winemaker(s)/viticulturist(s) Hennie Andrews ▪ 800ha/6ha (shiraz, sauv) ▪ 3 sauv + bought in shiraz/±750cs own label 67% red 33% white ▪ PO Box 1080 Bredasdorp 7280 ▪ hennie@braaicube.co.za ▪ **T +27 (0)82-940-3654**

Still making wine? 'Yes and no,' says Hennie Andrews, whose Napier farm has been sold. Still buying in grapes and working in his cellar at time of writing, h and wife Annatjie were looking for a new home, perhaps in Greyton, where he could continue as a small-scale winemaker.

Henry Shiraz ★★★ Previewed **10** a more modern take than most from this area: very ripe fruit, high but well-disguised alcohol (15%), berry compote & lashings oak. From Cape Agulhas grapes (previous from Wellington). **Fijnbosch Sauvignon Blanc** ★★★ Lemongrass & herbaceous notes on early-picked **11** previewed last edition. From Napier vines, vinified by Jean Daneel (Jean Daneel Wines). WO W Cape. — CvZ/MW

Zandvliet Wine Estate & Thoroughbred Stud

Location: Ashton ▪ Map/WO: Robertson ▪ Est 1867 ▪ 1stB 1975 ▪ Tasting & sales Mon-Fri 9–5 Sat 10-2 ▪ Closed Easter Fri/Sun, Dec 25/26 & Jan 1 ▪ Tour groups ▪ Private tastings presented by cellarmaster/winemaker in Zandvliet House by appt only — fee R55pp ▪ BYO picnic ▪ Owner(s) Paul & Dan de Wet ▪ Cellarmaster(s) Paul de Wet (1971) ▪ Winemaker(s) Jacques Cilliers (Dec 2011) ▪ Viticulturist(s) Dan de Wet (1993) ▪ 830ha/148ha (cab, shiraz, chard, cbard, sauv) ▪ 1,134t/45,000cs own label 47% red 49% white 5% rosé + 2,000cs for clients ▪ Export brands: Enon, Cogmanskloof ▪ Ranges for clients: Cogmanskloof Cape Muscat, Rijckholt (Netherlands); Villa San Giovanni ▪ PO Box 36 Ashton 6715 ▪ info@zandvliet.co.za ▪ www.zandvliet.co.za ▪ S 33° 50' 50.7" E 020° 2' 13.7" ▪ **T +27 (0)23-615-1146** ▪ F +27 (0)23-615-1327

Approaching 40 years of bottling wine, this fourth-generation branch of a clan deeply rooted in Robertson Valley is looking ahead, determined to reverse languishing per capita wine consumption by attracting the emerging youth market with affordable quality. Meanwhile, worldwide exports continue, bolstered by a five-year Chinese sales and distribution deal. New winemaker Jacques Cilliers is focusing on fine-wine, spearheaded by the revival of the flagship Kalkveld 'Hill of Enon' Shiraz. 'Kalkveld' describes lime-rich soil pockets enriching both Paul's wines and brother Dan's racehorses, including the legendary Pocket Power.

Zandvliet Estate range

★★★★ **Kalkveld Shiraz** New-French-oaked version. **07** (★★★★) drinks well: very ripe yet not overly sweet. As with perfumed **06**, oak is supportive, structural, adds savoury nuance; 15% alcohol tad warming.

★★★★ **Kalkveld Chardonnay** 100% new French oak sets this apart from standard bottling. **10** restrained & savoury, some earthy notes.

Kalkveld 'Hill of Enon' Shiraz Await new. **Shiraz** ★★ **09** for fans of full bore super-ripe reds, warmth from high alcohol better with food than solo. **Chardonnay** ★★★ Appealing **12** has sweet vanilla charm from brief sojourn in oak, undemanding flavours. **VLW Cape Vintage Shiraz** NEW ★★★ Fortified port-style **08** from shiraz, dusty ripe fruit, syrupy sweet with a charming Christmas pudding warmth.

Le Bistro range

Cabernet Sauvignon ★★★ Plum & prune aromas on ripe, accessible **10**; light-bodied for anytime enjoyment. **Chardonnay Unwooded** ★★★ Creamy **12** ripe & easy sipper with peach & pear flavours. **Sauvignon Blanc** ★★ Picked early, **12** is very dry & bracing. **Crème** ★★ Tropical quaffability from **12**'s combo colombard & sauvignon.

My Best Friend range

Red ★★ Strawberry compote, slightly sweet **09** easy everyday red. **Shiraz Rosé** ★★ Switches from slightly sweet to ultra-dry in **12**, with light berry tone. **Semi-Sweet** ★★ From chenin, **12** soft & uncomplicated curry companion. **White** ★★★ Lick of chenin's quince in step-up **12**, friendly almost-dry blend with chardonnay & two others. — DB/HJ

- **Zandwijk** *see* Kleine Draken
- **Zantsi** *see* Darling Cellars
- **Zaràfa** *see* Mountain River Wines
- **Z-Collection** *see* Zevenwacht
- **Zebra Collection** *see* Rooiberg Winery
- **Zee** *see* Anura Vineyards
- **Zellerhof** *see* Huguenot Wine Farmers
- **Zenith** *see* Kumala

Zevenwacht

Location: Kuils River ▪ Map/WO: Stellenbosch ▪ Est 1980 ▪ 1stB 1983 ▪ Tasting & sales Mon-Fri 8.30-5 Sat/Sun 9.30-5 ▪ Fee R32 incl glass ▪ Cellar tours by appt ▪ Closed Dec 25 ▪ Restaurant (see Restaurants section) ▪ Picnics in summer ▪ Facilities for children ▪ Gift shop ▪ Conferences ▪ Weddings/banqueting ▪ Walking & mountain biking trails ▪ 4x4 trail by appt ▪ Conservation area ▪ Mangwanani spa ▪ 4-star country inn (see Accommodation section) ▪ Owner(s) Harold Johnson ▪ Winemaker(s) Jacques Viljoen (May 2005), with Hagen Viljoen (Sep 2010) ▪ Viticulturist(s) Eduard van den Berg (Jan 2001) ▪ 473ha/150ha (cabs s/f, grenache, merlot, mourv, ptage, primitivo, shiraz, chard, chenin, gewürz, Muscat de F, rouss, sauv, sem, viog) ▪ 657t/50,000cs own label 48% red 48% white 4% rosé ▪ BWI, IPW ▪ PO Box 387 Kuils River 7579 ▪ info@zevenwacht.co.za ▪ www.zevenwacht.co.za ▪ S 33° 55' 46.0" E 018° 43' 38.2" ▪ **T +27 (0)21-900-5700** ▪ F +27 (0)21-903-3373

Harold Johnson, formerly a leading figure in the construction industry, bought Zevenwacht in 1992 and has since invested heavily in realising the property's potential. Wife Denise, a director, says: 'While we do have tourist facilities, management of our restaurant, banqueting, picnics and spa is all outsourced. Our focus has always been and will always be our wine.' Winemaker Jacques Viljoen, who started here as a junior in 2002 before taking full charge of the cellar in 2005, now has input from the acclaimed Chris Keet (previously of the sadly defunct Cordoba). 'We want to be measured against the best of the best. We won't be skimping on oak, but ultimately it's about respecting the fruit,' says Viljoen.

Flagship range

Cabernet Sauvignon 🔲 ★★★★ Cassis, attractive herbal quality on classically styled **10**. Medium bodied, with fresh acidity, fine tannins. **Merlot** ✓ ★★★★ **09** is a serious effort with red & black fruit, olive note, attractive oak. Medium bodied but greater heft than **08** (★★★★). Well balanced, with fresh acidity & fine tannins. **Syrah** ⊕ ★★★★ Unpretentious **08** shows red & black fruit, hint of pepper; medium body with fresh acidity, well-judged oak. **Chenin Blanc** 🔲 🔲 ★★★★ Citrus through peach & brush of vanilla on **11**. Good concentration, bright acidity but straightforward overall. **Sauvignon Blanc** 🔲 🔲 ★★★★ Ripe yellow fruit, slight sweaty note & soft acidity on **12**. Lacks poise of **11** (★★★★). **Semillon Straw Wine** 🔲 Await new vintage.

Z-Collection

★★★★ **CMC** Mainly cab & merlot, dash cab franc, **09** shows old-school styling: red & black fruit, some leafiness, dusty oak (16 months, 50% new). Medium bodied with fresh acidity, fine tannins. Finish is dry, pleasingly austere.

★★★★ **Gewürztraminer** ⊕ 🔲 🔲 Poised **11** (★★★★★) subtle lime & pot-pourri; juicy fruit, some spice, thick but not unctuous texture, gentle but sufficient acidity. Also-reviewed **10** almost unbearably rich & heady with plenty of Turkish Delight character.

SGM ★★★★ No viognier this time, so **09** is 74% shiraz with grenache & mourvèdre. Super-concentrated & smooth, with ripe black fruit & fynbos. Ambitious but arguably overdone.

Limited Release range

★★★★ **360° Sauvignon Blanc** 🔲 🔲 **11** rather lean & severe despite 5% older-barrel portion. Gunpowder note on the nose, intense lime, bracing acidity on the palate. Long dry finish.

Primitivo 🔲 ★★★★ Variety also known as zinfandel. **10** manages to retain surprising freshness despite 15.5% alcohol. Red & black fruit, slightly hollow.

The Tin Mine Collection

★★★★ **Red** ✓ 🔲 🔲 **10** (61% shiraz, rest grenache, mourvèdre, primitivo) continues positive trajectory for this label. Red & black cherry, some fynbos. Displays admirable lightness of touch.

★★★★ **White** 🔲 🔲 Unadulterated **11** a blend of 45% chenin, chardonnay, viognier & roussanne. Intense citrus & peach, hint of vanilla (6 months in oak, 50% new), fresh acidity.

7even range

Pinotage 🔲 🔲 ★★ Confected **11** shows dark cherry fruit, oak-derived coffee. **Rood** 🔲 ★★★ Was 'Zevenrood'. Cab-driven **09** is light bodied, with bright acidity & firm tannins. **Rosé** 🔲 🔲 ★★★ Plenty of strawberry, soft acidity on off-dry **12**, mainly from merlot. **Blanc** ⊕ 🔲 🔲 ★★ Was 'Zevenblanc'. Sauvignon-led **11** is lean, neutral, acidic. **Bouquet** 🔲 🔲 ★★★ 'Bouquet Blanc' last time. Viognier-led off-dry **12** equals jolly summer drinking. Note: range last listed as 'Lifestyle'. — CE

Zidela Wines

Location: Stellenbosch ▪ WO: Western Cape ▪ Est 2001 ▪ 1stB 2002 ▪ Closed to public ▪ Owner(s) Danie Kritzinger, Herman Nell & Jaco Kritzinger ▪ 70% red 25% white 5% rosé ▪ 5,000,000 litres for clients ▪ PO Box 3021 Matieland 7602 ▪ info@zidelawines.co.za ▪ www.zidelawines.co.za ▪ **T +27 (0)21-880-2936** ▪ F +27 (0)21-880-2937

This Stellenbosch negociant house is thrilled to have increased exports, particularly of bottled wines. Co-owner Jaco Kritzinger would like, however, to up the ante. He believes too many of South Africa's markets regard the country as a source of 'cheap' product, and plans to change this 'one importer at a time'.

Zidela range

Cabernet Sauvignon ⑦ ★★★ **10** appealing berry-toned sipper. Like following, with gentle tannic nip thanks to brief sojourn oak. **Merlot** ⑦ ★★ Leafy **10** has some mulberry whiffs, good grip. **Pinotage** Await next, as for **Shiraz, Chenin Blanc, Sauvignon Blanc. Bouquet Blanc** ⑦ ▨ ★★ **11** honest, softly sweet & grapey sipper from muscat ottonel. Discontinued: **Cabernet Sauvignon-Merlot-Petit Verdot.**

Suikerbosch range

Reserve Shiraz ⑦ ★★★ Juicy fruit centre, taut tannin structure & unusual orange rind highlight on **08. Shiraz-Merlot** 🍴 Await next, as for **Reserve Chardonnay, Golden Muscat. Rosé** 🍴 ▨ ★★ **11** authentic coral hue but lacks true rosé aromas/flavours. Discontinued: **Chenin Blanc.** — CvZ

Zoetendal Wines

Location/WO: Elim ▪ Map: Southern Cape ▪ Est 2002 ▪ 1stB 2004 ▪ Tasting, sales & cellar tours Mon-Fri 9-5 Sat by appt 9-1 ▪ Closed Easter Fri/Sun, Dec 25 & Jan 1 ▪ Conservation area ▪ Draaihoek self-catering guesthouse ▪ Owner(s) Johan & Elizan de Kock ▪ Cellarmaster(s)/winemaker(s)/viticulturist(s) Johan de Kock ▪ 790ha/8.5ha (shiraz, sauv) ▪ 39t/2,000cs own label 15% red 85% white ▪ Other export brand: Last Chance ▪ BWI, IPW ▪ PO Box 22 Elim 7284 ▪ info@zoetendalwines.co.za ▪ www.zoetendalwines.co.za ▪ S 34° 36'1.0" E 019° 47'20.9" ▪ **T +27 (0)28-482-1717** ▪ F +27 (0)28-482-1720

Hard to believe that one of South Africa's star winegrowing wards was born on the golf course. Back in 1996, Bredasdorp sheep and grain farmer Johan de Kock played a few rounds with then Nederburg cellarmaster Newald Marais, who had spotted winegrowing potential in the windswept plains around Elim. Johan planted his first vines that same year. He and wife Elizan's boutique wines have since pleased many a palate, including UK winewriter Oz Clarke's, who included the current sauvignon in his latest 250 top wines list.

Shiraz ⑦ ★★★★ Sweet fruit, hint char on firm **09.** Commendably dry & savoury, holds head high in area recognised for the variety. **Sauvignon Blanc** 🍴 ▨ ★★★★ Satisfying **11** back on track, its hallmark herbal character well balanced with creamy lees & a full spread of green & citrus flavours. Discontinued: **Milè.** — WB/GdB

Zonnebloem

Location: Stellenbosch ▪ WO: Stellenbosch/Western Cape/Coastal/Darling ▪ Est 1893 ▪ Wine sales at Die Bergkelder Wine Centre ▪ Owner(s) Distell ▪ Cellarmaster(s) Deon Boshoff (Feb 2010) ▪ Winemaker(s) Bonny van Niekerk (reds, Oct 2007) & Elize Coetzee (whites, Jun 2010), with Gerhard Viljoen (reds, Aug 2007), Melissa Williams (reds, Dec 2009), Bradley van Niekerk (whites) & Natasha Williams (whites, Aug 2008) ▪ Viticulturist(s) Annelie Viljoen (Jun 2008) ▪ (cab, merlot, shiraz, chard, sauv, sem) ▪ 9,000t/±220,000cs own label 59% red 41% white ▪ ISO 9002, Fairtrade ▪ PO Box 184 Stellenbosch 7599 ▪ info@zonnebloem.co.za ▪ www.zonnebloem.co.za ▪ **T +27 (0)21-809-7000** ▪ F +27 (0)21-886-4879

New energy is flowing through this venerable Cape brand, with an expanded range of Limited Edition wines, new labels for the flagship Laureat blend, an enthusiastic team of mostly young women winemakers led by the quietly confident Deon Boshoff, and wines on an upwards curve of quality. But this is not a brand to forget its roots — much of the fruit comes from third or fourth generation contracted growers, and family heritage features strongly on the new Lauréat packaging.

Limited Editions

★★★★ **Sauvignon Blanc** 🚫 **11** (WO Coastal) step up on **10** (★★★) & showing pleasing complexity in citrus — limes & naartjies — combining with green vegetal notes, balancing acidity. **12** preview (WO W Cape) also promising well.

★★★★ **Sauvignon Blanc-Semillon** NEW 🚫 Delicious 75/25 Bordeaux blend, entirely unwooded to preserve zippy grapefruit & gooseberry flavours; ex-tank **12**'s weight & length augur well. Coastal WO.

Cabernet Sauvignon NEW ★★★★ 100% new oak for this top-line version. Dark choc & spiced blackcurrant nose on **09** with whiffs of eucalyptus & herbs. Well-managed tannins, good length. **Pinotage** Await next.

Shiraz ★★★★ **09** sweet concentrated fruit with some meaty/hammy notes, more intense than **08** (★★★★). Dark chocolate, plums, damsons, currants all lifted by well-integrated acidity & all-new oak. Lots of drinking pleasure. **Chenin Blanc** ★★★☆ From Darling dryland vines, unwooded. **11** ripe honeyed entry with some leafy, appley hints. Concentrated yellow fruits with peaches, guavas & fresh lemons. Debut **09** (★★★★) shade more impressive. **10** sold out unreviewed. **Semillon** 🚫 ★★★★ **11** lots of fresh limes, orange citrus & subtle whiffs of fragrant blossoms & vanilla seeds. Crisp acidity & intensity suggest even more delight to come over time. Improves on **08** (★★★★). **09**, **10** sold out untasted. WO W Cape.

Zonnebloem range

> **Chardonnay** 😊 🍴 🚫 ★★★ Plenty of easy-drinking appeal in well-made, friendly **11**. Lime marmalade, oranges & melons with merest waft of oak (10%). WO W Cape, as next. **Blanc de Blanc** 😊 🍴 🚫 ★★★ All-day summer sipper **12** from chenin & sauvignon (80/20); tinned litchis & grapefruit; dry, brisk acidity, friendly (11.5%) alcohol.

Cabernet Sauvignon 🚫 ★★★ Stalky nose **10** with soft melange of black fruit. Dry wood tannins (staves & barrels), slightly bitter coffee finish, lacks classic style of previous. **Merlot** 🚫 ★★★ Bright dark fruit & chocolate notes, **10** also stewed plums, whiffs of spice, dry finish. **Pinotage** 🚫 ★★★ Plenty of dry wood tannins give stern backbone to **10**, offset by stewed plums & leather. **Shiraz** ⏱ 🚫 ★★★★ Rich, dark **10** packed with ripe, spicy fruit dusted with black pepper. Nice weight, but flavours don't linger. **Shiraz-Mourvèdre-Viognier** ✓ 🚫 ★★★★ Casserole aromas of dried & spiced meats, **10** broadens to blackcurrant sweetness with lively acidity & pleasing length. **Lauréat** 🚫 ★★★★ Enduring label switches to Bordeaux blend plus 10% shiraz in **10**. Sweet plum clafoutis aromas with some spiced cherries. Soft tannins surround black berries with pleasing grip on finish. **Sauvignon Blanc** 🍴 🚫 ★★★ Tinned grapefruit aromas on **12** with mineral/metallic edge. Palate is a mouthful of green peas, guavas & papaya. WO W Cape. Discontinued: **Viognier**. — CM

■ **Zonneweelde** *see* Slanghoek Winery

Zonquasdrift Estates

🍷 NEW

Location: Riebeek-Kasteel ▪ Map: Tulbagh ▪ WO: Swartland ▪ Est 2001 ▪ 1stB 2009 ▪ Tasting Mon-Fri by appt ▪ Closed all pub hols ▪ Sales at Riebeek Cellars ▪ Owner(s) Alexander & Antoinette Mettenheimer ▪ Cellarmaster(s) Sakkie Bester (Riebeek Cellars) ▪ Winemaker(s) Eric Saayman (Riebeek Cellars) ▪ Viticulturist(s) Gustav Andrag (Sep 2005) ▪ 350ha/47ha (shiraz, chard, chenin) ▪ 580t/50cs own label 100% white ▪ HACCP, IPW ▪ PO Box 7 Riebeek-Kasteel 7307 ▪ info@zonquasdrift.co.za ▪ S 33° 20′ 35.00″ E 018° 58′ 32.00″ ▪ **T +27 (0)22-448-1078/+27 (0)82-896-4430** ▪ F +27 (0)86-606-2049

When Alexander and Antoinette Mettenheimer bought Zonquasdrift farm in 2001, they realised the value of the chenin blanc vines dating back to 1962. A precious 50 cases are now made under the Zonquasdrift label by nearby Riebeek Cellars' Eric Saayman from a vineyard managed by Gustav Andrag as part of 47ha of mainly chenin, chardonnay and shiraz. Tastings (and tours of the historic Berg River property named for the bygone Zonqua tribe) by appointment; sales at Riebeek.

Chenin Blanc 🍴 ★★★★ Single-vineyard handled with care & allowed full (unoaked) expression: preview **11** lemon blossom perfume, stonefruit & lime, lovely intensity, weight & texture. A label to watch. — CE/CvZ

Zorgvliet Wines

Location/map: Stellenbosch ▪ WO: Banghoek ▪ Est/1stB 2000 ▪ Tasting & sales Mon-Fri 9–5 Sat/Sun 10–5 pub hols 10–4 ▪ Closed Good Fri & Dec 25 ▪ Fee R20pp, waived on purchase ▪ Cellar tours by appt ▪ Zorgvliet Picnic Sep-Apr ▪ Facilities for children ▪ Tour groups ▪ Gifts ▪ Conferences ▪ Walks/hikes ▪ Zorgvliet Country Hotel (17 rooms) ▪ Owner(s) Van der Merwe family ▪ Winemaker(s) Neil Moorhouse (Jan 2003) ▪ Viticulturist(s) Hannes

Jansen van Vuuren ▪ 131ha/46ha (cabs s/f, merlot, p verdot, pinot, shiraz, tannat, chard, chenin, sauv, sem, viog) ▪ 250t/12,500cs own label 50% red 40% white 7% rosé 3% MCC + 200t for clients ▪ PO Box 1595 Stellenbosch 7599 ▪ winecellar@zorgvliet.com ▪ www.zorgvlietwines.com ▪ S 33° 54′41.7″ E 018° 56′32.0″ ▪ **T +27 (0)21-885-1399** ▪ F +27 (0)21-885-1318

With his tenth harvest in 2012, winemaker Neil Moorhouse and the team at this family-owned winery in Stellenbosch's Banhoek Valley took time to reflect — and big changes are already afoot. At the time of writing, he was supervising the installation of four supersized 4,500L barrels, intended to soften and polish the red wines (flagship Richelle in particular) while imparting less oak character. 'We felt the toast and oak was more prominent than the fruit on older vintages, so we decided to alter things.' Though Neil had advocated larger, older oak, he wasn't anticipating as dramatic a stylistic move as this! '180-degree change' he says — but co-owner Mac van der Merwe believes it's the right thing.

Zorgvliet range

★★★★ **Cabernet Sauvignon** ⓘ Seriously styled mint-chocolate **08** has dabs cab franc & merlot, & plenty fruit to stay the distance, while assertive tannins from oaking & skins soften & integrate.

★★★★ **Cabernet Franc** ⓘ 🍷 Preview **09** shows variety's typically herbal aromas, which belie succulent red fruit flavours underpinned by structured tannins & fine acid, ensuring elegance. **08** was under Silver Myn.

★★★★ **Petit Verdot** 🍷 **08** (★★★★) is powerful, brooding, but shows restraint. Fine tannins are still perky despite padding of rich fruit. Savoury **07** shade more impressive.

★★★★☆ **Richelle 08** retains power, complexity of **07**. Cab still leads mix of all-Bordeaux varieties, plus dab tannat. Concentration & density, spice, integration & elegance all there in a classy package.

★★★★ **Sauvignon Blanc** 🍷 Powerfully crisp & pungent **12** tank sample assails the senses with flinty minerality in a lean dry body. Crunchy & refreshing, long.

★★★★ **Simoné** ⓘ 🍷 Enticingly smoky **10** (★★★★☆) semillon, sauvignon blend in convincing style. Even more impressive than **09**, with super-long, savoury acidity & precise minerality to finish.

Blanc de Blancs ⓘ ★★★★ Clean, crisp **08** chardonnay méthode cap classique sparkling is biscuity, bone-dry & focused, with pleasurable elegance & creaminess. **Natural Sweet Sauvignon Blanc** NEW ★★★ Muted richness on **10**. Brûlée & oatmeal over grapefruit marmalade. Varietal acidity noticeable on clean, dry finish. Discontinued: **Five-Thirty-Five**.

Silver Myn range

★★★★ **Argentum** 🍷 **10** (★★★★) mulberry earth & chalky grip on merlot-led Bordeaux quartet. Density & lengthy charm though not as invitingly juicy or integrated as **08**, also tasted pre-bottling. No **09**.

Sauvignon Blanc ☺ 🍷 🌀 ★★★ Pungent rhubarb & gooseberry, **12** vibrant & crisp yet rounded & textured. Splash semillon adds richness.

Cabernet Sauvignon 🍷 ★★★★ Grip takes hold on entry of **09** serious contender in elegance stakes. Richly fruited yet structured & firm, with ample appeal. **Merlot** ⓘ ★★★ Considerable tannins challenge baked plum fruit flavours in seriously structured **09**, giving overly stern finish. **Cabernet Franc Rosé** 🍷 🌀 ★★★ Cranberry tang on uncomplicated & appealing **12**. Rounded mouthfeel but dry cherry-driven finish. — FM

David Biggs

David has been writing about wine for more than 30 years, since attending two Gilbeys courses in 1979, before the establishment of the Cape Wine Academy. He has been a judge in every Veritas competition since its inception, regularly judges the Muscadel Award for Excellence and the Terroir Wine Awards, and is a founder member of the Wine-of-the-Month tasting panel. He qualified officially as a wine judge in 2000. In 2011 he was declared a 'Living Legend' in the Cape wine industry by the South African National Wine Show Association. He is a regular contributor to Good Taste magazine and runs the wine website www.davidbiggsonline.com.

Winifred Bowman

A qualified physiotherapist and biomedical scientist, and holder of a PhD in Education, Winnie developed an interest in wine during her student days at Stellenbosch University and later through frequent travels to international winegrowing areas. She is a Cape Wine Master, and judges wine regularly at local and international competitions. She also presents corporate and private wine tastings, teaches and writes about wine and food. Wine is Winnie's passion and she enjoys every moment talking about or tasting it.

Greg de Bruyn

Greg is an architect by profession, practicing in and around the Cape wine industry. He allowed wine to beguile him into leaving Johannesburg in 1999 to seek his future amongst the vines, first to establish and run a wine estate, and later as a specialist consultant in winery construction. He qualified as a wine judge in 1996 and a Cape Wine Master in 2000. Greg has sat on many of the major South African competitions and assessment panels, and has contributed to several publications and websites.

Christian Eedes

Christian Eedes is a freelance winewriter and founder of Whatidranklastnight.co.za. A Stellenbosch University graduate with an Honours degree in Philosophy, he has also completed a wine evaluation course and a small-scale winemaking programme run by that institution's Department of Viticulture & Oenology. He has judged at the Old Mutual Trophy Wine Show since 2007 and sits on numerous other competition panels.

Michael Fridjhon

Michael is South Africa's leading wine industry authority and the country's most widely published winewriter. A former advisor to the Minister of Agriculture and past chairman of the South African Wine Industry Trust, he is currently visiting professor of Wine Business at the University of Cape Town's Graduate School of Business. An internationally recognised wine judge, he is chair of the Old Mutual Trophy Wine Show, chair (2012) of the Five Nations Challenge in Sydney and co-chair (2007) of the International Wine Challenge. An honorary life member of the UK Circle of Wine Writers, he has authored or contributed to over 35 books and has been a taster for the guide since the early 1980s.

Higgo Jacobs

Before, during and after studying and qualifying in Law at Stellenbosch University, Higgo spent nine years on either side of the cellar door: first making wine, then marketing and exporting it. Today, certified with the Court of Master Sommeliers, he is general secretary and founding member of the South African Sommelier Association (SASA), co-ordinator of the Nederburg Auction selection tastings and tasting director for Top 100 SA Wines. He consults within the hospitality industry, is a senior judge at the International Wine Challenge (IWC), and tastes for local publications and competitions.

Tim James

Tim has been writing about wine long enough for him to realise that it's no longer just a hobby. With a home-base on www.grape.co.za, he contributes to various local and international publications, including a weekly column for the Mail & Guardian and frequent articles in the London-based World of Fine Wine. Tim is a Cape Wine Master and has twice won the SA Wine Writers Annual Award. He declines to participate in large competitive tastings but has been a taster (and associate editor) for this guide for many years. His book on SA wine is scheduled for publication this year.

Angela Lloyd

Writing, lecturing, broadcasting and making wine are some of Angela's undertakings during her more than 30 years' professional involvement with wine. Even so, it is still just one interest in her life though closely allied to another, cooking. When not tied to her laptop, Angela loves the outdoors: she grows vegetables, fruit and indigenous flowers in her and her husband's garden, while her daily walks with Syrah, their black Labrador, keep them both fit. Reading, cinema, theatre, music, rugby and cricket are other interests crammed into a busy life.

Cathy Marston

Cathy hails from Yorkshire, UK, and after completing her degree in English at Cambridge University, she joined Adnams Wine Merchants, passing all the Wine & Spirit Education Trust exams, culminating in Diploma. She came to South Africa in 2001, and opened and ran The Nose Restaurant & Wine Bar, selling it after seven successful years. Cathy now concentrates on tasting, writing for local and international publications, and wine education. She is an associate of the Institute of Wines & Spirits and is currently the only Approved Programme Provider in Africa for the Wine & Spirit Education Trust.

Fiona McDonald

Chronicling the dramatic changes that have taken place in the South African wine landscape for the past two decades has been not only a privilege but a pleasure for trained journalist Fiona. Editor of Wine magazine for eight years and a freelance wine writer for the past four, she got into wine 'by accident'. It started in the 1990s by helping a colleague organise The Mercury Wine Week for a number of years while working as a reporter and night news editor on the KwaZulu Natal newspaper. Fiona serves as a judge and jury president at various international wine competitions, among them the International Wine Challenge, International Wine & Spirit Competition, Decanter World Wine Awards and Concours Mondial de Bruxelles.

Ingrid Motteux

Love of wine and a growing aversion to hospital basements led Ingrid to give up a successful career in nuclear medicine to work first as a vineyard labourer, then as a lecturer and wine writer. Her wine interest took formal shape during more than a decade abroad, where she attained the UK WSET Diploma and, soon after, the Cape WSET Wine Judge certification. An associate of the Institute of Wines & Spirits, Ingrid judges for the International Wine Challenge and runs an independent wine consultancy, advising some of Africa's top game lodges.

Jörg Pfützner

German-born Jörg is an internationally trained and certified sommelier living in South Africa. Having worked at top restaurants in Hamburg and Cape Town, he started his own businesses: The Riesling Club, whose members have access to top European bottlings; and Fine Wine Events, which celebrates wine with specifically themed fine-wine and food tastings and festivals. Since completing his postgraduate diploma in Wine Business Management, Jörg continues to present and lecture locally and abroad, as well as manage a group of private cellars.

James Pietersen

As a Stellenbosch University student, James helped organise his law professor's cellar. 'In exchange, he opened a few great bottles and I fell in love with wine.' He's since pursued his passion, first as

Vineyard Connection's wine buyer, consultant to Singita Game Lodge and lately as the head sommelier for Belthazar in Cape Town, also responsible for the wine program at Balducci's restaurant. Further experience was gained as Trophy Wine Show judge and as a panelist for Wine magazine.

Christine Rudman

Christine's love affair with wine might have started late, in her 30s, when she joined Stellenbosch Farmers' Winery after a Johannesburg FMCG marketing career, but she rapidly made up for lost time. Enrolling in the Cape Wine Academy, she achieved her Cape Wine Masters qualification in 1986; left SFW to run the CWA for seven years; and has since been occupied with consultancy work, wine judging, lecturing and writing. She has written A Guide to the Winelands of the Cape, travels widely, tastes on international panels and looks forward to working with wine for years to come.

Dave Swingler

Co-author of One Hundred Wines – An Insiders' Guide to South African Wine and drinks contributor to Posh Nosh, Dave has been blending his love of wine and words for this guide since the 1990s. A long-standing member of the International Wine & Food Society, Dave was director of wine for the IWFS Cape Town Festival, is the South African consultant for its Annual Vintage Chart and current chair of the Cape Town branch. Dave has over the years consulted to restaurants, game lodges and convention centres, taught wine courses and contributed to various radio, print and other media.

Cathy van Zyl

Cathy started her wine journey on a bicycle: she asked her husband to ride South Africa's famed Argus Cycle Tour with her, he accepted if she attended a wine course with him. She has since notched up 15 more Cycle Tours and gone on to pass the Master of Wine examination. Cathy judges locally and internationally, occasionally contributes to wine journals and websites around the world, but spends most of her wine-time as associate editor of this guide.

Meryl Weaver

The Cape winelands lured Meryl away from her legal career and she remains happily under their spell. She is a Cape Wine Master, and recently further honed her skills by graduating from the Wine Judging Academy with distinction. She lectures for the Cape Wine Academy, conducts local wine tours for foreign journalists and presentations abroad on SA wine on behalf of Wines of South Africa. Meryl also judges at local competitions and for wine magazines.

Here we summarise the wines featured in the A–Z section, with their ratings, sorted first by wine style, in alphabetical order, and then by producer or brand. New wines in **bolder type**. **NS** = no star; **NT** = not tasted; **NR** = tasted but not rated; **D** = discontinued. Where wineries produce more than one version of a particular style, the number of versions is indicated in brackets after the name. A number of wines were tasted as pre-bottling barrel or tank samples, and therefore ratings are provisional. Refer to the A–Z for details. The rating summaries for sparkling wine below take into account the new, lower maximum permitted residual sugar level of 12 g/l (vs 15 previously) for bubblies labelled as 'Brut'. As a result, several wines identified by their producers as 'Brut' in the guide's A–Z directory are listed here as 'Off-dry/Semi-sweet' and not as 'Dry'.

Barbera
★★★★ Altydgedacht, Fairview, Hofstraat, Merwida

★★★☆ Idiom ★★★ Bovlei **NT** Hidden Valley

Biodynamic
★★★★☆ Reyneke (4) (Red blends, shiraz/syrah-based, Chenin blanc wooded, dry, Sauvignon blanc wooded, Sauvignon blanc unwooded)

★★★★ Woolworths (2) (Red blends, shiraz/syrah-based, Chenin blanc wooded, dry), Reyneke (3) (Pinotage, Shiraz/syrah, Red blends, Cape Bordeaux)

★★★☆ Creation

Blanc de noir
★★★★ Maison, Mellasat ★★★ Altydgedacht, Arra, Asara, Blaauwklippen, Boschendal, Groot Constantia, Lemberg, Lovane, Mount Abora, Peter Falke, Woolworths ★★★ Aan de Doorns, Culemborg, Klawer, Lynx, Nieuwedrift, Oude Kaap, Swartland, Tempel ★★ Abingdon, Boucheron, De Redley, Landskroon (2), Van Loveren ★★ Van Loveren **NT** Buitenverwachting, Lovane **D** Oudtshoorn

Bukettraube
★★★ Cederberg ★★★ Simonsvlei, Swartland ★★ Darling Cellars, Seven Sisters

Cabernet franc
★★★★★ Raka, Von Ortloff, Warwick

★★★★☆ BLANKbottle, Buitenverwachting, Nelson, Plaisir, Raats

★★★★ Alluvia, Anthonij Rupert, Avontuur, CK Wines, Claime d'Or, Doolhof, Druk My Niet, Knorhoek, La Petite Ferme, Longridge, Lovane, Raats, Rainbow's End (2), Ridgeback, Zorgvliet

★★★★ Benguela Cove, Hermanuspietersfontein, High Constantia, Hillcrest, KWV, Leopard Frog, Lynx, Maison de Teijger (2), Mont du Toit, Mooiplaas, Môreson, My Wyn, Oldenburg, Ormonde, Philip Jordaan, Spookfontein , Val de Vie, Vergenoegd, Woolworths ★★★ Audacia, Hannay, Idiom, Signal Hill, Whalehaven ★★★ Bushmanspad

Cabernet sauvignon
★★★★★ Delaire

★★★★☆ Belfield, Bilton, Boekenhoutskloof, Cederberg, Chateau Naudé, Conviction, Dalla Cia, De Meye, De Trafford, Delaire, Edgebaston, Eikendal, Ernie Els, Flagstone, Fleur du Cap, Glen Carlou, Glenelly, Grangehurst, House of Mandela, Journey's End, Knorhoek, Le Riche (2), Louis, Meerlust, Nederburg, Neil Ellis, Restless River, Rickety Bridge (2), Rudera (2), Rustenberg, Saxenburg, Springfield, **Stark-Condé** (2), Teddy Hall, **The Butcher Shop**, Thelema (2), Waterford, Webersburg

★★★★ Akkerdraai, Alluvia, Annandale, AntHill, Arra (2), Asara, Bartinney, Bergsig, Bilton, Bon Courage, Bon Terroir, Bonfoi, Botanica, **Brenaissance**, Buitenverwachting, Cape Chamonix, Cape Hutton, Cederberg, Clovelly, Darling Cellars, Delheim, Dombeya, Dornier, Druk My Niet, Edgebaston, Eerste Hoop, Eikendal, Excelsior, Fairview, Glen Carlou, Graceland, Graham Beck (2), Groenland, Guardian Peak, Hartenberg, Hathersage, Hoopenburg, Jordan, Journey's End, Kanonkop, Katbakkies, Klawer, Klein Constantia, Kleine Zalze (2), Kloovenburg, L'Avenir, La Motte, Laibach, Landskroon, Lanzerac, Le Bonheur, Le Riche, Linton Park, Lovane, Manley, Marianne, Marklew, MC Square, Meinert, MolenVliet, Mont du Toit, Mooiplaas, Morgenhof, Mount Vernon, Namaqua, Nederburg (2), Neil Ellis, Niel Joubert, Nitida, Noble Hill, Nuy, Oldenburg (Organic), Org de Rac (Organic), Overgaauw, Plaisir, Rainbow's End, Raka, Ridgeback, Savanha, **Silvermist**, South Hill, Springfontein, Stark-Condé (2), Sterhuis, Super Single Vineyards, The Butcher Shop, The Township Winery, The Winery of Good Hope (2), Topiary, Uitkyk, Usana, Vergelegen, Vergenoegd (2), **Vondeling**, Vriesenhof, Warwick, Welbedacht, Wellington Winery, Windmeul, Woolworths (3), Zorgvliet

★★★★ African Pride, Agterplaas, Alto, Altydgedacht, Amares, Anthonij Rupert (2), Anura, Arra, Avontuur, Backsberg, Beau Joubert, Bernheim, Boekenhoutskloof, Boschheim (2), Bosman, Bovlei, Brampton, Bushmanspad, Callender, Carisbrooke, **Catch Of The Day**, Chennells, Conradie, Constantia de Tulbagh, De Wetshof, Devonair (2), DeWaal, Dormershire (2), **Durbanville Hills**, Eaglevlei, Feiteiras, Fort Simon, Glenelly, Goede Hoop, Goedvertwedt, Grande Provence, Groenland, Groot Constantia, Haut Espoir, Havana Hills, Helderberg,

Hildenbrand, Hofstraat, Holden Manz, Hoopenburg, Hout Bay, Jacques Smit, Juno, Kaapzicht, Kanu, KWV (2), Kyburg, La Bri, La Kavayan, Laborie, Linton Park, Longridge, Lourensford, Lovane (2), Lutzville, Lyngrove, Lynx, MAN Vintners, McGregor, Middelvlei, Miravel (2), Mischa, Mitre's Edge, Mont Rochelle, Mountain Ridge, Nederburg, Neil Ellis Meyer-Näkel, Onderkloof , Opstal, Ormonde, Oude Kaap, **Perdeberg**, Pulpit Rock, **Rietvallei**, Robertson, Roodezandt, Rooiberg, Ross Gower, Rust en Vrede, Schalkenbosch, Simonsvlei, Slaley, Spookfontein , Springfield, Stellekaya, Stonewall, Swartland, SylvanVale, Teubes, The Berrio, The Butcher Shop, **The Rhino**, Tokara, Trajan, Ultra Liquors, Van Loveren, Viljoensdrift, Villiera, Walker Bay Vineyards, Waterkloof, Woolworths (2), Zevenwacht, **Zonnebloem**, Zorgvliet ★★★ Abbottshill, African Pride, Allesverloren, **Annex Kloof**, Arniston Bay, Audacia, Ayama, **Bellingham**, Bergsig, Blaauwklippen, Bloemendal, Boland (2), Bon Courage, Bonnievale, **Bonview**, Boplaas, Boschkloof , Botha, Bovlei, Brandvlei, Calais, Cloof, Crows Nest, Darling Cellars, De Meye, **Desert Rose**, Devonvale, **Die Mas**, Diemersfontein, Domaine Brahms, Doolhof, Douglas Green, Du Toitskloof , Elgin Vintners, Excelsior, Fairvalley, Fairview, Fleur du Cap, Galleon, **Govert**, **Herold**, Het Vlock Casteel, High Constantia, **Hunneyball**, Joubert-Tradauw, Kleine Draken (Kosher), Kleine Zalze, Koopmanskloof, Landskroon, **Le Manoir de Brendel**, Le Pommier, Leopard's Leap, Lindhorst, **Linton Park** (2), **Lovane**, Lutzville, Maastricht, Maison de Teijger (3), MAN Vintners, Meerendal, Merwida, Mon Rêve, Montagu Wine & Spirits, Montagu Wine Cellar, Mostertsdrift, **Mount Rozier**, Napier, Nederburg, Neethlingshof, New Beginnings, **Nuweland**, Nwanedi, Obikwa, Oewerzicht, Olifantsberg, Orange River, Ormonde, Osbloed, Painted Wolf, Perdeberg, Pulpit Rock, Retief, Rico Suter, Riebeek, Rietvallei, Saam, Savanha, Simonsig, Simonsvlei, Six Hats, **Southern Sky**, Spier (Organic), Stellar (Organic), Stellenbosch Hills, Stellendrift, StellenRust, Swartland, Thandi, Tulbagh Winery, Ultra Liquors (Organic), Upland (Organic), Vredenheim, Waterstone (2), Waverley Hills (Organic), Wines of Cape Town, **Women in Wine**, Zanddrift, Zandvliet, Zonnebloem ★★★ African Terroir (5), Alvi's Drift, Ashton, **Bayede!**, Belbon Hills, Breëland, Bushmanspad, Cape Dreams, Clairvaux, Culemborg, De Doorns, De Krans, De Villiers, Desert Rose, Drostdy-Hof, Du Preez (2), Durbanville Hills, DuVon, Eikehof, Goedvertrouw, **Hornbill** , **House of Mandela**, Jacobsdal, Klein Parys, Klein Roosboom , Kranskop, KWV, La Petite Provence, Ladismith, Louisvale, Montpellier, Moordenaarskop, Niel Joubert, Nietvoorbij, **Oneiric** (Organic), Org de Rac (Organic), Phizante Kraal,

Place in the Sun, Post House, Re'Mogo, Riebeek, Robertson, Roodezandt, Rooiberg, Rosendal, **Sauvignon.com**, Savanha, Seven Sisters, Simonsvlei, Slanghoek, Slowine, Somersbosch, Somerset Wines, Steenberg (Organic), Stellar (Organic), Stellenzicht, Tanagra, **The Hills**, Tukulu, Tulbagh Winery, United Nations, uniWines, Valley Vineyards, Vruchtbaar, Vukani, Wandsbeck, Waterstone (Organic), **Waverley Hills** (Organic), Wellington Winery, Welmoed, Welvanpas, William Everson, Windmeul, Wineways (Organic), Woolworths (3) (Organic), Zidela ★★ **African Terroir**, Barrydale, Beau Joubert, Bergwater, **Blomendahl**, Calitzdorp, Cape Rock, Cranefields, **Cronier**, De Wet, Goudini, Imbuko, Kleinfontein, Libby's Pride, **Lovane**, Maske, Mountain River, Namaqua, Nuy (Organic), **Org de Rac** (Organic), Oude Compagnies Post, Quest, Robertson, Savanha, Simonsvlei, Southern Sky, Stoumann's, Van Loveren, Vriesenhof , Waterstone, Windfall, Wineways (2) ★★ Blue Crane, Boplaas, **Boutique Baratok** (2), Groupe CDV, Langverwacht, Prospect1870, Southern Sky, Tulbagh Winery, **Van Loveren**, Waterstone ★ Jonkheer **NS** TTT Cellar, Withoek **NT** Abingdon, AlexKia, Benguela Cove, Bernheim, Black Pearl, Blomendahl, Botha, Camberley, Devon Hill, Escapades, **Fat Bastard**, Galleon, Hildenbrand, Jason's Hill, L'Olivier, La Petite Ferme, La Petite Vigne, Laibach, Landzicht (2), Le Grand Chasseur, Malanot, Melkboomsdrift, Mimosa, Mont Rochelle, Mooi Bly, Moordenaarskop, Mountain River, Origin, Remhoogte, Robertson, Spier (2), Stellendrift (2), **Stone Ridge**, Ultra Liquors, Waterstone, Wineways **NR Fernskloof**, Franschhoek Cellar, Seal Breeze **D** Allée Bleue, Arniston Bay, Blaauwklippen, Boschendal, Du'SwaRoo, Graham Beck, Hartswater, Jakob's Vineyards, Kumkani, La Couronne, Leeuwenjacht, Muratie, Oudtshoorn, Overhex, Perdeberg, Peter Falke, Pulpit Rock (Organic), Spier (Organic), Stellenzicht, Tokara, Wildekrans, Wines of Cape Town, Yonder Hill

Cape Riesling
★★★ Theuniskraal ★★ Calais, Goudini, Van Loveren **D** Nederburg

Carignan
★★★★ Fairview ★★★ Bovlei, **Koopmanskloof**, Withington **NT** BLANKbottle (2)

Chardonnay unwooded
★★★★★ De Wetshof (2), Diemersdal, GlenWood, Groote Post, Springfield, Van Zylshof, **Warwick**, Woolworths
★★★★ Arniston Bay, Bouchard Finlayson, Brampton, Constantia Uitsig, De Wetshof, **Delheim**, Doolhof, Eikendal, Franschhoek Cellar, **Glen Carlou**, Kloovenburg, La Couronne, Louisvale, McGregor, Meerendal, Rustenberg, Sterhuis, Withington, Woolworths ★★★ African Pride, Asara, Bellpost,

Bon Courage, Cloverfield, Dalla Cia, De Meye, **Eagle's Cliff** (Organic), Elgin Ridge (Organic), False Bay, Glenelly, Hildenbrand, Jordan, Karusa, Kleine Zalze, La Petite Ferme, Landskroon, Langverwacht, Libby's Pride, Lourensford (Chardonnay wooded), Middelvlei, Mont Rochelle, Nederburg, Neethlingshof, New Beginnings, **Newstead**, Riebeek, Rietvallei, Savanha, Seven Springs , Stellenzicht, The Butcher Shop, The Winery of Good Hope, **Women in Wine**, Woolworths ★★★ African Terroir (2) (Organic), AlexKia, Ayama, Backsberg, Blomendahl, Boland, Brandvlei, Burgershof, Cape Dreams, **Cloof**, De Krans, Eerste Hoop, Goudini, Graham Beck, Groupe CDV, **Kanu**, Koopmanskloof, Lutzville, **Malanot**, Mostertsdrift, Ormonde, Rooiberg, Schalkenbosch, Somerbosch (Organic), Stellar (Organic), **The Rhino**, **The Wine Fusion**, Tulbagh Winery, Walker Bay Vineyards, Wellington Winery, Wine Village-Hermanus, Zandvliet ★★ Boplaas, Bovlei, Leopard's Leap, Obikwa, Valley Vineyards (2), Welbedacht ★★ Die Mas, Groupe CDV, Ladismith, uniWines, Waterstone, Woolworths ★ Jonkheer (Organic), **Org de Rac** (Organic), Woolworths **NT** Ashton, Calais, Eagle's Cliff (Organic), Groot Parys (Organic), Highgate, Leeuwenberg, **Stone Ridge**, United Nations **NR Eaglevlei D** Morgenhof, Oudtshoorn (2), Woolworths

Chardonnay wooded

★★★★★ Boschendal, Cape Chamonix, Hamilton Russell, Jordan (2)

★★★★☆ Ataraxia, Bouchard Finlayson (2), Crystallum, De Wetshof, Glen Carlou, GlenWood, Groot Constantia, Hartenberg, Haskell, Julien Schaal, **Lanzerac**, Longridge, Meerlust, Môreson, Mulderbosch, Newton Johnson, Oak Valley, Paul Cluver, Rijk's, Rustenberg, Saxenburg, Springfield, Sterhuis, Sumaridge, The Winery of Good Hope, Uva Mira, Vergelegen, Vins d'Orrance, Waterford, Woolworths

★★★★ Almenkerk, Alvi's Drift, Amani, Anura, Bartinney, Bergsig, Bouchard Finlayson, Buitenverwachting, Callender, Cape Chamonix, Cape Point, Creation, Crystallum, De Wetshof (2), Delaire, DeMorgenzon, Dombeya, Edgebaston, Eikendal, Elgin Vintners, Fleur du Cap, Glen Carlou, Glenelly, Graham Beck, Grande Provence, Groote Post, Hartenberg, Haut Espoir, Havana Hills, Hoopenburg, House of Mandela, Iona, **JH Meyer**, Jordan, Journey's End (2), Kleine Zalze, Koelfontein, KWV (2), La Motte, La Petite Ferme, Lanzerac, Le Riche, Linton Park, Lourensford, Marklew, MC Square, **Meinert**, Merwida, Mont Rochelle (2), Mulderbosch, Muratie, Napier, Nederburg, **Neil Ellis**, Newton Johnson, Ormonde, Paul Cluver, Pulpit Rock, Quoin Rock, Restless River, Rijk's, Robertson, Rupert &

Rothschild, Rustenberg, Savanha, **Springfontein**, Stanford Hills, StellenRust, Thelema (2), **Tierhoek**, Tokara (2), Vergelegen, Von Ortloff, Vondeling, Vriesenhof, Warwick, Waterford, Weltevrede, William Everson, Windmeul, Woolworths (2), **Yardstick**, Zandvliet

★★★☆ Anthonij Rupert, Asara, **Babylonstoren**, Badsberg, **Bellingham**, Boland, Bon Courage, Boschendal, Boschkloof, **Brenaissance**, **Brothers**, Cape Classics, Chateau Naudé, Clos Malverne, Delheim, Diemersdal, Domaine des Dieux, Doolhof, Durbanville Hills, Eerste Hoop, Ernst Gouws, Fairview (2), Fat Bastard, **Flagstone**, Fort Simon, **Freedom Hill**, Goedverwacht (Organic), Groot Parys (Organic), Hildenbrand, Journey's End, Kaapzicht, **Kanu**, Kloovenburg (2), KWV, L'Avenir, La Bri, La Vierge, Laborie (2), **Ladera** (Organic), Lazanou (Organic), Le Bonheur, Lord's, Lorraine, Louisvale (2), Lourensford, Lyngrove, **Maison**, Mellasat, **Migliarina**, Mimosa, Morgenhof, **My Wyn**, Nabygelegen, Nederburg, Nelson, Niel Joubert, Nitida, **Noble Hill**, Oldenburg, Onderkloof, **Origin**, Ormonde, Osbloed, Overgaauw, Passages, Plaisir, Rickety Bridge, Riebeek, Rooiberg, Seven Springs , **Signal Gun**, Simonsig (2), Slaley, StellenRust, Stonewall, Thandi, Thelema, Tokara (Organic), Tukulu (Organic), Uitkyk, Van Loveren, **Veenwouden**, Waterkloof, Welbedacht, Winters Drift (Organic), Woolworths ★★★ Alkmaar, Anura, Avontuur, Backsberg, Darling Cellars, De Wet, De Wetshof, Douglas Green, Drostdy-Hof, Durbanville Hills, **Elgin Heights**, Fairvalley, Felicité, **Fernskloof**, Fleur du Cap, Goedertrouw, Goedverwacht, **Hillock**, Hoopenburg, Joubert-Tradauw, Klein Parys, Kranskop, **Kumala**, **Kumkani**, Louiesenhof, Lourensford (Chardonnay unwooded), Lutzville, MAN Vintners, Meerendal, **Mount Rozier**, Mount Vernon, Niel Joubert, Nuy, Olsen, **Oneiric**, Orange River, Overhex, Pulpit Rock, Rhebokskloof, Robertson, **Scrucap**, Simonsvlei, Springfontein, Steenberg, **Sumsaré**, Two Oceans, Viljoensdrift, Welmoed, Weltevrede (2), Woolworths (2), Zandvliet, Zonnebloem ★★★ Aaldering, African Terroir, Anthonij Rupert, Anthony Smook, **Ashton**, Calitzdorp, **Claime d'Or**, Cloverfield, Conradie, Du Preez, Du Toitskloof , Esona, Excelsior, Jonkheer, Klawer, KWV, **Linton Park**, Lord's, Nietvoorbij (Organic), Org de Rac (Organic), Oude Kaap, Robertson (2), Savanha, Six Hats, Slanghoek, Spier, Swartland, **Thembi & Co**, United Nations, Van Zylshof, Waterstone (2), Whalehaven, Wines of Cape Town (Organic), Woolworths (2) (Organic) ★★ **Abingdon** (Organic), African Terroir (Organic), **Barrydale**, Bonnievale, De Zoete Inval, Eikehof, Hathersage, Kingsriver, Montpellier, Mooi Bly, Rosendal, Simonsvlei, Walker Bay Vineyards ★★ **African Terroir**, Kleine Draken (Kosher), Montagu Wine & Spirits, Van Loveren (2) ★ Four Fields **NT**

Bergwater, Bloemendal, Bonfoi, Buffalo Creek, Clovelly, Crows Nest, Flagstone, Four Paws, Galleon, Goede Hoop, Hill & Dale, Imbuko, Jason's Hill (Organic), Mountain Oaks (Organic), Olifantsberg, Origin (2) (Organic), Rhebokskloof, Rietvallei, Spier, Stoumann's, Teubes, **Thembi & Co**, Val de Vie, Veenwouden, Vruchtbaar, Waterstone, Welvanpas, Windmeul, Wolfkloof, Zidela **NR** Neil Ellis **D** Amani (2), Bayede!, Beau Joubert, Bergsig, Clairvaux, Delaire, Delheim, Elemental Bob, Fort Simon, Graham Beck, Kumala, La Couronne, Namaqua, Stellenbosch Hills, Stellenzicht, Weltevrede, Woolworths (2)

Chenin blanc off-dry/semi-sweet (w & u/w)

★★★★★ Beaumont, Botanica, DeMorgenzon

★★★★☆ Ken Forrester, Rijk's, Spier, StellenRust

★★★★ Beaumont, Kanu, **Ken Forrester**, **Knorhoek, Lutzville,** Perdeberg, Rudera, Saam, Simonsig, Stark-Condé, Tierhoek, Woolworths (2) ★★★☆ Final Cut, **Flagstone,** Franschhoek Cellar, Glen Carlou, Katbakkies, Knorhoek, Painted Wolf, Saltaré, Trajan, Virgin Earth ★★★ Boschendal, Botha, **False Bay,** KWV, Landskroon (2), **Leopard's Leap,** Nederburg (2), Robertson, Simonsvlei ★★★ Brandvlei, Cape Classics, Cloverfield, Drostdy-Hof, Du Toitskloof, Goudini, Kanu, Nelson, Nuweland, Obikwa, Robertson, Summerhill, Valley Vineyards ★★ Bon Courage, Bottelary (2), **Ken Forrester,** Lutzville, Simonsvlei (2) ★★ Goudini, Leopard's Leap, Robertson (Light & low-alcohol), Simonsvlei, Waterstone, Woolworths (3), Zandvliet ★ **Hillock,** Woolworths **NT** Dagbreek, Landzicht, MAN Vintners, Waterstone **D** Hartswater, Seven Oaks, Zidela

Chenin blanc unwooded dry

★★★★ Annex Kloof, Babylon's Peak, Cederberg, Groote Post, L'Avenir, Laibach, Mooiplaas, Old Vines, Teddy Hall, **The Fledge**

★★★★ Arra, **Babylonstoren,** Barton, **Bellevue,** Bosman, Chateau Naudé, Darling Cellars, Ernie Els, Fairview, Hazendal, Kaapzicht, Kleine Zalze, L'Avenir, La Chataigne (Organic), Lazanou (Organic), Le Pommier, Mooi Bly (Organic), Mountain Oaks (Organic), Napier, Nederburg, Nieuwedrift, **Phizante Kraal,** Raats, Saam, **Scrucap,** Simonsvlei, Stellekaya, The Winery of Good Hope, Tukulu, Zonnebloem, **Zonquasdrift** ★★★ Alvi's Drift, Ayama, Backsberg, **Bellingham,** Boland, **Bottelary Hills,** De Meye, De Wet, Delheim, DeWaal, Dornier (2), Douglas Green, DuVon, Ernst Gouws, Fairview, Fish Hoek, **Freedom Hill,** Halala, Hawksmoor, Klein Parys, **Koopmanskloof,** Landskroon, **Leeuwenkuil,** Leopard's Leap, Lula Wines, Lyngrove, McGregor, Niel Joubert, Olsen (Chenin blanc wooded, dry), Orange River, Ormonde (2), Perdeberg, Pulpit Rock, Re'Mogo, Rhebokskloof, Rickety Bridge, Rietvallei,

Roodezandt, Seven Oaks, Seven Sisters, Simonsig, Slowine, Somerbosch, Spier, Stoumann's, **The Rhino,** TTT Cellar, Ultra Liquors, United Nations, uniWines, Veenwouden, Waterstone, Wedgewood, Woolworths (2) ★★★ Aan de Doorns, Badsberg, Bergsig (2), Blaauwklippen, Blomendahl, Bottelary, Bovlei, Brandvlei, Cloof, Culemborg, David Frost Signature, De Krans, Douglas Green, Dragonridge, Eagle's Cliff, Fairvalley, False Bay, Glenview, Groenland (Organic), Groot Parys (Organic), Groupe CDV, Klawer, Klein Parys, Kleine Zalze (2), Koopmanskloof, Langverwacht, MAN Vintners, Mellasat, Millstream, Monterosso, Mountain River, **New Beginnings,** Nuy, **Origin,** Oude Kaap (2), Overhex, Riebeek, Rooiberg, **Savanha,** Slanghoek, Somerset Wines (Organic), Stellar (Organic), Stettyn, Swartland, **The Grape Grinder,** Thembi & Co, Tread Lightly, Tulbagh Winery, Ultra Liquors, uniWines, Valley Vineyards (3), Van Zylshof, Vaughan Johnson, Waterstone, Welbedacht, Wellington Winery, Welmoed, Windmeul, Woolworths ★★ African Pride, Ashton, Calais, **Cronier,** Groupe CDV, Montagu Wine & Spirits, Montagu Wine Cellar, Napier, **Neethlingshof, Robert Stanford,** Simonsvlei, Six Hats, Skilpadvlei, Tulbagh Winery, Van Loveren (2), Vaughan Johnson, Waboomsrivier, Wineways ★★ **African Terroir, Bayede!, Boutique Baratok,** Drostdy-Hof, Groupe CDV (2), Ladismith, Maske, Montpellier, Stellenbosch Hills, Woolworths (2) ★ **The Hills,** Woolworths (2) (Light & low-alcohol, Light & low-alcohol) **NT** Belbon Hills (2), Botha, Cape Dreams, Catch Of The Day, Diners Club Bartho Eksteen , Domaine Brahms, Jacques Smit, Jason's Hill, Ken Forrester, Môreson, Nwanedi, Oude Denneboom, The Mason's, **Thembi & Co,** United Nations, Versailles, Vruchtbaar, Westbridge, Zidela **NR** Groot Parys **D** Nuy, Opstal, Overgaauw, Viljoensdrift, Wildekrans, Wines of Cape Town (2), Woolworths, Zidela

Chenin blanc wooded, dry

★★★★★ **Alheit,** Jean Daneel, **KWV, Sadie,** Spice Route

★★★★☆ Cederberg, **David,** Diemersfontein, **Donkiesbaai,** L'Avenir, Lammershoek, Oldenburg, Post House, Remhoogte (Biodynamic), Reyneke (Biodynamic), **Sadie,** Stone Ridge, Teddy Hall, The Winery of Good Hope

★★★★ AA Badenhorst, Andy Mitchell, Anthonij Rupert (Organic), Avondale (Organic), Bellingham, De Trafford (2), Delaire, DewaldtHeyns, **Doran, Druk My Niet, Eenzaamheid,** Fort Simon, Graham Beck, Jordan, Ken Forrester, Kleine Zalze, Maison, Mooiplaas, Morgenhof, **Mount Abora,** Mulderbosch, Mullineux (Light & low-alcohol), **Nederburg,** Old Vines, Raats, Remhoogte, Ridgeback, Rijk's (2), Rudera, **Signal Hill, Spioenkop,** Springfontein, The

Winery of Good Hope, Wildehurst, Windmeul (Biodynamic), Woolworths
★★★★ Aeternitas, Anura, Arniston Bay, Awendland, **Beau Joubert**, Black Bay, **Black Pearl**, **Boland**, **Chateau Naudé**, Crios Bríde, Fleur du Cap (Organic), Groot Parys (2) (Organic), Hazendal, Intellego, Longridge, MAN Vintners, **Meerhof**, Mulderbosch, Nabygelegen, **Paardebosch**, Painted Wolf, Raka, Rickety Bridge, **Riebeek**, Rudera, Springfontein, Star Hill, StellenRust, Sterhuis, Teddy Hall, The Winery of Good Hope, Villiera (2), Vruchtbaar, Waterford, Waterkloof, Wildekrans, Zevenwacht ★★★ 5 Mountains, Agterplaas, Anthonij Rupert, **Croydon**, Graham Beck, Hildenbrand, M'hudi, Malanot, Olsen (Chenin blanc unwooded dry), Super Single Vineyards, Welbedacht, Woolworths ★★★ Jacaranda, **Kumala**, **Linton Park**, Orange River, **Origin**, Vukani ★★ Koelenhof ★★ Hawksmoor, **Lord's NT** Allée Bleue, Barry Gould, BLANKbottle, Domaine Brahms, Jean Daneel, KWV, Lateganskop, Môreson (Organic), Mountain Oaks (2) (Organic), Origin (2), Robert Stanford, Spier, Swartland, SylvanVale **D** Fort Simon, Kumkani, KWV (Organic), Lazanou (Organic), Leopard Frog, Meerendal, Perdeberg

Cinsaut
★★★★☆ AA Badenhorst, Sadie
★★★★ Howard Booysen, Osbloed ★★★ BLANKbottle ★★ Landskroon **NT** BLANKbottle

Colombard
★★★★★ Micu Narunsky
★★★★ McGregor ★★★ Bon Courage, Montagu Wine Cellar, Nuy, Orange River, Rooiberg, Van Loveren ★★ Goedverwacht, Hartswater (2), Nuy ★★ Aan de Doorns, Langverwacht (Organic), **Stellar** (Organic), Woolworths **D** Clairvaux

Gamay noir
★★★ Asara ★★★ Kleine Zalze ★★ Altydgedacht

Gewürztraminer
★★★★☆ Zevenwacht
★★★★ Buitenverwachting, Paul Cluver
★★★★ Delheim, Simonsig, Weltevrede ★★★ Altydgedacht, Bergsig, Neethlingshof, Villiera ★★★ Bovlei ★★ **Montpellier NT** Belbon Hills, Groupe CDV **D** Woolworths

Grenache blanc
★★★★★ KWV, The Foundry
★★★★ Signal Hill
★★★ Bovlei

Grenache noir
★★★★☆ Neil Ellis, Vriesenhof
★★★★ Hermit on the Hill, Nederburg, Tierhoek, Woolworths

★★★★ Lynx ★★★ Franki's, Nuweland ★★★ **David**, **Hermit on the Hill NT** BLANKbottle, Diemersdal, Signal Hill **D** Anura, Six Hats

Hanepoot fortified
★★★★☆ Boplaas, Constantia Uitsig, **Signal Hill**
★★★★ Aan de Doorns, Calitzdorp (2), Ladismith, Muratie, Nuweland, Opstal
★★★★ Badsberg, De Wet, Die Mas, Du Preez, Eaglevlei, Mon Rêve, Orange River, Slanghoek, SoetKaroo, Swartland, Villiersdorp ★★★ Boplaas, Bovlei, Clairvaux, Du Toitskloof , Kaapzicht, **Namaqua**, Simonsvlei, Stoumann's, TTT Cellar, Vriesenhof ★★ Bergwater, Goudini, Waboomsrivier **NT** Belbon Hills, Klawer, Landzicht, Oudtshoorn **D** Montagu Wine Cellar, Tulbagh Winery

Hanepoot unfortified
★★★ Origin ★★☆ Culemborg, Overhex ★★ **Cape Classics**, **uniWines** (2) (Perlé wines, Perlé wines) **NT** Origin (2) (Light & low-alcohol, Light & low-alcohol), Zidela

Jerepigo red
★★★★☆ Blaauwklippen
★★★★ Badsberg, Laborie, Swartland
★★★★ Catherine Marshall, **De Krans**, Feiteiras, **SoetKaroo**, Solms-Delta ★★★ Camberley, Grundheim, **Montagu Wine & Spirits**, Orange River, Simonsvlei, Slanghoek, Stonewall ★★★ Botha, Hartswater, Montagu Wine & Spirits, Tulbagh Winery ★★ **Die Mas** ★ Stoumann's **NT** Landzicht, Oudtshoorn **D** Pulpit Rock

Jerepigo white
★★★★☆ Signal Hill
★★★★ Botha
★★★★ Feiteiras, Niel Joubert, Opstal, **Riebeek**
★★★ Backsberg, Calitzdorp, Montagu Wine & Spirits, Orange River, Sedgwick's Old Brown Sherry ★★★ Brandvlei, Chateau Naudé, Swartland ★★ Hartswater ★★ Ship Sherry **NT** Dellrust, Lateganskop, Oudtshoorn, Wellington Winery

Kosher
★★★ Kleine Draken ★★★ Backsberg (2) (Merlot, Pinotage) ★★ **Backsberg** (Natural Sweet, red), Kleine Draken (3) (Red blends, Cape Bordeaux, Natural Sweet, red, Sacramental wine) ★★ Kleine Draken (4) (Rosé off-dry/semi-sweet, Chardonnay wooded, Sauvignon blanc unwooded, Sparkling, Non-MCC, white, off-dry/semi-sweet) ★ Kleine Draken **D** Hill & Dale (2) (Red blends, shiraz/syrah-based, White blends, unwooded, dry), Kleine Draken (2) (Pinotage, Shiraz/syrah)

Late Harvest
★★★★ Landau du Val, Nederburg

★★★★ Delheim, Thelema (2) ★★★ Montagu Wine Cellar ★★ Jonkheer, Overmeer Cellars ★★ Robertson ★ Kellerprinz, Pick 'n Pay, Simonsvlei **D** KWV

Light & low-alcohol

★★★★☆ De Wetshof (Noble Late Harvest), **Durbanville Hills** (Noble Late Harvest), **Hermanuspietersfontein** (Noble Late Harvest), Miles Mossop (Noble Late Harvest), Neethlingshof (Noble Late Harvest), Springfontein

★★★★ Blaauwklippen (Noble Late Harvest), Mullineux (Chenin blanc wooded, dry), Paul Cluver (Riesling), Vondeling

★★★★ Blaauwklippen (Noble Late Harvest), Boschendal (Natural Sweet, white), Meerendal (Natural Sweet, white), Ridgeback ★★★ Origin (Hanepoot unfortified), **Somerset Wines** ★★★ Alvi's Drift (Sparkling, Non-MCC, rosé, off-dry/semi-sweet), Conradie (Perlé wines), De Grendel (Noble Late Harvest), Groupe CDV (Natural Sweet, white), Grünberger (2) (Natural Sweet, rosé, Natural Sweet, white), Lutzville (Natural Sweet, white), Obikwa (White blends, off-dry/semi-sweet (w & u/w)), Orange River (Rosé off-dry/semi-sweet), **Origin** (3) (Perlé wines, Sparkling, Non-MCC, white, off-dry/semi-sweet, Perlé wines), **Overhex** (2) (Perlé wines, Perlé wines), Robertson (Sauvignon blanc unwooded), Slanghoek (Rosé off-dry/semi-sweet), Solms-Delta (Sparkling, Non-MCC, red, off-dry/semi-sweet), **Somerset Wines** (2) (Natural Sweet, rosé, Natural Sweet, red) ★★ 4th Street (2) (Natural Sweet, rosé, Natural Sweet, white), **Arniston Bay** (White blends, off-dry/semi-sweet (w & u/w)), **Boplaas** (Muscadel, white, unfortified), Cold Duck (5th Avenue) (Sparkling, Non-MCC, rosé, off-dry/semi-sweet), Douglas Green (2) (Natural Sweet, white, Perlé wines), Drostdy-Hof (2) (Natural Sweet, rosé, Natural Sweet, white), Eve (Sparkling, Non-MCC, white, off-dry/semi-sweet), Flat Roof Manor (2) (Sauvignon blanc unwooded, Rosé off-dry/semi-sweet), Fleur du Cap (White blends, off-dry/semi-sweet (w & u/w)), Lutzville (Natural Sweet, rosé), Overhex (2) (Sparkling, Non-MCC, white, off-dry/semi-sweet, Sparkling, Non-MCC, rosé, off-dry/semi-sweet), Pearly Bay (4) (Rosé off-dry/semi-sweet, White blends, off-dry/semi-sweet (w & u/w), Sparkling, Non-MCC, white, off-dry/semi-sweet, Sparkling, Non-MCC, rosé, off-dry/semi-sweet), Riebeek (2) (Perlé wines, Perlé wines), Robertson (3) (Natural Sweet, rosé, Natural Sweet, white, Natural Sweet, red), Simonsvlei (Natural Sweet, rosé), JC le Roux (2) (Sparkling, Non-MCC, white, off-dry/semi-sweet, Sparkling, Non-MCC, red, dry), Van Loveren (7) (Natural Sweet, red, Natural Sweet, rosé, Natural Sweet, rosé, Natural Sweet, white, Sparkling, Non-MCC, white, off-dry/semi-sweet, Sparkling, Non-MCC, rosé, off-dry/semi-sweet, Sparkling, Non-MCC, red, dry), Versus (Natural Sweet, rosé), Woolworths (5) (Merlot, Natural Sweet, red, Natural Sweet, white, Rosé off-dry/semi-sweet, White blends, off-dry/semi-sweet (w & u/w)) ★★ **Arniston Bay** (2) (Red blends, other, Rosé off-dry/semi-sweet), Bergsig (Perlé wines), **Bonnievale** (Perlé wines), De Wet (Perlé wines), Douglas Green (Natural Sweet, rosé), Drostdy-Hof (Natural Sweet, red), Jonkheer (2) (Perlé wines, Perlé wines), Obikwa (Natural Sweet, red), Pick 'n Pay (Rosé off-dry/semi-sweet), Robertson (8) (Natural Sweet, red, Natural Sweet, rosé, Sauvignon blanc unwooded, Natural Sweet, rosé, Natural Sweet, white, Sweet red, Chenin blanc off-dry/semi-sweet (w & u/w), Sauvignon blanc unwooded), Swartland (Rosé off-dry/semi-sweet), JC le Roux (Sparkling, Non-MCC, red, off-dry/semi-sweet), **Van Loveren** (Rosé off-dry/semi-sweet), **Viljoensdrift** (Sparkling, Non-MCC, rosé, off-dry/semi-sweet), Woolworths (4) (Natural Sweet, rosé, White blends, off-dry/semi-sweet (w & u/w), Rosé off-dry/semi-sweet, Red blends, shiraz/syrah-based) ★ **4th Street** (Natural Sweet, red), **Bonnievale** (Perlé wines), Pick 'n Pay (White blends, unwooded, dry), Robertson (3) (White blends, unwooded, dry, Natural Sweet, rosé, Rosé off-dry/semi-sweet), Simonsvlei (Natural Sweet, rosé), Van Loveren (White blends, unwooded, dry), Woolworths (6) (Shiraz/syrah, Chardonnay unwooded, Chenin blanc off-dry/semi-sweet (w & u/w), Sauvignon blanc unwooded, Chenin blanc unwooded dry, Chenin blanc unwooded dry) ★ Robertson **NT** Botha (White blends, off-dry/semi-sweet (w & u/w)), Bottelary (Rosé off-dry/semi-sweet), Klawer (Sparkling, Non-MCC, rosé, off-dry/semi-sweet), Lutzville (Natural Sweet, red), Origin (5) (Rosé off-dry/semi-sweet, Hanepoot unfortified, Hanepoot unfortified, Sweet red, Sparkling, Non-MCC, rosé, off-dry/semi-sweet) **D** Robertson (3) (Sparkling, Non-MCC, white, off-dry/semi-sweet, Sparkling, Non-MCC, rosé, off-dry/semi-sweet, Sparkling, Non-MCC, red, dry)

Malbec

★★★★ Anura, Diemersfontein, High Constantia, Maison de Teijger, Mooi Bly, Mount Vernon, Paul Wallace, Plaisir, Raka, **Woolworths** (2)

★★★★ Blaauwklippen, Doolhof, Druk My Niet, Maison de Teijger, Umkhulu, **Vergenoegd** ★★★ **Bushmanspad**, Fairview, Hildenbrand, Hillcrest, Maison de Teijger, Neethlingshof, **Withington** ★★☆ Bellevue, **Bovlei**, Flagstone, Woolworths **NT** Annex Kloof, Audacia, Haut Espoir, Le Pommier, Signal Hill

Merlot

★★★★☆ Bein (2), Creation, Delaire, Dombeya, Eagles' Nest, **Hartenberg**, Laibach, Meerlust,

Oldenburg, Red Tape, Remhoogte, Saxenburg, Shannon, Thelema, Vergelegen, Yonder Hill
★★★★ Amani, Anthonij Rupert (2), Anura, Barton, Bein, Buitenverwachting, De Trafford, **De Wetshof**, DeWaal, Durbanville Hills (2), Eikendal, Fleur du Cap, GlenWood, Groenland, Groot Constantia, Hazendal, Hillcrest, Jordan, Kaapzicht, Ken Forrester, Laibach, Lanzerac, Linton Park, Marianne, Morgenhof, Nabygelegen, Nederburg, Nico van der Merwe, Noble Hill, Rainbow's End, Rickety Bridge, Ridgeback, Rust en Vrede, Rustenberg, Slaley, Steenberg, Stellekaya, Sumaridge, The Butcher Shop, The Winery of Good Hope, Veenwouden, Vergenoegd, Von Ortloff, Welbedacht, Wine Village-Hermanus, Woolworths (2), Zevenwacht

★★★★ Annandale, Asara, Backsberg, **Blaauwklippen**, Blueberry Hill, Boekenhoutskloof, Boland, Boschendal, **Botanica**, Bovlei, Catherine Marshall, Clos Malverne, De Meye, Devon Hill, Diemersdal, Dornier, Du Preez, Elgin Vintners, Ernst Gouws, Excelsior, Fairview, False Bay, **Flagstone**, Fort Simon, Fraai Uitzicht 1798, **Glen Carlou**, Glenelly, Graceland, Guardian Peak, Hofstraat, Hout Bay, **Jordan**, Kling, Kranskop, KWV, Kyburg, La Couronne, La Petite Ferme, Linton Park, Lourensford, Maison de Teijger, Manley, Meerendal (2), Meinert, Miravel, Mooiplaas, Muratie, Nederburg, Niel Joubert (Organic), Org de Rac (2) (Organic), Overgaauw, Painted Wolf, Passages, Quoin Rock, Raka, Remhoogte, Savanha, Spookfontein , StellenRust, Sterhuis, The Butcher Shop (2), **The Rhino**, Thelema, Tread Lightly, **Ultra Liquors**, Vergenoegd, Viljoensdrift, Waterkloof, Woolworths (2) (Organic) ★★★ Altydgedacht, Anthonij Rupert, Anura, Arra, Ayama, Beau Joubert, Bellingham (2), Bilton, Blaauwklippen, Blue Crane, Boland, Boschkloof , Botha, **Brenaissance** Cape Classics, D'Aria, Darling Cellars, De Grendel, De Villiers, Delheim, DeWaal, Doolhof, Du Preez, Dunstone, Ernie Els, Fairview, Fish Hoek, **Flagstone**, Flat Roof Manor, Fleur du Cap, Fort Simon, Fraai Uitzicht 1798, **Goede Hoop**, Groote Post, Havana Hills, **Herold**, Het Vlock Casteel, Hoopenburg, Journey's End, Klein Parys, Kleine Zalze, Kleinfontein, Kloovenburg, Koelenhof , KWV, L'Avenir, La Bri, Laborie, Leopard's Leap, Lindhorst, **Linton Park**, Lomond, Longridge, Lyngrove, Lynx, M'hudi, MAN Vintners, **Middelvlei**, Mon Rêve, Mont du Toit, Mont Rochelle, Mzoli's, **Namaqua**, Nederburg, Ormonde (2), Overhex, Perdeberg, Place in the Sun, Plaisir, Post House, Pulpit Rock, Quest, Retief, Rooiberg, Savanha (2), Seal Breeze, Slowine, Spier (Organic), Stellar (Organic), Stellenbosch Hills, Tulbagh Winery, **Ultra Liquors** (2), uniWines, Van Loveren, Villiera, Wellington Winery, **Weltevrede**,

Wines of Cape Town, Woolworths (3), Yonder Hill, Zonnebloem, Zorgvliet ★★★ Audacia, Backsberg (Kosher), Badsberg, Bayede! (2), Bellpost, Bloemendal, Blomendahl, Boland, Bovlei, **Desert Rose**, Die Mas, Domaine Brahms, Douglas Green, Drostdy-Hof, Du Toitskloof , Durbanville Hills, Eikehof, Excelsior, Goedverwacht, Hoopenburg, Kanu, Klawer, KWV, **L'Auberge**, La Petite Provence, Ladismith, Landskroon, **Le Manoir de Brendel**, Libby's Pride, Louisvale, Maison de Teijger, Maske, Mischa, **Mount Rozier**, Namaqua, Neethlingshof, Niel Joubert, Old Vines (Organic), **Org de Rac** (Organic), Oudtshoorn, Riebeek (2), Robertson (2), Savanha, Seven Sisters, Simonsvlei, Slanghoek, Somersbosch (Organic), Stellar (Organic), **The Wine Fusion**, uniWines, Valley Vineyards (2), **Versailles**, Vredenheim, **Wandsbeck**, Waterstone, Whalehaven, Windmeul, Wineways, **Women in Wine**, Wonderfontein (Organic), Woolworths (2) (Organic) ★★ African Pride, African Terroir (2) (Organic), Arniston Bay, Barrydale, **Bernheim**, **Bonview**, Boplaas, **Boutique Baratok**, Burgershof, Calitzdorp, Cape Dreams, **Cronier**, Culemborg, Glenview, Goudini, Graham Beck, Groupe CDV (2), Hill & Dale, Jason's Hill, Kleine Draken, Lutzville, Maison de Teijger, Robertson, Rooiberg, Stellendrift, Swartland, Waterstone, Welmoed, Wineways, Woolworths (2) (Light & low-alcohol), Zidela ★★ African Terroir (Organic), Bergwater, Cranefields, Jonkheer, Pulpit Rock, Tulbagh Winery, United Nations, Wineways (3), Woolworths ★ **Boutique Baratok** ★ Robertson **NT** AlexKia, Bonfoi, Bottelary, Buffalo Creek, Calais, Callender, Camberley (Organic), De Breede (Organic), Dellrust, Elberti, Escapades, Hartenberg (2), Hathersage, High Constantia (2), Holden Manz, Hornbill , Klein Parys, Klein Roosboom , Marklew, Mitre's Edge, Montagu Wine & Spirits, My Wyn, Nietvoorbij (Organic), Origin (Organic), Oude Compagnies Post, Rosendal (2), Ross Gower, Spier, Stellendrift, **Stone Ridge**, Tanagra, The Township Winery, Westbridge, Wineways, Wolfkloof, Wonderfontein **NR** Bergwater, Franschhoek Cellar, Obikwa **D** Belfield, Boschheim, De Krans, Morgenhof, Stellenzicht, Stony Brook, Wandsbeck, Wildekrans, Withington, Woolworths

Mourvèdre

★★★★☆ Beaumont

★★★★ Raka

★★★★ Fairview, Hawksmoor, Spice Route ★★★ Bovlei, MAN Vintners ★★★ Oude Compagnies Post ★★ Idiom **NT** BLANKbottle, Signal Hill **D** Stony Brook

Muscadel, red, fortified

★★★★☆ Boplaas, **Namaqua**, Rietvallei, Robertson

★★★★ Badsberg, Calitzdorp, De Wet, Nuweland, Nuy, Orange River

★★★★ Aan de Doorns, Bon Courage, **Boplaas**, **Clairvaux**, Du Toitskloof , **Karusa**, Klawer, McGregor, Rietvallei, Roodezandt, Rooiberg, Slanghoek, Van Loveren, Weltevrede ★★★ Boland, **Boplaas**, Klein Parys, KWV ★★★ BurCon, Jonkheer, Montagu Wine & Spirits, Wandsbeck **NT** Grundheim, Montagu Wine Cellar, TTT Cellar **NT** Ashton, Excelsior Vlakteplaas, Janeza, Landzicht, Montagu Wine & Spirits, Oudtshoorn, Wolvendrift, Wonderfontein **NR** Reiersvlei **D** Leeuwenjacht

Muscadel, white, fortified

★★★★☆ Alvi's Drift, Boplaas, Monis

★★★★ Calitzdorp, De Krans, De Wet, Graham Beck, Ladismith, Lutzville, Merwida, Nuy, Orange River, **Windmeul**

★★★★ Bon Courage, Boplaas, De Krans, Jonkheer, Klawer, Montagu Wine & Spirits, Weltevrede ★★★ De Wetshof, Excelsior Vlakteplaas, Jonkheer, La Couronne, McGregor, Montagu Wine Cellar, **Namaqua**, Withoek ★★★ Clairvaux, Grundheim, Oudtshoorn ★★ Montagu Wine & Spirits **NT** Calitzdorp, Landzicht, Montagu Wine & Spirits, Mostertsdrift, Robertson **D** Ashton

Muscadel, white, unfortified

★★★ Karusa ★★★ Thelema ★★ Boplaas

Muscat de Hambourg fortified

★★★★ Stellenbosch Hills

Muscat Ottonel unfortified

★★ Zidela

Natural Sweet, red

★★★★ Adoro ★★★ Blomendahl (2), Bosman ★★★ Somerset Wines ★★ Backsberg (Kosher), **Kanu**, Kleine Draken (Kosher), Robertson (Light & low-alcohol), Van Loveren (Light & low-alcohol), Wineways (2), Woolworths ★★ Drostdy-Hof (Light & low-alcohol), Obikwa (Light & low-alcohol), Robertson ★ 4th Street (Light & low-alcohol), Versus **NT** Lutzville (Light & low-alcohol), Wineways **NR** Rooiberg **D** Cape Hutton

Natural Sweet, rosé

★★★★☆ Groot Constantia

★★★ Seven Sisters, Villiersdorp ★★★ Fort Simon, Grünberger (Light & low-alcohol), Rooiberg, **Somerset Wines** ★★ 4th Street (Light & low-alcohol), Drostdy-Hof (Light & low-alcohol), Lutzville (Light & low-alcohol), Robertson (Light & low-alcohol), Simonsvlei (Light & low-alcohol), Van Loveren (2) (Light & low-alcohol, Light & low-alcohol), Versus ★★ Douglas Green (Light & low-alcohol), Robertson (2) (Light & low-alcohol, Light & low-alcohol), Woolworths ★ Robertson (Light &

low-alcohol), Simonsvlei **NT** Landzicht **D** Clairvaux, Oudtshoorn

Natural Sweet, white

★★★★☆ Badsberg, Buitenverwachting, Klein Constantia, Nederburg, Perdeberg, Quoin Rock

★★★★ Dornier, Stony Brook

★★★★ Boschendal (Light & low-alcohol), Cloof, **Highlands Road**, Meerendal (Light & low-alcohol), Ridgeback (Light & low-alcohol, Organic), Stellar ★★★ Arra, Kaapzicht, **Le Pommier**, Lord's, **Quando**, Rickety Bridge, Rooiberg, **Somerset Wines** (Light & low-alcohol), **Zorgvliet** ★★★ Groupe CDV (Light & low-alcohol), Grünberger (Light & low-alcohol), Lutzville (Light & low-alcohol), Theuniskraal ★★ 4th Street (Light & low-alcohol), Douglas Green (Light & low-alcohol), Drostdy-Hof (Light & low-alcohol), Goudini, Robertson (Light & low-alcohol), Van Loveren (Light & low-alcohol), Versus, Woolworths ★★ Obikwa, Robertson ★ Kleine Draken **NT** Bottelary Hills, Landzicht **D** Somersbosch, Vredenheim

Nebbiolo

★★★★☆ Steenberg (2)

★★★★ Du Toitskloof ★★★ Dagbreek **NT** Awendland, Idiom

Noble Late Harvest

★★★★★ Fleur du Cap, Nederburg, Paul Cluver, Signal Hill

★★★★★☆ Boekenhoutskloof, De Wetshof (Light & low-alcohol), Delheim, **Durbanville Hills** (Light & low-alcohol), **Hermanuspietersfontein** (Light & low-alcohol), Joostenberg, Jordan, Lourensford, Miles Mossop (Light & low-alcohol), Nederburg, Neethlingshof (Light & low-alcohol), Springfontein (Light & low-alcohol), Tokara, Villiera

★★★★ Badsberg (2), Beaumont, Blaauwklippen (Light & low-alcohol), Bon Courage, Eikendal, Fort Simon, Kanu, L'illa, **Longridge**, Mulderbosch, **Namaqua**, Post House, Signal Hill (3), Simonsig, Slaley, Slanghoek, StellenRust, Virgin Earth, Waterford, Woolworths

★★★★ Blaauwklippen (2) (Light & low-alcohol), Savanha ★★★ Altydgedacht, Du Toitskloof , Hildenbrand ★★★ De Grendel (Light & low-alcohol), Van Loveren **NT** Asara, Avontuur, Darling Cellars, Delaire, Groote Post, Ken Forrester, Morgenhof, Nelson, Shannon, Tokara, Vruchtbaar **D** Villiera

Non-muscat, red, fortified

★★★★ SoetKaroo

★★★ uniWines **NT** SoetKaroo

Non-muscat, white, fortified

★★★★ uniWines

★★★★ Haute Cabrière

Nouvelle
★★★ Darling Cellars

Organic

★★★★☆ Woolworths (Red blends, shiraz/syrah-based), Avondale

★★★★ Woolworths (2) (Red blends, Cape Bordeaux, Sauvignon blanc unwooded), Avondale (5) (Shiraz/syrah, Red blends, Cape Bordeaux, Red blends, shiraz/syrah-based, Chenin blanc wooded, dry, Sparkling, Méthode cap classique, white, dry), Org de Rac (Cabernet sauvignon), La Motte (Sauvignon blanc unwooded), Groot Parys (Vin de paille), **Joostenberg** (White blends, unwooded, dry), Laibach (Red blends, Cape Bordeaux), Porseleinberg (Shiraz/syrah), Bon Cap

★★★★ Woolworths (2) (Merlot, Chardonnay wooded), Org de Rac (2) (Merlot, Shiraz/syrah), Stellar (Shiraz/syrah), Org de Rac (Merlot), Stellar (Natural Sweet, white), Bon Cap (2) (Red blends, with pinotage, Sparkling, Méthode cap classique, white, dry), **De Breede** (Red blends, Cape Bordeaux), Groot Parys (3) (Chardonnay wooded, Chenin blanc wooded, dry, Chenin blanc wooded, dry), Elgin Ridge (Sauvignon blanc unwooded), Laibach (White blends, wooded, dry), Lazanou (5) (Shiraz/syrah, Chardonnay wooded, Chenin blanc unwooded dry, Viognier, White blends, unwooded, dry), Mountain Oaks (2) (Pinotage, Chenin blanc unwooded dry), **Reyneke** (2) (Red blends, shiraz/syrah-based, White blends, wooded, dry), **Silvermist** (Sauvignon blanc unwooded), Tukulu (Chardonnay wooded), **Waverley Hills ★★★** Woolworths (Rosé dry), Avondale (Rosé dry), Van Loveren (Port, red), **KWV** (White blends, off-dry/semi-sweet (w & u/w)), **Stellar** (5) (White blends, unwooded, dry, Cabernet sauvignon, Merlot, Rosé dry, Rosé dry), Org de Rac (Shiraz/syrah), Elgin Ridge (Chardonnay unwooded), Lazanou (Red blends, shiraz/syrah-based), Mountain Oaks (Red blends, Cape Bordeaux), Seven Oaks (Red blends, Cape Bordeaux), African Terroir (Viognier), Bon Cap (White blends, wooded, dry), Upland (Cabernet sauvignon), Waverley Hills (6) (Cabernet sauvignon, Shiraz/syrah, Red blends, shiraz/syrah-based, Red blends, other, White blends, wooded, dry, Sparkling, Méthode cap classique, white, dry) ★★★ Woolworths (5) (Cabernet sauvignon, Merlot, Shiraz/syrah, Chardonnay wooded, Sauvignon blanc unwooded), Origin (Red blends, shiraz/syrah-based), Woolworths (Sparkling, Non-MCC, white, off-dry/semi-sweet), **Stellar** (10) (Red blends, with pinotage, Pinotage, Chardonnay unwooded, Chenin blanc unwooded dry, Sauvignon blanc unwooded, White blends, off-dry/semi-sweet (w & u/w), Cabernet sauvignon, Merlot, Pinotage, White blends, off-dry/semi-sweet (w & u/w)), Org de Rac

(4) (Cabernet sauvignon, Chardonnay wooded, Merlot, Red blends, Cape Bordeaux), Bergwater (Shiraz/syrah), De Breede (Red blends, Cape Bordeaux), Groot Parys (Chenin blanc unwooded dry), **African Terroir** (4) (Cabernet sauvignon, Cabernet sauvignon, Shiraz/syrah, Chardonnay unwooded), Bon Cap (3) (Pinotage, Rosé dry, Sauvignon blanc unwooded), Upland (Port, red), **Waverley Hills** (3) (Cabernet sauvignon, Red blends, Cape Bordeaux, White blends, wooded, dry), African Terroir (3) (Cabernet sauvignon, Shiraz/syrah, Red blends, with pinotage) ★★ Woolworths (Pinotage), **Origin** (White blends, wooded, dry), **Stellar** (5) (Pinot noir, Shiraz/syrah, Sparkling, Non-MCC, white, dry, Pinotage, White blends, off-dry/semi-sweet (w & u/w)), Org de Rac (2) (Rosé dry, Cabernet sauvignon), **Bon Cap** (Port, red), Groot Parys (Rosé dry), **Mountain Oaks** (Red blends, with pinotage), African Terroir (2) (Pinotage, Sauvignon blanc unwooded), Bon Cap (Sparkling, Non-MCC, white, off-dry/semi-sweet), Waverley Hills (Rosé dry), African Terroir (5) (Merlot, Pinotage, Chardonnay wooded, Sauvignon blanc unwooded, Sparkling, Non-MCC, rosé, dry) ★☆ Woolworths (Colombard), **KWV** (Red blends, other), **Stellar** (2) (Colombard, Rosé off-dry/semi-sweet), African Terroir (Merlot), **Waverley Hills ★ Org de Rac** (2) (Rosé dry, Chardonnay unwooded), African Terroir (2) (Rosé dry, White blends, unwooded, dry) **NT** Origin (4) (Red blends, shiraz/syrah-based, Merlot, Chardonnay wooded), Bon Cap (Viognier), De Breede (Merlot), Groot Parys (Chardonnay unwooded), Mountain Oaks (6) (Red blends, Cape Bordeaux, Rosé dry, Chardonnay wooded, Chenin blanc wooded, dry, Chenin blanc wooded, dry, White blends, unwooded, dry) **NR** Groot Parys **D** Stellar (2) (Sauvignon blanc unwooded, White blends, unwooded, dry), Spier (2) (Cabernet sauvignon, Sauvignon blanc unwooded), Lazanou (Chenin blanc wooded, dry), Reyneke

Perlé wines

★★★ Conradie (Light & low-alcohol), **Origin** (3) (Light & low-alcohol, Light & low-alcohol), **Overhex** (2) (Light & low-alcohol, Light & low-alcohol) ★★ Ashton, Douglas Green (Light & low-alcohol), Du Toitskloof (Rosé off-dry/semi-sweet), Grünberger (2), Riebeek (2) (Light & low-alcohol, Light & low-alcohol), **uniWines** (2) (Hanepoot unfortified, Hanepoot unfortified), Wandsbeck ★★ Autumn Harvest Crackling (2), Bergsig (Light & low-alcohol), **Bonnievale** (Light & low-alcohol), Capenheimer, Darling Cellars, De Wet (Light & low-alcohol), Jonkheer (2) (Light & low-alcohol, Light & low-alcohol) ★ Autumn Harvest Crackling, **Bonnievale**

Petit verdot

★★★★ Asara, **Havana Hills**, My Wyn, Nederburg, Raka

★★★★ Anura, **BLANKbottle**, Darling Cellars, Doolhof, Hillcrest, Lovane, Nabygelegen, Rico Suter, Signal Hill, Zorgvliet ★★★ Bellevue, Maison de Teijger (2), Stellenzicht ★★★ **Definitum** ★★ TTT Cellar **NT** Calais, Du Preez, Haut Espoir, KWV **D** Môreson

Petite sirah/durif

★★★★ Fairview

★★★★ Spotswood

Pinot gris/grigio

★★★★ De Grendel, **Eagle's Cliff**

★★★★ Anthonij Rupert, Nederburg, The Township Winery ★★★ **Idiom**, **Spring Grove**, Usana ★★★ **Flagstone**, Flat Roof Manor, **Hill & Dale**, Origin, **Overhex** ★★ Fairview, Robertson, Two Oceans ★★ Obikwa, Van Loveren (Organic), **Waverley Hills** (Organic), **Woolworths NT** Woolworths

Pinot noir

★★★★★ Cape Chamonix, Newton Johnson

★★★★★ Bouchard Finlayson (2), Creation, Crystallum (2), **Iona**, Meerlust, Paul Cluver (2), Shannon, The Winery of Good Hope (2)

★★★★ Andy Mitchell, Botanica, Catherine Marshall (2), Creation, **Dalla Cia**, Domaine des Dieux, **Edgebaston**, Flagstone, **Glen Carlou**, Groote Post, Hamilton Russell, Kleine Zalze, **La Chaumiere**, La Vierge, Muratie, Newton Johnson, Oak Valley, Paul Cluver, Signal Hill (2), **Stark-Condé**, Strandveld, Sumaridge, **The Winery of Good Hope**, Topaz, Two Oceans, Virgin Earth, Vriesenhof , Woolworths (2), Yardstick

★★★★ Avontuur, **Backsberg**, De Grendel, De Wetshof, Elgin Vintners, Fryer's Cove, Glen Carlou, Grande Provence, Herold, **JH Meyer**, Lord's, **Maison de Teijger** (2), **Malanot**, Meerendal, **Peter Falke**, **Seven Springs**, Stark-Condé, Strandveld, Thandi, The Winery of Good Hope, Thelema, Waterford, Woolworths (2) ★★★ **Andy Mitchell**, Barrydale, Bon Courage, Ernst Gouws, Felicité, Haute Cabrière (2), Hoopenburg, **Maison de Teijger** (2), Nabygelegen, Robertson, **Scrucap**, The Butcher Shop, **The Hills**, Vriesenhof, Whalehaven, William Everson, **Woolworths** ★★★ Highlands Road, **Lemberg**, Maison de Teijger (2), **Mofam**, **Rietvallei**, Spookfontein , **The Wine Fusion** ★★ Goedvertrouw, Quando (Organic), **Stellar NT** Bouchard Finlayson, Callender, Herold, Longbarn, Spier, Springfield, Windfall, Woolworths **D** Anura, Beau Joubert, Klein Optenhorst

Pinotage

★★★★★ Cape Chamonix, Kanonkop

★★★★☆ Beyerskloof, DeWaal, Diemersfontein, Durbanville Hills, Fairview, Flagstone, Grangehurst, Kaapzicht, L'Avenir, Meerendal, Nederburg, Rijk's (2), Southern Right, Spier, Umkhulu, Windmeul

★★★★ Allée Bleue, Altydgedacht, Anura, Arra, Bayede!, Bosman, Chateau Naudé, Clos Malverne, Conradie, Croydon, De Zoete Inval, DeWaal, Diemersdal (2), Diemersfontein, Dornier, Eikendal, Hidden Valley, **Hornbill**, Kaapzicht, Kleine Zalze, KWV, Laibach, Lammershoek, Lanzerac (2), Longridge, Lyngrove, Maastricht, Meerendal, Môreson, Namaqua, Neil Ellis, Painted Wolf, Perdeberg, Pulpit Rock, Remhoogte (Biodynamic), Reyneke (Biodynamic), Rijk's, Rooiberg, Savanha, Scali, Simonsig, Slaley, Spice Route, Springfontein (2), Stanford Hills, StellenRust, Stellenzicht, Swartland, SylvanVale, **The Winery of Good Hope**, Tokara, Virgin Earth, Warwick, Welbedacht, Welgegund, Wellington Winery, Wildekrans, Woolworths

★★★★ Annex Kloof, Badsberg, Beaumont, Bellingham, Bergsig, Beyerskloof, Boland, Bovlei, Camberley, Cloof, Delheim, Domaine Brahms, Doolhof, **Eagle's Cliff**, Eaglevlei, **Eenzaamheid**, Fort Simon, Graham Beck, Hofstraat, Jonkheer, Klawer, Kleine Zalze, KWV, L'Avenir, Lemberg, Lindhorst, Malanot, MAN Vintners, Marklew, Meinert, Middelvlei, Misty Mountains, Mooiplaas (Organic), Mountain Oaks (Organic), Nederburg, Neethlingshof, **Neil Ellis**, **Olifantsberg**, Onderkloof , Painted Wolf, Raka, Rhebokskloof, Romond, Simonsvlei, Slaley, Spioenkop, Springfontein, Stellekaya, Stellenbosch University , Super Single Vineyards, Tempel, The Winery of Good Hope, Tukulu, Vriesenhof , Welgevallen, Whalehaven, **Wineways**, **Woolworths** ★★★ Aaldering, Allée Bleue, Anthonij Rupert, Anura, Arniston Bay, Arra, Avontuur, Barista, Bellevue, **Bellingham**, Bergsig, Blomendahl, Boer & Brit, Boland, Botha, Calitzdorp, Cape Dreams, Cloof, Clos Malverne, Darling Cellars (2), De Villiers, DeWaal, **Die Mas**, Douglas Green, Drostdy-Hof, Du Toitskloof , Durbanville Hills, Eagle's Cliff, Fairvalley, Fairview (2), False Bay, **Fernskloof**, Fish Hoek, **Flagstone**, Fleur du Cap, **Franschhoek Cellar**, Freedom Hill, Goede Hoop, Hawksmoor, **Hoopenburg**, Imbuko, Ken Forrester, Klein Parys, Knorhoek, Kumkani, L'Auberge, L'Avenir, Landskroon, **Lemberg**, Louiesenhof, Lyngrove, M'hudi, Malanot, MAN Vintners, Manley, Merwida, Mount Vernon, Nederburg, Niel Joubert, Nitida, Nuweland, Obikwa, Olsen, **Orange River**, Painted Wolf, **Passages**, Perdeberg, Pulpit Rock, Re'Mogo, Rickety Bridge, Rico Suter, Riebeek (2), Rooiberg, Saam, Saxenburg, **Silkbush**, Simonsvlei, Slanghoek, Spier, **Stanford Hills**, Stellenbosch Hills, Stellendrift, StellenRust, Stellenzicht, Swartland, **Teubes**, The Grape Grinder,

The Rhino, The Township Winery, **Thembi & Co**, Trajan, Tulbagh Winery (2), Two Oceans, uniWines, Viljoensdrift, Villiera, Vriesenhof , Vruchtbaar, Welbedacht, Wellington Winery, Windmeul, Woolworths (2), Zonnebloem ★★★ Aan de Doorns, Anura, Ayama, Backsberg (2) (Kosher), Bergheim, Bernheim, Bloemendal, Boland (Organic), Bon Cap (Organic), Bon Courage, Boplaas, Bovlei, Breëland, Burgershof, Culemborg, De Wet, Eagle's Cliff, **Freedom Hill**, Goudini, Graham Beck, Groupe CDV, Hawksmoor, Jacobsdal, Karusa, **Klein Parys**, Kleine Zalze, Koelenhof , **Koopmanskloof**, KWV, Ladismith, **Lateganskop**, **Le Manoir de Brendel**, Lutzville, **Malanot**, Marianne, McGregor, Montagu Wine & Spirits, Morgenhof, Neethlingshof, Oude Kaap, Overhex, Robertson, Schalkenbosch, Simonsvlei, Six Hats, Somersbosch (Organic), Stellar (2) (Organic), Tulbagh Winery, Valley Vineyards, Vukani, Waterstone (2), **Wineways**, Withington, Woolworths ★★ African Pride, African Terroir (3) (Organic), Alvi's Drift, Ashton, **Boutique Baratok** (2), **Govert**, Groupe CDV, Hill & Dale, Koopmanskloof, Mountain River (2), Namaqua, Oude Compagnies Post, Rhebokskloof, Simonsig (Organic), **Stellar** (Organic), Van Loveren, Welmoed, Wineways, **Woolworths** (2) (Organic), Zevenwacht ★☆ African Terroir, **Bayede!**, Blomendahl, Bovlei, Café Culture, **Imbuko** ★ Van Loveren, **Woolworths** ☆ Jonkheer, Wineways **NT** Bellevue, Beyerskloof, Bottelary Hills, Buffalo Creek, Calais, De Zoete Inval, Devon Hill, Devon Rocks, Escapades, Four Paws, Groot Constantia, Groupe CDV, Hawksmoor, Hazendal (2), Jason's Hill, Klein Parys, Le Grand Chasseur, Mountain River, New Beginnings, Nietvoorbij, Origin (2), Oude Compagnies Post, Spier (2), Stellenbosch University , SylvanVale, Teubes, **Thembi & Co**, United Nations, uniWines, Vredenheim, Waboomsrivier, Westbridge (2), Zidela, Zonnebloem **NR Reiersvlei D** Bilton, Boplaas, Kleine Draken (Kosher), Leeuwenjacht, Oudtshoorn (2), Wildekrans, Withington, Woolworths (2)

Port, pink
★★★ Boplaas ★★★ De Krans

Port, red
★★★★★ Boplaas, De Krans, JP Bredell
★★★★☆ Boplaas (3), De Krans, Vergenoegd
★★★★ Axe Hill (2), Bergsig (2), Boplaas (4), De Krans (2), Delaire, Jonkheer, JP Bredell, **Knorhoek**, KWV, Landskroon, **Lovane**, Monis, Morgenhof, Muratie (3), Overgaauw, Peter Bayly, Quinta, Simonsig, Swartland, The Butcher Shop
★★★☆ Allesverloren, Alto, Annandale, **Annex Kloof**, Backsberg, Beaumont, Bergsig, Beyerskloof, Boplaas, Calitzdorp, De Wet, Dellrust, Die Mas,

Douglas Green, Du'SwaRoo, Flagstone, Goede Hoop, Groot Constantia, Grundheim (2), Hout Bay, Jacques Smit, Kaapzicht, Louiesenhof, **Maison**, Monis, TTT Cellar, Villiera ★★★ Aan de Doorns, Anura, Badsberg, Beau Joubert, Boland, Bon Courage, Botha, Clairvaux, De Wet, De Zoete Inval, Du Toitskloof, Holden Manz, **Karusa**, Koelenhof , KWV, Louiesenhof, Montagu Wine & Spirits (2), My Wyn, Riebeek, Ultra Liquors (Organic), Van Loveren (Organic), Vergenoegd, Windmeul, **Zandvliet** ★★☆ Allée Bleue, Bernheim, Bovlei, Calitzdorp, **Elemental Bob**, Grundheim, **Peter Bayly**, Slanghoek, Somersbosch, Swartland (Organic), Upland (Organic), Wellington Winery, Withoek ★★ **Bon Cap** (Organic), Klawer, Montpellier, Oudtshoorn, **Reiersvlei**, Viljoensdrift, Villiersdorp, Withoek (2) ★☆ Bonnievale, TTT Cellar, Tulbagh Winery ★ Du'SwaRoo, McGregor, Nietvoorbij **NT** De Zoete Inval, Jean Daneel, JP Bredell (2), Landzicht, Montagu Wine & Spirits, Ridgeback, Robertson, Rooiberg **D** Goudini, Graham Beck, Oudtshoorn, Riebeek, Tulbagh Winery

Port, white
★★★ Axe Hill, Boplaas, De Krans, **Grundheim** ★★ Peter Bayly ★★ **Karusa NS** TTT Cellar **NT** My Wyn **D** Asara

Red blends, Cape Bordeaux
★★★★★ Dalla Cia, Fleur du Cap, Keets, Mvemve Raats, The Butcher Shop
★★★★☆ Anthonij Rupert, Bartinney, Beaumont, Buitenverwachting, Cape Chamonix, **Capelands**, Constantia Glen (2), Darling Cellars, **De Trafford**, Delheim, Diemersdal (2), Dornier, Druk My Niet, Eikendal, Ernie Els, Gabriëlskloof, Grangehurst, Groot Constantia, Hartenberg, Haskell, Havana Hills, Hermanuspietersfontein, Hidden Valley, Jordan (2), KWV, Laibach, Lovane, Lynx, Meerlust, Miles Mossop, Morgenster (2), Mulderbosch, Muratie, Nabygelegen, Nico van der Merwe, Nitida, Overgaauw, Peter Falke, Romond, Rupert & Rothschild, Saronsberg, Simonsig, Steenberg, Stellenbosch Ridge, StellenRust, **The Butcher Shop**, Thelema, Tokara, Vergelegen (3), Vergenoegd, Vilafonté (2), Warwick, **Waterford**, Woolworths (2), Yonder Hill
★★★★ Asara (Organic), Avondale (Organic), **Babylonstoren**, Backsberg, Belfield, Beyerskloof, Blaauwklippen, **BLANKbottle**, Bonfoi, Boschkloof , Bottelary Hills, Camberley (3), Capaia, CK Wines, Claime d'Or, Cloof (2), Constantia Uitsig, Creation, Damarakloof, De Toren (2), DeWaal, Dombeya, Durbanville Hills, Eagles'Nest, Eikendal, Epicurean, Glen Carlou, Grande Provence, Grangehurst, Hermanuspietersfontein, Hillcrest, Hout Bay, Iona, JP Bredell, Kaapzicht, Kanonkop, Kleinfontein, Knorhoek, La Petite Ferme (Organic), Laibach (Organic), Le Bonheur, Le Riche, Louis, Lourensford,

Meerhof, MolenVliet, Mooiplaas, Môreson, Morgenhof, Namaqua, Napier, **Nederburg** (3), Neethlingshof, Neil Ellis (2), Nelson, Noble Hill, Noble Savage, Oak Valley, Ormonde, **Raats**, Raka (Biodynamic), Reyneke (Biodynamic), Ridgeback, Rietvallei, Robert Stanford, Rupert & Rothschild, Russo, Rustenberg, Saltaré, Saronsberg, Spier, Spookfontein , Springfield, Stellekaya, Stony Brook (2), The Butcher Shop (2), The Drift, The High Road, Topaz, Uva Mira, Veenwouden, Vergelegen, Vergenoegd, Villiera, Von Ortloff, Vondeling, Vriesenhof , **Waterford**, Welbedacht, Woolworths (2) (Organic), Yonder Hill, Zevenwacht

★★★★ Allée Bleue, Amani, Anura, Ashton, Avontuur, **Beau Constantia**, Beau Joubert, BLANKbottle, Boer & Brit, **Bosman**, Buitenverwachting, Cape Chamonix, Clos Malverne (Organic), **De Breede** (Organic), De Grendel, Doolhof (2), Dornier, Druk My Niet, Eagles'Nest, Elgin Vintners, Emineo, Fundi (2), Groote Post, Hathersage, High Constantia, Holden Manz, Jakob's Vineyards, Kanu, Klein Constantia, **Kumkani**, L'Avenir, La Bri, La Vigne, Laborie, Le Joubert, Leopard's Leap, **Linton Park**, Louisvale, **Lovane**, Lynx, Maison de Teijger, Meerendal, Mimosa, Monterosso, **Mzoli's**, **Natte Valleij**, Neethlingshof, Nelson, Nick & Forti's, Nomada, **Rainbow's End**, **Rosendal**, **Scrucap** (2), Southern Sky, **Springfontein**, Steenberg, **Stellekaya**, Sterhuis, Stonewall, Stony Brook, **The Butcher Shop**, The High Road (2), The Winery of Good Hope, Thelema, Thunderchild, Two Oceans, Umkhulu (2), **uniWines**, Vuurberg, **Welbedacht**, Welgemeend (2), Welmoed, Woolworths (2), Yardstick, Zorgvliet

★★★ Aaldering, Agterplaas, Akkerdal, Alkmaar, Alluvia, Arniston Bay, Arra, Avontuur, Badgerberg, Barry Gould, Bayede!, **Beyerskloof**, Black Oystercatcher, Blomendahl, Bon Courage, Boschendal, **Brenaissance**, **Cronier**, Crows Nest, D'Aria, Diemersfontein, Doolhof, Douglas Green, Eagle's Cliff, Equitania, Four Fields, Gabriëlskloof, Havana Hills, Hermanuspietersfontein, Hillcrest, Hornbill , Idiom, Jacaranda, Jordan (2), Klein Parys, Kleine Zalze, La Vierge, La Vigne, Landskroon, Leeuwenjacht, Leopard Frog, Louiesenhof, Maison de Teijger, Malanot, MolenVliet, Morgenhof (2), Mostertsdrift (Organic), Mountain Oaks (Organic), Nico Vermeulen, Opstal, **Orange River**, **Origin**, Overgaauw, Passages, Ridgeback, Rosendal, Saxenburg, Schalkenbosch (Organic), Seven Oaks (Organic), Simonsvlei, Slaley, Slanghoek, Springfontein, Stellendrift, Thandi, **Ultra Liquors**, Van Zylshof, Vondeling, Walker Bay Vineyards, Wedgewood, Welgemeend, Woolworths ★★☆ Anura, Asara, Bellevue, Bernheim, Boschkloof , **Cronier**, Darling Cellars (Organic), De Breede (Organic), Diemersdal, Diemersfontein, Douglas

Green, **Elberti**, Glen Carlou, **Govert**, Jean Daneel, La Petite Provence, McGregor, **Montpellier**, Mount Rozier, Nietvoorbij (2), **Oneiric** (Organic), **Org de Rac** (Organic), Origin (3), Oude Kaap, Rhebokskloof, Riebeek, **Rosendal**, Simonsig, Somerset Wines, Sterhuis, Tanagra, uniWines, Van Loveren (Organic), Waverley Hills (Organic), Welgevallen, Windmeul, Wineways ★★ Bonnievale, Craighall, Goedverwacht, Hoopenburg, Ken Forrester, Kleine Draken (Kosher), KWV, Overhex, Perdeberg, Rooiberg, **Ultra Liquors**, Wineways, Woolworths ★★ **Boutique Baratok**, **La Couronne**, Swartland, Wineways (3) ★ Robertson, Tanagra **NT** Alto, Amani, Ashton, Awendland (2), Bernheim, BLANKbottle, Druk My Niet, Kronendal, Louiesenhof, Môreson (2), Mountain Oaks (Organic), Noble Hill, Old Vines, Origin, Rico Suter, Rosendal, Stellendrift, Tanagra, Ultra Liquors, Vendôme (2), Versailles, Viljoensdrift, Vredevol, Webersburg, Wedderwill, Windmeul, Wineways, Wolfkloof, Wolvendrift **NR** Equitania **D** Bellingham, Beyerskloof, Buitenverwachting, Elemental Bob (2), Flagstone (2), Goats do Roam, Goede Hoop, La Couronne, Main Street, Manley, Meinert, Oak Valley, Raats, Schalkenbosch, Ultra Liquors, Wildekrans, Wines of Cape Town, Woolworths, Zidela

Red blends, other

★★★★★ Ken Forrester, Nico van der Merwe

★★★★☆ Bilton, Bouchard Finlayson, De Trafford, Delaire, Druk My Niet, Ernie Els, Graham Beck, Jean Daneel, Keermont, Klein Constantia, **Lourensford**, Mont du Toit, **Nederburg** (2), Rust en Vrede, The Winery of Good Hope, Uva Mira, Val de Vie, Waterford, Zorgvliet

★★★★ Akkerdal, Allée Bleue, Amani, Anatu, Annandale (2), Ataraxia, Axe Hill, Backsberg (2), Beau Joubert, Bergsig, Black Oystercatcher, BLANKbottle, Boplaas, Boschendal, Bushmanspad, Capaia, Clovelly, De Krans, De Meye, Ernie Els, Fairview, Flagstone, Fundi, Graceland, Guardian Peak (2), Ken Forrester, KWV, **Le Bonheur**, Lingen, Marianne, MC Square, Micu Narunsky, Mont du Toit (2), Nederburg, Neil Ellis Meyer-Näkel, Newton Johnson, **Nietgegund**, Plaisir, Quoin Rock, Rico Suter (2), Rustenberg, Somersbosch, Stony Brook, Swartland, The Butcher Shop, The Goose, Tierhoek, TMV, **Veenwouden**, Virgin Earth, Waterford, Waterkloof

★★★★ Adoro, **Akkerdal**, Anthonij Rupert, Blaauwklippen, Casa Mori, Cederberg, Cloof, **De Krans**, Desert Rose, Dormershire, Durbanville Hills, **Eikendal**, **Fairview**, Faraway House, Four Paws, Fundi, Goats do Roam, Hartenberg, Haut Espoir, **Havana Hills**, Jacques Smit, Joostenberg, **Kanu**, Ken Forrester, Klein Gustrouw, Kumala, Kyburg, La Kavayan, La Motte, La Vierge, **Leopard Frog**, Lutzville, Micu Narunsky, Mont Destin, Morgenster

(2), Nabygelegen, Nederburg, Overgaauw, Rhebokskloof, Roodeberg, **Rustenberg**, Saxenburg, Sophie, Stellekaya, StellenRust, The Butcher Shop, Topiary, Uitkyk, Val de Vie, Veenwouden, Vergenoegd (3), Welvanpas, Woolworths (3), Zonnebloem ★★★ Allée Bleue, Arniston Bay, Avontuur, **Babylon's Peak**, Backsberg, Badsberg, Bayede! (2), **Blaauwklippen**, Blomendahl, Blue Crane, Bon Courage, Boschheim, Chateau Libertas, Clos Malverne, Darling Cellars, Delheim, Du Toitskloof , **Eenzaamheid**, Feiteiras, Franki's, **Govert**, Graham Beck, Groot Constantia, Hazendal, **Hermit on the Hill**, Idiom, Journey's End, Knorhoek, Kumala (3), Longridge, Mon Rêve, Mont du Toit, Mont Rochelle, Natte Valleij, Prospect1870, Raka, **Remhoogte**, Robertson, Schalkenbosch, Seven Oaks, Simonsig, Stonehill, **The Hills**, The Township Winery, Thelema, Van Loveren, Vaughan Johnson, Villiera (Organic), Waverley Hills (Organic), **Woolworths** ★★★ Aan de Doorns, **Allesverloren**, Angels Tears, Audacia, Blouvlei, Botha, Bottelary, Crows Nest, David Frost Signature, De Zoete Inval, Dornier, Du'SwaRoo, Goede Hoop, Goudini, Hill & Dale, **Hillock**, Idiom, **Klein Parys**, **Koopmanskloof**, Landskroon (2), Lynx, Melkboomsdrift, Millstream, Mountain Range, Mzoli's, **Napier**, Nederburg, Nuy, Oude Kaap (2), Oudtshoorn, **Somerset Wines**, Stettyn, Stoumann's, Tanagra, Tassenberg, TCB Wines, Theuniskraal, uniWines, Van Loveren, Versus, Villiersdorp, Vleiland, **Vriesenhof** , Waterstone (2), Zevenwacht ★★ Ashton, Beaumont, Bergwater, Boland, Bonnievale (2), Burgershof, Cloverfield, Cranefields, Culemborg, Eve, Landskroon, Leopard's Leap, Libby's Pride, **Main Street**, Mooiplaas, Mountain River, **Oude Compagnies Post**, Pick 'n Pay, Robertson, Skilpadvlei, Southern Sky, Swartland, Taverna Rouge, Van Loveren, Waterstone, Whalehaven, **Wildehurst**, Withington, Woolworths, Zandvliet ★★ Abbottshill, **African Terroir**, **Arniston Bay** (Light & low-alcohol), Barrydale, Bonne Esperance, Brandvlei, Herold, **Kumala** (Organic), **KWV** (Organic), Overmeer Cellars, Peter Bayly, Robertson, Roodezandt, **Stellenbosch Hills**, TTT Cellar, Woolworths (3) ★ Groupe CDV **NT** Bergwater, Buffalo Creek, Calais (2), Cape Rock (2), Groupe CDV, Hornbill , Janeza, Jason's Hill, Jean Daneel, La Petite Ferme, Montagu Wine Cellar, Retief (2), Rosendal, Seven Oaks, Signal Hill, Waterstone (3), Welvanpas, Westbridge **D** Anura, Arumdale, Bergsig, Blouvlei, Clairvaux, Cloof, Delaire, Du Preez, Elemental Bob (2), Knorhoek, Lemberg, Lourensford, Onderkloof , Swartland, Tierhoek, Wandsbeck, Wildekrans, Woolworths, Zoetendal

Red blends, shiraz/syrah-based

★★★★★ La Motte, Sadie

★★★★☆ AA Badenhorst, **Anatu**, Anwilka, Asara, Boekenhoutskloof, Creation, Fable, Glenelly, Graham Beck, Hoopenburg, **Iona**, Kronendal, Lammershoek, **Luddite**, Mont Destin, Post House, Rall (Biodynamic), Reyneke (Biodynamic), Rust en Vrede, Sequillo, **Strandveld**, The Butcher Shop, Welbedacht (Organic), Woolworths

★★★★ AA Badenhorst, **Akkerdal**, Alto, Amani, **AntHill**, Anwilka (Organic), Avondale (Organic), Ayama, BABISA, Babylon's Peak, Barton, Bellingham, Black Pearl, BLANKbottle (Organic), Bon Cap (Organic), Bosman, Bovlei, Cape Rock, Catherine Marshall, Cecilia, Crios Bride, Domaine des Dieux, Eagle's Cliff, **Eaglevlei**, Emineo, Goats do Roam, Graceland, Graham Beck, Grangehurst, Groenland, Guardian Peak, Havana Hills, Hawksmoor (2), Hermanuspietersfontein, Hermit on the Hill, Hidden Valley, Hughes Family, **Intellego**, KWV, La Motte, Landskroon, Lourensford, Malanot, Mary Le Bow, Meerhof, Middelvlei, MolenVliet (2), Mullineux, **Nederburg**, Newton Johnson, Nico Vermeulen (Shiraz/syrah), Noble Hill, Orangerie, Oude Denneboom, Painted Wolf, Post House, Rijk's, Saronsberg, Schalkenbosch, **Scrucap**, Sijnn, Solms-Delta, Spice Route, Spier, Stony Brook, Sumaridge, The Butcher Shop (2), The Winery of Good Hope (3), Val de Vie, Wildehurst, **Woolworths** (3), Zevenwacht

★★★☆ Akkerdal, **Alkmaar**, Annex Kloof, Anthonij Rupert, Arra (2), Auction Crossing, **Axe Hill**, Babylon's Peak, Beaumont, Bilton, Boekenhoutskloof, Boer & Brit, Boplaas, Boschendal, Boutros, **Brenaissance**, **Brothers**, Cape Rock, Darling Cellars, Diemersfontein, Edgebaston (2), **Eenzaamheid**, Ernie Els, Flat Roof Manor, Goats do Roam, Groenland, **Hermanuspietersfontein**, Heron Ridge, Idiom, **Joostenberg**, **Juno**, Kaapzicht, Kleine Zalze, Kloovenburg, Koelenhof , La Ferme Derik, La Vierge, Le Joubert (2), **Leeuwenkuil**, Leopard's Leap, Lievland, **Louis**, Lourensford, Lyngrove, Lynx, MAN Vintners, Mount Babylon, Mount Vernon, Naughton's, **Neil Ellis**, Nico van der Merwe, **Noble Hill**, Ormonde, Osbloed, Painted Wolf, **Plaisir** (Organic), **Reyneke** (Organic), Rickety Bridge, Ridgeback, **Roodeberg**, Rosendal, Schalkenbosch, Simonsvlei, Spice Route, Springfontein, Stellenbosch Hills, Stettyn, **Strydom**, The Butcher Shop, Thokozani, Trajan, uniWines, Val du Charron, Vredenheim, Waterford, Welgegund, Woolworths, **Yardstick**, Zevenwacht, Zonnebloem ★★★ Akkerdal, Almenkerk, Amani, Arniston Bay, Asara, Beau Joubert, Beaumont, Bellingham, Bernheim, **Blaauwklippen**, Blue Crane, Boekenhoutskloof, Boschheim, D'Aria, Doolhof, Eagle's Cliff, Eikendal, Freedom Hill, GlenWood, Hermit on the Hill,

Highlands Road, Idiom, **Kanu**, Karusa (2), Kleine Zalze (2), Kumala (Organic), Lazanou (Organic), Lindhorst (2), **MAN Vintners**, Manley, Muratie, Nederburg, Origin (2), Ridgeback, Rijk's, **Robert Stanford**, Simonsig, Skilpadvlei, **Somerbosch**, Teddy Hall, Thandi, **The Amistad Wine Company**, **The Grape Grinder**, **The Rhino**, Two Oceans, Waterford (Organic), Waverley Hills (Organic), Withington ★★★ Arniston Bay, Audacia, Blue Crane, Boschendal, Camberley, D'Aria, Drostdy-Hof (2), **Elberti**, Excelsior, Groupe CDV, Hazendal, **Jacaranda**, Joostenberg, Kanu, Koelenhof , **Lemberg**, Leopard Frog (Organic), Origin (2) (Organic), Oude Compagnies Post, Overhex, Rietvallei, **Savanha**, Teddy Hall, Valley Vineyards, Wine Village-Hermanus, Woolworths (2) ★★ Arniston Bay, **Bottelary**, De Wet, **Du'SwaRoo**, Govert, **Hoopenburg**, Kleine Zalze, KWV, **Lynx**, Malan Family, **Malanot**, Old Vines, **Origin**, Reiersvlei, Riebeek, Summerhill, Tulbagh Winery, Windfall ★★ **Malanot**, **Origin**, Prospect1870, **TTT Cellar**, Ultra Liquors, **Woolworths NT** Abbottshill, Croydon, Dellrust, Graham Beck (2), Haskell, Hazendal, Klawer, La Vierge, Nederburg, Orange River (Organic), Origin (2) (Organic), Retief, Saam, Simonsvlei, Somerbosch, Valley Vineyards, Zidela **NR** Cape Point **D** African Pride, Anura (2), Bellingham, DeMorgenzon, Du Preez, Freedom Hill, Hill & Dale (Kosher), Joostenberg, Kumkani (2), KWV, Waka Waka, Woolworths, Yonder Hill, Zidela

Red blends, with pinotage

★★★★☆ Beaumont, Beyerskloof, **Bosman**, Bottelary Hills, Kaapzicht (2), Lanzerac, Meinert, Remhoogte, Spier

★★★★ Altydgedacht, Alvi's Drift, Ashbourne, Beyerskloof, Brampton, Clos Malverne (2), **Credo**, Devon Hill, **Eaglevlei**, Emineo, Flagstone, **Goede Hoop**, Grangehurst, Idiom, Kaapzicht, Klein Parys, Post House, Rijk's, Simonsig, Springfontein, StellenRust, SylvanVale, Warwick, Welbedacht, **Wellington Winery**, **Wildekrans**, Windmeul

★★★★ Bon Cap (Organic), Cloof, Croydon, Domaine Brahms (2), Doolhof, **Durbanville Hills**, Eaglevlei, La Chataigne, **Leeuwenberg**, Lindhorst, Lyngrove, Maske, Mellasat, Nuweland, Raka, Remhoogte (2), **Rooiberg**, Slaley, Spier, Stellekaya, Stellenbosch University , Stellenzicht, **Truter Family**, Umkhulu, Val du Charron, Viljoensdrift ★★★ Anura, Arra, Ayama, **Bergsig**, Bernheim, Bottelary Hills, Cloof, **Croydon**, Doolhof, Douglas Green, Du Toitskloof (2), **Flagstone**, Freedom Hill (2), Fundi, Kaapzicht, Kanonkop, Kumala, **L'Avenir**, Lateganskop, Leopard Frog, Lorraine, Marianne, Mellasat, Middelvlei, Mostertsdrift, **Origin**, Oude Compagnies Post, Seven Sisters, Solms-Delta, Stellekaya, Umkhulu, **Waboomsrivier**,

Welbedacht, Welgemeend, **Woolworths** ★★★ African Pride (Organic), African Terroir (Organic), Cloof, Conradie, De Krans, Drostdy-Hof, Du Preez, Faraway House, **Hornbill** , Kumala, Leeuwenberg, Louiesenhof, Rooiberg, Simonsvlei, Slaley (Organic), **Stellar** (Organic), Stellenbosch Hills, Stellendrift, StellenRust, Two Oceans, Vruchtbaar, Waterstone ★★ **Boutique Baratok**, BurCon, De Doorns, Dragonridge, Groupe CDV, Jonkheer, **Montagu Wine & Spirits** (Organic), **Mountain Oaks** (Organic), Obikwa, Overhex, Pearly Bay, **Savanha**, Slanghoek, Stellendrift ★★ Douglas Green, Simonsvlei (2) ★ Skilpadvlei **NT** African Terroir, Belbon Hills, Bellevue, Bernheim, BLANKbottle, Bon Cap, Clos Malverne, Fairview, Kaapzicht, Marklew, Mountain River, Wedderwill, Wedgewood **D** Babylon's Peak, Flagstone, Koopmanskloof, Kumala, Kumkani, Rosendal, SylvanVale, Wildekrans (2)

Riesling

★★★★☆ Groote Post, Howard Booysen

★★★★ De Wetshof, Hartenberg, Nitida, Paul Cluver (2) (Light & low-alcohol), Spioenkop, The Drift, Woolworths (2)

★★★★ Altydgedacht, Fairview, **Howard Booysen**, Jordan, Klein Constantia, Nederburg, Ross Gower, Thelema, Villiera ★★★ Osbloed, Thelema ★★★ **Rosendal NT** La Vierge

Rosé dry

★★★★ Delaire, Grangehurst, Solms-Delta

★★★★ AA Badenhorst, Anatu, **Arumdale**, Blouvlei, **Croydon**, De Meye, De Wetshof, DeMorgenzon, **Desert Rose**, Dunstone, Hermanuspietersfontein, Highlands Road, Holden Manz, Jordan, Kanonkop, **La Couronne**, **La Ferme Derik**, Lammershoek, Morgenster, Nabygelegen, **Noble Hill**, Opstal, Romond, Schalkenbosch, Sijnn, Sophie, South Hill, **Tamboerskloof**, The Drift, Topiary, Waterford, Wildehurst ★★★ Allée Bleue, **Anatu**, Andy Mitchell, Anura (Organic), Avondale (Organic), Barton, Beaumont, Bein, Beyerskloof, Black Oystercatcher, Blomendahl, Brampton, Bushmanspad, Clouds, Dornier, Elgin Vintners, Feiteiras (2), Fort Simon, Goats do Roam, Hawksmoor (2), Herold, Hill & Dale, Hillcrest, Hout Bay, Ken Forrester, Klein Constantia, Kleine Zalze, La Petite Ferme, **La Petite Vigne**, Le Pommier, Lord's, Painted Wolf, **Rainbow's End**, Raka, Rickety Bridge, Robert Stanford, Ross Gower, **Scrucap** (Organic), Stellar (2) (Organic), Stonehill, Stony Brook, **Strandveld**, SylvanVale, The Butcher Shop, Tokara, Waterkloof (Organic), Woolworths (Organic), Zorgvliet ★★★ Asara, Avontuur, Beau Joubert (Organic), Bon Cap (Organic), Bosman, Claime d'Or, De Grendel, Diemersdal, Doolhof, Douglas Green, Dragonridge, Escapades, Fairview, Felicité, **Fernskloof**, Hildenbrand, Jacaranda, Joostenberg, Kleinfontein,

Koopmanskloof, Kumala (2), L'Avenir, **La Bourgogne**, La Chataigne, **Le Bonheur**, **Leopard Frog**, Mount Vernon, Muratie, **New Beginnings**, Niel Joubert, Perdeberg, Saronsberg, Savanha, Slaley, Slowine, **Spotswood**, Springfontein, Vergenoegd, Welgegund, Welmoed, Whalehaven ★★ African Pride, Ayama, Bernheim, De Krans, Du'SwaRoo, Durbanville Hills, Eerste Hoop, False Bay (Organic), Groot Parys (Organic), Groupe CDV (3), Kleine Zalze, Knorhoek, Koopmanskloof, Marianne, Mellasat, Mont Rochelle (Organic), Org de Rac (Organic), Overhex (2), **Plettenvale**, **Quando**, Re'Mogo, Ridgeback, Riebeek, Thandi (Organic), Waverley Hills ★★ Groupe CDV (2), Six Hats, Zandvliet ★ African Terroir (Organic), Koelenhof (Organic), **Org de Rac NT** Abbottshill, African Terroir, Blomendahl, Calitzdorp, Cape Dreams, Cloof, Dormershire, Groupe CDV, Haut Espoir, High Constantia (2), Kaapzicht, Land's End, Mitre's Edge (Organic), Mountain Oaks (Organic), New Beginnings, Origin, Oude Compagnies Post, Signal Hill, TTT Cellar, Wolfkloof **NR** Walker Bay Vineyards **D** Abingdon, Backsberg, Boschendal, Devonair, Eaglevlei, Flat Roof Manor, Holden Manz, Hoopenburg, Kloovenburg, Longridge, Lynx, Mountain River, Oak Valley, Onderkloof , Overgaauw , Rietvallei, Simonsvlei, Spier, Spookfontein , Vukani

Rosé off-dry/semi-sweet

★★★☆ Almenkerk, Cederberg, **Eaglevlei**, Sumaridge ★★★ **Babylonstoren**, Backsberg, Eikendal, Fish Hoek, Goedverwacht, Karusa, Ladismith, Lanzerac, Leeuwenjacht, Lourensford, Meinert, Mulderbosch, Nelson, Noble Savage, Saxenburg, uniWines, Wonderfontein, Woolworths (3) ★★★ Badsberg, Blaauwklippen, Blomendahl, Bovlei, Brandvlei, Darling Cellars, Delheim, Eagle's Cliff, Graça, Haute Cabrière, Hazendal, Kanu, **KWV**, Leopard's Leap, Lorraine, Lutzville, McGregor, Meerendal, Merwida, Mooiplaas, Morgenhof, Mountain Ridge, Nederburg, Orange River (Light & low-alcohol), **Pick 'n Pay**, Rooiberg, Seven Oaks, Slanghoek (Light & low-alcohol), StellenRust, **The Rhino**, Two Oceans, Van Zylshof, Viljoensdrift, Waterstone, Welvanpas, Winters Drift, Woolworths (2), Zevenwacht ★★ Angels Tears, Arniston Bay (2), Bellingham, Bergsig, Botha, **Chateau Beau Belle**, D'Aria, Darling Cellars, Douglas Green, Drostdy-Hof, Du Toitskloof (Perlé wines), Eve, **Flat Roof Manor** (Light & low-alcohol), **Goedverwacht**, Graham Beck, Havana Hills, **Hoopenburg**, Koelenhof , Louiesenhof, MAN Vintners, Millstream, Mostertsdrift, Nelson, Obikwa, Pearly Bay (2) (Light & low-alcohol), Rhebokskloof, Tulbagh Winery, Versus, Vredenheim, Welbedacht, Woolworths (3) (Light & low-alcohol) ★★ Arniston Bay (Light & low-alcohol), Ashton, Bon

Courage, Cellar Cask, Goudini, Hartswater, Jonkheer, Kleine Draken (Kosher), Pick 'n Pay (Light & low-alcohol, Organic), Stellar (Organic), Swartland (Light & low-alcohol), Theuniskraal, **Van Loveren** (Light & low-alcohol), Wineways, Woolworths (Light & low-alcohol), Zidela ★ **Overmeer Cellars**, Pulpit Rock, Robertson **NT** Benguela Cove, Bergwater, Bottelary (Light & low-alcohol), Bovlei, Buffalo Creek, Devon Rocks, Drostdy-Hof, Havana Hills, Mzoli's, Nietvoorbij, Origin (2) (Light & low-alcohol), Stoumann's, Thokozani, Van Loveren **D** Arniston Bay, Bellingham (2), Boland, Du Toitskloof , Imbuko, KWV, Lindhorst, Simonsvlei, Stettyn, Stony Brook, Wildekrans (2), Zidela

Roussanne

★★★★☆ Mischa, **The Three Foxes**
★★★★ Rustenberg, The Foundry
★★★☆ Bellingham, Painted Wolf

Ruby cabernet

★★★ Bellpost, Orange River, Robertson (2) ★★☆ Langverwacht, Lutzville ★★ Ladismith, McGregor ★★ Barrydale, Hartswater **NT** Kingsriver **D** Oudtshoorn

Sacramental wine

★★ Kleine Draken

Sangiovese

★★★★ Anura, The Three Foxes
★★★☆ Anthonij Rupert, Idiom, **Spring Grove** ★★★ **Bovlei**, Dragonridge, Fairview, Koelenhof , Monterosso, Raka

Sauvignon blanc unwooded

★★★★★ Fryer's Cove, Graham Beck, Tokara
★★★★☆ Ataraxia, Buitenverwachting, Constantia Glen, Constantia Uitsig, Corder, De Grendel, Delaire, Diemersdal (2), Durbanville Hills (2), Flagstone, Fleur du Cap (2), High Constantia, Iona, Kleine Zalze, Lomond, Nederburg, Noble Hill, Phizante Kraal, Quoin Rock (Biodynamic), Reyneke (Biodynamic), **Scrucap**, Southern Right, Spioenkop, Steenberg, Strandveld, Tokara, Vergelegen, Warwick
★★★★ African Pride, Allée Bleue, Altydgedacht, **Anthonij Rupert**, Anura, Bartinney, Benguela Cove, Boplaas, Boschendal, Bouchard Finlayson, Bramon , Brunia, Buitenverwachting, Cape Hutton, Catherine Marshall, Cederberg (2), Clouds, Constantia Mist, Creation, Dalla Cia, Darling Cellars, De Grendel, De Wetshof, Delaire, Domaine des Dieux, Driehoek, **Dunstone**, Durbanville Hills (2), Elgin Heights, Ernie Els, Escapades, Fryer's Cove, Groot Constantia, Groote Post (2), Hermanuspietersfontein (2), Hidden Valley, **Hillock**, Hout Bay, Izak van der Vyver, Jordan, Klein Constantia, KWV (3), La Motte (Organic), La Vierge, Lanner Hill, Lemberg, Lomond, Longridge, Louis, Lourensford (2), MAN Vintners, Meinert, Nederburg

(2), Neethlingshof, Neil Ellis, Nitida (2), Packwood, Paul Cluver, Perdeberg, Plaisir, Rivendell, Robert Stanford, Rustenberg, Saronsberg, Saxenburg, Sir Lambert, **Skaap**, South Hill, Spice Route, Spioenkop, Springfield (2), Steenberg, Sterhuis, Sumaridge, The Berrio, Thelema (2), Tierhoek, Tokara, Usana, Uva Mira, Van Loveren, Vergelegen, Villiera (2), Waterford, Waterkloof, Webersburg, Wedderwill, Woolworths (5), Zonnebloem, Zorgvliet

★★★☆ Adoro, Alluvia, Amani, Annandale, Anthonij Rupert, **Arumdale**, Avontuur (2), Bergwater, Black Oystercatcher, Bloemendal, Blomendahl, Bonnievale, Boschendal, Bottelary Hills, Brampton, Bushmanspad, **Callender**, Cave d'Or, Clos Malverne, Conradie, Crios Bríde, D'Aria, Darling Cellars, De Wetshof, Delheim, Diemersdal, Doolhof, **Eagle's Cliff**, Eagles'Nest, Edgebaston, Elgin Grove (Organic), Elgin Ridge (Organic), Elgin Vintners, Ernst Gouws, Excelsior, Fairview, False Bay, Fort Simon, Franschhoek Cellar, Garden Route, Glen Erskine, Graham Beck, Grande Provence, Hannay, Hartenberg, Hathersage, Havana Hills, Hazendal, Het Vlock Casteel, Hillcrest, **Hillock**, **Journey's End**, Kaapzicht, Karusa, Ken Forrester, Klein Constantia, Klein Gustrouw, Kling, Kloovenburg, Kumkani, L'Avenir, La Motte, La Petite Ferme, Laborie, Land's End, Langverwacht, Lanzerac, Lindhorst, Lomond, Longbarn, Lutzville, M'hudi, Maastricht, Meerendal, Misty Mountains, **Mofam**, Môreson, Morgenhof, **Mount Rozier**, Mulderbosch, Nederburg, **Neil Ellis**, **Newstead**, Nico Vermeulen, Noble Hill, **Nuweland**, Oak Valley, **Oneiric**, Ormonde (2), Overhex, **Painted Wolf**, Peter Falke, Post House, Quando, Raka, Ridgeback, Rietvallei, Ross Gower, Savanha, **Scrucap**, Seven Sisters, Seven Springs , Seven Steps, Signal Gun (Organic), **Silvermist** (Organic), Simonsig, Simonsvlei, Sophie, Spring Grove, Thandi, The Butcher Shop, The Goose (2), The Township Winery, Trajan, **Ultra Liquors**, Van Zylshof, Virgin Earth, Von Ortloff, Vondeling, Waterford, Waterstone, Welmoed, Weltevrede, Wolvenfontein, Zevenwacht, Zoetendal ★★★ Almenkerk (2), Alvi's Drift, Ayama, Backsberg, Bellevue, **Bellingham**, Bergsig, Blaauwklippen, **Bloemendal**, Blouvlei, Blue Crane, Boekenhoutskloof, Boland, **Boschkloof** , Botha, **Brenaissance**, **Brothers**, Camberley, Catch Of The Day, Cloof, COAV, Dâbar, Devon Hill, DeWaal, Douglas Green, Drostdy-Hof, Du Preez, Du Toitskloof , Durbanville Hills, Esona, False Bay, Fat Bastard, Flagstone, Fleur du Cap, Fort Simon, Four Paws, Freedom Hill, Galleon, Glen Carlou, GlenWood, Goede Hoop, **Goedverwacht**, Groenland, Helderberg, High Constantia, Hill & Dale, Hoopenburg, Imbuko, Klawer, Kleine Zalze, Knorhoek, Kranskop, KWV, L'Olivier, La Chataigne, Le Pommier, Lorraine, **Louis**, LuKa, Lutzville, Lyngrove, McGregor, Merwida, Miravel, Mooiplaas, Mount Vernon, Nederburg, Neethlingshof, Nelson, **Noble Savage**, Overgaauw, **PaardenKloof**,

Rietvallei (2), Rosendal (2), Sauvignon.com, Seal Breeze, Simonsvlei, Six Hats, Somerbosch, Spier, Springfontein, StellenRust, Stellenzicht, Stettyn, Stoumann's, Strandveld, **SylvanVale**, Teubes, Tulbagh Winery, Two Oceans, Uitkyk, Ultra Liquors, uniWines, Vaalvlei, **Val de Vie**, Versailles, **Waka Waka**, Welbedacht, Welgevallen, Windfall, Wines of Cape Town, Winters Drift, Woolworths (5), Zandfontein, Zonnebloem, Zorgvliet ★★★ Aan de Doorns, African Pride, **Andersons**, Angels Tears, Anura, Arniston Bay, Asara, Bilton, **Blue Crane**, Boland (Organic), Bon Cap (Organic), Bon Courage, Boplaas, Calais, Cape Classics, Cape Point, De Villiers, De Wet, Die Mas, Diemersdal, Dornier, Du Preez, Eagle's Cliff, Fairview, Fish Hoek, **Flagstone**, Goedvertrouw, Goedverwacht, Goudini, Havana Hills, Imbuko, Kanu, Koelenhof, Koopmanskloof, La Couronne, **La Petite Vigne**, Landskroon, Le Bonheur, Leopard's Leap, Linton Park (2), Louiesenhof, Louisvale, Lourensford, Misty Mountains, Monterosso, Mountain Ridge, Muratie, Nabygelegen, Namaqua, Niel Joubert, Onderkloof, **Orange River**, Oude Kaap, Oudtshoorn, Perdeberg, Re'Mogo, Rhebokskloof, Rickety Bridge, Robertson (3) (Light & low-alcohol), Savanha, Schalkenbosch, Seven Oaks, Simonsig, Simonsvlei, Slaley, Slanghoek, Slowine, Somerset Wines, Steenberg (Organic), Stellar (Organic), **Stellenbosch Hills**, **Stellenbosch University** , Stony Brook, TCB Wines, **The Amistad Wine Company**, **The Rhino**, The Township Winery, Tread Lightly, Tukulu, United Nations, uniWines, **Van Loveren**, Vredenheim, Wandsbeck, Waterford, Waterstone (2), **Welbedacht**, **Weltevrede**, Whalehaven, Windmeul (Organic), Woolworths (3) (Organic), Yonder Hill ★★ African Terroir (4) (Organic), Akkerdal, Badsberg, Beau Joubert, Boplaas, Bovlei, Brandvlei, Burgershof, Calitzdorp, Cape Dreams, Clairvaux, Corder, Craighall, Culemborg, Flat Roof Manor (Light & low-alcohol), Glenview, **House of Mandela**, Juno, **Ken Forrester**, Klein Parys, Klein Roosboom , Koelenhof , Ladismith, Lateganskop, Libby's Pride, Lievland, Lord's, Mischa, Nuy, Obikwa, Origin, Riebeek, Roodezandt, Rooiberg, Saam, Skilpadvlei, Stellenbosch Hills, Swartland, Tulbagh Winery, Valley Vineyards (2), Van Loveren, Viljoensdrift, Waboomsrivier, Walker Bay Vineyards, **Waterstone** (2), Wellington Winery, Wine Village-Hermanus, Wineways (2), Withoek ★★ Ashton, Barrydale, Bayede! (2), **Boutique Baratok**, Cloverfield, Goudini, Jonkheer (2), Kleine Draken (Kosher), **Montagu Wine & Spirits**, Mountain River (2), Robertson (2) (Light & low-alcohol, Light & low-alcohol), Wineways, Zandvliet ★ Boutique Baratok, Cronier, Montpellier, Wineways, Woolworths **NT Aaldering**, African Terroir, Alluvia, Badgerberg, Barry Gould, Belbon Hills, Boer & Brit, Bonfoi, Boschendal, **Bosman**, Buffalo Creek, Dellrust, Devon Rocks, Dormershire, DuVon, Elberti, Haut Espoir, Highlands Road,

Hoopenburg, Jason's Hill, Kingsriver, Klein Roosboom , Mimosa, Montagu Wine & Spirits, Môreson, Nomada, Nuweland, Origin (2), Rico Suter, Rosendal, Saam, Spier (2), Stanford Hills, Stellendrift, Sumsaré, Swartland, Tierhoek, United Nations, Welvanpas, William Everson, Wolvendrift, Zidela **NR** Awendland, Herold, Place in the Sun, **Reiersvlei**, Robertson **D** Amani, AntHill, Anura, Arniston Bay, Crystallum, DeWaal, Du Toitskloof , Fairvalley, Flagstone, Freedom Hill, Groot Constantia, Hermanuspietersfontein, Highlands Road, Kumala, Kumkani, Morgenhof, Namaqua, Oak Valley, Overhex (Organic), Spier (Organic), Stellar (Organic), Vukani, Wildekrans (3), Woolworths

Sauvignon blanc wooded

★★★★☆ Cape Chamonix (2), Cape Point, Diemersdal, **Nederburg**, Quoin Rock (Biodynamic), Reyneke (Biodynamic), Shannon, Waterkloof

★★★★ **Black Oystercatcher**, Bouchard Finlayson, Capaia, Cape Point, D'Aria, DeMorgenzon, Diners Club Bartho Eksteen , Eikendal, Hermanuspietersfontein, Hermit on the Hill (2), Jordan, Klein Constantia, Le Pommier, Meerendal, Nederburg, Neil Ellis, Newton Johnson, Rickety Bridge, Stony Brook, The Butcher Shop (2), **The Goose**, **Trizanne**, Zevenwacht

★★★★ Backsberg, Barton, Dombeya, Gabriëlskloof, Misty Mountains, Stark-Condé, Wildekrans ★★★ **African Terroir**, **Leeuwenberg**, Mont Rochelle, Steenberg ★★★ Marianne, Opstal **NT** Abingdon, Spioenkop, Stone Ridge **D** Peter Falke, Zorgvliet

Semillon unwooded

★★★★ Nederburg, Zonnebloem
★★★★ Bloemendal, Lutzville, Ormonde ★★★ Withington ★★★ **Origin D** Stellar

Semillon wooded

★★★★☆ Cederberg, Landau du Val, **My Wyn**, Nitida, Steenberg, Stellenzicht, Stony Brook

★★★★ Anthonij Rupert, Boekenhoutskloof, Fairview, Fleur du Cap, Franschhoek Cellar, GlenWood, KWV, **My Wyn**

★★★★ Constantia Uitsig, Escapades, Hildenbrand, Rickety Bridge ★★★ **Eaglevlei**, Hathersage, Haut Espoir, La Bourgogne, **Wine Village-Hermanus NT** Vergelegen, Woolworths **D** Creation

Shiraz/syrah

★★★★★ Boschendal, Cederberg, Delheim, Fable, Fairview, Mont Destin, Mullineux (2), Raka, Saronsberg, Simonsig

★★★★☆ Avontuur, **Belfield**, Boekenhoutskloof, Boschendal, De Grendel, De Trafford (2), Driehoek, Eagles' Nest, Fairview (3), GlenWood, Graham Beck, Groot Constantia, Groote Post, Hartenberg (3), Haskell, Hawksmoor, Iona, Julien Schaal, Lomond, Lourensford, Luddite, Metzer, **Mullineux**, Muratie, Nederburg, Nico van der Merwe, Quoin Rock, Rust

en Vrede, Rustenberg, Saxenburg (2), Scali, Signal Hill, **Simonsig**, Solms-Delta, Stark-Condé, StellenRust, Strandveld, Tamboerskloof, The Foundry, TMV, Vins d'Orrance, Waterford, Waterkloof

★★★★ Aeternitas, **Allegria**, Allesverloren, Andreas, Andy Mitchell, Annandale, Anura (2), Arra (Organic), Avondale (Organic), Axe Hill, **Babylonstoren**, Backsberg, Bellingham, Bilton, Bizoe, Blaauwklippen (2), Black Pearl, Boland, Bon Courage, Cederberg, Cirrus, Cloof, Creation, D'Aria, Darling Cellars, De Trafford, Delheim, DeMorgenzon, Dombeya, Dunstone, Elgin Vintners, Ernie Els, Flagstone, Gilga, Grande Provence, Hartenberg, Haskell, Haut Espoir, Hawksmoor, **Hermit on the Hill**, Heron Ridge, Hildenbrand, House of Mandela, Joostenberg, Kaapzicht, Katbakkies, Keermont, Kleine Zalze (2), Koelfontein, KWV, La Couronne, La Motte, La Vigne, Laborie, Ladera, Lammershoek (2), Land's End, **Leeuwenberg**, Linton Park, Lomond, Longridge, Maastricht, **Malanot**, Meerendal, Meerhof, Metzer, Middelvlei, Migliarina, Mischa, MolenVliet, Montagu Wine & Spirits, Mooiplaas, Mountain Ridge, Muratie, Nabygelegen, Namaqua, Nederburg, Neil Ellis, Nico van der Merwe, Nico Vermeulen (Red blends, shiraz/syrah-based), Niel Joubert, Nuy, **Oak Valley**, Oude Denneboom, Painted Wolf, Pax Verbatim, Plaisir (Organic), Porseleinberg (Organic), Post House, Quoin Rock, Rainbow's End (Biodynamic), **Reyneke** (Biodynamic), Rheboskloof, Rickety Bridge, Ridgeback, Rijk's (3), **Robert Stanford**, Robertson, Rooiberg, Rudera, Rudi Schultz, Rust en Vrede, Saronsberg, Spice Route (2), Star Hill, Stark-Condé, Steenberg, Stellekaya, Stellenzicht, Stony Brook, Super Single Vineyards, Swartland, Teddy Hall, **The Butcher Shop**, The Three Foxes, The Winery of Good Hope (2), Thelema, Topiary, Trizanne, Uva Mira, Val de Vie, Veenwouden, Vergelegen (2), Vergenoegd (2), Von Ortloff, Vondeling, Wedderwill, Welbedacht, Windmeul, Woolworths (2), Zonnebloem

★★★★ Aaldering, Allée Bleue, Alto, Amani, Amares, Andy Mitchell, **Annex Kloof**, Anthonij Rupert (2), Asara, Ayama (2), Babylon's Peak, **Bayede!**, Bellevue, Bellpost, Benguela Cove, Bergheim (2), Bernheim, Blaauwklippen, Blue Crane, Boekenhoutskloof, Boland, Bon Courage, Boplaas (2), Boschendal, Boschrivier, Bottelary Hills, Bovlei, Brampton, **Brenaissance**, **Brothers**, Camberley, **Cape Rock**, Chateau Naudé, **Claime d'Or**, Cloof, Clovelly, Delaire, Devon Hill, Devonvale, DewaldtHeyns, Diemersdal, **Diners Club Bartho Eksteen** , Dispore Kamma, Domaine Brahms, Doolhof, **Doran**, Du Preez, Durbanville Hills, DuVon, Eerste Hoop, Eikendal, Elgin Heights, Ernst Gouws, Excelsior, Fairview (2), Faraway House, Fish Hoek, Fort Simon, Franschhoek Cellar, Freedom Hill, Gabriëlskloof (2), Garden Route, Glen Carlou, Glenelly, Goede Hoop, Graceland, Groenland (2), Guardian Peak, **Hartenberg**,

Hazendal, Hermit on the Hill, **Heron Ridge**, Hoopenburg (2), Hout Bay, Jacques Smit, Jordan, Journey's End, Juno, Katbakkies, Kling, Kloovenburg, Knorhoek, Kranskop, Kumkani, KWV (2), Kyburg, La Bri, La Petite Ferme, Laborie (2), Landskroon (Organic), Lazanou (Organic), Lievland, Lindhorst, Linton Park, Lord's, Lorraine, Lourensford, Lutzville, Lyngrove, Lynx, Maison, MAN Vintners, Manley, MC Square, Meerendal, Metzer, Mont du Toit, Mont Rochelle, Mooiplaas, Mount Rozier, Naughton's, Nederburg, Neil Ellis, Nelson (2), Nick & Forti's, Nieuwedrift, Nitida, Nwanedi (Organic), Org de Rac (Organic), Perdeberg, Peter Falke, Pulpit Rock, Remhoogte, Rhebokskloof, Riebeek (2), Rietvallei, Robertson, Ross Gower, Saltaré, Savanha, Seven Springs , Seven Steps, Signal Gun, Signal Hill, Simonsvlei (4), **Skaap**, Slaley, Solo, Spier, Spring Grove (Organic), Stellar (Organic), Stellendrift, StellenRust, Stone Ridge, Stony Brook, The Butcher Shop, **The Mason's**, **The Rhino**, Thelema, Tokara, **Trajan**, **Uitkyk**, Umkhulu, Vondeling (Organic), **Waverley Hills** (Organic), Wellington Winery, Weltevrede, William Everson, Woolworths (3), Zandvliet, Zevenwacht, Zoetendal, Zonnebloem ★★★ Abbottshill, African Pride, Altydgedacht, AntHill, Arra, **Arumdale**, Ashton (2), Avontuur, Beau Joubert, Bonnievale, Boschkloof , Bovlei, Brunia, Bushmanspad, Cape Classics, Cape to Cairo, Catch Of The Day, **Chateau Beau Belle**, Chennells, Cloverfield, Corder, **Cronier**, Darling Cellars, David Frost Signature, De Meye (2), De Villiers, DeanDavid, Desert Rose, Devonvale, Diemersfontein, Dispore Kamma, Dormershire (2), Du Toitskloof , Du'SwaRoo, Durbanville Hills, Eaglevlei, Esona, **False Bay**, Fat Bastard, Fleur du Cap, Fort Simon, **Freedom Hill**, Goedverwacht, Graham Beck, Groupe CDV, Havana Hills (2), **Hill & Dale**, Hofstraat, Jordan, Karusa, Koelenhof , Kumala, **La Bourgogne**, La Chaumiere, La Terre La Mer, Ladismith, Landskroon, Le Fût, Le Manoir de Brendel, Le Pommier, **Leeuwenberg**, Leeuwenkuil, Leopard's Leap, **Linton Park**, **Louiesenhof**, Lyngrove, Marianne, Mischa, Misty Mountains, Mooi Bly, My Wyn, Namaqua, Nederburg, Neethlingshof, New Beginnings, Noble Hill, Nwanedi, Oldenburg, Olifantsberg, **Oneiric**, Orange River (Organic), Org de Rac (Organic), Ormonde (2), Oude Kaap, Perdeberg, Phizante Kraal, Place in the Sun, Rijk's, Robertson, Saam, Savanha, Schalkenbosch, **Scrucap**, **Silkbush**, Simonsig, Simonsvlei, Six Hats, Slaley, Slanghoek, Slowine, Somerbosch, Somerset Wines, **Southern Sky**, **Spotswood**, Stellenzicht, Strandveld, Swartland, **The Amistad Wine Company**, The Butcher Shop, The Goose, The Mason's, **The Wine Fusion**, The Winery of Good Hope, Thembi & Co, Tukulu, Tulbagh Winery (2), Ultra Liquors (4), Van Loveren, Virgin Earth, Vredenheim, Waterstone (Organic), Waverley Hills (Organic), Wellington

Winery, Welmoed, Welvanpas, Wildekrans, William Everson, Windmeul, Wines of Cape Town, Wonderfontein, Yonder Hill, Zanddrift, Zandfontein ★★★ African Pride, African Terroir (3) (Organic), Alvi's Drift, Arniston Bay, Audacia, Belbon Hills, **Bellingham** (Organic), Bergwater (2) (Organic), Blomendahl, **Bonview**, Botha, Calais, Cape Dreams, Crows Nest, DeWaal, Drostdy-Hof, Du Preez, Du'SwaRoo, Eagle's Cliff, Eerste Hoop, Eikehof, Excelsior, False Bay, Halala/Lula, Het Vlock Casteel, **Hillock**, **House of Mandela**, Imbuko, Jason's Hill, Kanu, Kingsriver, Koopmanskloof, **Kumala**, KWV, **Le Manoir de Brendel**, **Lemberg**, Libby's Pride, Lula Wines, Lutzville, Malanot, McGregor, Mellasat, Mitre's Edge, Niel Joubert, Obikwa, **Origin**, Overhex (2), Pulpit Rock, Riebeek, Robertson, Roodezandt, Rooiberg, Seal Breeze, Stellenbosch University , Stoumann's, **The Hills**, Two Oceans, Ultra Liquors, uniWines, Vaalvlei (2), Viljoensdrift, Wederom (2), Windfall, Wine Village-Hermanus (Organic), Woolworths (3) (Organic), Zidela ★★ African Pride, African Terroir (3), Barrydale, **Blomendahl**, Calitzdorp, Cape Classics (Sweet red), **Chateau Beau Belle**, Clairvaux, De Wet, Douglas Green, **Fernskloof**, Goudini, Jonkheer, Klein Parys, Langverwacht, Mountain River, Rhebokskloof, Savanha (Organic), Stellar (Organic), United Nations, Waterstone (2), Wineways, Zandvliet ★★ Bonnievale, **Boutique Baratok**, Cranefields, Die Mas, **Spotswood**, Wineways, Withoek ★ Jonkheer, **Van Loveren**, Woolworths **NT** Abingdon, Anthony Smook (2), Awendland, Bergwater, Black Pearl, Bonfoi, Camanga, Cameradi, Corder, Dellrust, Eaglevlei, Escapades, Final Cut, Freedom Hill, Galleon, GlenWood, Haut Espoir, Hawksmoor, Helpmekaar, Hermit on the Hill, Holden Manz, Journey's End, Klawer, Le Grand Chasseur, Lomond, Lovane, Malanot, Mimosa, Montpellier, Mountain River, Nietvoorbij, Onderkloof , Origin, Oude Compagnies Post, Rico Suter, Robertson, Rosendal, Rudi Schultz, Saam, Signal Hill, Sir Lambert, Spier (2), Stellenbosch Hills, Stone Ridge, StoneyCroft, Sumsaré, SylvanVale, Tanagra, Teubes, The Township Winery, The Winery of Good Hope, **Thembi & Co**, Topaz, TTT Cellar, Tulbagh Winery, Uitkyk, United Nations (3), Versailles, Villiera, Wandsbeck, Warwick, Waterstone, Westbridge, Zandvliet, Zidela **NR** Franschhoek Cellar, Joubert-Tradauw, **Reiersvlei D** Anatu, AntHill, Bayede!, Boplaas, Dormershire, Edgebaston, Fairvalley, Graham Beck (2), Groot Constantia, Holden Manz, Julien Schaal, Kleine Draken (Kosher), Kumkani, Leeuwenjacht, Leopard Frog, Nuy, Oudtshoorn (2), Perdeberg (Organic), Reyneke (Organic), Stellenzicht, Tierhoek, Wildekrans

Sparkling, Méthode cap classique, red, dry
★★★ Camberley, Nitida

Sparkling, Méthode cap classique, rosé, dry
★★★★☆ Villiera, Woolworths

★★★★ Ambeloui, **Ayama**, **Bon Courage**, Domaine des Dieux, Graham Beck (2), Klein Optenhorst, L'Avenir, Mount Babylon, **Saltaré**, Silverthorn, Simonsig, Steenberg, Tanzanite

★★★★ Allée Bleue, **Barrydale**, Boschendal, Groote Post, Karusa, Laborie, Pongrácz, **Rickety Bridge**, Ross Gower, JC le Roux, Twee Jonge/Krone, Weltevrede, **Woolworths** ★★★ **Francois La Garde**, Haute Cabrière, JC le Roux, Villiera, Woolworths ★★★ Namaqua, **Packwood NT** Du Preez, Môreson

Sparkling, Méthode cap classique, rosé, off-dry/semi-sweet

★★★★ Colmant

Sparkling, Méthode cap classique, white, dry

★★★★★ Bon Courage, Villiera

★★★★☆ Ambeloui, Boschendal, Colmant (2), Graham Beck, High Constantia, Klein Constantia, Lourensford, MC Square, Silverthorn (2), Simonsig (2), Twee Jonge/Krone, Woolworths

★★★★ Altydgedacht, Anura (Organic), Avondale (Organic), Avontuur, Bon Courage, Cape Chamonix, Cederberg, **Chabivin** (2), Darling Cellars, Du Preez, Eikendal, Francois La Garde (2), **Genevieve**, **Glen Carlou**, Graham Beck, Groot Constantia, Haute Cabrière (2), Hoopenburg, Hout Bay, Kumkani, KWV, La Motte, Laborie (2), Meerendal, Morgenhof, Muratie, Niel Joubert, Old Vines, Perdeberg, Pongrácz, Quoin Rock, Saltaré, Saronsberg, **Scrucap**, Signal Hill, Simonsig, **Simonsvlei**, Spier, Steenberg, Sterhuis, Tanzanite, **The House of GM**, JC le Roux, Twee Jonge/Krone, **Vergelegen**, Villiera, Weltevrede, **Wonderfontein**, Woolworths (3)

★★★★ Allée Bleue, **Ayama**, Backsberg, **Badgerberg** (Organic), Bon Cap (Organic), Boplaas, Bramon, Buitenverwachting, **Chabivin**, Constantia Uitsig, Crios Bríde, De Wet, Domaine des Dieux, Elgin Heights, Graham Beck (2), Hazendal, Longridge, Lovane, Mooiplaas, Môreson, My Wyn, Nico van der Merwe, Rhebokskloof, Saltaré, Saxenburg, Schalkenbosch, Stony Brook, Teddy Hall, **The Butcher Shop**, JC le Roux, Ultra Liquors (2), Van Loveren, Villiera (2), **Welbedacht**, Weltevrede, Woolworths, Zorgvliet ★★★ **Ayama**, Backsberg, De Grendel, De Wetshof, Haute Cabrière (2), Highlands Road, Kanu, Klein Parys, **Leopard Frog**, Montpellier, Nieuwedrift, Nitida, Pongrácz, Riebeek, **Robertson**, JC le Roux, Viljoensdrift, Virgin Earth (Organic), Waverley Hills (Organic), Weltevrede, **Windfall** ★★☆ **La Chaumiere**, **Skaap**, **Ultra Liquors**, Wildekrans ★★ **Diners Club Bartho Eksteen NT** Boer & Brit, De Zoete Inval, Jean Daneel, Karusa, Klein Roosboom , Le Grand Chasseur, Môreson (3), Somersbosch, Topiary **D** Karusa, KWV, La Couronne, Simonsig

Sparkling, Méthode cap classique, white, off-dry/semi-sweet

★★★★ Roodezandt, Saxenburg

★★★★ **South Hill** ★★★ Graham Beck, JC le Roux

Sparkling, Non-MCC, red, dry

★★★ Tulbagh Winery ★★ JC le Roux (Light & low-alcohol), Van Loveren **NT** Le Grand Chasseur **D** Robertson

Sparkling, Non-MCC, red, off-dry/semi-sweet

★★★ Solms-Delta ★★ JC le Roux ★ **Café Culture**

Sparkling, Non-MCC, rosé, dry

★★★★ Beyerskloof ★★★ **Knorhoek** ★★ African Terroir (Organic), Boplaas **NT** African Terroir, Origin **D** uniWines

Sparkling, Non-MCC, rosé, off-dry/semi-sweet

★★★ Bayede! ★★★ Aan de Doorns, Alvi's Drift (Light & low-alcohol), Bon Courage, Eve, Goedverwacht, Kloovenburg, Koelenhof , Orange River, Rhebokskloof, Stellenbosch Hills ★★ Arniston Bay, Cold Duck (5th Avenue) (Light & low-alcohol), De Wet, Oudtshoorn, Overhex (Light & low-alcohol), Pearly Bay (Light & low-alcohol), **Perdeberg**, Thandi, Van Loveren (2) (Light & low-alcohol) ★☆ Bergwater, Bovlei, KWV, Rooiberg, **Viljoensdrift** (Light & low-alcohol), Woolworths **NT** Ashton, Jason's Hill, Klawer (Light & low-alcohol), Origin **D** Robertson

Sparkling, Non-MCC, white, dry

★★★ Clos Malverne, Welmoed ★★★ **Altydgedacht**, **Bovlei**, Eve, Obikwa, Orange River, Overhex, **Perdeberg**, Riebeek ★★ Arniston Bay, Bonnievale, Goudini, KWV, Slanghoek (Organic), **Stellar** (Organic), Wines of Cape Town ★★ Tulbagh Winery, Van Loveren **NT** African Terroir, Bergsig, Goedverwacht, Klein Parys, Merwida, Origin **D** Drostdy-Hof, Robertson

Sparkling, Non-MCC, white, off-dry/semi-sweet

★★★ Du Toitskloof , Nederburg, JC le Roux ★★★ Badsberg, Botha, Koelenhof , Nuy, Opstal, **Origin** (Light & low-alcohol), Slanghoek, Swartland, Van Loveren, Vredenheim, Wines of Cape Town (Organic), Woolworths ★★ Bon Cap (Organic), Eve (Light & low-alcohol), Grand Mousseux, KWV, Overhex (Light & low-alcohol), Pearly Bay (Light & low-alcohol), Rhebokskloof, Rooiberg, Swartland, JC le Roux (Light & low-alcohol), Van Loveren (Light & low-alcohol), Woolworths ★★ Kleine Draken (Kosher), Rooiberg, Van Loveren, Woolworths **NT** African Terroir **D** KWV, Montagu Wine Cellar, Oudtshoorn, Robertson

Special Late Harvest

★★★★☆ Nederburg

★★★★ Robertson

★★★☆ Backsberg, Drostdy-Hof ★★★ Bergsig, Bon Courage, Fairview, Roodezandt, Slanghoek ★★☆ Badsberg, Bovlei, Van Loveren

Sweet red

★★★★☆ Signal Hill

★★★★ Dormershire ★★★ Fairview ★★☆ Arra, David Frost Signature, Perdeberg ★★ Bottelary, Cape Classics (Shiraz/syrah), **Kumala**, Louiesenhof, **Overhex**, Somerset Wines, Woolworths ★☆ BerRaz, Culemborg, Hartswater, **Pearly Bay**, Robertson (Light & low-alcohol), Simonsvlei, Tulbagh Winery, Wineways ★ Cellar Cask, Pick 'n Pay, Robertson **NT** Herold, Lynx, Origin

Sylvaner

★★★ Overgaauw

Tannat

★★★★ Mooi Bly

Tempranillo

★★★ De Krans

Tinta barocca

★★★★☆ Sadie

★★★ Boplaas, De Krans, **Jeu**, Nuweland ★★☆ Allesverloren, Boplaas, Swartland **NR** Reiersvlei

Touriga nacional

★★★★ De Krans

★★★★ Boplaas, Dagbreek ★★★ Bergsig ★★☆ Allesverloren, Calitzdorp ★★ Ladismith **NT** Du'SwaRoo **NR** Reiersvlei

Verdelho

★★★★ **Anura**, Feiteiras **D** Boschheim

Vin de paille

★★★★★ Fairview, Mullineux

★★★★☆ Alluvia, Hazendal, **Lemberg**, Rustenberg, The Winery of Good Hope, Tierhoek, TMV

★★★★ De Trafford, Goede Hoop (Organic), Groot Parys (Organic), Keermont, Lammershoek, **Maison**, Nuweland, Saronsberg, Vondeling

★★★☆ Fairview, Signal Hill, Simonsig ★★★ Fairview, Mellasat, Naughton's **NT** Orange River, Zevenwacht **D** La Bourgogne

Viognier

★★★★☆ Eagles'Nest

★★★★ Alvi's Drift, Backsberg, Beau Constantia, Bilton, Creation, De Grendel, Diemersfontein, Fairview, Flagstone, Fleur du Cap, Fort Simon, **Four Paws**, Gabriëlskloof, Idiom, Katbakkies, Kranskop, KWV, Lourensford, Lynx, **Nederburg**, Nick & Forti's, Pax Verbatim, Ridgeback, Saronsberg, The Foundry, The Winery of Good Hope

★★★★ Arra (2), **Babylonstoren**, Bellingham, Elgin Vintners, Kanu, Karusa, Klawer (Organic), **Lazanou** (Organic), Lemberg, Leopard Frog, Lorraine, **Maison**,

Niel Joubert, Noble Hill, Painted Wolf, Solo, Star Hill, Stonehill, **The Fledge**, Waterkloof ★★★ Abingdon (Organic), African Terroir (Organic), Anura, Auction Crossing, Ayama, Blaauwklippen, Brampton, **Chennells**, Cloof, Corder, DeWaal, Excelsior, Fairview, Graham Beck, Haut Espoir, Katbakkies, Mischa, My Wyn, Robertson, Six Hats, Wellington Winery ★★☆ **African Terroir**, Boplaas, Eerste Hoop, Kling, Le Joubert, **Montpellier**, **Welmoed** ★★ Arra, La Bri, Riebeek, Schalkenbosch, Wine Village–Hermanus ★☆ Spring Grove **NT** Abingdon (Organic), Bon Cap (Organic), Flagstone, High Constantia (2), Iona, **Jason's Hill**, La Ferme Derik, La Petite Ferme, Lynx, Montagu Wine & Spirits, Naughton's, Rhebokskloof, Riebeek, Spice Route, Stellenbosch University, Tamboerskloof, Topaz **D** African Pride, Babylon's Peak, Boschheim, Eaglevlei, Kumkani, Ladismith, Lindhorst, Niel Joubert, Rudi Schultz, Sterhuis, Zonnebloem

White blends, off-dry/semi-sweet (w & u/w)

★★★★☆ Woolworths

★★★★ Du Toitskloof, Hughes Family, Painted Wolf, The Butcher Shop, **The Wine Fusion**, Virgin Earth, Zevenwacht

★★★☆ Amani, Boschendal, Buitenverwachting (2), **Edgebaston**, Haute Cabrière, Slanghoek, **Woolworths** ★★★ Altydgedacht, Boschendal, Eikendal, **Kanu** (Organic), **KWV** (Organic), Nederburg, Onderkloof, Overhex, Robertson, Saxenburg (2), **Wandsbeck** ★★☆ Angels Tears, Arniston Bay, Bayede!, Beaumont, Bergwater, Boland, Boschendal, Douglas Green, Drostdy-Hof, Graça, Groupe CDV, Koelenhof, Kumala, KWV, Leeuwenjacht, Limelight, Malan Family, Montpellier, Obikwa (Light & low-alcohol), Robertson, Slanghoek (Organic), Stellar (2) (Organic), StellenRust (2), Tulbagh Winery, Zevenwacht ★★ **African Terroir** (2), **Arniston Bay** (Light & low-alcohol), Barrydale, Bovlei, Culemborg, De Krans, Du Toitskloof (2), Fleur du Cap (Light & low-alcohol), Jonkheer, **Kumala** (2), KWV, **Opstal**, Oude Kaap, Pearly Bay (Light & low-alcohol), Rooiberg (Organic), Stellar (Organic), Two Oceans, **Woolworths** ★★ Bonne Esperance, Kupferberger Auslese, Ladismith, Leopard's Leap, Morgenhof, Overmeer Cellars, Robertson, Simonsvlei, Swartland, Versus, Woolworths (2) (Light & low-alcohol) ★ Bonnievale, Cellar Cask, Robertson, Virginia ★ Drostdy-Hof, Pick 'n Pay **NS** Pick 'n Pay **NT** Botha (Light & low-alcohol), Landzicht **NR** Solms-Delta, TTT Cellar **D** Buitenverwachting, Clairvaux, Du Preez, Edgebaston, Manley, Morgenhof, Vergelegen, Wines of Cape Town, Woolworths

White blends, other, unwooded, dry

★★ Overhex

White blends, other, unwooded, off-dry/semi-sweet

★★★ Woolworths ★★ Pearly Bay

White blends, unwooded, dry

★★★★★ Nederburg

★★★★☆ Ashbourne, The Berrio

★★★★ Bouchard Finlayson, Groote Post (Organic), **Joostenberg** (Organic), Quando, Thokozani, Truter Family, Vendôme, **Woolworths**, Zonnebloem

★★★★ Ayama, Buitenverwachting, Cape Chamonix (Biodynamic), Creation (Biodynamic), Douglas Green, **Elgin Vintners**, Flagstone, Groot Constantia, Karusa, Lammershoek (Organic), Lazanou (Organic), Leeuwenjacht, Nabygelegen, Post House, Raka, **Rustenberg**, **The Wine Fusion** ★★★ Allée Bleue, Altydgedacht, Ayama, **Babylon's Peak**, Barrydale, Bloemendal, Bon Courage, Boschendal, Cloof, **De Zoete Inval**, Four Paws, Glen Carlou, Goats do Roam, Highlands Road, Jordan (2), Kaapzicht, Knorhoek, **Koopmanskloof**, Kumala, Ladismith, Longridge, Mooiplaas, Napier, Old Vines, Opstal, **Savanha**, Slowine, Springfontein (Organic), **Stellar** (Organic), **Strydom**, Teddy Hall, Theuniskraal, Villiera, Villiersdorp, Vondeling, Whalehaven, Woolworths, Zonnebloem ★★★ Arniston Bay (2), Asara, Ashton, Avontuur, Barton, Beau Joubert, Beyerskloof, Darling Cellars, Delheim, **Diemersfontein**, Doolhof (2), Goede Hoop, Hathersage, Hazendal, Jean Daneel, Joostenberg, **Kanu**, Kumala, Landskroon, **MAN Vintners**, Mountain Range, **Noble Hill**, Oude Kaap, Overgaauw, **Somerset Wines**, Stellenbosch Hills, Thandi, **The Rhino**, uniWines (2), Van Loveren, Vergenoegd, Waterstone, Welvanpas, Woolworths, Zandvliet ★★ African Pride, African Terroir, Breëland, D'Aria, Kumala (2), **La Bourgogne**, Mountain River, Origin (2), Overmeer Cellars, Schalkenbosch (2), Simonsvlei, Zandvliet ★★ African Terroir, Bonnievale, Bovlei, Drostdy-Hof, Eve, Groupe CDV, Nuy, Overhex, Pick 'n Pay, Robertson (3), Two Oceans, Van Loveren, Woolworths ★ African Terroir (Organic), Oom Tas, Pick 'n Pay (Light & low-alcohol), Robertson (2) (Light & low-alcohol), Van Loveren ★ African Terroir **NT** Bottelary Hills, Buffalo Creek, Grande Provence, Groupe CDV, Hildenbrand, Klein Parys, KWV, La Petite Ferme, Lateganskop (Organic), Mountain Oaks (Organic), Nico Vermeulen, Obikwa, Oude Denneboom, Rico Suter, Somersbosch, Stellendrift, Wedderwill, Withington, **Woolworths D** Backsberg, Bellingham (2), Bottelary Hills, Hartswater, Hill & Dale (Kosher), Joostenberg, Kumala, Nederburg, Nuweland, Oudtshoorn, Rustenberg (Organic), Stellar (Organic), Val de Vie, Van Loveren, Waka Waka, Woolworths

White blends, wooded, dry

★★★★★ AA Badenhorst, **Cape Chamonix**, **Cape Point**, David, **Fairview**, Flagstone, Miles Mossop, Nederburg, Nitida, Rall, Tokara

★★★★☆ Adoro, Anatu (Organic), Avondale (Organic), Bizoe, Black Oystercatcher, Cape Point, Constantia Uitsig, Darling Cellars, **DeMorgenzon**, **Ernst Gouws**, Fable, Groot Constantia, Hermanuspietersfontein, Lammershoek, **Lomond**, Lourensford, Mullineux, Nederburg, Oak Valley, Sadie (2), Scali, Sequillo, Sijnn, Spier, Steenberg (2), Sterhuis, Strandveld, Thelema, TMV, Vergelegen, Vins d'Orrance, Welgegund, Woolworths, Zorgvliet

★★★★ AA Badenhorst, Allée Bleue, Altydgedacht, Alvi's Drift, **Anatu**, **Babylon's Peak**, Backsberg, Bellingham, Bergheim, BLANKbottle (2), Boekenhoutskloof, Bosman, **Cape Rock**, **Celestina**, **Constantia Glen**, Delaire, Dornier, **Drostdy-Hof**, Escapades, Gabriëlskloof, Joostenberg, Keermont, Klein Constantia, La Ferme Derik (2), La Vierge, Lanner Hill, **Leeuwenkuil**, Lomond, Muratie, **Neethlingshof**, Newton Johnson, Nico van der Merwe, Orangerie, Ormonde, **Paardebosch**, Quoin Rock, Reginald James, **Rietvallei**, Trizanne, Val de Vie, Val du Charron, Vondeling, Waterford, Waterkloof, Welbedacht

★★★★ Anura, **Beau Constantia**, Bellingham, Boekenhoutskloof, **Credo**, D'Aria, De Grendel, Dragonridge, **Eerste Hoop**, Glen Erskine, Hermit on the Hill, La Ferme Derik, La Vigne (Organic), Laibach (Organic), Manley, **Metzer**, Morgenster, My Wyn, Perdeberg (Organic), Reyneke (Organic), Rijk's, Springfontein, Stellenbosch Hills, Stony Brook (2), Sumaridge, Tierhoek, Val de Vie, Vuurberg, Wellington Winery ★★★ Bon Cap (Organic), Doolhof, Druk My Niet, **Hildenbrand**, **Hillock**, Kumala, La Vigne, Nederburg, Ridgeback, Solms-Delta, Sterhuis, Thandi (Organic), **Waverley Hills** (Organic), Welmoed, **Whalehaven**, William Everson, **Yardstick** ★★★ Alvi's Drift, Bellpost, Bergheim, Craighall, Kumala, Nederburg, **Origin**, Two Oceans (Organic), Waverley Hills (Organic), Woolworths (2) ★★ **Elemental Bob**, Kumala, **Olifantsberg** (Organic), **Origin** (Organic), Van Loveren, Zevenwacht ★★ **Klein Parys NT** Abingdon, Benguela Cove, Druk My Niet, Graham Beck, Hermit on the Hill, Hildenbrand, Karusa, Malanot, Mountain Oaks, Nomada, Origin, Withington, **Woolworths NR** Solms-Delta **D** Alvi's Drift, Annex Kloof, Bellingham, Flagstone, Graham Beck, Hoopenburg, Kumkani (2), KWV, The Winery of Good Hope, Wildekrans, Woolworths

Zinfandel/Primitivo

★★★★ Blaauwklippen, Idiom

★★★★☆ Blaauwklippen, Glen Carlou, Zevenwacht

Overview

According to the latest available data (2011), South Africa is the 8th largest wine-producing nation by volume. France, with 18.4% of global production, is the biggest, followed by Italy (15.4%) and Spain (12.7%). South Africa, with ±967m litres (excluding grape juice and grape juice concentrate), currently contributes 3.6% of global volume, slightly down from 3.7% in 2010. This mirrors the continuing, albeit slower, downward trend in the number of wine-grape growers in South Africa (3,527 compared with 3,596). Interestingly, the overall number of wine cellars crushing grapes is slightly up — 582 vs 573 — thanks to a spike in the number of private cellars crushing grapes, from 493 in 2010 to 505. (Producing wholesalers crushing grapes are slightly down, to 25, while co-operatives — 'producer cellars' in officialese — dropped further, to 52). Though their number declined marginally in 258 in 2011, reversing a long-term trend, microcellars vinifying fewer than 100 tonnes still constitute ±44% of all producers and thus remain a potent force in the industry.

Vineyards

An adjustment of official figures meant that the slight rise in the extent of new vineyard establishment reported for 2010 in this guide, did not in fact materialising. Instead, the pace of replanting continued to slow, to 2,800 ha, and in 2011 fell by an bigger margin to 2,417 ha. (The rate of uprooting of vines also fell in 2011, to 3,722 ha). Planting for white wine continues to outstrip that for red, albeit by a reduced margin (1,332 ha vs 1,085), and chenin retains its entrenched position as most-planted

2001	2011
41% / 59%	44% / 56%

Red ● and white ○ grape varieties as % of total area

variety (498 ha added). Second most-planted white-wine variety is colombard, with 306 ha, followed consumer favourite sauvignon with a relatively modest 219 ha added; chardonnay is still 4th with 171 ha. Pinotage, with 409 ha, again outpaced shiraz (263 ha) as most-planted red-wine variety, followed by cab (128) and (supplanting pinot noir) merlot (64). As ever, much more chenin is uprooted than planted, but the variety still leads the overall hectareage table, with ±18% of the total 100,568 ha under vine. Cab, with 12%, remains the leading red. The percentage of very young vines, after many years' decrease, increased fractionally in 2011. Thus 7.9% of all vines are under 4 years, while 18.1% are older than 20, slightly more than previously.

Exports

Exports in 2011 declined for the third consecutive year, to 357,4 m litres or 43% of South Africa's total wine production (compared with 378,5 m litres or 48.5% in 2010), reflecting the troubled global

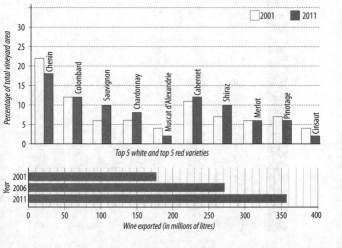

Top 5 white and top 5 red varieties

Wine exported (in millions of litres)

South African Wine Industry — Ten-Year Overview

	2002	2003	2004	2005	2006	2007	2008	2009	2010	2011
Number of wineries	428	505	561	581	576	560	585	604	573	582
Total vine area (excl sultana) (hectares)	96 233	98 605	100 207	101 607	102 146	101 957	101 325	101 259	101 016	100 568
Producing area 4 yrs & older (excl sultana) (hectares)	79 073	82 719	85 331	87 284	89 426	91 326	92 503	93 285	93 198	92 621
Avg yield (tons/hectare)	13.66	14.91	15.38	13.42	14.55	14.80	15.41	14.45	13.53	14.10
Avg grape price — producer cellars/co-ops (R/ton) (2010/2011 est)	1 333	1 624	1 458	1 387	1 362	1 434	1 522	1 918	1 806	1 821
Avg grape price — excl producer cellars/co-ops (R/ton)	3 953	4 041	4 133	3 593	3 128	2 971	3 173	3 917	3 949	3 801
Grapes crushed (millions of tons)	1.08	1.23	1.31	1.17	1.30	1.35	1.43	1.35	1.26	1.31
Total production (millions of litres)	834.2	956.0	1 015.7	905.2	1 013.0	1 043.5	1 089.0	1 033.41	984.8	1012.8
Domestic sales (millions of litres)	387.4	345.5	347.7	340.0	340.4	355.5	355.8	338.4	346.4	352.7
Consumption per capita (litres SA wine)	8.9	7.9	7.7	7.4	7.1	7.4	7.3	6.9	6.9	7.0
Export volume (millions of litres)	217.4	238.5	267.7	281.8	271.7	312.5	411.7	389.1	370.9	350.4
Stock (millions of litres)	209.3	336.8	363.7	339.4	403.1	425.2	357.2	361.7	351.0	417.5
Stock : sales ratio	0.35:1	0.57:1	0.59:1	0.54:1	0.65:1	0.64:1	0.47:1	0.49:1	0.48:1	0.59:1

economy. Chenin and (overtaking chardonnay) sauvignon top the list of most-exported varietal wines (bottled and bulk), with in-vogue pinks, cab, shiraz, pinotage and merlot also in demand. The top five markets for SA wine (packaged and bulk) remain, in descending order, the UK, Germany, Sweden, Netherlands and Denmark. When it comes to packaged wine only, the UK, Sweden, Netherlands and Germany still top the list, followed by the holy grail of many exporters, the US, displacing Denmark.

Local wine consumption

South African domestic per-capita wine consumption in 2011 increased fractionally for the second year in a row, from 6.93L to 6.97L. Note: The (official) figure of 7.03L given last edition was an estimate; actual consumption proved to be lower). But wine's combined market share (natural, fortified and sparkling) of ±16% remains substantially lower than beer (±57%). Brandy's ±6% share is stable, while whisky's ±6% represents steady incremental growth. Note: above market share percentages reflect revised official figures. Of natural wine sold in South Africa during 2011 (including imports), a slightly higher 49% is in glass, of which about half is in the standard 750ml bottle. Wine in bag-in-box accounts for ±25% of total sales, plastic containers ±23% and Tetra packs ±2%. Foil bags — the notorious *papsakke*, lately carefully regulated — represent less than 1% .

Note

Statistical data provided by SA Wine Industry Information & Systems (see below).

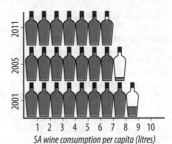

SA wine consumption per capita (litres)

Percentage market share (based on alcohol content) — Beverage — □2001 ■2011
Beer, Wine, Brandy, Whisky

Wine Industry Organisations

African Vintners Alliance Marketing: Vivian Kleynhans ▪ **T +27 (0)71-049-4109** ▪ ava@africanrootswines.com
Established to create an enabling environment for emerging black-owned wineries.

Agricultural Ethical Trade Initiative of SA (WIETA) CEO: Linda Lipparoni ▪ **T +27 (0)21-880-0580** ▪ F +27 (0)21-880-0580 ▪ linda@wieta.org.za; info@wieta.org.za ▪ www.wieta.org.za
Multi-stakeholder, non-profit, voluntary organisation established in 2002 to promote ethical trade in wine, fruit, cut flowers and general agriculture. WIETA has adopted a code of labour standards for the industry, and its main task is to support, enhance and promote members' ethical performance and best practice through training, technical assessments and ethical inspections to assess compliance. WIETA recently adopted an ethical seal which has been endorsed by the wine industry

in recognition of wine supply chains' ethical commitment to good working conditions on farms and in cellars.

ARC Infruitec-Nietvoorbij Research Institute Manager: Dr Johan van Zyl ▪ Acting PR: Derusha Rangasamy ▪ **T +27 (0)21-809-3100** ▪ F +27 (0)21-809-3400 ▪ infocape@arc.agric.za ▪ www.arc.agric.za
Internationally-regarded one-stop research institute, generating advanced technology for deciduous fruit- and grape-growers and related processors.

Biodiversity & Wine Initiative (BWI) See WWF-SA Biodiversity & Wine Initiative.

Cape Estate Wine Producers' Association (CEWPA) Secretary: Elsabe Ferreira ▪ **T +27 (0)21-863-1599** ▪ F +27 (0)21-8631552 ▪ elsabe@efpromosies.co.za

Cape Port Producers' Association (previously South African Port Producers' Association) Chair:

Carel Nel ▪ **T** +27 (0)44-213-3326 ▪ F +27 (0)44-213-3750 ▪ boplaas@mweb.co.za

Cape Winemakers Guild (CWG) Chair: Louis Strydom ▪ General Manager: Kate Jonker ▪ **T +27 (0)21-852-0408** ▪ F +27 (0)21-852-0409 ▪ info@capewinemakersguild.com ▪ www.capewinemakersguild.com
Independent, invitation-only association, founded in 1982 to promote winemaking excellence among its members. Since 1985, the CWG has held a highly regarded annual public auction. Established in 1999, the Nedbank CWG Development Trust provides social development investment for school children in the wineland areas, further education trough the Protégé Programme Bursary Fund and the mentorship of just-graduated winemakers through the Protégé Programme.

Chardonnay Forum of South Africa Chair: Matthew van Heerden ▪ matthew@uvamira.co.za ▪ **T +27 (0)21-880-1682 / +27 (0)82-520-9338** ▪ F +27 (0)21-880-1682

Chenin Blanc Association (CBA) Chair: Ken Forrester ▪ **T +27 (0)21-855-2374 / +27 (0)82-783-7203** ▪ F +27 (0)21-855-2373 ▪ ken@kenforresterwines.com ▪ www.chenin.co.za ▪ Manager: Ina Smith ▪ T +27 (0)82-467-4331 ▪ F +27 (0)86-672-8549 ▪ ina.smith@iafrica.com ▪ @CheninBlancAsso

Fairtrade Africa Southern Africa Network (FTA-SAN) Regional Coordinator: Mkhululi Silandela ▪ **T +27 (0)21-448-8911** ▪ m.silandela@fairtradeafrica.net ▪ www.fairtradeafrica.net
FTA-SAN represents Southern African Fairtrade producers in the global Fairtrade system on issues related to governance, new price setting, standards consultation and making standards more relevant to local farming practices. FTA-SAN supports producers with market access and promotes south-south trade and intra-Africa trade.

Fairtrade Label South Africa (FLSA) Executive Director: Boudewijn Goossens ▪ **T +27 (0)21-448-8911** ▪ info@fairtrade.org.za ▪ www.fairtradesa.org.za
The local marketing organisation for Fairtrade, FLSA was established in 2009 as an associate member of FLO and is the first organisation that promotes the Fairtrade label in a producing country, thus being a pioneer in the marketing of Fairtrade in the South. See also Southern Africa Fairtrade Network.

Garagiste Movement Coordinator: Tanja Beutler ▪ **T +27 (0)21-855-4275** ▪ F +27 (0)86-612-6118 ▪ tanja@topazwines.co.za

Institute of Cape Wine Masters Chair: Andy Roediger ▪ **T +27 (0)83-250-9821** ▪ Secretary: Margaret Fry ▪ T +27 (0)83-628-6511 ▪ F +27 (0)86-611-7150 ▪ capewinemasters@gmail.com ▪ www.capewinemasters.co.za
Successful completion of examinations set since 1983 by the Cape Wine & Spirit Education Trust and, latterly, the Cape Wine Academy, have qualified 82 Cape Wine Masters. Their Institute holds seminars, runs tasting workshops, charts trends and names a Wine Personality of the Year

Integrated Production of Wine (IPW) Manager: Daniël Schietekat ▪ **T +27 (0)21-889-6555** ▪ F +27 (0)866-903-224 ▪ daniel@ipw.co.za ▪ www.ipw.co.za
Innovative, widely supported initiative aimed at producing wine in an environmentally sustainable, profitable way by means of guidelines for both farm and cellar, embracing all aspects of grape production, winemaking and, now, biodiversity conservation. See also WWF-SA Biodiversity & Wine Initiative and Sustainable Wine South Africa.

Méthode Cap Classique Producers' Association Chair: Peter Ferreira ▪ **T +27(0)21-863-1599** ▪ F +27 (0)21-863-1552 ▪ elsabe@efpromosies.co.za ▪ bubblesferreira@gmail.com

Muscadel SA (previously Muscadel Association) Chair: Henri Swiegers ▪ **T +27 (0)23-344-3021** ▪ F +27 (0)86-617-9443 ▪ winemaker@badsberg.co.za ▪ Vice-chair: Nico Grundling ▪ **T +27 (0)23-344-3026** ▪ nico@slanghoek.co.za

Pinotage Association Chair: Beyers Truter ▪ T +27 (0)21-865-1235 ▪ F +27 (0)21-865-2683 ▪ reception@beyerskloof.co.za ▪ Manager: Elsabe Ferreira T +27 (0)21-863-1599 ▪ F +27 (0)21-863-1552 ▪ admin@pinotage.co.za ▪ www.pinotage.co.za

Sauvignon Blanc Interest Group of South Africa (SBIG) Secretary: Pieter de Waal ▪ **T +27 (0)83-357-3864** ▪ F +27 (0)21-948-3441 ▪ sbig@dw.co.za

Shiraz South Africa Chair: Edmund Terblanche ▪ **T +27 (0)82-770-2929** ▪ F +27 (0)21-876-3446 ▪ et.cellar@la-motte.co.za ▪ Secretary: Sandra Lotz ▪ **T +27 (0)21-863-1599 / +27 (0)82-924-7254** ▪ F +27 (0)86-267-4333 ▪ info@shirazsa.co.za

South African Black Vintners Alliance See African Vintners Alliance

South African Port Producers' Association (SAPPA) See Cape Port Producers' Association

South African Sommelier Association (SASA) Chair: Neil Grant ▪ General secretary: Higgo Jacobs ▪ info@sommeliers.org.za, memberships@sommeliers.org.za ▪ www.sommeliers.org.za
Membership driven, non-profit, voluntary private organisation established in 2012 to promote a culture of fine wine, food and service excellence in South Africa; formalise the profession of sommelier; and provide a forum for dialogue, exchange of ideas, knowledge and skills.

South African Wine Industry Information & Systems (SAWIS) Executive Manager: Yvette van

der Merwe ▪ T +27 (0)21-807-5703 ▪ F +27 (0)86-559-0274 ▪ info@sawis.co.za
Responsible for the collection, processing and dissemination of industry information. Administers the Wine of Origin (WO) system and manages the Information Centre, a comprehensive information resource base for the South African wine and brandy industry.

South African Wine Industry Trust (SAWIT)
Chair: Sharron Marco-Thyse ▪ CEO: Charles Erasmus ▪ T +27(0)21-889-8101 ▪ F +27 (0)86-503-6222 ▪ sawit@live.co.za ▪ www.sawit.co.za
The vision of SAWIT is the creation of a transformed wine industry that is sustainable and vibrant, populated by an empowered worker community that shares equitably in growth and prosperity.

Southern Africa Fairtrade Network (SAFN) See Fairtrade Africa Southern Africa Network

Sustainable Wine South Africa www.swsa.co.za ▪ Contact details as for individual organisations. Alliance between the Wine & Spirit Board (WSB), Integrated Production of Wine (IPW), Biodiversity & Wine Initiative (BWI) and Wines of South Africa (WOSA), driving the industry's commitment to sustainable, eco-friendly production.

Wine & Spirit Board Chair: Sibongile Nkomo ▪ Secretary: Hugo van der Merwe ▪ T +27 (0)21-889-6555 ▪ F +27 (0)21-889-5823 ▪ hugo@wsb.org.za
Mainly administers the Wine of Origin, Estate Brandy and Integrated Production of Wine (IPW) schemes.

Wine & Agricultural Ethical Trade Association (WIETA) See Agricultural Ethical Trade Initiative.

Wines of South Africa (WOSA) Chair: Johann Krige ▪ T/F +27 (0)21-884-4656 ▪ wine@kanonkop.co.za ▪ CEO: Su Birch T +27 (0)21-883-3860 ▪ F +27 (0)21-883-3861 ▪ info@wosa.co.za ▪ www.wosa.co.za, www.varietyisinournature.com
Generic marketing organisation, responsible for raising the profile of SA wine in key export markets. See also WWF-SA Biodiversity & Wine Initiative and Sustainable Wine South Africa.

Wine Industry Development Association (WIDA) Executive Manager: Denver Williams ▪ T +27 (0)21-872-9181 ▪ F +27 (0)2-872-4560 ▪ denver@wida.co.za ▪ www.wida.co.za
Promotes transformation through social development, human resource development and training, economic empowerment, and industrial relations, and protects the interests of vulnerable communities in the industry.

Wine Industry Network of Expertise & Technology (WINETECH) Executive manager: Gerard Martin ▪ T +27 (0)21-807-3099 ▪ F +27 (0)21-807-3385 ▪ marting@winetech.co.za
Coordinates the research, training and technology transfer programmes of participating institutions and individuals, to improve the competitiveness of the wine industry.

WWF-SA Biodiversity & Wine Initiative (BWI) Programme Manager: Martin Albertus ▪ T +27 (0)21-882-9085 ▪ F +27 (0)865-359-433 ▪ malbertus@wwf.org.za ▪ www.wwf.org.za/bwi ▪ Senior Extension Officer: Joan Isham ▪ T +27 (0)21-882-9085 ▪ F +27 (0)865-359-433 ▪ jisham@wwf.org.za ▪ www.wwf.org.za/bwi
Pioneering conservation partnership between the wine industry and conservation sector, aiming to protect places of outstanding conservation value and iconic species, and to maintain living and productive landscapes. This is achieved by steering expansion away from threatened natural vegetation and fostering a culture of sustainable production through wise land use practices. Demonstrating laudable commitment and buy-in, producers have set aside highly threatened natural areas well in excess of the industry's 100,568 ha vineyard footprint. Consumers can support accredited BWI members by buying wines displaying the colourful 'conservation in action' logo, depicting a sugarbird and a protea. See also Integrated Production of Wine and Sustainable Wine South Africa.

Winegrowing Areas

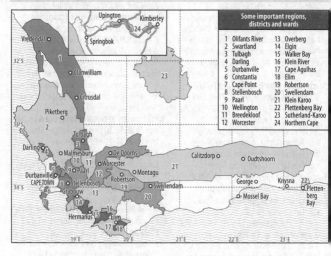

Some important regions, districts and wards	
1 Olifants River	13 Overberg
2 Swartland	14 Elgin
3 Tulbagh	15 Walker Bay
4 Darling	16 Klein River
5 Durbanville	17 Cape Agulhas
6 Constantia	18 Elim
7 Cape Point	19 Robertson
8 Stellenbosch	20 Swellendam
9 Paarl	21 Klein Karoo
10 Wellington	22 Plettenberg Bay
11 Breedekloof	23 Sutherland-Karoo
12 Worcester	24 Northern Cape

From modest beginnings in the Dutch East India Company's 17th-century gardens below Table Mountain, South Africa's vineyards now cover 100,568 ha and more than 100 official appellations. Changes to the Wine of Origin (WO) scheme of 1972/3 saw 'geographical units' incorporated into the WO classification alongside 'regions', 'districts' and 'wards' (the latter have the smallest footprint of the WO areas, following earlier amendments to the 'estate' legislation). Below are brief notes on the most important grape cultivation zones. Information supplied by Wines of South Africa (WOSA) and SA Wine Industry Information & Systems (SAWIS), and reflect 2011 data for the WO areas. **Note:** Area maps are not to the same scale.

Breedekloof Large (±12,620 ha) Breede River Valley district producing mainly for brandy industry and merchant trade, but also featuring some quality-focused boutiques and family estates with reputations for pinotage, chardonnay and semillon. Major varieties (ha): chenin (2,779), colombard (1,863), chardonnay (1,029), sauvignon (949), shiraz (830). See under Robertson for climate, geology etc.

Cape Point Small (32 ha), cool district on mainly western slopes of the Cape Peninsula. Recognised for sauvignon and semillon. Sauvignon (19), cab (5), shiraz (4), semillon (2), chardonnay (1). See also Constantia below.

Cape South Coast Recent 'umbrella' region (2,751 ha) for Cape Agulhas, Elgin, Overberg, Plettenberg

Bay, Swellendam and Walker Bay districts, and Herbertsdale, Napier and Stilbaai East wards.

Cederberg 70 ha ward in the Cederberg Mountain range, with some of South Africa's remotest and highest vineyards (950-1,100 m). Best known for shiraz (14 ha) and sauvignon (11). Chenin (9) chardonnay (8), cab (7).

1 Hout Bay   2 Constantia   3 Cape Point

Central Orange River
This ward along the Orange River (Gariep) is a production zone within the Northern Cape Geographical Unit. Altitude: 500–1,000 m; temp 25.3°C; rain: 250/208 mm; geology: granite, dolorite, shale, alluvial. Overwhelmingly a white-grape area but red plantings are increasing. Sultana (7,257),

colombard (2,443), chenin (933), villard blanc (182), muscat d'Alexandrie (167).

Constantia Premier viticultural ward on the eastern flank of the Cape Peninsula, cooled by south-easterly sea breezes. Recognised for whites generally, notably sauvignon, semillon and muscat. Altitude: 100–300 m; temp (Mean February Temperature, MFT) 20.6°C; rain:

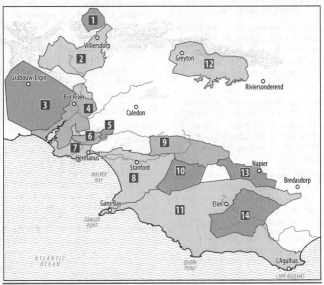

1 Elandskloof	4 Bot River	7 Hemel-en-	9 Klein River	12 Greyton
2 Theewater	5 Hemel-en-Aarde Ridge	Aarde Valley	10 Sunday's Glen	13 Napier
3 Elgin	6 Upper Hemel-en-Aarde	8 Walker Bay	11 Cape Agulhas	14 Elim

1 Voor Paardeberg	4 Simonsberg-Paarl
2 Wellington	5 Franschhoek
3 Paarl	

1 Polkadraai Hills	5 Stellenbosch
2 Bottelary	6 Simonsberg-Stellenbosch
3 Devon Valley	7 Jonkershoek Valley
4 Papegaaiberg	8 Banghoek

total/summer 1,056/335 mm; geology: granite (sandstone). Major varieties: sauvignon (169), cab (51), merlot (48), chardonnay (27), cab franc (24).

Darling District encircling the eponymous West Coast town, best known for the wines from its higher-lying ward, Groenekloof, long the source of top sauvignon; growing reputation for reds, especially shiraz. Groenekloof: cab (484), shiraz (355), sauvignon (311), chenin (204), pinotage (192) .

Durbanville Ward within the Tygerberg district, with solid reputation for striking merlot and sauvignon. The latter (400) is the dominant variety, followed by cab (283), merlot (235), shiraz (216) and chardonnay (98). Altitude: 150-350 m; temp 22.4°C; rain: 481/140 mm; geology: shale.

Elgin Cool upland district within the Cape South Coast region, yielding aromatic whites and elegant reds. Altitude: 200-250 m; temp 19.7°C; rain: 1,011/366 mm; geology: shale (sandstone). Sauvignon (348), pinot (99), chardonnay (97), shiraz (80), cab (68).

Elim Maritime ward within the Cape Agulhas district, its 146 ha of vineyards are arrayed around the old mission village of Elim near Africa's most southerly point. Sauvignon (80), shiraz (28), semillon (12), pinot noir (10), cab (6).

Franschhoek Valley A district with 1,276 ha under vine, recognised for cab and semillon. Sauvignon (202), cab (193), chardonnay (179), shiraz (176), merlot (116).

Hemel-en-Aarde See Walker Bay

Klein Karoo Scrubby semi-arid region, reliant on irrigation. Recognised for excellent 'ports', and fortifieds generally. Calitzdorp district: muscat d'Alexandrie (96), colombard (69), cab (24), chenin (24), chardonnay (17). Tradouw district: chardonnay (17), colombard (13), sauvignon (11), merlot (11), shiraz (10). Interesting stirrings in tiny Langeberg-Garcia

district (41), and Upper Langkloof (50) and Tradouw Highlands (10) wards.

Northern Cape See Central Orange River.

Olifants River Quality moves are afoot in this north-westerly Cape grape-growing region, particularly in the Bamboes Bay 'micro-ward' (just 5 ha) and Lutzville Valley district (3,025) nearer the coast, as well as the cool upland ward of Piekenierskloof (489). Inland, a climate conducive to organic cultivation is being exploited to that end. Altitude: 20-100 m; temp 23°C; rain: 139/47 mm; geology: mainly schist and alluvial deposits. Koekenaap ward (Lutzville Valley): chenin (286), colombard (210), sauvignon (167), cab (72), muscat d'Alexandrie (41). Piekenierskloof: pinotage (79), chenin (51), palomino (49), grenache noir (47), cab (45).

Orange River See Central Orange River

Paarl This district has many mesoclimates, soils and aspects, and thus succeeds with a variety of styles and grapes. Altitude: 100-300 m; temp 23.2°C; rain: 945/273 mm; geology: granite and shale. Paarl proper is recognised for shiraz and, more recently, viognier and mourvèdre grown on warmer slopes. Chenin (1,488), cab (1,007), shiraz (919), pinotage (529), cinsaut (413). The following are wards: Simonsberg-Paarl, on the warmer slopes of the Simonsberg, recognised for red blends, shiraz and chardonnay. Cab (303), chardonnay (206), sauvignon (185), shiraz (177), chenin (135). Voor Paardeberg, long an uncredited source of top-quality grapes, now becoming a star in own right. Cab (394), shiraz (292), chenin (222), merlot (204), chardonnay (98).

Philadelphia A ward of Tygerberg, cooled by the Atlantic air and noted for cab, merlot and Bordeaux-style reds. Cab (225), sauvignon (139), shiraz (65), merlot (65), chardonnay (37). See under Durbanville for climate, geology etc.

Robertson Traditionally a white-wine district, increasingly recognised for shiraz and cab. Chardonnay,

1 Montagu	5 Malgas	9 Langeberg-Garcia	12 Calitzdorp	15 Outeniqua
2 Stormsvlei	6 Buffeljags	10 Still Bay East	13 Prince Albert Valley	16 Upper Langkloof
3 Swellendam	7 Tradouw	11 Herbertsdale	14 Swartberg	17 Plettenberg Bay
4 Tradouw Highlands	8 Klein Karoo			

sauvignon and sparkling remain stand-outs. Altitude: 150-250 m; temp 23°C; rain: 280/116 mm; geology: shale and alluvial. Colombard (2,183), chardonnay (2,149), chenin (1,664), sauvignon (1,567), cab (1,464).

Stellenbosch To many, this intensively farmed district is the wine capital of South Africa. Key contributors to quality are the cooler mountain slopes, varied soil types and breezes off False Bay which moderate summer temperatures. Altitude: 200-400 m; temp

21.5°C; rain: 713/229 mm; geology: granite (sandstone). Jonkershoek Valley, a ward east of Stellenbosch town, is recognised for cab and cab blends. Cab (64), merlot (24), chardonnay (24), shiraz (19), sauvignon (15). Simonsberg-Stellenbosch, in the south-western foothills of the Simonsberg Mountain, is especially recognised for cab, cab blends and pinotage, and reds generally. Cab (325), sauvignon (196), merlot (172), shiraz (151), chardonnay (130). North-west of Stellenbosch town are four adjoining

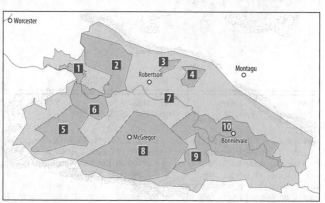

1 Eilandia	3 Hoopsrivier	5 Agterkliphoogte	7 Robertson	9 Boesmansrivier
2 Vinkrivier	4 Klaasvoogds	6 Le Chasseur	8 McGregor	10 Bonnievale

1 Swartland	4 Durbanville	7 Tulbagh
2 Darling	5 Malmesbury	
3 Philadelphia	6 Riebeekberg	

1 Lutzville Valley	6 Olifants River
2 Bamboes Bay	7 Citrusdal Mountain
3 Lamberts Bay	8 Citrusdal Valley
4 Vredendal	9 Piekenierskloof
5 Spruitdrift	10 Cederberg

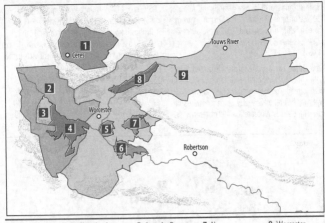

1 Ceres	**3** Slanghoek	**5** Aan-de-Doorns	**7** Nuy	**9** Worcester
2 Breedekloof	**4** Goudini	**6** Scherpenheuvel	**8** Hex River Valley	

wards: Papegaaiberg — chardonnay (28), sauvignon (23), chenin (21), pinotage (13), pinot gris (12); Devon Valley, recognised mainly for red blends — merlot (158), cab (145), sauvignon (108), shiraz (80), pinotage (65); Bottelary, noted for pinotage, shiraz and warm-blooded blends — chenin (459), cab (364), sauvignon (335), shiraz (276), pinotage (249); the most westerly ward, Polkadraai Hills — sauvignon (166), cab (158), shiraz (130), merlot (92), chenin (77); and Banghoek, the mountain amphitheatre above the village of Pniel — cab (75), shiraz (44), merlot (30), sauvignon (30), chardonnay (22). The remainder of the Stellenbosch district, as yet officially undemarcated, includes Stellenboschberg, Helderberg and Faure, recognised for red blends, chenin and sauvignon. Cab (1,732), shiraz (1,239), sauvignon (1,140), merlot (1,005), chenin (700).

Swartland Traditionally associated with full-bodied reds, but latterly also with chenin and Mediterranean-style red and white blends, this sunny district north of Cape Town has two wards, Malmesbury and Riebeekberg, plus a large unappellated area. Riebeekberg: chenin (225), shiraz (184), pinotage (170), chardonnay (159), cab (107). Malmesbury: cab (728), shiraz (561), chenin (503), pinotage (495), sauvignon (338). 'Swartland': chenin (1,947), cab (823), shiraz (807), pinotage (726), chardonnay (414). Altitude: 100–300 m; temp 23.3°C; rain: 523/154 mm; geology: granite and shale.

Tulbagh Inland district, traditionally known for sparkling and lightish whites, acquiring reputation for quality reds and serious white blends. Altitude: 160–400 m; temp 24°C; rain: 551/175 mm; geology: sandstone boulderbeds and shale. Chenin (256), colombard (194), shiraz (140), cab (138), chardonnay (84).

Walker Bay Highly regarded maritime district southeast of Cape Town, recognised for pinot noir, pinotage, sauvignon and chardonnay. Altitude: 100–250 m; temp 20.3°C; rain: 722/322 mm; geology: shale, granite and sandstone. Sauvignon (268), shiraz (131), pinot noir (107), chardonnay (92), cab (78). Bot River, Hemel-en-Aarde Ridge, Hemel-en-Aarde Valley, Sunday's Glen and Upper Hemel-en-Aarde Valley are wards.

Wellington Previously a ward in Paarl district, now itself a district in the Coastal region. Increasingly reputed for shiraz and gutsy red blends. Chenin (964), cab (776), shiraz (585), pinotage (392), merlot (313).

Worcester District producing chiefly for the brandy industry and merchant trade, but small quantities bottled under own labels often represent good quality/value. Recognised for everyday reds/whites and fortifieds. Chenin (1,888), colombard (1,067), chardonnay (588), shiraz (383), sauvignon (371). See under Robertson for climate, geology etc.

Wine of Origin-defined production areas
(New appellation/s in bold.)

Geographical Unit	Region	District	Ward
Eastern Cape	–	–	St Francis Bay
KwaZulu-Natal	–	–	–
Limpopo	–	–	–
Northern Cape	–	Douglas	–
	–	–	Central Orange River
	–	–	Hartswater
	–	–	Rietrivier (Free State)
	–	Sutherland-Karoo	–
Western Cape	Breede River Valley	Breedekloof	Goudini
			Slanghoek
		Robertson	Agterkliphoogte
			Boesmansrivier
			Bonnievale
			Eilandia
			Hoopsrivier
			Klaasvoogds
			Le Chasseur
			McGregor
			Vinkrivier
		Worcester	Aan-de-Doorns
			Hex River Valley
			Nuy
			Scherpenheuvel
	Cape South Coast	Cape Agulhas	Elim
		Elgin	–
		Overberg	**Elandskloof**
			Greyton
			Klein River
			Theewater
		Plettenberg Bay	–
		Swellendam	Buffeljags
			Malgas
			Stormsvlei
		Walker Bay	Bot River
			Hemel-en-Aarde Ridge
			Hemel-en-Aarde Valley
			Sunday's Glen
			Upper Hemel-en-Aarde Valley
		–	Herbertsdale
		–	Napier
		–	Stilbaai East
	Coastal	Cape Point	–
		Darling	Groenekloof
		Franschhoek Valley	–
		Paarl	Simonsberg-Paarl
			Voor Paardeberg
		Stellenbosch	Banghoek
			Bottelary
			Devon Valley
			Jonkershoek Valley

Geographical Unit	Region	District	Ward
Western Cape *(continued)*	Coastal *(continued)*	Stellenbosch *(continued)*	Papegaaiberg
			Polkadraai Hills
			Simonsberg–Stellenbosch
		Swartland	Malmesbury
			Riebeekberg
		Tulbagh	—
		Tygerberg	Durbanville
			Philadelphia
		Wellington	—
		—	Constantia
			Hout Bay
	Klein Karoo	Calitzdorp	—
		Langeberg-Garcia	—
		—	Montagu
		—	Outeniqua
		—	Tradouw
		—	Tradouw Highlands
		—	Upper Langkloof
	Olifants River	Citrusdal Mountain	Piekenierskloof
		Citrusdal Valley	—
		Lutzville Valley	Koekenaap
		—	Bamboes Bay
		—	Spruitdrift
		—	Vredendal
—	—	—	Cederberg
—	—	—	Ceres
—	—	—	Lamberts Bay
—	—	—	Prince Albert Valley
—	—	—	Swartberg

Boberg (fortified wines from Franschhoek, Paarl and Tulbagh). Source: SAWIS.

Grape Varieties

Below are brief notes on some of the grape varieties mentioned in the guide, and their contribution to the national vineyard (statistics from SA Wine Industry Information & Systems — SAWIS). See under Wine-growing Areas for details of the most widely planted and best-performing varieties in the major vine cultivation zones.

Red-wine varieties

Cabernet sauvignon Adaptable and internationally planted black grape making some of the world's finest and longest-lasting wines. And retaining some of its inherent qualities even when overcropped in less suitable soils and climates. Can stand alone triumphantly, but frequently blended with a wide range of other varieties: traditionally, as in Bordeaux, with cab franc, merlot and a few minor others, but also in SA sometimes partnering varieties such as shiraz and pinotage. Number of different clones, with differing characteristics. ±12% of total vineyard area.

Cabernet franc Like its descendant cabernet sauvignon, with which it is often partnered, a classic part of the Bordeaux blend, but in SA and elsewhere —

particularly in the Loire — also used for varietal wines. Tiny, stable vineyard area (±1%).

Carignan Hugely planted in the south of France, where it is not much respected. But there, as in SA, older, low-yielding vines can produce pleasant surprises. Insignificant vineyard area.

Cinsaut (noir) 'Cinsault' in France. Another of the mass, undistinguished plantings of southern France, which only occasionally comes up trumps. Used to be known locally as hermitage, the name reflected in its offspring (with pinot noir), pinotage. About 2% of vineyard area.

Gamay noir Although it produces some serious long-lived wines in Beaujolais, its use for (mainly) early- and easy-drinking 'nouveau' wines there, often using carbonic maceration, is the model mostly copied in SA. Insignificant vineyard area.

Grenache (noir) The international (ie French) name for the Spanish grape garnacha. Widespread in Spain and southern France, generally used in blends (as in Rioja and Châteauneuf), but occasionally solo. A favourite for rosés. When vigour restrained, capable of greatness, but this is rare. Tiny plantings here. (White/pink versions also occur.)

Malbec Once a significant part of Bordeaux's blend, now most important in Cahors in western France (where it is known as cot), and as Argentina's signature variety. In SA a few varietal and blended examples; very small plantings.

Merlot Classic blending partner (as in Bordeaux) for cabernet, fashionable around the world, where it tends to be seen as an 'easier' version of cab — although this is perhaps because it is often made in a less ambitious manner. Merlot varietal wines increasingly common in SA too. ±6% of vineyard area.

Mourvèdre Internationally known by its French name, though originally Spanish (monastrell). In Australia and California also called mataro. Particularly successful in some serious southern French blends, and increasingly modish internationally. Minuscule plantings here.

Nebbiolo Perhaps the greatest red grape to have scarcely ventured from its home — Piedmont in this case, where it makes massive, tannic, long-lived wines. Minute plantings here.

Petit verdot Use of this excellent variety in the Médoc limited by its late ripening. Now appearing in some local blends, and a few varietals. 0.7% of vineyard area.

Pinotage A 1920s cross between pinot noir and cinsaut ('hermitage'). Made in a range of styles, from simply fruity to ambitious, well-oaked examples. 6.5% of vineyard area.

Pinot noir Notoriously difficult grape to succeed with outside its native Burgundy, but South Africa, along with the rest of the New World, now produces some excellent examples. Slightly increasing 1% of the vineyard.

Ruby cabernet US cross between cabernet sauvignon and carignan, designed for heat tolerance. Rather rustic, used mostly in cheaper blends. ±2% of vineyard area.

Shiraz Better known as syrah outside South Africa and Australia (and on some local labels too). Internationally increasing in popularity, with northern Rhône and now also Australia as its major domiciles. Made here in a variety of styles — generally wooded. 10% of vineyard area.

Tinta barocca Elsewhere spelt 'barroca'. One of the important Portuguese port-making grapes, which is now its primary role in SA, usually blended. Also used for some varietal unfortified wines, and namelessly in some 'dry reds'. 0.2% of vineyard area.

Touriga nacional Important Portuguese port-making grape, now usefully grown here for similar ends, along with tinta franca, tinta roriz (tempranillo) and souzão. Tiny plantings.

Zinfandel The quintessential Californian grape (of European origin, and the same as Italy's primitivo), used here in a small way for some big wines. Tiny plantings.

White-wine varieties

Chardonnay In SA, as elsewhere, many new vineyards of this grape have come on-stream, with wines showing a wide range of styles, quality and price. Generally used varietally, but also in blends, and for sparkling. (Heavily) wooded in more ambitious wines. Steady 8% of vineyard area.

Chenin blanc SA has more chenin (locally also called steen) than even France's Loire Valley, the variety's home. Used here for everything from generic 'dry white' to ambitious sweet wines, to brandy. Increasing numbers of table-wine successes in recent years, as well as inexpensive but flavoursome easy-drinkers. ±18% of vineyard area.

Colombar(d) One of the mainstays of brandy production in South Africa, colombard (usually without the 'd' in SA) is also used for numerous varietal and blended wines, ranging from dry to sweet — seldom wooded. Steady ±11% of vineyard area.

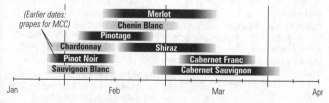

Approximate ripening dates in the Stellenbosch area for some important grape varieties

Gewürztraminer Readily identifiable from its rose-petal fragrance, best known in its Alsatian guise. In South Africa usually made off-dry. Insignificant vineyard area.

Hanepoot Traditional Afrikaans name for muscat d'Alexandrie, South Africa's most planted muscat variety (see also muscadel below). ±2% of vineyard area (some for raisins and table grapes), slowly declining.

Muscadel Name used here for both muscat de Frontignan and muscat blanc à petits grains (both red and white versions). The grape associated with the famous Constantia dessert wines of the 18th century today is used chiefly for dessert and fortified wines and for touching up blends. Red and white versions total about 1% of vineyard area.

Muscat See Hanepoot and Muscadel.

Riesling The name by itself now refers to the great German grape (as it does in this guide). Previously, the grape had to carry the prefix 'Rhine' or 'weisser', and the 'riesling' was an official SA synonym for the inferior crouchen blanc, also known as Cape riesling and mostly used anonymously in blends, occasionally varietally. Rhine riesling often off-dry here, in blends or varietally, some excellent botrytised dessert examples. Crouchen: 0.6% of vineyard area, steady; Rhine: small but steady 0.2%.

Sauvignon blanc Prestigious vine most associated with eastern Loire regions, Bordeaux and New Zealand — whose wines have helped restore fashionability to the grape. The SA version no longer a poor relation of these. Usually dry, but some sweet wines; sometimes wooded, more often not (former sometimes called fumé blanc/blanc fumé). 9.6% of vineyard area, still growing.

Semillon
Spelt sémillon in French. Sometimes heavily wooded, sometimes sweet, more often in blends. ±1% of vineyard area. Recent boutique vinifications of rare red version causing excitement.

Viognier Increasingly fashionable variety internationally, spreading out from its home in the northern Rhône, now showing promise here. Usually wooded. Still tiny plantings.

Competitions, Challenges & Awards

An increasing number of wine competitions, awards and challenges are run by liquor industry bodies, independent companies, publishing houses and individuals. Below are the main national events:

Absa Perold Cape Blend Competition See Perold Absa Cape Blend Competition.

Absa Top Ten Pinotage Competition Run annually by the Pinotage Association and a major financial institution to help set international quality targets for growers of pinotage. Local/overseas judges. See under Industry Organisations for contact details.

Amorim Cork Cap Classique Challenge Annual competition to appoint SA's top bottle-fermented sparkling wines. Mostly local judges. ▪ elsabe@efpromosies.co.za ▪ www.capclassique.co.za ▪ T +27 (0)21-863-1599 ▪ F +27 (0)21-863-1552

Best Value Wine Guide SA judges gather annually to select the best-value wines under R80 based on quality. Sponsored by Ultra Liquors, results are published in the Best Value Wine Guide, distributed with Getaway magazine. ▪ sasha.vanzyl@ramsaymedia.co.za ▪ www.bestvaluewineguide.co.za ▪ T +27 (0)21-530-3151

Cape Port & Wine Challenge Organised by the Cape Port Producers' Association (previously South African Port Producers' Association) to select the best bottling in each of the various port categories, and an overall winner. Local judges. ▪ info@boplaas.co.za ▪ www.sappa.co.za ▪ T +27 (0)44-213-3326 ▪ F +27 (0)44-213-3750

Classic Wine Trophy Established in 1998 to recognise ageworthy, classic SA wines. Staged under rules of the Office Internationale de la Vigne et du Vin (OIV) in partnership with La Revue du Vin de France. Overseas judges. ▪ info@classicwinetrophy.co.za ▪ www.classicwinetrophy.co.za ▪ T +27 (0)21-683-7479 ▪ F +27 (0)86-588-2989

Diners Club Winemaker of the Year Inaugurated in 1981, this prestigious competition features a different category each year. Local panel with some overseas representation. ▪ winemaker@dinersclub.co.za ▪ www.dinersclub.co.za ▪ T +27 (0)21- 795-5400 ▪ F +27 (0)21-794-8185

Michelangelo CCL Label International Wine Awards Well-established competition (1997) with strong international emphasis: 15 accredited wine judges from around the globe, and foreign as well as South African wines competing under international OIV rules for 12 trophies and double-gold, gold and silver medals. ▪ lorraine@michelangeloawards.com ▪ www.michelangeloawards.com ▪ T +27 (0)21-856-3194 / +27 (0)82-556-8679 ▪ F +27 (0)86-555-8061

Muscadel Award for Excellence Annual competition aimed at raising consumer awareness and recognising quality in the creation, packaging and promotion of SA's muscadel wines. Local judges. ▪

winemaker@badsberg.co.za ▪ T +27 (0)23-344-3021 ▪ F +27 (0)23-344-3023

Nedbank Green Wine Guide A three-part competition, recognising the best wine made from certified organically grown grapes, wines made from BWI certified farms and the producer with the best environmental practices. Results are published in the Nedbank Green Wine Awards booklet. Local judges. ▪ kathryn.frew@ramsaymedia.co.za ▪ www.greenwineawards.com ▪ T +27 (0)21-530-3308

Old Mutual Trophy Wine Show See Trophy Wine Show.

Perold Absa Cape Blend Competition Launched in 2011 and aimed at creating a signature style for Cape Blends (see SA Wine Styles section). Local judges. Contacts as for Absa Top Ten Pinotage.

SAPPA Port Challenge See Cape Port Challenge

South African Airways (SAA) Wine Awards Annual selection of wines to fly with the national carrier (drinkability in flight conditions an important consideration). The top red, white, bubbly and port each receive a trophy. Local and overseas palates. ▪ BongiSodladla@flysaa.com, YolandeSchutte@flysaa.com ▪ T +27 (0)11-978-9304 / +27 (0)11-978-5835; +27 (0))11-978-3982 / +27 (0)11-978-3115 ▪ F +27 (0)11-978-3115

South African Terroir Wine Awards Only wines that truly portray a specific terroir can enter, making this a highly exclusive competition. The best wines certified as from single vineyards, units registered for the production of estate wine, wards in SA's officially recognised winegrowing areas, as well as small districts that are not divided into wards, are awarded. SA's top 5 estate wines are also honoured. Seven local judges. ▪ mlab@iafrica.com ▪ www.terroirwineawards.co.za ▪ T +27 (0)21-975-8166

South African Young Wine Show Inaugurated 1975 to gauge the quality of embryo wines, prior to finishing and bottling, thereby also recognising wineries

which sell their products in bulk. The grand champion receives the General Smuts Trophy. Local judges. ▪ information@veritas.co.za ▪ www.youngwineshow.co.za ▪ T +27 (0)21-863 1599 ▪ F +27 (0)21-863-1552

Top 100 South African Wines National fine-wine and wine list challenge that aims to identify the best 100 wines of South Africa, as well as winning restaurants. The winners are showcased in a hardcopy book and on the website, and made available for tasting by the public both in SA and internationally. Local/overseas ▪ info@top100sawines.com ▪ www.top100sawines.com ▪ T +27 (0)21-787-9880 ▪ F +27 (0)86-627-5588

Trophy Wine Show Convened by Michael Fridjhon, sponsored by Old Mutual. Seeks to identify the best wines in SA and award trophies to the top gold medal winner in the major classes, as well as the top producer overall. Local and international judges. ▪ alex@outsorceress.co.za ▪ www.trophywineshow.co.za ▪ T +27 (0)1-482-9178 ▪ F +27 (0)11-482-9168

Veritas SA's biggest competition for market-ready wines, awarding double-gold, gold, silver and bronze medals across a wide range of categories. Local palates with some overseas input. ▪ information@veritas.co.za ▪ www.veritas.co.za ▪ T +27 (0)21-863 1599 ▪ F +27 (0)21-863-1552

Wine Magazine Nedbank Green Wine Awards See Nedbank Green Wine Awards.

Wine Magazine Ultra Liquors Best Value Wine Awards See Best Value Wine Guide.

Winemakers' Choice Awards Gives winemakers from all wine regions the opportunity to judge the products of their peers. A Diamond Award is given to all winning wines; trophies and a cash prize are also awarded to the best white and red on show. ▪ robyn@winemakerschoice.co.za ▪ www.winemakerschoice.co.za ▪ T +27 (0)21-887-2377 / +27(0)82-301-4509

Wine Education

Cape Wine Academy Long-established general wine education body. Based in Stellenbosch and Johannesburg with satellites in Durban, Pretoria, Bloemfontein, Namibia and Harare. Runs wine theory and tasting courses with examinations at several levels, as well as training for front-of-house sales staff and sommeliers . Also presents corporate tastings. ▪ www.capewineacademy.co.za ▪ Stellenbosch: T +27 (0)21-889-8844 ▪ F +27 (0)21-889-7391 ▪ michelle@capewineacademy.co.za ▪ Johannesburg:

T +27 (0)11- 024-3616 ▪ F +27 (0)11- 440 2157 ▪ marilyn@capewineacademy.co.za

University of Stellenbosch Garagiste Winemaking Course The premium short course for people interested in producing quality small-scale wines at home or simply expanding their wine knowledge. Attendees receive a set of notes; observe the use of garagiste winemaking equipment; taste different vinifications; bottle their own wine; and receive a certificate from Stellenbosch University. ▪ wdutoit@

sun.ac.za ▪ **T** +27 (0)21-808-2022 ▪ F +27 (0)21-808-4781

Wine Tasting Academy Run by Michael Fridjhon and the University of Cape Town's Graduate School of Business, this intensive 3-day tasting and wine judging course aims to increase the number of competent wine judges at work in the local industry. ▪ mf@reciprocal.co.za

WSET in South Africa The internationally recognised standard for wine education in 58 countries, the UK-based Wine & Spirit Education Trust's courses cater for beginners up to seasoned wine industry professionals. In-situ training for front-of-house staff is

also offered and, for those wanting to take their wine education to the very highest level, WSET is the direct path to the Master of Wine (MW) qualification. Courses offered throughout Africa. ▪ info@thewinecentre.co.za ▪ www.thewinecentre.co.za ▪ **T +27 (0)72-390-9166**

Service Excellence Training Runs wine courses for staff in the licensed restaurant trade to improve their knowledge of viticulture and wine service. ▪ mfine@icon.co.za ▪ www.bevtrainsa.co.za ▪ **T +27 (0)82-932-9430 / +27 (0)21-782-5472**

Selected Wine Shops

The following retail outlets, on-line emporia and specialist shippers stock a wide range of fine-wines and/or provide specialised services to the wine-consuming public. See our website, www.platteronline.com, for an expanded listing, including special facilities and programmes such as regular tastings, wine clubs and special offers.

Eastern Cape

Makro Port Elizabeth ▪ www.makro.co.za ▪ T +27 (0)41-397-8000 ▪ F +27 (0)41-397-8001

Metro Liquor Matatiele ▪ T +27 (0)39-737-3050 ▪ +27 (0)39-737-3374

Metro Liquor Port Elizabeth ▪ T +27 (0)41-451-2293 ▪ +27 (0)41-451-2391

Picardi Rebel Fig Tree Park (Port Elizabeth) ▪ figtree@picardirebel.co.za ▪ www.picardirebel.co.za ▪ T +27 (0)41-368-2840 ▪ F +27 (0)41-368-2420

Prestons (Walmer) ▪ T/F +27(0)41-581-1993

Spargs Liquor Mart (East London) ▪ tops27@spargs.co.za ▪ T +27 (0)43-711-7700 ▪ F +27 (0)43-748-4707

Ultra Liquors East London ▪ eastlondon@ultraliquors.co.za ▪ T +27 (0)43-743-5174/722-3476 ▪ F +27 (0)43-743-4283

Ultra Liquors Newton Park ▪ newtonpark@ultraliquors.co.za ▪ T +27 (0)41-364-1103/46 ▪ F +27 (0)41-364-2277

Free State

Metro Liquor Bloemfontein ▪ T +27 (0)51-434-1315 ▪ F +27 (0)51-434-3074

Metro Liquor Welkom ▪ T +27 (0)57-355-7741 ▪ F +27 (0)57-355-5047

Ultra Liquors Bloemfontein ▪ bloem@ultraliquors.co.za ▪ T +27 (0)51-447-3328 ▪ F +27 (0)51-447-3600

Garden Route

Picardi Rebel Beacon Isle (Plettenberg Bay) ▪ www.picardirebel.co.za ▪ T/F +27 (0)44-533-1225

Picardi Rebel George ▪ george@picardirebel.co.za ▪ www.picardirebel.co.za ▪ T +27 (0)44-887-0053 ▪ F +27 (0)44-887-0054

Picardi Rebel Lagoon Fine Wine & Liquors (Market Square, Plettenberg Bay) ▪ www.picardirebel.co.za ▪ T +27 (0)44-533-2440 ▪ F +27 (0)44-533-2442

Picardi Rebel Liquor Guys Knysna ▪ www.picardirebel.co.za ▪ T +27 (0)44-382-1614 ▪ F +27 (0)382-3307

Picardi Rebel Square (The Square, Plettenberg Bay) ▪ www.picardirebel.co.za ▪ T +27 (0)44-533-1340 ▪ F +27 (0)44-533-0574

Picardi Rebel Waterfront Drive (Knysna) ▪ waterfrontdrive@picardirebel.co.za ▪ www.picardirebel.co.za ▪ T/F +27 (0)44-382-3318

The Oak Barrel (Wilderness) ▪ nikki@silver.co.za ▪ T +27 (0)44-882-1201 / +27 (0)82-924-6196

34° South (Knysna) ▪ info@34south.biz, keith@34south.biz ▪ www.34south.biz ▪ T +27 (0)44-382-7331/302-5818 ▪ F +27 (0)866-328-454

Ultra Liquors George ▪ george@ultraliquors.co.za ▪ T +27 (0)44-874-5514 /10 ▪ F +27 (0)44-874-5511

Gauteng

Alpha Liquor Store (Roodepoort) ▪ T +27 (0)11-766-1086 ▪ F +27 (0)11-763-8741 ▪ tony@jumbomeats.com

Bamboo-Love Books See Love Books

Bootleggers Liquor Specialist ▪ Booysens: T +27 (0)11-493-2536 ▪ Fourways Crossing: T +27 (0)11-465-9777 ▪ Glenanda: T +27 (0)11-432-

3570 • Glenvista: T +27 (0)11-432-3093 • Lombardy: T +27 (0)11-882-6252

Boulevard Cellars • andrewpanayiotou7@gmail.com • T +27 (0)11-803-6808/6121 • F +27 (0)118-070-675

Central Liquors @ The Square (Boksburg) • centralliquors@telkomsa.net • T +27 (0)11-826-5070 • F +27 (0)11-826-7151

Love Books (Melville) • info@lovebooks.co.za • www.lovebooks.co.za • T +27 (0)11-726-7408 • F +27 (0)866-395-375

Metro Liquor Boksburg • T +27 (0)11-826-1420 • F +27 (0)11-826-1462

Metro Liquor Devland • T +27 (0)11-933-1667/8/9

Metro Liquor Hillfox (Weltevreden Park) • T +27 (0)11-679-5690/4076 • F +27 (0)11-679-3778

Metro Liquor Pretoria • T +27 (0)12-379-6050 • F +27 (0)12-379-7388

Metro Liquor Pretoria East • T +27 (0)12-809-0800 • F +27 (0)12-809-0786

Metro Liquor Springs • T +27 (0)11-817-1133 • F +27 (0)11-817-1607

Makro Centurion • www.makro.co.za • T +27 (0)860-305-999 • F +27 (0)860-405-999

Makro Crown Mines • www.makro.co.za • T +27 (0)11-309-1000 • F +27 (0)11-309-1089

Makro Germiston • www.makro.co.za • T +27 (0)860-304-999 • F +27 (0)860-408-999

Makro Silver Lakes • www.makro.co.za • T +27 (0)860-307-999 • F +27 (0)860-407-999

Makro Strubens Valley (Roodepoort) • www.makro.co.za • T +27 (0)860-302-999 • F +27 (0)860-402-999

Makro Vaal (Vanderbijlpark) • www.makro.co.za • T +27 (0)860-303-999 • F +27 (0)860-403-999

Makro Wonderboom • www.makro.co.za • T +27 (0)860-306-999 • F +27 (0)860-406-999

Makro Woodmead • www.makro.co.za • T +27 (0)860-301-999 • F +27 (0)860-401-999

Morara Wines & Spirits Emporium (Johannesburg) • maputsoe@mweb.co.za • www.morarajozi.co.za • T +27 (0)11-024-7957 • F +27 (0)86-512-1311

Norman Goodfellow's • www.ngf.co.za • Illovo: erick@ngf.co.za • T +27 (0)11-788-4814 • F +27 (0)86-628-8029 • Hyde Park: jeffg@ngf.co.za • T +27 (0)11-325-6462 / 5217 • F +27 (0)86-624-4434 • Melrose Arch: clinton@ngf.co.za • T +27 (0)11-684-2756/7 • F +27 (0)86-582-3273

Picardi Rebel Bedfordview • www.picardirebel.co.za • T +27 (0)11-615-9160 • F +27 (0)11-622-2475

Picardi Rebel Eco Boulevard (Centurion) • www.picardirebel.co.za • T +27 (0)12-661-1529 • F +27 (0)12-661-1516

Picardi Rebel Honeydew (Glen Dayson) • www.picardirebel.co.za • T +27 (0)11-475-4658 • F +27 (0)11-675-6404

Picardi Rebel Moreleta Park • www.picardirebel.co.za • T +27 (0)12-997-4250 • F +27 (0)12-997-4332

Picardi Rebel Morning Glen (Gallo Manor) • www.picardirebel.co.za • T +27 (0)11-802-0964 • F +27 (0)11-802-0965

Picardi Rebel Northmead • www.picardirebel.co.za • T +27 (0)11-849-5392 • F +27 (0)11-849-7332

Picardi Rebel Norwood • www.picardirebel.co.za • T +27 (0)11-728-6709 • F +27 (0)11-728-1632

Picardi Rebel Sandton • sandton@picardirebel.co.za • www.picardirebel.co.za • T +27 (0)11-884-2151 • F +27 (0)11- 884-1067

Solly Kramers Parkview • T +27 (0)11-486-2584 • F +27 (0)11-646-3663 • parkview@sollykramers.co.za • www.ultraliquors.co.za

Ultra Liquors Church Str West (Pretoria) • churchstreet@ultraliquors.co.za • T +27 (0)11-327-4613 • F +27 (0)12-327-2150

Ultra Liquors Corlett • corlett@ultraliquors.co.za • T +27 (0)11-887-1001/2/3 • F +27 (0)11-887-4947

Ultra Liquors Hazelwood • hazelwood@ulrtraliquors.co.za • T +27 (0)12-460-6012/4896 • F +27(0)12-460-6831

Ultra Liquors Meyerspark • meyerspark@ultraliquors.co.za • T +27 (0)12-803-4292 • F +27 (0)12-803-6953

Ultra Liquors Paul Kruger St (Eloffsdal) • paulkruger@ultraliquors.co.za • T +27 (0)12-335-2780/1 • F +27 (0)12-335-5820

Ultra Liquors Parkview • parkview@sollykramers.co.za • T +27 (0)11-486-2584 • F +27 (0)11-646-3663

Ultra Liquors Voortrekker Road (Pretoria) • voortrekker@ultraliquors.co.za • T +27 (0)12-335-0946/7/0939 • F +27 (0)12-335-6226

Vintages-The Wine Seller (Sandton) • T +27 (0)11-784-8676/7 • F +27 (0)11-784-8674 • thebutchershop@mweb.co.za • www.thebutchershop.co.za

Wine Cellar – Fine Wine Importers (Johannesburg) • debi@winecellar.co.za • www.winecellar.co.za • T +27 (0)11-027-9463

WineDirect (Midrand) • T +27 (0)11-312-4684 • F +27 (0)11-887-4553 • sales@

winedirectonline.co.za ▪
www.winedirectonline.co.za
Winesense Melrose Arch ▪ T +27 (0)11-684-1487 ▪ F +27 (0)11-684-2160

KwaZulu-Natal
Broadway Liquors & Wine Boutique (Durban North) ▪ T +27 (0)31-564-5044
Buxtons La Cave Liquors (La Lucia Mall) ▪ lacave@telkomsa.net ▪ T +27 (0)31-572-6073 ▪ F +27 (0)31-572-2619
Liberty Liquors (Durban) ▪ argyle@ libertyliquors.co.za ▪ www.libertyliquors.co.za ▪ T +27 (0)31-303-9857 ▪ F +27 (0)31-303-9864
Makro Pietermaritzburg ▪ www.makro.co.za ▪ **T +27 (0)33-846-3600** ▪ F +27 (0)33-346-0247
Makro Rossburgh ▪ www.makro.co.za ▪ T +27 (0)31-480-7000 ▪ F +27 (0)31-480-7060
Makro Springfield ▪ www.makro.co.za ▪ T +27 (0)31-203-2800 ▪ F +27 (0)860-409-999
Metro Liquor Empangeni ▪ T +27 (0)35-787-2604/6/8 ▪ F +27 (0)35-787-2605
Metro Liquor Newcastle ▪ T +27 (0)34-312-3654 ▪ F +27 (0)34-312-9493
Metro Liquor Pietermaritzburg ▪ T +27 (0)33-398-8900 ▪ F +27 (0)33-398-7980
Metro Liquor Pongola ▪ T +27 (0)34-413-1245 ▪ F +27 (0)34-413-2126
Marriott Gardens Liquor Store (Greyville) ▪ herveallen@hotmail.com ▪ **T +27 (0)31-309-2079** ▪ F +27 (0)31-309-2097
Meander Fine Wines (Lions River) ▪ meanderfinewines@yahoo.com ▪ www.meanderfinewines.co.za ▪ T +27 (0)33-234-2913 / +27 (0)83-452-3350
Picardi Rebel Cascade Centre (Pietermaritzburg) ▪ www.picardirebel.co.za ▪ T +27 (0)33-347-3852 ▪ F +27 (0)33-347-1019
Picardi Rebel Emapangeni ▪ www.picardirebel.co.za ▪ T +27 (0)35-772-5537 ▪ F +27 (0)35-772-5543
Picardi Rebel Glenwood (Durban) ▪ www.picardirebel.co.za ▪ T +27 (0)31-201-5487 ▪ F +27 (0)31-201-5488
Picardi Rebel Howick ▪ www.picardirebel.co.za ▪ T +27 (0)33-330-6636 ▪ F +27 (0)33-330-6638
Picardi Rebel Midlands Mall (Pietermaritzburg) ▪ www.picardirebel.co.za ▪ T +27 (0)33-342-1698 ▪ F +27 (0)33-342-1699
Picardi Rebel Shelly Beach ▪ www.picardirebel.co.za ▪ T +27 (0)39-315-1277 ▪ F +27 (0)39-315-1278
Parklane Cellars (Pietermaritzburg) ▪ cameron@ parklane.co.za, parklane@parklane.co.za, cellars@

parklane.co.za ▪ T +27 (0)33-342-3487 / +27 (0)83-628-1575 ▪ F +27 (0)33-342-6413
The Village Vineyard (Kloof) ▪ vineyard1@ retail.spar.co.za ▪ www.facebook.com/ TheVillageVineyard ▪ T +27 (0)31-764-6679/5112 ▪ F 031-764-7196
The Wine Cellar (Rosetta) ▪ info@ thewinecellar.co.za ▪ www.thewinecellar.co.za ▪ T +27 (0)33-267-7044/+27 (0)82-923-8781 ▪ F +27 (0)33-267-7044
Ultra Liquors New Germany ▪ newgermany@ ultraliquors.co.za ▪ T +27 (0)31-705-3777/ 3993 ▪ F +27 (0)31-705-6640
Ultra Liquors Tollgate (Mayville) ▪ tollgate@ ultraliquors.co.za ▪ T +27 (0)31-261-2233/67 ▪ F +27 (0)31-261-7980
Ultra Liquors Westville ▪ westville@ ultraliquors.co.za ▪ T +27 (0)31-266-4364/60 ▪ F +27 (0)31-266-4300

Limpopo
Makro Polokwane ▪ www.makro.co.za ▪ T +27 (0)860-009-550
Metro Liquor Brits ▪ T +27 (0)12-252-7318 ▪ F +27 (0)12-252-4777
Metro Liquor Polokwane (Magnesiet Str) ▪ T +27 (0)15-298-8800 ▪ F +27 (0)15-298-8666
Metro Liquor Tzaneen ▪ T +27 (0)15-307-1254 ▪ F +27 (0)15-307-1767
Ultra Liquors Polokwane ▪ polokwane@ ultraliquors.co.za ▪ T +27 (0)15-297-6808/6851 ▪ F +27 (0)15-297-6809

Mpumalanga
Makro Nelspruit ▪ www.makro.co.za ▪ T +27 (0)860-009-548
Metro Liquor Burgersfort ▪ T +27 (0)13-231-7891/2 ▪ F +27 (0)13-231-7018
Metro Liquor Bushbuckridge ▪ T +27 (0)13 799 0448/9 ▪ F +27 (0)13-799-0401
Metro Liquor Ermelo ▪ T +27 (0)17-819-7402 ▪ F +27 (0)17-811-6582
Metro Liquor Hazyview ▪ T +27 (0)13-737-6314 ▪ T +27 (0)13-737-6315
Metro Liquor Nelspruit ▪ T +27 (0)13-753-2146 ▪ T +27 (0)13-752-2915
Metro Liquor Witbank ▪ T +27 (0)13-656-2497 ▪ F +27 (0)13-656-6109
Picardi Rebel Witbank ▪ www.picardirebel.co.za ▪ T +27 (0)13-656-6697 ▪ F +27 (0)13-656-6692
Windmill Wine Shop & Cottages (R536 between Hazyview & Sabie) ▪ info@thewindmill.co.za ▪ www.thewindmill.co.za ▪ T +27 (0)13-737-8175 / +27(0)82-930-6289 ▪ F +27 (0)13-737-8966

Northern Cape

Metro Liquor Kimberley ▪ T +27 (0)53-833-4340 ▪ T +27 (0)53-832-0902

Zebrani Liquor City (Upington) ▪ T/f +27 (0)54-331-2831

North West

De Wijnwinkel (Wolmaransstad) ▪ gert@pop.co.za ▪ T +27 (0)83-262-0387 / +27 (0)18-596-1606 ▪ F +27 (0)18-596-2890

Picardi Rebel Rustenburg ▪ www.picardirebel.co.za ▪ T +27 (0)14-537-3414 ▪ F +27 (0)14-537-3410

Sharbel Wine (Broederstroom) ▪ phillip@sharbelwine.co.za, sales@sharbelwine.co.za ▪ www.sharbelwine.co.za ▪ T +27 (0)82-839-2957/ +27 (0)12-333-7921 ▪ F +27 (0)86-272-1314

Western Cape

Aroma Fine Wine Centres Constantia (Aroma Liquors Alphen): ▪ alphen@aroma.co.za ▪ T +27 (0)21-794-8693 ▪ F +27 (0)21-794-8694 ▪ Canal Walk (Century City): aromacwa@aroma.co.za ▪ T +27 (0)21-551-7511 ▪ F +27 (0)21-981-5411

Bergkelder Vinoteque Wine Bank See Die Bergkelder Vinoteque Wine Bank

Bottelary Hills Wine Centre (Stellenbosch) ▪ bhwc@telkomsa.net ▪ www.bhwc.co.za ▪ T +27 (0)21-865-2955 ▪ F +27 (0)21-865-2885

Caroline's Fine Wine Cellar (Cape Town) ▪ carowine@mweb.co.za, carowine3@mweb.co.za ▪ www.carolineswine.com ▪ Strand Str: T +27 (0)21-419-8984 ▪ F +27 (0)21-419-8985 ▪ V&A Waterfront: T +27 (0)21-425-5701 ▪ F +27 (0)21-425-5702

Chapmans Peak Wine & Spirits (Hout Bay, Cape Town) ▪ wine@cpws.co.za, lidia@cpws.co.za ▪ T +27 (0)21-790-1088 ▪ F +27 (0)21-790-1089

Darling Wine Shop ▪ www.darlingwine.co.za ▪ wineshop@darlingwine.co.za ▪ T +27 (0)22-492-3971/+27 (0)74-194-1711

De Wijngarten Wine Boutique (Bonnievale) ▪ dewijngarten1@telkomsa.net ▪ www.dewijngarten.co.za ▪ T +27 (0)23-616-2367 ▪ F +27 (0)23-616-3160

Die Bergkelder Vinoteque Wine Bank (Stellenbosch) ▪ info@bergkelder.co.za ▪ www.bergkelder.co.za ▪ T +27 (0)21-809-8280 ▪ F +27 (0)21-883-9533 ▪ See also under Die Bergkelder Wine Centre in the A–Z section

House of Wines (Franschhoek) ▪ info@how.za.net ▪ T/F +27 (0)21-876-4120

La Cotte Inn Wine Sales/Fromages de France (Franschhoek) ▪ info@lacotte.co.za ▪ www.lacotte.co.za ▪ T +27 (0)21-876-3775 ▪ F +27 (0)21-876-3036

La Verne Wine Boutique (Robertson) ▪ T +27 (0)23-626-4314 ▪ F +27 (0)23-626-1916 ▪ info@lavernewines.co.za ▪ www.lavernewines.co.za

Metro Liquor George ▪ T +27 (0)44-874-1370 ▪ F +27 (0)44-874-1377

Metro Liquor Oudtshoorn ▪ T +27 (0)44-272-0602 ▪ F +27 (0)44-279-1568

Metro Liquor Vuyani ▪ T +27 (0)21-364-4901 ▪ F +27 (0)21-364-4906

Makro Montagu Gardens ▪ www.makro.co.za ▪ T +27 (0)860-308-999 ▪ F (0)860-408-999

Makro Ottery ▪ www.makro.co.za ▪ T +27 (0)21-704-7400 ▪ F +27 (0)21-703-6348

Manuka Fine Wines (Somerset West) ▪ southeys@manuka.co.za ▪ www.manuka.co.za ▪ T +27 (0)21-851-6060 ▪ F +27 (0)86-665-1051

Mooiberge (Stellenbosch) ▪ winery@zetler.co.za ▪ www.zetler.co.za ▪ T +27 (0)21-881-3222 ▪ +27 (0)21 8813017

Old Cape Wine Shop Imhoff Farm (Kommetjie) ▪ info@ocws.co.za ▪ www.ocws.co.za ▪ T +27 (0)21-783-5054

Picardi Rebel Claremont (Main Rd) ▪ claremont@picardirebel.co.za ▪ www.picardirebel.co.za ▪ T +27 (0)21-671-9611 ▪ F +27 (0)21-683-9025

Picardi Rebel Mainstream Centre (Hout Bay) houtbaycellars@picardirebel.co.za ▪ www.picardirebel.co.za ▪ T +27 (0)21-790-7273 ▪ F +27 (0)21-791-3211

Picardi Rebel Longbeach Mall (Noordhoek) ▪ www.picardirebel.co.za ▪ T +27 (0)21-785-3323 ▪ F +27 (0)21-785-3318

Picardi Rebel Parklands Junction (Parklands) ▪ parklandsjunction@picardirebel.co.za ▪ www.picardirebel.co.za ▪ T +27 (0)21-556-1877 ▪ F +27 (0)21-556-8556

Picardi Rebel Rosmead Ave (Claremont) ▪ www.picardirebel.co.za ▪ T +27 (0)21-683-1406 ▪ F +27 (0)21-674-2094

Picardi Rebel Spearhead (Cape Town Foreshore) ▪ spearhead@picardirebel.co.za ▪ www.picardirebel.co.za ▪ T +27 (0)21-425-1664 ▪ F +27 (0)21-425-9443

Picardi Rebel Sun Valley ▪ www.picardirebel.co.za ▪ T +27 (0)21-785-2149 ▪ F +27 (0)21-785-2942

Picardi Rebel Tygervalley ▪ www.picardirebel.co.za ▪ T +27 (0)21-914-1649 ▪ F +27 (0)21-914-2420

Picardi Rebel Victoria Ave (Hout Bay) ▪ winebarrel@picardirebel.co.za ▪ www.picardirebel.co.za ▪ T +27 (0)21-790-0039 ▪ F +27 (0)21-790-0552

Picardi Rebel Willowbridge ▪ willowbridge@ picardirebel.co.za ▪ www.picardirebel.co.za ▪ T +27 (0)21-914-3506 ▪ F +27 (0)21-914-3508

Rubin's Liquor Store (Cape Town) ▪ ian@ rubins.co.za, orders@rubins.co.za ▪ T +27 (0)21-425-4692/3 ▪ F +27 (0)21-419-9405

Simon's Town Bottle Store (Cape Town) ▪ aaronlin@hotmail.com ▪ T +27 (0)21-786-1438 ▪ F +27 (0)21-786-1440

Something To Wine About (Rawsonville) ▪ nell.karlien@gmail.com ▪ +27 (0)23-349-1882 / +27 (0)82-461-3127 ▪ +27 (0)86-514-7893

Steven Rom Wine Merchants & Exporters (Cape Town) ▪ www.stevenrom.co.za, www.thewinemerchant.co.za ▪ mario@ stevenrom.co.za ▪ Sea Point: T +27 (0)21-439-6043 ▪ F +27 (0)21-434-0401 ▪ Three Anchor Bay: T +27 (0)21-439-1112 ▪ F +27 (0)21-434-0401 ▪ Kloof Street: T +27 (0)21-424-8476 ▪ F +27 (0)21-426-0546

The Vineyard Connection (Stellenbosch/ Muldersvlei) ▪ info@vineyardconnection.co.za, wine@vineyardconnection.co.za, lara@ vineyardconnection.co.za ▪ www.vineyardconnection.co.za ▪ T +27 (0)21-884-4360 ▪ F +27 (0)21-884-4361

The Wine Kollective (Riebeek Kasteel) ▪ espost@ telkomsa.net ▪ T +27 (0)22-448-1008 / +27 (0)82-776-9366

The Wine Shop at Constantia Uitsig (Constantia) ▪ www.constantia-uitsig.com ▪ wine@uitsig.co.za ▪ T +27 (0)21-794-1810 ▪ F +27 (0)21-794-1812

Ultra Liquors Goodwood ▪ goodwood@ ultraliquors.co.za ▪ T +27 (0)21-591-5581 / +27 (0)21-592-5812 ▪ F +27 (0)21-591-8492

Ultra Liquors Greenpoint ▪ greenpoint@ ultraliquors.co.za ▪ T +27 (0)21-434-4847/38/ 4302 ▪ F +27 (0)21-434-7548

Ultra Liquors Parow ▪ parow@ultraliquors.co.za ▪ T +27 (0)21-930- 2415/6/2453 ▪ F +27 (0)21-930-4007

Ultra Liquors Wynberg ▪ wynburg@ ultraliquors.co.za ▪ T +27 (0)21-762-5885/1473 ▪ F +27 (0)21-761-6005

Vaughan Johnson's Wine & Cigar Shop See A–Z section for details

Vino Pronto (Cape Town) ▪ sales@vinopronto.co.za ▪ T +27 (0)21-424-5587 ▪ F +27 (0)21-424-5587

Wade Bales Wine Society (Cape Town) ▪ info@ thewinesociety.co.za ▪ www.wadebaleswinesociety.co.za ▪ T +27 (0)21-794-2151 ▪ F +27 (0)21-794-2821

Wine & Company (Hermanus) ▪ wineandco@ whalemail.co.za ▪ www.wineandcompany.co.za ▪ T +27 (0)28-313-2047 / +27 (0)82-355-4346 ▪ F +27 (0)866-101-800

Wine Boutique (L'Agulhas) ▪ wine.boutique@ telkomsa.net ▪ T/F +27 (0)28-435-7931

Wine Cellar – Fine Wine Importers (incl insulated/secure maturation cellars) ▪ info@ winecellar.co.za ▪ www.winecellar.co.za ▪ T +27 (0)21-448-4105

Wine Concepts (Cape Town) ▪ www.wineconcepts.co.za ▪ Newlands: newlandshop@wineconcepts.co.za, michael@ wineconcepts.co.za, corlien@wineconcepts.co.za ▪ T +27 (0)21-671-9030 / +27 (0)87-807-7854 ▪ F +27 (0)21-671-9031 ▪ Kloof Str: kloofst@ wineconcepts.co.za ▪ T +27 (0)21-426-4401 ▪ F +27 (0)88-021-426-4401

Wines (Franschhoek) ▪ www.winescourier.com ▪ wines@project19.co.za, elsa@project19.co.za ▪ T +27 (0)21-876-3185 / +27 (0)83-458-9835 ▪ F +27 (0)866-393-919

Wine Village Hermanus ▪ wine@hermanus.co.za, winevillage@hermanus.co.za ▪ www.winevillage.co.za ▪ T +27 (0)28-316-3988 ▪ F +27 (0)86-509-4931

Online Wine Shops

Arriba Liquor Merchants ▪ www.arriba.co.za

Cape Ardor ▪ www.cape-ardor.com

Cape Wine Cellars ▪ www.capewinecellars.com

Cybercellar.com ▪ www.cybercellar.com

eWine ▪ www.ewine.co.za

Getwine ▪ www.getwine.co.za

Hermanuspietersfontein Wine Shop ▪ www.hpf1855.co.za

Manuka Wine Exports ▪ www.manuka.co.za

Michelangelo Int. Wine Awards Wine Shop ▪ www.michelangeloawards.com

The Wine Registry ▪ www.thewineregistry.co.za

SaleWine.co.za ▪ www.salewine.co.za

SA Wines ▪ www.sawines.com

Wine Cellar ▪ www.winecellar.co.za

Wine-Club ▪ www.wine-club.co.za

Wine Direct ▪ www.winedirectonline.co.za

Wine Village Hermanus ▪ www.wine-village.co.za

WineWeb ▪ www.wineweb.co.za

See also A–Z section for wineries' own online retail facilities.

Specialist Wine Shippers

Cape Grape & Wine Logistics ▪ motti@aspiring.co.za ▪ www.aspiring.co.za ▪ T +27 (0)21-881-3477 ▪ F +27 (0)21-881-3476

The Vineyard Connection ▪ info@ vineyardconnection.co.za, wine@ vineyardconnection.co.za, lara@ vineyardconnection.co.za ▪ www.vineyardconnection.co.za ▪ T +27 (0)21-884-4360 ▪ F +27 (0)21-884-4361

A-Code Numbers & Codes

Many wines appear on the market under brand names, with, at first glance, no reference to their producers or purveyors. However, consumers need not buy 'blind', and may trace a wine's provenance by checking the official 'A-number' which appears on the bottle or pack. This identity code tells you either who produced the wine, or who sourced it for resale. In the latter case, an enquiry to the merchant should elicit the source. The list keeps growing and being revised, and is too lengthy to reproduce in this guide. Via the online SAWIS portal (**www.sawis.co.za**), it is possible however to search the list of A-codes, as well as the certification codes issued for each wine by the Wine & Spirit Board, for details about the production area, variety and vintage.

Recent Cape Vintages

South African wines do not exhibit the major vintage variations seen in some winegrowing areas. There are, nevertheless, perceptible differences from year to year. Dry, hot summers are the norm but a variety of factors make generalisations difficult and possibly misleading.

2012 Unusually dry, hot January strained unirrigated vineyards; otherwise good to very good vintage for both reds and whites; moderate alcohol levels.

2011 Yet more variable than the last, impossible to generalise. As in 2010, producer's track record should guide the buying/cellaring decision.

2010 A real test of the winegrower's savvy, and one of the toughest recent harvests to call. Be guided by producer's track record.

2009 Perhaps one of the greatest vintages. Late, gruelling, but whites and reds both stellar.

2008 Long, wet, late and challenging but also unusually cool, favouring elegance in reds and whites.

2007 Elegant, structured whites; smaller red-grape berries gave intense colour and fruit concentration.

2006 Perhaps the best white-wine vintage in a decade — particularly expressive sauvignon and chenin. Fleshy, mild-tannined reds, with lower alcohols.

2005 Short, early and particularly challenging. Concentrated if alcoholic reds; mostly average whites, some stellar exceptions.

2004 Cooler dry conditions yielded elegant, often ageworthy wines with lower alcohols and yielding tannins.

2003 Outstanding, especially for reds — concentrated and structured, and often slow to show their best.

Older Vintages

2002 Challenging and patchy, but top producers show fine concentration and moderate alcohol levels. **2001** Some excellent reds — fruity and concentrated, best are long-lived. Flavourful if alcoholic whites. **2000** Powerful and concentrated reds, befitting a hot year; the best have kept very well. Whites generally less impressive and not for long ageing. **1999** Fat, alcoholic reds with ripe fruit for earlier drinking. Generally not too much excitement among the whites. **1998** Excellent red vintage with enough fruit for extended cellaring; whites generally not for keeping. **1997** Among coolest and latest vintages on record. Supple, elegant reds; some excellent and stylish whites. **1996** Generally awkward reds, not for keeping; whites, except for top NLHs, best drunk up. **1995** For many, the vintage of the 90s. Concentrated reds, some still maturing spectacularly. **1994** Hottest, driest vintage in decades; variable quality; new-clone cabs and early ripening reds fared well. **1993** Without serious mishaps; some excellent sauvignons; above-average reds. **1992** Coolish season, favouring whites, especially sauvignon; the reds (notably pinotage) very good; **1991** Dry, warm to hot, favouring early to mid-season ripeners; some long-lasting reds. **1990** Uneven year, alternately cool and warm; average whites and reds; not for further ageing. The **1980s**: even years (82, 84, 86) were usually more favourable for reds; uneven years, marginally cooler, favoured whites, but 'white' years 87 and, especially, 89 produced remarkable reds. The **1970s**: again, even years generally favoured reds. Best was 74; but top wines from some other vintages are still delicious. The **1960s** and earlier yielded some astonishingly long-lived wines, prompting a new look at the traditional 'dikvoet' winemaking style.

South African Wine Styles

Blanc de blancs White wine made from white grapes only; also used for champagne and méthode cap classique.

Blanc fumé or **fumé blanc** Dry white from sauvignon, usually but not necessarily wooded (nor smoked, smoky).

Blanc de noir A pink wine (shades range from off-white through peach to pink) made from red grapes. See also Rosé.

Blend See Varietal wine and Cape Blend.

Brut See Sugar or sweetness, and Sparkling wine.

Cap classique See Sparkling wine.

Cape Blend Evolving term, increasingly used to denote a (red) blend with pinotage, the 'local' grape making up a significant part of the assemblage; sometimes simply a blend showing a distinct 'Cape' character; occasionally used for chenin-based blends.

Carbonated See Sparkling wine.

Cultivar Grape variety (a contraction of 'cultivated variety').

Cuvée French term for the blend of a wine.

Demi-sec See Sugar or sweetness.

Dessert wine A sweet wine, often to accompany the dessert but sometimes pleasurably prior, as in the famous Sauternes/foie gras combo.

Dry to sweet See Sugar or sweetness.

Estate wine Term now reserved for wine originating from an officially registered 'unit for the production of estate wine' (see www.sawis.co.za for current list).

Fortified wines Increased in alcoholic strength by the addition of spirit, by SA law to minimum 15% alcohol by volume.

Grand cru See Premier Grand Cru.

Jerepiko or **jerepigo** Red or white wine, produced without fermentation; grape juice is fortified with grape spirit, preventing fermentation; very sweet, with considerable unfermented grape flavours.

Kosher See Winemaking terms section.

Late Harvest Sweet wine from late-harvested and therefore sweeter grapes. See Sugar or sweetness.

Méthode cap classique (MCC) See Sparkling wine.

Noble Late Harvest (NLH) Sweet dessert wine (still, perlé or sparkling) exhibiting a noble rot (botrytis) character, from grapes infected by the *botrytis cinerea* fungus. This mould, in warm, misty autumn weather, attacks the skins of ripe grapes, causing much of the juice to evaporate. As the berries wither, their sweetness and flavour become powerfully concentrated. SA law dictates that grapes for NLH must be harvested at a minimum of 28° Balling and residual sugar must exceed 50g/L.

Nouveau Term originated in Beaujolais for fruity young and light red, usually from gamay and made by the carbonic maceration method. Bottled soon after vintage to capture the youthful, fresh flavour of fruit and yeasty fermentation.

Perlant, perlé, pétillant Lightly sparkling, usually carbonated wine.

Port Fortified dessert with ever-improving quality record in Cape since late 1980s, partly through efforts of Cape Port Producers' Association which recommends use of word 'Cape' to identify the local product. Following are CPPA-defined styles: **Cape White**: non-muscat grapes, wood-aged min 6 months, any size vessel; **Cape Ruby**: blended, fruity, components aged min 6 months, up to 3 years depending on size of vessel. Average age min 1 year. **Cape Vintage**: fruit of one harvest; dark, full-bodied, vat-aged (any size); **Cape**

Vintage Reserve: fruit of one harvest in year of 'recognised quality'. Preferably aged min 1 year, vats of any size, sold only in glass; **Cape Late Bottled Vintage** (LBV): fruit of single 'year of quality', full-bodied, slightly tawny colour, aged 3–6 years (of which min 2 years in oak); **Cape Tawny**: wood-matured, amber-orange (tawny) colour, smooth, slightly nutty taste (white grapes not permitted); **Cape Dated Tawny**: single-vintage tawny.

Premier Grand Cru Unlike in France, not a quality rating in SA — usually an austerely dry white.

Residual sugar See Sugar or sweetness.

Rosé Pink wine, made from red or a blend of red and white grapes. The red grape skins are removed before the wine takes up too much colour.

Single-vineyard wine Classification for wines from officially registered vineyards, no larger than 6ha in size and planted with a single variety.

Sparkling wine Bubbly, or 'champagne', usually white but sometimes rosé and even red, given its effervescence by carbon dioxide — allowed to escape in the normal winemaking process. **Champagne** undergoes its second fermentation in the bottle. Under an agreement with France, SA does not use the term, which describes the sparkling wines from the Champagne area. Instead, **méthode cap classique** (MCC) is the SA term to describe sparkling wines made by the classic method. **Charmat** undergoes its second, bubble-forming fermentation in a tank and is bottled under pressure. **Carbonated** sparklers are made by the injection of carbon dioxide bubbles (as in fizzy soft drinks). See also Sugar or sweetness.

Special Late Harvest (SLH) SA designation for a lighter dessert-style wine. There is no legal stipulation for residual sugar content, but if the RS is below 20g/L, the label must state 'extra dry', 'dry', 'semi-dry' or 'sweet', as the case may be. The minimum alcohol content is 11% by volume.

Stein Semi-sweet white wine, usually a blend and often confused with steen, a grape variety (chenin blanc), though most steins are at least made partly from steen grapes.

Sugar or sweetness In still wines: extra-dry or bone-dry wines have less than 2.5g/L residual sugar, undetectable to the taster. A wine legally is dry up to 5g/L. Taste buds will begin picking up a slight sweetness, or softness, in a wine — depending on its acidity — at about 6g/L, when it is still off-dry. By about 8–9g/L a definite sweetness can usually be noticed. However, an acidity of 8–9g/L can render a sweet wine fairly crisp even with a sugar content of 20g/L plus. Official sweetness levels in SA wine are listed in the table opposite.

Varietal wine From a single variety of grape. Legislation requires the presence in the wine of 85% of the stated variety or vintage. Blends may name component parts only if those components were vinified separately, prior to blending; then they are listed with the larger contributor(s) named first. If any one of the blend partners is less than 20%, percentages for all the varieties must be given. Blends may be vinified separately in any recognised WO area; component areas may be named, as above except the threshold is 30%.

Vintage In SA primarily used to denote year of harvest. Not a quality classification (a 'vintage' port in Europe means one from an officially declared great port-grape year).

Wine	Sugar (g/l)
Still wines	
Extra-dry	≤ 2.5
Dry	≤ 5
Semi-dry	5 ≤ 12
Semi-sweet	> 5 <30
Late Harvest	≥ 20
Special Late Harvest (SLH)	–
Natural Sweet (or Sweet Natural)	> 20
Noble Late Harvest (NLH)	> 50
Naturally dried grape wine (straw wine)	> 30
Sparkling wines	
Brut nature	<3
Extra brut	<6
Brut	<12
Extra-dry	12–17
Dry	17–32
Semi-sweet	32–50
Sweet	> 50

Winetasting Terms

Short of a ready description? Here are a few frequently-used words, phrases and explanations that may be helpful. See also Winemaking terms; SA wine styles.

Accessible, approachable Flavours and feel of the wine are harmonious, easily recognised; it is ready to drink.

Aftertaste The lingering flavours and impressions of a wine; its persistence — the longer, the better.

Alcoholic 'Hot' or, in excess, burning character caused by imbalanced or excessive alcohol. Also simply spiritous.

Astringent Mouth-puckering sensation in the mouth, associated with high tannin (and sometimes acid); also bitter, sharp.

Aroma Smells in the bouquet, or nose, especially the odours associated with the grape rather than the winemaking process.

Attack First sensations on palate/nose — pungent, aggressive, quiet etc.

Austere Usually meaning unyielding, sometimes harsh. Sometimes, more favourably, to imply a notable restraint/refinement.

Backbone The wine is well formed, firm, not flabby or insipid.

Baked 'Hot', earthy quality. Usually from scorched/shrivelled grapes which have been exposed too long to the sun, or from too warm a barrel fermentation, especially in some whites.

Balance Desirable attribute. The wine's chief constituents — alcohol, acid, tannin, fruit and wood (where used) — are in harmony.

Bead Bubbles in sparkling wine; a fine, long-lasting bead is the most desirable. See also Mousse.

Big Expansive in the mouth, weighty, full-bodied, as a result of high alcohol or fruit concentration.

Bite or **grip** Imparted by tannin, acid and/or alcohol, important in young wines designed for ageing. If overdone can impart undesirable bitterness, harshness or spiry 'glow'.

Bitter Sensation perceived mainly on the back of the tongue, and in the finish of the wine. Usually unpleasant, though an accepted if not immediately admired character of certain Italian wines. Sometimes more positively associated with the taste of a specific fruit or nut, such as cherry-kernel or almond.

Body Fullness on the palate.

Botrytis/ed Exhibits a noble rot/botrytis character, from grapes infected by the *botrytis cinerea* fungus.

Bottle-age Negative or positive, depending on context. Positively describes development of aromas/flavours (ie complexity) as wine moves from youth to maturity. Much-prized attribute in fine whites

and reds. Negatively, bottle age results in a wine with stale, empty or even off odours.

Buttery Flavour and texture associated with barrel-fermented white wines, especially chardonnays; rich, creamy smoothness.

Claret Another name for a dry red Bordeaux or Bordeaux-like red.

Classic Showing characteristics of the classics of Bordeaux, Burgundy etc; usually implying balance, elegance, subtlety.

Coarse Rough, unbalanced tannins, acid, alcohol or oak.

Complexity Strong recommendation. A complex wine has several layers of flavour, usually developing with age/maturation. See Bottle age.

Concentration See Intensity.

Confected Over-elaborately constructed, artificial, forced; sometimes overly sweet.

Corked, corky Wine is faulty; its flavours have been tainted by yeast, fungal or bacterial infections, often but not necessarily from the cork. It smells damp and mouldy in its worst stages — but sometimes it's barely detectable. In a restaurant, a corked wine should be rejected and returned immediately; producers are honour-bound to replace corked wine.

Creamy Not literally creamy, of course; more a silky, buttery feel and texture.

Crisp Refers to acidity. Positively, means fresh, clean; negatively, too tart, sharp.

Deep and **depth** Having many layers; intense; also descriptive of a serious wine.

Dense Well-padded texture, flavour packed.

Deposits (also sediment or crust) Tasteless and harmless tartrates, acid crystals or tannin in older red wines. Evidence that wine has not been harshly fined, filtered or cold-stabilised.

Dried out Bereft of fruit, harder constituents remaining; tired.

Earthy Usually positive, wine showing its origins from soil, minerals, damp leaves, mushrooms etc.

Easy Undemanding (and hopefully inexpensive).

Elegant Stylish, refined, 'classic'.

Esters Scents and smells usually generated by alcohols and acids in wine. A wine may be 'estery' when these characteristics are prominent.

Extract An indication of the 'substance' of a wine, expressed as sugar-free or total extract (which would include some sugars). 18g/L would be low, light; anything much above 23g/L in whites is significant; the corresponding threshold for reds is around 30g/L.

Fat Big, full, ample in the mouth.

Finesse Graceful, polished. Nothing excessive.

Finish The residual sensations — tastes and textures — after swallowing. Should be pleasant (crisp, lively) and enduring, not short, dull or flat. See also Length.

Firm Compact, has good backbone.

Flabby Usually, lacking backbone, especially acid.

Flat Characterless, unexciting, lacks acid. Or bubbly which has lost its fizz.

Fleshy Very positive, meaning a wine is well fleshed out with texture and grape flavours.

Flowery, **floral** Flower-like (ie the smell of rose, honeysuckle, jasmine etc). Distinct from 'fruity' (ie smell/taste of papaya, cantaloupe, grape! etc).

Forward rather than shy; advancing in age too; mature.

Fresh Lively, youthful, invigorating. Closely related to the amount of acid in the wine and absence of oxidative character: a big, intensely sweet dessert without a backbone of acidity will taste flat and sickly; enough acid and the taste is fresh and uncloying.

Fruity See Flowery.

Full High in alcohol and extract.

Gamey Overripe, decadent, not universally unattractive; also meaty, 'wild'.

Gravel/ly With suggestions of mineral, earthy quality; also firm texture.

Green Usually unripe, sour; also herbaceous; sometimes simply youthful.

Grip Gripping, firm on palate, in finish. Acid, tannin, alcohol are contributors.

Heady Usually refers to the smell of a wine. High in alcohol; intense, high-toned.

Herbaceous Grassy, hay-like, heathery; can also indicate under-ripeness.

Hollow Lacking substance, flavours.

Honey or **honeyed** Sometimes literally a honey/beeswax taste or flavour; a sign of developing maturity in some varieties or more generally a sign of bottle-age.

Hot Burning sensation of alcohol in finish.

Intensity No flab, plenty of driving flavour; also deep colour.

Lean Thin, mean, lacking charm of ample fruit; also, more positively, compact, sinewy.

Lees/leesy Taste-imparting dead yeast cells (with grape skins and other solid matter) remaining with wine in tank/barrel (or bottle in the case of *méthode champenoise* sparkling wines) after fermentation. The longer the wine is 'on its lees' (*sur lie*) the more richness and flavour it should absorb.

Light/lite Officially wines under 10% alcohol by volume; also light in body (and often short on taste); a health-conscious trend in both reds and whites.

Lively Bouncy, fresh flavours.

Long or **length** Enduring; wine's flavours reverberate on the palate long after swallowing.

Maderised Oxidised and flat; colour is often brownish. Over-mature.

Meaty Sometimes suggesting a general savouriness; but also literally the aroma of meat — raw, smoked etc.

Mousse Fizz in sparkling wines; usually refers also to quality, size and effervescence of the bubbles. See also Bead.

Mouthfeel, **mouthfilling** Texture, feel; racy, crispness (fine with appropriate dishes) or generous, supple, smooth.

Neutral What it says, neither here nor there.

New World Generally implies accessible, bold, often extrovert (in terms of fruit and use of oak). **Old World** embraces terms like subtle, complex, less oaky, more varied and generally more vinous (than fruity). See also Classic.

Oaky Having exaggerated oak aromas/flavours (vanilla, spice, char, woodsmoke etc). Oak balanced by fruit in young wines may lessen with age, but over-oaked young wines (where fruit is not in balance) will become over-oaked old wines.

Palate Combination of flavour, taste and texture of a wine.

Pebbly See Gravelly.

Perfumed or **scented** Strong fragrances (fruity, flowery, animal etc)

Plump Well fleshed in a charming, cherubic way.

Porty Heavy, over-ripe, stewed; a negative in unfortified wine.

Rich Flavourful, intense, generous. Not necessarily sweet.

Robust Strapping, full-bodied (but not aggressive).

Rough Bull-in-a-china-shop wine, or throat sandpapering quality.

Round Well balanced, without gawkiness or jagged edges.

Sharp or **tart** All about acid, usually unbalanced. But occasionally sharpish, fresh wine is right for the occasion.

Short or **quick** Insubstantial wine, leaving little impression.

Simple One-dimensional or no flavour excitement.

Stalky Unripe, bitter, stemmy.

Stewed Over-ripe, cooked, soft, soggy fruit.

Structure Vague word, usually refers to the wine's make up (acid, tannin, alcohol) in relation to its ageing ability; if a wine is deemed to have 'the structure to age' it suggests these principal preservatives are in place.

Stylish Classy, distinguished; also voguish.

Supple Very desirable (not necessarily subtle), yielding, refined texture and flavours. See also Mouthfeel.

Tannic Tannins are prominent in the wine, imparting, positively, a mouth-puckering, grippy, tangy quality; negatively, a harsh, unyielding character.

Tension Racy, nervous fruity-acid play on the palate.

Terpene(s)/terpenoid Strong, floral compounds influencing the aromas of especially riesling, gewürztraminer and the muscats; with bottle-age, terpenes often develop a pungent resinous oiliness.

Texture Tactile 'feel' in the mouth: hard, acidic, coarse and alcoholic; or, smooth, velvety, 'warm'.

Toasty Often used for barrel-fermented or -aged wines showing a pleasant biscuity, charry character.

Vegetal Grassy, leafy, herby — in contrast to fruity, flowery, oaky. Overdone, a no-no.

Yeasty Warm bakery smells, often evident in barrel-fermented whites and *méthode champenoise* sparkling wines, where yeasts stay in contact with the wine after fermentation.

Winemaking Terms

A few brief reference explanations. See also sections Winetasting Terms, SA Wine Styles.

Acid and **acidity** The fresh — or, in excess, sharp or tart — taste of wine. Too little acid and the wine tastes dull and flat. In SA, winemakers are permitted to adjust acidity either by adding acid — at any stage before bottling — or by lowering the acid level with a de-acidifier. See also Volatile acid and Malolactic.

Alcohol Essential component of wine, providing fullness, richness and, at higher levels, sometimes an impression of sweetness. Also a preservative, helping keep wines in good condition. Produced by yeasts fermenting the sugars in the grape. Measured by volume of the total liquid. Most unfortified table wines in SA have between 11% and 14.5% alc by vol; fortifieds range from ±16% to 21%. A variation of up to 1% between the strength stated on the label and the laboratory analysis is permitted by local law. Various techniques (such as reverse osmosis and 'spinning cone', also the addition of water) exist to address the increasingly important issue of high alcohol levels in wine, and some are legal in SA (though not for export to, eg, Europe).

Barrels (**barrel-aged**; **barrel-fermented**) Wines are transferred into barrels to age, pick up oaky flavours etc. When must or fermenting must is put into barrels, the resulting wine is called barrel-fermented. A barrel or cask is generally a 225–500L oak container; *barrique* is a French word for a 225L barrel; a pipe, adapted from the Portuguese *pipa*, usually indicates a vessel of 530–630L; vat is a term generally used for larger (2,000–5,000L) wooden vessels.

Batonnage See Lees.

Biodynamic See Organic.

Blend A wine made from two or more different grape varieties, vintages, vineyards or containers. Some of the world's finest wines are blends.

Bottles While the 750ml (75cl) bottle is now the most widely used size of container for wine, it is by no means the only one. Smaller bottles (375 & 500ml) are popular with restaurants and airlines, and larger sizes are prized by collectors because of their novelty value and/or their tendency to promote slower wine ageing. The following are the larger bottle sizes (note: some no longer in production):

Capacity		Bordeaux	Champagne/Burgundy
litres	bottles		
1.5	2	Magnum	Magnum
3	4	Double magnum	Jéroboam
4.5	6	Jéroboam	Rehoboam
6	8	Impériale	Methuselah
9	12	—	Salmanazar
12	16	—	Balthazar
15	20	—	Nebuchadnezzar

Brettanomyces or **'brett'** Naturally occurring yeast, usually associated with red wine and regarded as a spoilage factor, because its growth triggers the formation of volatile acids, phenols and other compounds which, in sufficient concentration, impart a range of unpleasant characters, from barnyard to sweat to cheese. At low concentrations, can enhance complexity and character.

Carbonic maceration or **maceration carbonique** Method of fermenting wine without first crushing the grapes. Whole clusters with stalks etc are put into closed vat; intracellular fermentation occurs within the grape berries, which then burst.

Chaptalisation Originally French term for the addition of sugar to grape must to raise the alcohol of a wine. Selectively legal in northern Europe, where acid adjustments are not allowed as they are in SA. Winemakers in both hemispheres bend the rules.

Charmat Method of making sparkling wine in a sealed tank (*cuvée close*) under pressure. Easier, cheaper than *méthode champenoise*.

Chips See Oak chips.

Cold ferment 'Cold' is a relative term; applied to fermentation of mainly white wines in temperature-controlled tanks, it refers to a temperature around usually 13–16°C. The benefits, especially important in a warm country, include conserving the primary fruit aromas and ensuring fermentation is carried out steadily and thoroughly.

Cold soak or **cold maceration**. Red winemaking method carried out prior to fermentation. Skins and juice are held, usually for a few days, at a sufficiently cool temperature to prevent fermentation. The theory is that this extracts more favourable colour and aromas than after fermentation.

Cold stabilisation Keeping a wine at about –4°C for a week or more to precipitate tartaric acid and 'clean up' the wine, preventing later formation of (harmless) tartrate crystals in bottle. Some winemakers believe this process damages flavour and prefer to avoid it.

Disgorgement (*dégorgement* in French) Important stage in the production of traditionally fermented sparkling where accumulated sediment (or lees), which could cloud the finished wine, is removed from the neck of the bottle.

Dosage The sugar added to sparkling wine after the second fermentation.

Fermentation The conversion of sugar in grapes into alcohol and carbon dioxide, a function of enzymes secreted by yeasts. Wild yeasts occur in vineyards and wineries, but in modern Cape winemaking cultured yeasts are normally added to secure the process. Beyond about 15% of alcohol, yeasts are overwhelmed and fermentation ceases, although it usually is stopped (for instance by cooling, filtration or the addition of alcohol) before this stage. See also Malolactic.

Filtration Removes last impurities including **yeast** cells. Done excessively, can thin a wine. Some traditionalists bottle without cold- or protein-stabilisation or filtration.

Fining and **protein stabilisation** Fining is ridding wine of suspended particles by adding substances that attract and draw the particles from the wine.

Flash-pasteurisation See Kosher.

Free run After grapes have been de-stalked and crushed, juice runs freely.

Garage wine Generic term for wine made in minuscule quantities, sometimes literally in a garage; a grower of such wine is sometimes called a *garagiste*.

Glycerol Minor product of alcoholic fermentation; from the Greek for sweet. Has an apparent sweetening effect on even dry wines and also gives a viscous, mouthfilling character.

Icewine Sweet, concentrated wine from grapes picked and pressed while frozen. Not a recognised category for SA wine production.

Kosher Wine made 'correctly', i.e. under rabbinical supervision, to be suitable for use by religious Jews. Vinification and any initial movement of the wine must be done by an observant Jew. Flash-pasteurisation, increasingly by means of new flavour-preserving processes such as Thermoflash, renders the resulting *meshuval* wine (literally 'boiled' or 'cooked') fit for handling by non-Jews.

Leafroll virus Virus (or complex of viruses), widespread throughout the winegrowing world, which causes the vine to perform below its potential and thereby produce wine which is lower in colour, body and flavour than that derived from virus-free or 'cleaned-up' plants.

Lees Spent yeast cells and other matter which collect at the bottom of any container in winemaking. Yeast autolysis, or decomposition, can impart richness and flavour to a wine, sometimes referred to as leesy. Lees stirring or *batonnage* involves mixing the bed of lees in a barrel or tank through the wine, which is said to be *sur lie*; it is employed primarily on barrel-fermented white wines. The main effects of mixing lees and wine are to prevent off-odours developing from lack of oxygen, to limit the amount of wood tannin and oak character extracted, and to increase flavour.

Malolactic fermentation (malo) Occurs when bacteria convert malic into lactic acids. This reduces the acidity of a wine, a normal and healthy process, especially in reds — provided, of course, it occurs before bottling.

Maturation Ageing properties are closely related to tannin and/or fixed acid content of a wine. A relatively full red wine with tannin has lasting power. With age, it may develop complexity, subtlety and smooth mellowness. Lighter wines with lower tannins are drinkable sooner but probably will not reach the same level of complexity. A number of Cape whites mature well over several years, but most are best drunk in their fruity youth, up to 18 months.

Méthode champenoise Classic method of making champagne by inducing secondary fermentation in the bottle and producing fine bubbles. Due to French restrictions on terminology, Cape sparkling wines made in this way are called méthode cap classique (MCC).

Micro-oxygenation Technique enabling introduction of precise, controlled doses of oxygen to must/wine. Advocates claim softer tannins, more stable colours and other advantages.

Oak chips, either in older barrels or stainless steel tanks, are used increasingly in SA, as are oak **staves**. Still frowned on by some purists, the 'additives' approximate the flavour effects of a new barrel, far more cheaply, more easily handled.

Oak-matured See Barrels.

Organic viticulture/winemaking Increasingly popular alternative to 'conventional' or 'industrialised' winegrowing, emphasising natural and sustainable farming methods and cellar techniques. A variant is biodynamic viticulture, influenced by anthroposophy, focused on improving wine quality through harmony with nature and its rhythms.

Oxidation Change (usually for the worse) due to exposure to air, in whites often producing dark yellow or yellowish colour (called maderisation), altering, 'ageing' the taste. Controlled aeration is used to introduce acceptable and desirable development in wine.

Pasteurisation See Kosher.

pH A chemical notation, used in winemaking and evaluation. The pH of a wine is its effective, active acidity — not in volume but by strength or degree. The reading provides a guide to a wine's keepability. The optimum pH in a wine is somewhere between 3.1 and 3.4 — which significantly improves a wine's protection from bacterial spoilage, so permitting it to mature and develop if properly stored.

Racking Drawing or pumping wine off from one cask or tank to another, to leave behind the deposit or lees.

Reductive Wine in an unevolved, unoxidised state is said to be 'reductive'; usually with a tight, sometimes unyielding character. The absence of air (in a bottled wine) or the presence of substantial sulphur dioxide (anti-oxidant) levels, will inhibit both oxidation and reduction processes, which are linked and complementary.

Reverse osmosis A specialised filtration technique, now permitted in SA for various purposes, including the removal of water from wine. See also Alcohol.

Skin contact After crushing and de-stemming, white grapes may be left for a period with the juice, remaining in contact with skins (before being moved into the press, from which the grape juice is squeezed). Some winemakers believe the colours and flavours in and under the grape skins should be maximised in this way; others believe extended (or any) contact can lead to coarseness, even bitterness.

Spinning cone See Alcohol.

Sulphur dioxide (SO_2) Sterilising agent and preservative, near-ubiquitous in winemaking since antiquity, now strictly controlled. In SA, max total SO_2 level for dry wines is 150–160mg/L; for wines with 5+ g/L sugar it is 200mg/L; and botrytis-style wines 300 mg/L. Any wine with more than 10mg/L total SO_2 must carry the warning 'Contains sulphites' (or 'sulfites') on the label.

Sur lie See Lees.

Tannin Vital preservative in wine, derives primarily from the grape skins. Necessary for a red wine's longevity. A young wine's raw tannin can give it a harshness, but no red wine matures into a great one without tannin, which itself undergoes change, combines with other substances and mellows. Tannin leaves a mouth-puckering dryness about the gums, gives 'grip' to a wine. A wooded wine will usually also contain some wood tannin.

Tartrates Harmless crystals formed by tartaric acid precipitating in non-cold-stabilised wine. Because of lack of public acceptance, usually avoided through cold stabilisation.

Terroir Important, controversial (and in SA overused) French term embracing soil, climate, topography and other elements which constitute the natural environment of a vineyard site and give it a unique character.

Thermovinification/Thermoflash See Kosher.

Unfiltered See Filtration.

Virus or **virused** See Leafroll.

Volatile acid (VA) The part of the acidity which can become volatile. A high reading indicates a wine is prone to spoilage. Recognised at high levels by a sharp, 'hot', vinegary smell. In SA, most wines must by law be below 1.2g/L of VA; in practice, the majority are well below 1g/L.

Whole-bunch pressing or **cluster pressing** Some SA cellars use this age-old process of placing whole bunches directly in the press and gently squeezing. The more usual method is to de-stem and crush the berries before pressing. Whole-bunch pressing is said to yield fresher, cleaner must, and wine lower in polyphenols which, in excess, tend to age wines faster and render them coarser.

Wood-fermented/matured See Barrels.

Yeasts Micro-organisms that secrete enzymes which convert or ferment sugar into alcohol. See fermentation.

Wine Routes, Trusts & Associations

For localised information about regional official wine routes and wineries, contact these organisations:

Breedekloof Wine & Tourism ▪ T +27 (0)23-349-1791 ▪ F +27 (0)23-349-1720 ▪ info@breedekloof.com ▪ www.breedekloof.com

Constantia Valley Wine Route ▪ T +27 (0)21-794-0542 ▪ Karen Michalowsky: karen@constantiavalley.com ▪ Chair: Ian Kilbride ▪ ian@constantiavalley.com ▪ www.constantiavalley.com ▪ T +27 (0)21-795-5199

The Darling Wine & Art Experience ▪ T +27 (0)22-492-3430 (Shaun McLaughlin) ▪ F +27 (0)22-492-2693 ▪ mclaughlin@worldonline.co.za ▪ www.darlingtourism.co.za

Durbanville Boutique Wine Association ▪ T +27 (0)83-357-3864 ▪ F +27 (0)21-948-3441 info@durbanvilleboutiquewine.co.za ▪ www.durbanvilleboutiquewine.co.za

Durbanville Wine Valley Association ▪ T +27 (0)83-310-1228 ▪ info@durbanvillewine.co.za ▪ www.durbanvillewine.co.za

Elim Winegrowers ▪ T +27 (0)28-482-1880/+27 (0)82-551-2351 (Francis Pratt) ▪ wine@theberrio.co.za

Franschhoek See Vignerons de Franschhoek

Green Mountain Eco Route (Elgin/Bot River) ▪ T +27 (0)21-844-0975 ▪ F +27 (0)21-844-0970 ▪ info@greenmountain.co.za ▪ www.greenmountain.co.za

Helderberg See Stellenbosch

Hermanus Wine Route & Hemel-en-Aarde Winegrowers Association ▪ T +27 (0)83-305-7319, +27 (0)28-316-2761 (Frieda Lloyd) ▪ frieda@hermanuswineroute.com ▪ T +27 (0)72-673-1880, +27 (0)28-212-1127 (Carolyn Martin) ▪ carolyn@creationwines.com ▪ www.hermanuswineroute.com

Klein Karoo Wine Route ▪ T +27(0)44-272-7492 / +27 (0)82-214-5910 ▪ F +27 (0)86-528-4055 (Ellen Marais) ▪ info@kleinkaroowines.co.za ▪ www.kleinkaroowines.co.za

Northern Cape Wine Association See Orange River Wine Route

Olifants River Vodacom Wine Route ▪ See West Coast Wine Route

Orange River Wine Route ▪ T +27 (0)54-337-8800 (Karlien Kuhn/Elene Swanepoel) ▪ F +27 (0)54-332-4408 ▪ admin@orangeriverwines.com, info@owk.co.za

Paarl Wine Route ▪ T +27 (0)21-863-4886 ▪ F +27 (0)21-863-4883 ▪ info@paarlwine.co.za ▪ www.paarlwine.co.za

Robertson Wine Valley ▪ T +27 (0)23-626-3167 / +27 (0)83-701-5404 ▪ F +27 (0)23-626-1054 ▪ manager@robertsonwinevalley.com ▪ www.robertsonwinevalley.com

Stellenbosch American Express Wine Routes ▪ T +27 (0)21-886-4310 ▪ F +27 (0)21-886-4330 ▪ info@wineroute.co.za ▪ www.wineroute.co.za

Santam Swartland Wine & Olive Route ▪ T +27 (0)22-487-1133 ▪ F +27 (0)22-487-2063 swartlandinfo@westc.co.za ▪ www.swartlandwineandolives.co.za

Tulbagh Wine Route ▪ T/F +27 (0)23-230-1348/ 75 ▪ tulbaghinfo@lando.co.za ▪ www.tulbaghwineroute.com ▪ www.tulbaghtourism.co.za

Vignerons de Franschhoek ▪ T +27 (0)21-876-2861 ▪ F +27 (0)21-876-2768 ▪ marketing@franschhoek.org.za, office@franschhoek.org.za ▪ www.franschhoek.org.za

Walker Bay Wine Wander ▪ T +27 (0)28-316-3988 ▪ F +27 (0)28-316-3989 / +27 (0)83-509-4931 ▪ wine@hermanus.co.za

Wellington Wine Route ▪ T +27 (0)21-864-2479 ▪ F +27 (0)21-873-4607 ▪ wine@wellington.co.za ▪ www.wellington.co.za

West Coast Wine Route ▪ T +27 (0)82-611-3999 / +27 (0)27-201 3376 / F +27 (0)86-629-9852 ▪ wineroute@vodamail.co.za ▪ www.westcoastwineroute.co.za

Worcester Wine Route ▪ T +27 (0)23-342-8710 ▪ F +27 (0)23-342-2294 ▪ info@worcesterwineroute.co.za ▪ www.worcesterwineroute.co.za

Winelands Tourism Offices

For additional accommodation options, brochures and local advice, contact the information offices and/or publicity associations of the wine areas you plan to visit.

Breedekloof Wine & Tourism ▪ T +27 (0)23-349-1791 ▪ F +27 (0)23-349-1720 ▪ info@breedekloof.com ▪ www.breedekloof.com

Calitzdorp Tourism ▪ T +27 (0)44-213-3775 ▪ F +27 (0)86-569-1447 ▪ tourism@calitzdorp.org.za ▪ www.calitzdorp.org.za

Cape Town Tourism ▪ Contact Centre: T +27 (0)86-132-2223

V&A Waterfront Gateway Information Office ▪ T +27 (0)21-405-4500 ▪ F +27 (0)21-405-4524 ▪ info@

tourismcapetown.co.za ▪
www.tourismcapetown.co.za

Cape Town Tourism ▪ T +27 (0)21-487-6800 ▪
F +27 (0)21-487-6859 ▪ capetown@cape-
town.travel

Somerset West ▪ T +27 (0)21-840-1400 ▪ F +27
(0)21-840-1410 ▪ somersetnwest@cape-
town.travel

Elgin Valley Tourism T +27 (0)21-848-9838 ▪
F +27 (0)86-660-0398 ▪ info@elginvalley.co.za ▪
www.elginvalley.co.za

Franschhoek Wine Valley ▪ T +27 (0)21-876-
2861 ▪ F +27 (0)21-876-2768 ▪ info@
franschhoek.org.za, office@franschhoek.org.za ▪
www.franschhoek.org.za

Hermanus Tourism Bureau ▪ T +27 (0)28-312-
2629 ▪ F +27 (0)28-313-0305 ▪
hermanustourism@hermanus.co.za ▪
www.hermanustourism.info

McGregor Tourism ▪ T +27 (0)23-625-1954 ▪
info@tourismmcgregor.co.za ▪
www.tourismmcgregor.co.za

Northern Cape Tourism ▪ T +27 (0)53-832-2657
▪ F +27 (0)53-831-2937 ▪ northerncapetourism@
telkomsa.net ▪ www.northerncape.org.za

Paarl Tourism Association ▪ T +27 (0)73-708-
2835 ▪ F +27 (0)86-590-871 ▪ info@
paarlonline.com ▪ www.paarlonline.com

Paarl Tourist Information Centre ▪ T +27 (0)21-
872 4842 ▪ F +27 (0)21-872-9376 ▪ paarlinfo@
drakenstein.gov.za ▪ www.drakenstein.gov.za

Robertson Tourism Association ▪ T +27 (0)23-
626-4437 ▪ F +27 (0)23-626-4290 ▪ info@robert-
son.org.za ▪ www.robertsontourism.co.za

Route 62 ▪ T +27 (0)23-616-3563 ▪ F +27 (0)23-
616-3422 ▪ info@route62.co.za ▪
www.route62.co.za

Saldanha Bay Tourism Organisation ▪ info@
sbto.co.za, marketing@sbto.co.za, dave@sbto.co.za
▪ www.capewestcoastpeninsula.co.za

Saldanha: T +27 (0)22-714-2088 ▪ F +27 (0)22-
714-4240 ▪ saldanha@sbto.co.za

Hopefield: T/F +27 (0)22-723-1720 / +27 (0)73-
187-6764 ▪ hopefield@sbto.co.za

Langebaan: T +27 (0)22-772-1515 ▪ F +27 (0)22-
772-1531 ▪ langebaan@sbto.co.za ▪
www.langebaaninfo.com

Vredenburg: T +27 (0)22-715-1142 ▪ F +27 (0)22-
715-1141 ▪ vredenburg@sbto.co.za

Paternoster: T/F +27 (0)22-752-2323 ▪ paternos-
ter@sbto.co.za ▪ www.paternoster.info

St Helena Bay: T +27 (0)76-661-2046 ▪
sthelenabay@sbto.co.za

Stellenbosch 360 (formerly Stellenbosch Tourism
Information Association) ▪ T +27 (0)21-883-3584
▪ F +27 (0)21-882-9550 ▪ info@
stellenbosch360.co.za ▪
www.stellenboschtourism.co.za

Wellington Tourism ▪ T +27 (0)21-873-4604 ▪
F +27 (0)21-873-4607 ▪ info@wellington.co.za ▪
www.wellington.co.za

West Coast Peninsula Tourism Bureau See
Saldanha Bay Tourism Organisation

Worcester Tourism Association ▪ T +27 (0)23-
348-2795 / +27 (0)23-342-6244 / +27 (0)76-
200-8742 ▪ F +27 (0)23-347-4678 ▪ info@
worcestertourism.com ▪
www.worcestertourism.com

Specialist Wine Tours

**Adamastor & Bacchus Cape Gourmet Wine &
Culinary Tours** ▪ English, Afrikaans, Dutch, Norwegian, German ▪ www.adamastorbacchus.com ▪
johnford@iafrica.com, jarche@iafrica.com ▪ T +27
(0)21-439-3169 / +27 (0)83-229-1172 ▪ F +27
(0)86-604-5169

African Story Wine Tours ▪ English ▪ info@
africanstorytours.com ▪
www.africanstorytours.com ▪ T +27 (0)73-755-
0444 / +27 (0)79-694-7915

African Trax Tours ▪ English ▪ africantrax@
telkomsa.net ▪ www.africantrax.co.za ▪ T +27
(0)83-692-8873

African Wonder Tours ▪ .Afrikaans, English,
French, Italian, German ▪ info@
africanwonder.co.za ▪ www.africanwonder.co.za ▪
T +27 (0)82-325-1485 / +27 (0)78-780-4289

Amber Tours ▪ English ▪ lesleyc@wol.co.za ▪
www.ambertours.co.za, www.lesleycox.co.za ▪
T +27 (0)83-448-7016

Bizoe Wine Tours ▪ Afrikaans, English ▪ info@
bizoe.co.za ▪ www.bizoe.co.za ▪ T +27 (0)21-843-
3307 / +27 (0)83-709-3957 ▪ F +27 (0)86-653-
8186

Cape Floral Kingdom Vineyard Tours ▪ sbirch@
iafrica.com ▪ www.CFKvineyardtours.co.za ▪ T +27
(0)76-145-1996

Capefuntours ▪ English ▪ capefuntours@icon.co.za ▪
www.capefuntours.co.za ▪ T +27 (0)21-782-5472
/ +27 (0)82-932-9430 ▪ F +27 (0)21-782-5472

Cape Fusion Tours ▪ English ▪ cazcape@
mweb.co.za, info@capefusion.co.za ▪
www.capefusiontours.com ▪ T +27 (0)21-461-
2437 / +27 (0)83-235-9777 ▪ F +27 (0)86-672-
5877

Double Gold Wineland Tours ▪ English ▪ kimdg@cybersmart.co.za, kimdg@absamail.co.za ▪ T +27 (0)21-785-5094 / +27 (0)82-293-3176

D'Vine Wine & Dine ▪ pauline.nel@dvinewinedine.co.za ▪ www.dvinewineanddine.co.za ▪ +27 (0)73-972-7830 / +27 (0)21-975-4851 ▪ +27 (0)86-601-1238

Exclusively African Tours ▪ English, Dutch (German, Swedish, French on request) ▪ ian@travelxa.com ▪ www.holidaystosouthafrica.co.uk ▪ T +27 (0)21-5314887 ▪ F +27 (0)86-609-0896

Go! Shuttles & Tours ▪ English, German, Afrikaans, French and Italian ▪ info@goshuttle.co.za, nic@gotours.co.za ▪ www.gotours.co.za ▪ T +27 (0)72-368-3455 ▪ F +27 (0)86-548-2375

Gourmet Travels ▪ English, German ▪ rainer@gourmettravels.co.za ▪ www.gourmettravels.co.za ▪ T +27 (0)82-449-7666 ▪ F +27 (0)86-542-0542

Gourmet Wine Tours ▪ English ▪ sflesch@iafrica.com ▪ www.gourmetwinetours.co.za ▪ T +27 (0)21-705-4317 / +27 (0)83-229-3581 ▪ F +27 (0)21-706-0766

Greatest Cape Wine Tours ▪ English, French ▪ richard@greatestcape.co.za ▪ www.greatestcape.co.za ▪ T +27 (0)21-855-5244 / +27 (0)83-650-5661

Happy Holiday Wine Tours ▪ English, Afrikaans, German & French on request ▪ john@happyholiday.co.za ▪ www.happyholiday.co.za ▪ T +27 (0)84-705-1383

Janet Malherbe ▪ German, French & Flemish ▪ janetm@mweb.co.za ▪ www.janetmalherbe.webs.com ▪ T +27 (0)82-553-8928 ▪ T/F +27 (0)21-862-1484

Judy Krohn Private & Personal Tours ▪ English, German, Afrikaans ▪ judithk@lantic.net ▪ www.judykrohn.co.za ▪ T +27 (0)84-500-1941 / +28 (0)21-851-7009 ▪ F +27 (0)21-851-7009

Klaus Schindler ▪ German, English ▪ schindler@lando.co.za ▪ www.kapstadt.de/schindlers-africa ▪ T +27 (0)83-270-3449

La Route Des Vins ▪ English, French, Spanish ▪ pauline.demartini@gmail.com, info@laroutedesvins.co.za ▪ www.laroutedesvins.co.za ▪ T +27 (0)21-461-1069 / +27 (0)71-499-0768 ▪ F +27 (0)21-461-7689

Luhambo Tours ▪ English, Afrikaans, German ▪ info@luhambotours.com ▪ www.luhambotours.com ▪ T +27 (0)21-551-0467 / +27 (0)82-306-4141

Ocean & Vine Adventures & Tours ▪ English, translator on request ▪ wayne@wine.co.za, oceanv@netactive.co.za ▪ www.prowinetours.co.za ▪ T +27 (0)21-559-6906 / +27 (0)82-900-6999 ▪ F +27 (0)21-559-6906

Percy Tours ▪ English, Afrikaans & some French & German ▪ travel@percytours.com ▪ www.percytours.com ▪ T +27 (0)72-062-8500 / +27 (0)28-316-4871

Redwood Tours ▪ English, Afrikaans ▪ info@redwoodtours.co.za ▪ www.redwoodtours.co.za ▪ T +27 (0)21-886-8138 / +27 (0)82-443-6480

Southern Destinations ▪ English ▪ info@southerndestinations.com, vanessa@southerndestinations.com ▪ www.southerndestinations.com ▪ T +27 (0)21-671-3090 ▪ F +27 (0)21-674-7481

Taste the Cape Travel & Tours ▪ English, other languages upon request ▪ info@tastethecape.co.za ▪ www.tastethecape.co.za ▪ T +27 (0)21-715-3559 / +27 (0)79-812-0220

Tri Active Events Management (Green Mountain Eco Route) ▪ English, Afrikaans ▪ info@triactive.co.za ▪ www.triactive.co.za ▪ T +27 (0)21-844-0975 / +27 (0)83-456-2181 ▪ F +27 (0)21-844-0970

Tsiba Tsiba Wine Tours & Travel ▪ Dutch, English, French, German, Spanish ▪ info@tsibatsiba.co.za ▪ www.tsibatsiba.co.za ▪ T +27 (0)82-956-8104

Vineyard Ventures ▪ English, Afrikaans, German; other languages on request ▪ vinven@iafrica.com ▪ www.vineyardventures.co.za ▪ T +27 (0)21-434-8888 / +27 (0)82-920-2825 ▪ F +27 (0)86-579-9430

Vintage Cape Tours ▪ English, Afrikaans, Dutch, French, German, Italian, Spanish ▪ info@vintagecape.co.za, jade@vintagecape.co.za ▪ www.vintagecape.co.za ▪ T +27 (0) 84-513-3066 / +27(0)21-913-2358 ▪ F +27 (0)86-690-8572

Vintour ▪ German, English, Afrikaans ▪ helmut@vintour.co.za ▪ www.vintour.co.za ▪ T/F +27 (0)21-976-5709 / +27 (0)83-626-0029

Walker Bay Wine Wander ▪ English, Afrikaans, French, German ▪ wine@hermanus.co.za, travel@percytours.com ▪ T +27 (0)28-316-3988 / +27 (0)72-062-8500 ▪ F +27 (0)86-509-4931

Wanderer Wines ▪ English, German, French, Italian ▪ wines@wanderer.co.za ▪ www.wanderer.co.za ▪ T +27 (0)21-713-2264 / +27 (0)82-878-1176 ▪ +27 (0)86-648-0352

Wellington Wine Walk ▪ English, Afrikaans ▪ judy@winescapetours.com ▪ www.winewalk.co.za ▪ T +27 (0)83-313-8383

Wine Desk ▪ Foreign language specialist wine guides available in most languages for private tours ▪ info@winedesk.co.za, ligia@winedesk.co.za ▪ www.winedesk.co.za ▪ T +27 (0)82-822-6127 ▪ F +27 (0)86-607 2980

Wine Escapes ▪ info@wineescapes.co.za ▪ www.wineescapes.co.za ▪ T +27 (0)83-453-2670

Winemaker-led Tasting Tours ▪ English; translators on request with sufficient notice ▪ vitis@mweb.co.za ▪ www.winetastingtours.co.za ▪ T +27 (0)82-322-7333

Restaurants in the Winelands and Cape Town

Below are some dining out options in Cape Town and the winelands. These are paid entries. The venues supplied information on their cuisine, menus and attractions, which was then edited for consistency of style. For more restaurants among the vines, consult the A–Z section of the guide for wineries which offer light lunches, picnics etc. Look for the 🍽 symbol beside the individual entries. Unless stated to the contrary, all allow you to bring your own (BYO) wine — the corkage fee is indicated at the start of each entry. Should you wish to know about wheelchair access, please discuss with the relevant restaurant.

Index of restaurants
Listed alphabetically, with region.

Caledon
Boschrivier Restaurant see under Stanford

Camps Bay
Azure Restaurant The Twelve Apostles Hotel and Spa, Victoria Road, Camps Bay, Cape Town ▪ Member

of Leading Hotels of the World ▪ SA influenced, modern French cuisine ▪ Open daily for lunch 12.30–2.30 & dinner 6.30–10 ▪ Booking advised ▪ Children welcome ▪ Major credit cards accepted ▪ No BYO ▪ Owner The Tollman Family ▪ Executive chef Henrico Grobbelaar ▪ bookta@12apostleshotel.co.za ▪ www.12apostleshotel.com ▪ S 33° 58′ 59.37″ E 18° 21′ 31.43″ ▪ **T +27 (0)21-437-9000** ▪ F +27 (0)21-437-9055

Sea vistas from this cliffside restaurant and balcony are mesmerizing; dishes divert attention from ocean to plate. Fresh, organic ingredients are from hotel herb garden and local markets; fish is sustainable. Delight in creative, unexpected ingredient combos and tantalising tasting menus by exec chef Henrico Grobbelaar, or more traditional options (including deliciously creamy rice pudding with salted caramel and nuts) from owner Bea Tollman's cookbook. (See also Accommodation section.)

Cape Town

Aubergine Restaurant 39 Barnet Street, Gardens, Cape Town ▪ Classical cuisine with innovative twists & Asian influence ▪ Outdoor terrace ▪ Lunch Wed–Fri 12–2, 'Cinq à Sept' Mon–Sat 5–7 & dinner Mon–Sat 7–10 ▪ Closed Sun ▪ Booking advised ▪ Children 5+ welcome ▪ Major credit cards accepted ▪ No BYO ▪ Owner/chef Harald Bresselschmidt ▪ info@aubergine.co.za ▪ www.aubergine.co.za ▪ S 33.932 E 18.416 ▪ **T +27 (0)21-465-4909** ▪ F +27 (0)86-671-0835

Warmly sophisticated restaurant revolving round wine-pairing. A 10 000-bottle cellar (selected for food compatibility) allows chef/patron Harald Bresselschmidt's keen palate and culinary skills full scope. Whether fish, seafood, prime aged local meat or tasty vegetarian options, dishes accent flavour, aroma and texture, with degustation menus offering taste-teasers like fish liaison with wasabi aroma and fried oysters, and fig terrine with marzipan mousse, orange tuille and elderflower sorbet. *Eat Out* Top 10, 2010 & 3 stars *Rossouw's Restaurants* 2010 & '11.

Auslese 115 Hope Street, Gardens, Cape Town ▪ Wines paired with tapas-sized dishes in classic yet innovative style ▪ Booking essential, open for pre-booked functions only ▪ Children welcome ▪ Major credit cards accepted ▪ BYO by arrangement ▪ Owner/chef Harald Bresselschmidt ▪ info@auslese.co.za ▪ www.auslese.co.za ▪ S 33.932 E 18.418 ▪ **T +27 (0)21-461-9727** ▪ F +27 (0)86-671-0835

Wanting to match gems from your wine collection, but can't cook? Organising anything from corporate events to a private birthday party or wine launch? Aubergine's elegant venue in a refurbished historic house close to the restaurant, is custom-designed for functions. Owner Harald Bresselschmidt will tailor the occasion for you, creating delectable tapas-

style dishes to complement wines, either your own or from his 10 000-bottle cellar.

Azure Restaurant see under Camps Bay

Bascule Whisky, Wine and Cocktail Bar Cape Grace, West Quay Road, V&A Waterfront, Cape Town ▪ Bistro/Tapas ▪ Open daily 10am–close ▪ Major credit cards accepted ▪ No BYO ▪ Owner Cape Grace ▪ Executive chef Malika van Reenen ▪ bascule@capegrace.com ▪ www.capegrace.com ▪ S 33° 54′ 29″ E 18° 25′ 12″ ▪ **T +27 (0)21-410-7082** ▪ F +27 (0)21-419-7622

Savour the sophisticated setting on the quayside of the international yacht marina at Cape Town's Waterfront. By day a lively destination for a cappuccino or light lunch (tapas a speciality); by night, a vibrant venue where whisky connoisseurs and social butterflies gather to enjoy a shot of Cape Town's social energy. Over 400 whiskies and an impressive selection of the finest Cape wines on offer. (See also Accommodation section.)

Bistro Sixteen82 see under Constantia

Buitenverwachting Restaurant see under Constantia

Den Anker Restaurant Pierhead, V&A Waterfront, Cape Town ▪ French/Belgian cuisine ▪ Open daily 11am–10.30pm (kitchen); 11am–12pm (bar) ▪ Booking advised ▪ Children welcome ▪ Visa & MasterCard accepted ▪ No BYO ▪ Owner E de Visscher ▪ denanker@mweb.co.za ▪ www.denanker.co.za ▪ **T +27 (0)21-419-0249** ▪ F +27 (0)21-419-0251

Buzzing quayside venue that opened with the waterfront and grew with it. Latest update highlights Belgian beers, including exclusive Belgian-brewed Den Anker, with tastings and menu pairing as new drawcards (there's also a well-chosen winelist). Watch basking seals from indoors or terrace tables, where a tapas menu is a must. Evergreen best-seller is moule & frites but don't ignore seafood platters, steaks and SA specialities.

Harveys Restaurant at Winchester Mansions 221 Beach Road, Sea Point, Cape Town ▪ South African cuisine with a European twist ▪ Mon–Sat: breakfast buffet 7–10.30, à la carte breakfast 7–12, lunch 12–3, snacks 3–6 & dinner 7–10.30; Sun: Jazz brunch 11–2 (bookings only, no walk ins), snacks 4–6 & dinner 7–10.30 ▪ Booking advised ▪ Children welcome ▪ Major credit cards accepted ▪ Corkage R70 ▪ Owner Frances Wainford ▪ MD Nils Heckscher ▪ Executive chef Jochen Riedel ▪ welcome@winchester.co.za ▪ www.winchester.co.za ▪ S 33° 54′ 38.1″ E 18° 23′ 26.5″ ▪ **T +27 (0)21-434-2351** ▪ F +27 (0)21-434-0215

Bistro by day and restaurant by night, revamped and revitalised Harveys tempts guests with fresh and flavourful local cuisine lifted by international touches; pairing food and wine against a backdrop of local art at monthly Grapes, Gourmet & Gallery evenings. The hotel's tranquil piazza-style courtyard, enhanced by palm trees and fountains, is a perfect setting for romantic dinners under the stars, or lively Sunday jazz brunches. Excellent winelist, winner of a Diners Club 2011 Diamond Award. (See also Accommodation section.)

HQ Restaurant 100 Shortmarket Street, Heritage Square, Cape Town ▪ Steakhouse ▪ Open Mon–Sat 11.30am–10.30pm (kitchen), bar open till 2am ▪ Closed Sun, Dec 24 eve, Dec 25/26 & Jan 1 ▪ Booking advised ▪ Children welcome ▪ Major credit cards accepted ▪ No BYO ▪ Owners Jean Muller, Brendon Crew & Marc Langlois ▪ Executive chef Gretchen Morkel ▪ info@hqrestaurant.co.za ▪ www. hqrestaurant.co.za ▪ S 33° 55′ 14.88″ E 18° 25′ 5.88″ ▪ **T +27 (0)21-424-6373** ▪ F +27 (0)21-424-6374

Steak restaurant focused on a single meal of salad, sirloin and chips, loosely based on famous Parisian restaurant, L'Entrecote, in its homage to meat. Other than deciding how they'd like their steaks cooked, carnivores can relax - which allows them to concentrate on the concise, well-chosen winelist. Sizeable bar area opening into Heritage Square courtyard offers cocktails, comfortable lounge seating and party-packed live music evenings.

Josephines Cookhouse 13 Boundary Road, Newlands, Cape Town ▪ Authentic Italian fare, pizza, pasta ▪ Open Mon–Sat 9am–10pm ▪ Closed Sun & pub hols ▪ Booking advised ▪ Children welcome ▪ Major credit cards accepted ▪ Corkage R30 ▪ Owners Chris Coetzee, Tammy Botbyl, Peter Weetman, Stéfan Marais, Stephen Coetzee & Julie Galvin ▪ Executive chef Kyle Knight ▪ info@josephinescookhouse.co.za ▪ www.josephinescookhouse.co.za ▪ **T +27 (0)21-686-1437** ▪ F +27 (0)86-532-6961

Relaxed eaterie in a historic mill on the banks of the Liesbeek river next to Newlands rugby stadium. Leafy patio overlooking the Liesbeek for lazy summer afternoons; inviting wood-burning fireplace for cosy winter evenings. Expect fresh Italian-inspired fare: thin-based wood-fired pizzas setting a new level in appetising toppings; more-ish al dente pastas; grass-fed/free range meats: must-try favourite is free-range rib-eye, anchovy butter and hand-cut chips.

Nobu One&Only Cape Town, Dock Road, V&A Waterfront, Cape Town ▪ Japanese style with a contemporary South African twist ▪ Upper level lounge with selection of Sakes, plum wines and Sake/Shochu based cocktails ▪ Dinner Mon–Sun 6–11 (summer) & Tue–Sun (winter) ▪ Booking advised ▪ Children welcome ▪ Major credit cards accepted ▪ No BYO ▪ Owner Nobuyuki Matsuhisa ▪ Executive chef Fred Faucheux ▪ restaurant.reservations@oneandonlycapetown.com ▪ www.oneandonlycapetown.com ▪ S 33° 54′ 30″ E 018° 24′ 59″ ▪ **T +27 (0)21-431-5888**

Take your tastebuds on a fascinating taste journey from delicate to tantalisingly spice-rich dishes. Master-chef Nobuyuki 'Nobu' Matsuhisa's first restaurant in Africa incorporates local seafood and spices in classically-styled Japanese dishes. Do experience the signature black cod den miso and sashimi/sushi, and note the perfection of the sushi rice. American Express Platinum Fine Dining Award 2012; *Eat Out* Top 10, 2011; *Rossouw's Restaurants* 3 stars 2011 & '12. (See also Accommodation section.)

Petit Caveau Shop G11, Colosseum Building, Century City, Cape Town ▪ French-style bistro with Mediterranean influences ▪ Open Mon–Sat 7am–10.30pm ▪ Closed Sun, Easter Sun, Dec 26 & Dec 31 eve ▪ Booking advised ▪ Children welcome ▪ Major credit cards accepted ▪ No BYO ▪ Owners Marc Langlois, Jean Muller & Brendon Crew ▪ Executive chef Sibu ▪ marc@caveau.co.za ▪ www.caveau.co.za ▪ S 33° 53′ 37.49″ E 18° 30′ 22.56″ ▪ **T +27 (0)21-823-3033** ▪ F +27 (0)21-424-6374

Want a break from the corporate grind, frenetic shopping - or a casual meal in lively surroundings? Strategically located in the Colosseum Building within buzzing Century City, this popular wine bar and bistro offers over 40 wines by the glass to pair with fresh, seasonal à la carte menus or daily changing tapas options. Mediterranean-inspired specialities include a generous lamb burger with tatziki, humus and fries.

Pure see under Hout Bay

Reuben's One&Only Cape Town, Dock Road, V&A Waterfront, Cape Town ▪ Wholesome bistro-fare using local flavours ▪ Open daily for breakfast 6.30–11, lunch 12.30–3 & dinner 6–11 ▪ Booking advised ▪ Children welcome ▪ Major credit cards accepted ▪ No BYO ▪ Owner Reuben Riffel ▪ Executive chef Jason Millar ▪ restaurant.reservations@oneandonlycapetown.com ▪ www.oneandonlycapetown.com ▪ S 33° 54′ 30″ E 018° 24′ 59″ ▪ **T +27 (0)21-431-5888**

Celebrity chef Reuben Riffel's first urban restaurant reflects the modesty of the man. In the sophisticated surroundings of One&Only Cape Town, his deceptively simple, bistro-style fare shows the skilled combination of freshness and flavour you'd expect from one of SA's most-loved chefs. Portions are generous and choices wide: flame-grilled prime steaks, pan-seared market fish, signature chilli-salted squid and soy-braised pork belly share space on the inviting menu. American Express Platinum Fine Dining Award 2012. (See also Accommodation section.)

Savoy Cabbage Restaurant & Champagne Bar 101 Hout Street, Cape Town ▪ Contemporary cuisine ▪ Lunch Mon–Fri 12–2.30, Dinner Mon–Sat 7–10.30 ▪ Closed Sun ▪ Booking essential ▪ Major credit cards accepted ▪ Air-conditioned ▪ Corkage R45 ▪ Owner Caroline Bagley ▪ savoycab@iafrica.com ▪

www.savoycabbage.co.za ▪ S 33° 55' 12.31" E 18° 25' 05.45" ▪ **T +27 (0)21-424-2626** ▪ F +27 (0)21-424-3366

Heading for 14 years and as popular as ever, this city-centre venue boasts a string of accolades and plaudits from international critics. Expect exposed brick and high ceilings; evergreen favourites as menu fixtures; and daily-changing taste treats like 'Three little pigs' with pan-fried loin, smoked fillet and sticky glazed belly; or house-smoked Norwegian salmon on buckwheat crêpe, with grapefruit jelly and Keta caviar. Intelligent boutique winelist.

Signal Restaurant Cape Grace, West Quay Road, V&A Waterfront, Cape Town ▪ Cape cosmopolitan cuisine ▪ Open daily for breakfast 6–11, lunch 12–3 & dinner 6.30–10 ▪ Booking advised for breakfast & dinner ▪ Children welcome ▪ Major credit cards accepted ▪ Corkage wine & sparkling R80; Champagne R250 ▪ Owner Cape Grace ▪ Executive chef Malika van Reenen ▪ signal@capegrace.com ▪ www.capegrace.com ▪ S 33° 54' 29" E 18° 25' 12" ▪ **T +27 (0)21-410-7080** ▪ F +27 (0)21-419-7622

Explore Cape Town's tastes and flavours in masterly mixes of herbs, spices and sustainable local ingredients, at a table under a mirrored, chandelier-hung ceiling, with views over an international yacht marina to Table Mountain. Go wild with bobotie-spiced ostrich with almond crumble, or cardamom caramel, nyangbo ganache and banana ice-cream; or opt for tasting menus (both meat-orientated and vegetarian) offering wine-pairing from an excellent, terroir-orientated winelist. (See also Accommodation section.)

Societi Bistro 50 Orange Street, Gardens, Cape Town ▪ French & Italian influenced, bistro ▪ Mon–Sat 12–11 ▪ Closed Sun ▪ Booking advised ▪ Children welcome ▪ Major credit cards accepted ▪ Corkage R30 ▪ Owners Peter Weetman & Tammy Botbyl ▪ Executive chef Stéfan Marais ▪ info@societi.co.za ▪ www.societi.co.za ▪ **T +27 (0)21-424-2100** ▪ F +27 (0)21-424-1140

Societi is a neighbourhood 'local'. More than cuisine, it's a way of life: savouring an unhurried meal in the company of family and friends. To hospitable owners Tammy and Peter, the bistro is an extension of their home — 'and a sanctuary for Capetonians and visitors looking for a home from home'. Flavour-packed specialities change frequently, but perennial best-sellers are fillet au poivre and dreamy cheesecake.

Sotano 121 Beach Road, Mouille Point, Cape Town ▪ Mediterranean ▪ Open daily 7am-10.30pm (kitchen), bar 11am–11pm ▪ Booking advised — can only book inside ▪ Children welcome ▪ Major credit cards accepted ▪ No BYO ▪ Owners Jean Muller, Marc Langlois & Brendon Crew ▪ Executive chef Russell Jalil

▪ info@sotano.co.za ▪ www.sotano.co.za ▪ S 33° 54' 7.49" E 18° 23' 58.37" ▪ **T +27 (0)21-433-1757** ▪ F +27 (0)21-424-6374

Casual, Mediterranean-inspired eatery offering simple but delicious dishes from fresh seasonal produce. Enjoy sun-warmed views of the ocean and Mouille Point promenade while tucking into flatbreads, grilled linefish or lamb burgers. Smaller appetite? Nibble delicacies like squid tentacles from the inviting tapas menu. Sotano (Spanish for cellar) lives up to its name, so pair your choice with boutique or well-known labels from the well-chosen winelist.

The Square Restaurant Vineyard Hotel & Spa, Colinton Road, Newlands, Cape Town ▪ Eclectic contemporary cuisine ▪ Sushi prepared by skilled Sushi chefs ▪ Breakfast Mon–Sat 6.30-10.30, Sun & public holidays 7.30–11; lunch daily 12–2.30 & dinner daily 6–10 ▪ Booking advised ▪ Children welcome ▪ Major credit cards accepted ▪ Corkage R60 still wine, R75 sparkling wine ▪ eat@vineyard.co.za ▪ www.vineyard.co.za ▪ **T +27 (0)21-657-4500** ▪ F +27 (0)21-657-4501

Chef Alex Docherty's varied, eclectic cuisine is echoed by the tranquil ambience of this glass-roofed restaurant and sushi bar, softened by trees and soothing water fountain in the heart of the Vineyard Hotel. Sushi is now offered at lunch and dinner, while both classic and creative dishes feature on à la carte menus, matched by a multi award-winning winelist presenting major estates as well as 'off-the-beaten-track' choices. Diners Club Winelist Diamond Award 2009 - '11. (See also Accommodation section.)

Constantia

Bistro Sixteen82 Steenberg Vineyards, Steenberg Road, Tokai ▪ Contemporary bistro ▪ Open daily for breakfast 9–11.30, lunch 12–4 & tapas 4.30–8 ▪ Closed 2–25 July ▪ Booking advised ▪ Children welcome ▪ Major credit cards accepted ▪ Corkage R40 ▪ Owner Graham Beck Enterprises ▪ Executive chef Brad Ball ▪ reservations@bistro1682.co.za ▪ www.steenberghotel.com ▪ **T +27 (0)21-713-2211** ▪ F +27 (0)21-713-2201

Award-winning chef Brad Ball packs flavour into contemporary bistro dishes paired with acclaimed Steenberg wines in a striking modern space overlooking vineyards, reflection pools and sensory gardens. Hearty or healthy breakfasts, inviting tasting bar and lounge, lunch treats like sticky pork belly with salted caramel, or Hermon beef fillet, truffled cauliflower purée and veal jus. The popular tapas selection encourages deliciously more-ish early evening snacking. American Express Fine Dining Award 2011, Fleur du Cap Top 100 Restaurants 2011. (See also A–Z section.)

Buitenverwachting Restaurant Klein Constantia Road, Constantia, Cape Town ▪ Global cuisine ▪ Easter-

Oct: lunch Tue–Sat 12–3, tapas 12–5 & dinner 7–9; Nov–Easter: lunch Mon–Sat 12–3.30, tapas 3–5 & dinner 7–9.30; public holidays: phone to enquire ▪ Closed Sun, Mon (Easter–Oct), month of Jul & first 2 weeks in Aug ▪ Booking advised ▪ Children welcome ▪ Major credit cards accepted ▪ Corkage R25 for 1st bottle, thereafter R75 each; no BYO allowed for functions ▪ Owners Richard & Christine Mueller ▪ MD Lars Maack ▪ Executive chef Edgar Osojnik ▪ restaurant@ buitenverwachting.com ▪ www.buitenverwachting.com ▪ S 34° 2'23.28" E 18° 25'22.08" ▪ **T +27 (0)21-794-3522** ▪ F +27 (0)21-794-1351

'Flow' is the new buzzword at Buitenverwachting: flow from the picnic lawns through the inviting new coffee roasterie/shop and deli to the winetasting centre and revitalised central courtyard. Linger over pastries and coffee; enjoy wine with deli choices, platters and tempting tapas bites - or move into the relaxed restaurant to feast on exec chef Edgar Osojnik's flavour-fresh, superbly sauced classic and seasonal dishes. Tripadvisor Certificate of Excellence 2011 & '12. (See also A–Z section.)

Constantia Uitsig Restaurant Constantia Uitsig, Spaanschemat River Road, Constantia, Cape Town ▪ Italian & Mediterranean cuisine ▪ Open daily for lunch 12–2.15 & dinner 7–9.15 ▪ Closed eve of Dec 25 ▪ Booking advised ▪ Children welcome ▪ Major credit cards accepted ▪ BYO restricted to one bottle ▪ Corkage wine R50 & Champagne R90 ▪ Owner Constantia Uitsig Holdings (Pty) Ltd ▪ Executive chef Clayton Bell ▪ restaurant@uitsig.co.za ▪ www.constantia-uitsig.com ▪ S 34° 2'33.8" E 18° 25'21.7" ▪ **T +27 (0)21-794-4480** ▪ F +27 (0)21-794-3105

Consistency coupled with a relaxed ambience has kept this eatery on Cape Town's culinary map for 20 years. Flavourful food, enjoyed against a mountain and vineyard backdrop, makes regulars of both locals and visitors - including names like Wilbur Smith and Heston Blumenthal. Menus blend Italian and Mediterranean influences with hints of spice; specialities range from springbok carpaccio to a signature fruit pavlova. Trip Advisor top10 restaurants 2012; 2 stars in *Rossouw's Restaurants* 2012. (See also Accommodation & A–Z sections.)

Jonkershuis Constantia Restaurant Groot Constantia Wine Estate, Groot Constantia Road, Constantia ▪ Bistro/Cape Malay ▪ Mon–Sat 9–9, Sun 9-4 ▪ Closed Sun eve ▪ Booking advised ▪ Function room with historic charm ▪ Children welcome ▪ Major credit cards accepted ▪ Corkage R50 ▪ Owners Chris Coetzee, Peter Weetman, Tammy Botbyl & Laurence Burgess ▪ Executive chef Laurence Burgess ▪ info@ jonkershuisconstantia.co.za ▪ www.jonkershuisconstantia.co.za ▪ S 34° 01'37.03" E

18° 25'28.84" ▪ **T +27 (0)21-794-6255** ▪ F +27 (0)86-532-6961

Step into the past. The Jonkershuis next to the historic Groot Constantia manor house, surrounded by ancient oaks and legendary vineyards, breathes old-world charm as a bistro specialising in traditional Cape Malay dishes. Eat al fresco overlooking the Constantia valley and False Bay; in a courtyard under vines; or choose the welcoming interior, warmed by a double-sided fireplace. And don't miss the baked cheesecake. (See also A–Z section.)

La Colombe Restaurant Constantia Uitsig, Spaanschemat River Road, Constantia, Cape Town ▪ French cuisine influenced with Asian fusion ▪ Open daily for lunch 12.30–2.30 & dinner 7–9.30 ▪ Closed Sun eve (winter); Dec 31 lunch; Jan 1 ▪ Booking advised ▪ Children welcome ▪ Major credit cards accepted ▪ BYO restricted to one bottle per table of four guests ▪ Corkage wine R45 & Champagne R70 ▪ Owner Constantia Uitsig Holdings (Pty) Ltd ▪ Executive chef Scot Kirton ▪ lacolombe@uitsig.co.za ▪ www.constantia-uitsig.com ▪ S 34° 02'45.28" E 18° 25'12.55" ▪ **T +27 (0)21-794-2390** ▪ F +27 (0)21-794-7914

Assurance and subtle flavours are now the hallmarks of head chef Scot Kirton's menus. Perfectly-presented dishes retain their classic base, with creative play lifting seasonal ingredients: tasting menus titillate with delights such as aromatic Asian citrus oysters; umami broth (with steamed languiste, miso scallop and shitake sushi roll); smoked bone marrow; duck combo of confit brioche/rooibos-smoked breast, foie gras and quince 'Swissroll'. Excellent wine-pairing. 12th in *San Pellegrino* 50 Best Restaurants in the World 2010 & *San Pellegrino* 100 Best Restaurants 2011; 3 stars in *Rossouw's Restaurants* 2009 –'11; 10th in Eat Out/DStv Food Network Restaurant Awards 2012. (See also Accommodation & A–Z sections.)

Societi Brasserie Shop 1, Forest Glade House, Main Road, Tokai ▪ European with French influences ▪ Mon–Sat 9–9 ▪ Closed Sun ▪ Booking advised ▪ Children welcome ▪ Major credit cards accepted ▪ Corkage R30 ▪ Owners Chris Coetzee, Peter Weetman, Tammy Botbyl, Stéfan Marais & Julie Galvin ▪ Executive chef Stéfan Marais ▪ brasserie@societi.co.za ▪ www.societi.co.za ▪ **T +27 (0)21-712-1363** ▪ F +27 (0)86-532-6961

Welcoming Brasserie in the successful 'Societi' mould, this time with an appealing French twist. Ambience is friendly and unpretentious; hearty seasonal menus and daily specials reflect the best produce available from local artisanal suppliers. Savour classic brasserie fare like croque-monsieur and soupe à l'oignon gratinée; tuck into best-selling steak au poivre, risotto and home-made pasta. Large selection of bespoke local beers and well-priced winelist.

The River Café Constantia Uitsig, Spaanschemat River Road, Constantia, Cape Town ▪ Rustic café-style dining ▪ Open daily for breakfast 8.30–11.30, tea time menu 11.30–4.30 & lunch 12.30–4.30 ▪ Booking advised ▪ Children welcome ▪ Major credit cards accepted ▪ BYO restricted to one bottle for every four guests ▪ Corkage R30 ▪ Owner Constantia Uitsig Holdings (Pty) Ltd ▪ Executive chef Craig Anderson ▪ rivercafe@uitsig.co.za ▪ www.constantia-uitsig.com ▪ S 34° 02′ 45.28″ E 18° 25′ 12.55″ ▪ **T +27 (0)21-794-3010** ▪ F +27 (0)86-504-0108

Long a popular meeting place for sumptuous breakfasts (regulars rave about the deluxe version of eggs Benedict) and affordable café-style lunches. The mood is relaxed, service smiling, and menus are enlivened with daily specials. But don't ignore the Café classics. Favourites include tasty fish pie; pepper-sauced, butter-tender beef fillet to pair perfectly with Constantia Uitsig Red; and decadent hot chocolate fondant with homemade honeycomb ice-cream. (See also Accommodation & A–Z sections.)

Durbanville

Cassia Restaurant, Bar & Function Venue Nitida Wine Estate, Tygerberg Valley Road (M13), Durbanville ▪ Trendy/Continental ▪ Mon–Sat 9–9.30, Sun 9–3 ▪ Closed Sun eve ▪ Booking advised ▪ Children welcome ▪ Major credit cards accepted ▪ Corkage R40 ▪ Owners Warren Swaffield & Bernhard Veller ▪ info@cassiarestaurant.co.za ▪ www.cassiarestaurant.co.za ▪ **T +27 (0)21-976-0640/+27 (0)21-975-3825** ▪ F +27 (0)21-976-0645

Ideal for vistors wanting a true taste of the winelands, this welcoming wine estate eaterie, only 20 minutes from central Cape Town, is a firm favourite with locals. Portions are generous, views panoramic, décor stylish, and a sunny deck beckons. Best-selling speciality is Durbanville Wine Valley's regional dish — lamb sosaties with cumin pumpkin stampkoring and pumpkin pickle — which pairs happily with highly-rated Nitida wine. (See also A–Z section.)

Joostenberg Bistro see under Stellenbosch

Ke-Monate Wine Bar & Bistro Hooggelegen Farm, Vissershok Road, Durbanville ▪ Bistro/Tapas ▪ Open Tue–Sat 9am–11pm, Sun & public holidays 9am–4pm ▪ Closed Mon ▪ Booking advised ▪ Children welcome ▪ Major credit cards accepted ▪ Corkage R50 ▪ Owners MJ & Estani de Wit ▪ info@ke-monate.co.za ▪ www.ke-monate.co.za ▪ S 33° 49′ 221″ E 18° 36′ 672″ ▪ **T +27 (0)21-976-7343** ▪ F +27 (0)86-611-8747

The view-rich bistro on Hooggelegen farm, one of the oldest family-owned wine farms in Durbanville,

is all about enjoying good food with the farm's popular Signal Gun wines. For specialities, consult the blackboard, listing options from SA-inspired tapas bites to temptations like glazed pork burgers and pastry-wrapped venison. More-ish breakfast muffins, scones and croissants are freshly baked; Mexican dishes are the drawcard on Thursday evenings. (See also A–Z section for Signal Gun Wines.)

Elgin

Gordon Manuel @ The Venue South Hill Vineyards, 113 The Valley Road, Elgin ▪ Country gourmet ▪ Lunch Wed–Sun, dinner Sat ▪ Closed Mon–Tue & last 3 weeks of August ▪ Booking advised ▪ Children welcome ▪ Major credit cards accepted (excl. American Express) ▪ Corkage R50 ▪ Indoor & outdoor seating, ideal for exclusive weddings and functions ▪ Owner/executive chef Gordon Manuel ▪ restaurant@southhill.co.za ▪ www.southhill.co.za ▪ S 34° 13′ 59.48″ E 19°06′44.28″ ▪ **T +27 (0)21-844-0033**

Welcoming venue amid vineyards and apple orchards, owner-run with Gordon at the stoves and his wife Emma front-of-house. The small, focused menu, highlighting produce from the Overberg region, changes every Saturday to capture variety and freshness, while specialities like slow-roasted pork belly with Calvados jus and gourmet risottos remain best-sellers. Walls are alive with paintings: the restaurant has joined forces with Red! The Gallery. (See also Accommodation & A–Z sections.)

The Pool Room @ Oak Valley Oak Valley Estate, off the R321, Oak Avenue, Elgin ▪ Country cuisine ▪ Restaurant open for lunch Wed–Sun 12–3.30 & dinner Fri 6.30–10 ▪ Closed Mon/Tue & 15 Jun–15 Aug ▪ Deli open Wed–Sun 10–4 ▪ Private functions welcome ▪ Booking advised ▪ Children welcome (restaurant overlooks swimming pool) ▪ Wheelchair-friendly ▪ Major credit cards accepted (excl. American Express) ▪ No BYO ▪ Owners The AG Rawbone-Viljoen Trust ▪ Executive chef Nicole Precoudis ▪ wines@oak-valley.co.za ▪ www.oakvalley.co.za ▪ S 34° 9′313″ E 19° 3′849″ ▪ **T +27 (0)21-859-4110** ▪ F +27 (0)21-859-3405

Freshness rules and a custom-built grill takes centre stage. Relax on the terrace, relishing country inspired cuisine, with ingredients sourced from the farm where possible, and crafted into mouthwatering dishes by passionate chef Nicole Precoudis. Feast on grass-fed beef, acorn-fed pork, charcuterie, naturally grown vegetables and freshly baked artisanal breads from the wood-burning oven. Favourite lunchtime platter combines these delights with highly-acclaimed Oak Valley wines. (See also A–Z section.)

Franschhoek

Babel Restaurant see under Paarl

Backsberg Restaurant see under Paarl

Bistro Allée Bleue   T-junction R45 & R310, Groot Drakenstein ▪ Bistro style ▪ Open daily 8–5, and on special occasions in the evening ▪ Booking advised ▪ Children welcome ▪ Major credit cards accepted (excl. Diners Club) ▪ Corkage R45 ▪ Wine Tasting Courtyard for light al fresco meals in summer ▪ Both venues available for small private functions ▪ Picnic area ▪ Owners Wilfred & Elke Dauphin ▪ Executive chef Glenn Ferus ▪ info@alleebleue.com ▪ www.alleebleue.com ▪ S 33° 51′51.02″ E 18° 58′ 42.90″ ▪ **T +27 (0)21-874-1021** ▪ F +27 (0)21-874-1850

Expect a classic bistro menu incorporating the estate's fresh produce, herbs and olive oil. Parma ham-wrapped goats cheese with fig chutney, veal saltimbocca with wild mushroom and the speciality crowd-puller, a generous gourmet burger, form part of the weekly changing menu. Easily accessible from Franschhoek, Stellenbosch and Paarl, Bistro Allée Bleue, with its stylish crisp blue interior, is located at the entrance to the estate. (See also Accommodation & A–Z sections.)

cosecha Restaurant   Noble Hill Wine Estate, Simondium-Klapmuts Road, Simondium, Paarl ▪ Latin-inspired, Californian influences ▪ Open Wed–Mon 10–5 ▪ Closed Tue; 2 weeks in Aug ▪ Booking advised ▪ Children & friendly, well-behaved pets welcome ▪ Major credit cards accepted (excl. Diners Club) ▪ Corkage R50 ▪ Pepper and vegetable garden ▪ Owner Noble Hill Trust ▪ info@cosecharestaurant.com ▪ www.cosecharestaurant.com ▪ S 33° 49′38.31″ E 18° 56′12.57″ ▪ **T +27 (0)21-874-3844** ▪ F +27 (0)21-874-2948

Feast on traditional or contemporary Latin-inspired treats. Bringing the farm-fresh flavours of the family's southwestern roots to Cape Town, cosecha (harvest) reflects the al fresco eatery's location adjoining the crushing and sorting area. For breakfast, choose traditional huevos rancheros, lunch on tequila tagliatelle, beef enchiladas, or bocaditos (small plates) to share. Peppers and vegetables are grown on the farm and daily specials feature freshly picked ingredients. (See also A–Z section.)

Franschhoek Kitchen   Holden Manz Wine Estate, Green Valley Road, Franschhoek ▪ Pacific Rim ▪ Lunch 12–3, dinner 6pm to close ▪ Booking advised ▪ Children welcome ▪ Visa & MasterCard accepted ▪ Corkage R50 ▪ Owners Gerard Holden & Migo Manz ▪ Executive chef Cheyne Morrisby ▪ info@ holdenmanz.com ▪ www.holdenmanz.com ▪ **T +27 (0)21-876-2729** ▪ F +27 (0)21-876-4624

Drink in the panorama of vineyards and mountains, then feast on intensely-flavoured dishes, expertly paired with Holden Manz wines. Internationally-experienced exec chef Cheyne Morrisby offers Pacific Rim food without tired fusion: here cutting-edge Asia meets Franschhoek freshness, presented in picture-perfect style. Kitchen star is pork belly, to be relished with edamame purée, anchovy dauphinoise, soy/maple and lotus-root crisps. And don't miss the indulgent dessert trio. (See also Accommodation & A–Z sections.)

Fyndraai Restaurant @ Solms-Delta   Delta Road, off R45, Groot Drakenstein, Franschhoek Valley ▪ Traditional Cape cuisine ▪ Open Mon–Sun 9–5 ▪ Closed Dec 25 & Jan 1 ▪ Booking advised ▪ Children welcome ▪ Major credit cards accepted ▪ No BYO ▪ Owner Solms Family Trust, Astor Family Trust & The Wijn de Caab Workers Trust ▪ Executive chef Shaun Schoeman ▪ restaurant@solms-delta.co.za ▪ www.solms-delta.co.za ▪ www.facebook.com/solmsdelta ▪ Twitter @ solms_delta ▪ S 33° 52′23.8″ E 018° 59′21.3″ ▪ **T +27 (0)21-874-3937 ext. 115** ▪ F +27 (0)21-874-1852

Culinary heritage meets modern innovation. Built over the foundations of the original cellar, this glass-floored restaurant pays tribute to the cultures contributing to SA cuisine, with helpful glossary to explain unfamiliar terms. Afrikaner boerekos, influenced by 'Cape Malay' slaves and infused with plants used by early indigenous nomads, is invitingly plated for contemporary eye and taste appeal. For an overview, order the flavour-filled tapas platter. Winner in Cape Winelands District Municipality Mayoral Tourism Awards' Wine Tourism Destination of the Year 2011 and Great Wine Capitals' Best of Wine Tourism Innovative Wine Tourism Experience 2012. (See also A–Z section.)

Glen Carlou Restaurant   see under Paarl

Grande Provence — The Restaurant   Grande Provence Heritage Wine Estate, Main Road, Franschhoek ▪ Contemporary French with Asian influence ▪ Open daily for lunch 12–2.30 & dinner 7–9 ▪ Booking advised ▪ Children welcome for lunch ▪ Major credit cards accepted ▪ No BYO ▪ Owner Grande Provence (Pty) Ltd ▪ Executive chef Darren Badenhorst ▪ reservations@grandeprovence.co.za ▪ www.grandeprovence.co.za ▪ S 33° 53′57.6″ E 19° 06′ 10.5″ ▪ **T +27 (0)21-876-8600** ▪ F +27 (0)21-876-8601

Past elegance fuses with contemporary chic in this sophisticated, girder-exposed restaurant where creative menus from new exec chef Darren Badenhorst update French inspiration with an Asian twist, changing weekly to highlight fresh local produce. Treat your tastebuds to specialities like Cajun-spiced soft-shell crab; bone-marrow chicken ballotine with morel mushrooms and Japanese truffle in port jus; and recapture childhood memories with Grand Provence diddle daddle dessert. (See also Accommodation & A–Z sections.)

Haute Cabrière Restaurant Haute Cabrière, Lambrechts Road (Pass Road), Franschhoek ▪ Modern French & continental cuisine ▪ Lunch Tue–Sun; dinner Tue–Sat (Oct–Apr) & Fri–Sat (May–Sep) ▪ Terrace tables overlooking the valley ▪ Closed Mon & Jan 1 ▪ Booking advised ▪ Children welcome ▪ Major credit cards accepted ▪ No BYO ▪ Owner Clos Cabrière Ltd ▪ Executive chef Ryan Shell ▪ restaurant@cabriere.co.za ▪ www.cabriere.co.za ▪ S 33° 54' 26.14" E 19° 7' 3.05" ▪ **T +27 (0)21-876-3688** ▪ F +27 (0)21-876-3691

Inviting after a glamorous makeover that includes couches and handcrafted chandeliers, and revitalised by passionate young Chef Ryan Shell, this vaulted mountainside restaurant focuses on creating the perfect marriage of food and wine. Menus are influenced by the season, with dishes displaying wine-pairing at its most creative, combining diverse ingredients in flavours that complement and 'dance with' Haute Cabrière wines and Pierre Jourdan Cap Classiques. (See also A–Z section.)

Mange Tout & Country Kitchen Mont Rochelle Hotel & Mountain Vineyards, Dassenberg Road, Franschhoek ▪ **Mange Tout** — international cuisine: breakfast daily 7–10.30, lunch Sat–Sun 12.30–2.30 & dinner Wed–Sun 7–9.30 ▪ **Country Kitchen** —rustic bistro: Mon–Tue 10–9 & Wed–Sun 10–7 ▪ Booking advised ▪ Children welcome ▪ Major credit cards accepted ▪ No BYO ▪ Owners Erwin Schnitzler & Rwayitare family ▪ Executive chef Maki Mahki ▪ info@montrochelle.co.za ▪ www.montrochelle.co.za ▪ S 33° 92' 05.20" E 19° 10' 50.53" ▪ **T +27 (0)21-876-2770** ▪ F +27 (0)21-876-3788

Both elegant and rustic restaurants to suit your mood. Mange Tout offers spectacular valley views, varied menus with a delightfully French slant that reflect support of organic and free range farming, showcasing local produce in imaginative vegetarian options. Informal Country Kitchen specialises in tasty bistro fare, around the fire place in winter, celebrating summer on the terrace, or with a winelands picnic in the garden. Diners Club Diamond winelist award 2011; *Eat Out* Top 10 Tasting menu & Top 10 Best Hotel Restaurant 2010 (Mange Tout). (See also Accommodation & A–Z sections).

Pierneef à La Motte La Motte Wine Estate, R45, Main Road, Franschhoek ▪ Traditional Cape Winelands cuisine ▪ Open for breakfast Sat–Sun from 9, lunch Tue–Sun & dinner Thu–Sat ▪ Closed Mon; 3-week winter break & Christian religious holidays ▪ Booking advised ▪ Children welcome ▪ Major credit cards accepted ▪ Corkage R50 ▪ Owner Hanneli Rupert-Koegelenberg ▪ Executive chef Chris Erasmus ▪ pierneef@la-motte.co.za ▪ www.la-motte.co.za ▪ S 33° 53' 0.91" E 19° 4' 21.57" gate; S 33° 52' 55" E 19° 4' 24" helipad ▪ **T +27 (0)21-876-8800** ▪ F +27 (0)21-876-8855

Savour an interactive food and wine experience in a tranquil garden setting, where innovative Cape Winelands cuisine echoes the creativity of renowned South African artist, J.H. Pierneef. Ingredients and flavours, inspired by centuries of cooking, are transformed into new favourites: try tasty, best-selling Cape bokkom salad. Whether lunching al fresco, fine dining or at a chef's table, enjoy wine-pairing suggestions from an extensive winelist. *Eat Out* Top 20, 2012. (See also A–Z section.)

Rickety Bridge Restaurant in the Vines Rickety Bridge Wine Estate, R45, Main Road, Franschhoek ▪ Asian-influenced cuisine ▪ Open daily 11–3.30 ▪ Closed Jan 1 ▪ Booking advised in summer ▪ Children welcome ▪ Major credit cards accepted ▪ No BYO ▪ Owner Rickety Bridge ▪ Chef Melissa Bruyns ▪ functions@ricketybridge.com ▪ www.ricketybridge.com ▪ **T +27 (0)21-876-2129** ▪ F +27 (0)21-876-3486

Take a seat in the revamped old wine centre, overlooking vineyards. Sip crisp estate wine with a flavour-packed lunch, given extra zest by the setting and mountain views. The varied menu is Asian-influenced and strong in seafood, accenting home-made sauces, jams and pesto. Try the gourmet Franschhoek salmon trout burger: the home-made roll is beetroot-pink and the fishcake and lime aioli fresh, light and delicious. (See also Accommodation & A–Z sections.)

The French Connection Bistro 48 Huguenot Street, Franschhoek ▪ French bistro ▪ Open daily for lunch 12–3.30 & dinner 6.30–9.30 ▪ Closed for dinner on Dec 25 ▪ Booking advised ▪ Children welcome ▪ Major credit cards accepted ▪ Corkage R40 (1 bottle per 4 guests) ▪ Chef-Patron Matthew Gordon ▪ GM Jason Ratner ▪ info@frenchconnection.co.za ▪ www.frenchconnection.co.za ▪ S 33° 54' 36.49" E 019° 7' 8.31" ▪ **T +27 (0)21-876-4056** ▪ F +27 (0)86-591-4988

One of the most popular stops in the 'Gourmet Capital' of the Cape, Matthew Gordon's bistro on the Franschhoek main street offers a relaxed dining experience with friendly, informative service. Treat your palate to superb steaks (best-seller is fillet mignon with 3-mushroom sauce); slow-roasted crispy duck with raspberry vinegar jus; the freshest fish and top-quality produce. As dessert, go Gallic with classic crème brûlée. American Express Platinum Fine Dining Award 2006-2012; Diners Club International winelist award 2011; Tripadvisor Certificate of Excellence for 2012.

Hermanus
La Vierge Restaurant & Champagne Verandah
La Vierge Private Cellar, Hemel-en-Aarde Valley Road (R320), Hermanus ▪ Fresh country fare ▪ Open daily 12–5 ▪ Booking advised ▪ Ideal for weddings & corporate events ▪ Children welcome ▪ Major

credit cards accepted (excl. AmEx) ▪ No BYO ▪ Owner La Vierge (Pty) Ltd ▪ restaurant@lavierge.co.za ▪ www.lavierge.co.za ▪ S 34° 22′22.3″ E 19° 14′29.4″ ▪ **T +27 (0)28-313-2007** ▪ F +27 (0)28-312-1388 Spectacular vistas of the Hemel-en-Aarde Valley and Atlantic Ocean form a backdrop to 'real food' that delights without intimidating. This is country fare; fresh, local and home-made: don't skip sinful dessert. Appetising blackboard menus change regularly (watch for comfort food in winter) with seafood, crunchy baby green salads, duck and cherry pie, and aged fillet steak sauced in date and Stilton cream, among nostalgic specialities. (See also A–Z section.)

Hout Bay
Pure Restaurant Hout Bay Manor, Baviaanskloof Road, Hout Bay ▪ Classic French bistro, with a modern twist ▪ Dinner Tue–Sat 6.30-10.30, lunch Sun 12-3 ▪ Closed Sun eve & Mon ▪ Booking advised ▪ Children welcome ▪ Major credit cards accepted ▪ No BYO, extensive wine list ▪ Occasional Wine & Dine evenings with live band ▪ Owner Susan Struengmann ▪ Head chef Philip Arno Botes ▪ pure@ houtbaymanor.co.za ▪ www.pure-restaurant.co.za ▪ S 34° 04′32.01″ E 18° 36′06.38″ ▪ **T +27 (0)21-791-9393** ▪ F +27 (0)21-790-0118 This elegant octagonal restaurant, awash in soothing tones of shell and sand appropriate to its seaside setting, is an unexpected but delightful find in a graceful 1871 manor house. Creative young head chef Philip Arno Botes adds an earthy touch to flavour combos and inviting plating, rooting appetising dishes in fresh local produce. Unpretentious ambience, friendly service, and a Hout Bay wine on the well-chosen winelist. (See also Accommodation section.)

Kuils River
Zevenwacht Restaurant see under Stellenbosch

Montagu
Ma Cuisine — Mimosa Lodge 19 Church Street, Montagu ▪ French contemporary ▪ Open daily for breakfast 8-10 & dinner 7.30-8.30 (last table in) ▪ Booking essential ▪ Children by prior arrangement ▪ Major credit cards accepted ▪ Corkage R45 ▪ Owners Bernhard & Fida Hess ▪ Executive chef Bernhard Hess ▪ info@mimosa.co.za ▪ www.mimosa.co.za ▪ S 33 47.270 E 20 07.145 ▪ **T +27 (0)23-614-2351** ▪ F +27 (0)86-535-0722 Run by chef/patron Bernhard Hess, this multiple award-winning restaurant in an Edwardian guest house is known for fine dining in the French contemporary style. Creative 4-course set dinners change daily, depending on what's local and freshly available, enhanced by subtle sauces and gourmet touches. Wine and dine options showcasing local

wines allow you to explore the region's wines at your table. Special dietary needs catered for. American Express Platinum Fine Dining Award 2008-2012. (See also A–Z section for Mimosa Boutique Wines.)

Overberg
Gordon Manuel @ The Venue see under Elgin

Paarl
Babel Restaurant Babylonstoren, Klapmuts-Simondium Road (R45), Franschhoek ▪ Honest, organic produce from the 8 acre garden (tours offered) ▪ Lunch Wed–Sun 12-4 & dinner Fri–Sat 6.30-9 ▪ Closed Mon–Tue & Dec 25 ▪ Booking advised ▪ Garden glasshouse open daily for teas and light bites ▪ Children welcome ▪ Major credit cards accepted ▪ Corkage R30/wine & R50/sparkling wine ▪ Owners Karen Roos & Koos Bekker ▪ Executive chef Simone Rossouw ▪ F&B Manager Anelle van Tonder ▪ enquiries@ babylonstoren.com ▪ www.babylonstoren.com ▪ S 33° 49′21.00″ E 18° 55′48.00″ ▪ **T +27 (0)21-863-3852** ▪ F +27 (0)21-863-1727 Table decorations in the airy, glass-walled restaurant could be a cabbage leaf; the farm-to-fork menu is based on what's available in the garden, with local meats and cheeses. Signature dishes of garden-fresh red, green or yellow salads burst with nature's bounty; crispy pork belly comes with best-ever hand-cut chips. New is a conservatory serving sandwiches on woodfire-oven baked bread; irresistible cakes and fresh herbal teas. *Eat Out* Top 20, 2011; *Tatler* International Travel Awards, category: Food, Glorious Food 2011. (See also Accommodation & A–Z sections.)

Backsberg Restaurant Backsberg Estate Cellars, Klapmuts-Simondium Road, Klapmuts ▪ Country cuisine ▪ Open daily 9.30-3.30 ▪ Booking advised ▪ Children welcome ▪ Major credit cards accepted (excl. American Express & Diners Club) ▪ No BYO ▪ Owner Michael Back ▪ Executive chef Linda Abrahams ▪ restaurant@backsberg.co.za; info@backsberg.co.za ▪ www.backsberg.co.za ▪ S 33° 49′684″ E 18° 54′917″ ▪ **T +27 (0)21-875-5952/-5141** ▪ F +27 (0)21-875-5144 Relaxed, child-friendly venue that makes matching food and wine (including international award winners) an everyday pleasure. Filling farm burger; seasonal à la carte dishes. Bookings essential for signature spit-roasted Karoo lamb with roast potatoes every Sunday, or by pre-arrangement. Lawns with stunning mountain views, cosy indoor setting for colder days; live music on Sundays. Go home with farm-grown preserves, fresh supplies and tempting baked goodies. (See also A–Z section.)

Bosman's Restaurant Plantasie Street, Paarl ▪ Global cuisine ▪ **Bosman's Restaurant:** closed Mon-Wed from 1 Apr-20 Dec, no children under the age of

4 ▪ Bistro Allegro: open daily for breakfast & lunch, children welcome, closed to outside guests Mon–Wed from 1 Apr–20 Dec ▪ Booking advised ▪ Major credit cards accepted ▪ No BYO ▪ GM Anja Bosken ▪ Executive chef Roland Gorgosilich ▪ reserve@ granderoche.co.za ▪ www.granderoche.com ▪ S 33° 45'02" E 18° 57'35" ▪ **T +27 (0)21-863-5100** ▪ F +27 (0)21-863-2220

Dine finely in the gracious ambience of a magnificent manor house in the heart of the Boland winemaking region. Five-star Grande Roche Hotel is a hospitality legend boasting an array of awards and culinary accolades; Bosman's restaurant, under award-winning executive chef Roland Gorgosilich, offers creative cuisine complemented by fine wines from a superbly stocked cellar. Indulgent specialities include subtly spiced foie-gras-baumkuchen terrine and truffle-flavoured goats cheese. Diners Club Wine List Diamond Award & *Wine Spectator's* 'Best of Award of Excellence' 2011; SA Tourism Award No 1 Fine Dining Restaurant in SA, & *Eat Out* Top 10, 2010. (See also Accommodation section for Grande Roche Hotel.)

cosecha Restaurant see under Franschhoek

Delheim Restaurant see under Stellenbosch

Glen Carlou Restaurant Simondium Road, Klapmuts ▪ Contemporary cuisine with French & African influences, paired with Glen Carlou wines ▪ Lunch daily 11–3; Thu–Fri (Oct–Apr) tapas 4–7 & dinner 7–9 ▪ Closed Good Fri, Dec 25 & Jan 1 ▪ Booking advised ▪ Children welcome ▪ Major credit cards accepted ▪ BYO by arrangement, corkage R50 ▪ Weddings & events welcomed ▪ Contemporary art on display ▪ Wine tasting available daily ▪ Owner Hess Family Estates ▪ Executive chef Hennie van der Merwe ▪ restaurant@glencarlou.co.za ▪ www.glencarlou.co.za ▪ S 33° 48'34.44" E 18° 54'19.41" ▪ **T +27 (0)21-875-5528** ▪ F +27 (0)21-875-5314

Family-friendly venue with spectacular view from the sunlit veranda, or from behind glass in winter, the stylish interior cosily lit and fire-warmed. Geared for long, lazy Sunday lunching and quick weekday business lunches. Seasonal menus offer choices from succulent venison shanks to prawn tortellini with chorizo and saffron cream, and signature Asian-glazed pork belly. Enjoy best-selling pairing: crème brûlée with their Natural Sweet Chenin Blanc. (See also A–Z section.)

Joostenberg Bistro see under Stellenbosch

Marc's Mediterranean Cuisine and Garden 129 Main Street, Paarl ▪ Mediterranean cuisine/grill/pizza/mezze platters/specials ▪ Open daily for lunch, dinner Mon–Sat ▪ Closed Sun night, Easter Mon, 2 weeks during winter school holiday, Dec 26 & Jan 1 ▪ Booking advised ▪ Children welcome ▪ Major credit cards accepted ▪ Corkage R40 ▪ Owner Marc Friederich ▪ info@marcsrestaurant.co.za ▪ www.marcsrestaurant.co.za ▪ **T +27 (0)21-863-3980** ▪ F +27 (0)21-863-3990

This relaxed, bistro-style restaurant (now with an off-licence) celebrates its 10th anniversary with greater focus on selected Paarl wineries and wine-pairing: a natural progression for patron Marc, who is both internationally qualified chef and sommelier. Regulars swear by evergreen paella, prime quality steaks and Belgian chocolate mousse, but ultra-crisp, thin-based pizzas with deliciously flavourful (even low-carb) toppings are also flying: do try Alsatian flammekueche.

Polo Club Restaurant at Val de Vie Estate R301, Jan van Riebeeck Drive, Paarl ▪ Contemporary country cuisine ▪ Open Tue, Thu & Sun 9–4, Wed, Fri & Sat 9–9 ▪ Closed Mon ▪ Booking advised ▪ Children welcome ▪ Major credit cards accepted ▪ Corkage R40 ▪ Owners Jan Morne Bosch & Nicolas Hendrik Hendrikse ▪ restaurant@valdevie.co.za ▪ www.valdevie.co.za ▪ S 33° 48'15.0" E 18° 58'4.0" ▪ **T +27 (0)21-863-6174** ▪ F +27 (0)21-863-2741

Relish sophisticated bistro-style fare in this view-rich restaurant. Enjoy a relaxed family lunch at terrace tables overlooking the polo field, or dine finely in the elegant dining room, in front of the great fireplace. Invitingly-plated dishes range from pizzas (even a bambino Margherita) and toasted ciabatta sandwiches to bobotie wontons, Thai curries, and succulent steaks, perfectly paired with the estate's award-winning wines. (See also A–Z section.)

Spice Route Restaurant Spice Route, Suid-Agter Paarl Road, Suider-Paarl ▪ Contemporary, eclectic ▪ Open Mon–Thu, Sun & pub hols 11–6 (kitchen closes at 5.30); Fri-Sat 11–8.30 (kitchen closes at 8) ▪ Picnic baskets available ▪ Closed Dec 25 & Jan 1 ▪ Booking advised ▪ Children welcome ▪ Major credit cards accepted ▪ Corkage R50 ▪ Owners Andy Küng & Charles Back ▪ Executive chef Marion Kumpf ▪ restaurant@spiceroute.co.za ▪ www.spicerouterestaurant.co.za ▪ S 33° 45'50" E 18° 55'10" ▪ **T +27 (0)21-863-5222** ▪ F +2 (0)21-863-2591

The public face of hand-crafted wines, with a relaxed restaurant focused on wine-pairing, Spice Route is the nucleus of an artisanal centre. Already home to DV Artisan chocolate and Red Hot Glass studio, there's a microbrewery about to open. Savour subtly-spiced, deliciously wine-friendly dishes overlooking an edge-to-edge vista of mountains and vineyards, and do try slow-roasted pork belly on dark chocolate lentils with Spice Route Chakalaka. (See also A–Z section.)

The Goatshed Restaurant Fairview Wine & Cheese Farm, Suid-Agter Paarl Road, Suider-Paarl ▪ Farm-style Mediterranean ▪ Open daily 9–5 (kitchen closes at 4.30) ▪ Closed Dec 25 & Jan 1 ▪ Booking advised ▪ Children welcome ▪ Major credit cards accepted ▪ Corkage R50 ▪ Owners Andy Küng & Charles Back ▪ Executive chef Andy Küng ▪ goatshed@fairview.co.za ▪ www.goatshed.co.za ▪ S 33° 46' 22.00" E 18° 55' 24.50" ▪ **T +27 (0)21-863-3609** ▪ F +2 (0)21-863-2591

Named for Fairview's 800-strong goat herd, this rustic, hospitable restaurant in one of the farm's old wine cellars pulls the crowds with light and tasty lunches from locally-sourced seasonal produce, spilling on to a terrace in summer. Enjoy highly-rated Fairview wines with Chalmar beef, chicken pie and springbok salad; or pick a platter from some 25 farm cheeses with just-baked breads, including more-ish Goatshed ciabatta. *Eat Out* Top 10 Alfresco Restaurants 2010. (See also A–Z section.)

Plettenberg Bay

Bramon Wine Estate Restaurant N2, The Crags, Plettenberg Bay ▪ Global mezze tapas country style ▪ Open daily 11–5 ▪ Closed Dec 25 ▪ Booking advised ▪ Children welcome ▪ Major credit cards accepted (excl. American Express) ▪ No BYO ▪ Owners Thorpe, Gaggio & Reggio families ▪ Chefs Olivia Casper, Henna Losper, Sumi Adlam & Cheryl Mynhard ▪ peter@bramonwines.co.za ▪ www.bramonwines.co.za ▪ S 33° 57' 20.30" E 23° 28' 45.02" ▪ **T +27 (0)44-534-8007** ▪ F +27 (0)86-589-6816

Relaxing restaurant with a unique location: the wine estate farthest east of the Western Cape, slap in the middle of Plettenberg Bay. Set in vineyards, overlooking the elephant sanctuary and Tsitsikamma Mountains, it's an ideal spot for languorous lunches with wines from the estate. Indulge in piping hot homemade breads, fresh oysters and flagship bubbly, mezze treats (including dolmades from the vine), and decadent desserts. Winner of Knysna Culinary Oyster Festival 2010 & '11; Top on *Trip Advisor* 2011 & '12; Top 10 Restaurants in Garden Route 2010 & '11. (See also A–Z section.)

Robertson

Fraai Uitzicht 1798 Klaas Voogds East, on R60 between Robertson & Montagu ▪ Contemporary, fusion, Mediterranean influences ▪ Open Wed–Sun lunch from 12 & dinner from 6 (Mon–Tue dinner for resident guests only) ▪ Closed mid Jun–end Aug, Dec 24/31 & Jan 1 ▪ Booking advised ▪ Children 12+ welcome ▪ Major credit cards accepted ▪ No BYO ▪ Owners Karl Uwe & Sandra Papesch ▪ Executive chef Sandra Papesch ▪ info@fraaiuitzicht.com ▪ www.fraaiuitzicht.com ▪ S 33° 47' 43.23" E 20° 00' 17.87" ▪ **T +27 (0)23-626-6156** ▪ F +27 (0)86-662-5265

Share the pleasures of award-winning food and the best Robertson wines on the umbrella-shaded veranda or at the dining-room fire. Seasonal menus highlight fresh vegetables and just-picked herbs from the garden: pair hand-crafted Fraai Uitzicht 1798 Merlot with best-selling grilled steak tartare (seared-on-the-base fillet topped with herb-rich tomato and pinenut salsa). Or enjoy the wine in merlot syrup with a dreamy, freshly-baked Belgian chocolate fondant. American Express Platinum Fine Dining award — 11 years consecutively, latest 2013. *Rossouw's Restaurants* (highly recommended good food & more). (See also Accommodation & A–Z sections.)

Rosendal Restaurant Rosendal Winery & Wellness Retreat, Klaas Voogds West, Robertson ▪ French haut cuisine & continental — catering for any dietary requirements & ethnical preferences ▪ Open daily for breakfast 8–10, lunch 12–3 & dinner 7–9.30 ▪ Booking advised ▪ Children welcome ▪ Visa & MasterCard accepted ▪ Corkage R35 ▪ Owners Geir & Sissel Tellefsen ▪ Executive chef David Godin; sous chef Enoryt Appolis ▪ info@rosendalwinery.com ▪ www.rosendalwinery.com ▪ S 33° 48' 7.8" E 019° 59' 19.0" ▪ **T +27 (0)23-626-1570** ▪ F +27 (0)23-626-1571

Robust by day, elegant by night. Experience a fusion of French/SA cuisine from Rosendal's internationally-experienced kitchen team, paired with award-winning wines. Herb-rich, flavour-fresh dishes are served with a healthy portion of passion, while classics like vol au vent of snails or lamb with ratatouille and potatoes dauphinois share menu space with butter chicken curry, and desserts include rooibos crème brûlée, chocolate brownies and Malva pudding. (See also Accommodation & A–Z sections.)

Somerset West

96 Winery Road Restaurant see under Stellenbosch

Avontuur Estate Restaurant Avontuur Wine Estate, R44, Somerset West ▪ Contemporary country ▪ Open daily 9–4; dinner Wed, Fri & Sat (to be confirmed in winter) ▪ Closed Good Fri, Dec 25 & Jan 1 ▪ Booking advised ▪ Children welcome ▪ Major credit cards accepted ▪ No BYO ▪ Chefs/patrons Zunia Boucher-Myers & Melanie Paltoglou ▪ openhand@polka.co.za ▪ www.avontuurestate.co.za ▪ S 34° 1' 33.2" E 018° 49' 23.8" ▪ **T +27 (0)21-855-4296** ▪ F +27 (0)21-855-4600

Celebrating its 10th anniversary, this popular estate restaurant with hands-on, people-friendly chef/patrons, specialises in value-for-money, appetising food, served at shady tables with a view. Seasonal menus, centred round organic produce, add new dishes to old favourites: tender fillet and crispy duck have been joined by lighter options like preserved figs, brie and mascarpone; and smoked salmon trout with grilled prawns. End indulgently with deep-fried ice-cream. 4-star rated by the Tourism Grading Council. (See also A–Z section.)

Manuka Restaurant 196 Main Road, Somerset West, next to Southeys Vines ▪ Family dining, Mediterranean ▪ Open Mon–Wed 8–5.30, Thu–Sat 8–10pm, Sun 9–3.30 ▪ Closed Good Fri, Dec 25/26 & Jan 1 ▪ Booking advised ▪ Children welcome ▪ Major credit cards accepted ▪ Corkage R25 ▪ Owners Stephen & Alison Digby ▪ southeys@manuka.co.za ▪ www.manuka.co.za ▪ S 34° 04' 33.02" E 18° 50' 40.26" ▪ **T** +27 (0)21-851-6060/+27 (0)87-150-0729 ▪ F +27 (0)21-86-665-1051

Welcoming family restaurant in a garden setting complete with ducks and chickens. Relax under sun-umbrellas and enjoy breakfasts from croissants to hearty Manuka Full House; thin-based wood-fired pizzas with inventive toppings; steaks (go for the blockman's choice); salads and wraps. Fully licensed, with the well-stocked wine shop offering over 300 wines at close-to cellar door prices. Monthly wine dinners and weekly tastings every Saturday. Ample parking.

The Restaurant at Waterkloof Waterkloof Wines, Old Sir Lowry's Pass Village Road, Somerset West ▪ Contemporary, with a French fusion ▪ Lunch daily, dinner Mon–Sat ▪ Closed Sun eve, Good Fri, Dec 25 & Jan 1 ▪ Booking advised ▪ Children welcome, preferably for lunch ▪ Major credit cards accepted ▪ Corkage R55 ▪ Owner Paul Boutinot ▪ Executive chef Grégory Czarnecki ▪ restaurant@waterkloofwines.co.za ▪ www.waterkloofwines.co.za ▪ S 34° 5' 55.4" E 018° 53' 22.8" ▪ **T** +27 (0)21-858-1491 ▪ F +27 (0)21-858-1293

Here food is art, calling for unhurried appreciation; complemented by the estate's European-style wines and seamless service. Chef Grégory Czarnecki is from a 3-star Michelin background: savour 6-course degustation menus, close your eyes, and you could be in Paris. But why close them? You're seated in a lofty glass promontory flowing from state-of-the-art tasting lounge and cellar, overlooking the amphitheatre of Waterkloof vineyards and False Bay. Great Wine Capitals Best of Wine Tourism Awards 2012, highly scored across several categories. (See also A–Z section.)

Vergelegen Vergelegen Wine Estate, Lourensford Road, Somerset West ▪ **Vergelegen Restaurant** (à la carte/contemporary/global) Nov–Apr: lunch daily 12–3 & dinner Thu–Sat; May–Oct: lunch Wed–Sun 12–3 & dinner Fri–Sat; **Stables at Vergelegen** (bistro) open daily for breakfast 9.30–11.30, lunch 12–3 & selected light meals 12–4; Nov–Apr kitchen closes Fri–Sun at 7pm; **Camphor Forest Picnic** (luxury/elegant picnic) baskets available Nov–Apr between 12.15–1.30 ▪ Estate closed Good Fri, May 1 & Dec 25 ▪

Booking advised ▪ Camphor Forest Picnic & Stables specifically child-friendly ▪ Major credit cards accepted ▪ No BYO ▪ Owners Anglo American plc ▪ info@vergelegen.co.za ▪ www.vergelegen.co.za ▪ S 34° 04' 47.0" E 18° 53' 12.3" ▪ **T** +27 (0)21-847-1346 **Vergelegen Restaurant,** +27 (0)21-847-2156 **Stables Bistro/Camphor Forest Picnic** ▪ F +27 (0)21-847-1608

The crowd-pulling Vergelegen hospitality experience has a new family-friendly drawcard: the glass-fronted **Stables at Vergelegen,** where you enjoy bistro-style treats - from pastries to pizzas (junior sizes available), generous burgers, juicy plank steaks and delectable desserts - against a breathtaking mountain backdrop. At weekends nibble early-evening light bites while admiring sunsets or the moon rising over the mountain range. (Summer: Friday–Sunday). **Vergelegen Restaurant (formerly Lady Phillips)** Experience food and wine culinary adventures in the revamped restaurant, where award-winning classic wines are seamlessly paired with classically-grounded global cuisine. Relax outdoors on the newly-designed patio, sheltered by liquid amber trees and overlooking manicured lawns, or opt for a table in the stylish interior. **Camphor Forest Picnic** Chill out at an elegant picnic in the deep shadow of a centuries-old-camphor forest while the children are occupied on an exciting treasure hunt. (See also A–Z section.)

Stanford

Boschrivier Restaurant On the R326 between Caledon & Stanford ▪ Country cuisine ▪ Open Mon–Fri & public holidays 8–5, Sat 9–5 & Sun 10–1 ▪ Closed Dec 25 ▪ Booking advised ▪ Children welcome ▪ Major credit cards accepted ▪ BYO allowed, no corkage charged ▪ Owner NJT de Villiers ▪ Executive chefs Chaline & Helen Dramat ▪ drnjtdevilliers@mweb.co.za ▪ S 34° 23' 19.4" E 19° 37' 51.0" ▪ **T** +27 (0)28-341-0630 ▪ F +27 (0)23-342-2215

Take a break among vines and fynbos when travelling the R326 in the scenic Overberg region. Boschrivier farm, where the De Villiers family has farmed sheep for centuries, is midway between Stanford and Caledon. Vines were planted in 1998 and the tasting room and restaurant established. Accommodation in the farmhouse is available, and the restaurant offers English breakfasts and light meals, with generous hamburgers a speciality. (See also Accommodation & A–Z sections.)

Stellenbosch

96 Winery Road Restaurant Zandberg Farm, Winery Road, off the R44 between Somerset West & Stellenbosch ▪ Warm country style ▪ Lunch daily 12–3, dinner Mon–Sat 6.30–10 ▪ Closed Sun eve, Dec 26 & Jan 1 ▪ Booking advised ▪ Children welcome ▪ Major credit cards accepted ▪ Corkage R45 ▪ Owners Allan &

Ken Forrester, Martin Meinert & Natasha Wray ▪ Executive chef Natasha Wray ▪ wineryrd@ mweb.co.za ▪ www.96wineryroad.co.za ▪ S 34° 02' 746" E 18° 80'891" ▪ **T** +27 (0)21-842-2020 ▪ F +27 (0)21-842-2050

This warm, relaxing venue, opened in May '96 in the heart of the Helderberg countryside, is still true to its goal: 'to delight each guest with a superb dining experience'. Appetising menus, inspired by SA favourites and global flavours, centre round fresh ingredients, often organic and locally sourced. Carnivores note: meat is a speciality and best-selling signature dish is mouth-melting Hollandse pepper fillet. Excellent winelist. Top 100 winelist award 2012; Diamond Award & *Wine Spectator* Award of Excellence '11.

Avontuur Estate Restaurant see under Somerset West

Barouche Restaurant Blaauwklippen Vineyards, on the R44 between Stellenbosch & Somerset West, opposite Techno Park ▪ Modern cuisine ▪ Breakfast & lunch Mon–Sat 9–4 Sun & pub hols 9–3 ▪ Tapas evenings in summer Wed–Fri 4–7, High Tea Mon–Fri 2.30–5 ▪ Closed Mon/Tue in winter; Jan 1 ▪ Booking advised ▪ Children welcome ▪ Major credit cards accepted ▪ Corkage R45 ▪ Family Market every Sun 10–3 ▪ Horse-drawn carriage rides ▪ Picnics ▪ Cellar tours & wine tasting at the Wine Centre ▪ Weddings, functions & conferences ▪ Owners Blue Lion GmbH ▪ hospitality@blaauwklippen.com ▪ www.blaauwklippen.com ▪ S 33° 58'23.3" E 018° 50' 51.0" ▪ **T** +27 (0)21-880-8222 ▪ F +27 (0)21-880-1246

Family friendly, indoor-outdoor restaurant with tasty picnic barrel platters or à la carte menus with wine-matching suggestions. Special under-12 lunch treats and play area with pony rides to occupy kids while you savour palate-pleasing favourites like ostrich carpaccio with zinfandel dressing or aromatic bobotie. Be seduced by deep-fried ice cream and round-off lunch with a horse-drawn carriage ride. (See also A–Z section.)

Cuvée Simonsig Wine Estate, Kromme-Rhee Road, Stellenbosch ▪ Contemporary cuisine ▪ Lunch Tue–Sat 12–3 Sun 12–2; dinner Wed, Fri & Sat 7–10 ▪ Closed Mon; Wed eve (winter) ▪ Booking advised ▪ Children welcome ▪ Major credit cards accepted ▪ No BYO ▪ Owners Francois & Johan Malan ▪ Executive chef Lucas Carstens ▪ cuvee@simonsig.co.za ▪ www.cuveeatsimonsig.co.za ▪ S 33° 52'14.19" E 18° 49'34.92" ▪ **T** +27 (0)21-888-4932 ▪ F +27 (0)21-888-4909

Enjoy genuine hospitality and back-to-basics food in a quirky mix of nostalgia and Cape Dutch modernism. New exec chef Lucas Carstens sources local, farm-fresh and sustainable ingredients, and his

delight in diverse flavours shows in combos like white fish, assam prawn salsa and miso-tossed noodles, and Chalmar beef with Guinness butter emulsion. Chocoholics, indulge in the bitter chocolate fondant with cognac ice-cream and chocolate coffee beans. (See also A–Z section.)

Delaire Graff Restaurant Delaire Graff Estate, R310, Helshoogte Pass, Banhoek Valley, Stellenbosch ▪ Bistro-chic ▪ Lunch daily 12–2.30, dinner Mon–Sat 6.30–9.30 ▪ Closed Sun eve ▪ Booking advised ▪ Children welcome ▪ Major credit cards accepted ▪ No BYO ▪ Owner Laurence Graff ▪ Executive chef Christiaan Campbell ▪ reservations@delaire.co.za ▪ www.delaire.co.za ▪ S 33° 55'236" E 18° 55'207" ▪ **T** +27 (0)21-885-8160

A trio of attractions: the spectacular view, the striking art-rich décor that juxtaposes happily with the mountain and vineyard panorama, and signature wine-friendly 'bistro chic' from exec chef Christiaan Campbell. This implies beautifully presented yet simple seasonal dishes from 'green' farmers and organic suppliers, combined with flair and flavour. Delight in decadent dessert and end with tea. The selection's wide and the ceremony delightful. (See also Accommodation & A–Z sections.)

Delheim Restaurant Delheim Wine Farm, Knorhoek Road, off the R44 between Stellenbosch & Paarl ▪ Traditional German & South African cuisine ▪ Open daily: breakfast 9.30–11.30, lunch 12–3.30, snacks & cheese platters 3.30–4.30 ▪ Small private functions catered for ▪ Closed Easter Fri/Sun, Dec 25 & Jan 1 ▪ Booking advised ▪ Children welcome ▪ Major credit cards accepted ▪ No BYO ▪ Owners Sperling family ▪ restaurant@delheim.com ▪ www.delheim.com ▪ S 33° 52'10" E 18° 53'08" ▪ **T** +27 (0)21-888-4600 ▪ F +27 (0)21-888-4601

German gemütlichkeit reigns at this relaxed restaurant in a gorgeous garden setting with long-distance views of Table Mountain. Eat al fresco on the garden terraces in summer; or relish comfort food beside a winter fire. Take a hearty appetite: specialities range from German platters (with traditional onion pie) to ostrich bobotie; from merlot-marinated Karoo lambshank to traditional bratwurst. There's even a sophisticated mini-menu for kids. (See also A–Z section.)

Eight Spier, R310 Lynedoch Road, Stellenbosch ▪ Fresh farm-to-table fare ▪ Open Tue–Sun 10–4 ▪ Closed Mon ▪ Booking advised ▪ Children welcome: jungle gym, toys & healthy treats ▪ Major credit cards accepted ▪ No BYO ▪ Executive chef Lorianne Heyns ▪ info@spier.co.za ▪ www.spier.co.za ▪ S 33° 58'379" E 18° 46'944" ▪ **T** +27 (0)21-809-1188 ▪ F +27 (0)21-809-1134

Relish the freshly picked flavours of a farm-to-table eating experience, with produce sourced from Spier or nearby farmers. As its name implies, the airy eaterie strives for balance, cycles, harmony, infinity and abundance — expressed in delicious daily choices. Start with refreshing just-squeezed juices; be tempted by tasty biodynamic vegetable dishes and pasture-fed chicken (try best-selling pie), and indulge without guilt in flour-free organic chocolate cake. (See also A–Z section.)

Flavours at The Devon Valley Hotel Devon Valley Road, Devon Valley, Stellenbosch ▪ Contemporary Cape cuisine ▪ Open daily 6.30am–11pm ▪ Booking advised ▪ Children welcome ▪ Major credit cards accepted ▪ BYO not encouraged, corkage R30 ▪ Owner Louis Group Hotels, Spa's & Vineyards ▪ Executive chef Markus Schwemberger ▪ info@devonvalleyhotel.com ▪ www.devonvalleyhotel.com ▪ S 33° 54' 12.64" E 18° 48' 53.03" ▪ **T +27 (0)21-865-2012** ▪ F +27 (0)21-865-2610

Welcoming restaurant in a picturesque setting deep in the vineyards, celebrating classic, uncomplicated seasonal dishes with fresh, clean tastes that allow flavour priority. For maximum palate pleasure, marry the bold flavours of specialities like herb-crusted Karoo rack of lamb on potato rösti with pinotage jus, to the restaurant's award-winning winelist. Lunch menus are light and tasty, enlivened with daily specials to ensure freshness and variety. Diners Club Wine List Diamond Award 2009 -'11. (See also Accommodation section & A–Z for SylvanVale.)

Guardian Peak Winery & Grill Guardian Peak, Annandale Road, Stellenbosch ▪ South African food & wine experience ▪ Open Tue–Sat 9–5 & Sun 9–4; dinner Wed–Sat from 6 to close ▪ Closed Mon, Good Fri & Dec 25 ▪ Booking advised ▪ Children welcome ▪ Major credit cards accepted ▪ No BYO ▪ Owner Jean Engelbrecht ▪ info@guardianpeak.com ▪ www.guardianpeak.com ▪ S 34° 0' 40.48" E 18° 50' 31.29" ▪ **T +27 (0)21-881-3899** ▪ F +27 (0)21-881-3388

For a true Stellenbosch Winelands experience, succumb to the invitation of vineyard vistas from tables on a wide veranda. Breakfasts range from light and healthy to a hearty 'Kalahari Lion'; lunches and dinners are wine-inspired, to match hearty, wholesome dishes and prime-quality steaks. Do try a 'Portfolio Tasting' with wines from Guardian Peak's greater portfolio, sold under separate brands. (See also A–Z section for Guardian Peak, Stellenbosch Ridge, Cirrus & Donkiesbaai.)

Indochine Restaurant Delaire Graff Estate, R310, Helshoogte Pass, Banhoek Valley, Stellenbosch ▪ Asian-inspired cuisine ▪ Open daily for lunch 12–2.30 & dinner 6.30–9.30 ▪ Booking advised ▪ Children welcome ▪ Major credit cards accepted ▪ No BYO ▪ Owner Laurence Graff ▪ Executive chef Christiaan Campbell ▪ guest.relations@delaire.co.za ▪ www.delaire.co.za ▪ S

33° 55' 236" E 18° 55' 207" ▪ **T +27 (0)21-885-8160**

Asian-inspired cuisine is perfectly placed in this serene, art-studded ambience, under a flight of swallows suspended from the ceiling. Wrap-round views over Stellenbosch valley, a focused winelist and organic ingredients from the estate greenhouse, root you in the Cape. But picture-perfect, aromatic dishes like ponzu duck salad, slow-roasted pork belly, and Burmese linefish, with an array of side-dishes, waft your taste buds swiftly to the East. (See also Accommodation & A–Z sections.)

Joostenberg Bistro Klein Joostenberg, R304, Muldersvlei ▪ French bistro ▪ Open daily from 8–5 ▪ Closed Dec 25 & Jan 1 ▪ Booking advised ▪ Children welcome ▪ Major credit cards accepted ▪ Corkage R35 ▪ Owners Susan & Christophe Dehosse, Philip Myburgh ▪ Executive chef Christophe Dehosse ▪ bistro@joostenberg.co.za ▪ www.joostenberg.co.za ▪ **T +27 (0)21-884-4208** ▪ F +27 (0)21-884-4141

Craving freshly prepared traditional bistro dishes? Look no further. The specialities & best-selling dishes will set you salivating: coq au vin; bouillabaisse; pork sausages from own farm-reared pork, apple sauce and mash; terrine and jambon persillée — with highly rated Joostenberg wines. The venue is relaxed, spacious and family friendly, with tables set on a vine-shaded stoep in summer and beside a huge fireplace in winter. (See also A–Z section.)

Makaron Restaurant Majeka House, 26-32 Houtkapper Street, Paradyskloof, Stellenbosch ▪ Classic cuisine with quirky update ▪ Open daily for breakfast, lunch & dinner ▪ Booking advised ▪ Children welcome ▪ Major credit cards accepted ▪ Corkage R50 ▪ Owners Karine Dequeker & Lloyd van der Merwe ▪ Executive chef Tanja Kruger ▪ Restaurant manager/sommelier Josephine Gutentoft ▪ info@makaronrestaurant.co.za ▪ www.makaronrestaurant.co.za ▪ S 33° 58' 04.07" E 18° 51' 39.64" ▪ **T +27 (0)21-880-1549** ▪ F +27 (0)21-880-1550

Sit back in the stylish, streamlined dining room: the meal you'll savour will be as eye-catching and sophisticated. Exec chef Tanja Kruger sees food as fun, fresh and flavourful, combining prime local products in creative taste-treats. Try cauliflower custards, popcorn powder, popped wild rice and truffle caviar; pan-seared scallops, black pudding, pea pesto and yuzu pearls; and as dessert, asiette of chocolate, beetroot and pistachio. *Eat Out* Boschendal Style Award 2011; *Wine Spectator* 2012 Award of Excellence for winelist. (See also Accommodation section.)

Morgenhof Restaurant Morgenhof Wine Estate, Klapmuts Road (R44), Stellenbosch ▪ Country — fresh seasonal ▪ Breakfast Sat/Sun 9–11, lunch daily 12–3 (Nov–Apr) & 12–2.30 (May–Oct) ▪ Closed Mondays

(May–end Aug), Good Friday, Dec 25 & Jan 1 ▪ Booking advised ▪ Children welcome (kiddies menu) ▪ Major credit cards accepted ▪ No BYO ▪ Owner Anne Cointreau ▪ info@morgenhof.com ▪ www.morgenhof.com ▪ S 33° 53' 38.5" E 018° 51' 39.2" ▪ **T +27 (0)21-889-5510** ▪ F +27 (0)21-889-5266

Popular year-round venue where flavour sets seasonal menus from exec chef Siraaj Allie. Relax at garden tables in summer; under a vine canopy in winter sunshine; or banishing the chill beside log fires indoors, enjoying signature chicken salad; pan-fried calamari; seafood platters laden with grilled linefish, black tiger prawns and Patagonia squid; or opt for hearty winter lamb shank, Irish crushed potatoes and tasty jus. (See also Accommodation & A–Z sections.)

Red Leaf Restaurant Beyerskloof, Koelenhof Road, R304, Koelenhof, Stellenbosch ▪ Mediterranean ▪ Open Tue–Fri 9–3.30, Sat & pub hols 10–3, last Sun of month 11–3 ▪ Closed Mon, Easter weekend, Dec 25 & Jan 1 ▪ Booking advised on Sat ▪ Children welcome ▪ Visa & MasterCard accepted ▪ Corkage R30 ▪ Owners Corné Hendricks & Francisco Menezes ▪ Executive chef Francisco Menezes ▪ redleafrestaurant@vodamail.co.za ▪ www.redleafrestaurant.weebly.com ▪ S 33° 53' 28.0" E 018° 49' 23.6" ▪ **T +27 (0)21-865-2685** ▪ F +27 (0)21-865-2683

Family-friendly indoor/outdoor eaterie where décor accents the signature logo of Beyerskloof's best-selling brand. Here wine meets food, and not surprisingly, both focus on pinotage. This is the home of the Giant Pinotage Burger. Relax on the wooden deck, enjoy spectacular views over the vineyards, and tuck into a roll with outsize pinotage-infused pattie and extra-large chips, followed by pinotage brandy tart and pinotage-flavoured purple ice-cream. (See also A–Z section.)

Restaurant Barrique Vredenheim Estate, Vlottenburg, R310, Stellenbosch ▪ International, with a lot of local items ▪ Open Tue–Sat 12–4 & 6–late, Sun 12–4 ▪ Closed Mon, Dec 25 & Jan 1 ▪ Booking advised ▪ Children welcome ▪ Major credit cards accepted ▪ Corkage R25 ▪ Owners Karin & Peter Brittz ▪ barrique@vodamail.co.za ▪ S 33° 57' 37.52" E 18° 48' 27.60" ▪ **T +27 (0)21-881-3001** ▪ F +27 (0)21-881-3340

Join the Barrique 'family'. Run by hospitable Karin and Peter Brittz, this warmly welcoming restaurant, a byword for hands-on care and consistent service, ensures that patrons feel at home. Eat in the restored wine cellar, main restaurant or restful garden, feasting on traditional favourites like oxtail, butter-tender Italian-style rump, or pizzas from the wood-fired oven. And don't leave without sampling the deliciously old-fashioned tipsy tart. (See also A–Z section.)

Rust en Vrede Restaurant Rust en Vrede Wine Estate, Annandale Road (off R44), Stellenbosch ▪ Fine dining, contemporary take on the classics ▪ Dinner Tue–Sat from 7 to close ▪ Closed Sun/Mon, Good Fri & Dec 25 ▪ Booking advised ▪ Major credit cards accepted ▪ No BYO ▪ Owner Jean Engelbrecht ▪ Executive chef John Shuttleworth ▪ dining@rustenvrede.com ▪ www.rustenvrede.com ▪ S 33° 59' 54" E 18° 51'21" ▪ **T +27 (0)21-881-3757** ▪ F +27 (0)21-881-3000

Stylish fine dining in the original wine cellar, where décor and custom-designed tableware enhance creative four- and six-course menus, paired with wine. Executive chef John Shuttleworth brings enticing delicacy and tantalisingly original touches to perfectly-plated dishes, while internationally-acclaimed sommelier Joakim Hansi Blackadder adds his expertise to the wine-matching experience, complementing flavour and freshness with superbly-selected, often little-known wines. The result is a world-class gourmet triumph. *San Pellegrino* Top 100 restaurants in the world 2009 -'11; Best Chef 2010, Best Restaurant 2010, Best Service 2009 -'11; *Rossouw's Restaurants* 3 stars 2009 -'11. (See also A–Z section.)

Terroir Restaurant Kleine Zalze Wines, R44, Technopark, Stellenbosch ▪ Provençal ▪ Lunch daily 12–2.30, dinner Mon–Sat 7–9 ▪ Closed Sun eve ▪ Booking advised ▪ Children welcome ▪ Major credit cards accepted ▪ Corkage R50 ▪ Owner Kleine Zalze Wines ▪ Chef Michael Broughton ▪ terroir@kleinezalze.co.za ▪ www.kleinezalze.co.za ▪ S 33° 56' 16.51" E 18° 51' 06.70" ▪ **T +27 (0)21-880-8167** ▪ F +27 (0)21-880-0862

The terroir is decidedly Cape in flavour and setting; so are the food-friendly, highly-rated Kleine Zalze wines. Though deceptively simple dishes are French-inspired, fresh seasonal ingredients are local, showcasing chef Michael Broughton's award-winning culinary skill and impeccably judged sauces. The come-as-you-are ambience encourages lingering over chalkboard offerings such as miso glazed salmon with smoked potato, tempura tomatoes and truffled asparagus, or pork belly with braised apples and cider sauce. *Eat Out* Awards' Top 10 2006 -'07, '09 -'11, 2011 -'12. (See also A–Z section.)

The Big Easy Restaurant & Wine Bar 95 Dorp Street, Stellenbosch ▪ Up-market and contemporary ▪ Open for breakfast, lunch & dinner Mon–Fri 7.30–10pm, Sat/Sun & public holidays 8.30–10pm ▪ Retail store open daily from 9–5 (for proprietor's wines at cellar door prices) ▪ Closed Dec 25 ▪ Booking advised ▪ Children welcome ▪ Major credit cards accepted ▪ No BYO ▪ Owners Jean Engelbrecht, Ernie Els, Johann

Rupert, Paul Harris & Giuseppe Cuicci ▪ info@thebigeasy.co.za ▪ www.thebigeasyrestaurant.co.za ▪ S 33° 56′ 21.67″ E 18° 51′ 28.52″ ▪ **T +27 (0)21-887-3462** ▪ F +27 (0)21-887-3470

Relax and enjoy hearty meals in a laid-back ambience rich in history. Setting is a gracious Cape Dutch manor house with interleading rooms; service is friendly and efficient, and constantly changing menus celebrate seasonal flavours. Prime chargrilled rump, sirloin and fillet are best-sellers, sharing top spot with a speciality burger. But do try the mushroom risotto with truffle cream, and the sinful 70% chocoholic platter. (See also A–Z section.)

The Restaurant @ Clos Malverne Devon Valley Road, Devon Valley, Stellenbosch ▪ Global cuisine ▪ Open Tue–Sun 12–5 ▪ Closed Mon & Christian holidays ▪ Booking advised ▪ Children welcome ▪ Visa & MasterCard accepted ▪ No BYO ▪ Owner Seymour Pritchard ▪ Executive chef Nadia Louw Smith ▪ info@closmalverne.co.za ▪ www.closmalverne.co.za ▪ S 33° 54′ 67″ E 18° 48′ 810″ ▪ **T +27 (0)21-865-2022** ▪ F +27 (0)21-865-2518

Welcoming restaurant, glass-fronted to frame the valley vista, abuzz with regulars back for best-selling grilled fillet with truffle/bone marrow jus. Order it with flagship Auret from a sophisticated four-course menu that pairs Clos Malverne wines with invitingly-presented dishes, from tempura prawns with homemade (hot) chilli sauce to duck confit rolled in crisp phyllo. End meltingly with a caramel-centered chocolate fondant and new-release Pinotage Le Café. (See also A–Z section.)

Wild Peacock Food Emporium 32 Piet Retief Street, Stellenbosch ▪ Brasserie — Del Foods and Mediterranean ▪ Open Mon–Tue 7.30–6, Wed–Fri 7.30–10pm & Sat 8–4 ▪ Closed Sun & religious holidays ▪ Booking advised evenings ▪ Children welcome ▪ Visa & MasterCard accepted ▪ No BYO ▪ Owner Baker Family Trust ▪ sarah@wildpeacock.co.za ▪ www.wildpeacock.co.za ▪ S 33° 56′ 24″ E 18° 51′ 34″ ▪ **T +27 (0)21-887-7585** ▪ F +27 (0)86-577-3663

This enticing French-style brasserie-cum-deli oozes temptation, whether shopping for specialities like oysters, snails, fresh duck, quail, fish, free-range poultry, artisanal cheeses and fine wine, or sitting down to eat. Breakfasts are scrumptious; lunches deliciously light or a filling, flavoursome *plat de jour* (pots of Ma Baker's mussels are a must). Excellent, well-priced wine-by-the-glass selection, plus a specialised retail wine boutique focused on the Stellenbosch area.

Zevenwacht Restaurant Zevenwacht Wine Estate, Langverwacht Road, Kuils River ▪ Modern bistro / farm style dining ▪ Breakfast Mon–Fri 7–10, Sat/Sun & pub hols 8–11; lunch 12–3 & dinner 6–10 daily ▪ Garden picnics ▪ Booking advised ▪ Children

welcome ▪ Major credit cards accepted ▪ No BYO ▪ Owner Manie Wolmarans ▪ Head chef Justin Pillay ▪ restaurant@zevenwacht.co.za ▪ www.zevenwacht.co.za ▪ S 33° 55′ 47″ E 18° 43′ 43″ ▪ **T +27 (0)21-900-5800** ▪ F +27 (0)21-903-5257

Friendly, relaxed manor house restaurant beside a picturesque lake. Service is attentive and seasonal ingredients, locally sourced where possible, are combined in imaginative dishes: pan-fried chicken livers gratinated in red pepper Hollandaise with baby salad leaves; amarula panna cotta topped with warm strawberry compote and a crispy cocoa tuille. Consult the grill menu for free-range meat dishes: best-sellers are the mixed grill and gourmet burgers. (See also Accommodation & A–Z sections.)

Wellington

No. 6 @ Welbedacht Wine Estate Oakdene Road, Wellington ▪ Contemporary styled fusion ▪ Open Tue–Sun 10–late ▪ Closed Mon, Good Fri & Dec 25 ▪ Booking advised ▪ Children welcome ▪ Major credit cards accepted ▪ No BYO ▪ WiFi ▪ Owners Welbedacht Wine Estate ▪ Executive chefs John & Susanna Tecklenburg ▪ no.6@welbedacht.co.za ▪ www.schalkburgerandsons.co.za ▪ S 33° 34′ 39.8″ E 019° 1′ 12.8″ ▪ **T +27 (0)21-873-1877** ▪ F +27 (0)86-669-5641

This gregarious venue for winelovers, sports-lovers and Springbok supporters is a favourite haunt of sporting greats (note the memorabilia on the walls: Schalk Burger Snr and Jnr were the 8th father and son Springbok combo). Integrated into the Welbedacht wine cellar, the down-to-earth restaurant is closely linked to the surrounding vineyards and the wine that complements chef John Tecklenburg's flavourful dishes. Take a hearty appetite. (See also Accommodation & A–Z sections.)

The Stone Kitchen Dunstone Winery, Bovlei Road, Wellington ▪ Bistro ▪ Open Wed–Sun 9–4; open in summer for dinner on Thursdays ▪ Closed Dec 25/26 ▪ Booking advised ▪ Children welcome ▪ Major credit cards accepted ▪ Corkage R50 ▪ Owners Abbi & Lee Wallis ▪ food@dunstone.co.za ▪ www.stonekitchen.biz ▪ S 33° 38′ 01″ E 19° 03′ 41″ ▪ **T/F +27 (0)21-873-6770**

Stomp grapes during harvest. Relaxed bistro in the wine cellar, now in the care of estate owners Abbi and Lee Wallis, uses tanks and barrels as décor, allowing you a feet-on experience of winemaking. Daily-changing blackboard menus highlight fresh produce from the organic vegetable garden and surrounding farms. Enjoy farmhouse breakfasts, lingering lunches, or picnic under guava trees, surrounded by mountains. Great play area for children. (See also Accommodation section for Bovlei Valley Retreat & A–Z section.)

Accommodation in the Winelands and Cape Town

Featured below are some guest lodges, hotels, country inns, B&Bs and self-catering cottages in the winelands, many of them on wine farms (look for the ⌂ symbol beside the individual entries in the A–Z section of this guide). These are paid entries. The venues supplied information on their facilities and attractions, which was then edited for consistency of style. Unless stated to the contrary, all speak English and Afrikaans, have parking and gardens/terraces. Rates are for standard double rooms unless otherwise specified — for example per person (pp) or breakfast included (B&B). Tourism Grading Council of South Africa (TGCSA) ratings where provided. Should you wish to know about wheelchair access, please discuss with the relevant venue.

Index of accommodation

Listed alphabetically, with region.

Ashton
Pat Busch Mountain Reserve see under Robertson

Bonnievale
Bushmanspad Estate see under Montagu

Caledon
Boschrivier Farm House see under Stanford

Calitzdorp

The Retreat at Groenfontein Groenfontein Road, District Calitzdorp (20km from Calitzdorp, off Route 62) ▪ TGCSA 3 & 4-star guest house ▪ 8 rooms — garden & standard ▪ Low season: R500–R640 pps DB&B, single R650–R1,150 DB&B; High season: R710–R950 pps DB&B, single R910–R1,700 DB&B ▪ Visa & MasterCard accepted ▪ Restaurant (problem diets catered for — advise when booking) ▪ Pool ▪ Children & pets welcome ▪ Walking trails ▪ Birding ▪ River with rock pools ▪ Star gazing ▪ Secure parking ▪ Fireplace ▪

WiFi ▪ Safe ▪ French, German, Italian & Swedish spoken ▪ Owner Marie Holstensson & Grant Burton ▪ info@groenfontein.com ▪ www.groenfontein.com ▪ S 33° 26' 15.6" E 21° 47' 20.9" ▪ **T +27 (0)44-213-3880** ▪ F +27 (0)86-271-5373

A consistent award-winner, this welcoming, personally run 3 and 4-star graded Victorian farmhouse offers both standard and garden rooms. You'll enjoy personal pampering, hearty breakfasts and tasty dinners. The inviting lounge and dining room overlook sweeping lawns and the majestic Swartberg. Take leisurely walks, challenging trails, explore the rock pools in the bird-rich river, or simply laze at the pool, soaking up the peace and silence.

Camps Bay

The Twelve Apostles Hotel and Spa Victoria Road, Camps Bay, Cape Town ▪ TGCSA 5-star hotel; Member of Leading Hotels of the World ▪ 70 rooms ▪ Seasonal rates: R2,082.50–R2,562.50 pps B&B, single R3,965–R4,925 B&B ▪ Major credit cards accepted ▪ Azure Restaurant; The Café Grill; The Leopard Bar (live music) ▪ Banqueting & conferences (8 function rooms) ▪ Weddings ▪ Spa ▪ Gym ▪ 2 pools (1 heated) ▪ Cinema ▪ Garden hammocks ▪ Mountain biking ▪ Hiking trails ▪ Birding ▪ Picnics on mountainside ▪ Helipad ▪ Wine tasting ▪ Secure parking ▪ Shuttle service ▪ Children welcome ▪ Air-conditioning ▪ Ceiling fans ▪ TV ▪ DVD player ▪ iPod docking station ▪ WiFi ▪ Safe ▪ French & German spoken ▪ Owners The Tollman Family; Horst Frehse ▪ bookta@ 12apostles.co.za ▪ www.12apostleshotel.com ▪ S 33° 58' 59.37" E 18° 21' 31.43" ▪ **T +27 (0)21-437-9000** ▪ F +27 (0)21-437-9055

Spoil yourself. Set on the mountainside between Table Mountain National Park and Atlantic breakers, this 5-star boutique hotel has one of the world's most dramatic locations. Views are spectacular; light, airy, and peaceful rooms offer luxurious comfort, up-to-the-minute technology and 24-hour service; world-class facilities include newly renovated seven treatment-room spa and cinema. The V&A Waterfront and Cape Town's bikini beaches are a few minutes away. *Condé Nast Traveler* USA Gold List as one of the best places in the world to stay 2012 (with overall score of 90.5); *TripAdvisor* Travellers' Choice Top 25 Luxury Hotels and Top 25 Relaxation & Spa Hotels in Africa 2012; *Spa Traveller* Reader's Choice International, Best International Hotel Spa 2011; *Travel & Leisure's* one of the 500 Best Hotels 2011; *Telegraph* UltraTravel runner-up Best Hotel in Africa 2011; Diners Club Winelist Diamond Award 2011. (See also Restaurants section.)

Cape Town

Brooklands House Guest House 3 Surbiton Road, Rondebosch, Cape Town ▪ TGCSA 4-star guest house ▪ 4 en-suite rooms ▪ Seasonal rates: double from R495–R750 pps B&B, single R615–R890 B&B ▪ Major credit cards accepted ▪ Conferences ▪ Pool ▪ Boule court ▪ TV ▪ Ceiling fans ▪ Owners Philip & Sandra Engelen ▪ brooklands@mweb.co.za ▪ www.brooklands-guesthouse.co.za ▪ **T/F +27 (0)21-689-3594** ▪ Mobile +27 (0)82-659-6659

Charming Victorian villa, within walking distance of some 7 restaurants, near Newlands rugby and cricket grounds, and less than 15 mins drive from CT international airport. Breakfast in the sunroom overlooking the garden; dine by prior arrangement; in winter relax beside the drawing room fire. If you're planning Winelands excursions, consult your hosts, wine enthusiasts who planted a petit shiraz vineyard beside the boule court.

Cape Grace Hotel West Quay Road, V&A Waterfront, Cape Town ▪ TGCSA 5-star hotel ▪ 120 rooms ▪ Seasonal rates: R4,790–R5,730 per room B&B ▪ Major credit cards accepted ▪ Signal Restaurant; Bascule Whisky, Wine and Cocktail Bar ▪ Luxury yacht charters ▪ Conferences ▪ Communication Centre with 24-hour complimentary Internet access ▪ Weddings/functions ▪ Spa ▪ Sauna ▪ Gym ▪ Outdoor heated pool ▪ Secure parking ▪ Shuttle service ▪ Air-conditioning ▪ Underfloor heating ▪ Satellite TV ▪ DVD player ▪ iPod docking station ▪ WiFi ▪ Safe ▪ French, German, Korean, Portuguese, Swedish, Xhosa & Zulu spoken ▪ Owner Cape Grace ▪ info@capegrace.com ▪ www.capegrace.com ▪ S 33° 54' 29" E 18° 25' 12" ▪ **T +27 (0)21-410-7100** ▪ F +27 (0)21- 419-7622

Setting is a private quay of an international yacht marina, against the backdrop of Table Mountain, between Cape Town's working harbour and bustling Victoria & Alfred Waterfront. Ambience is gracious, capturing the essence of the Cape in furnishings and fabrics that combine local creativity with seductive luxury, reinforcing the warm atmosphere and personalised service that have for years defined the hotel. Cape contemporary restaurant and whisky bar. Showered with annual awards. Latest are: 2nd consecutive year Best Hotel in Africa in *Celebrated Living's* Readers' Choice Platinum List; ranked in top five City Hotels (Africa and the Middle East) *Travel + Leisure's* World's Best Awards 2012.

Hout Bay Manor see under Hout Bay

One&Only Cape Town Dock Road, V&A Waterfront, Cape Town ▪ TGCSA 5-star luxury hotel/resort ▪ 131 guest rooms & suites ▪ Low season from R5,350 per room B&B; High season from R6,250 per room B&B ▪ Major credit cards accepted ▪ 2 Restaurants: Nobu & Reuben's ▪ KidsOnly Club ▪ Conferences ▪ Weddings/functions ▪ Spa ▪ Sauna ▪ Fitness Centre ▪ Pool ▪ Wine tasting ▪ Secure parking ▪ Air-conditioning ▪ Fireplaces (Select Suites) ▪ Multi-media entertainment system, 42-inch flat screen TV, DVD/CD player, iPod docking station ▪ Complimentary WiFi ▪ Safe ▪ Nespresso machine ▪ Arabic, French & German spoken ▪ Owner Kerzner International ▪ reservations@ oneandonlycapetown.com ▪ www.oneandonlycapetown.com ▪ S 33° 54' 30" E 18° 24' 59" ▪ **T +27 (0)21-431-5888**

More than a hotel: a luxury urban waterfront destination, where pampering is the norm and personalised service standard, with two top restaurants and world-class spa. Stylish Afro-chic rooms and suites in the seven-story Marina Rise are the largest in Cape Town, offering magnificent views of Table Mountain and lively V&A Waterfront; those on a peaceful private island, each with balcony or terrace, overlook the waterway. 2012 Awards: *Travel + Leisure* World's Best Award: No 1 City Hotel in Africa and the Middle East and No 14 in the Top 100 Hotels; World Spa Awards, Best in Africa; *Trip Advisor* Travelers' Choice: Top 25 Luxury Hotels & Top 25 Trendiest Hotels, Africa. (See also Restaurants section.)

Steenberg Hotel   see under Constantia

The Twelve Apostles Hotel and Spa   see under Camps Bay

Vineyard Hotel & Spa   Colinton Road, Newlands, Cape Town ▪ TGCSA 4-star deluxe ▪ 207 rooms ▪ Double R875–R3,575 B&B; single R1,300–R6,700 B&B ▪ Major credit cards accepted ▪ 3 restaurants: The Square, Myoga & Splash Café ▪ Conferences ▪ Angsana Spa ▪ Health & fitness centre ▪ 2 pools: outdoor & heated indoor ▪ TV ▪ Air-conditioning ▪ Dutch, French, German & Xhosa spoken ▪ Owners Alexander & George Petousis ▪ hotel@vineyard.co.za ▪ www.vineyard.co.za ▪ **T +27 (0)21-657-4500** ▪ F +27 (0)21-657-4501

Start your Cape Town adventure from one of its most historic and beautiful settings — the 117 year-old Vineyard Hotel, on the eastern slopes of Table Mountain, near Kirstenbosch Botanical Gardens, the sporting mecca of Newlands, and a short drive from the city. Stroll the idyllic riverside estate, unwind at the internationally-known spa or indulge in top Cape wines and gourmet food at two award-winning restaurants. (See also Restaurants section for The Square.)

Winchester Mansions   221 Beach Road, Sea Point, Cape Town ▪ TGCSA 4-star ▪ 76 rooms ▪ Low season from R775 pps B&B, single supplement R445; High season from R1,175 pps B&B, single supplement R675 ▪ Major credit cards accepted ▪ Harveys Restaurant ▪ Conferences ▪ Weddings/functions ▪ Spa ▪ Pool ▪ Air-conditioning ▪ TV ▪ WiFi ▪ Safe ▪ French & German spoken ▪ Owner Frances Wainford ▪ MD Nils Heckscher ▪ welcome@winchester.co.za ▪ www.winchester.co.za ▪ S 33° 54' 38.1" E 18° 23' 26.5" ▪ **T +27 (0)21-434-2351** ▪ F +27 (0)21-434-0215

After 17 years MD Nils Heckscher jokes he's the only piece of furniture still around. This landmark hotel on the seafront, near the V&A Waterfront and with easy access to Cape Town International Airport, has shed its old-fashioned image to combine grace with modernity. Elegant rooms boast sea or mountain views; attractions include a pool, spa, buzzing bar, popular Harveys restaurant and full service conferencing. Trip Advisor Certificate of Excellence 2011. (See also Restaurants section.)

Constantia

Constantia Uitsig Country Hotel and Spa
Constantia Uitsig Wine Estate, Spaanschemat River Road, Constantia, Cape Town ▪ TGCSA 4-star hotel ▪ 16 rooms ▪ Seasonal rates: Garden twin R1,750–R3,600 per room B&B; Victorian double R2,050–R4,500 per room; Manor suite R2,500–R5,200 per room B&B ▪ Major credit cards accepted ▪ Three restaurants: Constantia Uitsig Restaurant, La Colombe & The River Café ▪ The Wine Shop ▪ Wine tasting ▪ Conferences ▪ Weddings/functions ▪ Spa ▪ Pool ▪ Mountain biking ▪ Walks/hikes ▪ Secure parking ▪ Air-conditioning ▪ Ceiling fans ▪ Fireplace — in some rooms ▪ TV ▪ WiFi ▪ Safe ▪ Owner Constantia Uitsig Holdings (Pty) Ltd ▪ reception@uitsig.co.za ▪ www.constantia-uitsig.com ▪ S 34° 2' 59.45" E 18° 25' 32.43" ▪ **T +27 (0)21-794-6500** ▪ F +27 (0)21-794-7605

A perfect resting place for the discerning traveller. This serene hotel, set among the vineyards of a private wine estate in the shadow of Table Mountain, is just 20 minutes from Cape Town city centre and the V&A Waterfront. Charmingly furnished rooms overlook tranquil gardens; heartfelt hospitality is backed by friendly service, and three restaurants on the estate offer a tempting choice of eating options. (See also Restaurants & A–Z sections.)

Hampshire House   10 Willow Road, Constantia ▪ TGCSA 4-star guest house ▪ 5 rooms ▪ Seasonal rates: R475–R650 pps B&B; single supplement R200–R300 ▪ Visa & MasterCard accepted ▪ Pool ▪ Secure parking ▪ Shuttle service ▪ Air-conditioning ▪ Ceiling fans ▪ Under-floor heating ▪ TV ▪ DVD player ▪ WiFi ▪ Safe ▪ Owners Ricky & Carole Chapman ▪ stay@ hampshirehouse.co.za ▪ www.hampshirehouse.co.za ▪ **T +27 (0)21-794-6288** ▪ F +27 (0)21-794-2934

Welcoming 4-star guesthouse, ideally placed for exploring the Cape Peninsula. Set in the peaceful Constantia wine valley, with six wineries just five minutes away, the lodge offers easy motorway access to Table Mountain, the Waterfront, Winelands, beaches and local restaurants. Five attractive, individually decorated en-suite bedrooms, both English and continental buffet breakfasts (Carole's fresh home-baked muffins are legendary), secluded swimming pool and secure off-street parking.

Steenberg Hotel 10802 Steenberg Estate, Tokai Road, Constantia, Cape Town • Tripadvisor 5-star rating • 24 rooms • Seasonal rates: from R2,365–R3,605 for standard luxury room B&B • Major credit cards accepted • Catharina's Restaurant; Bistro Sixteen82; Gorgeous by Graham Beck bubbly bar • Conferences • Weddings/functions • Luxury spa • Steam room • 2 pools • 18-hole golf course • Mountain biking • Walks/hikes • Birding • Cellar tours • Wine tasting • Secure parking • Shuttle service • Air-conditioning • Fireplace • Under-floor heating • Satellite TV • iPod docking station • Complimentary WiFi • Digital safe • Mini-Bar • Bathrobes • French & German spoken • Owners Graham Beck Enterprises • info@steenberghotel.com • www.steenberghotel.com • S 34° 04' 17.90" E 18° 25' 30.83" • **T +27 (0)21-713-2222** • F +27 (0)21-713-2251

De-stress deliciously at this boutique retreat. Small, special and exclusive, Steenberg's charm lies in its Cape Dutch heritage, sensitively converted for contemporary comfort in spacious en-suite rooms and butler-serviced suites, where décor reflects past eras. Set in manicured gardens against vineyards and mountain slopes, with sophisticated restaurant, award-winning winery, deluxe spa, swimming pools and golf course, it's a hard-to-leave base for exploring the Cape. *Condé Nast* US Readers' Choice Awards Top 100 and No.1 Hotel in Africa 2011; *Tripadvisor* Travellers Choice, Best Luxury Hotel in Africa 2011. (See also Restaurants section for Bistro Sixteen82 & A–Z section.)

Darling

Darling Lodge 22 Pastorie Street, Darling • TGCSA 3-star B&B; Greenwood Guide; Portfolio Collection • 6 rooms • Seasonal rates R400–R490 pps B&B, single R550–R670 B&B • Dinner available on request • Major credit cards accepted • Conferences • Weddings/functions • Pool • Golf • Walks/hikes • Birding • Wine tasting • Secure parking • Shuttle service • TV & fireplace in guest lounge • Ceiling fans • TV • WiFi • Safe • Tea/coffee making facilities • German, Swiss German & French spoken • Owners Stephan Moser & Oliver Studer • info@darlinglodge.co.za • www.darlinglodge.co.za • S 33° 22' 44.78" E 18° 22' 41.29" • **T +27 (0)22-492-3062** • F +27 (0)22-492-3665

Charmingly restored Victorian House in the gentle Darling Valley offers a welcoming blend of old and new in an environment of vineyards, pastures, wheatfields and spectacular wildflower displays. Enjoy the area's award-winning wines and olives in a gorgeous garden with inviting pool. An hour from Cape Town and minutes from the Atlantic Ocean. Winelands, beaches, whale-watching, golf, art galleries, Evita se Perron nearby.

Elgin

The Guest House @ South Hill South Hill Vineyards, 113 The Valley Road, Elgin • TGCSA 4-star self-catering guest house • 5 bedrooms • Honeymoon cottage • Seasonal rates: R470–R620 pps B&B; single R820–R900 B&B • Major credit cards accepted (excl. American Express) • Restaurant • Weddings/functions • Pool • Jacuzzi • Mountain biking • Walks • Bird watching • Boule court • Wine tasting • Under-floor heating • iPod docking station • WiFi • Owner Kevin King • info@southhill.co.za • www.southhill.co.za • S 34° 13' 59.48" E 19°06' 44.28" • **T +27 (0)21-844-0033/+27 (0)21-421-1367** • F +27 (0)21-421-2821

Luxuriate at this self-catering 4-star villa and romantic cottage surrounded by vines. Individually decorated en-suite bedrooms open onto private patio; state-of-the-art kitchen, dining and lounge area overlooks garden and vineyards; pizza oven encourages alfresco eating. Disinclined to cook? Besides gourmet meals, Gordon Manuel @ The Venue offers a fully-inclusive catering service. Enjoy leisure activities from tasting wine at South Hill to kayaking, quad biking and boule. (See also Restaurants & A–Z sections.)

Franschhoek

Akkerdal Akkerdal Estate, R45 Franschhoek Road, Franschhoek • 1 self-catering chalet (sleeps 4) • Seasonal rates from R350–R400 pp • Visa & MasterCard accepted • Wine tasting • Fully equipped kitchen • Private patio with braai area — wood supplied • Towels & bedding • Complimentary bottle of wine on arrival & bottled water • Air-conditioning • TV • No pets allowed • Owner Pieter Hanekom • franschhoek@terason.co.za • www.akkerdal.co.za • S 33° 52' 43.40" E 19° 2' 58.50" • **T +27 (0)21-876-3481** • F +27 (0)21-876-3189

Escape from city pressures to this peaceful two-bedroomed, self-catering chalet, sheltered by oaks beside the Berg river in picturesque Franschhoek valley. Taste carefully handcrafted Akkerdal wines; braai on the private patio watching the sun set over the mountains, glass in hand; or eat in the village. Franschhoek, known for its restaurants, is only 7km from the farm, and golf estates and luxury spas are minutes away. (See also A–Z section.)

Allée Bleue Kendall Cottage and Manor House T-junction R45 & R310, Groot Drakenstein • TGCSA 5-star MESE • **Kendall Cottage** accommodates 4 guests; 15 guests for cocktail-style function: R900 pps B&B, single supplement R1,200 • **Manor House** accommodates 4 guests; 40 guests for functions: R1,400 pps B&B, single supplement R1,700 • Major credit cards accepted (excl. Diners Club) • Bistro Allée Bleue • Picnics • Conferences • Weddings/functions • Cellar tours & wine tasting • Secure parking • Air-conditioning • Under-floor heating • Fireplace • TV • WiFi • Safe • German spoken • Owners Wilfred & Elke Dauphin • info@alleebleue.com • www.alleebleue.com

▪ S 33° 51'51.02" E 18° 58'42.90" ▪ **T +27 (0)21-874-1021** ▪ F +27 (0)21-874-1850

Allée Bleue provides three bed and breakfast accommodation options. **Kendall Cottage**, a Sir Herbert-Baker designed cottage, linking two en-suite bedrooms through a modern-meets-old lounge and bar area. The **Manor House**: Two contemporary modern-meets-old suites with en-suite bathrooms and the **Mill House** for standard en-suite options. Dinners by arrangement. (See also Restaurants & A–Z sections.)

Babylonstoren Farm Hotel see under Paarl

Basse Provence Country House R45 Main Road, Franschhoek ▪ TGCSA 4-star guest house/B&B ▪ 9 rooms ▪ R425–R550 pps B&B ▪ Major credit cards accepted (excl. Diners Club) ▪ Restaurant ▪ Conferences ▪ Weddings/functions ▪ Pool ▪ Cellar tours & wine tasting ▪ Secure parking ▪ Air-conditioning ▪ DSTV ▪ WiFi ▪ Safe ▪ Owner Rickety Bridge ▪ booking@basseprovence.co.za ▪ www.basseprovence.co.za ▪ **T +27 (0)21-876-2994** ▪ F +27 (0)21-876-3673

Huguenot heritage blends with modern luxury in this stylish 4-star sister accommodation to the 1855 Cape Dutch manor house at Rickety Bridge. Both manor and neighbouring country house have been totally refurbished, enhancing rather than losing their period charm. Inviting, delightfully comfortable suites under thatch and roof beams, with ingenious well-fitted corner bathrooms under the eaves, offer views of the vine-green valley and ageless mountains. (See also Restaurants section.)

Cabrière Cottage 47 Cabrière Street, Franschhoek ▪ 1 cottage, with 2 en-suite bedrooms ▪ Self-catering ▪ Low season from R800 & high season from R1,200 per cottage ▪ No credit card facilities — cash or prepayment via EFT ▪ Plunge pool ▪ Mountain biking ▪ Ceiling fans ▪ Fireplace ▪ DSTV ▪ DVD player ▪ iPod docking station ▪ Safe ▪ Owners Matthew & Nicky Gordon ▪ info@cabrierecottage.com ▪ www.cabrierecottage.com ▪ **T +27 (0)82-455-6411** ▪ F +27 (0)21-876-4444

Restful self-catering Cabrière Cottage, at the heart of the mountain-ringed Franschhoek village, offers visitors the ideal base for exploring all that the beautiful valley has to offer. The upmarket cottage, with private garden and plunge pool, has two comfortable en-suite bedrooms, spacious open-plan lounge with fireplace, and fully-equipped kitchen — plus the amenities expected by today's travellers: DSTV satellite television, iPod docking station and DVD player.

Holden Manz Country House Holden Manz Wine Estate, Green Valley Road, Franschhoek ▪ TGCSA 5-star country house ▪ 4 rooms ▪ Seasonal rates: R1,320–R2,178 pps B&B, afternoon tea included ▪ Visa & MasterCard accepted ▪ Franschhoek Kitchen restaurant ▪ Weddings/functions ▪ Spa with revitalising Africology products ▪ Pool ▪ Cellar tours ▪ Wine tasting ▪ Secure parking ▪ Air-conditioning ▪ Fireplace ▪ Under-floor heating ▪ TV ▪ iPod docking station ▪ WiFi ▪ Safe ▪ French & German spoken ▪ Owners Gerard Holden & Migo Manz ▪ info@holdenmanz.com ▪ www.holdenmanz.com ▪ S 33° 56'7" E 19° 6'54" ▪ **T +27 (0)21-876-2738** ▪ F +27 (0)21-876-4624

Ultimate tranquility. Expect light, space and striking contemporary art, juxtaposed against a vineyard and mountain backdrop. A play of colour, subtle in bedrooms overlooking vines; dramatic in a comfortable lounge; with a soothing koi pond to complete the picture. Plus added inducements: bountiful breakfasts next to the orchard, a pool where two rivers meet, vineyard spa to ensure well-being, and gourmet restaurant on the estate. (See also Restaurants & A–Z sections.)

Mont Rochelle Hotel & Mountain Vineyards
Dassenberg Road, Franschhoek ▪ 16 rooms & 6 suites ▪ Seasonal rates: R2,300–R3,500 per room B&B ▪ Major credit cards accepted ▪ Two restaurants: Mange Tout & Country Kitchen ▪ Conferences ▪ Weddings/functions ▪ Spa ▪ Sauna ▪ Gym ▪ Pool ▪ Jacuzzi ▪ Horse riding ▪ Mountain biking ▪ Hiking ▪ Boule court ▪ Cellar tours ▪ Wine tasting ▪ Secure parking ▪ Air-conditioning ▪ Under-floor heating ▪ TV ▪ DVD player ▪ WiFi ▪ Safe ▪ German spoken ▪ Owners Erwin Schnitzler & Rwayitare Family ▪ info@montrochelle.co.za ▪ www.montrochelle.co.za ▪ S 33° 92'05.20" E 19° 10'50.53" ▪ **T +27 (0)21-876-2770** ▪ F +27 (0)21-876-3788

Elegant boutique hotel with wrap-round views of vineyards and mountains, plus fine dining and rustic restaurants. Attention to detail is paramount: sink into comfort in individually decorated rooms and luxury suites, each with every convenience. Expect fresh flowers, homemade chocolates and a welcome drink upon arrival, daily local newspaper and scrumptious breakfast every morning. Diners Club Diamond Winelist award 2011; *Eat Out* 2010: Mange Tout awarded Top 10 tasting menu & Top 10 best hotel restaurant. (See also Restaurants & A–Z sections.)

Rickety Bridge Manor House Rickety Bridge Wine Estate, R45 Main Road, Franschhoek ▪ TGCSA 4-star guest house/B&B ▪ 3 en-suite bedrooms ▪ R550–R800 pps B&B ▪ Major credit cards accepted (excl. Diners Club) ▪ Restaurant ▪ Conferences ▪ Weddings/functions ▪ Pool ▪ Boule court ▪ Cellar tours & wine tasting ▪ Secure parking ▪ Air-conditioning ▪ Under-floor heating ▪ DSTV ▪ WiFi ▪ Safe ▪ Owner Rickety Bridge ▪ shani@ricketybridge.com ▪ www.ricketybridge.com ▪ **T +27 (0)21-876-2994** ▪ F +27 (0)21-876-3673

Enjoy gracious living in a gabled guest house. The ambience encourages it; the friendly, personalised service ensures it. Stylishly renovated 19th century rooms offer the luxury of a four-star hotel, with the added appeal of yellow-wood beams, Cape Dutch furniture and a Cape kitchen. Sleep late (easy to do), enjoy leisurely breakfast in the quaint breakfast room, or beside the pool in a purple-mountain setting. (See also Restaurants & A–Z sections.)

The Owner's Cottage at Grande Provence
Grande Provence Heritage Wine Estate, Main Road, Franschhoek ▪ TGCSA 5-star guest house ▪ 4 rooms & 1 deluxe suite ▪ Seasonal rates: R4,150–R7,000 per room B&B; exclusive use from 1 to 10 guests: one room/one couple from R13,000–R16,000 to five rooms/five couples from R29,000–R42,000; full breakfast & 3-course dinner included ▪ Major credit cards accepted ▪ Restaurant ▪ Conferences ▪ Swimming & spa pool ▪ Butler service ▪ Cellar tours ▪ Wine tasting ▪ Guided tour of The Gallery ▪ Air-conditioning ▪ TV ▪ WiFi ▪ Dutch, French & German spoken ▪ Owner Grande Provence (Pty) Ltd ▪ ownerscottage@grandeprovence.co.za ▪ www.grandeprovence.co.za ▪ S 33° 53′ 57.6″ E 19° 06′ 10.5″ ▪ **T +27 (0)21-876-8600** ▪ F +27 (0)21-876-8601

Indulge yourself. This superbly-appointed 5-star retreat merges history with ultimate luxury and contemporary comfort, cleverly concealing the technology demanded by high-powered travellers. Four rooms and deluxe suite in soothing charcoal grey and white ensure tranquility; a sunny conservatory and stylish lounge invite relaxation; on lush lawns a swimming pool and elevated spa beckon. Pamper yourself with butler service or book at the estate's gourmet restaurant. (See also Restaurants & A–Z sections.)

Whale Cottage Franschhoek 11 Akademie Street, Franschhoek ▪ TGCSA 4-star guest house ▪ 8 rooms ▪ Seasonal rates: R350–R590 pps B&B ▪ Visa & MasterCard accepted ▪ Small conferences, weddings & functions ▪ Pool ▪ Secure parking ▪ Air-conditioning ▪ TV ▪ WiFi ▪ German spoken ▪ Owner Chris von Ulmenstein, Whale Cottage Portfolio cc ▪ winelands@whalecottage.com ▪ www.whalecottage.com ▪ S 33° 54′ 41″ E 19° 07′ 22″ ▪ **T +27 (0)21-433-2100** ▪ F +27 (0)21-433-2101

Welcome to a whale of a stay at Whale Cottage Franschhoek, a country house with a delightful garden and babbling brook, in the heart of South Africa's mountain-ringed gourmet village. Top restaurants Reuben's and Le Quartier Français are 200m away. Besides beautiful mountain views, nearby attractions include tennis, golf, horse riding, mountain biking, walks/hikes, cellar tours, wine tasting and a convenient shuttle service.

Hermanus
Whale Cottage Hermanus 38 Westcliff Drive, Hermanus ▪ TGCSA 4-star guest house ▪ 6 rooms ▪ Seasonal rates: R350–R590 pps B&B ▪ Visa & MasterCard accepted ▪ Small conferences, weddings & functions ▪ Pool ▪ Secure parking ▪ Shuttle service ▪ Air-conditioning ▪ TV ▪ WiFi ▪ Safe ▪ German spoken ▪ Owner Chris von Ulmenstein, Whale Cottage Portfolio cc ▪ hermanus@whalecottage.com ▪ www.whalecottage.com ▪ S 34° 23′ 34″ E 19° 13′ 50″ ▪ **T +27 (0)21-433-2100** ▪ F +27 (0)21-433-2101

You'll have a whale of a stay at Whale Cottage Hermanus, a marine-themed beach house with magnificent views over Walker Bay, and of whales B & B (breaching and blowing). Hermanus is the whale capital of South Africa, and offers the best land-based whale watching in the world. Just a 1km walk to village centre and craft market. Welcome to a coastal home from home.

Hout Bay
Hout Bay Manor Baviaanskloof Road, Hout Bay ▪ TGCSA 5-star boutique hotel ▪ 19 rooms ▪ Seasonal rates from R1,920– R3,200 per room B&B ▪ Major credit cards accepted ▪ Pure Restaurant ▪ Conferences ▪ Weddings/functions ▪ Inzolo Wellness Suite ▪ Heated pool ▪ Secure parking ▪ Shuttle service on request ▪ Air-conditioning ▪ Under-floor heating ▪ TV ▪ iPod docking station on request ▪ WiFi ▪ Safe ▪ Xhosa & Zulu spoken ▪ Owner Susan Struengmann ▪ reservations@houtbaymanor.com ▪ www.houtbaymanor.com ▪ S 34° 2′ 34.76″ E 18° 21′ 38.46″ ▪ **T +27 (0)21-790-0116** ▪ F +27 (0)21-790-0118

Taste tranquillity at a gracious, beautifully restored 19th century manor house, set between mountains and beach in the self-proclaimed seaside 'Republic of Hout Bay'. Step into a vibrant mix of fabrics, art, colonial and ethnic touches extending from welcoming reception rooms to individually-decorated rooms and suites. Eat at Pure restaurant, pamper yourself with soothing spa treatments, laze at the pool or walk along pristine beaches. (See also Restaurants section.)

Knysna
Packwood Country Estate see under Plettenberg Bay

Kuils River
Saxenburg Guest Cottages see under Stellenbosch
Zevenwacht Country Inn see under Stellenbosch

Montagu
Bushmanspad Estate R60, Ashton — Swellendam ▪ TGCSA 4-star self-catering ▪ 5 cottages ▪ Seasonal rates: R750–R950 per cottage ▪ Major credit cards accepted (excl. Diners Club) ▪ Hiking ▪ Birding ▪ Fishing ▪ Wine tasting ▪ Secure parking ▪ Fireplace ▪ TV ▪ WiFi ▪ Dutch spoken ▪ Owner Menno Schaafsma ▪ info@bushmanspad.co.za ▪ www.bushmanspad.co.za ▪ S

33° 53' 55.0" E 020° 11' 46.7" ▪ **T +27 (0)23-616-2961** ▪ F +27 (0)23-616-3714

Escape to a wine estate high in the Langeberg Mountains, where en-suite cottages, easily accessible by car, are fully-equipped for self-catering. Breakfast in the 17th century farmhouse, taste wine in the 200 year-old cellar and braai on a wood fire in the barbeque area. Fish, swim, bird-watch and hike: or simply chill, enjoying 100 km vistas, breathtaking sunsets and peaceful nights under an African sky. (See also A–Z section.)

Les Hauts de Montagu 3km from Montagu on Route 62 to Barrydale ▪ TGCSA 4-star lodge ▪ 10 en-suite rooms ▪ Seasonal rates: R600–R850 pps B&B ▪ Visa & MasterCard accepted ▪ Weddings/functions ▪ Small chapel ▪ Pool ▪ 8 hiking trails ▪ Boule court ▪ Secure parking ▪ Ceiling fans ▪ Fireplace ▪ Under-floor heating ▪ TV ▪ WiFi ▪ Safe ▪ French spoken ▪ Owners Myriam & Eric Brillant ▪ info@leshautsdemontagu.co.za ▪ www.leshautsdemontagu.co.za ▪ S 33° 80' 58.96" E 20° 15'77.23" ▪ **T +27 (0)23-614-2514** ▪ F +27 (0)23-614-3517

Take time out in a peaceful 4-star lodge on a 600 ha olive farm on the slopes of the Langeberg, offering spectacular views of surrounding mountains and olive groves, and bird-rich hiking trails through fynbos. Romantic thatched cottages with spacious en-suite rooms have quaint Victorian bathtubs, plus outdoor showers that make the most of the view. Two hours from Cape Town on the scenic Route 62.

Overberg

The Guest House @ South Hill see under Elgin

Paarl

Babylonstoren Farm Hotel Babylonstoren, Klapmuts-Simondium Road (R45), Franschhoek ▪ TGCSA 5-star hotel ▪ 6 suites plus 3 x 1-bedroom cottages & 4 x 2-bedroom cottages ▪ Seasonal rates: R3,135–R4,400 per suite B&B (2 guests); R3,415–R4,900 per one bedroom cottage B&B (2 guests); R5,150–R7,365 per two bedroom cottage B&B (4 guests) ▪ Major credit cards accepted ▪ Babel Restaurant ▪ Conferences ▪ Weddings/functions ▪ Spa with plunge pool, steam room, sauna ▪ Gym ▪ Natural dam swimming pool ▪ Guided garden tours ▪ Horse riding ▪ Mountain biking ▪ Walks/hikes ▪ Bicycles ▪ Canoes ▪ Birding ▪ Boule court ▪ Cellar tours ▪ Wine tasting ▪ Secure parking ▪ Air-conditioning ▪ Ceiling fans ▪ Fireplace ▪ Under-floor heating ▪ TV ▪ DVD player ▪ WiFi ▪ Safe ▪ Owners Koos Bekker & Karen Roos ▪ Hotel Manager Elmine Nel ▪ reservations@babylonstoren.com ▪ www.babylonstoren.com ▪ S 33° 49' 21.00" E 18° 55' 48.00" ▪ **T +27 (0)21-863-3852** ▪ F +27 (0)21-863-1727

Relax, at one with nature, but with all modern extras (including spa and gym) on a 1692 farm where appealing en-suite guest accommodation echoes early whitewashed Cape Dutch farm buildings and a formal 8-acre fruit orchard was inspired by Cape Town's 17th century Company Gardens. Tour the garden, pick your own produce, and celebrate the seasons at Babel restaurant. Just 60 kms from Cape Town. *Visi* Designer of the Year Award 2011; *Conde Nast Traveller's* Hot List in the UK and USA 2011. (See also Restaurants & A–Z sections.)

Druk My Niet Wine Estate Bodal Road, Daljosafat, Paarl ▪ 3 self-catering cottages ▪ Rates per cottage per night: Protea R1,000 (sleeps 2), Guava R1,600 (sleeps 4) & Fynbos R2,600 (sleeps 6) ▪ Major credit cards accepted ▪ Weddings/functions ▪ Pool ▪ Walks/hikes ▪ Birding ▪ Cellar tours ▪ Wine tasting ▪ Secure parking ▪ Ceiling fans ▪ Fireplace ▪ DSTV ▪ DVD player ▪ iPod docking station ▪ WiFi ▪ Safe ▪ German spoken ▪ Owners Georg & Dorothee Kirchner ▪ carlien@dmnwines.co.za ▪ www.dmnwines.co.za ▪ S 33° 41' 25" E 19° 01'42" ▪ **T +27 (0)21-868-2393** ▪ F +27 (0)21-868-2392

Move back in time - with mod cons like washing machines, DStv and DVD - in charming Cape Dutch thatched cottages on a boutique wine farm, where original buildings (still extant) date back to 1692. The area is a biosphere rich in fynbos; the fully equipped self-catering cottages, from one-bedroomed to a refurbished larger cottage sleeping six, enjoy unspoiled vistas over farm vineyards and Paarl Valley. (See also A–Z section.)

Grande Roche Hotel Plantasie Street, Paarl ▪ TGCSA 5-star hotel; Satour 5-star silver ▪ 28 rooms ▪ Low season R2,270–R3,555 per room B&B; High season R3,210–R4950 per room B&B ▪ Major credit cards accepted ▪ Bosman's Restaurant & Bistro Allegro ▪ Conferences ▪ Weddings/functions ▪ Fitness Room ▪ 2 heated pools ▪ Tennis court ▪ Walks/hikes ▪ Wine tasting ▪ Secure parking ▪ Shuttle service ▪ Air-conditioning ▪ Fireplace ▪ Under-floor heating ▪ TV ▪ DVD player ▪ WiFi ▪ Safe ▪ German & Xhosa spoken ▪ GM Anja Bosken ▪ reserve@granderoche.co.za ▪ www.granderoche.co.za ▪ S 33° 45'02" E 18° 57'35" ▪ **T +27 (0)21-863-5100** ▪ F +27 (0)21-863-2220

The only SA member of Small Luxury Hotels of the World, this legendary 5-star estate hotel boasts numerous awards for pampering, beautiful gardens and award-winning cuisine at its elegant Bosman's restaurant. Overlooking vineyard and mountains, it's the ideal base for exploring the Cape, or simply unwinding at the pools, the fitness centre, on nearby golf courses, or visiting the numerous wine farms in close proximity. Diners Club Diamond winelist award & *Wine Spectator's* 'Best of Award of Excellence' 2011; SA Tourism No 1 Fine Dining Restaurant in SA & *Eat Out* Top 10, 2010. (See also Restaurants section.)

Mooi Bly Horse Shoe at Bo Dal Road, Dal Josafat, Paarl ▪ 5 self-catering cottages (each sleeping up to 6) ▪ Breakfast can be booked upfront ▪ From R220-R450 pppn, depending on length of stay, season & number of guests ▪ Visa & MasterCard accepted ▪ Pool ▪ Walks/hikes ▪ Cellar tours ▪ Wine tasting ▪ Fan ▪ Fireplace ▪ TV ▪ Dutch spoken ▪ Owners Wouters family ▪ info@mooibly.com ▪ www.mooibly.com ▪ S 33° 41′14″ E 19° 01′17″ ▪ **T/F +27 (0)21-868-2808**

'Mooi Bly' translates as 'keep well'. You'll not only keep well but stay well at these delightful thatched cottages on a family wine farm on the Du Toitskloof mountain slopes. Surrounded by vineyards, secluded in a large garden with swimming-pool, all are spacious, fully-equipped, charmingly furnished and serviced on a regular basis. Just 10 minutes to Paarl and Wellington and 30 to Stellenbosch and Franschhoek. (See also A–Z section.)

Plettenberg Bay

Packwood Country Estate Fisanthoek, Nr Harkerville, Plettenberg Bay ▪ TGCSA 4-star self-catering ▪ 3 self-catering cottages sleeping 2, 4 & 6; main country house available with fulltime housekeeper & cook when rented out as a whole ▪ Rates from R900-R3,500 per day ▪ Visa & MasterCard accepted ▪ Pool ▪ Horse riding ▪ Mountain biking ▪ Walks/hikes ▪ Birding ▪ Fishing ▪ Wine tasting ▪ Secure parking ▪ Fireplace ▪ Under-floor heating ▪ TV ▪ DVD player ▪ WiFi ▪ Safe ▪ Owners Vicky & Peter Gent ▪ vicky@packwood.co.za ▪ www.packwood.co.za ▪ S 33° 98′725″ E 23° 24′095″ ▪ **T +27 (0)44-532-7614** ▪ F +27 (0)86-510-0741

Taste country living at its best in a 4-star nature-lovers' paradise. Surrounded by Knysna's national park, three self-catering cottages and main country house (available with housekeeper-cum-cook), are set in 1000 acres of pasture, overlooking forest, mountains and ocean. Feast on farm-fresh produce from Jersey cream to free-range beef, plus Packwood wine; explore the Garden Route and pristine beaches; play golf at nearby courses, or simply unwind. (See also A–Z section.)

Robertson

Ballinderry, The Robertson Guest House 8 Le Roux Street, Robertson ▪ TGCSA 4-star guest house ▪ 7 rooms ▪ Low season: R400-R590 pps B&B; High season: R470-R680 pps B&B; single on request ▪ Major credit cards accepted ▪ Restaurant for stay-over guests ▪ Pool ▪ Secure parking ▪ Air-conditioning ▪ DSTV ▪ WiFi ▪ Safe ▪ Dutch/Flemish, French & German spoken ▪ Owners Luc & Hilde Uyttenhove ▪ info@ballinderryguesthouse.com ▪ www.ballinderryguesthouse.com ▪ S 33° 48′02.40″ E 19° 53′13.58″ ▪ **T +27 (0)23-626-5365** ▪ F +27 (0)86-742-8692

Relish fine wines and delectable food at this contemporary guest house in the heart of Robertson, where hands-on Belgian owners, Luc and Hilde, pamper guests with personal service. The thatched villa in a large and tranquil tropical garden offers five double rooms and two pool suites. Near the region's best-known wineries and an 18-hole golf course. Champagne breakfast included in room rates; dinner reservations essential.

Fraai Uitzicht 1798 Klaas Voogds East, on R60 between Robertson & Montagu ▪ TGCSA 4-star guest house ▪ 9 units consisting of luxury cottages & garden suites ▪ From R550 pps B&B ▪ Major credit cards accepted ▪ Restaurant ▪ Pool ▪ Walks/hikes ▪ Birding ▪ Cellar tours ▪ Wine tasting ▪ Secure parking ▪ Air-conditioning & under-floor heating ▪ Fireplace in cottages ▪ DSTV in cottages ▪ German, Xhosa & Zulu spoken ▪ Owners Karl Uwe & Sandra Papesch ▪ info@fraaiuitzicht.com ▪ www.fraaiuitzicht.com ▪ S 33° 47′43.23″ E 20° 00′17.87″ ▪ **T +27 (0)23-626-6156** ▪ F +27 (0)86-662-5265

This gem lives up to its name: 'Beautiful View'. Stylishly-appointed guest accommodation overlooks the Robertson valley, Sonderend Mountains, orchards and vineyards; some at your door. Take your pick: reed-ceilinged pool cottages have modern interiors, French doors and verandas; those at the historic wine cellar retain 1800's charm with open fireplaces and wooden ceilings; while individual suites, with private entrances, offer spacious bedrooms and modern en-suite facilities. (See also Restaurants & A–Z sections.)

Pat Busch Mountain Reserve Klaasvoogds West, Robertson ▪ Sleeping 45 people in variety of self-catering cottages ▪ Standard cottages from R200-R220 pps & Exclusive cottages from R350-R425 pps depending on length of stay/midweek/weekend/season; Farmhouse Erika incl. garden flat (sleeps up to 21) R2,500 per night ▪ Visa & MasterCard accepted ▪ Conferences ▪ Weddings/functions ▪ Ceiling fans ▪ Fireplaces ▪ Exclusive cottages include: spa bath ▪ Air-conditioning ▪ Tea/coffee making facilities ▪ Outdoor hammocks ▪ Mountain biking ▪ Walks/hikes ▪ 4x4 route ▪ Birding ▪ Swimming & fishing in mountain dams ▪ WiFi ▪ German spoken ▪ Owners Stephan & Lindi Busch ▪ cottages@patbusch.co.za ▪ www.patbusch.co.za ▪ S 33° 46′34″ E 19° 59′47″ ▪ **T +27 (0)23-626-2033** ▪ F +27 (0)86-573-2156

A world in one valley, part of a 2 000 ha pristine mountain reserve on the fynbos-covered kloofs and slopes of the Langeberg, just beyond Robertson and 1.5 hours from Cape Town. Great rates for self-catering accommodation in comfortable cottages, larger farmhouse and luxury air-conditioned units with spa baths. Hiking trails, birding and mountain biking, mountain dams for swimming and fishing.

Rosendal Winery & Wellness Retreat Klaas Voogds West, Robertson ▪ TGCSA 4-star guest house ▪ 8 rooms ▪ Seasonal rates from R495–R695 pps B&B ▪ Visa & MasterCard accepted ▪ Restaurant ▪ Weddings/functions ▪ Spa & Wellness Centre ▪ Pool ▪ Birding ▪ Fishing ▪ Wine tasting ▪ Ceiling fans ▪ Under-floor heating ▪ WiFi ▪ Safe ▪ French & Norwegian spoken ▪ Owners Geir & Sissel Tellefsen ▪ info@rosendalwinery.com ▪ www.rosendalwinery.com ▪ S 33° 48'7.8" E 019° 59'19.0" ▪ **T +27 (0)23-626-1570** ▪ F +27 (0)23-626-1571

Need a relaxing getaway? Head for the serenity of Klaas Voogds, to this four-star guest house with revitalising spa, where qualified therapists offer traditional treatments using products made from wine grapes, enriched with antioxidants. Elegant colonial-style accommodation in the original manor and farmhouse ranges from luxury spa rooms, to farm rooms and interlinking family rooms, all en-suite and overlooking vineyards, pond, pool or picturesque garden. (See also Restaurants & A–Z sections.)

The Robertson Small Hotel 58 Van Reenen Street, Robertson ▪ TGCSA 5-star hotel ▪ 10 suites ▪ Low season from R850 pps B&B, high season from R950 pps B&B; single supplement R200 ▪ Major credit cards accepted ▪ Reuben's at The Robertson ▪ The Wellness Room ▪ 2 pools ▪ Secure parking ▪ Air-conditioning ▪ Under-floor heating ▪ TV ▪ DVD player ▪ iPod docking station ▪ WiFi ▪ Electronic safe ▪ Complimentary mini-bar contents ▪ Wheelchair-friendly with suite specifically for the disabled ▪ Owners Tim Rands, Gys Naude & Marc Kent ▪ GM Riaan Kruger ▪ reservations@therobertsonsmallhotel.com ▪ www.therobertsonsmallhotel.com ▪ S 33° 48'00.8" E 19° 52 47.6" ▪ **T +27 (0)23-626-7200** ▪ F +27 (0)23-626-1680

Sophisticated outer-city hospitality at its best. Natural hues and rich textures cocoon air-conditioned luxury suites in tranquillity, while eclectic furnishings fuse modern design with space and comfort. The Victorian manor house is home to a cosy bar-lounge and state-of-the-art wine cellar, backdrop to signature restaurant, Reuben's at the Robertson. Manicured lawns and inviting pools encourage relaxation; the pampering wellness room will revitalise body and spirit. Best Luxury Country Hotel in South Africa — World Luxury Hotel Awards 2011.

Route 62
Les Hauts de Montagu see under Montagu

Somerset West
Eikendal Lodge see under Stellenbosch

Lyngrove Wines and Guesthouse see under Stellenbosch

Somerton Manor Guesthouse 13 Somerset Street, Somerset West ▪ TGCSA 4-star guesthouse ▪ 12 rooms ▪ Seasonal rates: R445–R845 pps B&B ▪ Major credit cards accepted ▪ Conferences ▪ Weddings/functions ▪ Spa ▪ Sauna ▪ Gym ▪ Pool ▪ Jacuzzi ▪ Secure parking ▪ Shuttle service ▪ Air-conditioning ▪ Ceiling fans ▪ Fireplace ▪ Under-floor heating ▪ TV ▪ DVD player ▪ WiFi ▪ Safe ▪ Dutch & German spoken ▪ Owner Antonie van den Hurk ▪ info@somerton.co.za ▪ www.somerton.co.za ▪ S 34° 09'92.7" E 018° 51'21.57" ▪ **T +27 (0)21-851-4682** ▪ F +27 (0)21-851-4672

Styled with Cape Dutch elegance, blending old-world charm with modern facilities. Luxurious en-suite bedrooms, jacuzzi, sauna, and heated-swimming pool; gym to keep toned. Wine from the cellar to enjoy in the tranquil garden, lapa, or on the veranda. A golfer's paradise: 20 courses nearby and reduced green fees at Erinvale golf club. 30 minutes from Cape Town international airport, with easy access to major tourist attractions.

Stanford
Boschrivier Farm House On the R326 between Caledon & Stanford ▪ Self-catering ▪ 4 rooms ▪ Rates on request ▪ Major credit cards accepted ▪ Restaurant ▪ Mountain biking ▪ Walks/hikes ▪ Fishing ▪ Canoeing ▪ Wine tasting ▪ TV ▪ Owner NJT de Villiers ▪ drnjtdevilliers@mweb.co.za ▪ S 34° 23'19.4" E 19° 37'51.0" ▪ **T +27 (0)76-736-0351/+27 (0)23-347-3313 Ext 3** ▪ F +27 (0)23-342-2215

Unwind in the peace of a typical veranda-shaded farmhouse in the heart of the Overberg, on a working winefarm dating back to 1659. Sleeps nine in four comfortable bedrooms with spectacular views; relaxing lounge with fireplace, modern kitchen and braai facilities. Self-cater, or breakfast in the farm restaurant; canoe on the dam or river, mountain-bike through the vineyards, or hike amid wild flowers and fynbos. (See also Restaurants & A–Z sections.)

Stellenbosch
Caledon Villa 7 Neethling Street, Stellenbosch ▪ TGCSA 3-star guest house ▪ Portfolio 'great comfort' ▪ National monument ▪ 15 rooms ▪ Seasonal rates: R420–R575 pps B&B ▪ Visa & MasterCard accepted ▪ Conferences ▪ Pool ▪ Secure parking ▪ Shuttle service ▪ Air-conditioning ▪ Ceiling fans ▪ Fireplace in some rooms ▪ TV ▪ WiFi ▪ Safe ▪ Dutch & German spoken ▪ Owners Johan & Ode Krige ▪ info@caledonvilla.co.za ▪ www.caledonvilla.co.za ▪ S 33° 56'15" E 18° 51'55" ▪ **T/ F +27 (0)21-883-8912**

Explore the historic heart of Stellenbosch with its restaurants, shops and art galleries on foot from this splendid Edwardian house. The owner's in-depth research into history, culture, genealogy, wine and art is reflected in the character and ambience of the Villa. Enjoy the colour-play of sunset on the mountains from the roof terrace and be assured of expert assistance in planning any outings and tours.

Clouds Wine & Guest Estate Helshoogte Road (R310), Stellenbosch ▪ TGCSA 5-star guesthouse ▪ 7 luxury rooms & 5 one-bedroom guest suites, each sleeping up to four persons (double sleeper couch in lounge) ▪ Seasonal rates from R800–R1,800 pps B&B ▪ Major credit cards accepted ▪ Conferences ▪ Weddings/functions ▪ Pool ▪ Walks/hikes ▪ Wine tasting ▪ Secure parking ▪ Air-conditioning ▪ Under-floor heating in bathroom ▪ Satellite TV ▪ DVD player ▪ iPod docking station ▪ WiFi ▪ Safe ▪ Tea/coffee making facilities ▪ Dutch spoken ▪ Owners P.E.C. Burema & J.C. van Harperen ▪ GM Marika Kok ▪ info@cloudsestate.co.za ▪ www.cloudsestate.co.za ▪ S 33° 55'20.3" E 018° 55'45.5" ▪ **T +27 (0)21-885-1819** ▪ F +27 (0)21-885-2829

Escape to a five-star getaway, set spectacularly at the summit of the Helshoogte mountain pass, minutes from picturesque Stellenbosch. Under new owners, guesthouse décor is changing to innovative and modern, making the most of the panoramic valley views. Guest suites for couples or families are fully equipped for self-catering, but a generous English breakfast plus daily sundowners are offered, and there are excellent restaurants nearby. (See also A–Z section.)

Delaire Graff Lodges & Spa Delaire Graff Estate, R310, Helshoogte Pass, Banhoek Valley, Stellenbosch ▪ TGCSA 5-star lodges ▪ 10 lodges ▪ Seasonal rates (B&B): Deluxe lodge R7,750–R9,350; Luxury lodge R8,600–R10,400; Presidential lodge R17,500–R21,200; Owners lodge R21,900–R26,500 ▪ Major credit cards accepted ▪ Delaire Graff & Indochine Restaurants ▪ Art collection ▪ Conferences ▪ Private cinema ▪ Spa ▪ Sauna ▪ Gym ▪ Pool ▪ Jacuzzi ▪ Walks/hikes ▪ Cellar tours ▪ Wine tasting ▪ Secure parking ▪ Shuttle service ▪ Each lodge has private heated pool, butler's kitchen, en-suite bedrooms & separate sitting area ▪ Air-conditioning ▪ Fireplace ▪ Under-floor heating ▪ LED flat screen TV ▪ DVD player ▪ iPad ▪ iPod docking station ▪ WiFi ▪ Safe ▪ German spoken ▪ Owner Laurence Graff ▪ lodge.reservations@delaire.co.za ▪ www.delaire.co.za ▪ S 33° 55'236" E 18° 55'207" ▪ **T +27 (0)21-885-8160**

Luxury meets serenity in private lodges on a working wine estate atop the Helshoogte pass linking Stellenbosch and Franschhoek. Centered round a main lodge with private cinema, gym, state-of-the-art spa and Asian-influenced restaurant, the soothing, faultlessly understated lodges, each with breathtaking view and heated pool, are both rich in art personally selected by connoisseur owner Laurence Graff, and fitted with an array of electronic conveniences. *Conde Nast Traveller* Hot List 2011; *Travel & Leisure* 'It list' 2011; Best of Wine Tourism award for accommodation 2011 & '12. (See also Restaurants & A–Z sections.)

Eendracht Hotel & Self-catering 161 Dorp Street, Stellenbosch ▪ TGCSA 3-star hotel ▪ AA Travel superior hotel ▪ 12 rooms; also 3 fully serviced, semi self-catering units in 1928 listed house ▪ Seasonal rates: Hotel R469–R849 pps B&B; Self-catering (per unit): Studio R329–R719; One-bedroom R399–R779; Two-bedroom R819–R1,469 ▪ Major credit cards accepted ▪ Pool ▪ Secure parking ▪ Air-conditioning ▪ TV ▪ DVD player ▪ Free WiFi ▪ Safe ▪ Owner Daniël Lutz ▪ info@eendracht-hotel.com ▪ www.eendracht-hotel.com ▪ S 33° 56'19.13" E 18° 51'46.15" ▪ **T +27 (0)21-883-8843** ▪ F +27 (0)21-883-8842

Experience the historic ambience of Dorp Street in the comfort of a delightfully restored, owner-run village hotel with award-winning service and friendly coffee bar offering breakfast, light lunch and traditional SA treats. Within easy walking distance of over 30 restaurants, antique shops, museums, and art galleries. Easy access to numerous golf courses; centrally placed for the Stellenbosch Wine Route; 30 minutes to CT International Airport. AA Accommodation Award — winner in small hotel/inn category 2009 –'11 and now part of the 'Hall of Fame'.

Eikendal Lodge Eikendal Vineyards, R44, between Somerset West & Stellenbosch ▪ TGCSA 4-star country house; AA Superior Small Country Retreat ▪ 9 rooms ▪ Rates from R620–R1,230 pps B&B; single supplement +10% ▪ Major credit cards accepted ▪ Restaurant ▪ Conferences ▪ Pool ▪ Mountain biking ▪ Walks/hikes ▪ Fly fishing ▪ Complimentary cellar tours & wine tasting ▪ Willie Haas cheetah outreach facility ▪ Secure parking ▪ Air-conditioning ▪ German TV ▪ Free WiFi ▪ Safe ▪ Owner Rudolf Saager ▪ info@eikendallodge.co.za ▪ www.eikendallodge.co.za ▪ S 34° 00'51.16" E 18° 49'42.42" ▪ **T +27 (0)21-855-3617** ▪ F +27 (0)21-855-3862

Re-charge in country-style luxury, experiencing a welcoming Winelands blend of fine wines and hospitality. Nine spacious en-suite rooms, each with private terrace, are surrounded by 'royalty', with noble cultivars at their door. Breakfast al fresco against the backdrop of the Helderberg; enjoy complimentary snacks and wine every evening. Meet cheetah cubs (seasonal); learn to fly-fish; hike through unspoiled fynbos; or take an enlightening cellar tour. (See also A–Z section.)

Laibach Vineyards Lodge Laibach Vineyards, R44, Klapmuts Road, Stellenbosch ▪ TGCSA 4-star self-catering ▪ 5 apartments ▪ R450 pps; single R750 ▪ Major credit cards accepted ▪ Pool ▪ Walks/hikes ▪ Wine tasting ▪ Secure parking ▪ Ceiling fans ▪ LCD satellite TV ▪ WiFi ▪ Safe ▪ Owners Laibach Family ▪ info@laibachwines.com ▪ www.laibachwines.com ▪ S 33° 50'41.67" E 18° 51'43.88" ▪ **T +27 (0)21-884-4511** ▪ F +27 (0)21-884-4848

Unwind among organic vines on a welcoming 50 ha working wine farm. Spacious, fully equipped self-catering apartments each with en-suite bathroom with shower, open on to a view-rich deck. Taste wines, enjoy vineyard walks, mountain bike or laze at the pool. Only 40 minutes from Cape Town, 20 from Franschhoek, 15 from Paarl and Stellenbosch. Beaches, golf courses, restaurants and wine estates within easy reach. (See also A–Z section.)

Lyngrove Wines and Guesthouse Raithby-Annandale Road (off Winery Road between Somerset West & Stellenbosch), Raithby ▪ TGCSA 5-star country house ▪ 9 rooms ▪ Seasonal rates: double R990–R1,500 per room B&B; single R560–R850 B&B ▪ Major credit cards accepted (excl. Diners Club) ▪ Conferences (8–10 delegates) ▪ Weddings/functions ▪ Pool ▪ Billiards room ▪ Tennis court ▪ Walks/hikes ▪ Wine tasting ▪ Secure parking ▪ Air-conditioning ▪ Satellite TV ▪ WiFi ▪ Safe ▪ stay@lyngrove.co.za ▪ www.lyngrove.co.za ▪ **T +27 (0)21-842-2116 ▪** F +27 (0)21-842-2118

Cast off care at this charming colonial-style country house surrounded by vineyards and magnificent mountains. The 5-star guesthouse, on a working wine farm just 20 minutes from Cape Town International Airport, offers all the luxuries you'll need while restoring your spirit. Leisure options range from a swimming pool and tennis court to nearby hiking and biking trails and golf courses. Ideal for weddings or conferences. (See also A–Z section.)

Majeka House 26–32 Houtkapper Street, Paradyskloof, Stellenbosch ▪ TGCSA 5-star country house ▪ 22 rooms ▪ Low season: double from R900 pps B&B, single from R1,370 B&B; High season: double from R1,150 pps B&B, single from R1,730 B&B ▪ Major credit cards accepted ▪ Makaron Restaurant ▪ Business centre & boardroom ▪ Library ▪ Sanctuary Spa with full range of treatments, sauna, steamroom & fitness centre ▪ 2 pools + 1 heated indoor pool ▪ Jacuzzi ▪ Mountain biking ▪ Walks/hikes ▪ Birding ▪ Secure on-site parking ▪ Air-conditioning ▪ DSTV ▪ DVD player ▪ iPod docking station ▪ WiFi ▪ Safe ▪ French spoken ▪ Owner Karine Dequeker & Lloyd van der Merwe ▪ reservations@majekahouse.co.za ▪ www.majekahouse.co.za ▪ S 33° 58'04.07" E 18° 51' 39.64" ▪ **T +27 (0)21-880-1549 ▪** F +27 (0)21-880-1550

Spectacular award-winning décor offsets absolute luxury and personal pampering at this 5-star boutique property in a secluded garden. Though a perfect base from which to explore the winelands, you might be tempted to stay put: the relaxing spa provides an extensive array of treatments (including SA's first healing Himalayan pure crystal salt bed), the indoor pool is magnificent and restaurant meals

are a gourmet experience. International A'Design Award and bronze medal in the interior design category 2012; *Eat Out* Boschendal Style Award, Makaron Restaurant 2011. (See also Restaurants section.)

Morgenhof Manor House Morgenhof Wine Estate, Klapmuts Road (R44), Stellenbosch ▪ 5 en-suite rooms ▪ Double R495 pps B&B, R990 per room B&B; single R695 B&B ▪ No charge for tour guides with parties ▪ Major credit cards accepted ▪ Restaurant (lunch only) ▪ Coffee, tea & handmade biscotti offered in rooms ▪ Free wine tasting at Morgenhof ▪ Conferences ▪ Weddings/functions ▪ Pool ▪ 24 hour security on estate ▪ French & German spoken ▪ Owner Anne Cointreau ▪ info@morgenhof.com ▪ www.morgenhof.com ▪ S 33° 53'38.5" E 18° 51'39.2" ▪ **T +27 (0)21-889-2034 ▪** F +27 (0)21-889-5266

Absorb the relaxed food and wine lifestyle on a wine estate dating back to 1692, now offering accommodation in the refurbished, gabled manor house. Five en-suite double rooms (those upstairs are smaller and more informal) and well-equipped, self-catering kitchen. Cosy coffee shop breakfasts included and lunch available at the estate restaurant. An inviting tourist base, centrally located on the R44 just 4 km from Stellenbosch. (See also Restaurants & A–Z sections.)

Natte Valleij Farm Natte Valleij, Klapmuts Road (R44), between Stellenbosch and Paarl ▪ TGCSA 3-star B&B & self-catering ▪ 2 cottages — both private with patio and BBQ — Vineyard cottage (sleeps 6) & Cellar cottage (sleeps 2 adults + 2 children) ▪ B&B R340–R360 pp; self-catering R220–R250 pp ▪ Owners Charles & Charlene Milner ▪ milner@intekom.co.za ▪ www.nattevalleij.co.za ▪ S 33° 50'3.6" E 018° 52' 43.2" ▪ **T +27 (0)21-875-5171**

Step into the past. Ideal for families or a group of friends, this historic wine farm in the prime wine-making 'Muldersvlei bowl' area, with a magnificent Cape Dutch homestead, was the original land grant of the area. Relaxing rural ambience; secluded pool set in the large garden. Wonderful walking through vineyards or the neighbouring game reserve where wildebeest, zebra, springbok, bontebok, gemsbok and eland graze. (See also A–Z section.)

Saxenburg Guest Cottages Polkadraai Road, Kuils River ▪ 3 self-catering apartments: bachelor, 1-bedroom & 3-bedroom ▪ R575 per room ▪ Major credit cards accepted ▪ The Guinea Fowl Restaurant ▪ Conferences ▪ Weddings/functions ▪ Pool ▪ Wine tasting ▪ Secure parking ▪ Air-conditioning ▪ Fireplace ▪ TV ▪ Safe ▪ German spoken ▪ Owners Adrian & Birgit Bührer ▪ info@saxenburg.co.za ▪ www.saxenburg.co.za ▪ **T +27 (0)21-903-6113 ▪** F +27 (0)21-903-3129

Shed stress in the idyllic surroundings of a view-rich working wine farm only 20 minutes from Cape Town

International Airport, 30 from Cape Town and 10 from Stellenbosch. Three inviting, colour-bright and fully secure Cape Dutch-style apartments share a swimming pool and are all fully equipped for self-catering (including barbeque facilities). Should you choose to relax rather than cook, book at the estate's popular restaurant. (See also A–Z section.)

Spier Hotel R310 Lynedoch Road, Stellenbosch ▪ TGCSA 4-star hotel ▪ 155 rooms ▪ Low season from R900 per room; High season from R1,850 per room ▪ Major credit cards accepted ▪ Restaurant ▪ Conferences ▪ Spa ▪ Pool ▪ Mountain biking ▪ Walks/hikes ▪ Wine tasting ▪ Secure parking ▪ Shuttle service ▪ Air-conditioning ▪ Ceiling fans ▪ Fireplace ▪ TV ▪ iPod docking station ▪ WiFi ▪ Safe ▪ Mini bar ▪ Xhosa spoken ▪ info@spier.co.za ▪ www.spier.co.za ▪ S 33° 58′ 379″ E 18° 46′ 944″ ▪ **T +27 (0)21-809-1100** ▪ F +27 (0)21-881-1134

More than a Winelands hotel, Spier is a destination, offering visitors a variety of authentic experiences, from sustainable food and highly-rated wine to outdoor activities in beautiful surroundings. This inviting public face is backed by pioneering work in social and ecological programmes to alleviate poverty and protect the environment. The hotel was one of South Africa's first to be Fair Trade in Tourism certified. Conde Nast World Savers Award 'Doing it all' Category 2011. (See also Restaurants & A–Z sections.)

Sugarbird Manor Devon Valley Road, Stellenbosch ▪ TGCSA 4-star guesthouse ▪ 9 rooms ▪ Seasonal rates: double R1,000–R1,450 per room B&B; single R700–R1,160 B&B ▪ Major credit cards accepted ▪ Conferences ▪ Weddings ▪ Pool ▪ Hiking ▪ DSTV ▪ Air-conditioning & ceiling fan ▪ Owner Ginny Povall ▪ reservations@sugarbirdmanor.co.za ▪ www.sugarbirdmanor.co.za ▪ S 33° 54′ 18.5″ E 18° 49′ 25″ ▪ **T +27 (0)21-865-2313/+27 (0)76-340-8296**

Comfortable meets chic; welcoming detail meets delightful destination. Eclectic in design, this 4-star guesthouse on a protea and wine farm adds a respectful twist of city sophistication to the Cape Wineland's country roots. Whether for a long holiday or short break, the 21 ha of gorgeous flowers and vineyards provides a perfect base for exploring the Winelands — or just chilling out in quiet luxury. (See also A–Z section for Botanica Wines.)

The Devon Valley Hotel Devon Valley Road, Devon Valley, Stellenbosch ▪ TGCSA 4-star hotel ▪ 50 suites ▪ Seasonal rates: from R468–683 pps B&B ▪ Major credit cards accepted ▪ Flavours Restaurant ▪ Conferences ▪ Weddings/functions ▪ 2 Pools ▪ Jacuzzi ▪ Walks/hikes ▪ Birding ▪ Boule court ▪ Wine tasting ▪ Secure parking ▪ Shuttle service ▪ Air-conditioning ▪ Fireplace ▪ TV ▪ WiFi ▪ Safe ▪ German spoken ▪ Owner

Louis Group Hotels, Spa's & Vineyards ▪ info@ devonvalleyhotel.com ▪ www.devonvalleyhotel.com ▪ S 33° 54′ 12.64″ E 18° 48′ 53.03″ ▪ **T +27 (0)21-865-2012** ▪ F +27 (0)21-865-2610

Hidden away in a shady, green and peaceful corner of the Stellenbosch Winelands, with unobstructed views of olive groves, vineyards and majestic mountains, this friendly 4-star hotel specialises in authentic 'handmade hospitality'. The 50 view-rich, stylish suites blend colonial charm with comfort and contemporary needs, while spacious luxury rooms and executive suites in the manor house are ideal for a romantic escape or rejuvenating retreat. Summit Hotels & Resorts™ 'Resort of the Year' 2011 by Preferred Hotel Group; Expedia Insiders Select Hotel Award 2010; Global Wine Capitals: Best of Wine Tourism award for accommodation category 2010. (See also Restaurants section & A–Z for SylvanVale.)

Zevenwacht Country Inn Zevenwacht Wine Farm, Langverwacht Road, Kuils River ▪ TGCSA 4-star country house ▪ 1 Honeymoon suite (Deluxe), 12 Country Inn suites, 7 three-bedroom Cottages & 1 four-bedroom self-catering Chalet — 38 rooms in total ▪ Low season from R315 pps B&B; High season from R455 pps B&B ▪ Major credit cards accepted ▪ Restaurant ▪ Picnics ▪ Conferences ▪ Weddings/functions ▪ Mangwanani Spa ▪ Sauna ▪ Pool ▪ Tennis court ▪ Mountain biking ▪ Walks/hikes ▪ 4x4 route ▪ Birding ▪ Cellar tours ▪ Wine tasting ▪ Secure parking ▪ Shuttle service ▪ Air-conditioning ▪ TV ▪ WiFi ▪ Safe ▪ Xhosa spoken ▪ Owner Harold Johnson ▪ info@zevenwacht.co.za ▪ www.zevenwacht.co.za ▪ S 33° 55′ 47″ E 18° 43′ 43″ ▪ **T +27 (0)21-900-5700** ▪ F +27 (0)21-906-1570

A choice of accommodation on a multi-faceted wine farm, from luxury suites in the Country Inn to vineyard cottages and self-catering chalet with spectacular views of Table Bay and False Bay. Restaurant in the historic manor house open daily for breakfast, lunch and dinner; garden picnics also available. Facilities for weddings, launches and conferences; cheesery, wine tasting centre, gift shop and Mangwanani African Day Spa. Superior Accommodation: Fine Country Estates. (See also Restaurants & A–Z sections.)

Wellington

Bovlei Valley Retreat Bovlei Valley Retreat Estate, Bovlei Road, Wellington ▪ TGCSA 4-star guest house ▪ 5 en-suite rooms in converted cottages and stables; 1 self-catering cottage ▪ Seasonal rates: R600–R800 pps B&B ▪ Major credit cards accepted ▪ The Stone Kitchen restaurant ▪ Weddings/functions ▪ Pool ▪ Walks/hikes ▪ Boule court ▪ Cellar tours ▪ Wine tasting ▪ Shuttle service ▪ Air-conditioning ▪ Under-floor heating ▪ TV ▪ DVD player ▪ iPod docking station ▪ WiFi ▪ Safe ▪ Owners Abbi & Lee Wallis ▪ info@bvr.co.za ▪

www.bvr.co.za ▪ S 33° 38'01" E 19° 03'41" ▪ **T/
F +27 (0)21-864-1504**
Idyllic retreat on a working wine, fruit and lavender
estate at the foot of the Limietberg mountains
exceeds 4-star expectations. Start your day with a
full English breakfast on a veranda with mountain
vistas; lunch lazily at the winery restaurant; take
afternoon tea in the rose and lavender-scented garden; taste wine with nibbles at sunset and experience fine dining in the Cape Dutch manor house.
(See also Restaurants section for The Stone Kitchen
& A–Z section for Dunstone Winery.)

Bradgate Manor House 2 Commissioner Street,
Wellington ▪ TGCSA 3-star B&B ▪ 6 en-suite rooms ▪
From R400–R450 pps B&B, single R550–R600 B&B ▪
Major credit cards accepted ▪ Pool ▪ Tennis court ▪
Cellar tours & wine tasting at Welbedacht Wine
Estate ▪ Secure parking ▪ Air-conditioning ▪ Fireplace
▪ TV ▪ DVD player ▪ WiFi ▪ Safe ▪ Owners Schalk &
Myra Burger ▪ myra@welbedacht.co.za ▪
www.bradgatemanor.co.za ▪ **T +27 (0)21-873-
1877**
Sojourn in Victorian splendour. Built in 1903 in
imposing British colonial style, Bradgate was
named after the home of England's nine-day
queen, Lady Jane Grey. It remained a private home
until the Burger family moved to Welbedacht wine
estate in 2001, renovating and adding modern conveniences, but leaving most of the family antiques
and paintings. This family feel and sense of period
permeates the manor. (See also Restaurants for
No.6 @ Welbedacht & A–Z sections.)

Druk My Niet Wine Estate see under Paarl

Grand Dédale Country House Doolhof Wine
Estate, Rustenburg Road, The Bovlei, Wellington ▪
TGCSA 5-star country house ▪ 7 rooms ▪ Low season
from R1,100 pps B&B, single supplement from R770;
High season from R1,375 pps B&B, single supple-
ment from R962.50 ▪ Major credit cards accepted
(excl. Diners Club) ▪ Restaurant ▪ Picnic baskets ▪
Library ▪ TV lounge ▪ Weddings/functions ▪ Spa ▪
Pool ▪ Mountain biking ▪ Walks/hikes ▪ 4x4 route ▪
Birding ▪ Cellar tours ▪ Wine tasting ▪ Secure parking
▪ Shuttle service ▪ Air-conditioning ▪ Under-floor
heating ▪ iPod docking station ▪ WiFi ▪ Safe ▪ French,
German & Italian spoken ▪ Business owners Angelo &
Tina Casu ▪ info@granddedale.com ▪
www.granddedale.com ▪ S 33° 37'34.9" E 19° 04'
58.6" ▪ **T +27 (0)21-873-4089** ▪ F +27 (0)21-
873-4188
Succumb to the peace of the original manor house
on this wine estate below the Bainskloof pass,

restored to blend history, 21st century comfort and
5-star luxury. Elegance characterises individually
decorated suites; loft living takes on a new charm in
bedrooms under thatch; and a stand-alone thatched
cottage is ideal for romantic get-aways. Expect
pampering, backed by discreet service, space,
sweeping views and delicious meals. (See also A–Z
section.)

Jacaranda Wine- and Guestfarm Old Hermon
Road, Voor Groenberg, Wellington ▪ 2 rooms in Manor
House & 2 cottage units ▪ Seasonal rates: double
R600–R650 per room B&B; single R500–R550 B&B ▪
No credit card facilities ▪ Lunch/dinner/picnics on
request ▪ Pool ▪ Air-conditioning in cottages ▪ Ceiling
fans ▪ TV ▪ WiFi hotspot ▪ French, German, Swiss-Ger-
man & Mandarin spoken ▪ Owners René Reiser & Birgit
Schmiederer-Reiser ▪ birgit@safinewines.co.za ▪
www.jacarandawines.co.za ▪ S 33° 36'49.2" E 019° 0'
16.1" ▪ **T +27 (0)21-864-1235/+27 (0)72-432-
6716**
Welcoming wine farm offering lunch, dinner, picnics
and wine tastings on request. Manor house guest
rooms blend old world appeal with a touch of Asia;
charming cottage units have romantic bedrooms
directly under the thatch, a private stoep, fully
equipped kitchen and braai facilities. Reading room,
tasting area and 15m pool at your disposal; biking,
golf courses and the Winelands right at your door-
step. (See also A–Z section.)

Worcester

Aan de Doorns Guesthouse Overhex Road,
Worcester ▪ 3-star guesthouse ▪ Seasonal rates from
R325–R375 pps B&B; single from R450–R550 B&B ▪
Visa & MasterCard accepted ▪ Restaurant ▪ Confer-
ences/weddings/functions (30 pax) ▪ Pool ▪ Golf ▪
Mountain biking ▪ Walks/hikes ▪ 4x4 route ▪ Birding ▪
Fishing ▪ Cellar tours ▪ Wine tasting ▪ Secure parking ▪
Ceiling fans ▪ Fireplace ▪ TV ▪ WiFi ▪ German spoken ▪
Owners Marita Schneider & Andries le Grange ▪ info@
aandedoorns-guesthouse.com ▪ www.aandedoorns-
guesthouse.com ▪ **T +27 (0)23-342-1402/+27
(0)72-408-9476** ▪ F +27 (0)86-670-7389
Be warmed by 'heritage hospitality' in a thatched
1860 farmhouse, still retaining its rustic charm. Generous breakfasts; old-fashioned bathrooms equalling
spacious en-suite and family bedrooms in size;
wood-burning stove and log fires to banish winter
chill; patio and pool for summer lazing. All this plus
a magnificent mountain-ringed location, positioned
at the gateway to the many wine-growing areas
and scenic routes waiting to be explored.

Disabled Access in SA Wineries

Now in its second decade, the guide's accessibility audit initiative is intended to verify that venues which are open to the public at set times, and aim to be disabled friendly, in fact are accessible — for not only wheelchairs but for all types of disability.

The audit project is carried out in stages in conjunction with disability consultant Guy Davies and his Disability Solutions team. The evaluations cover both new and recently upgraded venues, and the results are incorporated into the relevant producer entries in the A-Z section of this book, in the form of the universally recognisable 'wheelchair' icon, as well as in the look-up tables which accompany the maps.

Wineries open only by appointment are excluded, as it is felt that in these cases visitors can ascertain their individual requirements when making an appointment.

It is worth noting that the audits cover four aspects, namely parking, the tasting area, toilet facilities and cellar tours, if offered. The focus is on the tasting area, however, and in the A-Z directory we display the wheelchair icon for wineries whose tasting area is considered accessible.

While Guy's team bases its assessments on local building regulations, it tries to be sensitive to the practical implications for each winery. In an agricultural/rural setting it can sometimes be quite a challenge to ensure that access is not compromised. Many tasting facilities occupy beautiful historic buildings, which were originally designed and built with no thought to accessibility, and it is acknowledged that providing good access can be a challenge for many wineries.

Bear in mind that wineries which are not flagged as accessible in the A-Z or the map tables do not necessarily have deficient or non-existent disabled facilities; it might simply be that we are not yet in a position to comment on them. .

This edition, due to unforeseen last-minute developments, we were unable to include the latest audit results and we do apologise for any inconvenience caused. We're intending to continue next year, however, with Guy's assistance, and invite readers who have comments or suggestions about the project, or want to contact Guy, to do so either through the guide's offices or directly on telephone +27 (0)21-872-1101, mobile +27 (0)83-289-1199 or email guy@disabilitysolutions.co.za.

We'd like to take the opportunity to wish our readers pleasant and safe travels around the winelands. Do connect with us on Twitter (@ wineonaplatter) or Facebook (www.facebook.com/platterswineguide) and share your experiences with us. We're looking forward to hear from you.

The maps in this section show locales where wine is available for tasting/sale either at set times or by appointment. The larger-scale map below shows the areas covered by the maps, and the table starting on the next page lists some details for prospective visitors.

Areas covered by the maps

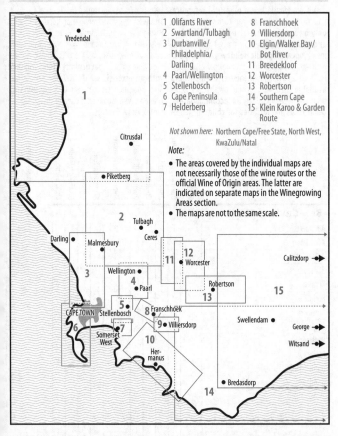

1 Olifants River
2 Swartland/Tulbagh
3 Durbanville/
  Philadelphia/
  Darling
4 Paarl/Wellington
5 Stellenbosch
6 Cape Peninsula
7 Helderberg
8 Franschhoek
9 Villiersdorp
10 Elgin/Walker Bay/
   Bot River
11 Breedekloof
12 Worcester
13 Robertson
14 Southern Cape
15 Klein Karoo & Garden
   Route

Not shown here: Northern Cape/Free State, North West,
KwaZulu/Natal

Note:
- The areas covered by the individual maps are not necessarily those of the wine routes or the official Wine of Origin areas. The latter are indicated on separate maps in the Winegrowing Areas section.
- The maps are not to the same scale.

Some distances from Cape Town (kilometres)

Calitzdorp	370	Paarl	60	Tulbagh	120
Franschhoek	75	Robertson	160	Vredendal	300
Hermanus	120	Stellenbosch	45	Worcester	110

Key for maps

═══ Main access roads		R62 R60	Road numbers
─── Roads			Towns
········ Gravel roads			

Details of Locales Shown on Maps

The tables below are intended to facilitate winery visits by providing summary information about all the winetasting venues which are open to the public, either at set times or by appointment, and appear on our winelands maps. Venues are listed by region, and details provided include a **map grid-reference**, if applicable; whether the particular venue is **open only by appointment** (T); **open on Saturdays and/or Sundays** (√ = at set times; T = by appointment); **open on public holidays** (× = closed all public holidays; otherwise assume open all or some holidays); and whether **meals/refreshments are available** (BYO = bring your own picnic). Other details include availability of **accommodation**, **cellar tours** and **facilities for children**. Venues

which are **friendly to individuals with reduced mobility**, as audited by our disability consultants, are highlighted. **Other languages spoken** (besides English and Afrikaans) are also noted (Danish = da, Dutch/Flemish = nl, French = fr, German = de, Hebrew = he, Hungarian = hu, Italian = it, Japanese = ja, Mandarin = mdr, Norwegian = nn, Portuguese = pt, Romanian = ro, Russian = ru, Setswana = tn, Spanish = sp, Swedish = sv, Swiss = gsw, isiXhosa = xh, isiZulu = zu). For more information, **particularly items marked with an asterisk**, see the A–Z and Restaurants/Accommodation sections. For **GPS coordinates**, where known, for wineries open to the public, see the relevant A-Z entries.

	Grid reference	Open by appt. only	Open Saturdays	Open Sundays	Open public holidays	Meals/refreshments	Accomodation	Cellar tours	Disabled friendly	Child friendly	Languages spoken
Breedekloof Map											
Aufwaerts		T				0					
Avondrood			T		×	T/BYO*	√	√		√	
Awendland		T				0		T			
Badsberg			√		×	T/BYO*		√*	√	√	
Bergsig			√			√		T		√	
Botha			√			BYO		T			
Breëland		T*				T/BYO*	√	T			
Dagbreek		T			×	BYO		T			
De Breede		T				0					
Du Preez			√		×	BYO		T*	√		
Du Toitskloof			√			BYO*		T	√		de
Goudini			√			√		T			
Jason's Hill			√			√		T	√	√	
Kirabo			T		×	T/BYO		√		√	
Ladera		T*				T*		T			sp
Lateganskop						0		T	√		
Lorraine					×	T/BYO*		√			
Merwida			√			0	√		√		
Mountain Oaks		T				0		T			
Mountain Ridge					×	BYO			√		
Olifantsberg		T*				0					
Opstal			√	T		√*		√	√	√	
Rico Suter		T				T/BYO*	√	T			de/fr/it
Seven Oaks		T				0					

	Grid reference	Open by appt. only	Open Saturdays	Open Sundays	Open public holidays	Meals/refreshments	Accomodation	Cellar tours	Disabled friendly	Child friendly	Languages spoken
Slanghoek			✓			T*		T	✓		de
TCB Wines					×	BYO	✓	✓			
uniWines			✓			BYO		✓*	✓		
Waboomsrivier					×	0		T*			
Cape Peninsula Map											
Ambeloui		T				0					
Beau Constantia			✓	✓	×	0					
Buitenverwachting			✓		×	✓		T	✓		
Cape Point			✓	✓		✓*			✓	✓	
Cape to Cairo		T				0					
Constantia Glen			✓	✓		✓*					
Constantia Mist	T*					BYO	✓				
Constantia Uitsig			✓	✓		✓	✓		✓		
Eagles' Nest			✓	✓		✓			✓		
Emineo		T				0					
Final Cut		T				0					
Groot Constantia			✓	✓		✓		✓	✓	✓	de/fr/nl
High Constantia			✓			T/BYO		✓			
Hout Bay		T				0		T		✓	de
Klein Constantia			✓			0			✓		fr/sv
Kling		T				0					
Mzoli's			✓	✓		✓					xh
Signal Hill			✓*		×	✓		✓			fr
Steenberg			✓	✓		✓*	✓	✓	✓		
Vaughan Johnson						0					
Durbanville, Philadelphia & Darling Map											
Altydgedacht			✓			✓		T		✓	
Bloemendal			✓	✓		✓		✓			
Capaia			T	T	×	0		✓			de
Cloof			✓			✓*		T	✓		
D'Aria			✓	✓		✓	✓				nl
Darling Cellars			✓			0		T	✓	✓	xh
De Grendel			✓	✓		✓		T	✓		
Diemersdal			✓			0		T			
Durbanville Hills			✓	✓		✓		✓*	✓	✓	
Four Fields		T				0		T			
Franki's		T			×	T/BYO	✓	T			
Groote Post			✓	✓		✓/BYO*		✓	✓	✓	
Hillcrest			✓	✓		✓		T			
Klein Roosboom			✓	✓		✓/BYO*		✓	✓		

	Grid reference	Open by appt. only	Open Saturdays	Open Sundays	Open public holidays	Meals/refreshments	Accomodation	Cellar tours	Disabled friendly	Child friendly	Languages spoken
Kronendal		T	✓			✓*		T	✓		
Meerendal			✓	✓		✓	✓	T	✓	✓	xh/zu
Nitida			✓	✓		✓			✓	✓	
Ormonde			✓			T/BYO*		T*	✓	✓	
Phizante Kraal			✓			0					
Russo		T			✗	0		✓			
Signal Gun			✓	✓		✓					
Wines of Cape Town		T				0					
Withington			✓	✓		0					
Elgin, Walker Bay & Bot River Map											
Alheit		T				0					
Almenkerk			✓	✓		✓/BYO*		✓*			nl/fr
Arumdale		T*				0					
Ashbourne		T				0		T			
Ataraxia			✓	✓*		0					
Barry Gould		T				T	✓	T		✓	
Barton			✓			0	✓	✓	✓		
Beaumont			✓			✓*	✓	✓	✓		
Belfield		T				0		T			
Benguela Cove			✓*			BYO					
Blomendahl		T				0					de
Boschrivier			✓	✓		✓/BYO	✓		✓		
Bouchard Finlayson			✓		✗	✓/BYO*		✓	✓		de/fr
Boutros			✓			0					
Catherine Marshall		T				T		T			
CharlesFox		T*	✓	✓		0		✓*		✓	
COAV		T				0					
Corder			T	T	✗	0					
Creation			✓	✓		✓		✓	✓	✓	de/fr
Dispore Kamma		T				0		T			
Domaine des Dieux			✓*	✓*		0					
Eerste Hoop		T*				0		T			
Elgin Ridge		T*				✓/BYO*		T*			fr
Elgin Vintners		T				0					
Feiteiras		T				0					pt
Gabriëlskloof			✓			✓		T		✓	
Genevieve		T				T					
Glen Erskine		T				BYO		T			de
Goedvertrouw		T				T	T			✓	
Hamilton Russell			✓			0		T			tn/xh

	Grid reference	Open by appt. only	Open Saturdays	Open Sundays	Open public holidays	Meals/refreshments	Accomodation	Cellar tours	Disabled friendly	Child friendly	Languages spoken
Hannay			T	T		T/BYO*		T			
Hermanuspietersfontein			✓	✓*		✓*	✓	T	✓		
Highlands Road			✓	✓		✓	✓	✓	✓	✓	
Hornbill			✓			✓		✓			
Iona			T		x	0		✓			
La Vierge			✓	✓		✓		T	✓		fr
Lothian		T				0	✓				sp
Luddite			T	T		0		T	✓		nl
Misty Mountains			✓			✓*		T			
Mofam			✓	✓		✓	✓			✓	
Mount Babylon		T				0		T			
Newton Johnson			✓		x	✓			✓		
Oak Valley			✓	✓		✓*	✓				it/fr
Oneiric		T*			x	BYO					
PaardenKloof		T*				0		T			xh
Paul Cluver			✓			✓*		✓			
Raka			✓			BYO		T			
Restless River		T			x	T/BYO*		T			
Rivendell			✓	✓		✓				✓	
Robert Stanford			✓	✓		✓*				✓	
Ross Gower		T				0	✓				fr/de
Shannon		T*				0					
South Hill			✓	✓		✓		✓			
Southern Right			✓			0		✓	✓		
Spioenkop		T			x	BYO	✓	T		✓	fr/nl
Spookfontein		T				0	✓	T			
Springfontein			T*			BYO	✓	✓*			
Stanford Hills		T*	✓		x	✓/BYO*	✓	✓	✓		
Sumaridge			✓	✓		✓	✓			✓	
Thandi			✓	✓		✓/BYO			✓	✓	
Vaalvlei		T*				0	✓				
Walker Bay Vineyards			✓	✓		✓/BYO		T	✓	✓	
Whalehaven			✓	✓		0		T			
Wildekrans			✓	✓		T*		✓	✓	✓	
William Everson		T				0	✓	T			
Wine Village-Hermanus			✓	✓		0			✓		
Winters Drift		T				0					
Franschhoek Map											
Akkerdal					x	0	✓				
Allée Bleue			✓	✓		✓	✓	T	✓	✓	de

	Grid reference	Open by appt. only	Open Saturdays	Open Sundays	Open public holidays	Meals/refreshments	Accomodation	Cellar tours	Disabled friendly	Child friendly	Languages spoken
Anthonij Rupert			✓	✓		✓			✓		
Blueberry Hill		T				0	✓				
Boekenhoutskloof					✗	0		✓			xh
Boschendal			✓	✓		✓		✓	✓	✓	
Cape Chamonix			✓	✓		✓	✓	T	✓		
Colmant		T*				0		T	✓		fr
Dieu Donné			✓	✓		✓		T*			
Eikehof		T				0		T			
Four Paws		T				0					
Franschhoek Cellar			✓	✓		✓/BYO		✓			
GlenWood			✓*	✓*		✓		✓	✓		
Grande Provence			✓	✓		✓	✓	✓*	✓		
Haut Espoir		T			✗	0		T	✓		
Haute Cabrière			✓	✓		✓		✓*			fr/de
Holden Manz			✓	✓		✓	✓	✓	✓		de
La Bourgogne			✓	✓		0		✓		✓	
La Bri			✓			✓/BYO*		✓			
La Chataigne			T	T	✗	0	✓				sv
La Chaumiere		T				0		T			
La Couronne			✓	✓		T*	✓			✓	
La Motte			✓			✓			✓	✓	xh
La Petite Ferme		T*			✗	✓	✓	✓			
La Vigne		T				0		T			
Landau du Val		T				0					
Le Manoir de Brendel			✓	✓		T*	✓			✓	
Leopard's Leap			✓			✓				✓	
Lynx			T	T	T	BYO		✓*			de/sp
Môreson			✓	✓		✓		✓			
Maison			✓	✓		✓					
Mont Rochelle			✓	✓		✓	✓	✓			
My Wyn			T	T	T	T*		✓			
Plaisir			✓	T*		✓*	T	✓	✓	✓	de
Rickety Bridge			✓	✓		✓	✓	✓	✓	✓	
Solms-Delta			✓	✓		✓		T			
Stony Brook			✓		✗	0	✓	✓			
The Amistad Wine Company		T*			✗	BYO	✓	T			
The House of GM		T			✗	T		T			
Topiary		T				T/BYO		T	✓		
Von Ortloff		T				0		T			de

	Grid reference	Open by appt. only	Open Saturdays	Open Sundays	Open public holidays	Meals/refreshments	Accomodation	Cellar tours	Disabled friendly	Child friendly	Languages spoken
Helderberg Map											
Aeternitas		T			×	0					
Anatu		T			×	0		T			fr/he
Avontuur			✓	✓		✓		T	✓		de/pt
BLANKbottle		T*				0					
Cape Classics		T				0					
Chennells		T*			×	0		T			de/sp
Conspirare		T				0					
Croydon			✓			T*		T	✓	✓	
Dellrust		T				0					
Eikendal			✓	✓		✓*	✓	✓	✓	✓	de
Elberti		T				0					
Equitania		T			×	BYO					
Fish Hoek						0					
Flagstone			✓			0		T	✓		
Grangehurst			✓*	✓*		0	✓				
Hathersage		T*			×	0					
Heron Ridge		T			×	T*		T			
Idiom		T*				0					it
Journey's End		T*				T/BYO*	✓	T			
JP Bredell			T			0					
Ken Forrester			✓	✓*		✓*	✓		✓		
Kumala						0					
Longridge			✓			✓		T			
Lourensford			✓	✓		✓		✓			
Lyngrove		T	✓	✓		✓*	✓				
Micu Narunsky		T				0					
Miravel		T			×	T	✓				nl/fr
Moordenaarskop		T				0		T			
Morgenster			✓	✓		✓					
Mount Rozier		T*				0	✓	T			
Onderkloof		T				0	✓	T			
Osbloed		T*				0		T*			
Pfeifer's		T				0					gsw/de
Post House			T		×	BYO	✓	✓	✓		
Romond		T*				0	✓	T*			
Skaap		T*			×	T*	✓			✓	nl
Somerbosch			✓	✓		✓		T	✓	✓	
Somerset Wines			✓		×	0					
Stonewall		T*				T					

	Grid reference	Open by appt. only	Open Saturdays	Open Sundays	Open public holidays	Meals/refreshments	Accomodation	Cellar tours	Disabled friendly	Child friendly	Languages spoken
The Winery of Good Hope		T			x	0					fr/sv
Vergelegen			✓	✓		✓		✓*	✓	✓	
Waterkloof			✓	✓		✓		T	✓		
Waterstone		T			x	0	✓	T			
Wedderwill		T*			x	BYO	✓	T	✓		de
Yonder Hill			✓*		x	✓*			✓		
Klein Karoo & Garden Route Map											
Andersons		T			x	0					
Axe Hill		T				0		T			
Barrydale			✓			BYO		T			
Bergwater			✓	✓		T/BYO	✓	T	✓		
Boplaas			✓			0		T		✓	
Bramon			✓	✓		✓		T	✓	✓	
Calitzdorp			✓			T/BYO		T			
De Krans			✓			✓/BYO*			✓	✓	
Domein Doornkraal			✓			✓*	✓				
Du'SwaRoo		T*			x	0					
Excelsior Vlakteplaas						0					
Fernskloof			✓	T*		BYO	✓			✓	sp
Garden Route			✓*			0			✓		
Grundheim			✓			0			✓		
Herold			✓			✓*	✓	✓	✓	✓	
Hillock			✓	✓		✓/BYO	✓	✓			
Jakkalsvlei			✓			✓/BYO					
Joubert-Tradauw			✓			✓	✓	✓	✓	✓	
Karusa			✓			✓		✓			
Ladismith			✓			✓		T			
LuKa						0					
Mimosa			✓	✓		✓	✓		✓	✓	de/gsw
Mons Ruber			✓			0	✓				
Montagu Wine & Spirits			✓			0			✓		
Montagu Wine Cellar			✓		x	0		T*	✓		
Newstead		T				T*					zu
Oudtshoorn			✓			BYO		T	✓		
Packwood					x	T*	✓				
Peter Bayly		T				0		T			
Plettenvale		T				0	✓				
Quinta		T				0					
Reiersvlei			✓			T*		✓			
SoetKaroo			✓			0			✓		de

	Grid reference	Open by appt. only	Open Saturdays	Open Sundays	Open public holidays	Meals/refreshments	Accomodation	Cellar tours	Disabled friendly	Child friendly	Languages spoken
Star Hill			✓	✓		✓	✓	T		✓	
The Goose		T				T	✓				
TTT Cellar			✓	T		BYO		✓	✓		
Withoek		T				0	✓	T			
KwaZulu-Natal Map											
Abingdon		T*	✓	✓		✓*	✓	T			
Highgate			✓	✓		✓				✓	de
Northern Cape, Free State & North West Map											
Bezalel			✓			✓*		✓		✓	nl
Die Mas			T	T		T/BYO*	✓	✓*		✓	
Douglas					✗	0		T			
Hartswater						0		T			
Landzicht					✗	T		T*			
Orange River			✓		✗	0		✓*	✓		
Olifants River Map											
Bellpost		T				0		T			
Cape Rock		T				BYO		T			
Cecilia		T				0					
Cederberg			✓			BYO	✓				
Desert Rose		T				0					
Driehoek		T				BYO	✓			✓	
Fryer's Cove			✓			T/BYO		✓			
Klawer			✓		✗	BYO			✓	✓	
Lutzville			✓			✓		✓	✓		de
Matzikama		T				0					
Melkboomsdrift						✓*	✓				
Namaqua			✓			✓*		✓*	✓	✓	
Seal Breeze			✓			T/BYO		✓	✓	✓	
Sir Lambert			✓			BYO	✓			✓	
Stellar					✗	BYO		T			
Stoumann's			T		✗	T		✓			
Teubes			✓			BYO	✓	T			
Tierhoek			T*		✗	BYO*	✓	✓			
Vleiland		T*				BYO					
Paarl & Wellington Map											
5 Mountains	G2		✓	✓		✓	✓	T			
African Terroir	C1	T*			✗	0		T*			fr
Alkmaar	G2		✓			0		T			
Andreas	G1	T*			✗	0	✓	T			sv

	Grid reference	Open by appt. only	Open Saturdays	Open Sundays	Open public holidays	Meals/refreshments	Accomodation	Cellar tours	Disabled friendly	Child friendly	Languages spoken
Anura	C7		✓	✓		✓		✓	✓		de
Arra	C8		✓			0					
Avondale	F6	T*				0		T	✓		
Avondvrede	C8	T				T					
Ayama	B2	T			×	T/BYO					it
Babylonstoren	D8		✓	✓		✓*	✓	T*			
Backsberg	D8		✓	✓		✓		T	✓		
Bayede!	E4		T	T	×	0					
Bergheim	E6	T				0					
Bernheim	D1, E3	T			×	0		T	✓		
Black Pearl	D5	T*				0	✓	T*	✓		
Blouvlei	G2		T		×	0		✓*			de
Boer & Brit	G2					0					de/fr/nl/sp/xh
Boland	E4		✓			0		T	✓		
Bosman	G1	T				0		T			
Boutique Baratok	E5		✓	✓	×	✓		✓			
Bovlei	G2		✓			0			✓		
Calais	F4	T*				0	✓				
Crows Nest	D3		T	T	T	T/BYO		✓		✓	
Damarakloof	A7	T*				0					
De Villiers	E6	T				0					
De Zoete Inval	E6	T				0					
Diemersfontein	F2		✓	✓		✓	✓	T			
Diners Club Bartho Eksteen	C3	T				T/BYO		T		✓	
Domaine Brahms	C3	T			T	0		T			
Doolhof	H1		✓	✓		✓*	✓	T	✓		
Doran	D1	T*	✓	✓		0					
Druk My Niet	F4	T			×	T/BYO	✓	T			de
Dunstone	H1		✓	✓		✓	✓	✓		✓	
Eenzaamheid	B5	T				0					
Fairview	D6		✓	✓		✓			✓		
Freedom Hill	F7		✓*	✓*		✓			✓		
Glen Carlou	D7		✓	✓		✓		T	✓	✓	de
Groot Parys	E5	T				0					nl
Hawksmoor	A7	T*				0	✓				fr/de/ja
Helpmekaar	F2	T*			×	0		T*			
Hildenbrand	G2		✓	T*		✓	✓		✓		de
Imbuko	F4		T		×	T*					
Jacaranda	F1		✓			T*	✓				fr/de/mdr
Jacques Smit	F2	T				0		T		✓	
Joostenberg	A8		✓	✓		✓		T	✓	✓	

	Grid reference	Open by appt. only	Open Saturdays	Open Sundays	Open public holidays	Meals/refreshments	Accomodation	Cellar tours	Disabled friendly	Child friendly	Languages spoken
Juno	E5		✓			✓					
Klein Optenhorst	H1	T				0					
Klein Parys	E5		✓			0		✓		✓	
Kleine Draken	D6				×	T*		T	✓		
KWV	E6		✓	✓		✓		✓	✓		de
La Ferme Derik	D3	T				0	✓	T			
Laborie	E6		✓	✓		✓	✓	✓*	✓		de
Landskroon	D6					T/BYO*	✓	T*		✓	
Lazanou	F1	T*				T*					
Le Fût	F5	T				0					
Le Joubert	E4	T				0					
Lindhorst	D7	T*				T*	✓	T	✓		
Linton Park	G1	T*			×	BYO		T*			
Longbarn	F2					0		T			
Marianne	C8		✓	✓		✓	✓	✓			de/fr
Maske	G2	T				BYO					de
Mellasat	G5		✓	✓		T*		T			
Mischa	F1	T			×	T	✓	T*			
Mon Rêve	D7	T				BYO		T		✓	fr/de
Mont Destin	C8	T			×	0		T			de/fr
Mont du Toit	G2		T		×	BYO*	✓	✓*			de
Mooi Bly	F4	T				BYO	✓	T			nl
Mount Vernon	C7		✓			✓*		✓			
Nabygelegen	H1		✓		×	T*	✓	✓			
Napier	G2		✓			✓*		✓	✓		
Nederburg	F5		✓	✓*		✓*		✓	✓		de
Nelson	D3	T			×	0	✓	T	✓	✓	
Niel Joubert	C8	T*			×	0					
Noble Hill	D8		✓	✓		✓		T	✓	✓	fr
Nwanedi	E3		✓	T		✓	✓	T			
Olsen	G5	T				T*					
Oude Denneboom	C2	T				0	✓				
Painted Wolf	E6	T*				T*					fr
Perdeberg	B3		✓			T/BYO*		T*			xh
Retief	E4	T			×	0					
Rhebokskloof	D3		✓	✓		✓		T	✓	✓	
Ridgeback	D3		✓	✓		✓	✓	T		✓	
Rudera	E4		T	T		0		✓*			
Rupert & Rothschild	D8		✓*			0		✓*	✓		
Scali	C1	T			×	0	✓	T			
Simonsvlei	D7		✓	✓		✓/BYO		T	✓	✓	

	Grid reference	Open by appt. only	Open Saturdays	Open Sundays	Open public holidays	Meals/refreshments	Accomodation	Cellar tours	Disabled friendly	Child friendly	Languages spoken
Southern Sky	E5	T				0					
Spice Route	D6		√	√		√					
Stone Ridge	D1	T				0					
Tempel	E3	T				0	√	T			de/fr/sv
The Mason's	E6	T				√*					
Thokozani	F2		√	√		√	√	T			
Upland	G3	T			T	0	√	T			
Val de Vie	F7		√	√		√*		T			
Val du Charron	H1		√	√		√	√	√	√		
Veenwouden	E3	T				0		T			
Vendôme	E6	T			X	0			√		
Versailles	E1	T				0		T			
Vondeling	C1	T				0		T			
Vrede en Lust	D8		√	√		√	√	T*	√	√	
Welbedacht	F1		√			√/BYO	√	√	√	√	de
Welgegund	G2	T				0	√				
Welgeleë	D7		√	√		T					
Welgemeend	C7		√		X	0		√	√		
Wellington Winery	E2		√		X	0		T	√		
Welvanpas	H1		√	√		√/BYO				√	nl
Windmeul	D3		√		X	√*		T	√		
Zanddrift	E6					0					
Robertson Map											
Arendsig		T				BYO	√	T			
Ashton			√			0	√	T	√	√	
Bon Cap				√		√	√	T	√	√	
Bon Courage			√			√			√	√	
Bonnievale			√			√*			√	√	
Buffalo Creek			√	T		0		√*			
BurCon			√	T		√	√		√		
Bushmanspad						BYO	√				nl
Cape Dreams		T				0		T			
Clairvaux					X	BYO		T	√		
Cloverfield						0		√			
De Wetshof			√			0		T*	√		
DuVon		T				0	√	T			
Esona			√			0					
Excelsior			√			T/BYO	√		√		
Fraai Uitzicht 1798			√	√		√*	√				de
Goedverwacht			√			T/BYO*		√			

	Grid reference	Open by appt. only	Open Saturdays	Open Sundays	Open public holidays	Meals/refreshments	Accomodation	Cellar tours	Disabled friendly	Child friendly	Languages spoken
Graham Beck			✓	✓		0			✓		
Janeza		T				0					
Jonkheer		T*			×	0	✓	T			
Kingsriver			✓	✓		✓/BYO	✓	✓			nl
Kleinhoekkloof		T*				0					
Koningsrivier		T				0		T			
Kranskop			✓			BYO		✓			de
Langverwacht					×	0		✓	✓		
Le Grand Chasseur		T			×	0		✓			
Lord's			T*	T*		0		✓			
McGregor			✓			BYO		T			
Mooiuitsig						0	✓	T			
Quando		T			×	0					de
Rietvallei			✓			✓*		T	✓		
Robertson			✓	✓		0		T			
Roodezandt					×	0		T	✓	✓	
Rooiberg			✓			✓/BYO			✓	✓	
Rosendal			✓	✓		✓	✓	✓	✓		nn
Springfield			✓			BYO		T			
Sumsaré		T*				BYO		T*		✓	
Tanagra		T*				0	✓	T			de
Van Loveren			✓	✓		✓	✓	✓	✓		
Van Zylshof			✓			0		T			
Viljoensdrift			✓	✓*		✓				✓	fr
Vruchtbaar		T			×	0		T			
Wandsbeck			T	T	×	0		T	✓		de
Wederom		T			T	T	✓	T			de
Weltevrede			✓			✓	✓	T	✓		
Windfall		T			×	BYO		T			
Wolfkloof		T				T/BYO		T			
Wolvendrift			✓			T		T	✓	✓	
Wonderfontein		T*				0					
Zandvliet			✓			BYO			✓		
Southern Cape Map											
Andy Mitchell		T				0		T			
Black Oystercatcher			✓	✓		✓*		✓		✓	
Brunia		T*				✓*					
Jean Daneel			✓			✓		T			de
Lismore		T				0				✓	
Oewerzicht		T				0	✓				

	Grid reference	Open by appt. only	Open Saturdays	Open Sundays	Open public holidays	Meals/refreshments	Accomodation	Cellar tours	Disabled friendly	Child friendly	Languages spoken
Strandveld			✓			BYO	✓	✓			
The Berrio		T*				T/BYO					
The Giant Periwinkle		T				0					
Zoetendal			T			0	✓	✓			
Stellenbosch Map											
Aaldering	D4		✓		✗	0		T			
Akkerdraai	E8		✓			0					de
Allegria Vineyards	B6	T				0	✓				nl/de/gsw
Alluvia	H5		✓	✓		T/BYO*	✓	T		✓	
Alto	E8		✓	✓		T*					
Amani	B6		✓			BYO		✓	✓	✓	
Amares	G4	T			✗	T*		T			nl
Annandale	E8		✓			BYO		✓	✓		
Asara	D6		✓	✓		✓	✓	T	✓	✓	de
Audacia	E7		✓			0			✓		
Bartinney	H5				✗	0		T	✓		
Beau Joubert	B6		T		✗	BYO	✓	T			
Bein	B6	T				0		T			de/fr
Bellevue	C3		✓			0					
Beyerskloof	E3		✓			✓		T	✓		
Bilton	E8		✓	✓		✓*		T*	✓	✓	
Blaauwklippen	E6		✓	✓		✓		T	✓	✓	de
Bonfoi	C5	T			✗	BYO			✓		
Boschheim	E5	T				0					de
Boschkloof	C6		✓			BYO		✓			
Botanica	D4	T*				✓*	✓				
Bottelary Hills	D3		✓	✓		0					
Brampton	F5		✓			✓*					
Brenaissance	D4	T				BYO	✓				
Camberley	H5		✓	✓		T/BYO	✓	T			
Cape Hutton	E7	T				T*		T			
Carisbrooke	C6				✗	0					
Casa Mori	D3	T				T		T			it/fr
Chabivin	E7		✓			✓*					fr
Chateau Beau Belle	C7	T*				T/BYO*	✓	T			
Cirrus	E8		✓*	✓*		0					
Clos Malverne	D4		✓	✓		✓		✓*			
Clouds	G5		✓			T*	✓				
Clovelly	D4	T				0		T			
Dalla Cia	E5		✓			✓					it

	Grid reference	Open by appt. only	Open Saturdays	Open Sundays	Open public holidays	Meals/refreshments	Accomodation	Cellar tours	Disabled friendly	Child friendly	Languages spoken
De Meye	E1		√	√		√*		T*	√		
De Toren	B6	T				0		T			
De Trafford	G8		√		×	0		√*			
Delaire	G5		√	√		√*	√	T*	√		
Delheim	F2		√	√		√	√	√	√	√	de
DeMorgenzon	C5		√	√		0		T			
Devon Rocks	D3	T				0	√	T			de/sv
Devonair	D3	T			×	0	√				
Devonvale	D3	T*				√	√		√		de/fr
DeWaal	C5		√*			0					
Die Bergkelder	E5		√			0		√	√		
Dombeya	E8		√	√		√*	√	T	√	√	
Donkiesbaai	E8		√*	√*		0					
Dormershire	A5		√		×	0		√			
Dornier	F7		√	√		√*	√	T	√	√	
Eaglevlei	E1		√	√		√*			√	√	
Edgebaston	F3	T				0					
Elgin Heights	C6	T				0					
Ernie Els	F8		√			√*		√	√		
Ernst Gouws	D1		√			0			√	√	de
Escapades	B4	T				0					
Fort Simon	C4		√		×	√*		T	√		
Francois La Garde	E5	T				0					
Gilga	D5	T				0					
Glenelly	F4		√			0		T	√		de/fr
Goede Hoop	C3		√			T/BYO*		√			
Graceland	E7	T*			×	0	√				
Groenland	B3		√			BYO		T	√		
Guardian Peak	E8		√	√		√					
Hartenberg	C4		√	√*		√		T	√	√	de
Haskell	E8		√	√		√*	√	T		√	
Hazendal	B3		√	√		√		√	√	√	de/ru
Hidden Valley	F8		√	√		√		√	√		
Hoopenburg	E1				×	BYO	√	√			
Jacobsdal	B6					0					
JC le Roux	D4		√	√*		√		√*	√		
Jordan	C5		√	√		√		T*	√		
Kaapzicht	B4		√			BYO	√	T			de
Kanonkop	F2		√			T/BYO*			√		
Kanu	E3				×	0					
Katbakkies	D5	T*			×	0					

	Grid reference	Open by appt. only	Open Saturdays	Open Sundays	Open public holidays	Meals/refreshments	Accomodation	Cellar tours	Disabled friendly	Child friendly	Languages spoken
Keermont	F8	T				0		T			
Klein DasBosch	F7	T				0					
Kleine Zalze	E6		√	√		√	√		√		
Knorhoek	F3		√	√		√*	√	√	√	√	
Koelenhof	D1		√			BYO		T	√	√	de
Koopmanskloof	C3	T*			×	0	√	T			
Kyburg	D4	T				0	√				fr/de
Laibach	F1		√*			0	√	T			
Lanzerac	G5		√	√		√	√	√		√	
L'Avenir	E3		√			BYO	√	T	√	√	fr
Le Bonheur	F1		√	√		0					
Le Pommier	H4	T*				√	√			√	
Le Riche	G6	T*			×	0		T			de
Lievland	F1		√	√		T*	√	√	√		
L'Olivier	D5	T				√					
Louiesenhof	E4		√	√*		√*	√		√	√	
Louisvale	D4				×	BYO		√	√		
Lovane	D6		√	√	×	0	√	√			
Malanot	E8	T*				0		T*	√		
Marklew	F1	T				0		T			
Meerlust	B8		√		×	0		T			
Meinert	D4	T*			×	0					de
M'hudi	B1	T				0	√				tn/xh/zu
Middelvlei	E4		√	√		√*	√	T	√	√	
Mitre's Edge	F1	T*				0	√	T			
MolenVliet	H4	T				0	√				
Monterosso	E4		T	T	T	0		√*			it/zu
Mooiplaas	B4		√			T/BYO*					
Morgenhof	F3		√	√		√	√	T	√	√	de/fr
Mostertsdrift	E4	T				T*		T		√	
Mulderbosch	C6		√	√		√*					fr
Muratie	F2		√	√		√	√	T			
Mvemve Raats	B6	T			×	0					
Natte Valleij	F1		√		×	0	√	√		√	
Neethlingshof	D5		√	√		√*		T	√	√	de
Neil Ellis	G5		√			√*			√		
Nico van der Merwe	B6	T				0					fr/de
Nietvoorbij	F4		T		×	0		T*			
Oldenburg	H5		√*			√*			√		
Origin	D3	T				0					fr/de
Overgaauw	D5		√*			BYO			√		

	Grid reference	Open by appt. only	Open Saturdays	Open Sundays	Open public holidays	Meals/refreshments	Accomodation	Cellar tours	Disabled friendly	Child friendly	Languages spoken
Peter Falke	E8		✓	✓		✓*		T			
Quoin Rock	F3		✓	✓		✓*					
Raats	B6	T			×	0					
Rainbow's End	H5	T				BYO		T			
Remhoogte	E3		✓			✓*	✓	T			
Re'Mogo	E4		✓			0			✓		
Reyneke	B6		T		T	0		✓*			
Rust en Vrede	E8		✓			✓		✓			
Rustenberg	G4		✓	✓		0			✓		
Saxenburg	A5		✓	✓		✓/BYO	✓				
Seven Sisters	D7	T				0					
Simonsig	E2		✓	✓		✓		✓*	✓	✓	
Skilpadvlei	C6		✓	✓		✓	✓		✓	✓	
Slaley	E2		✓			✓		T			
Sonklip	G5	T*				0		T			
Spier	C7		✓	✓		✓	✓		✓	✓	de/xh
Spotswood	F7	T				0					
Spring Grove	H4	T				0					
Stark-Condé	G6		✓	✓		✓			✓		ja
Stellekaya	E5				×	T*		✓	✓		zu
Stellenbosch Hills	D6		✓			0			✓		
Stellenbosch Ridge	E8		✓*	✓*		0					
Stellenbosch University	F6		T		×	0					
Stellendrift	C7	T				0		T			
StellenRust	E7		✓		×	✓/BYO*		T			xh
Stellenzicht	E7		✓	✓		0		T			
Sterhuis	C4	T				0		T	✓	✓	
Stonehill	D4	T				0					
StoneyCroft	D3	T				0					
Summerhill	E3				×	✓*		✓			
Super Single Vineyards	C5		✓			0					
SylvanVale	D4		✓	✓		✓	✓		✓	✓	de/xh
Tamboerskloof	F7				×	0		✓			
The Company of Wine People	C7		✓	✓		✓			✓	✓	xh
The Foundry	B8	T			×	0		T			
The High Road	E5		✓		×	0					
Thelema	G4		✓			BYO		✓			
Tokara	G4		✓	✓		✓		✓	✓		
Topaz	F2	T				0					de/fr
Uitkyk	F2		✓	✓		T/BYO*		✓	✓	✓	
Usana	C5	T				0					

	Grid reference	Open by appt. only	Open Saturdays	Open Sundays	Open public holidays	Meals/refreshments	Accomodation	Cellar tours	Disabled friendly	Child friendly	Languages spoken
Uva Mira	F8		√	√		√				√	
Vergenoegd	B8		√	√		√*		T	√	√	xh
Vilafonté	E5	T				0		T			
Villiera	D1		√			√/BYO*		√	√		fr
Vredenheim	D6		√			√	√		√		
Vriesenhof	F7		T		×	0		T			
Vuurberg	H4	T			×	0		T			
Warwick	F1		√	√		√*		T	√	√	
Waterford	F7		√			0		√	√		
Webersburg	E8		√			√	√	√	√		
Welgevallen	F5				×	0		√			
Westbridge	E1	T				T*	√				
Yardstick	C6	T				0					
Zevenwacht	B5		√	√		√	√	T	√	√	xh
Zorgvliet	H4		√	√		T*	√	T	√	√	

Swartland Map

	Grid reference	Open by appt. only	Open Saturdays	Open Sundays	Open public holidays	Meals/refreshments	Accomodation	Cellar tours	Disabled friendly	Child friendly	Languages spoken
AA Badenhorst		T			×	0	T	T			
Abbottshill		T				BYO		T			
Allesverloren			√			√*		T	√	√	
Annex Kloof			√	√	×	BYO		T			
Babylon's Peak		T				T/BYO*	√	T	√		
Dragonridge		T				T/BYO	√	T		√	
Farm 1120			√			√*					
Het Vlock Casteel			√			T*			√		
Hofstraat		T				0		T			
Hughes Family		T				0					sp
Kloovenburg			√	√*		BYO	√	√*	√		
Lammershoek		T				T/BYO		T			de
Meerhof		T				0					
Mount Abora		T				0					
Mullineux		T*	√	T		0		T*			
Nieuwedrift			√			T/BYO		√		√	
Orangerie		T				0		T			
Org de Rac			√			T/BYO		√			de
Paardebosch		T			×	BYO		T			
Pulpit Rock			√			√/BYO	√	T	√		
Riebeek			√	√		BYO		T			
Sadie		T				0					
Santa Cecilia			√	√		√*	√				
Sequillo		T*			×	0					

	Grid reference	Open by appt. only	Open Saturdays	Open Sundays	Open public holidays	Meals/refreshments	Accomodation	Cellar tours	Disabled friendly	Child friendly	Languages spoken
Swartland			✓			0			✓	✓	
Wildehurst			✓	✓		0		T			
Winkelshoek			✓			0			✓		
Tulbagh Map											
Blue Crane			T			0		T			
Constantia de Tulbagh		T			×	0		T			
Drostdy-Hof			✓			0			✓		
Fable		T				0					
Koelfontein			✓		×	BYO	✓				
Lemberg			✓	✓		T/BYO*	✓	✓			
Manley			✓			✓	✓	T			
Montpellier			✓		×	✓*	✓	✓		✓	
Oude Compagnies Post		T				0		T			
Rijk's			✓			0	✓	T	✓		
Saronsberg			✓			BYO		T			
Schalkenbosch		T			×	0	✓	T			de
Theuniskraal			✓			0			✓		
Tulbagh Winery			✓*	✓*		BYO		T	✓		
Twee Jonge/Krone			✓			0			✓		de
Waverley Hills			✓	✓		✓/BYO*		✓	✓	✓	
Zonquasdrift		T*			×	0					
Villiersdorp Map											
Badgerberg		T*				✓*					
Cranefields		T				0					
Faraway House		T				0					
Slowine			✓			✓			✓		
Villiersdorp			✓			✓			✓		
Worcester Map											
Aan de Doorns			✓		×	0		T*	✓		
Alvi's Drift		T				0		T			
Auction Crossing			✓		×	✓		T		✓	
Brandvlei			✓		×	0			✓		
Conradie			✓	✓		✓/BYO	✓	✓		✓	
De Doorns			✓			0			✓		
De Wet			✓		×	BYO		T	✓		
Eagle's Cliff					×	✓			✓	✓	
Nuy			✓			BYO			✓		
Overhex			✓	✓		✓*		T	✓	✓	
Stettyn			✓*		×	T/BYO*		T*	✓	✓	

Cape Peninsula

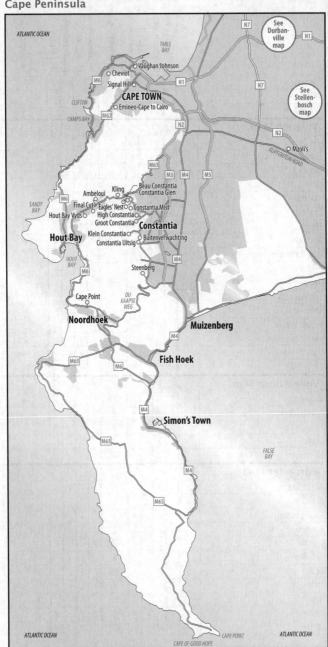

ATLANTIC OCEAN

TABLE BAY

See Durbanville map

N7

N1

N1

N7

N7

See Stellenbosch map

Cheviot

Vaughan Johnson

M6

Signal Hill

CAPE TOWN

N1

CLIFTON

Emineo-Cape to Cairo

N2

CAMPS BAY

M62

N2

Mzoli's

KLIPFONTEIN ROAD

M63

M3 M4 M5

Kling

Ambeloui

Beau Constantia
Constantia Glen

SANDY BAY

M6

Final Cut

Eagles' Nest

Constantia Mist

Hout Bay Vrds

High Constantia

Hout Bay

Groot Constantia

Constantia

Klein Constantia

Buitenverwachting

Constantia Uitsig

HOUT BAY

M6

M4

Steenberg

Cape Point

OU KAAPSE WEG

Noordhoek

Muizenberg

M4

M65

Fish Hoek

M6

M4

⌂ **Simon's Town**

M65

FALSE BAY

M4

M65

ATLANTIC OCEAN

ATLANTIC OCEAN

CAPE POINT

CAPE OF GOOD HOPE

Durbanville, Philadelphia & Darling

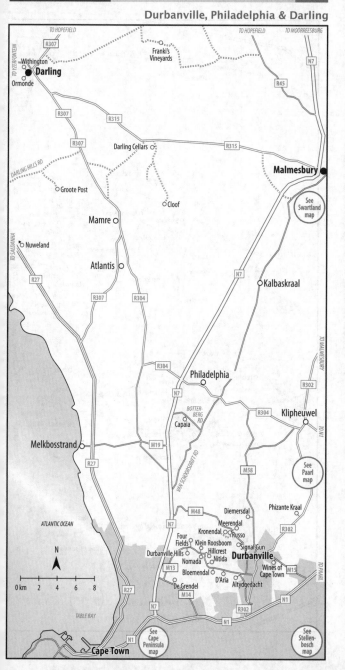

TO HOPEFIELD

TO HOPEFIELD

TO MOORREESBURG

R307

Franki's Vineyards

R307

Withington

● **Darling**

Ormonde

N7

R45

R307

R315

R307

DARLING HILLS RD

Darling Cellars

R315

R315

● **Malmesbury**

Groote Post

Cloof

See Swartland map

TO SALDANHA

Mamre

Nuweland

Atlantis

R27

R307

R304

Kalbaskraal

N7

R304

Philadelphia

TO MALMESBURY

R302

BOTTER-BERG RD

Klipheuwel

Capaia

R304

R27

M19

Melkbosstrand

VAN SCHOORSDRIFT RD

See Paarl map

TO N1

M58

M48

Diemersdal

Phizante Kraal

ATLANTIC OCEAN

Meerendal

R302

N7

Kronendal

Russo

Four Fields

Klein Roosboom

Signal Gun

Durbanville Hills

Hillcrest

Nitida

TO PAARL

N
▲

Nomada

Durbanville

M13

Bloemendal

D'Aria

Wines of Cape Town

0 km   2   4   6   8

De Grendel

M14

Altydgedacht

M15

R27

N7

R302

N1

TABLE BAY

N1

TABLE BAY

N1

● **Cape Town**

See Cape Peninsula map

See Stellenbosch map

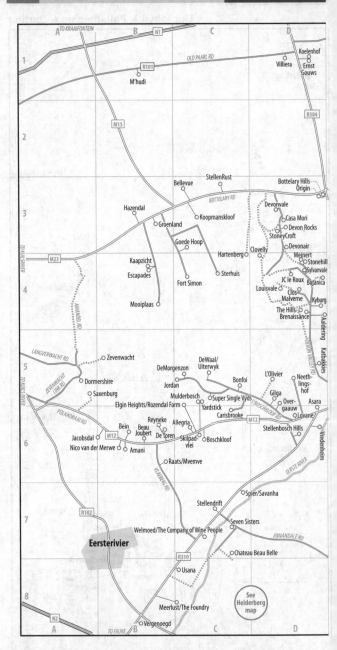

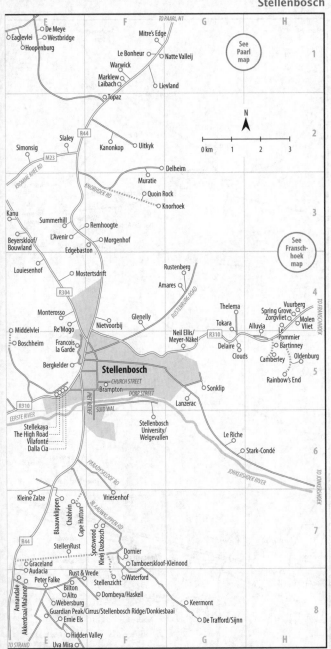

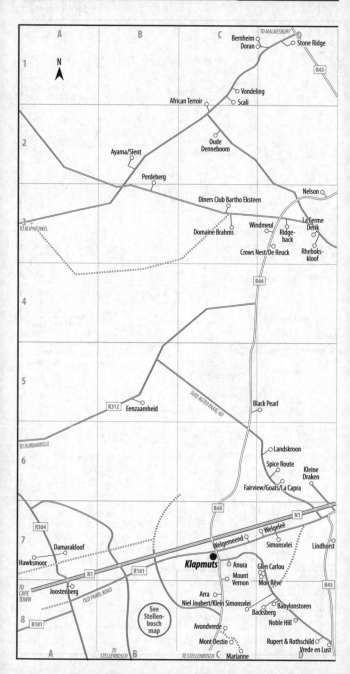

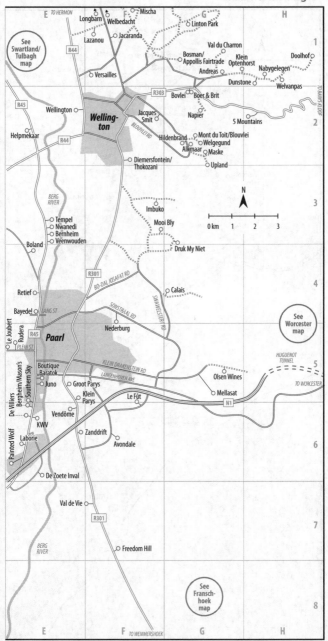

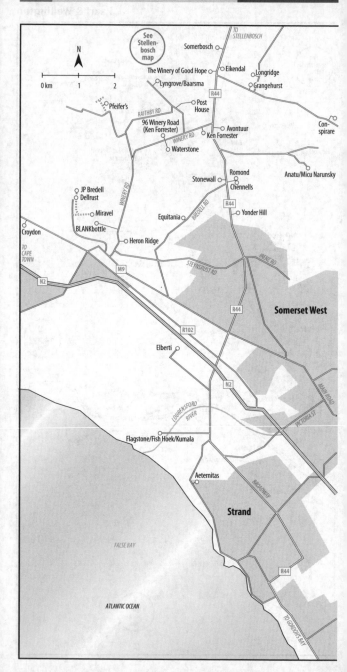

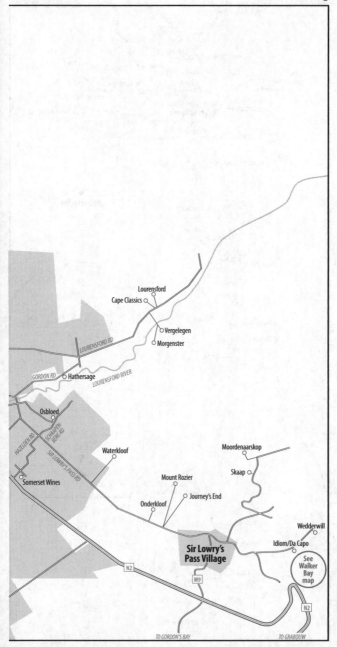

Lourensford

Cape Classics

Vergelegen

Morgenster

LOURENSFORD RD

GORDON RD   Hathersage

LOURENSFORD RIVER

Osbloed

HAZELDEN RD

SCHAPEN-BERG RD

SIR LOWRY'S PASS RD

Waterkloof

Somerset Wines

Moordenaarskop

Skaap

Mount Rozier

Journey's End

Onderkloof

Wedderwill

Sir Lowry's
Pass Village

Idiom/Da Capo

See
Walker
Bay
map

N2

M9

TO GORDON'S BAY

TO GRABOUW

N2

Franschhoek

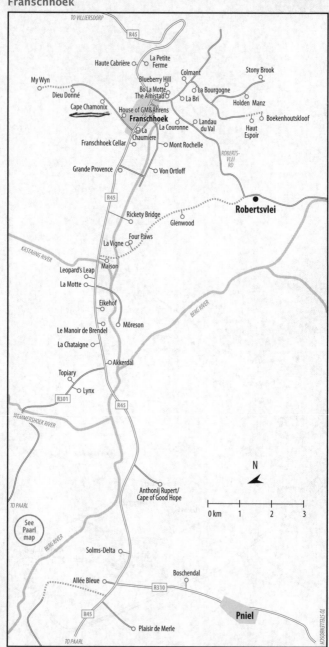

Elgin, Walker Bay & Bot River

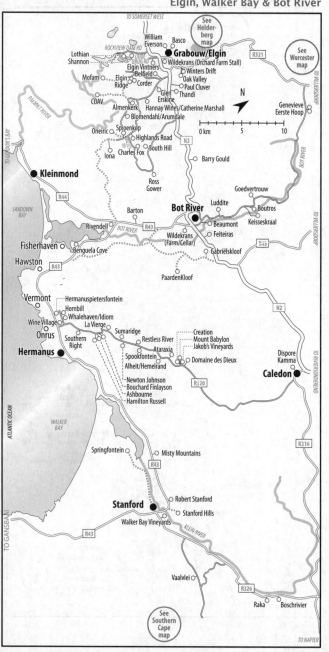

TO SOMERSET WEST

See Helderberg map

See Worcester map

William Everson

Basco

ROCKVIEW DAM RD

R321

Grabouw/Elgin

Lothian
Shannon

OUDE
BRUG RD

Wildekrans (Orchard Farm Stall)

Elgin Vintners

Winters Drift

Mofam

Belfield

Oak Valley

Elgin
Ridge

Corder

Paul Cluver

Glen
Erskine

Thandi

COAV

Almenkerk

Hannay Wines/Catherine Marshall

Genevieve
Eerste Hoop

Blomendahl/Arumdale

Oneiric

Spioenkop

N

TO VILLIERSDORP

Highlands Road

0 km   5   10

Iona

Charles Fox

South Hill

N2

BOT RIVER

PALMIET RIVER

Barry Gould

Ross
Gower

Kleinmond

Goedvertrouw

SANDOWN
BAY

R44

Barton

Luddite

Boutros

Bot River

Beaumont

Keisseskraal

TO GORDON'S BAY

Rivendell

BOT RIVER

R43

Beaumont

Feiteiras

Fisherhaven

Benguela Cove

Wildekrans
(Farm/Cellar)

Gabriëlskloof

R43

TO VILLIERSDORP

Hawston

R43

PaardenKloof

Vermont

Hermanuspietersfontein

Hornbill

Whalehaven/Idiom

Wine Village

La Vierge

Sumaridge

Creation

Onrus

Southern
Right

Restless River

Mount Babylon
Jakob's Vineyards

Dispore
Kamma

Hermanus

Ataraxia

Spookfontein

Domaine des Dieux

Caledon

TO RIVERSONDEREND

Alheit/Hemelrand

Newton Johnson
Bouchard Finlayson
Ashbourne
Hamilton Russell

R320

N2

R316

WALKER
BAY

ATLANTIC OCEAN

Springfontein

Misty Mountains

R43

TO GANSBAAI

Stanford

Robert Stanford

Stanford Hills

Walker Bay Vineyards

KLEIN RIVER

Vaalvlei

R326

Raka

Boschrivier

See Southern Cape map

TO NAPIER

Swartland

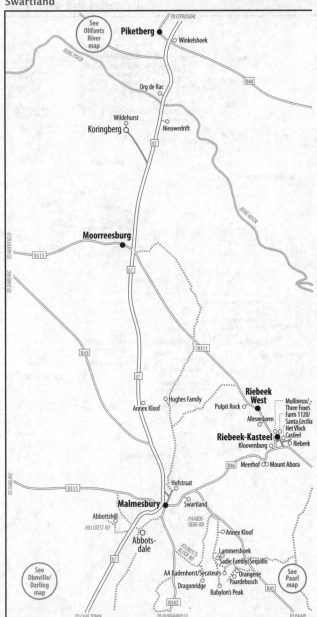

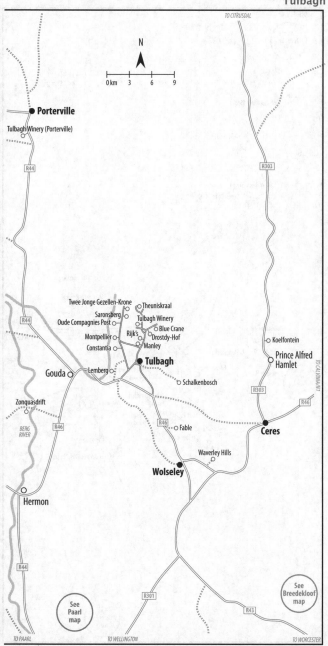

TO CITRUSDAL

N

0 km   3   6   9

Porterville

Tulbagh Winery (Porterville)

R44

R303

Twee Jonge Gezellen-Krone
Saronsberg
Oude Compagnies Post
Montpellier
Constantia
Rijk's
Theuniskraal
Tulbagh Winery
Blue Crane
Drostdy-Hof
Manley

R44

Tulbagh

Koelfontein

Prince Alfred
Hamlet

Gouda   Lemberg

Schalkenbosch

TO CALVINIA/N1

Zonquasdrift

BERG
RIVER

R46

R303

Fable

R46

Ceres

Waverley Hills

Wolseley

Hermon

R44

See
Paarl
map

R301

R43

See
Breedekloof
map

TO PAARL   TO WELLINGTON   TO WORCESTER

Breedekloof

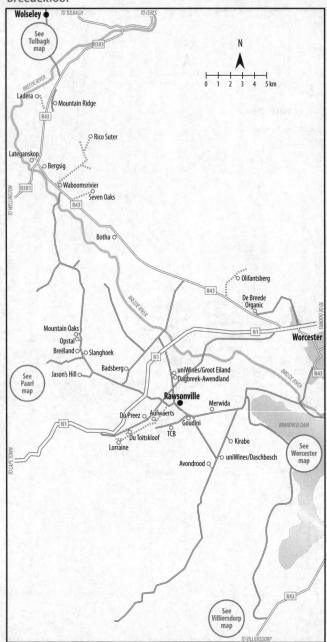

Worcester

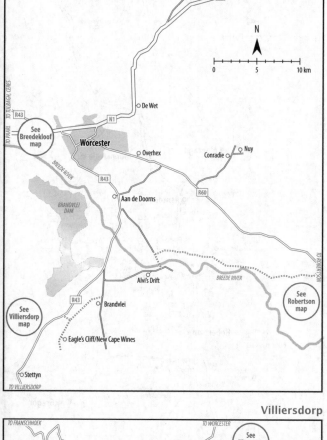

Villiersdorp

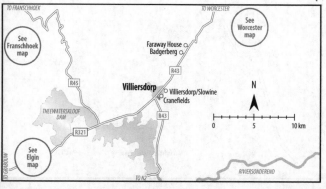

Robertson

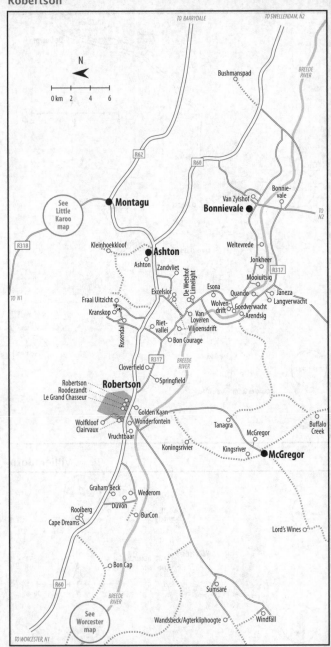

N

0 km 2 4 6

TO BARRYDALE

TO SWELLENDAM, N2

BREEDE RIVER

Bushmanspad

R62

R60

See Little Karoo map

R318

Montagu

Van Zylshof

Bonnie-vale

Bonnievale

TO N2

Kleinhoekkloof

Ashton

Weltevrede

Ashton

Zandvliet

Jonkheer

R317

De Wetshof
Limelight

Mooiuitsig

TO N1

Excelsior

Esona

Quando

Janeza

Langverwacht

Fraai Uitzicht

Wolven-
drift

Goedverwacht

Kranskop

Van
Loveren

Arendsig

Riet-
vallei

Rosendal

Viljoensdrift

Bon Courage

Cloverfield

R317

BREEDE
RIVER

Robertson

Springfield

Robertson
Roodezandt
Le Grand Chasseur

Golden Kaan

Wolfkloof
Clairvaux

Wonderfontein

Tanagra

McGregor

Buffalo
Creek

Vruchtbaar

Koningsrivier

Kingsrivier

McGregor

Graham Beck

Wederom

Rooiberg

DuVon

Cape Dreams

BurCon

Lord's Wines

Bon Cap

R60

BREEDE
RIVER

Sumsaré

See
Worcester
map

Wandsbeck/Agterkliphoogte

Windfäll

TO WORCESTER, N1

Olifants River & West Coast

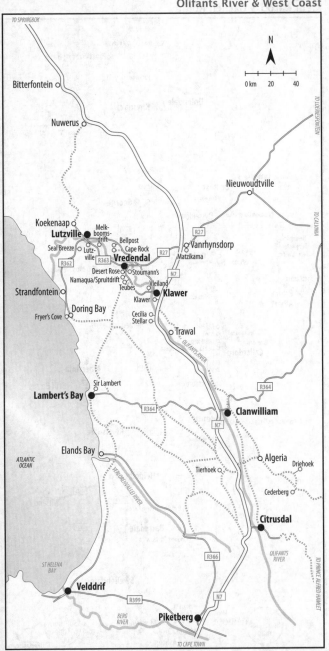

Klein Karoo & Garden Route

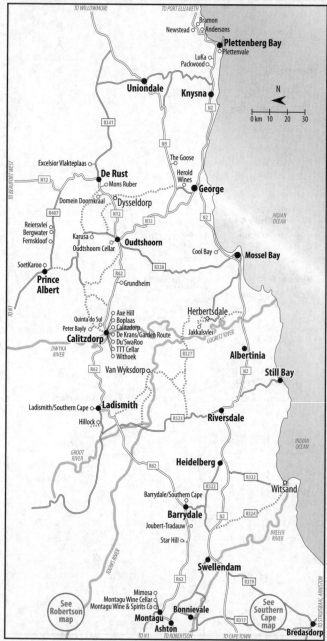

KwaZulu-Natal

Southern Cape

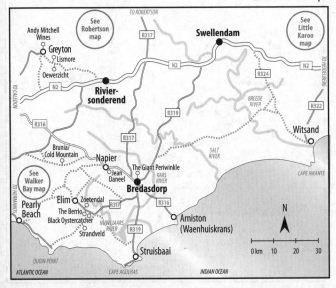

Northern Cape, Free State & North West

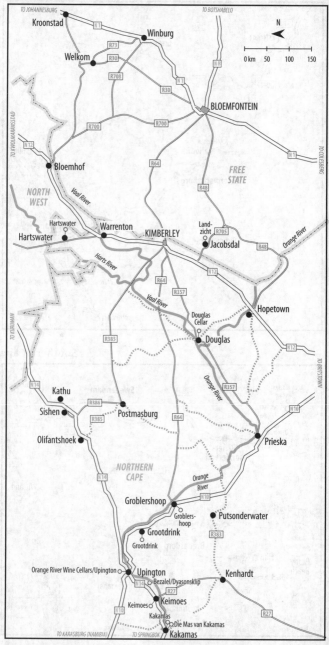

On the nose!

Intimidated or just uninitiated?
Help is now in the palm of your hand. Navigate any
South African wine moment with the Platter's apps
for iPhone® and Android®.

Search Platter's vintages and producers. Save favourites,
share discoveries and rate the wines. See for yourself -
the GPS-enabled maps will lead you to producers and
wine experiences that make South Africa one of the
great wine destinations of the world.

Visit us at www.wineonaplatter.com
or www.wine-oh.info